Austria

THE ROUGH GUIDE

There are more than one hundred Rough Guide titles
covering destinations from Amsterdam to Zimbabwe

Forthcoming titles include
Bangkok • Japan
Jordan • Los Angeles • Tokyo

Rough Guide Reference Series
Classical Music • European Football • The Internet • Jazz
Opera • Reggae • Rock Music • World Music

Rough Guide Phrasebooks
Czech • French • German • Greek • Hindi & Urdu • Hungarian • Indonesian
Italian • Japanese • Mandarin Chinese • Mexican Spanish • Polish
Portuguese • Russian • Spanish • Thai • Turkish • Vietnamese

Rough Guides on the Internet
http://www.roughguides.com

ROUGH GUIDE CREDITS

Text editor: Olivia Eccleshall
Series editor: Mark Ellingham
Editorial: Martin Dunford, Jonathan Buckley, Samantha Cook, Jo Mead, Kate Berens, Amanda Tomlin, Ann-Marie Shaw, Paul Gray, Sarah Dallas, Chris Schüler, Helena Smith, Caroline Osborne, Judith Bamber, Kieran Falconer, Orla Duane, Ruth Blackmore, Sophie Martin (UK); Andrew Rosenberg (US)
Production: Susanne Hillen, Andy Hilliard, Judy Pang, Link Hall, Nicola Williamson, Helen Ostick, James Morris

Cartography: Melissa Flack, Maxine Burke, Nichola Goodliffe
Picture research: Eleanor Hill
Online editors: Alan Spicer, Kate Hands (UK); Geronimo Madrid (US)
Finance: John Fisher, Celia Crowley, Neeta Mistry
Marketing & Publicity: Richard Trillo, Simon Carloss, Niki Smith (UK); Jean-Marie Kelly, SoRelle Braun (US)
Administration: Tania Hummel, Alexander Mark Rogers

ACKNOWLEDGEMENTS

The authors would like to thank Olivia Eccleshall for encouragement, patience and all-round unflappability, Jonathan Buckley for his encyclopedic knowledge of central European culture, Marion Telsnig of the Austrian National Tourist Office for graciously answering the most bizarre of queries, and Vivienne Heller for getting the whole project under way in the first place.

Jonathan Bousfield: thanks also to Franca-Maria Kobenter and Claudia Krakolinig of Karntner Tourismus, Heiner Kolbe of the Salzburg State Tourist Board, Maria Altendorfer in Salzburg, Anton Bittner in Klagenfurt, Carmen Fender in Solden, Evy Halder in Bregenz, Karin Hauser in Spittal an der Drau, John and Helga Hinsby in Huntingdon, Marianne Hinterndorfer in Bregenz, Alexandra Kossler in Hall, Michael Kreissl in Lienz, Gerhard Kusternigg in Millstatt,

Herbert Lackner in Launsdorf, Harald Londer in St Veit, Lauren Nadrag in Ossiachersee, Heinz Sillober in Innsbruck, Malcolm and Emma Wilkinson in Blackheath, and Barbara Wille-Folie in Schwaz.

Rob Humphreys: a big thankyou to Val for research, Gordon on the ground, so too Kate, Stan and Josh; also to Bettina Fischer in Vienna, to Sylvie Wenzl in Linz, and to Roman Wiche in the Austrian Youth Hostel Association.

Thanks also go to Narrell Leffman and Nick Thomson for Basics research; Nichola Goodliffe, Maxine Burke and Kingston Presentation Graphics for providing the maps; James Morris for typesetting; Susanne Hillen and Nicola Williamson for production; Nikky Twyman for proofreading; and Lisa Pusey and Eleanor Hill for picture research.

PUBLISHING INFORMATION

This first edition published July 1998 by
    Rough Guides Ltd, 62–70 Shorts Gardens,
    London WC2H 9AB.
    Distributed by the Penguin Group:
Penguin Books Ltd, 27 Wrights Lane, London W8 5TZ.
Penguin Books USA Inc., 375 Hudson Street, New York 10014, USA.
Penguin Books Australia Ltd, 487 Maroondah Highway, PO Box 257, Ringwood, Victoria 3134, Australia.
Penguin Books Canada Ltd, 10 Alcorn Avenue, Toronto, Ontario, Canada M4V 1E4.
Penguin Books (NZ) Ltd, 182–190 Wairau Road, Auckland 10, New Zealand.
Typeset in Linotron Univers and Century Old Style to an original design by Andrew Oliver.
Printed in England by Clays Ltd, St Ives PLC.
Illustrations in Part One and Part Three by Edward Briant.
Illustrations on p.1 and p.481 by Henry Iles.

Austria

THE ROUGH GUIDE

written and researched by

Jonathan Bousfield and Rob Humphreys

with additional accounts by

Kev Reynolds

THE ROUGH GUIDES

We set out to do something different when the first Rough Guide was published in 1982. Mark Ellingham, just out of university, was travelling in Greece. He brought along the popular guides of the day, but found they were all lacking in some way. They were either strong on ruins and museums but went on for pages without mentioning a beach or taverna. Or they were so conscious of the need to save money that they lost sight of Greece's cultural and historical significance. Also, none of the books told him anything about Greece's contemporary life – its politics, its culture, its people, and how they lived.

So with no job in prospect, Mark decided to write his own guidebook, one that aimed to provide practical information that was second to none, detailing the best beaches and the hottest clubs and restaurants, while also giving hard-hitting accounts of every sight, both famous and obscure, and providing up-to-the-minute information on contemporary culture. It was a guide that encouraged independent travellers to find the best of Greece, and was a great success, getting shortlisted for the Thomas Cook travel guide award,

and encouraging Mark, along with three friends, to expand the series.

The Rough Guide list grew rapidly and the letters flooded in, indicating a much broader readership than had been anticipated, but one which uniformly appreciated the Rough Guide mix of practical detail and humour, irreverence and enthusiasm. Things haven't changed. The same four friends who began the series are still the caretakers of the Rough Guide mission today: to provide the most reliable, up-to-date and entertaining information to independent-minded travellers of all ages, on all budgets.

We now publish a hundred titles and have offices in London and New York. The travel guides are written and researched by a dedicated team of more than a hundred authors, based in Britain, Europe, the USA and Australia. We have also created a unique series of phrasebooks to accompany the travel series, along with an acclaimed series of music guides, and a best-selling pocket guide to the Internet and World Wide Web. We also publish comprehensive travel information on our Web site:

http://www.roughguides.com

HELP US UPDATE

We've gone to a lot of effort to ensure that this new edition of The Rough Guide to Austria is accurate and up-to-date. However, things change – places get "discovered", opening hours are notoriously fickle, restaurants and rooms raise prices or lower standards, extra buses are laid on or off. If you feel we've got it wrong or left something out, we'd like to know, and if you can remember the address, the price, the time, the phone number, so much the better.

We'll credit all contributions, and send a copy of the next edition (or any other Rough Guide if you prefer) for the best letters.

Please mark letters: "Rough Guide Austria Update" and send to: Rough Guides Ltd, 62–70 Shorts Gardens, London WC2H 9AB, or Rough Guides, 375 Hudson St, 9th Floor, New York NY 10014. Or send email to: mail@roughguides.co.uk
Online updates about this book can be found on Rough Guides' Web site at http://www.roughguides.com

Jonathan Bousfield was forced into his first pair of lederhosen at the age of 9 and has been a regular visitor to Austria ever since. In between times he has been the rock critic of the *European* newspaper and has worked on the (now defunct) *Rough Guide to Yugoslavia*, as well as the *Rough Guide to Bulgaria*. He is currently working on the *Rough Guide to Croatia*.

Rob Humphreys joined the Rough Guides in 1989, having worked as a failed actor, taxi driver and male model. He has travelled extensively in central and eastern Europe, writing guides to Prague, the Czech and Slovak Republics, and St Petersburg, as well as London. He has lived in London since 1988.

CONTENTS

Introduction x

• CHAPTER 2: LOWER AUSTRIA 138–191

• CHAPTER 3: BURGENLAND 192–209

• CHAPTER 4: STYRIA 210–250

• CHAPTER 5: CARINTHIA AND THE EAST TYROL 251–301

• CHAPTER 6: SALZBURG AND THE SALZBURGER LAND 302–348

PART THREE CONTEXTS 481

LIST OF MAPS

MAP SYMBOLS

══	Major road	▲	Mountain peak
──	Minor road	⁄ ⁄	Mountain pass
- - - -	Track		Gorge
══	Railway	ⓘ	Information centre
─ ─	Chapter division boundary	⊠	Post office
▬ ▬	National boundary	★	Bus station
───	River	🄿	Parking
	Waterfall	Ⓤ	U-Bahn
⌂	Monastery	Ⓢ	S-Bahn
✡	Synagogue		Fortifications
♔	Castle		Built up area
	Museum		Building
∴	Ruin	⊞	Church
	Gardens		Cemetery
	Swimming pool		Jewish Cemetery
▲	Campsite		Park
■─■	Cable car		National Park
			Swamp

INTRODUCTION

I t's the spectacular, snowcapped mountains of regions like the Tyrol that provide the most familiar images of **Austria** – a landscape of jagged peaks and rampaging rivers, giving way to green pastures studded with onion-domed churches. Yet Austria is by no means all alpine vistas: the country stretches across central Europe for some 700km, from the shores of the Bodensee in the west to the edge of the flat Hungarian plain in the east. Far removed from the archetype are the wetlands and reed beds of Burgenland, and the dramatic sequence of stopes that carve their way up the Erzberg in Styria. In Upper and Lower Austria in particular, a predominantly low-key landscape of gentle rolling hills and vineyards can come as something of a surprise to first-time visitors. Yet this fertile, low-lying northern half of the country is, in fact, where the majority of Austrians live and work, many of them within commuting distance of the capital, **Vienna** – the country's chief tourist destination after the alpine regions.

For all its bucolic charm and fondness for the days of empire, when Vienna sat at the centre of the vast, multinational Habsburg dynasty, Austria today is thoroughly modern, clean, efficient and eminently civilized, with uniformly excellent tourist facilities. Like neighbouring Switzerland, it's also a supremely law-abiding nation, where no one jaywalks or drops litter, and the trains and trams run on time. Whether you're staying in one of the popular skiing, hiking or spa-resorts, or in an out-of-the-way Gasthof, you're likely to experience *"Gemütlichkeit"* – a typically Austrian term expressing a mixture of cosiness and hospitality – at some point during your visit.

Looking at the country at the close of the twentieth century – stable, conservative and wealthy – you wouldn't think that Austria had spent the first half of the century struggling to find a national identity. After all, it was only in 1918, when the Habsburg Empire disintegrated, that the idea of a modern Austrian nation was born. The new republic, with a population of just eight million reluctant citizens, was riven by left- and right-wing political violence and, as a result, the majority of Austrians were wildly enthusiastic about the Anschluss with Nazi Germany in 1938. The price of Austria's participation, and ultimately defeat, in World War II, however, was Allied occupation. For ten years the country was split, like Germany, into Soviet, American, British and French zones. As a gesture of détente, the Soviets agreed ultimately to withdraw their troops, in return for Austria's "permanent neutrality". At this point, Austria turned over a new leaf, and recast itself as a model of consensus politics, with an almost Scandinavian emphasis on social policy as the guiding principle of national life. Postwar stability saw the growth of a genuine patriotism, while the end of the Cold War put the country, and its capital, back at the heart of Europe.

In 1995, Austria became a full member of the European Union, a move that for many was a sign that the country had finally entered the mainstream of European politics. From time to time, Austria's more reactionary elements have attracted widespread media attention, most notably during the Waldheim affair, when the wartime record of the president was called into question, and in the recent rise of the Far Right under the charismatic Jörg Haider. But the reality is that the Socialist party retains the strongest influence in government, as it has for much of the postwar period, and the country's political stability, for the most part, continues intact.

Where to go

There's a lot to be said for concentrating on just one or two regions, rather than trying to cover a bit of everything in one trip – you could happily spend a week or two in any one of the Austrian provinces, or *Länder*. Austria's unique combination of outdoor attractions and classic urban centres ensures that you can pack a lot of variety into your stay: take in some fresh air at a high altitude, linger over one of the country's world-class art collections, make the most of a musical heritage second to none, or select any number from the list of recommended highlights below.

Without a visit to **Vienna** you'll return home with only half the picture. Built on a grand scale as seat of the Habsburg Empire, it's a place that positively drips with imperial nostalgia. The pickings are rich, with the old palaces of the Hofburg and Schönbrunn high on the list, as are the cultural offerings from the gargantuan art collection at the Kunsthistorisches Museum and the hi-tech applied-arts displays of the MAK. Equally compelling, nowadays, are the ghosts of Vienna's golden age at the turn of the nineteenth century, when the likes of Freud, Klimt, Schiele and Schönberg frequented the city's cafés. The city boasts some wonderful Jugendstil and early modernist buildings and a bevy of traditional fin-de-siècle cafés patrolled by waiters in tuxedos. Last, but by no means least, Vienna is by far the best place in the country for nightlife, and that means everything from top-class opera to techno.

Salzburg is no less intoxicating. Its Altstadt contains the country's most concentrated ensemble of Baroque architecture, and the Hohensalzburg fortress is arguably the country's most impressive medieval castle. A substantial musical pedigree is ensured by the city's status as the birthplace of Mozart and venue of the Salzburg Festival, one of the world's most renowned celebrations of classical music and theatre. Of Austria's other regional capitals, **Innsbruck** combines both a buzzing nightlife and close proximity to some of the Tyrol's highest peaks to make it one of Austria's most popular destinations. Its attractive and largely medieval city centre focuses on the Hofkirche, site of the memorial to sixteenth-century Habsburg strongman Emperor Maximilian I. In the Styrian capital, **Graz**, main attractions include the town centre, the fine-art collections of the Landesmuseum Joanneum and the Baroque Eggenberg Palace. Austria's second largest city is also a good base from which to venture out into the vineyards and pumpkin fields of the rural southeast.

Explorations down back streets of Austria's small **medieval towns**, many of which are still enclosed by their original walls, will reward you with hidden arcaded courtyards, tinkling fountains and overflowing flower boxes: Freistadt in Upper Austria, Hall in the Tyrol and Friesach in Carinthia present the pick of the bunch. Lower Austria has the country's highest concentration of **monasteries**, ranging from the Baroque excess of Melk, Altenburg and Zwettl to the likes of Heiligenkreuz, built on the cusp of the stylistic transition from Romanesque to Gothic. For unadulterated Romanesque architecture, head for Gurk in Carinthia; for Rococo floridity, Wilhering in Upper Austria is hard to beat. Austria also holds a bewildering variety of **castles and chateaux**, from fortified seats such as Forchtenstein in Burgenland to luxury aristocratic piles like Artstetten in Lower Austria. The two finest imperial palaces are the magnificent Baroque residence of Schönbrunn, on the outskirts of Vienna, and Schloss Ambras, the archduke Ferdinand of Tyrol's Renaissance treasure-trove near Innsbruck.

Musical pilgrimages are possible to the birthplaces or resting places of such luminaries as Beethoven, Bruckner, Haydn, Liszt, Mozart, Schönberg and Schubert. The country's top **music festivals**, among them the Salzburg Festival, the Haydn Festival in Eisenstadt and the chamber music festival in Lockenhaus, draw international performers and audiences alike. At both the Bregenz Festival and the operetta festival in Mörbisch, floating stages host top-class performances against a shimmering backdrop.

Austria's main **lakeland area** is the Salzkammergut, where the Wolfgangsee, Mondsee, Traunsee and Hallstättersee offer a combination of water-based pursuits and stunning scenery. To the south, the Carinthian lakes of the Wörthersee, Ossiachersee and Millstättersee boast good bathing, boating and windsurfing facilities. In the far east of the country, the reed-encircled Neusiedlersee, Austria's only steppe lake, provides a total contrast, and an opportunity to marry beach culture with a spot of bird-watching.

Austria forms one of Europe's most mountainous countries, yet an excellent network of transport links puts even the dizziest of heights within reach. Key summer **hiking** areas are the alpine regions of western Austria, stretching from northeastern Styria and eastern Carinthia through the Salzkammergut, Salzburger Land, Tyrol and Vorarlberg. For **snow sports**, the Salzburger Land, Tyrol and Vorarlberg boast the highest concentration and widest range of modern, fully equipped resorts.

Finally, a great deal of Austria's industrial heritage has been put to good touristic effect, and many of the **show-mines** count among top attractions. If you have time to visit only one of them, pick from the following: the iron-ore workings at Eisenerz in Styria, the salt mine at Bad Dürrnberg in the Salzburger Land, the salt mine above Hallstatt in the Salzkammergut, the lead mine at Bad Bleiberg in Carinthia, and the silver mine at Schwaz in the Tyrol.

When to go

The best time to visit Austria depends on whether you're aiming for urban or rural parts. Most of the mountain resorts, for example, have **two distinct tourist seasons**, one for winter sports enthusiasts, the other for summer hikers. In between times, you may find many of the tourist facilities closed. More urban centres, however, act as **year-round tourist destinations**, with the number of visitors swelling during peak holidays and annual festivals – Vienna pulls in crowds over Christmas, New Year and, of course, Fasching (the ball season), while the Salzburg Festival ensures a steady stream of well-heeled visitors in July and August.

For the best of the warm weather, plan to go between **April and October** – Austrian summers, in particular, are reliably warm, but not overpoweringly so. If you're skiing, you can pretty much guarantee a good covering of snow from **November onwards to April**. Away from the ski resorts, winter travel can't really be recommended, since the weather can be pretty wet and miserable. Weather conditions vary only slightly across the country, with the alpine regions decidedly cooler, the lowland regions in the north and east enduring more continental conditions of colder winters and hotter summers, and the southeast of the country enjoying longer, warmer, almost Mediterranean summers. Be aware that whatever the season, if you're at a high altitude, the weather can change quickly and dramatically. The possibility of a thundery shower exists at any time of the year.

AUSTRIA'S CLIMATE

Average maximum/minimum daily temperatures in degrees Celsius/and monthly rainfall in millimetres.

Innsbruck

	Jan	Feb	March	April	May	June	July	Aug	Sept	Oct	Nov	Dec
Max Temp	1	4	11	16	20	24	25	24	21	15	8	2
Min Temp	-7	-5	0	4	8	11	13	12	10	5	0	-4
Rainfall	54	49	41	52	73	110	110	108	81	67	53	46

Klagenfurt

	Jan	Feb	March	April	May	June	July	Aug	Sept	Oct	Nov	Dec
Max Temp	-1	3	9	15	20	23	25	24	20	14	6	1
Min Temp	-9	-7	-2	3	7	11	13	12	10	5	0	-4
Rainfall	41	45	39	71	88	125	125	104	83	89	75	52

Vienna

	Jan	Feb	March	April	May	June	July	Aug	Sept	Oct	Nov	Dec
Max Temp	1	3	8	15	19	23	25	24	20	14	7	3
Min Temp	-4	-3	-1	6	10	14	15	15	11	7	3	-1
Rainfall	39	44	44	45	70	67	84	72	42	56	52	45

THE

BASICS

GETTING THERE FROM BRITAIN AND IRELAND

The easiest way to get to Austria from Britain is by plane, with flights from London to either Vienna or Salzburg taking around two hours. Trains represent a viable alternative if you're keen on overland travel and like the idea of being able to stop off en route; without stopping off, it takes just under 24 hours to get from London to Vienna, slightly less to Salzburg or Innsbruck. Travelling by bus is the cheapest option, but also the most time-consuming.

BY PLANE FROM BRITAIN

Vienna and Salzburg are the only Austrian destinations served by direct scheduled flights from the UK. Travellers bound for provincial capitals like Graz, Klagenfurt and Innsbruck must first fly to Vienna and connect with an internal flight. If you're heading for western Austria, you might also consider Munich and Zürich as potential gateways to the country.

Both Austrian Airlines and British Airways run three or more daily **scheduled flights** from London to Vienna. Austrian Airlines fly out of Heathrow (Terminal 2), while British Airways fly from both Heathrow (twice daily; Terminal 1) and Gatwick (twice daily; North Terminal). Lauda Air flies daily from Gatwick (North Terminal) to Salzburg and Vienna; it's also the only carrier flying direct from Manchester to Vienna.

All the above airlines offer **economy fares** to Vienna and Salzburg year-round for £200 or so. Fares to other Austrian destinations (Innsbruck,

Graz or Klagenfurt) can turn out to be quite pricey: the cheapest return fare to Graz, for example, hovers around the £300 mark. These tickets are non-changeable, non-refundable, valid for one month and must include at least one Saturday night in Austria; you can book them up to the day before you travel (subject to availability).

Though none of the above airlines offers **Apex fares** from London to Vienna as a matter of course, they do pop up from time to time. It's always worth asking, as Apex tickets tend to be £20 or so cheaper. Depending on the specific conditions that apply, they must be bought 7 to 21 days in advance, and you may or may not be offered a fifty percent refund if you cancel before the deadline.

Discounted flights, usually with one of the scheduled airlines, are available from the many low-cost flight agents who advertise in the various London freebie magazines, *Time Out*, the *Evening Standard* and the quality Sunday papers. Tickets to Vienna and Salzburg can go for as little as £100 return and will certainly bring the price of the flight below £150 (although airport tax will mean shelling out an additional £15 or more).

Bear in mind that all these **fares** vary slightly according to **season** – tending to be highest from April to October and in the two weeks around Christmas. During the skiing season (roughly December to early April), there are some **charter flights** serving Innsbruck direct, and available seats are sold off through ticket agents, sometimes for as little as £100.

VIA ZÜRICH AND MUNICH

Zürich airport is on the main rail network, with several Austria-bound expresses passing through every day – the train journey to Innsbruck, for example, takes just under four hours. There are six buses a day from Munich airport to Innsbruck, and numerous express trains from Munich train station (a short trip from the airport by the S-Bahn suburban railway) to Salzburg (Munich–Salzburg by train 2hr; Munich–Salzburg by bus 2hr 30min). **Scheduled flights** from London to Zürich or Munich tend to work out a bit cheaper than those to Vienna: a London–Zürich return with Swissair, for example, currently costs £160, provided you spend at least one weekend away, and cheaper fares can be found if you contact ticket agents.

Bear in mind, however, the cost of onward travel from Zürich or Munich to Austria: a Zürich–St Anton return train ticket, for example, currently costs £50; a Zürich–Innsbruck return £70; a Munich–Salzburg return by train £50; and a Munich–Innsbruck return by bus £40.

PACKAGES AND CITY BREAKS

Package-holiday deals can be worth considering, saving you the hassle of finding accommodation when you arrive or phoning abroad yourself to try and organize it. Prices generally work out as equivalent to or less than if you organize everything yourself – and, as a general rule, you'll get a better class of accommodation for your money if it's block-booked as part of a package than if you were to arrange accommodation independently and pay for it on a per-night basis.

WINTER PACKAGES

In the **alpine areas** of Austria (Vorarlberg, the Tyrol, the Salzburger Land, much of Carinthia and northwestern Styria), almost any settlement within chairlift distance of a serviceable slope has

AIRLINES

Austrian Airlines, 10 Wardour St, London W1V 4BJ (☎0171/434 7350).

British Airways, 156 Regent St, London W1R 5TA (☎0171/828 4895); plus regional offices (all enquiries ☎0345/222111).

Lauda Air, Units 1 & 2, 123 Buckingham Palace Rd, London SW1W 9SH (☎0171/630 5924).

Swissair, 10 Wardour St, London W1V 4BJ (☎0171/434 7300).

DISCOUNT FLIGHT AGENTS

Campus Travel, 52 Grosvenor Gardens, London SW1W 0AG (Europe ☎0171/730 3402); 541 Bristol Rd, Selly Oak, Birmingham B29 6AU (☎0121/414 1848); 61 Ditchling Rd, Brighton BN1 4SD (☎01273/570226); 37–39 Queen's Rd, Clifton, Bristol BS8 1QE (☎0117/929 2494); 5 Emmanuel St, Cambridge CB1 1NE (☎01223/324283); 53 Forest Rd, Edinburgh EH1 2QP (☎0131/225 6111, telesales ☎668 3303); 122 George St, Glasgow G1 1RS (☎0141/553 1818); 166 Deansgate, Manchester M3 3FE (☎0161/833 2046, telesales ☎273 1721); 105–106 St Aldate's, Oxford OX1 1DD (☎01865/242067). Student/youth travel specialists, with branches also in YHA shops and on university campuses all over Britain.

Council Travel, 28a Poland St, London W1V 3DB (☎0171/437 7767). Flights and student discounts.

Flightbookers, 177–178 Tottenham Court Rd, London W1P 0LX (☎0171/757 2000); Gatwick Airport, South Terminal inside the British Rail Station (daily 7am–10pm; ☎01293/568300); 34 Argyle Arcade, off Buchanan Street, Glasgow G1 1RS (☎0141/204 1919). Low fares on an extensive offering of scheduled flights.

North South Travel, Moulsham Mill Centre, Parkway, Chelmsford, Essex CM2 7PX (☎01245/492882, fax 356612). Friendly, competitive travel agency, offering discounted fares worldwide – profits are used to support projects in the developing world, especially the promotion of sustainable tourism.

STA Travel, 86 Old Brompton Rd, London SW7 3LH; 117 Euston Rd, London NW1 2SX; 38 Store St, London WC1E 7BZ (Europe ☎0171/361 6161); 25 Queen's Rd, Bristol BS8 1QE (☎0117/929 4399); 38 Sidney St, Cambridge CB2 3HX (☎01223/366966); 75 Deansgate, Manchester M3 2BW (☎0161/834 0668); 88 Vicar Lane, Leeds LS1 7JH (☎0113/244 9212); 36 George St, Oxford OX1 2OJ (☎01865/792800); and branches in Aberdeen, Birmingham, Canterbury, Cardiff, Coventry, Durham, Glasgow, Loughborough, Nottingham, Sheffield and Warwick. Worldwide specialists in low-cost flights and tours for students and under-26s, though other customers also welcome. Also offices abroad.

Trailfinders, 215 Kensington High St, London W6 6BD (European ☎0171/937 5400); 58 Deansgate, Manchester M3 2FF (☎0161/839 6969); 254–284 Sauchiehall St, Glasgow G2 3EH (☎0141/353 2224); 22–24 The Priory Queensway, Birmingham B4 6BS (☎0121/236 1234); 48 Corn St, Bristol BS1 1HQ (☎0117/929 9000). One of the best-informed and most efficient agents for independent travellers; all branches open daily until 6pm, Thursday until 7pm.

undergone tourist development to some degree, and the range of Austrian destinations offered by the large package-tour companies is huge. Even for non-skiers, a winter package presents a good way of enjoying alpine Austria at its snowy best.

The factors that will influence your choice of resort are covered in more detail under "Skiing and snowboarding" on p.48. Suffice to say here that a winter package is usually cheaper than a ski trip organized independently, especially if any extras (such as lift passes, boot and pole rental, lessons) are included in the price of the holiday. There's also a growing number of all-inclusive holidays on offer, in which you'll get full board as well as most of your drinks free. Accommodation is usually in a **hotel** or **pension**, although the number of **self-catering apartments** on offer is on the increase.

The **season** for winter packages runs from mid-December to early April, with the **peak** periods occuring between late December and early January, and early February to mid-March. Staying in a small two-star hotel, a week in one of the cheaper resorts (such as Alpbach, Mayrhofen or Söll) at the beginning or end of the season **costs** as little as £300–320, rising to £400 in mid-February. Prices in more fashionable resorts like Kitzbühel and St Anton aren't much higher, provided you stick to simple bed-and-breakfast accommodation, although rates rise steeply once you break into the three- and four-star hotel bracket, where rooms are also much more likely to be offered on a half-board basis. A free lift pass is included in some deals; otherwise, expect to spend an additional £90–130 per week on a lift pass, plus £70 per week on equipment hire and £70–100 per week on skiing lessons (depending on your requirements).

SUMMER PACKAGES

Generally speaking, the Austrian destinations offered by the major package companies in their summertime "Lakes & Mountains" brochures are the same as those offered to skiers over the winter. Although most of the summer packages focus on mountainous, western Austria, you can use your package resort as a jumping-off point for **side-trips** to set-piece destinations like Innsbruck and Salzburg. Some of the bigger **alpine centres** (Kitzbühel, Zell am See and the like) are situated on major road and rail routes as well, and are therefore good bases from which to explore a large swath of western Austria.

Staying in less accessible **alpine valley resorts** – Alpbach, Söll, Pfunds and Galtür are among the most idyllic – means you'll be dependent on local bus routes (which are adequate, but time-consuming), on coach tours offered by the local rep, or on self-organized car rental, if you want to roam further afield. It's also worth mentioning that the kind of après-ski **nightlife** that lightens up the alpine resorts in winter is usually conspicuous by its absence in summer, during which a fair proportion of bars and restaurants close down. Perhaps the best **rural/urban mix** is provided by the resorts of the **Salzkammergut** (St Wolfgang and St Gilgen are the most popular; Traunkirchen is a quieter alternative), which provide immediate access to a wide range of both lake and mountain scenery, and are within striking distance of Salzburg.

Many of the summer-package operators assume that their clients are interested in **walking** to some degree, and will either provide a range of free guided rambles as part of the package or point you in the direction of the short guided walks offered by local tourist offices over the summer. If you want to tackle a more demanding walking itinerary and prefer to do so in the company of a guided group, specialist operators like Ramblers Holidays and Waymark offer a selection of seven- and fourteen-day walking holidays, catering for a range of abilities. Most involve overnight accommodation in a hotel, with daily expeditions into the mountains, although some guided hut-to-hut walks are available (for more on which, see p.33). Some of the big tour operators (notably Thomson) also offer walking tours, such as a walk along a stretch of the Danube Valley – these are usually easy-going affairs involving three to four hours' optional walking per day, with non-walkers and baggage transferred by bus to the next stop-off point.

The **season** for summer packages usually runs from mid-May to late September, with the cheapest deals falling in the first week or two of the season. The peak period, from late July to late August, is the most expensive time of the year to travel. **Prices** per person for seven days (assuming half-board in a double room in a three-star hotel) start at about £300–350 across the whole of Austria in mid-May, even in such traditionally expensive resorts as Kitzbühel and Seefeld. By July and August, the cheapest seven-day holidays will cost something in the region of £400–450, while peak-period prices for seven days in four-star hotels can rise to £550–650.

PACKAGE AND SPECIALIST OPERATORS

Airtours, Wavell House, Holcombe Rd, Helmshore, Rossendale, Lancashire BB4 4NB (☎01706/260000). Winter and summer packages in all major resort areas.

Anglo-Dutch Sports, 30a Foxgrove Rd, Beckenham BR3 5BD (☎0181/289 2808). Seven-day cycling tours along the Danube.

Austria Travel, 46 Queen Anne's Gate, London SW1 (☎0171/222 2430). City breaks in Vienna and Salzburg, as well as tailor-made holidays in regional centres such as Bad Ischl, Badgastein and Zell am See. Their *Summer Experience* brochure lists German language courses in a number of centres in Austria, including Vienna, Kitzbühel, Graz and Melk.

Austrian Holidays, 5th Floor, 10 Wardour St, London W1 (☎0171/434 7399). Austrian package-tour specialist run by Austrian Airlines. City breaks in Vienna, Salzburg, Innsbruck and Graz.

Cresta Holidays, Tabley Court, Victoria St, Altrincham, Cheshire WA14 1EZ (☎0161/927 7000). City breaks in Vienna, Salzburg and Innsbruck.

Crystal Holidays, Crystal House, Arlington Rd, Surbiton, Surrey KT6 6BW (☎0181/399 5144). Impressive choice of winter and summer packages. Also available are city breaks in Vienna and two-centre holidays combining a few days in Salzburg with an Austrian (or Slovenian) alpine resort.

Danube Travel, 6 Conduit St, London W1R (☎0171/493 0263). City breaks in Vienna, as well as Vienna–Budapest–Prague combinations.

First Choice, First Choice House, Peel Cross Rd, Salford, Manchester M5 2AN (☎0990/557755). A wide range of summer destinations, including mountain village resorts in the Tyrol and lakeside resorts in the Salzkammergut.

Habsburg Heritage Cultural Tours, 158 Rosendale Rd, London SE21 (☎0181/761 0444). Highbrow cultural tours, including tailor-made visits to Eisenstadt for the Haydn Festival (September) or Feldkirch for the Schubert Festival (June), as well as Danube cruises (Regensburg–Vienna–Budapest).

Inghams, 10–18 Putney Hill, London SW15 (☎0181/780 4444). Big range of skiing and Lakes & Mountains holidays, concentrating on the Tyrol and Salzburger Land.

Made to Measure, 43 East St, Chichester, West Sussex (☎01243/533333). Luxury package-tour specialist.

Martin Randall Travel, 10 Barley Mow Passage, London W4 (☎0181/742 3355, fax 742 7766). Small-group cultural tours, led by experts on art, archeology or music. Tours include "Salzburg Festival", "Eisenstadt" and "Christmas in Vienna".

Most summer packages involve travelling to Austria by plane, although the holidays offered by **coach travel** specialists (notably Shearings and Wallace Arnold) are worth considering – the range of destinations on offer is essentially the same. Most of the coach-based packages include a (free) pick-up service from the area of the UK in which you live, but the subsequent journey across Europe can be gruelling: you may have to spend one night on the coach on both your outward and return journeys, though some options allow for overnight stops in hotels. An advantage of a coach-based package is that they tend to be slightly cheaper, with a nine-day peak-season trip, staying in Kitzbühel or a Salzkammergut resort, weighing in at around £380–420.

CITY BREAKS

Several tour operators offer **city breaks** in Vienna, Salzburg and Innsbruck. Most of these are simple flight-and-accommodation deals, with prices depending on the grade of hotel you choose (most companies offer a choice). Three nights' accommodation in a three-star hotel in Vienna, Salzburg or Innsbruck, plus return flights from London, can cost anything from £230 to £350 depending on the season. It's worth bearing in mind, too, that city breaks to Innsbruck and Salzburg often use Munich airport: your transfer from there to your hotel will be included in the price of the holiday, but it will add an extra couple of hours to your journey time. If you've more money to spend, it's worth checking agents specializing in **cultural or historical tours** (such as Martin Randall, Page & Moy and Habsburg Heritage) who arrange such extras as opera and theatre tickets, visits to music festivals, as well as flight and accommodation – for which, of course, you pay a hefty (if all-inclusive) price. **Cruises** along the River Danube – which include a few leisurely days in Austria, and take in neighbouring countries as well – are offered by a couple of operators, notably Peter Deilman and Habsburg Heritage.

Mondial Travel, 32 Links Rd, West Wycombe, BR4 0QW (☎0181/777 7000). Specialists in flights and accommodation for central and eastern Europe.

Page & Moy, 136–140 London Rd, Leicester LE2 1EN (☎0116/250 7979). Short breaks to Vienna including tickets to opera performances.

Peter Deilman River & Ocean Cruises, Suite 404, Albany House, 324/326 Regent St, London W1R 5AA (☎0171/436 2607). Danube cruises from Passau to the Black Sea, taking in Vienna and Budapest en route.

Ramblers Holidays, PO Box 43, Longcroft House, Frethern Rd, Welwyn Garden City, Hertfordshire AL8 6PQ (☎01707/320226). Long-established and reputable walking-holiday specialist offering organized trips to the Alps.

Shearings, Miry Lane, Wigan, Lancashire WN3 4AG (☎01942/824824). Coach holidays in spring and summer centred on Tyrolean and Salzkammergut resorts. Also walking tours in Upper Austria, and ten-day "Habsburg Cities" tours taking in Vienna, Prague and Budapest.

Sunworld, 71 Houghside Rd, Pudsey LS28 9BR (☎0870/601 0425). Lakes & Mountains holidays in the Salzkammergut and the Tyrol. Kitzbühel-based mountain-biking packages also on offer.

Tall Stories, 67a High St, Walton on Thames, Surrey KT12 1DJ (☎01932/252002). Summer-activities packages based in Zell am See, involving mountain biking, paragliding, canyoning and snowboarding on the Kitzsteinhorn Glacier.

Thomson, Greater London House, Hampstead Rd, London NW1 (☎0990/502565). Full range of skiing options, and probably the widest range of Lakes & Mountains-style packages. Also on offer are a seven-day Salzkammergut walking tour, a seven-day Danube Valley walking tour, and a seven-day Danube cruise between Passau and Vienna.

Time Off, Chester Close, Chester St, London SW1 7BQ (☎0171/235 8070). City breaks to Vienna, as well as Vienna–Budapest and Vienna–Prague combinations.

Travelscene, 11–15 St Ann's Rd, Harrow, Middlesex (☎0181/427 8800). City breaks to Vienna, Salzburg and Innsbruck.

Wallace Arnold, Gelderd Rd, Leeds LS12 6DH (☎0113/231 0739 or 0181/686 9833). Coach holidays in summer to Tyrolean and Salzkammergut resorts.

Waymark Holidays, 44 Windsor Rd, Slough SL1 2EJ (☎01753/516477). Walking holidays in the Tyrol and cross-country-skiing groups.

Worldwide Journeys/Eurocity Breaks, 243 Euston Rd, London NW1 (☎0171/388 0888). City breaks in Vienna and Salzburg.

BY TRAIN

Which train route you choose really depends on which part of Austria you're visiting. The most direct route from **London to Vienna** is from London's Victoria Station, via the Ramsgate–Ostend catamaran service to Brussels, then southeast through Germany via Köln and Nürnberg, entering Austria at Passau. At the moment, there's a direct train service from Ostend to Vienna from June to September (making it possible to leave London at 11am and arrive at Vienna's Westbahnhof at 9.30am the next morning), but in the winter months you must change at Brussels. The direct summer service may be discontinued, however, so check before you set out. Travelling Eurostar from London to Brussels allows you to head off nearly four hours later from London Waterloo, and still catch the same Brussels–Vienna service.

If you're aiming for **Salzburg** or **Innsbruck**, you'll probably follow the same route as above, before changing at Nürnberg or Munich. It's also possible to approach Innsbruck and **western Austria** through France and Switzerland (either Paris–Basel–Zürich, or Brussels–Strasbourg–Basel–Zürich). Changing trains in Paris can be time-consuming, although this route – for some reason – often works out cheaper than the others when buying standard tickets.

However you choose to travel, it will entail spending at least one night on the train. Although you can simply crash out on the seats, you won't get much sleep as the border guards and ticket inspectors wake you up at regular intervals. To travel in more comfort, it's best to book a **couchette** before you leave. Couchettes are mixed-sex and allow little privacy, but you do get the chance of an unbroken night and free rolls and coffee in the morning. For your very own compartment, you'll need to book a berth in a **sleeper**. Sleeper compartments are either two-berth or three-berth (the latter being slightly cheaper). If you're travelling alone,

---

however, you will not be required to share with passengers of the opposite sex.

TICKETS AND PASSES

Buying a rail ticket from the UK to anywhere in continental Europe can be complicated, with prices often depending on which day of the week, even which time of day, you begin your outward journey. The **standard rail ticket** from London to Vienna is a whopping £332 return, with an optional further £16 each way for a couchette. Tickets are available from London's Victoria Station and some travel agents, are valid for two months, and allow an unlimited number of stopovers en route. Provided you spend at least one weekend away, however, and commit yourself to travelling on a particular train (and cross-Channel ferry) on the first stage of your outward journey from London, the price shrinks to £275 return. Travelling to Innsbruck (assuming you spend at least one weekend away) costs £298 return if you go via Brussels and Munich; £260 via Brussels, Basel and Zürich; or £238 via Paris, Basel and Zürich.

Further reductions are sometimes available from Wasteels, who sell **discounted tickets** on the Ramsgate–Ostend route, bringing the price for a London–Vienna return down to around £200. Everyone is eligible for these discounts, when available, and there are no restrictions.

At the moment, it's actually not that expensive to travel via **Eurostar**, which goes from Waterloo International in London to the continent via Ashford (itself 1hr from London) in Kent and the Channel Tunnel. They currently offer a £59 London–Brussels return fare (journey time 3hr 15min), which, when added to the Brussels–Vienna return fare, gives a grand total of £286. You can book right up to the last minute, subject to availability: the only snag is that you must travel mid-week and book your return journey on Eurostar. Prices and frequencies do change regularly and should be checked; cheaper Apex fares are available if you book two weeks in advance.

If you're planning to travel extensively within Austria, or if you're visiting Austria as part of a more extensive trip round Europe, it may be worth buying an **InterRail Pass**. Passes are available from major train stations and some travel agents; the only restriction is that you must have been resident in Europe for at least six months. The pass entitles you to free travel on most European rail networks (including Austrian railways), as well as half-price discounts on British trains and on the Channel ferries, and discounts on the Eurostar service (see above). Inter-Rail Passes for the **under-26s** are divided into seven regional zones, and you can either buy a ticket for all of them (£279 for one month) or assemble a package of zones that suits you best. Austria (together with Germany and Switzerland) is in zone C, and to get there you'll need to pass through zone B (France, Belgium and Holland). A one-month pass valid for both these zones currently costs £224. The zonal system doesn't apply to those **aged 26 and over**, who can instead purchase an Inter-Rail 26+ Pass (£275 for one month), which is valid for most European countries, including Austria, but not France, Switzerland, Italy or Belgium – thereby making it impossible to travel from the UK to Austria without having to purchase a full-price ticket for at least part of the journey. A return ticket from one end of Belgium to the other can be bought in advance from the International Rail Centre at Victoria Station in London, and will cost around £70.

The **Eurodomino Freedom Pass** offers unlimited train travel within any one of 24 European countries, including Austria. The passes are available for any three, five or ten days' travel within a one-month period; prices vary depending on the country, but include most high-speed train supplements. You can buy as many separate country passes as you want. A three-day pass for Austria costs £73 (£55 for under-26s, £36.50 for under-15s); a five-day pass, £82 (£61 for under-26s, £41 for under-15s); and a ten-day pass, £146 (£112.50 for under-26s, £73 for under-15s).

Eurotrain, the youth rail specialist, offers discounted rail fares for under-26s on a variety of European routes. They also offer **Explorer Tickets**, which allow you to travel to a specified destination along one route, stopping off anywhere along the way, and to return on a different route.

Offers with stops in Austria include the "Venetian Explorer" (£219: London–Amsterdam–Cologne–Munich–Innsbruck–Verona–Venice–Milan–Lyon–Paris–London) and the "Eastern Explorer" (£256: London–Amsterdam–Hanover–Berlin–Prague–Budapest–Vienna–Salzburg–Switzerland–Basel–Luxembourg–Brussels–London).

The **Rail Europe Senior Card**, available to those over 60 at a cost of £5, gives a thirty percent discount on rail travel between – but not within – 25 European countries, and includes Eurostar and rail-connected sea crossings. However, before you can purchase this card, you must have a British Rail Senior Card (£18); both are valid for a year.

BY BUS

The only Austrian destination served by a regular **bus** service from the UK is **Vienna**. There's a direct service run by **Eurolines** from London's Victoria Coach Station at least three times a week (currently Mon, Fri & Sat). The bus sets off at around 10am, arriving in Wien-Mitte/Landstrasse roughly 22 hours later. Tickets currently cost £71 single and £109 return (£119 in July & Aug), with a fare of £64 single and £99 return (£109 in July & Aug) for those under 26. The tickets are valid for six months from the date of issue, but there are no stop-offs allowed on the journey. The trip is bearable (just about) and a bargain, but only really worth it if you absolutely can't find the extra cash for the flight or train. Definitely worth considering, however, is a **Euro Explorer** ticket, which allows you to travel on Eurolines services on a circuit comprising London–Budapest–Vienna–Bratislava–London for £126. These tickets are also valid for six months. Eurolines also offers a youth pass for Europe-wide travel, for either thirty (£199) or sixty days (£249), between sixteen European cities: London, Amsterdam, Berlin, Brussels, Budapest, Copenhagen, Florence, Frankfurt, Hamburg, Lyon, Milan, Munich, Paris, Prague, Rome and Vienna.

If you're heading for Salzburg or Innsbruck by bus, the only viable option is to take the **Eurolines** service to Munich (four times weekly), before picking up an onward rail or bus service to Austria from there. Those travelling to Austria west of Innsbruck should also consider the Eurolines service to Zürich (currently Wed & Fri), a good hub from which to pick up onward road and rail transport. Both London–Munich and London–Zürich fares are £94 return (£104 July & Aug), £84

> ### BUS INFORMATION
> **Eurobus**, PO Box 3026, Wokingham, Berkshire RG40 2YP (☎0118/936 2321, fax 936 2322).
>
> **Eurolines**, ticket office opposite Victoria Station at 52 Grosvenor Gardens, London SW1W 0AU (bookings and enquiries ☎0990/143219, Luton ☎01852/404511). Tickets can also be purchased from any National Express agent.

return (£94 July & Aug) for the under- 26s. In both cases you'll need to budget an extra £40–50 for a return rail or bus ticket to Austria.

A new hop-on, hop-off bus service, **Eurobus**, also with zone-pass ticketing, is being marketed towards backpackers (a 16–38 age range is suggested in the marketing literature). Continental Europe is divided into three zones: Austria (Vienna and Salzburg) is included in the Northern Zone, along with Paris, Reims, Brussels, Amsterdam, Berlin, Prague, Munich and Basel. Ticket passes have different rates for under-26s and for those over 26: each separate zone is £119/£129, while any two zones are £199/£229, and all zones are £269/£299. The pass is valid for four months from the first day of travel; routes are circular, going in one direction only and departures are daily. An extra London–Paris ticket has to be bought for a one-zone pass (£28) or a two-zone one (£14), but is included in the all-zone pass.

BY CAR

Though with two or more passengers it can work out relatively inexpensive, **driving to Austria** is not the most relaxing option – unless you enjoy pounding along the motorway systems of Europe for the best part of a day and a night.

> ### CROSS-CHANNEL INFORMATION
> **Holyman Sally Ferries** (reservations ☎0990/595522). Fast catamarans from Ramsgate to Dunkerque and Ostend.
>
> **Hoverspeed** (reservations ☎0990/240241). Dover to Calais; Folkestone to Boulogne.
>
> **Le Shuttle**, Customer Services Centre (☎0990/353535). Folkestone–Calais by train through the Tunnel.
>
> **P&O European Ferries** (reservations ☎0990/980980). Dover–Calais.
>
> **Stena Line** (☎0990/707070). Dover–Calais.

The quickest way of taking your car over to the continent is to drive to the **Channel Tunnel**, near Folkestone, where **Le Shuttle** operates a 24-hour service carrying cars, motorcycles, buses and their passengers to Coquelles, near Calais. At peak times, services run every fifteen minutes, and the journey lasts about 35 minutes. It is possible to turn up unannounced and buy your ticket at the toll booths (after exiting the M20 at junction 11a). Rates depend on the time of year, time of day and length of stay (the cheapest ticket is for a day-trip, followed by a five-day return); it's cheaper to travel between 10pm and 6am, while the highest fares are reserved for weekend departures and returns in July and August. As an example, a five-day trip at an off-peak time starts at £89 (passengers included) in the low season and goes up to £129 in the peak period. Frequencies may change and prices, of course, must be checked each time.

The alternative cross-Channel options for most travellers are the conventional **ferry and hovercraft** links between Dover and Calais or Boulogne, and Ramsgate and Dunkerque or Ostend. Fares vary enormously with the time of year, month and even day that you travel, and the size of your car. If you book in advance, the cheapest standard fare on the Dover–Calais run, for example, can be as little as £100 return for a carload (including passengers). However, turn up without a booking on an August weekend and you'll pay more than twice that.

Once you've made it onto the continent, you've got something in the region of 1200km of driving ahead of you. Theoretically, you could make it in ten hours, but realistically it will take at least sixteen hours of solid driving. If you're heading for Salzburg, central Austria, eastern Austria and Vienna, the most direct route from Ostend or Calais is via Brussels, Köln, Frankfurt and Nürnberg. For Innsbruck and the Tyrol, Brussels–Köln–Stuttgart probably represents the fastest route. It costs nothing to drive on motorways in Belgium and Germany, but Austria itself has recently introduced charges for travelling on an auto-bahn. All cars using the Austrian autobahn must display a sticker or *Vignette* (available at border crossings and petrol stations); the cheapest version is valid for ten days and costs öS70 (£3.50– 4).

If you're travelling by car, you'll need proof of ownership, or a letter from the owner giving you permission to drive the car. A British or other EU driving licence is fine; all other drivers must hold an International Driving Licence. You also need a red warning triangle in case you break down, a first-aid kit (both these are compulsory in Austria), and a "Green Card" for third-party insurance cover at the very least. An even better idea is to sign up with one of the national motoring organizations like the AA or the RAC, who offer continental breakdown assistance for an additional fee, and in extreme circumstances will get you and your vehicle brought back home if necessary.

FLIGHTS FROM IRELAND

There are **direct flights** from Dublin to Vienna operated by Tyrolean Airlines (booked through Swissair in Dublin) twice a week, currently Mondays and Thursdays. Fares start at around IR£240, peaking at IR£270 in summer. Low-cost flight agents such as Joe Walsh Tours and USIT can offer **non-direct flights** from Dublin to Vienna with other carriers (such as British Airways via London, Air France via Paris, or Aer Lingus/Lauda Air via Manchester) , with prices hovering around the IR£230 mark.

Ther are no direct flights to Austria from Belfast, although a number of non-direct options are available. British Airways offer a Belfast–Vienna fare of IR£280 return travelling via Heathrow, and flight agents can often come up with cheaper options (for example, flying with KLM via Amsterdam) for around £240.

All the above prices are for economy tickets, which are usually non-changeable, non-refundable, and assume you're prepared to travel midweek and stay a Saturday night. Note that airport tax will add an extra IR£10–20 onto all prices quoted.

AIRLINES IN IRELAND

Aer Lingus, Northern Ireland reservations ☎0645/737747; 40–41 O'Connell St, Dublin 1; 13 St Stephen's Green, Dublin 2; 12 Upper St George's St, Dun Laoghaire (centralized reservations at Dublin airport ☎01/705 3333); 2 Academy St, Cork (☎021/327155); 136 O'Connell St, Limerick (☎061/474239); Minicom/Text telephone ☎01/705 3994.

British Airways, 1 Fountain Centre, College St, Belfast BT1 6ET (reservations ☎0345/222111, bookings and travel agency services ☎0345/326566). BA doesn't have a Dublin office; Aer Lingus acts as their agents (reservations ☎1-800/626747).

TRAVEL AGENTS AND TOUR OPERATORS IN IRELAND

Joe Walsh Tours, 69 Upper O'Connell St, Dublin 2 (☎01/872 2555); 8–11 Baggot St, Dublin 2 (☎01/676 3053); 117 St Patrick St, Cork (☎021/277 959). General budget-fares agent.

Neenan Travel, 12 South Leinster St, Dublin 2 (☎01/676 5181). European city breaks.

Student & Group Travel, First Floor, 71 Dame St, Dublin 2 (☎01/677 7834). Student and group specialists.

Thomas Cook, 11 Donegall Place, Belfast (☎01232/242341); 118 Grafton St, Dublin 2 (☎01/677 1721). Package-holiday and flight agent, with occasional discount offers.

Travel Shop, 35 Belmont Rd, Belfast 4 (☎01232/471717). General discount agent.

USIT, Fountain Centre, College St, Belfast BT1 6ET (☎01232/324073); 10–11 Market Parade, Patrick St, Cork (☎021/270900); 33 Ferryquay St, Derry (☎01504/371888); 19 Aston Quay, Dublin 2 (☎01/602 1600 or 679 8833); Victoria Place, Eyre Square, Galway (☎091/565177); Central Buildings, O'Connell St, Limerick (☎061/415064); 36–37 George's St, Waterford (☎051/872601). Student and youth specialists for flights and trains.

GETTING THERE FROM NORTH AMERICA

Austrian Airlines and Delta fly direct to Vienna from the US, and many other airlines have flights to Vienna via other major European cities. A direct flight from the east coast of the States takes nine hours. Another option is to buy a cheap flight to London or Frankfurt and make your way overland from there (see p.3 for details of getting to Vienna from Britain and Ireland).

Though in the account that follows we've quoted fares that are offered direct from the airlines, it's always worth contacting **discount travel agents** or **consolidators,** who buy up blocks of tickets from the airlines and sell them at a discount, to see about cheaper flight options.

The **high season** for travel is summer (for most airlines and tour operators June through to mid-September), and the weeks around Christmas and New Year, when fares are roughly $1000. **Low season**, when tickets can be as much as $400 cheaper, is generally from the beginning of November to mid-March (excluding Christmas and New Year, when prices are again hiked up and seats are at a premium). **The shoulder season**, which sees a rise in cost from low season by about $150, runs from mid-March to the end of May and from mid-September to the end of October.

FLIGHTS FROM THE USA

Barring special offers (advertised in newspapers and often with only a small window of time in which to make your bookings), the cheapest options available from the airlines are **Apex fares**. These generally need to be bought – and paid for – 21 days in advance and entail certain restrictions as to length of stay, such as a seven-night minimum and a three-month maximum. There are also winter **Super Apex** tickets, sometimes known as "Eurosavers", which are slightly cheaper than an ordinary Apex, but limit your stay to between seven and 21 days. Some airlines also issue **Special Apex** tickets to people younger than 24, often extending the maximum stay to a year. Many airlines offer youth or student fares to **under-26s**; a passport or driving licence are sufficient proof of age, though these tickets are subject to availability and can have eccentric booking conditions. It's worth remembering that most cheap return fares involve spending at least one Saturday night away and that many will only give a percentage refund if you need to cancel or alter your journey, so make sure you check the restrictions carefully before buying a ticket.

You can normally cut costs further by going through a **specialist flight agent** – either a **consolidator**, who buys up blocks of tickets from the airlines and sells them at a discount, or a **discount agent**, who in addition to dealing with discounted flights may also offer special student and youth fares and a range of other travel-related services such as travel insurance, rail passes, car rentals,

NORTH AMERICAN TOLL-FREE AIRLINE ENQUIRIES

Air Canada US: ☎1-800/776 3000; Canada: ☎1-800/555 1212.

Air France US: ☎1-800/237 2747; Canada: ☎1-800/667 2747.

Alitalia US: ☎1-800/223 5730; Canada: ☎1-800/361 8336.

Austrian Airlines US & Canada: ☎1-800/843 0002.

British Airways US: ☎1-800/247 9297; Canada: ☎1-800/668 1059.

Canadian Airlines US: ☎1-800/426 7000; Canada: ☎1-800/665 1177.

Czech Airlines US: ☎1-800/223 2365.

Delta Airlines US & Canada: ☎1-800/241 4141.

KLM US: ☎1-800/374 7747; Canada: ☎1-800/361 5073.

Lauda Air US & Canada: ☎1-800/645 3880.

Lufthansa US & Canada: ☎1-800/645 3880.

SwissAir US: ☎1-800/221 4750; Canada: ☎1-800/267 9477.

DISCOUNT AGENTS, CONSOLIDATORS AND TRAVEL CLUBS IN THE US AND CANADA

Council Travel, Head Office, 205 E 42nd St, New York, NY 10017 (☎1-800/226 8624, 888/COUNCIL or 212/822 2700). Other offices include: 530 Bush St, Suite 700, San Francisco, CA 94108 (☎415/421 3473); 10904 Lindbrook Drive, Los Angeles 90024 (☎310/208 3551); 1138 13th St, Boulder, CO 80302 (☎303/447 8101); 3300 M St NW, 2nd Floor, Washington, DC 20007 (☎202/337-6464); 1153 N Dearborn St, Chicago, IL 60610 (☎312/951 0585); 273 Newbury St, Boston, MA 02116 (☎617/266 1926). Nationwide US organization that mostly, but by no means exclusively, specializes in student/budget travel.

New Frontiers/Nouvelles Frontières, 12 E 33rd St, New York, NY 10016 (☎1-800/366 6387 or 212/779 0600); 1001 Sherbrook E, Suite 720, Montréal, PQ H2L 1L3 (☎514/526 8444). French discount-travel firm. Other branches in LA, San Francisco and Québec City.

STA Travel, 10 Downing St, New York, NY 10014 (☎1-800/781 4040 or 212/627 3111); 7202 Melrose Ave, Los Angeles, CA 90046 (☎213/934 8722); 51 Grant Ave, San Francisco, CA 94108 (☎415/391 8407); 297 Newbury St, Boston, MA 02115 (☎617/266 6014); 429 S Dearborn St, Chicago, IL 60605 (☎312/786 9050); 3730 Walnut St, Philadelphia, PA 19104 (☎215/382 2928); 317 14th Ave SE, Minneapolis, MN 55414 (☎612/615 1800), are just some branches. Worldwide specialists in independent travel; also student IDs, travel insurance, car rental, rail passes, etc.

Travac, 989 6th Ave, New York NY 10018 (☎1-800/872 8800). Consolidator and charter broker, with another office in Orlando.

Travel Avenue, 10 S Riverside, Suite 1404, Chicago, IL 60606 (☎1-800/333 3335). Full-service travel agent that offers discounts in the form of rebates.

Travel Cuts, 187 College St, Toronto, ON M5T 1P7 (☎1-800/667 2887 or 888/238 2887; from US 416/979 2406); 180 MacEwan Student Centre, University of Calgary, Calgary, AB T2N 1N4 (☎403/282 7687); 12304 Jasper Ave, Edmonton, AB T5N 3K5 (☎403/488 8487); 1613 rue St Denis, Montréal, PQ H2X 3K3 (☎514/843 8511); 555 W 8th Ave, Vancouver, BC V5Z 1C6 (☎888/ FLY CUTS or 604/822 6890); University Centre, University of Manitoba, Winnipeg, MB R3T 2N2 (☎204/269 9530), etc. Canadian student-travel organization.

Unitravel, 11737 Administration Blvd, Suite 120, St Louis, MO 63146 (☎1-800/325 2222). Consolidator.

tours and the like. Bear in mind, though, that penalties for changing your plans can be stiff. Remember too that these companies make their money by dealing in bulk – don't expect them to answer lots of questions. Some agents specialize in **charter flights**, which may be cheaper than anything available on a scheduled flight, but again departure dates are fixed and withdrawal penalties are high (check the refund policy). If you travel a lot, **discount travel clubs** are another option – the annual membership fee may be worth it for benefits such as cut-price air tickets and car rental.

Don't automatically assume that tickets purchased through a travel specialist will be cheapest – once you get a quote, check with the airlines and you may turn up an even better deal. Be advised also that the pool of travel companies is swimming with sharks – exercise caution and *never* deal with a company that demands cash up front or refuses to accept payment by credit card.

Prices quoted below assume midweek travel (count on $50–60 extra at weekends), exclude taxes and are subject to change. Austrian Airlines offers the most extensive service, with **non-stop daily flights** from New York and Atlanta to Vienna, and direct service from Washington DC and Chicago via New York or Atlanta. From Vienna, you can fly onwards to Graz, Innsbruck, Klagenfurt, Linz or Salzburg at no extra cost. At the time of writing, their midweek Apex round-trip fares from New York range from $651 to $1042, depending on season; from Chicago, $751 to $1142; from Atlanta, $731 to $1122; from Washington DC, $703 to $1102; and from LA (with the first leg of the journey with Delta, the second with Austrian Airlines), $891 to $1282. But be on the lookout for any special offers. You might be able to find an Austrian Airlines round-trip fare from New York for as little as $385. Delta flies non-stop from New York or Atlanta to Vienna for the same fare as Austrian Airlines. Lauda Air flies four times weekly from Miami to Vienna via Munich, starting at $751 (low season) up to $1142 (high season).

Numerous European-based airlines – Lufthansa, KLM, Swissair, British Airways, CSA/Czechoslovak Airlines, Air France and Alitalia – fly from major US cities to Vienna with stop-offs at their gateway cities (Frankfurt, Amsterdam, Zurich, London, Prague, Paris and Rome, respectively).

The airlines are fiercely competitive, however, and you're not likely to find any difference between their fares and those of Austrian Airlines quoted above.

Another option, especially for hikers or skiers heading to western provinces, like the Tyrol (Innsbruck) or Vorarlberg (Bregenz and the Bodensee, the Bregenzerwald), is to take a round-trip flight to **Munich** and make your own way from there. Regular Apex fares to Munich are only in the region of $50–70 cheaper than those to the nearest Austrian city, but you might catch one of Lufthansa's limited special offers and get a midweek round-trip ticket from New York to Munich for as little as $298.

FLIGHTS FROM CANADA

Though there are **no direct flights** from Canada to Austria, there are many competitively priced one-stop options. Flights take about eleven hours from Montréal, twelve from Toronto and fourteen from Vancouver. The best deals are usually on European carriers such as Air France, Lufthansa, KLM or Swissair, which fly from major Canadian cities to **Vienna** via Paris, Frankfurt, Amsterdam and Zurich respectively. At the time of writing, KLM offer the best value, with a special low-season fare of CDN$775 (from Toronto or Montréal) or CDN$1040 (from Vancouver). In peak season, however, you'll pay around CDN$1430 (from Toronto/Montréal) or $1810 (from Vancouver). Alternatively, you can fly from Toronto on Air Canada or Canadian Airlines for around CDN$1050 (low season) or CDN$1480 (high season), but you will have to switch planes and carriers in a European city, most likely London, Frankfurt or Zurich.

PACKAGE TOURS AND CITY BREAKS

It may be worth your while checking deals with **specialist agents**. Though specialist tours often don't include air fares, they do map your itinerary and activities, fix you up with experienced guides, and – essential if you're planning your trip around any of Austria's major music festivals – organize the purchase of opera and symphony tickets and the like.

Although we've given phone numbers of specialist operators (see box opposite), you're better off making tour reservations through your local travel agent. An agent will make all the phone calls, sort out the snafus and arrange flights and insurance – all at no extra cost to you.

RAIL AND BUS PASSES

If you're planning on doing a decent amount of travelling in Europe, you may want to look into getting a **train pass** to get you into Austria. A regular **Eurail Pass** can span from fifteen days (the

two fares available are $376 for under-26s/$538 for "first class" or over-26s) to three months ($1059/$1512). This covers seventeen countries: Austria, Belgium, Denmark, Finland, France, Germany, Greece, Hungary, Ireland (Republic), Italy, Luxembourg, Netherlands, Norway, Portugal,

NORTH AMERICAN SPECIALIST TOUR OPERATORS

All prices quoted below exclude taxes and are subject to change. Where applicable, round-trip flights are from New York and accommodation is based on single person/double occupancy.

Adventures on Skis (☎1-800/628 9655 or 413/568 2855). Customized tours and set packages to all the major ski resorts; seven nights in Innsbruck $849–1179 (land/air).

American-International Homestays, Inc (☎1-800/876 2048 or 303/642 3088). B&B accommodation with English-speaking families in Vienna, Salzburg or Innsbruck from $59 (single) or $89 (double) per night.

Cross Culture (☎413/256 6303). Offers back-to-back, nine-day "Viennese Waltzes" ($2650) and "Mozart's Salzburg" ($2700) tours. Total sixteen-day land/air cost, including concert/opera tickets, is $4480. Also hiking and biking tours.

Delta Vacations (☎1-800/872 7786). Fly-drives and city breaks to Vienna, Salzburg and Innsbruck.

Elderhostel (☎1-617/426 8056). Specialists in educational and activity programmes, cruises and homestays for senior travellers (companions may be younger). Offer courses in Vienna and Salzburg, as well as a Danube study cruise, all under the auspices of UNESCO. Also a cycling tour along the Danube.

Eastern Europe Tours (☎1-800/641 3456 or 206/448 8400). Most of their organized tours take in other countries as well as Austria, but they do offer a three-night city package to Vienna starting around $300 (land only) and an eight-day "Panorama of Austria" tour, which takes in Vienna, Graz, Klagenfurt, Innsbruck and Salzburg, and costs from $1905 (land/air).

European Travel Services formerly Lotus Travel. (☎1-800/675-0559; 714/850-9876) Customized tour operator specializing in central and eastern Europe. Discounted flights, accommodation (standard hotel rates under $100 per night), concert tickets, bike trips, etc.

Europe Train Tours (☎1-800/551 2085 or 914/698 9426). Bus tours of Austria, as well as packages centred around Vienna and Salzburg. Their speciality is customized tours.

Fugazy International (☎1-800/828 4488). Group tours that include Vienna, or personalized packages to Vienna, with guided tours. The fifteen-day Vienna/Hungary tour is $3000, based on double occupancy, all-inclusive.

Great Composer Tours (☎1-800/228 SONG). Beethoven and Schubert "pilgrimages", at $4200 for ten days, including sightseeing trips, museum tours, accommodation and meals, but not air fare.

Herzerl Tours (☎1-800/684 8488). Food, wine, spas and music are the focus of some of the many cultural tours on offer. A week-long Viennese cooking tour (including air fare, accommodation, classes, some meals, concert tickets and various other sundries) is $2375; an Austrian wine tour covers more of the country and costs $2450 for seven days.

Holiday Tours Ltd (☎1-800/234 2895). Art, architecture, arts and crafts, cooking, horticulture, gay/lesbian and other special-interest excursions in Austria. Nine-day Schubert tour is $1800; Viennese cooking tours go for $2200 (land/air).

Holidaze Ski Tours (☎1-800/526 2827 or 732/280 1120). Several ski packages, including seven-night "Salzburg Ski Safari" from $785 (land/air).

International Gay Travel Association (☎1-800/448 8550). Trade group that will provide lists of gay-owned or gay-friendly travel agents, accommodation and other travel businesses.

Smolka Tours (☎1-800/722 0057 or 732/576 8813). Specialists in Austrian group or fully independent travel, including cultural, hiking and biking itineraries, visits to the Salzburg Easter and summer music festivals, music packages and opera tours. Four-day River Danube cruises from $520; farmstays in the Salzburger Land from $30 a night.

Van Gogh Tours (☎1-800/435 6192 or 781/721-0850). Nine-day guided bicycle tour called "The Trail of Mozart", through Vienna and Salzburg, at $1250 for bike rentals, meals, and accommodation in three- and four-star hotels.

Spain, Sweden and Switzerland. Probably the best value for your money is the **Flexipass**, which gives you any ten days ($444/$634) or fifteen days ($585/$836) of train travel over a two-month period in any of the seventeen Eurail Pass countries. Also available are the **Austrian Railpass**, which grants any three days' unlimited train travel in a fifteen-day period ($98/$145) with up to five extra days at $15/$21 a day; and the **European East Pass**, for any five days in one month ($195) in Austria, Czech Republic, Hungary, Poland and Slovakia with the option of a maximum of five extra days at $21 a day.

Eurobus Passes are another worthwhile option (see p.9). They're available from STA Travel

RAIL CONTACTS IN NORTH AMERICA
CIT Tours, 9501 W Devon Ave, Suite 502, Rosemont, IL 60018 (☎1-800/223 7987).
Rail Europe, 226 Westchester Ave, White Plains, NY 10604 (US: ☎1-800/438 7245; Canada: ☎1-800/361 7245).
ScanTours, 3439 Wade St, Los Angeles, CA 90066 (☎1-800/223 7226 or 310/636-4656).

and are valid for four months. The rates for under-26s are: $210 (zone 1), $350 (two zones), $470 (all three zones). For over-26s, the rates rise to $225 (zone 1), $400 (two zones) and $525 (three zones).

GETTING THERE FROM AUSTRALIA AND NEW ZEALAND

BY PLANE

There's a good selection of airlines that can get you to Austria from Australia and New Zealand, but the only direct flights are with Lauda Air from Sydney to Vienna – all other airlines include either a transfer or stopover in the carrier's home city. Given the high cost of flights in general from Australasia, however, a "Round the World" fare is a good option. Destinations in western Austria are also served by flights to Munich, from where you can continue your journey by land. Several rail and bus passes can be bought before you leave should you intend to expand your trip into Europe.

Air fares are seasonal, with low season from mid-January to the end of February and October to the end of November; high season is mid-May to the end of August, and December to mid-January. There is no price variation during the week. Flying time is long – between twenty and thirty hours – and can be physically and mentally taxing, so you may want to consider a **stopover**.

Tickets purchased direct from the airlines tend to be expensive – travel agents offer better deals and have the latest information on limited special offers, such as free stopovers and fly-drive/accommodation packages. Flight Centres and STA (which offer fare reductions for ISIC card-holders and under-26s) generally offer the lowest fares. Flights to Europe are generally cheaper via Asia than the USA.

Most airlines have a set fare ("common rated") from major eastern Australian cities, while from Perth and Darwin you'll pay between A$100 and A$200 less via Asia, or A$200–400 more via Canada and the US. Fares from Christchurch and Wellington are between NZ$150 and NZ$300 more than from Auckland.

From Australia, Lauda Air team up with Ansett to provide a connecting service from state capitals via Sydney to Vienna for around A$1899–2299. In addition, several airlines can take you to Vienna or Munich via a transfer in their Asian hub-cities; Air France, Swissair–Ansett,

Thai Airways, Cathay Pacific, Alitalia, Malaysia Airlines and Singapore Airlines all offer reasonable deals, for around A$1999–A$2399

From New Zealand, Lauda Air, in conjunction with Air New Zealand, have a good through-service to Vienna from Auckland, Christchurch and Wellington for about NZ$2299–2799. Good deals on flights to either Vienna or Munich are also offered by Malaysia Airlines, Alitalia, Thai Airways, Cathay Pacific and Singapore Airlines, via their Asian hubs, for around NZ$2399–2799. Alternatively, United Airlines fly to Vienna or Munich via LA from Auckland starting at NZ$2599.

If you want to fly to another European gateway and then travel overland to Austria, you'll find

---

AIRLINES IN AUSTRALIA AND NEW ZEALAND

Air France Australia ☎02/9321 1000; NZ ☎09/303 3521. Daily flights via Paris from major Australasian cities (code-share with Qantas).

Alitalia Australia ☎02/9247 1308; NZ ☎09/379 4457. Three flights per week to Vienna and Munich via Bangkok and a transfer in Rome from major Australasian cities (code-share with Qantas and Cathay Pacific).

Britannia Airways Australia ☎02/9251 1299. Several flights per month to London during their charter season, via Bangkok and Abu Dhabi from Sydney, Brisbane, Cairns and Auckland.

Garuda Australia ☎1800/800873; NZ ☎09/366 1855. Three flights a week to London, Amsterdam and Frankfurt with a transfer/stopover in Jakarta/Denpasar, from major Australasian cities.

KLM Australia ☎02/9231 6333 or 1800/505747. Two flights a week each to Vienna, Innsbruck, Munich and Zurich, via Amsterdam–Singapore from Sydney and via either Sydney–Singapore–Amsterdam or LA–Amsterdam from Auckland.

Lauda Air Australia ☎02/9251 6155; NZ (Lufthansa) ☎09/303 1529. Three flights a week to Vienna via Sydney from major Australasian cities with onward connections to Innsbruck and Graz (code-share with Ansett and Air New Zealand).

Malaysia Airlines Australia ☎13 2627; NZ ☎09/373 2741. Twice-weekly flights to Vienna and Munich, with a transfer or stopover in Kuala Lumpur, from major Australasian cities.

Singapore Airlines Australia ☎13 1011; NZ ☎09/379 3209. Several flights a week to Vienna and Munich, with a transfer in Singapore, from major Australasian cities.

Swissair Australia ☎02/9232 1744; NZ ☎09/358 3925. Several flights a week to Zurich from major Australasian cities, with onward connections to Innsbruck, Munich and Vienna.

Thai Airways Australia ☎13 1960; NZ ☎09/377 3886. Several flights a week to Munich from Sydney, Brisbane, Cairns, Melbourne, Perth and Auckland.

United Airlines Australia ☎13 1777; NZ ☎09/379 3800. Several flights a week to Vienna or Munich from Sydney and Auckland via LA.

DISCOUNT TRAVEL AGENTS

Anywhere Travel, 345 Anzac Parade, Kingsford, Sydney (☎02/9663 0411).

Brisbane Discount Travel, 260 Queen St, Brisbane (☎07/3229 9211).

Budget Travel, 16 Fort St, Auckland, plus branches around the city (☎09/366 0061 or 0800/808040).

Destinations Unlimited, 3 Milford Rd, Auckland (☎09/373 4033).

Flight Centres Australia: 82 Elizabeth St, Sydney, plus branches nationwide (☎13 1600); NZ: 205 Queen St, Auckland (☎09/309 6171), plus branches nationwide.

Northern Gateway, 22 Cavenagh St, Darwin (☎08/8941 1394).

STA Travel Australia: 702 Harris St, Ultimo, Sydney; 256 Flinders St, Melbourne; other offices in state capitals and major universities (nearest branch ☎131776; fastfare telesales ☎1300/360960). NZ: 10 High St, Auckland (☎09/309 0458; fastfare telesales ☎09/366 6673), plus branches in Wellington, Christchurch, Dunedin, Palmerston North, Hamilton and at major universities.

Thomas Cook Australia: 175 Pitt St, Sydney; 257 Collins St, Melbourne; plus branches in other state capitals (local branch ☎131771; telesales ☎1800/063913); NZ: 96 Anzac Ave, Auckland (☎09/379 3920).

Tymtro Travel, Level 8, 130 Pitt St, Sydney (☎02/9223 2211 or 1300/652969).

lowest fares are with Britannia Airways to London and Amsterdam during their limited charter season (Nov–March) from A$1290/NZ$1799 to A$1799/NZ$2050; or with Philippine Airlines via Manila, and Garuda via either Jakarta or Denpasar, to Frankfurt from A$1500/NZ$1899 to A$1900/NZ$2400.

There are a number of **Round the World** (RTW) fares that include Vienna or Munich, offering a range of stopovers. The cheapest is with Qantas/Air France, allowing four stops in each direction for around A$1599/NZ$1999. Offering greater flexibility are Cathay Pacific/United's "Globetrotter" for A$2349/NZ$2999 to A$2899/NZ$3449 and British Airways/Qantas' "Global Explorer" for A$2499/NZ$2399 to A$3099/NZ$2999; both allow six free stopovers, with the option of additional stopovers for A$100/NZ$110. Thai Airways, in conjunction with Cathay Pacific, Air New Zealand and Varig Brazilian, offer unlimited stop-overs – except within the USA and Canada – for a flat rate of A$3199/NZ$3200. All fares are valid for one year.

SPECIALIST TOURS

If you're interested in Austrian art and architecture, music, or activities like skiing or hiking, and prefer to have all the arrangements made for you before you leave, then seeking the help of a **specialist agent** is a good way to plan your trip. Unfortunately, there are few pre-packaged tours that include airfares from Australasia, but most specialist agents will be able to assist with flight arrangements as well. In turn, many of the tours we've listed (see box below) can also be arranged through your local travel agent.

SPECIALIST AGENTS

Adventure World Australia: 73 Walker St, North Sydney (☎02/9956 7766 or 1800/221931), plus branches in Brisbane and Perth; NZ: 101 Great South Rd, Remuera, Auckland (☎09/524 5118). Offer Vienna city packages from A$280 (twin share) including accommodation, city tour and concert tickets; day tours from Vienna to Salzburg from A$189 and the Vienna Woods from $69; also agents for Lauda Air and an array of international adventure companies that offer trips to Austria.

Australians Studying Abroad, 1st Floor, 970 Armadale, Victoria (☎03/9509 1955 or 1800 645 755). Twenty-day all-inclusive tour delving into the art and culture of Vienna, Prague and Budapest for around A$4500 (land only).

CIT, 263 Clarence St, Sydney (☎02/9267 1255), plus offices in Melbourne, Brisbane, Adelaide and Perth. Hotel and tour packages, including round-trip coach tours from Vienna via Graz, Franz-Josefs-Hohe, Salzburg and Melk, for A$950 (twin share).

Danube Travel, 106 Chapel St, St Kilda, Melbourne (☎03/9525 4733). Have an extensive range of tours and accommodation throughout Austria, from budget to first class, including Danube cruises from A$100 and hydrofoil trips from Vienna to Budapest for A$135.

European Travel Office,122 Rosslyn St, West Melbourne (☎03/3329 8844); 133 Castlereagh St, Sydney (☎02/9267 7727); 407 Great South Rd, Auckland (☎09/525 3074). Two-night accommodation and concert packages from A$280 (twin share), half-day Vienna city tours from A$60 and day boat trips on the Danube from A$150.

Peregrine Adventures, 258 Lonsdale St, Melbourne (☎03/9663 8611), plus offices in Brisbane, Sydney, Adelaide and Perth. Seven- and eight-day walking and cycling holidays following the Inn and Danube rivers, from A$1095 (twin share; land only).

Snow Bookings Only, 1141 Toorak Rd, Camberwell, Melbourne (☎1800/623266). Accommodation packages from A$535 for seven nights; ski hire and passes extra.

Travel Plan, 72 Chandos St, St Leonards, Sydney (☎02/9438 1333). All-inclusive skiing holidays in the Arlberg, Zell am See and Salzburger Land. Accommodation packages from A$550 (twin share; ski hire and passes extra).

The Ski Travel Company, 21 Sydney Rd, Manly NSW (☎02/9977 7677 or 1800/251934). Customized ski holidays in St Anton, Lech, Kitzbühel and surroundings.

Walkabout Gourmet Adventures, PO Box 52, Dinner Plain, Melbourne (☎03/5159 5556). Leisurely, food-and-wine-focused walking tours through Bavaria, the Austrian Alps and the Dolomites.

RAIL AND BUS PASSES

If you're planning to visit Austria as part of a wider European trip, it's worth looking into the variety of **rail and bus passes**, many of which have to be bought in your home country before you leave. If you don't want to spend time in any one place, **Eurail** and **Eurail Youth Passes** allow unlimited travel through seventeen countries. A Youth Pass costs A$510/NZ$600 for fifteen consecutive days, A$665/NZ$876 for 21 days, A$825/NZ$932 for one month, A$1165/NZ$1259 for two months, and A$1440/NZ$1575 for three months; if you're 26 or over, you'll have to buy a first-class pass, which costs A$730/NZ$870 for fifteen days, A$950/NZ$1125 for 21 days, A$1170/NZ$1380 for one month, A$1665/ NZ$1885 for two months, and A$2050/NZ$2255 for three months. A more flexible alternative, allowing for extended stop-offs along the way, is the Eurail **Flexipass**, valid for travel on non-consecutive days within a two-month period at a cost of A$605/A$860 or NZ$715/NZ$1020 (youth/first class, or under-26/over-26, rates) for ten days, and A$790/A$1140 or NZ$935/1345 for fifteen days. A scaled-down version of the Flexipass, the **Europass** allows travel in France, Germany, Italy, Spain and Switzerland for (youth/first class) A$295/A$440 or NZ$350/NZ$525 for five days in two months, on up to A$700/A$1030 or NZ$830/NZ$1220 for fifteen days in two months; there's the option of adding adjacent, "associate", countries (Austria, Hungary, Benelux, Portugal and Greece) for approximately A$50/NZ$60 (the cost shrinks with the number of associate countries added). If you just want to explore Austria on its own, the **Austrian Railpass** allows for unlimited travel for four days in ten for (youth/adult) A$210/A$280. Also available are **Eurobus Passes**, which cost around (youth/adult) A$200/A$260 for two weeks, A$280/A$370 for one month and A$370/A$500 for two months.

All of the above passes can be obtained from **CIT** (see box, p.17), **Flight Centres** (see box, p.16) or from **Thomas Cook World Rail** (Australia: ☎1800/422747; NZ: ☎09/263 7260).

RED TAPE AND VISAS

Citizens of EU countries (and of Iceland, Norway and Switzerland) need only a valid national identity card to enter Austria. Since Britain has no identity card, however, British citizens do have to take a passport. EU citizens can stay for as long as they want, but if they're planning on staying permanently they should register with the local police. Citizens of the US, Canada, New Zealand and Australia require a passport, but no visa, and can stay up to three months.

Visa requirements do change, however, and it is always advisable to check the current situation before leaving home. A list of Austrian embassies abroad is given below; addresses of foreign embassies and consulates in Vienna and other major cities are given in this guide.

CUSTOMS

Customs and duty-free restrictions vary throughout Europe, with subtle differences even within the European Union. British and Irish travellers returning home directly from another EU country do not have to make a declaration to customs at their place of entry. In other words, British and Irish citizens can effectively take back as much **duty-paid** wine or beer as they can carry (the legal limits being 90 litres of wine or 110 of beer).

However, there are still restrictions on the volume of tax- or **duty-free** goods you can bring in or take out of the country. In general, **residents of EU countries** travelling to other EU states are permitted a duty-free allowance of 200 cigarettes, one litre of spirits and five litres of wine; for **non-EU residents**, the allowances are usually 200 cigarettes, one litre of spirits and 2.25 litres of wine.

Residents of the US and Canada can take up to 200 cigarettes and one litre of alcohol back home, as can **Australian** citizens, while **New Zealanders** must confine themselves to 200 cigarettes, 4.5 litres of beer or wine, and one litre of spirits. Again, if in doubt consult the relevant – or your own – embassy.

HEALTH AND INSURANCE

No specific inoculations or health precautions are necessary for a trip to Austria. Minor complaints can be dealt with at any pharmacy (*Apotheke*); pharmacy hours are usually Monday to Friday 8am to 5pm (sometimes with a break for lunch) and Saturday 8am to 3pm. Cities and larger towns will have a duty pharmacy where medicines can be obtained outside opening hours. Details of duty pharmacies are posted in all pharmacy windows.

For serious complaints, head for the casualty department of the nearest hospital (*Krankenhaus*), or call an ambulance (☎144). As members of the EU, **citizens of the UK and Ireland** receive free hospital treatment in Austria on production of their passport. Nationals of other countries should check whether their government has a reciprocal health agreement with Austria.

Though not compulsory, **travel insurance** including medical cover is good idea. Check before shelling out, however, that you are not already covered: many credit cards (particularly American Express) have certain levels of medical or other insurance included if you use them to pay for your trip. Many private medical schemes also cover you while abroad. If you have a good "all risks" home insurance policy, it may well cover your possessions against loss or theft even when overseas.

Few regular travel insurance policies cover injuries incurred during relatively high-risk activities such as **skiing**, and if you're travelling to Austria on a winter sports holiday you'll have to take out specific insurance cover.

UK COVER

Most travel agents and tour operators will offer you travel insurance – those policies offered by Campus Travel or STA in the UK, and USIT in Ireland, are usually reasonable value. If you feel the cover is inadequate, or you want to compare prices, any insurance broker, bank or specialist travel insurance company should be able to help: call Columbus Travel Insurance (☎0171/375 0011) or Endsleigh Insurance (☎0171/436 4451). Two weeks' cover for a trip to Austria should cost around £20.

Expect to pay £25–30 per person for two weeks' winter sports cover; special deals are usually available for families.

US AND CANADIAN COVER

Before buying an insurance policy to travel in Austria, check that you're not already covered. **Canadian provincial health plans** typically provide some overseas medical coverage, although they are unlikely to pick up the full tab in the event of a mishap. Holders of official **stu-**

TRAVEL INSURANCE COMPANIES IN NORTH AMERICA

Most travel agents will arrange travel insurance at no extra charge. The following insurance companies can be called directly.

Access America ☎1-800/284 8300.

Carefree Travel Insurance ☎1-800/323 3149.

Desjardins Travel Insurance Canada only: ☎1-800/463 7830.

STA Travel ☎1-800/777 0112.

Travel Guard ☎1-800/826 1300.

Travel Insurance Services ☎1-800/937 1387.

TRAVEL INSURANCE COMPANIES IN AUSTRALIA AND NEW ZEALAND

Covermore, 32 Walker St, North Sydney (☎02/9202 8000 or 1800/25 1881).

Ready Plan, Australia: 141 Walker St, Dandenong, Melbourne (☎03/9791 5077 or 1800/33 7462); New Zealand: 10th Floor, 63 Albert St, Auckland (☎09/379 3208).

dent/teacher/youth cards are entitled to accident coverage and hospital in-patient benefits. **Students** may also find that their student health coverage extends during the vacations and for one term beyond the date of last enrolment. **Homeowners' or renters'** insurance often covers theft or loss of documents, money and valuables while overseas.

If you do need travel insurance, most travel agents will arrange it. The insurance companies we've listed (see box) can be called directly.

Travel insurance **policies** vary: some are comprehensive while others cover only certain risks (accidents, illnesses, delayed or lost luggage, cancelled flights, etc). In particular, ask whether the policy pays medical costs up front or reimburses you later, and whether it provides for medical evacuation to your home country.

The best **premiums** are usually to be had through student/youth travel agencies – STA policies, for example, come in two forms: with or without medical coverage. The current rates are US$45/US$35 (for up to seven days); $60/$45 (eight to fifteen days); $110/$85 (one month); $140/$115 (45 days); $165/$135 (two months); and $50/$35 for each extra month. If you're planning to do any "dangerous sports" (skiing, mountaineering, etc), be sure to ask whether these activities are covered: some companies levy a surcharge.

Most North American travel policies apply only to items lost, stolen or damaged while in the custody of an identifiable, responsible third party – hotel porter, airline, luggage consignment, etc. Even in these cases, you will have to contact the local police within a certain time limit to have a complete report made out so that your insurer can process the claim.

AUSTRALASIAN COVER

Comprehensive **travel insurance policies** are generally put together by the airlines, major travel agents and some banks in conjunction with insurance companies. All are fairly similar in premium and coverage that includes medical expenses, loss of personal property and travellers' cheques, cancellations and delays, as well as most adventure sports, except mountaineering with ropes, bungy jumping (some policies) or unassisted diving without an Open Water licence. Make sure all your intended activities are covered as it may be necessary to tailor a policy to suit your requirements. Ready Plan and Covermore (see box) give the best value-for-money coverage. A normal policy costs around A$190/NZ$220 for one month, A$270/NZ$320 for two months and A$330/NZ$400 for three months.

INFORMATION AND MAPS

There are branches of the Austrian National Tourist Office in most large foreign countries (a selection of addresses is given on p.24), although most prefer to deal with the public by telephone rather than admit personal callers – ring ahead and check before trying to visit them in person. The staff are, as a rule, very helpful, and can usually supply brochures, accommodation lists and maps covering specific towns and resorts, providing you're focused about your interests.

Within Austria itself, most settlements of any size have a tourist office, although they come under an assortment of names: *Information*, *Verkehrsamt* and *Fremdenverkehrsverein* are the most common. All are helpful and well organized, and staff usually speak English. They will supply a surfeit of brochures

---

```

## TRAVEL BOOKS AND MAP OUTLETS

### BRITAIN AND IRELAND

**Aberdeen Map Shop**, 74 Skene St, Aberdeen AB10 1QE (☎01224/637999). Mail order.

**Austick's City Bookshop**, 91 The Headrow, Leeds LS1 6OJ (☎0113/243 3099). General bookshop with a wide range of travel books and maps.

**Blackwell's Map and Travel Shop**, 53 Broad St, Oxford OX1 3BQ (☎01865/792792). Specialist outlet.

**Call of the Wild**, 21 Station St, Keswick, Cumbria CA12 5HH (☎01768/771014). Adventure travel with international maps reflecting the mountaineering/walking slant; some more general maps available.

**Daunt Books**, 83 Marylebone High St, London W1M 3DE (☎0171/224 2295); 193 Haverstock Hill, NW3 4QL (☎0171/794 4006).

**Easons Bookshop**, 40 O'Connell St, Dublin 1 (☎01/873 3811).

**Fred Hanna's Bookshop**, 27–29 Nassau St, Dublin 2 (☎01/677 1255).

**Heffers Map Shop**, 3rd Floor, in Heffers Stationery Department, 19 Sidney St, Cambridge, CB2 3HL (☎01223/568467). Mail order available from here; more maps and travel literature at their excellent bookshop at 20 Trinity St.

**Hodges Figgis Bookshop**, 56–58 Dawson St, Dublin 2 (☎01/677 4754).

**James Thin Melven's Bookshop**, 29 Union St, Inverness, IV1 1QA (☎01463/233500). Established 1849; map department with all foreign maps; mail-order specialist.

**John Smith and Sons**, 57–61 St Vincent St, Glasgow, G2 5TB (☎0141/221 7472). Specialist map department in long-established bookseller's; full range of foreign maps; mail-order service.

**The Map Shop**, 30a Belvoir St, Leicester LE1 6QH (☎0116/2471400). Domestic and foreign maps; mail order available; 15 High St, Upton-upon-Severn, Worcestershire WR8 0HJ (☎01684/593146). Free catalogue sent; mail order available.

**National Map Centre**, 22–24 Caxton St, London SW1H 0QU (☎0171/222 2466).

**Stanfords**, 12–14 Long Acre, London WC2E 9LP (☎0171/836 1321); maps by mail or phone order are available on this number. Other branches in London are located within Campus Travel at 52 Grosvenor Gardens, SW1W 0AG (☎0171/730 1314), and within the British Airways offices at 156 Regent St, W1R 5TA (☎0171/434 4744). Outside London: 29 Corn St, Bristol BS1 1HT (☎0117/929 9966).

**The Travel Bookshop**, 13–15 Blenheim Crescent, London W11 2EE (☎0171/229 5260).

**Latitude**, 34 The Broadway, Darkes Lane, Potters Bar, Hertfordshire EN6 2HW (☎01707/663090). Mail-order catalogue available.

**Newcastle Map Centre**, 55 Grey St, Newcastle upon Tyne NE1 6EF (☎0191/261 5622). Ordnance survey stockists also keep a good range of foreign maps.

**Waterstone's**, 91 Deansgate, Manchester M3 2BW (☎0161/832 1992). Particularly good map department in this branch of the UK-wide chain of bookshops; mail-order service. In Ireland, Queens Building, 8 Royal Ave, Belfast BT1 1DA (☎01232/247 355), 7 Dawson St, Dublin 2 (☎01/679 1415); and 69 Patrick St, Cork (☎021/276522).

covering local attractions and activities, but local maps are sometimes sold to the public rather than given away. Local tourist offices almost always book accommodation for personal callers, sometimes for a small fee, a deposit, or both. Opening hours can be long, as late as 9pm in the larger cities during the summer and in alpine resorts during winter; outside this period, and in smaller towns and remote areas, times are likely to be more limited, often including a long lunch break (typically Mon–Fri 8am–noon & 2–5pm). It's worth visiting tourist offices even outside the advertised opening hours, as many of them either maintain touch-screen computer information points in a lobby outside (often accessible 24hr, or at least from 6am or 7am until midnight) or leave a stock of leaflets and maps in a rack outside.

## MAPS

The **maps** in this guide, together with the free plans you'll often pick up from tourist offices and hotels, should be sufficient to help you find your way around the towns and regions. Otherwise, the best maps are by Freytag & Berndt, who produce a 1:500,000 map of the whole country; or by Generalkarte, whose series of eight 1:200,000 regional maps are useful for
```

USA

Book Passage, 51 Tamal Vista Blvd, Corte Madera, CA 94925 (☎415/927 0960).

The Complete Traveler Bookstore, 3207 Fillmore St, San Francisco, CA 92123 (☎415/923 1511); 199 Madison Ave, New York, NY 10016 (☎212/685 9007).

Elliot Bay Book Company, 101 S Main St, Seattle, WA 98104 (☎206/624 6600).

Forsyth Travel Library, 226 Westchester Ave, White Plains, NY 10604 (☎1-800/367 7984).

Map Link Inc., 30 S La Patera Lane, Unit 5, Santa Barbara, CA 93117 (☎805/692 6777).

The Map Store Inc.,1636 I St NW, Washington, DC 20006 (☎202/628 2608).

Phileas Fogg's Books & Maps, #87 Stanford Shopping Center, Palo Alto, CA 94304 (☎1-800/533 FOGG).

Rand McNally, 444 N Michigan Ave, Chicago, IL 60611 (☎312/321 1751); 150 E 52nd St, New York, NY 10022 (☎212/758 7488); 595 Market St, San Francisco, CA 94105 (☎415/777 3131), etc. Rand McNally now has more than twenty stores across the US; call ☎1-800/333 0136 ext 2111 for the address of your nearest store, or for direct-mail maps.

Travel Books & Language Center, 4437 Wisconsin Ave, Washington, DC 20016 (☎1-800/220 2665).

Sierra Club Bookstore, 6014 College Ave, Oakland, CA 94618 (☎510/658 7470).

Traveler's Bookstore, 22 W 52nd St, New York, NY 10019 (☎212/664 0995).

CANADA

Open Air Books and Maps, 25 Toronto St, Toronto M5R 2C1 (☎416/363 0719).

Ulysses Travel Bookshop, 4176 St-Denis, Montréal H2W 2M5 (☎514/843 9447).

World Wide Books and Maps, 1247 Granville St, Vancouver V6Z 1G3 (☎604/687 3320).

AUSTRALIA AND NEW ZEALAND

Bowyangs, 372 Little Bourke St, Melbourne (☎03/9670 4383).

The Map Shop, 16a Peel St, Adelaide (☎08/8231 2033).

Perth Map Centre, 891 Hay St, Perth (☎08/9322 5733).

Specialty Maps, 58 Albert St, Auckland (☎09/307 2217).

Travel Bookshop, Shop 3, 175 Liverpool St, Sydney (☎02/9261 8200).

Worldwide Maps and Guides, 187 George St, Brisbane (☎07/3221 4330).

---

lengthier touring. Both Freytag & Berndt and rival firm Kompass produce numerous **walking maps**, or *Wanderkarten* (ranging in scale from 1:50,000 to 1:30,000 depending on the area), which cover most areas of western, alpine Austria and many rural parts of the east as well. The best walking maps of Austria's mountain areas, however, are those belonging to the 1:25,000 *Alpenvereinskarte* series, produced by the Austrian Alpine Association. In addition, many bookshops and tourist offices in Austria sell local walking and cycling maps produced by smaller publishers.

Both the Austrian National Tourist Office and relevant local tourist offices should be able to provide plans of the larger **towns and cities**, though they may charge for them. Kompass also produce good maps of Graz, Innsbruck, Salzburg, Vienna and other regional centres in their Kompass-Stadtplan series, each marked with public transport routes; Freytag & Berndt's plans of Innsbruck, Salzburg and Vienna are similarly serviceable. The latter's 1:20,000 spiral-bound *Buchplan Wien* map is the most comprehensive map of the Austrian capital, while Falkplan's fold-out map, with a good large-scale section of the city centre, is a worthy alternative.

COSTS, MONEY AND BANKS

Although Austria is by no means a budget destination, it is not quite as expensive as people imagine. It's true to say that there are few bargain deals around, and even the cheapest coffee and cake at a traditional café will cost you dearly, but restaurants on the whole are moderately priced, as are rooms in most pensions and hotels. That said, if you have the money, Austria has plenty of luxury shops, hotels and restaurants ready to relieve you of it.

MONEY

The **currency** in Austria is the Austrian Schilling, or *österreichische Schilling* (abbreviated to öS within Austria, occasionally written as ATS or AS in English), which is divided into one hundred *Groschen*. Coins come in the denominations öS20, öS10, öS5 and öS1, plus 50 and 10 Groschen; notes are öS5000, öS1000, öS500, öS100, öS50 and öS20.

The Austrian economy is in a quite healthy condition, despite what some Austrians would have you believe, and the Schilling is a relatively strong currency. Generally speaking, the **exchange rate** hovers between öS18 and öS20 to the pound sterling, and around öS12 to the US dollar.

AVERAGE COSTS

Accommodation will be your biggest single expense, with the cheapest reasonable double rooms in a pension going for about öS500–700 (£25–35/$38–53). Within that price range, you should be able to get somewhere pretty comfortable and clean.

After you've paid for your own room, count on a **minimum** of £20/$32 a day, to buy your breakfast, a takeaway lunch, a budget dinner and a beer or coffee, but not much else. Eating sit-down meals twice a day, visiting museums and drinking more beer and coffee (especially coffee) will mean allowing something in the range of £40/$64 a day; if you want to go to the opera or a nightclub, then you could easily double that figure.

Tipping is expected in the more upmarket hotels, taxis and in most cafés, bars and restaurants, usually up to the nearest öS5 or öS10 depending on how much you've spent and how good the service. In more expensive restaurants, you'll find the bill arrives with a fifteen percent service charge already tacked onto the total.

TRAVELLERS' CHEQUES AND CREDIT CARDS

Travellers' cheques are the safest and easiest way to carry money. They're available for a small commission (usually one percent of the amount ordered) from any bank and some building societies, whether or not you have an account, and from branches of American Express and Thomas Cook.

Even if you have travellers' cheques, it's a good idea to take a **credit card** with a PIN number as well; it will come in handy both as a backup source of funds and as a way to save on exchange-rate commissions. You can pay with plastic in most hotels, shops and restaurants, though it's not as widely used as in the UK or the US and you may find that many smaller rural establishments insist on cash. With MasterCard and Visa, it is also possible to withdraw cash at certain Austrian banks from the 24-hour **cashpoint**/automatic teller machines (**ATMs**); check with your bank before you leave home. You can also pay for goods and services by **Eurocheque** pretty much everywhere.

CHANGING MONEY

The best place to change money is at a **bank**, which should give you a more favourable rate of exchange and take a lower commission than a hotel

or exchange booth. The process takes a little bit longer, however, and, of course, restricts you to normal banking hours. The main Austrian high-street banks are Creditanstalt, Bank Austria and Die Erste Banke; there's nothing to choose between them.

Banking hours vary, but are generally Monday to Friday 8am to 12.30pm and 1.30 or 2pm to 3 or 4pm. Banks stay open until 5.30pm on Thursdays. Outside these hours, you will have to rely on the **Wechselstube**, or exchange booths. Those with the longest hours (typically daily 8am–8pm) are usually found at big-city train stations and at airports. There are also 24-hour automatic exchange machines dotted around the bigger towns, accepting notes of most major currencies, although commission rates may be more punitive than those charged in a bank.

EMERGENCIES

When you buy your **travellers' cheques**, make a note of the emergency phone number given. On your trip, keep a record of all cheque serial numbers and note which ones you spend – and report any loss or theft immediately. All being well, you should get the missing cheques reissued within a couple of days. Things can be trickier if you lose your credit card: your bank should be able to give you details of the number to call if this happens, but you won't be provided with a replacement card until you get home.

Assuming you know someone who is prepared to send you the money, the quickest way to have funds sent out to you in an emergency is to do it through **Western Union**, who will wire the money to you in a couple of hours (some banks will also do this): get your sponsor to phone ☎0800/833833 in the UK; ☎1-800/325 6000 in North America; ☎1800/649565 in Australia; or ☎09/302 0143 in New Zealand.

If you have a few days' leeway, you can simply get your bank to wire your money to an Austrian bank, a process that shouldn't take more than a couple of days. If you can last out for a week, then an **international money order**, exchangeable at any post office, is by far the cheapest way of sending money.

If you're in really dire straits, you can get touch with your consulate in Vienna (some countries also maintain consulates in regional capitals like Salzburg, Innsbruck, Graz and Bregenz – details are given in the relevant sections of this book), who will usually let you make one phone call home free of charge, and will – in worst cases only – repatriate you, but will never, under any circumstances, lend money.

GETTING AROUND

Public transport in Austria is on the whole well organized, if not particularly cheap. Train and bus routes tend to complement each other rather than compete, with services timed to connect with each other wherever possible. You can reach most areas of the country by public transport, although rural villages may only be served by one bus per day. Getting around on Sundays and public holidays can be problematic: most train services (especially InterCity and international services) continue as usual, but there's less in the way of local trains, and many rural bus services cease altogether.

Most parts of Austria – including the big cities – operate a zonal **travelcard** (*Zeitkarte* or *Netzkarte*) system covering all forms of public transport in that particular area. Ticket durations and prices vary considerably from one place to another, and depend on how many zones in a particular region they cover, but it's safe to assume that, if you're staying in one area and are planning to explore the outlying region by a combination of rail and bus, then it will be much cheaper to buy a 24-hour ticket (*Tageskarte*) or seven-day ticket (*Wochenkarte*) for the relevant zone than to buy tickets for each individual journey. Travelcards of longer duration (a month-long season ticket is a *Monatskarte*) are also available in most regions. Travelcards can be bought from both train and bus stations. A 24-hour pass for the whole of the Vorarlberg, for example, costs öS140, and a seven-day pass öS250. There are also (cheaper) passes for specific regions within the Vorarlberg, and reductions for children and OAPs.

BY TRAIN

Austrian Federal Railways – Österreichische Bundesbahnen, or "ÖBB" – run a punctual, clean and comfortable rail network, which includes most towns of any size. Trains marked "EC" (EuroCity international expresses) or "IC" (Austrian InterCity expresses) are the fastest. Those designated "E" (*Eilzug*) are "semi-fast trains" stopping at most intermediate points, while the *Regionalzug* is the slowest form of service, stopping at all stations. Both InterRail and Eurail passes are valid for the ÖBB network, as well as for the majority of small, privately owned railways that augment it – the three that you're most likely to come across are the Zillertalbahn (from Jenbach to Mayrhofen), the Murtalbahn (from Unzmarkt to Tamsweg via Murau) and the Graz–Köflacher-Bahn (from Graz to Köflach and from Graz to Wies-Ebiswald). Passes are less likely to be valid for the tourist-oriented mountain railways, such as the Schafbergbahn (see p.355) or the Achenseebahn (see p.430), although they may secure a reduction – be sure to ask about this, as regulations change.

Fares are calculated according to distance, with the first 100km costing öS156; 200km costing öS276; 500km, about öS580 (although prices on EC trains are twenty percent higher). **Tickets** (*Fahrschein*) are bought either from the ticket office in the train station (*Bahnhof*; a main station in a big city is called the *Hauptbahnhof*) or on the train itself (usually on payment of a small supplement; around öS30). If travelling from a small, unstaffed halt, however, tickets can be bought on the train without paying the extra supplement. When buying tickets from a ticket office, credit cards are only accepted on purchases exceeding öS200. Return tickets are rarely cheaper than two singles, but are valid for two months and allow for unlimited stop-offs en route. Single tickets are only valid for four days. InterCity and EuroCity trains can get crowded at weekends, especially over the summer, when making a reservation is a good idea; reserving a seat costs öS30 extra.

If you don't have an InterRail or Eurail Pass, it's worth buying a regional public transport *Netzkarte*, or enquiring about one of the numerous **money-saving options** offered by ÖBB for the whole or part of the rail network. Most useful of these is the *Puzzle* ticket (öS1090, under-26s öS660), which allows four days' free travel over a ten-day period in one of four zones: west (covering Vorarlberg, Tyrol and Salzburg), south (Salzburg, Carinthia and Styria), north (Upper Austria, Lower Austria, Vienna and Burgenland) or east (Lower Austria, Vienna, Burgenland and Styria). A *Bundesnetzkarte*, covering one month's unlimited travel anywhere in the country, weighs in at öS4300. Less frequent travellers might prefer to invest in a *Kilometerbank*, which involves paying in advance for a number of kilometres (currently öS2400 for 2000km, öS3540 for 3000km, öS5850 for 5000km; valid for twelve months), which can then be used up as and when needed. The advantage of the *Kilometerbank* is that it can be shared between as many as six people. Those staying in Austria long-term might also consider the *Vorteilscard*, which for öS1190 a year entitles the bearer to fifty percent reductions on all rail travel.

Train **times** are displayed in the ticket halls and on the platforms of all stations. Yellow *Abfahrt* posters list departures, and white *Ankunft* posters list arrivals. A train **timetable** (*Kursbuch*, or *Fahrpläne*) covering the whole country comes in compact paperback form and is available from station ticket offices at a cost of öS100. Some smaller regional timetables are available for around öS15 each, though leaflets detailing specific routes are free from some stations and tourist offices.

For **telephone information** on train times and prices, call ☎1717 if you're in Vienna, Graz, Linz, Salzburg, Klagenfurt, Innsbruck or Bregenz. Elsewhere, call ☎1717 prefixed by the code of the city that's nearest.

BY BUS

Austria's *Bahnbus* and *Postbus* system fills most of the gaps left by the rail network. As a general rule, *Bahnbus* services (run by the ÖBB) depart from train stations, and *Postbus* services (run by the Post Office) stop outside the post office, though often either service calls in at both. Bus **fares** work out slightly cheaper than train fares, costing around öS130 per 100km; along routes served by both forms of transport, however, you'll find that trains are almost invariably quicker. Buses come into their own on routes serving out-of-the-way, alpine villages, where they constitute a valuable lifeline for the local community, carrying mail as well as ferrying the local kids to and from school. Indeed, bus timetables often reflect the needs of the school

day, with a flurry of departures in the early morning and early afternoon, compared to fewer services later in the day. Generally, bus services are less frequent on Sundays and public holidays, and in some areas cease altogether on these days.

Bus **schedules** (*Fahrpläne*) for a particular route are usually displayed at bus stops (*Bushaltestelle*); larger towns will have a bus station (*Busbahnhof*, usually next to either the post office or the main train station), where a complete range of arrivals and departures is listed. A full timetable (*Kursbuch*) covering the whole of Austria is available for öS230 from the ticket windows at bus stations, but it's divided into five volumes (each covering a separate geographical region) and weighs a tonne; individual volumes are sold for öS15–60, depending on the region covered. Happily, free booklets containing local timetables are often available from both bus stations and tourist offices.

Tickets are usually bought from the bus driver, although it's possible to buy them in advance from the ticket window at a bus station. Twenty-four-hour travelcards (*Tageskarten*) for a particular route or zone are often cheaper than buying individual return tickets. A *Tageskarte* can usually be bought from the bus driver, though travelcards of longer duration (*Netzkarten*) must be purchased from the ticket office of a bus or train station.

BY SHIP

Passenger **ships** ply many of Austria's lakes and waterways, notably the Salzkammergut lakes, the Carinthian lakes and the stretch of the Danube Valley between Vienna and Linz. Operating times may well be seasonal (most lake steamers tend to run from April or May to Sept), and ships are invariably slower and more expensive than other forms of public transport – it's as a means of enjoying some relaxed sightseeing that they really come into their own. Most ship services are run by private companies, though public transport passes (InterRail and Eurail passes, Austrian regional travelcards) are valid on some – including the stretch on the River Danube – but by no means all of the services.

DRIVING

Austria's roads are in general impeccably maintained, and there's an extensive system of **autobahns** linking all main cities and providing onward routes to neighbouring countries. Autobahns are sometimes designated by name (the Salzburg–Villach *Tauern Autobahn*, for example), but more often by number. Note that the Austrian **numbering system**, in which autobahns are prefixed by the letter A, conflicts with the European numbering system, whereby all main continental routes are prefixed with the letter E – you'll therefore find that the main A1 Salzburg–Vienna autobahn is also marked on most maps as the E60. Main roads (*Bundesstrasse*) are usually marked in red on maps and designated by number; minor roads are usually marked in yellow and have no number.

All Austria's autobahns are subject to a single **toll**, which involves buying a *Vignette* (windscreen sticker) from the petrol stations or shops found at border posts when entering the country. You can also buy them from post offices and *Tabak* shops once inside the country. A ten-day *Vignette* costs öS70 (and you'll need to buy a ten-day one even if you're merely passing straight through the country); a two-month *Vignette* öS140; and twelve-month *Vignette* öS550 (motorbikers get a fifty percent reduction on the twelve-month *Vignette*, but not on the others). You don't need a *Vignette* at all if you intend to stick to normal main roads; however, those caught driving on Austria's autobahns without displaying a valid *Vignette* will be subject to an öS1100 fine.

Speed limits are 50kph in built-up areas, 100kph on normal roads and 130kph on motorways. You have to be 18 to drive in Austria, but most **driving rules** are otherwise fairly standard. Seatbelts must be worn (in the back seats as well, if you're in a car that has them fitted).The wearing of crash helmets is compulsory for motorbike riders. The permissible alcohol limit is 0.8 percent – roughly two glasses of wine or two pints of beer.

Many car insurance policies cover taking your car to Europe; check with your insurer while planning your trip. However, you're advised to take out extra cover for motoring assistance in case your car breaks down. If you are driving a car abroad and you are already a member of the AA, RAC or equivalent body, you can make use of the **breakdown services** offered by both the main Austrian motoring organizations, the Österreichischer Automobile, Motorrad und Touring Club (ÖAMTC; ☎120), and the Auto-, Motor- und Radfahrerbund Österreichs (ARBÖ; ☎123). Callout charges hover around the öS1000 mark.

As far as **parking** is concerned, most urban areas have time-limited parking zones (*Kurzparkzone*), allowing a parking time of ninety minutes up to three hours. You'll need to purchase

a sticker (*Parkschein*) from a *Tabak* shop or petrol station, which you then display on the windscreen, although in a very few places you may be able to park for a limited time for free.

ALPINE ROUTES

Most of the major **alpine routes** are kept open year-round, whatever the weather, but it's a good idea to carry **snow chains** in winter months if you're traversing alpine areas not served by autobahns. Road signs showing a white tyre on a blue background indicate that snow chains are compulsory. Several scenic, high-altitude mountain roads are only open during snow-free months, and **tolls** (*Mäute*) are levied for their use. The Grossglockner Hochalpenstrasse, which links the Salzburger Land with Carinthia and passes Austria's highest mountain along the way, is one of the most popular; opening times and prices for this and other scenic toll roads are detailed throughout this book.

Many of Austria's steep, winding transalpine roads are unsuitable for **caravans** or other **trailers**. The box below details the major routes on which trailers are banned; you should refer to a good motoring map for details of the many minor roads in the Alps that are closed to trailers. Alternatively, contact your home motoring organization for details of which routes are recommended for trailers, or simply stick to the autobahns.

PRINCIPAL ALPINE ROAD ROUTES CLOSED TO TRAILERS

Enns Gorge (Weyer Markt–Hieflau)

Flexen Pass (Rauzalpe–Zürs–Lech–Warth)

Gerlos Pass (Zell am Ziller–Krimml)

Grossglockner Hochalpenstrasse
(Zell am See–Heiligenblut)

Hochtannberg Pass (Au–Warth)

Holzleiten Sattel (Nassereith–Telfs)

Loibl Pass (Klagenfurt–Slovenia)

Plöcken Pass (Kötschach–Italy)

Pötschenhöhe (Bad Ischl–Bad Aussee)

Seeberg Sattel, Carinthia
(Eisenkappel– Slovenia)

Seeberg Sattel, Styria
(Bruck an der Mur–Mariazell)

Silvretta Hochalpenstrasse (Partenen–Galtür)

Timmelsjoch Pass (Obergurgl–Italy)

Würzen Pass (Villach–Slovenia)

CAR RENTAL AGENCIES

BRITAIN

Avis (☎0990/900500).
Budget (☎0800/181181).
Eurodollar (☎01895/233300).
Europcar/InterRent (☎0345/222525).

Hertz (☎0990/996699).
Holiday Autos (☎0990/300400).
Thrifty (☎0990/168238).

IRELAND

Avis Northern Ireland (☎0990/900500); Republic (☎01/874 5844).

Budget Northern Ireland (☎0800/181181); Republic (☎0800/973159).

Europcar Northern Ireland (☎0345/222525); Republic (☎01/874 5844).

Hertz Northern Ireland (☎0990/996699); Republic (☎01/676 7476).

Holiday Autos Northern Ireland (☎0990/300400); Republic (☎01/872 9366); freefax (☎1800/729366).

USA AND CANADA

Alamo (☎1-800/522 9696).
Auto Europe (☎1-800/223 5555).
Avis (☎1-800/331 1084).
Budget (☎1-800/527 0700).
Dollar (☎1-800/421 6868).

Enterprise Rent-a-Car (☎1-800/325 8007).
Europe by Car (☎1-800/223 1516).
Hertz (☎1-800/654 3001; in Canada ☎1-800/263 0600).
Thrifty (☎1-800/367 2277).

AUSTRALIA

Avis (☎1800/225533).
Budget (☎1300/362 848).
Hertz (☎13/3039).

NEW ZEALAND

Avis (☎09/526 2847).
Budget (☎09/375 2222).
Hertz (☎09/309 0989).

CAR RENTAL

All of the big international **car rental** companies have offices in most Austrian towns and at airports, and it's fairly easy to book a car in your home country before you travel (see box above) – it's almost always cheaper to book from home and pick the car up at the airport. Typical charges with the multinationals range from around öS850 per day with unlimited mileage for a small compact, to öS1800 per day for something at the top end of the range. Cars rented within Austria should come with a valid *Vignette* (a windscreen sticker showing that autobahn tax has been paid, see opposite) – it's a good idea to check that this is in order before driving off. You need to be over 21 to rent a car.

CYCLING

Austria is a bicycle-friendly country, with **cycling** lanes in all major towns. There are also a large number of designated cycle routes out in the countryside; these include stretches of pedestrian- and cycle-only pathway, but more often consist of a separate lane by the roadside.

Most well-touristed places in Austria boast a couple of **bike rental** (*Fahrradverlieh*) outlets – usually requiring production of a passport or other photo-accompanied ID. All but the smallest train stations rent out bikes for öS90 per day, öS50 if you have a valid rail ticket. They can be returned to a different station to the one you set out from for an extra fee of öS50. Train stations don't always have the widest choice of bikes, however, and for something more specialized, like a **mountain bike**, it's often better to go to another bike rental operator, where prices may be up to öS50 per day higher. Details of where to rent bikes in the larger towns and resorts are given throughout this book.

ACCOMMODATION

Despite profiteering in main tourist centres like Vienna and Salzburg, accommodation need not be expensive in Austria. Although it can be a scramble in July and August, and (in skiing areas) between late December and April, finding a room doesn't present too many problems.

The majority of **tourist offices** will book accommodation on behalf of personal callers (most refuse to do so for those enquiring by phone or by fax); other offices will supply you with an accommodation list and point you in the direction of a public telephone. Of the tourist offices who do book accommodation for you, some charge a small fee (usually not more than öS20–30) and/or a deposit – in general, it's in the large urban centres (Vienna, Salzburg and Innsbruck, for example) that this extra charge is levied. The bigger tourist offices have accommodation lists on an information board (or touch-screen computer) either in the lobby or on the wall outside, for those who arrive during closing hours; these are often accompanied by a courtesy phone so you can call up whichever hotel or pension takes your fancy.

Inevitably, accommodation **prices** are subject to seasonal variations. In most areas rates are highest in July and August, with a shoulder season comprising April to June and September; in ski resorts, prices peak from December to March. Some areas (notably alpine resorts that remain popular throughout the year) have a peak season

in both summer and winter, and offer cheaper prices in spring and autumn. Throughout this guide, we've quoted **peak summer prices**, though an indication of what you might expect to pay in winter has been provided in alpine resorts where relevant.

HOTELS AND PENSIONS

A high standard of cleanliness and comfort can be taken for granted in most Austrian hotels. **Hotels** call themselves either a Hotel or Gasthof (plural Gasthöfe) – there's little difference between the two terms, although use of the word Gasthof (originally used to describe a country inn offering both refreshment and lodging) is intended these days to connote a traditional, cosy feel. Most hotels and Gasthöfe have restaurants offering food and drink throughout the day; a **Hotel-Garni** is a hotel that offers breakfast but no other meals. A **Gästehaus** is usually a small B&B hotel, not to be confused with a **Gasthaus**, which is merely a restaurant – unless, of course, it's followed by the words "mit Unterkunft" (with lodging). The label **Pension** denotes a bed-and-breakfast hotel that, although self-contained, occupies one or more floors, but not the whole, of a larger building. Pensions tend to be small, family-run affairs, but there are no hard-and-fast rules as to what they look like or what they offer: those in the big cities tend to occupy large apartment blocks, while those in country areas may well be in traditional, rustic houses. One other oft-used piece of terminology worth looking out for is the word *Komfortzimmer* ("comfort room"), which is used to describe rooms that have both en-suite bath/shower facilities and TV.

COSTS AND STANDARDS

Hotels and pensions are graded on a **five-star scale**. The most basic, one-star places, offering simple rooms with shared toilets and bathrooms, are in very short supply, as well as rarely quoted in Austrian tourist-office literature. Most budget

ACCOMMODATION PRICE CODES

All **hotels and pensions** in this book have been graded according to the following price categories. All the codes are based on the rate for the least expensive double room during the **summer season**. In those places where winter is the high season, we've indicated winter room rates in the text.

① under öS400   ④ öS800–1000   ⑦ öS1400–1600
② öS400–600   ⑤ öS1000–1200   ⑧ öS1600–1800
③ öS600–800   ⑥ öS1200–1400   ⑨ over öS1800

accommodation falls into the two-star category, offering rooms usually with en-suite shower and toilet (although some have en-suite toilet but shared shower) and a simple continental breakfast – typically a pot of coffee, bread rolls and jam. Generally speaking, pensions tend to fall into this category; some of Vienna's inner-city pensions, however, are luxury hotels in all but name. In two-star hotels and most pensions, you can expect to pay öS500–700 for a double with bathroom; slightly less for rooms with shared facilities.

Once beyond the two-star bracket, prices rise rapidly. Rooms in three-star places usually come with en-suite shower, telephone and TV (often with a range of satellite programmes, including a couple of English-language channels like CNN or the BBC), together with a larger range of breakfast food, often an as-much-as-you-can-eat buffet comprising cereals, cold meats and pastries. You should expect to pay öS700–1200 for a double in this category. Once you break into the four- and five-star brackets, you can expect bigger rooms, an expanded range of creature comforts, like more luxurious furnishings and large baths to wallow in, and additional facilities like swimming pool, gym and sauna. Anything between öS1200 and öS2500 for a double is not unusual, with prestigious luxury hotels in Vienna and other big cities exceeding even this.

Credit cards are not accepted in many small hotels and pensions, but you can pay by Eurocheque almost everywhere.

PRIVATE ROOMS AND FARMHOUSES

Staying in a **private room** (*Privatzimmer*) is a widely available option in Austria whereby you stay in the house of a local family. While in many cases you'll be sharing a bathroom and eating your breakfast with the family, in others it's not that different from staying in a pension – you might be in a reasonably self-contained part of the house, and

rooms can come with en-suite shower and toilet (and perhaps even a TV). Most tourist offices keep extensive lists of all the private rooms offered locally, and tourist office staff will usually book one on your behalf; in well-travelled, rural areas where the locals depend a great deal on tourism, roadside signs offering *Zimmer frei* (vacancies) are fairly common. Most private rooms are let on a bed-and-breakfast basis, with a continental breakfast often served in your host's kitchen, but do check to make sure that the price you're quoted includes breakfast. Prices for a double room are between öS400 and öS600. Single travellers shouldn't have difficulty in finding a room, although they'll pay sixty to seventy percent of the price of a double.

Most tourist offices in small-town and rural Austria also book bed-and-breakfast rooms in local **farmhouses**. Promoted nationally under the rubric *Urlaub am Bauernhof* (farmhouse holidays), this kind of tourism is little different to staying in a private room, save for the fact that you'll be on a working farm and may be able to observe – or help out – as the animals are fed or cheese is made in an alpine dairy. Most farmhouses offer either double rooms, family-size apartments (typically sleeping four to six) or a mixture of both. Double rooms in farmhouses cost no more than comparable private rooms, while apartments usually offer even better value, often working out at öS150 or less per person per night. Prices usually include breakfast, but not always; some of the farmhouse apartments have self-catering facilities. A drawback, however, is that most of the farms offering rooms prefer guests to stay for about a week; you may get away with a stay of three or four days, especially if you're travelling outside the peak season, but anything less than this tends to be discouraged. Farmhouse accommodation is increasingly popular, and if you're travelling in July or August it's a good idea to book in advance before you travel: most tourist offices (addresses, phone and fax numbers of which are

HOSTELLING ASSOCIATIONS

AUSTRIA

Österreichischer Jugendherbergsverband, Schottenring 28, 1010 Wien (☎0222/533 5353).

Österreichisches Jugendherbergswerk, Helferstorferstrasse 4, 1010 Wien (☎0222/533 1833).

ENGLAND AND WALES

Youth Hostel Association (YHA), Trevelyan House, 8 St Stephen's Hill, St Alban's, Hertfordshire AL1 2DY (☎017278/45047). London information office: 14 Southampton St, London WC2 7HY (☎0171/836 1036).

IRELAND

Youth Hostel Association of Northern Ireland, 22 Donegall Rd, Belfast BT12 5JN (☎01232/324733).

An Oige, 61 Mountjoy St, Dublin 7 (☎01/830 4555).

SCOTLAND

Scottish Youth Hostel Association, 7 Glebe Crescent, Stirling FK8 2JA (☎01786/451181).

USA Hostelling International-American Youth Hostels (HI-AYH), 733 15th St NW, Suite 840, PO Box 37613, Washington, DC 20005 (☎202/783 6161).

CANADA

Hostelling International/Canadian Hostelling Association, Room 400, 205 Catherine St, Ottawa, ON K2P 1C3 (☎1-800/663 5777 or 613/237 7884).

AUSTRALIA

Australian Youth Hostels Association, 422 Kent St, Sydney (☎02/9261 1111).

NEW ZEALAND

Youth Hostels Association of New Zealand, PO Box 436, Christchurch (☎03/379 9970).

included throughout this book) will gladly send you a list or an illustrated brochure covering local options. Most farms are in quite remote areas, so you're likely to need your own transport if you want to enjoy a farmhouse holiday to the full.

HOSTELS

Youth hostels (*Jugendherberge* or *Jugendgästehaus*) are fairly widespread in Austria – around a hundred in all. They're run by two separate national organizations, the Österreichischer Jugendherbergsverband and the Österreichischer Jugendherbergswerk, although both are HI (Hostelling International) affiliated. There are also several hostels run by church organizations or private individuals, which are found in big cities like Vienna, Salzburg and Innsbruck. High standards of cleanliness and organization can be taken for granted, but such factors as room size, number of people per dorm and range of facilities vary widely. Rural hostels tend towards the hearty and basic, with large numbers of bunk beds crammed into a small number of rooms; that said, many large resorts and cities have almost hotel-like hostels, which contain a mixture of both multi-bed dorms and well-appointed double rooms with en-suite facilities. Overcrowding, however, can be a problem – especially during school holidays, when

hostels everywhere are besieged by kids – so book in advance whenever possible.

Rates hover between öS130 and öS240 depending on how plush the hostel. Expect to pay something nearer the lower rate for a rural hostel with dorm accommodation; the higher rate for a city hostel with lower person-per-dorm ratios or accommodation in double rooms. HI-affiliated hostels usually charge an extra öS20–30 if you're a non-member. Sheet sleeping bags are obligatory, and the cost of hiring one is often included in the overnight charge. A very simple breakfast – two rolls, jam and coffee – is also usually included in the price. In addition to breakfast, many hostels serve meals and snacks throughout the day in cafeteria-like surroundings, often at very competitive prices. Most hostels close during the day, and you're expected to check in either in the morning (around 8–9am) or in the evening (typically between 5 and 10pm); you may also be expected to vacate the premises at 9am on the dot, so be prepared. Most hostels also operate a curfew after 10 or 11pm, although in lots of cases you'll be given a key (often on payment of a small deposit) enabling you to come and go as you please. For a full list of HI-affiliated hostels in Austria, buy the HI handbook *Guide to Budget*

Accommodation, which costs £6.99, or write to both the Austrian youth hostel organizations in Austria (note that neither organization will give out information on hostels run by the other). If you're doing a lot of hostelling, it's well worth joining the hostelling organization of your home country (see box). This entitles you to stay in a hostel for a lower, members' rate.

MOUNTAIN HUTS

Highland areas of Austria are equipped with an extensive network of *Hütte*, or **mountain huts**, catering for hikers and mountaineers. More than 500 of these are run by the Austrian Alpine Association (Österreichischer Alpenverein, or ÖAV; see p.47), and an additional 500 are either privately owned or belong to smaller mountain clubs. Originally intended as simple refuges, most huts these days are rather like mountain inns, offering a range of accommodation. Mixed-sex dormitories (bring your own sheet sleeping bag) are the norm, although two-bed rooms or family rooms are often available. The hut warden provides meals and sells assorted drinks – tea, coffee, hot chocolate, beer, wine and schnapps – but prices are likely to be higher than those charged down in the valley.

Most huts are open from the beginning of July to mid-September; a few open in late May or June, and some may be open for longer periods to provide accommodation during the spring ski-touring season. Huts are at their busiest from mid-July to mid-August, but booking in advance is rarely necessary. If you arrive to find that all the beds are taken, you'll be allocated an emergency bed (*Notlager*) – a mattress on the floor. Expect to **pay** around öS100 for a *Notlager* bed; öS70–300 for a dorm bed; öS250–450 for a bed in a two-person room. A rudimentary breakfast (comprising bread, jam and tea or coffee) is available for an extra öS100 or so. Members of the ÖAV (they have a branch in Britain; see p.47) receive a fifty percent reduction on the price of a bed in all ÖAV-administered huts. A list (in German) of all huts, their opening dates, facilities and the like, can be found in the book *Der Alpenvereinshütten* (8th edition £15 for members, £18 for non-members), available from the UK branch of the Austrian Alpine Club.

CAMPING

Austria's high standards of accommodation are reflected in the country's **campsites**, the vast majority of which are clean, well-run affairs offering laundry facilities, shops and snack bars, as well as toilet and shower facilities. The only drawback is their tendency towards over-regimentation, with a plethora of rules and regulations – it's usually forbidden to light fires, make noise between certain hours, and some sites lock the gates for a couple of hours at lunchtime ensuring that no vehicle can get in or out. The larger sites often provide a wealth of activities and sports facilities – especially the lakeside sites of the Salzkammergut and Carinthia – and are good places to enjoy a family break; if you want to avoid a holiday-camp atmosphere, however, opt for a smaller, rural site. While most places cater just for tents and caravans, some sites offer four- to six-person bungalows. Sites usually open May to September only, although a great many in the winter resorts of western Austria never close. Prices are subject to seasonal variations, rising slightly in July and August, when you can expect to pay about öS60–80 per person, öS40–60 per pitch, plus öS20–50 per vehicle. Use of electricity is usually öS30–50 extra.

Caravanners should note that some transalpine roads are considered unsafe for caravans. The principal routes to avoid are listed on p.28.

EATING AND DRINKING

Austrian cuisine revolves around a solid pork- and veal-based repertoire, of which *Wiener Schnitzel* is the most famous example. Main meals tend to be meat-heavy affairs, however, and don't reflect the variety offered by Austria's main contribution to global gastronomic culture – the consumption of endless varieties of coffee, cakes and sweets. Partaking of the calorific delights in the cake-filled cafés and coffeehouses is an essential part of the Austrian experience – whatever consequences this might have for your waistline.

The kinds of venues where you will do your eating and drinking tend to overlap, making precise definitions difficult. Many cafés and coffeehouses offer breakfast and lunchtime menus alongside the expected range of drinks and sweets, while bars and other night-time drinking venues often have a wide choice of hot evening food. Similarly, many of the less grand restaurants are good places in which to simply sit and enjoy a beer.

AUSTRIAN FOOD AND DRINK GLOSSARY

Basics

Abendessen	supper/dinner	*Käse*	cheese
Auflauf	omelette	*Knödel*	dumplings
Beilagen	side dishes	*Kren*	horseradish
Brot	bread	*Löffel*	spoon
Butter	butter	*Messer*	knife
Ei	egg	*Mittagessen*	lunch
Frühstuck	breakfast	*Nachspeise*	dessert
Gabel	fork	*Öl*	oil
Gebäck	pastries	*Pfeffer*	pepper
Hauptgericht	main course	*Reis*	rice
Honig	honey	*Salat*	salad

Salz	salt
Semmel	bread roll
Senf	mustard
Spätzle or *Nockerl*	
	pasta noodles
Speisekarte	menu
Suppe	soup
Tasse	cup
Teller	plate
Vorspeise	starter
Zucker	sugar

Vegetables (*Gemüse*)

Blaukraut	red cabbage	*Lauch*	leek
Bohnen	beans	*Maiskolben*	corn on the cob
Champignons	button mushrooms	*Paprika*	green or red peppers
Erbsen	beans	*Paradeiser*	tomatoes
Erdäpfel	potatoes	*Kohlsprossen*	Brussels sprouts
Fisolen	green beans	*Rote Rübe*	beetroot
G'röste	fried grated potatoes	*Pilze*	mushrooms
Gurke	gerkhin/cucumber	*Pommes Frites*	chips/French fries
Karfiol	cauliflower	*Sauerkraut*	pickled cabbage
Karotten	carrots	*Spargel*	asparagus
Knoblauch	garlic	*Spinat*	spinach
Kohl	cabbage	*Zwiebeln*	onions

Meat (*Fleisch*) and poultry (*Geflügel*)

Eisbein	pig's trotters	*Hirsch*	venison	*Puter*	turkey
Ente	duck	*Huhn*	chicken	*Rindfleisch*	beef
Fasan	pheasant	*Innereien*	innards	*Schinken*	ham
Gans	goose	*Klabfleisch*	veal	*Schweinefleisch*	pork
Hackfleisch	mincemeat	*Kuttelfleck*	tripe	*Speck*	bacon
Hammelfleisch	mutton	*Lamm*	lamb	*Taube*	pigeon
Hase	hare	*Leber*	liver	*Zunge*	tongue
Hirn	brains	*Nieren*	kidneys		

Fish (*Fisch*)

Aal	eel	*Krabben*	prawns	*Scholle*	plaice
Fogosch	pikeperch	*Krebs*	crab	*Seezunge*	sole
Forelle	trout	*Lachs*	salmon	*Thunfisch*	tuna
Hecht	pike	*Makrele*	mackerel	*Tintenfisch*	squid
Hummer	lobster	*Matjes*	herring		
Karpfen	carp	*Muscheln*	mussels		

Common terms

Am Spiess	on the spit	*Gebraten*	roasted	*Heiss*	hot
Blau	rare	*Gedämpft*	steamed	*Kalt*	cold
Eingelegte	pickled	*Gefüllt*	stuffed	*Kümmelbraten*	roasted with
Frisch	fresh	*Gegrillt*	grilled		caraway seeds
Gebacken	fried in	*Gekocht*	cooked	*Powidl*	plum sauce
	breadcrumbs	*Hausgemacht*	homemade	*Geräucht*	smoked

Fruit (*Obst*)

Ananas	pineapple	*Grapefruit*	grapefruit	*Ribisel*	redcurrants
Apfel	apple	*Heidelbeeren*	bilberries	*Rosinen*	raisins
Banane	banana	*Himbeeren*	raspberries	*Trauben*	grapes
Birne	pear	*Kirschen*	cherries	*Zwetschgen*	plums
Brombeeren	blackberries	*Marillen*	apricots		
Erdbeeren	strawberries	*Pflaumen*	plums		

Desserts (see also "Coffee and cakes" box on p.38)

Baiser	meringue	*Marillenknödel*	sweet apricot dumplings
Bienenstich	honey and almond tart	*Mohr im Hemd*	chocolate steamed pudding
Buchteln	sweet dumplings		with cream
Käsekuchen	cheesecake	*Palatschinken*	pancakes

Austrian specialities

Backhendl	chicken fried in breadcrumbs	*Schweinshaxe*	pork knuckle
Bauernschmaus	platter of cold sausage, pork	*Stelze*	leg of veal or pork
	and ham	*Tafelspitz*	boiled beef, potatoes and
Beuschel	chopped lung		horseradish sauce
Brettljause	platter of cold meats and bread	*Tiroler Gröstl*	potatoes, onions and flecks
Debreziner	paprika-spiced sausage		of meat fried in a pan
Grammelknödel	pork dumplings	*Tiroler Knödel*	dumplings with pieces of
Kärntner Käsnudl	large parcel of pasta dough		ham, often eaten in a soup
	filled with cheese	*Wiener Schnitzel*	breaded veal
Kasspätzln	pasta noodles with cheese	*Zwiebelrostbraten*	slices of roast beef topped
Schinkenfleckern	ham with noodles		with fried onions
Schlipfkrapfen	ravioli-like pasta parcels		
	with a meat and/or potato filling		

continued over/

Drinks

Apfelsaft	apple juice	Kir	white wine with	Sauermilch	sour milk
Bier	beer		blackcurrant	Schnapps	spirit
Flasche	bottle	Korn	rye spirit	Sekt	sparkling wine
Gespritzer	white wine with	Kräutertee	herbal tea	Sturm	new wine
	soda	Milch	milk	Tee	tea
Glühwein	mulled wine	Mineralwasser	mineral water	Traubensaft	grape juice
Grog	hot water with	Obstler	fruit schnapps	Trocken	dry
	rum and sugar	Orangensaft	orange juice	Wasser	water
Kaffee	coffee	Roséwein	rosé wine	Weisswein	white wine
Kakao	cocoa	Rotwein	red wine	Zitronentee	tea with lemon

BREAKFASTS, STREET FOOD AND SNACKS

Breakfast (*Frühstuck*) in Austria usually comprises a pot of tea or coffee, together with a couple of rolls with butter and jam – this is what you'll get if you're staying in a youth hostel, private room, pension or inexpensive hotel. One step up, a "full continental breakfast" means you should get a bit of choice, perhaps cold meats and cheeses and, if you're really lucky, a hot egg-based snack. Most hotels at mid-range and above offer a buffet breakfast, which means you can gorge yourself on as much cereal, muesli, eggs, bread, rolls, cheese and meats as you can eat. Most cafés will have a set breakfast menu (again, usually a pot of coffee and a couple of bread rolls and/or pastries) for around öS45–60, and you can of course order extra bits and pieces separately. If you're self-catering, then fresh bread rolls (*Semmeln*) bought from a supermarket or bakery (*Bäckerei*) are delicious, as are *Kipferl*, croissant-style pastries.

Austrian **street food** centres on the ubiquitous *Würstelstand*, or sausage stand, which sells hot sausage (*Wurst*) as well as a few other things – usually French fries, soft drinks, canned beer and occasionally burgers. Numerous varieties of Wurst are available: *Frankfurter*, *Bratwurst* (fried sausage) or *Burenwurst* (boiled sausage) are the most common, but you could also try a *Debreziner*, a spicy Hungarian sausage, a *Currywurst*, which speaks for itself, a *Käsekrainer*, a sausage filled with blobs of molten cheese, or a *Bosna*, a thin and spicy Balkan sausage. To accompany your sausage, you usually get a roll (*Semmel*) and some mustard (*Senf*), which can be either *scharf* (hot) or *süss* (sweet).

For a cheap sit-down meal, chains like Wienerwald (an upmarket fried chicken joint) and Nordsee (serving fish-based snacks) are well represented in most major towns, and offer a reasonably authentic central European alternative to the international burger chains. *Prima* is the biggest chain of **self-service** (*Selbstbedienung*) restaurants, with branches throughout Austria, and big town-centre department stores often have a self-service restaurant of their own. They're a good place to get a cheap meal, although surroundings are pretty unatmospheric, and they're usually only open in the daytime, closing at around 5–6pm. Train-station buffets usually offer reasonably inexpensive meals of the schnitzel and chips variety, although they're not always the kind of place that you'd want to sit down in for long.

RESTAURANTS AND MAIN MEALS

The main meals of the day can often be taken in a café (see p.39), although a larger choice of dishes will be offered by a **restaurant** or a **Gasthof** – the latter traditionally describing an inn, though nowadays use of the word merely implies that the establishment has a homely, traditional feel. A **Stübe**, or **Stüberl** ("small room" or "parlour"), also denotes an eating venue with a traditional or cosy atmosphere. Other words for restaurant to look out for are **Gasthaus** and **Gastwirtschaft**. In mountain areas you can eat in an atmospheric, pine-clad *Hütte*, or *Almhütte* (literally "meadow-hut"), which will offer a modest range of food and drink to skiers in winter and walkers in summer.

For many Austrians, lunch rather than dinner is the day's principal repast, although this doesn't usually affect the choice of food that you'll be offered in the evening. As a general rule, restaurants and Gasthöfe are open for lunch between noon and 2pm, and for dinner between 6pm and 9.30pm, although in cities and tourist resorts many establishments remain open until 11pm or midnight.

Eating out need not be expensive. Standards are generally high wherever you choose to eat, and price differences from one establishment to the next are usually reflected in the decor, the choice of items on the menu, and the way in which the food is presented, rather than in the quality of ingredients. A hearty soup will set you back something in the region of öS50–80, wherever you choose to eat. A main course of the schnitzel variety (with accompanying veg or salad) will cost öS90–130 in the more unassuming restaurants, and will rarely rise above a ceiling of öS200–220 in plush establishments. The cheapest main courses on offer are often the combinations of cheese and pasta-style noodles (such as *Kasspätzln* or *Käsnudl*; see "What to eat" below) so characteristic Austrian rural cuisine. They're usually priced somewhere in the öS80–120 bracket, and even the most upmarket restaurants will have at least one basic, inexpensive dish of this kind on the menu.

Most places will have a full menu (*Speisekarte*) of individually priced dishes, as well as a two- or three-course **set menu** (often chalked up on a board outside), which is often much better value. A Mittagsmenü is a lunchtime set menu, and a Tagesmenü is a set menu that's available all day.

WHAT TO EAT

The basis of Austrian cooking is what is known as *gute bürgerliche Küche* – literally "good burghers' cuisine", so called in order to distinguish it from the noodles-and-cheese dishes that once formed the diet of the peasantry. As a result, the kind of food you'll find on restaurant menus today is often rather uniform, revolving as it does around a set repertoire of solid, meat-based dishes.

Light meals and starters (*Vorspeise*) include *Frittatensuppe*, a clear soup containing small strips of pancake, *Gulaschsuppe*, a much more substantial, paprika-rich beef-and-vegetable soup, and *Serbische Bohnensuppe* (Serbian bean soup), a spicy affair that makes a good lunchtime meal on its own. Another common lunchtime item is *Bauernschmaus*, a platter of cold meats, slices of sausage and bread.

Most common of the **main dishes** (*Hauptspeise*) are the schnitzel dishes (pan-fried cutlet, based on veal (*Kalb*) and pork (*Schwein*): *Wiener Schnitzel*, a veal or pork cutlet fried in breadcrumbs, is the most famous, although *Pariser Schnitzel* (fried in batter) and *Natur Schnitzel* (schnitzel fried on its own or with a creamy sauce) are also ubiquitous. The other classic Austrian

dishes you'll find almost anywhere are *Backhendl*, chicken fried in breadcrumbs, *Schweinsbraten*, slices of roast pork, *Zwiebelrostbraten*, slices of roast beef liberally covered with fried onions, and *Tafelspitz*, a quintessentially Viennese dish of boiled beef, potatoes and horseradish sauce. Main courses like these usually come served with potatoes and either vegetables or a salad. In addition, most restaurants offer one or two regional dishes reflecting local rustic cuisine. The most common of these is the combination of pasta noodles and alpine cheese that goes under the name of *Kasspätzln* in Vorarlberg and the Tyrol, and *Käsnockn* in the Salzburger Land. Two provinces whose **regional cuisine** has a particular impact are Carinthia, where *Käsnudl* (large pieces of ravioli-like dough filled with cheese) almost enjoys the status of a national dish, and the Tyrol, where *Schlipfkrapfen* (ravioli-like parcels with meat and/or potato filling), *Tiroler Knödel* (dumplings with small pieces of ham) and *Tiroler Gröstl* (pieces of onion, meat and potato fried in a pan) are specialities. Two traditional Austrian working-class dishes that sometimes appear on menus are *Schweinshaxe* (pork knuckle) and *Stelze* (leg of veal or pork). On a healthier note, look out for *Eierschwammerl*, chanterelle mushrooms that appear in various guises on menus in the autumn. The prevalence of *Gulyas* (goulash) is a Hungarian legacy, while the Italians make their presence known with dishes featuring *Nockerl*, the Austrians' heavy version of pasta – *Schinkenfleckerl*, flecks of ham baked in pasta, is especially popular.

You'll find **fish** featured all over Austria, but especially in areas near lakes or mountain streams. Trout (*Forelle*) is by far the most common dish, although native pike (*Hecht*), carp (*karpfen*) and pikeperch (*Fogosch*) are also popular. **Game** (*Wild*) is popular throughout the year, but especially in autumn when the bulk of the hunting takes place. Most restaurants in rural Austria will offer a special game menu in the second half of October, although many establishments (especially top-of-the-range ones) will offer game dishes outside this period. The most common dishes are *Hirsch* (venison), *Gems* (chamois) and *Reh* (roe deer), and sometimes *Wildschwein* (wild boar) crops up. **Seasonal menus** are also worth looking out for in May, when dishes featuring freshly harvested *Spargel* (asparagus) appear almost everywhere, and in November, when the period around St Martin's Day (November 11) is marked by the serving of roast *Gans* (goose).

Austria is hardly a paradise for **vegetarians**. Upmarket establishments usually have a couple of imaginative vegetarian choices on the menu (*Strudel* containing vegetables, spinach or cheese feature fairly often), but in most smaller restau-rants and Gasthöfe you might have to rely on omelettes. Note that apparently meat-free soups (such as the sweet and not-at-all-foul-smelling *Knoblauchsuppe*, or garlic soup) are very often based on meat stock – ask restaurant staff to be

COFFEE AND CAKES

Coffee

On average, the Austrians drink almost twice as much coffee as beer (over a pint a day per head of the population). Austrian coffee culture is at its most developed in Vienna and the east of the country, where the varieties of coffee on offer are legion – when ordering, few Austrians ever ask for a straight *Kaffee* (if you do order a "Kaffee", you'll get a *Verlängerten* – see below). Cities like Salzburg, Graz and Innsbruck possess coffeehouses as grand and dripping in atmosphere as those of the capital, but outside these urban centres you mustn't expect the full range of beverages to be offered.

Once you've selected the type of coffee you want, prefix it with the word kleiner (small) or grosser (large). The grander the coffeehouse, the more likely your infusion will come served on a little silver tray with a glass of water.

Brauner	Black coffee with a small amount of milk	*Mazagran*	Coffee served with an ice cube and laced with rum
Einspänner	The traditional Viennese coffee, served in a glass and topped with whipped cream (*Schlagobers*)	*Mélange*	Equal measures of frothed milk and coffee
Eiskaffee	Iced coffee with ice cream and whipped cream	*Mokka*	Black coffee flavoured slightly with mocha
Fiaker	A coffee with a shot of rum	*Pharisäer*	Coffee in a glass topped with whipped cream, served with a small glass of rum on the side
Kaffee Crème	Coffee served with a little jug of milk		
		Schwarzer	Black coffee
Kapuziner	Austrian version of a cappuccino	*Türkische*	Coffee grains and sugar boiled up together in individual copper pots to create a strong, sweet brew
Konsul	Black coffee with a spot of cream		
Kurz	Viennese version of an espresso	*Verlängerten*	Slightly weaker than normal coffee, served with optional milk

Cakes

Many cafés will have *Torten* piled high in a display cabinet, in which case you can simply point to the one that takes your fancy. The best cafés still bake their own cakes, and all can be served with a help-ing of *Schlagobers*. The following are some of the more common choices.

Apfelstrudel	Apple and raisins wrapped in pas-try and sprinkled with icing sugar	*Linzertorte*	Jam tart made with almond pastry
Dobostorte	A rich Hungarian cake made up of alternate layers of biscuit sponge and chocolate icing sugar	*Mohnstrudel*	A bread-like roly-poly pudding with a poppyseed and raisin filling
Esterházytorte	Several layers of cream and sponge coated in white icing with a feather design on top	*Sachertorte*	The most famous of the Viennese cakes, and in some ways the least interesting – a chocolate sponge cake coated in chocolate, most often with a layer of apricot jam beneath the chocolate coating
Guglhupf	Sigmund Freud's favourite, at its most basic a simple sponge cake baked in a fluted ring mould and cut into slices		
		Topfenstrudel	Like an *Apfelstrudel*, but with a sweet curd cheese filling

sure of what's in them. Regional dishes like *Kärntner Käsnudl* and *Kasspätzln* (see p.37) are usually completely meat-free, although some traditional noodles-and-cheese combinations include small pieces of ham – again, it's a good idea to ask before ordering.

The main alternative to Austria's stolid meat-and-potatoes cuisine is provided by **pizzerias**, which crop up in most settlements of any size – largely good-quality, inexpensive, authentic affairs producing pizzas on traditional Italian lines, and usually offering a wide range of pasta dishes as well. Most medium-to-large-sized towns will have a Chinese restaurant, while other cuisines – notably Mexican and Indian – are increasingly represented in the big cities. Chinese restaurants in particular are often good places to look for a cheap Mittagsmenü, or set lunchtime menu.

Obviously in a country with such a famous sweet tooth, there's no shortage of rich **desserts** (*Mehlspeisen*) on most menus. Apart from the omnipresent *Apfelstrudel*, *Palatschinken* (pancakes) filled with jam and/or curd cheese are a regular feature. Look out, too, for *Topfenstrudel*, a delicious cheesecake/strudel combination, *Marillenknödel*, sweet apricot dumplings, and the politically incorrect *Mohr im Hemd* – literally "Moor in a shirt" – a chocolate pudding with hot chocolate sauce and whipped cream. See also "Coffee and cakes" opposite.

CAFÉS

For urban Austrians, daytime drinking traditionally centres around the **café** or the **Kaffeehaus**. There's no real difference between the two: the name "*Kaffeehaus*" suggests some historical pedigree – a relaxing, urban café, furnished with a stock of the day's newspapers, in the vein of the grand, atmospheric Viennese cafés – but cafés, too, offer essentially the same range of food and drink. Both serve alcoholic and soft drinks, cakes and a wide range of different coffees (see "Coffee and cakes" opposite). Places where cakes and pastries are baked on the premises often call themselves a *Café-Konditorei*, or Kaffee-Konditorei. Many places also serve substantial lunches and main evening meals, although the fare on offer may be slightly more expensive than that offered by a straightforward restaurant. Cafés and coffeehouses often open as early as

7am and continue until early evening; those in big cities remain open until 11pm or later.

BARS AND HEURIGEN

Although some cafés stay open quite late in the evening, most night-time drinking centres on a growing number of **bars** and **Musikcafés** – bars in which taped music or a live DJ play an important part, though this doesn't usually mean that there will be any dancing. Most stay open until 1–2am; in cities and alpine resorts opening hours may extend further, especially on Friday and Saturday nights. An alternative place to do your drinking is in one of Austria's many **Heurigen**, the wine taverns found predominantly in the former villages of Vienna's outer suburbs, on the slopes of the Wienerwald, and in the many wine regions of Lower Austria, Burgenland and Styria. The word *heurig* means "this year's", as it was here that the vintner would encourage tastings in order to try and sell a few bottles of his (exclusively white) wine. In the good old days, people used to bring their own picnics to consume and sat on wooden benches in the vintner's garden whilst sampling the wine, but nowadays, most *Heurigen* provide a self-service (usually, but not exclusively, cold) buffet of traditional peasant fare. Traditionally, a visit to a *Heuriger* is accompanied by *Schrammelmusik*, sentimental fiddle, guitar and accordion music, though today such music only features at the more touristy ventures in Vienna. Real *Heurigen* are only permitted to open for 300 days in any one year, and may only sell wine and food produced on the premises. If the *Heuriger* is open, the custom is to display a *Buschen*, or bunch of evergreen boughs, over the entrance, with a sign telling you it's *ausg'stekt* ("hung out"). Those that still abide by the strict *Heurigen* laws generally have a sign saying *Buschenschank*, though it has to be said that some have now attained restaurant licences in order to open all year round. A display board at the centre of the smaller villages lists those *Heurigen* that are currently open; otherwise the local tourist office will have the details.

WHAT TO DRINK

Most Austrian **beer** is a high-quality brew of the light, continental-lager type. Beers that you'll encounter throughout Austria, not just in their home region, are *Gold Fassl* from Vienna, *Gösser* from Leoben in Styria, *Stiegl* from Salzburg, *Villacher* from Villach and *Puntigamer* from Graz. Smaller breweries still have big influence locally – *Murauer*, from Murau in Styria, and *Fohrenburg*, from Bludenz in Vorarlberg, are well worth looking out for. Many Austrian breweries produce speciality beers alongside their regular brews, such as *Märzen*, a slightly stronger, maltier concoction than the norm, and *dunkeles Bier* (dark beer), similar to stout. In addition, many Austrian bars serve foreign beer on draught, especially the excellent Czech brands Budvar and Pilsener Urquell, as well as international favourites like Guinness. Beer is generally drunk by the half-litre, or *Krügerl*, but you can also ask for a third of a litre, or *Seidl*, a fifth of a litre, *Pfiff*, and occasionally a *Mass*, or litre jug. Draught beer is *Bier vom Fass*, and is cheaper than buying either Austrian or imported bottled beers – of which most bars offer an impressive selection. Bottled *Weissbier* (wheat beer) is worth trying: it's extremely fizzy, and you must pour it painfully slowly to avoid creating a vast head.

Wine runs beer a close second as Austria's favourite alcoholic tipple. A wide range is available in bars, restaurants and cafés everywhere, but in the main wine-producing areas, the best place to try the local vintage is in a *Heuriger* or a *Buschenshenk* (wine tavern; see p.39). Wine is drunk by the *Viertel* (a 25cl mug) or the *Achterl* (a 12.5cl glass). The majority of wine produced in Austria is white, the dry, fruity *Grüner Veltliner* being the most popular. Look out, too, for *Sturm*, the half-fermented young wine that hits the streets and bars in autumn. Most red wine hails from Burgenland, where the most sought-after is *Blaufränkisch*.

Common to the **apple**-growing areas of Austria – mostly Styria and Carinthia – is a drink called *Most*, drier than cider and slightly less alcoholic. Austrians are also extraordinarily fond of **spirits**, particularly *Schnapps*, made in a variety of delicate fruit flavours and occasionally known as *Obstler*. Many towns and villages produce their own brand of *Obstler* – especially in the south, where fruit orchards abound – and it's a good idea when you're drinking or dining out to ask which local variety the staff recommend.

COMMUNICATIONS

Most post offices (*Postämte*) are open Monday to Friday 8am to noon and 2 to 6pm; those in larger towns often stay open during lunchtime, in addition to a couple of hours on Saturday morning (8–10am). Vienna, and cities like Graz, Salzburg and Innsbruck, have at least one post office that is open 24 hours a day, seven days a week. Addresses of these are given in the relevant parts of this guide.

Air mail (*Flugpost*) between Austria and the UK usually takes three or four days, about a week to reach the US, and ten days to Australia and New Zealand. For stamps (*Briefmarken*) for postcards within the EU, you may be able to go to a tobacconist (*Tabak*), though for anything more complicated or further afield, you'll probably have to go to a post office in order to have your letter or parcel weighed.

Poste restante (*Postlagernd*) letters can be sent to any post office, if you know the address. To collect mail, go to the counter marked *Postlagernde Sendungen* – mail should be addressed using this term rather than "poste restante". It will be held for thirty days (remember to take your passport when going to collect it).

TELEPHONES

Austrian **phone booths**, usually dark green with a bright-yellow roof and logo, are easy enough to

DIALLING CODES

To Austria

From Australia and New Zealand ☎0011 43	From Britain and Ireland ☎00 43	From North America ☎011 43

The dialling codes for individual Austrian towns and cities are provided throughout the guide. (When dialling from abroad, don't include the 0 that precedes each regional code.) Note that the Vienna city code is 1 when phoning from abroad; but 0222 when phoning from elsewhere in Austria.

From Austria

Australia ☎0061	Ireland ☎00353	New Zealand ☎0064	North America ☎001	UK ☎0044

Information

Local directory enquiries ☎1611   **International operator** ☎1616

spot and to use, some even having instructions in four languages (including English). The dialling tone is a short and then a long pulse; the ringing tone is long and regular; engaged is short and rapid. Although the minimum charge is öS1, you're likely to need much more than that in order to make even a **local call**, since Austria has one of the most expensive telephone systems in the world.

You can make an **international call** from any phone; it's easiest to do so with a **phone card** (*Telefonkarte*) rather than fumbling for change. *Telefonkarten* are available from all post offices, tobacconists and some other shops, in öS50, öS100 and öS200 denominations. The other option is to go to one of the larger post offices and use their **direct phone service** facility: a booth will be allocated to you from the counter marked *Fremdgespräche*, which is where you pay once you've finished. The post office is also the place to go if you want to make a collect call (*Rückgespräch*).

The number of digits in **telephone numbers** in Austria can vary wildly from region to region. Often, a telephone number is followed by a hyphen and a couple of additional digits – this merely denotes that it's an extension number that can be dialled direct.

THE MEDIA

Heavily subsidized by the state, the Austrian media is for the most part conservative and lacking in cut and thrust. The only locally produced English-language newspaper is the monthly *Vienna Reporter*, a thin broadsheet available in the capital, with good local news and selective listings.

The **Austrian press** is pretty uninspiring, with nearly half the population reading either the *Neue Kronen Zeitung* or *Kurier* tabloids, both of which are fairly right-wing. Of the qualities, *Der Standard*, printed on pink paper, is more liberal compared with the rather strait-laced *Die Presse*. Both of the above are considered to be Vienna-centric by folk outside the capital, hence the pop-

ularity in western Austria of two major regional dailies, the Salzburg-based *Salzburger Nachtrichten*, and Innsbruck's *Tiroler Tageszeitung*, both of which are fairly conservative. Newspaper stands in city centres, large train stations and well-touristed resorts stock a variety of **English-language newspapers**. You can usually get the European edition of the British broadsheet the *Guardian*, printed in Frankfurt, by mid-morning the same day. Similarly, the *International Herald Tribune* is widely available the same day. Other papers tend to be a day or so old.

Vienna boasts a good weekly **listings** tabloid, *Falter*, which is lively, politicized and critical, and comes out on a Friday. Although it's entirely in

German, it's easy enough to decipher the listings. Outside Vienna, regional dailies like the *Salzburger Nachrichten* or the *Tiroler Tageszeitung* will have limited listings of what's on in their particular area; otherwise, local editions of the *Kurier* or *Neue Kronen Zeitung* are the best places to look. If your German is up to it, most cafés and bars, and the traditional Viennese coffeehouses, have a selection of newspapers and magazines for patrons to browse through.

Austrian **television** is unlikely to win any international awards for cutting-edge programming or presentation. The two state-run channels are ORF 1 and ORF 2; other channels regularly accessible include the ARD and ZDF German channels, which are more or less indistinguishable from the Austrian

ones. Many hotels and pensions have satellite TV, bringing the joys of CNN and MTV to your room.

The state-run **radio** channels all feature a lot of chattering, though Ö1 (87.8/92FM) offers a good dose of classical music, in addition to news in English and French at 8am. State-run Blue Danube Radio (103.8FM) is the sort of channel you'll either love or hate, mixing AOR and transatlantic chat with the odd bit of news and weather in English, German and French; after 7pm, Blue Danube changes to U4 ("ooh-fear"), playing alternative and ambient music throughout the night. The BBC World Service broadcasts in English on 100.8FM in Vienna, though you'll have to revert to short wave in order to receive it anywhere else in the country.

OPENING HOURS, PUBLIC HOLIDAYS AND SIGHTSEEING

Opening hours in Austria are strictly controlled, and it can be difficult to obtain even the most basic provisions in the evening or at weekends. Most shops are open Monday to Friday 8.30am–6pm, Sat 8am–noon – except on the first Saturday of the month (known as the *Langersamstag*, or "long Saturday"), when hours are 8am–5pm. In smaller communities, shops may well close for an hour or two at lunchtime. Shops at the main train stations and airports are sometimes open late into the evening and at weekends, but you can't buy much at these places save for newspapers, sweets, soft drinks, cigarettes and rudimentary snacks.

HOLIDAYS

On national public holidays (see box), banks and shops will be closed all day. Museums and galleries will, somewhat confusingly, either be closed or open for free; for example, the vast majority are open for free on October 26, whereas most are closed on December 25. During the school summer holidays – July and August – you'll find that many theatres and other businesses in Vienna and some provincial centres close for all or some of the period.

MUSEUMS, GALLERIES AND CHURCHES

There are no hard-and-fast rules governing museum and gallery opening times in Austria. They're often closed on Mondays, especially in Vienna,

but check opening times within the text of this guide before setting out.

Museums and galleries in Austria go under a number of different names. Designations like *Historischesmuseum* and *Archäologischesmuseum* are fairly self-explanatory, although in the major provincial capitals you'll also come across *Landesmuseum* (provincial museum; also *Landesgalerie*), which deals more specifically with the history of a whole province. Those at Graz (Styria), Innsbruck (the Tyrol) and Bregenz (Vorarlberg) provide a comprehensive introduction to the art and culture of the surrounding region. A *Stadtmuseum* (town museum) is usually more local-

---

PUBLIC HOLIDAYS
January 1 (*Neues Jahr*)
January 6 (Epiphany/*Dreikönigsfest*)
Easter Monday (*Ostermontag*)
May 1 (Labour Day/*Tag des Arbeits*)
Ascension Day (6th Thursday after Easter/ *Christi Himmelfahrt*)
Whit Monday (6th Monday after Easter/ *Pfingstmontag*)
Corpus Christi (*Fronleichnam*)
August 15 (Assumption Day/*Maria Himmelfahrt*)
October 26 (National Day/*Nationalfeiertag*)
November 1 (All Saints' Day/*Allerheiligen*)
December 8 (Immaculate Conception/*Maria Empfängnis*)
December 25 (*Weihnachtstag*)
December 26 (Boxing Day)

ized in its focus, while a *Heimatmuseum* (literally "homeland museum") is likely to include material on regional customs and crafts — as is a *Volkskunstmuseum* (folklore museum). One of the best introductions to traditional Austrian culture is a *Freilichtmuseum*, or open-air museum, in which wooden farmhouses and other rustic buildings have been assembled and frozen in time — the best of these are at Stübing just outside Graz, Grossgmain near Salzburg, and Maria Saal in Carinthia.

Many of Austria's castles, palaces and aristocratic residences now hold local museums or displays relating to their erstwhile princely owners — *Schloss* is a loose term that can mean either castle or palace, while *Burg* tends to describe a hilltop fortress. Finally, Austria's industrial heritage is often dramatically showcased in a *Schaubergwerk*, or show-mine. Those that deserve special mention are the former iron-ore workings at Eisenerz in Styria, the Terra Mystica lead-mine near Villach in Carinthia, and the silvermine at Schwaz in the Tyrol.

Labelling in English and other languages other than German is fairly patchy, even in the big city museums, and you may have to buy a small **English-language brochure** (typically öS30–50) in order to get the best out of the attraction. Some sights, especially castles, former palaces, monasteries and show-mines, are only accessible by **guided tour** (*Führung*). Tours usually depart on the hour (again, timings are given throughout this book where relevant), although some establishments only go ahead with the tour if a sufficient number of people have turned up (usually around five). By the same token, you may be turned away from a tour if it's already oversubscribed. Big attractions may offer tours in English, but in most cases you'll have to tag along with a German-speaking guide and hope that he or she is prepared to give an English summary at intervals.

When quoting **entrance fees** throughout this guide, we've given the full adult rate. Bear in mind, however, that museums, and other attractions, often give a **reduction** of about fifty percent to students (on production of a valid student card) and children under the age of 16. Very young children are often admitted free, although the cutoff age for this varies from place to place.

Churches in city centres and well-touristed areas usually stay open daily from 7am to 7pm or later, but many of those in suburbs or rural areas only allow you to peep in from the foyer, except just before and after mass. Again, if a church has set opening times, we've said so in the text of the Guide. The churches and chapels of Austria's many historic **monasteries** and **abbeys** are usually (but not always) accessible to all-comers, although they're sometimes subject to an entrance fee. Abbeys like those at Melk (Lower Austria), St Florian (Upper Austria) and Admont (Styria) house some of the best of Austria's Gothic and Baroque religious art, as well as sumptuous libraries and *Prunkräume* (state rooms), although again these are subject to an entrance fee.

FESTIVALS

Vienna and Salzburg tend to hog the limelight as far as cultural festivals are concerned, but many provincial centres also host festivals of music and theatre that attract top international performers and enjoy a global reputation. There is also a full calendar of local religious festivals, many of which have their roots in rural folk customs dating from the pre-Christian era.

CULTURAL FESTIVALS

Annual **cultural festivals** occupy an important place in the Austrian calendar. The Salzburg Festival is perhaps the most renowned, and least accessible, of a long list of festivals, ranging from classical music to operetta, from jazz to film. We've listed the most important of these (see box), while further information on how to obtain tickets is included in the relevant sections of the Guide.

FOLK AND RELIGIOUS FESTIVALS

Austria retains a surprising number of rural festivals, which, despite their pagan origins, were taken over by the Catholic Church and vigorously promoted during the Counter-Reformation, in order to wean the populace away from Protestantism.

The year kicks off on the night of January 5–6 with one of the oddest of Austria's folk practices, the **Perchtenlaufen**, when folk dressed as

Perchten – kindly spirits wearing elaborate head-dresses – parade through the streets in the hope of ensuring good fortune and good harvests in the coming year. It's celebrated in various locations in the Salzburger Land and western Austria: the Pongauer Perchtenlauf (whose venue changes every year; see p.334) is the most renowned fest. The same night sees the **Glöcklerlaufen** in the Salzkammergut town of Ebensee, a related ritual in which the men of the community don giant tissue-paper head-dresses illuminated from within by lanterns. Both *Perchten* and *Glöckler* costumes are a common sight in regional museums.

January and early February sees the height of **Fasching**, or the carnival season, which officially starts on November 11 and comes to an end on Shrove Tuesday (*Faschingsdienstag*). The weeks in the run up to Shrove Tuesday are marked by lavish society balls in Vienna and Salzburg. On Ash Wednesday, families greet the arrival of Lent by eating *Heringschmaus*, a platter of various dried, salted and pickled fish. Also in February, but at four-year intervals, are two Tyrolean New Year fertility rituals, which echo the costumed parades of the *Perchtenlaufen*: the *Schemenlaufen* in the town of Imst and the *Schellerlaufen* in nearby Nassereith.

The three great movable feasts of spring and early summer, **Easter** (*Oster*), **Whitsun** (*Pfingsten*) and **Corpus Christi** (*Fronleichnam*), all provide the excuse for long-weekend holidays and family outings. Corpus Christi is marked by religious processions in the Salzkammergut towns of Traunkirchen and Hallstatt – in both cases, celebrants take to the waters of nearby lakes in flotillas of tiny boats. The summer solstice is the occasion for the lighting of bonfires on high mountains in some areas on the night of June 21–22 (known as the *Bergfeuer* in Ehrwald, see p.454; or the *Sonnwendfeier* in the Gasteinertal, see p.338). In alpine parts of Austria, September and October see the **descent of the cattle herds** from the high mountain pastures where they spend the summer. Festivals marking the event – usually called *Alpabtrieb* or *Almabtrieb* – are held in many areas, notably Zell am Ziller (see p.425) on the first weekend in October, and Mayrhofen (see p.428) on the second weekend of the same month. **All Saints' Day** (*Allerheiligen*) on November 1 is taken seriously across the country, with hordes

ANNUAL CULTURAL FESTIVALS

BREGENZ
Bregenzer Festspiele (late July to late Aug). Opera performed outdoors on a floating stage on the Bodensee.

EISENSTADT
Haydn Festival (Sept). Featuring large-scale orchestral works and smaller chamber pieces by Haydn, and involving top international performers.

FELDKIRCH
Schubertiade (June). Orchestral and chamber music with a strong Schubert bias.

GRAZ
Styriarte (mid-June to mid-July). Classical music.
Steirischer Herbst (late Sept to late Oct). Avantgarde music, theatre, film and art.

LINZ
Ars Electronica (Sept). Electronic and avantgarde music.
Bruckner Festival (early Sept to early Oct). Orchestral music by Bruckner and contemporary composers. Opens with a big laser and fireworks display.

MÖRBISCH
Seefestspiele (mid-July to late Aug). Operetta performed on an open-air stage on the shores of the Neusiedlersee.

MILLSTATT
Internationale Musikwoche (July–Aug). Classical chamber music.

SALZBURG
Mozartwoche (Jan). Mozart-penned classical music.
Sommer Szene (June & July). Experimental theatre, dance and rock.
Salzburger Festspiele (July & Aug). Theatre, opera and symphonic music, usually featuring some Mozart.
Salzburger Jazz Herbst (Nov). International jazz festival.

VIENNA
Wiener Festwochen (May to mid-June). Opera, music and theatre.
Klangbogen Wien (July to early Sept). The city's big summer music festival, which includes a two-week Jazzfest in July.
Viennale (late Oct). The trendy film festival.
Wien Modern (late Oct to early Nov). Contemporary classical music.
Mozart Festival (Dec). A big pull for visitors in the run-up to Christmas.

WIESEN
Festglände (June–Sept). Series of open-air rock festivals, dubbed the "Austrian Woodstock", held 15km southwest of Eisenstadt.

heading out to the cemeteries to pay their respects to the dead.

The feast of **St Barbara**, patron of miners and tunnellers, is celebrated in mining areas (such as at the Styrian towns of Leoben and Eisenerz) with parades and special church services, either on the day itself (December 4) or on the nearest Sunday. Also at the beginning of December, Christmas preparations get under way with **Christmas markets** (*Christkindlmärkte*) taking place in the cities. The biggest of these is in front of the Rathaus in Vienna, although big markets also take place in the Domplatz in Salzburg and in Innsbruck's old town. **St Nicholas' Day** on December 5 sees a procession in Innsbruck and, on the night of December 5–6, a custom known

as the **Krampuslaufen** (when demonically masked males run through the streets to symbolize the evil spirits chased away by the goodly St Nicholas himself) takes place in many areas, notably Zell am See (see p.342). **Christmas** (*Weihnacht*) is usually a private, family affair, although in some areas carol singers go from house to house in order to symbolize the visit of the three wise men to Bethlehem; a record of their visit is chalked above the door of each household, using the letters K, M and B to denote Kaspar, Melchior and Balthazar – you're bound to encounter some of these strange chalk marks as you travel around Austria, because it's considered unlucky to wipe them off until the following year's visit.

SPORTS AND OUTDOOR ACTIVITIES

Whatever the season, if you're looking for an active outdoor holiday you'll be spoilt for choice in Austria. In summer, well-maintained footpaths and expansive mountain scenery make it something of a paradise for walkers. Fast-flowing alpine rivers and tranquil lakes offer a great range of water-based pursuits, and most holiday resorts of any size cater to tennis, swimming and golf enthusiasts. In winter, wherever you are in alpine parts, you'll be in striking distance of a winter sports centre of one sort or another. Winter sports have deep roots in Austria, and locals will ski or snowboard anywhere there's a serviceable slope. The season generally lasts from early December to early April, though skiing and snowboarding are possible all the year round in a small number of high-mountain areas.

WALKING

Austria offers some of the finest walking terrain in Europe. Variety is the order of the day, with lowland walks in the east of the country, and gently rolling hills in southern Styria, Upper Austria and Lower Austria, contrasting sharply with the more challenging, alpine regions of central and western Austria. Tracks are for the most part well marked and well maintained, and numerous, well-positioned signposts often include an estimation of how long a particular route will take.

In alpine Austria, much of the tourist infrastructure developed for the winter sports crowd is available for ramblers and hikers in the summer, and the basic forms of mountain lift (cable cars, gondolas and chairlifts; see "Skiing and Snowboarding", p.49) are often pressed into service from late spring until early autumn in order to convey sightseers and walkers to higher altitudes. Walks that require spending a night or more on the mountain utilize the network of mountain huts (Hütte), which provide rudimentary dorm accommodation in mountain areas (see p.33). Some huts are privately owned, but most are run by the Österreichischer Alpenverein or their affiliates. Details of some all-day mountain walks and more ambitious hut-to-hut walks are included in this guide.

PLANNING YOUR WALK

Whatever level of walking you intend to do, a good **map** is essential. There's usually a wide choice of maps on sale in tourist offices, bookshops and souvenir shops once you arrive; details of map-buying options outside Austria are given on page 22. Whichever map you buy, walking routes will be marked according to a rigid **colour scheme**: tracks marked in blue designate easy routes, while red ones are intermediate, and black ones difficult. Tracks marked in blue are usually on the flat, or involve an ascent gentle enough to be accessible to most people with average mobility. Those in red usually involve steeper gradients, but they shouldn't pose too many problems to people of reasonable fitness. Those in black may have been designated as such for a number of reasons: they might be high-altitude tracks prone to year-round snow and ice; involve a sheer drop on one or both sides of the track, therefore requiring a good head for heights; or include stretches where a certain amount of scrambling or climbing is necessary (such stretches are usually protected with cables). On no account should you set off to tackle a black route unless you're an experienced walker, or you're in the company of someone who is. One good way of getting an introduction to walking in the Alps – especially black routes, or walks on glaciers, neither of which you should attempt on your own – is to join one of the many **guided walks** organized by tourist offices throughout Austria in the summer. Sometimes these are free, but you can usually expect to pay öS80–120 per person for a half-day walk.

THE AUSTRIAN ALPINE CLUB

Österreichischer Alpenverein, Wilhelm-Griel-Strasse 15, Innsbruck (☎59547, fax 575 528).

UK branch: Austrian Alpine Club, PO Box 43, Welwyn Garden City, Hertfordshire Al8 6PQ (☎01707/324835).

Members are entitled to a fifty percent reduction on accommodation in all alpine huts run by the ÖAV. Membership costs £29 per year (£22 for those aged 15–18 and over 60; £9 for under-15s).

Always check the weather forecast before setting out, as mountain weather can change rapidly. Even if you're merely going on a cable-car ride to the summit of some local peak in order to enjoy the view and embark on a brief amble, it's worth taking a pullover and a waterproof jacket at the very least. For anything more ambitious than this, windproof and waterproof clothing is essential. Choosing the right footwear is of prime importance, too: trainers are only really adequate for a short walk on the flat, and you'd be foolish to attempt walks of any duration in alpine regions without a good pair of walking boots.

Be extra vigilant when crossing mountain streams, patches of snow or exposed rocks. Some trails have sections safeguarded with ropes or cables, while signs announcing *nur für Geübte* warn that the route is for experienced walkers only. Avoid straying onto glaciers and snowfields unless accompanied by a mountaineer who is experienced in glacier travel and has the necessary equipment to deal with crevasse rescue. You should never embark on a walk that can't reasonably be completed well before dusk. Gauging distance that can be covered depends on many variables, inlcuding terrain, fitness levels, weight being carried and so on. Reasonably fit people carrying a light rucksack should be able to manage 4.5km per hour on the flat, plus an additional hour for every 350m of ascent. Don't be too proud to turn back should the weather deteriorate or the route become difficult or dangerous.

For those on all-day or **hut-to-hut walks**, the list of what to take with you increases. Although signposts and waymarks are frequent in most areas, it is prudent to carry a map and compass – and know how to use them. A first-aid kit, whistle and torch should also be taken in case of emergencies. Carry food for the day, including emergency rations and at least one litre of liquid per person. Leave a note of your itinerary and expected time of return with a

responsible person, and when using mountain huts enter the route details in the book provided. If unable to reach the destination at which you're expected, try to send a message to prevent the mountain rescue team being called out. If you do get into trouble, the **International Distress Signal** is six quick blasts on a whistle (or flashes with a torch) followed by a minute's pause. Then repeat. The response is three signals followed by a minute's silence. Mountain rescue can be very expensive, and it won't be covered by most regular travel **insurance** policies. If you're devoting all or most of your holiday to serious walking in the Alps, it's a good idea to ask a travel agent or insurance company about getting specific cover for what you're doing. Membership of the Austrian Alpine Club includes worldwide mountain accident rescue cover.

LAKE AND RIVER ACTIVITIES

Austria's many lakes serve as centres of warm-weather sporting action – predominantly the lakes of the Salzkammergut, the Wörthersee, Ossiachersee and Millstättersee in Carinthia, and the Neusiedler See in Burgenland. All of the above are well equipped with **windsurfing** schools and **sailing** schools, the latter usually offering a range of courses in a variety of craft. Courses in all disciplines tend to last a week, although shorter, two-day crash courses are often available. Expect to pay around öS2000 for a seven-day course, öS900 for a crash course. Courses will be in German and, although not all instructors speak English, most schools will make an effort to tailor their courses to suit your needs if you show persistent interest. Most sailing and windsurfing schools will also rent out surfboards and boats to those who already have experience – addresses of schools are given throughout this book. On the larger lakes, **water-skiing** and **paraskiing** are usually on offer.

Scuba diving is a popular activity in the lakes of the Salzkammergut, although each lake only allows diving in designated areas, and at certain times of the year (transgressors will be fined). Addresses of places where you can find out more, hire equipment or join diving courses, are provided in the relevant sections of the Guide.

RAFTING

Rafting is an increasingly popular activity on the fast-flowing rivers of the Tyrol, and involves sharing a large dinghy with a ten- to fifteen-strong group of people and hurtling downstream. The dinghy will be captained by a local guide, and safety equipment (such as lifejackets) will be provided. A trip usually costs around öS550–600 per person depending on duration, and you can often choose between travelling a mild stretch of the river, or a more fast-flowing one – children under a certain age may be excluded from the latter. The main centres for rafting are the towns of Imst and Landeck on the River Inn, Taxenbach near Zell am See, and the village of Sölden in the Ötztal. (Most tourist resorts in western Austria run regular trips to these centres, so you don't have to stay in the Inn Valley or the Ötztal in order to take part.) These areas are also popular for **canoeing** and **kayaking**, and it's fairly easy to rent equipment and obtain advice on which stretches of the river you can use once you arrive – local tourist offices are the obvious starting point for enquiries, although other contact addresses are given in this book where relevant.

FISHING

It's relatively easy to indulge in a spot of **fishing** on Austria's lakes and rivers, even if you're only spending a day or two in a particular area. Tourist offices should be your first point of contact when enquiring about where to fish and where to hire equipment. You'll have to buy a fishing **licence** – the tourist office will sell you one, or at least point you in the direction of a local sports shop where they're available. The cost of a licence often depends on whether you're intending to fish from dry land or from a boat: for the former, expect to pay öS200–250 per day, öS700–1000 per week.

SKIING AND SNOWBOARDING

Almost all Austrians know how to ski, and for those living in alpine areas skiing represents (for much of the year at least) the major recreational activity. The emphasis is very much on **downhill skiing**, although **nordic** (cross-country) skiing is practised almost anywhere there's enough snow to make it practicable. The increasing popularity of **snowboarding** is injecting the Austrian skiing scene – and the après-ski scene – with a new vigour. Most resort areas have a mixture of terrain suitable for different ability levels, with runs coded by colour: blue runs are for beginners, red runs for intermediates, and black for advanced skiers only.

PLANNING YOUR TRIP

Most places in alpine Austria will have nursery slopes and a ski school of sorts, and if you're a

beginner (or you're travelling with children who are new to skiing) you can learn to ski or snowboard almost anywhere. However, it's a good idea to pick a resort where the nursery slopes are in the valley floor near the hotels, rather than some distance away, and where easy runs (which a beginner might progress onto after a few days) are within good striking distance. It may also be worth avoiding resorts (notably in the Arlberg region) that are traditionally popular with advanced skiers and where beginners may feel out of place. The relatively laid-back, small-scale village resorts like Alpbach, Niederau and Obergürgl in the Tyrol, and Neukirchen in the Salzburger Land, are enduringly popular with first-time skiers; that said, glitzy, fashionable and traditionally more expensive Lech in the Vorarlberg is just as good a place to learn. All of the above feature regularly in the package-holiday brochures. If you're travelling independently, Kals in the East Tyrol is a good place for young families and children learning to ski – it's not a destination offered by package companies.

Intermediate skiers have a much wider choice, with most Austrian resorts of any size offering extensive intermediate areas linked together by interconnecting lift networks. You'll find a wide and varied skiing terrain at your disposal at Söll, Ischgl, Mayrhofen and Kitzbühel in the Tyrol; and at St Johann and Saalbach–Hinteglemm in the Salzburger Land. Saalbach–Hinterglemm also boasts several runs for the **advanced** skier, and the Badgastein region is worth investigating, although the most challenging terrain is to be found in the Arlberg region, Austria's top destination for off-piste skiing. St Anton provides the best access to the Arlberg slopes, although St Christoph, Lech and Zürs are sufficiently nearby to be serviceable bases.

All-year skiing is possible on a number of high-mountain **glaciers**, except during particularly hot summers if conditions get too slushy. The main glacier areas are the Dachstein, accessible from Schladming in Styria; the Kitzsteinhorn, accessible from Zell am See–Kaprun in the Salzburger Land; Sölden in the Ötztal; and Stubai, accessible from Fulpmes or Innsbruck in the Tyrol.

Your choice of resort will also depend on whether you're looking for a lively place with lots of nightlife or a more laid-back, traditional village. As a general rule, a resort that is at the same time a sizable town (Zell am See, Badgastein, Kitzbühel) is going to see more night-time action than a small village. Village resorts like Alpbach, Niederau and Wagrain have preserved their unspoilt, rural character, and in places such as these après-ski tends to be confined to your hotel-bar. Villages like Söll, Sölden and Ischgl, on the other hand, have experienced much more indiscriminate tourist development, and bars and discos are correspondingly thick on the ground. Some of these places (notably Söll) have earned a largely undeserved reputation as lager-lout resorts in the past, and such alarmist reports shouldn't dissuade you from spending a family holiday there. The swishest nightlife is to be found in high-society resorts like Kitzbühel and Lech–Zürs – bear in mind that food and drink prices will be correspondingly high.

LIFTS, PASSES AND BASIC COSTS

Access to the slopes is provided by a variety of **lifts**. The most common of these are the *Seilbahn*, or single-cabin **cable car**, the *Gondelbahn*, or **gondola** (a succession of smaller cabins suspended from the same cable), and the *Sesselbahn*, or **chairlift**. You'll also encounter the *Standseilbahn*, or **funicular**, and the more rudimentary *Schlepplift*, or **T-bar lift**. Single journeys on any of these can be quite expensive, so you'll need to buy a **ski pass**, which entitles you to unlimited use of all the various lifts in your area over a certain period of time. A variety of passes are usually available, ranging in duration from one-day to six-day, thirteen-day, one-month and occasionally longer.

Prices of ski passes vary wildly from one area to the next, and are usually dependent on how fashionable the resort is, and how wide an area the pass covers. Wherever you are in Austria, one-day ski pass prices rarely fall below the öS350 mark, and most are in the öS400–450 range (although the cost of a one-day pass is often graded according to how early in the day you buy it). A six-day ski pass for the low-key resort of Alpbach in the Tyrol, covering the slopes above Alpbach and the nearby village of Reith, costs around öS1400, whereas a six-day ski pass for more trendy St Anton covers the whole of the Arlberg region (embracing nearby resorts Zürs and Lech) and weighs in at a hefty öS2200 – wide-ranging passes such as these are undoubtedly worth it if you're an experienced skier keen to cover a lot of ground.

Assuming you're not already kitted out, **rental** of skis (or snowboard) and boots for six days will probably set you back öS1400 or more. If you're a beginner, you'll also have to budget for **tuition**, with six-days' worth of lessons (usually about 4hr

---

---

of tuition a day) costing something in the region of öS1300–1800. Beginners' snowboarding courses usually last about three days and cost upwards of öS1400.

SNOWBOARDING

Snowboarding is becoming the dominant winter activity for increasing numbers of younger Austrians, although not all the resorts in the country are geared up with the kind of facilities – a fun-park featuring obstacles and jumps, or a half-pipe (a kind of cross between a ski piste and a bobsleigh run) – specifically designed with snowboarding in mind. A well-equipped resort favoured by Austrian snowboarders but rarely featured in holiday brochures is Axamer Lizum, just southwest of Innsbruck; if you're staying in the Tyrolean capital, it's relatively easy to pop out there for the day. Schladming is a good place to learn how to snowboard, while St Anton and Zell am See are both well equipped to deal with the demands of the more experienced. The glacier above Zell am See's sister resort Kaprun is a good spot for all-year snowboarding. It's easy to rent snowboard gear and sign up for some lessons in all the above-mentioned resorts, and Schladming, St Anton and Zell am See–Kaprun all feature regularly in the package-holiday brochures.

NORDIC SKIING

Most alpine resorts will offer the chance to sample *Langlauf*, or **nordic** (cross-country) skiing, utilizing prepared trails (known as *Loipe*) down in the valley floor below the main alpine ski slopes. Both Ramsau above Schladming and Ehrwald–Lermoos in the Tyrol offer the most challenging network of trails, although other resorts shouldn't be discounted if all you want to do is take a few lessons and try the sport out. Few companies offer specific nordic packages in Austria – save for Waymark Holidays (see "Package and specialist operators", p.6) – but you can always book a standard skiing package to a mainstream resort like Ischgl, Kitzbühel or Schladming, and then register for a nordic skiing course once you arrive.

SKIING AS A SPECTATOR SPORT

The main venues for **international skiing competitions** in Austria are Schladming, St. Anton and Kitzbühel, each of which hosts World Cup downhill and slalom races in January (contact local tourist offices for precise dates). The most famous of these is the Hahnenkamm downhill in Kitzbühel, which usually takes place mid-January for women and the end of January for men – the latter is an important date in the society calendar. Austria's most important ski-jumping sites are Bischofshofen in the Salzburger Land and the Bergisel just outside Innsbruck; again the big international World Cup meetings are usually scheduled for January, and you should check with local tourist offices for details.

POLICE, TROUBLE AND SEXUAL HARASSMENT

The Austrians are a law-abiding lot, almost obsessively so. Few people drop litter, and no one jaywalks. That said, crime does, of course, exist and is on the rise, so it's as well to take the usual precautions.

Almost all problems encountered by tourists in Austria are to do with **petty crime**. Reporting thefts to the **police** is straightforward enough, though it'll take some time to wade through the bureaucracy. The Austrian police (*Polizei*, known in some areas as *Gendarmerie*) – distinguishable by their dark-green uniforms and army-style officers' caps – are armed, and are not renowned for their friendliness, but they usually treat foreigners with courtesy. It's important to carry ID with you at all times (ideally your passport, or at least a driving licence). Making photocopies of your passport and tickets is a very sensible precaution.

There are few specific areas in which **female travellers** might feel uncomfortable. In **Vienna**, large sections of the **Gürtel ring road** double as a red-light district, and as such are best avoided. The area just southwest of the main train station in **Graz** has a similar reputation. Big-city train stations (particularly the Südbahnhof in Vienna) can be unsavoury after dark. Even so, none of these places are strictly speaking no-go areas. ÖBB (Austrian railways) have introduced *Damenabteilen* (women-only sections) on some InterCity and EuroCity expresses, especially those that involve travel late at night. You'll have to ask about these at station ticket offices when buying your ticket.

EMERGENCY PHONE NUMBERS
Fire ☎122.
Police ☎133.
Ambulance ☎144.

TRAVELLERS WITH DISABILITIES

Like most western European countries, there are now regulations in force in Austria which mean that all public buildings must provide wheelchair access. As a result, the country is becoming gradually more accessible for travellers with special needs.

Wheelchair access to **hotels** is by no means universal, however, and is more likely to be a feature of upmarket establishments than the more inexpensive places. Unfortunately, there's no currently available list of Austria-wide hotels that are geared up for wheelchairs, so you'll have to ring up local tourist offices and ask them which establishments are *Rollstuhlfreundlich* (wheelchair-friendly). Access to the **public transport** system is quite good providing you plan your trip in advance.

Nationwide, an increasing number of ÖBB **rail** services (marked by a wheelchair symbol in timetables) are equipped for wheelchair-bound travellers, and you'll be seated in a place with plenty of room and a wheelchair-accessible WC close at hand. The main drawback is that you have to book your trip at least three days in advance. Wheelchair access to trains is provided by all manned stations – the service isn't available from unstaffed wayside halts. People who aren't wheelchair-bound but who lack full mobility will be helped onto the train by station staff – although you're expected to register with staff at least thirty minutes before the time of departure.

Access to **urban transport** in the big cities is more patchy – only Vienna is in any way geared up for disabled travellers. In the capital, only the new U3 and U6 subway lines are fully equipped with lifts, escalators and a guidance system for the blind. Trams are not at all user-friendly, but some of the newer buses in Vienna "kneel" to let people on and off. For a clearer picture, phone for the leaflet (in English) *Vienna for Guests with Handicaps* from the Austrian tourist board before you set off. This describes the level of access to U-Bahn stations, hotels and many tourist sights, and contains lots of other useful pieces of information. Leaflets covering other cities are sadly lacking.

CONTACTS FOR TRAVELLERS WITH DISABILITIES

AUSTRALIA

ACROD (Australian Council for Rehabilitation of the Disabled), PO Box 60, Curtin, ACT 2605 (☎02/6282 4333).

BRITAIN

Holiday Care Service, 2nd Floor, Imperial Building, Victoria Rd, Horley, Surrey RH6 9HW (☎01293/774535). *Information on all aspects of travel.*

RADAR, 12 City Forum, 250 City Rd, London EC1V 8AS (☎0171/250 3222; Minicom ☎0171/250 4119). *A good source of advice on holidays and travel abroad.*

IRELAND

Irish Wheelchair Association, Blackheath Drive, Clontarf, Dublin 3 (☎01/833 8241). *National voluntary organization working with people with disabilities with related services for holidaymakers.*

NEW ZEALAND

Disabled Persons Assembly, 173–175 Victoria St, Wellington (☎04/801 9100).

NORTH AMERICA

Directions Unlimited, 720 N Bedford Rd, Bedford Hills, NY 10507 (☎1-800/533 5343). *Tour operator specializing in custom tours for people with disabilities.*

Mobility International USA, PO Box 10767, Eugene, OR 97440 (Voice and TDD ☎503/343 1284). *Information and referral services, access guides, tours and exchange programmes. Annual membership $25 (includes quarterly newsletter).*

Society for the Advancement of Travel for the Handicapped (SATH), 347 5th Ave, New York, NY 10016 (☎212/447 7284). *Non-profit-making travel industry referral service that passes queries onto its members as appropriate.*

Travel Information Service (☎215/456 9600). *Telephone-only information and referral service.*

Twin Peaks Press, Box 129, Vancouver, WA 98666 (☎206/694 2462 or 1-800/637 2256). *Publisher of the Directory of Travel Agencies for the Disabled ($19.95), listing more than 370 agencies worldwide; Travel for the Disabled ($19.95); the Directory of Accessible Van Rentals ($9.95) and Wheelchair Vagabond ($14.95), loaded with personal tips.*

DIRECTORY

ADDRESSES The name of the street always comes before the number of the building. In Vienna, an additional number (denoting the district within the city) precedes the name of the street.

BEACHES Austria's many lakes usually have bathing beaches, and some rivers – notably the Danube in and around Vienna – provide popular bathing areas as well. You can't just swim anywhere, though, and bathing is usually restricted to a specific area known as a *Strandbad* (plural *Strandbäder*), where you'll find a stretch of waterfront, a grassy area on which to lay your towel, changing cubicles and a snack stall or café. Some *Strandbäder* are free, but most charge about öS30–40 per day.

CIGARETTES are rarely sold in restaurants or bars, and you might have trouble stocking up late at night. Your best bet is to buy them from tobacconists (*Tabak*) during normal shop opening hours, or from the vending machines that are to be found outside the *Tabak*s.

ELECTRIC POWER 220 volts, out of round, two-pin plugs. Equip yourself with an adapter before leaving home if you want to use your hairdryer, laptop, etc. while travelling.

LAUNDRY Launderettes (*Schnellwäscherei*) are fairly easy to find in most towns, and addresses of big-city launderettes are included under "Listings" in this guide.

LEFT LUGGAGE The bigger train stations have coin-operated lockers (*Schliessfächer*) costing from öS30 to 60 for 24 hours. Most train stations (not the small ones) have a left-luggage counter (*Gepäckaufbewahrung*) costing between öS30 and öS60 per item.

LOST PROPERTY Lost-property offices (*Fundämte*) are usually located at the local police station.

SWIMMING Most Austrian towns of any size will have somewhere where you can swim. A *Freibad* is an open-air pool; a *Hallenbad*, an indoor pool; and an *Erlebnis-Hallenbad*, an adventure pool, which will probably feature water slides, whirlpool effects and so on. Spa-resorts like Badgastein will have public swimming pools filled with mineral-rich waters from the local thermal springs. Entrance fees are rarely steep, ranging from about öS40 for a small-town *Freibad* to about öS70 for a big-city *Erlebnis-Hallenbad*.

TIME Normally one hour ahead of GMT, six hours ahead of Eastern Standard Time and nine hours ahead of Pacific Standard Time. Austrian Summer Time lasts from the beginning of April to the end of September.

TIPPING When paying in restaurants, cafés and bars, it's customary to add a tip of around five to ten percent – even for a single drink at the bar.

TOILETS As a general rule, free (and invariably spotless) public toilets are found in all town centres in Austria, and are usually located somewhere near the main square. Otherwise, head for the nearest train station.

PART TWO

THE

GUIDE

VIENNA

Most people visit **Vienna** with a vivid image of the city in their minds: a monumental vision of Habsburg palaces, trotting white horses, old ladies in fur coats and mountains of fat cream cakes. And they're unlikely to be disappointed, for the city positively feeds off imperial nostalgia – High Baroque churches and aristocratic mansions pepper the Innere Stadt, monumental projects from the late nineteenth century line the Ringstrasse, and postcards of the emperor Franz-Josef and his beautiful wife Elisabeth still sell by the sackful. Just as compelling as the old Habsburg stand-bys are the wonderful Jugendstil and early modernist buildings, products of the era of Freud, Klimt, Schiele, Mahler and Schönberg, when the city's famous coffeehouses were filled with intellectuals from every corner of the empire. Without doubt, this was Vienna's golden age, after which all has been decline: with the end of the empire in 1918, the city was reduced from a metropolis of over two million, capital of a vast empire of fifty million, to one of barely more than 1.5 million and federal capital of a small country of just eight million souls.

Given the city's twentieth-century history (for more on which, see below), it's hardly surprising that the Viennese are as keen as anyone to continue plugging the good old days. The visual scars from this turbulent history are comparatively light – even Hitler's sinister wartime *Flacktürme* (anti-aircraft towers) are confined to the suburbs – though the destruction of the city's enormous Jewish community, the driving force behind the city's fin-de-siècle culture, is a wound that has proved harder to heal. The city has struggled since to live up to its glorious past achievements, and has failed to shake off a reputation for xenophobia. Yet for all its problems, Vienna is still an inspiring city to visit, with one of the world's greatest art collections in the **Kunsthistorisches Museum**, world-class orchestras and a superb architectual heritage. It's also an eminently civilized place, clean, safe (for the most part) and peopled by citizens who do their best to live up to their reputation for *Gemütlichkeit*, or "cosiness". And despite its ageing population, it's also a city with a lively nightlife, with plenty of late-opening *Musikcafés* and drinking holes. Even Vienna's restaurants, long famous for quantity over quality, have discovered more innovative ways of cooking and are now supplemented by a wide range of ethnic restaurants.

Most first-time visitors spend the majority of their time in Vienna's central district, the **Innere Stadt**. Retaining much of its labyrinthine street layout, it's the city's main commercial district, packed with shops, cafés and restaurants. The chief sight here is the **Stephansdom**, Vienna's finest Gothic edifice, standing at the district's pedestrianized centre. Tucked into the southwest corner of the Innere Stadt is the **Hofburg**, the former imperial palace and seat of the Habsburgs, now housing a whole host of museums, the best of which is the Schatzkammer, home to the crown jewels.

The old fortifications enclosing the Innere Stadt were torn down in 1857, and over the next three decades gradually replaced by a showpiece boulevard called the **Ringstrasse**. Nowadays, the Ringstrasse is used and abused by cars and buses as a ring road, though it's still punctuated with the most grandiose public buildings of late-imperial Vienna, one of which is the **Kunsthistorisches Museum**. Beyond the Ringstrasse lie Vienna's seven **Vorstädte**, or inner suburbs, whose outer boundary is marked by the traffic-clogged *Gürtel* (literally "belt"), or ring road. The highlight out here is the **Belvedere**, where you can see a wealth of paintings by Austria's

Hermannskogel
(542m)

Leopoldsberg
(425m)

Kahlenberg
(484m)

HÖHENSTRASSE

Am
Cobenzl

Bellevuehöhe
(388m)

GRINZING

HEILIGENSTADT

Geymüllerschlössl

DÖBLING
19

HERNALS
17

WÄHRING
18

W i e n e r w a l d

OTTAKRING
16

THE GÜRTEL

Kirche am
Steinhof

RUDOLFSHEIM
15

PENZING
14

Westbahnhof

Technisches
Museum

HIETZING
13

Schönbrunn

MEIDLING
12

Lainzer
Tiergarten

Hermesvilla

Lainzer
Tor

LIESING 23

① Postal District Numbers

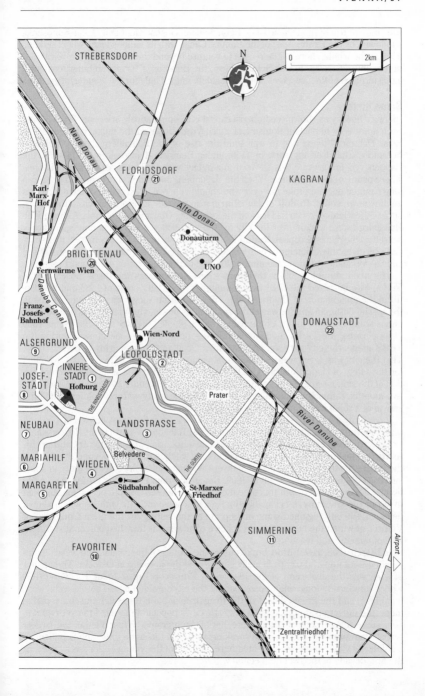

STREBERSDORF

N

0   2km

Neue Donau

FLORIDSDORF
㉑

KAGRAN

Karl-
Marx-
Hof

Alte Donau

Donauturm

BRIGITTENAU
⑳
Fernwärme Wien

UNO

Danube Canal

Franz-
Josefs-
Bahnhof

DONAUSTADT
㉒

Wien-Nord

ALSERGRUND
⑨

LEOPOLDSTADT
②

INNERE
STADT ①
Hofburg

JOSEF-
STADT
⑧

THE RINGSTRASSE

Prater

River Danube

NEUBAU
⑦

LANDSTRASSE
③

MARIAHILF
⑥

Belvedere

THE GÜRTEL

WIEDEN
④

MARGARETEN
⑤

Südbahnhof

St-Marxer
Friedhof

Airport

SIMMERING
⑪

FAVORITEN
⑩

Zentralfriedhof

pre-eminent trio of modern artists – Egon Schiele, Gustav Klimt and Oskar Kokoschka – followed by the **Prater**, east of the Danube Canal, with its famous ferris wheel and funfair. On the whole, there's little reason to venture beyond the *Gürtel* into the *Vororte*, or outer suburbs, except to visit **Schönbrunn**, the Habsburgs' former summer residence, a masterpiece of Rococo excess and an absolute must if only for the wonderful gardens.

Some history

Vienna's history as showpiece imperial capital is a comparatively brief one. From having been a not very important Roman fort called **Vindobona** on the military border of the River Danube, Vienna had to wait until the rise of the Babenberg dynasty before it became a capital of any sort. In 1156, under Heinrich II Jasomirgott (1141–72), the Babenbergs' margravate was elevated to a duchy, with the ducal palace situated somewhere near Am Hof in Vienna. When the Babenberg male line came to an end in 1246, a long-running dispute broke out over who should rule over the region. In the end, it was a little-known count, **Rudolf of Habsburg**, who proved victorious, much to the annoyance of the Viennese, who had backed the loser, King Otakar II of Bohemia. Although the Habsburgs were to rule over the city for the next 640 years, Vienna only sporadically served as the dynastic capital. **Rudolf IV** (1356–65) was one of the few to treat it as such, and was given the nickname "The Founder" after he established the city's university and laid the foundation stone of the future cathedral during the course of his short reign.

The main stumbling block to Vienna's development was the threat posed by the Turks, who besieged the city twice. Although it is the later siege of 1683 that has captured the imagination of historians, the **1529 Turkish siege** was a much closer-run thing. The Ottoman empire was at the zenith of its power, and Vienna was defended by only a small garrison under Count Salm. Having shelled the city and killed some 1500 of its citizens, the Turks suddenly withdrew – quite why, no one knows. During the **1683 siege**, the city garrison of 10,000 men faced an Ottoman army of over 200,000. That the city was saved was no thanks to its emperor, Leopold I (1658–1701), who fled for the safety of Upper Austria. This time the Turks' defeat was assured by a combination of the sultan's greed – he tried to force the city to surrender by besieging it for over two months, rather than storming it and sharing the booty with his soldiers – and the arrival of a relief force under Polish King Jan Sobieski.

It was only after the Turks had been beaten back from the gates of Vienna a second time that the city finally established itself as the Habsburgs' permanent *Residenzstadt,* or *Kaiserstadt*. Over the next hundred years, an outpouring of **Baroque art and architecture** transformed the city, which could now safely spread out beyond the walls of the Innere Stadt. During the Napoleonic era, Vienna was besieged twice more in short succession – in 1805, and again in 1809. Emperor Franz I (1792–1835) followed tradition by fleeing to safety, but this time the city surrendered on both occasions, and had to suffer the ignominy of occupation by French troops. In 1815, with Napoleon almost defeated, the city regained some of its pride as the setting for the great **Congress of Vienna**, at which the new European balance of power was thrashed out, amidst a great deal of dancing and feasting.

In March 1848, **revolution** broke out on the streets of the capital, and wasn't extinguished until imperial troops brutally suppressed the uprising in October. The upshot of it all was the accession of the 18-year-old **Emperor Franz-Josef I** (1848–1916), whose immensely long reign encompassed the city's golden age. The old walls were torn down and the great edifices of the **Ringstrasse** built: the court museums, parliament, the university, to name but a few. The city's population swelled to over two million, some ten percent of whom were Jewish immigrants, giving Vienna the largest Jewish community in the German-speaking world. At the same time, anti-Semitism as a politically viable force was invented here, in front of the young Hitler's very eyes, in the first decade of the twentieth century.

In the 1920s and early 1930s, Vienna became renowned for its enlightened municipal socialism, during a period that has since gone down in history as *Rotes Wien*, or **Red Vienna**. However, for much of the century the city, rather like Berlin, had the misfortune of serving as a weather vane of European history. The political battles between Left and Right fought out on the streets of Vienna mirrored those in Berlin, and the weekend Hitler enjoyed his greatest electoral victory in the Reichstag, Austro-fascism was declared in Vienna. In 1938, Vienna was the first foreign capital to fall to the Nazis, greeting the Führer with delirious enthusiasm, and sounding the death knell on the city's 200,000 Jews. For a decade after the war, Vienna, like Berlin, was under **Allied occupation**, divided into French, American, British and Soviet sectors, with the Innere Stadt as an international zone, in which all four powers patrolled the streets "four in a jeep", as the period became known.

Since the withdrawal of the four Allied powers in 1955, Vienna has lived a fairly peaceful existence, best known as one of the three cities that serve as UN headquarters and as host to international conferences. However, the opening up of eastern Europe and the break-up of Yugoslavia have had a profound effect on the city, with an estimated ten percent of the population now made up of immigrants. Although most Viennese can trace their ancestry back to the far corners of the old empire, many voters are fearful of the newcomers. The impact on voting patterns has been marked, with 1996 proving something of a watershed: the Socialists lost overall control of the city council for the first time in its history, while the far right Freedom Party (FPÖ) gained a staggering 27 percent of the vote.

Arrival, information and city transport

For all its grandiosity, Vienna is surprisingly compact: the centre is just a kilometre across at its broadest point, and you can travel from one side of the city to the other by public transport in less than thirty minutes. Although the **Danube** is crucial to Vienna's identity, most visitors see very little of the river, whose main arm flows through the outer suburbs to the northeast of the centre.

Arrival

The city's **international airport**, Flughafen Wien-Schwechat, lies around 20km southeast of the city. It's connected to the centre by S-Bahn line S7; **trains** leave every thirty minutes between 5am and 10pm, taking 25 minutes to reach Wien-Mitte, where most people alight, and terminating at Wien-Nord. This is the cheapest way of getting into town, costing around öS17, plus the price of a travel pass for the central zone (see p.61), which you can buy at the same time. **Buses** from the airport to the City Air Terminal bus station underneath the *Hilton Hotel* (adjacent to Wien-Mitte), are even more frequent, leaving every twenty minutes from 6.30am until 11.30pm, and every thirty minutes throughout the night; they take around twenty minutes to reach the city centre, and cost öS70 one way. There are also hourly buses to the Südbahnhof and Westbahnhof (see below). Taxis to the centre take twenty minutes or so and charge around öS400.

Arriving in Vienna by train from the west, you'll end up at the **Westbahnhof**, five U-Bahn stops west of Stephansplatz in the city centre. Trains from eastern Europe, Italy and the Balkans terminate at the **Südbahnhof**, to the south of the city centre; you can either walk five minutes west to Südtiroler Platz U-Bahn station, or hop on tram D into town. Of Vienna's other stations, **Franz-Josefs-Bahnhof**, in the northern suburb of Alsergrund, serves as arrival point for services from Lower Austria and the odd train from Prague (take tram D into town), while Wien-Nord (U-Bahn Praterstern), in Leopoldstadt, is used exclusively by local and regional trains, including the S-Bahn to the airport (see above).

> The telephone code for Vienna is ☎0222 from the rest of Austria
> and ☎01 from outside the country.

International, long-distance buses arrive at Vienna's **main bus terminal** beside Wien-Mitte, on the eastern edge of the city centre (U-Bahn Landstrasse). If you arrive on one of the **DDSG boat** services from further up the Danube, or from Bratislava or Budapest, you'll find yourself disembarking at the Reichsbrücke, some way northeast of the city centre; the nearest station (U-Bahn Vorgartenstrasse) is five minutes' walk away, one block west of Mexicoplatz.

Information

The main **tourist office** of the Vienna Tourist Board (*Wiener Tourismusverband*) is at Kärntnerstrasse 38 (daily 9am–7pm; ☎513 8892). It's a small office, with few leaflets on display, but if you have a specific enquiry, or just need directions, the staff will happily help out. It's worth asking for the latest *Museums* leaflet, listing all the current opening times, plus the *Young Vienna Scene* booklet, which contains some useful information, despite its cringe-making youthspeak. Other leaflets include the tourist board's monthly *Programm* for opera, concert and theatre schedules, and upcoming exhibitions and events. There are also **information desks** at the airport (24hr) and at the Westbahnhof (daily 7am–10pm) and Südbahnhof (6.30am–10pm).

The English-language monthly broadsheet *The Vienna Reporter* (öS25) carries selective **listings**, but for a more comprehensive rundown you need the weekly tabloid *Falter* (öS28), which comes out on Wednesdays. Even if your German isn't great, you should be able to decipher the pull-out *Wienprogramm & Lexicon* section, which contains the week's listings.

City transport

Vienna's Innere Stadt is best explored on foot, but for covering larger distances you'll need to use the enviable **public transport system**, the Wiener Linien. Predictably enough, the trams and buses are punctual and the rapidly expanding U-Bahn clean and very quick. The whole system runs from between 5 and 6am to between midnight and 1am; the only other way of getting home in the small hours is to catch one of the Nightline **night buses**. These run every thirty minutes from 12.30am to 4am, and all 22 routes pass through Schwedenplatz at some point. **Taxis** are plentiful and fairly reliable, too, with the minimum charge around öS25, followed by an extra öS10 or so per kilometre or couple of minutes. You can catch a cab at one of the taxi ranks around town, flag one down or phone ☎31300, 40100 or 60160. The most expensive way to get about, of course, is by **Fiaker**, one of the horse-drawn soft-top carriages driven by bowler-hatted, multilingual coachmen. There are *Fiaker* ranks at Stephansplatz, Heldenplatz, Michaelerplatz and Albertinaplatz. It's best to settle on the price and duration of your ride beforehand; the going rate is öS400 for twenty minutes, or öS1000 for an hour.

Tickets

A single-journey **ticket** (*Fahrschein*), standard for all forms of public transport (excluding night buses), costs öS17 from machines and ticket booths (*Vorverkäufe*) at U-Bahn stations, and also from tobacconists (*Tabak-Trafik*). When you enter the U-Bahn, or board a tram or bus, you must punch your ticket in one of the blue machines. You can then make one journey, during which you can change buses, trams or U-Bahn lines as many times as you like, as long as you proceed in a logical direction without any "breaks".

If you're planning on making more than two journeys a day, you should invest in a **travel pass**, or *Netzkarte*, which allows travel on all trams, buses, U- and S-Bahn trains within the city. You can buy a 24-hour ticket (öS50) or a 72-hour ticket (öS130) from machines and booths at all U-Bahn stations; when buying your ticket from a machine, select the central zone, or *Kernzone* (*Zone 100*), which covers the whole of Vienna. You must punch your single *Netzkarte* at the beginning of your first journey – your 24 or 72 hours starts from that point.

The much-touted **Wien-Karte** (Vienna Card; öS180) gives various discounts at local attractions, as well as being a 72-hour *Netzkarte*. In addition, you get discounts at such sights as the Hofburg and Schönbrunn, plus selected restaurants and shops. If you're in Vienna for a long weekend and intend to do quite a bit of sightseeing, then the ticket will probably pay for itself.

Another option is a **strip ticket**, or *Streifenkarte*. The bargain is the green *Umwelt-Streifennetzkarte* (öS265), which is valid for eight (not necessarily consecutive) days' travel, calculated from the hour of purchase. It can be used by one or more people – one person for eight days, two people for four, and so on – simply punch one strip on the card for each person in the group. To do this you must fold the card over before inserting it in the blue machines, starting with strip 1. The other *Streifenkarten* available are the four-journey (öS68) and eight-journey (öS136) tickets.

If you're staying in Vienna longer than three days, it might be worth buying a **weekly card**, or *Wochenkarte* (öS142), available only from the ticket offices at U-Bahn stations. The pass runs from 9am Monday to Monday, so there's no need to punch the ticket. When you buy your first *Wochenkarte*, you need to ask for a *Zeitkarte*, which you must sign on the back, and onto which you must attach your (self-adhesive) *Wochenkarte*. The **monthly ticket**, or *Monatskarte* (öS500), which runs for a calendar month, works in much the same way. Note that none of the passes are valid on **night buses**, for which you must buy a separate ticket costing öS25.

The Viennese being a law-abiding bunch, there are few **ticket inspectors**, but if you are caught without a valid ticket or pass, you'll be handed an on-the-spot fine of öS500 (on top of the appropriate fare).

GUIDED TOURS

Vienna Sightseeing Tours run a variety of **bus tours** around the city and surrounding districts. Their standard city tour (daily 10.30am, 11.45am & 3pm; 1hr 15min; öS220) takes you round the Ringstrasse; pick up a leaflet at the tourist office or any hotel or pension. Alternatively, you can save yourself the commentary by hopping on tram #1 or #2, which circumnavigate the Ringstrasse clockwise and anticlockwise respectively.

Every Saturday (11.30am and 1.30pm) and Sunday (9.30am, 11.30am and 1.30pm) from May to October, you can leap aboard a 1920s **tram** outside the Otto-Wagner-Pavillon on Karlsplatz and go on an hour-long guided tour, run by Wiener Linien; tickets cost öS200 and are available from Karlsplatz U-Bahn.

Most appealing are the walking tours organized by Vienna's official tourist guides – you'll find details, such as whether the tours are in German or English, in the monthly Wiener Spaziergänge leaflet from the tourist office. These cover a relatively small area in much greater detail, mixing historical facts with juicy anecdotes in the company of a local specialist. Subjects covered range from Jugendstil architecture to Jewish Vienna – the weekly Third Man tour takes you round the locations associated with the eponymous 1948 film (☎220 6620). Tours cost around öS110 and last about ninety minutes. Simply turn up at the meeting point specified.

The U- and S-Bahn

Vienna's **U-Bahn**, currently boasting five lines (U1–4 and U6), is by far the fastest way of getting around the city. Not all U-Bahn lines are underground: the U4 and U6 lines run partly on the old overground Stadtbahn created in the 1890s, and both lines retain some of their original stations and bridges designed by Otto Wagner.

The **S-Bahn**, or *Schnellbahn* in full, is of most use to Viennese commuters, though it's also the cheapest way of getting to and from the airport and is useful for day-trips to places in Lower Austria. S-Bahn trains are less frequent than U-Bahn trains – running every fifteen to thirty minutes – and are strictly timetabled.

Trams and buses

Vienna has one of the world's largest networks of **trams** – the *Strassenbahn* or *Bim*, after the noise of the bell), as they're known colloquially – with more than thirty routes crisscrossing the capital. After the U-Bahn, trams are the fastest and most efficient way of getting around, running every five to ten minutes. They're fairly punctual, though some lines don't run on weekends or late at night so be sure to check the timetables posted at every stop (*Haltestelle*).

Buses (*Autobusse*) mostly ply the narrow backstreets and outer suburbs and, despite having to battle with the traffic, are equally punctual. In the heart of the Innere Stadt, where there are no trams and only two U-Bahn stations, there are several very useful bus services:

#1A, which winds its way from Schottentor to Stubentor; #2A from Schwedenplatz through the Hofburg to Burgring; and #3A from Schottenring to Schwarzenbergplatz.

Accommodation

As you might expect, Vienna has some of the most opulent, historic **hotels** in Europe, with mesospheric prices to match. However, reasonably priced central accommodation can be found, especially in the numerous **pensions**. These are not necessarily inferior in quality to hotels – in fact some are a whole lot better. Vienna also has plenty of space in official HI and independent **hostels**, although these can be booked up months in advance, so try and ring ahead to make a reservation before you leave. The city's tourist offices (see p.60) can book **private rooms** for upwards of öS300 per person per night (with a minimum of three nights' stay) for a small commission. Inveterate **campers** have a wide choice of peripheral sites. If you arrive without a booking, any of the tourist offices can make a reservation for you, for which they charge around öS35. Our recommendations are divided by district, and listed alphabetically.

Hotels and pensions

Hotels and pensions in Vienna as a rule adhere to the standards of efficiency, modernity and cleanliness you'd expect in Austria. Although you can stay right in the Innere Stadt without breaking an arm and a leg, the cheapest places tend to be in the districts beyond the Ringstrasse. This is no bad thing, as the seventh (Neubau) and eighth (Josefstadt) districts have a wider choice of restaurants and bars than the central tourist zone. **Breakfast** is included in the price at most hotels and pensions, though what it comprises can differ enormously.

The Innere Stadt

Pension Aclon, 1, Dorotheergasse 6–8 (☎512 7940-0, fax 513 8751); U-Bahn Stephansplatz. Family-run pension in an incredible location – next door to the wonderful *Café Hawelka* – on the third floor with an elderly up-only lift (öS1). Nicely furnished rooms, some with shower and toilet. ④.

Hotel Austria, 1, Wolfengasse 3 (☎515 23, fax 515 23-506); U-Bahn Schwedenplatz. Plush family-run hotel, somewhat characterless but pleasantly located in a quiet cul-de-sac off Fleischmarkt, with some cheap rooms without en suite facilities. ⑤.

Pension Aviano, 1, Marco d'Avianogasse 1 (☎512 8330, fax 512 8330-6); U-Bahn Karlsplatz. Part of *Pertschy* pension chain. Squeezed onto the top floor of a building just off Kärntnerstrasse. Low ceilings, but roomy rooms, all en suite, with TV and fluffy, floral decor. ⑤.

Pension City, 1, Bauernmarkt 10 (☎533 9521, fax 535 5216); U-Bahn Stephansplatz. On the second floor of a wonderful late-nineteenth-century building and run by a friendly woman proprietor. Tastefully decorated rooms, all en-suite. ⑤.

ACCOMMODATION PRICE CODES

All **hotels and pensions** in this book have been graded according to the following price categories. All the codes are based on the rate for the least expensive double room during the **summer season**. In those places where winter is the high season, we've indicated winter room rates in the text. For more on accommodation, see p.30.

① under öS400	④ öS800–1000	⑦ öS1400–1600
② öS400–600	⑤ öS1000–1200	⑧ öS1600–1800
③ öS600–800	⑥ öS1200–1400	⑨ over öS1800

Palais Liechtenstein

Allgemeines Krankenhaus

Josephinum

Freud-Museum

Rossauer Kaserne

Ringturm

LAZARETTGASSE

SPITALGASSE

BERGGASSE

WÄHRINGERSTRASSE

HÖRLGASSE

Schottering

Votivkirche

MARIA-THERESIEN-STRASSE

Börse

ALSERSTRASSE

Schottentor

SCHOTTENRING

WIPPLINGERSTRASSE

ESSLINGGASSE

UNIVERSITÄTSTRASSE

Universität

SCHOTTENGASSE

Schottenstift

Maria am Gestade

LANDESGERICHTSSTRASSE

LANGE GASSE

SKODAGASSE

GRILLPARZERSTRASSE

TIEFER GRABEN

STRASSE

Rathaus

RATHAUSSTRASSE

Rathaus park

Burgtheater

Palais Ferstel

Kirche am Hof

KOHLMARKT

TUCHLAUBEN

DR-KARL-LUEGER-RING

Rathaus

Minoritenkirche

INNERE STADT

JOSEFSTÄDTERSTRASSE

JOSEF-STADT

Parlament

Bundeskanzleramt

Herrengasse

Peters-kirche

GRABEN

AUERSPERGSTRASSE

Volksgarten

Michaeler-kirche

Justizpalast

Heldenplatz

Hofburg

Michaelerkirche

Jüdisches Museum

LERCHENFELDER STRASSE

Lerchenfelder Strasse

DR-K-RENNER-RING

MUSEUMSTRASSE

Naturhistorisches Museum

Kaisergruft

NEUSTIFTGASSE

Volkstheater

Volkstheater

BURGRING

Burggarten

Hotel Sacher

BURGGASSE

SPITTELBERG

MARIA THERESIEN-PLATZ

Kunsthistorisches Museum

Burggarten

Staatsoper

Museumsquartier

MESSEPLATZ

OPERNRING

SIEBENSTERNGASSE

BABENBERGER STRASSE

Schillerplatz

KÄRNTNER

NEUBAU

Akademie der bildenden Künste

NEUBAUGASSE

Babenberger-strasse

FRIEDRICHSTRASSE

Secession

Karlsplatz

LINDENGASSE

Neubaugasse

MARIAHILFERSTRASSE

Theater-an-der-Wien

Karlsplatz

OPERNGASSE

GUMPENDORFER STRASSE

Haus des Meeres

Majolikahaus

Naschmarkt

WIENZEILE

WIEDER HAUPTSTRASSE

GUSSHAUS-

LINKE

WIENZEILE

RECHTE

Kettenbrückengasse

CENTRAL VIENNA

Schönbrunn   Schönbrunn

LEOPOLDSTADT

LANDSTASSE

Praterstern
Wien-Nord
Volksprater
Riesenrad
Strauss-Museum
Planetarium
Nestroyplatz
Ruprechtskirche
Altes Rathaus
Stadttempel
Urania
Schwedenplatz
Postsparkasse
Post Office
Former Kriegsministerium
KunstHausWien
Jesuitenkirche
GEORG-KOCH-PLATZ
Stephensdom
Dominikanerkirche
MAK
Hundertwasserhaus
Stephans-platz
Figarohaus
Landstrasse/Wien-Mitte
Wien-Mitte
Stubentor
Deutschordenskirche
Stadtpark
Strauss Monument
Kursalon
Wittgensteinhaus
Stadtpark
Rochusgasse
Musikverein
Konzerthaus
Historisches Museum der Stadt Wien
Soviet War Memorial
Gardekirche
British Embassy
Karlskirche
Unteres Belvedere
Palais Schwarzenberg
Rennweg
△ Oberes Belvedere

ACCOMMODATION

Aclon	20	Kugel	9
Altstadt Vienna	8	Lerner	4
Anna	10	Lindenhof	11
Astra	1	Mozart	16
Austria	27	Neuer Markt	23
Aviano	24	Nossek	17
Baltic	2	Orient	5
Bosch	32	Pertschy	19
Burgenland	12	Post	28
City	25	Praterstern	31
Esterházy	13	Quissana	15
Falstaff	3	Rathaus	6
Dr Geissler	29	Riedl	30
Goldenes Einhorn	14	St Stephan Appartement	22
Graben	21	Wandl	18
Kärntnerhof	26	Wild	7

0   500m

VIENNA'S POSTAL DISTRICTS AND ADDRESSES

Vienna is divided into 23 *Bezirke*, or postal districts, which spiral outwards from the first district (the Innere Stadt), in a clockwise direction, with only the odd geographical hiccup. When writing addresses, the Viennese write the number of the district first, followed by the name of the street, and then the house number; most residential addresses also include an apartment number, separated from the house number by a slash. For example: 9, Löblichgasse 11/14, denotes apartment no. 14 at no. 11 Löblichgasse in the ninth district.

Pension Dr Geissler, 1, Postgasse 14 (☎533 2803, fax 533 2635); U-Bahn Schwedenplatz. Anonymous modern pension on the eighth floor; all rooms with satellite TV, some en suite. ③.

Graben Hotel, 1, Dorotheergasse 3 (☎512 1531-0, fax 512 1531-20); U-Bahn Stephansplatz. The foyer is suitably lugubrious, with heavy velvet drapery, but all the rooms are modernized and smart, with en-suite shower and toilet. Location is great. ⑦.

Hotel Kärntnerhof, 1, Grashofgasse 4 (☎512 1923, fax 513 2228-33); U-Bahn Schwedenplatz/ Stephansplatz. Characterful rooms, though some are a bit dingy, so take a look first. Cheaper rooms are without en-suite facilities. ④.

Pension Lerner, 1, Wipplingerstrasse 23 (☎533 5219, fax 533 5678); U-Bahn Schottentor/ Herrengasse. Bright, simple rooms with shower, toilet, satellite TV, plus nice high ceilings and fans. Big buffet breakfasts served until 11am. ④.

Pension Neuer Markt, 1, Seilergasse 9 (☎512 2316, fax 513 9105); U-Bahn Stephansplatz. Very popular pension on the second floor of a lovely old patrician building. All rooms with bath or shower, some with views over Neuermarkt. ⑤.

Pension Nossek, 1, Graben 17 (☎533 7041-0, fax 535 3646); U-Bahn Stephansplatz. Large pension on three floors of an old building on the Graben; book in advance. ⑤.

Hotel Orient, 1, Tiefer Graben 30 (☎533 7307, fax 535 0340); U-Bahn Herrengasse. Vienna's equivalent of a Tokyo "love hotel", with rooms rented by the hour and per night. Couples come for the mind-boggling exotic decor, and the wide range of themed rooms from inexpensive to more than öS2000. ④–⑨.

Pension Pertschy, 1, Habsburgergasse 5 (☎534 49, fax 534 4949); U-Bahn Stephansplatz. Flagship of the *Pertschy* chain, with rooms off a series of plant-strewn balconies looking onto a lovely old courtyard. All rooms with high ceilings, tasteful furnishings and TV. ⑤.

Hotel Post, 1, Fleischmarkt 24 (☎515 83-0, fax 515 83-808); U-Bahn Schwedenplatz. Civilized, central hotel with big old rooms and modern furnishings, some without shower and toilet. ④.

Pension Riedl, 1, Georg-Coch-Platz 3 (☎512 7919, fax 512 7919); U-Bahn Schwedenplatz/Wien-Mitte. Bright, cheerful pension on the fourth floor of a wonderful fin-de-siècle building, overlooking the Postsparkasse. Rooms are small, but all have toilet and shower, and you get breakfast in bed. ④.

Hotel Römischer Kaiser, 1, Annagasse 16 (☎512 7751-0, fax 512 7751-13); U-Bahn Karlsplatz. Turn-of-the-century family-run hotel on a delightfully narrow side street off Kärntnerstrasse. New furnishings are successfully combined with the originals, though some rooms feature plainer, modern decor. Cable TV and en-suite rooms throughout. ⑨.

St Stephan Appartement-Pension, 1, Spiegelgasse 1 (☎512 2990-0, fax 512 2990-20). Incredible location in the Braun building overlooking Graben. An antique lift takes you up to the fourth floor, where there are just six doubles, each furnished in keeping with the period and with creaky parquet flooring. All have TV, shower, toilet and cooking facilities. No breakfast. ⑥.

Hotel Wandl, 1, Petersplatz 9 (☎534 55-0, fax 534 55-77); U-Bahn Stephansplatz. Modernized nineteenth-century hotel with uniformed staff, and period fittings in the grandiose dining room and in the high-ceilinged rooms. ⑤.

The Vorstädte

Altstadt Vienna, 7, Kirchengasse 41 (☎526 3399-0, fax 523 4901); U-Bahn Volkstheater. A cut above most other pensions, with laid-back staff, relaxing lounge and full-on buffet breakfast. Beautifully decorated en-suite rooms with high ceilings, and a great location, near Spittelberg and within easy walking distance of the Ring. ⑧.

Pension Anna, 7, Zieglergasse 18 (☎523 0160, fax 523 0160-39); U-Bahn Webgasse. First-floor pension run by a friendly couple. The startling light-blue decor doesn't extend into the fourteen bedrooms, all of which have en-suite shower and toilet. ⑤.

Pension Astra, 8, Alserstrasse 32 (☎402 4354, fax 402 4662-46); U-Bahn Alserstrasse. Mid sized pension on the mezzanine of an old patrician building. Friendly staff and a range of modernized rooms, from simple doubles without shower or toilet to roomy apartments. ④.

Pension Baltic, 8, Skodagasse 15 (☎405 0173); U-Bahn Alserstrasse. Variable rooms, but all of them large, with endearing creaky parquet floors and crudely added showers. ③.

Pension Bosch, 3, Keilgasse 13 (☎798 6179, fax 799 1718); S-Bahn Rennweg. Decent pension near the Südbahnhof, in a quiet backstreet behind the Belvedere, and an easy tram ride into town. ③.

Hotel Burgenland, 6, Esterhazygasse 26 (☎587 0381); U-Bahn Neubaugasse. Just off Mariahilferstrasse, and a bit gloomy inside, but offering fairly spacious rooms all with en-suite shower and toilet. ③.

Pension Esterhazy, 6, Nelkengasse 3 (☎587 5159); U-Bahn Neubaugasse. Basic rooms, but clean and close to Mariahilferstrasse. There's no reception as such and no breakfast – it's simply a place to crash. ②.

Pension Falstaff, 9, Müllnergasse 5 (☎317 9127, fax 317 9186-4); tram D. Highly regarded, comfortable pension with plain rooms, in a late nineteenth-century building. ②.

Hotel Goldenes Einhorn, 5, Am Hundsturm 5 (☎544 4755); U-Bahn Margaretengürtel. Inexpensive family-run place with fourteen rooms. In a residential area just within the Gürtel but well connected to the centre. Booking essential. ②.

Hotel Kugel, 7, Siebensterngasse 43 (☎523 3355, fax 523 1678); U-Bahn Neubaugasse. Jovial ownership and good location within spitting distance of Spittelberg's numerous restaurants and bars. Plain rooms, and continental breakfast only, in the *gemütlich* peasant-style breakfast room. ④.

Pension Lindenhof, 7, Lindengasse 4 (☎523 0498, fax 523 7362); U-Bahn Neubaugasse. On the first floor of a turn-of-the-century building at the Spittelberg end of this long street. Lovely, up-only lift (öS1) and appealing rooms with creaky parquet flooring. ③.

Pension Mozart, 6, Theobaldgasse 15 (☎ & fax 587 8505); U-Bahn Neubaugasse/ Babenbergerstrasse. No-frills pension on the mezzanine of a Jugendstil building, handy for both the Mariahilferstrasse and the Westbahnhof. ③.

Hotel Praterstern, 2, Mayergasse 6 (☎214 0123, fax 214 7880); U-Bahn Nestroyplatz. Turn-of-the-century hotel with some nice period touches and a pleasant outdoor courtyard. Simply furnished rooms with shower and toilet. ②.

Pension Quisisana, 6, Windmühlgasse 6 (☎ & fax 587 3341, fax 587 3341); U-Bahn Neubaugasse/ Babenbergerstrasse. Wonderful late nineteenth-century pension, a short stroll from the Kunsthistorisches, and run by a friendly old couple. Rooms are small but clean, and there's a continental breakfast in the adjoining café. ③.

Hotel Rathaus, 8, Lange Gasse 13 (☎406 0123, fax 408 4272); U-Bahn Lerchenfelder Strasse. Clean, comfortable and quiet hotel a few blocks west of the Rathaus, with some cheap singles without en-suite bathroom. ⑤.

Hotel Regina, 9, Rooseveltplatz 15 (☎404 46-0, fax 408 8392); U-Bahn Schottentor. Huge Ringstrasse hotel next door to the Votivkirche, with gloriously heavy Viennese decor in the public areas and in some of the rooms. ⑨.

Pension Wild, 8, Lange Gasse 10 (☎406 5174, fax 402 2168); U-Bahn Lerchenfelder Strasse. Backpackers' favourite, a short walk from the Ring in a student district behind the university. Booking essential. ②.

Hostels, student halls and camping

Vienna's official **Hostelling International** *Jugendherbergen* are efficient, clean and, occasionally, even friendly. However, with just one exception, they're all a long way from the centre. Most of the beds are in segregated dorms, but some do have bunk-bed doubles. Prices vary slightly, but are around öS150 a night, including a simple continental breakfast. If possible, you should make an advance **reservation** as soon as you know when you might be arriving, as places can be booked out months in advance; at the very least, you should ring before turning up. The biggest practical drawback to the official hostels is that they throw you out each day at 9am in order to clean, and won't let you back in until 3 or 4pm. The lure of the **independent hostel**, then, is that while the prices are much the same as the HI hostels, there is generally no curfew and no lockout. Such places do tend to be a bit more run-down and cramped, though.

From July to September, there are dorm beds, doubles and even single rooms available in *Studentenheime* or **student halls** of residence. Prices tend to be a little higher than in the hostels (and breakfast is often not included), but there's no curfew or lockout.

Finally, Vienna's **campsites** are all quite far out from the centre, on the perimeters of the city, and so for committed campers only. Pitches cost around öS60, plus a fee of around öS60 per person.

Hostels

Jugendgästehaus Brigittenau, 20, Friedrich-Engels-Platz 24 (☎332 8294-0, fax 330 8379); tram N from U-Bahn Schwedenplatz or Dresdner Strasse. Huge modern hostel in a dour working-class suburb, with dorms and en-suite bunk-bed doubles. Curfew 1am; 24hr reception.

Jugendgästehaus Hütteldorf-Hacking, 13, Schlossberggasse 8 (☎877 0263, fax 877 0263-2); S- and U-Bahn Hütteldorf. A 271-bed dorm-only hostel way out in the sticks, but convenient for those who wish to explore the wilds of the Lainzer Tiergarten and Schönbrunn. Nightlife is somewhat curtailed by the 11.45pm curfew.

Kolpingfamilie Wien-Meidling, 12, Bendlgasse 10–12 (☎835487, fax 812 2130); U-Bahn Niederhofstrasse. Modern hostel easily reached by U-Bahn from the centre. Beds in the big dorms go for under öS100 (without breakfast). Curfew 1am; 24hr reception.

Jugendherberge Myrthengasse/Neustiftgasse, 7, Myrthengasse 7/Neustiftgasse 85 (☎523 6316, fax 523 5849); bus #48A or 10min walk from U-Bahn Volkstheater. The most central of all the official hostels, with 243 dorm beds divided between two addresses, round the corner from each other. Book well in advance and go to the Myrthengasse reception on arrival. Curfew 1am.

Hostel Ruthensteiner, 15, Robert-Hamerling-Gasse 24 (☎834693); U-Bahn Westbahnhof. In easy walking distance of the Westbahnhof, with dorm beds, singles and doubles (discounts for HI members). Open all year. No curfew.

Schlossherberge am Wilhelminenberg, 16, Savoyenstrasse 2 (☎458503-7000, fax 458503-702); bus #146B or #46B from S-Bahn Ottakring or tram J terminus. Offering 164 beds in a beautiful location next to a Neoclassical mansion in the Vienna Woods, but not a great base from which to sample the nightlife. Curfew 11.45pm. Dorm beds and doubles (③) available.

Turmherberge "Don Bosco", 3, Lechnerstrasse 12 (☎713 1494); U-Bahn Kardinal-Nagl-Platz. Without doubt the cheapest beds in town (öS70 without breakfast), in a church tower in the back end of Landstrasse. Curfew 11.25pm. Open March–Nov.

Hostel Zöhrer, 8, Skodagasse 26 (☎430730, fax 408 0409); U-Bahn Josefstädter Strasse or trams #5 and #33. Small private hostel centrally located with dorms and bunk-bed doubles. No curfew and no lockout. Open all year.

Student halls

Auersperg, 8, Auerspergstrasse 9 (☎432 5490); U-Bahn Lerchenfelder Strasse. Excellent, central location, just off the Ring. Singles and doubles with or without shower and toilet. ②.

Haus Döbling, 19, Gymnasiumstrasse 85 (☎347631-16); tram #38. Prices vary slightly according to whether you want "hotel service" or not. ①.

Josefstadt, 8, Buchfeldgasse 16 (☎406 5211); U-Bahn Rathaus. Tucked behind the Rathaus in a quiet backstreet. All rooms have en-suite shower. ②.

Porzellaneum, 9, Porzellangasse 30 (☎317 7282); tram D. Functional singles, doubles and quads for öS175 per head, popular with backpackers. No breakfast, but showers, courtyard and lounge with TV. ①.

Campsites

Camping Rodaun, 23, An der Au 2 (☎884154); tram #60 from U-Bahn Hietzing to its terminus, then 5min walk. Nice location by a stream in the very southwestern outskirts of Vienna, near the Wienerwald. Open April to mid-Nov.

Wien West I, 14, Hüttelbergstrasse 40 (☎914 2314); bus #151 from U-Bahn Hütteldorf, or a 15min walk from tram #49 terminus. In the plush, far-western suburbs of Vienna, close to the Wienerwald. Open mid-July to Aug.

Wien West II, 14, Hüttelbergstrasse 80 (☎914 2314); directions as for *Wien West I*. Just one bus stop on from *Wien West I*, but much larger, and with bungalows to rent (öS400; sleep four people; April–Oct). Closed Feb.

The Innere Stadt

The **Innere Stadt**, Vienna's first district, has been the very heart of the place since the Romans founded Vindobona here in 15 BC. It was here, too, that the Babenburg dukes built their powerbase in the twelfth century, and from 1533 the Habsburgs established the **Hofburg**, their imperial residence (dealt with in detail under a separate section on p.84). In fact, the city occupied pretty much the same space until the zigzag fortifications, which had protected the city on two occasions against the Turks, were finally taken down in the mid-nineteenth century.

The focus of the Innere Stadt is the magnificent cathedral, the **Stephansdom**, whose spire also acts as a useful landmark. Close by are the chief shopping streets of **Kärntnerstrasse**, **Graben** and **Kohlmarkt**, which get progressively more exclusive the nearer you get to the Hofburg. There's a steady ebb and flow of folk along these streets at most times of the day, but the **Kaisergruft**, the last resting place of the Habsburgs, just off Kärntnerstrasse, is the only sight that gets heavily clogged up with tour groups. Head off into the rest of the Innere Stadt, with its baffling medieval lanes, hidden courtyards and *Durchhäuser* (literally, "through-houses"), and you'll soon lose the crowds.

Stephansplatz and around

The geographical heart of the Innere Stadt is **Stephansplatz**, the lively, pedestrianized square that surrounds the hoary Gothic bulk of **Stephansdom**. As such, it's one of the best places for watching Viennese streetlife, from the benign young flame-haired punks who lounge around on the benches by the U-Bahn escalators to the beleaguered folk in eighteenth-century costumes wearily flogging tickets for up-and-coming classical concerts. The smell of horse dung wafts across the square from the *Fiakers* lined up along the north wall of the cathedral.

Apart from the cathedral, the dominant feature of the square is the **Haas Haus**, probably the singly most inappropriate building in the Innere Stadt and one which, not surprisingly, caused something of a furore when it was first unveiled in 1990. The real disappointment is that the architect, Hans Hollein, is clearly gifted – his equally uncompromising jewellery stores along Graben and Kohlmarkt are minor masterpieces. Here, though, the metal-coated glass and polished stone facade lacks subtlety, and the protruding turret is a veritable carbuncle; to cap it all, the interior is an unimaginative mini-shopping centre.

The Stephansdom

The **Stephansdom**, distinguished by the multicoloured chevrons on its roof, dominates the Viennese skyline as it has done for centuries. An obvious military target, it has endured two Turkish sieges, Napoleonic bombardment and, in the later stages of World War II, the attentions of American bombers and Russian artillery. That it sur-

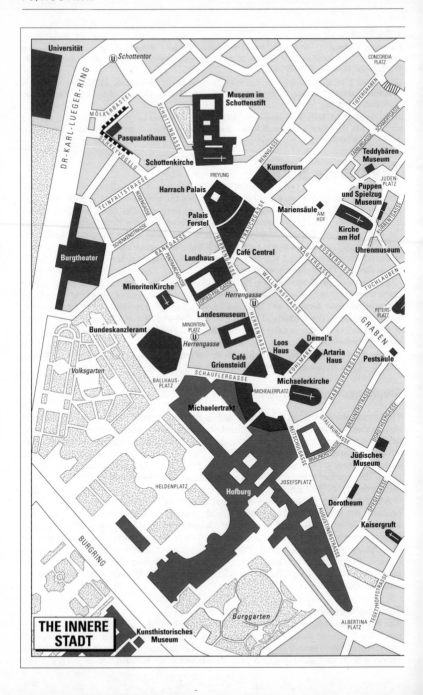

Universität

Ⓤ Schottentor

CONCORDIA PLATZ

DR·KARL·LUEGER·RING

MÖLKERBASTEI

SCHREYVOGELG

SCHOTTENGASSE

TIEFERGRABEN

SCHWERTGASSE

Pasqualatihaus

Schottenkirche

Museum im Schottenstift

RENNGASSE

FREYUNG

Kunstforum

FÄRBERGASSE

Teddybären Museum

JUDEN-PLATZ

Harrach Palais

TEINFALTSTRASSE

ROSENGASSE

SCHENKENSTRASSE

Palais Ferstel

STRAUCHGASSE

Mariensäule AM HOF

Puppen und Spielzug Museum

KURRENTGASSE

Kirche am Hof

BOGNERGASSE

Burgtheater

BANKGASSE

PENITENZGASSE

Landhaus

HERRENGASSE

Café Central

WALLNERSTRASSE

NAGLERGASSE

Uhrenmuseum

TUCHLAUBEN

MinoritenKirche

LEOPOLD·FIGL·GASSE

Herrengasse

Landesmuseum

MINORITEN-PLATZ

Ⓤ Herrengasse

HERRENGASSE

PETERS-PLATZ

GRABEN

Bundeskanzleramt

Volksgarten

Café Griensteidl

BALLHAUS-PLATZ

SCHAUFLERGASSE

KOHLMARKT

Loos Haus

Demel's

Artaria Haus

Pestsäule

HABSBURGERGASSE

Michaelerkirche

MICHAELERPLATZ

Michaelertrakt

REITSCHULGASSE

BRAUNERSTRASSE

STALLBURGGASSE

DOROTHEERGASSE

Jüdisches Museum

HELDENPLATZ

JOSEFSPLATZ

Hofburg

Dorotheum

AUGUSTINERSTRASSE

SPIEGELGASSE

Kaisergruft

BURGRING

Burggarten

ALBERTINA PLATZ

TEGETHOFFSTRASSE

THE INNERE STADT

Kunsthistorisches Museum

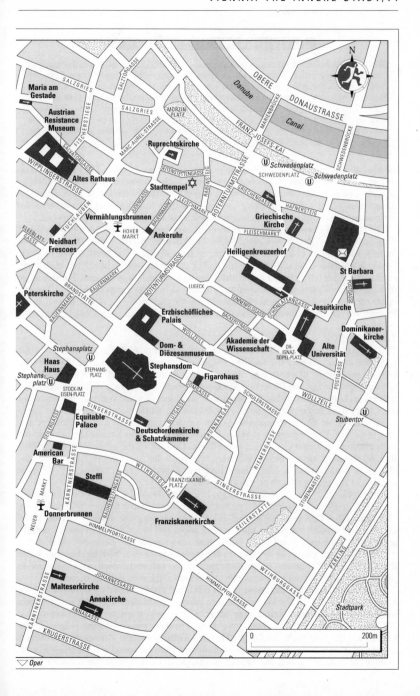

VISITING THE STEPHANSDOM

Although the cathedral opening hours are daily 6am to 10pm, tourists are discouraged from sightseeing during the religious services. In practice, this means visiting times are restricted to Monday to Saturday 9am to noon and 1pm to 5pm and Sunday 12.30pm to 5pm. Entrance is free, though to have a proper look at anything beyond the transept, you really need to join a guided tour (*Domführung*). These run Monday to Friday 10am and 3pm, Saturday 10am, 3pm and 7pm, Sunday 3pm, and cost öS40; you meet just inside the cathedral by the main door. Additional charges are made for the catacombs, the Pummerin and the Steffl (see below).

vived at all is a miracle, and it's dear to Viennese hearts as a result. The first church on this site was a Romanesque basilica, begun in 1137, but replaced after a fire in 1193 by an early-Gothic variant, which was itself reduced to rubble in the fire of 1258. The foundation stone of the current building was laid in 1359 by Rudolf IV, but it wasn't until the early twentieth century that the choir and several of the chapels were completed.

The cathedral's most magnificent feature is the sublime south tower (daily: March–Oct 9am–5.30pm; Nov–Feb 9am–4.30pm; öS20) – nicknamed "**Steffl**" (Little Stephen) by the locals – which soars to a not-so-little height of around 137m. The north tower, or Eagle Tower (daily 9am–6pm; öS40 for the lift, öS20 if you walk), was to have been built along similar lines, but fell victim to cost-cutting during the build-up to the first Turkish siege of 1529, its half-finished stump eventually receiving a copper cupola in 1556. You can climb (or take the lift) up the north tower to see the cathedral's great bell, known as the **Pummerin** (*Boomer*), though the Steffl, a blind scramble up 533 steps, has better views.

THE INTERIOR

The first thing that strikes you as you enter the gloomy, high-vaulted interior of the cathedral is that, despite the tourists, Stephansdom is still very much a place of worship. At peak times of worship, it can be difficult to get a seat in the area immediately to your right, facing the **Pötscher Madonna**, which sits below a delicate late-Gothic baldachin. Legend has it that the Madonna, an object of great veneration even today, wept tears from her unusually large eyes during the Battle of Zenta against the Turks in 1697, and in so doing miraculously secured victory against the infidels. Another saviour of the city, Prince Eugène of Savoy, hero of the campaigns against the Turks in the early eighteenth century, is buried in the **Tirna Chapel**, on the other side of the cathedral, off the north aisle – he's mostly here, that is, for his heart lies in Turin. Sadly, the chapel is usually shut behind heavy iron gates, which prevent even the slightest glimpse of the prince's tomb on the south wall.

The highlight of the cathedral, though, is without doubt the early sixteenth-century carved stone **Pilgram pulpit**, with portraits of the four Church fathers, sculpted by the Moravian Anton Pilgram, who "signed" his work by showing himself peering from a window below the pulpit stairs. The filigree work above and below the staircase is masterly, as are the salamanders and toads (sadly now under protective perspex), symbolizing good and evil, pursuing one another up the banister towards a barking dog who keeps them all at bay. Pilgram can be spotted again on the wall of the north aisle, this time in polychrome, peeping out below another of his works, the now defunct organ case.

Beyond the transepts, the **choir** is roped off, and only visitable by guided tour (see box). At the far end of the Women's Choir, however, you should just be able to make out the winged **Wiener Neustädter Altar**, a richly gilded masterpiece of late-Gothic art, whose central panels, sculpted from wood, are only revealed during religious festivals. Below the altar to the left lies the **Donor's Tomb**, adorned with sandstone effigies of Rudolf IV and his wife Catherine of Bohemia (they're actually buried in the catacombs), once richly gilded and peppered with precious stones. In the Apostles' Choir to the south stands the glorious red-marble **Tomb of Emperor Friedrich III**. In amongst the 240 statues, 32 coats of arms and numerous scaly creatures that decorate the tomb is the emperor's mysterious acronym AIEOU (for more on which, see p.189).

THE CATACOMBS

A stairway in the north transept leads down into the **catacombs** (guided tours every 30min Mon–Sat 9–11.30am & 12.30–4.30pm, Sun 1–4.30pm; öS35), which, initially at least, are a bit disappointing, having been over-restored in the 1960s. It's here that Rudolf IV and his wife rest with other early Habsburg rulers, sundry priests, bishops and archbishops. Beyond a small chamber filled with bronze caskets holding the entrails of the later Habsburgs is the entry to the damp, dimly lit labyrinth of eighteenth-century catacombs, which were closed in 1783 after the stench became too overpowering. Around 16,000 locals are buried here, their bones piled high in more than thirty rooms; in the final chamber, there's a particularly macabre pile left over from a medieval plague pit. You exit from the catacombs via a secret staircase, which deposits you outside the cathedral beside the place where Mozart's body was blessed before being buried in St Marxer Friedhof (see p.111).

The Dom- and Diözesanmuseum

The square was badly bombed in the war, and few of the other buildings are worthy of mention, though you might want to visit the **Dom-** and **Diözesanmuseum** (Tues, Wed, Fri & Sat 10am–4pm, Thurs 10am–6pm, Sun 10am–1pm; öS40) on the first floor of the Zwettlhof; access is via Stephansplatz 6 on the north side of Stephansplatz. This is basically the dumping ground for a mishmash of the cathedral's most valuable treasures, church plate and artwork. There are some arresting medieval sculptures in wood and some kitsch Baroque pieces, like the Madonna shrine, whose cloak opens up to reveal God (forming her body), surrounded by a host of worshippers' faces. The highlight, though, is the dimly lit treasury of monstrances and macabre reliquaries, including St Leopold's hipbone, a piece of the Virgin Mary's belt and the cranium of St Stephen.

The Schatzkammer des Deutschen Ordens

A much more intriguing ecclesiastical treasure trove can be seen at the **Schatzkammer des Deutschen Ordens** (Treasury of the Teutonic Knights; May–Oct Mon, Thurs & Sun 10am–noon, Wed 3–5pm, Fri & Sat 10am–noon & 3–5pm; Nov–April closed Fri am & Sun; öS25), spread over five rooms on the second floor of the Deutschordenshaus – you enter from Singerstrasse 7, one block south of Stephansplatz. The treasury's varied collection, assembled by seven centuries of Grand Masters, ranges from the mundane – seals, coins and crosses – to the bizarre: an adder's tongue used for testing food for poison, and a red coral salt-cellar tree hung with the fossils of sharks' teeth. The Order's military past is represented by a collection of exotic arms and armour, including a wiggly sixteenth-century Malaysian sword and scabbard, and a poisoned dagger with a handle carved out of rhino horn into the Goddess of Death, with sapphire eyes and ruby eyebrows.

The Figarohaus

To get to the **Figarohaus** (daily except Mon 9am–12.15pm & 1–4.30pm; öS25), home of Vienna's Mozart Museum, immediately east of the cathedral, pass through the Durchhaus at Stephansplatz 5a, and enter at Domgasse 5. Here, on the first floor, Mozart, Constanze and their son, Karl Thomas, lived for three years, during which the composer enjoyed his greatest success. It was Mozart's swankiest accommodation in Vienna – it even had a billiards room. The composer Johann Nepomuk Hummel stayed here as Mozart's live-in pupil for two and a half years, and Josef Haydn – who opined that Mozart was "the great-

MOZART IN VIENNA

It's almost as difficult to avoid images of Wolfgang Amadeus Mozart (1756–91) in Vienna as it is in his home town of Salzburg. For it was in Vienna that Mozart spent the last decade of his life, during which he composed nearly all his most famous works. Mozart moved to Vienna in March 1781 after a summons from his employer, the irascible archbishop of Salzburg, Count Colloredo, who was visiting his sick father in the city. Within three months Mozart had resigned from his post as court organist to the archbishop, or "arch-oaf" (*Erzlimmel*) as he called him, causing a rift with his overbearing father, who was assistant *Kapellmeister* in Salzburg. The relationship was further strained when Mozart, against his father's wishes, moved in with the all-female Weber family, and grew particularly attached to one of the daughters, Constanze. In August 1782 Mozart eventually married the 19-year-old Constanze in the Stephansdom. Their union appears to have been happy, despite most biographers' misogynist attacks on Constanze as unworthy of his genius. Mozart himself hated to be parted from her, if his letters – "I kiss and squeeze you 1,095,060,437,082 times" – and the fact that he rarely left her side, are anything to go by.

After giving many concerts as conductor and pianist, Mozart turned his hand again to opera, enjoying his greatest success in July 1782 with what is now the least known of his major operatic works, Die Entführung aus dem Serail. It was after hearing Die Entführung for the first time that the Emperor Josef II is alleged to have said: "Too beautiful for our ears, and an awful lot of notes, dear Mozart"; to which Mozart replied, "No more notes than necessary, Your Majesty!" Such tales have led to a popular belief that Mozart and Josef were constantly feuding over artistic issues: in his letters, however, Mozart's criticisms of the notoriously stingy emperor were on purely financial matters.

Mozart's next opera, Le Nozze di Figaro, was premiered in May 1786 to a decidedly mixed reception, running for just nine performances. This was partly because its subject matter, in which a lecherous count is prevented from seducing a servant girl by an alliance between the serving classes and his own long-suffering wife, was controversial – as a play it had already been banned in Paris and Vienna. Josef II obviously liked it, however, inviting the cast to give a special performance at his summer residence at Laxenburg. And Figaro's subversive overtones went down a storm in Prague, where Mozart premiered two later operas, Don Giovanni and La Clemenza di Tito, both of which were written in Vienna. Mozart's final work was his Requiem, which was commissioned anonymously by an "unknown messenger" in the last year of Mozart's life. Only after Mozart's death did the patron's identity become known: it was the recently widowed Count Franz Walsegg-Stuppach, who wished to pass the composition off as his own. In the end it became Mozart's own Requiem, still unfinished when he died during the night of December 4–5, 1791, after two weeks of rheumatic fever. Few biographers have forgiven Constanze for not attending the funeral service at the Stephansdom; others assert that she was too distraught to attend. She has also been criticized for having the Requiem completed by one of Mozart's pupils, Sussmayr, so as to get the final payment – though this seems fair enough for a widow left with two children to raise and apparently it was Mozart's suggestion on his deathbed.

Yet more anecdotes surround the generally accepted rivalry with the Kapellmeister Antonio Salieri, though this, too, has been overplayed. Salieri was primarily an opera composer, while Mozart, at least until 1786, was known chiefly as an instrumental composer and virtuoso pianist. Some went as far as to suggest that Salieri himself poisoned Mozart, an allegation strenuously denied by Salieri on his deathbed years later, but to no avail: Alexander Pushkin dramatized it, Nicolai Rimsky-Korsakov made it into an opera, and most famously Amadeus, Peter Shaffer's play on the subject, was made into an Oscar-winning film by Milos Forman. For the story of how Mozart was condemned to a pauper's grave, see p.111.

est composer that I know in person or by name" – was a regular visitor. Sadly, however, there's not a lot to see inside, and only one of the rooms retains the original decor of marble and stucco (the Camesina family, who owned the property, were stucco artists). There are none of Mozart's personal effects, no period furniture, no atmosphere; just a few fac-similes of his scores and reproductions of the composer and his circle of friends. Nevertheless, it's worth a visit, if only for the building's lovely courtyard, the views along Blutgasse, and the chance to hear some of Mozart's music on the headphones provided.

Kärntnerstrasse and around

As its name suggests, **Kärntnerstrasse** lies along the old road from Vienna to the southern Austrian province of Carinthia (Kärntner), and beyond to the Adriatic. Widened in the nineteenth century, badly bombed in World War II and pedestrianized in the 1970s, it retains only a few reminders of the days when it was home to the city's luxury retail trade. Nevertheless, it's still a favourite street for promenading, and for window-shopping – the stratospheric prices mean you can do little else.

One exception is **J. & L. Lobmeyr** (Mon–Fri 9am–6pm, Sat 9am–1pm), at no. 26, which, as well as flogging expensive glass and crystal, also houses an informal glass museum. The assistants are quite happy for you to wander through to the back of the shop, where you'll find the stairs that lead to the second-floor balcony. The wonderful, mostly antique, exhibits here include an incredible range of chandeliers, culminating in a copy of the 1960s chandelier that graces the New York Metropolitan Opera. Downstairs, in the shop itself, you'll see glassware sets still made to designs by Adolf Loos and Josef Hoffmann for the Wiener Werkstätte (see p.106).

The Neuer Markt and the Kaisergruft
Kärntnerstrasse's most interesting sights lie off the street itself, most conspicuously in the **Neuer Markt** to the west, formerly the city's medieval flour market, now a car park. The centrepiece of the square is the **Donnerbrunnen**, a Baroque fountain designed by Georg Raphael Donner. The nudity of the figures perched on the edge of the fountain – they represent the four Austrian tributaries of the Danube – was deemed too risqué by the Empress Maria Theresa, who had the lead statues removed in 1770 to be melt-ed down into cannon. They were returned unharmed in 1801, and in 1873 replaced by bronze copies: the young male figure of Traun, in particular, depicted dipping his triton into the waters, clearly showed rather too much buttock for contemporary tastes, hence the judiciously placed fig leaf.

The square's grim-looking Kapuzinerkirche hides one of the premier sights in Vienna: its crypt, the **Kaisergruft** (daily 9.30am–4pm; öS30), which has been the unlikely resting place of the Habsburgs (with just a few notable exceptions) since 1633. The crypt is entered from a doorway to the left of the church. While a monk relieves you of your money, notices demand a respectful "*Silentium!*" – but don't let them kid you, this place is a tourist attraction above all else. Inside, though the crypt isn't gloomy, it is, nevertheless, an intriguing insight into the Habsburgs' fascination with death. As you enter the burial vault, you're confronted with the monster Baroque sar-cophagi of Leopold I and Josef I, both designed by Johann Lucas von Hildebrandt, and the latter sporting ghoulish skulls in full head armour and bat wings. Those of Karl VI and his wife are his'n'hers designs by Rococo artist Balthasar Ferdinand Moll: his sits on lions, with toothy skulls sporting crowns at each corner; hers sits on eagles, with women in mourning veils at each corner. The main focus and highlight of the crypt is Moll's obscenely large double tomb for the Empress Maria Theresa and her husband, Franz Stephan, immediately to the left as you enter. Over 3m high and wide, 6m long, and smothered in Rococo decorations, the tomb depicts the imperial couple sitting up in bed, as if indignantly accusing one another of snoring. Immediately below their feet lies the simple copper coffin of their son, Josef II, to whom such pomposity was anath-ema. It was he who instigated the idea of a reusable coffin, and issued a decree enforc-ing its use in all funerals – not surprisingly, given the Viennese obsession with elaborate sendoffs, the emperor was eventually forced to back down. Several more of Maria Theresa's sixteen children lie in the shadow of their mother, in ornate Rococo coffins, as does the only non-Habsburg among the crypt's 143 occupants, Karoline Fuchs-Mollard, the empress's governess.

It's all downhill aesthetically after Maria Theresa, though the gloomy postwar bunker of the **New Vault** features some jazzy concrete vaulting. Star corpses here include Maximilian I, Emperor of Mexico, who was executed in 1867, and Marie Louise, Napoleon's second wife. Their son, the duke of Reichstadt – or "L'Aiglon" – who died of tuberculosis at the age of 21, was also buried here until 1940, when Hitler had his remains transferred to Paris as a gesture of goodwill. Finally, there's **Franz-Josef I**'s sarcophagus, permanently strewn with fresh flowers. Even more revered, though, is his wife, Empress Elisabeth, who was assassinated in 1898, her tomb draped in Hungarian wreaths and colours. On the other side of the emperor is the coffin of their eldest son, Crown Prince Rudolf, who committed suicide in 1889 (see p.182). The **chapel** beyond contains the Kaisergruft's most recent arrival, the empress Zita, who died in 1989 in exile and was buried here with imperial pomp and circumstance.

Graben and Kohlmarkt

The prime shopping streets of **Graben** and **Kohlmarkt** retain an air of exclusivity that Kärntnerstrasse has lost. Their shops, many of which are preserved in aspic, as if the Empire lives on, advertise branches in places such as Karlsbad, Leipzig and Prague. Others still sport the *K.K.* or *k.u.k* emblem – *kaiserlich und königlich* (Imperial and Royal) – the Austrian equivalent of "By Appointment to Her Majesty the Queen", flaunted by the shops of upper-crust London. In between these old-fashioned stores are several Art-Nouveau edifices and trendy new designer jewellers produced by the doyen of modern Austrian architecture, **Hans Hollein**.

Graben
Graben – its name translates as "ditches" – was once a moat that lay outside the Roman camp. It was filled in sometime in the thirteenth century and, like Kärntnerstrasse, was widened at the beginning of the nineteenth century, from which era most of its buildings date. The most conspicuous monument on Graben is the **Pestsäule**, or plague column, a towering, amorphous mass of swirling clouds, saints and cherubs, covered in a cobweb of netting to keep the pigeons off. Ostensibly erected to commemorate the 1679 plague, this monument – like similar ones throughout the Empire – was raised on the initiative of the Jesuits, to celebrate deliverance from the Protestant or Turkish "plague". The Pestsäule, in addition to the Hildebrandt-designed Bartolotti-Partenfeld palace, at no. 11 on the corner of Dorotheergasse, are the only survivors of the Baroque era on Graben. More arresting, though, are the shop fronts by Hans Hollein from the 1960s and 1970s, in particular the **Schullin** (now Deutsch) jewellers, Graben 26, a polished marble facade spliced by a seam of gold which trickles down into the doorframe.

Set back slightly from Graben, occupying a little square of its own, is the **Peterskirche**, completed by Hildebrandt in 1733, and without doubt the finest Baroque church in the Innere Stadt. From the outside, the great green oval dome overwhelms the church's twin towers; inside, the dome's fresco by Johann Michael Rottmayr is faded beyond recognition, leaving the High Baroque side altars and the trompe l'oeil painting in the choir to create a sense of theatrics. The lavish gilded pulpit is truly magnificent, but the most dramatic work of art is the monument designed by Lorenzo Matielli, opposite, depicting St John of Nepomuk being thrown off Prague's Charles Bridge by some nasty-looking Czech bullyboys, with Václav IV in Roman garb directing the proceedings.

The Jüdisches Museum

Just off Graben, up Dorotheergasse, is the city's intriguing **Jüdisches Museum** (daily except Sat 10am–6pm, Thurs until 9pm; öS70), halfway up in the Palais Eskeles at no. 11. Vienna was home to the first Jewish Museum in the world, founded in 1896 but forcibly closed by the Nazis in 1938; it wasn't until 1989 that it was finally re-established. Lavishly refurbished with money from the city council, the museum now boasts state-of-the-art premises, including a swanky café and bookshop.

On the ground floor, the covered courtyard is dominated by a giant glass cabinet of Judaica etched with quotations from the Torah and other sources, whose prophetic nature is revealed on the walls, over which are scattered photographic images from the Holocaust. On the whole, though, the curators have rejected the usual static display cabinets and newsreel photos of past atrocities. Instead, the emphasis of the museum's excellent temporary exhibitions on the first floor is on contemporary Jewish life.

On the second floor, visitors enter a seemingly empty room, with a quote from Marxist Jewish critic Walter Benjamin in large letters on the white walls: "the past can only be seized as an image which flashes up at the instant when it can be recognised and is never seen again." It's a bold conceit, which the museum tackles admirably by employing a series of free-standing glass panels imprinted with holograms – ranging from the knob of Theodor Herzl's walking stick to a short clip capturing an everyday instance of anti-Semitism from 1911. These ghostly images, accompanied by judiciously selected sound bites (in German and English) on Zionism, assimilation and other key issues, pithily trace the history of Vienna's Jewry, juxtaposing the enormous achievements of the city's Jews – from Gustav Mahler to Billy Wilder – with its justified reputation as a hotbed of anti-Semitism.

Taking something of a different tack, the third floor contains the museum's *Schaudepot*, or storage depot. The displays of Hanukkah candelabra and other ritual objects in large movable glass cabinets, are deliberately haphazard – they constitute all that is left of the pre-1938 Jewish Museum and the community it served, and include many items pulled from the burnt embers of the city's synagogues, torched in *Kristallnacht*.

Kohlmarkt

Even more than Graben, **Kohlmarkt** is the last bastion of luxury retailing, perhaps best expressed by the various outlets of **Demel**, a very *k.u.k.* establishment, which still advertises itself as an imperial and royal confectioners. Established in 1786 as *Zuckerbäckerei* to the Habsburgs, its very famous and opulent Kaffee-Konditorei, dating from 1888, is at no. 14, while opposite is Demel's small seafood deli outlet. Another Viennese institution is the **Artaria Haus**, a Jugendstil building set back from the street at no. 9, and faced in marble by Max Fabiani in 1901, the bolted slabs on the first floor anticipating Otto Wagner's Postsparkasse (see p.106). The bookshop of the master mapmakers, Freytag & Berndt, occupies the ground floor, while Artaria & Co itself, publishers of music by the likes of Haydn, Mozart and Beethoven, live on the first floor.

Michaelerplatz

At the far end of Kohlmarkt lies **Michaelerplatz**, dominated on one side by the exuberant arc and green dome of the neo-Baroque **Michaelertrakt**, the southern gateway into the Hofburg (see p. 84), begun in the 1720s by Fischer von Erlach's son, but only completed in the 1890s. Its curving balustrade bears a lively parade of eagles, giant urns and trophies, while the gate's archways are framed by gargantuan statues of Hercules and, at either end, fountains overburdened with yet more ungainly statuary.

The centre of the square is now occupied by a collection of archeological remains uncovered during work on the nearby U-Bahn station of Herrengasse. LED texts in several languages explain the significance of the rubble that lies exposed in a designer concrete trench (another of Hollein's works); most of what you see are nineteenth-century heating ducts – hardly heart-stopping stuff.

Much more significant is the **Loos Haus**, on the corner of Kohlmarkt and Herrengasse, which caused an uproar when it was built in 1910–11 by Adolf Loos. Franz-Josef despised this "house without eyebrows" – in other words, without the sculpted pediments that sit above the windows of most Viennese buildings. Work on the building was temporarily halted due to the protests, and only allowed to continue after Loos had acquiesced to adding bronze flower boxes.

The Michaelerkirche

The oldest building on Michaelerplatz, and the inspiration for its name, is the **Michaelerkirche**, built in the thirteenth century, though the Neoclassical facade, added in 1792, somewhat obscures this fact. Inside, the church retains its plain Gothic origins, but it's the later additions that are of more interest, in particular the *Fall of Angels*, a Rococo cloudburst of cherubs and angels rendered in alabaster, tumbling from the ceiling above the high altar.

From November to April you can get a closer look at this by simply walking in via the west door; from May to October, however, you can only do so by entering from the *Durchgang* via the south door and paying a small fee (Mon–Sat 10.30am–4.30pm, Sun 1–5pm; öS25). After picking up a confusing information sheet in English, you may then explore the church and the interesting exhibition that spreads out into the adjoining monastery. From a doorway in the north choir aisle, you can also descend into the church's labyrinthine **crypt**, which stretches the length and breadth of the building. A brief guided tour (Mon–Fri 11am and 3pm; öS20) reveals piles of paupers' bones and numerous musty coffins taken from the now defunct graveyard, many with their lids off revealing desiccated bodies, still clothed and locked in a deathly grimace.

Herrengasse

Herrengasse was the preferred address of the nobility from the time the Habsburgs moved into the Hofburg until the fall of the dynasty in 1918. Its name dates from the sixteenth century, when the Diet of Lower Austria built its **Landhaus**, which still stands at no. 13. Vienna was for centuries the capital of Lower Austria – the region surrounding the city – but in 1986 the small provincial town of St Pölten took over the mantle (see p.159), making the Vienna Landhaus redundant.

Opposite the Landhaus is the grandiose Italianate **Palais Ferstel**, built in the Ringstrasse style by Heinrich Ferstel in 1860 and home to Vienna's most famous *Kaffeehaus*, **Café Central**, restored in 1986 primarily as a tourist attraction (though a very beautiful one at that). At the turn of the century, the café was *the* meeting place of the city's intellectuals, including the first generation of Austrian Socialists – Karl Renner, Viktor Adler and Otto Bauer – who were occasional chess adversaries of Leon Trotsky, who also whiled away several years here before World War I. At the entrance to the café is a life-size papier-mâché model of the moustachioed poet Peter Altenberg, another of the café's fin-de-siècle regulars.

Further up Herrengasse, past the café, is the entrance to the **Freyung Passage** – built in the 1860s as part of the Palais Ferstel – an eminently civilized, lovingly restored shopping arcade, which links Herrengasse with Freyung. The focus of this elegant marble passage is a glass-roofed, hexagonal atrium, with a fountain, crowned by a statue of the Donaunixen (Danube Mermaid), whose trickling water echoes down the arcade.

Minoritenplatz

On the opposite side of Herrengasse, hidden away round the back of the Hofburg, **Minoritenplatz** is a peaceful, cobbled square entirely surrounded by Baroque palaces, now transformed into ministries and embassies. At its centre is the fourteenth-century **Minoritenkirche**, whose stunted octagonal tower is one of the landmarks of the Innere Stadt (the top was knocked off by the Turks during the 1529 siege). Inside, the church is impressively lofty, but it's the tacky copy of Leonardo da Vinci's *Last Supper*, on the north wall, that steals the show – only close inspection reveals it to be a mosaic. The work was commissioned in 1806 by Napoleon, who planned to substitute it for the original in Milan, taking the latter back to Paris. By the time it was finished, however, Napoleon had fallen from power and the emperor Franz I bought it instead, though it wasn't until 1847 that it arrived back in Vienna.

On the south side of the square stands a magnificent palace built for the Emperor Karl VI by Hildebrandt as the Court Chancery, and now the **Bundeskanzleramt** (Federal Chancery), home of the Austrian Chancellor and the Foreign Ministry, whose main entrance opens onto Ballhausplatz. It was in this palace that Prince Metternich presided over the numerous meetings of the Congress of Vienna in 1814–15, and here, in the Chancellor's office, that the Austro-fascist leader, Engelbert Dollfuss, was assassinated during the abortive Nazi putsch of July 25, 1934.

Freyung and the Mölker Bastei

The Freyung Passage from Herrengasse brings you out onto **Freyung** (meaning "Sanctuary") itself, a misshapen square centred on the Austria-Brunnen. Unveiled in 1846, the fountain bears bronze nymphs representing Austria and the key rivers in the Habsburg Empire at the time: the Danube, Po, Elbe and Vistula. In addition to the **Harrach Palais**, adjacent to the Freyung Passage, and the **Kunstforum** – two museums hosting temporary exhibitions – the Freyung also boasts the **Museum im Schottenstift** (Thurs–Sat 10am–5pm, Sun noon–5pm; öS40), on the first floor of the monastery, through the archway by the church, whose prize exhibit is the fifteenth-century winged altarpiece that used to reside in the Schottenkirche. Thirteen out of the original sixteen panels survive, set in a new, purpose-built mini-chapel: one side depicts scenes from the life of the Virgin; the reverse side (shown only in the two or three weeks leading up to Easter) features the Passion – a leaflet in English explains the significance of each panel. The vivid use of colour, the plasticity of the faces and the daring stab at perspective single this out as a masterpiece of late-Gothic art. As a bonus, you also get to see the inside of the vast Prälatensaal, decked out in pink and yellow Biedermeier style around 1830 by Josef Kornhäusel, and now the setting for the Schottenkirche's somewhat inferior Baroque high-altar painting.

The **Mölker Bastei**, one of the few remaining sections of the old zigzag fortifications that once surrounded the Innere Stadt, can be found on Schreyvogelgasse, to the west of Freyung. The sloping cobbled lane below the fortifications should be familiar to fans of the movie *The Third Man*, for it's in the doorway of no. 8 that Harry Lime (played by Orson Welles) appears for the first time. High up on the Bastei itself, at no. 8, is the **Pasqualatihaus** (daily except Mon 9am–12.15pm & 1–4.30pm; öS25), where Beethoven lived on and off from 1804 onwards (he stayed at over thirty addresses during his 35 years in Vienna). The composer's apartment is now a museum (for more on Beethoven, see p.121), though there's no indication of how the place might have looked at the time he lived there. Perhaps this is just as well – according to one visitor it was "the darkest, most disorderly place imaginable . . . under the piano (I do not exaggerate) an unemptied chamber pot . . . chairs . . . covered with plates bearing the remains of last night's supper". Instead, you're left to admire Ludwig's gilded salt and pepper pots and battered tin sugar container, or sit down and listen to some of his music through headphones.

Am Hof and around

Am Hof is the largest square in the Innere Stadt, an attractive, tranquil spot, marred only by the surface protrusions of its underground car park. The name – *Hof* means both "royal court" and "courtyard" – dates from medieval times, when this was the headquarters of the Babenbergs, who lorded it over Vienna until the Habsburgs took the reins in 1273. The centrepiece of the square is the rather forbidding, matt-black **Mariensäule** (Marian column), erected by the emperor Ferdinand III as a thankyou to the Virgin for deliverance from the Protestant Swedish forces in the Thirty Years' War. At the base of the column, blackened cherubs in full armour wrestle with a dragon, lion, serpent and basilisk.

Dominating the square is the **Kirche am Hof**, from whose balcony the Austrian Emperor Franz I proclaimed the end of the Holy Roman Empire in 1806, on the orders of Napoleon. The church's vast Baroque facade, topped by a host of angels, belies the fact that this is, for the most part, a fourteenth-century structure. Inside, it's quite frankly a stylistic mess, with the old Gothic church struggling to get out from under some crude later additions.

Pass under the archway by the Kirche am Hof, head down Schulhof, and you'll come to the **Uhrenmuseum** (daily except Mon 9am–4.30pm; öS50), a clock museum ranged over three floors at Schulhof 2. Founded in 1917, this is the world's oldest museum of its kind, but, sadly, it lacks the crucial information in either German or English to bring the collection alive. Nevertheless, you'll find every kind of time-measuring device from sophisticated seventeenth-century grandfather clocks to primitive wax candles containing tiny lead balls, which drop onto a metal dish as the candle melts. Other exhibits include the smallest pendulum clock in the world, which fits inside a thimble, and a wide selection of eighteenth-century *Zwiebeluhren*, literally "onion clocks", set within cases shaped like fruit, musical instruments and the like.

For most people, the **Puppen und Spielzeug Museum** (Doll and Toy Museum; daily except Mon 10am–6pm; öS60), next door on the first floor of Schulhof 4, holds more appeal, further enhanced by the building's well-preserved Baroque interior. It's an old-fashioned kind of a place, with ranks of glass cabinets and no buttons to press for younger kids. The majority of the exhibits are dolls, with just a small selection of teddies, toys and trains. Also on show are a toy marionette stage, a Punch and Judy booth, a shadow screen and a dolls' toy shop, grocer's and house, complete with miniature Jugendstil coffee set. Off Am Hof, a short way down Drahtgasse, another toy museum, this time the **Teddybären Museum** (daily 10am–6pm; öS45), holds a private collection of antique teddy bears from all over the world. As well as the cuddly variety, there are china bears, bears on carousels and one of the very earliest battery-operated bears from before World War I, whose eyes light up in a way that would give most kids nightmares.

Judenplatz, the Altes Rathaus and Maria am Gestade

Taking either of the two alleyways that lead north from Schulhof brings you to **Judenplatz**, one of the prettiest little squares in Vienna. As the name suggests, this was the site of the city's first Jewish ghetto, dating as far back as the twelfth century, when the square itself was known as Schulhof. It remained at the heart of the Jewish community on and off for centuries, and even today there's an orthodox Jewish prayer room at no. 8. The oldest house on the square, **Zum grossen Jordan** (The Great Jordan), at no. 2, bears a sixteenth-century relief of the Baptism of Christ, commemorating the pogrom of 1421, when the Jews were driven out of Vienna: the lucky ones fled to Hungary, the rest were burnt at the stake, or – to avoid that fate – killed by the chief rabbi, who then committed suicide. Judenplatz was due to have a memorial to the Holocaust, by British sculptor Rachel Whiteread, erected in the centre of the square.

JEWS IN VIENNA

"Nine tenths of what the world celebrated as Viennese culture of the nineteenth centu-
ry was a culture promoted, nurtured or in some cases even created by Viennese Jewry."
Stefan Zweig, *The World of Yesterday*, 1942

Most Jews have mixed feelings about Vienna: the city that nurtured the talents of such Jewish geniuses as Sigmund Freud, Gustav Mahler and Ludwig Wittgenstein also has a justifiable reputation as a hotbed of anti-Semitism. The city where the father of Zionism, Theodor Herzl, spent much of his adult life, is also seen by many as the cradle of the Holocaust, where Hitler spent five years honing his hatred; where in 1986, Kurt Waldheim was elected president, despite rumours that he had participated in Nazi atrocities in the Balkans; and where, as recently as 1996, Jörg Haider's FPÖ achieved the largest percentage of the electorate of any extreme right-wing party in Europe.

Jews have lived in Vienna intermittently for something like a thousand years, yet like most of the Diaspora they have been tolerated only when it suited the powers that be. They have been formally expelled twice, first in 1420, when the community was accused of supporting the Czech Hussite heretics (the real incentive for the expulsion was to boost the royal coffers by appropriating the Jews' property). The following year, those that remained – around 200 of them – were burnt at the stake. Apart from a few individual exceptions, Jewish resettlement only took off again at the beginning of the seventeenth century, when Ferdinand II established a walled ghetto east of the Danube (now Leopoldstadt). For around fifty years Jewish life flourished in the ghetto, but as the Counter-Reformation gathered pace, there was increasing pressure from Catholics to banish the Jews altogether. Finally in 1670, Emperor Leopold I once more expelled the community.

The city suffered financially from the expulsion, and with the Turks at the gates a small number of Jewish financiers and merchants were hastily granted the status of *Hofjuden*, or "Court Jews", and permitted to resettle. The most famous of the Court Jews was Samuel Oppenheimer, who was appointed chief supplier to the imperial army by Leopold I in 1677. Despite the elevated status of the Court Jews, their position was precarious, and it wasn't until Josef II's 1781 *Toleranzpatent* that they were allowed to take up posts in the civil service and other professions and to build their own synagogue. At the same time, the *Toleranzpatent* began the process of assimilation, compelling Jews to take German names and restricting the use of Yiddish and Hebrew.

After the 1848 revolution, all official restrictions on Jews were finally abolished. At this point, there were only around 2000 Jews living in Vienna. In the next sixty years, thousands arrived in the city from the Habsburg provinces of Bohemia, Moravia and Galicia, the majority of them settling, initially at least, in Leopoldstadt. By 1910, there were approximately 180,000 Jews – almost ten percent of the total population and more than in any other German-speaking city. Though the majority of them were far from well off, a visible minority formed a disproportionately large contingent in high-profile professions like banking, medicine, journalism and the arts. The Rothschilds were one of the richest families in the empire; virtually the entire staff on the liberal newspapers, *Neue Freie Presse* and the *Wiener Tagblatt*, were Jewish; the majority of the city's doctors were Jews, as were most of the leading figures in the Austrian Socialist Party. Other prominent Viennese Jews were the writers Arthur Schnitzler, Robert Musil, Stefan Zweig and Josef Roth, and the composers Arnold Schönberg, Alban Berg and the Strauss family.

Those Gentiles who found themselves sinking into poverty after the stock market crash of 1873 desperately needed a scapegoat. They eagerly latched onto anti-Semitism, which began to be promoted by the Christian Social Party under Karl Lueger, the city's populist mayor from 1897 to 1910. Perversely, however, this virulent anti-Semitism helped to save more Jews than in other more tolerant places, causing thousands to flee the country even before the 1938 Anschluss; by 1941, a total of 120,000 Viennese Jews had escaped. Nevertheless, some 65,000 died in the Holocaust. Now, the community of around 7000 – many of them immigrants from the former eastern bloc – is enjoying something of a renaissance, much of it centred once again in Leopoldstadt, maintaining a dozen synagogues and several schools across the city.

However, objections from local residents and traders were later joined by protests from within the Jewish community, after excavations revealed the smoke-blackened remains of the medieval Or-Sarua Synagogue, which was burnt to the ground in 1421. Whiteread's project has now been permanently shelved, and it remains to be seen what, if anything, will be erected here.

One block north of Judenplatz, on the other side of busy Wipplingerstrasse, lies the **Altes Rathaus**, a dour-looking Baroque palace that served as the city's town hall until 1885. The main courtyard is undistinguished but for Donner's wonderful **Andromeda Brunnen** from 1741, which depicts the Greek myth in lead relief. The reason to come here, though, is to visit the highly informative **Austrian Resistance Museum** (Mon, Wed & Thurs 9am–5pm; free), which has a permanent exhibition on the Austrian anti-Fascist resistance, with labelling in German and English throughout. The bulk of the displays cover resistance to the Nazi regime, but there's also a brief summary of the political upheavals of the interwar republic, including a detailed section on the rise of Austro-fascism in the 1930s. Despite the high level of popular support for the Nazis, the Austrian resistance remained extremely active throughout the war, as a result of which 2700 of its members were executed and thousands more were murdered by the Gestapo.

One of Vienna's finest Gothic churches, **Maria am Gestade**, up Salvatorgasse, is topped by an elaborate filigree spire depicting the Virgin's heavenly crown, a stunning sight after dark when lit from within. With its drooping, beast-infested pendants and gilded mosaics, the stone canopy of the slender west facade is also worth admiring, best viewed from the steps leading up from Tiefergraben. The unusual interior – the nave is darker and narrower than the choir and set slightly askew – is a product of the church's cramped site, lying as it does on the very edge of the old medieval town. Much of what you see, both inside and out, is the result of nineteenth-century over-restoration, as the church caught fire in 1809 when it was used by the Napoleonic forces as an arms depot.

The Hoher Markt and around

It's difficult to believe that the **Hoher Markt**, now surrounded by dour, postwar buildings and packed with parked cars, is Vienna's oldest square. Yet this was the heart of the Roman camp, Vindobona, a conduit of which you can see beneath the shopping arcade on the south side of the square (Sat & Sun 11am–1pm; öS25; you enter through the arcade's sushi bar). The square's centrepiece is Fischer von Erlach's **Vermählungsbrunnen**, or Marriage Fountain, depicting the union of Mary and Joseph by the High Priest, for which there is no biblical evidence and few iconographical precedents. Even more remarkable is the ornate bronze baldachin and gilded sunburst, held aloft by Corinthian columns with matching rams'-head urns, under which the trio shelter.

The real reason folk crowd into Hoher Markt, however, is to see the glorious Jugendstil **Ankeruhr**, a heavily gilded clock designed by Franz Matsch in 1914, which spans two buildings owned by the Anker insurance company on the north side of the square. Each hour, a gilded cut-out figure, representing a key player in Vienna's history, shuffles across the dial of the clock, and at noon tour groups gather to watch the entire set of twelve figures slowly stagger across to a ten-minute medley of slightly mournful organ music. The identities of the figures, which range from Marcus Aurelius to Josef Haydn, are revealed on the clock's street-level plaque. Before you leave, check out the brackets on the underside of the clock bridge, which feature Adam, Eve, the Devil and an angel.

There's one other sight worth seeking out in the streets around Hoher Markt: the secular medieval **Neidhart Frescoes** (daily except Mon 9am–12.15pm & 1–4.30pm; öS25), at Tuchlauben 19, discovered in 1979 during rebuilding works. Executed around 1400, the wall paintings are patchy but jolly, some of them illustrating the stories of the *Minnesinger* (aristocratic minstrel) Neidhart von Reuenthal, others depicting a snowball fight, a ball game, dancing and general medieval merriment.

The Bermuda Triangle

Since the 1980s, the area around the Ruprechtskirche has been known as the **Bermuda Dreieck**, or Bermuda Triangle, the idea being that there are so many bars in these few narrow streets that you could get lost for ever. And it's true: there are a staggering number of designer bars, late-night drinking holes, music venues and restaurants literally piled on top of one another, particularly along Seitenstettengasse and Rabensteig. The night-time clientele tends to be young(ish) and moneyed, well turned out but not that trendy. During the day, however, the scene is pretty muted, and you're more likely to rub shoulders with tourists who've come to appreciate the area's narrow cobbled streets and the two main sights: the Ruprechtskirche, the city's oldest church, and the Stadttempel, the only synagogue to survive *Kristallnacht*.

Ironically, it was the building restrictions in force at the time the **Stadttempel** (daily except Sat; free) was built in 1826 that enabled it to be the only synagogue (out of 24) to survive *Kristallnacht*. According to the laws enacted under Josef II, synagogues had to be concealed from the street – hence you get no hint of what lies behind Seitenstettengasse 2–4 until you've gone through the security procedures (take your passport) and passed through several anterooms to the glass doors of the temple itself. Despite its hidden location, it suffered some damage in 1938 when this predominantly Jewish area was torched, and it has since been lavishly restored. Designed from top to bottom by Biedermeier architect Josef Kornhäusel, it's a perfect example of the restrained architecture of the period, its top-lit, sky-blue oval dome delicately dotted with golden stars, and its two-tiered curving women's gallery supported by yellow Ionic pillars. The slightly sinister presence of police with dogs and machine guns outside on Seitenstettengasse is a sad consequence of the terrorist attack on the Stadttempel in 1983, which killed three people, and the continuing vandalism of Jewish property that takes place in Austria.

Round the corner from the Stadttempel on Ruprechtsplatz stands the ivy-covered **Ruprechtskirche**, its plain, stout architecture attesting to its venerable age. Founded as long ago as the eighth century, the current building dates partly from the twelfth century and has been much altered and expanded since. Inside, the vivid reds and blues of the modern stained glass are a bit overwhelming, detracting from the church's uniquely intimate ambience. Mass is still said here, and the space is also frequently used for art exhibitions.

Fleischmarkt to Dr-Ignaz-Seipel-Platz

One block south of the Bermuda Triangle, **Fleischmarkt**, the old meat market, straddles Rotenturmstrasse and extends east as far as Postgasse. Greek merchants settled here in the eighteenth century, and following the 1781 *Toleranzpatent* built their own Greek Orthodox church on Griechengasse. On Fleischmarkt itself, there's another, more imposing **Griechische Kirche**, a stripy red-brick affair redesigned in mock-Byzantine style in 1861 by Ringstrasse architect Theophil Hansen, its decorative castellations glistening with gilt. Opening hours are erratic, and you may not be able to get past the gloomy, arcaded vestibule – the best time to try is on a Sunday – to see the candlelit interior, pungent with incense and decorated with icons and gilded frescoes. Next door to the church is the popular inn, *Griechenbeisl*, a Viennese institution for over five centuries, and now something of a tourist trap.

At the end of Fleischmarkt, turn right into Postgasse past another neo-Byzantine edifice, the Greek-Catholic **Church of St Barbara**, and the Italianate **Dominikanerkirche**, and you'll come to Bäckerstrasse. One block west lies **Dr-Ignaz-Seipel-Platz**, named after the anti-Semitic leader of the Christian Socials, who became the country's chancellor in 1922. The east side is taken up by the **Alte Universität**, founded by Rudolf IV in 1365, and thus the second oldest university (after Prague) in the German-speaking world. By the eighteenth century, the university had outgrown its original premises, and a more fanciful Baroque extension – now the **Akademie der Wissenschaften** (Academy of Sciences) – was built on the opposite side of the square. The building's barrel-vaulted Freskenraum, decorated with frescoes by Franz Maulbertsch, is occasionally open to the public during summer vacation for exhibitions (Mon–Fri 10.30am–5.30pm).

Next door is the **Jesuitenkirche** (also known as the Universitätskirche), whose flat facade rises up in giant tiers that tower over the square. Begun in 1627 at the peak of the Jesuits' power, this church smacks of the Counter-Reformation and is by far the most awesome Baroque church in Vienna. Inside, the most striking features are the red and green barley-sugar spiral columns, the exquisitely carved pews and the clever trompe l'oeil dome – the illusion only works from the back of the church: walk towards the altar and the painting is revealed as a sham.

The Hofburg

His gaze wandered up high walls and he saw an island – gray, self-contained, and armed – lying there while the city's speed rushed blindly past it.
                                        Robert Musil, *The Man Without Qualities*

Enmeshed in the southwest corner of the Innere Stadt, the **Hofburg** (Court Palace) is a real hotchpotch of a place, with no natural centre, no symmetry and no obvious main entrance. Its name is synonymous with the Habsburgs, the dynasty which, at its zenith, ruled a vast multinational empire, stretching the length and breadth of Europe. Nowadays, apart from the tiny proportion that has been retained as the seat of the Austrian president, the palace has been taken over by various state organizations, museums and, more prosaically, a conference centre.

Two of Vienna's most famous attractions keep the Hofburg at the top of most visitors' agendas: the **Wiener Sängerknaben** (Vienna Boys' Choir), who perform regularly in the Burgkapelle, and the **Spanische Reitschule** (Spanish Riding School), who trot their stuff in the Winter Reitschule. Getting to see either of them takes considerable time and money, however, which you might well be better off spending elsewhere. The tourist office leaflet, *Spanische Reitschule/Wiener Sängerknaben*, explains the intricate schedules of both institutions. The other chief sights are the dull **Kaiserappartements**, where the emperor Franz-Josef I (1848–1916) and his wife Elisabeth lived and worked, the **Schatzkammer**, with its superb collection of crown jewels, and the **Prunksaal**, Fischer von Erlach's richly decorated Baroque library. The palace also boasts several excellent museums and galleries: the **Albertina**, home to one of the world's great graphics collections; several departments of the Kunsthistorisches Museum – the **Hofjagd- und Rüstkammer** (Court Hunting and Arms Collection), the **Sammlung alte Musikinstrumente** (Collection of Early Musical Instruments) and the **Ephesos Museum** (Ephesus Museum); and the **Museum für Völkerkunde** (Museum of Ethnology).

The Kaiserappartements

Of all the sights within the Hofburg, it is the **Kaiserappartements** (daily 9am–5pm; öS70; combined ticket with Hofsilber- und Tafelkammer öS90) that are the most disappointing. Virtually every room is decorated in the same style: creamy-white walls and ceiling with gilded detailing, parquet flooring and red furnishings. There aren't any guided tours in English to bring these mundane surroundings to life, nor is there any information or labelling in the rooms themselves. To give you an idea of the paucity of treasures on display, the empress Elisabeth's gymnastic equipment is one of the highlights of the rooms.

The Kaiserappartements' current state is a legacy of their last full-time imperial occupant, the emperor Franz-Josef, who, though a stickler for pomp and protocol at official functions, was notoriously frugal in his daily life (the simple iron bedstead on which he slept is on view). Rising at 4am, he would eat a simple breakfast of coffee, *Semmel* and a slice of ham (except during Lent); lunch was invariably *Tafelspitz*, or boiled rump. He distrusted telephones, cars, electricity and modern plumbing, and his only concession to modern life was his use of the telegraph. If you're looking for opulence, you need to visit Maria Theresa's apartments at Schönbrunn (see p.115).

Beyond the ticket office for the Kaiserappartements are six rooms devoted to the **Hofsilber- und Tafelkammer** (daily 9am–5pm; öS65), the "Court Silver and Porcelain Collection". You really have to be seriously into dinner services to get the most out of it, though if you're visiting the Kaiserappartements anyway it doesn't cost much more to get a combined ticket. Among star exhibits is the eighteenth-century, green and gold Sèvres Service, originally made up of 290 separate pieces, given to Maria Theresa by Louis XV, and the monster Milanese centrepiece in gilded bronze, which stretches for 33m along a table strewn with classical figures and (more) gilded bronze and crystal urns. For the sake of variety, check out the stone jugs and salvers, with which the emperor and empress used to wash the feet of twelve ordinary men and women every year on Maundy Thursday.

The Schatzkammer

Of all the Hofburg museums, the imperial **Schatzkammer** (daily except Tues 10am–6pm; öS60), or Treasury, is far and away the most rewarding. Here you can see some of the finest medieval craftsmanship and jewellery in Europe, including the imperial regalia and relics of the Holy Roman Empire, not to mention the Habsburgs' own crown jewels, countless reliquaries and robes, goldwork and silverware. You can wander at will around the twenty or so rooms, but, since the labelling is in German only, you might consider renting a headphone commentary (öS30) or signing up for an English guided tour (usually 1 daily; öS30).

Centre stage in room 2, you'll find the stunning golden **Crown of Rudolf II** (later to become the Austrian imperial crown), studded with diamonds, rubies, pearls and, at the very top, a huge sapphire. The mother of all cots resides in room 5, an overwrought, silver-gilt cradle with silk and velvet trimmings, made in 1811 for the short-lived **duke of Reichstadt**, or King of Rome, son of Napoleon and his second wife, Marie Louise, daughter of the emperor Franz I. The poor boy must have had nightmares from the golden eagle that hovers over the cot.

Among the remnants of the **Habsburgs' private jewellery**, in room 7, there are some serious stones on display, like the 2680-carat Colombian emerald the size of your fist, carved into a salt cellar in Prague in 1641, and the huge garnet, "La Bella", which forms the centre of a double-headed eagle, along with an amethyst and an opal, set in enamel. Another notable treasure is the solid gold Turkish crown of the rebel King of Hungary, István Bocskai, from 1605, inlaid with pearls and precious stones. Room 8 contains the so-called "**inalienable heirlooms**", two pieces collected by Ferdinand I, which the Habsburgs were very keen to hold onto: a fourth-century agate dish, stolen from Constantinople in 1204 and thought at the time to be the Holy Grail, and a 2.43metre-long narwhal's horn, which was originally believed to have come from a unicorn.

The highlights of the whole collection, however, are the **crown jewels of the Holy Roman Empire** in room 11. The focal point is the octagonal imperial crown itself, a superb piece of Byzantine jewellery, smothered with pearls, large precious stones and enamel plaques. Legend has it that the crown was used in the coronation of Charlemagne, the first Holy Roman Emperor, in 800, but it now seems likely that it dates back only to that of Otto I, in 962. Also on display here is the legendary **Holy Lance**, with which the Roman soldier pierced the side of Christ. The lance – which actually dates from the eighth century – was alleged to have magic powers, so that who-ever possessed it held the destiny of the world in their hands. It was in front of this exhibit that the young Hitler is supposed to have had a mystical revelation, which changed the course of his life (and therefore of twentieth-century history), though the story is probably apocryphal.

The last four rooms (13–16) of the Schatzkammer house the substantial dowry that came into Habsburg hands in 1477, when the emperor Maximilian I married the only daughter and heiress of the duke of Burgundy. By so doing Maximilian also became Grand Master of the **Order of the Golden Fleece**, the exclusive Burgundian order of chivalry founded in 1430, whose insignia are displayed here: heavy mantles embroi-dered with gold thread, a collar of golden links, from which the "fleece" would hang, and the ram emblem, worn by the 24 knights of the order at all times.

The Burgkapelle

The **Burgkapelle** (guided tours Jan–June & mid-Sept to Dec Tues & Thurs 1.30–3.30pm, Fri 1–3pm; öS15), up the stairs above the entrance to the Schatzkammer, was built in the late 1440s by the emperor Friedrich III. Despite numerous alterations over the centuries, the interior retains its Gothic vaulting, carved ceiling pendants, and much of its fifteenth-century wooden statuary protected by richly carved baldachins. It's a favourite venue for society weddings, but the pub-lic only get to see it on guided tours. In any case, the real point of going there is to hear the Hofmusikkapelle, made up of members of the *Wiener Sängerknaben*, or **Vienna Boys' Choir**, supplemented by musicians from the Staatsoper, sing Mass for the tourists on Sunday mornings (and on religious holidays) at 9.15am. To find out about how to get tickets, see p.134.

Founded back in 1498 by the emperor Maximilian I, the choir was closely linked to the imperial family, for whom they used to perform (famous *Sängerknaben* include Schubert and Haydn). In 1918, the choir went under with the dynasty, but was revived in 1924 and, dressed in ludicrous sailors' uniforms and caps, has since become a major Austrian export. There are, in fact, four choirs, who take it in turns to work, rest, play and tour the world.

The Spanish Riding School

The Habsburgs' world-famous **Spanische Reitschule** originated with the Archduke Karl, brother of Maximilian II, who established several studs at Lipizza, northeast of Trieste (now the Slovene town of Lipica) in the 1570s. By cross-breeding Spanish, Arab and Berber horses, the Lipizzaner strain was born, and subsequently supplied the Habsburgs with all their cavalry and show horses. However, it was only properly expanded by the Spanish-bred Emperor Karl VI, who gave the riding school a perma-nent home in the Hofburg. After World War I, the stud was moved to Piber near Graz (see p.227), though the silver-white stallions are now bred at both places.

The Spanish Riding School is such an intrinsic part of Vienna's Habsburg heritage industry, it's difficult not to feel a certain revulsion for the whole charade. That said, to witness the Lipizzaners' equestrian ballet is an unforgettable experience; certainly those with any interest in horses will feel compelled to see at least a rehearsal. Performances take place regularly in the splendidly Baroque **Winterreitschule** (Winter Riding School), on the west side of Reitschulgasse, purpose-built by Josef Emanuel Fischer von Erlach in 1735.

Access to the Winterreitschule is either from the north side of Josefsplatz or from underneath the Michaelertor. The complicated public schedule of training sessions and performances is written up outside both entrances. There are one or two

performances (*Vorführungen*) a week (usually Sun 10.45am and, less frequently, Wed 7pm) between March and June and September and December, though for at least a month of the latter period the school is usually on tour. Seats **cost** öS240–800, and standing room is öS190. Even at those prices, the performances are booked solid months in advance; to be sure of a place, you must **write in advance** to: Spanische Reitschule, Hofburg, A-1010 Wien.

From mid-February to June and from late August until early October, the school also holds **training sessions** (*Morgenarbeit;* Tues–Sat 10am–noon), which are open to the public. Seats cost öS100 and are sold at the Michaelertor entrance box office; the queue for tickets is at its worst early on, but by 11am it's usually easy enough to get in. Another option, between April and June, and occasionally in the autumn, is to catch one of the training sessions with music (*Morgenarbeit mit Musik;* Sat 10am), for which tickets cost öS240. Cheapest of all is to watch a **video** on the riding school, which is shown daily from 10am to 6pm in the Palais Palffy, Josefsplatz 6; tickets cost öS50.

The Prunksaal

If the Karlskirche (see p.103) is Johann Bernhard Fischer von Erlach's sacred master-piece, then the **Prunksaal** (June–Oct Mon–Sat 10am–4pm, Sun 10am–1pm; Nov–May Mon–Sat 10am–noon; closed for the first three weeks of Sept; öS50) is his most stunning secular work. The library was begun in 1723, the year of his death, and, like so many of his projects, had to be finished off by his son, Josef Emanuel. It's by far the largest Baroque library in Europe, stretching the full eighty-metre length of the first floor of the central wing of the Hofburg facing onto Josefsplatz. Now part of the Nationalbibliothek, ccess to the Prunksaal is via the monumental staircase in the southwest corner of the square.

Not an architect to be accused of understatement, Fischer von Erlach achieves his desired effect by an overdose of elements: massive marble pillars and pilasters, topped by gilded capitals, gilded wood-panelled bookcases, carved balconies accessed by spiral staircases and, from floor to ceiling, more than 200,000 leather-bound books, including the 15,000-volume personal library of Prince Eugène of Savoy. The space is divided by a transverse oval dome, which is decorated with Daniel Gran's magnificent fresco, with the winged figure of Fame holding a rather misshapen pyramid. Among the many celestial groups there's a model of the library, to which the woman depicted as Austrian magnanimity is pointing. At the lowest level, Gran has painted trompe l'oeil balconies, on which groups of figures hold scholarly discussions. If you're really keen to work out what's going on, there's an inexpensive guide to the dome fresco available (in English) at the ticket desk.

There are several antique globes in the Prunksaal itself, but if that has only whetted your appetite, you can view lots more in the two rooms of the **Globenmuseum** (Mon–Wed & Fri 11am–noon, Thurs 2–3pm; öS15), situated on the third floor. The museum also displays a selection of the library's map collection. Check out the upside-down map of the world from 1154, and the sixteenth-century charts, one of which features a magnificent sea dragon happily swimming in the South Atlantic, while another depicts a bevy of parrots in the *terra incognita*, now known to us as South America.

The Augustinerkirche

Masked by Picassi's bland facade, the **Augustinerkirche** (Mon–Sat 10am–6pm, Sun 1–6pm), to the south of Josefsplatz, is one of the oldest parts of the Hofburg, dating back as far as the 1330s. Inside, the church has taken a beating over the years, though it retains its lofty Gothic vaulting. The chief attraction is Antonio Canova's Neoclassical **Christinendenkmal**, in the right-hand aisle, a lavish memorial to Maria Christina, favourite daughter of Maria Theresa, erected in 1805 by her husband, Albrecht, Duke of Saxony-Tetschen. A procession of marble mourners heads up the steps for the open door of the pyramidal tomb, while a winged spirit and a sad lion embrace on the other side, and another genius holds aloft the duchess's medallion. They'd be disappointed if they ever got inside, as she's actually buried in the Kaisergruft. Canova himself was so taken with his creation that he repeated it in a design for Titian's tomb, which was eventually used for his own mausoleum in Venice.

Several more monumental tombs can be found in the **Georgskapelle**, a self-contained, two-aisled chapel, built in the fourteenth century to the right of the chancel. In the centre of the chapel lies the empty marble tomb of the emperor Leopold II, whose brief reign of less than two years ended in 1792. Balthasar Ferdinand Moll's gilded wall tomb to Count Leopold Daun, on the far wall, is significantly more extravagant, and includes a relief of the 1757 Battle of Kolín in which Daun trounced the Prussians. To get to the Georgskapelle, you must pass through the Lorettokapelle, at the far end of which lies the **Herzgrüftel** (Little Heart Crypt), where, arranged neatly on two semi-circular shelves, are 54 silver urns containing the hearts of the later Habsburgs.

The Albertina and around

At the far end of Augustinerstrasse, beyond the Augustinerkirche, the **Albertina** is a mishmash of a building, incorporating parts of the former Augustinian monastery, the late eighteenth-century Taroucca Palace and the southernmost bastion of the Hofburg. There are steps up to the bastion, which overlooks the back of the Staatsoper and is surmounted by a grand equestrian statue of the Archduke Albrecht, who vanquished the Italians at the Battle of Custozza, one of his few bright moments in the otherwise disastrous Austro-Prussian War of 1866. Founded in 1768 by Albrecht, duke of Saxony-Teschen (after whom the gallery is named), the Albertina boasts one of the largest collections of **graphic arts** in the world, with approximately 50,000 drawings, etchings and watercolours, and more than 1.5 million printed works. With such a vast archive, the gallery can only hope to show a tiny fraction at any one time, which it does by putting on a series of temporary exhibitions (Tues–Fri 10am–6pm, Sat & Sun 10am–4pm; öS50) devoted to one artist, period or theme. Within its catalogue, it has some 43 drawings by Raphael, 70 by Rembrandt, 145 by Dürer – more than any other gallery in the world – and 150 by Schiele, plus many more by the likes of da Vinci, Michelangelo, Rubens, Bosch, Pieter Brueghel the Elder, Cézanne, Picasso, Matisse, Klimt and Kokoschka.

The Philipphof, a typically ornate Ringstrasse-style building that was home to the exclusive Jockey Club, originally stood to the northeast of the Albertina. However, during the air raid of March 12, 1945, the building received two direct hits, killing several hundred people sheltering in the basement. The lot remained vacant until the 1980s, when the city council commissioned Alfred Hrdlicka to erect a Holocaust memorial – a controversial move given the site's history and its extreme prominence. An almighty row meant that at the time of the planned unveiling – the fiftieth anniversary of the Anschluss and *Kristallnacht* – the **Monument Against War and Fascism** was three years behind schedule. Hrdlicka's final design makes no direct mention of the Holocaust, but shows, among other things, a crouching Jew scrubbing the pavement, recalling the days following the Anschluss, when some of the city's Jews were forced to clean up anti-Nazi slogans with scrubbing brushes dipped in acid.

The Neue Burg

The last wing of the Hofburg to be built – completed in 1913 – was the **Neue Burg**, a piece of pure bombast designed in heavy neo-Renaissance style by Gottfried Semper and Karl von Hasenauer half a century earlier. Semper planned another new palatial

VISITING THE NEUE BURG MUSEUMS

A single ticket (öS30) covers the **Hofjagd** und **Rüstkammer**, the **Sammlung alter Musikinstrumente** and the **Ephesos Museum**. Free radiophone commentary (in German) is available for the first two collections, and access to all three is via the main entrance. The **Museum für Völkerkunde** has its own separate entrance, and requires a separate ticket (öS60). All the above museums open daily except Tuesday 10am to 6pm.

wing to mirror the Neue Burg and enclose Heldenplatz (Heroes' Square). In the end, time (and money) ran out, leaving Heldenplatz as a wide, slightly meaningless, expanse, which nonetheless affords a great view across to the Rathaus and Parlament buildings on the Ringstrasse. The Neue Burg is now home to the Nationalbibliothek's main reading room, an offshoot of the Naturhistorisches Museum and three departments of the Kunsthistorisches Museum. For the Viennese, though, it's for ever etched in the memory as the scene of Hitler's victorious return to Vienna on March 15, 1938, when thousands gathered here to celebrate the Anschluss. Hitler appeared on the central balcony of the Neue Burg and declared: "As Führer and Chancellor of the German nation and the German Reich I hereby announce to German history that my homeland has entered the German Reich."

The Court Hunting and Arms Collection

The **Hofjagd- und Rüstkammer** boasts one of the world's finest assemblages of armour, mostly dating from the fifteenth century to the seventeenth. Chronologically, the collection begins in room 1, where you can view two dog-snout-shaped visors – devised to replace the closed helmet, in which it was extraordinarily difficult to breathe – from the estate of Duke Ernst of of Austria (1377–1424), who was responsible for starting the weaponry collection. The museum continues in an anticlockwise direction, past a splendid array of jousting equipment (side gallery A), made for the knights of Emperor Maximilian I, and a display of High Renaissance **costume armour** (room 3), which was meant only for show, its design deliberately imitating the fashionable clothes of the time: puffy sleeves, decorative bands inlaid with gilded silver, and slightly comical pleated skirts.

There's some fabulous sixteenth-century **Milanese armour** crafted by Filippo Negroli in room 4, including an iron shield embossed with a Medusa head, and a suit of armour with a cap complete with naturalistic ears and curly hair. The museum's other great weaponry freak was the manic collector Archduke Ferdinand of Tyrol (1525–95), who ordered the bank-breaking **Adlergarnitur** (eagle armour) in room 5, with its exquisite gilded garniture. Yet more richly decorated suits of armour fill room 7, including the "rose-petal" garniture ordered by Maximilian II for the tournament held in Vienna in 1571 to celebrate his brother Karl's wedding; equally fancy suits were created for his two sons, Rudolf and Ernst. There's more Milanese craftsmanship in room 8, including a rapier whose hilt features numerous Moors' heads. A vast array of elaborate hunting rifles and pistols, dating from the early seventeenth century to the nineteenth, concludes the exhibition.

The Collection of Early Musical Instruments

If you've absolutely no interest in instruments of death, however beautifully crafted, you can skip the entire collection and head straight for the **Sammlung alter Musikinstrumente**. The Archduke Ferdinand of Tyrol is again responsible for many of the rare pieces, such as the unique set of six sixteenth-century **dragon-shaped**

shawms, in room 10. The vertically strung **calvicytherium**, in room 11, richly inlaid with ivory, ebony, tortoiseshell and mother-of-pearl, was actually played by the emperor Leopold I, who was a musician and composer in his own right. Room 12 is loosely based around Josef Haydn, featuring instruments from his day, plus a quadruple music stand for a string quartet; the extraordinarily lifelike beeswax bust of the composer sports a wig of real human hair. The **tortoiseshell violin**, decorated with gold and ivory, in room 13, was bought by Maria Theresa for the Schatzkammer, and, like many such showpieces, is totally unsuitable for playing. Also in this room is an early nineteenth-century **glass harmonica** of the variety invented by the American statesman Benjamin Franklin. Next door, the ornate **Marmorsaal** (room 14) – still occasionally used as a concert venue – contains several instruments associated with famous composers: a harpsichord owned by Haydn, a square piano used by Schubert, and a grand piano given to Beethoven by the famous piano-makers Erard Frères.

Eye-catching exhibits in room 15 include a **crystal flute**, and a violin that doubled as a walking stick. An aluminium violin and a "**dummy keyboard**" – stringless, for silent practice – can be found in room 16, and in the final room there's an entire late nineteenth-century orchestra, as well as a grand piano designed by Theophil Hansen and given to the emperor Franz-Josef for his wife, Elisabeth, to play.

The Ephesos (Ephesus) Museum
From 1866, until a ban on the export of antiquities from Turkey stopped the flow early this century, Austrian archeologists made off with a lot of first-class relics from the ancient city of Ephesus. It wasn't until 1978 that the loot was finally publicly displayed in the **Ephesos Museum**, occupying one half of the Neue Burg's monumental staircase. The most significant find of the lot is the forty-metre-long **Parthian Frieze**, sculpted in high relief around the second century AD, shortly after the Roman victory in the Parthian Wars. The relief formed the outer walls of a pantheon in honour of the commander of the Roman forces, Lucius Verus, who was joint emperor of the Roman Empire, along with his adoptive brother, Marcus Aurelius. The adoption of the two brothers by Antoninus Pius (himself adopted by the emperor Hadrian) is depicted at the end of the corridor on the right.

The Museum of Ethnology
In the section of the Neue Burg nearest the Ring, the **Museum für Völkerkunde** houses a bewildering array of secular and religious artefacts from around the world. Unfortunately, large sections of the museum are likely to be closed for renovation over the next few years as it drags itself into the 21st century. The ground-floor galleries, despite being badly in need of modernization, contain some interesting pieces from the **Far East**: check out the cheek-whipping device from China, dried frog from Korea, and Japanese reed raincoat with matching rice straw boots. The ground floor also houses the Africa section, including one of the world's finest collections of bronze sculptures from **Benin**, bought at auction in London, where the former kingdom's finest art treasures were sold following the British invasion of 1897. The new displays upstairs are a great deal more enticing to look at, beginning with the **Polynesia** section, much of it brought back from Captain Cook's expeditions, and then snapped up at auction in 1806 by the emperor Franz I – who could resist the Hawaiian firelighter shaped like a giant penis? The highlight of the Americas section is undoubtedly the stunning sixteenth-century gilded **Aztec feather headdress** of the emperor Montezuma II, who was stoned to death by his own people for his passivity in the face of Cortés, the Spanish imperialist.

Ringstrasse

On Christmas Eve 1857, the emperor Franz-Josef I announced the demolition of the zigzag fortifications around the old town and the building of a **Ringstrasse**, a horseshoe of imperial boulevards to be laid out on the former glacis (the sloping ground between the walls and the suburbs). Twelve major public buildings were set down along its course between 1860 and 1890 – among them the court opera house and theatre, two court museums, the imperial parliament, the city university and town hall – all at no cost to the taxpayer. By the end of World War I, though, the Habsburgs were no more: as Edward Crankshaw wrote, the Ringstrasse "was designed as the crown of the Empire, but it turned out to be a tomb".

Today Vienna's Ringstrasse looks pretty much as it did in last days of the Habsburgs, studded with key landmarks. The monumental public institutions remain the chief sights: heading anticlockwise, they include the **Börse**, **Votivkirche**, **Rathaus**, **Burgtheater** and **Parlament** buildings, the two monster museums – the **Naturhistorisches** and **Kunsthistorisches** – and the **Staatsoper**. Countless other cultural institutions occupy prime positions on the Ring and neighbouring Karlsplatz, most notably, the **Musikverein**, the city's premier concert venue, the glorious Jugendstil **Secession** building, and three more excellent museums: the **Akademie der bildenden Künste**, the **Historisches Museum der Stadt Wien**, and the **MAK** (Museum of Applied Art). Last, but not least, Karlsplatz also boasts Vienna's most imposing Baroque church, the **Karlskirche**.

The Votivkirche

The first public building on the Ringstrasse – begun in 1854, even before the emperor had ordered the demolition of the city ramparts – was the **Votivkirche**, a monumental church built by the Vienna-born architect Heinrich Ferstel in the style of the great Gothic cathedrals of Cologne and Chartres. Built opposite the spot where a Hungarian tailor, János Libényi, had tried to stab the emperor Franz-Josef the previous year – he was thwarted only by the emperor's collar and cap – the church was to be "a monument of patriotism and of devotion of the people to the Imperial House". For all its size, there is something spiritually lacking in the Votivkirche. Built partly to serve the large influx of soldiers to the capital following the 1848 revolution, the church has no natural parishioners, and the gloomy interior, badly damaged in World War II, remains underused and little-visited. The one monument worth a look is the sixteenth-century marble tomb of Count Salm, who commanded Vienna during the Turkish siege of 1529.

Rathausplatz

Rathausplatz is the Ringstrasse's showpiece square, framed by no fewer than four monumental public buildings – the Rathaus, the Burgtheater, Parliament and the university – all completed in the 1880s. The most imposing building of the four is the cathedralesque **Rathaus** – strictly speaking the Neues Rathaus – a powerful symbol of the city's late nineteenth-century political clout, designed by the German architect Friedrich von Schmidt in imitation of Brussels' town hall. To get a look at the ornate interior, you must join a 45-minute guided tour in German (Mon, Wed & Fri 1pm; ☎52550). Concerts are occasionally held in the main Arkadenhof and, in July and August, free opera and classical concerts are beamed onto a giant screen on the main facade. Restaurants set up stalls selling food and beer, though these are as nothing compared to the number of stalls set up during the famous **Christkindlmarkt** (mid-Nov to Christmas). As well as selling various kitsch Christmas presents, the market runs workshops for making and baking presents, and there are sideshows for kids.

EXPLORING THE RINGSTRASSE

Blighted by heavy traffic, the **Ringstrasse** is not much fun to stroll along nowadays. In addition, the boulevard's sheer size – 5km from end to end – and its uneven distribution of sights precludes exploration on foot. You're better off adopting a hit-and-run approach, making forays from the nearest U-Bahn or tram stop. The best way to circumnavigate and appreciate the scale of the Ring is by **tram** – #1 goes round in a clockwise direction, and #2 runs anticlockwise. From the trams, only Karlsplatz lies entirely hidden from view. Each section of the Ring is **individually named** (eg Schottenring, Dr-Karl-Lueger-Ring, etc); the account on pp.92–106 works **anticlockwise** starting with the Votivkirche.

Directly opposite the Rathaus, the **Burgtheater** seems modest by comparison – until you realize that the sole function of the theatre's two vast wings was to house monumental staircases leading to the grand boxes. In practical terms, though, the design by Gottfried Semper and Karl von Hasenauer was none too successful. Less than a decade after the opening night in 1888 the theatre had to close in order to revamp the acoustics, which were dreadful, and to modify the seating, some of which allowed no view of the stage at all. The auditorium was gutted by fire during the liberation of Vienna in April 1945, and has since been totally modernized. Thankfully, the staircase wings survived, and still boast their sumptuous decor, including ceiling paintings by Franz Matsch and Gustav Klimt. The easiest way to get to see the Burgtheater is to go to a performance; however, in July and August, when the theatre's closed, you can sign up for a guided tour (Mon, Wed & Fri 1, 2 & 3pm; öS50).

The **Universität** – strictly speaking the Neue Universität – is the most unassuming of the four public buildings on Rathausplatz, built in neo-Renaissance style by Heinrich Ferstel in the 1870s. Sadly, it's no longer possible to view the paintings, commissioned for the university's main hall, which caused possibly the biggest scandal in the institution's history. When the first picture, *Philosophy* by Gustav Klimt, was unveiled in March 1900, its tangled mass of naked, confused humanity prompted 87 professors to sign a petition of protest. The scandal drew 34,000 onlookers to see the painting in just two months. In the end, Klimt returned his fee and claimed back the paintings. All three were placed in Schloss Immendorf for safekeeping during World War II, but were destroyed in a fire started by retreating SS troops on May 5, 1945.

On the south side of Rathausplatz stands the Neoclassical **Parlament**, one of five major Ringstrasse buildings by the Danish architect Theophil von Hansen. From street level, it's difficult to see past the giant Corinthian portico and its accompanying wings and pavilions. Stand back, though, and it becomes clear that the main body of the building is mostly hidden behind the projecting facade. The main pediment frieze shows the emperor Franz-Josef I reluctantly granting the seventeen peoples of the empire a deeply undemocratic constitution. In front of the building, a gargantuan statue of Athena, goddess of wisdom, sporting a natty gilded plume in her helmet, presides over a fountain served by four writhing mermen. The attic of the main building, meanwhile, is peppered with 76 classical statues, 66 reliefs and 4 bronze chariot groups – these are best viewed from the sides of the building, where you'll find porticoes held up by caryatids modelled on the Erechtheion on the Acropolis. If you want to see inside the building, you can simply turn up for one of the free guided tours (Mon–Fri 11am and 3pm; mid-July to Aug also 9 & 10am and 1 & 2pm).

The Naturhistorisches Museum

The **Naturhistorisches Museum** (daily except Tues 9am–6pm; first floor closes at 3pm in the winter; öS30) is the first of the pompous neo-Renaissance museums that stand on the other side of the Ringstrasse from the Hofburg. Whereas most European cities have tried to pep up their natural history collections with automated dinosaurs, ecological concerns and the like, the hard sell has, so far, passed Vienna by, and little has changed here since the museum opened in 1889. The display cabinets are over a century old, as is the exclusively German labelling – places as distant as Illyria (present-day Slovenia) and Galicia (part of present-day Ukraine) are still described as if part of Austria – the dim panes of glass are almost pre-industrial, and the stuffed animals have all succumbed to a uniform, musty, grey hue.

The ground floor kicks off with five rooms of minerals (I–V), of little interest to non-specialists. The adjacent paleontology section is currently under wraps, with the exception of room X – a huge hall decorated with caryatids struggling with weird, prehistoric beasts – where you can find the skeleton of a diplodocus and various fossils. The prehistoric civilizations section begins in room XI with the **Venus of Willendorf**, by far the most famous exhibit in the entire museum. This tiny fertility symbol – a stout, limestone figure with drooping breasts – stands just a few centimetres high, but is something like 25,000 years old, and as such is an object of some fascination. Sadly, what you actually see is a replica (the real thing is far too precious to be put on display), accompanied by another much larger reproduction.

The west wing includes finds from the prehistoric Beaker folk and various implements, jewellery and arms from Iron Age burial tombs at Halstatt in the Salzkammergut (see p.368). There's some impressive Thracian silver jewellery, a reconstructed funereal chariot from the Iron Age, and a staggering collection of human skulls. The *Kindersaal*, beyond, is the museum's one concession to modernization, though this tired children's playroom, built in the 1970s, isn't going to impress kids brought up on interactive, hands-on displays. Zoology occupies the top floor, progressing from starfish, corals and seashells in the east wing to a bevy of bears, cats and monkeys in the west.

The Kunsthistorisches Museum

In a city somewhat overloaded with museums, the **Kunsthistorisches Museum** stands head and shoulders above the rest. Thanks to the wealth and artistic pretensions of successive Habsburg rulers, it contains not only the fourth largest collection of paintings in the world, but also Egyptian, Greek and Roman antiquities, plus sundry *objets d'art* from this millennium. So numerous are the exhibits that several of the museum's departments are now housed in the Neue Burg wing of the Hofburg (see p.89).

VISITING THE KUNSTHISTORISCHES MUSEUM

The museum's **opening times** are Tuesday to Sunday 10am to 6pm; the picture gallery is also open until 9pm on Thursdays, while some of the ground-floor galleries close at dusk in winter. **Tickets** cost öS100, a lot of money for what is supposed to be a public institution, though it does include entry into the museum's temporary exhibition. There's no readmission into the museum, and even if you spend the whole day here you'll be pushed to see everything, so it's best to concentrate on just one or two areas. You'll also be extremely hungry, since the only place to eat is the architecturally superb, but overpriced **café** in the upper foyer, which has only a limited menu. **Guided tours** of the museum in English set off daily at 3pm and cost öS30.

The paintings of the first-floor Gemäldegalerie are arranged in parallel rooms around two courtyards: the Italians, plus a few French and Spanish, lie to one side; the Germans, Dutch and Flemish, to the other. The larger rooms, which face onto the courtyards, sport Roman numerals (I–XV), while the smaller outer rooms use the standard form (1–24), though the latter are often unmarked. It would be difficult to concoct a more confusing numerical system, but at least both wings are laid out (vaguely) chronologically. The ground floor is laid out entirely chronologically using only Roman numerals.

Most people come here to see the sixteenth- and seventeenth-century art in the Gemäldegalerie, in particular the collection of **Bruegels** – the largest in the world – which forms part of a superlative early Netherlandish and Flemish section. Thanks to the Habsburgs' territorial acquisitions, the museum is also loaded with **Venetian** works, by the likes of **Tintoretto**, **Veronese** and **Titian**, and a goodly selection of **Velázquez** portraits. In addition, there are numerous works by **Rembrandt**, **Cranach** and **Dürer**, and whole rooms devoted to **Van Dyck** and **Rubens**. Lastly, don't miss the unrivalled collection of Mannerist works from the court of Rudolf II, especially the surrealist court painter, **Giuseppe Arcimboldo**.

The Gemäldegalerie

The **Gemäldegalerie** (Picture Gallery), on the first floor, has around eight hundred paintings on display at any one time, a mere tenth of the museum's total catalogue. It's easy to become overwhelmed by the sheer volume of art. Unlike most big galleries, the Kunsthistorisches makes no attempt to cover a broad span of art history – the collection has changed very little since the Habsburgs bequeathed it. Consequently, British and French artists, and the early Italian Renaissance, are all underrepresented, and the collection stops at the late eighteenth century.

BRUEGEL

The great thing about the museum's Bruegels is the breadth and range of the collection, from innovative interpretations of religious stories to allegorical peasant scenes. Though well connected in court circles in Antwerp and, later, Brussels, **Pieter Bruegel the Elder** (*c.*1525–69) excelled in these country scenes, earning himself the soubriquet "Peasant Bruegel" – the story goes that he used to disguise himself in order to move freely among the peasantry. A classic example of the genre is his *Children's Games*, an incredibly detailed picture with more than 230 children playing 90 different games. Perhaps the most beguiling of all Bruegel's works within the peasant genre are the cycle of seasons, commissioned by a rich Flemish banker. Three (out of six) hang in this room: *The Gloomy Day*, *The Return of the Herd* and, the most famous of the lot, *Hunters in the Snow*, in which Bruegel perfectly captures a monochrome wintry landscape.

Several of Bruegel's peasant works clearly have a somewhat high-handed moral message, too, as in the *Peasant Dance*, where the locals revel irreverently, oblivious to the image of the Madonna concealed in the top right-hand corner. Similarly, the *Peasant Wedding* comes over less as a religious occasion than as another excuse for gluttony. Even in Bruegel's overtly religious paintings, the biblical events are often subordinated to the whole. In *The Procession to Calvary*, the typically vigorous Bruegelian crowd seem utterly unmoved by the tragedy quietly unfolding in their midst. Gruesome characters, revealing the influence of Bosch, inhabit *The Fight Between Carnival and Lent*, a complex painting in which the orgy of Shrove Tuesday is contrasted with the piety of Ash Wednesday. *The Tower of Babel* (inspired, it's thought, by the Colosseum in Rome) is more straightforward, illustrating the vanity of King Nimrod – the detail on both the tower and the city below it is staggering.

DÜRER, CRANACH AND HOLBEIN

If you head off into the smaller side rooms, you come to the excellent German collection, in particular the so-called "Danube School", an extremely loose title used to group together various sixteenth-century German-speaking painters inspired by the landscape around the Danube. The collection begins in room 16 with a colourful *Adoration of the Trinity* by **Albrecht Dürer** (1471–1528). Amidst his gilded throng are the donor, Matthäus Landauer (lower row, to the left), his son-in-law (lower row, to the right) and, with his feet firmly on the ground, Dürer himself (bottom right). The frame (a modern copy of the original) bears closer inspection, too, with those not heading for heaven being chained up and devoured by the Devil. Dürer also appears, somewhat incongruously dressed in black, in the centre of his *Martyrdom of the Ten Thousand*; amid scenes of mass murder, he strolls deep in conversation with his recently deceased friend, the humanist Conrad Celtes.

A prime example of the Danube School of painting is *The Crucifixion* by **Lucas Cranach the Elder** (1472–1553), in room 17; one of his earliest works, with its gory depiction of Christ, spattered with, and vomiting up, blood, set against a rugged Danubian landscape. His depiction of the *Stag Hunt of Elector Frederick the Wise*, in which numerous stags are driven into the water so the royals can pick them off with crossbows, is almost playful, and his son, Lucas Cranach the Younger (1515–86), contributes an equally jolly scene of slaughter in *Stag Hunt of the Elector John Frederick*, which hangs close by.

The portraits in room 18 by **Hans Holbein the Younger** (1497–1543) date from his period as court painter to the English King Henry VIII. One of his first royal commissions was a portrait of Jane Seymour, lady-in-waiting to Henry VIII's second wife, Anne Boleyn, who, after the latter's execution, became his third wife (she died giving birth to Henry's one and only son, the future Edward VI).

ARCIMBOLDO, BRUEGHEL AND VAN DYCK

In room 19, you enter the court of Rudolf II (1576–1612), the deeply melancholic emperor who shut himself up in Prague Castle surrounded by astrologers, alchemists and artists. It is Rudolf, whose portrait by **Hans von Aachen** (*c*.1551–1615) hangs in the room, we have to thank for the Bruegels and Dürers in the museum. One of Rudolf's favourite court artists was **Giuseppe Arcimboldo** (1527–93), whose "composite heads" – surrealist, often disturbing, profile portraits created out of inanimate objects – so tickled the emperor that he had portraits made of every member of his entourage, right down to the cook. Among the four in the Kunsthistorisches, all of which are allegorical, are *Water*, in which the whole head is made of sea creatures, and *Fire*, where it's a hotchpotch of burning faggots, an oil lamp and various firearms.

Room 19 also contains several works by the son of "Peasant Bruegel", **Jan Brueghel the Elder** (1568–1625), whose detailed still lifes of flowers were highly prized, his luminous paintwork earning him the nickname "Velvet Brueghel". One of his most famous, non-flowery paintings is his reverential *Adoration of the Kings*, a beautifully detailed work that's a firm favourite on Christmas cards. **Anthony van Dyck** (1599–1641) predominates in the adjacent room (XII): some pieces, like *The Apostle Philip*, date from the time when van Dyck was working closely with Rubens, hence the characteristic, "ruffled" brushstrokes; others – mostly portraits – from after van Dyck's appointment as court painter to the English King Charles I.

RUBENS, REMBRANDT AND VERMEER

Thanks to the Habsburgs' long-term control of the southern Netherlands, the Kunsthistorisches Museum boasts one of the largest collections of paintings by **Peter Paul Rubens** (1577–1640), spread over three rooms (rooms 20, XIII and XIV). Perhaps the best known of all his works here is *The Fur*, in room XIII, a frank, erotic testament to the artist's second wife, Hélène Fourment, who was 37 years his junior. Rubens was clearly taken with his 16-year-old wife, who appears as an angel, saint or deity, in two other of his late works: the *Ildefonso Altar* and the *Meeting Near Nördlingen*. The loose brushwork and painterly style in these two bears comparison with Titian's late work in room I, and Rubens pays tribute to the Italian in his *The Worship of Venus*, a veritable cherub-fest set in a classical landscape.

Rubens' Baroque excess is a million miles from the sparse, simple portraits of **Rembrandt van Rijn** (1606–69), five of which hang in room XV. There's a sympathetic early portrait of his mother, the year before she died, depicted in all the fragility and dignity of old age, and a dreamlike later study of his son, Titus, reading. The other three are self-portraits from the 1650s, when Rembrandt was beginning to experience financial difficulties. Next door, in room 24, is the museum's one and only painting by **Jan Vermeer** (1632–75), *Allegory of the Art of Painting*. The bright light from the onlooker's left, the yellow, blue and grey, the simple poses, are all classic Vermeer trademarks, though the symbolic meaning, and even the title, of the work have provoked fierce debate.

NORTHERN ITALIAN PAINTINGS

Over in the west wing, the museum boasts an impressive selection of Venetian paintings, especially works by **Titian** (*c*.1490–1576), which span all sixty years of his artistic life. Very early works like *The Gypsy Madonna* in room I reveal Titian's debt to Giovanni Bellini, in whose studio he spent his apprenticeship. The colours are richer, the contours softer, but the essentially static composition is reminiscent of Bellini's own *Young Woman with a Mirror* (see below). The largest canvas in room I is Titian's *Ecce Homo*, from his middle period, in which, amidst all the action and colour, Christ is relegated to the top left-hand corner.

In *Girl in a Fur* and the portrait of Benedetto Varchi, Titian shows himself equally capable of sparing use of colour, allowing the sitter's individual features maximum effect. By contrast, Titian's very last portrait, of the art dealer Jacopo Strada, whom the painter disliked, is full of incidental detail, colour and movement. Towards the end of his life, Titian achieved a freedom of technique in his own personal works (as opposed to those produced for commission by his studio), in which "he used his fingers more than his brush" according to fellow painter Palma il Giovane. A masterpiece of this period is the *Nymph and Shepherd*, painted without a commission, using an autumnal palette and very loose brushwork.

Bellini's *Young Woman with a Mirror* hangs in the adjacent room 1, along with a sculptural *St Sebastian* by his brother-in-law, **Andrea Mantegna** (*c*.1431–1506), and three fragments of an altarpiece by Antonello da Messina, who is credited with introducing oil painting to northern Italy. Next door, in room 2, the subject matter of the *Three Philosphers* is almost as mysterious as its painter, **Giorgone** (*c*.1478–1511), about whom we know little other than that he was tall, handsome and died young, possibly of the plague; as for the painting, no one's sure if it depicts the Magi, the three stages of man's life or some other subject. Giorgone's sensuous portrait *Laura* – fur and naked breasts are a recurring theme in the gallery – is one of his few works to be certified and dated on the back.

Colourful, carefully constructed, monumental canvases by **Paolo Veronese** (1528–88) fill the walls of room II – the *Anointing of David* is a classic example, with the subject matter subordinated to the overall effect. In room III, there are several impressive portraits by **Tintoretto** (1518–94), and a voluptuous *Susanna and the Elders*, full of contrasts of light and shade, old age and youthfulness, clothing and bare flesh. Another work that draws your attention is the series of horizontal panels depicting scenes from the Old Testament with refreshing immediacy and improvised brushstrokes.

RAPHAEL, THE MANNERISTS AND CARAVAGGIO

In room 3, the scene shifts across northern Italy to the Mannerist school of Emilia. **Antonio Correggio** (*c*.1494–1534) puts his bid in for the gallery's most erotic painting with *Jupiter and Io*, in which the latter is brought to the verge of ecstasy by Jupiter in the form of a cloud. *Self-Portrait in a Convex Mirror* by **Parmigianino** (1503–40) was just the sort of tricksy art that appealed to Rudolf II, in whose collection it appeared in 1608. There's a masterly study in Renaissance harmony and proportion in room 4, with the *Madonna in the Meadow*, painted by **Raphael** (1483–1520) at the tender age of 22. Further on, a typically icy *Holy Family* by **Agnolo Bronzino** (1503–72) hangs in room 7.

Caravaggio (1573–1610) was nothing if not controversial. His chief artistic sin, in the eyes of the establishment, was his refusal to idealize his biblical characters, frequently using street urchins as his models, as in his *David with the Head of Goliath*; he also painted his own self-portrait as the severed head of Goliath. He may have managed to outrage more than a few of his religious patrons, but his works had a profound effect on seventeenth-century artists like Rubens and Bruegel, both of whom at one time or another owned the *Madonna of the Rosary*, now in room V.

VELÁZQUEZ, BELLOTTO AND CANALETTO

If the Italians start to get you down – and there is a lot of less-than-fantastic seventeenth-century art out there – head for the Spaniards in rooms 9 and 10. The museum's smattering of works by **Diego Velázquez** (1599–1660), most of them gifts from the Spanish Habsburgs to the Austrian side of the family, include one of Queen Maria-Anna of Spain, whose hairdo is twice the size of her face, and two of Charles II of Spain, though neither is as grotesque as the early portrait by Juan Carreño de Miranda – it's scary to think that he probably looked even worse in real life. The most famous of Velázquez's works are those of the Infanta Margarita Teresa, who was betrothed to her uncle, the future Emperor Leopold I, from the age of 3, and the one of the sickly Infante Philip Prosper, first-born son of Philip II, who died shortly after the painting was finished.

Lastly, you might want to take a look at the eighteenth-century views of Vienna in room VII, commissioned by the court from **Bernardo Bellotto**, to see how little the view from the Upper Belvedere has changed over the centuries. The Viennese insisted on calling Bellotto "Canaletto", though he was in fact the latter's nephew and pupil. For real **Canalettos** (1697–1768), you must go next door, to room 13, where his views of Venice hang alongside those of his compatriot Francesco Guardi.

The ground-floor galleries

The **ground-floor galleries** kick off with the Egyptian and Near Eastern Collection (I–VIII), passes through Greek and Roman Antiquities (IX–XVIII) and heads off into Sculpture and Decorative Arts (XIX–XXVII). However, for what seems like an eternity now, rooms XXVIII onwards, and the Coin Cabinet, have been closed for renovations, with eight rooms from this collection remaining open.

EGYPTIAN AND NEAR EASTERN COLLECTION

Immediately to the right as you enter the museum are the purpose-built galleries of the **Egyptian and Near Eastern Collection**, beginning in room I, which is devoted to the **Egyptian death cult**. The entrance to the room is guarded by two statues of the fearsome, lion-headed goddess, Sekhmet; the museum owns just four out of the six hundred that once formed a colossal monument to the deity erected at Thebes by Amenophis III. In the room itself, there's only one actual mummy, wrapped in papyrus leaves, but there are numerous wooden inner coffins in the shape of mummies, smothered with polychrome symbols and hieroglyphs. Below the mummy cases are the tiny canopic jars, used for storing the entrails removed during mummification, with lids carved in the shape of animal deities. Another display cabinet to make for, in room III, contains the mummies of various animals, including cats, falcons, snakes, crocodiles and a bull's head, alongside figurines evincing the strength of Egyptian animal cults.

The Kunsthistorisches Museum owns some superb examples of **Egyptian sculpture**, beginning in room V with an unusual depiction of a lion tucking into a bull, and Isis, sporting cow's horns, a solar disc and a vulture headdress, breastfeeding Horus. Horus appears in his adult, falcon-headed form in a rather wonderful duo in room VII, seated alongside King Horemheb, who was the power behind the throne of Tutankhamen. Also in this room is a winsome blue pottery hippo, whose body is tattooed with papyrus leaves, lotus flowers and a bird. Room VIII contains one of the collection's most prized possessions, the so-called **Reserve Head** from around 2450 BC, a smooth, stylized head carved in limestone, which exudes an extraordinary serenity.

GREEK AND ROMAN ANTIQUITIES
The **Greek and Roman Antiquities** begin in room X, though one of the most prominent statues here – the **Youth of Magdalensberg** – is in fact a sixteenth-century bronze copy of the Roman original, something that was only discovered in 1983 when research was being conducted into the methods used in the casting. At the centre of the large, arcaded room XI, is the magnificent fourth-century AD **Theseus Mosaic**, discovered in a Roman villa near Salzburg. Theseus and the Minotaur are depicted in the middle of a complex geometric labyrinth, out of which the hero escapes with the help of the red thread given to him by Ariadne, who is pictured abandoned to the right.

Those in search of **Greek vases** need look no further than room XIV, which contains an excellent selection from early Geometric vases from the eighth century BC to the sophisticated black- and red-figure vases of the Classical period. Among the many onyx cameos in the adjoining room XV is one of the finest in the world, the **Gemma Augusta**, a mere 19cm in height. The upper scene depicts the emperor Augustus in the guise of Jupiter, seated on a bench alongside Roma, with the emperor's star sign, Capricorn, floating between them.

The last three small rooms (XVI–XVIII) contain **gold work**, much of which, strictly speaking, postdates the collapse of the Roman Empire. The chain of honour with 52 pendants is an excellent example of early Germanic gold, its centrepiece a bead of smoky topaz, mounted with two tiny pouncing panthers. The most impressive haul is the treasure from Nagyszentmiklós (Sînicolaul Mare) in Romania, 23 pure gold vessels, weighing a total of 20kg, with runic inscriptions that continue to fox the experts.

SCULPTURE AND DECORATIVE ARTS
The majority of the **Sculpture and Decorative Arts** galleries have been under wraps for some time now, but the seven rooms that remain open give a fair indication of the wealth of the collection. Most of the exhibits were collected or specially commissioned for the various **Kunstkammern** (Chambers of Marvels), which became *de rigueur* among German-speaking rulers during the Renaissance – the most avid collectors were the archduke Ferdinand II of Tyrol (see p.413) and the emperor Rudolf II.

Room XIX contains objects made from precious and semi-precious stone, and sets the slightly vulgar tone of much of the collection. Prime examples are the gold vase holding tulips made from agate, jasper, chalcedony and rock crystal, or the gold chain, inset with rubies and made up of 49 portraits of the Habsburgs carved in shell. Most of the exhibits have no function, but the rock-crystal dragon-lions were something of a party piece: liquid poured into their tails would gush through a shell through nozzles in the beast's breasts.

In room XXV you can see an elaborate piggy bank belonging to the archduke Ferdinand II of Tyrol, but the most famous exhibit in the entire collection is Benvenuto Cellini's **Saliera**, in room XXVII, a slightly ludicrous sixteenth-century salt cellar, in which the gold figures of Neptune and Earth appear to be engaged in some sort of erotic seesaw.

The Messepalast (Museumsquartier)

If you stand between the two big museums with your back to the Hofburg, you are confronted with the **Messepalast** (Trade Fair Palace), built in the eighteenth century as the imperial barracks by Johann Bernhard Fischer von Erlach, but greatly enlarged following the 1848 revolution. This vast complex of buildings was earmarked way back in the 1980s to become a new **Museumsquartier**, which its backers hoped would rival the likes of the Centre Pompidou in Paris, housing, among other things, the city's collection of modern art, currently on show at the Palais Liechtenstein (see p.113).

So far, however, only a few museums and galleries have made it here, chief amongst which is the the **Österreichisches Tabakmuseum** (Austrian Tobacco Museum; Tues–Fri 10am–5pm, Sat & Sun 10am–2pm; öS50), an exhaustive collection of *objets d'art* and smoking paraphernalia housed in the Klosterhof (accessible from Mariahilferstrasse). Funded by the state tobacco monopoly, Austria Tabak, the overall tone is celebratory – you can even smoke whilst inside the museum. Ask for the English notes, in order to identify the various snuffboxes made out of gold, agate, ivory, tortoiseshell, mother-of-pearl and horn, and the huge pile of pipes, ranging from simple clay versions to the Giant Pipe of the Waldviertel, an ornamental monstrosity made for the emperor Franz-Josef in 1910.

The Staatsoper

That the **Staatsoper** (State Opera House) was the first public building to be completed on the Ringstrasse – opening in May 1869 with a performance of Mozart's *Don Giovanni* – is an indication of its importance in Viennese society. Prestigious past directors include Gustav Mahler, Richard Strauss, Herbert von Karajan and Claudio Abbado, though each one had notoriously difficult relationships with the opera house. The building itself was designed in heavy Italian Renaissance style – even the Viennese deferred to Italy as the home of opera – and has a suitably grandiose exterior, with a fine loggia beneath which carriages could draw up. There are guided tours (öS50) of the interior, schedules for which are listed beneath the arcade on the east side of the building, though the main auditorium is pretty undistinguished, having been destroyed in an air raid in 1945. In any case, for less than the price of the tour, you can buy one of the hundreds of standing-room tickets (*Stehplätze*) that are sold each day on a first-come, first-served basis (and limited to one ticket per person).

Akademie der bildenden Künste

Set back from the Ring, on Schillerplatz to the southwest of the Staatsoper, the **Akademie der bildenden Künste** (Academy of Fine Arts; Tues, Thurs & Fri 10am–2pm, Wed 10am–1pm & 3–6pm, Sat & Sun 9am–1pm; öS30) occupies an imposing neo-Renaissance structure built by Theophil von Hansen in 1876. The Academy itself was founded in 1692, and its main purpose continues to be teaching, but the school also houses a small, much-overlooked study collection. To see the paintings, follow the signs to the **Gemäldegalerie**: turn right after the porter's lodge, head up the stairs to the second floor, then right again to the end of the corridor. The **Aula** – straight ahead as you pass through the main entrance – is also worth a glimpse, both for its decor and for the regular wacky student installations.

Badly lit and indifferently hung, the Academy's collection is tiny compared with the Kunsthistorisches Museum. Nevertheless, it does have one star attraction: *The Last Judgment* triptych by **Hieronymus Bosch** (*c.*1450–1516). The action in the left panel, Paradise, is a taster for the central panel, the Last Judgment itself, most of which is taken up with strange, half-animal diabolic figures busy torturing sinners in imaginatively horrible ways; the right panel, Hell, looks even less fun. Overall, the possibility of salvation seems painfully slim, with only a lucky few having made it to the small corner of the painting given over to heaven.

Flemish and Dutch paintings make up the core of the Academy's collection, with an early Rembrandt portrait, a self-portrait by Van Dyck aged just 14, and preparatory studies for the Jesuit Church frescoes in Antwerp by Rubens, among the finest works. After Bosch, the other outstanding masterpiece is the *Family Group in a Courtyard* by **Pieter de Hooch** (c.1629–84), with its sublime tranquillity and clever play on perspective. The Italian works are disappointing in comparison, with the exception of Titian's *Tarquin and Lucretia*, a late work replete with loose brushwork and brooding, autumnal colours. Other works to look out for are Murillo's sentimental *Two Boys Playing Dice*, a *Crucifixion* by Memlinc, Lucas Cranach the Elder's moralistic-erotic *Ill-Matched Couple*, and paintings by Guardi and Lorrain. In the final corridor, there's a brief selection of twentieth-century Austrian art, including works by Friedensreich Hundertwasser, Fritz Wotruba and Herbert Boeckl.

Karlsplatz

Overlooked by the city's most awesome Baroque church, several key Ringstrasse institutions, the gilded **Secession** building and Otto Wagner's wonderful Art Nouveau pavilions, **Karlsplatz** should be one of Vienna's showpiece squares. Instead, the western half is little more than a vast traffic interchange, with pedestrians relegated to a set of seedy subways that stretch north as far as Oper. The problem is there has never been any grand, overall plan at Karlsplatz – the **Naschmarkt** was held here until the 1890s, but when it moved to the nearby **Wienzeile** the heart was ripped out of the square. The city council provided a site for the Secession, but the avenue that should have connected it with the **Karlskirche** never materialized. As a result, it's actually impossible to stand back and admire the Secession building without seriously endangering your life. The latest abomination is Adolf Krischanitz's Kunsthalle, a mustard-yellow and blue pre-fab steel box used for large-scale art exhibitions.

Secession

In 1898, Joseph Maria Olbrich completed one of the most original Jugendstil works of art in Vienna, the headquarters for the **Secession** movement (see box, p.102). The dome of gilded bronze laurel leaves is the most startling feature – the Viennese dubbed it the "golden cabbage" – though all the building's decorative details are unusual. On the sides, three wise owls suddenly emerge from the rendering, while the main entrance is adorned with a trio of Medusas, a pair of salamanders and copious gilded foliage; above is the group's credo "For every age its art; for art its freedom", replaced after being removed by the Nazis. Don't miss the tortoises at the feet of the ornamental bowls, Georg Klimt's bronze doors with snake handles, and Arthur Strasser's bronze statue of an overweight Mark Antony on a chariot drawn by panthers.

The main hall upstairs stages provocative contemporary art installations, while downstairs in the basement Gustav Klimt's **Beethoven Frieze** is on permanent display (Tues–Fri 10am–6pm, Sat & Sun 10am–4pm; öS30). The frieze was intended to last only for the duration of the fourteenth exhibition held in 1902 – in the end it was preserved but not shown to the public again until 1986. With much of the mural consisting of huge blank spaces framed by floating maidens, the frieze looks strangely half-finished. In between the blank spaces are three painted sections: *Longing for Happiness*, where the weak, represented by three naked emaciated figures, appeal to a knight in golden armour; *Hostile Forces*, which features a slightly comical giant ape, with a serpent's tail and wings, and his three daughters, the Gorgons, backed up by the figures of Disease, Madness and Death, and surrounded by decorative sperm and ovaries; and finally *Ode to Joy*, which culminates in an embracing couple, offering, in Schiller's words, "this kiss to all the world". There's an excellent English commentary available, which explains in greater detail the symbolism behind the frieze; also on display are Klimt's preparatory sketches.

A BRIEF GUIDE TO THE VIENNESE SECESSION

In 1897, a number of artists broke away from the Künstlerhaus, Austria's leading mainstream artists' association, and set up their own organization, which they named the **Secession**. The second half of the nineteenth century had seen the ossification of the arts in Vienna, exemplified in architecture by the heavy-handed historicism of the Ringstrasse, and in painting by the flattery of Hans Makart. Broadly speaking, the aims of the new group were to regenerate the arts in Vienna, and to promote "art for arts sake", in particular the latest style, Art Nouveau, known in German as Jugendstil ("youth-style"). "We want to declare war on sterile routine, on rigid Byzantinism, on all forms of bad taste," declared the critic Hermann Bahr, one of the literary champions of the movement. The other major thrust, which sat less happily with the Secession's other commitments, was to strip off the mask of historicism and, as Otto Wagner put it, "to show modern man his true face".

The first president of the Secession was the artist Gustav Klimt, who became the group's driving force over the next eight years. Klimt had begun his career as a promising young master of the old ideology. In the movement's striking, purpose-built headquarters, in full view of the Künstlerhaus, he now helped put on a series of exhibitions of new work. Initially, the reception among Viennese critics and the public was good, but the movement ran into trouble when Klimt exhibited *Medicine* here, part of his controversial mural intended for the university. The ensuing public scandal, and the mixed reception given to the group's fourteenth exhibition in 1902, eventually prompted Klimt, along with a number of his followers, to secede from the Secession and retreat from public life for several years.

Between 1898 and 1903, the Secession group published *Ver Sacrum*, a successful arts journal employing lavish Jugendstil typography and layout. Instrumental in its production and design were two of the Secession's co-founders, Josef Hoffmann and Kolo Moser, who went on to pursue their interest in applied art, forming the craft-based Wiener Werkstätte in 1902. Hoffmann and Moser left the Secession in 1905 with Klimt, but the threesome later worked together to organize the Kunstschau exhibitions of 1908 and 1909, which in many ways represented the swan song of the Secessionists.

Though only a peripheral character in the Secessionist organization, the architect Otto Wagner was a seminal figure in the Viennese art world throughout the period – as Hermann Bahr wrote, "without Wagner, there would be no Secession, no Klimt group, no applied art". Wagner not only completed more buildings than any other Secession architect, he also designed the entire Stadtbahn system from 1894 to 1901 – many of his stations are extant on the U4 and U6 metro lines. As such, he remains the most high-profile exponent of the Secession style, though his works in fact range from nineteenth-century historicism to twentieth-century modernism.

Last, but not least, it's worth mentioning the architect Adolf Loos, who published two articles in Ver Sacrum, one of which was a stinging attack on Ringstrasse architecture. Loos' relationship with the Secession was brief, however, and in 1908 he published a thinly veiled criticism of the movement in an article entitled "Ornament is Crime".

The Karlsplatz pavilions, Künstlerhaus and Musikverein

Another Jugendstil masterpiece in Karlsplatz is Otto Wagner's duo of entrance pavilions for the now defunct **Station Karlsplatz**, erected in 1899. Wagner broke with his usual design here, partly in deference to the presence of the nearby Karlskirche, adding gold trimmings and a sunflower motif. The green, wrought-iron framework, which was a feature of all his Stadtbahn stations, forms an essential part of the overall design, framing a series of thin marble slabs and creating a lovely, curving, central canopy. Today, one of the pavilions has been converted into a café (daily 10am–7pm), while the other holds exhibition space for the Historisches Museum (May–Oct daily except Mon 9am–12.15pm & 1–4.30pm; öS25).

From the terrace between the pavilions, you can also admire two key institutions on the north side of Karlsplatz, both executed in Ringstrasse style. The neo-Baroque

Künstlerhaus was built in 1881 as the exhibition hall of Austria's leading artists' association (from which the Secession group split in 1897); its diminutive extension was converted into a mid-scale theatre in the 1970s. Next door stands the **Musikverein**, Vienna's number-one concert hall, designed by the ubiquitous Theophil von Hansen in the 1860s. The classical terracotta exterior apes the opera house with its front loggia, but you need to attend a concert in the Grosser Saal to appreciate the unbeatable acoustics and the sumptuous decor with its parade of gilded caryatids. Home to the world-famous Vienna Philharmonic, the Musikverein's most prestigious event is the annual New Year's Day concert, which is transmitted live around the world to an estimated 1.3 billion viewers.

The Karlskirche

Rising majestically above everything around it, the **Karlskirche** (Mon–Sat 9–11.30am & 1–5pm, Sun 1–5pm), designed by Johann Bernhard Fischer von Erlach and completed by his son Johann Michael in 1737, is, without doubt, the city's finest Baroque church. A huge Italianate dome with a Neoclassical portico, flanked by two giant pillars modelled on Trajan's Column, and, just for good measure, a couple of hefty Baroque side towers, it's an eclectic and rather self-conscious mixture of styles, built to impress. Even surrounded by the mess that is now Karlsplatz, the church is an awesome sight – and must have been even more so when there was nothing between it and the Hofburg except the open space of the glacis.

The church is dedicated to the sixteenth-century saint, Carlo Borromeo, though the fact that the emperor and saint shared the same name no doubt played a part in Karl VI's choice, conveniently glorifying both of them at the same time. The Karlskirche's dual nature – votive and imperial – is nowhere more evident than with the columns, imperial symbols whose reliefs illustrate the life of Borromeo. The interior is surprisingly sparse and light, allowing a much better appreciation of Johann Michael Rottmayr's vast fresco than you get of the artist's work in the Peterskirche. The subject is the apotheosis of Carlo Borromeo, along with a bit of Counter-Reformation Luther-bashing – see the angel setting fire to the German's Bible. Everything else in the church finds it rather hard to compete with the sublime beauty of the dome, though Fischer von Erlach's sunburst above the main altar is definitely worth a closer look.

The Historisches Museum der Stadt Wien

Housed in an unprepossessing modernist block to the side of the Karlskirche, the **Historisches Museum der Stadt Wien** (daily except Mon 9am–4.30pm; öS50) is an uneven collection, but it does contain, among other things, an excellent fin-de-siècle section – which alone more than justifies a visit – and excellent temporary exhibitions are often held on the ground floor.

The historical rundown on the city kicks off on the ground floor with the Roman and Gothic section – like much of the museum rather a ragbag assortment. You could happily skip this and head upstairs to the **Baroque** section on the first floor, with a selection of paintings including minor works by all the key artists of the period. Also exhibited are a smattering of spoils from the city's two Turkish sieges of 1529 and 1683: a vast red silk banner, Turkish horse plumes sporting crescent moons, and the odd turban. Before you head upstairs, take a look at the model of Vienna shortly before the old zigzag fortifications were torn down in 1857.

On the top floor, by far the most interesting section in the whole museum, the centrepiece is another model of Vienna, this time after the construction of the great Ringstrasse buildings of the late nineteenth century, accompanied by "before" and "after" photos. To the side is an entire living/dining room designed in 1903 by the modernist architect **Adolf Loos** for his first marital home on nearby Bösendorferstrasse.

Despite his diatribes against ornament of any kind, Loos loved rich materials – marble, mahogany and brass – and created for himself a typically plush interior. Nearby hangs **Gustav Klimt**'s *Pallas Athene* from 1898, marking his first use of gold, which was to become a hallmark of his work.

Dotted around the next two rooms are various other works of art from Vienna's golden age at the turn of the century. The copy of Max Klinger's nude statue of Beethoven, which formed the centrepiece of the Secession exhibition of 1902, is displayed here, albeit without its coloured marble drapery and seat. Carl Moll contributes two gloomily Expressionist views of the interior of his Haus Moll, designed by fellow Secessionist Josef Hoffmann. There are several glass cabinets – including one designed by Kolo Moser – stuffed with Wiener Werkstätte produce, but it's the five works by **Egon Schiele** that really stand out. A typically distraught study of sunflowers from 1909 and the harrowing *Blind Mother II* hang beside a fondly painted view of the artist's bedroom in Neulengbach, a clear homage to Van Gogh, executed shortly before his brief imprisonment on a charge of "displaying an erotic drawing in a room open to children". The characteristically angular portraits of the art critic and collector Arthur Roessler and his wife Ida – loyal friends and patrons throughout Schiele's life – are among the artist's earliest commissioned portrait oils.

The Naschmarkt and Linke Wienzeile

The **Naschmarkt** (Mon–Sat 9am–6pm), which stretches away to the southwest of Karlsplatz, is now the city's premier source of fruit and vegetables, and one of the few places where you get a real sense of the city's multicultural make-up: Turks, Arabs, Slavs and Chinese stallholders vie for customers all the way to the Kettenbrückengasse metro station. On Saturdays, the market extends even further west as the weekly flea market joins in. The Linke and Rechte Wienzeile, which run parallel to each other on either side of the market, now function as a six-lane motorway, but there are a couple of sights along the Linke Wienzeile to make a stroll through the market doubly rewarding. First off, at no. 6, there's the **Theater-an-der-Wien**, which opened in 1801 under the directorship of Emanuel Schikaneder, who is depicted above the main portico as the bird-catcher Papageno from Mozart's *Die Zauberflöte* (Magic Flute), for which he wrote the libretto. Beethoven's opera *Fidelio* premiered here on November 20, 1805, exactly a week after the French had marched into Vienna. Under such extreme conditions – French soldiers made up much of the audience – it's hardly surprising that the opera flopped, running for just three performances.

A good 500m further west on the same side are two of Otto Wagner's most appealing Secession buildings from 1899: the apartment blocks of **Linke Wienzeile 38** and **40**. The right-hand building (no. 38) is richly embossed with gold palm leaves and medallions, but the other is more unusual, its pollution-resistant cladding of majolica tiles giving rise to the nickname **Majolikahaus**. To contemporary eyes, the facade looks highly decorative, but what mattered to the Viennese was that – as with the Looshaus – there was virtually no sculptural decoration, and no mouldings or pediments above the windows. Instead, Wagner weaves an elaborate floral motif – a giant, spreading rose tree or a vine of sunflowers – on the tiles themselves.

Schwarzenberg Platz and the Stadtpark

Faced with the din of cars and trams whizzing across its cobbles, it's difficult to believe that the large, rectangular, traffic intersection of **Schwarzenberg Platz**, one block east of Karlsplatz, was once a fashionable address. At the southern end of the square, dramatically floodlit at night and spurting water high into the air, stands the **Hochstrahlbrunnen** (High Jet Fountain), erected in 1873 as a celebration of the city's nascent modern water-supply system. Once the focal point of the square, it's now thoroughly upstaged by the bombastic **Russen Heldendenkmal** (Russian Heroes' Monument), which rises up behind the jet of water. A giant curving colonnade acts as the backdrop to the central column, crowned by the Unknown (Soviet) Soldier in heroic stance, flag aloft, sporting a gilded shield and helmet; on the red granite plinth are the names of the fallen and a quote from Stalin (after whom the square was briefly renamed in 1945). For the Viennese, though, it's more a grim reminder of the brutality of the liberators and the privations suffered by those in the city's postwar Russian zones.

Opened in 1862 as the city council's first public park, the **Stadtpark** is best known for Edmund Hellmer's eye-catching **Strauss Monument** from 1925, with its statue of the "Waltz King", Johann Strauss the Younger, violin in hand. Gilded from head to toe and dramatically floodlit at night, the composer stands framed by a stone arch of naked, swirling naiads. Tour groups turn up at regular intervals to admire the monument, while the benches close by are a favourite spot for Vienna's elderly population. Vienna's younger generation hangs out here, too, smoking, drinking on the grass and selling dope; the authorities occasionally move the scene on a few hundred metres or so, but without any great enthusiasm.

The MAK

One of the most enjoyable museums in Vienna is the **Österreichisches Museum für angewandte Kunst** (Austrian Museum of Applied Art), better known simply as the **MAK** (Tues, Wed & Fri–Sun 10am–6pm, Thurs 10am–9pm; öS90), north of the Stadtpark. The highlights of its superlative, highly eclectic selection of *objets d'art*, stretching from the Romanesque period to the twentieth century, are Klimt's *Stoclet Frieze* and the unrivalled collection of Wiener Werkstätte products. But what really sets it apart is the museum's provocative redesign, completed in 1993, in which the MAK gave some of Austria's leading designers free rein to create a unique series of rooms. At the ticket office in the beautiful, glass-roofed courtyard, with its double-decker loggia, you'll be given a plan of the museum in German and English. On the wall of each room there's a slightly pretentious, bilingual introduction by the designer, and a leaflet in English cataloguing and explaining each exhibit. Temporary exhibitions are held, for the most part, in the museum annexe, whose main entrance is on Weiskirchnerstrasse. If you've got the time and energy, don't neglect the museum's crowded **Studiensammlung** (Study Collection), in the basement.

The ground floor

To follow the collection chronologically, you should begin with the **Romanik, Gotik, Renaissance** room, on the ground floor, where the minimalist display cabinets are beautifully offset by deep cobalt-blue walls. Aside from a few pieces of furniture and some very early thirteenth-century ecclesiastical garments, most of the exhibits are items of Italian sixteenth-century majolica, decorated with mythological scenes and grotesque faces. The main focus of the room next door – **Barock, Rokoko, Klassizismus** – is a room within a room. Acquired by the museum in 1912, the mid-eighteenth-century Porcelain Room was removed piece by piece from the Palais Dubsky in Brno and reassembled here. It derives its name from the ceramics that have been used to decorate everything right down to the wall panelling, candelabra, chandeliers and table-tops.

There's a slight chronological hiccup as you cross the main courtyard to the **Renaissance, Mittelalter** room, from which point the rooms' designers begin to impose themselves more emphatically. This particular room consists of two long, central glass cabinets hung from the ceiling displaying Bohemian, Silesian and Venetian glass, with examples of Italian, French and Flemish lacework set against a black background all along the walls. The Empire-style **Biedermeier** room is much quirkier.

A parade of early nineteenth-century Viennese chairs, arranged as if for a game of musical chairs, occupies the central space, while, up above, the cornice is broken by fast-moving, multilingual LED text. To take it all in, sit down on the aluminium mock-Biedermeier sofa.

The museum's *pièce de résistance*, though, in terms of design, comes in the **Historismus, Jugendstil, Art Deco** room – a wordy title for what is a very simple conceit. Two parallel shadow screens, running the length of the room, create a corridor down which you can stroll, whilst admiring the changing geometry of chair design over the last hundred years in silhouette. If you want a 3-D look at the chairs, you can simply go round the back of the screens. Next door, the final ground-floor room is devoted to tiles and carpets from the **Orient**, covering the walls and floors to create a peaceful, mosque-like atmosphere.

The first floor

Three rooms on the **first floor** are given over to the permanent collection. One room is devoted to the **Wiener Werkstätte** (Vienna Workshops), founded in 1903 by the architect Josef Hoffmann, the designer Kolo Moser and the rich Jewish textile merchant Fritz Waerndorfer. The range and scope of the WW is staggering, and just about every field in which they were active is represented here from jewellery and metalwork, primarily by Dagobert Peche and Hoffmann, to an upper gallery containing the WW's prolific fashion offshoot. One of the finest works is Kolo Moser's wood-inlaid writing-desk, which includes a retractable armchair that can be slotted into place to make the whole thing appear like a chest of drawers.

The **Jugendstil, Art Deco** room is dominated by Gustav Klimt's working designs for his *Stoclet Frieze*, a series of mosaics commissioned in 1904 for the dining room of the Palais Stoclet in Brussels. Predominantly gold, with Byzantine and Egyptian overtones, the frieze marks the climax of Klimt's highly ornamental phase – the finished product was inlaid with semi-precious stones. Aside from the Klimt, there's furniture by the likes of Otto Wagner and Kolo Moser, along with contemporaries Charles Rennie Mackintosh and Margaret Macdonald, and an amazing selection of Bohemian glass. A staircase leads up to an entire room of contemporary applied art. More recent work is displayed in the adjacent **20. Jahrhundert, Architektur, Design**, including a monochrome room installation by Jasper Morrison, architectural models by the Austrian deconstructionists Coop Himmelblau, and a wonderful cardboard armchair by Frank Gehry, who is best known as architect of Bilbao's Guggenheim Museum.

The Postsparkasse

The final segment of the Ringstrasse, from Stubentor to Urania, was the last to be laid out, erected mostly in the decade before World War I, and contains one of Vienna's most celebrated pieces of modern architecture, the **Postsparkasse** (Mon–Wed & Fri 8am–3pm, Thurs 8am–5.30pm), completed in 1912 by Otto Wagner. The building still functions as a savings bank, and from the outside it looks something like a giant safety deposit box, its otherwise smooth facade studded with aluminium rivets, used to hold the thin grey marble slabs in place. Aluminium – an architectural first at the time – is also used for the delicate glazed canopy over the entrance and, most famously, for the heating cowls, which rise up into the main banking hall like giant curling tongs. Sadly, some of the interior furnishings have been carelessly modified, but the curved glass ceiling and the thick glass tiles in the floor survive intact. There's also a model of the building and regular exhibitions on modern architecture on display in the main banking hall.

The Vorstädte

A horseshoe of seven districts – the third to the ninth – form the inner suburbs known as the **Vorstädte**. Neatly confined between the Ringstrasse and the Gürtel, they have remained predominantly residential, though each one is cut through with a busy commercial thoroughfare, the largest of which is the city's main shopping drag, **Mariahilferstrasse**, which divides the sixth and seventh districts. Sights in the Vorstädte are widely dispersed, so it pays to be selective. The one sight that no visitor should miss is the **Belvedere**, in the third district, with its formal gardens and twinset of Baroque palaces, which house some wonderful works of art. Two other sights that positively heave with visitors in summer are the wacky **Hundertwasserhaus**, also in the third district, and the **Freud Museum** in the ninth. Even for those not keen on military paraphernalia, the **Arsenal** is worth visiting for its quasi-Moorish architecture alone, and the two branches of the city's **Museum moderner Kunst** boast undervisited permanent collections of twentieth-century art.

Hundertwasserhaus and KunstHausWien

In 1983 the ageing hippie artist Friedensreich Hundertwasser was commissioned to redesign some council housing on the corner of Löwengasse and Kegelgasse, in an unassuming residential area of Landstrasse, Vienna's third district. Following his philosophy that "the straight line is godless", he transformed the dour apartment block into **Hundertwasserhaus** (tram N to Hetzgasse from Schwedenplatz U-Bahn), a higgledy-piggledy, child-like jumble of brightly coloured textures that caught the popular imagination, while enraging the architectural establishment. It certainly runs the gamut of styles: a frenzy of oriel windows, loggias, ceramic pillars, glass embellishments, a gilded onion dome, roof gardens and even a slice of the pre-1983 building.

Understandably, the residents were none too happy when hordes of pilgrims began ringing on their doorbells, asking to be shown round, so Hundertwasser obliged with an even tackier shopping arcade opposite, called **Kalke Village**, providing a café (with a stream running along the bar) and information centre to draw the crowds away from the apartments (closed to the public), while simultaneously increasing the sales outlets for his artwork. Here, you can get the full Hundertwasser experience, the most disconcerting aspect of which is his penchant for uneven floors.

There's another of Hundertwasser's Gaudiesque conversions, **KunstHausWien** (daily 10am–7pm; Mon öS40 Tues–Sun öS80), three blocks north up Untere Weissgerberstrasse, though it has been less successful at attracting visitors; it features another shop and café, and a gallery devoted to Hundertwasser's own paintings. The gallery also hosts temporary exhibitions (another öS80 combined ticket öS120) by other headline-grabbing contemporary artists. Hundertwasser's most recent project, the rebuilding of a rubbish incineration plant, Fernwärme Wien, is visible from the U-Bahn to Heligenstadt.

The Belvedere

The **Belvedere** is the finest palace complex in the whole of Vienna, at least from the outside. Two magnificent Baroque mansions, designed in the early eighteenth century by Lukas von Hildebrandt, face each other across a sloping formal garden, commanding a superb view over central Vienna. The man for whom all this was built was **Prince Eugène of Savoy**, Austria's greatest military leader, whose campaigns against the Turks helped push them back from the gates of the city. Today, the loftier of the two palaces, the **Oberes Belvedere**, houses one of the most popular art galleries in Vienna, with an unrivalled collection of paintings by Gustav Klimt, Egon Schiele and Oskar Kokoschka. A single ticket (öS60) lets you into both parts of the Belvedere (daily except Mon 10am–5pm); take tram #71 one stop from Schwarzenbergplatz – or just walk – to get to the **Unteres Belvedere**, from where you can either walk through the garden or jump on tram D from the Ringstrasse to get to the Oberes Belvedere.

The Unteres Belvedere

Completed in 1716, at the bottom of the formal gardens, the **Unteres Belvedere** (Lower Belvedere) is a relatively simple, one-storey garden palace, built for Prince Eugène's personal use, rather than for affairs of state or entertainment. Inside, however, it preserves more of its original, lavish decor than the Oberes Belvedere, and for that reason alone it's worth exploring the **Barock-Museum** now installed in its rooms.

The highlight of the palace is the richly decorated **Marmorsaal** (Marble Hall), which extends over two floors at the central axis of the building. The whole hall is a hymn to Prince Eugène's military prowess, white stucco trophies and reliefs contrasting with the rich red marbling. Extra depth is given to the walls through trompe l'oeil niches and balconies, and to the ceiling by illusory moulding, leading up to Martino Altomonte's fresco featuring Prince Eugène himself enjoying his apotheosis in the guise of Apollo. At ground level, you can admire the original lead statues from the Donnerbrunnen on Neuermarkt, sculpted by Georg Raphael Donner (1693–1741).

At the far end of the wing lies the **Groteskensaal**, with a decor of grotesque birds and beasts, and fanciful floral murals. Displayed here is a series of bizarre, hyperrealist "character heads", carved by the eccentric sculptor Franz Xaver Messerschmidt (1732–83), each depicting a different grimace. Next comes the **Marmorgalerie**, a richly stuccoed white-and-red reception room built by Prince Eugène to house his trio of classical statues from Herculaneum (now in Dresden). By far the most mindblowing room, though, is the adjacent **Goldkabinett**, a cabinet of mirrors, dotted with oriental vases and adorned with yet more grotesques painted onto a vast expanse of gaudy, 23-carat-gold panelling. Dominating this small room is the *Apotheosis of Prince Eugène*, an explosion of marble by Balthasar Permoser, in which a tangle of figures struggles to stay on the plinth.

The Goldkabinett marks the end of the Barock-Museum, but there are further artistic treasures in the former orangery, down the steps from the palace. Converted into stables by Maria Theresa, the orangery now houses the **Museum mittelalterlicher Kunst** (Museum of Medieval Art), housing a collection of sculptures and paintings, the greater part of which dates from the fifteenth century.

The Oberes Belvedere

Purpose-built for the lavish masked balls, receptions and firework displays organized by the prince, the **Oberes Belvedere** (Upper Belvedere), completed in 1724, is at least twice as big and twice as grand as the Unteres Belvedere from the outside. Guests would pull up in their coaches underneath the central *sala terrena*, which was glassed in during the nineteenth century and now serves as the ticket office and entrance area of the museum. To the right is the trompe l'oeil-frescoed **Gartensaal**, the first in a series of ground-floor rooms used for temporary exhibitions; to the left lies the bookshop and the changing displays of **art after 1918**, beyond which lies the café. There isn't enough space to display all the gallery's post-1918 works; instead, temporary exhibitions are mounted around a particular theme, with a representative sample of paintings on show. Some of these are taken from the permanent galleries upstairs, so you may not find things on the first floor exactly as described below.

Most visitors head straight upstairs to the **Marmorsaal**, a lighter and loftier concoction than the one in the Unteres Belvedere; it was here that the Austrian State Treaty of 1955 was signed, guaranteeing the Allied withdrawal in return for Austria's neutrality. There's a painting of the event in the hall, in which you can pick out the chief representatives of the four Allied powers: Molotov for the Soviets, Pinay for the French, Macmillan for the British and Dulles for the Americans.

The permanent collection of **art around 1900** begins in the room to the right of the Marmorsaal with the *Plain at Auvers*, painted by **Vincent van Gogh** a month before his suicide in 1890. Alongside it hangs the trainless *Rack Railway on the Kahlenberg*, painted by fellow depressive Richard Gerstl, in a similar, though slightly less intense, style; **Egon Schiele's** *Interior 1907* also pays homage to the Dutch genius. **Auguste Rodin's** bust of Mahler, and a small terracotta study for the Victor Hugo Monument, in which the author is overwhelmed by allegorical figures from his own imagination, can also be found in this room.

GUSTAV KLIMT

The first of the gallery's works by **Gustav Klimt** (1862–1918) is in the second room, along with works by his contemporaries, Kolo Moser, Carl Moll and Max Kurzweil. Klimt's ethereal, slightly aloof *Portrait of Sonja Knips*, from 1898, marked his breakthrough as an independent artist, and was the first of several portrait commissions of the wives of the city's wealthy Jewish businessmen. Two later examples hang in the adjacent room: the *Portrait of Fritza Riedler*, from 1906, in which Klimt's love of ornamentation comes to the fore, and the *Portrait of Adele Bloch-Bauer I*, painted at the height of his "golden phase" in 1908, with the subject almost engulfed in gilded Mycenaean spirals and Egyptian eyes.

The culmination of Klimt's golden age is his monumental work *The Kiss*, displayed behind a protective glass shield and depicting Klimt himself embracing his long-term partner, Emilie Flöge. Klimt's use of gilding – derived partly from his father, who was an engraver – proved extremely popular, and the painting was bought for the Austrian state during the *Kunstschau* of 1908, a rare seal of official approval for an artist whose work was mostly frowned upon by the establishment. Sharing the room with *The Kiss* are eight landscapes on square canvases painted at the Flöge family house on the Attersee in the Salzkammergut. As a way of relaxing, he liked to paint landscapes alfresco straight onto canvas, without preliminary sketches. The results are rich, almost flat, one-dimensional tapestries of colour – some almost pointillist – which are easy on the eye and sold extremely well in the salons.

The final room of Klimt's work is from his later period, when, having dispensed with gold, he was influenced by Japanese art and the primary colours of Fauvists such as Matisse. The results can be seen in the doll-like *Portrait of Adele Bloch-Bauer II*, painted in 1912. Klimt regularly worked on several canvases at once, often painting his models in the nude before clothing them, as is clearly demonstrated in *The Bride*, discovered unfinished in his studio at his death.

EGON SCHIELE

Klimt actively supported younger artists like **Egon Schiele** (1890–1918) – to whom the next two rooms are devoted – introducing them to his patrons, allowing them to exhibit in shows he organized, and even, in the case of Schiele, passing on his young models after he'd finished with them. Such was the case with the 17-year-old Wally Neuzil, with whom Schiele enjoyed a four-year affair. *Death and the Maiden* is a disturbingly dispassionate farewell portrait to Wally, painted in 1915, the year they split up. In it, Wally clings to Schiele, depicted in deathly, detached decay. Also in this room is one of Schiele's most famous erotic oil paintings, *The Embrace*, a double nude portrait of the artist and his model.

Schiele went on to marry Edith Harms, who came from a respectable middle-class family, and is depicted in *The Artist's Wife*. Edith's pregnancy in spring 1918 was the inspiration for *The Family*, Schiele's last great painting, which remained unfinished at the time of his death from the influenza epidemic that had claimed Edith's life, and that of their unborn child, just three days earlier (and Klimt's eight months before that). Schiele is the father figure, the child is Schiele's nephew, Toni, but Edith had reservations about posing nude and is clearly not the model for the mother.

The next room holds portraits commissioned by their sitters, among them one of Eduard Kosmak, an amateur hypnotist, which may explain his somewhat intense stare. Displayed alongside Schiele's works is **Richard Gerstl**'s manic *Laughing Self-Portrait* from 1908, a deeply disturbing image given that its subject was deeply depressed at the time – his lover, Mathilde, had gone back to her husband, the composer Arnold Schönberg. Gerstl committed suicide the very same year at the age of 28.

OSKAR KOKOSCHKA AND OTHERS
The works by **Oskar Kokoschka** (1886–1980), on permanent show in the last two rooms, mostly date from his first ten creative years when he lived in Vienna. After 1915, Kokoschka only occasionally returned, usually staying with his mother, an affectionate portrait of whom hangs in the first room. Kokoschka's several portraits displayed here contrast sharply with those of Schiele: "A person is not a *still* life" Kokoschka insisted, and he encouraged his sitters to move about and talk, so as to make his portrayals more animated. The last room features more work by Kokoschka, including his *Still-Life with Dead Mutton* from 1909, painted in the kitchen of the art collector Dr Oskar Reichel, who had commissioned him to paint a portrait of his son. There's a smattering of other artists' works in this room, too, among them a characteristically dark, intense work by **Emil Nolde**, a Cubist offering from **Fernand Léger** and **Max Oppenheimer**'s evocative *Klingier Quartet*.

HISTORICISM, REALISM, IMPRESSIONISM
The seven rooms in the west wing, on the other side of the Marmorsaal, are given over to late nineteenth-century paintings. The first few rooms are crowded with works by French Impressionists, among them Manet and Monet, and their immediate predecessors, like Camille Corot. Less well-known, and less well thought of now, is the Austrian artist **Hans Makart** (1840–84), whose influence went far beyond painting. He was a high-society figure and, appropriately enough, the room devoted to his works has been decked out with sumptuous furnishings much as Makart's own studio was. On one side hangs the gigantic, triumphant flesh-fest of *Bacchus and Ariadne*; on the opposite wall in long vertical panels are four of the *Five Senses*, featuring typically sensuous Makart nudes.

In the adjacent room, you can admire more work by Makart, whose fame eclipsed several of his more innovative contemporaries, among them **Anton Romako** (1832–89), so much so that the latter's death was rumoured to be suicide. Compared with Makart's studied flattery, it's easy to see why Romako's uncomfortably perceptive psychological portraits were less popular. Romako's most famous work, *Tegetthoff at the Naval Battle of Lissa*, hangs in the final room, and again reveals his unconventional approach; there's no hint of heroics, but simply fear and foreboding in the expressions of the crew.

The Museum des 20. Jahrhunderts

A short distance south of the Südbahnhof, which lies on the other side of the Landstrasser Gürtel from the Oberes Belvedere, stands the **Museum des 20. Jahrhunderts** (daily except Mon 10am–6pm; öS25, more if there's a temporary exhibition). The gallery hosts large contemporary art exhibitions on the ground floor, while maintaining a permanent collection upstairs of international modern art, dating from the 1960s to the present day. The first-floor collection, mostly derived from previous exhibitions held in the gallery, is arranged in "-isms", with pretentious (and unintentionally hilarious) commentaries in German and English. The works displayed here are the kind that give modern art a bad name: two prime examples are Bertrand Lavier's *Crashed Peugeot 103* or the three entirely grey paintings by Roman Opalka. However, armed with a sense of humour, you can enjoy such treats as Pino Pascali's giant furry blue spider.

The Arsenal (Heeresgeschichtliches Museum)

Further south still, down Arsenalstrasse, lies the city's former **Arsenal** (daily except Fri 10am–4pm; öS40), a huge complex of barracks and munitions factories, built on strategic heights above the city in the wake of the 1848 revolution. At the same time, the emperor Franz-Josef I ordered the construction of the city's first purpose-built museum, the **Heeresgeschichtliches Museum** (Museum of Military History), designed to glorify the imperial army. The winning design is a wonderful red-brick edifice, completed in neo-Byzantine style by the Ringstrasse architect Theophil Hansen in 1856. The ticket office is in the vaulted foyer, or **Feldherrnhalle** (Hall of the Generals), which is crowded with life-size marble statues of pre-1848 Austrian military leaders. To follow the collection chronologically, you should begin in the **Ruhmshalle** (Hall of Fame) on the first floor, a huge domed hall of polished marble, gilded, arcaded and decorated with worthy frescoes depicting Austrian military victories over the centuries.

The rich pickings to be had during the **Turkish Wars** proved a useful incentive to the imperial troops fighting the Ottomans, and a fine selection of trophies is displayed in the **west wing**, including the vast tent of the Grand Vizier. Among the most impressive are the horsetails that formed the insignia of the Ottoman army, and the Great Seal of Mustafa Pasha. To continue chronologically, you need to retrace your steps and walk to the far room of the **east wing**, which deals with the **Napoleonic Wars**. The room closer to the Ruhmshalle is filled with splendid early nineteenth-century military uniforms, and concludes with paintings of the disastrous **Austro-Prussian War**, which the Habsburgs lost at Königgrätz in 1866.

A large section of the ground-floor west wing is taken up with the glorious **uniforms of the imperial army**, and their opponents, but by far the most famous exhibits in this wing relate to the **archduke Franz Ferdinand**. In particular, you can view the splendid Gräf & Stift convertible in which the archduke and his wife, Sophie, were shot dead on June 28, 1914. Even more macabre is the archduke's reverentially preserved blood-stained light-blue tunic and his unblemished, slightly comical hat with green feathers. The final rooms of the wing are devoted to **World War I** memorabilia. There are some great posters and paintings, including Albin Egger Lienz's chilling tribute *To the Unknown Soldier*, whose repetitive image of advancing infantry perfectly captures the mechanical slaughter of modern warfare.

The St Marxer Friedhof

In the 1780s, the emperor Josef II closed all the inner-city cemeteries and decreed that all burials, for health reasons, should take place outside the city walls. The first of these out-of-town graveyards, founded in 1784, was the **St Marxer Friedhof** (St Mark's Cemetery; daily 7am–dusk), by the Landstrasser Gürtel (tram #18 or #71). Planted with a rather lovely selection of trees, the cemetery today gives little indication of the bleak and forbidding place it must have been when, on a rainy night in December 1791, **Mozart** was given a pauper's burial, in an unmarked mass grave with no one present but the grave-diggers.

Though to contemporary minds the bare facts of Mozart's final journey seem a particularly cruel end for someone considered by many to have been the greatest composer ever, the reality is less tragic. In the immediate period after Josef II's reforms, mass burials were the rule; only the very wealthy could afford to have a family vault, and the tending of individual graves was virtually unknown. Funeral services took place in churches (Mozart's in the Stephansdom), and it was not customary for mourners to accompany the funeral cortege to cemeteries. In fact, bodies were only allowed to be taken to the cemetery after nightfall, where they were left in the mortuary overnight for burial the next day. By the mid-nineteenth century, however, the Viennese had adopted the lavish tastes for funerals and monuments for which they remain famous to this day. It was in this context that it became a scandal that no one knew where Mozart was buried. In 1844, his wife Constanze returned to try and locate the grave, but to little avail as graves were usually emptied every eight years to make way for more corpses. The most Constanze could find out was that he had probably been buried three or four rows down from the cemetery's central monumental cross. In 1859, the **Mozartgrab** was raised around this area, featuring a pillar, broken in half to symbolize his untimely death.

To get to the Mozartgrab, head up the main avenue and bear left. You'll also find the graves of several other eighteenth-century artists here – a plan at the entrance to the cemetery locates the most famous graves.

Alsergrund

Alsergrund – Vienna's large, roughly triangular ninth district to the north of the Innere Stadt – is dominated by its medical institutions and associations. A vast swath of land is taken up with the **Allgemeines Krankenhaus** (General Hospital), established by Josef II in 1784, and now more than double its original size. The following year, Josef founded the **Josephinum**, an academy for training military surgeons, next door. Since then, various university science faculties have relocated here, and the area remains popular with doctors and medical students, as it has done since **Freud**'s day – his museum is now Alsergrund's chief tourist attraction. Alsergrund also boasts one of the few aristocratic summer palaces to survive into the modern era, the **Palais Liechtenstein**, now Vienna's premier modern art museum.

Josephinum

Founded in 1785 to the northeast of the Allgemeines Krankenhaus, the **Josephinum** (Mon–Fri 9am–3pm; öS10) is housed in an austere silver-grey palace, set back from Währinger Strasse behind a set of imposing wrought-iron railings (take any tram heading up Währinger Strasse from U-Bahn Schottentor). Having observed at first hand the primitive techniques used by army surgeons during his military campaigns, the emperor Josef II decided to set up an Institute for Military Surgery. The institute was closed in 1872, and now houses, among other things, a museum containing a remarkable collection of anatomical wax models, the "*Wachspräparate Sammlung*", commissioned by Josef II from a group of Florentine sculptors in 1780. The serene, life-size human figures are for the most part presented as if partially dissected, revealing the body's nerves, muscles and veins in full technicolour. Equally beautiful are the original display cases, fashioned from rosewood and fitted with huge, bobbly, hand-blown panes of Venetian glass.

The Freud Museum

Sigmund Freud moved to the second floor of Berggasse 19 in 1891 and stayed here until June 4, 1938, when he and his family fled to London. His apartment, now the **Freud Museum** (daily: July–Sept 9am–6pm; Oct–June 9am–4pm; öS60), is a place of pilgrimage, even though Freud took almost all his possessions – bar his library, which he sold

– with him into exile. As a result, an exhibition of photographs, rather like a giant family album, with captions in English and German, is pretty much all there is to see. His hat, coat and walking stick are still here, and there's home movie footage from the 1930s, but the only room with any original decor – and consequently any atmosphere – is the waiting room, which contains the odd oriental rug, a cabinet of antiquities, and some burgundy-upholstered furniture, sent back from London by his daughter Anna after the war.

The Palais Liechtenstein (Museum moderner Kunst)

Hemmed in by nineteenth-century apartment blocks, the Baroque **Palais Liechtenstein** (daily except Mon 10am–6pm; öS45) comes as something of a surprise, hidden away down the backstreet of Fürstengasse (tram D three stops from Schottentor U-Bahn). It's built on a giant scale, with an imposing entrance hall, two grandiose marble staircases, and frescoes by the likes of Johann Michael Rottmayr and Andrea Pozzo. Though the Liechtenstein family used to house their own vast art collection here, it's still a somewhat overblown and incongruous (albeit temporary) setting for Vienna's **Museum moderner Kunst** (Museum of Modern Art).

There's a good showing of 1960s **Pop Art** in the huge rooms on the first floor, including a whole room devoted to the Pope of Pop Art, **Andy Warhol**. The greater part of the gallery's collection, though, is housed in the more cramped rooms on the second floor. **Oskar Kokoschka**'s portrait of his friend, the feisty journalist Karl Kraus, kicks off the proceedings in room A. Kokoschka was closely associated with the Dresden Brücke group, led by **Ernst Ludwig Kirchner**, whose sickly green *Grünes Haus* reveals his debt to the French Fauvists as clearly as does the self-portrait by Alexei Jawlensky, a painter from Munich's *Blaue Reiter* group. The influence of African art is discernible in room B in André Derain's *Crouching Figure* and **Pablo Picasso**'s bronze head of Fernande Olivier, both sculpted in 1907. Room C features three works by the Czech **František Kupka**, a pioneer of abstract art, while room E contains Surrealist works by Réne Magritte, Giorgio de Chirico, Max Ernst and Man Ray, and a tender portrait from 1960 by Picasso of Jacqueline Roque, who became his second wife the following year.

Abstract paintings by Paul Klee and Vassily Kandinsky, and a colourful mobile by kinetic artist Alexander Calder, are the highlights of room F. Next door, in room G, a very small and squiggly Jackson Pollock and an attenuated Alberto Giacometti statue rub shoulders with two "over-paintings" – in which works by great artists are painted over in thick, usually black, paint – by **Arnulf Rainer**, one of Austria's leading contemporary artists. There's more Rainer in room H, along with works by the leading figures of **Wiener Aktionismus**, Vienna's very own, very often extremely violent version of 1960s performance art. Their last happening, *Art and Revolution* by Günter Brus, in which Brus urinated and dipped his penis into a foaming beermug, resulted in a six-month prison sentence for "degrading Austrian symbols" (presumably the beermug) and a "gross and public violation of public morality and decency".

Schuberts Geburthaus

Further north, at Nussdorfer Strasse 54, stands **Schuberts Geburthaus** (daily except Mon 9am–12.15pm & 1–4.30pm; öS25), the unassuming, two-storey house where the composer was born in 1797. Inside, the charming courtyard has been lovingly restored, with wooden balconies festooned with geranium-filled flower boxes. As so often with Vienna's musical memorials, however, there has been no attempt to reconstruct Schubert's family home, which would have consisted of just one room and a kitchen (the latter survives). In any case, Schubert would have had very little recollection of the place as the family moved down the road, to Säulengasse 3, when he was 4 years old. So, beyond admiring the composer's broken spectacles and his half-brother's piano, there's little to do here but listen to the excerpts from his music on the headphones provided.

FRANZ SCHUBERT

Of all the composers associated with Vienna, Franz Schubert (1797–1828) fulfils more Romantic criteria than most. He died of syphilis at the age of just 31 (younger even than Mozart), he really was penniless (unlike Mozart, who was just a spendthrift), and he never lived to hear any of his symphonies performed (the first one wasn't published until fifty years after his death). The picture would be complete had he died whilst writing his *Eighth (Unfinished) Symphony* – in fact, he abandoned it before he died, and went on, instead, to complete a *Ninth Symphony*.

Schubert was born the eleventh child of an impoverished teacher. At the age of 9 or 10, he was sent to study with the organist at the local church on Marktgasse, where he had been baptized. He went on to become the church organist, and composed his first mass for the church at the age of 17. In between times, he served as a chorister at the Burgkapelle, where he studied under Antonio Salieri, Mozart's famous court rival, before working as an assistant teacher at his father's school for three years. At the end of this period, he became a freelance musician, thanks to financial help from his friends, and spent two summers as music tutor for the Esterházys. His intensely lyrical chamber music, copious songs – in one particularly productive year he wrote 145 of them – and piano works were popular amongst the Viennese bourgeoisie, and he performed at numerous informal social gatherings, which became known as "*Schubertiaden*".

In his personal life, he was fairly dissolute: a heavy drinker, who frequented "revolutionary" circles, he remained unmarried, his sexual appetite confined to prostitutes. Towards the end of his short life, he fulfilled a lifetime's ambition and met up with his hero Beethoven, though there are no reliable details of the encounter. He was one of the torchbearers at the great composer's funeral, and was buried, according to his wishes, three graves away from him in Währinger Friedhof the following year (he now lies with Beethoven in the Zentralfriedhof; see p.123).

To reach the museum, take tram #38 or #39 five stops from U-Bahn Schottentor. Schubert's brother's house – 4, Kettenbrückengasse 6, near the Naschmarkt – in which the composer died, has been made into a similarly unenthralling museum; times and prices as for Schuberts Geburthaus.

The Vororte

Vienna's vast outer suburbs, or **Vororte**, have a scattering of interesting sights, many of them outdoor attractions, that call for a targeted approach, relying on the transport system to get you around. Top of the list, and one of Vienna's most popular tourist attractions after the Hofburg, is the Habsburgs' former summer residence, **Schönbrunn**, to the west of the city centre. The palace boasts some of the best Rococo interiors in central Europe, while the surrounding **Schlosspark** is home to the **Tiergarten**, Vienna's zoo, the **Schmetterlinghaus** (Butterfly House) and the **Palmenhaus** (Palm House). Further west is the much wilder parkland of the **Lainzer Tiergarten**, a former royal hunting ground that's now a haven for wildlife.

After Schönbrunn, the most popular attraction in the suburbs is the **Prater**, the vast city park and funfair on the east bank of the Danube Canal, famous, above all, for its giant ferris wheel, or *Riesenrad*. Another possible day-trip can be made to the **Wienerwald** (Vienna Woods), the forested hills that stretch from the alpine foothills to the southwest of Vienna right up to the doorstep of the capital and offer glorious views over the entire city. Finally, there's the **Zentralfriedhof**, Vienna's awesome Central Cemetery, featuring the graves of Beethoven, Schubert, Brahms, Schönberg and the Strauss family.

Schönbrunn

Compared with the hotchpotch that is the Hofburg, the Habsburgs' summer residence of **Schönbrunn** is everything an imperial palace should be: grandiose, symmetrical and thoroughly intimidating. Built over the course of the eighteenth century to a design by Johann Bernhard Fischer von Erlach, it contains nearly 1500 rooms and, in its day, would have housed more than a thousand servants.

The exterior is plain, but inside, there's a superb array of Baroque and Rococo **Prunkräume** (State Rooms), dating from the time of the empress Maria Theresa, the first of the Habsburgs to make Schönbrunn the official imperial summer residence. There's also a fine collection of imperial carriages in the outbuilding of the **Wagenburg**, plus temporary exhibitions in the **Orangerie**. In the **Schlosspark**, you'll find the **Tiergarten** far more uplifting than most inner-city zoos, which combines easily with visits to the nearby **Schmetterlinghaus** and **Palmenhaus**.

Prunkräume

Compared to the sterility of the Hofburg's state apartments, Schönbrunn's **Prunkräume** are a positive visual feast. That said, not every room is worthy of close attention, so don't feel bad about walking briskly through some of them. Whichever tour you're on (see box below), the entrance is via the **Blauerstiege** (Blue Staircase) on the ground floor of the west wing. If you're on the "Imperial Tour", you'll miss the nine private apartments of Franz-Josef – no great loss – entering at **Elisabeth's Salon**, which smack even less of her personality than those in the Hofburg. The decor, in fact, mostly dates from the time of the empress **Maria Theresa**, a century or so earlier, and the walls of the next three rooms are lined with portraits of the the empress's numerous offspring. Two of her sons went on to become emperors, Josef II and Leopold II, but the most famous of the lot was her youngest daughter, **Marie Antoinette**, who married Louis XVI and followed him to the guillotine in 1793. Under her portrait in the nursery is the only piece of furniture sent back to Vienna by the French after her execution.

The first of the more elaborate state apartments is the **Spiegelsaal** (Mirror Hall), where, in 1762, the 7-year-old Mozart performed a duet with his older sister, Nannerl, in the presence of the empress Maria Theresa and family, and famously "sprang on the lap of the empress, put his arms round her neck and vigorously kissed her", according to his father. From here, both tours take in the splendid **Great Gallery**, a vast long hall,

---

VISITING SCHÖNBRUNN

Approaches to the palace suffer from the roar of traffic from the nearby Linke Wienzeile and Schönbrunner Schloss Strasse. Consequently, the best way to **get there** is to head straight for the Meidlinger Tor on Grünbergstrasse from U-Bahn Schönbrunn, rather than struggle along the multilane freeway to the main gates. You could also continue one stop further on the U-Bahn to Hietzing, and dive into the park via the Hietzinger Tor on Hietzinger Hauptstrasse. This enables you to peek at the nearby Hofpavillon Hietzing, the imperial family's private U-Bahn station (Tues–Sun 9am–12.15pm & 1–4.30pm; öS25), built in extravagant Jugendstil by Otto Wagner in 1899 (and put into use only twice).

To visit the Prunkräume (April–Oct: daily 8.30am–5pm; Nov–March 8.30am – 4.30pm), head for the ticket office on the ground floor of the east wing. Here, you'll be allocated a visiting time; if the palace is busy, you may have to wait several hours, in which case you should head off into the gardens or visit one of Schönbrunn's other sights. There's a choice of two tours: the "Imperial Tour" (öS80), which takes in 22 state rooms (skipping the palace's most magnificent Rococo delights), and the "Grand Tour" (öS110), which includes all forty rooms. For both tours, you're given a hand-held audioguide in English.

SCHÖNBRUNN

LINZER STRASSE

Technisches Museum

MARIAHILFERSTRASSE

SCHLOSSALLEE

CUMBERLANDSTRASSE

S Penzing

Auer-Welsbach-Park

PENZINGER STRASSE

LINKE WIENZEILE

Schönbrunn

HADIKGASSE

Schönbrunn River

U

Wien

SCHLDSSSTRASSE

SCHÖNBRUNNER

Schlosstheater

Orangerie

Hofpavillon

Meidlinger Tor

U Hietzing

Wagenburg

Schönbrunn

HIETZINGER HAUPTSTRASSE

Prunkäume

GRÜNBERGSTRASSE

Hietzinger Tor

Schlosspark

Schmetterlinghaus

Schöner Brunnen

Palmenhaus

Obelisk

MAXINGSTRASSE

Botanischer Garten

Tiergarten

Neptunbrunnen

Römische Ruine

Swimming Baths

Tiroler Garten

Kleine Gloriette

GLORIETTEGASSE

Gloriette

Werkbundsiedlung

HIETZING

MAXINGSTRASSE

Friedhof Hietzing

Barracks

GASSMANNSTRASSE

SCHÖNBRUNNER ALLEE

N

ELISABETHALLEE

0   500m

▽ Lainzer Tiergarten

heavy with gilded stucco embellishments and originally lit by over 4000 candles. Of the three ceiling frescoes by Guglielmo Guglielmi glorifying the Habsburgs, the last – depicting Austria's military prowess – was destroyed by bombing in World War II, and is therefore a copy.

It's worth venturing from here into the **Little Gallery**, which lies through the three arches to the south of the Great Gallery, to take a peek at the two chinoiserie rooms – one round, one oval – to either side. The parquet flooring is sublime, as are the oriental lacquer panels set into the wainscoting, and the numerous pieces of blue-and-white Chinese porcelain, that give the rooms their names. The final room for those on the "Imperial Tour" is the **Ceremonial Hall**, displaying five large paintings by pupils of the court painter Martin van Meytens. The majority are concerned with recording the elaborate festivities that accompanied the wedding of Maria Theresa's eldest son, Josef II, to Isabella of Parma, in 1760. The magnifying glass, over the section that depicts the wedding's opera performance, helps you pick out Mozart and his father from the crowd, though the family didn't in fact arrive in Vienna until two years after the event.

It was next door in the beautiful surroundings of the **Blue Chinese Salon**, on November 11, 1918, that the last Habsburg, Emperor Karl I, signed the document renouncing "all participation in the affairs of state" – though he refused to abdicate formally and would later attempt to regain the Hungarian half of his title. The lightness of this room is in complete contrast to the next, the oppressively opulent **Vieux-Laque Room**, with its black-and-gold lacquer panels, exquisite parquetry and walnut wainscoting. During his two sojourns at Schönbrunn, Napoleon is thought to have slept in the neighbouring walnut-panelled **Napoleon Room**, lined with Brussels tapestries depicting the Austrian army in Italy.

Despite its name, only three items in the remarkable **Porcelain Room**, designed by Isabella of Parma, are genuine Meissen porcelain: the chandeliers, the clock and the wall bracket. The rest of the decor is carved from wood and painted over in blue and white to appear like porcelain. Further on, the **Millions Room** – the most precious of all the rooms in Schönbrunn – is so called because it's estimated that Maria Theresa paid over a million silver florins to have it decorated. Unfortunately, the priceless miniature seventeenth-century Persian watercolours of life in the Moghul court are somewhat overwhelmed by the richly gilded cartouches set into the Caribbean rosewood panelling.

The **Memorial Room** is dedicated to Napoleon's son, known variously as the duke of Reichstadt, king of Rome, or simply "L'Aiglon" ("The Little Eagle"). After the emperor Napoleon's demise in 1815, the boy was kept a virtual prisoner here in the palace. Passing quickly through the next few rooms, you reach **Maria Theresa's Bedroom**, though the empress never actually slept in the room's red velvet and gold-embroidered four-poster bed. Instead, the room was used exclusively for *levees* – a kind of official breakfast in bed – during her frequent pregnancies. This was also the modest little room in which Franz-Josef was born in 1830. The last few rooms of the "Grand Tour", last used by the **Archduke Franz Karl** (Franz-Josef's epileptic father), and his wife, the archduchess Sophie, are of little interest, decked out as they are in the usual red damask and white panelling, and stuffed full of Habsburg portraits.

The Wagenburg

The main exhibition space of the **Wagenburg** (April–Oct daily 9am–6pm; Nov–March daily except Mon 10am–4pm; öS30), to the west of the main courtyard, is crowded with nineteenth-century carriages, which are of limited interest to the non-specialist. The best thing to do is pass quickly to the far end of the hall, where, below the gallery, there's an odd assortment of carriages and sleighs used to transport the imperial offspring. The most poignant is the phaeton designed for Napoleon's son "L'Aiglon", with mudguards in the shape of eagle's wings; the bees that decorate the sides of the carriage were the Bonaparte family symbol. The highlights of the collection, though, lie beyond the gallery, where you'll find the Baroque and Rococo carriages of the Habsburgs. The most outrageous is the **coronation carriage of Franz Stephan**, enormously long, dripping with gold plate, and fitted with windows of Venetian glass. The ornate carriage opposite, painted entirely in black, was used during oath ceremonies for the new emperor, which coincided with periods of official mourning for the previous incumbent. Somewhat incredibly, the relatively modest **red-leather litter,** studded with over 11,000 gold-plated nails and buckles, was used solely for transporting the Archduke of Austria's hat from Klosterneuburg to Vienna and back for the aforementioned ceremonies. The richly carved, gold-plated carousel or **racing sleigh of Maria Theresa** is the sole survivor of a whole set built in the shape of giant scallops for the special ladies' tournament held in the Winter Reitschule in 1743.

Schlosspark

Even if you've no interest at all in visiting the interior of Schönbrunn, it's worth coming out here to enjoy the glorious **Schlosspark** (daily 6am–dusk), concealed behind the palace. The lower section is laid out in the formal French style, with closely cropped trees and yew hedges forming an intricate network of gravel paths. The first thing that strikes you, however, is the central axis of the **parterre**, decorated with carefully regimented flowerbeds, leading to the **Neptunbrunnen** (Neptune Fountain), and, beyond, to the triumphal arch of the Gloriette, the focal point of the park. If you do nothing else in the Schlosspark, you should make the effort to climb up the zigzag paths to the **Gloriette**, built to celebrate the victory of the Habsburgs over the Prussians at the 1757 Battle of Kolín, and now housing a swanky café (May–Oct daily 9am–5pm), from which – if you can get a window table – you can enjoy the view down to the palace.

Hidden amongst the foliage to the east of the Neptunbrunnen are various architectural follies, sprinkled throughout the park in the late eighteenth century. Particularly fine are the **Römische Ruine** (Roman Ruins), built as a stage set for open-air concerts and theatre, a tradition that continues to this day in August and September. Close by the ruins is the outlet of the original **Schöner Brunnen**, a small grotto pavilion in which the nymph, Egeria, dispenses mineral water from a stone pitcher into a giant scallop basin. Further east stands an obelisk, topped by an eagle and an orb, and supported at the base by four, originally gilded, long-suffering turtles.

A substantial segment of the palace gardens is taken up by the **Tiergarten** (daily: Feb & Oct until 5pm; March until 5.30pm; April until 6pm; May–Sept 9am–6.30pm; Nov–Jan until 4.30pm; öS90), which, originating in the royal menagerie founded by Franz Stephan back in 1752, is the world's oldest zoo. Here, the imperial couple would breakfast among the animals, in the octagonal pavilion designed for them by Jean-Nicholas Jadot, and decorated with frescoes by Guglielmi depicting Ovid's *Metamorphoses*. The pavilion is now a very good restaurant and, along with several of the original Baroque animal houses, makes this one of the most aesthetically pleasing zoos any captive animal could hope for. The nicest feature of the zoo, by far, is the **Tirolergarten**, on whose woody slopes perches a wonderfully large timber-framed farmhouse from the Tyrol. The original Tirolergarten was the dreamchild of the Archduke Johann, younger brother of Franz II, who was fond of the Alps and commissioned two Tyrolean houses and an alpine garden in which the imperial famliy could dispense with the formalities of court life and "get back to nature". If you're thinking of admiring either the butterflies of the nearby **Schmetterlinghaus** (daily: May–Sept 10am–5pm; Oct–April 10am–3.30pm in good weather; öS40) or the tropical plants of the **Palmenhaus** (daily: May–Sept 9.30am–6pm; Oct–April until 5pm; öS40), then it's worth forking out for a "KombiKarte" (öS140), covering all three attractions.

The Technisches Museum

The **Technisches Museum**, on the opposite side of Auer-Welsbach-Park from the main gates of Schönbrunn, was conceived in the last decade of Habsburg rule, and opened in 1918. The whole place has been closed for some years, and was closed at the time of writing, so it's difficult to predict what the new museum will look like inside. However, the collection will undoubtedly continue to cover a wide range of subjects from the history of the postal system to atomic physics. The most popular exhibits, particularly with youngsters, are the steam locomotives, and primitive flying machines from the late nineteenth century. Vienna's **IMAX cinema**, next door, has daily showings of less-than-brilliant films, specially shot to show off the 180-degree projection system; tickets currently start at a hefty öS110 for an hour-long sitting.

Lainzer Tiergarten

In the far west of Vienna, some 3km beyond Schönbrunn, lies the former imperial hunting reserve of **Lainzer Tiergarten**, enclosed within a 25-kilometre-long wall by the emperor Josef II in the late eighteenth century. Since 1923, however, the reserve has been the wildest of Vienna's public parks – with virtually no traffic allowed inside its boundaries and no formal gardens – and serves as the place in summer to escape the urban sprawl. It may not boast the views of Wienerwald, but you're more likely to spot wildlife here, including wild boar, wolves and, most easily, deer; in addition, the famous Lipizzaner horses of the Spanische Reitschule spend their summer holidays in the park.

The park's chief sight, the **Hermesvilla** (Wed–Sun 9am–4.30pm; öS50), built in 1882 by the emperor Franz-Josef in an effort to ingratiate himself with his estranged wife (see box, p.120), is just ten minutes' walk from the main gates of Lainzer Tor, at the end of Hermesstrasse. Carl von Hasenauer was employed to design the building, and Gustav Klimt and Hans Makart among those commissioned to decorate the interior; there was even a purpose-built exercise room in which the empress could indulge in her daily gymnastics. In the end, though, the villa failed to entice Elisabeth back to Vienna, and she stayed there only very occasionally. The house is now used to host exhibitions put on by the Historisches Museum der Stadt Wien. Even if the particular show doesn't grab you, the well-preserved interior is rewarding, though there's no information on the Hermesvilla's imperial days, nor anything specific on the empress Elisabeth herself.

This section of the Lainzer Tiergarten is open year-round; the rest of the park is only open from Easter to October (Wed–Sun 8am–dusk); the St-Veiter Tor and the Adolfstor entrances, to the north of Lainzer Tor, are only open on Sundays and public holidays. To get to the Lainzer Tor, take tram #60 or #61 from Hietzing U-Bahn to Hofwiesengasse, then it's a fifteen minutes' walk or bus #60B down Hermesstrasse.

Kirche am Steinhof

Despite its limited opening hours, anyone with even a passing interest in Jugendstil architecture should make the effort to visit the **Kirche am Steinhof** (guided tours in German Sat 3pm; öS30), completed in 1907 by Otto Wagner as a chapel for the city's main psychiatric hospital. The church occupies a fantastic site on the commanding heights of the Baumgartner Höhe; to get there, take bus #47A from Unter-St-Veit U-Bahn. Like the Karlskirche (see p.103), the church is topped by a giant copper dome and lantern, both of which were originally gilded, and features two belfries capped with copper statues of seated saints. Inside, the church is deliberately organized on a north–south axis, rather than the usual east–west configuration, in order to allow more light through the glorious

EMPRESS ELISABETH

Elisabeth (1837–98) was born into the eccentric Wittelsbach dynasty that produced the likes of **"Mad" King Ludwig II of Bavaria**, one of Elisabeth's cousins. She enjoyed a carefree, if sheltered upbringing, only to find herself engaged to the Habsburg **Emperor Franz-Josef I** – another cousin – at the age of just 16, after an entirely public, two-day courtship. In choosing Elisabeth instead of her older sister Hélène, Franz-Josef went against the wishes of his mother, the **archduchess Sophie**. Sophie took her revenge, preventing Elisabeth from fulfilling her role either as empress or as mother to her children, by hand-picking her ladies-in-waiting and having the children removed from her care as soon as they were born. Later, Elisabeth was to advise her daughter "marriage is an absurd institution. At the age of fifteen you are sold, you make a vow you do not understand, and you regret for thirty years or more that you cannot break it."

By 1860, having dutifully produced a male heir, Elisabeth had given up on the marriage. She encouraged Franz-Josef to get a mistress, introducing him to the actress Katharina Schratt, "very much as a woman might put flowers into a room she felt to be dreary", as Rebecca West put it. Elisabeth's sudden departure to Madeira, however, was more specifically a reaction to discovering that Franz-Josef had infected her with venereal disease. She sought solace in riding, and spent much of her lonely life travelling around Europe, under the pseudonym the Countess Hohenhelms. As she herself put it, "When we cannot be happy in the way that we desire there is nothing for it but to fall in love with our sorrows."

Elisabeth's marriage to Franz-Josef was the wedding of the century, but despite public appearances it was a disaster from the start. The issue of their relationship divided folk: either Franz-Josef was a boorish, unimaginative prig, who visited brothels during their honeymoon, or Elisabeth was a frigid, neurotic, narcissistic brat, obsessed with her looks. Sisi, as Elisabeth was and still is affectionately known, won over people's hearts with her beauty. Yet many Viennese grew to resent her absences from the capital and were appalled at her pro-Hungarian sentiments.

In the 1870s, the growing insanity of her cousin King Ludwig spurred her to roam Europe in search of an elixir to cure madness. When Ludwig, and then her only son Rudolf, committed suicide within a few years of each other, she became convinced that she too was mentally unstable. From then on, she dressed only in black, and carried a black fan that she used to hide her newly forming wrinkles. She crisscrossed Europe, never staying in one place for long, and went on interminable cruises – she had an anchor tattooed on her shoulder – alarming her companions by asking to be tied to the ship's mast during storms.

By 1897, Elisabeth's health began to deteriorate rapidly – a condition partly brought on by anorexia – to the extent that she could barely walk. Despite her poor health, and her obsession with madness and death, few would have predicted her final demise. On September 10, 1898, the empress was assassinated by an Italian anarchist, Luigi Luccheni, on Lake Geneva. A local newspaper had unwisely announced the arrival of the empress, who was attempting to travel incognito. As she was about to board a steamer to go to tea with Baroness Rothschild, Luccheni rushed up and stabbed her in the heart. Like the empress, Luccheni had also been wandering aimlessly around Europe, in his case looking for someone famous to kill. He was fixed on assassinating the Duke of Orléans, but when he failed to turn up in Geneva as planned, resolved to attack the Austrian empress instead. Naturally enough, thousands turned out for Sisi's funeral in Vienna. Over the years, her martyrdom has ensured that the myth and intrigue around her life remain as compelling as ever.

mosaic windows, designed by Kolo Moser. The focus of the interior is very much on the main altar, with its eye-catching, cage-like gilt baldachin, against a backdrop mosaic featuring St Leopold and sundry other saints. Sadly, the church is little used nowadays; it's too cold for services during the winter, and even in summer there are few takers amongst the patients.

The Geymüllerschlössl

In the first decade of the early nineteenth century, the wealthy banker Johann Heinrich von Geymüller had a luxury summerhouse – known today as the **Geymüllerschlössl** (March–Nov Thurs–Sun 10am–5pm; öS30) – built in the sleepy village (now suburb) of Pötzleinsdorf. The house is no standard Biedermeier residence, but is, in fact, an exotic mixture of Gothic and Moorish elements executed by an unknown architect. It now houses the MAK's (see p.105) collection of early nineteenth-century furniture, as well as temporary Biedermeier exhibitions, which are staged on the ground floor. The first-floor rooms house the collection of clocks bequeathed, along with the house in 1965, by Dr Franz Sobek. The clocks – fascinating though they are – are a sideshow to the overall effect of the painstakingly restored Biedermeier decor, the most startling of which is the Salon mit Panoramatapete, a drawing room equipped with period furniture made from ebony and gold and upholstered in deep blue, and dominated by the panoramic murals of idealized, oriental landscapes. To get to the Geymüllerschlössl, take tram #41 to its terminus from Volksoper U-Bahn.

Karl-Marx-Hof

If there is one housing complex that has come to symbolize the interwar municipal socialism of "Red Vienna", it is the **Karl-Marx-Hof**, the kilometre-long, peach-and-salmon-coloured "people's palace", whose distinctive giant archways greet you as you exit from Heiligenstadt U-Bahn, in the city's northern suburbs. Though right-wing critics charged that these housing complexes were built as fortresses by the socialists to protect their workers in case of civil war, their fragility was proved on February 12, 1934, when the World War I artillery of the Austro-fascist government reduced much of the Karl-Marx-Hof to rubble in a few hours. It took another four days for the government forces to flush the last defenders out, however. This is only the most famous of the battles of the civil war, which began in Linz, and was fought just as keenly and bloodily in numerous other working-class housing estates in Vienna and other Austrian cities.

Heiligenstädter-Testament-Haus

Beethoven moved out to the **Heiligenstädter-Testament-Haus**, Probusgasse 6 (daily except Mon 9am–12.15pm & 1–4.30pm; öS25), in 1802 on the advice of his doctor, who hoped the country air would improve his hearing. It was here he wrote his "Heiligenstadt Testament" – a facsimile of which is at the museum – addressed but never sent to his brothers. In it he apologizes for appearing "unfriendly, peevish, or even misanthropic", talks honestly about his deafness – "a sense which in me should be more perfectly developed than in other people" – and the pain and embarrassment it brought him: "I was on the point of putting an end to my life – the only thing that held me back was my art." It reads like a will, though it was more of a confession, the cathartic soliloquy of someone who's reached rock bottom. Despite his personal distress, while resident at Probusgasse Beethoven completed his joyful *Second Symphony*, "brought home right from the meadows of Heiligenstadt, so full is it of summer air and summer flowers".

Beethoven changed addresses more times even than Mozart (see p.74), and spent a further four summers at various addresses in Heiligenstadt. The house in Probusgasse, however, is one of the best preserved of all his residences, and probably the most rewarding of the city's three memorial museums to the composer. Confusingly, there are, in fact, two museums situated here. The official municipal one, on the far side of the shady, cobbled courtyard, occupies the rooms rented by Beethoven, and contains a lock of the composer's hair and his death mask. On the opposite side of the courtyard is the rival **Beethoven Ausstellung** (Tues, Thurs & Sat 10am–noon & 1–4.30pm;

öS10), run by the elderly lady who lives at no. 5, on behalf of the Beethoven Society. There's more of an attempt at recreating some period atmosphere here, and there's an information sheet in English detailing the exhibits. To reach the museum, take bus #38A to Armbrustergasse from U-Bahn Heiligenstadt, or walk from the tram #37 terminus.

The Wienerwald

The forested hills of the **Wienerwald** (Vienna Woods) stretch from the northern tip of the city limits to the foothills of the Alps, away to the southwest – few other capitals can boast such an impressive green belt on their doorstep. In the eighteenth century, the wealthier folk used to move out into the villages on the vine-clad slopes of the Wienerwald for the duration of the summer. With the arrival of public transport, even those without such means could just hop on a tram to the end of the line, and enjoy a day in the countryside. Still today, the Wienerwald remains a popular weekend jaunt, and throughout the summer, the wine gardens of the local *Heurigen* (for more on which, see p.130) are filled not only with tour groups, but also with the Viennese themselves, who come here to sample the new wine.

The most popular place from which to admire the view over Vienna is **Kahlenberg** (484m), the higher of the two hills that rise to the north of the city. There's a café, with a magnificent terrace and a viewing platform, though the whole place is mobbed at weekends. According to tradition, this was where Polish King Jan Sobieski celebrated mass in 1683, before leading the army down the mountain to relieve the city from the Turks. The Baroque Josefskirche nearby, in which the event is supposed to have taken place, is now run by the Poles, and the church's Sobieski Chapel is a Polish national shrine. The most striking thing about the plain interior is the hundreds of rosaries, pendants and lucky Madonna and Child talismans, which hang on the walls from floor to ceiling.

Tradition notwithstanding, it has been proved fairly conclusively that the aforementioned mass actually took place on the neighbouring peak of **Leopoldsberg** (425m), just over 1km by road east of Kahlenberg. To confuse matters further, the two hills swapped names after the Leopoldskirche was built on what is now Leopoldsberg in 1693. This is certainly a more beguiling spot in which to relax and enjoy the view. There's a much more pleasant courtyard and café, shaded by pine trees, and a more dramatic view from the restored ramparts, built by the Babenbergs in 1135. The church itself is also better looking than the one on Kahlenberg, and has a historical display of prints and documents relating to the Turkish siege.

There are several ways of **approaching the Wienerwald**. Tram #38 deposits you in the centre of Grinzing. If you walk up Cobenzlgasse, turn right up Krapfenwaldgasse and then straight on at the crossroads, up Mukenthalerweg, you'll find yourself on the right path to Kahlenberg. To avoid the worst of the crowds and the traffic, though, it's probably better to start walking from the terminus of tram D in Nussdorf, following Beethovengang past the Beethoven memorial, then up Kahlenberger Strasse. Either way, it's a good 3km uphill to Kahlenberg itself. Alternatively, bus #38A from Heiligenstadt U-Bahn will take you all the way to Kahlenberg, Cobenzl and (less frequently) Leopoldsberg.

The Prater

The only good reason to venture onto the eastern bank of the Danube Canal is to visit the **Prater** (derived from the Spanish *prado*). This large, flat tract of land, taking up almost half of the island formed by the various arms of the Danube, first opened to the public in 1766 by Josef II, includes vast acres of mixed woodland, sports stadiums, racecourses, a miniature railway, allotments, a trade-fair centre, a planetarium, an amusement park and, most famously of all, the Vienna's giant ferris wheel, or *Riesenrad*. In sum, the Prater is vast, and its backbone is the chestnut-lined Hauptallee, which runs dead straight for 5km.

By far the busiest section of the Prater is the northwest end, where you'll find the park's permament funfair, known as the **Volksprater** (Easter–Oct daily 8am–midnight). Tourists flock here for the *Riesenrad*, but the Viennese come here for the other rides, a strange mixture ranging from hi-tech helter-skelters and white-knuckle affairs to more traditional fairground rides like ghost trains and dodgems. Taking a ride on the giant **Riesenrad** (April daily 10am–11pm; May–Sept daily 9am–midnight; Oct daily 10am–10pm; Nov & Christmas–Jan 6 until 6pm; rest of Dec Sat & Sun only; öS45), built in 1898 by the British military engineer Walter Basset, is one of those things you simply have to do if you go to Vienna; it's also a must for fans of the film *The Third Man*, as the place in front of which Orson Welles does his famous "cuckoo clock" speech. Be prepared for the fact that the wheel doesn't so much spin as stagger slowly round, as each gondola fills up with passengers; once you've done a complete circuit, you've had your twenty-minute ride.

The easiest way of approaching the Prater is from the northwest, from Wien-Nord station (U-Bahn Praterstern), the terminus for tram #5 and O, and a stop on tram #21. Alternatively, tram N from U-Bahn Schwedenplatz has its terminus right by the Hauptallee, a third of the way down from the ferris wheel. Getting around the Prater, you can walk, jog, rollerblade, cycle, take a fiacre, or rent one of the pedal carriages, which seat two adults (plus two kids if you wish). Another possibility is to buy a one-way ticket on the miniature railway or *Liliputbahn*, which will get you almost halfway down the Hauptallee.

The Johann-Strauss-Museum

Fans of the "Waltz King" might like to head for the **Johann-Strauss-Museum** (daily except Mon 9am–12.15pm & 1–4.30pm; öS25), on the first floor of Praterstrasse 54 (U-Bahn Nestroyplatz), where the composer lived from 1863 until the death of his first wife, the singer Jetty Treffz, in 1878. In contrast to most of the city's musical museums, some attempt has been made here to recreate a period interior: one room, decorated with ceiling panels of cherubs, contains his grand piano, house organ and standing desk at which he used to compose. There's also a fascinating collection of ephemera from the balls of the day, with various gimmicky dance cards – one laid out in the form of a staircase – and quirky ball pendants, which were kept as a sort of memento of the evening. Strauss is, of course, best known for having written the city's signature tune, *An der schönen, blauen Donau* (known to the English-speaking world as *The Blue Danube*). Originally scored for male chorus, not orchestra, complete with ludicrous lyrics, it wasn't at all well received after its inept first performance. Only when Strauss took it to Paris, and performed it with an orchestra, did it become a stratospheric success.

Vienna's cemeteries

In a city where some people still keep a separate savings account in order to ensure an appropriately lavish funeral, it comes as little surprise that Vienna's chief cemetery, the **Zentralfriedhof** (Central Cemetery), is one of the biggest in Europe. Larger than the entire Innere Stadt, and with a much greater population – 2.5 million – than the whole of the city, it even has its own bus service to help mourners get about. Opened in 1874, at the height of Viennese funereal fetishism – when having *eine schöne Leich* ("a beautiful corpse") was something to aspire to – it's still very much a working graveyard. It's particularly busy on Sundays and on religious holidays, most notably All Saints' Day (November 1), when up to a million Viennese make the trip out here and leave candles burning in remembrance on virtually every grave. To get there, take tram #71 from Schwarzenbergplatz and get out at the monumental Jugendstil Zweite Tor.

Most of the so-called **Ehrengräber** (Tombs of Honour) are in Gruppe 32A, to the left, as you approach the central Jugendstil church. Centre stage is a memorial to Mozart, though he was buried in St Marxer Friedhof (see p.111). At a respectful distance lie the graves of Beethoven and Schubert, who were disinterred from Währinger Friedhof in 1889 and reburied here. Other composers to look out for include **Christoph Willibald Gluck, Johannes Brahms, Hugo Wolf** and the entire **Strauss** clan. The sunken roundabout in front of the main church is the illustrious **Prezidentsgruft**, containing the remains of the presidents of the Second Republic. Close by, in Gruppe 32C, you'll find more intriguing incumbents like the composer **Arnold Schönberg**, and his mentor **Alexander Zemlinsky**, both of whom died in exile in the USA.

A majority of Vienna's most famous personages are to be found in the Zentralfriedhof, but there are a few notable exceptions. Gustav Klimt, for example, is buried in the **Friedhof Hietzing** (March, April, Sept & Oct daily 8am–5pm; May–Aug until 6pm; Nov–Feb 9am–4pm), ten minutes' walk from Hietzing U-Bahn up Maxingstrasse, in the western suburbs. Other notables buried here include Klimt's friend the artist Kolo Moser, Engelbert Dollfuss, the Austro-fascist leader murdered by the Nazis in 1934, Katharina Schratt, the emperor Franz-Josef's mistress, the composer Alban Berg, and Otto Wagner, whose rather pompous tomb was designed by the architect himself, but is devoid of even a hint of Jugendstil motifs. Egon Schiele is buried in the nearby **Friedhof Ober-St-Veit**; take bus #54B or #55B from Ober-St-Veit U-Bahn. Devotees of the Gustav Mahler need to head for **Grinzinger Friedhof**, where the composer was buried in 1911, having converted to Catholicism earlier in his career in order to make himself more acceptable to the anti-Semitic Viennese music establishment. His modernist tombstone, designed by Josef Hoffmann, was commissioned by his widow, Alma Mahler-Werfel, who lies close by. Other notable corpses here include the one-armed pianist Paul Wittgenstein (brother of philosopher Ludwig). To get to the Grinzinger Friedhof, take tram #38 to its terminus.

Cafés and restaurants

More so than anywhere else in Austria, Vienna has a huge variety of places to **eat and drink**, from *Beisln*, the Viennese version of a local pub, to upmarket restaurants, as well as a wide range of cuisines, from Mongolian to South Indian. Even the country's ubiquitous protein-heavy food is given a new lift in the capital thanks to the popularity of *Neue Wiener Küche*, the Viennese version of *nouvelle cuisine*, which uses fresh produce to give a slightly Mediterranean bent to traditional dishes.

Vienna is, of course, also home of the *Kaffeehaus*, and has by far the largest selection in the country. While the rest of the world queues up for fast food, the Viennese *Kaffeehaus* implores you to slow down; as the sign in one such café says, "sorry, we do not cater for people in a hurry." For the price of a small coffee, you can sit for as long as you like without being asked to move on or buy another drink. Understandably, then, the price of this first drink is astronomical and will regularly set you back around öS35.

Eating and drinking establishments are divided into **Kaffeehäuser**, incorporating snack bars and *Kaffee-Konditorei,* and **restaurants**, which includes some of the city's *Beisln*. Phone numbers have been given only for those restaurants where it's advisable to **book a table**. Lastly, some places have what is known as a *Schanigarten*. Don't get too excited, however, as this is rarely much of a garden; simply a few tables alfresco.

Cafés

The Viennese take their cafés seriously – on average they drink twice as much coffee as beer – and the capital's *Kaffeehäuser* are by no means a uniform bunch. As well as the traditional *Kaffeehaus* – the smoky type, with a wide range of newspapers to read, and a waiter in a tuxedo – there's also the *Kaffee-Konditorei*, where the coffee is a mere sideshow to the establishment's cakes and pastries. In the last decade or so, new modern variants on the old *Kaffeehaus* have begun to appear, too. These places generally eschew the tuxedos, heavy Viennese cooking and *Torten*, and consequently attract a younger crowd. In addition, there are also several more modest, stand-up snack counters listed below.

The Innere Stadt

Aida, branches at 1, Stock-im-Eisen-Platz 2; 1, Bognergasse 3; 1, Rotenturmstrasse 24 (all U-Bahn Stephansplatz). The largest Viennese *Konditorei* chain serving a staggering selection of calorific cakes and coffee in rather dodgy decor. Varied hours, but usually Mon–Sat 7am–8pm, Sun 9am–8pm.

Alt Wien, 1, Bäckerstrasse 9; U-Bahn Stephansplatz. Bohemian *Kaffeehaus* with *Beisl* decor, posters on nicotine-stained walls, and a dark, smoky atmosphere even on the sunniest day. Daily 10am–3am.

Anker (Treff zum Nestroy), 1, Bräunerstrasse 4–6; U-Bahn Stephansplatz (hundreds of branches across Vienna). *Anker* are the largest bakery chain in the country, producing excellent bread, rolls and pastries. This branch also does hot food: breakfast until 11am, full Austrian cuisine thereafter. Mon–Fri 7.30am–6pm.

Central, 1, Herrengasse 14; U-Bahn Herrengasse. The most famous of all Viennese cafés, resurrected in the 1980s and still the most architecturally interesting (see p.78). Trotsky was once a regular. Piano music 4pm to 7pm. Mon–Sat 9am–8pm.

Demel, 1, Kohlmarkt 14; U-Bahn Herrengasse. The king of the *Kaffee-Konditorei* – and one of the priciest. The cake display is a work of art, as is the interior. Daily 10am–6pm.

Engländer, 1, Postgasse 2; U-Bahn Stubentor. Stylish minimalist *Kaffeehaus* with a long pedigree – viz the erstwhile Jewish maitresse on the wall – serving *Neue Wiener Küche* at reasonable prices. Daily 8am–2am.

Frauenhuber, 1, Himmelpfortgasse 6; U-Bahn Stephansplatz. One of the oldest *Kaffeehäuser* in Vienna – Beethoven was a regular – with vaulted ceiling, deep burgundy upholstery and an excellent menu. Mon–Fri 8am–11pm, Sat 8am–4pm.

Hawelka, 1, Dorotheergasse 6; U-Bahn Stephansplatz. Small, smoky bohemian café run by the same couple since it opened shortly after World War II; you'll have to fight for a table. Mon–Sat 8am–2am, Sun 4pm–2am.

Kleines Café, 1, Franziskanerplatz 3; U-Bahn Stephansplatz. Cosy little café, one of the first of the crossovers between the new and the traditional *Kaffeehaus,* designed by the Viennese architect Hermann Czech in the 1970s. Mon–Sat 10am–2am, Sun 1pm–2am.

Landtmann, 1, Dr-Karl-Lueger-Ring 4; U-Bahn Herrengasse. One of the poshest of the *Kaffeehäuser* – and a favourite with Freud – with impeccably attired waiters, and a high quota of politicians and Burgtheater actors. Daily 8am–midnight.

Lukullus-Bar, 1, Graben 19; U-Bahn Stephansplatz. Stand-up buffet at the rear of the flagship outlet of the Julius Meinl delicatessen/supermarket chain, where you can eat traditional hot dishes and lighter snacks. Mon–Sat 8am–5pm.

MAK Café, 1, Stubenring 5; U-Bahn Stubentor. Not strictly speaking a traditional *Kaffeehaus*, but it does have a wonderfully high coffered ceiling. This is a trendy hangout, as you might expect from the MAK (see p.105). The food is pricey, with a Mediterranean edge. Daily except Mon 10am–2am.

Museum, 1, Friedrichstrasse 6; U-Bahn Karlsplatz. Adolf Loos designed this L-shaped café way back in 1899, and it was a favourite haunt of Klimt, Kokoschka and Schiele, among others. It's changed a lot since then, but remains endearingly well worn and is still popular with art students. Daily 7am–11pm.

Prückel, 1, Stubenring 24; U-Bahn Stubentor. The *Prückel* has lost its ornate interior, but the dowdy 1950s refurbishment looks appealingly dated now, and still draws in lots of elderly shoppers and dog-owners from the nearby Stadtpark. Daily 9am–10pm.

Sacher, 1, Philharmonikerstrasse 4; U-Bahn Karlsplatz. For all its fame, the *Sacher* is a bit of a letdown. The decor is imperial red and gold, but the room is small and the *Sachertorte* overrated – practically the only folk who come here nowadays are tourists. Daily 6am–midnight.

Schottenring, 1, Schottenring; U-Bahn Schottentor/Schottenring. Situated on the corner of Börsegasse, this L-shaped *Kaffeehaus*, with its high stuccoed ceiling, is an oasis of calm on the Ringstrasse. Daily 8am–11pm.

Schwarzenberg, 1, Kärntner Ring 17; U-Bahn Karlsplatz. Opulent café with rich marble, ceramic and wood-panelled decor, plus huge mirrors and a great cake cabinet. Live music Tues–Fri 8–10pm, Sat & Sun 4–7pm & 8–10pm. Daily 7am–midnight.

Sluka, 1, Rathausplatz 8; U-Bahn Rathaus. Lovely little *Kaffee-Konditorei* tucked under the arches by the Rathaus. White wood, gilded panelling, mirrors and chandeliers – a Ringstrasse classic. Mon–Fri 8am–7pm, Sat 8am–5.30pm.

Trzśniewski, 1, Dorotheergasse 1; U-Bahn Stephansplatz. Minimalist sandwich bar that's a veritable Viennese institution, serving mouthwatering slices of rye bread (*Brötchen*) topped with fishy, eggy and meaty spreads – wash it all down with a *Pfiff*. Stand-up tables and a few seats. Mon–Fri 8.30am–7.30pm, Sat 9am–1pm.

Zum schwarzen Kameel, 1, Bognergasse 5; U-Bahn Herrengasse. A terribly smart, convivial deli that's yet another Viennese institution, with stand-up tables only. Mon–Sat 9am–7pm.

The Vorstädte

Benno, 8, Alserstrasse 67; U-Bahn Alserstrasse. Very popular studenty café with groovy music, half a 2CV sticking out of the wall, lots of board games and a menu of toasted baguette munchies for under öS75. Daily 11.30am–2am.

Café Berg, 9, Berggasse 8; U-Bahn Schottentor. Relaxed modern mixed gay/straight café with an attractive assortment of chairs and great *Neue Wiener Küche*. Daily 10am–1am.

Europa, 7, Zollergasse 8; U-Bahn Neubaugasse. Lively, spacious café that attracts a trendy crowd, who love the posey window booths. Food is tasty mixture of Viennese and Italian. Daily 9am–4am.

Das Käuzchen, 7, Gardegasse 8; U-Bahn Volkstheater. Spittelberg café with zany decor, toasted snacks and more substantial fare. Daily 8am–2am.

Lux, 7, Spittelberggasse 3; U-Bahn Volkstheater. Pared-down modern version of a *Kaffeehaus*, with a friendly bistro feel and an eclectic menu featuring tofu-based dishes, pizzas and pancakes. Daily 10am–2am.

Luxor, 9, Grünentorgasse 19; tram D. Lively neighbourhood café-bar with lugubrious decor, a column of water on the bar, an aquarium and the odd pinball machine. Mon–Thurs 9am–2am, Fri & Sat 9am–4am.

Nil, 7, Siebensterngasse 39; tram #49. Trendy Egyptian café hung with lanterns, offering simple Arab dishes and backgammon. Mon–Thurs 10am–midnight, Fri 10am–2am, Sat 5pm–2am, Sun 5pm–midnight.

Stadlmann, 9, Währinger Strasse 26; U-Bahn Schottentor. Sepia-coloured *Kaffeehaus*, with unrenovated red velvet alcoves, brass chandeliers and mirrors. Mon–Fri 8am–9pm. Closed Aug.

Stein, 9, Währingerstrasse 6; U-Bahn Schottentor. The king of the new generation of posey designer cafés, on the corner of Kolingasse, with minimalist decor, funky music, online facilities, trendy loos, baguettes, veggie food and breakfasts served until 8pm. Mon–Sat 7am–1am, Sun 9am–1am.

Westend, 7, Mariahilferstrasse 128; U-Bahn Westbahnhof. Conveniently located directly opposite Westbahnhof, this traditional *Kaffeehaus* is the best possible introduction to Vienna for those who've just arrived by train. Daily 7am–11pm.

Restaurants

Overall prices in Vienna's restaurants, and particularly in the Innere Stadt, are slightly higher than in the rest of Austria. That said, outside the most exclusive places, you can still eat very reasonably at most restaurants. The only truly budget option is to eat at one of the city's student canteens, or *Mensen*, which are open to the general public

MENSEN

If you're on a tight budget, then it's worth considering using the city's numerous university canteens, or **Mensen**, which are open to the general public (you get an extra discount with student ID). It might not be cordon bleu, but the food is generally perfectly decent traditional Viennese fare, and you usually get a couple of courses for under öS45 – about half what you'd pay in a restaurant.

Afro-Asiatisches Institut, 9, Türkenstrasse 3; U-Bahn Schottentor. Vienna's most multiethnic clientele, but not great for veggies; situated on the ground floor through the archway. Mon–Fri 11.30am–2pm.

Katholische Hochschulgemeinde, 1, Ebendorferstrasse 8. Two choices of set menu (occasionally veggie). Mon–Fri 11.30am–2pm. Closed Easter & Aug to mid-Sept.

Musikakademie, 1, Johannesgasse 8. Small central *Mensa* with a pleasant summer courtyard; not great for veggies. Mon–Fri 7.30am–2pm.

Neues Institutsgebäude, 1, Universitätsstrasse 7; U-Bahn Schottentor. This is the main university *Mensa*; take the dumb-waiter lift to floor 6 and then walk up another flight of stairs – there's a nice view over to the Votivkirche. Mon–Fri 8am–7pm.

Technische Universität, 4, Wiedner Hauptstrasse 8–10; U-Bahn Karlsplatz. Big *Mensa* on the first floor (follow the yellow B signs) of the building behind the main university block on Karlsplatz. Mon–Fri 11am–2.30pm.

(lunchtime only). The next best option is to head for a *Beisln*, or city pub, where the standard Austrian dishes on offer won't set you back too much. Outside the centre, the **Spittelberg** area, behind the Messepalast (Museumsquartier), has the highest concentration of cafés and restaurants, though there are further options dispersed more widely throughout the surrounding district of **Neubau** (seventh district), and in neighbouring **Josefstadt** (eighth district).

The Innere Stadt

Achilleus, 1, Köllnerhofgasse 3; U-Bahn Schwedenplatz. Strangely Austrian-looking, excellent Greek restaurant. Daily 11.30am–3pm & 5.30pm–12.30am.

Arche Noah, 1, Seitenstettengasse 2; U-Bahn Schwedenplatz. Vienna's most central kosher restaurant with solid Jewish specialities and, of course, *gefilte Fisch*. Daily 11.30am–3.30pm & 6.30–11pm.

Bizi, 1, Rotenturmstrasse 4; U-Bahn Stephansplatz. Devise your own pizza toppings, assemble your own salad, or choose one of the main dishes and/or roasted vegetables. Take-away or sit-down. Daily 11am–midnight.

Brezlg'wölb, 1, Ledererhof 9; U-Bahn Herrengasse. Wonderful candlelit cave-like restaurant with deliberately zany decor. Hidden in a cobbled street off Drahtgasse, it serves the usual Austrian favourites plus specials like Greek salad. Daily 11.30am–1am.

Danieli, 1, Himmelpfortgasse 3 (☎513 7913); U-Bahn Stephansplatz. Italian joint with a bare-bricks Pompeii look and a nice big conservatory at the back. Huge pizzas, fresh fish and meat dishes, too. Daily 9am–2am.

Figlmüller, 1, Wollzeile 5; U-Bahn Stephansplatz. *The* place to eat *Wiener Schnitzel* (see p.37), though they're not cheap at öS145 a go. Wash it down with wine (there's no beer). Daily 8am–10.30pm, Sat 8am–3pm. Closed Aug.

Gösser Bierklinik, 1, Steindlgasse 4; U-Bahn Stephansplatz. Ancient inn with wooden booths for drinking, and a more formal back-room restaurant serving traditional Austrian food. Mon–Sat 10am–midnight.

Gulasch-Museum, 1, Schulerstrasse 20; U-Bahn Stubentor. Not a museum at all: just an inexpensive *Beisl* specializing in goulash. Daily 9am–midnight.

Ilona-Stüberl, 1, Bräunerstrasse 2; U-Bahn Stephansplatz. Gypsy-music-free Hungarian restaurant with lashings of goulash on offer. Mon–Sat noon–3pm & 6–11pm.

Inigo, 1, Bäckerstrasse 18; U-Bahn Stubentor. Inexpensive *Beisl* overlooking the Jesuit church, with an interesting menu including a fair proportion of soya-based veggie dishes. Mon–Thurs 8am–midnight, Fri 8am–1am, Sat 10am–8pm, Sun 10am–midnight.

K2, 1, Rotgasse 8; U-Bahn Schwedenplatz. Designer sushi bar attached to *Kiang* restaurant (see below). Mon–Sat 11.30am–3pm & 6pm–midnight.

Kiang, 1, Rotgasse 8; U-Bahn Schwedenplatz. Vienna's best-known designer Chinese restaurant decked out in loud primary colours with huge fish-bowl windows. The food is prepared right in front of your nose. Mon–Sat 11.30am–2pm & 6pm–1am.

Kuckuck, 1, Himmelpfortgasse 15 (☎512 8470); U-Bahn Stephansplatz. Tiny, vaulted restaurant, with lots of cuckoo clocks (hence the name), antique furniture and regional cookery. Good-value lunch menu at öS190 for two, but otherwise more than double that. Daily 6pm–1am.

Lale, 1, Franz-Josefs Kai/Rabensteig; U-Bahn Schwedenplatz. Stylish Turkish place on the edge of the Bermuda Triangle. Mon–Thurs & Sun 11.30am–midnight, Fri & Sat 11.30am–1am.

Mongolian Barbecue, 1, Fleischmarkt 4; U-Bahn Schwedenplatz. All-you-can-eat buffet grill of beef, lamb, pork, turkey and horse meat for öS220. Daily noon–2.30pm & 5.30pm–midnight.

Naschmarkt, branches at 1, Schottengasse 1 (U-Bahn Schottentor); 1, Schwarzenbergplatz 16 (U-Bahn Karlsplatz). Perfectly decent self-service Austrian restaurant chain, where you can eat as much or little as you like. Hours vary, but the Schwarzenbergplatz branch is Mon–Fri 6.30am–9pm, Sat & Sun 9am–9pm.

Nordsee, branches at 1, Kärntnerstrasse 25; 1, Kohlmarkt 6 (both U-Bahn Stephansplatz). Fish and seafood self-service restaurant, with everything from rollmop rolls to fish and chips, lobster and salad. Take-away or eat-in. Varied hours: Kärntnerstrasse branch is daily 9am–11pm.

Oswald und Kalb, 1, Bäckerstrasse 14 (☎512 6992); U-Bahn Stephansplatz. Wonderful, dimly lit *Gasthaus* specializing in moderately priced Styrian dishes. Daily 6pm–midnight.

S'Palatschinkengartl, 1, Salzgasse 8; U-Bahn Schwedenplatz. Inexpensive pancake place serving savoury and sweet varieties on the edge of the Bermuda Triangle. Daily 11am–midnight.

Salzamt, 1, Ruprechtsplatz 1; U-Bahn Schwedenplatz. Typical of Vienna's modern *Beisln*: popular, minimalist and serving up excellent traditonal Viennese food in a *nouveau* way. Tables outside in summer. Daily 5pm–4am.

Siddhartha, 1, Fleischmarkt 16 (☎513 1197); U-Bahn Schwedenplatz. Strangely normal decor for this Buddhist vegetarian restaurant, which is no bargain, but has a cheap weekday lunch menu. Daily 11.30am–3pm & 6–11pm.

Wrenkh, 1, Bauernmarkt 10 (☎533 1526); U-Bahn Stephansplatz. Very fashionable, designer vegetarian restaurant, with most main dishes over öS100. Mon–Sat 11am–1am.

Zu den drei Hacken, 1, Singerstrasse 28; U-Bahn Stephansplatz. Old-style *Beisl* with cheap fare with a Styrian bent – quite a boon in this part of town. Mon–Sat noon–midnight. Closed Aug.

The Vorstädte

Altes Jägerhaus, 2, Aspernallee, Prater; bus #77A. Lively Prater *Beisl*, at the far end of the Hauptallee, serving typical hearty fare you can wash down with Budvar beer. Wed–Sun 10am–11pm.

Amerlingbeisl, 7, Stiftgasse 8; U-Bahn Volkstheater. Spacious, modern *Beisl* that's a popular drinking hole with Vienna's younger generation. Good range of veggie food and salads; breakfast served from 9am. Shady courtyard and occasional live music. Daily 9am–2am.

Bier Oase, 9, Liechtensteinstrasse 108; tram #5, #47 or #48. Friendly little *Beisl* with ten beers on tap and numerous exotic bottled brands. Simple and inexpensive pub food available, too. Summer Mon–Fri 11am–midnight, Sat 7pm–midnight; winter Mon–Fri from 5pm only.

Bombay, 7, Neustiftgasse 65; bus 13A and 48A. Friendly south Indian restaurant (a rarity in Vienna) with veggie or meat thalis for öS110. Daily 11am–3pm & 6pm–midnight.

Drechsler, 6, Linke Wienzeile 22; U-Bahn Kettenbrückengasse. Laid-back, scruffy Mariahilf *Kaffeehaus*, by the Naschmarkt; popular with the younger generation of Viennese, especially clubbers attracted by the early opening hours. Mon–Fri 3.30am–8pm, Sat 3.30am–6pm.

Glacisbeisl, 7, Messeplatz 1; U-Bahn Volkstheater. Hidden in the entrails of the Messepalast, this is a popular venue in summer. Good vegetarian selections. March & April Mon–Sat 10am–midnight; May–Dec daily, same times.

Hunger-Künstler, 6, Gumpfendorferstrasse 48 (☎587 9210); U-Bahn Kettenbrückengasse. Candle-lit but unpretentious Mariahilf restaurant serving Vorarlberg specialities and plenty of veggie options. Daily 6pm–1am.

Ilija, 8, Piaristengasse 36; tram J or bus #13A. Croatian restaurant that serves up delicious fried squid, grilled kebabs and the like. Mon–Sat 11am–3pm & 6pm–1am.

Legume, 9, Währinger Strasse 57; tram #40, #41 or #42. Plain lunchtime-only vegetarian diner attached to a health-food shop of the same name; set three-course menu for around öS100. Mon–Fri 11.30am–2.30pm.

Lusthaus, 2, Hauptallee (☎728 9565); bus #77A. Eighteenth-century rotunda at the far end of Hauptallee that makes a perfect food halt whilst exploring the Prater. May–Sept Mon–Fri noon–11pm, Sat & Sun noon–6pm; shorter hours in winter and closed Wed.

Orlando, 8, Florianigasse 20; U-Bahn Rathaus, tram #5 or bus #13A. Nice little Italian place with nautical decor, plenty of fish and great pasta (no pizza), and Italian muzak for authenticity. Daily noon–11pm.

Phönixhof, 7, Neustiftgasse 55; bus #13A and #48A. Relaxed, evening-only *Beisl* that's a real favourite with the locals. Daily 6pm–2am.

Plutzer Bräu, Schrankgasse 2; U-Bahn Volkstheater. Spacious designer-beer bar in Spittelberg, good for a quiet lunch, or a much more boisterous evening drink. Inexpensive. Daily 11am–2am.

Pontoni, 7, Burggasse/Halbgasse; tram #5 or bus #48A. A modish crowd frequent this *nouveau* stripped-down *Beisl*; the food is traditional but imaginatively presented and freshly prepared. Daily 11am–2pm & 5pm–1am.

Ritter, 6, Mariahilferstrasse 73; U-Bahn Neubaugasse. Vast, high-ceilinged V-shaped Mariahilf café popular with veteran card-players and shoppers. Mon–Sat 7am–11pm, Sun 8am–11pm.

Savoy, 6, Linke Wienzeile 36; U-Bahn Kettenbrückengasse. Wonderfully scruffy, but ornate fin-de-siècle decor, packed with bohemian bargain-hunters during Mariahilf's Saturday flea market. Mon–Fri 5pm–2am, Sat 9am–6pm, Sun 9pm–2am.

Schnattl, 8, Lange Gasse 40 (☎405 3400); U-Bahn Rathaus. Innovative, but expensive *Neue wiener Küche* cooked by Herr Schnattl himself; call to reserve a table in the courtyard. Mon–Sat 11.30am–2.30pm & 6pm–midnight, Sun 6pm–midnight.

Schnitzelwirt, 7, Neubaugasse 52; tram #49. After *Figlmüller* (see p.127), *the* place to eat Wiener Schnitzel – they're just as humongous and cheaper, too. Very popular with backpackers. Mon–Fri 10am–10pm, Sat & Sun 10am–2.30pm & 5–10pm.

Schweizerhaus, 2, Strasse des 1 Mai 116; U-Bahn Praterstern. Czech-owned in the Prater; known for its draught beer and Czech specialities such as tripe soup and roast pork. March–Oct daily 10am–11pm.

Siebenstern Bräu, 7, Siebensterngasse 19; tram #49. Popular modern *Bierkeller*, which brews its own beer and serves a range of others on tap. The food is solid Viennese; the pan-fried dishes come with the pan, and the black bread is delicious. Mon–Sat 4pm–1am, Sun 11am–midnight.

Spatzennest, 7, Ulrichsplatz 1; bus #13A and #48A. Traditional Viennese *Beisl* with a good "salad and vegetable lovers' menu". Daily except Fri & Sat 10am–midnight.

Speri, 6, Gumpendorfer Strasse 11; U-Bahn Karlsplatz/Babenbergerstrasse. One of the classics of the *Kaffeehaus* scene, in Mariahilf; L-shaped, with billiard tables and still a hint of shabbiness despite its renovation. Mon–Sat 7am–11pm, Sun 3–11pm.

Spittelberg, 7, Spittelberggasse 12; U-Bahn Volkstheater. A chic brasserie with some veggie options and delicious crepes for dessert. Daily 6pm–late.

Stadtbeisl, 9, Währinger Strasse 59; tram #40, #41 or #42. Funky arty *Beisl* in the trendy w.u.k. arts complex, with a varied menu, half-veggie/half-organic meat dishes. Daily 11am–2am.

Vega, 7, Neubaugasse 81; tram #46. Strangely sterile vegetarian restaurant serving Viennese dishes redone with soya, a few Indian staples and draught Budvar. Tues–Sun 11.30am–3pm & 6–11pm.

Wegenstein, 7, Lerchenfelder Strasse 73 (☎526 7872); tram #46. Three generations of owners have made this is a real, local, family-run Wiener *Beisl*, no messing. Mon–Fri 8am–midnight, Sat 9am–2pm.

Witwe Bolte, 7, Gutenberggasse 13; U-Bahn Volkstheater. Long-established Wiener *Beisl* in the charming backstreets of Spittelberg, famous for having been visited by Josef II – incognito – in the eighteenth century. Lovely summer garden. Daily 11am–midnight.

Wratschko & Schmid, 7, Neustiftgasse 51; bus #13A and #48A. Lively, wood-panelled café-restaurant with lovely etched-glass partitions and a good range of food. Daily 5pm–1am.

Vienna's Heurigen

The city's traditional **Heurigen** are located out in the wine-producing villages, at the foot of the Wienerwald, that now form the outer suburbs of Vienna. These are good places to go in fine weather, preferably during late summer and autumn, and the areas to head for are listed in the box below. In addition, however, Vienna boasts a handful of centrally located wine-taverns known as **Stadtheurigen**, often housed in the cellars of the city's monasteries. These are not real Heurigen at all, but are still great places to drink wine and eat the simple food on offer.

Stadtheurigen

Augustinerkeller, 1, Augustinerstrasse 1; U-Bahn Karlsplatz. Vast array of green and black striped booths in the cellars underneath the Albertina. Fast service and hearty Viennese food; a tad touristy, but fun – prices are cheaper in the day. Schrammelmusik from 6.30pm. Daily 11am–midnight.

Esterházykeller, 1, Haarhof 1; U-Bahn Herrengasse. Snug, brick-vaulted wine-cellar with a limited range of hot and cold snacks. Situated off Naglergasse. Inexpensive. Mon–Sat 11am–10pm.

Melker Stiftskeller, 1, Schottengasse 3; U-Bahn Schottentor. Vast, high-ceilinged wine-cellar owned by the famous Melk monks. Mon–Sat 5pm–midnight.

Urbani-Keller, 1, Am Hof 12; U-Bahn Herrengasse. Well-known, slightly pricey Heuriger with live Schrammelmusik. Daily 6pm–1am.

Zwölf-Apostelkeller, 1, Sonnenfelsgasse 3; U-Bahn Stephansplatz. An attractive seventeenth-century building with bars housed in three levels of cellars. The place to drink wine, but often difficult to find a space; cold food only. Daily 4.30pm–midnight. Closed July.

SELECTED HEURIGEN

Grinzing is the most famous of Vienna's *Heuriger* village-suburbs, and consequently the most touristy. There are numerous *Heurigen* on the main street of Sandgasse, but to avoid the worst of the crowds head further up Cobenzlgasse. Next most popular are the nearby areas of **Heiligenstadt** and **Nussdorf**. Less touristy alternatives include Sievering and Neustift am Walde, or you can cross over the Danube and head for the village of Stammersdorf. There are no specific listings for the villages, as the opening times of most *Heurigen* are unpredictable (most don't open until mid-afternoon). Part of the fun of visiting a *Heuriger* is to simply set off to one of the districts and take potluck.

Below are single recommendations intended to serve as starting points for each district:

Grinzing
Altes Presshaus, 19, Cobenzlgasse 15; tram #38 to the end terminus.

Heiligenstadt
Mayer am Pfarrplatz, 19, Pfarrplatz 2: bus #38A from U-Bahn Heiligenstadt.

Neustift am Walde
Huber, 19, Rathstrasse 15: bus #35A from U-Bahn Nussdorfer Strasse.

Nussdorf
Schübel-Auer, 19, Kahlenberger Strasse 22; tram D to the end terminus.

Sievering
Haslinger, 19, Agnesgasse; bus #39A from U-Bahn Heiligenstadt to the end stop.

Stammersdorf
Wieninger, 21, Stammersdorfer Strasse 78; tram #31 to the end terminus.

Riesenrad, Vienna

Belvedere Palace, Vienna

St Marxer Friedhof, Vienna

Melk abbey

Tram car, Vienna

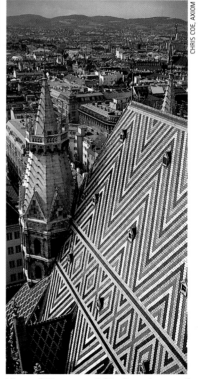
View of Vienna and Stephansdom roof

Logs in the Waldviertel

Storks' nest, Burgenland

Open-cast mine workings, Erzberg

Guns in the Zeughaus, Graz

Detail in the library at Admont

Heiligenblut and the Grossglockner

Bars, clubs and live venues

Surveys have shown that a vast majority of the Viennese are safely tucked up in bed by as early as 10pm. Meanwhile, however, a hard core stay up until very early in the morning – in fact it's quite possible to keep drinking round the clock. Vienna's late-night **bars** are concentrated in three main areas, the most famous of which is the so-called **Bermuda Triangle**, or *Bermuda Dreieck*, which focuses on Rabensteig, Seitenstettengasse, Ruprechtsplatz and the streets around. The emergence of the Triangle in the 1980s helped kick-start Vienna's nightlife out of its stupor, though, sadly, the area has become a victim of its own success: prices have gone up and more moneyed punters now predominate. That said, such is the variety packed into these few streets that you're bound to find somewhere that appeals.

The two other areas worth exploring are the **Naschmarkt**, where late-night licences abound, and Neubau's **Spittelberg** area – the narrow streets between Burggasse and Siebensterngasse, behind Messepalast – which has the highest concentration of late-night drinking holes, many of which double as restaurants and cafés.

Vienna's **club** scene is very small indeed for a city of 1.5 million. Dance culture, such as one would find in, say, London, is restricted to just a few venues. Aside from discos, the majority of Vienna's clubs are, in fact, bars, which either occasionally, or regularly, have live bands. But a more interesting phenomenon peculiar to Vienna is the *Musikcafé*, where resident DJs spin discs (both danceable and non-danceable) while the punters simply chill out and drink. As it's so difficult to differentiate between what is a bar, what's a club and what's a live venue, we've simply organized the listings by area. To find out what's on at Vienna's clubs, check out the *Musik-U* section in the weekly listings tabloid *Falter*. Drink prices are relatively high – bars in the Bermuda Triangle tend to charge öS40 and upwards for a *Krügerl* (half-litre) – but in those clubs where there is an admission charge, it's rarely more than öS100–150.

The Bermuda Triangle

First Floor, 1, Seitenstettengasse 1; U-Bahn Schwedenplatz. As the name suggests, an upstairs bar, with a vast array of aquariums and packed with a well-dressed, moneyed crowd. Mon–Sat 7pm–4am, Sun 11pm–4am.

Jazzland, 1, Franz-Josefs-Kai 29; U-Bahn Schwedenplatz. Vienna's main trad-jazz venue, just below the Ruprechtskirche. Tues–Sat 7pm–2am, occasionally Sun & Mon.

Krah Krah, 1, Rabensteig 8; U-Bahn Schwedenplatz. Crowded bar known for its excellent selection of draught beers; snacks also on offer, and occasional live jazz. Daily 11am–2am.

Roter Engel, 1, Rabensteig 5; U-Bahn Schwedenplatz. Stylish café-bar designed by deconstructionist mob, Coop Himmelblau, in 1979. Live music most nights; sets at 9.30pm (Fri & Sat at midnight, too). Mon–Wed 3pm–2am, Thurs–Sat 3pm–4am, Sun 5pm–2am.

Steh-Achterl, 1, Sterngasse 3; U-Bahn Schwedenplatz. A loud, young crowd fill this black UV and candlelit cellar, which features a male stripper on Wednesdays. Daily 6pm–2am, Fri & Sat until 4am.

The rest of the Innere Stadt

Aera, 1, Gonzagagasse 11; U-Bahn Schwedenplatz. Relaxing café upstairs serving tasty snacks, and dimly lit cellar downstairs where live bands perform. Daily 10am–2am.

American Bar (*Kärntner Bar*), 1, Kärntner Durchgang; U-Bahn Stephansplatz. Small, dark late-night bar off Kärntnerstrasse with surprisingly rich interior by Adolf Loos. Shame about the strip club next door. Daily Jan–May & Sept–Dec noon–4am; June–Aug from 6pm only.

LESBIAN AND GAY NIGHTLIFE

Vienna's **lesbian and gay scene** is pretty limited for your average Western European capital, prehaps reflecting the conservatism inherent in the country at large. Only the merest handful of bars and clubs, scattered across the city, are at all open about their existence. The traditional "gay district" around Naschmarkt is a mixture of old-style closet clubs, where you have to ring the bell to gain entry, and more relaxed venues. The social and political heart of the gay community is focused on the **Rosa-Lila Villa**, 6, Linke Wienzeile 102 (U-Bahn Pilgramgasse), which proudly flies the rainbow flag and proclaims itself as a *Lesben und Schwulen Haus*.

The best gay clubs are the one-nighters like the mixed gay/lesbian *Kinky Disco*, every Saturday at Volksgarten, 1, Burgring 1, and *Heaven*, every Thursday at U4, 12, Schönbrunner Strasse 222. In addition, check out the following:

Alfi's Goldener Spiegel, 6, Linke Wienzeile 46; U-Bahn Kettenbrückengasse. Naff but popular gay men's bar with restaurant; entrance is on Stiegengasse. Daily except Tues 9pm–4am.

Alte Lampe, 4, Heumühlgasse 13; U-Bahn Kettenbrückengasse. Long-established gay bar south of the Naschmarkt, with live piano and lots of Viennese schmaltz. Daily 9pm–4am.

Café Berg, 9, Berggasse 8; U-Bahn Schottentor (also reviewed on p.126). Cool café with mixed gay/straight clientele, especially during the day. The food's good, and you can pick up flyers about up-and-coming gay events. Daily 10am–1am.

Café Savoy, 6, Linke Wienzeile 36; U-Bahn Kettenbrückengasse (also reviewed on p.129). Even more than the *Berg*, this scruffy fin-de-siècle café is by no means exclusively gay, but things pick up in the evening. Mon–Fri 5pm–2am, Sat 9am–6pm, Sun 9pm–2am.

Café Willendorf, 6, Linke Wienzeile 102; U-Bahn Pilgramgasse. Café-restaurant inside the *Rosa-Lila Villa*, with a nice leafy courtyard. Another good place to pick up information about events. Daily 7pm–2am.

Eagle Bar, 6, Blümelgasse 1; U-Bahn Neubaugasse. Vienna's cruisy leather bar for gay men. Daily 9pm–4am.

Frauencafé, 8, Lange Gasse 11; U-Bahn Lerchenfelderstrasse. Vienna's only permanent women-only space is a small, but friendly café. Mon–Sat 8pm–1am.

Why Not?, 1, Tiefergraben 22. Late-night gay/lesbian bar and disco. Wed–Sun 11pm–5am.

Flex, 1, Donaukanal/Augartenbrücke; U-Bahn Schottenring. Hip-hop bar down by the canal, overlooking Wagner's Schützenhaus, with music from 9pm. Daily 3pm–late.

Krebitz, 1, Salzgries 9; U-Bahn Schwedenplatz. A small slice of post-industrial cool, with the occasional live band, low-key DJ, table football and pinball. Daily 6pm–2am.

Lindbergh, 1 Mahlerstrasse 11; U-Bahn Karlsplatz. Soul, retro and house at this clubby venue. Daily 9pm–4am.

P1, 1, Rotgasse 9; U-Bahn Stephansplatz. Big city-centre disco playing commercial dance music to a youngish crowd. Mon–Thurs & Sun 9pm–4am, Fri & Sat 9pm–6am.

Pavillon, 1, Burgring 1; U-Bahn Volkstheater. Strange location right by the Hofburg for this trendy garden café, which attracts clubbers heading for the *Volksgarten* (see opposite). Daily 8pm–2am.

Porgy & Bess, 1, Spiegelgasse 2; U-Bahn Stephansplatz. Venue for up-and-coming jazz bands. Mon–Fri 7pm–2am, Sat & Sun 8pm–4am.

Tiffany, 1, Robert-Stolz-Platz 4; U-Bahn Karlsplatz. New addition to the club and live music scene, specializing in techno and trance. Mon–Sat 9pm–4am, Sun 5pm–midnight.

Volksgarten, 1. Burgring 1; U-Bahn Volkstheater. Situated in the park of the same name, Vienna's trendiest club and a firm favourite with the dance crowd; the outdoor dance floor is a summertime treat. Daily 8pm–5am.

The Vorstädte and beyond

Arena, 3, Baumgasse 80; U-Bahn Erdberg. It's a long trek out to this former slaughterhouse on the corner of Französengraben, but there's a real variety of stuff that goes on here – all-night raves, outdoor concerts, films – so check the listings before setting out. Daily 7pm–late.

B.A.C.H., 16, Bachgasse 21; tram #46 from U-Bahn Thaliastrasse. A favourite of the alternative crowd, but a way out; DJs and occasional live bands. Mon–Thurs & Sun 8pm–2am, Fri & Sat until 4am.

Blue Box, 7, Richtergasse 8. *Musikcafé* with resident DJs and a good snack menu. Live music from 8pm. Mon 6pm–2am, Tues–Thurs 10am–2am, Fri & Sat 10am–4am.

Blues Man, 19, Glatzgasse 4; U-Bahn Nussdorferstrasse. Reasonably priced, relaxed blues and jazz café just the other side of the Gürtel from Alsergrund; live music most nights from 9pm. Mon–Sat 6pm–2am.

Chelsea, 8, U-Bahnbögen 29–31, Lerchenfelder Gürtel; U-Bahn Thaliastrasse. Punky Anglophile haunt with regular live music; situated underneath the U-Bahn. Mon–Sat 7pm–4am, Sun 4pm–4am.

Donau Bar, 7, K. Schweighofergasse 10; U-Bahn Neubaugasse. Ambient/jungle *Musikcafé* with in-house DJ and strange monochrome projections on the walls. Daily 9pm–4am.

Fischer Bräu, 19, Billrothstrasse 17; U-Bahn Nussdorferstrasse. Very civilized micro-brewery pub, which produces a great, lemony, misty beer. Lots of tasty snacks and more substantial pub fare to be consumed in the bare-boards interior or the shady courtyard. Strictly speaking just outside Alsergrund, but worth the trek. Daily 4pm–1am.

Jazzpelunke, 6, Dürergasse 3; U-Bahn Kettenbrückengasse. Newish jazz venue with live acts from trad to modern, located near the Naschmarkt. Mon–Fri 6pm–2am, Sat & Sun 11am–2am.

Nachtasyl, 6, Stumpergasse 53–55; U-Bahn Westbahnhof. Darkened beer hall managed by an expatriate Czech, and the odd live music. Daily 8pm–4am.

Stehbeisl, 6, Windmühlgasse 6; U-Bahn Babenbergerstrasse. Small amiable rock/folk bar off Mariahilferstrasse with occasional live music and cheap pub snacks. Mon–Thurs & Sun 6pm–2am, Fri & Sat 6pm–4am.

Szene Wien, 11, Hauffgasse 26; tram #71 from Schwarzenbergplatz. Live music venue run by a radical bunch from Simmering. Daily 6pm–late.

Tunnel, 8, Florianigasse 39; tram #5. Large, clean-living student establishment with café upstairs and frequent live bands down in the cellar. Daily 9am–2am.

U4, 12, Schönbrunnerstrasse 222; U-Bahn Meidling-Hauptstrasse. Dark, cavernous disco, mostly rock/indie, with frequent gigs; a mecca of the alternative crowd. Gay/lesbian night Thursday. Mon & Tues 11pm–4am, Wed–Sun until 5am.

w.u.k., 9, Währinger Strasse 59; tram #40, #41 or #42. Formerly squatted old red-brick school, now legitimate arts venue with a great café and a wide programme of events, including live music; check the *Falter* listings. Daily 11am–2am.

The performing arts

Vienna prides itself on its musical associations, and classical music and opera, in particular, are heavily subsidized by the Austrian state. The season runs from September to June, though smaller concerts are held throughout the year in the city's churches and palaces. The chief cultural festival – featuring opera, music and theatre – is the **Wiener Festwochen**, which lasts from early May until mid-June. The city's film festival, or **Viennale**, and the **Wien Modern** festival of contemporary classical music both take place towards the end of October. But by far the busiest time of the year is **Fasching**, Vienna's ball season, which begins on November 11, and continues until Ash Wednesday the following year. To find out what's on in Fasching, pick up a *Wiener Ballkalender* from the tourist office in the months leading up to and during the season.

Information and tickets

To find out **what's on** in general, pick up the tourist board's free monthly listings booklet *Programm*, which gives the programmes of the big opera and concert houses, plus a day-by-day concert guide, ball calendar and details of the current art exhibitions. The weekly listings tabloid *Falter* also lists classical concerts under its *Musik-E* section.

Ticket **prices** vary enormously in Vienna: the Staatsoper is a case in point, with seats ranging from öS50 to over öS2000. For some events – most notably the Vienna Boys' Choir and the New Year's Day Concert – it's not so much the price as the availability that's a problem. However, the big state venues offer cheap *Stehplätze*, or **standing-room tickets**, which can cost as little as öS20 each and usually go on sale one hour before the performance; some venues also offer unsold tickets at a discount to students, around an hour or thirty minutes before the show starts.

The cheapest way of **buying tickets** is to go to the venue's own box office. You can buy direct from the big four state theatres – Staatsoper, Volksoper, Burgtheater and Akademietheater – or from their shared central box office, the *Bundestheaterkassen*, by the Staatsoper at 1, Hanuschgasse 3 (☎51444-2955; Mon–Fri 9am–5pm, Sat & Sun 9am–noon; U-Bahn Karlsplatz; *www.austria-info.at/kultur/wswv/index.html*). There's also a box office on the Kärntnerstrasse side of the Staatsoper, which sells half-price tickets for musicals plus other events, and several on the Kärtner Ring, such as *Flamm* at 1, Kärntner Ring 3 (☎512 4225).

Opera and classical music

Vienna has a musical pedigree second to none, boasting one of Europe's top opera houses in the **Staatsoper**, served by one of its finest orchestras, the **Wiener Philharmoniker**, whose New Year's Day Concert (*Silvesterkonzert*) in the Musikverein is broadcast across the globe. When the big state theatres are closed in July and August, opera and classical music concerts captured on film are also shown for free every evening outside the Rathaus.

The most famous musical institution in the city is the **Wiener Sängerknaben**, or Vienna Boys' Choir, who perform mass at the Burgkapelle in the Hofburg every Sunday from mid-September to June at 9.15am. Tickets for the mass (öS60–280) are sold out weeks in advance, though some are held over each week and go on sale on Fridays between 4 and 6pm (you need to be there at least half an hour before the box office opens). To book in advance, write to Hofburgkapelle, Hofburg, A-1010 Wien, Austria, stating which Sunday mass you wish to attend. The other option is to settle for one of the free *Stehplätze*, which are distributed before mass; get there for 8.30am to be sure of a ticket. Be warned, however, that the choir remain out of sight up in the organ loft for the whole of mass.

Opera and operetta

Kammeroper, 1, Fleischmarkt 24 (☎513 0851); U-Bahn Schwedenplatz. Vienna's smallest opera house, hidden in the backstreets of the Innere Stadt and performing a variety of works from Rossini to Britten. In July and August, when the theatre is closed, the Kammeroper stages Mozart operas in the theatre at Schönbrunn.

Staatsoper, 1, Opernring 2 (☎51444-2955); U-Bahn Karlsplatz. Vienna's largest opera house stages around forty operas a season played in rep. It's a conservative place, but attracts the top names, and has the benefit of the Wiener Philharmoniker in the pit. With over 500 *Stehplätze* a night, it is also one of the most accessible opera houses in the world.

Volksoper, 9, Währinger Strasse 78 (☎51444-2955); U-Bahn Volksoper or tram #40, #41 or #42. Vienna's number-two opera house, which specializes in operetta, but also branches out into Janáček, Shostakovich and the late Romantics; over 100 *Stehplätze* a night.

Classical music

Bösendorfer Saal, 4, Graf Starhemberg-Gasse 14 (☎504 6651); U-Bahn Taubstummengasse. Chamber-music concert hall belonging to the famous Austrian piano manufacturers.

Konzerthaus, 3, Lothringerstrasse 20 (☎712 1211); U-Bahn Karlsplatz. Early twentieth-century concert hall designed by Viennese duo Helmer & Fellner. Three separate halls: the Grosser Saal, Mozart-Saal and Schubert-Saal.

Kursalon, 1, Johannesgasse 33 (☎713 2181); U-Bahn Stadtpark. The best place to hear Strauss and other popular tunes. April–Oct only.

Musikverein, 1, Bösendorferstrasse 12 (☎505 8190); U-Bahn Karlsplatz. Two ornate concert halls in one building, gilded from top to bottom inside. The larger of the two, the Grosser Saal, has the best acoustics in the country, while the smaller hall, the Brahms-Saal, is used mainly for chamber concerts; *Stehplätze* available for the Grosser Saal.

Theatre and musicals

Obviously for the non-German speaker, most of Vienna's theatres and satirical cabarets have limited appeal. However, there are a couple of English-speaking theatre groups: International Theatre, 9, Porzellangasse 8 (☎319 6272; tram D), and Vienna's English Theatre, 8, Josefsgasse 12 (☎402 1260; U-Bahn Lerchenfelderstrasse). There are also a few theatres that specialize in musicals, several puppet theatres, where language is less of a problem, and, of course, the Burgtheater, whose interior alone is worth the price of a ticket.

Straight theatre and musicals

Burgtheater, 1, Dr-Karl-Lueger-Ring 2 (☎51444-0); U-Bahn Herrengasse. Vienna's most prestigious theatrical stage puts on serious drama in rep. The foyer and staircases are spectacular; the auditorium was modernized after bomb damage in 1945.

Raimund Theater, 6, Wallgasse 18 (☎59977-27); U-Bahn Westbahnhof. Late nineteenth-century theatre, where *Beauty and the Beast* was enjoying a long run at the time of going to press.

Ronacher, 1 Seilerstätte 9 (☎51402); U-Bahn Stephansplatz. Beautifully refurbished turn-of-the-century music hall that puts on a variety of dance shows and musicals.

Theater-an-der-Wien, 6, Linke Wienzeile 6 (☎58885); U-Bahn Karlsplatz/Kettenbrückengasse. Historic, early nineteenth-century theatre, specializing in musicals.

Volkstheater, 7, Neustiftgasse 1 (☎523 2776); U-Bahn Volkstheater. Modern plays and classics and even the odd operetta.

Puppet theatre

Lilarum, 14, Philipsgasse 8 (☎894 2103); U-Bahn Hietzing. Puppet theatre opposite Schönbrunn, with several performances a day Friday–Sunday.

Schönbrunner Schloss-Marionettentheater, 13, Schloss Schönbrunn, Hofratstrakt (☎817 3247). String-puppet theatre in Schönbrunn specializing in Mozart operas – try and catch a different show if you can. Performances Wednesday–Sunday 4 & 8pm.

Cinema

Austrian cinema is not really up there with the greats, and unless your German is up to scratch you're best off sticking to British and American films. One film that's fun to see, and regularly gets a screening here, is *The Third Man* – **Der Dritte Mann** – made in 1949, set amidst the rubble of postwar Vienna and starring Orson Welles. The best place to check out the week's cinema listings is *Falter*, the city's weekly tabloid. *OF* means it's in the original (without subtitles); *Omengu* means it's in original with English subtitles; *OmU* means it's in the original with German subtitles, but should not be confused with *OmÜ*, which means it's in the original, but has a live voiceover German translation; and *dF* means it's dubbed into German.

Burg-Kino, 1, Opernring 19; U-Bahn Babenbergerstrasse. Cinema on the Ringstrasse that regularly shows films in the original.

De France, 1, Schottenring 5; U-Bahn Schottenring. Another Ringstrasse cinema that shows films in the original.

Filmhaus Stöbergasse, 5, Stöbergasse 11–15; bus #12A or #14A. Art-house cinema south of the Naschmarkt.

Filmmuseum, 1, Augustinerstrasse 1; U-Bahn Karlsplatz. Vienna's main art-house cinema, on the ground floor of the Albertina, with a very esoteric programme.

Imax Filmtheater, 14, Mariahilferstrasse 212; U-Bahn Schönbrunn or tram #52 and #58. Specially made films to show off the 400-square-metre wrap-round screen's awesome scope.

Star-Kino, 7, Burggasse 71; bus #48A. Art-house cinema specializing in old black-and-white movies.

Top Kino Center, 6, Rahlgasse 1; U-Bahn Babenbergerstrasse. Specializes in original-language films.

Votiv-Kino, 9, Währinger Strasse 12; U-Bahn Schottentor. Popular, central, two-screen art-house cinema.

Listings

Airlines Air Canada 1, Krugerstrasse 11 (☎515 5531); Air France 1, Kärntnerstrasse 49 (☎514 1818); Alitalia 1, Kärntner Ring 2 (☎505 1707); Austrian Airlines 1, Kärntner Ring 18 (☎505 5757); British Airways 1, Kärntner Ring 10 (☎505 7691); Delta 1, Kärntner Ring 17 (☎512 6646); Lauda Air 1, Opernring 6 (☎51477); Qantas 1, Opernring 1 (☎587 7771); South African Airways 1, Opernring 1 (☎587 1489); *TWA* 1, Opernring 1 (☎587 6868). The nearest U-Bahn for all the above airlines is Karlsplatz.

American Express 1, Kärntnerstrasse 21–23; U-Bahn Stephansplatz.

Books Shakespeare & Co, 1 Sterngasse 2; U-Bahn Schwedenplatz. Ramshackle, friendly English-language bookstore with a great selection of novels, art books and magazines.

Embassies and consulates Australia, 4, Mattiellistrasse 2–4 (☎512 8580); Canada, 1, Laurenzerberg 2 (☎531 3830); Czech Republic, 14, Penzinger Strasse 11–13 (☎894 3111); Hungary, 1, Bankgasse 4–6 (☎533 2631); Ireland, 3, *Hotel Hilton*, Landstrasse Hauptstrasse 2 (☎715 4246); Slovakia, 19, Armbrustergasse 24 (☎318 9055); Slovenia, 1, Niebelungengasse 13 (☎586 1304); South Africa, 19, Sandgasse 33 (☎322 4693); UK, 3, Jauresgasse 12 (☎713 1575); USA, 9, Bolzmanngasse 16 (☎31339).

Exchange Outside normal banking hours, the exchange booths at the airport (daily 6.30am–11pm), Westbahnhof (daily 7am–10pm) and Südbahnhof (daily 6.30am–10pm) are open. Banks with 24hr automatic exchange machines include Bank Austria, Stephansplatz 2; Creditanstalt, Kärntnerstrasse 7; Die Erste Banke, Graben 21.

Hospital Allgemeines Krankenhaus, 9, Währinger Gürtel 18–20; U-Bahn Michelbeuern-AKH.

Laundries 8, Josefstädter Strasse 59 (tram J or bus #13A); 9, Nussdorferstrasse 80 (tram #37 or #38).

Lost property *Fundamt*, 9, Wasagasse 22 (Mon–Fri 8am–noon); if lost on public transport phone ☎7909-105; lost on Austrian Railways phone ☎5800-32996 or 5800-35656.

Maps Freytag & Berndt, 1, Kohlmarkt 9; U-Bahn Stephansplatz. Flagship store of Austria's most prestigious map-makers, with loads of maps, as well as guides on Vienna and the rest of the world in English, including a large selection of *Rough Guides*.

Markets Naschmarkt, 6 & 7, Linke & Rechte Wienzeile (Mon–Sat); U-Bahn Karlsplatz/ Kettenbrückengasse: Vienna's most exotic fruit and veg market, with Turkish, Balkan, Chinese, Middle Eastern and Austrian produce, take-away stalls plus clothes and sundries. On Saturday mornings, there's a flea market (*Flohmarkt*) extension west of Kettenbrückengasse U-Bahn. Spittelberg, 7, Spittleberggasse (April–June, Sept & Oct every third weekend; Aug & Dec daily); U-Bahn Volkstheater: artsy, craftsy market in the narrow streets of the Spittelberg area.

Police The main police station in the first district is at Deutschmeisterplatz 3.

Post office The main post office is at Fleischmarkt 19 (U-Bahn Schwedenplatz). It's open 24hr, seven days a week.

Soccer Vienna's top soccer team, SK Rapid, play at the Gerhard Hanappi Stadion on Keisslergasse in Hütteldorf (U-Bahn Hütteldorf); FK Austria, their main rivals, play at the Franz Horr Stadion on Fischofgasse in Favoriten (tram #67, three stops from U-Bahn Reumannplatz); big international games are played at the Prater Stadion in the Prater (U-Bahn Praterstern).

Swimming The Amalienbad, 10, Reumannplatz 23 (U-Bahn Reumannplatz) has a wonderful Art-Deco interior, particularly the sauna; the Jörgerbad, 17, Jörgerstrasse 42–44 (tram #43), is also very beautiful inside. The Krapfenwaldbad, 19, Krapfenwaldlgasse 65–73 (bus #38A), is an outdoor pool up in the foothills of the Wienerwald (May–Sept) with great views; so too is the Schafbergbad, 18, Josef-Redl-Gasse (bus #42B).

travel details

Trains

Vienna (Franz-Josefs Bahnhof) to: Eggenburg (hourly; 1hr–1hr 20min); Gmünd NÖ (every 2hr; 2hr–2hr 20min); Klosterneuburg-Kierling (every 30min; 15min); Krems an der Donau (hourly; 1hr–1hr 15min); Tulln (every 30min; 30–45min).

Vienna (Südbahnhof) to: Baden (every 30min; 30min); Bruck an der Leitha (every 30min; 25–35min); Bruck an der Mur (hourly; 1hr 55min); Graz (every 2hr; 2hr 40min); Klagenfurt (every 2hr; 2hr 5min–2hr 25min); Laa an der Thaya (hourly; 2hr); Leoben (every 2hr; 2hr 15min); Mödling (every 15min; 25min); Neusiedl am See (every 2hr; 50min); Semmering (hourly; 2hr); Villach (every 2hr; 4hr 25min–4hr 50min); Wiener Neustadt (every 30min; 50min).

Vienna (Westbahnhof) to: Bregenz (8 daily; 10hr); Feldkirch (8 daily; 7hr 40min); Innsbruck (every 2hr; 5hr 20min); Kufstein (every 2hr; 3hr 15min–3hr 35min); Linz (1–2 hourly; 1hr 50min–2hr); Melk (every 1–2hr; 1hr); Pöchlarn (every 1–2hr; 1hr 15min); St Anton (8 daily; 6hr 45min); St Pölten (1–2 hourly; 40min); Salzburg (1–2 hourly; 3hr–3hr 20min); Wels (hourly; 2hr 10min).

Vienna (Wien-Nord) to: Flughafen Wien-Schwechat (every 30min; 30min); Petronell-Carnuntum/Hainburg Ungartor (hourly; 1hr 5min–1hr 15min); Retz (every 2hr; 1hr 5min).

LOWER AUSTRIA

Lower Austria (Niederösterreich) is by far the largest and most populous of all the Austrian Länder, yet it is also the least explored by tourists. One problem is that, apart from the foothills that form the border with Styria, the landscape doesn't conform to the alpine image of Austria. Most visitors don't come all the way to Austria to roam the gently rolling countryside that characterizes much of Lower Austria, or the unrelenting flat Hungarian *puszta* that extends east of Vienna. Only the famously un-blue Danube, which splits the region in two, attracts tourists in any great number, particularly along the most scenic stretch known as the Wachau, justifiably the most popular destination in the Land.

Lower Austria's other big problem is that it has something of an identity crisis. Along with Upper Austria, it forms the country's historic heartland – together these regions give their name to the entire country. But while Upper Austria has Linz as its regional capital, Lower Austria's natural capital is Vienna. Indeed, Vienna doubled as the regional capital until 1986, when its place was taken by the small provincial town of St Pölten. Vienna still dominates the region, however, and serves as the main transport hub, which means that much of Lower Austria can be easily visited on day-trips from Vienna. However, to do so would be to skim the surface, and to miss out on the slow pace of life that makes the region so appealing.

The **Wachau** is definitely better visited over a couple of days than as a rushed day-trip from Vienna. You could easily spend a whole day just exploring **Krems**, the medieval town that marks the entrance to the valley. From Krems, the river cuts its way through steep, vine-clad hills, emerging some 40km later at **Melk**, whose cliff-top monastery gets more visitors than any other in the country. Both the above places are less than an hour by train from the capital, but to explore the valley's smaller wine-producing villages – something that's possible by road, rail or river – or the cliff-top castles in between, it's worth setting aside a day or two.

Some of the more remote areas are, in any case, simply too far away to be reached comfortably in a day. This is particularly true of the alpine foothills around the mountain spa-resort of **Semmering**, and along the **Ybbstal**, which lies along the southern border with Styria. It's also true of the **Waldviertel**, the little-visited agricultural region in the northwest that's considered something of a rural backwater by most Austrians. The Cold War helped to keep it that way for over forty years, and tourists who do make it here appreciate the region precisely for its soporific qualities and gentle, rural

---

ACCOMMODATION PRICE CODES

All **hotels and pensions** in this book have been graded according to the following price categories. All the codes are based on the rate for the least expensive double room during the **summer season**. In those places where winter is the high season, we've indicated winter room rates in the text. For more on accommodation, see p.30.

① under öS400	④ öS800–1000	⑦ öS1400–1600
② öS400–600	⑤ öS1000–1200	⑧ öS1600–1800
③ öS600–800	⑥ öS1200–1400	⑨ over öS1800

charms. It takes a day or two to get used to the relaxed pace of life in the region's numerous tiny, walled towns, like **Drosendorf** or **Zwettl**, which have changed surprisingly little over the last two hundred years.

The **Wienerwald**, which stretches away southwest of Vienna, is another area that needs to be taken at a leisurely pace, allowing time for a walk in the densely wooded hills: the spa-town of **Baden** or neighbouring **Mödling** are the perfect launching pads. There are, of course, one or two places that can be happily visited on a day-trip, **Wiener Neustadt** being a case in point. Less than an hour by train from Vienna, its attractions are easily covered in a day and its appeal as an overnight stop limited. With a population of just 50,000, the young capital of **St Pölten** is never going to compete on equal terms with Vienna, though it's worth a day-trip if only to look at the new Landhausviertel, built to house the new regional administrative headquarters.

Up the Danube: Klosterneuburg and Tulln

The first place of interest up the Danube from Vienna is the glorious monastery of **Klosterneuburg**, separated from the capital only by a thin wedge of the Wienerwald. Beyond Klosterneuburg, you reach the wide plain of the Tullnerfeld, a patchwork of vineyards and fields of maize and sunflowers, with the hills of Wienerwald becoming ever more distant to the south. **Tulln**, the birthplace of celebrated artist Egon Schiele, is the first stop for boats heading upriver (see box below). Thanks to Austria's efficient public transport system, both the above places make for day-trips from Vienna.

Klosterneuburg

Just north of Vienna's city limits, hidden from the capital by the hills of the Wienerwald, the village of **KLOSTERNEUBURG** is one of the quickest and easiest day-trips from Vienna. Chief attraction is its imposing Augustinian monastery, the oldest and richest in Austria, whose Baroque domes and neo-Gothic spires soar above the right bank of the Danube. It was founded in the twelfth century by the Babenberg Duke Leopold III, who, so the story goes, vowed to build an abbey on the spot where he found his wife's veil, which had been carried off by the wind from a nearby castle. Leopold himself was canonized in 1485, and later became the patron saint of Austria, making Klosterneuburg a popular place of pilgrimage. Having withstood the Turkish siege of 1683, Klosterneuburg enjoyed a second golden age under the Emperor Karl VI (1711–40), who planned a vast imperial palace here, along the lines of the Escorial in Spain. The project was never fully realized, but the one wing that was completed gives some idea of Karl's grandiose plans.

BOATS UP THE DANUBE

On Saturdays and Sundays, from April to October, the Donaudamfschiffahrtsgesellschaft (DDSG) run a daily boat up the Danube from Vienna to Dürnstein. The boat leaves from Vienna's Reichsbrücke at 9am, calling at Tulln at 11.45am and Krems at 2.10pm. DDSG, and several other companies, also run daily sailings along the most picturesque section of the river known as the Wachau, which lies between Krems and Melk. The DDSG boat from Dürnstein calls in at Krems on the way back downstream at 4.35pm, reaching Tulln at 6.20pm, and arriving two hours later in Vienna. These were the correct times at the time of going to print, however, you should check with the local tourist office before setting out. Note that a boat launch in German is a *Schiffsstation*.

The monastery

To reach the monastery, which is clearly visible from the train station, head up Hundskehle, and then take the steps to your left. To go inside, you must sign up for a German-only **guided tour** (Mon–Sat hourly 9–11am & 1.30–4.30pm, Sun 11am & 1.30–4.30pm; Nov–March no 9am tour; öS50); the ticket office is right by the entrance to the monastery at Rathausplatz 20. The tour starts with the **Stiftskirche**, which still hints at its origins as a Romanesque basilica, despite overzealous nineteenth-century restoration. Neo-Gothic finials and other details obscure the west front of the church, but the south door, with its blind arcading, is still much as it would have been in the Babenbergs' day. Inside, the church is a riot of seventeenth-century early Baroque, replete with frescoes and mountains of stucco-work. The most impressive craftsmanship is in the chancel: the richly gilded choirstalls, the exuberant high altar and, above all, Johann Michael Rottmayr's *Assumption*, without doubt the pick of the frescoes.

To the north of the church are the **medieval cloisters**, built at the end of the thirteenth century. The central courtyard is encroached upon, in the southwest corner, by the Freisingerkapelle, a dinky little L-shaped chapel containing the episcopal tomb of its namesake, who died in 1410. More intriguing is the polygonal wellhouse, which juts out into the courtyard from the eastern cloister, and boasts some fine tracery over the portal; the highlight, though, is the magnificent, giant bronze candelabra, crafted in Verona in the twelfth century.

The monastery's outstanding treasure, however, is the **Verdun Altarpiece**, in the Leopoldskapelle to the east of the cloisters. This stunning winged altar, completed in 1181 by Nicholas of Verdun, comprises more than fifty gilded enamel plaques depicting biblical scenes from both Old and New Testaments. Sadly, you can't get close enough to appreciate the detail, but the overall effect is dazzling. The top half of St Leopold is buried in the Wiener Werkstätte casket underneath the altar; his legs are buried beneath the nearby wrought-iron grille.

You can get some idea of the Spanish-bred Emperor Karl VI's big plans for Klosterneuburg from the **Residenztrakt**, to the east of the medieval buildings. Plans were drawn up in 1730 for a vast imperial edifice, enclosing four inner courtyards, in deliberate imitation of the Escorial in Spain, which the Habsburgs had recently lost to the Bourbons. The building was intended to sprout numerous domes, each to be capped by a crown representing one of the Habsburg lands. In the end, the money ran out even before the completion of the first courtyard, and the roof sports just two domes, one capped with the imperial crown, the other with the archducal hat of Niederösterreich. The showpiece of the Baroque wing is the **Marmorsaal** (Marble Hall), with its giant oval dome, supported by coupled composite columns, and decorated with frescoes by Daniel Gran glorifying the Habsburg dynasty.

KAFKA IN KIERLING

While you're in the vicinity of Klosterneuburg, you might be interested to know that the Prague-born writer Franz Kafka died of tuberculosis in Sanatorium Hoffmann (now converted into flats), in the nearby village of **Kierling** on June 3, 1924, at the age of 40. Die-hard devotees can catch a bus from outside the train station to Hauptstrasse 187, and visit the place in which he spent the last few weeks of his life, correcting proofs of his collection of short stories, published as *The Hunger Artist*. The **Kafka-Gedenkraum** (Mon–Sat 8am–noon & 1–5pm; free), on the second floor, is not, in fact, the very one in which he died, as that overlooked the garden and is currently occupied. To gain entry to the room, you must retrieve the key from flat D along the corridor. Inside there are photos of Dora Dyment, who nursed him in his sickness, and whom he intended to marry, and of the old sanatorium, plus lots of books about (and by) Kafka.

After the tour, it's worth taking a stroll round the outlying monastic buildings, particularly those surrounding the **Leopoldhof**, a secluded little cobbled courtyard to the northwest of the monastery church, with an attractive, late-Gothic oriel window on one side. The main courtyard, Stiftsplatz, to the south of the church, centres on a lovely Gothic **Lichtssäule** (Lighted Column), once a common sight in Austrian towns, now a rare, surviving example.

Practicalities

The easiest way to get to Klosterneuburg from Vienna is on S-Bahn line S40; trains depart from Franz-Josefs Bahnhof every half-hour, taking just twelve minutes to get to Klosterneuburg-Kierling (the nearest station to the monastery). If you're peckish, or have time to kill before your tour departs, the *Stiftscafé* (daily 9am–6pm), next door to the monastery, offers reasonable food, and a chance to sample the local wine. The upper floor of the pricier *Stiftskeller* restaurant is open all day, though the Keller itself is only open from 5pm. A much more congenial place to have an evening meal, though, is the *Römerhof*, up the Stadtplatz, at the beginning of Kierlinger Strasse, which offers a range of beers on tap, all the usual pub snacks and a range of *Spätzle* dishes.

It's easy enough to find **accommodation** in Klosterneuburg itself. *Hotel Schrannehof* (☎02243/32072, fax 32072-13; ④), on Niedermarkt, opposite the train station, is a nicely modernized hotel that has retained plenty of original features. For a cheaper option, head for the *Hotel-Pension Höhenstrasse*, Kollersteig 6 (☎02243/52757; ③), which enjoys a quiet location a kilometre or so south of the town centre (and closer to the Klosterneuburg-Weidling train station). The nearest **youth hostel** (☎02243/83501; May–Sept) is about 3km west of Klosterneuburg, beyond Kierling in Gugging; frequent local buses ply the route. The *Donaupark* **campsite** (☎02243/52757; Feb–Nov) is efficiently run, and conveniently located by the Danube, on the other side of the railway tracks from the Klosterneuburg-Kierling train station. If you have any queries, there's a **tourist office** (summer daily 9am–7pm; winter Mon–Fri 9am–noon; ☎02243/32038, fax 86773) in the train station.

Tulln

TULLN, a quiet provincial town situated in the fertile plain roughly 25km northwest of Vienna, has an ancient history dating back to its foundation as the Roman naval fort of Comagena. Its main claim to fame today, however, is as the birthplace of the painter Egon Schiele (1890–1918), who was born above Tulln's main train station, where his father was stationmaster.

The Town

On the hundredth anniversary of the artist's birth, Tulln finally honoured its most famous son by opening an **Egon-Schiele-Museum** (daily except Mon 9am–noon & 2–6pm; öS40) in the town's former prison by the banks of the River Danube. Before you set off round the exhibition, be sure to pick up the free booklet in English from the ticket desk. The ground floor is filled with reproductions of his works, and photographs from his brief life. One of the original cells has been transformed to represent the Neulengbach prison cell in which Schiele was incarcerated for 24 days in 1912. He was charged with displaying erotic drawings in a room open to children, and sentenced to three days in prison (by a judge who was himself a collector of pornography); since he had already served more than that in the course of his remand, he was immediately released. On the walls are reproductions of the watercolours he executed whilst a prisoner, mostly angst-ridden self-portraits and simple interiors of his tiny cell.

The museum's modest collection of Schiele originals is displayed on the first floor. There's a goodly selection of pencil sketches, among them numerous nudes, a ghostly *Madonna and Child* in chalk and an early oil painting from 1908 of Trieste harbour, a favourite destination of the artist, who, as the offspring of an employee of the railways, benefited from cheap train tickets. In the attic, you'll find one of the artist's sketchbooks and the powerfully energetic *Ruined Mill at Mühling*, painted in oil in 1916, when Schiele was employed as a clerk in a POW camp for Russian officers.

The town's brand-new museum complex, the **Tullner Museen** (Wed–Fri 3–6pm, Sat 2–6pm, Sun 10am–6pm; öS30), housed in the former Minorite monastery, three blocks west down Albrechtsgasse, is a bit of a disappointment, despite its stylish new premises. The main courtyard, sporting an elegant glass roof, houses the town's collection of historic fire engines from the horse-drawn carts of the eighteenth century to the diesel monsters of the 1970s. Other displays tell the story of the town's uneventful history, while the basement is given over to the less-than-impressive archeological finds dug up during the renovation of the cloisters. You're better off taking a quick peek inside the adjacent Baroque **Minoritenkirche**, which has been lovingly restored and is positively gleaming with white and gold paint. Be sure to check out the church's sacristy, with its cabinets of inlaid wood and Rococo ceiling decoration, and the brick-built Loreto chapel, a mock-up of Mary's house in Nazareth, complete with obligatory Black Madonna and Child, surrounded by cherubs.

The town's most impressive Roman remain is the bulky **Römerturm**, built under the emperor Diocletian (284–305 AD), on the riverfront beyond the Schiele Museum. Also worth a once-over is the **Pfarrkirche St Stefan**, two blocks east of the main square of

Hauptplatz. Underneath this bulky Baroque church, the original Romanesque basilica can still be seen at ground level. Particularly fine is the west portal, which boasts thirteenth-century mug shots of the apostles. Best of all, though, is the **Karner** (Charnel House) to the east of the church, one of the best-preserved Romanesque buildings in Austria, dating to 1250. The hexagonal rib vaulting looks clumsily restored, but the series of weird and wonderful animals and beasts that decorate the walls, above the blind arcading, are fantastic, as are the devilish characters with outsized ears and noses that accompany them.

Finally, if you've time to kill while waiting for the next train back to Vienna, you might as well visit **Egon Schieles Geburtszimmer** (June–Sept daily except Mon 10am–noon & 3–5pm; öS20), occupying two rooms on the first floor of the main train station (Bahnhof Tulln), which has changed very little since Schiele's childhood. However, there's not a great deal to see beyond a reconstruction of the bedroom in which the artist was born in 1890, and a small model railway – understandably, trains were a major feature of Schiele's childhood, and a few of his early drawings of trains are reproduced here.

Practicalities

Fast trains from Vienna's Franz-Josefs Bahnhof take just 25 minutes to reach Bahnhof Tulln, the **main station**, some fifteen minutes' walk southeast of the town centre. S-Bahn trains depart more frequently, taking 45 minutes, but terminating at Tulln-Stadt, less than five minutes' walk south of the centre. Tulln's **tourist office** (May–Oct Mon–Fri 9am–noon & 2–6pm, Sat & Sun 1–6pm; Nov–April Mon–Fri 9am–noon; ☎02272/5836), on the east side of Minoritenplatz, will furnish you with a free map and can organize **private rooms** for you. By the river to the west of the Tullner Museen, you'll find the town's simple **youth hostel**, called the *Alpenvereinsherberge* (☎02272/2692; May–Oct). Other **accommodation** options are more limited: the venerable *Zur Rossmühle*, Hauptplatz 12 (☎02272/2411, fax 2539; ④), is Tulln's finest hotel, with an attractive plant-strewn interior; the family-run *Römerhof* (☎02272/2954, fax 0663/355989; ③), on Langenlebarner Strasse, is much plainer inside and out, but perfectly comfortable. The town's *Donaupark* **campsite** (☎02272/2954) is set amidst the leisure facilities to the east of the town centre. The best place for a bit of no-nonsense Austrian **food** is the *Albrechtsstuben*, Albrechtsgasse 24, east of Minoritenplatz.

Krems an der Donau

Some 75km northwest of Vienna, **KREMS AN DER DONAU** sits prettily on the terraced, vine-clad slopes of the left bank of the Danube. Site of a twelfth-century Babenberg mint, in the course of the thirteenth century Krems became a wealthy provincial wine-growing town. The architectural fruits of this boom period, which lasted until the seventeenth century, are clearly visible in the narrow streets of the Altstadt. In 1995, Krems' 1000th anniversary prompted a frenzy of much-needed restoration and culminated in the building of a swanky new arts centre and a post-graduate university, which together look set to enhance the town's cultural life.

Krems

Present-day **KREMS** is actually made up of three previously separate settlements, Krems, Und and Stein, giving rise to the side-splitting local joke, "Krems Und Stein sind drei Städte" ("Krems and Stein are three towns"). Most people restrict their wandering to Krems proper, but, in many ways it's Stein that has most successfully retained its medieval character.

KREMS AN DER DONAU

STEIN

Stein-Mautern Train Station

STEINER-WEG

STEINER KELLERGASSE

STEINER KELLERGASSE

Grosser
Passaurhof

Frauenbergkirche

Mauthaus
4
SCHURER-
PLATZ

Pfarrkirche

RATHAUS-
PLATZ

LUDWIG-V.-
KÖCHEL-PLATZ

STEINER DONAULÄNDE

Minoritenkirche
5

Salzstadel

STEINER LANDSTRASSE

Kremser
Tor

Kunst-
Halle-
Krems

DR.-KARL-DORREK-STRASSE

KASERNSTRASSE

i

UNDSTRASSE

STEINER LANDSTRASSE

MEYERECK-STRASSE

REIFBASSE

STEINER DONAULÄNDE

STEINER DONAULÄNDE

7

Schiffsstation

TREPPELWEG

River Danube

ACCOMMODATION

Gästehaus Anna-Maria Rameis	5
Gästehaus Einzinger	4
Gasthof Karl Jell	1
Hotel Alte Poste	2
Hotel am Förthof	3
Hotel unter den Linden	6
Youth Hostel	7

Krems' main thoroughfare, **Landstrasse**, three blocks north of the train station, is a busy, pedestrianized shopping street studded with old buildings. The finest of these is the **Bürgerspitalskirche**, originally built in 1470 on the site of the old Jewish ghetto as the town's hospital chapel. Over the doorway is the AEIOU motto of the emperor Friedrich III (see p.189), while the inside boasts some attractive lierne vaulting. On the opposite side of the street stands the sixteenth-century **Rathaus**, whose Renaissance origins are glimpsed in the corner oriel window facing onto Kirchengasse. Further west along the main street, at Oberer Landstrasse 10, it's worth peeping into the exquisite arcaded courtyard of **Fellnerhof**.

To the north of Landstrasse, the quieter, hilly cobbled streets and squares boast some of Krems' finest late-medieval buildings. The largest of the squares, Pfarrplatz, is dominated by the **Pfarrkirche**, originally a late-Romanesque church, enlarged at the end of the seventeenth century – you can see this most clearly in the tower. The interior is a perfect example of High Baroque drama, with trompe l'oeil masonry and gold covering just about everything, including the entire pulpit and the high altar: an explosion of gilded saints and cherubs set against the background of an enormous sunburst. The ceiling frescoes are by local-born Baroque artist Johann Martin Schmidt, known as "Kremser Schmidt", whose works can be found in churches and museums all over town.

A covered stairway known as the "Piaristen Stiege", on the far side of Pfarrplatz, leads up to the imposing late-Gothic **Piaristenkirche**. The church boasts some fine stellar vaulting, and several Baroque altarpieces by Kremser Schmidt, but it's worth the climb up the stairs, above all, for the stupendous view across town. From here, you can descend via **Hoher Markt**, perhaps the prettiest of Krems' cobbled squares, which slopes down to the wonderfully scruffy-looking **Palais Gozzo**, a honey-coloured medieval palace with a loggia on the ground floor. Round the corner, at Margarethenstrasse 5, is the **Sgraffitohaus**, which, as its name suggests, is smothered in sixteenth-century sgraffito decoration depicting medieval folk frolicking and feasting.

West of Pfarrplatz lies the town's recently overhauled **Weinstadt Museum** (March–Nov Tues 9am–6pm, Wed–Sun 1–6pm; öS40), atmospherically located in the former Dominican monastery on Körnermarkt. Most of the museum amounts to little more than a mildly diverting trot through the history of the town and, in particular, its viticulture. However, you do get the chance look around the thirteenth-century monastery, whose cloisters feature unusual zigzag trefoil arcading, and whose church – now used for temporary exhibitions – is refreshingly free of Baroque clutter and boasts the remnants of its original medieval frescoes. The museum also allows you the opportunity to take a closer look at some of **Kremser Schmidt**'s artworks and sculptures. There's something dark and tortured about Schmidt's work that makes it compulsive viewing. Born in nearby Grafenwörth in 1718, he trained under local artisans and set up his own workshop in Krems, eschewing the cosmopolitan art scene of the capital, and it's this attachment to his provincial roots that sets his work apart from the more academic painters of the Austrian Baroque.

Landstrasse, and the old medieval town of Krems, officially terminate at the strangely hybrid **Steiner Tor**, a monstrously belfried fifteenth-century town gate, flanked by two cone-capped bastions. Appropriately enough, the district of **UND** links Krems, in the east, with Stein, to the west. There's no reason to pause in Und, unless you wish to visit the town's tourist office (see p.148), housed in the former Capuchin monastery. And if you're keen to sample some of the region's wines, you can sign up for a **wine-tasting** tour of the monastery's cellars (daily 11am–7pm; öS130).

Stein

The **Kremsor Tor**, ten minutes' walk west of the Steiner Tor, confusingly, signals the beginning of **STEIN**. As you approach the gateway, it's difficult to miss the **Kunst-Halle-Krems** (daily except Mon 10am–6pm; öS80), the town's vast new arts venue, which hosts major modern art exhibitions, stages shows in the nearby Minoritenkirche (see below) and puts out a series of events on Friday and Saturday evenings.

Stein is much quieter than Krems, its narrow main street, **Steiner Landstrasse**, a sequence of Renaissance town houses and crumbling old facades, opening out every 100m or so into small cobbled squares that face onto the Danube. The first church you come to is the impressive thirteenth-century shell of the **Minoritenkirche**, whose high-vaulted, late-Romanesque interior was used as a tobacco warehouse, and now stages art exhibitions, organized by the Kunst-Halle-Krems. At the southern end of Minoritenplatz stand two sixteenth-century **Salzstädels** (salt barns), sporting the distinctive red-and-white quoins, or cornerstones, that are characteristic of many of Stein's old buildings.

Further along Landstrasse, the Pfarrhof stands out due to its rich Rococo stuccowork, followed shortly afterwards by the Gothic **Pfarrkirche**, which sports a classic Baroque onion dome. Steps round the east end of the church climb sharply to the fourteenth-century **Frauenbergkirche**, now a chapel to Austrian war dead. From here, you get a great view across Stein and the Danube to the domes of the hilltop monastery of Göttweig to the south. It's worth continuing a little further along Steiner Landstrasse to appreciate Stein's two other winsome squares, Rathausplatz and Schürerplatz, and its remarkable parade of Renaissance houses: in particular, the **Grosser Passauerhof**, with its half-moon battlements, and the **Mauthaus**, which boasts faded trompe l'oeil frescoes, and a lovely false oriel with ribbed supports.

Kremser Schmidt lived in the prettily gabled Baroque house close by the squat **Linzer Tor**, which marks the western limit of the old town of Stein. If you're heading back to Krems, the backstreet of Hintere Fahrstrasse provides an interesting alternative to Steiner Landstrasse.

Practicalities

The town's **tourist office** is situated in the former Und monastery, halfway between Krems and Stein at Undstrasse 6 (May–Oct Mon–Fri 9am–6pm, Sat & Sun 10am–noon & 1–6pm; Nov–April Mon–Fri 8.30am–noon & 1.30–5pm; ☎02732/82676, fax 70011). If you want to stay in the centre, then it's worth considering the **private rooms** on offer through the tourist office. Situated one block south is the town's **youth hostel**, Ringstrasse 77 (☎02732/83452; April–Sept), a favourite with passing cyclists. The nearest **campsite** is close by, overlooking the Danube (☎02732/84455; April–Oct), though if you've your own transport the tiny campsite in Senftenberg (☎02719/2319, fax 2319-18; April–Nov), 7km northwest of Krems, is much quieter. Wherever you stay the night, you should ask your hosts for a **Gästepass**, which costs nothing but allows you small discounts at various places – from swimming pools to museums – in Krems and elsewhere in the Wachau–Niebelungengau area of the Danube Valley.

Hotels and pensions

Gästehaus Anna-Maria Rameis, Steiner Landstrasse 16 (☎02732/85169, fax 85169-8). Modernized sixteenth-century house in Stein, with a pleasant inner courtard; rooms with or without en-suite facilities. ②.

Gästehaus Einzinger, Steiner Landstrasse 82 (☎02732/82316, fax 82316-6). Another reasonably priced option, situated in a converted Renaissance house in Stein, with a beautiful arcaded courtyard. ③.

Gasthof Karl Jell, Hoher Markt 8–9 (☎02732/82345, fax 83952-22). Rooms above an old vintner's at the top of Hoher Markt, with an excellent wine cellar/restaurant. ④.

Hotel Alte Poste, Obere Landstrasse 32 (☎02732/82276, fax 84396). Krems' premier Altstadt hotel, a 500-year-old building with a spacious cobbled and arcaded courtyard, offering reasonably priced and very comfortable en-suite rooms. Closed Jan & Feb. ④.

Hotel am Förthof, Förthofer Donaulände 8 (☎02732/83345, fax 83345-40). Old Biedermeier hotel, to the west of Stein on the banks of the Danube, with a justly famous gourmet restaurant. Traffic noise can be a problem, so choose your room carefully. ⑤.

Hotel unter den Linden, Schillerstrasse 5 (☎02732/82115, fax 82115-20). Perfectly located in the quiet neighbourhood of Und, with a lovely shady *Gastgarten*; cheaper rooms have shared facilities. ③.

Eating and drinking

A convenient place to **eat** in town is *Gozzoburg zu den 3 Raben*, at the bottom of Hoher Markt (closed Tues); at the more upmarket *Graffito*, Margarethenstrasse 5, it's worth trying the house *Nudeln*, while the Turkish-run *Halil*, Pfarrplatz 8, serves decent pizza and pasta. If you're en route from Krems to Stein, the swanky café-restaurant in the Kunst-Halle-Krems is a convenient fuelling point. The *Stadtcafé*, on Südtirolerplatz, overlooking the Steiner Tor, is the town's most Viennese of *Kaffeehäuser*. On a warm, summer's evening, it's worth heading out of town to one of the numerous *Heurigen* in the suburbs and outlying villages: one of the more central is *Erich Hamböck*, Kellergasse 31, in Stein. For some indoor distraction in the evening, the varied programme of events at the Kunst-Halle-Krems is probably your best bet, or, on Friday and Saturday nights, the cellar *Kremser Jazz Club*, at Körnermarkt 13 (closed July & Aug).

Göttweig

As you walk around the upper reaches of Krems and Stein, you're repeatedly treated to tantalizing glimpses of **Göttweig**, the palatial hilltop monastery some 5km south of the Danube. The original monastery, founded by the bishop of Passau in the eleventh century, was destroyed by fire in 1718; the imposing Baroque complex you see today is the partial realization of an even more grandiose plan by Johann Lukas von Hildebrandt. To get to see the interior of the monastery, you must join a guided tour (April–Oct daily 10 & 11am, 2, 3 & 4pm; öS55), in German only, lasting 45 minutes.

Even if you don't fancy the guided tour, you're free to visit the pastel-pink **Stiftskirche** (daily 6am–noon & 1.15–6.15pm), which overlooks the manicured lawns of the main courtyard. The church's Tuscan loggia, flanked by two symmetrical square towers, adds a Palladian touch to the unfinished exterior. Inside, the church is a bit of a mess: Gothic in scale, clumsily converted to Baroque, and then given a dubious pink-and-blue colour scheme in the nineteenth century. The richly gilded Baroque furnishings are the most attractive feature, particularly the inlaid choirstalls, topped by gilded filigree, and the main altarpiece, flanked by turquoise and gold barley-sugar columns. Note, too, the thoroughly upstaged, but surviving medieval stained-glass windows above the main altar.

Guided tours begin with Göttweig's most celebrated Baroque masterpiece, Hildebrandt's light and airy **Kaiserstiege** (Imperial Staircase), which boasts spectacular views north to Krems. The staircase is lined with pilasters featuring wonderful atlantes, wrestling with their togas, in the place of capitals, and niches containing urns, symbolizing the twelve months, and statues representing the four seasons, all by Kremser Schmidt. Completed in just four months, the ceiling fresco by Paul Troger glorifies the emperor Karl VI, who looks slightly ludicrous in the guise of the sun-god Apollo in his heavenly chariot. The best of the rest of the state rooms, which host changing exhibitions taken from the abbey's treasury and art collection, is the **Altmannsaal**, the former banqueting hall, in which feasting guests would have been observed in turn by the guests partying on the trompe l'oeil balcony of the *Wedding at Cana* ceiling fresco.

To get to the monastery, you can either catch one of the infrequent buses from Krems, or take the train to Klein-Wien (every 2hr; 10min), from which it's a stiff, but pretty, kilometre-hike through the woods. The *Stiftsrestaurant*, in the grounds of the monastery, serves traditional fare and has a terrace looking north to the Danube; down in Klein-Wien, the *Landgasthof Schickh* (☎02736/7218, fax 7218-7; ④), next to the train station, has a rather more adventurous (and expensive) menu, featuring lobster and crayfish, and an old train carriage for a café.

The Wachau

Krems marks the beginning of the most picturesque, tortuously winding stretch of the Danube, known as the **Wachau**. Vine-bearing, ruin-encrusted hills roll down to the river on both sides, and in springtime the banks are a mass of apricot blossom. Marking the upstream end of the Wachau is **Melk**, arguably Austria's most spectacular monastery, a stunning Baroque confection that towers over the town and river below, and which merits its own separate section (see p.154). Inevitably, given the above attractions, the Wachau – less than 40km in length – is by far the most popular section of the river, and, indeed, the most heavily touristed bit of Lower Austria.

To really appreciate the joys of the Wachau, you need to travel slowly, preferably by bike, boat or train, rather than by car. Bike is by far the most popular mode of transport for visitors of all ages, with a well-marked **cycle path**, the *Donauradweg*, linking all the villages north of the river. A single-track rail line also hugs the northern bank, stopping at every village along the way. Finally, there are frequent sailings along this stretch of the **Danube**; for more details pick up a leaflet from one of the tourist offices. Although there are no bridges over the river between Mautern and Melk, there are numerous little boats, known as *Rollfähre*, attached to high wires stretched across the Danube, which carry cars, bicycles and pedestrians from one side of the river to the other.

Dürnstein

The tiny, walled town of **DÜRNSTEIN**, 9km upstream from Krems, is probably the most photographed spot in the Wachau, thanks to the beautiful ice-blue and white Baroque tower that overlooks the river. Its one other great claim to fame is that the English king Richard the Lionheart was imprisoned in the castle above the town, and escaped thanks to the perseverance of his minstrel, Blondel (see box, p.152). This has guaranteed a steady trickle of English-speaking tourists since tourism first began, and is now fairly shamelessly exploited by the town.

Dürnstein's pretty little main street, Hauptstrasse, is peaceful and pedestrian-friendly. To get to the **Stiftskirche** (daily 9am–noon & 1–5pm; öS20) of the former Augustinian monastery, head south off Hauptstrasse to Klosterplatz. Once you've bought your ticket, cross the rather nasty mustard-and-grey main courtyard, and turn left through the ornate ceremonial portal, whose obelisks, symbolizing eternity, are echoed in the church's trademark main tower. The interior is less richly decorated, except around the high altar, with its unusual tabernacle, featuring a large golden globe embellished with reliefs. Instead of frescoes, the church's vaulting is adorned with delicate, plain white stucco reliefs of scenes from the New Testament. To get a closer look at the famous tower, walk out onto the terrace overlooking the river.

The **Burgruine**, in which Richard is alleged to have been kept prisoner, is a stiff fif-teen-minute climb up the steps that lead off beside the Steiner Tor. Founded in the eleventh century, it was trashed in 1645 during the Thirty Years' War by the passing Swedish army, and is now nothing to shout about. The view from the top, however, is quite stunning, the richly decorated church tower perfectly contrasting with the deep green foliage of the south bank of the river, with Göttweig and Weissenkirchen both vis-ible in the distance.

The train station is just east of the Altstadt; close by is the tourist office (April–Oct Thurs–Sat 2–6pm; ☎02711/219, fax 442), with a free phone from which you can book accommodation. Hauptstrasse is lined with private rooms (look out for "Zimmer frei" signs) and pensions. *Pension Altes Rathaus* (☎02711/252; ③) is a lovely sixteenth-century sgraffitoed building with an inner courtyard at Hauptstrasse 26; *Pension Böhmer*, (☎02711/239; ③), at no. 22, is another good bet. You can also stay in some considerable luxury at the excellent, family-run *Gasthof Sänger Blondel* (☎02711/253, fax 253-7, ⑤), a

THE KIDNAPPING OF RICHARD THE LIONHEART

During the Third Crusade, the English **King Richard I** managed to upset several of his fellow crusaders, one of whom was the Babenberg Duke Leopold V, whose standard Richard uprooted and threw in a ditch at the siege of Acre, in 1191. It was an action he lived to regret, for on his way home, the following year, he was shipwrecked in the Adriatic, and forced to travel incognito across Babenberg territory. Despite growing a beard and travelling under a false name, Richard attracted attention to himself on several occasions: either due to his good looks, by throwing his money around carelessly, or because of the splendour of his gloves. He was eventually arrested at an inn in Erdberg (now a suburb of Vienna), imprisoned in Dürnstein and ransomed by Leopold.

Here the tale falters and legend takes over, as Richard's loyal French minstrel, Blondel, wanders through the land looking for his master. Having made it to Dürnstein, Blondel, according to one version of the tale, "called to mind a song which they had made between them two and which no one knew save the king". On hearing the tune, Richard joined in, and Blondel returned to England to break the news. Two English knights then arrived, paid the ransom and delivered Richard back to England, where he got a distinctly cool reception from his brother John, who had already announced his death. Some chroniclers even suggest that it was at Dürnstein that Richard got his nickname "Lionheart". So the story goes, a hungry lion was set loose on the king after it was discovered that he had seduced the daughter of the jailer. Undaunted, Richard wrapped his cloak around his arm and thrust it down the lion's throat, tore out its heart and ate it.

In the end, though, it was Richard who had the last laugh in his feud with Leopold. He got his revenge by complaining to the pope, who promptly excommunicated Leopold for harming a "Soldier of Christ". As if that weren't enough, poor Leopold fell off his horse a few days later and broke his leg in such a way that it needed amputating. No surgeon was willing to do the job, so Leopold himself took an axe to it and chopped it off in three blows. Unfortunately, it was too late, and Leopold died before he could make it up with the Vatican.

---

pretty, wisteria-strewn villa overlooking Klosterplatz, and, at a considerable cost, at the town's seventeenth-century riverside *Neues Schloss* (☎02711/212, fax 351; ⑨), which has its own sauna and pool.

Food at the *Sänger Blondel* (closed Mon), where main dishes are öS150 or more, is superb; *Goldener Strauss*, Hauptstrasse 18, offers simpler dishes for öS85 and upwards. The *Alter Klosterkeller* (closed Tues), set in the vineyards on Anzuggasse, just east of the Altstadt, is the town's most popular *Heuriger*.

Weissenkirchen in der Wachau

Nowhere else in the Wachau enjoys quite the same idyllic situation as Dürnstein, but the wine-producing village of **WEISSENKIRCHEN**, 6km upstream, has even more charm and character. Set back slightly from the river amidst sloping vineyards, its narrow matrix of streets is centred on a small cobbled square, overlooked by the eye-catching, pink sixteenth-century Teisenhoferhof, whose pretty little arcaded courtyard, hung with vines and corn on the cob, is home to an eighteenth-century winepress and the **Wachaumuseum** (April–Oct daily except Mon 10am–5pm; öS20). Amidst folk artefacts from the region and Romantic nineteenth-century landscape paintings of the Wachau, there are several works by Kremser Schmidt, including some Bacchanalian etchings and a rare self-portrait of the artist and his family. A covered stairway leads up from the square to the Gothic **Pfarrkirche**, which rises up above the town's terracotta jumble of rooftops, and was fortified against the Turks in 1531. A couple of superb Gothic statues, in particular an artless fifteenth-century *Pietà*, adorn the interior, and there's a tiny modern statue, *Schmerzensmann* (Grieving Man), in a niche on the south side of the church's smaller tower, sculpted in 1990 by a Bavarian priest.

There are some picturesque places to **stay overnight** in Weissenkirchen, most notably the *Raffelsbergerhof* (☎02715/2201, fax 2201-27; ⑤; May–Oct only), an old arcaded sixteenth-century shipmaster's house filled with antiques, and with a lovely garden out the back. The **tourist office** (April–Oct Mon–Sat 10am–noon & 4–7pm), in the Teisenhoferhof, can give you the full rundown. The Teisenhoferhof is also part of the *Ludwig Stüberl*, an unpretentious inn where you can eat and drink for very little.

Spitz an der Donau

Another 6km brings you to **SPITZ AN DER DONAU**, a larger and more disparate village. Like most in the region, it makes its money nowadays from a combination of viticulture and tourism. Less than a century ago, however, the river would have played a much more important part in local life, through fishing and as a means of transport, a story told in more detail by the **Schifffahrtsmuseum** (April–Oct Mon–Sat 10am–noon & 2–4pm, Sun 10am–noon & 1–5pm; öS40), housed in an old Baroque mansion, up the road to Ottenschlag, and once owned by a wine-producing monastic order. Amidst the old oars, winches and boats, there's an instructive model showing how, before the advent of steam, three large barges needed a team of more than forty horses to pull them upriver. The building itself is quite something, too, retaining several fancy stone doorways and fine stucco ceilings. Spitz's **Pfarrkirche** is also worth seeking out, primarily for its remarkable parade of fourteenth-century sculptures of Christ and the apostles.

Spitz's **train station** is in the north of the village, near the Pfarrkirche, and rents out bikes. The local **tourist office** (April–Oct Mon–Sat 11am–noon & 3–8pm, Sun 3–7pm), by the car ferry, can book **private rooms** for you. Alternatively, the late-nineteenth-century **hotel** *Haus Prankl* (☎02713/2323; ③), on the southern edge of the village, is a good choice for an overnight stay, as is the family-run *Wachauerhof* (☎02713/2303, fax 2403; ④), on Hauptstrasse. Either of these places will also fill you with unpretentious, inexpensive local food.

Aggstein and Maria Langegg

By far the most awesome of the numerous ruined castles that crown the hills of the Wachau is **Aggstein**, perched some 300m above the right bank of the Danube, some 5km south of Spitz (where you need to cross the river). Built in the twelfth century, and sacked by (among others) the Turks, the castle was, as Patrick Leigh Fermor calls it, a "gap-toothed hold of the Kuenringers" – a family of robber-barons who used to mug passers-by. The place is not entirely in ruins, retaining large parts of the outer defences intact and a keep, up which you can climb for an incredible view down to the Danube. The old castle kitchens now serve as a simple summertime café-restaurant, with tables outside in the main courtyard.

If you're up for it, it's only 3km by foot (and about 7km by road) inland from Aggstein to the Baroque pilgrimage church of **Maria Langegg**, nothing special to look at from the outside, but a feast of trompe l'oeil painting inside. Not only do the ceiling frescoes play tricks on the eye with their perspective, but the paintings along the north and south walls are framed by illusionistic side altars; ditto the impressive high altar, whose medieval *Madonna and Child* is set within a putti- and cloud-spattered sunburst. As you leave, note the delightful Rococo organ, with its delicate gold filigree and giant clock suspended between the organ pipes.

Melk

Strategically situated at the western entrance to the Wachau, some 40km upstream from Krems, the town of **MELK** boasts by far the most spectacular Baroque monastery in Austria. Dramatically perched on a high granite bluff overlooking the Danube, the palatial mustard-yellow abbey dominates the landscape from whichever direction you approach, dwarfing the town into insignificance. Initially a Roman border post and later a tenth-century Babenberg fortress, the site was handed to the Benedictines in 1089. Very little of the medieval structure survives; what draws in a staggering half a million tourists a year is the flamboyant Baroque pile built in its place in the first half of the eighteenth century.

Stift Melk

Melk's early renown was based on its medieval scholarship (discussed in some detail in Umberto Eco's monastic detective story *The Name of the Rose*), and its possession of some very valuable relics, including the body of the Irish missionary St Koloman, who was revered for his powers of healing. The abbey was gutted by fire during the Turkish invasion of 1683, and lay in ruins until Melk's ambitious abbot Berthold Dietmayer commissioned local architect Jakob Prandtauer to design a new showpiece **monastery**. The project was so overblown that Dietmayer initially faced a rebellion by his own monks, and the abbot had to prove that the monastery could afford the work before building could recommence. The abbey continues to function today, with around 34

ACCOMMODATION
Goldener Stern 1
Hotel Stadt Melk 2
Weisses Lamm 3
Youth Hostel 4

monks (only half of whom are resident); the monastery school, with some seven hundred boys and girls, remains one of Austria's most prestigious academic institutions.

Access to the **Stift** (Palm Sunday–May & Sept–early Nov 9am–5pm; May–Sept 9am–6pm; early Nov–Palm Sunday guided tours only 11am & 2pm) is via the main gates to the east. You can walk through several of the courtyards and take a peek at the abbey church without paying, but to see inside the monastery, you must buy a ticket (öS50 without a guide, öS65 with a guided tour) at the top of the Kaiserstiege in the southwest corner of Prälatenhof (the second courtyard), or from the monastery's information point on the south side of the Vorhof (the first courtyard).

The Kaisergang, Marmorsaal and Bibliothek

The **Kaisergang**, at the top of the Kaiserstiege, is a vast gallery – over 190m in length – designed to provide access to the 88 imperial chambers, some of which now house the abbey museum. Unfortunately, the abbey's most precious trio of treasures is only sporadically on public display, and is usually just represented by photographs: the Melker Kreuz, a fourteenth-century cross, containing a piece of Christ's cross and studded with aquamarines, pearls and gems; the eleventh-century portable altar of Swanhild, portraying the life of Christ in walrus horn; and a thirteenth-century reliquary of the lower jaw and tooth of St Koloman. The only work of art from the museum that you can be sure of seeing is the winged altarpiece from around 1502 by Jörg Breu the Elder, one of the "Danube School" of artists that included Lucas Cranach the Elder and Albrecht Dürer. The altar panels tell the story of Christ, employing the exaggerated facial expressions that were the hallmark of the Danube School.

The rest of the abbey museum, which is basically a propaganda exercise by the monastery and its school, can be happily passed over in order to reach the two rooms by Prandtauer that make the visit to Melk worth the effort. The first is the red-and-grey **Marmorsaal** (Marble Hall), featuring Paul Troger's superb fresco depicting the Enlightenment. Troger specialized in fresco paintings, and his masterly handling of perspective makes the ceiling appear much higher than it really is. Despite its name, the only furnishings in the hall made from real marble are the doorframes. To get to Prandtauer's **Bibliothek** (Library), you must first take a stroll outside across the curvaceous terrace, from whose balcony you can admire the the town below and the Danube in the distance. The library's ancient tomes – re-bound in matching eighteenth-century leather and gold leaf – are stacked up to the ceiling on beautifully carved shelves of aspen, walnut and oak. Troger's colourful fresco – a cherub-infested allegory of Faith – has kept its original hue thanks to the library's lack of lighting and heating. From the library, you descend a cantilevered spiral staircase to the Stiftskirche.

Stiftskirche

The **Stiftskirche**, designed by Jakob Prandtauer in 1702 and completed in 1738 after his death, occupies centre stage at Melk, dominating the monastery complex with its fanciful symmetrical towers and octagonal dome. From the balconies above the side altars to the acanthus-leaf capitals of the church's fluted pilasters, the red stucco interior drips with gold paint. The Galli da Bibiena family of Italian theatrical designers is responsible for the stunning all-gold pulpit, and the design of the awesome high altar with its gilded papal crown suspended above the church's patron saints, Peter and Paul. The airy frescoes and side-altar paintings are mostly by Johann Michael Rottmayr, who, along with Troger, was responsible for importing High Baroque art to Austria from Italy.

It's impossible not to notice the grisly reliquaries that lie in the church's side altars, some of them featuring full-scale skeletons reposing in glittering garments. However, the most hallowed bones, those of St Koloman (presumably not including his jaw), are hidden away from the public gaze inside the sarcophagus in the north transept. Beyond this lies the entrance to the **Babenbergergruft**, where the remains of the long line of Babenberg rulers were traditionally thought to have been buried. In 1969, however, the remains were exhumed and examined, after which it was concluded that only Adalbert (1018–55), Ernst (1055–75) and possibly Heinrich I (994–1018) were actually interred here.

The Altstadt

Melk's **Altstadt** is hardly much bigger than the monastery, and, inevitably, with such enormous numbers of tourists passing through, it suffers from overcrowding. However, there are a few good-looking buildings that repay a stroll around the town. Pretty painted shutters adorn the chemist's, next door to the **Rathaus**, and there are a couple of dinky turrets on the old bakery at the corner of Sterngasse, but the single most attractive structure is the **Altes Posthaus**, built in 1792, at Linzerstrasse 3–5. The facade features stucco reliefs of horses' heads, agricultural tools, an eagle holding a post horn in its beak and so on, while the roof balustrade is dotted with urns spouting golden cacti and, as its centrepiece, a double-headed crowned eagle. For a glimpse of old Melk that few tourists get to see, seek out the vine-covered **Haus am Stein**, set back in its own courtyard behind Kremser Strasse.

Practicalities

Melk's **train station** is at the head of Bahnhofstrasse, which leads directly into the Altstadt. If you're travelling by train along the other bank of the Danube, the nearest station is Emmersdorf an der Donau, a walk of 3km from Melk. The **tourist office**, on Abbe-Stadler-Gasse (April–Oct Mon–Sat 9am–7pm, Sun 10am–2pm; Nov–March Mon–Fri 9am–noon & 1–4pm; ☎02752/230732), can book **private rooms** for you, though most are out of the centre. Most folk come to Melk on a day-trip, so **hotel** prices, even in the Altstadt, are surprisingly reasonable. The *Goldener Stern*, Sterngasse 17 (☎02752/3390; ②), offers clean doubles with shared facilities, and serves reliable pub food on a pleasant terrace, while the *Weisses Lamm*, Linzerstrasse 7 (☎02752/4085; ②), has simple rooms with shower and toilet. Rooms at the back of the plush *Hotel Stadt Melk*, Hauptplatz 1 (☎02752/2475, fax 2475-19; ④), have views onto the abbey, and all are fully en suite; the hotel also has the town's finest restaurant, and a sauna. In addition to the *Goldener Stern,* a good local to go to for lunch is *Gasthaus Melkerstüberl*, slightly off the tourist track at Wienerstrasse 7, with a three-course Tagesmenü for öS95.

Melk's **youth hostel** is just ten minutes' walk from the tourist office, at Abt Karl-Strasse 42 (☎02752/2681, fax 4257; March–Oct). A similar distance in the opposite direction is the town's **campsite**, *Melker Camping* (☎02752/3291; March–Nov), adjacent to the *Schiffsstation* on the Danube.

Schallaburg

Schloss Schallaburg (May–Oct Mon–Fri 9am–5pm, Sat & Sun 9am–6pm; öS80), 4km south of Melk, is a popular day-trip: you can even get a discount **Kombi-Karte** (öS115) covering entry to the castle and the monastery at Melk. Part ruined medieval keep, part Renaissance chateau, the building is a strange hybrid. Its most celebrated (and much-photographed) treasure is the unusual, and strikingly beautiful, terracotta arcading in the **Grosser Arkadenhof**. Each pillar is richly decorated with atlantes and caryatids, each spandrel with cartouches, and each keystone with grotesques, while slightly comical busts emerge from along the entablature. Unfortunately, nothing else in the Schloss can quite compete with this sixteenth-century Italianate masterpiece, though the exhibitions staged within the castle are usually excellent. Buses to Schallaburg are pretty infrequent, however; hiring a bike from Melk station is a more sensible idea.

The Danube beyond Melk

The **Danube Valley west of Melk** can't hope to compete scenically with the magic of the Wachau, though the hillier north bank tries hard enough, boasting the spectacularly sited pilgrimage church of **Maria Taferl**, and numerous other riverside castles along the way. The noble seat that receives the greatest number of tourists is **Artstetten**, resting place of the ill-fated Archduke Franz Ferdinand and his wife, Sophie Chotek, who were assassinated at Sarajevo in 1914. The only other truly compelling sight along the river is **Pöchlarn**, the pretty little town where Oskar Kokoschka (1886–1980) was born.

Artstetten

While the rest of the Habsburg dynasty lie in Vienna's Kaisergruft, the Archduke Franz Ferdinand (1863–1914) is buried in a private chapel beneath the majestic, onion-domed **Schloss Artstetten** (April–Oct daily 9am–5.30pm; öS50), 10km west of Melk, on the opposite bank of the river. The reason for this lies in the archduke's morganatic marriage to Sophie Chotek, which he embarked upon in 1900 against the wishes of his uncle, the emperor Franz-Josef I. As crown prince, and heir to the imperial throne, Franz Ferdinand was expected to marry a princess of royal blood, not a mere countess,

---

NIBELUNGENLIED

The stretch of the Danube between Melk and Persenbeug is known as the Nibelungengau, after the **Nibelungenlied**, the great epic German poem, written around the end of the twelfth century, and based on Scandinavian legends about the destruction of the Burgundian kingdom by the Huns in the fifth century AD.

Nibelung himself was the mythical king of Nibelungenland (Norway), who, along with his twelve paladins, all giants, guarded a mythical hoard of treasure. Siegfried, prince of the Netherlands and hero of the first part of the poem, kills Nibelung and the giants and gains possession of the hoard, which he gives as a dowry to his new wife Kriemhild of Burgundy. Siegfried then helps Kriemhild's brother, Gunther, King of Burgundy, to gain the hand of Brunhild of Iceland. This is no simple task as Brunhild has announced that she will only marry a man who can beat her at the javelin, shot put and long jump. Siegfried, who rather handily possesses a cloak of invisibility, helps Gunther to cheat and therefore marry Brunhild. After the marriage, Kriemhild tells Brunhild how Siegfried aided Gunther. Brunhild, furious, gets Gunther's retainer (and the big baddy of the poem), Hagan, to murder Siegfried, grab the treasure, and bury it in the Rhine. The plan is to recover it later, but by the end of the poem everyone's dead, so the treasure is lost for ever. The second part of the poem tells of Kriemhild's subsequent marriage to Attila the Hun (known as Etzel in the poem). She invites the Burgundians en masse to the Hunnic court, where Hagan, rather rudely, kills Etzel's son. Kriemhild then decapitates Gunther and Hagan with her own hands, but is herself killed by Old Hildebrand of Bern, who is horrified by her behaviour.

Thanks to Wagner, whose *Ring* cycle is based on a version of the tale, most people associate the myths with the Rhine Valley, though much of the action, in the second part of the poem, takes place along the Danube, as first Kriemhild, and then Gunther, Hagan and the rest of the Burgundians, travel en route to meet Etzel. (Most people also think of the Nibelungen as dwarfs, although in the myths the term is used for whoever possesses the treasure). The topography in the poem is pretty vague, but Pöchlarn (dubbed Nibelungenstadt by the local tourist authorities) features as the residence of Margrave Rüdiger, who puts on a four-day feast for Kriemhild and her entourage "in colored tents all over the meadows", and escorts her to her meeting with Etzel, downriver at Tulln, where he "allowed not the king to caress his bride in secret".

like Sophie, who ranked lower than more than thirty archduchesses (she had even been lady-in-waiting to one of them). As a result, Sophie was forbidden to accompany her husband to any official court function, including the court opera and theatre; at official banquets, her place was laid, but remained unoccupied. As a result of this rigid and humiliating court protocol, the archduke and his family spent as little time as possible in Vienna, preferring instead to hole up in their Bohemian properties and, to a lesser extent, in Schloss Artstetten.

Apart from the wonderful majolica-clad bathroom (c.1869), very little of the chateau's original decor remains. Instead, the rooms now house the exhaustive and somewhat sycophantic **Franz Ferdinand-Museum**, which includes the archduke's *Schussliste*, cataloguing the more than 270,000 wild animals he bagged – everything from pigeons to tigers – during his globe-trotting hunting expeditions (in 1911 alone, he clocked up 18,709 kills). Naturally enough, the museum carefully documents the archduke's final hours in Sarajevo in 1914, when he and his wife, who was allowed to accompany her husband on an official visit for the first time as a special favour, were assassinated by the Bosnian Serb Gavrilo Princip. In the main courtyard, there's a replica of the Gräf & Stift convertible in which they were killed (the original is in Vienna; see p.111). On hearing of the tragedy, the emperor Franz-Josef is alleged to have said: "God will not be mocked. A higher power has put back the order I couldn't maintain." Franz Ferdinand and his wife were refused burial in the Kaisergruft, alongside the rest of the Habsburgs, and now lie in Artstetten's subterranean crypt; every half-hour, visitors are permitted a brief glimpse of the modest marble sarcophagi.

Artstetten is hard to get to without your own set of wheels. The nearest **train station** is 3km away in Klein Pöchlarn, which is linked by ferry to Pöchlarn, on the south bank (see opposite). You can picnic happily in the chateau's English-style gardens, or enjoy a reasonably priced **meal** at the excellent local *Schlossgasthof* (☎07413/8303, fax 8486; ③), which also has large en-suite rooms above it, should you need a **bed** for the night.

Maria Taferl

It's impossible to miss the Baroque pilgrimage church of **Maria Taferl**, which occupies a magnificently ostentatious position high above the Danube, 5km upstream of Klein Pöchlarn. The church gets its name from the *Taferl* (board), containing a crucifix, that was attached to an oak tree that once stood on this spot. In 1633, so the story goes, a local farmer tried to fell the oak with an axe, but succeeded only in hacking both his legs to bits. At this point, he spotted the crucifix, fell to his knees and prayed for forgiveness. His legs were immediately healed and, after several further miracles and apparitions over the course of the next thirty years, the foundation stone of Maria Taferl was eventually laid in 1660. Today, just about every tour group heading along the Danube Valley pauses here at some point, so you're unlikely to have the spot to yourself; but the effort of getting here is amply rewarded both by the stupendous views, and by the church's glorious interior. Although the original cruciform plan survives, the interior was finished off in High-Baroque style by Carlo Lurago and Jakob Prandtauer. The latter is responsible for the central cupola, whose fresco, though not of the highest quality, creates a pleasing overall effect with its trompe l'oeil masonry. There's plenty of gold throughout the church, from the acanthus-leaf capitals to the filigree work on the organ and the particularly fine pulpit. There's also a **Schatzkammer** (May–Oct daily 9am–5pm; öS20) inside the church, containing a copy of the miraculous *Pietà* carved from the original oak tree, not to mention a rain gauge made from the wedding dress of the empress Elisabeth, while the nearby **Mechanische Krippe** (April–Oct daily 9am–5pm; öS10) contains a mechanized Bethlehem scene set beneath a copy of the church.

The nearest train station to the village of Maria Taferl is 3km below the church, in the village of **Marbach an der Donau**. There are numerous places to stay in the village, but you're really much better off back in Artstetten, or across the river in Pöchlarn.

Pöchlarn

PÖCHLARN is a pretty little walled town of winding, narrow streets, which features in the *Nibelungenlied* (see box, p.157), though its chief claim to fame nowadays is as the birthplace of **Oskar Kokoschka**. At Regenburgerstrasse 29, to the west of the Altstadt, stands the house in which the artist was born in 1886 – it was not, in fact, the family home, but a sawmill belonging to one of his uncles – now the **OK-Dokumentation** (May–Sept daily except Mon 9am–noon & 2–5pm; öS30). The courtyard displays reproductions of the artist's most famous works, many of which are scattered around the art museums of the world, but some of which can be seen in the Belvedere in Vienna (see p.107). On the ground floor, the museum puts on temporary exhibitions from its own collection, mostly little-known drawings, sketches and watercolours, but interesting nonetheless. In the attic of the old house, there's also an exhibition (in German only) on Kokoschka's prolific and very long life. Perhaps the most startling exhibit is the bullet that had to be removed from the artist's skull by military surgeons during World War I. Kokoschka left Austria before the end of the war, and from there on led a peripatetic existence, returning only sporadically to his homeland. During the 1930s, he lived in exile in Prague, and later London, eventually becoming a British citizen in 1947. He died at the age of 94 in Montreux, Switzerland.

With regular boats connecting the town with Klein Pöchlarn on the north bank, Pöchlarn makes a good base for exploring the surrounding district. The town's **tourist office** (April–Oct Mon–Sat 9am–5pm; ☎02757/2310), in the Rathaus at Regensburgerstrasse 11, can book **private rooms**. Alternatively, you can **stay** in a simple room, with en-suite shower and toilet, above the pleasant *Futtertrögl* restaurant on Kirchenplatz (☎02757/2395; ②); or opt for the recently modernized, family-run *Hotel Moser* (☎02757/2448, fax 2833; ④), opposite the train station, whose rooms are fully en suite. There's a **campsite** (May–Oct), by the *Schiffsstation*, north of the Altstadt.

St Pölten and around

It's only forty minutes by train from Vienna to **ST PÖLTEN**, but most visitors simply pass through on their way to or from the capital. The biggest town in Lower Austria, with a population of over 50,000, St Pölten is small and provincial at heart – it only really began to expand with the arrival of the railway in 1860. Today, as the new regional capital, or *Landeshauptstadt*, St Pölten is enjoying another period of growth, with a whole new administrative quarter, known as the *Landhausviertel*, currently being built by the banks of the Traisen, in order to accommodate the new regional government offices, which have been in the process of moving here from Vienna since 1986. As well as being an easy day-trip from Vienna, St Pölten is a useful base for exploring the nearby monasteries of Herzogenburg and Lilienfeld, not to mention Melk (see p.154), or for taking a trip on the spectacular railway to Mariazell (see p.235).

The Town

The tourist board have dubbed St Pölten "Barockstadt in Donauland"; something of a misnomer, given that the town is neither overwhelmingly Baroque, nor particularly near the Danube. If anything, St Pölten's most noteworthy piece of architecture is the little-heralded Jugendstil **Stöhr Haus**, a startlingly beautiful building dominated by a grand curvaceous gable, across the road from the train station at Kremser Gasse 41. The relief on the gable depicts a snake drinking from a golden bowl held by a Greek goddess with golden hair, while the rest of the exterior decoration is predominantly vegetal: mini cabbages, gilded berries and green and gold foliage. The house was designed in 1899 by Joseph Maria Olbrich, architect of the Secession building in Vienna (see p.101), for Ernst Stöhr, a local artist, poet and musician who was one of the chief ideologues of the Secession movement.

The town's chief claim to Baroque fame rests with the spectacular interior of its **Dom**, on Domplatz, originally built in the middle of the thirteenth century as the abbey church of the neighbouring Augustinian monastery. The rather dour exterior gives no indication of the exuberant Baroque makeover that took place inside under the supervision of Jakob Prandtauer, the architect responsible for Melk (see p.154), in the first half of the eighteenth century. There's a rich autumnal flavour to the interior, the red, orange, brown and fawn marbling combining with the gilded stucco-work to great effect. The ceiling frescoes in the nave, mainly by Daniel Gran and Bartolomeo

Altomonte, are dramatically framed by trompe l'oeil masonry; the best fresco of the lot is the one above the main altar depicting the archangel and a mob of cherubs smiting the sinful with a bolt of lightning. It takes time to take in the full extent of the rich decoration: the pulpit, smothered in gilded drapery, reliefs and cherubs, is crowned by an entire Crucifixion scene; more frescoes hide in the cupolas of the side aisles; and the organ features a splendid turbaned and gilded statue of David with his harp. The only bit of the medieval cathedral to have survived is the rib-vaulted **Rosenkranzkapelle**, whose capitals are carved with mischievous grimacing faces and strange creatures; the chapel can be reached by an entrance in the middle of the choir stalls.

St Pölten's other Baroque masterpiece is the **Institut der Englischen Fräulein**, on Linzer Strasse, whose light pink palatial facade, thought to be by Prandtauer, is punctuated with fluted white pilasters and niches filled with statuary and crowned by gilded sunbursts. Inside, the tiny Institutskirche, divided into two domed spaces, has been beautifully restored, from its magnolia stucco-work to its Altomonte and Paul Troger frescoes.

After Prandtauer's two masterworks, the town's spacious traffic-free main square, **Rathausplatz**, can't help but be something of a disappointment, despite its recent face-lift. The ubiquitous plague column – an amalgam of clouds, cherubs and saints – and the frothy pink Rococo facade of the Franziskanerkirche are both upstaged by the raspberry-coloured **Rathaus**, built to Renaissance dimensions, but now looking distinctly ill-proportioned in its more recent Baroque dressing. The trawl through the town's history in the nearby **Stadtmuseum** (Tues–Sat 9am–5pm, Sun 9am–noon; öS20), housed in the former Carmelite monastery on Hess Strasse, is also something of a letdown. The changing art exhibitions staged in the museum's "Dokumentationszentrum für moderne Kunst" are occasionally worth a look, but the biggest surprise is the Czech MiG-21 sitting in one of the museum courtyards.

A much better (albeit partisan) account of the town's recent history can be gleaned from the small two-room **Museum am Hof** (Wed, Fri & Sat 9am–noon; free), in the courtyard of no. 4, on the opposite side of the street. Labelling is in German only, but you can get a feel for the town's strong Socialist tradition from the copious photographs and mementoes. If your German's up to it, the old Socialists who run the place will give you eyewitness accounts of many events, and show you the museum's archive footage of the Führer's triumphant drive through the town following the 1938 Anschluss.

There are plans, too, for some kind of permanent exhibition, on the history of the town's Jews, to be housed in the **former synagogue** (Mon–Fri 9am–4pm), southeast of the town centre at Dr-Karl-Renner-Promenade 22. Built in late-Jugendstil style in 1912, the synagogue was damaged by local anti-Semites during *Kristallnacht*, and restored only in the 1980s. Its sheer size is testament to the prewar strength of the local Jewish community, which numbered over four hundred in St Pölten alone. The synagogue is currently home to the Institute for the History of the Jews in Austria, who use the place for various talks and events. If you're interested in seeing the inside of the building, or learning more about the town's Jewish history, ring the bell at the side entrance at Lederergasse 12.

Landhausviertel

More than ten years after its promotion to regional capital status, St Pölten's new **Landhausviertel** (also known as "Regierungsviertel") is finally beginning to take shape on the left bank of the River Traisen, a short walk southeast of the town centre. It's difficult not to be impressed by the sheer aplomb with which this small provincial town has redefined itself. It has to be said, however, that the modern, boxy architecture has a rather grey and cold feel to it, epitomized by the central, glass-covered Landhaus-Boulevard. This is the quarter's commercial zone; though, as with most shopping precincts, it's a soulless place dominated by franchises, with a Billa supermarket slap bang in the middle of the boulevard, as if to underline the point.

All large projects must have their phallic symbol, and the Landhausviertel is no exception. So, for an overview of the whole administrative district, you can ride by glass lift to the top of the 62 metre-tall **Klangturm** (Mon–Fri 9am–6pm, Sat & Sun 2–6pm; öS20), a see-through iron, steel and glass "sound tower", designed by Ernst Hoffmann, that transforms itself into a red- and blue-lighted beacon at night; "sound events" and further attractions are planned for the near future. The shiny stainless-steel- and glass-encased **FestSpielHaus**, designed by Klaus Kada, is another building that looks at its best when lit up at night.

By far the funkiest building in the whole complex, however, is Hans Hollein's **Shedhalle** (Tues–Fri 9am–1pm, Sat & Sun 10am–4pm; öS60), with its distinctive wavy glass canopy held up by giant coloured biros, and its zigzag roof. Eventually, the Shedhalle will be joined by the new Landesmuseum (still in the process of being built), but in the meantime it puts on temporary exhibitions, and gives a taster of what's to come in its warehouse-style main gallery, which displays a sample of the range of the museum's collection, from pickled fish to plastic shoes.

Practicalities

Staff at the **tourist office** (Easter–Sept Mon–Fri 8am–6pm, Sat 9.30am–6.30pm, Sun 1.30–6.30pm; Oct–Easter Mon–Fri only; ☎02742/353354), in the Rathaus, are very helpful, and there's a free telephone outside for booking accommodation – there's another one outside the **train station**.

Given the general absence of tourists in St Pölten, you should have few problems getting a **room**, though there's not much choice if you want to stay close to the centre. *Gasthof Graf* (☎02742/52757; ④), opposite the train station, is convenient and comfortable enough, but the Jugendstil *Hausereck*, Schulgasse 2 (☎02742/73336, fax 78386; ④), has a much cosier atmosphere and is the one to head for. The cheapest options in and around the town centre are *Mariazellerhof*, Mariazellerstrasse 6 (☎02742/76995, fax 76995-8; ③), which has decent enough en-suite rooms, and *Fuchs*, Europaplatz 7 (☎02742/72946; ②), which offers rooms with or without en-suite facilities but is a bit run-down. The nearest **campsite** is the *Freizeitzentrum Megafun* (☎02742/251510; open all year), 3km northeast of the centre by a lake, on the banks of the Traisen.

Traditional local **food** is best eaten at *Weissenbeck*, on Ranzonigasse, which offers a two-course weekday menu for öS75. *Cerny*, a self-service cafeteria on Kremser Strasse, specializes in tasty fish dishes, but lacks atmosphere. For that and excellent Austrian food, head for the *Palais-Restaurant*, situated on the first floor of the Renaissance palace on Riemerplatz, which has a filling three-course fixed menu for around öS180. Equally reliable, though much cheaper, are the pizzas and pasta available at *Pizzeria Duomo*, Wienerstrasse 36 (closed Sun), which also has some Greek dishes on the menu.

St Pölten has a fairly busy **cultural calendar**, especially now that its boasts a state-of-the-art theatre in the FestSpielHaus. The latter's programme is adventurous compared to many Austrian theatres, but is still almost entirely comprised of classical concerts, operas and ballets, with only an infrequent foray into more eclectic styles – more often than not jazz, though even rap or flamenco have been featured. Operettas, musicals, new theatre and children's shows are put on in the Theater der Landeshauptstadt, on Rathausplatz (closed July & Aug). For **nightlife**, it's easy enough to hop on a train to Vienna, though occasionally one-off raves prompt the human traffic into flowing in the opposite direction (look out for flyers in the tourist office).

Around St Pölten

Given that St Pölten's distractions are limited, there's a lot to be said for spending the afternoon visiting one of the nearby monasteries, **Herzogenburg** and **Lilienfeld** (or Melk, see p.154), which are a short train ride away, or the **Schloss Pottenbrunn**, which you can reach easily by local bus or bike. St Pölten is also the starting point for the **Mariazellerbahn**, the spectacular narrow-gauge railway that takes two and a half hours to wind its way south to the Styrian pilgrimage centre of Mariazell (see p.235). Trains run regularly throughout the year, and are occasionally pulled by steam locomotive (pick up a leaflet from the train station to get the current schedule).

Pottenbrunn

The easiest day-trip from St Pölten is **Schloss Pottenbrunn** (May–Oct daily except Mon 9am–5pm; öS50), 6km northeast of the town centre in a former village, now outlying suburb, of the same name. The Schloss itself is a remarkable building, a moated sixteenth-century pile with an arcaded balcony wrapped round the upper floor of the main body of the chateau and the tower. The annual exhibitions staged in the chateau are consistently good, and there's a permanent **Zinnfigurenmuseum**, featuring more than 35,000 tin soldiers, many of them arranged into fifty battle dioramas illustrating various crucial armed engagements in Austrian history, from the 1683 Turkish siege of Vienna to the Battle of Leipzig in 1813, when Prince Karl von Schwarzenberg trounced Napoleon.

Herzogenburg

The remarkable copper-crowned tower of the Augustinian monastery at **HERZOGENBURG** rises majestically out of the flat landscape, 4km north of Pottenbrunn. The bishop of Passau founded the monastery in the thirteenth century, though the current, scruffy-looking, pinky-brown buildings date from the early eighteenth century, when the monastery was completely rebuilt by three of Austria's greatest Baroque architects: Johann Bernhard Fischer von Erlach, Jakob Prandtauer and his cousin Josef Munggenast. To get to see Fischer von Erlach's magnificent **Festsaal**, which contains a vast celestial fresco by Altomonte glorifying the prince-bishops of Passau, the richly stuccoed library and the outstanding Gothic art collection, you must sign up for one of the hour-long guided tours (April–Oct daily 9am–noon & 1–5pm; öS40), in German only.

The **Stiftskirche**, by contrast, is open to all comers, and is, in many ways, the highlight of the monastery. The rich, playful, pink, grey and gold interior is lined with Corinthian columns and pilasters wrapped in spiralling painted garlands, and decorated from top to bottom in trompe l'oeil frescoes, mostly by Altomonte. The nave gradually narrows, forcing your eye to focus on Daniel Gran's main altarpiece, which is crowned by a copper ducal cap and gilded sunburst. As you leave, look up at the wonderful, richly gilded, pastel-green Baroque organ case, within which you should just be able to make out a trompe l'oeil statue of David with his harp.

Saurierpark

If you're looking to entertain your children with something other than Baroque monasteries, visit the **Saurierpark** (March–Oct daily 9am–6pm; öS50), or dinosaur park, 20km or so northeast of St Pölten. Set in shady woodland on the left bank of the River Traisen, the park lies roughly 1.5km from the train station in **TRAISMAUER**; walk through town, cross the river, and head right up Ing. Toder-Gasse. Jurassic Park it's not, but with numerous life-sized fibreglass models of dinosaurs concealed in the undergrowth, it's unlikely to disappoint younger children, who can happily explore the maze of pathways looking for their favourite prehistoric friend.

Lilienfeld

With its beautiful setting amidst forested alpine foothills, the Cistercian monastery in the village of **LILIENFELD**, 20km south of St Pölten, makes for a fine day-trip (you may need to change trains in Traisen). Although from a distance you wouldn't guess it, the abbey retains much of its Romanesque and Gothic architecture, dating back to its foundation in 1202 by Duke Leopold VI. The striking main portal of the **Stiftskirche** is a perfect example of this transitional style; sixteen slender marble columns form what the Austrians call a *Trichterportal* ("funnel portal"), whose arches are very slightly pointed, heralding the beginning of the Gothic style. Inside, the three-aisled basilica features simple quadripartite vaulting and crocket capitals typical of the transitional phase. The matching black-and-gold Baroque furnishings provide a striking contrast to the church's pinkish-white stone; the wooden inlay of the choirstalls is particularly fine, topped by a parade of gilded cherubs and angels. You're free to take a look at the church's interior through iron railings, and explore the monastery's thirteenth-century cloisters, but in order to walk round the church or visit the rest of the monastery – including the Baroque library and the groin-vaulted medieval dormitory – you must sign up for one of the hour-long guided tours (on the hour, Mon–Sat 8–11am & 2–4.30pm, Sun 2–4.30pm; öS40).

The Ötscher and the Ybbstal

The southwest corner of Lower Austria hides the Land's most spectacular, unspoilt scenery, dominated by the region's largest peak, the colossal **Ötscher** (1893m), which provides an impressive snowcapped backdrop as you approach from the north. The chief summer and winter resort here is **Lackenhof**, situated just below the Ötscher. To the west is the peaceful meandering **Ybbstal**, once home to numerous hammer forges, driven by the River Ybbs, and supplied with iron ore from the Styrian town of Eisenerz (see p.239). Nowadays, the Ybbstal's economy relies solely on agriculture, supplemented by a modicum of tourism.

Lackenhof

LACKENHOF, nestling amongst meadows on the west side of the Ötscher, is the region's busiest resort. It's by no means an unattractive or overdeveloped village, but the chief reason for being here is either to go walking or skiing in the surrounding mountains. The longest and most frequent of the various lifts is the Ötscher chairlift (daily: summer 8–11.30am & 1–4.30pm; winter 9am–4pm), to the east of the tourist office, which takes you as far as the *Ötscherschutzhaus* (1420m), from which it's about an hour's hike to the summit, or back down to Lackenhof.

The **tourist office** (daily 8am–noon & 2–5pm; ☎07480/5286, fax 5242) is on the old village square of Lindenplatz, and can help you find a **private room**. You can stay in the simple *Ötscherschutzhaus* (☎07480/5249; ②), at the top of the chairlift; near the bottom of the chairlift, the *Gasthof Schützenwirt* (☎07480/5202, fax 5202-4; ③) is a comfortable but relatively inexpensive option. For a real treat, head for the *Bio-Hotel Jagdhof* (☎07480/5300-0, fax 5300-8; ⑧), a mini health farm where you'll be treated to delicious organic, wholefood cooking. There's also a **campsite** (☎07480/5276; open all year), behind the *Gasthof zur Ötscherwiese*, beyond the chairlift, and a typically efficient and clean **youth hostel** (☎07480/5251, fax 5338; closed April to mid-May & Nov) a short walk north of the tourist office, on Ötscherweg.

Ybbstal

By far the prettiest town in the Ybbstal is **WAIDHOFEN AN DER YBBS**, situated at the northwestern head of the valley. The machicolated tower of the town's neo-Gothic Schloss creates a striking first impression, with several onion domes rising up from the Altstadt beyond. Built around 1407, the castle was saved from dereliction in the 1880s by the Rothschild family, who employed the German Friedrich von Schmidt, architect of the Vienna Rathaus (see p.92), to create a mock-medieval fantasy. It's now home to the local college of forestry and closed to the public. The rest of the Altstadt revolves around two parallel and picturesque squares, Oberer and Unterer Stadtplatz, both lined with handsomely gabled Gothic and Renaissance houses.

Waidhofen is also the starting point for the narrow-gauge **Ybbstalbahn**, which winds its way for more than 40km through the beech- and pine-forested valley to **LUNZ AM SEE**, 14km or so west of Lackenhof. Lunz is a leisurely little village, with a superb sgraffitoed sixteenth-century Rathaus, better known as the **Ammonhaus**, decorated with a frieze featuring Jonah cheerily waving as he's swallowed by the whale. The main activities here are swimming, rowing and sunbathing at the nearby **Lunzer See**, ten minutes' walk east of the village, in whose calm waters the wooded mountainsides are perfectly reflected.

Practicalities

Waidhofen's main **train station** is a fifteen-minute walk north of the Altstadt (bus #1 covers the distance roughly every hour). You'll find the **tourist office** (Mon, Tues, Thurs & Fri 8.30am–noon & 2–5pm, Wed & Sat 8.30am–noon; ☎07442/511255) in the big sixteenth-century stone tower on Platz. *Gasthof zum goldenen Hirschen* (☎07480/52132; ③), on Unterer Stadtplatz, is as good a place as any to hole up, and has a nice atmospheric *Stube* serving inexpensive traditional food. Elsewhere in the Ybbstal, by the church in the village of **Göstling**, 11km before Lunz on the rail line from Waidhofen, is the rustic, vine-clad and highly recommended *Hotel zum goldenen Hirschen* (☎07484/2225, fax 2225-28; ③). In Lunz, the *Hotel zum Zellerhof* (☎07486/5349, fax 5349-20; ④), a sixteenth-century inn on Seestrasse, is a good place to **stay**, with an idyllic inner courtyard and an excellent restaurant, and there's a **campsite** (☎07486/5413; open all year) beside the lake.

The Weinviertel and Waldviertel

The huge swath of Lower Austria that lies between the Danube and the Czech border is probably the least-visited area in the whole country. The northeastern half, the so-called **Weinviertel**, may be the country's agricultural heartland and chief wine-producing region, but its flat, featureless landscape holds little of any great interest to the tourist. The rolling countryside of the **Waldviertel**, to the west, however, has much more to offer. Less forested than its name would suggest, it's a pleasantly undulating region of prettily meandering river valleys harbouring sleepy, but picturesque walled towns. **Retz** and **Drosendorf** are probably two of the most attractive destinations in the Thayatal, hard by the Czech border, while **Eggenburg**, on the edge of the Weinviertel and Waldviertel, is a possible base for the more central **Kamptal**, a valley punctuated by two exceptionally fine monasteries, **Altenburg** and **Zwettl**.

Weinviertel

The only conceivable reason to find yourself in the flat, northeastern corner of the **Weinviertel** is if you happen to be heading for the Czech Republic. The road from Vienna to Brno (Brünn) is a particularly miserable one, with **Poysdorf** the only place of any size – in many ways, you'd be far better off continuing for 15km to Mikulov (Nikolsburg), a much more interesting town on the Czech side of the border. Poysdorf's local cemetery contains a passionate memorial to 120 victims of the **Brno Death March** of May 1945, when the city's 23,000 German-speakers were forced to walk across the border, taking only what they could carry (and no money or jewellery).

The violent expulsion of ethnic Germans from the border regions of Czechoslovakia that took place after World War II is more thoroughly explored in the fascinating **Südmährer Heimatsmuseum** (April–Oct Sun 2–5pm; free), housed on the top floor of the Altes Rathaus, on the main square in **LAA AN DER THAYA**, 22km west of Poysdorf, flush with the Czech border. Laa is also home to Austria's ubiquitous Hubertus Bräu, and the inspiration behind the small **Biermuseum** (May–Oct Sat & Sun 2–4pm; free), located in one wing of the scruffy Schloss, in the northeastern corner of the town. With two giant duty-free shops, situated in no-man's-land within walking distance of the town centre, it's a miracle that there are any shops left at all in Laa. If you need to **stay the night**, there's just the fully en-suite *Hotel zum Brüdertor* (☎02522/8286, fax 8156; ④), on Nordbahnstrasse, or the simple rooms with shared facilities in the *Gasthof Helmut Koffler* (☎02522/2386; ②), on Stadtplatz.

Retz

Another 30km or so west of Laa lies the walled town of **RETZ**, a place of considerable charm, on the border between the Weinviertel and the Waldviertel. The town's showpiece **Hauptplatz** is a beautifully proportioned, sloping, cobbled rectangle, lined with pastel-coloured buildings, among them the salmon-hued sixteenth-century **Verderberhaus**, whose castellated bulk acts as a sort of gateway to the square. At the western end of this vast space is the town's freestanding, ochre-coloured sixteenth-century **Rathaus**, a suitably imposing building with a strikingly tall Renaissance tower. Underneath the Rathaus, you can gain access to the town's vast complex of underground **Weinkeller**, 1km of which you can visit on a guided tour (March–Dec daily 10.30am, 2 & 4pm; öS70). Unfortunately, the rest of the building is only rarely open to the public – the Rococo **Rathauskapelle** for services only; the **Ratsaal**, on the first floor, with its frescoes by Kremser Schmidt, only when the Stadtmuseum (Sun 10am–noon; öS10) is open.

Wandering the backstreets of Retz, you should head for the **Dominikanerkirche**, in the southwest corner of the Altstadt, which sports an exquisite early Gothic stone tympanum over the north door, featuring Mary, Jesus and a fine collection of lions. Inside, particularly fine Baroque and Rococo furnishings include the richly gilded pulpit, replete with cherubim, and the organ loft, from which gold flames appear to be escaping. Retz's most famous monument, though, is its eighteenth-century **Windmühle**, one of the country's few remaining windmills. To reach it, pass under the Verderberhaus and the medieval Znaimer Tor, turn left up Windmühlgasse, and follow the signs up through the vineyards.

Practicalities

The **tourist office** (April–Oct daily 9am–noon & 1–5pm; ☎ & fax 02942/2700), at no. 30 in the northeastern corner of the square, can book private rooms, though none are actually in the Altstadt. The two other **accommodation** possibilities in Retz are the *Althof Retz* (☎02942/3711-0, fax 3711-55; ⑤), a nicely converted castle hotel in the northwest of town – whose restaurant offers a very reasonable Mittagsmenü for öS85 – and the more modest en-suite rooms above the *Gasthof zum weissen Löwen* (☎02942/2418; ③), on Hauptplatz. The nearest **campsite** is *Hubertus Campingplatz* (☎02942/3238; open all year), 4km towards the Czech border in the village of Ober-Retzbach.

If you want to sit outside and admire the square, head for the *Cyrill Blei* **café**, attached to an old established bakery, right by the tourist office. A good place to sample the **local wines** is at the *Vincenz Liebl* bar on Klostergasse, while for inexpensive Austrian **food**, you'll find most main dishes well under öS100 at *Gasthaus Brand* on Windmühlgasse (closed Wed & Sun evening). Lastly, for a daytime or night-time meal or drink, it's worth checking out the *Schlossgasthaus* (closed Mon), which occupies one wing of the peeling, ivy-covered Schloss Gatterburg, in the southeastern corner of the Altstadt.

Retz is only 5km from the Czech border, and twenty minutes by train from Znojmo (Znaim); the **train station** is ten minutes' walk southeast of Hauptplatz. If you're **driving into the Czech Republic**, you must use the Kleinhaugsdorf–Hatĕ crossing, not the Mitteretzbach–Hnanice crossing, which is for Czech and Austrian passport holders only.

Hardegg

To the northwest of Retz, the wiggling River Thaya briefly marks the Czech–Austrian border. At the heart of this wonderful, woody gorge studded with rocky outcrops is the peaceful little town of **HARDEGG**, hard by the Czech border. It's a landscape full of drama, made all the more so by the forbidding presence of the town's medieval **Burg** (April to mid-Nov daily 9am–5pm; öS50), which occupies the highest bluff of all, splitting the town in two. Built in the eleventh century, the castle was partially restored in the late nineteenth century by Johann-Carl von Khevenhüller-Metsch, loyal companion of the **emperor Maximilian of Mexico** (1832–67), who is the subject of the castle museum. Younger brother of Franz-Josef, Maximilian foolishly accepted the offer of the throne of Mexico in 1864. Even more unwisely, he proceeded to alienate his conservative supporters by refusing to repeal the liberal reforms passed by Juárez, and was eventually executed by firing squad some three years later. There's a model of the *Novara*, in which he set sail for Mexico, a copy of Max's heavy, gilded imperial crown, and photos of Khevenhüller's funeral, which took place in Hardegg in 1905 (he's buried in the family vault underneath the castle's lovely stellar-vaulted chapel).

During the Cold War, Hardegg had to endure an uncomfortable proximity with the Iron Curtain. Nowadays, pedestrians and cyclists can cross the reopened **Thayabrücke** (mid-April to Oct daily 8am–8pm) and enjoy a day exploring the Podyjí National Park on the Czech side. If you set out early enough, you could make it all the way to Vranov nad Dyjí (Frain) and back, a journey of about 16km. There are one or two weekday buses from Retz to Hardegg, though you might be better off hiring a bike or walking. There are a few **private rooms** available in Hardegg, one simple pension, *Gasthof Hammerschmiede* (✆ & fax 02949/8263; ②), and a tiny **campsite**, *Waldbad Hardegg* (✆02949/8450; June–Aug), next door to the local swimming pool.

Geras

GERAS, 20km southwest of Hardegg, is a small town dominated by its palatial, magnolia-painted Premonstratensian abbey, which was founded around 1150 but entirely rebuilt in the Baroque period by Josef Munggenast. Unfortunately, to visit the interior, the highlight of which is the showpiece **Marmorsaal**, with its ceiling fresco by Paul Troger, you must sign up for a guided tour (Easter–Oct Tues–Sat 10 & 11am, 2, 3 & 4pm, Sun no 10am tour; öS50), in German only. However, without going on a tour you can still visit the **Stiftskirche**, arguably the finest work by Munggenast in the entire complex. The interior, though by no means large, is lavishly decorated in faux pink and grey marble, and trompe l'oeil ceiling frescoes. Oval paintings, interspersed with windows crowned by open-topped pediments, line both walls of the church, but the most striking feature of all is the Rococo ornamental icing, composed mostly of gilded acanthus leaves strewn over the choirstalls, the organ and even the pews.

Geras is on the branch line from Retz to Drosendorf; from the **train station**, it's a fifteen-minute walk south into town. The **tourist office** (Mon–Thurs 8am–4pm, Fri 8am–noon; ✆02912/216, fax 216-9) is on the main street, in the *Stadtgemeinde*, Haupstrasse 16, and can arrange **private rooms**. The most unusual **place to stay**, however, is in the *Alter Schüttkasten* (✆02912/332-0, fax 332-33; ④), a converted seventeenth-century monastic granary on the northern fringe of the village, with a good restaurant, and comfortable rooms with lots of exposed beams. You can also stay, more cheaply, in the monastery's *Meierhof* (☎ & fax as above; ②; March–Sept), a converted dairy, off the road to Kottaun. If you've children in tow, you might like to visit the **Naturpark** (Easter–Oct daily 9am–7pm; Nov–Easter Sun 9am–4pm; öS25), where you can see some rare woolly pigs, goats, sheep and rabbits, and feed some (fairly tame) wild boars and red deer. Beyond the Naturpark is the tiny *Edlersee* **campsite** (☎02912/52552; open all year), with an adjacent open-air swimming pool and bikes for hire.

Drosendorf

Geras makes a good base for exploring the area, but, without doubt the prettiest place in which to hole up is the tiny walled town of **DROSENDORF**, perched above one of the Thaya's numerous S-bends, 10km to the northwest, by the Czech border. Confusingly, it's Drosendorf Stadt (not Drosendorf Altstadt) that's the walled town, made up of little more than the long, leafy **Hauptplatz**, at the eastern end of which stands the town's sixteenth-century **Rathaus**, with its shapely gable and richly sgraffitoed facade. In the sixteenth-century Bürgerspital, east of the main square, you'll find the small **Stadtmuseum** (daily 11am–noon & 5–7pm; free), housing a moderately interesting collection of artefacts, including the old night watchman's horn, pike and uniform from the turn of the century.

Buses arrive at Hauptplatz, while the **train station** is ten minutes' walk to the southeast, off the road to Geras. As for **accommodation**, the town's sgraffitoed Renaissance *Schloss Drosendorf* (☎02915/2321, fax 2321-40; ③), in the southeastern corner of the town, is surprisingly affordable. Failing that, you've a choice between the two excellent family-run Gasthöfe on the main square: the *Goldenes Lamm* (☎02915/2327, fax 2327-37; ④) or *Die Traube* (☎02915/2227; ④). If you leave the town via the Raabser Tor, and follow the signposts, you'll quickly come to the town's **youth hostel**, at Badstrasse 25 (☎02915/2257; April to mid-Oct), and, beyond to the pleasant riverside **campsite** (☎02915/2285; open all year). Note that the Oberthürnau–Vratěnín border crossing, 4km nothwest of Drosendorf, is only open from 8am to 8pm.

Raabs an der Thaya

Public transport west of Drosendorf is pretty thin on the ground, so if you want to continue along the Thayatal, you're best off walking or cycling the 13km upstream to **RAABS AN DER THAYA**. The medieval **Schloss Raabs** (Wed, Sat & Sun 10am–5pm; öS50), which hovers above the town, makes quite an impression as you approach from the west, but is only really worth visiting if the current exhibition takes your fancy. The footpath from Drosendorf to Raabs along the Thaya takes you past the vast, sprawling **Ruine Kollmitz**, some 4km southeast of Raabs itself. With two towers and its huge main gate and drawbridge still intact, the ruin is well worth a visit. There's a small exhibition in one room, with press cuttings from the 1920s when the Hungarian Bolshevik Béla Kun was exiled close by. The castle can also be reached from the main road via Kollmitzdörfl and the Böhmische Mauer gateway.

Raabs **train station** is on the south bank of the Thaya, to the southeast of Hauptplatz. **Private rooms** can be arranged through Raabs **tourist office** (June–Sept Mon–Fri 9am–noon & 1–5pm, Sat 9am–noon; 02846/365), in the Rathaus, at the eastern end of the triangular Hauptplatz. The late-nineteenth-century *Hotel Thaya* (☎02846/202, fax 202-20; ③), opposite the Rathaus, has **rooms** in a modern wing overlooking the castle and the river, and there are two other very inexpensive Gasthöfe to choose from on Hauptplatz, most of whose rooms have shared facilities only. Raabs has better connections with the rest of the Waldviertel, with regular buses and trains to Göpfritz an der Wild, on the main line from Vienna to Gmünd, and to Horn.

Eggenburg

Despite its convenient location halfway between the Danube and the Czech border on the main line from Vienna to Gmünd, the walled town of **EGGENBURG** is too far from the likes of Altenburg to act as a base unless you have your own vehicle. Nevertheless, there are plenty of good reasons for visiting Eggenburg, not least because it's home to the **Österreichische Motorradmusem** (Mon–Fri 8am–4pm, Sat & Sun 10am–5pm; öS60), at the top of Museumgasse, one block east of the train station. The forecourt, littered with scores of old bikes and even a vintage Viennese tram, gives a fair indication of the scale of the enterprise – there are more than three hundred pristinely restored motorbikes inside. The museum kicks off with a parade of sleek, black inter-war BMWs and ends with a posse of great British bikes, including classic 1950s café racers like the BSA Gold Star. In between, there's every conceivable type of bike, from a couple of Laurin & Klements from before World War I to the fabulous three-seater Böhmerland 600, built in 1929 and the longest motorbike ever in production.

At the bottom of Museumgasse is the **Krahuletz-Museum** (daily 9am–5pm; öS40), opened back in 1902 to house the mineral and fossil collection of local-born geology professor, Johann Krahuletz (1848–1928). The subject matter might not grab you, but this is a well-laid-out museum that succeeds in making what could be a deathly subject as interesting as possible. You can look into a microscope and inspect fifteen different types of crystal at close quarters, and there are plenty of other hands-on exhibits aimed to appeal to children in particular. The local museum, occupying the first floor, is less interesting, though it does contain an exceptionally fine collection of (mostly eighteenth- and nineteenth-century) clocks and watches. Special exhibitions are staged on the top floor, along with a permanent display on the Iron Age.

Museums aside, Eggenburg has a very attractive **Altstadt**, to the north of the Krahuletz-Museum up Kremserstrasse. The most remarkable single building on the Hauptplatz is the sixteenth-century **Gemalte Haus**, smothered with sgraffito scenes from the Bible which extend round the corner into Kremserstrasse. Unfortunately, the town's Gothic **Pfarrkirche**, west of the main square up Kirchengasse, is usually kept closed, but you can still make out the church's fine lierne vaulting, and the gilded figures peeping out from amidst the Gothic tracery of the pulpit, by peeping through the beautiful wrought-iron railings. Outside the church, follow the signs to the **Beinhaus**, by the foundations of the old Karner, and switch the light on to see the gruesome wall of bones and skulls illuminated within. To view Eggenburg's fortifications at their most impressive, head up Judengasse from the church, where the walls stand 10m high on either side of the **Kanzlerturm** (April–Oct Sat & Sun 10am–noon & 2–6pm; öS20), which houses a museum to the local *Bürgerkorps*, and allows you access up onto the walls.

Practicalities

Eggenburg **train station**, ten minutes' walk south of the Altstadt, has frequent connections to Gmünd and Vienna, but to get here from Horn you must change at Sigmundsherberg. There are a couple of **private rooms** available through the **tourist office** (daily 9am–5pm; ☎02984/3400, fax 3400-5), housed within the Krahuletz-Museum, situated halfway between the station and Hauptplatz. Otherwise, **accommodation** choices boil down to the large, comfortable *Stadthotel*, Kremserstrasse 8 (☎02984/3531-3533, fax 3531-101; ③), and two small B&Bs, the more central of which is the one run by Herr Podschlapp, at Wasserburgerring 13 (☎02984/3293; ②). Take-away pizza (and delicious Yugoslav *burek*) can be had from *Imbiss Ingrid*, on Kremserstrasse, and standard Austrian **food** from *Gasthaus zum goldenen Kreuz*, on Hauptplatz, which offers a Tagesmenü for under öS100. Eggenburg lies on the edge of the Weinviertel, so if you fancy visiting one of the **Heurigen** in the neighbouring villages of Stoizendorf or Röschitz, to the east, pick up a timetable from the tourist office to see which ones are currently open.

Horn and around

With a host of attractions all within spitting distance, **HORN**, 14km west of Eggenburg, is the obvious place from which to explore the central Waldviertel. Aesthetically, however, it can't really compete with the nearby towns of **Gars am Kamp** or Eggenburg, though it is a tad livelier. Apart from the obligatory Renaissance **Sgraffitohaus**, on Hauptplatz, depicting, among other things, Joseph with Potiphar's wife tugging at his monochrome dreamcoat, there's the local sixteenth-century Schloss, set in pleasant wooded grounds off Wienerstrasse. The interior has been tastefully converted into the **Höbarthmuseum** (Palm Sunday–Oct daily except Mon 9am–noon & 2–5pm; öS50), though its collection of agricultural machinery is an acquired taste. More memorable than either of the above is Paul Troger's light and feathery fresco decorating the main dome of the Baroque pilgrimage church of **Maria Dreieichen**, 4km southeast of Horn, on the road to Eggenburg (even this is no match for Troger's work in nearby Altenburg).

The Schloss also houses the town's **tourist office** (times as above; ☎02982/2372-1, fax 2372-4), which can arrange **private rooms** in the vicinity. The nicer of the town's two **Gasthöfe** is the family-run *Gasthof zum weissen Rössl* (☎02982/2398, fax 2398-51; ③) on Hauptplatz itself. A **bar and café** crawl in Horn should begin with a drink at *The Corner*, on Florianigasse, followed by a game of pool or billiards and some Zwettler Bier at the *Carambol*, down Thurnhofgasse, finishing up either in *Twister*, by the pizza place on the road to Vienna, or in *Brooklyn*, the only disco for miles around, southwest of the town off Zwettler Strasse. Horn's **train station**, ten minutes' walk east of the town centre off the Vienna road, is not in fact on the main line from Gmünd to Vienna, but there are frequent connections to the nearest station – that is, Sigmundsherberg – 7km to the northeast.

Altenburg

The chief reason for staying in Horn is to visit the Benedictine abbey in **ALTENBURG**, 5km to the southwest. Having been trashed in 1645 by the Swedes, Altenburg was transformed in the 1730s by Josef Munggenast into one of the finest Baroque monasteries in the entire country, on a par with Melk, yet it receives a fraction of the visitors. It's certainly more difficult to get to without your own transport, with buses between Horn and Altenburg restricted to schooldays only. Given the riches within, however, it really is worth getting to, even by foot or bike, and signing up for the guided tour (May–Oct Tues–Sat 10.30am, 2 & 3pm, Sun 11am & 2pm; öS60), in German only. Without the tour you'll only be able to view the **Stiftskirche**, whose tower rises to the west of the main Prälatenhof. The church's phalanx of red marble pilasters, turquoise pendentives and generous sprinkling of light-giving lunettes create a splendid overall impression, but it's Paul Troger's apocalyptic fresco, adorning the main cupola, that steals the show, with its rich colouring and pin-sharp detailing. God is depicted commandeering his archangels in the final battle against the forces of evil, represented here by a very nasty-looking bunch of devils, a huge fire-breathing dragon and the many-headed beast from Revelations.

The guided tour begins with the **Alter Kloster**, in which archeologists have discovered patches of frescoes, a sixteenth-century oven decorated with biblical tiles, and other sections of the medieval monastery. Most folk come here, though, to admire the combined artistry of Munggenast and Troger, as revealed in the **Kaiserstiege**, in the marble-clad **Festsaal** and, above all, in the magnificent **Bibliothek**, whose trio of domes sports three superbly vibrant Troger frescoes, their subject matter ranging from Jesus arguing with the rabbis in the synagogue to Solomon receiving the Queen of Sheba. The library's most startling feature, however, is the sea-blue Corinthian columns, topped by gilded capitals and dramatically set off against the heavy red marble cornice and plinth. But perhaps the most remarkable chamber in the whole complex is the barrel-vaulted **Krypta**, where Troger's students practised the art of "grotesque" painting, decorating the walls and ceilings in fanciful arabesques and fabulous images based around the theme of death. Considering the subject matter, the murals are full of action: there's Death as Neptune, Death as Mercury, and a wonderful scene featuring skeletons picking off cherubs with their bows and arrows.

Greillenstein

Five kilometres west of Altenburg, and no easier to reach by public transport, **Schloss Greillenstein** (daily: April–Oct 9.30am–5pm; July & Aug until 6pm; öS40) makes for another memorable day-trip from Horn. Built in the late sixteenth century by the parvenu Hans Georg III von Kuefstein, Greillenstein is still owned by the family, one of whom conducts guided tours if there are enough visitors; if not, you'll be free to explore the place on your own, and will be given some explanatory notes in English. The chateau was once famous for its hi-tech **Wasserspielanlage** (Watergames Park), built in 1720, employing some 1.5km of pipes to pump water down a seventy-step waterfall at the bottom of which was a fearsome dragon fountain. The Wasserspielanlage has long since gone, but the Baroque statues that adorned it can still be seen on the ground floor of the chateau. The dragon fountain now stands in the courtyard, which has a three-tiered loggia along one side, along with two grotesque huntsmen statues who used to lurk in the woods, while a collection of nine dwarfs shelter in a nearby room. Several more exotic Baroque sculptures dot the balustrade in front of the chateau, including a series of sphinxes, tussling cherubs and shaggy lions, while a pair of African servants flank the main entrance, naked except for their crowns, fig leaves and swords. The main rooms of the chateau harbour a few fine Renaissance ceilings, some wonderful seventeenth-century portraits of Turks, and the occasional modern art exhibition, but little else of note.

Rosenburg and Gars am Kamp

Medieval **Schloss Rosenburg** (April to mid-Nov daily 9am–5pm; öS30), situated high above the River Kamp, 5km south of Horn, has one distinct advantage over Greillenstein, and that is accessibility. It's also a much more commercial enterprise. It's not the architecture but the **displays of falconry** (*Flugvorführung*; daily 11am & 3pm; öS65, or öS85 if performed to music by horse-riders), held in the castle's wonderful seventeenth-century arcaded tiltyard, that pull in the crowds. That said, it's not a bad-looking pile, if a mite over-restored in the nineteenth century. The entry fee allows you to wander round the tiltyard, see a dull exhibition on the Hoyos family (who own the place), and visit the *Burgtaverne* in the second courtyard, which does a decent öS98 Tagesmenü. There's not an awful lot to see inside the castle – the highlight is probably the Mannerist strap-work ceiling in the library – but to do so you must join a guided tour (öS65, *Kombi-Karte* covering falconry displays öS100–120). From the **train station** to the castle, it's a one-kilometre hike across the railway bridge over the Kamp and up through the woods of the Graslhöhle.

The modest *Landgasthof Mann* (☎02982/2915, fax 2915-7; ③) is the only place you can **stay** in Rosenburg. Alternatively, you could head 5km down the verdant **Kamptal** to the spa-town of **GARS AM KAMP**, which specializes in treatments using peat. The town's landmark *Hotel Gars* (☎02985/2666, fax 2666-745; ⑧) is a handsome imperial yellow building, with an excellent KaffeeKonditorei and a top-class restaurant (three-course menus start at öS250), but rooms don't come cheap. Less formal and a third of the price is the nearby *Rathauskeller Winghofer* (☎02985/2294; ②), or the secluded *Waldpension* (☎02985/2365; ③), a grand turn-of-the-century villa on Wolzniczakgasse, off the road to Krems. The *Café-Konditorei Ehrenberger*, on Dreifaltigkeitsplatz, offers a filling two-course Tagesmenü for around öS100. If you're around for a few days, ask at the **tourist office** (Sat 10am–noon & 2–4pm, Sun 10am–noon), in the Rathaus, about the open-air opera performances that take place in the medieval Burgruine overlooking the town from the opposite bank.

Zwettl

Deep in the heart of the rolling, forested hills of the Waldviertel, 50km west of Horn, **ZWETTL** boasts the region's second finest monastery after Altenburg. The town itself is also very appealing, with a well-preserved, partially walled **Altstadt**, centred on a series of interconnecting squares, lined with prettily painted and gabled sixteenth- and seventeenth-century houses. The most distinguished edifice is the sgraffitoed **Altes Rathaus** (May–Oct Fri 2–5pm, Sat & Sun 10am–noon & 2–5pm; July & Aug also Tues–Thurs 2–5pm; öS30), worth exploring more for its architecture than the Stadtmuseum it now contains. A more recent addition to the main square is the **Hundertwasserbrunnen**, by the eponymous maverick. All his usual trademark touches are evident – ceramic tiles, baubles and wonky paving, and even a roof garden – though for a notorious self-publicist it's remarkably understated.

Stift Zwettl

Stift Zwettl, the Cistercian monastery for which the town is most famous, is actually situated a good 3km downstream from Zwettl. Founded in 1159 by Hadmar I von Kuenring, the abbey retains much of its original twelfth-century architecture, though it was greatly enlarged and embellished during the Baroque period by the likes of Josef Munggenast and Paul Troger, the pair responsible for Altenburg. Unfortunately, the monastery's spendid **Bibliothek**, by the aforementioned duo, is often closed to the public, but by signing up for a 45-minute **guided tour** (May–Oct Mon–Sat 10 & 11am, 2 & 3pm, Sun 11am, 2 & 3pm; July & Aug also daily at 4pm; öS50), at the door marked *Pforte*, you can get to see a reconstructed Romanesque latrine, the chapterhouse and the **medieval cloisters**, which span the stylistic shift from Romanesque to Gothic.

The abbey's real jewel, however, is the **Stiftskirche**, which you can view without a guided tour. The church's landmark 93-metre-high tower, built in grey granite, cuts a striking figure amidst the uniform imperial yellow of the surrounding monastic complex, its undulating facade peppered with urns, obelisks and statuary in a lighter stone – particularly fine are the cherubs holding giant burning hearts, and the archangel dealing a death blow to a winged devil. Inside, the architectural bare bones of the original Gothic hall church remain more or less unchanged. The furnishings, however, are predominantly High Baroque, reaching their climax in the choir, whose entrance is flanked by matching pulpit and choir organ, both heavily gilded and littered with putti and angels. Beyond lie the **choirstalls**, richly inlaid with exquisite marquetry, their entablatures occupied by a parade of gilded saints. Finally, your eye is drawn to the extraordinary **high altar**, an explosion of red, brown and orange stucco marbling, white statuary and gilded sunburst and crown. The unusual central statue of Christ crucified on an oak tree in full foliage, itself carved from oak, is a reference to Hadmar's New Year's Eve dream, in which the Virgin told him to found his abbey wherever he might find an oak tree in full bloom. The church does have one piece of late-Gothic art that's worth a glance: the **winged altar of St Bernhard**, in the second chapel in the north aisle, centred on a statue of Christ standing up on the Virgin's lap, with eight scenes from the life of Bernhard, founder of the Cistercian order, by Jörg Breu of the Danube School. The church's fine Baroque **organ** is put to good use every year at the monastery's annual Orgelfest, from late June to late July.

Practicalities

Zwettl's **train station** is north of the Altstadt, and there are frequent trains to and from Schwarzenau, on the main Vienna–Gmünd line. Transport to and from Stift Zwettl is limited to one or two buses a day, so you might be better off hiring a bike or walking. A small number of **private rooms** are available through the **tourist office** (Mon–Fri

TRUPPENÜBUNGSPLATZ ALLENTSTEIG

If you're travelling from Horn to Zwettl, it's impossible to miss the vast military zone of the **Truppenübungsplatz Allentsteig**, which stretches more than 30km at its widest point. The area was handed over to the military by Hitler shortly after the Anschluss, since it contained the village of Döllersheim, where Hitler's paternal grandmother, Maria Anna Schicklgruber, was buried. Hitler was very keen to destroy all evidence of his ancestry, so Döllersheim was used for target practice, and by the end of the war it had been totally destroyed.

Hitler's paranoia dated back to 1930, when he received a letter from the son of his half-brother, Alois Junior, attempting to blackmail him by hinting at dark secrets in his family history. Hitler immediately dispatched his lawyer, Hans Frank (later to become Nazi governor of Poland), to investigate. The rumour was that Maria Anna had become pregnant after sleeping with a 19-year-old Jewish lad named Frankenberger while she was working as a maid in the Frankenberger house in Graz. The illegitimate product of this union was Hitler's father, Alois Schicklgruber, born in Döllersheim parish in 1837. Money was sent to Maria Anna from Graz even after she had married Georg Hitler and moved to the Waldviertel. Even though Hans Frank could find no conclusive proof either way, Hitler was clearly rattled by the story; hence his determination to wipe Döllersheim and its parish records off the face of the earth in 1938, and his decision to instruct the Gestapo to make further enquiries in 1942.

8am–12.30pm & 2–5pm; ☎ & fax 02822/52233) on the main square. Most of the town's other **accommodation** possibilities are on Landstrasse, and all are fairly modest Gasthöfe or B&Bs: *Schwarzer Kater* (☎02822/52410; ②) is closest to the centre at no. 15, followed by *Jagastüberl* (☎02822/52453; ②), at no. 61. For more luxury, you need to head out of town, either to the modern *Schwarz-Alm* hotel, restaurant and conference centre (☎02822/53173, fax 54273-11; ⑤), in the village of Gschwendt, 5km to the southwest, or to *Schloss Rosenau* (☎02822/58221, 58221-8; ⑤), a pretty Baroque chateau 8km west of Zwettl, that's also home to the national Freimaurermuseum Museum of Freemasonry). Back in Zwettl, you can eat heartily and quaff some of the local *Zwettler Bier* at the *Gasthof zur goldenen Rose*, a late sixteenth-century inn overlooking the town's plague column. There are several **campsites** to the east of Zwettl, along the banks of the River Kamp, the nearest one being *Camping Lichtenfels* (☎02826/7492; May–Sept), 9km east.

Gmünd

Hard by the Czech border, on the main line from Prague to Vienna, **GMÜND** – often written "Gmünd (NÖ)" to distinguish it from Gmünd in Carinthia – is an obvious place to halt your journey, whichever direction you're heading. The main square, **Stadtplatz**, makes for a pretty introduction (or farewell) to the Waldviertel, with its dinky Renaissance **Altes Rathaus** sporting a shapely Baroque gable and tall onion-domed steeple, and now housing a florist's and the **Stadtmuseum** (May–Sept Sun 9am–noon; öS20). Stadtplatz also has two exceptionally lovely **Sgraffitohäuser**, from the same period as the Rathaus, which understandably tend to feature on almost every picture of the town produced by the local tourist board. Both houses are castellated, but only the right-hand house features lively mythological scenes: Actaeon has been transformed into a stag by Diana, as a punishment for stumbling upon the goddess and her nymphs bathing naked; below, Medea is nonchalantly slaughtering one of her children (appropriately enough, the building itself is now a butcher's). On the south side of the square, the **Glas- und Steinmuseum** (Glass and Rock Museum; May–Sept Mon–Fri 9am–noon & 1–5pm, Sat & Sun 9am–noon; öS20) is mildly diverting. Skip the rocks and the snakes in formaldehyde that occupy the ground floor, and head instead for the history of the local glass industry, as revealed on the top two floors, where there's a decent selection of turn-of-the-century glassware and jewellery.

A good place to picnic and explore is the **Naturpark Blockheide**, where a series of strangely shaped sandstone protrusions are dotted about the woods to the northeast of the town centre. It's roughly ten minutes' walk from Stadtplatz to the park: cross the river from Braunauplatz, east of the main square, and follow the signs. Another popular activity in summer is to ride on the narrow-gauge **Waldviertler Schmalspurbahn**, which winds its way through the forests via Weitra (see below) to Gross Gerungs, 43km to the south. Eight normal trains a day make the journey throughout the year; steam trains run along the line most weekends from June until October.

Practicalities

From Gmünd **train station**, it's about ten minutes' walk north up Bahnhofstrasse to Stadtplatz, where you'll find the **tourist office** in the Glas- und Steinmuseum (times as on p.173; ☎02852/52506). The latter can arrange private rooms, which are a good option given that **accommodation** in Gmünd is somewhat overpriced, particularly the (albeit very comfortable) *Goldener Stern* (☎02852/54545, fax 54548; ⑨) at Stadtplatz 15. Better value is the excellent *Gasthof Werner Pauser*, Bahnhofstrasse 44 (☎02852/53860, fax 54807; ③), whose restaurant does tasty local carp dishes. For a choice of pizzas, and the usual Austrian fare, washed down with local Schrems beer, head for the *Caroussel*, at Stadtplatz 10.

The **Czech border crossing** is about 200m northwest of Stadtplatz, up Litschauerstrasse. You can walk into the neighbouring town of České Velenice (which was merely a suburb of Gmünd until the border split the town in two in 1920), in around fifteen to twenty minutes, though there's not a lot to see there. The main road from Prague to Vienna passes 6km to the north of Gmünd, at Neunagelberg, where there's a **youth hostel** (☎02859/7476; closed mid-Dec to mid-Jan), by the lake to the north of the main road. Gmünd's lakeside **campsite**, *Camping Assangteich* (☎02852/ 51552; May–Sept), is ten minutes' walk south of the train station on Albrechtserstrasse.

Weitra

The walled town of **WEITRA**, 16km to the southwest, is an easy day-trip from Gmünd and a much more peaceful place to spend the night. The sloping main square, **Rathausplatz**, is prettier, too, and is entered from the east via a lovely little crenellated Renaissance gateway, the **Obere Tor**. As in Gmünd, the most eye-catching building is the **Sgraffitohaus**, its central allegorical cartoon depicting the stages of a man's life in decades from birth to one hundred years of age. On the opposite side of the square, another sgraffitoed house features a gloriously wild dragon being done in by St George.

From Rathausplatz, take a stroll up Schlossgasse to the Fürstenberg-owned **Schloss** (daily except Tues 10am–12.30pm & 2–5.30pm; öS85), a late sixteenth-century affair, with a gabled, triple-decker loggia in its main courtyard. The local museum inside is unremarkable, but the view from the main tower is impressive, and the pretty little Schlosstheater (still in use) is worth a glance, built in the eighteenth century but enlarged in twiddly, gilded neo-Rococo style in 1885. Weitra is home to Austria's oldest brewery, Weitra Bräu, founded in 1321, and the cellars of the chateau now house an exhibition on the Fürstenbergs' brewing concerns, and an staggering array of beer mats and glasses from all over Europe.

The much-heralded **Museum Alte Textilfabrik** (May, June & mid-Sept to Oct Thurs & Fri 2–5pm, Sat & Sun 10am–noon & 2–5pm; July to mid-Sept daily except Mon 10am–noon & 2–5pm; öS35), in an old textile factory fifteen minutes' walk northeast of the Altstadt in the suburb of Brühl, is fairly low-key compared with the Schloss, though the temporary exhibitions on the top floor are occasionally worth catching.

The **train station** is five minutes' walk southeast of the Altstadt, with eight regular trains a day from Gmünd, and steam trains on weekends between June and October. Weitra is an easy day-trip from Gmünd, though you may prefer to **stay** overnight at *Gasthof Karl Waschka* (☎02856/2296, fax 2296-41; ③), one of two Gasthöfe to be found on Rathausplatz, or at the superb *Brauhotel Weitra*, also on Rathausplatz (☎02856/ 2936, fax 2936-222; ④). **Private rooms** can be organized through the **tourist office** (May–Oct Mon–Fri 8am–noon & 1.30–5.30pm, Sat 10am–noon & 5–7pm; ☎02856/2998, fax 3150), in the Rathaus. The best place to accompany your meal with the local beer is at the aforementioned *Brauhotel*.

Marchfeld and around

To the east of Vienna lies the featureless plain of the **Marchfeld**, whose name is derived from the River March, which forms the border between Slovakia and Austria. In Roman times, however, it was the **Danube**, to the south, that formed the region's natural border or *Limes*, strengthened by a series of forts along its banks. The main camp along this stretch of the Danube was Carnuntum, 40km or so east of Vienna, which now boasts the best Roman remains in the country, and is by far the most popular sight in the district.

As a border region, the Marchfeld has seen more than its fair share of battles over the centuries. It was at the **Battle of Marchfeld** in 1278 that Rudolf of Habsburg defeated King Otakar II of Bohemia, and thus secured the Austrian lands – roughly Upper and Lower Austria – and Styria for the dynasty. And in 1809 the Marchfeld was the scene of two of the bloodiest battles in the Napoleonic Wars. In May, at the **Battle of Aspern** (now within Vienna's city limits), Napoleon suffered his first ever defeat at the hands of the Habsburg archduke Karl: Austrian losses amounted to an unhealthy 23,000, but the French lost nearly half of their entire army, with 43,000 being killed or taken prisoner. Austrian victory was short-lived, and two months later at the **Battle of Deutsch-Wagram**, despite losing another 34,000 soldiers, Napoleon reversed the result and defeated the Austrians, whose casualties exceeded 50,000.

GÄNSERNDORF SAFARIPARK

Strategically situated within easy driving distance of the Czech Republic, Slovakia, Hungary and, of course, Vienna, **Gänserndorf Safaripark** (Easter–Oct Mon–Fri 9am–4.30pm, Sat & Sun 9am–5.30pm), in the Marchfeld, 4km south of Gänserndorf itself, is really only of any interest if you've got children to entertain. To get to, and to get the most out of, the place, you need your own car, which you can then drive round the safari area, where a collection of listless lions and hyperactive monkeys, among other animals, have a modicum of room in which to roam free. Taking your car in will set you back öS140 per person; the cheaper option, however, is to take the safaribus (öS32). In addition to the Safaripark, there are a conventional zoo, or Arbenteuer Park, and various "shows", featuring circus acts, parrots, snakes, tigers, sea lions, panthers and leopards. You can either pay extra for each show, or buy an all-inclusive ticket (öS175), which allows you into the Safaripark, the zoo and any of the shows. Kids are unlikely to leave disappointed, but the experience is less edifying for adults.

THE LAST EMPEROR

Emperor Karl I was born in 1887 at Schloss Persenbeug in Lower Austria, and spent a carefree, privileged childhood typical of a Habsburg archduke. As the emperor Franz-Josef I's great nephew, Karl hardly expected to become emperor himself. However, when the heir to throne, Archduke Franz Ferdinand, was assassinated in Sarajevo in 1914, Karl was unexpectedly elevated to the status of crown prince. Two years later, in the midst of World War I, Franz-Josef died at the age of 86, and Karl somewhat reluctantly took up the reins of power.

The emperor Karl's brief reign is best known for his bungled attempt at negotiating a separate peace for the empire in March 1917, using as an intermediary Sixtus of Bourbon-Parma, brother of his wife, Zita, and a soldier in the Belgian army. When the whole affair became public knowledge in the spring of 1918, it caused a great deal of embarrassment all round, particularly in view of the fact that the young emperor had agreed that Alsace-Lorraine should be returned to the French (without asking the Germans). In the end, on Armistice Day, ensconced in Schönbrunn with the empire crumbling around him, Karl agreed to sign a document relinquishing "all participation in the affairs of state", a compromise formula which avoided an official abdication. The very same day, the family left for the imperial hunting lodge at Eckartsau in the Marchfeld, where, two days later, Karl was forced to agree to withdraw from Hungarian state affairs, though again he refused to abdicate outright.

When the Austrian republic's first parliament convened in March 1919, Karl was given an ultimatum: abdication, exile or prison. He chose exile, and he and his family left Eckartsau for Switzerland, under British escort. Shortly afterwards, the Austrian government passed a law confiscating the family's property and banishing them from the country, unless they renounced their rights to the throne. Restoration in Austria was out of the question, but the situation in Hungary was much more hopeful. The Communist regime of Béla Kun had fled, and Karl's former naval chief, Admiral Horthy, had seized power and declared himself regent. However, when Karl travelled incognito overland across Austria to meet Horthy face to face in Budapest, in March 1920, the admiral refused to hand over power. The "Easter Bid" was a resounding failure, but in October the same year Karl made a last, desperate attempt to regain the Hungarian half of his empire, flying secretly into Sopron, in western Hungary, accompanied by his pregnant wife. After a brief skirmish with Horthy's forces in the suburbs of Budapest, Karl was forced to admit defeat for a second time, and sailed, once more under British escort, into permanent exile on the island of Madeira, where he died of pneumonia less than six months later at the age of 35. The irrepressible Zita outlived her husband by 77 years, dying in her late nineties in 1989.

Of course, monarchists are eager to point out that Karl was, in fact, by no means the last Habsburg. In the 1930s, Karl's eldest son, Otto, kept the dynastic cause going from the family's refuge outside Brussels. An apocryphal story has it that when asked if he would be watching the Austria–Hungary football match, Otto replied, "Who are we playing?" Eventually, in the 1960s, he renounced his claim to the throne (though his brothers still refused), handing it onto his son, Karl, and was therefore able to pay a few brief visits to his homeland. In the 1980s, Otto became a Euro MP for Bavaria, where he continues to live in exile. Austria has recently rescinded the law banning the Habsburgs from the country unless they abdicate their claims to the throne, but a return of the monarchy looks as unlikely as ever.

Archäologischer Park Carnuntum

Carnuntum was founded as a permanent military camp for the XV Legion around 40 AD, and in the course of the next century became the military and civil capital of the Roman province of Upper Pannonia, with a population of over 50,000. The emperor Marcus Aurelius used it as his chief military base during his campaign against the

Marcomanni and Quadi tribes (171–173 AD), and twenty years later the local commander Septimius Severus was declared emperor by the Pannonian legions. Carnuntum's other moment of glory was in 307 AD when Diocletian staged a conference of emperors there. Around 400 AD the town was abandoned by the Romans and soon afterwards sacked by the Goths.

Today, its Roman remains spread across 5km between the villages of **Petronell** and **Bad Deutsch Altenburg**. In order to impose some logic to the disparate sites, the whole area has been dubbed the **Archäologischer Park Carnuntum**, and divided into three zones (from east to west): Kernzone I, centred on Bad Deutsch Altenburg, where the most important finds are now displayed in the Archäologisches Museum Carnuntinum; Kernzone II, centred on the military camp, or Legionslager-Lagerstadt; and Kernzone III around Petronell-Carnuntum (as the village is now known), where the civilian town (Zivilstadt Carnuntum) was situated. In the account below we've reversed the order of the zones to reflect the fact that most visitors approach the park from Vienna. If you don't have your own car, the best way to visit the sights is on foot, or by bike, which you can hire from Petronell or Bad Deutsch Altenburg train stations.

Petronell-Carnuntum

To get your bearings in **PETRONELL-CARNUNTUM**, it's best to head straight for the main excavation site and **information centre** (April–Oct Mon–Fri 9am–5pm, Sat & Sun 9am–6pm; öS35, *Kombi-Karte* öS80 includes entry to the museum in Bad Deutsch Altenburg), at the west of Hauptstrasse, opposite the rather attractive Romanesque Rundkapelle; here, you can pick up a map of the sites and lots of other useful info. Your ticket allows you entry to the nearby excavation site of the **Antikes Wohnstadtviertel** (ancient civil town) of Carnuntum, but unless you buy a guidebook or pay the extra öS45 for an audioguide (in English) you won't get much out of the ruins, which rarely rise above foundation level. At the far end of the site's sloping field, you can, however, view an excellent example of Roman engineering, where a substantial slice of the *Limes* road and accompanying drainage system have been preserved, not to mention a full-scale reconstruction of the classical facade of the town's Temple of Diana. Beyond the excavation site lie the slightly more intriguing foundations of the **Grosse Therme** (public baths), a vast complex thought to have been significantly embellished in preparation for the 307 AD conference.

If you're pushed for time, though, you're probably best off skipping the excavation site altogether and heading off to the more substantial ruins in Kernzone III. The most impressive of these, and the one that features in nearly all the area's promotional literature, is the **Heidentor**, a gargantuan gateway that stands in the fields a kilometre or so to the southwest of the village, beyond the railway tracks and route 9. Signs from the Heidentor will lead you to the nearby **Amphitheater II**, an out-of-town theatre even in Roman times, which was capable of seating 13,000 on its grassy banks. A lot more impressive, however, is the smaller **Amphitheater I**, situated off the road to Bad Deutsch Altenburg, in the military camp (Kernzone II), to the east of Petronell, where much more of the Roman stonework has been preserved, including the entrance tunnels.

Bad Deutsch Altenburg

The chief sight in the spa-town of **BAD DEUTSCH ALTENBURG** is the **Archäologisches Museum Carnuntinum** (closed mid-Dec to mid-Jan daily except Mon 10am–5pm; öS60), overlooking the Kurpark at the far eastern end of the main street, Badgasse. The museum is a pleasure to visit, thanks in part to the lovely building in which it's housed, purpose-built by Friedrich Ohmann in 1904 to look something like a giant Roman villa. All the museum's labelling is in German, but luckily, if your German isn't up to it, some of the finds are impressive enough without any additional information. The museum's finest individual piece is the marble *Dancing Maenad ("Tanzende Mänade")*, whose finely carved drapery reveals her beautifully formed (and much-photographed) buttocks. In the foyer, there's also an interesting (mostly reconstructed) Mithraic relief, from the male-only cult popular among Roman legions before the advent of Christianity. The relief depicts the Persian deity Mithras slaying a cosmic bull, while a scorpion grasps its genitals and a dog licks its wounds (the bull's blood was seen as life-giving, and initiates to the cult had to bathe in the stuff in subterranean tombs).

While you're in Bad Deutsch Altenburg, it's worth strolling up the nearby hill, known as the Kirchenberg, to take a closer look at the town's landmark **Marienkirche**, a bizarre Gothic edifice made up of three elements that look like they belong to separate churches. The octagonal west tower is remarkably small and features a series of grimacing gargoyles, while at the opposite end of the church is a fanciful presbytery, prickling with delicately carved finials, which looks like it should form part of a much larger church. Between the two is the older Romanesque nave, which is much plainer and sits much lower than either the tower or the chancel.

Practicalities

The **train station** in Petronell is a short walk south of the village centre, while the one in Bad Deutsch Altenburg is a similar distance southwest of the spa. It takes about an hour to reach either station on S-Bahn line 7 from Wien-Mitte or Wien-Nord, making the whole area an easy day-trip from Vienna. There's a **tourist office** (April–Oct daily 9am–5pm; ☎02163/3555, fax 3556) in Petronell, opposite the main excavation site; there's another (Mon–Fri 8am–noon & 12.30–4pm) in the *Kurhotel* on Badgasse in Bad Deutsch Altenburg.

As for **accommodation**, the *Gasthof zum Heidentor* (☎02163/2201; ②), in Petronell, has rooms, each with en-suite facilities and TV; the *Hotel Marc Aurel* (☎02163/2285, fax 2285-60; ③) offers plusher rooms, though no TV. A better bet, however, is Bad Deutsch Altenburg, with a nice leafy Kurpark and, being a spa-town, a much wider choice of places. The cheapest option is *Pension Mittermayer*, Badgasse 20 (☎02165/62874; ②), where most of the rooms have shared facilities only, though the en-suite rooms at *Pension Madel* (☎02165/62763; ②) are only slightly more expensive. All the above places have restaurants attached, where you can get decent, reasonably priced Austrian food.

Hainburg

Squeezed between two hills that signal the end of Austrian territory, the little walled town of **HAINBURG**, 3km east of Bad Deutsch Altenburg, is another good base for exploring the area. As befits a border town that is still every bit the gateway into Austria from Slovakia and northern Hungary, Hainburg boasts extensive fortifications, including three substantial gateways, the largest of which is the colossal thirteenth-century **Wiener Tor**.

The *Hotel zur goldenen Krone* (☎02165/62105-0, fax 62105-10; ③), on the main square, is a bit dowdy but very friendly; alternatively, there's the more homely *Gasthof zu drei Raben* (☎02165/62407; ②), on Ungarstrasse. The best place to eat out is *Zur alten Bampress*, an excellent *Stadtheuriger* on Ungarstrasse (closed Thurs), with a lovely courtyard. Hainburg has two **train stations**: Hainburg-Donau Frachtenbahnhof, to the west of town, and Hainburg Ungartor, closer to the centre, east of the Altstadt.

Rohrau

The composer Josef Haydn was born in **ROHRAU**, a one-street village 4km south of Petronell, on the banks of the River Leitha. The **Haydn-Geburthaus** (daily except Mon 10am–5pm; öS20) is a lovely thatched cottage, with a delightful arcaded courtyard covered with vines and a cosy, folksy feel to it. This creates something of a false impression, as it was clearly a hovel when Haydn was born here in 1732 (the original building, built by Haydn's father in 1728, burnt down in 1899). By all accounts, Haydn had a pretty miserable childhood – with "more floggings than food", according to one of his letters – and was no doubt relieved when he was sent off to nearby Hainburg at the tender age of 8, eventually becoming a choirboy at the Stephansdom in Vienna (for more on Haydn's life, see p.198). Few of his personal belongings have made their way here, apart from a baptismal bowl and a rather attractive tortoiseshell snuff box.

In order to make ends meet, Haydn's mother was for a while employed as a cook at the nearby **Schloss Harrach** (Easter–Oct Tues–Sun 10am–5pm; öS58). The present, rather plain, late-Baroque moated chateau is still occupied, in part, by the Harrachs, though the public are allowed to admire their extensive private art collection displayed on the first floor, along with the family's Meissen porcelain and Chinese vases. The bulk of the art collection came into the family thanks to a couple of illustrious ancestors: Ferdinand Bonaventura (1636–1706), who served as imperial ambassador in Madrid, and Aloys Thomas (1669–1742), who served as Viceroy of Naples. However, despite the smattering of big-name painters – there are some minor works and sketches by the likes of Van Dyck, Rubens, Teniers and Jan Breughel the Elder – there are few masterpieces here.

Bruck an der Leitha

When the River Leitha formed the historical border between Austria and Hungary under the Habsburgs, the walled town of **BRUCK AN DER LEITHA**, 9km southwest of Rohrau, served as the main border post. Now most folk simply pass through the town en route to the Neusiedler See, but it's a more promising place to stay than Rohrau if you're in the area. The town walls are particularly impressive as you approach from Vienna, and the spacious central **Hauptplatz** boasts a parade of monuments – a Marian column, a Trinity column, punctuated by two fountains – overlooked by a handsome silver-white Pfarrkirche. The Pompeiian-red **Schloss Harrach**, east of the main square at the end of Stefaniegasse, though closed to the public, has a nice park for a picnic.

The town's **tourist office** (Mon 9am–noon & 1–5pm, Tues & Wed 9am–noon, Fri 9am–6pm; May–Oct also Sat 10am–noon) is by the church on Hauptplatz, and can furnish you with a map of the town and help with other enquiries. Unfortunately, **accommodation** options are all outside the old walled town: the two closest to the centre are the *Ungarische Krone* (☎02162/62777, fax 623759; ③), a three-star hotel with all mod cons on the other side of the Leitha off Parndorferstrasse, or the excellent *Pension Josef Eitler* (☎02162/63206; ②), further down Parndorferstrasse at no. 173. *Café Haas*, on the east side of Hauptplatz, is a really nice, classy café-restaurant and pizzeria with tables outside overlooking the square. The best place to sample the local wine is in the lovely ivy-strewn *Schanigarten* of the secluded *Harrachkeller*, on Schlossgasse.

The Wienerwald area

The gentle wooded hills of the **Wienerwald** (Vienna Woods) stretch from the suburbs of Vienna itself southwest to the alpine foothills that form the border between Lower Austria and Styria. As such, they have been a favourite weekend destination for the Viennese, who can simply hop on a tram to get there (see p.60 for details). In many ways, this accessibility is the woods' chief virtue. Compared to the country's sublime alpine peaks, the Wienerwald's scenery is pretty low-key. The main resorts, such as **Mödling** and the spa-town of **Baden**, cling to the eastern edge of the Wienerwald, and make for easy day-trips from the capital; if you want to spend a day or two walking in the woods themselves, you're best off overnighting at either of the above places.

Mödling bei Wien

Like Baden (see below), **MÖDLING**, 15km south of Vienna, makes great play of its associations with Beethoven, who stayed here in the summer of 1819. Even if you've no interest in the composer, Mödling is a very pretty little town, which has preserved a remarkable number of sixteenth- and seventeenth-century houses in its minuscule Altstadt.

From the **train station**, to the east of town, it's a ten-minute walk along **Hauptstrasse** to Freiheitsplatz on the northeastern edge of the old town. Beethoven rented three rooms nearby at Hauptstrasse 79, now the **Beethoven-Haus**, whilst he worked on, among other things, the *Diabelli Variations* and the *Missa Solemnis*. "From behind the closed door of one of the parlours we could hear the master working on the fugue of the Credo, singing, yelling, stamping his feet", some friends, who dropped in on him, recalled; "when we had heard enough of this almost frightening performance and were about to depart, the door opened and Beethoven stood before us, his features distorted to the point of inspiring terror. He looked as though he had just engaged in a life and death struggle with the whole army of contrapuntists, his everlasting enemies." The following year Beethoven intended to stay in Mödling again, but was refused lodgings "on account of his strange behaviour". At the time of writing, the house was undergoing renovation work, which should be completed by the time you read this; enquire at the Stadtmuseum, halfway down Hauptstrasse, for the current opening times.

From Freiheitsplatz, head up Herzoggasse, which is flanked by attractive houses bearing frescoes and sgraffiti, into the pedestrianized main square, **Schrannenplatz**, with its distinctive fountain decorated with ornamental pineapples, and, beyond, the town's dinky little sixteenth-century **Rathaus**, sporting a tiny loggia at one corner. A short hike up Pfarrgasse will bring you to the town's huge **Pfarrkirche St Othmar**, built in the fifteenth century to double as a defensive stronghold. Close by stands a distinctive circular tower-like charnel house, featuring a superb knotted Romanesque portal, and sporting a Baroque onion dome.

A network of paths crisscrosses the adjacent Wienerwald: from the other side of the town's river, to the south, you can explore the woods of the **Naturpark Föhrenberge**, which is punctuated with numerous monuments, the most famous of which is the Neoclassical Husarentempel. An easy two-kilometre walk west along the river from Mödling is the popular tourist attraction of the **Seegrotte Hinterbrühl** (daily: April–Oct 8.30am–noon & 1–5pm; Nov–March 9am–noon & 1–3.30pm; öS50), a former gypsum mine, which fell into disuse when it was flooded in 1912. Later, the caves were used by the Nazis as a work camp for building fuselages for jet fighters. Guided tours (in a variety of languages including English) are quite fun – but cold, so wrap up before you enter – and finish with an atmospheric boat ride through the flooded mineshafts.

You can pick up **tourist information** from either the Stadtmuseum (Mon–Fri 9am–noon, Sat & Sun 10am–noon & 2–6pm), or the post office (Mon–Fri 8am–4pm), on the main square. There's a wide range of **accommodation**, from intimate pensions such as *Haus Monika* (☎02236/257359, fax 257355; ③), Badstrasse 53, in the villa quarter to the south of the Altstadt, to the plush *Babenbergerhof* (☎02236/22246, fax 22246-6; ⑤), in the heart of the Altstadt at Babenbergergasse 6. If you're staying the night in Mödling, be sure to check out what's on at the town's stylish theatre/cinema, Mödlinger Bühne, on Babenbergerstrasse.

Laxenburg

Though not strictly speaking in the Wienerwald, the former imperial residence of **LAXENBURG** is within striking distance of the woods, 5km or so east of Mödling. The town's links with the Habsburgs go back to the fourteenth century, when Duke Albrecht III built the **Altes Schloss**, but the place really came into its own four hundred years later under the reign of Maria Theresa, who built the **Neues Schloss** (also known as the Blauer Hof and now headquarters of the suspicious-sounding International Institute of Applied Systems Analyses), overlooking the town's Schlossplatz. Laxenburg quickly became the family's favourite country retreat, a place in which the stifling court formalities of Vienna could be abandoned. According to one of Josef II's numerous decrees, each guest was "free to do as he will, to ride, to drive, to join in the hunt or to stay at home". Not surprisingly, it was also much frequented by the reclusive Empress Elisabeth, who gave birth to her only son, Rudolf, in the Blauer Hof in 1858 (for more on Rudolf, see pp.182–3).

The chief attraction nowadays is the beautifully landscaped and extensive grounds of the **Schlosspark** (dawn–dusk; öS13), whose woods are dotted with various follies: a Neoclassical temple, a grotto, a jousting arena and, at the centre of a wooded *étoile*, the Grünes Lusthaus, a summer pavilion decorated with frescoes, where Maria Theresa's husband, Franz Stephan, used to play cards. The largest folly of the lot is the **Franzensburg** (guided tours Easter–Oct at 11am, 2 & 3pm; öS50), a mock Gothic castle, described in 1814 by an English visitor as "an imperial toy . . . a little building provided with numerous turrets and watch-towers, loop-holes, irongates, and portcullises". Built in the park's artificial lake, on one of the islands linked by bridges and a little raft on a chain, the castle was conceived by the emperor Franz I as a sort of romantic retreat, based loosely on the dynasty's original seat in Switzerland. There's a café in the castle courtyard, and regular open-air theatre performances on summer weekends. Alternatively, you can go on a guided tour of the interior, which features lots of arms and armour, portraits and busts of the Habsburgs, quasi-medieval furnishings and even a faux dungeon, complete with fake prisoner.

If you're not picnicking in the park, the *Laxenburgerhof* does bargain three-course lunches for around öS75, or else there's a pizzeria in the former Kaiserbahnhof, built in neo-Gothic style in 1845. If you're camping, Laxenburg makes for a good base, especially as a convenient launching pad for day-trips to Vienna. The **campsite** (☎02236/71333; May–Oct), situated ten minutes' walk out of town along the road to Münchendorf, has an adjacent outdoor pool and a gate into the Schlosspark. There are hourly buses to Wien-Mitte, and regular trains to the Südbahnhof, though the Laxenburg-Biedermannsdorf **train station** is a good two-kilometre walk from the campsite.

Heiligenkreuz

The majority of monasteries in Austria enjoy spectacular, cliff-top locations, but the Cistercians have always preferred well-watered, wooded spots for their abbeys, and **HEILIGENKREUZ**, which nestles unassumingly in the undulating landscape of the Wienerwald, 14km west of Mödling, is no exception. Don't let that put you off, however, for Heiligenkreuz is easily one of the finest examples of Romanesque–Gothic architecture in the country, and boasts, in addition, some very fine Baroque furnishings, courtesy of Italian sculptor Giovanni Giuliani.

Though the monastery was founded in the twelfth century by Duke Leopold III, who planned to establish a burial place for the Babenberg dynasty, the whole complex looks thoroughly Baroque from the outside, having been extensively rebuilt after being looted by the Turks in 1683. The main courtyard features a bevy of fantastically bushy beech trees and a splendidly animated Baroque Trinity column and fountain sculpted by Giuliani. Only on the eastern side of the courtyard do you get the first hint of the monastery's medieval origins, in the plain Romanesque facade of the **Stiftskirche**. To gain full access to the church, you must join one of the guided tours, which set off hourly (in German only; Mon–Sat 10am, 11am & 2–4pm, Sun 11am & 2–4pm; öS45). Inside, the church is the product of two distinct building periods: the plain round arches of the nave are Romanesque, while the lofty, vaulted presbytery is Gothic. The

Baroque choirstalls, by Giuliani again, are outstanding, each one decorated with a lime-wood relief from the Life of Christ, and crowned by cherubs and busts of eminent aristocrats, priests and bishops. They're put to good use by the brothers, who come here to sing five times a day.

The guided tours begin with the monastery's beautifully preserved thirteenth-century **cloisters**, lined with more than three hundred slender pink marble columns, which, like the church itself, perfectly illustrate the transition from the rounded arches of the Romanesque style to the pointed arches of the Gothic. Several chapels are connected to the cloisters, among them the **Kapitalkapelle**, where many of the Babenberg dynasty are buried, and the polygonal Brunnenkapelle, which echoes noisily to the sound of its fountain. Best of the lot is the ghoulish **Totenkapelle**, decked out with black and gold furnishings by Giuliani, including a macabre set of four candelabra, supported by skeletons in shrouds. The guided tours end with a stroll round the **sacristy**, an extraordinarily rich Baroque concoction, furnished with stunning inlaid wooden cabinets and decorated with frescoes framed by pink and white stucco-work.

THE MAYERLING TRAGEDY

Numerous theories continue to be put forward as to why Rudolf chose to take his own life. The Viennese, who love to sentimentalize the tragedy, tend to claim it was all for love, yet Rudolf was a notoriously fickle womanizer, and Maria Vetsera just one in a long line of pretty mistresses. The plot thickens when you consider that the previous summer Rudolf had proposed a suicide pact to his long-term mistress Mizzi Caspar, but was turned down. On the very night before his suicide, Rudolf spent the evening with Mizzi Caspar, before leaving to meet Maria at Mayerling. It's true that his marriage to Princess Stephanie of Belgium – arranged by his father for political reasons – was a dismal failure, but it wasn't enough to drive him to suicide, and certainly didn't prevent him from keeping bachelor digs at the Hofburg where he could receive his numerous mistresses. One plausible theory is that, in 1887, he contracted a venereal disease, which he believed to be incurable. Worse still, it's thought that he had infected Stephanie, causing her to become infertile (having failed to produce a male heir to the throne).

Others contend that it was a political act, born of frustration with his lack of any part in the decision-making process of government. Franz-Josef allowed his son little real power and, in any case, disagreed with him on most issues. Rudolf, who was never close to his father, tended to mix with liberals opposed to his father's ministers' policies, and even wrote anonymous, critical articles to the liberal *Neues Wiener Tagblatt*. There were even rumours at the time that Rudolf had been assassinated by his political opponents or French secret agents, a version of events upheld by the late Empress Zita as recently as 1982. Another possible explanation is that Rudolf, having written to the pope to seek an annulment of his marriage, had been snubbed by the pontiff, who had returned the petition directly to Franz-Josef. Finally, on January 26, 1889, Rudolf and his father are known to have had a fierce argument – what it was about we shall never know.

Four days later, Rudolf and Maria's bodies were discovered by Rudolf's hunting partner, Count Hoyos, who had got no answer when he called in at Mayerling. The first official version of events was that Rudolf had died of apoplexy, but after the post-mortem it was admitted that he had shot himself. As suicides were denied a Christian burial, the pathologists in charge were wise enough to suggest that "the act was committed in a moment of psychological unbalance", thus allowing the Catholic authorities an escape clause. Rudolf's request to be buried in the nearby village of Alland alongside his mistress was denied, and he was buried in the Kaisergruft amid much pomp and circumstance. Maria Vetsera's presence at Mayerling was never acknowledged by the Habsburgs, though rumours abounded. Some 36 hours after the incident, her fully clothed corpse, in the first stages of rigor mortis, was wedged upright between her two uncles in a carriage, transported to Heiligenkreuz and secretly buried in the cemetery there.

Mayerling

Mystery still surrounds the motives behind the suspected double suicide of **Crown Prince Rudolf** (1858–89), eldest son of the emperor Franz-Josef I and heir to the throne, and his half-Greek, 17-year-old mistress, Baroness Maria Vetsera, which took place in the early hours of the morning on January 29, 1889, at Rudolf's hunting lodge at **MAYERLING**, 2.5km southwest of Heiligenkreuz. Subject of a ballet, several films and countless books, the event has captured the popular imagination for over hundred years – as recently as 1988, an Austrian businessman confessed to having stolen Maria's coffin after becoming obsessed with Mayerling.

Although the site of the lodge is only half an hour's walk from Heiligenkreuz, it's hardly worth the effort. Franz-Josef had the building demolished shortly after the incident, and a neo-Gothic chapel (April–Sept Mon–Sat 9am–12.30pm & 1.30–6pm; Oct–March closes 5pm), run by Carmelite nuns, erected in its place. Despite the fact that there's very little to see, folk still flock to the chapel, where they're relieved of a few Schillings, and ushered into the two side rooms that contain furniture and a bit of carpet from the old hunting lodge, plus photos and portraits of the tragedy's leading protagonists.

Baden bei Wien

Just 25km south of Vienna, the spa-town of **BADEN** is an easy day-trip from the capital, accessible either by train or via its own tram link. This compact little town, peppered with attractive Neoclassical buildings in varying shades of magnolia and ochre, comes across as deeply provincial, a haven of peace for its elderly spa patients. But back in the eighteenth and nineteenth centuries, Baden was the most fashionable spa-town in the Habsburg Empire, the favourite summer holiday retreat of none other than Emperor Franz II (1792–1835). Baden's distinctively Biedermeier appearance, however, is largely the result of a building frenzy – much of it under the direction of the architect Josef Kornhäusel – prompted by a devastating fire in 1812. A swim in Baden's hot thermal baths is highly recommended and, as the town lies on the very edge of the Wienerwald, the walking and picnicking possibilities are a further enticement.

Hauptplatz and around

The small, triangular **Hauptplatz**, at the centre of Baden's pedestrian zone, gives you an idea of the modest scale of things in Baden. Almost dwarfing the surrounding buildings, including Kornhäusel's Neoclassical **Rathaus** from 1815, is the central plague column, erected a hundred years earlier, and crowned with a gilded sunburst. Even the last of the Holy Roman Emperors, Franz II, chose an unassuming three-storey building – now the **Kaiserhaus**, on the east side of the square – as his summer residence. The last of the Habsburgs, Emperor Karl I, also stayed here, during World War I, when Baden became the Austrian army headquarters. (Baden later reached its nadir in the decade after World War II, when it was used as the Soviet army headquarters.)

From 1804 onwards, Baden became a favourite retreat of Beethoven's, too; he made a total of fifteen visits, staying at various addresses, one of which, at nearby Rathausgasse 10, has been turned into the **Beethoven Schauräume** (Tues–Fri 4–6pm, Sat & Sun 9–11am & 4–6pm; öS25). In the 1820s, Beethoven was well known around the spa as the local eccentric; as one friend recalls, "his hair was coarse and bristly . . . and when he put his hand through it, it remained standing in all directions which often looked comical." On one occasion he even got himself arrested, in the nearby town of Wiener Neustadt, after a local resident had been so frightened by his dishevelled appearance that she had called the police. On being arrested, the composer said "I am Beethoven", to which the constable replied, "You are a tramp, Beethoven doesn't

BADEN BEI WIEN

Kaiser-Franz-Josef-Museum (500m)

Ruine Rauheneck (1 km)

0   400m

Lokalbahn

Beethoven-Tempel

Udinebrunnen
Stadttheater
Pfarrkirche
Kaiserhaus

Beethoven Schauräume
Rathaus
Lokalbahn (Train Station)

Frauenbad

Städtische Arena
Kurhaus

Sauerhof

Schloss Weikersdorf

Rollett-Museum

Thermalstrandbad

Main Train Station

PALFFYGASSE
WIENERSTRASSE
MÜHLGASSE
GERMERGASSE
FLAMMINGGASSE
MAUTNER-MARKHOF
WELTZERGASSE
GRILLPARZERSTR
FRANZ RING
KAISER
SPIEGELGASSE
ANTONSGASSE
VÖSLAUERSTRASSE
STIFTGASSE
MÖNCHGASSE
HILDEGARDGASSE
VON WOYZEKOFF-PLATZ
PALFFYG
ANNAGASSE
STRASSERNGASSE
BAHNGASSE
PFARRGASSE
GRABENGASSE
WASSERGASSE
BRETTGASSE
RAINERGASSE
THERESIENG
RENNGASSE
HAUPT-PLATZ
RATHAUSGASSE
JOSEFS-PLATZ
ERZHERZOG RAINER RING
GRÜNER MARKT
BRAITNERSTRASSE
VÖSLAUERSTRASSE
BRUSATTI-PLATZ
ROLLETTG
SOTTENBRUNNG
JOHANNESGASSE
SCHWECHAT
WEILBURGSTRASSE
THERESIG
SAUERHOFSTRASSE
SCHMIDTGASSE
WEIKERS-DORFERPLATZ
ELISABETHSTRASSE
ANDREAS-HOFER-ZEILE
HOCHSTRASSE
MITTERBERGSTRASSE
MOZARTSTRASSE
SCHUBERTG
SCHUBERTG
MARCHETSTRASSE
PELZGASSE
Mühlbach
Dobihoffpark
HABSBURGERSTRASSE
MARGBURGERSTRASSE
SANDWIHLGASSE
SCHLOSSGASSE
DOBIHOFFGASSE
HELENENSTRASSE
WEILBURGSTRASSE
SCHWECHAT
KARLSGASSE
BERGSTEIGGASSE
ELISABETHSTRASSE

N

ACCOMMODATION
Gästehaus am Kurpark   1
Hotel Rauch   4
Hotel Schloss Weikersdorf 3
Pension Margit   2
Villa Inge   5

S&M IN BADEN

The staid spa-town of Baden is the unlikely setting for *Venus im Pelze* ("Venus in Furs"), an account of sexual slavery written by **Count Leopold von Sacher-Masoch** (1835–95). Born the son of the chief of police in Lemberg, Galicia, the count was allegedly influenced as a child by the brutality of the prisons. As an adult, he became professor of history at Graz University, and wrote several historical and folkloric novels. His renown today, however, rests on his affair in the 1860s with "Baroness Bogdanoff", or "Wanda" (real name Fanny Pistor), to whom the count willingly signed away his freedom – becoming her manservant, taking the name of Gregor, and embarking upon "a liaison, marked materially by a prodigality in which furs and foreign travel were to be conspicuous". She agreed to wear furs "as often as possible, especially when in a cruel mood", while he agreed to "comply unreservedly with everyone of her desires and commands". After six months of slavery, the two parted company, but the affair had inspired the count to write *Venus im Pelze*, which was published in 1870. In 1873 the count married Aurore Rümelin, who changed her name to Wanda in honour of the book's heroine. "Gregor" and Wanda became involved in a weird *ménage à trois* with a fake Polish count, Anna von Kottowitz, who turned out to be a chemist's assistant.

We have the count to thank for the term "sadomasochism", though he himself never coined the phrase. That was left to one of Freud's early mentors, Richard von Krafft-Ebing (1840–1902), who first used the term – with reference to Sacher-Masoch's numerous writings on the S&M theme – in his *Psychopathia Sexualis*, published in Latin in 1886 (but later translated into seven languages), about which the emperor Franz-Josef I once quipped, "it's about time someone brought out a decent book on Latin grammar". The same year, Sacher-Masoch split from Wanda, and he married his children's governess in 1887. He died in 1895, depressed by the decline of his reputation and by Krafft-Ebing's use of his name to designate a sexual perversion.

look like that." It wasn't until later that night that the town's musical director was finally called out to identify him, and the mayor sent him back to Baden in the state coach.

Woefully, the three small rooms Beethoven rented out contain no mementoes of the composer's three sojourns here (there's a section on later, lesser-known Badenites to pad things out). It was in these rooms that Beethoven wrote parts of his *Missa Solemnis* in 1821, and, two years later, finished his *Ninth Symphony*, though he had to get a friend to persuade the landlord to take him back on the promise of good conduct. The landlord agreed on condition that Beethoven pay for a set of new shutters (the previous set, on which Beethoven had scrawled financial and musical calculations, had been sold by the landlord for a piece of gold).

The Kurpark and longer walks

The focus of Baden the spa, as opposed to Baden the town, is the ochre-coloured Kurhaus (now a casino) and summer theatre, north of Hauptplatz by the **Kurpark**, which is laid out on the steep slopes of the Wienerwald. This is by far the nicest bit of Baden, and the place to head for if you're intent on a spot of walking or picnicking, as the park's web of paths can quickly transport you high above the town. In its lowest reaches, closest to the town, the park is formally arranged, with the focus on the bandstand and the **Udinebrunnen**, an eye-catching fountain featuring a gilded water sprite emerging from a vast rockery replete with oversized frogs, serpents, fish and the sprite's giant stepfather. In fine weather, concerts take place in the nearby bandstand (May–Sept daily except Mon 4.30pm). Higher up the park, various monuments emerge from the foliage: statues of Johann Strauss and his chief rival Josef Lanner, a temple to Mozart, and, biggest of the bunch, the **Beethoven-Tempel**, a Neoclassical rotunda from 1927, sporting some dubious modern frescoes and graffiti, but the best of all views across the spa.

For a more physically taxing walk, follow the signs to the offbeat **Kaiser-Franz-Josef-Museum** (April–Oct daily except Mon 1–7pm; öS30), roughly half an hour's walk through the woods from the bandstand, in a northwesterly direction. Although it advertises itself as a museum of folk art and craftwork, the collection is a lot more eclectic than you might imagine. The reconstructed smithy is par for the course, but the mousetrap from the room in which the commander in chief of the imperial forces during the Thirty Years' War, Albrecht von Waldstein, was murdered in 1634 is rather more unusual. In addition, there's a whole collection of arms and uniforms from the seventeenth to the twentieth century, banknotes, Habsburg memorabilia, a paper theatre, cake moulds, two penny farthings, and more.

Baden is also a perfect starting point for a full day's **hiking** in the Wienerwald. From the western end of Weilburgstrasse, a path leads up to the twelfth-century rubble of the Ruine Rauheneck. Beyond here lies the Kalternberger Forst, whose main peak is the Hoher Lindkogel (834m), 6km across the forested hills to the west; the hike there and back is relatively easy and takes about six hours non-stop.

The Rollett-Museum and Doblhoffpark

A bizarre collection of exhibits fills the **Rollett-Museum** (daily except Tues 3–6pm; öS20), ten minutes' walk southwest of Hauptplatz on Weikersdorfer Platz. It's worth trekking out here for the building alone, designed in extravagant neo-Renaissance style in 1905 as the town hall for Weikersdorf, only to become redundant seven years later when Weikersdorf was subsumed into Baden. The most fascinating section of the collection within is the array of skulls, busts, brains and death masks – plus a wax model of Marie Antoinette's hand, and a plaster cast of Goethe's – amassed by Franz-Josef Gall (1758–1828), the founder of phrenology, a pseudo-science that claimed a person's talents or criminal traits could be traced to the size of certain areas of the brain. The rest of the museum is a hotchpotch: some crystals, an Egyptian sarcophagus and a cabinet of curios from the world tour of local nineteenth-century bigwig Josef von Doblhoff.

If you'd prefer something less mentally taxing, head for the vast hot thermal **open-air swimming pool** complex, which hides behind the 1920s facade of the Thermalstrandbad on Helenenstrasse. After your dip, you can relax in the nearby **Doblhoffpark**, a lovely mix of formal gardens and English park, with a large rosarium, a pergola and a huge, bushy plane tree at the centre. To the north is the Schloss Weikersdorf, built in the sixteenth century – you should be able to sneak a look at the arcaded courtyard – and seat of the Doblhoff family from 1741 until 1966 (it's now a hotel; see "Practicalities"). Finally, if you've time to spare, check out the latest contemporary art exhibitions in the low-slung Neoclassical **Frauenbad** (daily except Mon 10am–noon & 3–7pm), on Josefplatz.

Practicalities

S-Bahn and regular trains from Vienna's Südbahnhof arrive at Baden's **main train station**, ten minutes' walk southeast of the town centre. Lokalbahn trams, distinguishable by their Prussian blue-and-cream livery, depart from Vienna's Staatsoper and arrive at the **station on Josefsplatz**. Baden's **tourist office** (Easter–Oct Mon–Sat 9am–12.30pm & 2–6pm, Sun 9am–noon; Nov–Easter Mon–Fri 8am–noon & 1–5pm; ☎02252/86800-310) is attractively ensconced in the Leopoldsbad, a magnolia-coloured Biedermeier building on Brusattiplatz.

There's a wide choice of **accommodation** in Baden, though much of it is in the higher price categories, with the handful of **private rooms** on offer through the tourist office the only truly inexpensive option. The rooms at *Hotel Rauch*, Pelzgasse 3 (☎02252/44561; ④), have nice high ceilings and en-suite facilities; *Pension Margit*, Mühlgasse 15–17 (☎02252/89718; ②), though slightly further from the centre, is another typical Baden building, and has some cheaper rooms with shared facilities; *Gästehaus am Kurpark*

(☎02252/89104, fax 89104-16; ②), as the name suggests, is a modern villa inside the Kurpark and enjoys views over the spa. There are several pleasant garden villas along the leafy boulevard of Weilburgstrasse, such as *Villa Inge*, at no. 24–26 (☎02252/43171; ③), but the nicest place to stay is, without a doubt, the *Hotel Schloss Weikersdorf* (☎02252/48301, fax 48301-150; ⑥), a converted Renaissance castle in the Doblhoffpark (see opposite). The cheaper rooms here are in the modern annexe, though all guests get free use of the sauna and pool.

The *Café Central*, on Hauptplatz, is a big traditional *Kaffeehaus* in the Viennese style, and a great place for watching life go by. The *Central* offers reasonably priced **food**, as does *Café Damals*, Rathausgasse 3, but if the weather's fine you're best off packing a picnic and heading off into the woods. The *Gasthaus zum Reichsapfel* is a homely inn just east of the Pfarrkirche, down Spiegelgasse, offering a range of beers and traditional pub fare; for a more formal setting (and fancier versions of the same dishes), try the *Badner Stüberl*, Gutenbrunnstrasse 19 (closed Tues). Baden is a sedate place at the best of times, and by nightfall spa patients are tucked up in bed, while everyone else heads for the town's casino (daily 3pm–3am; öS250) – you'll need jacket and tie to get in.

Wiener Neustadt

Considering that an estimated 52,000 bombs fell on the industrial town of **WIENER NEUSTADT**, 50km south of Vienna, during the latter stages of World War II, killing 790 civilians and destroying some 88 percent of the town's buildings, the place doesn't look that bad. The pedestrianized town centre is pleasant enough, if a little soulless. Sections of the ancient walls, erected by the Babenberg Duke Leopold V when he founded the town in 1194, have survived, and, in the local Militärakademie, there are reminders, too, of the town's fifteenth-century heyday, when it served briefly as the Habsburgs' chief residence under Emperor Friedrich III (1440–93).

The Town

Despite being the largest town in Lower Austria after St Pölten, Wiener Neustadt has a surprisingly compact Altstadt. Dominating the skyline is the town's Romanesque **Dom**, situated a couple of blocks north of Hauptplatz, the town's marketplace (Mon–Sat). Heavily restored in the late nineteenth century, the church's west front still makes a powerful impression; the Gothic interior, distinguished if only for its chancel, which is slightly askew, is equally awesome in scale. The furnishings are mostly Baroque, but patches of medieval fresco survive, and there's a wonderful set of fifteenth-century statues of the twelve apostles adorning the pillars of the central aisle.

One of the best-preserved sections of the old town walls – paid for, incidentally, by the ransom money extracted from England for the release of Richard the Lionheart (see p.152) – lies to the northwest of the Dom, around the **Reckturm** (May–Oct Tues–Thurs 10am–noon & 2–4pm; Sat & Sun 10am–noon; free), a corner tower now housing a small collection of medieval arms and armour. The collection of exhibits at the stylish **Stadtmuseum** (Tues & Wed 10am–5pm, Thurs 10am–8pm, Fri 10am–noon, Sun 10am–4pm; öS30), in the nearby Dominican monastery on Petersgasse, is marginally more interesting, and includes the golden, lidded goblet donated to Wiener Neustadt by Matthias Corvinus after he had captured the town.

The Militärakademie, Wappenwand and Georgskapelle

The town's most intriguing sight is hidden within the prestigious local **Militärakademie** (Military Academy), established in 1752 in the old imperial residence on the southeast corner of the town centre. The building began life as a thirteenth-century castle, but was considerably enlarged by Emperor Friedrich III, when

ACCOMMODATION

Gasthof Friedam	1
Hotel Corvinus	3
Hotel Zentral	2
Youth Hostel	4

WIENER NEUSTADT

he decided to establish his court here in the 1450s. Sadly, an earthquake in 1768, and the bombing raids of World War II, destroyed much of the building's original appearance, but it's still worth visiting, if only for the surreal experience of being guided round by one of the soldiers on duty. To get inside, you must announce yourself to the guard at the Südtor (if the gate is closed, ring the bell).

On the west side of the main courtyard is the **Wappenwand**, or Heraldic Wall, an impressive display of noble might, in which the castle chapel's central window is framed by carved reliefs of over one hundred coats of arms from all of Friedrich's territories and connections, real or imagined. At the base of the wall is a statue of Friedrich, with his cryptic monogram, **AEIOU** (see box).

Behind the Wappenwand, on the first floor, Friedrich built the **Georgskapelle**, dedicated to the emperor's favourite saint, George, in whose honour he founded a new order of chivalry. Though heavily restored inside – the soldier will show you photos of the extent of the bomb damage in 1945 – the chapel has miraculously retained a set of superb fifteenth- and sixteenth-century stained-glass windows, which were wisely stored underground for the duration of the war. Otherwise, only the marble font and one column, decorated with colourful frescoes, survive from the original church. Friedrich's son, Maximilian I (1493–1519), was born here in 1459, and spent his childhood playing mock jousts and war games outside the castle gates; his remains are buried beneath a modern graveslab behind the main altar, though his splendid mausoleum lies in Innsbruck (see p.410).

One other work of art from Friedrich's day that's worth seeking out is the beautiful red marble tombstone of the emperor's beloved Portuguese wife, Eleonore, which lies in the church of **Neukloster**, a short walk north of the Militärakademie. To get to see the tombstone, you must collar one of the monks or priests, as it lies behind the main altar, and can only be reached through the sacristy (try and arrive just before or after Mass). Opposite her finely carved tombstone are the graveslabs of the three of her five children who died in infancy.

Practicalities

The **train** and **bus station** are next door to each other ten minutes' walk southwest of the Hauptplatz, where you'll find the **tourist office**, housed in the Rathaus (Mon–Fri 8am–noon & 1–4pm, Sat 8am–noon; ☎02622/23531-468, fax 23531-498). Wiener Neustadt sees few tourists, so the choice of **accommodation** is fairly limited; it's the sort of place that's best visited on a day-trip from Baden or Vienna. If you do need to stay, the simple, family-run *Gasthof Friedam* (☎02622/23552; ②) is a local pub with rooms, located in the backstreets, fifteen minutes' walk west of the train station at Schneeberggasse 18. Of the town's two hotels, *Hotel Zentral* (☎02622/23169, fax 237935; ④), on the main square at Hauptplatz 27, has greater character than the more modern eyesore, *Hotel Corvinus* (☎02622/24134, fax 24139; ⑦), on Ferdinand Porsche-Ring; both offer en-suite facilities, but only the *Corvinus* has a sauna and steam bath. The town also has a **youth hostel** (☎02622/29695), situated in the park near the distinctive chalice-shaped water tower, south of the Militärakademie. Reception is open from 7am to 10am, and from 5pm to 8pm, but you'd be well advised to ring ahead before tipping up as the place is often full.

Zum weissen Rössl, by the Rathaus, is a traditional pub serving inexpensive and fill-ing **food**, though it closes around 8pm. Another possibility is the *Laguna Azzurra*, on the corner of Bahngasse and Beethovengasse, which does large pizzas for less than öS100, and Italian fish and meat dishes for a bit more. You can soak in the scene from the tables outside at the *Café Bernhart*, a traditional *Kaffeehaus* on the east side of Hauptplatz, but for the real thing, head for the smoke-filled booths of *Café Wenninger*, Neunkirchnerstrasse 36, near the Militärakademie, a sepia-coloured *Kaffeehaus* with lots of newspapers, and a chance to play backgammon and billiards.

For **nightlife**, the locals tend to catch the train to Vienna, though *K&K*, opposite the Neukloster on Ungargasse, has the occasional live band, a pleasant covered courtyard to relax in, an adjoining *gelateria*, as well as tasty snacks. *Gruft* is a Goth/trip-hop hang-out on Frauengasse, north of the Dom, while *Triebwerk*, on Neunkirchnerstrasse, is a popular weekend indie/drum-and-bass venue.

AEIOU

The mysterious acronym **AEIOU**, which became the emperor Friedrich III's personal logo, was emblazoned on everything from library books to new buildings, and can still be seen at several locations across Austria, most notably on his tomb in Vienna's Stephansdom, and his mausoleum in Graz's Domkirche. Composed of all the vowels of the Roman alphabet (in which the letters "u" and "v" are both rendered as "V"), it is open to various interpretations, ranging from the obvious *Austria Erit In Orbe Ultima* (Austria will be last in the world), to the ingenious *Aquila Electa Iovis Omnia Vincit* (The chosen eagle conquers all things). Friedrich himself revealed the German version to be *Alles Erdreich Ist Österreich Untertan* (The whole world is subject to Austria), though some wags put forward the more appropri-ate *Aller Erst Ist Österreich Verloren* (In the first place, Austria is lost), since Friedrich had great difficulty in keeping hold of his Austrian lands, losing Vienna to the Hungarian king Matthias Corvinus in 1485 and his beloved Wiener Neustadt the following year.

Beyond Wiener Neustadt: Schneeberg, Semmering Pass and Raxalpe

South and west of Wiener Neustadt, you begin to enter the alpine foothills that form the border between Lower Austria and Styria. The main autobahn to Graz heads south through the undulating countryside of the Bucklige Welt (literally "Bumpy World"), but the more spectacular route by road and rail is via the Semmering Pass. As the nearest alpine resort to the capital, **Semmering** has long been a popular holiday destination with the Viennese, though it's really the rail journey there that is the main attraction. In addition, the two highest mountain ranges in the vicinity, the evil-sounding **Raxalpe** and the more benevolent **Schneeberg**, can be ascended via chairlift and cog railway respectively.

Puchberg-am-Schneeberg

The **steam cog railway**, which climbs Lower Austria's highest mountain range of Schneeberg, has been a popular day-trip since its completion in 1897. The railway departs from the village of **PUCHBERG-AM-SCHNEEBERG**, itself accessible by regular train from Wiener Neustadt 30km to the west. The cog railway (Zahnradbahn) then wiggles its way along 9km of track ascending over 1200m to the top station of Hochschneeberg (1796m), a journey of just under one and a half hours (May–Oct 2–5 trains daily; öS250 return). The view from the top is pretty impressive, but if the weather's clear it's worth walking onwards to one of the nearby viewpoints: the highest peak of the **Schneeberg** range, **Klosterwappen** (2076m), is an hour's hike from the top of the railway, and gives views over to the Raxalpe (see opposite); the right-hand fork is less strenuous, and will take you to the *Fischerhütte* restaurant, and beyond, to the Kaiserstein (2061m).

If you're planning a **day-trip** from either Wiener Neustadt or Vienna, it's worth picking up the Zahnradbahn leaflet, which lists train connections. If you want to do some hiking from the top station, or simply want to take it easy, it's probably best to stay the night somewhere near Puchberg. En-suite **rooms** at the traditional *Gasthof-Pension Hausmann* (☎02636/2231; ②) are good value, while *Pension Bruckerhof* (☎02636/2315, fax 2315-5; ③) has comfortable rooms with geranium-festooned balconies.

Semmering

The rail line over the 985-metre **Semmering Pass** to Mürzzuschlag is another spectacular feat of engineering. Completed in 1854, it was one of the first railways to forge its way across an alpine pass, employing seventeen tunnels and numerous switchbacks and viaducts; the most scenic stretch of track is the final section between Payerbach and **SEMMERING**. A pleasant, if somewhat amorphous resort, Semmering lies strung out along the northern slopes of the pass, and is dotted with attractive turn-of-the-century villas. Hovering at around 1000m, and famed for its clean air, it has also been a very popular spa with the Viennese for nearly 150 years.

There are two **tourist offices** in Semmering: one concerned mostly with the resort's spa facilities (Mon–Thurs 8am–noon & 1–4pm, Fri 8am–noon), twenty minutes' walk along Hochstrasse by the vast *Jugendstilhotel Panhans*, and a more general one at the Passhöhe (Mon 8.30am–2pm, Tues–Fri 8.30am–4pm; ☎02664/2539, fax 2335), by the main road at the top of the pass. There's an enormous choice of **accommodation** along Hochstrasse. *Pension Daheim* (☎02664/2220; ②) is a characteristic wooden villa, set amidst pine trees. Several notches up in the luxury stakes, but not much more expensive, the welcoming *Hotel Belvedere* (☎02664/2270; ④) comes highly recommended: guests have free use of the hotel's sauna and pool, and the hotel restaurant is excellent.

Höllental and Raxalpe

The River Schwarza cuts a very narrow and dramatic defile, known as the **Höllental** (Valley of Hell), between the limestone massifs of Schneeberg, to the north, and the **Raxalpe**, to the south. The twenty-kilometre section between Reichenau and Schwarzau is popular with cyclists (and car drivers), but most folk only make it as far as the **Raxseilbahn** (öS155 return), Austria's first ever cable car, which opened in 1926, and sets off from just beyond the village of Hirschwang, 3km west of Reichenau. The cable car climbs just over 1000m, leaving you half an hour's hike from the Jakobskogel (1737m), and around two hours from the highest peak of the range, **Heukuppe** (2007m), on the Styrian side of the Raxalpe. If you want to ascend Schneeberg from the Höllental, you'll have to rely on your legs: a marked path sets off from *Naturfreundhaus Weichtal*, 6km beyond the Raxseilbahn; it takes roughly two hours to reach the summit of Klosterwappen (see opposite).

As buses along the Höllental are infrequent, your best bet if you want to explore the valley is to hire a **bike** from the train station at Payerbach (Semmering train station doesn't offer bike rental). Just south of Payerbach, in the hamlet of **Kreuzberg**, you can **stay** at the *Alpenhof* (☎02666/2911, fax 2670; ②), a surprisingly rustic villa designed by the Austrian father of modernism, Adolf Loos, in the 1930s, with good views over the surrounding countryside.

travel details

Trains

Gmünd (NÖ) to: Weitra (8 daily; 20min).

Horn to: Gars am Kamp (hourly; 15min); Krems an der Donau (hourly; 1hr); Rosenburg (hourly; 10min).

Krems an der Donau to: Emmersdorf (every 1–2hr; 50min); Dürnstein (up to hourly; 10min); Gars-Thurnau (hourly; 55min); Marbach-Maria Taferl (1–3 daily; 1hr 25min); Rosenburg (hourly; 1hr); St Pölten (every 40min–1hr; 35–45min); Spitz an der Donau (up to hourly; 25min); Tulln (hourly; 40min); Weissenkirchen (up to hourly; 20min).

Retz to: Drosendorf (every 2hr; 1hr); Geras (every 2hr; 45min); Znojmo (3–6 daily; 20min).

St Pölten to: Herzogenburg (1–2 hourly; 12min); Melk (1–2 hourly; 15–20min); Mariazell (7 daily; 2hr 40min); Pöchlarn (1–2 hourly; 20–25min); Tulln (every 2hr; 1hr).

Vienna (Franz-Josefs Bahnhof) to: Eggenburg (hourly; 1hr–1hr 20min); Gmünd NÖ (every 2hr; 2hr–2hr 20min); Klosterneuburg-Kierling (every 30min; 15min); Krems an der Donau (hourly; 1hr–1hr 15min); Tulln (every 30min; 30–45min).

Vienna (Südbahnhof) to: Baden (every 30min; 30min); Bruck an der Leitha (every 30min; 25–35min); Laa an der Thaya (hourly; 2hr); Mödling (every 15min; 25min); Payerbach-Reichenau (hourly; 1hr 30min/2hr); Semmering (hourly; 2 hr) Wiener Neustadt (every 30min; 50min).

Vienna (Westbahnhof) to: Melk (every 1–2hr; 1hr); Pöchlarn (every 1–2hr; 1hr 15min); St Pölten (1–2 hourly; 40min);

Vienna (Wien-Nord) to: Bad Deutsch Altenburg (hourly; 1hr 10min); Hainburg Ungartor (hourly; 1hr 15min); Petronell-Carnuntum (hourly; 1hr 5min); Retz (every 2hr; 1hr 5min).

Waidhofen an der Ybbs to: Lunz am See (5–8 daily; 1hr 25min).

Wiener Neustadt to: Payerbach-Reichenau (every 30min; 30min); Puchberg-am-Schneeberg (hourly; 45min); Semmering (hourly; 1hr).

Buses

Horn to: Drosendorf (Mon–Sat 1–2 daily; 1hr); Laa an der Thaya (Mon–Fri 3 daily; 1hr 20min); Raabs an der Thaya (1–2 daily; 1hr 15min); Vienna (1–4 daily; 2hr 30min).

Krems an der Donau to: Melk (3–4 daily; 1hr).

Mödling to: Heiligenkreuz (Mon–Fri 10 daily, Sat 5 daily, Sun 7 daily; 15min); Laxenburg (Mon–Fri every 30min, Sat & Sun hourly; 20min).

BURGENLAND

The diminutive province of **Burgenland** is the easternmost and the least Austrian Land of all. An integral part of Hungary from the seventeenth century, it was only handed over to Austria at the end of World War I, after a controversial plebiscite (see box on p.194) left the region's natural capital, Ödenburg (Sopron), in Hungary. Naturally enough, with an awkward salient virtually squeezing Burgenland in two, the province faced enormous problems, not just in terms of communications but in forging any sense of collective identity. Add to these the Russian occupation and the imposition of the Iron Curtain after World War II, and it's easy to see why the last decade or so has been by far the best yet in the region's history. Burgenland has long been a predominantly German-speaking region – hence why it was handed over to Austria in the first place – and the residual **Hungarian**-speaking community now makes up less than five percent of the total population. In fact, the Hungarians are outnumbered by the region's ten percent **Croatian** minority, whose ancestors were encouraged by the local Hungarian lords to settle here in the sixteenth century, to revitalize an area devastated by the Turkish army. However, apart from the odd bilingual sign, and the names of some of the border villages, you'd hardly even notice the presence of the Croatians, whose assimilation continues apace.

In the absence of Ödenburg, the small provincial town of **Eisenstadt** took over the regional administrative role. What brings most people to the town nowadays, however, is its affiliation with **Josef Haydn**, who spent some thirty years here in the second half of the eighteenth century, under the patronage of the powerful Hungarian **Esterházy family**. After Eisenstadt, the most popular destination in Burgenland is the nearby reed-fringed **Neusiedler See**, the country's largest inland lake and the only one in Europe with no natural outlet. For the Austrians, this is the closest the country gets to a coastline, and many come here purely and simply for a fix of beach culture. The **wine-growing** villages around the See have a distinctly Hungarian feel to them, as does the flat *puszta* (steppe) landscape and the consistently warm weather – it can be baking hot here in summer. The rest of Burgenland, south of the region's 5km thin "waist", receives a tiny fraction of the tourists that pack the resorts of the Neusiedler See – and with some justification. The rolling, forested countryside is attractive enough, but there are very few places you'd go out of your way to visit.

ACCOMMODATION PRICE CODES

All **hotels and pensions** in this book have been graded according to the following price categories. All the codes are based on the rate for the least expensive double room during the **summer season**. In those places where winter is the high season, we've indicated winter room rates in the text. For more on accommodation, see p.30.

① under öS400	④ öS800–1000	⑦ öS1400–1600
② öS400–600	⑤ öS1000–1200	⑧ öS1600–1800
③ öS600–800	⑥ öS1200–1400	⑨ over öS1800

They may have shared an empire, but when the ruling dynasty fell in 1918, Austria and Hungary were at each other's throats in no time, arguing over their mutual border. The disputed territory comprised the four predominantly German-speaking border districts of western Hungary: **Pressburg** (Bratislava), **Wieselburg** (Moson), **Ödenburg** (Sopron) and **Eisenburg** (Vasvár). With no historical collective term for this area to hand, the Austrians, in the process of staking their claim, had to invent a name for the proposed province. They eventually decided on "Burgenland", not because of the number of castles in the region, but because of the endings of the four provinces.

Pressburg, however, was already occupied by the Czechs, and with only a forty percent German population, was soon disregarded; in addition, the rail line running through Wieselburg was deemed too strategically important to Hungary, and the district then taken out of the equation. In September 1919, therefore, just Eisenburg and Ödenburg provinces were added to the Austrian Republic as part of the Treaty of St Germain. At this point, however, the Allies wavered in their support of the treaty. To begin with, they had strongly supported the Austrian claim, preferring the Social Democrat government in Vienna to Béla Kun's Bolsheviks in Budapest. However, when Béla Kun and his Communists fell from power and were replaced in November 1919 by the authoritarian regime of Admiral Horthy, the Allies' support for the left-wing government in Vienna weakened. Matters were complicated by the fact that the Austrians, who had been deemed an "enemy state" by the Allies, had been disarmed. Not so the Hungarians, who had been dubbed a "successor state" and who promptly refused to withdraw their troops, saying they were not a party to the treaty.

Eventually, in July 1921, the Hungarians themselves were forced to sign the Treaty of Trianon, agreeing to secede Burgenland. Once more, however, the Hungarians resisted and, under the noses of the Allied troops supposedly overseeing the transfer, drove the Austrians back out of the area. Yielding to the Hungarian military pressure, the Allies advised the Austrians to give up Ödenburg in exchange for the rest of the district. To add a little spice to the course of events, the exiled Habsburg Emperor Karl I turned up in Ödenburg on October 20, 1921, in the vain hope of resuscitating the Hungarian monarchy (see p.176). A plebiscite was finally agreed upon, whereby Ödenburg and eight surrounding rural communes would vote. The Austrians wanted the Hungarians to withdraw their troops before the plebiscite took place, and for the area to be occupied by Allied troops, but the Hungarians refused, in the end withdrawing less than a week before the December vote. Voting lists were therefore drawn up by, and the administration remained in the hands of, the Hungarians. In Ödenburg, the Hungarians got over seventy percent of the vote, but in the rural districts they narrowly lost. As a result, Burgenland lost both its natural centre and its capital. On January 1, 1922, the last border change resulting from World War I was completed, as Hungary formally accepted Ödenburg, now Sopron.

Eisenstadt and around

For a provincial capital – albeit of Austria's second smallest Land – **EISENSTADT** is a tiny little place, with a population of just 11,000. Situated some 50km southeast of Vienna, where the Leithagebirge fuse gently with the Hungarian *puszta*, it became the regional capital only by default in 1921 (see box). Nowadays, the town is known, above all, for its associations with the composer **Josef Haydn**, who was in the employ of the local bigwigs, the Esterházys, for most of his adult life. Haydn may be the main draw nowadays, but the town also has a well-preserved **Jewish ghetto** and an excellent new Jewish **museum**.

EISENSTADT

CARL MOREAU-STR.

GLORIETTE ALLEE

FRANZ-SCHUBERT-PLATZ

❸

Schloss
Esterházy

Haydnhaus

Rathaus

JOSEF-HAYDN-GASSE

Landesmuseum

❶

Jüdisches
Museum

❷

DOMPLATZ

UNTERBERGSTRASSE
ESTERHÁZYSTRASSE

ESTERHÁZY-PLATZ

H A U P T S T R A S S E

KALVERIENBERGPLATZ

PFARRGASSE

Bergkirche

BANKGASSE

ST-ROCHUS-STRASSE

Domkirche

ST-ANTONI-STRASSE

HOTTERWEG

RUSTERSTRASSE

JOSEF-REICHL-GASSE
BAHNSTRASSE

GASSE

N

HANS SIEBENHIRTER-GASSE

DR-KARL-RENNER-STRASSE

GARTENGASSE

KIRCHACKERG.

WÖRMSER STR.

ÖDENBURGERSTRASSE

BAHNSTRASSE

❹

LASCHOBERSTRASSE

❺

**Train
Station**

RUSTERSTRASSE

ACCOMMODATION

Das sportliche Haus	4
Gasthof Ohr	5
Gasthof zum Eder	2
Gasthof zum Haydnhaus	1
Hotel Burgenland	3

0   200m

The Town

Eisenstadt's Altstadt comprises a mere three streets. **Domplatz**, the southernmost of the three, is open to traffic and used primarily as the local bus station; its fifteenth-century Domkirche was only given cathedral status in 1960 and, apart from its gilded pulpit and organ, is nothing special. **Hauptstrasse**, the pedestrianized main street, is prettier; among its striking facades is that of the Rathaus, with shapely Baroque gables, three oriel windows and lively folk paintings of the seven virtues.

Schloss Esterházy

Nothing prepares you for the sheer scale of the **Schloss Esterházy** (guided tours May–Oct daily except Mon 9am–5pm; Nov–April Tues–Fri only; öS50), which presides over Esterházy-Platz, at the western end of Hauptstrasse. The Schloss was built as a medieval fortress with bulky corner towers, later received a Baroque conversion, and was finally redesigned in Neoclassical style (though you can't actually see the fancy, colonnaded north facade overlooking the gardens). The result is a strange building, a sort of oversized French country chateau, daubed in a fresh coat of imperial ochre-yellow paint set off by smart green shutters. Most of the rooms are now used as offices by the provincial government, but a few are open for an hour-long guided tour, which sets off on the hour and is usually in German, so ask for the English notes.

To be perfectly frank, the only room worth seeing is the one that kicks off the guided tour, the **Haydnsaal**, its coved ceiling smothered with more than thirty colourful frescoes, its walls lined with painted roundels of Hungarian heroes. The acoustics are tremendous, and Haydn himself conducted numerous performances of his own music here. If you can catch a live performance, do – it'll also save you having to endure the second half of the guided tour. This takes you round the **Esterházy Museum**, which contains Esterházy family treasures, and traces the history of the clan, who still own the Schloss and remain among the wealthiest landowners in the country. At the end of this endurance test, you emerge in another fine concert hall, the **Empiresaal**, which takes its name from the Neoclassical pastel green, blue and brown trompe l'oeil decor.

Unterberg

A hundred metres or so west of the Schloss lies the old Jewish quarter of **Unterberg**, established as a walled ghetto back in medieval times, and for centuries home to a relatively large Jewish population. All 446 of the town's Jews were deported to the camps shortly after the Anschluss in 1938, and today there are just two Jewish families left in Eisenstadt, though Unterberg has since been repopulated. The remarkable thing about the district, however, is that despite the human destruction wrought on the community, the ghetto itself – comprised of five streets and two cemeteries to the north of Esterházystrasse – remains more or less physically intact. As you enter the ghetto's main street of Unterbergstrasse, you can even see one of the two stone piers between which a chain was placed on the Jewish Sabbath (a practice that was continued right up until 1938).

ÖSTERREICHISCHES JÜDISCHES MUSEUM

Further up Unterbergstrasse on the right, at no. 6, is the **Österreichisches Jüdisches Museum** (Austrian Jewish Museum; May–Oct daily except Mon 10am–5pm; öS50), in the house that once belonged to Samson Wertheimer. Wertheimer was chief administrator of financial affairs to three successive Habsburg emperors, became first rabbi of Eisenstadt, and was appointed Landesrabbiner (Chief Rabbi) of the Hungarian Jewry in 1693 by Emperor Karl VI.

The museum stages temporary exhibitions on the ground floor, while the **permanent exhibition** on the first floor is a fairly standard rundown on Judaism, plus models of a few of Vienna's now demolished synagogues and of Eisenstadt's old ghetto. Captions are exclusively in German, with the only English-language information in the museum's pricey catalogue. All the more reason, then, to head for the **multimedia catalogue** room, which has two televisual presentations in German and English. The first is a history of the Jews in Burgenland, while the second describes the horrors of the Nazi period, and catalogues recent neo-Nazi attacks on the region's surviving Jewish cemeteries.

Also on the first floor is the **Wertheimer'sche Schul**, Wertheimer's private synagogue, built in the early eighteenth century, but whose trompe l'oeil decor dates from the early nineteenth. It was one of the few in the Third Reich to survive *Kristallnacht*, perhaps because by then Eisenstadt had already been cleared of Jews, and was used in the decade after World War II by Jewish soldiers of the Red Army.

BURGENLÄNDISCHES LANDESMUSEUM

Another wealthy Jewish burgher's former home – the rather attractive house with the corner oriel at the junction of Unterbergstrasse and Museumgasse – has been converted into the **Landesmuseum** (daily except Mon 9am–noon & 1–5pm; öS30). As usual, there's no information in English, but the building itself is a lovely, rambling mansion, with a plant-filled rooftop loggia, and, in the cellar, a whole series of impressive Roman mosaics, the largest of which features Bellerophontes killing the lion Ceres. The local history section on the first floor is particularly strong on the territorial dispute after World War I, with propaganda posters from the period, such as Death in Hungarian costume playing the fiddle over Ödenburg. Finally, you shouldn't miss Franz Liszt's plush-ly furnished Blauer Salon, transferred here in its entirety from the Schottenhof in Vienna, where the local-born composer stayed when in the capital from 1869 to 1886.

Haydn's Eisenstadt: the Haydnhaus and Bergkirche

The house that Haydn bought in Eisenstadt, where he kept chickens, two horses and probably a cow, is now the **Haydnhaus** (Easter–Oct daily 9am–noon & 1–5pm; öS20), on Josef-Haydn-Gasse. This was Haydn's home on and off from 1766 to 1788, though there's no attempt here to recreate his abode in any way. With no information at all in English (unless you buy the pricey catalogue) and only a few battered sections of one of the composer's own organs to look at, this is one for all but the most fanatical to skip.

A better way of paying your respects to Haydn is to head for the squat, Baroque **Bergkirche** (April–Oct daily 9am–noon & 1–5pm; Nov–Feb by appointment only; öS20; ☎02682/62638), which, as its name suggests, is located on raised ground 500m west of the Schloss, on the other side of Unterberg. The church interior is a trompe l'oeil fantasy in pinks and greys, but the reason most folk come here is to visit the pur-pose-built **Haydn-Mausoleum**, erected by the Esterházys at the west end of the church in 1932 in order to receive Haydn's decapitated corpse. At the time his head was still in Vienna's Gesellschaft der Musikfreunde, to which it had been bequeathed in 1895, having been stolen by one of Haydn's friends, a keen phrenologist, shortly after the composer's burial in Vienna in 1809. Finally, in 1954, Haydn's head was reunited with his body, and the whole of Haydn now lies in the marble tomb under the mourn-ful gaze of four lounging cherubs.

The Bergkirche's other star attraction (covered by the same ticket) is the **Kalvarienberg** (Calvary Hill), accessible from the outside on the eastern side of the church. Here, steps lead up to a small chapel, beside which a turnstile lets you into a labyrinth of mini-chapels begun in 1701, recounting the story of the Passion through a series of theatrical tableaux of full-size statues. First, you enter a subterranean grotto, then you wind your way round the outside up to the Crucifixion tableau on top of the church (with great views over Burgenland), and finally back down to the Entombment on the other side.

Practicalities

Eisenstadt's **train station** is just ten minutes' walk southeast of the town centre; **buses** arrive and depart from Domplatz. You'll find the **tourist office** (May–Oct daily 9am–5pm; Nov–April Mon–Fri 9am–noon & 2–5pm; ☎02682/67390, fax 67391) in the east wing of the Schloss, but they only have a handful of **private rooms** to offer at the height of the summer season; the regional Burgenland tourist office is located next door (times as above; ☎02682/63384-16, fax 63384-20). For inexpensive **accommodation**, try *Das sportliche Haus*, Hotterweg 67 (☎02682/62326-12, fax 62326-10; ②), a functional place aimed at visiting sports teams. Two clean and unpretentious Gasthöfe in the cen-tre, both with en-suite facilities, are *Gasthof zum Haydnhaus*, Josef-Haydn-Gasse 24 (☎02682/64636; ③), and *Gasthof zum Eder*, Hauptstrasse 25 (☎02682/62645, fax 62645-5; ③). The excellent cooking at the *Gasthof Ohr*, Rusterstrasse 51 (☎02682/62460, fax 62460-9; ④), is a major part of its appeal; all rooms also have en-suite facilities and TV. Top-notch accommodation is available at the *Hotel Burgenland*, on Franz-Schubert-Platz (☎02682/696, fax 65531; ⑦), which boasts a swimming pool and sauna. If you're **camp-ing**, it's probably best to pitch your tent at one of the sites on the western shores of the Neusiedler See, and come to Eisenstadt on a day-trip.

A nice place to **eat and drink** alfresco, and enjoy a view of the Schloss, is the reasonably priced *Schlossrestaurant*, directly opposite in the former stables, on

JOSEF HAYDN

"Well, here I sit in my wilderness, forsaken like a poor waif, almost without any human society, melancholy, full of the memories of glorious days gone by – alas, long gone! And who knows when these days shall return? Those wonderful parties . . . . Here at Estoras [Esterháza], no one asks me: 'Would you like some chocolate, with or without milk? Will you take some coffee, black or café Liègois? What may I offer you, my dear Haydn? Would you like a vanilla or pineapple ice?'"
Letter to Maria Anna von Genzinger, February 9, 1790, from Josef Haydn

Of the big three classical composers, **Josef Haydn** (1732–1809) is seen as coming a poor third to Mozart and Beethoven, despite the fact that his music was in many ways just as radical – not only did he entrench the symphony, the string quartet and the sonata in the cultural landscape, he also experimented with the rigid Baroque symmetry of classical music, often developing a single theme in a way that prefigured much nineteenth-century music. Part of the problem undoubtedly lies in the ordinariness of both Haydn's character and his life – during his lifetime, he acquired the nickname "Papa Jo" for his generally amiable personality (notwithstanding his boorish behaviour towards his wife).

Haydn was born in the Lower Austrian village of Rohrau (see p.178). His father, a master wheelwright who played the harp, recognized his son's musical talents, and at the age of 8 Josef joined the choir of the Stephansdom in Vienna, where he was a pupil for the next nine years. At this point, in 1749 Haydn's voice broke, and he was kicked out of the choir, his little brother Michael becoming the new star pupil. Haydn then endured a difficult, poverty-stricken decade as a freelance musician, which finally ended with his appointment in 1758 as music director for Count von Morzin, a rich Bohemian nobleman. Two years later, Haydn made the biggest mistake of his life, as he later saw it, and married Maria Keller, the daughter of a hairdresser, with whom he could neither get on nor conceive children. She showed virtually no interest in his work, and is alleged to have used his manuscripts as pastry-pan linings and curl papers.

More auspiciously, in 1761 Haydn was appointed assistant Kapellmeister to the Esterházy family at Eisenstadt. Haydn's patron, Prince Paul Anton Esterházy, was a keen music lover – he even published his own songbook, Harmonia Celestis – but he died the following year. Luckily, he was succeeded by Prince Nikolaus (Miklós) "the Ostentatious", another music fan and a lavish entertainer. After a visit to Versailles in 1764, Prince Nikolaus decided to establish his own version of the French chateau, on the other side of the Neusiedler See from Eisenstadt. Although equipped with a theatre, opera house and a marionette theatre, the palace – named Esterháza (Fertöd) – was intended only as a summer residence. In the end, however, it became a more or less permanent home for Prince Nikolaus and for Haydn, now the family's chief Kapellmeister, who was, in any case, glad of the chance to escape his wife and sleep with his mistress, the young Italian mezzo-soprano, Luigia Polzelli.

In 1790, Prince Nikolaus died; his successor, Anton, was less interested in music (and had less money). The family's court orchestra was disbanded, but as a sign of respect for his loyalty the Esterházys continued to pay Haydn's salary and allowed him to keep his title. He immediately moved to Vienna, embarked on two long tours of England, and enjoyed late, but great acclaim, letting his hair down and earning himself a great deal of money at the same time. His final years were plagued by illness, and he died during the second French occupation of Vienna. Such was his renown that – so the story goes – Napoleon placed a guard of honour outside his house, and a French Hussars officer came and sang an aria from The Creation at his deathbed.

Esterházy-Platz. Alternatively, *Silberfuchs*, near the Bergkirche on Kalvarienbergplatz, offers a good range of Austrian dishes and daily specials for around öS75. Another good bet is the *Burgenländische Gasthausbrauerei*, Pfarrgasse 22, where you can wash down your food with the new micro-brew, Haydnbräu.

Regular **concerts** are held in the Haydnsaal of the Schloss Esterházy, and there's an annual festival of Haydn's music called the **Haydntage**, held in the first half of September.

Schloss Forchtenstein and Wiesen

Even in a border region renowned for its castles, the fourteenth-century **Schloss Forchtenstein** (March & Nov Sat & Sun 9am–4pm; April–Oct daily 9am–4pm; öS55), 20km southwest of Eisenstadt, stands head and shoulders above the rest. On the one hand, it occupies an absolutely unassailable position on the eastern slopes of the Rosaliengebirge, with the most stupendous views across the *puszta*. On the other, it contains one of the finest arms collections in the country, courtesy of the Esterházy family, who have owned the property since 1622. It was the only fortress in what was formerly western Hungary not to be captured by the Turks in the 1680s. When the Turkish threat receded, however, Forchtenstein was deemed too uncomfortable for regular use, and became the family arms depot, and as early as 1815, a museum. The weapons remain *in situ*, as if the family's private troops might rush in at any moment and gird themselves up, and are displayed along with Turkish spoils and numerous family portraits. Forchtenstein makes a rewarding day-trip from Eisenstadt (or Wiener Neustadt), but public transport connections are pretty dire, and would need careful planning. The *Burgstüberl*, outside the castle gates, cooks up simple, inexpensive fish and meat dishes.

Burgenland's (and the country's) biggest open-air music events take place in the Festglände, near the village of **WIESEN**, 5km north of Schloss Forchtenstein. Thousands of punters descend on the "Austrian Woodstock" for a series of summer rock festivals, ranging from a reggae *Sunsplash* to a *Jazz Fest*. For more information about the above, contact the Tourismusbüro Region Rosalia, Brunnenplatz 4, Mattersburg (☎02626/63467).

The Neusiedler See

Eisenstadt is close enough to the **Neusiedler See** (Fertö to the Hungarians) to make a day-trip to the its western shores perfectly possible, though you'll get more out of the area by staying over for a night or two. It's quite unlike anywhere else in Austria. Fringed by giant reed beds and vineyards, and set amidst the flat steppe landscape of the *puszta*, the area feels more Hungarian than any other part of Burgenland. The lake itself is a strange ecological phenomenon: it has no major water source feeding into it – the water just sits on the surface of the land, with a slightly saline quality to it. The water is never much more than one or two metres deep – it has been known to dry up completely (lastly in the 1860s) – and, if the wind blows persistently in one direction, it can literally take the lake with it, leaving one shore bereft. The lake's shallowness means, of course, it warms up very quickly in summer, making it a perfect spot for **windsurfing**. Its reed beds, meanwhile, are home to a wide variety of **bird life**, and the Seewinkel wetlands to the east of the lake are especially popular with ornithologists. Another activity that's big around these parts is **cycling**: a cycle path winds its way through the reed beds, passing through Hungary along the southern shore in order to make the full circuit of around 100km. You can also take your bike on one of the many boats that crisscross the See in summer months, and on the special Fahrradbus that does a partial circuit of the lake from Mörbisch to Illmitz (see box, p.201).

Neusiedl am See is the chief town and transport hub, but the two most photogenic places around the See are the prosperous wine-producing town of **Rust**, and the neighbouring village of **Mörbisch**, flush with the Hungarian border. If you're more

NEUSIEDLER SEE

△ Vienna

Parndorf

N

Jois

Neusiedl am See

Breitenbrunn

Winden am See

Weiden am See

Purbach

Gols

Donnerskirchen

Mönchhof

Halburn

Podersdorf

Frauenkirchen

△ Eisenstadt

Oggau

△ Tadten & Andau

SEEWINKEL

Zicksee

Rust

St. Andrä

Neusiedler See

Lange
Lacke

Illmitz

△ Eisenstadt

Mörbisch

Apetlon

Wallern

△ Tadten & Andau

△ Sopron

Fertörákos

Pamhagen

Mosonmagyaróvár △

△ Sopron

0   10 km

HUNGARY

Fertöd

GETTING AROUND AND ACROSS THE NEUSIEDLER SEE

Train services link a few of the villages on the western shore with Eisenstadt and Neusiedl am See, as well as some of the villages of the Seewinkel. Elsewhere, you'll have to rely on buses. Particularly useful is the **Fahrradbus**, which carries both pedestrians and cyclists and plies its way from Mörbisch to Illmitz every day, calling at all the lakeside villages in between (pick up a timetable from the tourist office). **Boat services** are provided by a number of companies from May until October; the Mörbisch–Illmitz route is one of the most frequent (May–Oct every 30min 8.30am–5pm). **Bike hire** (*Radverleih*) is available from Neusiedl am See train station and from numerous outlets in each of the resorts; a day's rental ranges from öS60 to öS150, depending on the bike. It's also worth asking at one of the region's tourist offices about any special deals on combined tickets covering boat, bus and/or train travel.

  Although the southern shore of the lake is in Hungary, it's easy enough to cross the border; simply take your passport with you. The Mörbisch–Fertörákos border point (daily: April, May & Oct 8am–8pm; June–Sept 6am–midnight) is for pedestrians and cyclists only, while the Pamhagen–Fertöd border crossing (open daily all year; 6am–midnight) is for cars, too.

interested in beach culture, then head for **Podersdorf am See**, on the eastern shore, as this is the only place with both village and resort on the lake. All the other villages around the See are separated from the shoreline by several kilometres of reed beds, and therefore have split personalities: the old village centre, usually surrounded by vineyards, and home to numerous *Heurigen* or *Buschenschänken*, and the modern development on the See itself, usually featuring a campsite, a restaurant, a small beach, and an open-air swimming pool among copious other leisure facilities. To gain access to the See, you usually have to pay an entrance fee of up to öS50 per day, though if you're staying overnight in the region, then you are entitled to a **VIP-Card** (pronouced "Vip"), which gives you free parking and entry to most of the resorts around the See, plus reductions for bike hire and other charges; take your accommodation receipt to the nearest tourist office to receive your card. The best time to visit the Neusiedler See is from April until October, as many of the facilities close down in winter.

Rust and around

By far the prettiest place on the Neusiedler See is **RUST**, 13km east of Eisenstadt. While most other settlements are strung out along a single main street, Rust is a proper town, albeit a very small one, built from the profits of the local wine trade, and with a well-preserved Altstadt centred on the lovely cobbled square of **Rathausplatz**. The Rathaus itself, a seventeenth-century building decked out in Pompeiian red, is just one of the square's many perkily painted houses, each of which features big barn doors, and geraniums spilling out from windows flanked by French shutters. Above all, though, Rust is famous for its **storks**, whose nests perch permanently on the chimneys of just about every house in the Altstadt. Each year towards the end of March, these huge birds return to the very same chimney top, lay their eggs and rear their young, leaving around late August for warmer climes.

  Overlooking the main square is the venerable **Fischerkirche** (Easter, April & Oct Mon–Sat 11am–noon & 2–3pm, Sun 11am–noon & 2–4pm; May–Sept Mon–Sat 10am–noon & 2.30–5pm, Sun 11am–noon & 2–5pm; öS10), a tiny Gothic church set into the old town walls, and dating, in parts, to the thirteenth century. The interior is richly painted with medieval patterning and frescoes depicting the Crucifixion, and the cute little Baroque organ of 1705 is the oldest in Burgenland. The rather handsome Baroque tower beyond the Fischerkirche belongs to the local Protestant church, testifying to the historic strength of Hungarian Calvinism in the area.

Like all the settlements around the See, Rust has a small lakeside development, 2km away through the reed beds. Here, you'll find Rust's **campsite** (☎02685/595; April–Sept), plus a marina, beach and all the usual facilities for bike hire, windsurfing and so forth. Rust has one other nearby attraction, of interest mostly to those with children: the **Märchenpark and Zoo** (March–Oct daily 9am–6pm; öS100), a kilometre or so west of Rust on the road to Eisenstadt. Along with the kangaroos, wild boar, deer and the like, there are various "animal shows", and rides of all kinds from waterboat slides to ghost trains.

Rust's **tourist office** (May–Sept Mon–Fri 8am–noon & 3–6pm, Sat 9am–noon, Sun 10am–noon; Oct–April Mon–Thurs 8am–noon & 1–4pm, Fri 8am–noon; ☎02685/6475, fax 502-10), housed in the Rathaus, can organize private rooms – if it's closed, there's a free phone for booking **accommodation** outside the office underneath the archway. Budget recommendations include *Stadt Rust* (☎02685/268; ②), on Rathausplatz, some of whose rooms have shared facilities only, and *Arkadenhof* (☎02685/246, fax 6480; ③), on Franz-Josef-Platz, just outside the Altstadt. One of the choicest places to stay in the Altstadt is the sixteenth-century *Rusterhof* (☎02685/6416, fax 6416-11; ⑥; May–Dec only), also on Rathausplatz; the rooms all have self-catering facilities, the restaurant is excellent and booking ahead is pretty much essential.

The nicest **places to eat** cheaply, and enjoy a taste of the local wine, are the various *Buschenschänken* in the Altstadt. A good one, with a typical vine-clad, cobbled courtyard is *Kicker*, on Haydngasse. The atmospheric cellars of the *Rathauskeller* (closed Wed), underneath the Rathaus, are also good place to while away the evening.

Mörbisch am See

MÖRBISCH, 5km south of Rust, is a classic one-street village, its whitewashed houses strung out like a ribbon along Hauptstrasse. Off the main street, beautifully scented, cobbled courtyards, filled with potted plants and hung with vines and dried corn cobs, lead down to back lanes on the edge of the vineyards that press in on the village from all sides. You can visit one of these traditional houses (and its wine cellars) by following the signs to the **Heimathaus** (Easter–Oct daily 9am–noon & 1–5pm; öS10), Hauptstrasse 53; to get the key (and a guided tour in German), you must call in at the house across the courtyard.

Mörbisch is best known for its **Seefestspiele**, the annual open-air operetta festival that takes place on the See at the **Seebühne**, or floating stage, 2km east of centre, from the middle of July to the end of August. For information or tickets, contact either the festival box office in Eisenstadt (☎02682/66210, fax 66210-14) or, after the middle of June, the box office in Mörbisch (☎02685/81810, fax 8334). Sharing the lakeside with the Seebühne are all the usual waterfront facilities, including an especially good children's swimming pool. Cyclists and pedestrians can **cross into Hungary** at Mörbisch (daily: April, May & Oct 8am–8pm; June–Sept 6am–midnight), but car drivers must use the 24-hour border crossing at Klingenbach, more than 20km away by road.

Mörbisch **tourist office**, Hauptstrasse 27 (May, June & Sept Mon–Fri 9am–5pm, Sat 9am–1pm; July & Aug Mon–Sat 9am–6pm; ☎02685/8420, fax 8430-9), can assist with the bewildering array of **accommodation** on offer. Try booking into *Fischl*, Hauptstrasse 93 (☎02685/8292; ②), or *Das Schmidt* (☎02685/8294, fax 8294-13; ④; Easter–Oct only), the large hotel on Raiffeisenstrasse, parallel to Hauptstrasse, which sports a nice arcaded balcony round the back; its rooms have en-suite facilities and views over to the See. The lakeside *Seehotel* (☎02685/8217, fax 8811; ③) is the only hotel in the thick of the beach resort, while *Seepension Stephanie* (☎02685/13815; ②) is hidden away in the thick of the reed beds, off the Seestrasse. The

Gemeindegasthaus, Hauptstrasse 22, opposite the tourist office, serves good local **food**, with a pleasant *Gastgarten* out the back, and there are numerous other *Buschenschänken* to choose from.

Purbach am Neusiedler See

PURBACH, the most appealing of the villages to the north of Rust, also has the advantage of a **train station** and frequent **bus** services to Eisenstadt and Neusiedler See. The town's emblem is a stone statue of a bearded, turbaned Turk, known as the **Purbacher Türke**, to be found on the town's northern battlements (you'll need to ask a local for directions). It's by no means the only reminder of the Turkish threat: the double gateway of the **Türkentor** now protects the village from the main road, while two Turkish cannonballs can be seen within a glass-fronted niche (inscribed with the jokey warning "Türkennot") set into the wall of the picturesque old inn, *Purbachhof*, on Schulgasse.

The town's **tourist office** (May–Sept daily 9am–noon & 3–6pm; ☎02683/5920) is at Hauptgasse 38. You can enjoy a memorable night's **accommodation** at the aforementioned *Purbachhof* (☎ & fax 02683/5564; ④), or in *Am Spitz* (☎02683/5519, fax 5519-20; ③), a tastefully converted monastery, set amidst its own vineyards above the village, a kilometre or so to the west. At Purbach's outlet to the See, 4km southeast through the reeds, there's a **campsite** (☎02683/5170; April–Oct), with a **youth hostel** attached, as well as all the usual leisure facilities. Of the village's numerous *Buschenschänken*, perhaps the prettiest of the lot is the thatched *Martinschenke*, Bodenzeile 16. Considerably more expensive is the upmarket *Nikolauszeche* (closed Tues & Wed lunchtime), housed in another beautiful old building, directly opposite, with a typical cobbled courtyard.

Neusiedl am See

NEUSIEDL AM SEE, the tacky, one-street town at the northern tip of the lake, is the only place with a frequent train service to and from Vienna; it's also a good place to get your bearings and pick up some information about the area – otherwise, its attractions are distinctly limited. The most interesting sight here is the **Kultur und Aktions Haus**, an arts squat on Untere Hauptstrasse, which puts on raves and other events, and looks like it landed here by mistake from Vienna. If you've time to kill, you could do worse than check out the staggeringly large private collection of bygone farming equipment at the **Pannonisches Heimatmuseum** (May–Oct Tues–Sat 2.30–6.30pm, Sun 10am–noon & 2.30–6.30pm; free), at Kalvarienbergstrasse 40, off Untere Hauptstrasse.

Neusiedl's **tourist office** (June & Sept Mon–Fri 8am–noon & 1–4.30pm; July & Aug Mon–Fri 8am–7pm, Sat 10am–noon & 2–6pm, Sun 4–7pm; Oct–May Mon–Thurs 7.30am–noon & 1–4.30pm, Fri 7.30am–1pm; ☎02167/2229, fax 2637) is conveniently

---

THE RAABERBAHN

The railway to the east of the Neusiedler See belongs to the **Raab-Oedenburg-Ebenfurther Eisenbahn** (ROeEE), established in 1872 and known as the Raaberbahn for short. This private line, whose trains sport a smart green and yellow livery, survived both the redrawing of the borders after World War I and the imposition of the Iron Curtain in 1945. The line, whose engines only changed over from steam to diesel in 1980, was electrified in 1986, and runs from Neusiedl am See to Fertöszentmiklós, in Hungary, situated on the company's other line from Ebenfurth in Austria to the Hungarian city of Györ (Raab). Rail passes are valid, and the ticketing is fully integrated into the Austrian and Hungarian state-run railway systems.

located in the Rathaus on the main street. **Trains** from Vienna, and most buses, arrive at the main train station, some 2km northwest of the town centre (your train ticket covers the bus into town); the Bad Neusiedl-am-See station, three blocks south of the main street, is served only by slow Raaberbahn trains.

If you need to grab a bite to **eat**, or **stay** the night, the *Rathausstüberl* (☎02167/2883, fax 2883-7; ③), situated directly behind the Rathaus, is hard to beat: it serves up a fresh fish of the day, for öS75 or so, has a shady, vine-covered courtyard and clean en-suite rooms. Neusiedl has the only official HI **youth hostel** in the area (☎ & fax 02167/2252; March–Nov), fifteen minutes' walk from the station and the centre, at Herberggasse 1, off Wienerstrasse.

Podersdorf am See

PODERSDORF, 12km south of Neusiedl, is the only town that can really claim to be "am See". Don't come here expecting the charms of Rust, however; Podersdorf is basically a convenient and serviceable place from which to gain easy, reed-free access to the water. It also happens to be the most popular destination in the whole of Burgenland, and the best spot from which to watch the sun set over the See. Swimming, boating, windsurfing, cycling, horse-riding and bird-watching are the chief attractions, though the village does boast a **Windmühle** (July & Aug; daily 6–7pm; öS25), on the southern edge of town, off the road to Illmitz.

Podersdorf has two **tourist offices**: the main one is at Hauptstrasse 2 (July & Aug Mon–Fri 7.30am–noon & 1–6pm, Sat 8am–noon & 1–6pm, Sun 8am–noon; Sept–June Mon–Fri 7.30am–noon & 1–4.30pm, Sat 9am–noon & 2–4pm, Sun 9am–noon; ☎02177/2227, fax 2170); the summer-only office (July & Aug, times as above; ☎02177/3400-20) is by the See, next door to *Tauber* restaurant. Either office can book **private rooms**, and the main one has a computer screen outside showing the current state of room vacancies. In the especially busy months of July and August, you're best off getting the tourist office to book **hotel** accommodation for you, as vacancies can be thin on the ground. Most places are fairly simple, modern and functional, though some have pleasant inner courtyards and balconies: two such B&Bs are *Pension Steiner*, Seestrasse 33 (☎ & fax 02177/2790; ②), which doubles as a *Heuriger*, and *Arkadenhof*, at no. 13 (☎02177/2402; ③). If you want a room overlooking the See, book in at the modern *Gästehaus Preiner*, on Seeweingärten (☎ & fax 02177/2346; ②), or the nearby *Gasthof Seewirt* and its adjacent annexe, *Haus Attila*, on Strandplatz (☎02177/2415, fax 2465-30; ④). Podersdorf's **campsite** (☎02177/2279, fax 2279-16; April–Oct) is a vast, efficiently run site spread out along the shore to the southwest.

When **eating** out, try some of the local fish, especially the carp, zander and eel. *Pfandlwirt*, by the campsite, serves its fish "in the pan" (hence the name), and *Gasthof Kummer*, near the seasonal tourist office, regularly offers a range of fish dishes, *gebacken* (in batter), *serbisch* (spicy) or *blau* (natural), while the *Seewirt*, mentioned above, has an excellent restaurant specializing in local cuisine. The cheapest and most convivial places to spend the evening, though, are the town's numerous *Heurigen*: try the *Heuriger zum 18er*, Seestrasse 40, a typical wine tavern with check tablecloths and a vine-strewn courtyard.

Frauenkirchen and Halbturn

If you're looking for a bit of cultural distraction around Podersdorf, pay a visit to the outstandingly beautiful **Basilika** in **FRAUENKIRCHEN**, 8km to the east. Built in the fourteenth century, and subsequently destroyed by the Turks on several occasions, the pilgrimage church was redesigned in High-Baroque style in 1702 by Francesco Martielli with Esterházy money. Inside, it's the cross-vaulted ceiling that makes the greatest initial impression, its frescoes framed by rich white and gold stucco-work. The richly carved pulpit, crowded out with polychrome angels and cherubs of varying sizes, also features an almost comical, disembodied gilded arm bursting out of the side and brandishing a crucifix. The choirstalls, with their painted panels and carved choirboy heads, also bear closer inspection, as does the ostentatious gilded high altar.

The pretty, pale-blue Baroque **Schloss** (May–Oct daily 9am–6pm; öS60) in **HALBTURN**, 5km northeast of Frauenkirchen, provides another welcome distraction. Designed in 1710 by Johann Lukas von Hildebrandt as a palatial hunting lodge for the Harrach family, and boasting a fresco by Franz Anton Maultbertsch, it now hosts temporary exhibitions taken from the imperial collections of the Österreichische Galerie. The chateau's formal gardens are perfect for a picnic, and there's a *Schlosstaverne* for those without provisions.

The Seewinkel

Podersdorf is also a good base for exploring the nearby **Seewinkel**, the marshy grasslands to the south, dotted with tiny, saltwater lakes, which provide a haven for a wide variety of flora and fauna. Much of the area has been granted protected national park status, and there's a solar-powered **Nationalparkhaus** (☎02175/3442; April & Oct Mon–Fri 9am–5pm, Sat & Sun noon–5pm; May–Sept Mon–Fri 9am–6pm, Sat & Sun 10am–5pm; Nov–March Mon–Fri 8am–4pm), just outside **ILLMITZ**, 11km south of Podersdorf. Here, you can buy expensive binoculars, cheap local apple juice and head up the viewing tower to try and spot one of the estimated 250 different species of bird that live in the marshlands. Exhibitions, videos and talks are held in the centre, and, though most information is in German, there are folk who speak English on hand to advise on where to go and what to see. If you prefer, you can sign up for one of the centre's organized excursions, which cost öS100 per person and usually last around three and a half hours.

One of the easiest places to spot some birdlife is around the **Lange Lacke**, 4km east of Illmitz, home to greylag geese, bitterns, great white egrets and spoonbills. The Lange Lacke tends to dry up completely in high summer, but not so the **Zicksee**, to the northeast, which is deeper than most of the other lakes, and, consequently, a popular place to swim. The grassy beach on the eastern shore is more sheltered, much shadier and generally a lot more laid-back than the one at Podersdorf. The lake is a short walk from the nearby **train station** at St Andrä Am Zicksee, and has a **campsite** (☎02175/2144; May–Sept). If you've come to the Seewinkel in search of the elusive great bustard, Europe's heaviest bird, the place to try and find it is in the swampy meadows 8km southeast of St Andrä, beyond the village of **Tadten**.

Southern Burgenland

Burgenland is very nearly split in two by the Sopron salient given to Hungary in 1922 (see p.194). At the region's "waist" there's barely 5km of Burgenland between the Hungarian border and Lower Austria. Add to this the thickly forested Rosaliengebirge and Ödenburgergebirge that form a continuous arc of hills from Sopron to Wiener Neustadt, and southern Burgenland starts to feel like a separate province. While Eisenstadt and the Neusiedler See feel as if they're teetering on the edge of the Great Plain of Hungary, southern Burgenland is a patchwork of gently rolling hills, forests, vineyards and rich farmland. There are very few places here that you'd go out of your way to visit, but if you're heading south to Slovenia or Styria the road that winds its way down the length of Burgenland is a pretty enough route to take. **Raiding**, the birthplace of Franz Liszt, receives a trickle of pilgrims, while **Lockenhaus**, hard by the Hungarian border, hosts a world-famous festival of chamber music. The museum in **Bernstein** dedicated to serpentine is of more general interest, as is the landmark castle at **Güssing**, in the far south of the province.

Raiding

The Hungarian composer Franz Liszt (1811–86) was born in the village of **RAIDING**, some 40km south of Eisenstadt, where his father was steward of the Meier estate. The family home, now the **Liszt Geburthaus** (Easter–Oct daily 9am–noon & 1–5pm; öS20), like the Meier estate itself, belonged to the Esterházy family. Over the entrance to the lovely sixteenth-century whitewashed cottage, set in its own beautiful walled garden, is an old Hungarian inscription commemorating Liszt Ferenc, unveiled in the composer's presence (there's a picture of the ceremony in the museum), and a more recent one in German. Liszt spent the first eleven years of his life here, before the family moved to Vienna (where he studied under Czerny and Salieri), and eventually to Paris, to further the Wunderkind's promising musical career as "one of the great renovators of nineteenth-century music" – as the English notes say. As usual, there's very little attempt to recreate the interior as it would have been in Liszt's day, but, to the strains of his *Piano Concerto No. 1*, you get to see a lot of photographs of the wild-looking Liszt, who spent much of his life as a roaming virtuoso.

Buses to Raiding are pretty infrequent, but the nearest **train station**, Raiding-Lackendorf, is 2km north of the village; alternatively, you could hire a bike from the station at Deutschkreuz, 10km northeast of Raiding.

Lockenhaus and around

LOCKENHAUS, at the foot of the Günsergebirge, 25km southwest of Raiding, is as good a place as any to stop off if you're passing this way. The town's focal point is its gargantuan Baroque **Pfarrkirche**, overlooking the main square, whose interior features a wild, technicolour high relief of winged cherubs clinging to giant acanthus leaves on the north wall and, on the opposite wall, a gruesome, full-scale Crucifixion scene, played out against a mural of Jerusalem. Check out the church's crypt, too, which contains several ornate red marble tombs belonging to the local Hungarian bigwigs, the Nádasdy family, into which the notorious "Blood Countess", Elizabeth Báthory, married (see box).

The medieval fortress of **Burg Lockenhaus** (daily: April–Sept 7.30am–6pm; Oct & Nov 8am–5pm; Dec–March 8am–4pm), which rises up out of the woods high above the town, is Burgenland's oldest, built around 1200 to defend the region against the Mongols. Much of the interior has been converted into a hotel (see below), including the cross-ribbed Rittersaal, while another part is used for art exhibitions (May–Oct daily 8am–5pm; öS50). The Festsaal is used for concerts and forms the centrepiece of the town's world-famous *Kammermusikfest*, established by the Latvian-born violinist Gidon Kremer in 1981, and held annually in late June/early July. The single most intriguing room, though, is the mysterious **Kultraum**, lit by a single shaft of light from the ceiling and thought to have been used for some sort of chivalric ceremony based on sun worship. Last, but not least, the castle has a **Griefvogelstation** (April–Oct daily 10am–5pm; öS50), home to numerous well-trained birds of prey, who put on regular demonstrations of their talons.

The **Hungarian border** is just 2km east of Lockenhaus, and, if you want to visit the nearby Hungarian town of Köszeg, there's a border crossing 8km further east at Rattersburg. If you just want to look over into Hungary, you could enjoy a full day's hike along the marked path to **Geschriebenstein** (884m), 10km south of Lockenhaus, the highest peak in the Günsergebirge, with a lookout tower from which there are glorious views over the Great Plain of Hungary.

Lockenhaus has a good **tourist office** (April–Oct Mon–Fri 8am–noon & 1–4.30pm; ☎02616/2247, fax 2314), at Hauptstrasse 21, with a smattering of private rooms to offer. The most memorable **place to stay** is, of course, in the *Burghotel Lockenhaus*

(☎02616/2394, fax 2766; ④), though make sure you get one of the atmospheric medieval rooms, and not one in the modern annexe. If the Burg is full, or your budget's not up to it, *Gasthof Schlögl* (☎02616/2225, fax 2225-16; ②), on Hauptplatz, is a good fall-back.

THE BLOOD COUNTESS

Born in 1560, **Countess Elizabeth** was the offspring of two branches of the noble Báthory family. She shared a tendency towards fainting spells and fits of uncontrollable rage with other **Báthory** family members, like her uncle, Prince "Crazy" Gábor. As a child Elizabeth was intelligent and well educated, being fluent in Latin, Hungarian and German at a time when many nobles, including the ruling prince of Transylvania, were barely literate. Brought up in the family seat at Nagyecsed, a humble town near the Hungarian–Romanian border, she witnessed at the age of just 9 the rape and murder of her sisters by the local peasantry, and absorbed from her surviving relatives the notion that peasants were little more than cattle – to be harshly punished for any act of insubordination.

As was customary in the sixteenth century, Elizabeth's marriage was arranged for dynastic reasons, and an illegitimate pregnancy hushed up. Betrothed in 1571 – the same year that her cousin István became Prince of Transylvania – she was married four years later, at the age of 15, to 21-year-old Ferenc Nádasdy. In the course of the next decade, Ferenc was usually away fighting Turks, earning his reputation as the "Black Knight", while Elizabeth grew bored at the family's castles in Sárvár, Kereshtur and Lockenhaus. She began to torture serving women, an "entertainment" that gradually became an obsession. With the assistance of her maids Dorothea Szentes and Anna Darvulia (who was also her lover), Elizabeth cudgelled and stuck pins into servants to "discipline" them; even worse, she forced them to lie naked in the snowy courtyard and then doused them with cold water until they froze to death. Ferenc balked at this on his return (although he, too, enjoyed brutalizing servants, so it wasn't until after his death in 1604 that Elizabeth started torturing and murdering without restraint.

Her victims were invariably women or girls, and – most importantly – always peasants. Killing peasants could be done with impunity. Poor women could always be enticed into service and, should word of their deaths leak out, the authorities would hardly believe the accusations of the victims' parents against the countess. With the assistance of Szentes, Darvulia, Elizabeth's son's former wet-nurse Helena Jo, and one man, the diminutive Fizcko, the countess allowed her sadistic fantasies full rein. On occasion she bit chunks of flesh from servants' breasts and necks – probably the origin of the legend that she bathed in the blood of virgins to keep her own skin white and translucent.

In this fashion Elizabeth murdered over six hundred women and might well have continued undetected had Darvulia not died. Grief-stricken, the countess formed an attachment to a local widow, Erzsi Majorová, who encouraged her to seek aristocratic girls for her victims. Enquiries by their parents could not be so easily ignored by the authorities, who in any case by now had their own motives for investigating *die Blutgräfin*: Ferenc Nádasdy had loaned the Habsburg crown 17,000 gulden, which Elizabeth had persistently, and vainly, demanded back – if she were to be found guilty of serious crimes, this debt would be forfeited. Among Elizabeth's other adversaries were her son Paul, who had grown up apart from her at Sárvár, and one Count Thurzo, both of whom were anxious to prevent the confiscation of the Báthory estates and so gathered evidence against her.

On December 29, 1610, Thurzo's men raided Aachtice Castle, another family seat (now in Slovakia), and on entry almost tripped over the corpse of a servant whom Elizabeth had just bludgeoned for stealing a pear. Thurzo secretly imprisoned the "damned woman" in her own castle immediately, so that (in his words) "the families which have won such high honours on the battlefield shall not be disgraced . . . by the murky shadow of this bestial female". Due to his cover-up, knowledge of the scandal was mainly confined to court circles, although when Elizabeth died in 1614 the locals protested at her burial in Aachtice cemetery. She was later reburied at Nagyecsed in the precincts of the family vault. Due to her sex (then considered incapable of such deeds) and rank, records of her trial were hidden and mention of her name subsequently prohibited by royal command.

Bernstein and around

BERNSTEIN, 15km west of Lockenhaus, means "amber" in German, and most likely got its name from the ancient "Amber Road" that linked the Baltic to the Adriatic, and passed through the town. Confusingly, the gemstone for which Bernstein is best known, however, and the subject of the town's **Felsenmuseum** (March–Dec daily 9–11.30am & 1.30–5.30pm; öS50), is **serpentine**, which was first commercially mined here in the mid-nineteenth century. Despite the lack of information in English, this is an intriguing museum, decked out like a dimly lit mineshaft, and glistening with all sorts of startling crystals and gemstones. On the first floor, you get to see what the local serpentine, which turns spinach-green when polished, can be made into at the hands of Otto Potsch, the sculptor who set up the museum. Potsch's slightly kitsch carved animals might not be everyone's cup of tea, but the craftsmanship is first class.

The main road runs right through Bernstein, so you're better off spending the night back in Lockenhaus, or continuing further south – unless, that is, you're up for staying in the medieval *Burg Bernstein* (☎03354/6382, fax 6520; ⑥; May–Oct), which sits above the village. This family-owned castle is the real thing, a wonderfully rambling place, complete with dungeon, ghosts and a candlelit dining hall with an Italian stucco-work ceiling; rooms have real fires, lots of antiques and few mod cons.

Most people seem to go to the walled town of **STADTSCHLAINING**, 12km south of Bernstein, to attend some conference at the UNESCO-funded Austrian Study Centre for Peace and Conflict-Resolution, which resides in the town's little medieval **Burg Schlaining**. You can also visit the castle on a thirty-minute guided tour (Easter–Oct daily except Mon 9am–noon & 1–5pm; öS30), which takes you up the round tower and past a bit of folk art and the odd leftover from the days of the Batthyány family, who sold it off to a local railway magnate in 1849. After the tour, you can eat, drink and relax in the dry moat, now part of the castle's *Burgtaverne*. Stadtschlaining does have one other, rather more intriguing sight: the **Friedensbibliothek** (Mon–Thurs 8am–5pm, Fri 8am–noon; free), housed in the town's former synagogue, across the Hauptplatz from the Burg through an archway at no. 3. The building has been lovingly restored, and its barrel-vaulted ceiling is richly decorated with trompe l'oeil plasterwork, so settle down with a book (there are plenty in English) and take some time out.

Some 10km south of Bernstein, the main road bypasses the smart spa-town of **BAD TATZMANNSDORF**. Other than to take the waters, there are two main reasons you might want to pause here: to have a swim in the lovely open-air pool, on Josef-Holzel-Allee, off Bahnhofstrasse, or to visit the neighbouring **Burgenlandisches Freilichtmuseum** (daily 9am–5pm; öS10). Neatly laid out in an orchard, with a few sheep, hens and goats for added authenticity, this laid-back open-air folk museum holds around fifteen, mostly thatched buildings that were commonplace in the nineteenth century. If your appetite is whetted, there's a better selection of folk buildings near Güssing (see opposite).

Güssing and around

At the very foot of Burgenland (though not quite the toe), more than 50km south of Bad Tatzmannsdorf, the little town of **GÜSSING** (Németújvár) lies wrapped round the base of a medieval castle – a striking sight as you approach from the north. **Burg Güssing** (May–Oct daily 9am–5pm; öS50) itself contains a half-decent art collection, including works by Dürer and Cranach, plus an array of Turkish and Hungarian arms and armour; it also hosts special exhibitions, stages open-air events in its main courtyard, and has an inexpensive restaurant with great views over the surrounding countryside. The **Franziskanerkirche**, on Hauptplatz in the town centre below, is filled with gilded Baroque altarpieces, but its fame rests on its **Batthyánysche Gruft**, the Batthyány family mausoleum, which has a separate entrance set into the south wall of the church.

Access to the ornate, eighteenth-century lead sarcophagus commissioned by one of the Batthyány from eminent sculptor Balthasar Ferdinand Moll, has to be arranged through the tourist office (see below). If you're here at the weekend, call in at the **Auswanderer Museum**, Stremtalstrasse 2 (May–Oct Sat & Sun 2–6pm; öS20), which tells the story of the thousands of Burgenländer who emigrated to North America in the half century leading up to World War I (Fred Astaire's father among them).

Güssing **tourist office** (Mon–Thurs & Sat 9am– noon, Fri 9am–noon & 3–6pm; ☎03322/42311-23, fax 42311-41) is at Hauptplatz 7, and can book private rooms for you. Other **accommodation** is limited, but *Hotel Josef Fabiankovits*, Hauptstrasse 49 (☎03322/42341, fax 43466; ②), and *Gasthof-Pension Kedl*, Urbersdorf 33 (☎03322/42403, fax 42403-14; ②), both have decent en-suite facilities. If you're just breaking your journey, the *Stadt Café* is a stylish *Kaffeehaus* on the main street, or you can get full Austrian cuisine and pizzas at the *Gasthof zur Burg*, further down the street on Marktplatz.

Gerersdorf and Naturpark Güssing

It's only a six-kilometre drive from Güssing through the cornfields and vineyards to the privately run **Freilichtmuseum** (Mon & Wed–Fri 8am–3pm, Sat & Sun 10am–noon & 3–6pm; öS40), in the village of **GERERSDORF**, to the northwest. This is an excellent open-air folk museum, where around twenty, mostly thatched farm buildings – from beehives and dovecotes to fruit presses and pigsties – have been reassembled. There's no information in English, but the German explanations are easy enough to follow.

Five kilometres to the northeast of Güssing, a large section of forest has been turned into a haven for rare and endangered species. Wild horses, red deer, water buffalo, European bison and several other unusual types of cattle roam freely here, and can be spotted from the park's observation towers. The best time to see the animals at the **Naturpark Güssing** (free) is towards dusk, when they come out to feed. To reach the park, you'll need your own car: take the road east to Urbersdorf, and skirt the Stausee to the north.

travel details

Trains

Eisenstadt to: Neusiedl am See (hourly; 35min); Purbach am Neusiedler See (hourly; 20min); Vienna Meidling (Mon–Fri hourly; 1hr 10min).

Neusiedl am See to: Frauenkirchen (Mon–Fri 10–12 daily, Sat & Sun 7 daily; 25min); Pamhagen (Mon–Fri 10–12 daily, Sat & Sun 7 daily; 40min); Purbach am Neusiedler See (Mon–Fri hourly, Sat & Sun 9 daily; 15min); St Andrä am Zicksee (Mon–Fri 10–12 daily, Sat & Sun 7 daily; 30min); Vienna Südbahnhof (every 2hr; 50min).

Buses

Bernstein to: Bad Tatzmannsdorf (Mon–Fri 3–5 daily; 15min).

Eisenstadt to: Forchtenstein (3–4 daily; 30min); Rust (hourly; 1hr); Vienna (8 daily; 1hr 10min).

Neusiedl am See to: Podersdorf am See (Mon–Fri hourly, Sat & Sun every 2–3hr; 20min).

Rust to Vienna (7 daily; 2hr).

STYRIA

Styria (Steiermark) reaches up from Austria's southeastern corner deep into the centre, across some of the most varied terrain the country has to offer. A gently undulating landscape to the south, rich in vineyards, orchards and fertile, arable land, gives way to the industrialized ribbon of the middle **Mur Valley** further north. Beyond here, in the increasingly alpine west and far north, a lack of classic skiing terrain ensures that imposing mountain ranges like the **Tauern** and the **Hochswab** preserve their laid-back, rural atmosphere.

Marketed today, reasonably enough, as the "green heart of Austria" by the local tourist board, Styria was historically the **industrial** powerhouse of the nation, with the rich iron-ore deposits of the **Erzberg** fuelling the iron and steel workshops of the Mur Valley. During the seventeenth- and eighteenth-century heyday of Habsburg expansion, this iron-based industrial might ensured a constant supply of weaponry to armies engaged in the struggle against the Ottoman Empire. Due to its position on the fringes of the Hungarian plain, Styria was, like Vienna, exposed to Turkish attacks from the fifteenth century onwards. The provincial capital, **Graz**, became the key military stronghold in a line of defences that kept the Turks out of central Europe, and for a while it rivalled Vienna, Innsbruck and Prague as a centre of political, cultural and religious influence.

Still the main target for most visitors to the province, Graz is one of Austria's most promising urban centres, an elegant and prosperous city with a rich choice of cultural diversions and a buzzing nightlife. It's also an ideal base for exploring the relatively little-visited region of **southern Styria**, whose agricultural villages and rural market towns have little in common with the alpine Austria of the tourist brochures. Wine-producing communities are scattered throughout the region, most notably in the villages towards the Slovene border, while apple-growing sustains the settlements northeast of Graz. Undisputed king of the south Styrian farming scene, however, is the pumpkin, whose seeds are milled to produce the province's most characteristic culinary product, pumpkin oil (*Kürbisöl*). This dark, nutty-flavoured liquid, not unlike sesame oil, is as ubiquitous as salt and pepper in the region's restaurants.

The abundance of local rail links means that for those dependent on public transport many of the south's outlying attractions can be reached on day-trips from the Styrian capital. Roads and a minor rail line run southwest from Graz towards **Deutschlandsberg**, an important market centre for the local wine industry and site of a fine castle, but there's probably more to see along the main southbound road and rail

---

ACCOMMODATION PRICE CODES

All **hotels and pensions** in this book have been graded according to the following price categories. All the codes are based on the rate for the least expensive double room during the **summer season**. In those places where winter is the high season, we've indicated winter room rates in the text. For more on accommodation, see p.30.

① under öS400	④ öS800–1000	⑦ öS1400–1600
② öS400–600	⑤ öS1000–1200	⑧ öS1600–1800
③ öS600–800	⑥ öS1200–1400	⑨ over öS1800

route to Slovenia, which passes by the historic town of **Leibnitz** and the nearby wine village of **Ehrenhausen**, home to the extraordinary **Eggenberg Mausoleum**. Near the Austrian–Slovene border at **Spielfeld**, another minor road and rail route veers off towards **Bad Radkersburg**, a quaint if sleepy border town in the far southeast. Another popular road and rail itinerary heads eastwards from Graz towards the south-ernmost finger of Burgenland and the Hungarian frontier at Szentgottard, passing through **Feldbach**, a convenient point from which to visit Styria's most impressive medieval fortress, **Schloss Riegersburg**. Just beyond Feldbach, a branch rail line from Fehring to Wiener Neustadt winds through the hills of the Styria–Burgenland border to **Hartberg** (buses from Graz are quicker and more direct, but not quite so scenic), another attractive historical town nestling beneath vine-bearing hills.

Northern Styria is really a tale of two regions: the Mur Valley, where workaday towns like Leoben and Judenburg proclaim the area's industrial heritage, and the much more appetizing mountain regions that lie to the north and west. Many travellers, hurtling at speed between Vienna and the lakes of Carinthia, only see the former, which is a shame: while it's true that the Mur Valley towns possess a certain historical pedi-gree, the real excitment lies off the beaten track in the side-valleys that carve their way through a sequence of rocky massifs. Important transport hubs, **Bruck an der Mur** and **Leoben** are good starting points for trips into the valleys fringing the Hochschwab Mountains, where the pilgrimage centre of **Mariazell** and the mysterious, pine-shrouded mining town of **Eisenerz** are main points of interest. Further west, the hill-top town of **Judenburg** is worth a quick visit, before pressing on to relatively isolated medieval settlements like **Oberzeiring**, **Oberwölz** and **Murau**. Travelling by road or rail from Graz towards Salzburg, Linz and the north, you'll pass through the **Enns Valley** in Styria's northwestern corner, worth visiting for its alpine scenery alone – here, the Benedictine abbey at **Admont** and the region's one major winter resort, **Schladming**, are the obvious places to stop off.

Graz

With a population of over 250,000, **GRAZ** ranks as Austria's second city, and yet has always been overlooked by visitors en route to the more widely publicized delights of Salzburg and Innsbruck. This is partly due to the city's lack of an alpine hinterland, although the Styrian capital's geographical situation – straddling the River Mur and sur-rounded by rolling hills – is undeniably attractive. Until the seventeenth century, Graz was a genuine rival to Vienna, as home to the Leopoldine line of the Habsburg family and an assemblage of aristocrats who swarmed around their court. The elegant palaces and town houses that line the narrow streets of the city centre bear testimony to Graz's Baroque heyday, as do the museum collections of the **Landesmuseum Joanneum** – among Austria's best – and the lavish state rooms of **Schloss Eggenberg**, just outside the town. In addition, the **Austrian Open-Air Museum**, 18km north near the village of Stübing, provides an excellent overview of Austria's rural traditions.

Some history

The **Schlossberg** above Graz has been fortified since at least the twelfth century, pos-sibly earlier – the name "Graz", derived from the Slav word *gradec*, or fortress, suggests that the Slovenes were here several centuries beforehand – but the town itself didn't really come into its own until 1379, when **Duke Leopold III**, head of a junior branch of the Habsburg family, adopted Graz as his capital. The dukes of Styria subsequently based themselves here, ensuring Graz's status as a centre of imperial power – Leopold's grandson **Friedrich III**, crowned Holy Roman Emperor in 1452, divided his time between three capitals: Graz, Wiener Neustadt and Linz. The town gained vital

strategic significance: from the fifteenth century onwards, Graz was crucial to the defence of central Europe against the **Turks**, who first ventured into Styria in 1478 and remained a near-constant threat for the next two hundred years. For a time, the impregnable citadel of Graz was far more secure than Vienna, and the town benefited greatly from the influx of military architects, freebooters and warrior-aristocrats grown fat on the profits of the Turkish wars. Painters and craftsmen flocked here from northern

Italy to decorate the palaces and town houses of Graz's sixteenth-century elite, and **Baroque styles** were adopted here a generation earlier than elsewhere in Austria.

Intellectuals, too, were drawn to Graz: as traditional Catholicism all but ebbed away in **post-Reformation Styria**, Graz became an important local centre for Protestant theologians and liberal-leaning academics. The astronomer Johann Kepler taught mathematics in one of Graz's Protestant schools in the 1590s, although a change in

> The telephone code for Graz is ☎0316.

the religious climate eventually forced him, along with many others, to seek sanctuary in the more tolerant court of Emperor Rudolf II in Prague. The man who pulled down the curtain on Styrian Protestantism was Archduke Ferdinand (who, as Emperor Ferdinand II, was to become the principal architect of the re-Catholicized Habsburg monarchy), a fanatically pious, Jesuit-educated 18-year-old when he became governor of Styria in 1595. By expelling preachers, demolishing churches, burning books and harrying Protestant-leaning magnates, Ferdinand soon dragged Styria back into the **Catholic** fold. Lorded over by the Jesuits who had been introduced to the city by Ferdinand's father Karl, Graz was to become a major seat of Catholic learning.

On becoming emperor in 1619, Ferdinand moved his court to Vienna, and after the defeat of the Turks outside Vienna in 1683, the city on the Danube began to replace Graz as Austria's main political, cultural and commercial centre. Graz has loitered on the fringes of history ever since, although stout defence in the face of **Napoleon's armies** in 1809 endowed the place with a modicum of civic pride.

By the late nineteenth century, Graz's mild climate had made it a popular retirement choice for ageing army officers and civil servants, and its reputation as a conservative town swarming with pensioners has since proved hard to shake off. Nowadays, however, partly due to the presence of a 37,000-strong student population, it's a rich and culturally varied city, with plenty of night-time diversions. There's a distinct and internationally respected local school of **architecture**, which specializes in producing audaciously modern buildings on a human scale; although few of its products are tourist attractions in themselves, they certainly give the town a contemporary feel. Further evidence of the town's commitment to modern culture is provided by the *Steirische Herbst*, or **Styrian Autumn**, a festival of avant-garde music, theatre, art and film, which takes place every October.

Arrival, information and transport

Graz's **train station** is on the western edge of town, a fifteen-minute walk or short tram ride (#1, 3, 6 or 7) from the central Hauptplatz. Buses arrive either at the train station or at the **bus station** at Andreas-Hofer-Platz, a couple of blocks west of the Hauptplatz. Graz **airport**, 9km south of the centre, is served by about six buses a day from the train station, between 6am and 6pm (öS55). A taxi doing the same trip will cost about öS200.

There's a **tourist office** on platform one of the train station (Mon–Fri 9am–6pm, Sat 9am–3pm), and a bigger one a couple of hundred metres southeast of the Hauptplatz at Herrengasse 16 (Mon–Fri 9am–6pm, Sat 9am–3pm, Sun 10am–3pm; ☎835241-11, fax 832739), either of which can provide free town plans and a wealth of brochures and advice.

Graz is served by an integrated network of local **buses** and **trams**. A single ticket costs öS20 and is valid for one hour, including any number of changes. A 24-hour ticket costs öS40; and a seven-day ticket, öS90. Tickets can be bought from *Tabak* shops, or from ticket machines at the main tram stops.

Accommodation

Budget accommodation is hard to come by in what is a prosperous, business-oriented town, although both branches of the tourist office will book **private rooms**; beware that almost all of these are a lengthy bus ride from the centre. The town's **youth hostel**, four blocks south of the station at Idlhofgasse 74 (☎914876, fax 914876-88), offers a range of accommodation in a pristine modern building. It's a good idea to book ahead. There are two **campsites** about 6km southwest of town, of which *Camping Central*, Martinhofstrasse 3 (☎281831; bus #32 from Jakominiplatz), is the easier to get to by public transport.

HOTELS AND PENSIONS

Erzherzog Johann, Sackstrasse 3–5 (☎811616, fax 811515). Atmospheric, old-fashioned city-centre hotel, with high standards of service and comfort. ⑨.

Gasthof Schmid Greiner, Grabenstrasse 64 (☎681482). Though difficult to reach, it's the cheapest option in the city, with rickety old rooms (all without en-suite facilities). It's 2km north of the centre and no public transport passes by; take tram #4 or #5 to Theodor-Korner-Strasse, then walk two blocks uphill to find Grabenstrasse. ②.

Grand Hotel Wiesler, Grieskai 4–8 (☎9066, fax 9066-76). Graz's best (and most expensive) hotel, decorated in turn-of-the-century styles, just across the river from the Hauptplatz. ⑨.

Grazerhof, Stubenberggasse 10 (☎824358, fax 819 63340). Good mid-range choice in the heart of town, although some of the rooms are on the poky side. ④.

Ibis, Europaplatz 12 (☎978, fax 978-300). Best of the tower-block-style modern business hotels, just outside the train station, with en-suite facilities, satellite TV and telephone in all rooms. ⑥.

Iris, Bergmanngasse 10 (☎322081, fax 322081-5). Pleasant pension in nineteenth-century apartment block within walking distance of both city centre and university district. It's on a noisy road, but the relative calm of the Stadtpark is nearby. ④.

Mariahilf, Mariahilferstrasse 9 (☎913163, fax 917652). Nice old hotel just across the river from the centre, with a range of widely differing rooms. Those without en-suite facilities (⑤) can seem a bit threadbare; others are quite roomy and atmospheric. (⑦).

Rückert, Rückertgasse 4 (☎323031). Pension housed in a suburban villa amid quiet, leafy streets 2km east of the centre. Take tram #1 from the train station, Hauptplatz or Jakominiplatz to Teggethofplatz, then walk down Hartenaugasse to Rückertgasse. ③.

Strasser, Eggenburger Gürtel 11 (☎913977, fax 916856). Drab apartment building 5min walk south of the station, and therefore handiest place for a quick departure. Rooms with en-suite facilities can be quite comfortable; those without, a bit cramped and gloomy. ③.

Zu den 5 Lärchen, Griesplatz 6–7 (☎912406-0, fax 912635-7). Uninspiring but comfortable modern building on the west side of the river, a 15min walk from the central sights. Most rooms have TV and en-suite facilities. ③.

Zur Stadt Feldbach, Conrad-von-Hötzendorf-Strasse 58 (☎829468, fax 847371). Nineteenth-century apartment block 1km south of the centre. Take trams #4 or #5 from Hauptplatz or from Jakominiplatz to Jakominigürtel. ③.

The City

Most of what you'll want to see in Graz is concentrated on the east side of the River Mur, where the **Hauptplatz** and the neighbouring streets of Herrengasse, Sporgasse and Sackstrasse provide the core of a busy downtown area. Immediately above hangs the **Schlossberg**, site of Graz's medieval fortress, while the **Stadtpark**, to the east, provides the town with an attractive promenading ground. The main **public transport hubs** are on the east bank of the river, too: the Hauptplatz itself, as key crossroads for various tramlines; and **Jakominiplatz**, 500m southeast, where tramlines and local bus routes converge. There's little to see on the west bank of the river, save for a couple of Baroque churches and the princely residence of Schloss Eggenberg, some 4km from the centre.

The Hauptplatz and Herrengasse

Everything in Graz revolves around the **Hauptplatz**, a triangular market square bordered by seventeenth- and eighteenth-century facades. In the middle stands a statue of Emperor Franz-Josef's uncle **Archduke Johann**, who did much to modernize Graz in the early

CENTRAL GRAZ

University
Schlossberg
Freilichtbuhne
Funicular
Station
Glockenturm
Leechkirche
Volkskundemuseum
SAURAUGASSE
Stadtpark
Schauspielhaus
Forum Stadtpark
KARMELITER
PL.
Uhrturm
Burg
Stadtmuseum
Neue
Galerie
HOFGASSE
Maria-Hilf
Kirche
Domkirche
ERZHERZOG-JOHANN-ALLEE
LEONHARDGASSE
Kunsthaus
Mausoleum
Rathaus
Stadtpfarrkirche
Landes-
museum
Landhaus and Zeughaus
Opera
Alte
Galerie

0   500 m

nineteenth century, founding a Technisches Universität, sponsoring the construction of the Graz–Mürzzuschlag railway, and donating his art collection and other items to form the basis of the Landesmuseum, which now bears his name. Despite disgracing the family by marrying a postmaster's daughter from Bad Aussee, he was one of the few nineteenth-century Habsburgs to enjoy true mass popularity (for more on him, see p.365).

At the southern end of the Hauptplatz, where the nineteenth-century, neo-Renaissance **Rathaus** looms, Herrengasse leads towards the much more interesting **Landhaus** at no. 16, built in the 1550s to house the Styrian Diet. Designed by the military architect Domenico dell'Allio, who also worked on the fortification of the Schlossberg, it's quite an unassuming building when viewed from outside; you can wander in at any time to see the the Italianate arcading of the inner courtyard that makes this one of the best examples of Renaissance architecture in Austria. Next door, the **Zeughaus**, or armoury (April–Oct Mon–Fri 9am–5pm, Sat–Sun 9am–1pm; öS30), was built in 1642 to provide the citizenry with a readily available stock of weapons in case of Turkish attack, and is preserved very much in its original form. With over 30,000 helmets, breastplates, swords, pikes and other items on show, it's an impressive, if ultimately quite numbing, display of the town's erstwhile military might.

A little way further along Herrengasse, a fine eighteenth-century bell tower sits atop the **Stadtpfarrkirche**, an elegant jumble of Baroque and neo-Gothic styles that's home to an *Assumption of the Virgin* attributed to Tintoretto on the right-hand side of the nave. Equally striking is the postwar stained glass by Albert Birkle behind the altar: one panel (in the window to the left) clearly portrays Hitler and Mussolini watching over the flagellation of Christ.

The Landesmuseum Joanneum

The only real attraction in the grid of nineteenth-century streets west of Herrengasse is the **Landesmuseum Joanneum**, a vast collection housed in two separate, though neighbouring, buildings and bequeathed to the city by the public-spirited Archduke Johann in 1811. The **natural history section** (Mon–Fri 9am–6pm, Sat & Sun 9am–noon; öS30), entered from either Raubergasse or Kalchberggasse, embraces geology, zoology and botany; its endless glass cases filled with rocks and stuffed animals, however, can't really compete with the attractions of the art collection in the **Alte Galerie** (Mon–Fri 10am–5pm, Sat & Sun 10am–1pm; öS55), round the corner at Neutorgasse 45. The ground floor is rich in Gothic devotional work, much of it rescued from decay in the village churches of Styria, and credited to anonymous artists known only by the name of the place where their work was found. The "Master of St Lambrecht" is a good example; his *Cavalry Battle of St Louis of Hungary*, depicting the saintly monarch's victory over the Turks in 1377 (a victory attributed to the miraculous powers of the Virgin of Mariazell; see p.235), is a vivid evocation of the horrors of medieval warfare. The prolific fifteenth-century Tyrolean master Michael Pacher (see p.354) is represented by the two-panel *Scenes from the Life of Thomas à Becket*, showing his martyrdom and funeral. Sixteenth- and seventeenth-century works on the first floor include a *Judgement of Paris* by Lucas Cranach the Elder, and a grippingly macabre *Triumph of Death* by Pieter Breughel the Younger. The rest of the collection focuses on the Austrian Baroque, with a representative selection of work by the "big four" – Rottmayr, Maulbertsch, Tröger and Kremser Schmidt – together with sculptures by the Graz-born J.T. Stammel.

The Mausoleum of Ferdinand II and the Domkirche

On the northern side of Herrengasse, Stempfergasse leads into a neighbourhood of narrow alleyways that dogleg their way up the hill towards the **Mausoleum of Ferdinand II** (Mon–Thurs & Sat 11am–noon & 2–3pm; öS20), a dome-encrusted structure that was begun in 1614 when the intended incumbent was a healthy 36 years old. Designed by the Italian Pietro de Pomis, who spent most of his life working for a Styrian aristocracy greedy for Italian style, the mausoleum skilfully blends a variety of styles, coming over as a cross between Classical temple and Baroque church. Inside, Ferdinand is entombed alongside a sarcophagus intended for both his parents, Emperor Karl II and Maria of Bavaria, although only Maria is actually buried here (her husband lies in the Abbey of Seckau; see p.241). The fine stucco-work on the ceiling and some of the frescoes were added by Fischer von Erlach in the 1690s.

Next door is the **Domkirche**, or cathedral, which has preserved much of its late-fifteenth-century Gothic character. It was built by Emperor Friedrich III, whose coat of arms and whose motto, AEIOU (usually taken to stand for *Austria Erit In Orbe Ultima*, or "Austria will be last in the world", although see p.189 for other possible versions), adorn the west portal. Inside, there's a fifteenth-century Crucifixion on the right-hand side of the nave, but most of the other decorations are Baroque. The elaborate side altars are largely the work of local Jesuit craftsmen; the Jesuits were also responsible for gaining possession of the two fifteenth-century reliquary chests, each bearing ivory reliefs depicting allegories of Love, Death and Time among other moralizing subjects, which now stand at the entrance to the choir. Made to contain the dowry of Paola di Gonzaga, Duchess of Mantua, in advance of her wedding to Leonhard of Görz (a big cheese in Lienz; see p.294) in 1470, the chests ended up in the abbey at Millstatt (see p.288) – an abbey that was comprehensively asset-stripped by the Graz Jesuits when they took it over in the seventeenth century.

The Burg, Sporgasse and the Steirisches Volkskundenmuseum

Immediately north of the cathedral lies the **Burg**, once the residence of Friedrich III, who briefly made Graz one of three imperial capitals in the mid-fifteenth century (he also maintained courts at Wiener Neustadt and Linz). Now much rebuilt and given over to local government offices, there's nothing specific to visit here save for the double spiral of a fifteenth-century Gothic staircase, found in the archway at the end of the first courtyard. Another archway leads eastwards through the wall of the Burg directly into the Stadtpark (see opposite), while Hofgasse heads west from the Burg towards **Sporgasse**, a busy shopping street that winds its way along the flanks of the Schlossberg. Among the many historic town houses that also line the Sporgasse, the **Palais Saurau** at no. 25 features an elegant seventeenth-century portal, and a Turkish figure throwing himself from a small upper window.

In its upper reaches Sporgasse becomes Paulustorgasse, where the **Steirisches Volkskundenmuseum**, or "Styrian Folklore Museum", at no. 13 (April–Oct Mon–Sat 9am–4pm, Sun 9am–noon; öS30) houses the usual collection of traditional costumes and reconstructed house interiors, alongside a curious Baroque sculpture of the bearded female St Kümmernis. According to a legend of Portuguese origin, the young woman in question prayed for facial hair in an attempt to repel the advances of a husband forced upon her by her heathen father. Crucified by way of punishment, she went on to become an important symbol of piety during the Catholic upsurge of the Counter-Reformation.

Sackstrasse and the Schlossberg

Leading out of the northern end of the Hauptplatz, **Sackstrasse** is one of Graz's most attractive streets, where former town houses of the nobility preside over the bustle of shoppers and rumble of trams. The plain exterior of the seventeenth-century **Palais Herberstein** at no. 16, built as a pied-à-terre for the Eggenberg family (see p.222), hides a marvellous staircase, which ascends towards ceiling frescoes depicting mythological scenes, as well as the luxurious Rococo interiors of the second floor, which now provide an absorbing backdrop to the paintings of the **Neue Galerie** (Tues–Sat 10am–6pm, Sun 10am–1pm; öS40), a municipal collection of nineteenth- and twentieth-century works that includes a sprinkling of Klimts and Schieles. The **Palais Khuenberg** next door at no. 18 was the birthplace of ill-starred Archduke Franz-Ferdinand in 1863, and currently houses the **Stadtmuseum** (Tues 10am–9pm, Wed–Sat 10am–6pm, Sun 10am–1pm; free), notable largely for the excellent model of Graz as it looked in 1800. From here it's worth popping over the road to peep inside the portals of **Palais Attems** (now the offices of Graz's principal cultural festivals, *Styriarte* and the *Steirische Herbst*) at no. 17, where intricately patterned stucco mouldings overlook an imposing Baroque staircase.

From Schlossbergplatz, halfway down Sackstrasse, a balustraded stone staircase zigzags up to the **Schlossberg**, a wooded hill overlooking the town. For the less energetic, it can also be reached by means of the Schlossbergbahn funicular, which departs from Sackstrasse's northern end (every 15min 9am–10pm; öS30 one way). The Schloss from which the hill derives its name was the key point in the city's defences from the Middle Ages onwards, and held out stoutly against Napoleon's armies in 1809, although its destruction was made a condition of the subsequent Treaty of Vienna. Now only two main features survive, the first of which is the sixteenth-century **Uhrturm**, or clock tower, near the top of the staircase from Sackstrasse, whose steep overhanging roof figures prominently in the town's tourist literature – unusually, the clock's big hand is the hour hand. Uphill to the north, near the summit of the funicular, is the **Glockenturm**, or bell tower, set amidst parklands that are ideal for a picnic or a ramble.

The Stadtpark, the university district and the Augarten

Paths descend southwards from the Schlossberg towards Sporgasse, whence you can soon get back to the Hauptplatz; or eastwards to the **Stadtpark**, a leafy barrier that divides the city centre from the residential suburbs beyond. Laid out on the site of the town fortifications after their demolition in 1784, it's a popular area for a daytime stroll, and a smattering of cafés ensures it remains lively well into the evening. An unassuming pavilion in the middle of the park houses the **Forum Stadtpark**, an important centre for avant-garde artists in the 1960s. The temporary exhibitions held here (Mon–Sat 2–6pm, Sun 11am–3pm; free) are always worth checking out. Continuing southwards from here, you'll soon come across the popular and sumptuous *Promenade Café*, just outside the Burgtor, the medieval gate where Hofgasse leads back into the city centre. Across the road from the café is the **Kunsthaus** (daily 11am–6pm; prices vary), a modern venue for top-notch contemporary art exhibitions.

Immediately east of the Stadtpark lies the **university district**, an initially unwelcoming grid of nineteenth-century apartment blocks around Graz University, which only really comes to life in the evenings – largely thanks to the numerous bars and eateries catering for a youngish clientele. The imposing, nineteenth-century bulk of the main university building itself lies just off Halbärthgasse, but the surrounding area is short on real sights. Worth a brief visit, however, is the **Leechkirche**, a few steps east of the park on Rittergasse, a delicate Gothic church with a delightful thirteenth-century relief of the Madonna and Child above the main portal. Before becoming the parish church for Graz University, the Leechkirche belonged to the Teutonic Order of Knights, and there's a fine grave relief of one of their number inside.

Returning to the Stadtpark, the broad sweep of the Burgring (later the Opernring) heads downhill towards the southern fringes of the city centre, passing the nineteenth-century **opera house** before arriving at **Jakominiplatz**, an important public transport interchange. There's little of interest beyond here save for the **Augarten**, a stretch of riverside park patrolled by pram-wielding parents and strolling pensioners. Lurking at the park's northwestern end at Friedrichgasse 41 is the Oktagon, a turn-of-the-century building that originally served as a bathhouse and is now the **Museum der Wahrnemung** (Museum of Perception; Mon, Wed, Fri & Sat 2–7pm, Thurs 2–9pm, Sun 11am–7pm; öS30). The museum aims to demonstrate the fallibility of human senses through a series of visual tricks, installations and sound-and-light-generated environments. Rather like a fairground hall of mirrors, it's a fun place to take the kids.

West of the river

Graz west of the River Mur attracts few tourists, although the area around Annenstrasse and Südtirolerplatz is a popular shopping area for the locals. Beyond here, the grid of streets between the river and the train station becomes increasingly drab and unappealing. There's one worthwhile church just across the river from the town centre: the **Maria-Hilf-Kirche**, a popular pilgrimage church on Mariahilferstrasse, with a stupendous twin-domed facade and a rather less exciting interior, which nevertheless contains an altar picture of the Virgin painted by Pietro de Pomis, who is buried inside the church.

Schloss Eggenberg

Situated some 4km west of the town centre at the end of Eggenberger Allee (you can reach it by tram #1 from the Hauptplatz or the train station – get off at Schloss Strasse), the Baroque **Schloss Eggenberg** was built for one of the region's most important families. Hailing from Bad Radkersburg in southeast Styria, the Eggenbergs became leading financiers in Graz before using their wealth to fund military careers. Ruprecht von Eggenberg led Austrian armies against the Turks in the late sixteenth century, and his son Hans Ulrich became Ferdinand II's chief minister. Accorded the title of prince in 1623 and appointed governer of Inner Austria (Styria, Carinthia and present-day Slovenia) two years later, Hans Ulrich was desperate for a residence that would match his status. Pietro de Pomis, who was already working on Ferdinand II's mausoleum in Graz, was the man for the job. Recognizing the post-Renaissance pretensions of Ferdinand II's new generation of courtly followers, de Pomis came up with a building that served as an allegory of universal order. Among the Schloss's more obvious symbols are the four towers marking the points of the compass, the 365 windows, and the 24 state rooms, one for each hour of the day.

A ticket to the grounds (daily 9am–6pm; öS2) allows you to amble around a landscaped **park** boasting deer and peacock, and take a peek at the palace's elegant galleried courtyard. A ticket to the Schloss itself (öS80) includes entrance to the palace's three **museum collections** (all open daily 9am–noon & 1–5pm) as well as a **guided tour** (daily 11am, noon, 2pm, 3pm & 4pm) of the **Prunkräume**, or state rooms.

The museums

Of the three, the **Collection of Pre- and Early History** is probably the most interesting. There's a wealth of local finds from Hallstatt-period Celtic settlements, notably the metre-high bronze *situlae* (big ceremonial jars) decorated with either abstract patterns or rows of grazing animals. Pride of place goes to the eighth-century BC **Strettweg chariot**, a small but impressively ornamented bronze wheeled platform unearthed in a burial mound near the Styrian town of Judenburg. In the centre of the platform, a female deity holds up a bowl, while hunters, mounted warriors and impressively endowed male fertility figures cavort around her. Less gripping are the Roman-era domestic implements that make up the rest of the collection, most of which were culled by Habsburg-era archeologists from the towns of Ptuj and Celje, both now in Slovenia.

Aside from a couple of Egyptian mummies and a range of ancient Greek vases, the **Münz- und Antiken Kabinett** (Coin and Antiquity Room), the second of the three collections, is given over to a bewildering array of golden ducats and silver Talers adorned with the heads of leading Austrian aristocrats – many of whom had the right to mint their own coins up until the nineteenth century. Worth looking out for are seventeenth-century pieces stamped with the imposing profile of Hans Ulrich von Eggenberg himself. Finally, a modest **Jagdmuseum** (Hunting Museum; the third collection) displays stuffed examples of a variety of alpine beasts, and didactic posters from the inter-war years showing, among other things, the best parts of a stag's body to aim for when shooting.

The state rooms

Lasting almost one hour and conducted in German (a few explanatory words in English will be provided on request), the guided tour of the **state rooms** provides useful insights into the princely world of the Eggenbergs, although ultimately there's a limit to the number of Bohemian glass chandeliers and Baroque velvety wallcoverings that the human eye can assimilate. Visitors troop round a series of bedrooms, reception rooms and themed rooms (such as the Porcelain Room, with

Chinese plates set into the wall, or the Romulus and Remus Room decorated with scenes from Roman mythology), but the highlight is the **Planetensaal**, or room of the planets, with paintings depicting signs of the zodiac and a figure of the sun-god Helios symbolizing Emperor Leopold I.

Eating and drinking

As befits a city of Graz's size, there are plenty of city-centre **restaurants** catering for a variety of tastes, none of which needs break the bank – although real bargains are more usually found on the west bank of the River Mur towards the train station, or in the university district to the east.

There are several classic coffeehouses in the centre, while night-time **drinking** revolves around two specific areas: the so-called **Bermudadreieck**, or "Bermuda Triangle", which comprises the streets of Prokopigasse, Färbergasse and Engegasse immediately east of the Hauptplatz; and the university district, east of the city centre beyond the Stadtpark. The Stadtpark itself harbours a couple of cafés and bars that shouldn't be ignored, especially on summer evenings when it's pleasant to sit outside.

Fast food

There's usually a Würstelstand open 24 hours a day on the Hauptplatz or just outside the train station. Also just outside the station, the *Annenpassage* subterranean shopping mall holds various fast-food joints offering sandwiches and French-bread pizzas during the daytime. In the city centre, *Fenster zum Kleinen Hunger*, Engegasse 4, is a hole-in-the-wall place serving up pizza slices and burgers; *Focaccia*, Paradiesgasse 1, doles out excellent if dainty sandwiches made using the Italian bread; and *Pizza Catharina*, Sporgasse 32, is a good place for an eat-in pizza or a take-away slice. There's a branch of the self-service restaurant *Wienerwald* between the town centre and the train station at Annenstrasse 41, offering cheap chicken burgers, pick-and-mix salads or more substantial schnitzel-type dishes.

Restaurants

Bosporus, Sparbersbachgasse 22. Turkish restaurant in a dull part of town 10min east of the centre, but serving good-value food. Much patronized by the local immigrant community.

Café El Greco, Schmiedgasse 18. Although hardly a budget choice, with typical entrées weighing in at around öS160, the Greek menu is varied and excellent and there's live bouzouki music most nights.

Café Pizzeria Galliano, Harrachgasse 22. Stylish bar and eaterie in the heart of the university district offering a comprehensive range of mid-priced pizzas.

Café Wolfzettl, Heinrichstrasse 17. No-nonsense neighbourhood café a couple of blocks east of the Stadtpark, offering cheap soups and schnitzel-and-chips-type dishes. Handy if you're in the university district.

Gambrinuskeller, Farbergasse 6–8. One of the more moderately priced establishments in the city centre, specializing in grilled meats and Balkan dishes such as kebabs, stuffed peppers, *pasulj* (spicy bean stew) and *djuveč* (lamb and vegetable stew).

Gandhi Tandoori, Hans-Sachs-Gasse 8. Reasonable range of mid-priced Indian specialities in a central location, with a good choice of vegetarian dishes.

Glockenspielkeller, Mehlplatz 3. Hearty, mid-priced Austrian staples popular with city-centre sightseers. Outdoor seating on a pleasant pedestrianized square.

Landhauskeller, Schmiedgasse 9 (☎830276). Top-quality Austrian and Styrian fare in atmospheric medieval surroundings. Outdoor seating in courtyard during summer. Closed Sun.

Mangolds, Griesgasse 11. A self-service health-food restaurant a couple of blocks west of the river, but with limited opening hours: closes 8pm Mon–Fri, 4pm Sat; closed Sun.

Weinstube zur Alten Press, Griesgasse 8. Cosy place one block west of the river, offering a small range of cheapish Austrian and Styrian dishes.

Zum Goldenen Fassl, Griesplatz 32. An unpretentious beer hall in a rather drab district 15min from the centre, with a restaurant serving good-value Chinese food. Worth checking out if you're on the west bank of the river.

Zur Goldenen Pasteten, Sporgasse. Traditional Styrian food on several floors of a late-medieval town house. Slightly more expensive than other central restaurants, this is a popular venue for a business lunch or a special family meal.

Cafés

Hofcafé Edegger Tax, Hofgasse 8. The sumptuous refuge of the city's more sedate citizens, this is the nearest thing that Graz has to the classic Viennese coffeehouse. Not cheap.

Hot, Paradeisgasse. A quiet spot between the Hauptplatz and the Hauptbrücke, with tables set out on the first floor of a galleried Renaissance courtyard.

Kaiserhof, Kaiserfeldgasse 1. Another long-established upmarket café dripping with fin-de-siècle atmosphere.

Operncafé, Opernring 22. Popular city-centre café, mixing old-fashioned elegance with modernist decor, thereby attracting a mixed, young and old, crowd.

Promenade, Erzherzog-Johann-Allee. Neoclassical pavilion in the Stadtpark with an attractive, hi-tech interior. Good range of lunches and snacks – the *Kürbiscremesuppe* (cream of pumpkin soup) is typically Styrian. Usually open after midnight.

Schubert Kino Café, Mehlplatz 2. Attached to the Schubert Kino cinema, this is a popular outdoor place on sunny days. Less enticing out of season.

Sörger, Sporgasse 4. A *Kaffee-Konditorei* serving excellent sweets and cakes. A large outdoor seating area makes it popular with city-centre shoppers.

Bars

Admiral Sportwetten Café, Gleisdorfergasse 1. A cross between bar, betting shop and amusement arcade, this relays most major sporting events (including English soccer) on a big screen. There's another branch on Europaplatz opposite the train station.

Bier Baron, Heinrichstrasse 56. A 10min walk east of the Stadtpark, but worth the extra effort. A large pub-style venue with over twenty varieties of German, Austrian and Czech beer on tap.

Café Art Scherle, Stockergasse 30. Roomy late-night café with bohemian leanings – the walls are covered with art and theatre posters. One of the best places on the west bank of the river.

Café Harrach, Harrachgasse 24. An enduringly popular student hangout one block away from the university, offering a bohemian pub atmosphere and simple snacks.

Café Shunko, Sporgasse 29. Upmarket bar with cocktail-lounge atmosphere midway between the Hauptplatz and the Stadtpark. Closes around 1am.

Dizzy Pub, Färbergasse 7. Centrally located Irish pub offering Guinness and Kilkenny on tap, and Celtic-flavoured music on tape.

Fink, Freiheitsplatz 2. Popular, twentysomething bar up the hill from the Bermuda Triangle area. Usually heaving after 10pm.

Girardikeller, Leonhardgasse 3. An unpretentious cellar-bound drinking venue catering for a young, studenty crowd, many of whom are drawn here at lunchtime by the cheap, schnitzel-type fare.

Hoppala, Prokopigasse 8. A modern cellar-bar just behind Herrengasse, providing a comfortable and not too noisy venue for either daytime or night-time drinking.

Immervoll, Neubaugasse 6. Swish and roomy café-bar west of the River Mur that also serves as a billiard club. Slightly set back from the street, it's reached by passing through an old factory gateway.

Jedermann, Leonhardgasse 3. Stylish *Musikcafé* with in-house DJs offering predominantly jazz- and funk-based tunes. Doesn't really fill up until about 11pm.

M1, Färberplatz. Smart drinking venue in the heart of the Bermuda Triangle area, on the third floor of a tastefully designed example of contemporary Graz architecture. Roof terrace in summer.

Park House, Stadtpark. A pavilion in the park usually open until 2am. DJs provide rock and dance music most nights, and live bands often play on Sundays. There's a snack menu featuring tasty salads.

Tom's Bierklinik, Färbergasse 1. Loud and smoky cellar bar with a wide range of local and international brews on draught and a dizzying array of bottled beers from around the world.

Vinum, Herrengasse 3. Small bar on the main shopping street specializing in Styrian wines. Outdoor seating in summer.

Entertainment

Graz's two main cultural institutions are the Opera, Kaiser-Josef-Platz 10 (☎8008), for **classical music**, **opera** and **ballet**, and the Schauspielhaus, Hofgasse 11 (☎8005), for **theatre**; both are closed in August. Tickets and programme information for both venues are available from the *Tageskasse*, Kaiser-Josef-Platz (Mon–Fri 8am–8pm; ☎8000).

As far as **popular music** is concerned, *Forum Stadtpark* sometimes hosts alternative rock gigs and rave-style events; *Kulturhauskeller*, Elisabethstrasse 30 (☎381058), often has live jazz or folk. Touring rock acts play at either the *Orpheum*, Orpheumgasse 8 (☎913478); or *Theatro*, Neubaugasse 6 (☎916027), which is also a jazz and fringe theatre venue.

Two central **discos** offering a diet of Eurotechno and chart music are *2night*, Sackstrasse 27 (open Wed–Sat), and *Thalia*, Opernring 58 (open Thurs–Sat). The best way to find out what's going on in Graz is to leaf through the local editions of national newspapers like *Der Kurier* or *Neue Kronen Zeitung* – or enquire at the tourist office.

Listings

Airport information ☎2902.

Architecture Guided tours of buildings belonging to the Graz school of architecture are organized by Haus der Architektur, Engelgasse 3–5 (☎323500).

Bike rental At the train station.

Car rental Avis, Schlögelgasse 10 (☎812920); Budget, Bahnhofgürtel 73 (☎916966); Europcar, Wienerstrasse 15 (☎914080); Hertz, Andreas-Hofer-Platz 1 (☎825007).

Cinemas Kino Geidorf, Geidorfplatz, offers first-run international movies, as well as art-house films in the adjoining studio cinema.

Consulates Great Britain, Schmiedgasse 10 (☎826105). The nearest consulates for other nationalities are in Vienna.

Exchange There's a 24hr service at the main post office.

Hospital Krankenhaus der Elisabethinen, Elisabethinergasse 14 (☎9063). In emergencies, call ☎144.

Laundry Putzerei Rupp, Jakoministrasse 34.

Motoring organizations ARBÖ, Kappelenstrasse 45 (☎27160); ÖAMTC, Girardigasse (☎504261).

FESTIVALS IN GRAZ

Graz's most important annual event involving high culture is **Styriarte**, a festival of top-quality opera and orchestral music that takes place from mid-June to mid-July. A variety of venues are used, including the Freilichtbuhne (open-air stage) on the Schlossberg. Information is available from the Styriarte Kartenbüro, Sackstrasse 17 (☎812941-22).

The **Steirischer Herbst**, or "Styrian Autumn", takes place in October and focuses on the avant-garde in art, contemporary classical music, jazz, film and theatre. A great opportunity to catch up on experimental and ground-breaking work in all fields of culture, it is nevertheless a pretty cerebral affair. Exhibitions and performances take place in venues all over town, and programmes and booking forms can be obtained in advance from the Steirischer Herbst Informationsbüro, Sackstrasse 17 (☎823007).

Pharmacy Bärenapotheker, Herrengasse 11 (☎830267). Names and addresses of duty pharmacies are posted in the windows of all pharmacies.

Police At the main train station (☎888 2775). In emergencies, call ☎133.

Post office Neutorgasse 46 (open 24hr).

Swimming pools There's a large open-air pool at the Augartenbad, 1.5km south of the centre on the Schönaugürtel (tram #5 from Hauptplatz to Schönaugürtel); and there are both open-air and indoor pools at Bad Eggenberg, 3km west of centre near Schloss Eggenberg (tram #1 from Hauptplatz or the train station).

Taxis ☎2801; ☎1716.

Train information ☎1717.

Travel agents ÖKISTA, Brandhofgasse 8 (Mon–Fri 9am–5pm).

Around Graz

The **Österreichisches Freilichtmuseum**, or Austrian Open-Air Museum, is a one-of-a-kind collection of vernacular architecture in an extremely attractive setting some 18km north of Graz. About eight trains a day make the twenty-minute journey from the Styrian capital to **Stübing**, the nearest settlement to the museum. Two other possible day-trips from Graz are the Lipizzaner stud farm at **Piber** and the Hundertwasser-decorated parish church at **Bärnbach**. Both small villages lie just north of the town of **Köflach**, about 40km west of Graz, which is served by regular trains on the privately owned Graz-Köflacher-Bahn (all rail passes valid).

The Austrian Open-Air Museum

Strung out along a pine-fringed vale, the **Österreichisches Freilichtmuseum** (April–Oct daily 9am–5pm; öS50) preserves more than eighty outstanding examples of village architecture. The whole thing is about 2km long, so you'll need a couple of hours in order to take everything in. Indeed there's such a bewildering array that the English-language guidebook sold at the entrance (öS25) is a worthwhile investment.

Beginning with the easternmost provinces, the museum tackles Austrian architecture by region, so it's the thatched-roofed farmhouses of **Burgenland** that command initial attention. Encrusted with vines, and with verandahs running along their south-facing sides, these single-storey buildings have more in common with the architecture of Hungary and the Pannonian Plain than with the alpine, timber-built farmhouses that follow. Of these, there are numerous examples of **Rauchstubenhäuser**, farmhouses in which the living room was built around an open hearth, and which were once widespread across eastern Styria, Carinthia and Salzburg province. The most curious variation on this theme is the **Rauchhaus** from Siezenheim near Salzburg, a chimneyless dwelling in which smoke from the hearth was allowed to escape through slats in the ceiling. Grain was stored in the loft to be dried by the ascending smoke. Further along, the characteristic Tyrolean farmstead familiar from picture-postcard views of the Alps is represented by the **Hansler Farm** from Alpbach, a large square-shaped structure embracing both animal stalls and living quarters, with a wide gabled front and flower-decked balconies outside, and intricate wood panelling inside. At the far end of the complex stands the **Bregenzerwald Alphütte**, or alpine dairy, where cheese was made and stored during the summer before being taken down into the valley in the autumn.

You can go inside the houses, where traditional **crafts** such as breadmaking, spinning and weaving are demonstrated by volunteers over the weekends, weather permitting. An **Erlebnistag**, or activity day, takes place on the last Sunday in September, featuring traditional food, folk dancing and displays of traditional agricultural machinery.

It's a twenty-minute walk to the museum from Stübing train station: turn left out of the station and bear right at the southern end of the village. There's a café-restaurant at the entrance to the museum, and a couple of Gasthöfe serve decent lunch fare back in the village.

Piber and Bärnbach

The **Gestüt**, or stud farm, at PIBER has provided Lipizzaner horses for the Spanish Riding School in Vienna (see p.87) since 1920, when it was moved here from the village of Lipizza (now Lipica in Slovenia). The farm can only be visited by signing up for one of the 75-minute guided tours (daily: Easter–Oct at 9am and 2pm; öS100; ☎03144/3323). After watching a video providing a brief introduction to the farm's history, you can linger in the stables, and observe the horses grazing on the pastures above the village. Although the horses are renowned for their pure white coats, they are born almost black, gradually lightening as they get older.

A further 2km northeast, the village of **BÄRNBACH** huddles around the **Pfarrkirche St Barbara**, a church of postwar construction, which was extensively renovated in 1987 by Hundertwasser. The church displays several of Hundertwasser's playful, decorative trademarks, notably the use of bright hues and shiny reflective surfaces to jazz up the exterior. It's also rich in metaphor: its churchyard is encircled by a series of gates representing the different faiths of the world, and inside a glass altar is filled with twelve different kinds of soil to symbolize the twelve tribes of Israel.

Piber is 3km out of Köflach, while Bärnbach is a further 2km out along the same road. From Köflach train station, there are about seven buses a day (fewer Sat & Sun) to Bärnbach, passing through Piber on the way. Should you miss any of the buses, it's easy enough to walk to Piber from the station: head down Bahnhofstrasse to the town's Hauptplatz, turn right, then left onto Piberstrasse, which takes you to the village and the stud farm after thirty to forty minutes. If you're visiting Bärnbach on its own, it's possible to get off the train at Bärnbach station (one stop before Köflach) and walk the 2km north into the village.

Deutschlandsberg and around

Hourly trains on the branch line running from Graz to Wies-Ebiswald make the forty-kilometre (55min) journey to **DEUTSCHLANDSBERG**, centre of the Schilcher wine region. It's a pleasant enough trip through rolling hills, although the railway bypasses **Stainz**, an attractive market town 35km southwest of Graz and a tempting stopping-off point for those travelling by road.

Deutschlandsberg is a charming rural backwater, with a neat quadrant of downtown streets grouped around a spacious Hauptplatz. The town's one major sight is **Schloss Landsberg** on a height above the town, half an hour's walk away. To get there, leave the Hauptplatz at the western end, cross the railway tracks and keep going until you reach a well-signposted right turn. The original twelfth-century keep is now a magnificent ruin, standing in sombre isolation from the outer buildings of later construction, all the subject of recent renovation. Inside, the **Burgmuseum** (Mon–Sat 9am–noon & 2–5pm; öS55) houses local Neolithic finds, and an entertaining, if rather fanciful, recreation of the castle torture chamber.

Practicalities

The **train station** is on the eastern fringes of the town centre, a short walk down Frauenthalerstrasse from the **tourist office** at Hauptplatz 35 (Mon–Fri 9am–noon & 2–4pm, Sat 9am–noon), which can book **private rooms**. Most atmospheric of the

WINE IN STYRIA

The best-known **wines** to come out of Styria are the dry white **Gewürztraminers** of the southeast, cultivated around Klöch, a village north of Bad Radkersburg, and the towns of Riegersburg and Hartberg. A variety of other whites are grown around Leibnitz and Ehrenhausen, and **Schilcher**, a medium dry rosé, is produced in the countryside near Deutschlandsberg and Stainz.

All this has encouraged local tourist authorities to promote the idea of the **Weinstrasse**, or wine-road, a suggested touring itinerary that links together the main vine-growing villages of a particular area. The most travelled of these routes in Styria are the **Schilcherstrasse**, which runs from Stainz southwards to Deutschlandsberg and on to Ebiswald near the Slovene border; the **Sausaler Weinstrasse**, which covers a small group of hilltop villages in the Sausal Gebirge just west of Leibnitz; the **Südsteirische Weinstrasse**, starting in Ehrenhausen and zigzagging its way west along the Austrian–Slovene border; and the **Klöcher Weinstrasse**, which heads from Bad Radkersburg northwards to Fehring. Local wine-makers sell their produce from a **Buschenschank** (the local equivalent of the Viennese *Heuriger*; see p.130), often no more than a converted garage with a few chairs and tables set out. There you can buy wine by the glass or the bottle, and enjoy a bite to eat, although food may amount to a simple platter of bread and cold meats.

Autumn is a good time to visit, when **wine festivals** take place in Leutschach on the last weekend of September, Gamlitz on the first weekend of October, and Leibnitz on the second weekend of October. Contact Leibnitz tourist office for details about both festivals.

town's limited range of **hotels** is *Gasthof Kollar-Göbl*, Hauptplatz 10 (☎03462/2642-0, fax 2642-15; ③), an attractive old inn that doubles up as one of the town's better cafés. Just outside the entrance to the Schloss at Burgstrasse 19, *Burghotel* (☎03462/5656, fax 5656-22; ④) offers rooms with TVs and minibars, together with the dubious attractions of the karaoke bar and *Cordon Rouge* nightclub. There are several **eating and drinking** options on and around the Hauptplatz: *Knobelbecher*, Hauptplatz 3, offers plain Austrian cooking and a very reasonably priced Italian menu; while *Café-Pub zur Schmieden*, Am Neuen Platz (access via an alleyway behind Hauptplatz 9), does a good line in toasted sandwiches as well as more substantial steaks. *Arkadencafé*, Frauenthalerstrasse 5, is a nice combination of old-style coffeehouse and modern bar.

Leibnitz and around

Despite being the main market centre for the wine-growing regions of the south, **LEIBNITZ** doesn't quite have the charm of some of Styria's other provincial towns, and it may be better to base yourself somewhere like Ehrenhausen (see p.230) if you're looking for a taste of the rural south. That said, Leibnitz has a historical pedigree second to none, and there are a few **ancient sites** in the environs of town. The Celts were the earliest known inhabitants, settling on the nearby **Frauenberg** hill, although it was the Romans who really put the town on the map, founding **Flavia Solva** (Flavia named after the emperor Titus Flavius Vespasian, and Solva, the Celtic name for the local River Sulm) around 70 AD. Commanding a convenient crossing point over the River Mur, the settlement flourished as a trade centre before succumbing to the barbarian invasions of the early fifth century. It was only with the bishop of Salzburg's decision to build a castle on the **Seggauberg** in the 860s that the area began to recover, and the town of Leibnitz grew at the foot of the hill as the Middle Ages ensued.

Antique attractions aside, Leibnitz is more of a gateway to the Styrian wine country than a tourist town in itself: the regional tourist office here (see opposite) is a good source of information on the villages to the south and east, and will book rooms in Ehrenhausen and the smaller settlements beyond. Leibnitz is also a useful launching pad for trips to the village of **Grossklein**, home to a small but rewarding museum of Celtic culture.

The Town and Flavia Solva

Leibnitz centres on the **Hauptplatz**, a bustling shopping area with a church at each end, neither of which really merits a visit. The town's main attractions lie further afield; Rudolf-Hans-Bartsch-Gasse heads west from the Hauptplatz towards the **Seggauberg**, a wooded hill on the other side of the Sulm. Fifteen minutes' walk up the hill is **Schloss Seggau**, built by the archbishops of Salzburg in the thirteenth century. The Renaissance touches added by the region's subsequent rulers, the bishops of Seckau, can be appreciated by venturing into the elegant, galleried courtyard. Numerous Roman stone reliefs from Flavia Solva, many of them family gravestones, have been built into the walls of the Schloss. Visits to the state rooms, including the bishopric of Seckau's picture gallery, are possible only by prior arrangement (☎03452/82435).

Immediately south of Seggauberg rises another hill, the **Frauenberg**, site of a Baroque pilgrimage church and the **Tempelmuseum** (April–Oct daily 10am–noon & 2–4pm; öS20, combined ticket including Flavia Solva öS30), built above a Roman-period temple of Isis. Associated with religious cults ever since the Celts first settled the hill a thousand years before Christ, the Frauenberg became a temple district in Roman times serving the people of Flavia Solva down in the valley. There's not much to see here save for the temple foundations and a few sculptural fragments, but the hillside setting is evocative.

The remains of **Flavia Solva** itself lie some 3km southeast of Leibnitz just beyond the suburb of Wagna. The **museum** (daily except Mon 10am–noon & 1–6pm; öS25) is short on star exhibits, but houses a representative collection of Roman jewellery, ceramics and gravestones. Entrance to the museum allows access to a familiar grid pattern of excavated streets outside. To get to the museum, take Schmiedgasse out of the Hauptplatz then bear left into Marburgerstrasse, or take one of the hourly Wagna–Leitring buses from Leibnitz train station.

Practicalities

Leibnitz's **tourist office** (Mon, Tues, Thurs & Fri 9am–noon & 1–4.30pm, Wed & Sat 9am–noon; ☎03452/82620, fax 71560) is at Hauptplatz 24, in a courtyard behind the town hall. **Private rooms** can be booked here; otherwise the best of the **hotels** are *Pension Lang*, Bahnhofstrasse 22 (☎03452/82552, fax 71606; ③), with TV in all rooms and a good-value buffet breakfast; and *Gasthof Sailler*, Hauptplatz 5 (☎03452/72516; ③), which offers a similar deal in an older, more central building. There's a **campsite** next to a sports centre in the town park west of the city centre; follow signs to the Freizeitzentrum (a sports and recreation complex) to get there.

Most **eating and drinking** venues are to be found on the Hauptplatz or along Grazergasse to the north. *Gasthof Sailler* (see above), and *Gasthaus Alte Post*, Grazergasse 7, both have reasonably priced Austrian standards; *China Restaurant Singapore*, Grazergasse 37, offers a pretty standard range of oriental cuisine enlivened by Malaysian favourites. *Café-Pub Rondo*, Grazergasse 18, is a good place for a night-time drink.

The Celtic museum at Grossklein

Twelve kilometres southwest of Leibnitz, just off the Leibnitz–Deutschlandsberg road, the village of **GROSSKLEIN** is home to the small but well-laid out **Museum der Hallstattzeit** (Museum of the Hallstatt Period; daily except Mon 10am–noon & 2–4.30pm; öS30). Recalling the Celtic culture of the Late Bronze Age (a period named after the village of

Hallstat; see p.368), the museum assembles a host of ornaments, weapons and implements retrieved from extensive eighth-century BC burial grounds located north and west of the village. Four of the graves are believed to be those of local princelings, and it's in one of these that the museum's star exhibits were found: an exquisite ceremonial bronze face mask, and a bronze pair of hands engraved with geometric patterns. Elsewhere in the museum, there are a series of tableaux re-creating scenes from Hallstatt-era daily life, and an impressive collection of *Zisten* – large, lidded bronze containers decorated with animal and bird shapes.

The eight daily **buses** plying the Leibnitz–Arnfels–Leutschach route pass through Grossklein.

Ehrenhausen and around

Ten kilometres south of Leibnitz, the small village of **EHRENHAUSEN** lurks beneath a wooded crag chosen by the Eggenbergs as the site of the sixteenth-century fortress that served as a base for their campaigns against the Turks. The Eggenberg coat of arms hangs over Ehrenhausen's **Pfarrkirche**, centrepiece of an attractive village Hauptplatz. Most of the cherub-laden interior is the result of an eighteenth-century remodelling, although the high altar features a sculpted Pietà from the 1430s. On the right side of the nave, a stone relief marks the tomb of Christoph von Eggenberg, shown here kneeling in prayer and flanked by wife Helena and six childen.

Christoph's son Ruprecht lies in the **mausoleum**, which dominates the village from a hilltop to the south and is accessible by a stairway from the southern end of the village square. A key to the mausoleum should be collected from the parsonage next door to the church before embarking on the climb. Having made his name by leading the Austrian army against the Turks at the Battle of Sisak in 1593, Ruprecht von Eggenberg engaged Italian architect Pietro de Pomis (who worked on the Mausoleum of Ferdinand II in Graz; see p.219) to design a suitably imposing funerary monument shortly before his death in 1611. The results are certainly impressive, with an elegant pastel blue facade flanked by towering, fancifully clad warriors. Austrian master builder Fischer von Erlach was drafted in by Ruprecht's descendants some eighty years later to plan an interior rich in late-Baroque imagery. Held aloft by Corinthian columns wreathed in vines, the cupola shelters four angels brandishing, respectively, a skull, an hourglass, a burning torch and an extinguished torch – all serving as reminders of our mortality. The Eggenbergs' castle, a short distance above the mausoleum, still looks imposing enough; unfortunately it's private property and sightseeing is not encouraged.

Practicalities
There are plenty of private **rooms** in the environs of both Ehrenhausen and neighbouring Gamlitz, 3km to the east. They can be booked through the tourist office in Leibnitz (see p.229), as well as through the small, irregularly open **tourist office** in Ehrenhausen town hall on the Hauptplatz. As for **hotels**, there's little to choose between the two nice old inns on Ehrenhausen's main square, both offering good-value, comfortable rooms: *Zum goldenen Löwen*, Hauptplatz 28 (☎03453/2312; ②), and *Zur goldenen Krone*, Hauptplatz 24 (☎03453/2640; ②). Either of these is also a good place to have a main **meal** or a quick snack and a **drink**. If you want a change from Austrian food, *Jakobs Pizzeria*, five minutes away on Hauptstrasse, has an inexpensive selection of pizzas.

Around Ehrenhausen
West of Ehrenhausen, Bundesstrasse 69 offers a scenic drive through a succession of villages sheltering beneath steeply banked vineyards. **GAMLITZ**, 3km away, is one of the most picturesque: it has a **tourist office** at Marktplatz 41 (☎03453/3922, fax 4482) as well as its own **Schloss**, which now holds a **museum of the wine industry**. Eleven

kilometres further on, **LEUTSCHACH**, with a **tourist office** at Hauptplatz 8 (☎ & fax 03454/6311), is another rustic wine-producing centre with a sprinkling of private rooms and *Buschenschänken*, or wine-taverns. From here, you can continue onwards to **EBISWALD** 20km to the west, where a right fork heads for the **Radlpass** and the **Slovene frontier**; alternatively, you can follow a minor road that meanders back towards Ehrenhausen through the extremely picturesque vineyard communities of **Sulztal** and **Ratsch**.

Bad Radkersburg

Nestling in flatlands of the far southeastern corner of Styria, where corn and pumpkins proliferate, **BAD RADKERSBURG** was once an important market centre for goods brought down the River Mur, and a crucial strongpoint in the Habsburgs' defences against the Ottoman Turks. Now that the main trade routes have shifted 35km to the west, the town has drifted into a provincial torpor, somewhat cut off from the main currents of Austrian life. The remains of sixteenth-century fortifications offer some reminder of the town's past glories, but today it's best enjoyed for its rural, market-town feel.

On the opposite side of the River Mur is the Slovene town of Gornja Radgona, easily reached by a bridge immediately to the south of the town centre. You can walk over without any problem, providing you have a passport handy.

The Town

Bad Radkersburg's main point of reference is **Langgasse**, a bustling shopping street that bisects the town from north to south. A few steps east of here in the former armoury is the **Heimatmuseum**, at Emmenstrasse 9 (Mon–Fri 9am–noon & 1–4pm; öS20), a fairly standard collection of local crafts and old farm tools, enlivened by a few oddities, as well as exquisitely painted targets used by nineteenth-century rifle associations, and the Negau helmet, an impressive bronze headpiece manufactured by local Celts in the first century BC.

Further south along Langgasse, Kirchgasse leads through to the fifteenth-century **Pfarrkirche**, surrounded by the tombs of the knights who once defended this area against the Ottomans. Inside, a Gothic altarpiece shows Christ the Shepherd cradling a lamb. Just beyond is the **Hauptplatz**, ringed by elegant sixteenth-century mansions, many of which harbour leafy courtyards. More old houses, groaning under red-tiled roofs, are to be found along Murgasse to the south, beyond which you'll emerge onto the remains of the town's seventeenth-century **fortifications**. Remaining town walls girdle the town centre on the southern, eastern and northern sides, although there's little to savour apart from the sight of several protruding bastions, and a certain sense of crumbling grandeur.

Practicalities

Bad Radkersburg's **train station** is 1km north of town. Some trains are met by a local bus, which goes direct to the Hauptplatz (which is also the place to catch regional buses), otherwise it's quite easy to walk: turn left outside the station and then take a right into Bahnhofstrasse. The **tourist office** at Hauptplatz 14 (April–Oct Mon & Fri 9am–noon & 3–7pm, Tues & Thurs closes 6pm, Wed closes 5pm; Nov–March Mon, Tues & Thurs 9am–noon & 2–5pm, Wed & Fri closes 4pm; ☎03476/2545, fax 2545-25) allocates **private rooms**. Some of these are central, but many are in the suburb of Altneudörfl, 1km out of town. You'll pass several "Zimmer frei" signs on the way into town along Bahnhofstrasse, which are a good option if you've arrived too late to hit the tourist office.

Among the numerous **pensions** in town are the *Altneudörflerhof*, Altneudörfl 127 (☎ & fax 03476/2253; ①), with comfy, balconied rooms in a quiet suburb 1km west of town; *Gästehaus Ferk*, Murgasse 11 (☎03476/2584; ①), offering en-suite rooms in an old house in the town centre; and *Pension Horvath*, Bahnhofstrasse 1 (☎03476/2128; ②), a family-run place between the town and the train station.

There's a **hostel**, the *Radlerherberge Kapuzinerbastei* (literally "cyclists' hostel", although they won't turn away non-cyclists), at Südtirolerplatz 6 (no phone: contact the town tourist office to reserve a place), which offers dorm beds for öS170 in a converted Gothic fortress tower. A **campsite** (☎03467/267725) lies at the western end of the town park, about 800m from the centre, well signposted from the southern end of town.

As far as **eating and drinking** are concerned, plenty of daytime cafés cluster around the Hauptplatz. *Gasthof zum Türkenloch*, Langgasse 10, is an atmospheric place offering standard Austrian food and good local beer in a late-medieval town house. The more modern *Hermann*, Langgasse 40, is a popular *Kaffee-Konditorei*-cum-restaurant-cum-pizzeria.

Feldbach, Schloss Riegersburg and Blumau

A workaday agricultural town, **FELDBACH** is that place people pass through en route to the area's most important attraction, the **fortress of Riegersburg**, most only staying in town for as long as it takes to catch a bus. Feldbach is worth more than that, if only because of a curious fortification, the Tabor, sole reminder of the town's medieval past.

The train station – also the departure point for buses to Riegersburg – stands some five minutes' north of a humdrum Hauptplatz. Between the two is the **Pfarrkirche St Leonhard**, a standard Gothic/Baroque hybrid notable for its remarkable modern clock tower, a gaudily decorated concrete pylon visible for kilometres around. Girdling the church are the remains of the **Tabor**, a fortified quadrant of buildings erected in the early 1500s to provide the local populace with a safe haven in the event of enemy attack. Built as a defence against the Turks, the Tabor was subsequently used as a refuge from marauding *haiduks*, Hungarian peasant bandits who raided the prosperous towns of eastern Austria in the early seventeenth century. The Tabor now houses a decidedly odd array of local **museums** (all open Mon–Fri 9–11am & 2–7pm, Sat & Sun 9am–noon; combined entrance fee öS30). These include an old smithy, a Styrian fishery museum featuring a variety of historic nets, a fire brigade museum, a geology museum, and an ethnographic collection showcasing antique agricultural implements, local costumes and a reconstructed eighteenth-century schoolroom.

Two kilometres north of the town on the Riegersburg road (and served by Feldbach–Riegersburg buses) is **Schloss Kornberg**, a Renaissance chateau that boasts a pentagonal galleried courtyard. It's now the venue for themed historical exhibitions and trade fairs: the tourist offices in Graz or Feldbach will have details.

Both Feldbach and nearby Riegersburg can be visited as a day-trip from Graz. Should you wish to stay in the area and haven't got time to press on to Riegersburg itself, the **tourist office** on the Hauptplatz (Mon–Fri 9am–noon & 1–5pm, Sat 9am–noon) will have a list of local **private rooms**. Two reasonable **hotels** off the southern end of the Hauptplatz are *Gasthof zum Weltmeister*, Grazerstrasse 17 (☎03152/2422; ②), and *Gasthof Hödl Kaplan*, Grazerstrasse 12 (☎03152/2338; ③).

Schloss Riegersburg

Ten kilometres north of Feldbach, **SCHLOSS RIEGERSBURG** is a breathtaking sight, dominating a landscape of rolling cornfields and pasturelands from a sheer crag of volcanic basalt some 200m above the valley floor. The original fortress was built in

1122 by Rüdiger von Hohenberg to keep the Magyars at bay, although its current extent, including over 3km of walls and numerous gateways and bastions, dates from the seventeenth century, when the Turks were the major threat. It was acquired in 1822 by the Liechtenstein family, who still use parts of the building as a residence.

Pathways lead up from Riegersburg village through a succession of gates and outer fortifications, passing vine-bearing terraces and a memorial to the World War I dead, before arriving at the **Wenzelstor**, the entrance to the inner fortress. The **museum** (April–Oct 9am–5pm; öS90) doesn't differ a great deal from any of Austria's other castle museums with its array of weapons, suits of armour and the odd cannon, but it's an excellently presented collection nevertheless. There's an understandable emphasis on the history of the **Liechtensteins** themselves: originally from Mödling near Vienna, they were influential in Habsburg court circles throughout the Middle Ages. However, their subsequent rise to princely status owed a lot to **Karl I** (1569–1627), whose statesman-like visage peers from many of the display cabinets in the museum. Despite being brought up as a Protestant, Karl chose to support the ultra-Catholic Ferdinand II in the religious disputes that foreshadowed the outbreak of the **Thirty Years' War**, and was responsible for rounding up and prosecuting rebellious Protestant nobles in Bohemia after 1620. Rewarded with vast tracts of land (often land confiscated from the rebels), Karl was made a prince for his efforts, although it was the family's acquisition of the crown lands of Vaduz and Schellenberg (the present-day Principality of Liechtenstein) in 1712 that secured their hereditary monarchical status. The museum exhibition ends with a tour of some of the castle's state rooms, most sumptuous of which is the fifteenth-century **Rittersaal**, whose ceiling and portals display stunningly intricate wood panelling.

Practicalities

Riegersburg is 13km south of the Graz–Wiener Neustadt motorway, although there are no direct buses from either of these two towns. For those dependent on public transport, the best way to get here is to take one of the eight daily trains from Graz to Feldbach, where there are six bus departures a day to Riegersburg. There's a small **tourist office** just outside the lowest of the castle's many gates, which will direct you to the limited selection of **private rooms** in the village. There are several Gasthöfe in the village offering solid Austrian **food** and good-value **accommodation**. Rooms at the *Gasthof Hasslhof*, Riegersburg 20 (☎03153/201; ①), are basic but comfortable, and have shared bathrooms; while those at the *Gasthof zur Riegersburg*, Riegersburg 29 (☎03153/216, fax 7357; ③) are a shade more luxurious with en-suite facilities.

Blumau

A minor road heads northeast of Riegersburg towards the provincial town of Fürstenfeld, 20km distant, and the village of **BLUMAU**, 10km beyond, a small spa-resort which can also be reached via the branch rail line that leaves the main Graz–Szentgotthard line at Fehring and heads north towards Hartberg (see p.234). Blumau was a pretty unremarkable place until the opening in 1997 of the ambitious resort complex of the *Rogner Bad Blumau* (☎03383/5100; ⑦), designed by visionary eccentric **Friedensreich Hundertwasser**, whose unorthodox but enduringly popular architectural creations can also be seen in Vienna (p.107) and Bärnbach (p.227). More of a self-contained village than a hotel, the resort draws a regular stream of Hundertwasser-inspired day-trippers, as well as those seeking the cure. Indeed it's an impressive sight, with an irregular jumble of rainbow-coloured accommodation blocks linked by winding, crazily-paved pathways to the swimming and spa facilities. Some of the hotel's roofs have been grassed over, mirroring the contours of the surrounding low hills.

Hartberg

Sprawling at the foot of the vine-covered Ringkogel, **HARTBERG**, near the Burgenland border, is one of the most pleasant small towns in Styria, combining a well-preserved historic town centre and an overwhelming sense of rural calm. It's little visited, which is surprising given its location just 4km west of the A2 autobahn from Graz to Wiener Neustadt (it's also accessible by train from either city, although the buses are quicker), and the relative wealth of tourist facilities on offer here.

At the southern end of a dainty Hauptplatz, the **Pfarrkirche St Martin** contains an impressive array of Baroque altars, notable for the striking contrast between the dark-grey pillars and pediments of their frames and their fussy gilt embellishments. Lurking behind the church is a squat round tower known as the **Karner**, or Charnel House, a Romanesque baptistry originally used to house the bones of the local dead. Inside are some fine thirteenth-century frescoes, if garishly painted over by nineteenth-century restorers. An *Apocalypse* near the ceiling portrays sinners being driven into the mouth of hell by a demon, while just below four princes riding fanciful beasts symbolize the worldly pursuit of wealth and power.

Just west of the main square, the **Stadtmuseum** on Herrengasse (Wed & Sat 9–11am) displays a few prehistoric implements and everyday utensils from the Roman settlement at Löffelbach 3km west of town. Just up the road from here is **Schloss Hartberg**, a largely modernized Renaissance building that now hosts art exhibitions. A pathway leads from the forecourt of the Schloss to the **Stadtpark**, which runs alongside crumbling remnants of the town's fortifications.

Practicalities

Hartberg's **train station** is some twenty minutes' walk east of town; head down Bahnhofstrasse and turn left in order to reach the centre. **Buses** use the forecourt of the post office, 300m east of the main square along Wienerstrasse.

The main **tourist office** (Mon–Fri 9am–noon & 2–5.30pm, ☎03332/64213) is at Ressavarstrasse 23 just behind the Schölbingerturm, a medieval tower easily spotted if you're approaching the town centre from the east. There's a smaller tourist office in the Rathaus on the main square, although opening times are less reliable. Either of them will provide a list of **private rooms**, although you may have to phone them up yourself to check on vacancies. Most private rooms are to be found above town on the slopes of the Ringkogel, a lovely spot, although the walk uphill can be tough if you're heavily laden with baggage. Worth recommending is Theresia Oswald, Ring 272 (☎03332/63772), who has a large house with excellent self-contained rooms, most of which have fine views of the valley below, for öS200 per person.

With such a wealth of good private rooms you may not need to fall back on Hartberg's **hotels**. Among them, *Zur Sonne*, Hauptplatz 9 (☎03332/62342; ③), is a nice old inn on the main square; *Gasthof Zsifkovics*, St Johannerstrasse 9 (☎03332/62337; ②), is near the station and a bit lacking in atmosphere, although with TV in all the rooms it's not bad value; *Zum Alten Gerichtshof*, Herrengasse 4 (☎03332/62615; ③), is the largest and swishest of the central hotels. There's a municipal **campsite** (May–Sept) just south of the centre and well signed from the main road through town, with open-air and indoor swimming pools a stone's throw away.

All of the above hotels have reasonable **restaurants**. In addition, *Zum Brauhaus*, Wienerstrasse 1, has good Austrian food; *Casa Mulino*, Hauptplatz 5, offers Italian cuisine to a youngish clientele. *Hotel zur Sonne* is probably the nearest thing that Hartberg has to a daytime café, while night-time **drinking** takes place in *Noarnkastl*, Wienerstrasse 10, a friendly bar on the main street that also serves snack food; *Zum Bierkrug*, Grazerstrasse 4, a nice wood-panelled place with a wide range of beers on tap; or *KHW*, Herrengasse 22, a *Musikcafé* with rock music from DJs or local live bands.

Bruck an der Mur and around

Despite **BRUCK AN DER MUR**'s importance as a road and rail junction straddling major north–south and east–west routes, the town itself is an unassuming place that betrays few signs of its role as northeastern Styria's main business and shopping centre. Situated at the confluence of the Mur and the Mürz, Bruck's strategic importance was recognized by both the Romans, who established a small garrison here in the first century AD, and King Ottokar of Bohemia, the remains of whose thirteenth-century fortress lie in ruin on the Schlossberg overlooking town.

Most travellers pass through Bruck in order to change trains on the way to or from Graz, or to catch a bus to Mariazell in the mountains to the northeast. The limited sights offered by Bruck itself can easily be digested in the space of an hour or two, but the town's atmosphere makes it a not unpleasant place to stay if you get stranded.

From the train station at the southern end of town, Bahnhofstrasse leads down towards the foot of the **Schlossberg**, where a couple of pathways ascend towards the meagre remains of **Schloss Landskron** and an excellent view across the red roofs of the town centre. A five-minute walk down Herzog-Ernst-Strasse brings you to the main square, Koloman-Wallisch-Platz, lined by an attractive ensemble of ochre-hued town houses. The square's most impressive feature is the intricate Gothic arcading of the **Kornmesserhaus** on the southeast corner, built for wealthy ironmonger Pankraz Kornmess in the final years of the fifteenth century. Standing above the square to the north, the Gothic **Pfarrkirche** has lost much of its medieval character inside, although there's an attractive piece of local wrought-ironwork in the shape of the sixteenth-century sacristy door, on the left side of the chancel.

Practicalities

A small pavilion in the middle of Koloman-Wallisch-Platz holds Bruck's **tourist office** (Mon–Fri 10am–noon & 2–5pm, Sat 10am–1pm; ☎03862/51811), which will help you find a **private room**, although most of these are in outlying villages. There's not much to choose between the two inexpensive **hotels** in the centre; *Pension Malissa*, Koloman-Wallisch-Platz 9 (☎03862/51158; ②), and *Zum schwarzen Adler*, Mittlergasse 23 (☎03862/51331; ③), are both small places offering functional rooms with en-suite facilities. The **youth hostel**, at Theodor-Korner-Strasse 37 (☎03862/53456, fax 56089), a ten-minute walk west of Koloman-Wallisch-Platz, occupies a former medieval hospital.

There are plenty of **eating and drinking** opportunities on and around the Koloman-Wallisch-Platz. *Gasthof zur Post Riegler* on the corner of the Platz and Schiffgasse is a good mid-range restaurant serving local dishes, such as *Steirergröstl* (small pieces of pan-fried potato, onion and ham), with main courses starting at around öS90; *Pizza Mann*, Mittlergasse 32, offers a reasonably authentic range, plus take-away slices. *Na Und*, Mittlergasse, is a cosy pub-like drinking venue, while *California Café Pub*, Am Grazer Tor, is a slightly more upmarket venue with a cocktail-bar feel.

Mariazell

There are two ways of getting from Bruck to the attractive settlement of **MARIAZELL**, 50km to the north, both of which involve a fairly scenic ride through the eastern spur of the Hochschwab Mountains. The most direct (and the one served by regular buses) takes the A20 Bundesstrasse north towards the small ski resort of **Aflenz** 16km away, before gradually climbing into the high pasturelands of northeastern Styria. The other route involves heading for Mürzzuschlag, 40km northeast of Bruck, before turning north onto the A23, an attractive drive up the increasingly narrow Mürz Valley, which passes through the village of **Neuberg an der Mürz**, grouped around the evocative ruins of a fourteenth-century **Cistercian abbey**.

Ranged on a hillside and encircled by pine-covered mountains, Mariazell would be worth a visit even without the religious associations that have made it Austria's most important place of pilgrimage. The local population of 2000 welcomes more than a hundred times that number of visitors every year; although most come to visit the miraculous statue of the Madonna and Child inside the **Basilica** that dominates the town, Mariazell's alpine charms are also a powerful draw. The town is far from being a winter sports centre comparable with the big package resorts of the Tyrol, but the presence of the 1266-metre **Bürgeralpe** immediately to the east and the 1626-metre **Gemeindealpe** to the northwest ensure good skiing in winter and excellent walking conditions for the rest of the year.

The town has been a religious centre ever since the Benedictine monks from St Lambrecht (see p.245) established a priory here in 1157, although it's not known when, or exactly why, the site became associated with the miraculous healing powers of the Virgin Mary. The town was certainly on the pilgrimage circuit by 1377, when King Louis of Hungary attributed his victory over the Turks to the intervention of the Virgin of Mariazell. The cult was subsequently adopted by the Habsburgs as a symbol of the supranational, Catholic unity of the empire, and it remains popular with believers from all over central Europe. Crowds throng the town centre on Saturdays and Sundays throughout the summer, with special ceremonies taking place on August 15 (Assumption) and September 8 (Birth of the Virgin).

About five buses a day run up to Mariazell from Bruck via Aflenz, and there are a couple of daily buses from Graz. For those approaching Mariazell from the north, a branch line (served by about five trains a day) connects Mariazell train station – actually 1.5km away in the village of St Sebastian – with St Pölten on the main Vienna–Salzburg line.

The Town

Girdled at a discreet distance by a ring of souvenir stalls, the **Basilica** looms over all else in Mariazell from its lofty position at the top of the Hauptplatz. Outwardly, it's not immediately attractive: begun in the thirteenth century and enlarged in the seventeenth to accommodate ever-increasing numbers of visitors, it sports a single Gothic spire squeezed awkwardly between later Baroque domes. Once inside, pilgrims congregate around the **Gnadenkapelle**, or Chapel of Miracles, halfway down the nave, where a twelfth-century statue of the Virgin and Child stands behind a silver grille. With the Virgin herself a curiously doll-like figure dressed in billowing silver skirts, the pair's image has become a trademark for the village as a whole, repeated endlessly on souvenirs and devotional prints. More sumptuous still is the **high altar**, designed by leading Baroque architect Fischer von Erlach and featuring a serpent crawling across a silver-plated globe, overlooked by a cherub-encircled Crucifixion. Elswhere the Basilica is stuffed with tombs and relics, the most macabre of which are the glass caskets on either side of the nave holding the remains of third-century saints Paulilus and Modestus, their fragile skeletons shrouded in bejewelled robes. Stairways on either side of the porch are decorated with nineteenth-century devotional paintings commissioned from local artisans by the grateful recipients of the Virgin's miraculous healing powers. Most of them follow a set formula, depicting the Virgin of Mariazell hovering benignly above the sickbeds of the faithful. The church **treasury** (daily except Mon 10am–5pm; öS50), approached from the southeastern side of the basilica, houses a treasure trove of ecclesiastical silverware, and a painting of the Virgin given to the church by Louis of Hungary in thanks for his deliverance from the Turks.

The Bürgeralpe and Erlaufsee

There's not much else to Mariazell save for Wienerstrasse, the main shopping street which leads north from the Hauptplatz, passing the terminal for the cable car (öS90 return) to the

Bürgeralpe, which commands superb views towards the Hochschwab range to the south-west. Continuing along Wienerstrasse, the road eventually descends into the neighbouring village of **St Sebastian**, site of Mariazell's train station and starting point for the forty-minute walk to **Erlaufsee**, along a well-signed path that starts just behind the station. On summer weekends an antique tram-locomotive makes the trip from the train station to the lake six times a day (öS50 one way, öS80 return). The lake itself is a charming spot, fringed by a shingle beach where pedalos and rowing boats can be rented.

Practicalities

Mariazell's **bus station** is on Dr-Leber-Strasse just below the Hauptplatz, while **trains** terminate in St Sebastian, fifteen minutes' walk away to the north. The **tourist office**, Hauptplatz 13 (May–Sept Mon–Sat 9am–12.30pm & 1.30–5.30pm, Sun 9am–noon; Oct–April Mon–Fri 9am–12.30pm & 1.30–5pm, Sat 9am–noon; ☎03882/2366, fax 3945), will arrange **private rooms** in Mariazell or St Sebastian. There's a large, 140-bed **youth hostel** ten minutes south of the Hauptplatz, at Fischer-Erlachweg 2 (☎03882/2669-0, fax 2669-88).

Of the town's numerous **pensions**, those offering the best deals include *Weisser Engel*, Grazerstrasse 9 (☎03882/2874; ②), with basic rooms with shared bathrooms in a modern block of flats; *Marienheim*, Abelplatz 3 (☎03882/2545; ②), offering much the same deal but in slightly cosier surroundings; and *Frühstuckspension Maria Zechner*, Wienerstrasse 25 (☎03882/2581, fax 4621-12; ②), with rooms with en-suite facilities in an old apartment building on the main street.

Plenty of **eating** establishments surround the Basilica, none of them charging too exploitative prices. You might try *Gasthof zum Jägerwirt*, Hauptplatz 2, a good place for schnitzel-based meals or a hearty bowl of goulash; or *Goldene Krone*, Hauptplatz, which has a good range of main meals as well as salad-based snacks. *Zum alten Brauhaus*, Wienerstrasse 5, is a good place to sample Styrian food, and is also one of the best places to **drink** in town, serving the excellent local Girrer beer on tap. *Café Liane*, Wienerneustadtstrasse 3, is a friendly bar usually open past midnight.

Leoben and around

Nineteen kilometres west of Bruck, **LEOBEN** has been a centre of the Styrian iron industry since the Middle Ages, processing the ore brought down the hills of Eisenerz 25km to the north. The steelworks in the suburb of Donawitz still blights the northern approaches to the town, but central Leoben, enclosed by a curve of the River Mur, remains surprisingly industry-free. There are few essential sights here, save perhaps for the Gothic murals of the **Stiftskirche** in the nearby suburb of **Göss**, but the town does serve as a useful introduction to the iron-dominated heritage of central Styria. Industrial archaeology figures prominently in the **Steirische Eisenstrasse** (Styrian Iron Road), an itinerary contrived by the local tourist authorities to breathe new life into Styria's decaying industrial heartland, which heads northwards from Leoben through **Vordenberg** to Eisenerz, before heading down to the Enns Valley towns of Hieflau, Grossreifling and Altenmarkt.

The Town

Leoben's **train station** is fifteen minutes' walk north of town; cross the River Mur and head down Franz-Josef-Strasse to reach the pedestrianized **Hauptplatz**, lined with elegant seventeenth-century facades. Most imposing of these is the **Hacklhaus**, at Hauptplatz 9, a stately maroon-and-cream edifice, whose stucco adornments, executed in 1660, include four female figures serving as allegories of the seasons. Immediately to the west stands the **Stadtpfarrkirche St Xaver**, an imposing monument to the Jesuits who once held sway here, containing an impressive array of black-and-gold framed Baroque altars. Behind the church in a former Jesuit college lies the **Stadtmuseum** (Mon–Thurs 10am–noon & 2–5pm; öS20), strong on local mining history, although there's also a room devoted to Leoben's brief flirtation with world history, the Treaty of Leoben, signed here by Napoleon in 1797. After a whirlwind campaign in northern Italy, the wily Corsican marched into Styria in spring 1797 and, having set up camp in Leoben, looked set to advance on Vienna. After negotiations in the Benedictine nunnery in Göss (see below), the Austrians secured Napoleon's withdrawal by ceding their possessions in the Low Countries to the French.

Leoben's most venerable attraction is the Romanesque **Stiftskirche** in the southern suburb of **Göss**, ensconced among the outbuildings of an erstwhile Benedictine nunnery. Late fourteenth-century frescoes adorn the choir, while older work is visible in the nearby **Bischofskapelle**. Across the road from here is the brewery responsible for Styria's most ubiquitous ale, Gösserbrau. The nearby *Brauhaus Göss*, Turmgasse 3, is a convenient place to stop off, have a bite to eat and sample the local brew. To get to Göss, turn right at the southern end of the Hauptplatz and then left into Gösserstrasse, which runs along the banks of the River Mur. Otherwise, take one of the regular municipal buses from Leoben train station.

Practicalities

Leoben's **tourist office**, Hauptplatz 12 (Mon–Thurs 9am–noon & 1.30–5pm, Fri 9am–noon; ☎03842/44018, fax 42581-24), has a small list of **private rooms**. Cheapest of the central **hotels** is *Zum Möhren*, Kärntnerstrasse 227 (☎03842/42207; ②), which has a number of rooms with shared bathrooms; those with en-suite facilities are more expensive. *Hotel Kindler*, Straussgasse 7–11 (☎03842/43202-0; ③), is a good mid-range choice; all rooms come with en-suite facilities, TV and telephone. Best-value rooms with en-suite facilities are 2km outside the centre at *Brauhaus Göss*, Turmgasse 3 (☎03842/22100; ②), handy if you're visiting the Stiftskirche.

Most **eating and drinking** venues are on the Hauptplatz or along Kirchgasse and Zellergasse, two alleyways behind the Stadtpfarrkirche. *Arkadenhof-Restaurant schwarzer Adler*, Hauptplatz 11, has some reasonably priced Austrian staples. Another traditional eatery, but slightly more expensive, is *Turmstub'n*, Kirchgasse 7, while *Trattoria da Francesco*, Zellergasse 1, is an intimate spot for authentic Italian food. For night-time drinking, try *Eden Pub*, Kirchgasse 8, the *Cafe Seitenblick* next door, or any of the bars along Zellergasse.

Vordenberg and the Erzbergbahn

Regular trains, as well as buses, make their way from Leoben train station towards **VORDENBERG**, a settlement that straggles along either side of the Vorden-berger-bach. There's a **tourist office** at Hauptstrasse 85 (☎03849/9119) and two nice old guesthouses along the sinuous main street: *Zur Post*, Hauptstrasse 86 (☎03849/274, fax 892; ②), and the *Schwarzer Adler*, at no. 98 (☎03849/264; ②). The town used to be a mining settlement, and the area around the village is dotted with the winching towers of abandoned mine workings. It's also the start of the **Erzbergbahn**, a narrow-gauge railway originally built to carry ore from Eisenerz (see opposite) down the valley towards Leoben. A tourist-oriented rail service runs between Vordernberg and Eisenerz between May and September; otherwise regular Leoben–Eisenerz buses are the best means of embarking on the journey. Five kilometres above Vordenberg, the road crosses the 1232-metre **Präbichl Pass**, beyond which fleeting glimpses of the extraordinary ore-bearing **Erzberg** herald the descent into Eisenerz.

Eisenerz

It's not often that a landscape scarred by industry proves strikingly attractive, and yet the Erzberg ("ore mountain"), rising above **EISENERZ**, is perversely beautiful, carved into a ziggurat shape by decades of open-cast mining, its colour shifting from ochre to red to purple as the sunlight flits across its slopes. First mined by the Celts, iron ore from Eisenerz fed an armaments industry that helped push Habsburg power southwards and eastwards against the retreating Turks. It continued to provide Austria's iron and steel industry with almost all of its requirements until the 1980s, when the mine here finally ceased production, a victim of cheaper imports from the Third World. Now blighted by high unemployment, Eisenerz has a tired and world-weary feel, although the town is beginning to turn its industrial heritage to good touristic effect. The Erzberg is now a show-mine, while in Eisenerz itself the presence of one of Austria's few remaining fortified churches and an absorbing town museum, combined with some excellent alpine scenery all around, ensures that there are plenty of other things to do too.

The Town

Surveying the attractive town houses of downtown Eisenerz from a hillock to the south is the walled **Pfarrkirche St Oswald**, fortified in the sixteenth century against the advancing Ottoman Turks. The Turks never got this far, but the fortifications proved their worth in 1599 when the Protestant townsfolk warded off an attack led by the Catholic Bishop of Seckau. The church itself dates from the thirteenth century, but it gained its current late-Gothic character from an extensive face-lift in the 1470s. It's full of reminders of Eisenerz's mining history: the relief of Adam and Eve above the door as you enter shows Adam dressed in medieval mining gear, while inside a wooden sculpture of a miner high up in the roof strikes a bell every hour. The church's most impressive feature is the **organ loft**, an ornate piece of late-Gothic stonework carved with interweaving patterns (reminiscent of intricate wickerwork) across which wild beasts frolic.

Below the church lies an attractive main square, **Bergmannsplatz**, grouped around a sixteenth-century **Rathaus** decorated with abstract sgraffito motifs. Beside the Rathaus is the **Krippenhaus** (literally the "crib-house"), where exhibitions of the typically Austrian craft of constructing *Krippen*, or Nativity scenes are held during Advent and at other times of the year (ask at the tourist office for details – see p.240).

The museum

Two hundred metres north of Bergmannsplatz on Schulstrasse, the **Stadtmuseum** (Mon–Fri 9am–5pm, Sat & Sun 10am–noon & 2–5pm; öS36), situated in the Kammerhof, occupies the former hunting lodge of Franz-Josef and is still owned by the descendents of his ill-starred nephew, Archduke Franz Ferdinand. There's a wealth of material on local crafts and costumes here, but it's the section on Eisenerz's mining history that is most interesting. Miners originally belonged to a highly respected medieval guild, whose uniform, the *Maximilianische Tracht*, is on display here. A white, hooded tunic with leather rear flaps (the so-called *Arschleder*, or "arse-leather", necessary for negotiating the wooden slides that linked one mine gallery to another), this garment served as the miners' uniform from the late Middle Ages until the mid-nineteenth century, when it was replaced by more military-style black outfits, still in use today on ceremonial occasions. To illustrate the importance of such ceremony, several paintings show the torchlight parade of 1841, held to celebrate Emperor Ferdinand IV's visit to the town. The special, velvet-seated wagon on which the august Habsburg was conveyed into the mine itself is also on display. In a bizarre variation on the *Krippen* theme, there's a glass case holding a model of the mine workings with a carved figure of St Barbara in the middle. Barbara is the patron saint of miners, and her feast day on December 4 (the *Brauchtumfest*) is still marked in Eisenerz with parades in traditional uniforms.

The Erzberg

A tourist centre at the eastern end of the town, just east of Bergmannsplatz, is the start-ing point for trips into the Erzberg itself. The **tour** (May–Oct daily 10am–3pm; öS140) involves a ninety-minute underground voyage with German-language commentary. Drilling machines are noisily demonstrated, while model dwarf-figures – looking rather like out-of-place garden gnomes – highlight traditional folk beliefs in the spirits that live in the mountain. Claustrophobic types might prefer a bumpy though scenic one-hour ride around the terraces of the Erzberg in the "Hauly", an enormous dumper truck designed to transport prodigious amounts of ore (same times; öS160, combined ticket for mine tour and Hauly öS250).

Practicalities

The town's **train station**, where **buses** also terminate, is a five-minute walk north of the centre. There are no hostels or campsites nearby, but the Eisenerz **tourist office** at Schulstrasse 1 (May–Oct Mon–Fri 9am–1pm & 3–5pm; ☎03848/3700, fax 3505) can help with **private rooms**, of which the town has a small selection. Among the **hotels**, *Frühstuckspension Krapf*, Schlingerweg 3 (☎03848/3457; ①), has excellent-value rooms (some with en-suite facilities) some ten minutes' walk south of the centre with views towards the Erzberg; *Rasthaus an der Eisenstrasse*, Vordenbergerstrasse 20 (☎03848/4590; ②), is another source of cheap rooms, most with shared bathrooms, five minutes' walk southeast of the centre. *Gasthof zur Post*, Lindmoserstrasse 10 (☎03848/2232; ②), is an attractive old inn in the town centre with TV and en-suite facilities in each room, while the *Eisenerzer Hof*, Hieflauerstrasse 17 (☎03848/2551; ②), between the train centre and the station, offers the same comforts but in slightly less atmospheric surroundings.

Both the *Gasthof zur Post* and the *Eisenerzer Hof* have restaurants serving standard Austrian **food**, the latter with good-value main courses from öS70 upwards. Another place with good-value lunchtime options is *Fleischerei Moser*, Dr-Karl-Renner-Strasse 7, while the nearby *Heiligen Geist Stub'n*, Dr-Karl-Renner-Strasse 4, has a dependable range of traditional schnitzels.

Barbara Stub'n Tagescafé, Bergmannplatz 2, is the place to sip coffee and eat cakes; the *Eisenerzer Hof* has a *Café City Pub* that's open late; and *Pizzeria Amici*, Krumpentalerstrasse, has a disco on Fridays and Saturdays.

Eisenerzer Ramsau and the Leopoldsteinersee

Eisenerz is hardly a winter sports resort, but there's one of sorts at **Eisenerzer Ramsau**, a side-valley that begins at the southern end of town (take Krumpentalerstrasse from the centre) and stretches uphill for a couple of kilometres. There's a big chalet-style **hotel**, the *Pichlerhof*, Schlingerweg 199 (☎03848/3414; ③), which can hire out gear for cross-country skiing in winter, or serve as a base for walk-ing in summer.

Three kilometres north of town there's a turning for the **Leopoldsteinersee** (served by local buses from Eisenerz train station), a popular local beauty spot a fur-ther kilometre away, dramatically situated below the sheer rock face of the **Seemauer**. There are a couple of cafés at the northern end, and a bathing area with a shingle beach 1.5km away at the southern end, where several trails lead off to skirt round the forested slopes of the 1871-metre Pfaffenstein.

Seckau

Beyond Leoben, the main road and rail route to western Styria and Carinthia continues to ascend the Mur Valley, passing a string of settlements which, despite their economic importance, harbour few attractions. **KNITTELFELD**, 30km west of Leoben, is just such a town, and the only reason to stop off here is to visit the Benedictine **Abbey of Seckau**, situated in a secluded side-valley 16km to the north: with seven buses a day (Mon–Sat only) making the trip from Knittelfeld train station, the abbey is relatively easy to get to from here. Originally an Augustinian foundation, the abbey served as the ecclesiastical capital of Styria until the diocese was moved to Graz in 1782. Dominating an arcaded Baroque courtyard is a fine twelfth-century Romanesque basilica, inside of which lies the Mausoleum of Karl II (father of Ferdinand II), fashioned by Lugano artist Alessandro de Verda and completed in 1612. Elsewhere in the church, the Sakramentskapelle holds a twelfth-century Veneto-Byzantine image of the Virgin fashioned from alabaster.

Judenburg and around

Dramatically situated on a hilltop overlooking the Mur Valley, **JUDENBURG** was Styria's leading mercantile centre in the late Middle Ages, controlling the trade routes between Vienna, southern Germany and northern Italy. Like most other Mur Valley towns, Judenburg grew rich on the export of iron (and, oddly, the lavender trade), and was by the fifteenth century an important site for the manufacture of weaponry. The town's name is thought to derive from one of its early medieval rulers, Jutho, although popular tradition subsequently identified it with the large Jewish colony that settled here in the thirteenth century. A pogrom in 1496 forced them to flee the town, and there's little trace of their culture today.

The Town

The scene of lively markets on Saturdays and Mondays, Judenburg's Hauptplatz is dominated by the 75-metre-high **Stadtturm** (May & June Fri–Sun 10am–6pm; July–Sept daily 10am–6pm; Oct Fri–Sun 10am–5pm; öS20), built in the fifteenth century as a symbol of the town's commercial wealth, although its appearance has drastically altered since then as a result of repeated fires and rebuildings. It's now the venue for temporary historical exhibitions, and there's a viewing gallery near the top offering a panorama of the local countryside. Beside it is the sixteenth-century **Pfarrkirche**, where the heavy-handed flourishes of the Baroque interior are lightened by a Gothic statue of the Madonna and Child, carved locally around 1420.

Kaserngasse heads eastwards from the Hauptplatz to the **Stadtmuseum** at no. 27 (July & Aug Mon–Fri 9am–noon & 3–5pm, Sat 9am–noon; Sept–June Mon–Fri 9am–noon; donation), a rather old-fashioned display of miners' uniforms, tools used by local ironmongers, and the intricate wooden moulds used by tilemakers. There's a reasonable collection of folk art on show, though, including a seventeenth-century wooden Christ figure, which was carried through the town on feast days.

A little further along Kaserngasse, Langganggasse descends to the banks of the Mur, from which the dainty, whitewashed **Magdalenakirche** is clearly visible on the other side of the river. Built around 1350, the church still preserves its original stained glass, together with exuberant frescoes, notably a *Crucifixion* and *Annunciation* on the north wall of the choir.

Practicalities

Judenburg's **train station** is 500m north of the centre. Turn right into Gussstahlwerkstrasse, cross the river, and take one of the paths leading up into the old town to reach the Hauptplatz. The **bus station** is much nearer at hand, just off Burggasse one block west of the Hauptplatz. The **tourist office** (Mon–Fri 9am–12.30pm & 2–5pm; ☎03572/85000), Hauptplatz 1, has a small list of **private rooms**, all within walking distance of the town centre. There's a **youth hostel** 200m east of the main square at Kaserngasse 22 (☎03572/87355, fax 87355-88). Two centrally located **hotels** are *Gasthof Reichsthaler*, Burggasse 22 (☎03572/82448-9; ①), with several budget-priced rooms with shared bathrooms, and more expensive ones with en-suite facilities; and *Pension Karlbauer*, Herrengasse 4 (☎03572/83415, fax 83415-50; ②), a smaller, more intimate place where all the rooms come with shower and WC. Slightly more expensive but still good value is *Gasthof Murblick*, Sensenwerkgasse 11 (☎03572/83671; ②), near the Magdalenakirche on the north bank of the Mur and with excellent views of the old town.

For food,*Gasthof Gruber*, Hauptplatz, offers a broad range of standard Austrian dishes and is a good daytime café, too; *Pizzeria San Marco*, Weyergasse 1, is the most authentic of several pizza outlets in the town centre; and *Willy's Café*, near the train station at Gussstahlwerkstrasse 24, is a lively **drinking** venue with good snack food, which stays open until 3am. *Disco-Pub Pharao*, Grünhüblgasse 1, is a late bar 1.5km east of the Hauptplatz.

Oberzeiring

Eight kilometres beyond Judenburg, a minor road leaves the main westbound route to head northwards towards Liezen in the Enns Valley, crossing the easternmost spur of the Tauern range. After about 10km, a left turn leads to the highland village of **OBERZEIRING**, an ancient silver-mining centre, which provided Judenburg with much of its former wealth. It's nowadays a minor health resort, utilizing the cool dry air of old mine workings to ease the suffering of those with respiratory problems. The village **show-mine** (May–Oct daily 9.45am–4pm; öS60) involves a short tour of some of the underground workings and a few museum exhibits, ranging from medieval coin-minting equipment to funerary urns used by the Illyrians, a Balkan tribe who penetrated this far north in the ninth century BC.

Getting to Oberzeiring is pretty straightforward, with hourly buses from Judenburg. The **tourist office** in the centre of the village can arrange **private rooms**, and there are a couple of good **hotels**: *Gasthof-Pension Berghof*, Berghofstrasse 3 (☎03571/2236; ③), is a pleasant, chalet-style building with en-suite facilities and TV in all rooms; and *Silberhof*, Hauptstrasse 22 (☎03571/2812; ⑤), is an altogether more upmarket establishment, which specializes in rest cures. There's a **campsite** at Bachstrasse 19 (☎03571/2438).

Unzmarkt and Oberwölz

Continuing westwards from Judenburg along the Mur Valley, the industrial character of much of central Styria is gradually left behind, with both road and railway winding their way up an increasingly narrow valley studded with farmsteads and rural villages. There's an important parting of the ways at **UNZMARKT**, where the main rail line begins to wheel south on its way towards Klagenfurt and Villach, and the privately owned Murtalbahn (see box) continues to follow the Mur Valley westwards to Murau and Tamsweg. Unzmarkt itself is worth a brief stop, if only to enjoy the views on offer from the **pilgrimage church of Frauenburg** on a hill north of town, an easy twenty-minute walk from the train station. Next to the church are the ruins of a thirteenth-century fortress once owned by warrior-aristocrat and minstrel Ulrich von Liechtenstein, an important figure in the history of Murau (see opposite), who died here in 1276.

THE MURTALBAHN

The **Murtalbahn**, the privately owned **narrow-gauge railway** that provides a public transport service between Unzmarkt and Tamsweg, also operates tourist-oriented, steam-hauled services in summer. Trains run between Murau and Tamsweg every Tuesday from early June to mid-September; return tickets cost öS180. An extra service in August runs from Murau to Stadl, a picturesque village between Murau and Tamsweg, every Saturday for öS120 return.

Committed anoraks will enjoy the **engine-driver training sessions**, which take place at Murau station every Thursday morning between early July and early September, offering all comers the chance to ride up and down for a few minutes in the driver's cab. However, it's not cheap, at öS600 for fifteen minutes or öS1600 for 45 minutes. Interested parties should register at Murau tourist office on the day.

At **Niederwölz**, 10km beyond Unzmarkt, a minor road heads northwards to the village of **OBERWÖLZ**, another 10km away up the valley of the Wölzer Bach. It's hard to imagine that this isolated settlement of a thousand souls was once a prosperous medieval mercantile centre that grew rich on the profits of the salt and silver trades. Much of the village's fourteenth-century fortifications, including three gates and two towers, still survives, enclosing an endearing jumble of old houses. At its centre stands the **Stadtpfarrkirche St Martin**, a Romanesque structure with Gothic additions embellished by a *Last Judgment* painted around 1500 on the south outer wall. The nearby **Sigmundskirche**, originally the chapel of a fourteenth-century hospital, has some intricate rib vaulting towards the back of the nave.

For those dependent on public transport, Oberwölz is just about feasible as a day-trip from either Judenburg or Murau, provided you're up early enough and you time your return journey carefully. Three daily buses run up to Oberwölz from Niederwölz train station on the Murau–Unzmarkt line (currently at 6.58am, 9.13am & 1.52pm; the last bus back from Oberwölz is at 1pm); and two buses a day go to Oberwölz from **Scheifling-Lind** train station (at 8.30am & 5.45pm), on the main Bruck–Judenburg–Klagenfurt line.

If you want to stay in Oberwölz, the **tourist office** on the Hauptplatz (Mon–Fri 9am–noon & 2–5pm; ☎ & fax 03581/420) has information on **private rooms**, and there are a couple of good Gasthöfe: the *Graggober*, Stadt 56 (☎03581/315, fax 315-4; ③), is an attractive chalet-style building, while *Zum Möhren*, Stadt 17 (☎03581/7389; ②), is a more modern affair with sauna and solarium on site.

Murau and around

Of all the provincial towns in Styria, **MURAU** is probably the most attractive, with a photogenic jumble of houses arranged alongside the clear, fast-flowing waters of the young River Mur. Despite the town's isolation from the main tourist routes, a sprinkling of historic churches set against an attractive alpine backdrop make a detour here worthwhile. Getting to Murau by public transport is relatively simple, with regular services on the Murtalbahn narrow-gauge railway running up to town from Unzmarkt on the main Bruck–Klagenfurt line.

Courtly poet and unruly magnate **Ulrich von Liechtenstein** built a castle here in 1250, establishing a market at the foot of the castle soon afterwards. The Murau branch of the Liechtenstein line came to an end when Christoph von Liechtenstein died childless in 1580, but the subsequent marriage of his widow **Anna Neumann** (see box, p.244) to leading magnate Georg Ludwig zur Schwarzenberg ensured Murau's

ANNA NEUMANN

Daughter of a local merchant, Anna Neumann (1535–1623) had already been widowed once (she'd married local knight Johannes Jakobus von Thenhausen in 1557) before catching the eye of Christoph von Liechtenstein in 1566. When Liechtenstein died without an heir in 1580, Anna's combined inheritance – from both the Liechtenstein family and her own – made her one of the most powerful, and most eagerly courted, women in Styria. Three more childless marriages followed before the "Black Widow of Murau" eventually married, at the age of 88, the 29-year-old Georg Ludwig zur Schwarzenberg, signing over her property rights to him. The marriage was ordered by Archduke Ferdinand of Styria, the future Emperor Ferdinand II, who wanted to see the Schwarzenbergs (important allies in his campaigns against the Protestants) firmly established in the Murau area.

Widely resented for her ability to accumulate wealth from a succession of husbands without ever providing them with children, Anna Neumann was dubbed a witch by Catholic propagandists, who feared her influence as a supporter of local Protestantism. Neumann's marriage to Schwarzenberg, an enthusiastic supporter of the Counter-Reformation, suggests that she'd given up the cause towards the end of her life.

continuing prosperity. The town's importance as a trading post on the transalpine routes between Italy and Germany is now a thing of the past, and although traditional trades like wood-carving are still practised here, the town is now largely known as a beer-making centre. The local Murauer Bier is served in all the establishments, and the Murauer Doppelmaltz, a dark stout, is also well worth trying.

The Town

A compact town centre is grouped around the triangular **Schillerplatz**, bordered by the elegant town houses of late-medieval merchants. At the western end of the square, a covered walkway leads up to the thirteenth-century **Pfarrkirche St Matthäus**, whose southern face is decorated with a faded but still recognizable fresco of St Christopher holding aloft the boy Jesus. At ground level, plaques marking the graves of sixteenth-century burghers are built into the wall, and an iron grille offers glimpses of the charnel house, home to a chaos of skulls and bones. The frescoes that fill the interior are also faded, but on days when sunlight streams in through the windows the effect can be quite stunning. The oldest works, an *Entombment* and an *Annunciation* dating from the 1370s, are on the south side of the nave. Much of the finest work is to be found in the north transept, where the medieval view of life and mortality is summed up by a picture of Eve standing beside the tree of life – a white mouse and a black mouse nibble at the tree's roots, while a figure of death aproaches in the background. The east wall of the north transept is decorated with a memorial to the house of Liechtenstein, painted sometime in the 1570s: Christ's ascent to heaven from Mount Tabor is displayed at the top; just below, successive generations of the family are shown kneeling at the grave of Otto von Liechtenstein. Below this, a series of panels depicts different branches of the family. Christoph von Liechtenstein and Anna Neumann are shown in the top left panel.

A covered wooden stairway leads from the church to the **Schloss Obermurau** perched on the hill above. Originally built as a fortress by Ulrich von Liechtenstein in 1250, the Schloss was converted into a princely residence by Georg Ludwig zur Schwarzenberg in the 1630s. It's still owned by the Schwarzenberg family, and guided tours of the Schloss's state rooms are frustratingly infrequent (mid-June to mid-Sept Wed 3pm, Fri 10am; öS30). However, you can peer inside a fine arcaded courtyard, where one wall is adorned with a seventeenth-century sundial incorporating a figure of Atlas shouldering a globe.

Heading east out of Schillerplatz along Grazerstrasse, an alley to the left leads down to the village graveyard and the **Annakirche**, a Gothic chapel that holds yet more excellent frescoes, most of which date from around 1400. There's a fine *St George and Dragon* on the north side of the nave, alongside a *Crucifixion* and *Resurrection*. St Anne herself is depicted on the south wall of the choir, flanked by the infant Jesus and the Virgin Mary. Don't miss the seventeenth-century wooden pews, decorated with curious, griffin-like forms.

A little further out along Grazerstrasse is the **Kapuzinerkirche**, once serving a Capuchin monastery founded by Georg Ludwig zur Schwarzenberg in order to bolster the Counter-Reformation. His grave, alongside that of Anna Neumann, is inside on the left. Next door is the **Heimatmuseum** (donation requested), which documents the contemporary woodcarving industry, and looks back in time at the merchants of the Middle Ages who exported felt and iron across the Alps to Italy and southern Germany.

The oldest church in Murau is the twelfth-century **Ägydikirche**, 1km from the centre on the main eastbound road. It's an endearingly simple, squat structure with a wooden steeple, and there are yet more frescoes inside, including a fifteenth-century picture of St Aegidius on the north wall of the choir, and some thirteenth-century scenes from the Life of the Virgin in the nave.

Practicalities

Murau's **tourist office** (Mon–Fri 9am–12.30pm & 2.30–6pm, Sat 8.30am–noon; ☎ & fax 03532/2720), immediately outside the train station on Bahnhofplatz, will provide a list of the town's numerous **private rooms**. Murau's **youth hostel** is near the train station at St-Leonhard-Platz 5 (☎03532/2395; closed Nov & Dec); and there's one inexpensive old-fashioned Gasthof in the centre of town, the *Bärenwirt* at Schwarzenbergstrasse 4 (☎03532/2079; ②), offering simple doubles, some with en-suite facilities. For something a little more comfortable, *Gasthof Ferner*, north of the centre at Roseggerstrasse 9 (☎03532/2318, fax 2318-5; ④), is a family-run **hotel** whose spacious rooms boast en-suite facilities, telephone and TV; while the *Paradise Hotel zum Brauhaus*, Raffaltplatz 17 (☎03532/2437, fax 3897; ④), is a stylish, modern business hotel with balconied rooms overlooking the River Mur.

For **food**, *Grilltreff*, Grazerstrasse 14 (closed Sat & Sun), is the place to go for a quick sausage-based snack. *Fleischerei Imbissstube*, Schwarzenberggasse 1, offers solid sausage-salad-and-chips-type sit-down meals from öS70, while the restaurant of the *Bärenwirt* is another inexpensive restaurant serving up Styrian staples from öS80. *Yang*, A.-Neumann-Strasse 29, is a friendly if fairly standard Chinese restaurant, with Tagesmenüs starting at öS70 and main meals from öS100.

There are a couple of places for a daytime **drink** around the main square; *Stadtcafé*, Schillerplatz 5, has a good range of ice cream and cakes to go with your coffee; *Café zur Krone*, Raffaltplatz, is a cosy bar with a suite of elegant rooms suitable for a quiet evening drink; while the more rowdy, riverside *Café-Pub Vis-a-Vis*, Grazerstrasse 10, attracts a youngish crowd.

Bikes can be hired from the train station or from Intersport Pintar, at Schwarzenbergstrasse 7.

St Lambrecht Abbey

Seven buses a day (Mon–Sat) travel from Murau to the **Stift St Lambrecht**, a Benedictine foundation of eleventh-century vintage set in verdant uplands some 15km southeast of the town. The twin-towered **Stiftskirche** is largely Gothic, although the main portal displays surviving fragments of the original Romanesque structure. The Baroque interior is dominated by Valentin Khautt's **high altar** of 1632, a stuccoed, marble-effect ensemble of statues surrounding a painting of the *Assumption*, and crowned by a figure of St Michael. Also inside the abbey courtyard is the smaller **Peterskirche**, housing a winged altar bearing a *Crucifixion* and various saints by the fifteenth-century Master of St Lambrecht. The abbey buildings (May–Oct 10am–4pm; öS30) house an art collection rich in Gothic wood sculpture, and a collection of stuffed birds.

The Enns Valley

Rising in the Salzburger Land and emptying into the Danube just east of Linz, the River Enns cuts through the mountainous northwestern corner of Styria to create one of the more attractive subalpine itineraries in this part of Austria. Although the market town of **Liezen** is the valley's main commercial centre, there are few obvious tourist destinations save for the rustic village of **Admont**; and the sophisticated winter sports centre of **Schladming**, which provides access to the slopes of the region's most impressive peak, the **Dachstein**.

The mountains of central Styria render the Enns Valley slightly isolated from the rest of the province, but both the A9 autobahn and a main Linz- and Salzburg-bound rail route provide access to the region, leaving the Mur Valley at St Michael and heading northwest through the **Eisenerzer Alpen** before reaching the lower Enns Valley at the village of **Selzthal**, a transport hub that's otherwise pretty unremarkable. From here, the Salzburg-bound road and rail routes lead westwards to the upper Enns Valley and Schladming, while a secondary road and branch line lead to Admont, just east of Selzthal.

Approaching the area from Eisenerz to the southeast, you'll pass through the former iron-working town of **Hieflau** (where rail travellers must change trains) before proceeding to Admont through the **Gesäuse**, a fifteen-kilometre-long gorge where the River Enns forces its way between forested hillsides and rugged cliffs.

Admont

A sleepy agricultural community set against the backdrop of the **Haller Mauern** Mountains to the north, **ADMONT** owes its place on the tourist map to the library and museum collections of the **Benedictine abbey** that stands at the centre of the village. However, Admont's charm doesn't end there: surrounded by pasturelands and wooded hills, it's an excellent place for a rural breather.

Founded in the eleventh century by **Hemma von Friesach**, the same Carinthian noblewoman who established the monastery at Gurk (see p.271), the abbey at Admont has gone through numerous reincarnations over the centuries. Remodelled in the Baroque style in the seventeenth century, it was almost completely destroyed by fire in 1865, and today you are greeted by a rather grim-looking neo-Gothic reconstruction. Happily, the sumptuous **library** (April–Oct daily 10am–1pm & 2–5pm; öS60) was largely untouched by the conflagration, and it's this that most visitors come to see. Built in 1774, the library's interior decorations add up to a vast allegory of human learning: ceiling frescoes by Bartolomeo Altomonte show figures representing the arts, the natural sciences and theology, while the busts of famous intellectuals that hover above the ornate library shelves embrace the gamut of cultural endeavour from Socrates to Dürer. Focus of the library at ground level is the ensemble of four limewood figures by Graz sculptor Josef Stammel, representing Death, Justice, Heaven and Hell. Display cases contain some of the library's most valued possessions, including some beautifully illustrated medieval manuscripts and an original 1516 copy of Erasmus's ground-breaking translation of the New Testament.

Upstairs, a **natural history museum** houses an odd collection of local flora and stuffed or pickled beasts, with South American butterflies standing incongruously beside trays of preserved Styrian apples. The abbey's extensive **art collection** is currently undergoing reorganization, but is due to reopen sometime in 1998.

Practicalities

Admont's **tourist office**, Hauptplatz 4 (Mon 8am–noon, Tues–Fri 8am–5pm; ☎03613/2164, fax 3648), will direct you to **private rooms** in both Admont and the neighbouring village of **Hall** (500m north). *Jugendherberge Röthelstein* (closed Oct & Nov), Austria's most impressive **youth hostel**, is situated on a hill just south of the town in an elegant Renaissance Schloss commanding excellent views across the valley. Among **hotels** in the village, *Gasthof Admonterhof*, just outside the station on Bahnhofstrasse (☎03613/2323; ②), provides rooms with en-suite facilities and TV in a clean if unremarkable building; *Gasthof Zeiser*, Hauptstrasse 6 (☎03613/2147; ③), offers a similar deal but in slightly more central surroundings; and *Gasthof Traube*, Hauptstrasse 3 (☎03613/2440, fax 2440-6; ③), has rooms with TV, minibar and telephone along with a good-value breakfast buffet. Admont's **campsite** occupies a pleasant riverside location, 500m north of the village in Hall.

Most **eating and drinking** takes place along the Hauptstrasse: *Café Wagner*, Hauptstrasse 5, is a good place for a quick sandwich or sausage; *Gasthaus Kamper*, at no. 19, has good-value Austrian staples, cheap lunchtime choices and nice outdoor seating; while *Pizzeria Marktcafé*, at no. 20, has a wide range of pizzas from öS100 and is probably the best place for an intimate evening drink. The *Stiftskeller*, a swish modern café-restaurant in the abbey grounds, offers top-notch local specialities (such as *Ennstaler Nock'n-Reindl* – noodles in ham and cream sauce) from about öS110, although it tends to close by 8pm on weekdays. *Pub Gesäuse-Eingang*, Hauptstrasse 4, is a late-opening bar with snack food; *Café-Pub Pfiff*, Hauptstrasse 7, is rowdier and rockier in its musical tastes.

Schladming and around

Fifteen kilometres west of Admont at **Selzthal**, the route forks, with the A9 autobahn and a main rail route heading north into Upper Austria (see Chapter 8), and another route continuing westwards up the Enns Valley towards Salzburg and Innsbruck. After passing the uninteresting, semi-industrialized town of **Liezen**, the latter route arrives at another major junction 15km upstream, where a branch line and a secondary road leave the Enns Valley at **Stainach** to climb towards Bad Aussee and the Salzkammergut (see Chapter 7). Continuing west, the valley narrows as impressive mountain ranges – the Dachstein to the north and the **Niedere Tauern** to the south – make their presence felt.

The valley floor is dotted with attractive villages (each harbouring a Gasthof or two), any of which would make an excellent base for hikes into the surrounding highlands, but it's really only **SCHLADMING**, 35km beyond Stainach, that's fully geared up for alpine tourism. Cradled by the southern slopes of the Dachstein, this is Styria's leading winter sports centre and an excellent base for walking, with the 1894-metre-high **Planai** towering over the town to the south and the mountain village of **Rohrmoos** only 5km to the southwest. Both destinations are accessible via cable car and chairlift from Schladming itself; indeed the downhill run from Planai (a regular venue for World Cup competitions since 1972) ends dramatically just outside the town centre. In addition, the nordic skiing resort of **Ramsau**, and the cable-car ride up the **Dachstein**, are both only a short bus ride away. From December to April Schladming is an important package holiday centre, and independent travellers will find that accommodation is both heavily booked in advance and more expensive than during the rest of the year.

Originally a silver-mining centre, Schladming was the focus of a miners' and peasants' rebellion in 1525, and the insurgents were punished by having their town razed to the ground. Thus, little of Schladming's medieval character remains, apart from a few surviving traces of the town wall.

The Town

With its smart shops, flower-bedecked buildings and beautiful background scenery, Schladming is an attractive and relaxing base from which to explore the mountains, but there's not that much in town itself worth seeing. Standing at the western end of a pedestrianized Hauptplatz is the **Rathaus**, a curious red-brick structure with crenellated roof, built for Augustus von Saxe-Coburg-Gotha in the 1890s as a hunting lodge, allegedly in imitation of the British neo-Gothic style. Much of the town north and east of here is modern, reflecting Schladming's rapid, tourism-inspired, postwar growth, although a jumble of narrow streets west of the Hauptplatz preserves a more village-like feel. One of the nicest houses in this area is the seventeenth-century **Bruderhaus** on Talbachgasse, a traditional wooden building that originally served as a municipal hostel for old miners and widows. It's now the **town musem** (daily 3–6pm; öS30) with the customary display of local crafts and costumes. The **Pfarrkirche**, north of here on Salzburger Strasse, boasts an elegant Romanesque spire, but little else to shout about.

The most direct route to higher altitudes is the two-section **Planaibahn** (daily 9am–5pm; one-section return öS90, two-section return öS150), a cable car that ascends to the summit of the Planai from a terminal just east of the Hauptplatz. At the western end of town, the **Rohrmoos-Hochwurzen** chairlift (daily 8.30am–noon & 1–5pm; return öS110) provides access to pleasant alpine meadows (and ski slopes in winter) to the southwest.

Practicalities

Schladming **train station** is 500m west of town; turn right out of the station building, cross the river and keep straight on to reach the **tourist office** on the corner of Erzherzog-Johann-Strasse and Langegasse (☎03687/22268, fax 24138). There you can get advice on Schladming's pensions, private rooms and holiday apartments, as well as **accommodation** in nearby villages. Recommended in the centre is *Haus Fischbacher*, Schulgasse 590 (☎03687/23428), offering balconied en-suite **private rooms**. There's a **youth hostel** just east of the main square at Coburgstrasse 253 (☎03687/24531, fax 24531-88). *Zirngast*, Rechte Ennsau 633 (☎03687/23195), is an all-year-round riverside **campsite** north of the centre: from the train station, head for the tourist office as above, turn left down Langegasse and cross the river a second time.

Schladming has a wealth of **hotels** to suit all pockets, although bear in mind that prices are twenty to thirty percent more expensive in the winter season. *Haus Pilz*, Augasse 30 (☎03687/23349; ②), is a small pension in a quiet area east of centre, between the River Enns and the Planaibahn. A nice, chalet-style building, *Pension Talbach*, Griesgasse 455 (☎03687/23321; ③), sits beside the stream after which it was named, just west of the centre. *Haus Barbara*, Coburgstrasse 553 (☎03687/22077; ③), offers rooms with en-suite facilities, most with balconies, near the Planaibahn. All rooms at the old-fashioned, town-centre hotel *Kirchenwirt*, Hauptstrasse 27 (☎03687/22435; ③), have en-suite facilities, telephone and TV. The atmospheric *Alte Post*, Hauptplatz 10 (☎03687/22571; ⑦), is an old coaching inn offering all the creature comforts.

Daytime snacks of the sausage variety can be obtained from either *S'würstl*, Hauptplatz 41, or *Bosna*, Salzburgerstrasse 95. More substantial **eating** options are provided by *Kirchenwirt*, Salzburgerstrasse 27, offering local Styrian dishes in a wood-panelled room; *Vorstadt Stüb'n*, Salzburgerstrasse, which serves up standard Austrian fare alongside a wide selection of Styrian wines; *Taalbachschenk*, Hammerfeldweg, beside the Talbach, which concentrates on grills and stays open until 2am; and *Liesi's Landhausstüberl*, Vorstadtgasse 117, with unpretentious Austrian favourites such as *Steirische Käsnock'n* (noodles in cheese sauce), and occasional folk music evenings. *Papageno*, Salzburgerstrasse, is the place to go for pizza- and pasta-based dishes.

Kaffee-Konditorei Landgraf, Hauptplatz 37, is both the town's main daytime café and a relaxed evening **drinking** venue. *Gasthof Braustüb'n*, Siedergasse, serves beer brewed on the premises (*Schwalbenbräu*, a form of *Weizenbier*), as well as filling soups and stews from around öS70. *Ferry's Pub*, Steirergasse 3, is not really a pub, but more of a stylish (and quite expensive) bar with pizzeria attached; the less pretentious *Sport Café*, Parkgasse 481, is the place to play pool, billiards and darts; and *Hanglbar*, Salzburgerstrasse 96, is a cosy bar with lively, pub-like atmosphere, open till 3am. Two centrally located bars that host mildly tacky **discos** in the evening are *Sonderbar*, Salzburgerstrasse, and *May Be*, Ramsauerstrasse.

Ramsau and the Dachstein

Immediately north of Schladming, a minor road climbs up towards **Ramsau am Dachstein** – really a string of small hamlets rather than a single village, occupying a south-facing terrace of pastureland suspended high above the Enns Valley. Dotted with wooden farmhouses and grazed by sheep, cows and goats, it's an idyllic, yet highly touristed area, offering an enticing vision of rural prettiness beneath the shadow of the 2995-metre-high **Dachstein**.

The road up from Schladming ends beneath the Dachstein itself, where a cable car conveys visitors to the **Hunerkogel**, some 300m beneath the summit. Eleven buses a day make the journey from Schladming to the hamlet of Ramsau-Ort, seven of which go all the way to the Dachstein cable-car terminal. The last bus back from the cable car is at 5.50pm, or 4.50pm between October and June. The area around Ramsau is full of **guesthouses** and **private rooms**; the tourist office in Schladming is the best place to make enquiries.

The first place you reach after climbing out of Schladming is **RAMSAU-KULM**, a hamlet famous for its fifteenth-century **church** decorated with frescoes of the time. Pictures of St Christopher carrying the young Jesus, and St George killing the dragon, adorn the north wall of the nave, while in the choir both the *Martyrdom of St Sebastian* and the *Annunciation* are given lively treatment.

Further up the valley is **RAMSAU-ORT**, a major centre for nordic skiing in winter, and gentle walks in spring and summer. The **Pfarrkirche** is Evangelical rather than Catholic, a reminder that Protestantism survived in these isolated upland regions from the sixteenth century onwards, despite the success of the Counter-Reformation elsewhere in Austria. Among the village communities north of Schladming, Protestantism is still the dominant faith.

Three kilometres beyond Ramsau Ort, a left fork continues to hug the mountainside, while the right fork ascends towards the Dachstein cable-car station. The cable car (daily: July & Aug 8am–5.50pm; Sept & Oct 8am–4.50pm; Nov–June 8.30am–4.50pm; öS250 return) ascends to the 2700-metre-high Hunerkogel, where you can look across the Dachstein glacier and the mountains of the Salzkammergut to the north, and the Tauern range to the south.

travel details

Trains

Bruck an der Mur to: Graz (hourly; 40min); Judenburg (12 daily, 50min); Klagenfurt (10 daily; 2hr 10min); Leoben (hourly; 15min); Unzmarkt (8 daily; 1hr); Vienna (hourly; 2hr); Villach (10 daily; 2hr 40min).

Eisenerz to: Hieflau (8 daily; 25min).

Graz to: Bruck an der Mur (hourly; 40min); Deutschlandsberg (10 daily; 1hr); Ehrenhausen (14 daily; 55min); Feldbach (8 daily; 1hr); Hartberg (4 daily; 2hr 40min); Innsbruck (3 daily; 6hr 15min); Kitzbühel (3 daily; 5hr 5min); Köflach (10 daily; 1hr); Leibnitz (14 daily; 45min); Linz (2 daily; 3hr 30min); Salzburg (3 daily; 4hr 15min); Schladming (6 daily; 2hr 45min); Selzthal (9 daily; 2hr 5min); Spielfeld-Strass (14 daily; 1hr); Stainach-Irdning (8 daily; 2hr 10min–2hr 40min); Vienna (9 daily; 2hr 30min).

Hieflau to: Eisenerz (8 daily; 25min).

Leibnitz to: Ehrenhausen (14 daily; 10min); Graz (14 daily; 45min).

Mariazell to: St Pölten (5 daily; 2hr 40min).

Schladming to: Graz (6 daily; 2hr 45min); Salzburg (3 daily; 1hr 45min).

Selzthal to: Admont (7 daily; 20min); Hieflau (7 daily; 40min); Schladming (9 daily; 1hr 10min).

Spielfeld-Strass to: Bad Radkersburg (8 daily; 50min).

Unzmarkt to: Murau (Mon–Sat 5 daily; 45min).

Buses

Bruck to: Aflenz (hourly; 30min); Mariazell (5 daily; 1hr 40min).

Feldbach to: Bad Radkersburg (1 daily; 1hr 10min); Riegersburg (8 daily; 25min).

Graz to: Feldbach (3 daily; 1hr 30min); Grossklein (2 daily; 1hr 30min); Hartberg (8 daily; 1hr 15min); Köflach (10 daily; 1hr 30min); Mariazell (2 daily; 2hr 20min); Voitsberg (1 daily; 1hr 15min).

Hartberg to: Graz (8 daily; 1hr 15min); Stubenberg (8 daily; 40min); Weiz (7 daily; 1hr).

Judenburg to: Oberzeiring (10 daily; 55min).

Knittelfeld to: Oberzeiring (2 daily; 1hr); Seckau (7 daily; 30min).

Leibnitz to: Grossklein (8 daily; 25min).

Leoben to: Eisenerz (5 daily; 1hr); Vordenberg (hourly; 20min).

Mariazell to: Graz (2 daily; 2hr 20min); Mürzzuschlag (1 daily Sat & Sun; 2hr); St Sebastian (8 daily; 20min).

Murau to: St Lambrecht (7 daily; 20min).

Niederwölz to: Oberwölz (3 daily; 30min).

Schiefling-Lind to: Oberwölz (2 daily; 50min).

CARINTHIA AND THE EAST TYROL

Carinthia (Kärnten) is regarded by the Austrians (and a great many Germans and Italians, too) as one of central Europe's most enticing vacation spots. Austria's southernmost province, it enjoys warm summers and exudes a relaxed, Mediterranean feel; this, together with an impressive combination of lake and mountain scenery, makes it the perfect place for an outdoor holiday.

Carinthia lacks a historic urban centre capable of competing with the likes of Vienna, Salzburg, Graz or Innsbruck, but the provincial capital **Klagenfurt** is a relaxed, unassuming city and provides a good base for exploring the surrounding area. The city's main claim to fame is its position on the eastern shores of the **Wörthersee**, an enduringly popular summer playground that annually attracts a fashionable, affluent crowd, together with hordes of attendant wannabes. Flashy lakeside settlements **Pörtschach** and **Velden** are the main resorts, offering all kinds of water-based activities and swollen with visitors from June onwards through the summer. To the north of Kagenfurt lie the broad, fertile valleys of the Glan and Gurk rivers, tracing an area liberally sprinkled with historical remains. Ruins on the **Magdalensberg** recall periods of Celtic and Roman settlement, while the pilgrimage church in the nearby village of **Maria Saal** stands as testament to the missionary energies of the archbishops of Salzburg, who began the process of converting Carinthia to Christianity in the eighth century. Close at hand are Carinthia's medieval capital **St Veit an der Glan**, now a picturesque market town, and the sixteenth-century stronghold of **Hochosterwitz**, a breathtakingly situated hilltop castle. Further north, but still within reach of day-trippers from Klagenfurt, lie the charming medieval town of **Friesach** and the important ecclesiastical centre of **Gurk**, famed for its splendid Romanesque cathedral.

Western Carinthia revolves around the province's second city, **Villach**, a lively and sophisticated place with an engaging historic centre. It's an important transport hub, commanding links to Salzburg, Italy and Slovenia, and also acts as the gateway to two more lakes, the **Faakersee** and the **Ossiachersee**. In contrast to the brash and upmarket Wörthersee, the lakes in this part of Carinthia are much more oriented towards family holidays, offering a wealth of campsites and apartment-style accommodation. North of Villach

---

ACCOMMODATION PRICE CODES

All **hotels and pensions** in this book have been graded according to the following price categories. All the codes are based on the rate for the least expensive double room during the **summer season**. In those places where winter is the high season, we've indicated winter room rates in the text. For more on accommodation, see p.30.

① under öS400   ④ öS800–1000   ⑦ öS1400–1600
② öS400–600   ⑤ öS1000–1200   ⑧ öS1600–1800
③ öS600–800   ⑥ öS1200–1400   ⑨ over öS1800

the main road and rail routes to Salzburg pass **Spittal an der Drau**, a small town built around the imposing Renaissance Schloss Portia, and the jumping-off point for two popular tourist targets – the lakeland paradise of the **Millstättersee** and the tiny medieval town of **Gmünd**. Both Spittal and Gmünd are within striking distance of the **Hohe Tauern**, Austria's highest mountain range, shared with the Salzburger Land and the Tyrol, although if you want to immerse yourself fully in the alpine experience you should continue north-westwards to the skiing and mountaineering centre of **Heiligenblut**, a village standing in the shadow of the most imposing Hohe Tauern peak of all, the **Grossglockner.**

The southern slopes of the Hohe Tauern are also accessible from the **East Tyrol** (Osttirol), which borders Carinthia to the west. Geographically isolated by the Tauern range from the rest of the Tyrol, this compact knot of alpine valleys and mountains remains surprisingly untouched by the winter package-holiday trade. Mountain-ringed **Lienz**, small and provincial though it is, serves as regional centre, and offers a good mixture of urban tourism and alpine pursuits, while in the highland villages to the north – notably **Matrei** and the captivatingly beautiful **Kals** – the character of this undervisited region shines through. The area's international atmosphere owes a great deal to the proximity of **Italy** and **Slovenia**.

CARINTHIA

Carinthia was an important centre of Celtic and Roman culture until the sixth-century arrival of the **Slavs**, who settled on the Zollfeld, the fertile valley north of present-day Klagenfurt. The area remained predominantly Slav until the eighth century, when local tribes asked the Bavarians for assistance in their struggles against the **Avars**, a race of Turkic interlopers from the east. The Bavarian presence – strengthened by the missionary zeal of priests sent by the bishops of Salzburg – increased over the next century, leading to the Christianization of the province and an influx of German-speaking settlers.

Still considered by the Slovenes to be a cradle of their civilization, there's no doubt that the Slav heritage has left its mark on Carinthia. Local place names (most names ending in *-ach* are of Slavic origin) and Slavic-sounding surnames bear testimony to the non-Germanic roots of a large part of the population. After World War I, the infant state of Yugoslavia laid claim to southern Carinthia, sparking a dispute that was settled by the Plebiscite of October 10, 1920, when a majority of the locals opted for the Austrian Republic. October 10 became a sacred date for right-wing nationalists thereafter: on that day in 1972, bilingual road signs in areas with a mixed Slovene German population were removed overnight by extremists. The anniversary now never passes without an undercurrent of tension.

Today, locals who speak the **Slovene language** are hard to find – only 14,000 Carinthians considered it to be their mother tongue according to the 1991 Census – although they still occupy a belt of territory in the south of the province stretching from Bleiburg westwards to the Faakersee. The picture is complicated by the existence of the **Wends**, a group related to the Slovenes who nevertheless claim to be descended from a different group of Slav settlers originating from Dalmatia. Their language, Windisch, is still spoken in the Faakersee and Rosental areas southeast of Villach, and church services in the area are often bilingual.

THE KÄRNTEN CARD

A worthwhile investment for anyone spending a reasonable length of time in Carinthia in the summer is the **Kärnten Card** (available mid-May to early Oct only), which allows the bearer free use of all public transport (including lake steamers, chairlifts and cable cars) and free entry to the vast majority of museums and tourist attractions (Minimundus at Klagenfurt being one of the few major exceptions). Valid for a three-week period, it's available from all the region's tourist offices and costs öS345.

Klagenfurt

Nestling among the low hills of southern Carinthia, sedate and prosperous **KLAGENFURT** may lack the historical and cultural pedigree of a Salzburg, Innsbruck or Graz, but it's an absorbing provincial capital nevertheless. It's a small, easily digestible city, whose appeal lies mostly in its proximity to the Wörthersee, just 3km west of the centre – the lakeside **Europapark**, site of the much-visited **Minimundus**, is a major tourist draw. In addition, a fairly absorbing provincial **museum** and a varied choice of restaurants and nightlife make this a good urban base for touring much of rural Carinthia.

Founded in the twelfth century by the Von Spannheims, a family of soldier-aristocrats from the Rhineland, Klagenfurt achieved regional pre-eminence after the intervention of Emperor Maximilian I, who ordered its redevelopment as provincial capital in 1518. Italian architect **Domenico dell'Allio** (who also worked on the Landhaus in Graz; see p.218) was responsible for the town's layout, creating the grid-iron street plan still very much in evidence today. The town was a Jesuit base in the seventeenth century, and became Carinthia's

ACCOMMODATION

Blumenstöckl	5
Jugendgästehaus Kölping	3
Liebetegger	2
Moser-Verdino	1
Sandwirt	4
Seeblick	7
Stadt Eger	6
Wörthersee	8

> The telephone code for Klagenfurt is ☎0463.

ecclesiastical capital in 1787, when Graf von Salm, Bishop of Gurk, moved the bishopric here in recognition of Klagenfurt's growing importance. As was the case with so many Austrian cities, the town walls were demolished in 1809 on the insistence of the victorious Napoleon – their outline is traced by a quadrangular ring road today. But, despite heavy damage in World War II, Klagenfurt's city-centre buildings retain many of their inner court-yards, now harbouring cafés and boutiques, which lend the place considerable charm.

Arrival and information

Both **train** and **bus stations** are on the southern fringes of the centre on the Südbahngürtel. From here it's a straightforward ten-minute walk down Bahnhof-strasse to the town centre, or buses #40, #41 or #42 will take you to Heiligengeistplatz on the centre's western fringe. The airport is 3km to the northeast, linked to the cen-tre by buses #45 and #42.

Heiligengeistplatz, 100m west of the central Neuer Platz, is the main hub for **city bus transport**, with most municipal services either starting there or passing through. A single journey costs öS20; a 24-hr ticket, öS45. Tickets are purchased from the driver or *Tabak* stores.

The main **tourist office** (May–Sept Mon–Fri 8am–8pm, Sat & Sun 10am–5pm; Oct–April Mon–Fri 9am–6pm; ☎537223, fax 537295) is in the Rathaus on Neuer Platz. There's also an information kiosk (May to mid-Oct daily 10am–8pm) outside Minimundus on the western approaches to the city, clearly signposted off the A2 auto-bahn from Villach.

Accommodation

Both the main tourist office and the kiosk outside Minimundus will check vacancies in hotels and book **private rooms**, although the latter are in short supply; there are a handful of rooms in the Klagenfurt suburbs for around öS200–250 per person, and a few slightly cheaper ones in Viktring, 6km to the southwest (bus #80, #81 or #82).

Klagenfurt's downtown **hotels** include few real budget options, although there are three good **youth hostels** (two of which only open in summer) and a well-appointed **campsite**, *Camping Strandbad* (☎21169, fax 21169-93; bus #12; May–Oct), just behind the municipal Strandbad in the lakeside Europapark.

Hotels

Blumenstöckl, 10-Oktober-Strasse 11 (☎57793, fax 57793-5). For those who want comfortable rooms with en-suite facilities and multi-channel TV, bang in the city centre, this is probably the best-value choice. A fine old building with an arcaded courtyard. ⑤.

Kohlweg, St Veiterstrasse 122 (☎42418). Small, plain hotel 1.5km north of the centre, offering adequate rooms with shared facilities. ②.

Liebetegger, Völkermarkterstrasse 8 (☎56935, fax 56835-6). An unspectacular family-run hotel, although it's conveniently located, just east of the town centre. There's a choice of rooms with en-suite facilities (③), or without (②).

Moser-Verdino, Domgasse 2 (☎57878, fax 516765). Luxurious city-centre hotel, offering comfort-able rooms with bathrooms and satellite TV. Computer and emailing facilities make it a good place for doing business. ⑦.

Müller, Rankengasse 21 (☎21254). Small, family-run pension with functional rooms. It's over 2km west of the centre, but is ideally located for the forested parklands of the Kreuzbergl – and you can just about walk to the lakefront from here, too. Rooms come with en-suite facilites (③), or without (②).

Sandwirt, Pernhartgasse 9 (☎56209, fax 514322). Central, upmarket hotel offering all the creature comforts. Nowadays holder of a *Best Western* franchise, it's strong on international uniformity rather than local colour. ⑦.

Seeblick, Villacherstrasse 348 (☎21196). Overlooking the lake, 4.5km west of the centre, but with a main road and railway roaring past it. The waterfront, Minimundus and the Europapark are all near at hand. ③.

Stadt Eger, Karfreitstrasse 20 (☎54320, fax 54709). Unpretentious place, conveniently placed three blocks south of Neuer Platz between the centre and the train station, with small but adequate rooms. ③.

Wörthersee, Villacherstrasse 338 (☎21158, fax 21158-8). Lakefront hotel in a fanciful nineteenth-century castellated building, with its own beach. All rooms have en-suite facilities and TV. Rooms come with a lake view (⑥), or without (③).

Hostels

Jugendgästehaus Kolping, Enzenberstrasse 26 (☎56965, fax 56965-32). A large modern block only 10min walk east of the centre, with two- and three-bedded rooms with en-suite showers. Open July 10–Sept 10.

Jugendherberge Klagenfurt, Neckheimgasse 6 (☎230020, fax 230020-20). An attractively designed piece of contemporary architecture 3km west of the centre, within walking distance of the lakefront. It's in a modern, suburban area of town with a lot of student accommodation, so there are some good cheap bars and pizzerias in the immediate vicinity. Open all year round, it offers accommodation in four-bed dorms with en-suite showers, and a few self-contained doubles. Reception is open 7–9am and 5–10pm. Take bus #12.

Mladinski Dom, Mikschallee 4 (☎35651, fax 35651-11). Slovene-run student hostel (the name simply means "youth hostel"), 1.5km east of the centre, open from the first week in July to the first week in September. Beds in three-person rooms, plus a limited number of doubles and singles. Bus #70 or #71.

The City

Klagenfurt centres on **Neuer Platz**, a broad flagstoned square whose focus is a statue of the grotesque **Lindwurm**, the mythical beast central to a local George-and-the-Dragon-style folk tale – and very much the city's trademark. Sixteenth-century sculptor Ulrich Vogelsang based the head of the beast on a locally unearthed prehistoric rhino skull (now displayed in the Landesmuseum), which perhaps accounts for its rather comic, gaping visage. The Lindwurm is faced by a statue of a club-wielding, Hercules-like hero, added later by Michael Hönel – creator of the spectacular high altar at Gurk (see p.271).

From here Kramergasse leads north to **Alter Platz**, heart of a pedestrianized shopping district where most of Klagenfurt's more historic town houses lie. Oldest of these, the **Haus zur goldenes Gans** stands at the western end of Alter Platz, a squat, medieval structure whose sloping buttresses were built to withstand the minor earthquakes that once shook the area. Behind it loom the twin towers of the **Landhaus**, seat of the Carinthian provincial government although built as an arsenal in the 1580s. Staircases lead from the galleried inner courtyard to the **Wappensaal**, or heraldic hall (April–Sept Mon–Fri 9am–12.30pm & 1–5pm; öS10), the walls of which are covered with the coats of arms of the Carinthian nobility. The trompe l'oeil ceiling paintings by local artist **Josef-Ferdinand Fromiller** (1693–1760) portray nobles paying homage to Emperor Karl VI, father of Maria Theresa. There's more work by Fromiller adorning the ceilings of the **Stadtpfarrkirche St Egyd**, north of Alter Platz on Pfarrplatz, a fourteenth-century edifice studded with aristocratic grave plaques. The main attraction is, however, the church **tower** (May–Sept Mon–Fri 10am–5.30pm, Sat 10am–12.30pm; öS10), which rewards a stiff climb with a fine view of Klagenfurt and surrounding hills.

The Landesgalerie, Domkirche and Diözesianmuseum

The main aim of the **Landesgalerie**, just east of Neuer Platz on Burggasse (Mon–Fri 9am–6pm, Sat 10am–noon; öS20), is to provide a showcase for Carinthian artists. The idealized nineteenth-century landscapes of Markus Pernhart, such as *Climbers Surveying the Grossglockner*, and the more expressionist rural views of locally born mid-twentieth-century painter Herbert Boeckl, provide some respite from the otherwise mediocre offerings.·

Three blocks south of here, on Lidmanskygasse, the attractive facade of Klagenfurt's **Domkirche** fronts an interior that's a competent if uninspiring exercise in Baroque. You'd do best to press on to the **Diözesianmuseum**, just round the corner at Lidmanskygasse 10 (May to mid-June & mid-Sept to mid-Oct Mon–Sat 10am–noon; plus 3–5pm mid-June to mid-Sept; öS40), which harbours altarpieces and statuary retrieved from churches across the province. Pride of place belongs to Austria's oldest piece of stained glass, the twelfth-century *Magdalenscheibe*, a portrayal of Mary Magdalene which once adorned the Magdalenakirche in the village of Weitensfeld, near Gurk.

The Landesmuseum

A block south of Lidmanskygasse, the **Landesmuseum**, at Museumgasse 2 (Tues–Sat 9am–4pm, Sun 10am–1pm; öS30), provides a thorough lesson in Carinthian history and culture. The overview begins in the entrance hall with the *Fürstenstein*, or prince's stone, a rudimentary throne made from the base of a Roman column and originally located in the village of Karnburg, 7km north of town. Rather like the *Herzogstuhl* (see p.267), the stone was used in ceremonies intended to confirm the authority of the German-speaking dukes of Carinthia over the Slav peasants of the Zollfeld. The first floor has a rather pedestrian and unimaginatively presented geology and natural history collection, although it's worth looking out for the *Lindwurmschädel*, the fossilized rhino skull which served as a model for the Lindwurm statue in Neuer Platz.

On the second floor, Hallstatt-era finds from Frög bei Rosegg (5km south of Velden) shed light on the region's thriving Celtic culture, including a display case full of exquisitely modelled, miniature lead horse-riding figures, rather like an army of toy soldiers. On a somewhat larger scale is the Roman-era Dionysus mosaic from Virunum (near present-day Maria Saal), first-century capital of the province of Noricum, depicting Dionysus surrounded by a colourful array of maenads, satyrs, birds and peacocks. Each corner of the mosaic bears an image of Medusa's head – intended as charms to protect the household from evil. Elsewhere in the museum, there's a fine collection of Gothic devotional paintings, and a couple of pictures relating to the Order of St George once based in Millstatt (see p.288), most notably the *Siebenhirter-Tafel*, which depicts the swearing-in ceremony of Johann Siebenhirter as Grand Master of the Order by Pope Paul II and Emperor Friedrich III in 1469.

Further on, the **ethnographic section** sheds light on some fascinating Carinthian folk customs. Commanding immediate attention are the captivatingly demonic *Partl* masks – still made by craftsmen in rural Carinthia, such masks are donned on the eve of St Nicholas' Day in most parts of Carinthia to represent the bogeyman figure who supposedly visits badly behaved children. There's also a costume representing the *Häbergass*, an imaginary beast that throws children into a basket on his back before taking them home to be eaten. Nearby are the paper lanterns in the shape of churches used to celebrate the feast of Maria Lichtmess (Candlemass), on February 2, in the village of Eisenkappel in southeast Carinthia. Children process through the streets carrying the lanterns, which are then placed in the river and left to float downstream – a practice believed to protect children from mishaps.

It's a short walk south from the Landesmuseum to the **Robert-Musil-Museum**, at Bahnhofstrasse 50 (Mon–Fri 10am–noon & 2–5pm, Sat 10am–noon; öS40), where manuscripts, books and other personal effects are displayed in the birthplace of novelist

Robert Musil (1880–1942). Musil never actually spent much time in Klagenfurt, however, having been sent away to school at an early age. He is primarily known for the vast, unfinished panorama of Viennese society on the eve of World War I *The Man Without Qualities*.

Northwest of the centre

On the other side of the city centre, north of Alter Platz, the **Stadtgalerie**, at Theatergasse 4 (Mon–Fri 10am–7pm, Sat 10am–5pm, Sun 10am–3pm), is the town's principal venue for major touring art exhibitions. A few steps west, Theatergasse becomes Theaterplatz, opening out to reveal the striking Art-Nouveau **Stadttheater**, Carinthia's main venue for serious drama, classical music and opera. From here Radetzkystrasse strikes northwestwards, with the verdant strolling areas of the **Goethepark** on the right and the **Schillerpark** on the left. Occupying stately villas in the Goethepark are two more venues for touring art exhibitions (check at the tourist office to find out what's on): the **Stadthaus Galerie**, Theaterplatz 4 (Mon–Fri 10am–1pm & 4–7pm, Sat 10am–1pm), and the **Kunstverein für Kärnten** (same hours; prices vary).

Radetzkystrasse continues towards Prof-Dr-Kahler-Platz 1km further west, where pathways lead up to the **Kreuzbergl**, an area of partly wooded hilly parkland crisscrossed by paths. Sheltering at the base of the hills on the northern side of the square is a small **Botanischer Garten** (May–Sept daily 9am–6pm; Oct–April Mon–Thurs 7am–4pm, Fri 7am–1pm; free), a cramped but beautifully laid out collection of native and exotic plants. Lurking at the back of the garden is the entrance to the **Bergbaumuseum** (April–Oct daily 9am–6pm; öS80), a mining museum housed in tunnels that served as air-raid shelters in World War II. There are well-presented displays of local minerals and drilling equipment from the lead-mining centre of Bad Bleiberg (50km west of here in the hills above Villach), as well as a dinosaur egg from China, but the potted history of Carinthian mining on offer lacks the punch of Austria's several show-mines; a visit to Bad Bleiberg itself (see p.280) would be a better bet if you have the time.

Europapark, Minimundus and the lakefront

From central Klagenfurt, buses #10, #11 and #12 head due west along Villacherstrasse towards the lakefront 3km away. The street runs along the banks of the **Lendkanal**, built in the late Middle Ages to connect landlocked Klagenfurt to the lake. Between mid-May and late September, a **passenger trimaran** runs along the Lend (contact the tourist office for prices and times), leaving town from the eastern end of Villacherstrasse and arriving near the lakefront some twenty minutes later.

Stretching back from the lakefront for about one kilometre is the **Europapark**, a grassy expanse that harbours one of southern Austria's top tourist attractions, **Minimundus**, at Villacherstrasse 241 (daily: April 30 & Oct 1–19 9am–5pm; May, June & Sept 9am–6pm; July & Aug 8am–7pm, Wed & Sat until 9pm; öS110). With profits going to Rettet das Kind, the Austrian equivalent of Britain's Save the Children, it's a popular family-oriented attraction centred around 1:25 scale models of the world's famous buildings – with a smattering of model trains and boats. A large open-air garden dotted with flowerbeds contains more than 160 models, including many obvious international landmarks (the Eiffel Tower, Big Ben, the White House and the like), although there's a sufficient number of less instantly recognizable choices – such as Bulgaria's Rila Monastery and a Yemenite royal palace – to make the official English-language guide booklet (öS30) a worthwhile investment.

Just north of Minimundus, **Happ's Reptilienzoo**, Villacherstrasse 237 (daily: May–Oct 8am–6pm; Sept–April 9am–5pm; öS70), provides haven for snakes, lizards and crocs, together with an aquarium, home to some piranhas, and an outdoor model dinosaur garden.

The lakefront

The Europapark stretches westwards from Minimundus as far as the lakefront just under 1km away, where Klagenfurt's marvellously old-fashioned municipal **Strandbad** (öS35) attracts bathers with its deckchair-covered lawns, long wooden piers and pedalos for rent. One incongruous concession to modernity is the nude sunbathing platform (open to men only on Tues, Thurs & Sat, women only on the other four days), separated from other bathers by a screen. Just north of the Strandbad is the ship station, where regular ferries depart for Velden, Pörtschach and other lakeside settlements between May and October.

The mouth of Lendkanal separates the Europapark from the southern shores of the Wörthersee. A footbridge at the southern end of the Strandbad leads over the canal, and from here foot and cycle paths follow the shore southeast, crossing the Glanfurt stream before arriving at the gently sloping lakeside lawns of **Strandbad Maiernigg**, a quieter alternative to the much larger Strandbad in the Europapark. From here, a path leads uphill to the west for about 1km in order to reach the **Gustav Mahlers Komponierhäuschen** (July–Sept daily 10am–4pm; öS10), the idyllic garden-shed-like retreat where the composer spent his days writing while holidaying in a nearby lakeside villa. Inside, there's a reconstruction of the desk area where he worked on symphonies 5, 6, 7 and 8, although the best reason to venture this far is to get a feel for the densely wooded lakeside environment from which he drew inspiration.

Eating, drinking and nightlife

Klagenfurt is at first glance a relatively quiet place, with most of the best eating venues hidden away from the main thoroughfares in charming alleyways and courtyards. The streets around Pfarrplatz – Herrengasse, Pfarrhofgasse and Osterwitzgasse – are the best places to look. In general Klagenfurt's **restaurants** provide a good introduction to Carinthian cuisine, with most places offering a mixture of local *Nud'l* dishes, Austrian staples, and fresh fish from the Wörthersee. For **snacks**, the one city-centre Würstelstand is in the bus station on Heiligengeistplatz, while *Cemal's Döner Kebab*, Lidmanskygasse 5, is a dependable source of good-quality Turkish fast food, and *Pizza Uno*, Herrengasse 1, is a good place to eat a stand-up slice or pick up a takeaway.

There's a healthy sprinkling of **drinking** venues, a large proportion of which are concentrated in the area around Herrengasse and Pfarrplatz. Most of these keep buzzing until around 1 or 2am throughout the week, except on Sundays, when the city centre can seem eerily deserted. The town also quietens considerably during periods of good summer weather, when locals abandon Klagenfurt's bars in favour of trendier Wörthersee venues in lakeside towns like Pörtschach and Velden.

Despite its status as the provincial capital, Klagenfurt is not a place in which to gorge yourself on **entertainment**, although the Stadtheater, Theaterplatz 4 (box office Tues–Sat: July & Aug 9am–noon & 5–7pm; Sept–June 9am–noon & 4–6pm; ☎54064), has an all-year programme of opera, highbrow drama and ballet.

The best **clubbing** venues in the region are *Fun Factory*, 2km south of the centre at Südring-Gerberweg 46, and, rather more distant, *Die Fabrik*, 15km west of town in the Wörthersee village of Saag (see p.263). Both usually stick to a diet of mainstream techno, though special themed nights and party-style events are arranged over the summer.

Restaurants

151, Wörthersee Suduferstrasse 151. Five kilometres out of town on the road to Maria Wörth, this is a stylish place offering top-notch Austrian cuisine to a smart clientele. Expect to pay about öS500 a head. The swish bar is a good place for an intimate evening drink.

A la Carte, Khevenhüllerstrasse 2 (☎516651). Northwest of the centre, an outwardly unspectacular restaurant that offers top-class French-Austrian cuisine and excellent fish. No official dress restrictions, but you'll feel out of place in jeans and teeshirt. Reservations advisable. Open until 9.30pm only. Closed Sun & Mon.

Gasthof zum heiligen Josef, Osterwitzgasse 7. Inexpensive mainstream Austrian food, including all the most popular schnitzel dishes, as well as Wörthersee fish. A good range of cheap soups and salads make this a lunchtime favourite.

Landhauskeller, Landhaushof. A popular daytime venue due to its plentiful outdoor seating in the Landhaus courtyard. Food is mid-priced Austrian. Closed Sun.

Maria Loretto, on the Wörthersee, just south of the main Strandbad. Mid-to-high-priced restaurant occupying an attractive lakeside villa, with plentiful outdoor seating facing the water. It's a good place for fresh trout and other Wörthersee fish, although the menu includes all the usual Austrian and Carinthian regulars as well. Closed Mon.

Rathausstüberl, Alte Rathausgasse. Cosy central place in an alleyway linking Alter Platz with the Pfarrplatz, providing cheap Carinthian *Nud'ln*, good-value schnitzel-based standards, and some good lunchtime choices, like salad platters and soups. Closed Sun.

Rote Lasche, Villacherstrasse 21. Renowned vegetarian restaurant 500m west of the centre, as famous for its decor, crowded with works by local artists, as it is for its food – an imaginative and constantly changing menu of inexpensive veggie delights. Closed Sun.

Zauberhütt'n, Osterwitzgasse. Mid-priced restaurant with a mixed Austrian and Italian menu and occasional performing magician.

Zum Augustin, Pfarrhofgasse 2. Roomy and atmospheric eating and drinking venue with wooden bench seating a few steps west of the Pfarrkirche, offering hearty and inexpensive Carinthian *Nud'l* dishes. A good place for a beer, too.

Cafés and bars

Gallo Nero, Pfarrgasse 6. Popular and youthful subterranean café-bar with a useful pizza- and baguette-oriented bar menu.

In Vino Veritas, Burggasse. Relaxed, elegant bar with outdoor seating in one of central Klagenfurt's leafy courtyards, with occasional live music on summer weekends.

Kamot, Bahnhofstrasse 9. Cool jazz bar two blocks east of Neuer Platz with live music some nights (admission sometimes charged, depending on the stature of the artist).

Mayer Lanski, Herrengasse 8. Flash teenage and twentysomething venue with booming music, packed at weekends.

Segafredo, Alter Platz. Popular because of its location more so than anything else, a modern café-bar with plenty of outdoor seating on the pedestrianized central thoroughfare; a nice place for a drink by day – the cakes and ice creams are good, too – and by night.

Spektakel, Pfarrplatz 16. Cosy bar with cramped, pub-like indoor boozing area, and outdoor seating in a pleasant courtyard. Entrance also from Wienergasse 7. Open until 4am at weekends.

Ungekünstlt, Herrengasse 3. Busy but friendly place with a small area of outdoor seating, just off Herrengasse in an arcade that harbours a couple of other bars.

VIP, Domgasse. Chic bar with twenty-to-thirty-something, dressy clientele, and slightly higher prices than elsewhere. A good place to sip *prosecco* and enjoy piped cocktail-bar sounds.

Listings

Airport Flughafen Annabichl, 3km northeast of town, is served by buses #42 and #45 from Heiligengeistplatz. Information ☎415000.

Bike rental At the train station.

Car rental Avis, Villacherstrasse 1c, and at the airport (☎55938, fax 504032); Budget, at the airport (☎46226, fax 47924); Hertz, Villacherstrasse 4 (☎56147).

Cinemas The Wulfenia, Luegerstrasse 5 (☎22288), is a modern multiscreen cinema with first-run Hollywood films (usually dubbed in German), while the smaller Kammerlichtspiele, Adlergasse 1 (☎54051), offers more art-house choices, sometimes in the original language.

Hospital Klagenfurter Krankenhaus, St-Veiter-Strasse 47 (☎538).

Pharmacies Most central are the Adler Apotheke, Neuer Platz 9, and the Lendorf Apotheke, Seltenheimerstrasse 2. Signs in pharmacy windows give names and addresses of duty pharmacies, which open on a rota basis.

Post office The main post office (Mon–Fri 7.30am–8pm) is at Pernhartgasse 7. The post office next to the train station at Bahnhofplatz 5 is open 24hr daily.

Sailing Kärntner Yachtsportschule, Villacherstrasse 1a, on the lakefront (☎511111). Offers boat hire and tuition.

Swimming pools Erlebnis Hallenbad, on the corner of Gabelsbergerstrasse and Lastenstrasse. Has water slides, whirlpools and children's areas. Open Sept–June. ·In summer, head for the Strandbad on the Wörthersee lakefront (see p.264).

Train information ☎1717.

Travel agent Kärntner Reisebüro, Neuer Platz 2 (☎56400).

Windsurfing Kärntner Yachtsportschule (see "Sailing" above). Board hire and a range of courses.

Around the Wörthersee

Both a high-society playground and sedate retreat for affluent oldies, the **Wörthersee** stretches west from Klagenfurt for 20km, squeezed between low hills with the Karawanken Alps a distant backdrop to the south. The lake has long been regarded as a laid-back, small-scale Austrian version of the French Riviera, a status that dates back to the 1860s when the region was first linked to Vienna by rail. It soon became the favoured vacation spot for Vienna-based businessmen and industrialists, many of whom embarked on the construction of lakeside holiday homes in which to while away the *Sommerfrische*, or summer holiday. Many of these villas – playfully embellished with details like little spires, balustrades and oriel windows – now function as hotels, so that today's Wörthersee is a curious mixture of nineteenth-century elegance and end-of-the-millennium hedonism.

Klagenfurt commands the eastern approaches to the lake, but lacks the high-society reputation enjoyed by the Wörthersee's other main centres – **Velden** on the western shore, and **Pörtschach** to the north. Both of these have a better choice of daytime activities and night-time diversions, but they're also two of the most expensive lakeside resorts in the country. Standing in the shadow of the wooded **Pyramidenkogel**, settlements on the **southern shore** of the lake receive slightly less sun, and are that bit less fashionable as a result. **Maria Wörth**, with its attractive lakeside churches, is the most pleasing of the settlements on this part of the lake, while **Reifnitz** and **Dellach** offer plenty of accommodation and a sprinkling of lakeside activities, but not much else.

Each of the resorts along the lakeshore has an attractive waterside esplanade of one sort or another; elsewhere most of the shore is private property, so public rights of way enabling you to walk or cycle along the lakefront, or simply stop off for a spot of sunbathing, are few and far between. Many hotels have access to small stretches of the lakefront where guests are allowed to bathe, however, and there are numerous municipal or privately owned **Strandbäder** where you can loll around on the grass or swim in the lake on payment of a fee. As a general rule, **cycling** is best on the north side of the lake, where there are more opportunities for getting off the busy main road and onto specific cycle- and pedestrian-only paths. **Water-based activities** such as windsurfing and sailing are easily arranged.

Getting around the lake by boat is no problem in season, which usually runs from the first week in May to the end of October. **Boats** run from Klagenfurt to Velden and back, calling at intermediate points on both sides of the lake, four times a day at the beginning and the end of the season, rising to ten times a day in July and August. Compared to buses and trains, boat travel is pricey (for example, Klagenfurt–Velden costs öS120 single, öS180 return; Klagenfurt–Pörtschach costs öS70 single, öS120 return), but it can be the easiest way to get from one side of the lake to the other.

Pörtschach

Situated midway between Klagenfurt and Velden on the northern shore of the lake, **PÖRTSCHACH** is traditionally the Wörthersee's most exclusive resort. But while prices here are higher than anywhere else in Carinthia, the resort caters for a wide range of ages and tastes. Whether you're looking for a night of bar-hopping or a slow stroll along the lakefront, it's an invigorating place to be. There's not a lot to the town itself save for a main road, the shop- and café-lined Hauptstrasse, which runs through the town from east to west. Immediately south of here, a small peninsula juts out into the lake, where a promenade along the water's edge is lined with terrace cafés and kiosks offering boat hire and windsurfing. At the tip of the peninsula, beyond the high-rise *Hotel Park*, you'll find the landing stage for Wörthersee passenger boats, and a large Strandbad (daily: May, June & Sept 9am–7pm; July & Aug 9am–8pm; öS55) occupying a partly wooded offshore island accessible by footbridge.

Arrival, information and accommodation

Pörtschach's **train station** is a few steps north of the Hauptstrasse: walk down the access road from the station and you'll see the **tourist office** diagonally opposite to the left at Hauptstrasse 153 (April–Oct Mon–Fri 8am–6pm, Sat & Sun 9am–5pm; Nov–March Mon–Thurs 8am–4pm, Fri 8am–1pm; ☎04272/2354, fax 3770), where you can pick up a town map and addresses of sporting facilities, and book **accommodation**. Bear in mind you don't come to Pörtschach to save money; as a general rule, any hotel near the water will be expensive, and a room with a lake view extortionate. There are plenty of comfortable mid-priced pensions, however, for about öS300–400 per person in the residential streets north of the railway tracks, with prices falling to around öS250 per head the further east you go. **Private rooms** start at about öS250 per person, although families and people travelling in groups will find **apartments** (stays of more than three days preferred) a cheaper option.

Gästehaus Gulle-Kohlweiss, Goritschacherweg 29 (☎04272/3669; ②), on a hillside 1.5km east of town, has utilitarian, modern rooms (most are ensuite) and offers residents free use of a lakeside bathing area five minutes downhill, while *Pension Waldschlössl*, Karawankenblickstrasse 9 (☎04272/2235; ②), on the hillside north of the town centre, has adequate doubles with en-suite facilities, and a couple of singles which share a bathroom. *Hotel-Pension Auguste*, Augustenstrase 12 (☎04272/2272, fax 3004-

---

PÖRTSCHACH ACTIVITIES

Bike rental At the train station (öS90 per day), or from United Sports, Hauptstrasse 198 (☎04272/2339; öS120 per day).

Boat rental In front of the *Hotel Park*.

Heliskiing Wasserschischule Martin Ramusch, directly in front of the *Hotel Park* (☎0664/330 7674). Expect to pay around öS500 per trip.

Hiking There are plenty of easy walks in the hills north of town. The tourist office sells a local *Wanderkarte* for öS30.

Sailing Segel-Surfschule Schweiger, 10-Oktober-Strasse 33 (☎04272/2655); or try the boathouse just west of the *Strandhotel*

Prüller. Seven-day sailing courses from öS2000.

Tennis Tennis Center Werzer (☎04272/3334). Court rental öS120 to öS160 per hour. Coaching (öS1950 for five days, öS1600 for an intensive weekend) also available.

Waterskiing Wasserschischule Martin Ramusch, see under "Heliskiing".

Windsurfing Segel-Surfschule Schweiger, see under "Sailing"; or the boathouse just west of *Strandhotel Prüller*. Seven-day surfing courses from öS1350; tuition for shorter periods at an hourly rate of öS300. Also board hire.

57; ③), is a modern building bang in the centre of town, 100m from the lake, with functional but fully equipped rooms. *Villa Miralago*, Hauptstrasse 129 (☎04272/2430, fax 2430-4; ④), is a lovely nineteenth-century lakeside villa on the eastern side of the peninsula, with period rooms, water's-edge gardens and a boathouse – price depends on which way your room faces. *Strandhotel Prüller*, Annastrasse 33–35 (☎04272/2353, fax 2353-201; ⑦), is a standard well-appointed lakefront hotel with its own bathing area, and modern rooms with en-suite facilities and TV. There's a **campsite** on the lakefront at **Töschling**, a small settlement 2km west of Pörtschach. Klagenfurt–Pörtschach–Velden buses and local trains (not expresses) stop nearby.

Eating and drinking

Despite Pörtschach's stylish reputation, places to **eat** are on the whole fairly uniform. All the hotels along the lakefront have restaurants with outdoor terraces, most of which offer a range of standard Austrian cuisine, together with local fish, at a reasonable (though hardly budget) price. The restaurant of the *Strandhotel Prüller*, Annastrasse 33–35, is as reasonable as any. *La Cassetta*, at the western end of the Hauptstrasse, serves up pizzas and spaghettis that won't break the bank, while the *Seerose*, Hauptstrasse 165, specializes in grilled meats at a reasonable price. *Franzl*, near the train station at Hauptstrasse 160, is a good place to try traditional Austrian food, and the more upmarket *Schloss Leonstain*, Hauptstrasse 228, is the best place to sample the fresh fish.

Most **nightlife** revolves around the **Monte-Carlo-Platz**, which becomes one vast open-air bar at the height of summer. The busy *Rainer's Bar* has a reputation for attracting the dressed-up crowd, with *Montesol* just over the road offering a slightly funkier alternative. *Anna W*, just west of here at Hauptstrasse 218, has a slightly younger, dressed-down crowd.

The biggest **clubbing** venue on the lake is *Fabrik*, a five-kilometre taxi ride west of Pörtschach in the tiny village of **Saag**.

Velden

Hugging the bay at the western end of the lake, brash and bustling **VELDEN** is larger and more crowded than Pörtschach, and less attractive as a result. It's another place where sybaritic youth mingle with strolling pensioners and sightseeing coach parties. Most visitors, coach or no coach, gravitate at some stage towards the central **Europaplatz**, where Velden's casino provides the fulcrum of the town's social life. The casino was opened in 1989, its attractive spire-like protrusions making it something of a landmark. From Europaplatz, Am Corso leads south towards the transport hub of Karawankenplatz, from where Seecorso leads round the lake. Overlooking Seecorso is the **Schloss**, close to the hearts of many Austrians and Germans as the backdrop to a popular 1980s television soap opera, *Schloss am Wörthersee*. Built for leading Carinthian magnate Bartholomäus von Khevenhüller in 1590, it was largely destroyed by fire in 1762, and most of what you now see is the result of an 1891 rebuilding. Previously used as an exhibition venue and luxury hotel, it was bought by German millionaire Günther Sachs (erstwhile husband of Brigitte Bardot) in 1990, but despite the millions since invested in its restoration it's not yet clear what he's going to do with it.

Arrival, information and accommodation

From Velden's **train station**, walk downhill along Bahnhofstrasse, turn right into Klagenfurterstrasse and keep going to reach the central ribbon of Europaplatz, Am Corso and Karawankenplatz. **Buses** from Klagenfurt and Villach pick up and drop off at Villacherstrasse, a five-minute walk west of Karawankenplatz. The **tourist office**, on

---

VELDEN ACTIVITIES

Bike rental At the train station (mountain bikes öS200 per day, öS150 on production of a train ticket valid for that day); and at the AGIP petrol station, Villacher Strasse (mountain bikes öS180 per day).

Golf Velden Golf Club at Oberdorf 70, Velden-Köstenberg (☎04274/7045). Eighteen-hole course open April–Nov. Green fee öS600.

Fishing Information from *Café Moro*, Am Korso 8 (☎04274/2279). Sample prices: one-day permit for öS250, seven days for öS600.

Sailing Segelschule Wörthersee, Seecorso 40 (☎04274/2691). Courses tailored to suit all abilities; expect to pay around öS2000 for couple of hours' tuition a day over a five-day period.

Squash *Hotel Tropic*, Klagenfurterstrasse 40 (☎04274/2037). Court hire: öS180 for an hour.

Swimming Casino-Bad, on the Casino's own piece of lakefront, is the trendy place to hang out (öS90), but the nearby Strandbad Wrann (öS60) and Strandbad Leopold (öS45) are just as good.

Tennis Tennis-Center, Bahnhofstrasse 20 (☎04274/4910). Outdoor courts öS150 per hour, indoor öS180 per hour.

Waterskiing All the Strandbäder offer waterskiing, as do a couple of places along the Seecorso. Expect to pay around öS120 per round.

Windsurfing Segelschule Wörthersee, see under "Sailing".

Karawankenplatz (May, June & Sept Mon–Sat 8am–7pm, Sun 10am–6pm; July & Aug Mon–Sat 8am–8pm, Sun 10am–7pm; Oct–April Mon–Sat 9am–5pm, Sun 10am–5pm; ☎04274/2103, fax 51078), has lists of **private rooms** and holiday **apartments** (the latter only really open to those contemplating a stay of four or more days) in Velden and surrounding villages, but they might not ring the places on your behalf to check vacancies. The nearest **campsite** is the *Weisses Rössl* at Auen (see p.266), accessible on Velden–Maria Wörth–Klagenfurt buses.

Best of the local **pensions** are *Gästehaus Teppan*, Sternbergstrasse 7 (☎ & fax 04274/2563; ②), a modern house with small balconied rooms just uphill from Villacherstrasse, the main road westwards out of town, and *Frühstückspension Urania*, on Mühlweg 2 (☎ & fax 04274/2696; ③), a residential street southwest of the centre and only minutes from the lake. One of the best **hotel** deals on the lakefront is *Seehaus Ogris*, Seecorso 34 (☎04274/2079; ④), a simple family hotel with en-suite facilites and TVs in all rooms. Of the luxury places, the characterful *Mösslacherhaus*, Karawankenplatz 1 (☎04274/2020, fax 2020-30; ⑤), is a delightful cross between central European villa and English country house, offering rooms with en-suite facilities and TV, and use of a private Strandbad a few steps away.

Eating and drinking

Good, cheap Austrian **food** is thin on the ground in Velden, but there's a growing range of ethnic restaurants to fill the gap. Among the most popular are *Xjangiang-Hof*, Am Corso 2a, a passable Chinese restaurant with a large, reasonably priced menu and outdoor seating in a big courtyard, and two pizzerias: the cheap-and-cheerful *Pizzeria Domino*, Bahnhofstrasse 5, and the slightly more expensive *Pizzeria da Leopoldo*, Seecorso 18, a chic place that stays open beyond midnight. For something indigenous, *Mozartstuben*, uphill from the lakefront to the south at Augsdorferstrasse 36, knocks out no-nonsense schnitzel-and-chips dishes as well as traditional Austrian working-man's recipes like *Schweinshaxe* (pork knuckle). For good-quality Austrian fare and the best in Carinthian *Nud'l* dishes, there's little to choose between the two central Gasthof-restaurants *Alte Post*, Europaplatz 4–6, and the slightly more upmarket *Hubertushof*, Europaplatz 1.

Most **drinking** revolves around Europaplatz, where the outdoor tables of the Casino's own café vie for custom with three fashionable near-neighbours: the *American Bar* (also known as *Schinakel*), a society hangout of long standing, and relative new-comers *Krugerl* and *Café Gig*. The *Stehbar*, a little further west underneath the Volksbank, features live bands playing easy-listening rock, while *Monkey Circus*, on the corner of Klagenfurterstrasse and Bahnhofstrasse, has Mexican beers and nibbles. Straightforward techno-oriented **clubs** include *Starlight Disco*, next to the fairly self-explanatory *Mexican Bar Laredo* on Villacherstrasse, and *Red Bull*, about 1km out of town along Klagenfurterstrasse.

Schloss Rosegg and the Wildpark

You can walk, cycle or catch a bus (eight daily from Villacherstrasse) to the village of **ROSEGG**, 4km southwest of Velden, site of a Neoclassical **Schloss** (more of a country villa than a castle) built by Habsburg diplomat Graf Orsini-Rosenberg in 1770 for his Italian mistress Lucrezia – and currently owned by the Liechtenstein family. It's visited for the linden-lined avenues of its landscaped **park** (dawn–dusk; free), and the **Figurenkabinett Madame Lucrezia** (May–Oct daily 9am–5pm; öS50), where the wax figures of Orsini-Rosenberg and his paramour mingle with other historical personages – including a portly Napoleon. But, if the weather's fine, your time would be better spent among the white wolves, deer and monkeys of **Wildpark Rosegg** (daily 9am–5pm; July & Aug open till 6pm; öS70), a short walk south of the Schloss.

The southern shore

Eight daily Klagenfurt–Velden buses speed along the Wörthersee Süduferstrasse, which runs from Klagenfurt to Velden along the **southern shore** of the lake, where a string of attractive if rather low-key settlements nestle beneath the wooded foothills of the Pyramidenkogel.

Ten kilometres west of Klagenfurt, **REIFNITZ** is the first place of any size, a quiet town with a municipal Strandbad and couple of café-restaurants on the lakefront. In recent years, it has gained notoriety for an annual meeting of Golf GTI fans, who assemble here from all across Europe over the *Pfingsten* (Whitsun) weekend. An unofficial affair conducted without the blessing of the local authorities, it basically involves a great deal of exuberant engine-revving, as enthusiasts trundle up and down the coast road in their vehicles. For the rest of the year, however, Reifnitz is a cheap and small-scale alternative to Pörtschach and Velden. The **tourist office**, on the main road through town (May–Oct Mon & Tues 8am–6pm, Wed–Fri 7.30am–6pm, Sat & Sun 9.30am–12.30pm & 1–6pm; ☎04273/2240), will fix you up with a **private room** or **pension**; alternatively, *Hotel-Pension Uschnig*, Seenstrasse 22 (☎04273/2294, fax 2294-4; ②–③), is a large B&B 500m from the lake with sparsely furnished but comfortable rooms, some with en-suite facilities. **Sailing** and **windsurfing** equipment rental and tuition can be organized at Segelschule Otto Stornig (☎04273/2371) on the lakefront.

From the centre of Reifnitz a road heads south then west towards the summit of the 850-metre **Pyramidenkogel**, 7km distant and topped by a futuristic **viewing tower** (daily: April & Oct 10am–6pm; May & Sept 9am–7pm; June 9am–8pm; July & Aug 9am–10pm; öS60), where you can patronize the expensive café and savour a sweeping panorama of the Carinthian countryside. There are well-signposted **paths** up to the Pyramidenkogel from either Reifnitz or Maria Wörth (see p.266); the steep ascent through the forest takes a couple of hours. There's also one direct **bus** a day (April–Oct) from Klagenfurt to the Pyramidenkogel, passing through Reifnitz on the way.

Maria Wörth and beyond

Four kilometres west of Reifnitz, the hotels and holiday apartments of **MARIA WÖRTH** crowd onto a promontory jutting into the lake, presided over in picturesque fashion by the spires of two medieval chapels. The larger of the two, at the eastern end of the promontory, is the twelfth-century **Pfarrkirche SS Primus und Felician**. The two early Christian martyrs are portrayed on either side (Primus on the left) of the *Virgin and Child* which graces the Baroque high altar. On the south wall of the nave, a late-Gothic altar panel shows St Jerome (Hieronymus) in the company of the ape. On a knoll opposite, the **Winterkirche**, whose inside walls bear traces of twelfth-century frescoes depicting the Apostles, holds a striking stained-glass window showing the Madonna, behind the altar.

Maria Wörth's **tourist office** (May & Oct Mon–Fri 10am–noon & 1–4.30pm, Sat & Sun 10am–noon & 2–4.30pm; June & Sept Mon–Fri 10am–noon & 1–5pm, Sat & Sun 10am–noon & 2–5pm; July & Aug daily 9am–6pm; ☎04273/2240, fax 3703) is just inland from the churches at Am Corso 110, on the second floor of a block containing shops and restaurants. Maria Wörth is too small to have a stock of private rooms, but the village's **pensions** tend to offer better value than those in Pörtschach on the opposite side of the lake. *Gasthaus Erika*, St-Anna-Weg 14 (☎04273/2701; ②), attractively perched on the hillside, is a modern house in traditional style with simple balconied rooms, some with en-suite facilities, cheaper ones without. *Pension Martha*, Primusweg 6 (☎04273/2574; ②), at the western end of the village, is larger and more impersonal, but has access to a private Strandbad.

West of Maria Wörth, the Velden-bound road passes through the straggling settlements of **DELLACH** and **AUEN**. Dellach stands beside one of Carinthia's best eighteen-hole **golf courses** (it's a scenic course, too, on high ground with views back towards the lake), and most of the hotels in the village do a profitable line in golf packages from March to October – the Maria Wörth tourist office has details. Immediately beyond Dellach, Auen is the site of the southern shore's best **campsite**, *Camping Weisses Rössl* (☎04274/2898), on a hillside above the lake and with free access to a water's-edge bathing area.

North of Klagenfurt

The area **north of Klagenfurt** is the historic heartland of Carinthia, for successive waves of immigrant cultures – Celtic, Roman, Slav and finally Bavarian – have moved in to stamp their identity on the fertile basin around the Glan and Gurk rivers. It's a territory laden with historic remains: the Celts settled the hummocks around the Zollfeld, where the remnants of a Celtic town lie on the slopes of the **Magdalensberg**. The Romans superseded, building the now-vanished city of **Virunum**, in the valley below. Stones from Virunum were used to build the pilgrimage church at **Maria Saal**, 10km north of Klagenfurt, once an important religious centre and now the site of the Carinthian Open-Air Museum. North of Maria Saal lies the rather more substantial market town of **St Veit an der Glan**, former capital of Carinthia, and a good base from which to visit **Hochosterwitz** castle, a startlingly attractive hilltop fortress, while the main northbound route continues onwards to **Friesach**, one of Austria's best-preserved small medieval towns. Lying slightly off the main north–south route are **Gurk** to the west, site of the province's most impressive cathedral, and **Hüttenberg** to the east, a former mining town that now harbours an intriguing ethnographic museum honouring local-born explorer Heinrich Harrer.

All of the above can be treated as day-trips from Klagenfurt. The main Vienna-bound rail line and Bundesstrasse 83 provide access to the area, striking north through the **Zollfeld** just beyond the Klagenfurt city limits, an area of rich corn-bearing farmland bordered by conifer-covered hills. If you're dependent on public transport, you'll find Maria Saal, St Veit, Hochosterwitz and Friesach fairly easy to get to, as they're all served by frequent **trains**. Less frequent **buses** run to Magdalensberg, Gurk and Hüttenberg.

Maria Saal

Back in the eighth century, when pagan Carinthia was a land of opportunity for any ambitious, evangelizing cleric, the great Bishop (and later St) Virgil of Salzburg dispatched the monk Modestus to the Zollfeld to lead the conversion – and Germanization – of the local Slavs. Modestus chose the hillock now occupied by the village of **MARIA SAAL** as his base, and this sleepy, rustic spot still revolves around the hilltop church he founded.

Arriving at Maria Saal's small **train station**, you can clearly see the famous **Wallfahrtskirche** on the high ground 500m to the east. A fifteenth-century structure built atop St Modestus's original foundation, the church is notable for the Roman gravestones pilfered from the ruins of nearby Virunum and built into its outer walls, especially around the south porch. Among the most expressive of these are one showing two horses pulling a wagon, and another showing a she-wolf suckling Romulus and Remus (the latter embedded inside the porch). Within the impressively lattice-vaulted interior, the high altar containing statuettes of the Madonna and Child serves as the main focus for pilgrims, although significantly more engaging is the Arndorfer altar in the northern apse, showing the Coronation of the Virgin, flanked by saints George and Florian. Outside the church, an octagonal charnel house features two storeys of arcading, the lower storey bearing medieval frescoes showing the Deposition.

Arndorferstrasse leads downhill northeast from the church towards a T-junction presided over by the **Pestkreuz**, a sixteenth-century wayside cross. A short walk west of here is the **Freilichtmuseum** (May–Oct daily except Mon 10am–6pm; öS50), occupying an attractive, partly wooded site on the edges of town and containing more than thirty farmsteads and other buildings collected from all over Carinthia. A German-language guidebook (öS50) gives the full rundown, but an obvious highlight is the water-wheel-operated sawmill complex in a dell to the west. Above the sawmill is the humble *Holzknechthütte*, the improvised shelter with tree-bark roof in which the woodcutters dwelt while away working in the forest.

Enclosed by railings 1.5km north of Maria Saal, beside the old road to St Veit (which runs parallel to the modern Bundesstrasse), the **Herzogstuhl** is a granite throne about 2m high, assembled from bits of Roman-era masonry from much-plundered Virunum. Dating from the ninth century, it was used in ceremonies to confirm the authority of the dukes of Carinthia over the local populace. The venerable seat is not much to look at, but exudes a powerful whiff of history nevertheless. It's easily reached by car, and buses on the Klagenfurt–Maria Saal–St Veit run stop just next to it. If you're on foot, simply turn right outside Maria Saal train station and keep going.

Practicalities

Local trains stop in Maria Saal, as well as a few of the expresses, and it's also on the Klagenfurt–St Veit bus route. The **tourist office**, just downhill from the church at Am Platzl 7 (☎04223/2214), can fix you up with one of a small number of **private rooms**. The nearest pension-type accommodation is *Gasthof Fleissner* (☎04223/2218; ②), 2km north in the village of **Zollfeld**. Both *Café zum Dom* and the more expensive *Gasthof Sandwirt*, on the Hauptplatz next to the church, offer good-quality Austrian food. For a quick lunch, *Jausenstazion Rauter*, just outside the entrance to the Freilichtmuseum, offers a range of Würst and cold cuts.

The Magdalensberg

Ten kilometres north of Maria Saal, a minor road leaves the main northbound route near the village of **St Michael am Zollfeld** to snake its way up to the summit of the 1059-metre **Magdalensberg** to the east. The hilltop is now occupied by the **pilgrimage church of Saints Helena and Magdalena**, a late-Gothic affair with some intricate stellar vaulting inside and a high altar whose panels tell the story of Helena's discovery of the Holy Cross and its re-erection by Emperor Heraclius. The church is the starting point of the annual *Vierbergelauf*, or "Four Mountains Walk", which takes place on the night of the first full moon after Easter. Up to 5000 people attend midnight Mass on the Magdalensberg before embarking on a torchlit hike that takes in three hills on the other side of the valley – the Ulrichsberg, Veitsberg and Lorenziberg.

Such rituals have their origins deep in the Celtic past, when spiritual life often centred on the area's hilltop shrines. The strength of Celtic culture in the area is evinced by the remains of a **Romano-Celtic town** 1.5km below the summit of the Magdalensberg, by the side of the road up to the summit. The site (May–Oct daily 9am–7pm; öS40) is arranged on terraced slopes around a central grassy area that once served as a forum. The Celts who settled the area in the first century BC grew rich from the gold, amber and iron found in the nearby hills, and iron implements like axe heads and horse bits are proudly displayed in cabinets in the former trade and residential quarter, to the right of the forum. A Roman takeover took place early in the first century AD, and it's thought that the settlement here served as Roman regional capital before the city of Virunum was constructed in the valley below. Indeed, many of the finer remains here were built under Roman stewardship: the **painted house** to the right of the forum bears a cycle of pictures relating to Dionysus – the use of the "Pompeii red" pigment suggests that it was executed by a craftsman who learnt his trade in the Italian south. On the other side of the forum, the reconstructed **council chamber** (where leaders of local Celtic tribes were summoned to assemblies) now holds a display of both Celtic and Roman jewellery and the *Jungling von Magdalensberg* (Young Man of Magdalensberg), a copy of a statue unearthed by farmers here in the Middle Ages, which was sent to Spain in the sixteenth century, and promptly lost – our knowledge of the statue comes from a seventeenth-century replica in the Kunsthistorisches Museum in Vienna.

Two daily buses (Mon–Sat only) head up the Magdalensberg from St Veit between Easter and October, stopping some 500m below the Romano-Celtic site.

St Veit an der Glan

Standing at the northern end of the Zollfeld, the peaceful market town of **ST VEIT AN DER GLAN** bears little evidence that it served as the capital of Carinthia until 1518. Generously sprinkled with medieval and Baroque town houses, and preserving portions of its medieval town walls, it's riddled with picturesque corners and serves as a good place for a brief stop on your way to Magdalensberg or Hochosterwitz (see opposite). The town comes to life during the last week of September, when the **Wiesenmarkt**, a medieval-styled fair featuring street entertainment and a bewildering array of stalls, pulls in as many as 500,000 visitors. Both the Wiesenmarkt and the *Pfingsten* (Whitsun) holiday are celebrated with marching displays by the **Trabanten**, a kind of honorary home guard comprised of local citizens who parade through town in antiquated uniforms.

Your best approach is to head for the elongated, rectangular **Hauptplatz** and indulge in a relaxed amble around the largely pedestrianized network of alleyways and courtyards around it. The **Pfarrkirche St Veit** at the northern end of the square is worth popping into for a glimpse of the colourful high altar (1752) by local master Johann Pacher, which features gilded figures of the Virgin flanked by saints Dominicus and Clara. The other end of the Hauptplatz is overlooked by the fine Baroque facade of the **Rathaus**, behind which lies an attractive arcaded courtyard decorated with sgraffito dragon, snake and bird designs. Next door, with a collection of railway uniforms and antiquated ticket machines, the **Verkehrsmuseum**, or transport museum, Hauptplatz 29 (daily 9am–noon & 2–6pm; öS40), will primarily interest rail enthusiasts, though the model railway on the top floor might have broader appeal. It's certainly more fun than the **Stadtmuseum** in the Herzogsburg, or ducal palace, north of here on Burggasse (Mon–Fri 10am–noon & 2–6pm, Sat 10am–noon; öS30), offering a mundane collection of coins, traditional furnishings, old shooting targets and Trabanten uniforms.

Practicalities

Buses and trains both stop at the **train station** at the northern end of town. From there, turn left onto the main road and walk straight for ten minutes before bearing right into the old town. The **tourist office**, in the Rathaus (Mon–Fri 9am–noon & 2–6pm, Sat 9am–noon; ☎04212/5555-13, fax 5555-80), has a limited list of private rooms in town. Of the local **hotels**, *Gasthof Steirerhof*, Klagenfurterstrasse 38 (☎04212/2442; ②), is a basic but bearable place with rooms with shared toilet and shower facilities, while the *Weisses Lamm*, Unterer Platz 4 (☎04212/2362; ④), is a traditional town-centre Gasthof with cosy rooms with en-suite facilties and a nice restaurant in the courtyard.

Those in search of **eating** and drinking venues shouldn't have to stray too far from the Hauptplatz and vicinity. The *Rathauscafé*, Hauptplatz 31, is a good place for inexpensive pizza- or pasta-based lunches, while the nearby *Moser*, Spitalgasse 6, has a good range of mid-priced Carinthian *Nud'l* dishes. Top-quality Carinthian fare is the order of the day at the slightly more upmarket *Puckelsheim*, Erlgasse 11. *Cantina Toscana*, Klagenfurterstrasse, has a big garden, Sicilian staff and a good reputation for authentic Italian food. For **drinking**, *Baradies*, Hauptplatz 24, is a long, narrow bar with ten varieties of beer on tap and a lively, youngish clientele. *Adele*, Hauptplatz 29, is a more laid-back watering hole offering jazz sessions on Friday nights and Sunday lunchtimes and serving a wide range of bar food, while *Kral*, Erlgasse, attracts a younger, more grungey crowd.

Hochosterwitz and around

North of St Veit, Bundestrasse 83 cuts through low hills, climbing out of the Glantal before descending to trace the course of the River Gurk. The railway ultimately follows the same route after initially veering east to pass within striking range of the region's most awe-inspiring sight, the hilltop fortress of **Hochosterwitz**. Situated 10km east of St Veit, though clearly visible long before you arrive, the fortress sits fairy-tale-like on the rock (it's said that it served as the inspiration behind the castle in Disney's *Snow White*), its turret-encrusted outer fortifications winding their way around the craggy slopes. This spot has been fortified since the early Middle Ages, but the current castle was largely the work of the governor of Carinthia, Georg von Khevenhüller, who purchased the site in 1571 and whose bust adorns the sixth gate on the approach to the fortress. Picturesque though the effect, his construction efforts had a serious purpose – the lowlands around St Veit and Klagenfurt were constantly under threat of Turkish raids at the time. Hochosterwitz still belongs to the Khevenhüllers, whose current head lives in a house in the valley below.

The **fortress** (Easter–Oct daily 8am–6pm; öS90) is approached via a pathway that ascends through fourteen fortified gates, which once controlled access to Hochosterwitz's impregnable inner sanctum. Many of the gates are decorated with impressive busts and reliefs; the first, the **Fähnrichtor** (Ensign's Gate), bears the arms of the Khevenhüllers – featuring an acorn, symbol of the family's original fifteenth-century residence near Villach, Eichelberg (Acorn Hill) – together with the child Jesus with a lamb. The inner fortress at the top of the hill is a bit of a disappointment; there's not much, save for a café in the central courtyard and a patchy **museum**, inadequately labelled in German. Amongst the old weapons and family portraits lining the walls is a piece of paper bearing the signature of King James I of England – it's an entry taken from Hans von Khevenhüller's *Stammbuch*, the kind of diary-cum-album in which aristocrats of the day kept records of the dignitaries they'd met in the course of their travels.

There's a lift up to the fortress for those who don't fancy the climb; lift tokens (öS40) are available from the castle ticket office beneath the first gate.

Practicalities

Hochosterwitz lies 2km south of the village of **Launsdorf**, on the Klagenfurt–Vienna rail route (all trains except inter-city ones stop here): turn right outside the **train station** and keep going – you'll soon see the fortress. Those with their own transport should follow Bundesstrasse 82, which leaves Bundesstrasse 83 at St Veit and heads east towards Brückl; a well-signposted turn leads to the fortress, which is a further 1km off the road. St Veit–Brückl buses pick up and drop off at this turnoff.

There's nowhere to stay around the castle, so it's best to treat Hochosterwitz as a day-trip from Klagenfurt, St Veit or Friesach. As for **eating and drinking**, *Gasthaus Tatzer* next to the castle car park offers solid Austrian cuisine and good-value Tagesmenüs from around öS100. Otherwise, it's best to eat in Launsdorf, where *Gasthof zur Post*, just opposite the train station on the Hauptstrasse, serves up service-able if uninspiring Austrian and Carinthian dishes, while *Pizzeria Mama Mia*, a little further west at Hauptstrasse 1, is renowned for its fresh fish from the Adriatic, and has a range of authentic, inexpensive pizzas and Italian dishes too. For those who have a car, *Gasthof Prettner*, Zollfeldstrasse 3, in the village of **St Donat** (6km southwest of Hochosterwitz on the road back towards Klagenfurt), is one of the best local venues for good Carinthian cooking at a moderate price.

The Gurktal

Twenty kilometres north of St Veit, at **Pöckstein**, a secondary road leaves Bundesstrasse 83 to explore the **Gurktal** to the west, a narrow ribbon of pastureland squeezed between the pine-carpeted hills of the Gurktaler Alpen. The Gurktal's main attraction is the village of **Gurk** and its cathedral, although **STRASSBURG**, 10km up the valley, is worth a brief stop in order to explore its hilltop **Schloss**, which over-looks the town from the north. This largely Renaissance castle was home to the bish-ops of Gurk until the bishopric was moved south to Klagenfurt in 1787, and its arcad-ed courtyard now plays host to classical concerts over the summer. There's also a **folklore museum** (April–Oct Mon–Fri 9am–noon & 2–5pm; öS30), showing the usual selection of craft implements and traditional wooden furniture, as well as some intriguing photographs of ritualistic Carinthian sports. These include *Kugelwerfen*, a quaintly pointless exercise in which a big wooden ball is thrown through village streets along a pre-agreed route at Easter time; and *Kranzelreiten*, a more straight-forward horse race that takes place at Whitsun in the village of Weitensfeld, 15km west of Strassburg. Dating from the Middle Ages, the race recalls a time of plague when young men indulged in equine contests to decide who had first choice of the vil-lage's few surviving virgins. There's a fairly inessential hunting section (costing an additional öS10) displaying the customary trophy animal heads, including those of stags Hansi and Mischko, who used to live in the castle grounds (they died peaceful deaths). The Schloss café-restaurant is a good place to enjoy a quality bite to **eat** before journeying further.

Gurk

Four kilometres beyond Strassburg, the dainty farming village of **GURK** is dominated by the imposing twin towers of its stately Romanesque cathedral. It's been an ecclesiastical focal point ever since Carinthian noblewoman Hemma of Gurk established a Benedictine convent here in 1043. Gurk was the last of a long line of churches and abbeys founded by this extraordinarily energetic and pious woman, and her tomb here quickly became an object of veneration for pilgrims. Hemma's convent was soon taken over by the archbishops of Salzburg, who were eager to consolidate their control over a region whose conversion to Christianity they had overseen. Gurk was upgraded to become a bishopric, necessitating the construction of a new cathedral to replace Hemma's church, and Bishop Roman I (1131–67) set about building a wondrous edifice that survives more or less intact form today. Located in a side-valley some distance from the main north–south trade routes, however, Gurk's status as spiritual capital of Carinthia was something of an anomaly. In 1787 Bishop Salm relocated the episcopal court to Klagenfurt, and the village of Gurk settled back into rural slumber. Gurk is not really geared up for tourist accommodation, although the **tourist office** in the centre of the village (May–Oct Mon–Sat 8am–noon & 2–5pm; ☎04266/8520, fax 8520-4) might find you a private room if you wish to stay. The *Kronenwirt*, just outside the cathedral's west gate, is a good place to pick up a hearty Austrian lunch.

THE CATHEDRAL

Despite later additions, notably the seventeenth-century onion domes that now grace the two towers, the **cathedral** is still essentially the same three-aisled basilica that was built by Bavarian masons between 1140 and 1200. Constructed from local iron-bearing limestone, the whole building exudes a curious, golden-yellow luminescence. Before venturing inside, it's worth wandering round to look at the tympanum above the south porch, which bears a figure of Christ, carved around 1150, holding aloft a book whose pages are inscribed with the words *ego sum hostium* – "I am the gate". On the east end of the cathedral, a small twelfth-century relief mounted high on the wall of the central apse shows a lion (symbolizing Christ) attacking a basilisk (representing the forces of darkness).

Entering the cathedral via the west door, you come face to face with thirteenth-century frescoes in the porch, showing scenes from Genesis on the left-hand side, and New Testament scenes on the right. From here an imposing Romanesque doorway, rich in abstract carving, leads through to the nave, where your eyes are drawn towards George Raphael Donner's **cross altar** of 1740, halfway up the nave, which features an expressive *Pietà* cast in lead. To the left of the altar, in the north aisle, the celebrated Romanesque **Samson tympanum** (1200) bears a relief of the biblical strongman breaking the jaws of a lion. At the east end of the cathedral, Michael Hönel's **high altar** (1626–32) shows the Ascension of the Virgin surrounded by an array of highly stylized statuettes – St Hemma kneels above the Virgin's head to the right. During Lent the high altar is covered by what amounts to an enormous painted curtain, the **Gurker Fastentuch**, or Gurk Lenten cloth, executed by Konrad von Friesach in 1458, and featuring 99 bible scenes. Despite being one of the great masterpieces of Austrian late-Gothic art, the cloth remains in storage for the rest of the year, although pictures of it are always on display in the cathedral. In the **crypt**, a shrine to St Hemma, flanked by eighteenth-century statues, has been built above the eleventh-century sarcophagus. In the southeast corner of the crypt you'll find a rock shaped vaguely like a seat, traditionally sat upon by women who wish to conceive a child. One of the most impressive parts of the cathedral, the first-floor **bishop's chapel**, at the west end of the nave, is only accessible by guided tour (April–Oct daily at 1pm; öS30). It's famous for its frescoes, painted in 1230 and restored in 1263 after a fire, depicting Old Testament scenes in vibrant turquoises, greens and ruddy browns.

Just north of the cathedral entrance is the infant-oriented **Zwergenpark**, or gnome park (daily: May & June 10am–6pm; July & Aug 9am–6pm; Sept & Oct 10am–5pm; öS60), a tawdry display of garden gnomes with a tiny stretch of miniature railway on which the kids can ride.

Friesach

Girdled by an impressive ensemble of hilltop ruins and enclosed within still-moated town walls, **FRIESACH** is one of Carinthia's more enticing small towns. Like most places in this part of Austria, it was settled by Slavs in the sixth century, before their gradual displacement by Bavarians and Franks. Ninth-century Holy Roman Emperor Louis (Ludwig) the German gave the town to the archbishops of Salzburg, who established a thriving market here, and by the thirteenth century it was the most important urban centre in Carinthia. Richard the Lionheart passed through town on his way to the Crusades in 1192, although Friesach's main claim to fame in this period was the famous **Tourney** in 1224, when Duke Leopold VI of Austria invited the flower of central European chivalry to a gathering later immortalized in the poems of knight and minstrel Ulrich von Liechtenstein (lord of nearby Murau in Styria; see p.243). The event is nowadays remembered in the **Stadtfest** of May 30, when the locals dress up in medieval costumes and the streets fill with stalls selling food and drink.

The Town

Dwarfing Friesach's attractive **Hauptplatz**, the Gothic bulk of the largely nineteenth-century **Stadtpfarrkirche** is probably worth giving a miss in favour of the **Dominikanerkirche** further northeast, which looks equally plain on first inspection, but is much more rewarding inside. There's a lively fourteenth-century sculpture of the Crucifixion on the north side of the nave and, behind it, a seventeenth-century *Pietà*, the whole scene surrounded by brightly coloured, fruit-laden foliage. To the right of the altar stands another fine piece of medieval wood sculpture, the delicate *Friesacher Madonna* of 1320, while on the north side of the choir the Johannes altar of 1500 bears a central relief featuring Christ flanked by saints George and Florian, and wings showing scenes from the life of St John – including his exile on the island of Patmos and an attempt by Roman soldiers to boil him in oil.

West of the Hauptplatz, pathways lead up towards part-ruined stretches of the town's medieval fortifications. One of the better-kept bits, to the northwest, is the **Petersberg**, where the surviving keep of a thirteenth-century fortress now holds the **Stadtmuseum** (May–Oct daily 10am–5pm; öS40), with archeological, art and craft exhibits on five floors. Most interesting are the Gothic altarpieces on the second floor – one of which was produced by the local workshop of Konrad von Friesach in 1435 (he of the *Gurker Fastentuch*; see p.271) – and the fifth-floor display of medieval copperware, featuring a fifteenth-century doctor's blood-letting beaker, decorated with an Adam-and-Eve motif.

Practicalities

From the **train station** on the eastern fringes of town, it's a straightforward five-minute walk down Bahnhofstrasse to the Hauptplatz, where the **tourist office**, at no. 1 (May–Oct Mon–Fri 9am–noon & 2–6pm, Sat 9am–noon; Nov–April Mon–Fri 10am–noon & 3–5pm; ☎04268/4300, fax 4280), will point you in the direction of the very few **private rooms** in town. Of the town's main **hotels**, grouped around the Hauptplatz, *Zum Goldenen Anker*, Bahnhofstrasse 3 (☎04268/2313; ②), is the most basic, a traditional downtown Gasthof offering a couple of rooms with shower and TV, and a couple of cheaper ones with facilities in the hallway, while the *Friesacherhof*, Hauptplatz 4 (☎04268/2123, fax 2123-15; ③), offers rooms with en-suite facilities together with satellite TV and phone.

Cheapest place to **eat** is probably *Gasthof zum Mohren*, a few steps north of the Hauptplatz on Wienerstrasse 12, offering cheap Würst and soups, and a range of schnitzels from öS80. Otherwise, restaurants in the hotels lining the Hauptplatz have more style: both the *Friesacherhof* and *Metnitztalerhof* offer a tempting array of Carinthian specialities alongside some more expensive game and fish dishes, and both have plenty of outdoor seating in summer. There's not a great choice of spots for a **drink**, although the Hauptplatz hotels are good places to sit outside during the summer. For indoor drinking, try the *Stadtcafé* on Herrengasse, a comfortable coffee-and-cakes venue, or the thirteenth-century wine cellar of the *Metnitztalerhof*.

Hüttenberg

On arrival in **HÜTTENBERG**, a historic iron-ore-mining village in the hills east of Friesach, it's difficult at first to believe you're still in Austria. A massive picture of the Buddha hangs from a cliff at the southern entrance to town, marking the starting point of the Tibetan-inspired **Lingkor**, a pathway that leads up the hillside and is supposed to aid meditation and prayer. That such Eastern esoterica should exist here at all is largely down to the local-born mountaineer and explorer **Heinrich Harrer** (see box, p.274), whose exploits – including the epic walk to Tibet from northern India that made him famous – are remembered in Hüttenberg's Heinrich Harrer **museum**. Hüttenberg's mining past also plays a role in the place's appeal, although it's difficult to imagine that this tranquil, rural environment of forest-fringed valleys was once a thriving centre of industry. A century ago, more than seven hundred people worked in the mines of **Knappenberg** – now the site of a **show-mine** – in the hills above Hüttenberg; and a further 800 worked in the blast furnaces of **Heft**, 2km up the valley to the east. By 1978 the whole mining and smelting operation had been wound down, the locally produced metal priced out of the market by cheap foreign imports. Mining traditions are celebrated, however, in the **Reiftanz**, which takes place on the first Sunday after Whitsun every three years (the next one is in spring 2001). In addition to a lot of processing around in traditional miners' uniforms and a good deal of alcohol-fuelled merrymaking, the *Reiftanz* centres on an age-old ceremony in which the social hierarchy is symbolically reversed – and local dignitaries have the honour of being lightly whipped on the backside by mining representatives.

Hüttenberg isn't accessible by train, but its position on Bundesstrasse 92 from Klagenfurt to Neumarkt in Steiermark ensures that it's not too difficult to reach. **Buses** from either Klagenfurt or St Veit head for the town of **Brückl** 22km south of the village, where you can change to a Brückl–Hüttenberg bus, which calls in at Hüttenberg village centre before heading uphill to Knappenberg.

The Town

Housed in a modern pavilion at the southern end of town, below the Lingkor, the **Heinrich-Harrer-Museum** (April–Oct daily 10am–5pm; öS100, combined ticket with Knappenberg mine öS160) was blessed by the Dalai Lama himself when it first opened in 1992. The special throne that was built for the Dalai Lama, together with Tibetan costumes, prayer wheels and trumpets made from human bones (those made from the bones of young girls or holy men are considered especially lucky) are displayed on the upper floor of the building. Downstairs, various totems associated with the Harrer cult are assembled, among them his mountaineering boots, golf clubs and an old tennis racket – Harrer introduced tennis to Tibet, making a clay court out of dried yak droppings. A well-organized ethnographic collection follows, largely made up of the items collected

HEINRICH HARRER

Explorer, all-round sportsman, mountaineer and one of the great popularizers of Tibetan culture in the West, Heinrich Harrer (born 1912) is one of contemporary Austria's most compelling figures. He's best known for his book *Seven Years in Tibet*, a stirring account of his adventures in the 1940s, recently filmed for Hollywood with Brad Pitt taking the role of Harrer himself. The release of the film in autumn 1997 looked set to put Harrer, and Hüttenberg, on the global map, but unfortunately things soured after revelations (courtesy of the German magazine *Stern*) that Harrer had been a member of the SS in the late 1930s.

That the Nazis were keen to recruit Harrer comes as no surprise: in the blue-eyed world of alpine sport, he was a demigod. Born in Obergossen near Knappenberg, he developed a passion for mountaineering and skiing early on, becoming so proficient that he was drafted into the Austrian Olympic skiing team in 1936. Together with three colleagues, Harrer made the first successful assault on the north wall of the Eiger in 1938 (subsequently immortalized in Harrer's book, *The White Spider*), an exploit which made Harrer internationally famous and secured his place on an Austro-German Himalayan expedition the following year. By this time, he was a Party member and had become skiing instructor to the SS. He even got married in an SS uniform. What's unclear is whether he was a committed believer, an ambitious careerist or merely the passive recipient of a status bestowed on him by a regime keen to associate itself with sporting heroes.

Fortuitously, Harrer was on the other side of the world scrambling around Himalayan foothills when World War II broke out. As a citizen of the German Reich, however, he was interned by the British at Dehra Dun in northwestern India, but escaped in April 1944 to embark on the adventure that made him famous. Together with colleague Peter Aufschneiter, he crossed the Himalayas in search of Tibet, a country which had long exerted a fascination over the Germans, who believed it to be the original home of the Aryan race. Two years later, he finally reached Lhasa, and somehow found a role for himself in this strange environment, becoming the Mr Fix-It that locals called for whenever some aspect of Western technology or culture needed explaining. He was in the process of teaching monks how to skate when he was summoned by an intrigued Dalai Lama (then a child), and they've been friends ever since. Once back in Europe, the success of the book *Seven Years in Tibet* and the documentary film of the same name enabled Harrer to finance further expeditions, starting with a trip to the Amazon in 1953. For the next three decades, he was constantly on the road, visiting Africa, South America and the Far East, pausing only briefly in 1958 to become the Austrian golf champion. He now lives in semi-retirement in Liechtenstein.

by Harrer on his travels through South America, Borneo and Africa – odd, though eminently practical, are the wooden head supports used by the Turkana tribesmen of Kenya to prevent their extravagant hairstyles from becoming tousled during sleep.

From here, Hüttenberg's main street leads north to Reiftanzplatz, bordered by charming late-medieval houses, one of which shelters the mildly diverting **Helga Riedel Puppenmuseum**, or doll museum (May–Sept daily 10am–noon & 1–5pm; öS35), a collection of exquisitely modelled figurines. Most are grouped together in scenes inspired by local author Dolores Vieser's rather whimsical novel of nineteenth-century Carinthian life, *Der Bänderhut* (*"The Ribboned Hat"*).

Knappenberg and Heft

Ranged across the hillside 4km east of Hüttenberg, and served by local bus, **KNAPPENBERG** (the name means "miners' hill") flourished as a centre of iron-ore mining from the days of the Celts until 1978. Some of the underground galleries have now been converted into a **Schaubergwerk** (tours depart hourly May–Oct daily 10am–4pm; öS100, combined ticket with Harrer Museum öS160), in which visitors are taken on a short walking tour and given several ear-splitting demonstrations of how different drilling tools worked. The ticket includes entry to the **museum** next door, a modest display that features miners' ceremonial uniforms, a model of the charcoal-fired smelting kilns once used by the Celts, and several cabinets full of crystals and minerals.

Two kilometres east of Hüttenberg, the hamlet of **HEFT** is dominated by a semi-ruined nineteenth-century **blasting furnace**, an impressive piece of industrial heritage whose smelting towers bring to mind the fortifications of a medieval castle. Parts of the complex have been restored and modernized to house artists' studios, and high-profile **exhibitions** are held there over the summer (May–Oct). Hüttenberg's tourist office will provide details of what's on.

Practicalities

Most people visit Hüttenberg on a day-trip from elsewhere, though the town's **tourist office**, operating out of the Heinrich-Harrer-Museum (same times; ☎04263/247, fax 784), can book **private rooms** in either Hüttenberg or Knappenberg if you choose to stay overnight. **Hotels** are a bit scarce, too: *Zur Post*, Reiftanzplatz 14 (☎04263/212; ②), is the sole Gasthof in Hüttenberg, but only has four rooms, two of which have en-suite shower and WC. In Knappenberg, *Gasthaus Steller* (☎04263/264; ②) is a similarly small, five-room pension near the Schaubergwerk. Six kilometres south of Hüttenberg, a minor road heads east up into the hills to **LÖLLING-GRABEN**, another 6km distant, site of the best **hotel** in the area, *Landgasthof Neugebauer* (☎04263/407, fax 757; ③), which has snazzy rooms, complete with TV and phone, as well as a highly regarded **restaurant** offering a mixture of Austrian standards and Carinthian specialities.

Best places to **eat** in Hüttenberg are the *Gasthaus Zois*, Münichsdorferplatz 9, serving all the usual schnitzels and, at lunchtime, an excellent *Bauernschmaus*, or cold meat platter, or the restaurant of *Zur Post*, which offers similarly hearty Austrian fare.

Villach and around

Sprawling across a lush plain near the confluence of the Drau and Gail, with the Karawanken Alps to the south, **VILLACH** ranks as Carinthia's most attractive provincial town. Local place names – like Villach itself, and suburbs of Vassach, Fellach and Pogöriach – are evidence of the area's Slavic origins, which gave way to German influences in the late Middle Ages, when courtly families like the Diedrichsteins and the Khevenhüllers built town houses here to take advantage of its growing importance as a trade centre. While Villach's standing has since rested more on its role as a major rail and motorway junction, its core of medieval and Renaissance buildings present a convincing argument for a stay of a day or two. Nightlife in Villach is also generally better than that in its larger local rival Klagenfurt, and it's a good urban base from which to explore nearby mountains and lakes. **Schloss Landskron**, on the northern fringes of town, presents one obvious excursion, as do **Mount Dobratsch** and the Terra Mystica show-mine at **Bad Bleiberg**, both to the west. **Warmbad Villach**, 3km south of town, is a modern spa-resort, which offers plenty of swimming pools and sporting activities. Although they're important resort areas in their own right, both the **Ossiachersee** and **Faakersee** are so close to Villach (and easily accessible by bus) that it's possible to stay in town and head out to a lakeside beach during the daytime.

Most important event on the folklore calendar is the **Villacher Kirchtag**, which falls on the first weekend in August, when people from all over Carinthia, Slovenia and northern Italy descend on the town to indulge in a weekend of folk music and outdoor drinking, culminating in a Saturday-night parade through town in traditional dress.

The telephone code for Villach is ☎04242.

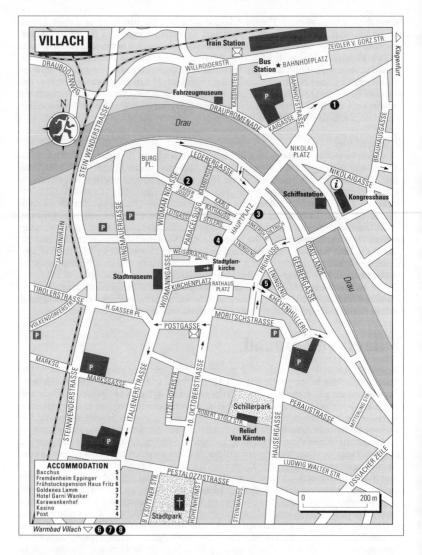

VILLACH

Train Station

Bus Station ★ BAHNHOFPLATZ

ZEIDLER V. GORZ STR.

△ Klagenfurt

DRAUBODENWEG

WILLROIDERSTR.

Fahrzeugmuseum

KASSINSTEIG

BAHNHOFSTRASSE

P

N

STEIN WENDERSTRASSE

Drau

DRAUPROMENADE

KAIGASSE

❶

BRAUHAUSGASSE

NIKOLAI PLATZ

BURG PL.

LEDERERGASSE

NIKOLAIGASSE

❷

BAMBERGER

ⓘ

WIDMAN N GASSE

KAISER JOSEF P.

LEITGASSE

PARACELSUSG.

KARLG.

RATHAUSG.

SEILERG.

HAUPTPLATZ

❸

ANKERSH.

DIETRICH

LENINGENG.

Schiffsstation

Kongresshaus

NIKOLAIGASSE

RINGMAUERGASSE

P

JAKOMINIRAIN

P

WEISBRIACHG.

❹

Stadtpfarr- kirche

FREIHAUSG.

LENINGENG.

GERBERGASSE

ORAHLANDE

Drau

Stadtmuseum

WIDMANNGASSE

KIRCHENPLATZ

RATHAUS PLATZ

❺

KHEVENHÜLLERG.

TIROLERSTRASSE

H. GASSER PL.

MORITSCHSTRASSE

P

VOLKENDORFERSTR.

POSTGASSE

P

MARKSG.

P

MARKSGASSE

ITALIENERSTRASSE

LITZELHOFERSTR.

10. OKTOBERSTRASSE

ROBERT STOLZ STR.

MITTERLING STR.

STEINWENDERSTRASSE

Schillerpark

PERAUSTRASSE

HAUSERGASSE

P

Relief Von Kärnten

LUDWIG WALTER STR.

OSSIACHER ZEILE

0   200 m

PESTALOZZISTRASSE

B. V. SUTTNER STR.

HOHENHEIMSTR.

STEINWANDG.

ACCOMMODATION

Bacchus	5
Fremdenheim Eppinger	1
Frühstuckspension Haus Fritz	6
Goldenes Lamm	3
Hotel Garni Wanker	7
Karawankenhof	8
Kasino	2
Post	4

Stadtpark

Warmbad Villach ▽ ❻❼❽

Arrival, information and accommodation

The **bus** and **train stations** are on Bahnhofplatz, just north of the centre. Walk south along Bahnhofstrasse and take the second left, Nikolaigasse, to reach the **tourist office**, at Europaplatz 2 (Mon–Fri 8am–6pm, Sat 9am–noon; ☎24444, fax 24444-17). They will provide a free city map and can book you into one of few **private rooms**, though none are particularly convenient for the centre. Apart from a couple of inexpensive inner-city choices, most of the cheaper **hotels and pensions** are in Warmbad

Villach (bus #1 from Bahnhofplatz) or farther-flung suburbs. On the whole, the nearby **Faakersee** (see p.280) is better served with private rooms and traditional pensions.

Hotels in central Villach

Bacchus, Khevenhüllergasse 13 (☎24192, fax 24192-8). A good mid-range downtown choice offering modern rooms with en-suite facilities and TV. ④.

Fremdenheim Eppinger, Klagenfurter Strasse 6 (☎24389). Cosy family-run pension north of the river, ideally situated for the train station and not too far from the centre. Most rooms have en-suite facilities, although a few cheaper ones share a hall shower. Breakfast not included. ②.

Goldenes Lamm, Hauptplatz 1 (☎24105, fax 24105-56). Straightforward central Gasthof offering some rooms with shared facilities (③), though most come with en-suite shower and WC (④).

Kasino, Kaiser-Josef-Platz 4 (☎24449, fax 24449-4). An affordable city-centre choice just west of the Hauptplatz. Rooms are sparsely furnished but come with en-suite shower and WC. ③.

Post, Hauptplatz 26 (☎26101, fax 26101-420). Classic central Gasthof occupying the sixteenth-century town house of the counts of Khevenhüller, with swish, modern and comfortable rooms. ⑥.

Hotels in Warmbad Villach

Frühstückspension Haus Fritz, Jesenfeldrain 7 (☎25581). Small, modern apartment block with balconied rooms in residential streets just northwest of Warmbad Villach train station. Rooms come with en-suite facilities. ②.

Hotel Garni Wanker, Warmbader Strasse 42 (☎33684). Nice alpine-style house on the main street just north of the Warmbad Villach train station. All rooms have en-suite facilities and TV, and there's a pleasant garden. The hotel offers a couple of four- or five-person family apartments too. ③.

Karawankenhof, Kadischenallee 8 (☎3003, fax 3003-89). Modern spa-hotel with spacious rooms, indoor and outdoor swimming pools, extensive grassy lawns, sauna and on-site doctors – everything you need in order to take the cure. ⑦.

The Town

The largely pedestrianized warren of arcades and alleyways around the **Hauptplatz** still holds an evocative, late-medieval atmosphere, making it an enticing area in which to wander. Raised on a terrace at the southern end of the Hauptplatz, the fourteenth-century **Stadtpfarrkirche Hl. Jakob** is home to a fine collection of sixteenth-century tombs. To the right of the high altar in the Diedrichstein chapel, Sigismund von Diedrichstein (lord of Finkenstein castle, south of Villach) is shown in full armour with his symbol, a snake, positioned above his head. To the left, the chapel and tomb of Christoph von Khevenhüller, master of Landskron castle, features a relief of the deceased together with wives Elizabeth and Anna-Maria. Along the south wall of the nave is an expressive relief of the tutor to Christoph's son, Dr Martin Siebenburger, who was allowed a last resting place here in the church by way of thanks. From the same era is the stone pulpit from 1555 carved in the form of the tree of Jesse, with the venerable Israelite himself shown lying at the base. Just outside the church, the **Stadtpfarrturm**, or bell tower, is worth scaling for an excellent panorama of the surrounding mountains (May & Oct Mon–Sat 10am–6pm; June & Sept Mon–Sat 10am–6pm, Sun noon–6pm; July & Aug Mon–Thurs & Sat 10am–6pm, Fri 10am–9pm, Sun noon–6pm; öS20). A short distance to the west on Widmanngasse, the **Stadtmuseum** (May–Oct Mon–Sat 10am–4.30pm; öS30) regales visitors with a well-presented if modest collection of local Bronze and Iron Age finds, together with some Gothic altar panels.

Tucked away in an area of attractive nineteenth-century villas southeast of the centre, the **Schillerpark**, on Peraustrasse, harbours a low modern pavilion containing the **Relief von Kärnten** (May–Oct Mon–Sat 10am–4.30pm; öS20), a vast 1:10,000-scale relief map of Carinthia – a rainy-day attraction, but hardly essential viewing other days.

The banks of the **Drau** just north of the centre are good for strolling or cycling along, with a sprinkling of cafés overlooking the river. On the northern side, the privately owned **Fahrzeugmuseum**, or motor museum, at Draupromenade 12 (mid-June to mid-Sept daily 9am–5pm; mid-Sept to mid-June Mon–Sat 10am–noon & 2–4pm; öS50), contains an engaging jumble of vehicles. Early Vespas and Lambrettas rub shoulders with more eccentric machines like the Messerschmit, KR175, a half-bike half-bubble car that somehow never made it as an icon of consumerism, while a couple of classic Porsches will satisfy the sports-car fetishists. But it's the less glamorous motors that are more compelling, such as the 1936 Fiat Topolino, which along with the German Volkswagen was an important step in bringing motoring to the masses.

Warmbad Villach

Three kilometres south of the city centre, **Warmbad Villach** is a chic, modern spa-resort where the mild radioactivity of natural thermal springs serves to reinvigorate limbs and soothe away stress. It's also an important sport and recreation centre, offering the best of the city's parks, swimming pools and tennis courts (see "Listings" p.280). If you're serious about taking the cure, you can stay in one of the bigger, more expensive hotels, like the *Karawankenhof*, that offer swimming pools, a range of treatments, and in-house medical staff. Alternatively, stay in a more modest pension and use central spa facilities at the **Kurzentrum** (☎37000) in the resort centre.

City buses (#1) and southbound local trains (not expresses) run from Villach train station to the Warmbad Villach halt in the centre of the resort. There's a **tourist office** across the way on Warmbaderstrasse (Mon–Fri 8am–noon & 2–6pm, Sat 9am–noon; ☎37244, fax 33966), which will advise on private rooms and pensions – though the main tourist office back in central Villach deals with these as well.

Eating, drinking and entertainment

Most of the central Gasthöfe offer reasonably good-value Austrian and Carinthian **food**, and it's well worth looking out for boards advertising set menus, especially at lunchtime. Fairly central **snacking** options include traditional Austrian sausage-fare from the Würstelstand just north of the Hauptplatz by the bridge, chickenburgers at *Wienerwald* on the corner of Gerbergasse and the Hauptplatz; and open sandwiches and filled rolls from *Panino* at the northern end of the Hauptplatz.

The main **drinking** area, which remains animated well into the early hours at weekends, is the pedestrian zone, stretching westwards from the Hauptplatz, where a variety of bars lurk in the alleyways around Lederergasse and Paracelsusgasse.

Restaurants

Café Burgmayr, Widmanngasse 25. A good source of inexpensive lunchtime meals of the basic schnitzel or pizza variety.

Da Francesco, Kirchenplatz 11. Central Gasthof serving a cheap-and-cheerful schnitzel menu, with most main dishes costing under öS100.

Hotel Post, Hauptplatz. Top-notch Austrian and modern European cuisine in the city centre's most evocative Gasthof. Expect to pay öS400–500 per head.

India King, Gerbergasse 33. Mid-priced Indian restaurant offering a dependable if predictable range of dishes.

Kabon, Hans-Gasser-Platz 7. Funky pasta and sushi bar that's good for a quick sit-down meal or a takeaway.

Pizzeria Trieste, Weissbriachgasse 14. One of several Italians in the central pedestrianized area, with a range of pizzas and spaghettis for under öS100.

S'Dachl, Lederergasse. Mid-priced restaurant specializing in fresh fish and Balkan-style grilled meats, with a pleasant outdoor arcaded area with seating near the river.

Tostenwirt, Lederergasse 25. A good place to try traditional Carinthian *Nud'l* staples, as well as new variations on the same theme, such as *Villacher Paradiesnud'l* – noodles with tomato and ham filling.

Villacher Brauhof, Bahnhofstrasse 8. Large restaurant and beer hall run by the local brewery, offering good-value Austrian food and a few Carinthian specialities.

Cafés and bars

Café Nino, Hauptplatz 28. Indoor bar behind the *Panino* fast-food outlet, which is good for either daytime or night-time drinking and also serves bar lunches.

Kukuwaia, corner of Leitgasse and Paracelsusgasse. Relaxing, refined café-bar with a nice mixture of comfy chairs and bar stools, and slightly higher prices then elsewhere.

Martina, Lederergasse 21. Cosy café-bar in the heart of the pedestrian zone which soon gets crowded with a good mixture of age groups.

Rathauscafé, Rathausplatz. A good place to sit outside during the daytime, with busy indoor bar area for late-night drinking.

Testa Rossa, Nikolaigasse 5. Popular café-bar just north of the river with occasional live music.

Viduli, Postgasse 6. Narrow, smart and self-consciously trendy designer bar just south of the pedestrian zone.

Entertainment

The modern Kongresshaus on Europaplatz (☎23561), just behind the tourist office, is the main venue for **classical** concerts, big **theatrical productions** and **musicals**. Smaller-scale drama takes place in the Studiobühne im Kellertheater, Freihausplatz (☎205205). Advance bookings for both of the above – as well as for other major cultural events in the region – can be made through Kartenbüro Knapp, Freihausgasse 3 (☎27341). The Evangelical church in the Stadtpark sometimes holds concerts of religious music.

Venues for **pop-rock** concerts and rave-style happenings tend to change, although posters and flyers in the Kartenbüro, the main ticket office for such events at Lederergasse 27, will have details of anything going on during your stay.

The main venue for **clubbing** is *Disco Fun* (admission öS40–60), fifteen minutes southeast of the centre at Ossiacherzeile 39, a large subterranean complex featuring an area for old-time dancing, an area for techno and house, and a couple of quieter bar areas. The nearby *Squash-Center*, also on Ossiacher Zeile, holds infrequent rave parties in summer.

Listings

Bike rental At the train station; also from Das Radl, Italienstrasse 22b (☎26954), or Sports Unlimited, Gerbergasse 3 (☎26998), both of which have a bigger choice of mountain bikes.

Car rental Avis, Ossiacher Zeile (☎24737); Hertz, Hans-Gasser-Platz (☎26970).

Cinema Stadtkinocenter, Rathausplatz (☎27000). Big multiscreen showing top international (dubbed) movies.

Hospital Landeskrankenhaus Villach, Nikolaigasse 43 (☎208).

Motoring organization ÖAMTC, Kärntnerstrasse 25 (☎34200, emergency breakdown service ☎120).

Pharmacy Kreis-Apotheke, Hauptplatz 9.

Police Bundespolizeidirektion Villach, Trattengasse 34 (☎2033).

Post office Hauptpostamt, Willroiderstrasse, next to the train station (daily 7am–10pm).

Swimming Erlebnistherme, Kadischenallee 25–27, Warmbad Villach, is an indooor pool with water slides, whirlpools and other fun features (öS105; bus #1 from Bahnhofplatz). For outdoor bathing, there are four small lakes strung out in the northern suburbs of Villach – the St Leonhardersee, Vassachersee, Magdalenesee and Silbersee (all accessible by city buses from the Bahnhofplatz) – each of which has a small Strandbad. Otherwise, head for the nearby Faakersee or Ossiachersee.

Tennis Tenniscamp Warmbad Villach, Warmbachweg 16 (☎32564, fax 312920); outdoor and indoor courts from öS120 per hour.

Train information ☎1717.

Travel agents Kärntner Reisebüro, Gerbergasse 12 (☎29888); Alpe Adria Touristik, Bahnhofplatz 6 (☎22536).

West of Villach: Dobratsch and Bad Bleiberg

A long, high ridge rising to the west of town, the 2166-metre **Dobratsch** is an easily identifiable landmark from whichever direction you approach Villach. Its upper reaches are accessible via a toll road, the **Villacher Alpenstrasse** (cars öS180, motorbikes öS90, bicycles free), which commences just southwest of town in the suburb of Möltschach and climbs steeply out of the valley before proceeding westwards along the ridge. About 8km out of Villach, the road passes the **Alpengarten** (mid-June to Aug daily 9am–6pm; öS20), a large collection of alpine flowers and plants native to the region. Eight kilo metres further on, the road terminates at **Rosstratten**, where a chairlift ascends to the 1957-metre **Höhenrain** (also accessible as an hour-long walk). Here, you can savour impressive views in all directions, or follow marked paths to the **Ludwig-Walter-Haus** (90min distant) just below the summit of Dobratsch itself.

Nestling below Dobratsch to the north, the erstwhile lead-mining settlement of **BAD BLEIBERG**, about 15km west of Villach, is reached by a minor road that leaves town from the suburb of Fellach. Mining stopped here in 1993, due to exhaustion of the ore deposits, and the galleries have now been transformed into one of Austria's most imaginative show-mines, **Terra Mystica** (daily: April 23–June & Sept 16–Oct 10am–3pm; July–Sept 15 10am–5pm; Nov–April 5 groups of ten or more by appointment only; öS185). A ninety-minute guided tour begins with a short video, in German, about the history of the mine, followed by a descent into the mine workings by wooden slide. Here, images are projected onto the cavern walls to create a highly effective underground son et lumière, with a German commentary (English leaflet available on request) on the creation of the earth and humans' relationship with the environment, plus an account of the cult of St Barbara, patron saint of miners, and jokey treatment of subterranean creatures like dwarfs and goblins.

There's a small museum in the show-mine's reception area displaying ceremonial mining uniforms and diagrams of the mine workings. Most valuable item here is probably the banner presented to the Bleiberg miners by Prince Eugene of Savoy in 1717, after several of their number had served as sappers in the Habsburg armies – most memorably helping to blow up Turkish positions during the siege of Belgrade.

In addition to the regular show-mine tour, you can choose between two **guided walks** (3hr 30min or 5hr; öS500 and öS600 respectively) through deeper sections of the mine, in the company of a trained geologist (ring a day in advance to book a place; English-speaking guides are usually available; ☎04244/2255-10). The price includes a packed lunch, and the chance to indulge in *Bergmeditation* (mine meditation) – a few quiet moments spent in the depths of the mine is said to be an excellent cure for stress.

The Faakersee and around

Less than 10km southeast of Villach, the placid waters of the **Faakersee** offer a popular escape from the city on hot summer weekends. Despite its small size (its widest point is little more than 2km across), the Faakersee is far from being just a

FAAKERSEE ACTIVITIES

Bike rental At Faak am See train station for öS90 per day; also at the Fahrradcenter, Strandbad Egg, which has a bigger choice of mountain bikes for around öS150 a day.

Boat rental Rowing boats, pedalos and electroboats from virtually all the campsites and Strandbäder. Expect to pay öS80–120 per hour depending on type of boat.

Fishing Information from Faak am See tourist office. Permits cost around öS150 per day, öS600 per week.

Rock climbing Informationsbüro am Kanzianiberg, 5km southwest of Faak on the road to Finkenstein fortress (☎04227/4366). Two-hour introductory course for beginners öS350; other courses by negotiation.

Sailing Surf- und Segelschule Pepi, *Hotel Karnerhof*, Egg (☎04254/3258). Rental of small craft and a variety of courses, with prices starting from around öS2000 for seven days' of tuition.

Windsurfing Surf- und Segelschule Pepi (see under "Sailing"). Board rental and a range of courses – for example, a seven-day beginners' course for öS2000.

glorified daytime beach for the Villach-based hordes, functioning quite happily as a resort in its own right. A main selling point are the string of campsites that run along the southern and eastern shores, each with its own stretch of shingle beach and water sports facilities. It's fairly easy to get to the lake from Villach by **bus**, with some services going round the lake in a clockwise direction, others anticlockwise. **Trains** on the Villach–Rosenbach–Ljubljana route stop at the lake's biggest town, Faak am See.

DROBOLLACH, nearest of the Faakersee communities to Villach, isn't much more than a strip of houses along the road set back slightly from the lake. It's from the lakeside walks around Drobollach, however, that you'll enjoy the Faakersee at its prettiest, with views south towards the Karawanken mountains, notably the 2143-metre Mittagskogel, which boldly marks the border with Slovenia. There's a **tourist office** (mid-June to mid-Sept Mon–Fri 9am–12.30pm & 1.30–7pm, Sat 10am–noon & 3–7pm, Sun 3–7pm; mid-Sept to mid-June Mon–Fri 9am–12.30pm & 1.30–5pm; ☎04254/21850, fax 4515) on the main street, in the Gemeindeamt. From here a path leads through meadows to the Strandbad (öS30), where there's a small shingle beach, a couple of cafés and the opportunity to hire pedalos and rowing boats.

Four kilometres south of Drobollach, on the road that circumnavigates the lake, **FAAK AM SEE** is another small settlement set back by a kilometre or so from the waterfront, where you'll find a Strandbad and boat-rental facilities. It's the only Faakersee town that's accessible by rail from Villach: from the **train station** on the southern side of town turn left then bear right to get to the village centre, where the **tourist office**, in the Gemeindeamt (June & Sept Mon–Fri 8am–6pm, Sat 10am–noon & 2–4pm; July & Aug Mon–Fri 8am–7pm, Sat 9am–noon & 1–4pm, Sun 10am–noon; Oct–May Mon–Fri 9am–5pm; ☎04254/2110-0, fax 3855), will fix you up with a **private room**. Besides the lake, the only attraction in town is the vast model railway at **Miniwelt**, just east of the train station (May, June & Sept daily 1–6pm; July & Aug daily 10am–noon, 1–6pm & 7–9pm; Dec 25–Jan 5 daily 1–5pm; Jan 6–April 30 Sat & Sun 1–5pm).

From Faak the lakeside road continues east then north, passing a series of big, family-oriented **campsites** ranged along the shoreline before arriving in **EGG**, 5km away. Another attractive if undramatic little resort, it's a popular centre for windsurfing, as well as being home to the best of the restaurants around the Faakersee – the *Gasthof Tschebull*, on the main road at Seeuferstrasse 26, is renowned for its fresh fish.

Finkenstein

A road heads south out of Faak am See towards the partly ruined hilltop castle of **Finkenstein**, some 5km away. The spot was fortified by the Finkenstein family in the twelfth century, but with the death of the Finkenstein line the castle fell into the hands of the Habsburgs, after which Emperor Maximilian I sold it in 1512 to his finance minister Sigmund von Diedrichstein. The castle is now home to a café and restaurant, and the impressive view of the Drautal, taking in Villach, the Faakersee and the fortress of Landskron on the opposite side of the valley (see below), ensures a steady stream of sightseers. Built into the western hillside of the castle is the **Burgarena Finkenstein**, an open-air concert venue with terraced seating in the ancient Greek style. Big-name opera stars and a smattering of ageing rock has-beens perform here over the summer.

Schloss Landskron

Six kilometres northeast of Villach, just off the road to the Ossiachersee, **Schloss Landskron** dominates the northern side of the Drautal from its hilltop perch. The castle was a stronghold of Christoph von Khevenhüller in the sixteenth century. As a staunch Protestant, Christoph was to endure the confiscation of all his lands, however, and Landskron was handed over to the solidly Catholic Diedrichsteins. Though imposing from a distance, the castle is now largely ruined, the only habitable section housing a café and (fairly expensive) restaurant. Most people come here to sip coffee and admire the view towards the Karawanken mountains to the south, but there's also an **Adlerschau**, or eagle show (May–Sept daily 11am and 3pm; öS60. Just below the castle gates, **Affenberg**, or Ape Mountain (May–Oct daily 9am–noon & 1–5.30pm; 20min tours depart at 30min intervals; öS60), is a small reserve containing a forty-strong community of Japanese macaques. **Buses** on the Villach–Ossiach route pass by the access road to the castle, whence it's a twenty-minute walk uphill. Private cars can be driven right up to the castle gates, although a **toll** (öS25 per vehicle) is charged on the access road.

The Ossiachersee

Just beyond Landskron and only 8km from central Villach, the **Ossiachersee** has a completely different atmosphere from its near-neighbour the Wörthersee (see p.261). Squeezed between wooded hills, the settlements along the lake lack the hustle and bustle of places like nearby Pörtschach and Velden, and generally cater for a quieter bunch of tourists looking for family-oriented holidays. There's a wealth of campsites, small pensions and outdoor, water-based activities; nightlife is meanwhile fairly low-key, revolving around a few cosy restaurants and rustic bars.

The northern shore, served by Bundesstrasse 94 and the Villach–Feldkirchen–St Veit rail route, can get traffic-clogged in summer, and resort towns like **Annenheim**, **Bodensdorf** and **Sattendorf** lack any real character. However, the presence of the **Gerlitzen** mountain immediately to the north – served by the Kanzelbahn gondola from Annenheim – makes this a good spot for walking. The southern shore of the lake, reached from Villach by bus, is an endless procession of lake-clinging campsites, punctuated by the villages of **St Andrä**, **Ostriach** and **Ossiach**. The last, site of a historic abbey and a summer music festival, is probably the main destination these parts for visitors. There's a well-signposted cycle route all the way round the lake, although this joins the main road for long stretches.

Boat transport links the main settlements on both shores from mid-May to early October, with eight daily sailings in August – the high season – and three to four daily at other times. A single ticket costs öS80, but a better option is the **Kreuzfahrt ticket** at öS130, which is valid for two and a half hours, during which time you can hop off and on as many times as you wish.

OSSIACHERSEE ACTIVITIES

Bike rental At Bodensdorf and Sattendorf train stations, or at *Camping Kölbl*, Ostriach 184 (☎04243/8223); *Seecamping Berghof*, Heiligengestade (☎04242/41133), has a range of mountain bikes for around öS150 per day.

Kayaking *Campingplatz Lampele*, Ossiach (☎04243/2563).

Scuba diving Tauchschule Ing. Patterer, Heiligengestade (☎04242/45663); Diving Center Ossiachersee, *Hotel Aichelberghof*, Annenheim (☎0664/130 1266).

Tennis *Camping Martinz*, Ossiach (☎04243/436); Tennis Center Annenheim (☎04248/2578). You'll pay around öS100–120 per hour.

Waterskiing Helmut Schabus, *Strandhotel Fünfhaus*, Ostriach 85 (☎04243/432); Arno Blasge, next to *Hotel Seerose*, Bodensdorf (☎04243/613); and *Seecamping Berghof*, Heiligengestade (see under "Bike rental"). Expect to pay about öS100 per trip. All three places also organize beginners' courses.

Windsurfing *Seecamping Berghof*, Heiligengestade (see under "Bike rental"); *Strandpension Prinz*, Ossiach (☎04243/2271). Expect to pay about öS100 for board rental, or öS1300–1500 for a seven-day course of tuition.

The main **tourist offices** around the lake are in Bodensdorf and Sattendorf on the northern shore, and in Ossiach on the southern shore. Each of them will book private **rooms** or rooms in B&B-style **pensions** within their area. Tourist offices can also fix you up with the many four- to six-person **apartments** (with per person prices working out as cheaply as öS150) on offer around the lake – for these you're expected to stay a resonable length of time, preferably a week.

The northern shore

Travelling westwards along the northern shore, the first settlement of any note is **ANNENHEIM**, a small village whose houses creep up the sides of the **Kanzelhöhe**, the wooded ridge to the north. The **Kanzelbahn** gondola (daily 9am–12.30pm & 1–5pm; öS165 return) ascends the ridge, connecting with the **Gipfelbahn** chairlift, which continues to the 1909-metre **Gerlitzen** – also accessible by a toll road from Bodensdorf (see below). An attractive area of alpine meadow and the starting point for a number of scenic walks, the Gerlitzen also commands one of the best views in Carinthia, with Villach and the Faakersee laid out to the southwest, the Wörthersee to the southeast, and the Karawanken and the Julian Alps (the triple-peaked Triglav, Slovenia's highest mountain, is relatively easy to make out).

A **campsite**, the *Campingbad Ossiachersee* (☎04248/2757), edges the lake at the western end of the village, though the site is largely unshaded. The *Aichelberghof* **restaurant**, on the lakefront by the ship station, is a good place to dine on fresh trout or simply to hang out and drink.

Another 5km east, the much larger **BODENSDORF** commands the lion's share of the lakeside facilities along the northern shore, and serves as the departure point for a panoramic **toll road** (cars öS50, motorbikes öS25), which winds its way up to the summit of the Gerlitzen. There's a **tourist office** in the Gemeindeamt, at the northern end of the village just off the main road (June & Sept Mon–Fri 7am–6pm; July & Aug Mon–Fri 7am–7pm; Oct–May Mon–Fri 9am–noon & 1–4pm; ☎04243/8383-23, fax 8383-33), which lists plenty of **private rooms** in Bodensdorf itself and also handles accommodation in Steindorf (see p.284). Among **hotels** and **pensions**, *Frühstückspension Fischer*, Burgweg 32 (☎04243/2748, ②), is a modern house with small but neat balconied rooms (most with en-suite facilities, some cheaper ones without) at the western end of town; *Frühstückspension Blasge*, Erlenweg 2 (☎ and fax 04243/613; ②), occupies a partly wooded spot uphill from the centre; and *Sonnenhotel Garni*, Helmut-Wobisch-Weg 4 (☎04243/616, fax 2676; ④), is a slightly more upmarket place on an attractive, reedy part of the lakefront 1km northeast of town, offering balconied rooms with en-suite facilities, satellite TV and phone.

At the head of the lake, **STEINDORF** has a small Strandbad, a small campsite and plenty of rooms (bookable through the tourist office in Bodensdorf). From here, a minor road veers southwards towards the southern shore, while both Bundesstrasse 94 and the rail line continue east towards the market town of **Feldkirchen** 7km distant, then proceed to **St Veit an der Glan** (see p.268).

The southern shore

In general, the southern shore is quieter and more characterful than the north. Heading east from Villach, the lakeside road passes through the hamlet of **HEILI-GENGESTADE**, site of *Camping Berghof* (☎04242/41133), the lake's most highly rated site and home to a tennis school and a large water activities centre. The next village along, **OSTRIACH**, is home to a further three enormous **campsites**: *Camping Kölbl* (☎04243/8223), *Terrassen Camping* (☎04243/8171) and *Camping Parth* (☎04243/2744), all visible from the main road and all enjoying a stretch of the lakeshore. There are a couple of other nice places to stay in the vicinity: *Frühstuckspension Rosenheim*, Ostriach 73 (☎ & fax 04243/438; ②), a wooden, balconied house with a small outdoor pool, about five minutes' walk from the lake, and *Strandhotel Fünfhaus*, Ostriach 85 (☎04243/432, fax 432-250; ③), a large lakeside hotel with its own waterside stretch of lawn and a waterskiing school.

Ostriach fades into **OSSIACH**, the lake's most popular settlement largely because the former Benedictine abbey adds distinction to its pretty, lakeside setting. The abbey **church** (mid-May to mid-Sept daily 9am–noon & 1.30–6pm; öS20) is renowned for the cake-icing stucco-work of its interior, and serves as a concert venue during the "Carinthian Summer" festival of chamber music, which runs from June to August – information and tickets are available from **Carinthischer Sommer**, A-9570 Ossiach, Stift (☎04243/2510, fax 2353). There's a windsurfing school at *Strandpension Prinz*, just west of the abbey, and a large grassy Strandbad (öS35) beyond. Ossiach's **tourist office**, in the Gemeindeamt on the main road in the village centre (June to mid-Sept Mon–Fri 7am–7pm, Sat & Sun 9am–7pm; mid-Sept to May Mon, Wed & Thurs 7am–noon & 1–5.30pm, Tues & Fri 7am–noon; ☎04243/8420, fax 8763), will fix you up with a **private room** in either Ossiach or Ostriach, and will also give advice on the numerous pensions. Most evocative place to stay in Ossiach is the *Gasthof Seewirt* (☎04243/2268, fax 3168; ④), a sixteenth-century house down on the lakefront near the abbey. The **restaurant** of the *Gasthof zur Post*, on the main road, has a good selection of Austrian dishes, while *Pizzeria Mamma Mia*, on the lane from the main road towards the abbey and lakefront, offers good-value pizzas and pastas, in addition to a couple of fish dishes. Lower down the lane, *Naturgasthof Schlosswirt* has the best range of **vegetarian** food on the lake, with dishes like rice with spinach and tofu weighing in at around öS100. The *Disco Regina*, at the western end of the village, provides somewhere to go after closing time.

Spittal an der Drau and the Millstättersee

About 40km northwest of Villach, lying just off the main road and rail route to Salzburg, the **Millstättersee** lacks the nightlife, high-society reputation and high prices of the Wörthersee, but it holds the usual mixture of bathing, windsurfing, boating and other activities. The biggest of the three main settlements along the shore is **Seeboden**, at the western end of the lake, but by far the nicest is **Millstatt**, on the northern side, which boasts a historic abbey and a wealth of charming nineteenth-century villas, many now converted into hotels. **Döbriach**, at the eastern end, is a smaller version of Seeboden, offering accommodation and lakeside activities, but little else. There's little tourist development on the south side of the lake – only a few hotels and no real centres.

Four kilometres west of the lake, commanding the approaches to it, the historic town of **Spittal an der Drau** is an important provincial centre straddling the main Villach–Salzburg road and rail routes. The tourist office in Spittal can book **rooms** throughout the Spittal and Millstättersee region, making it a useful tourist gateway to the region; likewise, tourist offices on the lake can book rooms in Spittal.

Spittal an der Drau

SPITTAL AN DER DRAU owes its existence to the paternalism of twelfth-century aristocrats, the Ortenburgs, who established a *Spittal*, or hospice, here to care for the local poor and provide a waystation for travellers on their way across the mountain passes to the north. The hospice that gave the town its name no longer exists, and nowadays Spittal is instead largely visited for **Schloss Porcia**, a fine Renaissance chateau built by Gabriel von Salamanca, a Spanish nobleman who served as imperial treasurer in the sixteenth century. The Schloss was sold to the Austro-Italian Porcia family in 1662, although the Salamancas are still remembered by the annual **Salamancafest** in late June, when the townsfolk don sixteenth-century garb and street stalls dole out food and drink.

Spittal is the starting point of a cable car to the nearby **Goldeck** peak, and a good base from which to visit the Millstättersee. It's also the obvious place from which to catch buses to Gmünd (see p.290), 15km to the north.

The Town

Surrounded by a small park, the centrally located **Schloss Porcia** was built over seven decades from 1527 onwards. Its galleried inner courtyard is now a venue for theatre performances and concerts over the summer. Occupying the upper two floors of the Schloss, the **Museum für Volkskultur** (daily 9am–6pm; öS45) is divided up into thematically arranged rooms, devoted to such topics as education, religion, mining, village crafts and so on, each with explanatory texts in English. There's an intriguing section on winter sports, displaying the snowshoes with which locals used to get about in winter, together with the fanciful assertion that it was from footwear such as this that modern skis evolved (skis were in fact imported from Scandinavia at the turn of the century). Finally, the Fürstenzimmer contains the kind of Baroque and Rococo furnishings that might once have decorated the Porcia family home, as well as a portrait of the last of the Salamancas, Countess Catharina. According to popular myth, the miserly Catharina murdered a servant girl who had discovered the location of her secret horde of cash, and was condemned to wander the castle in ghostly form as a result.

About twenty minutes' walk south of the town centre, the **Goldeckbahn** cable car (usually operative mid-May to Oct and Dec–March) provides access to the 2142-metre Goldeck, which rises above the valley floor to the southeast. The cable car runs first to

---

SPITTAL ACTIVITIES

Bike rental At the station, from öS90 per day.

Mountaineering Alpintreff, Khevenhüllerstrasse 13 (☎04762/5045), offers mountaineering trips to the Ankogel region, including overnight stay in a hut from öS1800 per person.

Rock climbing Alpintreff (see under "Mountaineering"), has courses for children and beginners from June to September, for around öS350 for day.

a middle station, from where there's chairlift to the Bergstation, starting point for numerous trails, including the walk to the Goldeck summit just above. There's also a toll road to a point just south of the summit, leaving the valley floor at the village of **Kamering**, 12km down the valley on the Villach road.

Practicalities

Spittal's **train** and **bus stations** are 500m southwest of the centre, on Südtirolerplatz. Walk down Bahnhofstrasse and head right across the Stadtpark to reach the **tourist office** (Mon–Fri 9am–6pm, Sat 9am–1pm; ☎04762/3420, fax 3470), lurking on the far side of Schloss Porcia. You can book accommodation throughout the Millstättersee region here, as well as **private rooms** in Spittal itself.

Hotels include the family-run *Brückenwirt*, An der Wirtschaftsbrücke 2 (☎04762/2772; ②), on the banks of the Lieser stream just east of the centre, offering basic but comfy rooms with en-suite facilities. *Antoniushöhe*, Fratresstrasse 17 (☎04762/2590, fax 35480; ③), is a traditional, wooden-balconied Gasthof on a hillside northwest of town, offering neat rooms with en-suite facilities. The modern, attractively designed *Edlingerwirt*, Villacherstrase 88 (☎04762/5150, fax 50400; ④), 2km east of the centre, on the way into town from the Spittal-Ost exit of the autobahn, has en-suite rooms with satellite TV. *Ertl*, Bahnhofstrasse 26 (☎04762/20480, fax 20485; ⑥), is a comfortable business hotel next to the train station, offering rooms with en-suite facilities, satellite TV, phone and minibar.

There's a moderately good choice of eateries in town and a healthy sprinkling of bars, making Spittal a better bet for evening diversions than the lakeside resorts of the nearby Millstättersee. For **food**, probably the best places to enjoy a well-prepared, good-value Carinthian *Nud'l* dish is *Zum Spitt'l*, on Edlingerstrasse. The centrally located *Altdeutsche Weinstube*, on Neuer Platz, has a pleasant garden out the back, and also serves a standard range of Carinthian *Nud'l* dishes, as well as much more expensive fish and steaks. Across the park from Schloss Porcia, the *Bella Italia*, Schillerstrasse 3, is an Italian café-restaurant with inexpensive and fairly authentic pizzas and pastas, while *Formosa*, Kirchgasse 5 (entry also from Hauptplatz), is the best of the Chinese restaurants, with a good-value Mittagsmenü from around öS70. *Beim Rabl*, Bogengasse 14, is a smart, top-quality, though not too pricey, restaurant with a wide range of traditional Austrian as well as Carinthian dishes. *Gösser Bräu*, Villacherstrasse, is a big, brewery-owned restaurant with straightforward and dependable schnitzel and *Nud'l* dishes, and a large beer garden at the back for an evening **drink**. A popular daytime coffee-and-cake venue, *K.ü.K. Hofcafé*, Hauptplatz 4, attracts a smart, youthful crowd by night. *Hannes Café*, on Bogengasse, is a low-key but moderately trendy bar that's good for an intimate drink, while *Suzanna's Bier Pub*, on Bogengasse, is more of a smart European bar than a true pub, but it's cosy, friendly and not too expensive. The *Joker Pub*, on Hofgasse, is a friendly, intimate venue with some convincingly pub-like features, and outdoor seating in a Renaissance courtyard – there's a late-night disco-bar, *Voodoo*, next door. The atmospheric cellar-*Musikcafé* Petzl Bräu, on Bogengasse, has in-house DJs providing a techno-jungle-trip-hop soundtrack.

Seeboden and around

A five-kilometre journey over the hill from Spittal, **SEEBODEN** is a bustling little resort town at the western end of the Millstättersee – even though the only attraction is the lakefront, and the hotels that serve it. There's a big municipal **Strandbad** at the northeast end of town, otherwise visitors tend to head for the village of **TREFFLING** in the hills to the north, where **Burg Sommeregg** provides a home for the popular **Foltermuseum**, or museum of torture (May–Oct daily 10am–6pm; öS65), which is about a 45-minute walk from the centre of Seeboden – head out of town on the Spittal road and turn right when you see the sign for Treffling. With its flashy lighting and grisly tableaux, the museum goes for titillation rather than education, though a display detailing the good works of Amnesty International is prominently situated near the entrance, suggesting some moral purpose to the collection. Before Maria Theresa and her son Josef II began the slow process of reform, torture had been a standard means of extracting confessions in Austria as elsewhere; methods illustrated here include the Saw, popularized by the Spanish Inquisition, which sliced people in half from the rump upwards, and the Iron Maiden, a metal human-shaped cabinet with sharp spikes on the inside, into which suspected miscreants were placed. Smaller, more humiliating than painful punishments prove equally sobering, like the grotesque, animal-like *Schandmasken*, or "masks of shame", which petty criminals were forced to wear before being paraded through the streets, and the stocks and gags into which nagging wives were forced.

Treffling is also the starting point for walks up the 2088-metre **Tschernock** – also accessible by road as far as the **Hansbauer-Alm** just below the summit – a popular local beauty spot and vantage point.

Practicalities

Spittal–Millstatt **buses** drop off near the **tourist office**, at Hauptstrasse 93 (Mon–Fri 9am–5pm, Sat 9am–1pm; ☎04762/81210, fax 82834), where you can enquire about **private rooms** in Seeboden, or rooms and **apartments** in the farmhouses of nearby Treffling. Of the local **hotels**, *Haus Goldeckblick*, Ertlhöhe 33 (☎047662/81420; ②), is a modern building with functional balconied rooms, on the hillside north of the tourist office, while *Pension Elizabeth*, Steinerstrasse 43–47 (☎04762/81701, fax 81701-19; ③), is a mid-priced bargain occupying a traditional, balconied house near the lake, offering rooms with en-suite facilities and TV, and an owner who organizes mushroom-picking hikes. *Sporthotel Royal*, Seehofstrasse 23 (☎04762/81714, fax 81705-705; ⑤), is a large and well-appointed modern lakefront hotel, which also runs the best of the windsurfing schools and offers tennis packages in the summer. **Campsites** on the lakefront include *Strandcamping Winkler*, Seepromenade 33 (☎04762/81927, fax 81822), a big grassy site with bathing area and plenty of sporting activities, while *Camping Lieseregg* (☎04762/2723, fax 33857), 2km northwest of town along Liesereggerstrasse, is a quieter place in the countryside.

Millstatt

Four kilometres east of Seeboden, **MILLSTATT** is where Millstättersee tourism first took off in the mid-nineteenth century. The resulting building boom produced a spate of elegant lakeside holiday villas which, now transformed into hotels or family homes, lend the town a sedate, refined air. This, combined with an attractive lakeside

---

MILLSTATT ACTIVITIES

Bike rental Reisebüro Burgstaller, Marktplatz 19 (☎04766/2012-2).

Boat rental At the Strandbad, and at various points along the lakeside promenade.

Tennis *Hotel Seevilla*, for öS110 per hour.

Sailing Strobl, Seemühlgasse 56, or on the Seepromenade next to the *Marchetti Hotel* (☎04766/2263, fax 3637); öS1600 for a four-day course.

Scuba diving Tauchschule Millstatt, *Hotel Seewirt*, Kaiser-Franz-Josef-Strasse 49 (☎04766/2110).

Swimming There's an indoor Hallenbad (daily 10am–6pm; öS80) on the lakefront.

Walking From June to September, there's a *Wanderbus* taking walkers to a different Carinthian mountain destination each day of the week. Check in the Millstatt tourist office for details.

Waterskiing Strobl (see under "Sailing").

Windsurfing Strobl (see under "Sailing").

---

promenade and a large municipal Strandbad, makes Millstatt the most enticing of the lake's resorts. The attractive hillside villages within reach above town help to broaden its appeal, while the historic **abbey** in the centre hosts an annual fix of high culture during the **Internationale Musikwochen** – from May to October, chamber music performances take place in the abbey, its courtyard and in the town's modern congress centre. Information and tickets can be obtained from Musikwochen Millstatt, Stiftgasse 1, A-9872 Millstatt (☎04766/2165, fax 3479), or from the tourist office.

The abbey

Much the town's main feature, the **abbey**, just uphill from the lakefront, began life as an eleventh-century Benedictine foundation, but was handed over in 1469 to Emperor Friedrich III's **Order of the Knights of St George**. Friedrich had established the Order in 1462, in part to give thanks for military successes in Vienna, where he'd been besieged in the Hofburg by the town's own citizens. The Order's golden age, however, was to come under Friedrich's son Maximilian I, who extracted enormous propaganda from his association with the cult of St George, who was regarded as a symbol of chivalry and courage. After Maximilian's death in 1511, the Order began to lose its importance, not least because its declared foe – the Ottoman Turks – rarely came within skirmishing distance of Millstatt anyway. Emperor Ferdinand II gave the abbey to the **Jesuits** in 1612, in preparation for the re-Catholicization of what had become a predominantly Protestant area. They used the abbey's revenue to fund Graz University, and high taxes imposed on the local community led to a peasant rebellion in 1737, which was brutally put down.

The abbey **church** still preserves a few Romanesque touches, notably the tympanum above the west porch, which depicts a donor presenting Christ with a model of the church. Inside, Urban Görtschauer's medieval *Last Judgement* fresco, to the right of the high altar, is particularly striking. Many of the abbey's treasures were dispersed after the abolition of the Jesuit order in 1773, which is why a number of Millstatt's treasures are now found in Graz or Klagenfurt rather than in the monastery's small **Stiftsmuseum** (May–Sept daily 9am–noon & 2–6pm; öS30). Alongside pictures relating to the Order of St George, some copies of ecclesiastical manuscripts, and the red marble tombs of medieval clerics, is one of the three ornately decorated wedding chests of Paola Gonzaga, which contained her dowry at her marriage in 1477 to Leonhard von Görz, master of Lienz Castle (see p.296). All three chests were presented to the Order of St George in Millstatt on Paola's death, but two were subsequently expropriated by the Jesuits, and are displayed in the Domkirche in Graz (see p.219).

Practicalities

Buses from Spittal stop near the lakeside promenade, just below the abbey. Walk up through the abbey complex to reach the **tourist office**, on Marktplatz (Mon–Fri 7.30am–6pm, Sat & Sun 10am–noon & 4–6pm; ☎04766/3700, fax 3700-8), which will check vacancies in **private rooms** in town or, if you have your own transport, in the rural suburb of **Obermillstatt**, which occupies a terrace of rich farmland above town to the north. The tourist office also has information on **apartments** by the lake or on hillside farms.

Other **accommodation** choices include *Haus Brigitte*, Grossdombra 18 (☎04766/3051; ①), a small, family-run place overlooking Millstatt from the village of Grossdombra, 1km uphill to the north; take Kalvarienberggasse (which becomes Laubendorferstrasse) out of the Marktplatz to get there. Set back slightly from the lake in a villa-crowded residential street east of the Marktplatz, *Villa Waldheim*, Mirnockstrasse 110 (☎ & fax 04766/2061; ②), represents good value for a taste of nineteenth-century atmosphere; it's a friendly, family-run place with creaking floorboards and Biedermeier furnishings. *Villa Margarethe*, Mirnockstrasse 72 (☎04766/2654, fax 2654-7; ③), is another pleasant pension in a suburban house just east of the centre, by the lake with its own stretch of shoreline (also offers a few big family apartments). Most evocative (and reasonably priced) of the nineteenth-century villas on the lake, *Seevilla*, Seestrasse 68 (☎04766/2102, fax 2221; ⑤), has traditionally furnished rooms, a private bathing area, sauna and tennis courts. The nearest **campsite** is *Terrassencamping Pesenthein* (☎04766/202122, fax 202120), on the lakefront 3km to the east.

There's little to choose between the generally excellent, and reasonably priced, hotel **restaurants** that line the lakeside promenade, most of which are also good places to sample the local freshwater fish. The *Hotel Forelle* has a particularly nice waterside terrace. Though many close in winter, the restaurant of the *Hotel Seewirt*, slightly inland at Kaiser-Franz-Josef-Strasse 49, stays open year-round. Elsewhere in the town centre, *Pizzeria Pepino*, just across the way from the Strandbad, is an inexpensive and lively place that stays open until 11pm – by which time most other places have closed – and *Hotel Post*, Mirnockstrasse 38, offers high-quality Austrian cuisine in comfortable surroundings, as well as a good-value lunchtime buffet.

Best of the **drinking** venues are *Café Columbia* on Georgsritterplatz, a good choice both day and night, which also serves cheap pizzas and wonderful ice creams, and the café of the *Hubertusschlössl* hotel on Seestrasse, which has a nice lakeside terrace. The bar of the *Ritterkeller* **disco** on Marktplatz stays open until 4am.

Beyond Millstatt: Döbriach

Eight kilometres beyond Millstatt, **DÖBRIACH** marks the Millstättersee's eastern extent, a resort village full of modern apartment hotels that spreads over the flatlands where the Riegerbach enters the lake. There's a string of pay-to-enter bathing areas along the lakeshore, many of which also offer boat rental and other sporting activities. The **tourist office**, about 1km east of the lake on the Hauptplatz (☎04246/7878), has a list of **private rooms** and **apartments**, though a stay of more than three days is expected in the latter; otherwise there are plenty of **pensions** in the ② bracket – try the traditional *Haus Kärnten*, Seestrasse 41 (☎04246/7122), trimmed with window boxes, or the more modern and functional *Haus Mayer*, Seestrasse 11 (☎04246/7813), both about ten minutes away from the lake on the main street leading inland. There's a wealth of **campsites** on or near the lakefront, all of which are well equipped, have access to bathing areas and lay on events for kids in summer: *Burgstaller* (☎04246/7774, fax 7774-4) is one of the biggest; *Ebner* (☎04246/7735-18, fax 7735-13), is smaller and less animated.

DÖBRIACH ACTIVITIES

Sailing Strandbad Burgstaller, Seepromenade 50 (☎04246/7763), or Sacher, Parkbad Döbriach (☎04246/7768). Both offer courses for all abilities; you'll pay öS2100 and up for a week's tuition.

Tennis Courts available at either the Parkbad or *Camping Burgstaller*, for öS90–110 per hour.

Waterskiing Strandbad Sittlinger, Seepromenade 52 (☎04246/7118).

Windsurfing Strandbad Burgstaller or Sacher (see under "Sailing"). Both places rent boards and run courses: you'll pay around öS350 for a day or afternoon introductory course; öS2100 and upwards for seven days.

Gmünd and around

The Salzburg-bound A10 autobahn heads north from Spittal up the Liesertal, continuing onwards to the **Katschberg tunnel**, which marks the border between Carinthia and the Salzburger Land. The obvious place to stop off en route is the medieval townlet of **Gmünd**, 15km north of Spittal and served by frequent local buses. An engaging destination in its own right, Gmünd is also a good base from which to visit the **Maltatal**, a highland valley nestling beneath an eastern spur of the Hohe Tauern range.

On leaving the Drautal, the autobahn advances up the Liesertal on concrete stilts, while the old Bundesstrasse (served by local buses) sticks to the valley floor, meandering along the forest-fringed course of the river. Twelve kilometres out of Spittal, the road passes through **TREBESING**, an important centre for family-oriented tourism dubbed "Austria's First Babydorf" by energetic local boosters. An unfashionable spa-resort with an ageing clientele until a decade ago, the village is now packed with hotels and pensions offering facilities for infants and their respite-seeking parents. An **information bureau** on the main road (dawn–dusk; ☎04732/3000) allocates accommodation. Trebesing's bigger hotels offer on-site baby-minding facilities and a range of activities for children, while the smaller Gasthöfe and pensions make use of the central nursery facilities provided by the village. *Trebesinger Hof Babyhotel*, Trebesing 1 (☎04372/2350; ④), is one of the larger, better-equipped establishments. The resort's only drawback is its popularity – it's teeming with toddlers.

Gmünd

Founded by the archbishops of Salzburg in the eleventh century to protect the trade routes that gave them a firmer hold on Carinthian life, **GMÜND** preserves much of its medieval character. Small, compact and traversed by cobbled alleyways spanned by little arches, it shelters a profusion of small galleries and craft shops, together with a brace of idiosyncratic museums.

Lined with medieval houses colourwashed in pastel shades, Gmünd's pretty Hauptplatz stretches from north to south, with the old town gates standing guard at each end. Alleyways leads westwards from the Hauptplatz to the building known as "Im Loch", a former jailhouse, which now holds the **Eva Faschaunerin Ausstellung** (May–Oct daily 9am–noon & 2–6pm; öS40), a collection recalling the local murderer who was the last person to be executed in the district. According to the prosecution, Eva killed her husband, Jakob Kary Hörlbauer, on a March day in 1770, by putting arsenic – mined locally for use in the dyeing industry – in his supper. She was executed in November 1773. Telling her story through a series of tableaux and (German-language) texts, the museum serves as a powerful evocation of eighteenth-century

Carinthian life. There's a recreation of the kitchen where the dirty deed was done, and of the rack where she was tortured into confession.

A short distance south of the Eva Faschaunerin museum, the thirteenth-century **Pfarrkirche Maria Himmelfahrt** boasts a rather bland Baroque interior; of greater interest, the **Karner**, or charnel house, outside is decorated with fourteenth-century frescoes depicting scenes of the New Testament, including a vibrant *Adoration of the Magi* in which Christ's manger is watched over by quaintly rendered farm animals. A few steps west of the church is the **Porsche-Automuseum** (daily: mid-May to mid-Oct 9am–6pm; mid-Oct to mid-May 10am–4pm; öS50), a must for anyone who enthuses over cars, and an intriguing slice of history for anyone who doesn't. Assembled by local collector Helmut Pfeifhofer, the well-arranged exhibit documents the output of the prolific Austrian-born designer Ferdinand Porsche. The oldest of the cars on show is the 1924 taxi built by the Austrian branch of Daimler, where Porsche worked as technical director immediately after World War I. From 1934 he worked in Stuttgart on the development of the VW Beetle, but allied bombing forced Volkswagen to disperse their production facilities to more isolated locations in 1944, and Porsche and his design team relocated to the village of Karnerau, 2km north of Gmünd. They stayed here until 1950, though Porsche himself was imprisoned by the French for two years immediately after the war due to his work on military vehicles. It was in Karnerau that the classic Porsche 356 sports car was first built, several rare examples of which are on display.

Standing at the northern end of town on an easily scaled hillock are the remnants of the thirteenth-century **Alte Burg**, where representatives of the Salzburg archbishops once held sway. Habitable portions are occupied by a restaurant and café-bar. Rock and jazz concerts take place in the castle courtyard on summer weekends. Further north, 1km out of town beside the main Bundesstrasse, is the oddity known as the **Geteilte Kirche**, or divided church. Comprising two buildings divided by a country lane, the church began life as a small roadside chapel and became an increasingly popular shrine in the eighteenth century. Unfortunately, there was no space to enlarge it, so an additional building was constructed on the opposite roadside, allowing the priest to conduct services on one side while the congregation sat on the other.

Practicalities

Buses come to rest in the Hauptplatz, just opposite the **tourist office** at no. 20 (☎04732/2197, fax 2197-21), which has a small number of **private rooms** at its disposal. Best of the **hotels** is the *Kohlmaier*, Hauptplatz 7 (☎04732/2149, fax 2153; ③), a lovely old Gasthof whose traditionally furnished rooms have en-suite facilities and TV; if it's full, *Gasthof zur Post*, Hauptplatz 17 (☎04732/2212; ③), is a comfortable alternative.

For **food**, the *Kohlmaier* is very much the focus of local life, offering a range of Austrian cuisine at medium prices, as well as being a good place to have a **drink**. The restaurant at the *Gasthof zur Post* has good food if slightly higher prices. *Café-Konditorei Nussbaumer*, also on Hauptplatz, is the town's main daytime coffee-and-cakes venue, while *Café 99*, just opposite, has a slightly younger clientele and is a good place to go in the evening.

The Maltatal

Heading northwest from Gmünd, a minor road ascends the **Maltatal** towards the **Kölnbrein reservoir**, 32km away at the head of the valley. It's a popular route, largely because it provides access to some desolate alpine uplands in the shadow of the 3246-metre Ankogel and its foothills, but also because the reservoir at the end boasts one of Austria's most impressive pieces of civil engineering, the **Kölnbreinsperre** (Kölnbrein Dam). Reaching the area is easy if you have your own transport, though the last 15km of the journey is via toll road, the **Malta-Hochalm-Strasse** (May to mid-Oct; öS120 per vehicle). Public transport of a sort exists during the Hochalm-Strasse's period of operation, with a weekly bus running from Gmünd to the dam (currently Tues; check at the Gmünd tourist office for details). It's a highly scenic ride, as the narrow road negotiates tortuous switchbacks, passing through several tunnels along the way. Traffic lights control the flow of traffic by day in order to minimize the risk of collisions; they don't work after 6pm, when greater vigilance must be exercised.

The Hochalm-Strasse culminates beside the elegant curve of the dam, built in the 1970s to collect glacial waters from the ring of mountains that forms the Hohe Tauern range's easternmost spur. Above the dam sits the curiously barrel-shaped **Panoramaturm**, a "panoramic tower" holding café, restaurant, hotel and the **Tauernschatzkammer**, a small exhibition of crystals (free), which includes a film about the Hohe Tauern National Park and a ten-minute video telling the story of the dam's construction. Guided **tours** of the dam interior are available throughout the summer (times are posted at the entrance of the Tauernschatzkammer; öS40), worth considering for the eerie atmosphere that reigns within the dam wall, rather than the barrage of mind-boggling statistics about how many cubic metres of concrete were needed in order to build it. The tours last 45 minutes and are conducted in German, although guides might give an English summary if requested.

A broad track leads westwards around the reservoir from the dam, providing walkers with good views of the surrounding mountains. A popular walk suitable for the moderately fit day-tripper is the hike to the **Osnabrücker Hütte** (2hr one way), which lies just beyond the western end of the reservoir on the shoulder of the Ankogel. A slightly more demanding itinerary, involving steeper ascents, is the walk from the dam to the **Katowitzer Hütte** (3hr 30min one way), which lies on the slopes of the Hafnergruppe to the southeast. To pick up this trail, walk back down the Hochalm-Strasse from the dam for about 1km until you see a sign leading uphill to the left.

Heiligenblut and the Grossglockner

Northwest of Spittal, both the main Salzburg-bound rail line and the A106 Bundesstrasse head up the Mölltal towards the imposing mountains of the **Hohe Tauern**. At **Obervellach**, a road splits off to the west and veers towards the Mölltal, climbing towards the chocolate-box alpine village of **Heiligenblut**, which shelters beneath Austria's highest peak, the **Grossglockner**. Both rail line and Bundesstrasse continue straight on from Obervellach towards the **Tauern tunnel**, emerging in the Gasteinertal and the Salzburger Land (see Chapter 6) on the other side. Car drivers must pay for their vehicle to be transported through the tunnel by rail; wagons carrying the cars operate from 6.30am to 10.30pm southbound, and from 6am to 10pm northbound (öS190 one way, öS320 return).

Heiligenblut

One of the most attractively situated villages in the Austrian Alps, **HEILIGENBLUT** is little more than a narrow strip of houses clinging to the west side of the valley, with the snow-clad summit of the 3798-metre **Grossglockner** in the distance to the north. It's a scene dominated by the tall spire of the cream-and-ochre **Pfarrkirche St Vinzenz**, a fifteenth-century structure that's very much the village trademark. The church was built by monks from Admont in Styria to hold a vial purported to contain the blood of Christ – hence the village's name, which translates as "holy blood". According to legend, the vial was brought to the area from Byzantium by St Briccius, who was consumed by an avalanche when attempting to cross the Alps, leaving the holy relic to be recovered by rescuers. It's now contained in an extravagantly pinnacled Gothic reliquary inside the church to the left of the choir. The high altar, an early sixteenth century affair featuring the Virgin flanked by saints Barbara and Catherine, is thought to be the work of Wolfgang Asslinger, a member of Michael Pacher's studio.

The slopes east of the village provide ample **skiing** terrain (suitable largely for intermediates; a one-day lift pass costs öS350, seven-day öS1600), and some of the lifts that serve them are open in July and August for summer walkers. A cable car leaves the village centre (just opposite the *Hotel Post*) for the 1750-metre **Rossbach**, from where you can take another cable car to the 2600-metre **Schareck**, or a funicular through a tunnel to the **Fleisalm**, an area of alpine meadow below the 2989-metre **Gjaidtroghöhe**.

Practicalities

Buses stop just above the **tourist office** on the main street (Mon–Fri 9am–12.30pm & 2–5.30pm, Sat 9am–12.30pm & 2–4pm; ☎04824/2001-21, fax 2001-43), where you can enquire about vacancies in **private rooms**, pensions and apartments. Cheapest **pension** in the centre is probably the *Bergkristall*, near the Rossbach cable-car station at Hof 71 (☎04824/2005, fax 2005-33; ①), which has some rooms with shared facilities, as well as more expensive ones with en-suite shower and WC. There are plenty more good-value pensions down in the valley bottom: *Margit*, Hadergasse 3 (☎04824/2011; ②), and *Edelweiss*, Hadergasse 17 (☎ & fax 04824/2083; ②), are two comfy, family-run B&B places. If you want a central **hotel** with all the creature comforts, the most atmospheric is the *Villa Kaiser-Franz-Josef*, Hof 45 (☎04824/2084, fax 2084-13; ⑦), also featuring a sauna and gym, in a large, timber-balconied traditional house. There's a **youth hostel** just downhill from the centre, at Hof 36 (☎ & fax 04824/2259; Jan–Sept), and a **campsite**, *Möllfluss* (☎04824/2129), lower down still in the valley bottom.

For **eating**, the *Dorfstube*, on the main street, features an inexpensive menu of Austrian regulars and pizzas, while the *Hotel Post* has a much wider range of local cuisine and only slightly higher prices.

The Grossglockner Hochalpenstrasse

The main excursion from Heiligenblut is to drive or journey by bus along the **Grossglockner Hochalpenstrasse**, a scenic toll road (mid-May to late Oct; cars öS350, motorbikes öS250, bus passengers pay a small fee included in the price of their ticket) that heads northeast from the village, rising above the Möll Valley towards the **Grossglockner Pass** (just east of the mountain similarly named), which marks the border between Carinthia and the Salzburger Land. It's a tortuous but spectacular ascent, occasionally allowing glimpses of the Grossglockner itself, a mountain first conquered in 1799, when Count Salm, bishop of Gurk and an enthusiastic promoter of alpinism, led a party of locals to the summit. Most sightseers turn left a few kilometres short of the top to enjoy a side-trip along the **Gletscherstrasse** to **Franz-Josefs-Höhe**, an itinerary more fully described on pp.345–346. One **bus** a day (three in July and Aug) serves the Franz-Josefs-Höhe, commencing in Lienz and passing through Heiligenblut on the way. Once there, you can pick up a connecting service to the lakeside resort of **Zell am See** (see Chapter 6) on the northern side of the pass.

EAST TYROL

Separated from the rest of the Tyrol by Italy, the **East Tyol** (Osttirol) is usually approached from Carinthia, tha Land with which it has the best transport links. Despite possessing some of the most dramatic mountain scenery in Austria, the the East Tyrol has, strangely, never enjoyed the same level of tourist development as northern Tyrol

...es in East Tyrol are featured in the package-holiday brochures, so trav-
...n tackling the pistes here will have to make arrangements independently.
...bably the most versatile base, with the **Zettersfeld** east of town providing
...rrain suitable for beginners and intermediates – descents of the Hochstein to
th... ...west prove more demanding. Lienz is also a big enough town to possess a modicum o. nightlife. The same can't be said of the three main resorts to the north – **Matrei**,
Prägraten and **St Jakob** – small villages that are nonetheless good for beginners and
intermediates. **Kals** is an emerging resort suitable for beginners and families, with nursery slopes just outside the village and several hotels catering for small children. **Ski
passes** for the East Tyrol's winter resorts are slightly cheaper than those elsewhere in
Austria: expect to pay öS280–300 for one day (children about half as much). Combined
ski passes for the Glockner–Dolomiten area are available if you fancy travelling across to
the ski regions in western Carinthia; they cover Kals, Matrei, Prägraten, St Jakob, Sillian,
Lienz, Heiligenblut and Mallnitz, and cost öS1600 for a week (half as much for children).

or the Salzburger Land – and therein lies its appeal. Towns like the local administrative
capital **Lienz** and villages like **Kals** and **Matrei** are perfectly equipped for skiing and
walking, but are spared the large numbers of Eurotourists that regularly descend on
places like Seefeld, Mayrhofen and St Anton. To outsiders, the East Tyrol seems marvellously unspoilt, though locals have sometimes felt a little left out of the main currents
of Austrian life. The separation of East Tyrol from the rest of the province, following
the award of the South Tyrol to Italy in 1919, was a big blow for the region, producing
feelings of isolation only partially alleviated by the building of the Grossglockner
Hochalpenstrasse in 1936 and the **Felber Tauern** tunnel in 1967.

Lienz can be reached by rail either from Innsbruck in the west (with trains running
through a corner of Italy to get here) or from Spittal an der Drau to the east. The
Felber Tauern tunnel presents the region's main road link with Austria north of the
Alps, with two daily buses making the journey here from Kitzbühel and Kufstein in
northeastern Tyrol. It's also possible to get here from Zell am See via the
Grossglockner Hochalpenstrasse in summer, with bus passengers changing at the
Franz-Josefs-Höhe.

Lienz

Standing at the confluence of the Drau and Isel, **LIENZ** sprawls beneath the ragged,
hostile slopes of the **Lienzer Dolomiten**, strangely beautiful peaks that adopt a pinkish hue in the early morning sun. Located at the southern end of two important
transalpine routes – the Felber Tauern and the Grossglockner Pass – the town has long
been an important staging post for those travelling onwards to Italy. The Romans were
the first to recognize this spot's potential, planting the settlement of **Aguntum** some
5km east of the modern town, near the village of Dölsach, where its scant remains can
still be seen. Settled by German-speaking tribes in the ninth century, medieval Lienz
enjoyed a brief period of importance as the seat of the powerful **counts of Görz**, from
what is now Gorizia in Italy, until 1500, when the last of the counts, Leonhard, died without an heir. The territory then fell to Emperor Maximilian I, who incorporated Lienz
and its environs into the Tyrol. Both **Schloss Bruck**, erstwhile residence of the counts
of Görz, and the **Stadtpfarrkirche St Andrä**, where Leonhard was entombed, provide
modern sightseers with a focus, although World War II air raids put an end to the
town's other medieval remnants.

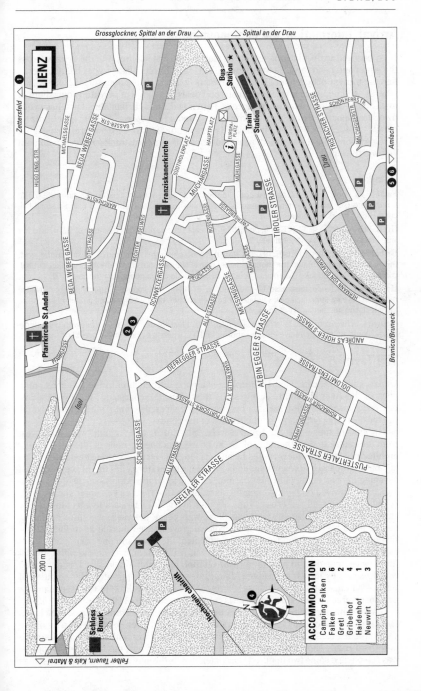

LIENZ

Grossglockner, Spittal an der Drau △   △ Spittal an der Drau

Zettersfeld △ ➊

▷ Amlach

Felber Tauern, Kals & Matrei ▷

Brunico/Bruneck ▷

Schloss Bruck

Pharrkirche St Andrä

Franziskanerkirche

Bus Station ★

Train Station

EUROPA PLATZ

HAUPTPLATZ

SÜDTIROLERPLATZ

Hochstein chairlift

ACCOMMODATION

Camping Falken	5
Falken	6
Gretl	2
Gribelhof	4
Haidenhof	1
Neuwirt	3

200 m

0

Streets: HUGO ENGL-STR, MICHAELSGASSE, BEDA WEBER GASSE, J. GASSER-STR, MARCHER STR, BILLROTHSTRASSE, RECHTER ISELWEG, MUCHARGASSE, ROSENGASSE, SCHWEIZERGASSE, KREUZGASSE, MESSINGGASSE, ALLEESTRASSE, DÉFREGGER STRASSE, MÜHLGASSE, ZWERGGASSE, TIROLER STRASSE, ALBIN EGGER STRASSE, ANDREAS HOFER-STRASSE, DOLOMITENSTRASSE, A. ROHRACHER STRASSE, F.V. OTTER WEG, ADOLF PURTSCHER STRASSE, SCHLOSSGASSE, ISELTALER STRASSE, PUSTERTALER STRASSE, HERMANN VON GILMWEG, TRISTACHER STRASSE, SCHÖNHERRSTR, WALCHEGGERSTR, PEARRGASSE, BEDA WEBER GASSE, N

Arrival, information and accommodation

Both **bus** and **train stations** are on Tirolerstrasse, just southeast of the centre. Cross the street and head towards the modern flagstoned Europaplatz to your left in order to find the **tourist office**, at no. 1 (Mon–Fri 8am–6pm, Sat 9am–noon; ☎04852/6526-5, fax 5265-2), which gives out free town maps and deals in a range of **private** rooms, both in town and in the neighbouring villages of **Thurn** and **Amlach** (suitable if you have your own transport). There's a **campsite**, *Komfort-Camping Falken*, Eichholz 7 (☎04852/64022, fax 64022-6), in the fields 1km south of town. To get there, turn left out of the station, take the next left, pass underneath the railway tracks and carry on until you see the sign.

Hotels

Falken, Eichholz 1 (☎71022, fax 64022-6). In the fields south of town, next to the campsite of the same name (see above), offering comfortable rooms with en-suite bathroom, TV and a small balcony. Buffet breakfast included in the room price. ④.

Gretl, Schweizergasse 32 (☎62106, fax 61979). Cheapest centrally located source of B&B, offering simple rooms with en-suite facilities. ②.

Gribelhof, Schlossberg 10 (☎62191, fax 70030). Overlooking the town from a hillside to the west, this is a wonderfully situated traditional Gasthof whose simple rooms have en-suite facilities and balconies. To get there, take the road to Schloss Bruck and keep on going past the castle. ②.

Haidenhof, Grafendorferstrasse 12 (☎62440, fax 62440-6). A relaxing, comfortable hotel, whose rooms all have en-suite facilities, satellite TV and telephone. Attractively located amidst fields on the hillside in the northern part of town. ④.

Neuwirt, Schweizergasse 22 (☎62101, fax 62101-33). Pleasant downtown Gasthof with plain, functional rooms, all of which have en-suite shower and TV. There's a good buffet breakfast, too. ④.

The Town

Lienz's attractive, café-filled **Hauptplatz** is a good introduction to the laid-back ambience of the Austrian south. A few steps west along Muchargasse, the **Franziskanerkirche** harbours a few garishly restored Gothic frescoes, but it's better to head for the town's two major sights on the fringes of the centre.

The first of these, the **Stadtpfarrkirche St Andrä**, a ten-minute walk northwest from the centre to the other side of the River Isel, is a fine example of fifteenth-century architecture, picturesquely ringed by an arcaded cemetery. Its entrance guarded by an age-battered pair of Romanesque lions, the church interior bears the heavy imprint of seventeenth- and eighteenth-century intervention, although impressive medieval paintings have survived on pillars lining the nave; one to the right as you enter shows a red-robed St Andrew on the cross, while another to the left carries a fourteenth-century cautionary image of Death trampling those who gorge themselves with meat during fasting periods. Two impressive late-medieval graves in red marble lie in the aisles – that of Graf Leonhard von Görz on the left side of the nave, and one of his successors as lord of the local castle, Michael Freiherr von Wolkenstein, over on the right. Amidst the arcades outside, the **war memorial chapel**, built after World War I, is decorated with frescoes by local-born painter Albin Egger-Lienz (see opposite). His rendition of Jesus – an emaciated figure whose skimpy loincloth leaves little to the imagination – was considered so shocking that priests refused to celebrate Mass here until the 1980s.

A fifteen-minute walk due west from the Hauptplatz along Schweizergasse, **Schloss Bruck** (Easter–Oct daily except Mon 10am–5pm; öS60) overlooks the town from the partly wooded flanks of the Schlossberg. Outwardly, the tower, with its Romanesque windows, is the only sign of the castle's thirteenth-century origins; the rest of what you see was remodelled some two hundred years later. Inside, the jumble of domestic furnishings and agricultural implements that crowds the rooms of the **Heimatmuseum** is far out-shone by the fifteenth-century frescoes in the Schloss's **chapel**, painted by Simon von Taisten for Count Leonhard. Leonhard and his wife, Paola von Gonzaga, feature promi-nently: they're shown kneeling in the depiction of the *Death of the Virgin*, on the left of the nave, as well as in the scene with St Elizabeth on the right, while also putting in an appearance with the *Madonna and Child* in the high altar. The castle's other main high-light is the **picture gallery**, which trots through a series of underachieving East Tyrolean artists before arriving at the canvases of **Franz von Deferegger** – an influential nine-teenth-century realist whose paintings elevated the status of the Tyrolean peasant to that of a subject fit for art – and the more disturbing paintings of his spiritual successor, **Albin Egger-Lienz** (1868–1926). Born near Lienz (hence the adopted surname), Albin shared Deferegger's love of the Tyrol and its people, and early on portrayed their sufferings in a hard, muscular style. He was also profoundly affected by World War I, having served on the Italian front, and his subsequent work was filled with spiritual pessimism and allu-sions to death. Egger-Lienz's work was extremely influential in Italy, but his lack of a high profile elsewhere in Europe – especially in Austria – is hard to explain. His application for a teaching post at the Vienna Academy in 1910 was turned down on the insistence of ill-fated Archduke Franz-Ferdinand, who fancied himself as an arbiter of public taste.

Into the mountains

The jagged outline of the Dolomites provide an impressive backdrop to the town, but their upper reaches are inaccessible to all but the most experienced rock climbers. Most skiing and walking takes place on the more hospitable heights to the north, most notably the **Zettersfeld**, a large area of upland meadow served by cable car (mid-June to early Oct Fri–Mon, Tues & Sun 9am–noon & 1–5pm; öS140) from the northern edge of town, at the end of Zettersfeldstrasse – a free minibus sometimes runs here from the train station in summer. At the top, a chairlift continues to the 2214-metre **Steinermandl**, starting point for walks up to the **Neualpseen**, a group of small moun-tain lakes surrounded by desolate moorland.

At the western end of town, next to the access road to Schloss Bruck, the two-stage **Hochsteinbahn** chairlift (mid-June to mid-Sept Wed–Sun 9am–noon & 1–5pm; öS120 return) rises to the 1016-metre **Moosalm**, site of the **Venedigerwarte** viewing tower and a farmyard zoo, for children, before continuing to the 1511-metre **Sternalm**, whence reasonably fit walkers can consider striking uphill towards the 2023-metre **Hochsteinhütte** above.

Eating and drinking

Notwithstanding a fair sprinkling of ethnic restaurants and typically Austrian Gasthöfe, **eating** out in Lienz is definitely a Tyrolean experience, with regional specialities like *Tiroler Gröstl* and *Schlipfkrapfen* dominating most menus. Proximity to Italy ensures a high standard of northern Italian cuisine, *haute* and otherwise: *Pizzadiele* on the Hauptplatz is a good place to pick up a pizza-slice **snack**. The outdoor cafés of the Hauptplatz help to turn **drinking** here into an almost Mediterranean experience in summer, and there's a wide choice of bars to boot.

Restaurants

Adlerstüberl, Andrä-Kranz-Gasse 7. Lienz's oldest restaurant, serving up a mid-priced range of Austrian and traditional Tyrolean food.

El Paso, in the Rosenpassage, just off Rosengasse. Restaurant with "fun" cantina atmosphere, offer-ing a fairly perfunctory range of Mexican standards, as well as jacket potatoes and steaks. Often fea-tures a good-value Mittagsmenü.

Edlinger, Schlossberg 6. Just downhill from the castle, serving grilled meats and a reasonable choice of fish, for medium prices.

Haidenhof, Grafendorferstrasse 12. Hotel restaurant north of town with mid-priced Tyrolean specialities as well as the full range of Austrian dishes. The outdoor terrace provides a great view of the Dolomites on the opposite side of the valley.

La Cucina della Mamma, Südtirolerplatz. Best of the Italians, with a not-too-pricey range of pizzas and pasta dishes served in wood-panelled, subterranean rooms.

Neuwirt, Schweizergasse 22. The best place to go for fish, and not too expensive, with plenty of outdoor seating.

Cafés and bars

Becks, alleyway off Rosengasse. Funky drinking venue that's always packed.

Café Wha, Schweizergasse 3. Popular, youthful hangout with alternative-rockish background music and a nice sideline in toasted sandwiches and soups.

City-Café Glanzl, Hauptplatz. Lienz's classic daytime coffeehouse and patisserie.

Dancingbar Joy, Hauptplatz. Subterranean disco-bar catering for a slightly older age group than the Stadtkeller (see below) – a convivial place to hang out in the early hours.

s'Eck, Hauptplatz 20. Best of the cafés with outdoor seating on the main square, plus a refined upstairs café and a pub-like beer cellar in a lovely medieval vaulted space downstairs.

s'Stöckl, Zwergergasse 2. Loud and friendly pub focused on a small circular bar.

Stadtkeller, Tirolerstrasse 30. Biggest of Lienz's discos, a predominantly techno-friendly venue in a cellar opposite the tourist office.

North of Lienz

North of Lienz, the main road ascends the Iseltal towards the **Felber Tauern**, an important route that tunnels from south to north through the Hohe Tauern and emerges near Mittersill in the Salzburger Land (see Chapter 6). **Matrei in Osttirol**, a small skiing and hiking resort, is the main centre along the way, although many of the side-valleys feeding the Isel are equally deserving of a visit. On the eastern side of Matrei, a road up the **Kalsertal** leads to the picturesque village of **Kals**, which lies in the southeastern shadows of the Grossglockner. To the west, both the **Defereggental** and the **Virgental** harbour a series of small ski villages worth a quick side-trip in summer.

The Defereggental

Twenty kilometres northwest of Lienz, the village of **Huben** stands at an important cross-roads, as the main road continues north towards Matrei and the Virgental (see p.300), and a secondary road splits off to the northeast and Kals. A third road branches off due west into the **Defereggental**, a photogenic narrow valley slotted between two impressive mountain chains, the Defereggengebirge to the south and the Lasörlinggruppe to the north. Twenty-five kilometres out of Huben, the village of **ST JAKOB** is a popular local skiing spot in winter. The two-stage **Mooserberg** gondola, 2km west of the village, provides access to an expanse of unspoilt alpine pastureland above the valley to the south. Six kilometres beyond St Jakob, the road splits: the left fork (served by twice daily buses in summer) heads for the Italian border at the **Staller Sattel Pass**, 6km away, and a very steep descent towards Bruneck/Brunico; the right fork (May–Oct only) continues up the Defereggental as far as *Alpengasthof Oberhaus*, on the border of the Hohe Tauern National Park (see p.341) and the starting point for several walking trails.

Kals

From Huben, the road to **KALS** zigzags its way uphill from the Iseltal to the **Kalsertal**, an appealing subalpine vale strewn with wooden farmsteads and tumbledown barns. Properly speaking, Kals itself is the collective name for a grouping of three hamlets: Kals-Lesach, Kals-Ködnitz and Kals-Grossdorf. You encounter the rustic huddle of farms that calls itself **Lesach** 10km out of Huben – it's bypassed by the main road, but buses stop here. There's more in the way of facilities 2km further, in **Ködnitz**, site of the Kals **tourist office** (Mon–Fri 8.30am–noon & 2–6pm, Sat 8.30am–noon; ☎04876/211, fax 433), a couple of shops and the **Ruprechtskirche**, which has a sixteenth-century mural of the Crucifixion inside. **Grossdorf**, barely 1km up the valley from Ködnitz, is where most tourist development has been concentrated, with a smattering of chalet-style hotels and plenty of farmhouses offering apartments. At the entrance to Grossdorf, the fourteenth-century **Georgikapelle**, a small whitewashed edifice dwarfed by its own spire, presides serenely over the cow pastures.

Into the mountains

It's Grossdorf that commands most of the routes into the mountains, with the **Glocknerblick** chairlift ascending to the heights west of the village, where views towards the Grossglockner to the northeast are the main draw. Eight kilometres north of Grossdorf up the Dorfertal, the café-restaurant at the **Kalser Tauernhaus** is another popular destination for both sightseers and walkers, where trails continue north up the Dabaklamm defile to the Dorfersee, with the Grossglockner to the right and the Granatspitze to the left. The road to the *Kalser Tauernhaus* lies within the Hohe Tauern National Park and is closed to private cars, but you can walk or take a bus from Kals-Ködnitz.

The **Kalserglocknerstrasse** toll road heads eastwards from Kals-Ködnitz up to the **Gasthof Lucknerhaus**, about 5km distant, whence several trails lead up onto the slopes of the Grossglockner. The most important, climbing to the 3454-metre *Erzherzog-Johann-Hütte* on the southeast shoulder, is one for experienced walkers or those accompanied by local guide.

Kals as a whole is a good base for mounting supervised assaults on the peaks of the Hohe Tauern: **mountain guides** can be contacted through *Haus Zeiner*, Kals-Ködnitz 31 (mid-June to Sept Mon–Sat 8.30–10.30am & 5–7pm, Sun 5–7pm; ☎04876/263). Among the many trips offered, an ascent of Grossglockner in a four-person group would cost öS1400 each.

Practicalities

The **tourist office** in Kals-Ködnitz will sort out **private rooms** and apartments throughout the area; late arrivals should be able to find a place by heading straight for Kals-Grossdorf and looking for "*Zimmer Frei* signs". Of the various **hotels and pensions** nearby, *Haus Oberlohr*, in Kals-Lesach (☎04876/266, fax 325; ①), offers rooms with shared facilities in a nice wood-clad farmhouse, while the *Ködnitzhof*, Kals-Ködnitz (☎04876/201, fax 201-2; ②), has adequate rooms, some en suite. The *Hotel Krone*, Kals-Grossdorf (☎04876/241, fax 448; ④), is a well-appointed modern building, and the *Jenshof*, Kals-Grossdorf (☎04876/520, fax 520-81; ⑤), is a "baby" hotel complete with playground, baby-listening devices and babysitting facilities. Five kilometres uphill to the east, the *Alpengasthof Lucknerhaus* (☎04867/291, fax 5555; ③) is an ideal base for walking; you might feel a bit cut off here, but it does have a reasonable restaurant.

Matrei and around

Thirty kilometres north of Lienz, just off the main road to the Felber Tauern, **MATREI** is a pleasantly sleepy, meadow-fringed resort, a good alternative to the skiing centres of the Salzburger Land and the Tyrol and equally satisfying in summer. The two-stage **Goldried** chairlift on the eastern side of the village provides the main local excursion, although there are plenty of easy walks into the **Virgental**, which curves away to the east. Nearest of these is the walk to the historic **Nikolaikirche**, its whitewashed form clearly visible in a meadow 2km southwest of Matrei. The church is unusual in preserving a Romanesque choir on two levels, the upper, balustraded storey coloured by frescoes of the period.

There's a **tourist office** on the village square (Mon–Fri 9am–noon & 3–6pm, Sat 9am–noon; ☎04875/6527, fax 6527-0), which will help with **private rooms** and advise on vacancies in local ski-oriented hotels – note that many of these close in late spring and autumn. The *Hotel Goldried*, Goldriedstrasse 15 (☎04875/6113; ④), is an imaginatively laid-out cluster of buildings on a hillside, with outdoor pool. There's also a **campsite**, the *Edengarten*, at the southern end of the village. The **restaurant** of the *Hotel Rauter*, Rauterplatz, has a delicious and not-too-expensive range of top-quality Austrian food, and there are always a couple of vegetarian choices on the menu.

The Virgental

West of Matrei, a minor road runs up the verdant **Virgental** towards the village of **Virgen**, where the *Neuwirt* on the main road is a good place to stop off for some traditional Tyrolean food. Two kilometres further on, the village of **Obermauern** shelters below the small **Wallfahrtskirche unserer lieber Frau**, which is decorated with frescoes by Simon van Taisten – the man responsible for most of the work in the chapel at Schloss Bruck (see p.296). West of here, the road enters **Prägraten**, a small winter sports centre cowering beneath the Venedigergruppe massif to the north. Most buses from Lienz terminate here, although three daily services (summer only) proceed as far as **Ströden** at the head of the valley, where a three-kilometre walking trail leads to the **Umbalfälle**, a romantic spot popular with local day-trippers.

travel details

Trains

Klagenfurt to: Friesach (10 daily; 45min–1hr); Launsdorf-Hochosterwitz (6 daily; 35min); Maria Saal (8 daily; 10min); Salzburg (3 daily; 3hr 10min); St Veit an der Glan (22 daily; 15–20min); Vienna (8 daily; 4hr); Villach (30 daily; 25–40min).

Lienz to: Innsbruck (3 daily; 4hr 30min); Spittal an der Drau (10 daily; 1hr).

Spittal an der Drau to: Lienz (10 daily; 1hr); Villach (14 daily; 25–35min).

Villach to: Klagenfurt (30 daily; 25–40min); Pörtschach (16 daily; 20–25min); Salzburg (10 daily; 2hr 50min); Spittal an der Drau (14 daily; 25–35min); Velden (20 daily; 10–15min); Vienna (8 daily; 4hr 25min).

Buses

Gmünd to: Spittal an der Drau (14 daily; 30min).

Klagenfurt to: Bad Kleinkirchheim (3 daily; 1hr 30min); Graz (2 daily; 3hr 30min); Hüttenberg (3 daily; 1hr 30min); Magdalensberg (1 daily; 1hr); Maria Saal (16 daily; 25min); Maria Wörth (8 daily; 25min); Pyramidenkogel (1 daily; 30min); Reifnitz (10 daily; 20min); St Veit an der Glan (16 daily; 55min); Velden via Maria Wörth (8 daily; 40min); Velden via Pörtschach (6 daily; 40min).

Lienz to: Franz-Josefs-Hohe (late June & Sept 1 daily; July & Aug 3 daily; 2hr 15min); Heiligenblut (3 daily; 1hr 10min); Kals (6 daily; 55min); Kitzbühel (2 daily; 2hr); Kufstein (2 daily; 3hr); Lucknerhaus (3 daily; 1hr 20min); Matrei (8 daily; 40min); Prägraten (8 daily; 1hr 10min); St Jakob (6 daily; 1hr 10min); Ströden (3 daily; 1hr 15min); Staller Sattel (2 daily; 1hr 40min).

Spittal an der Drau to: Franz-Josefs-Hohe (July & Aug 2 daily; 3hr 30min); Gmünd (14 daily; 30min); Heiligenblut (3 daily; 2hr); Millstatt (20 daily; 30min); Seeboden (20 daily; 20min).

Velden to: Klagenfurt via Maria Wörth (8 daily; 40min); Klagenfurt via Pörtschach (6 daily; 40min); Rosegg (8 daily; 10min); Villach (6 daily; 30min).

Villach to: Drobollach (8 daily; 20min); Egg (8 daily; 25min); Faak am See (8 daily; 30min); Millstatt (4 daily; 1hr 20min); Ossiach (6 daily; 30min); Ostriach (6 daily; 25min); Pörtschach (6 daily; 50min); Velden (6 daily; 30min).

Ferries

Klagenfurt to: Maria Wörth/Pörtschach/Velden (May–Oct: 4 to 10 daily, depending on season; 45min/55min/1hr 45min).

Villach to: St Niklas (end April to early Oct 1 to 6 daily, depending on season; 45min).

SALZBURG AND THE SALZBURGER LAND

The borders of the modern **Salzburger Land** roughly correspond to the area ruled by the prince-archbishops of Salzburg (although the archbishopric was a typically feudal entity, comprising motley holdings dotted throughout central Austria and southern Germany), up until the Principality's incorporation into Austria in 1816. The **River Salzach**, which rises in the lofty heights of the Hohe Tauern range before flowing east then north towards Salzburg, eventually joining the River Inn in Upper Austria, gives the area a measure of geographical cohesion; and it's the main transport routes along the Salzach Valley that link the provincial capital, **Salzburg**, with much of its hinterland. As a tourist destination, the Salzburger Land offers a good mixture of both the urban and the alpine, with its splendid Baroque capital proving the main focus for many visitors. Music is an important draw in a city that was the birthplace of **Mozart**, and the annual **Salzburg Festival**, held in July and August, is a world-renowned feast of classical music and theatre. South of Salzburg, the narrow confines of the Salzach Valley and a sequence of exhilarating mountainscapes provide a dramatic setting for historic towns like **Hallein** and **Werfen**, while further south, **Radstadt, St Johann im Pongau, Badgastein** and **Zell am See** serve as the best bases from which to explore the countryside – most notably the lofty heights of the **Hohe Tauern** range.

In **winter**, snow sports take hold in the south of the province, with Radstadt, St Johann im Pongau, Badgastein and the package resort of Saalbach-Hinterglemm providing a wealth of white slopes. The most versatile area is around Zell am See, where a glacier above the neighbouring settlement of Kaprun provides year-round skiing and snowboarding. All the Land's winter sports centres make equally good hiking bases in **summer**. A key destination for hikers is the Hohe Tauern National Park, which preserves the unspoilt highland areas above the towns of Badgastein and Zell am See.

In the past, the Salzburger Land was divided into districts known as **Gaue** (*Gau* in the singular): the Flachgau north of Salzburg, the Tennengau to the south, the Pongau in the middle Salzach Valley, the Lungau in the far southeast, and the Pinzgau, which runs from Zell am See westwards along the Upper Salzach Valley. Each developed its

---

ACCOMMODATION PRICE CODES

All **hotels and pensions** in this book have been graded according to the following price categories. All the codes are based on the rate for the least expensive double room during the **summer season**. In those places where winter is the high season, we've indicated winter room rates in the text. For more on accommodation, see p.31.

① under öS400	④ öS800–1000	⑦ öS1400–1600
② öS400–600	⑤ öS1000–1200	⑧ öS1600–1800
③ öS600–800	⑥ öS1200–1400	⑨ over öS1800

own folkloric traditions, and regional differences still provide the people who live here with an important badge of regional identity. This is partly expressed in several surviving **folk festivals**, which include the **Pongauer Perchtenlauf**, when costumed figures rampage through the streets of one of four Pongau towns (see p.334), **Krampus** festivities in Zell am See (see p.343), and the **Samsonumzug** in the Lungau town of Tamsweg, in which an effigy of Samson is paraded through the streets on important summer feast days (see p.332–333).

SALZBURG

Up until 1816, **SALZBURG** led a separate life to the rest of Austria, existing as an independent city-state ruled by a sequence of powerful **prince-archbishops**. An ambitious and cultured bunch, they turned the city into the most Italianate city north of the Alps. Spread out below the brooding presence of the Hohensalzburg fortress, the churches, squares and alleyways of the compact Altstadt today recollect a long-disappeared Europe. For many, Salzburg is the quintessential Austria, offering the best of the country's Baroque architecture, subalpine scenery and a musical heritage largely provided by the city's most famous son, **Wolfgang Amadeus Mozart**, whose bright-eyed visage peers from every box of the ubiquitous chocolate delicacy, the *Mozartkügel*. Salzburg's captivation with Mozart is perhaps best reflected in the world-famous **Salzburg Festival**, a five-week celebration of opera, orchestral music and theatre that begins in late July, although there's a wide range of (not always Mozart-related) musical events on offer throughout the year. Souvenirs recalling the Salzburg-based musical *The Sound of Music* dangle round the city's neck like some bad-taste medallion, with coach tours and shows on the same theme providing an entertainingly lowbrow alternative to the more highbrow events.

Standing at the centre of a prosperous, economically booming region, Salzburg also represents Austria at its most **conservative**. Writer Thomas Bernhard, an acerbic critic of the postwar state who spent his formative years in Salzburg, called his home town "a fatal illness", whose Catholicism, conservatism and sheer snobbery drove its citizens to a state of terminal misery. The city certainly has a strong bourgeois ethos, easy to discern in the snooty cafés and refined restaurants of the city centre, and in a pre-Lenten ball season that rivals that of Vienna. But if high culture and high society don't really turn you on, you can always take solace in the city's alternative nightlife or join the crowds at the football stadium – the local team, Casino Salzburg, is one of the few outfits outside Vienna that enjoys a genuine mass following.

Salzburg is popular with tourists all year round – there's no real low season here – and **accommodation** tends to be either overpriced or oversubscribed. Once you've found yourself a place to stay, however, you'll find the city to be an easily manageable, hassle-free place to explore. The local bus and rail network makes Salzburg a convenient base from which to visit the lakes of the **Salzkammergut** (see Chapter 7) to the east, and the historic towns of **Hallein** and **Werfen** to the south. It's also handily placed for much of southeast Germany: Munich is only ninety minutes away by train.

Some history

Although Salzburg was an urban centre of some importance under both Celts and Romans (who called it Juvavum), it was the pioneering missionary activity of eighth-century holy men who really put the city on the map. Sponsored by the Bavarians who were eager to extend their influence into the area, Frankish monk **St Rupert** was the first to establish a church here, in around 700, using it as a base from which to evangelize to Germanic tribes in the Danube basin and the neighbouring alpine valleys. He also presided over the foundation of a monastery and a nunnery on the heights

△ Linz Vienna

▷ Linz, Vienna

UPPER AUSTRIA

N

Strasswalchen

A1

Attersee

Traunsee

Mondsee

158

SALZBURG

Wolfgangsee

Hallein

Bad Ischl

Tennengau

SALZKAMMERGUT

berg

Salzach

162

Abtenau

Hallstätter
See

A10

Eisriesenwelt

Werfen

Bischofshofen

Radstadt 146

Enns

Schladming

St Johann

Schwarzach

Wagrain

STYRIA

Liechtensteinklamm

Gasteinertal

Dorfgastein

Grossarl

98

162

Bad Hofgastein

A10

Stubnerkogel
2246 m

Badgastein

St Michael
im Lungau

Tamsweg

Böckstein

Graukogel
2492 m

Katschbergtunnel

Sportgastein Tauerntunnel

Lungau

CARINTHIA

0   10 km

▷ Murau, Graz

▷ Admont, Graz

▽ Villach

▽ Villach

> The telephone code for Salzburg is ☎0662.

(subsequently dubbed the **Mönchsberg** and **Nonnberg**) overlooking the city. The most illustrious of Rupert's early successors was the Irish monk and missionary **St Virgil**, who extended the influence of the bishopric as far as Carinthia in the southeast during the second half of the eighth century. Accorded the status of **princes** by the Holy Roman Emperor Rudolf of Habsburg in 1228, the city's ecclesiastical rulers were also major feudal landowners, administering territories scattered over present-day Austria, southern Germany and northern Italy. Additionally, the city's position on the River Salzach gave it a controlling influence on the transport of **salt** from the mines at Hallein upstream, and it was from this trade that Salzburg's prince-archbishops obtained much of their wealth – salt revenues helped **Archbishop Leonhard von Keutschach** (1495–1519) transform Hohensalzburg fortress into the impressive monument you see today. The city's Baroque appearance owes most to the ambitions of **Archbishop Wolf Dietrich von Raitenau** (1587–1612), a great-nephew of Pope Pius IV, who purposefully recast Salzburg on the model of Rome, employing artists and craftsmen from south of the Alps to do the job. A worldly figure whose love affair with Salome Alt was an open secret, Wolf Dietrich quarrelled with Bavaria over salt revenues in 1612. His defeat led to his overthrow and imprisonment in the Hohensalzburg, where he died in 1617. The transformation of the city, however, was continued by his successors **Marcus Sitticus von Hohenems** (1612–19), who began the construction of both the cathedral and his own pleasure-palace at Schloss Hellbrunn, and **Paris Lodron** (1619–53), responsible for the the archiepiscopal city-centre palace, the Residenz. **Johann Ernst von Thun** (1687–1709) was an early patron of Austria's outstanding eighteenth-century architect **Johann Bernhard Fischer von Erlach** (1656–1723), who was responsible for two of the city's finest churches, the Dreifaltigkeitskirche and Kollegienkirche.

The old central Europe of semi-feudal statelets to which Salzburg belonged was largely swept away by the campaigns of Napoleon, with the last of the prince-archbishops, Hieronymus Graf Colloredo, fleeing in 1800 as French troops prepared to take the city. After a brief period of Bavarian rule, the city was definitively awarded to Austria by the **Congress of Vienna** in 1816. For much of the nineteenth century, Salzburg was a provincial centre of declining importance. However, the founding of the **Mozarteum** in 1870 helped to put the place back on the cultural map. Serving as both a music school of growing repute and an important archive of Mozart's works, the Mozarteum initiated various small-scale musical festivals which were grouped together in 1920 to form the backbone of the prestigious **Salzburg Festival**.

Arrival, information and transport

Salzburg is divided by the River Salzach into the **linkes Salzachufer** (left bank), on the western side of the river, and the **rechtes Salzachufer** (right bank), on the east. On the left bank, the **Altstadt** holds the concentration of historic sights, though most points of arrival are across the river. That said, central Salzburg is reasonably compact, and it's relatively easy to get around on foot.

The **Hauptbahnhof** is north of the centre on Südtirolerplatz, a 25-minute walk from the Altstadt (buses #1, #2, #5, #6, #51 and #55 run from the station to either F-Hanusch-Platz or Rudolfskai, both on the fringes of the Altstadt). The main **bus station** is in front of the train station, although most services also stop on Mirabellplatz, nearer the centre. Salzburg's **airport** is 3km west of the centre on the Innsbrücker Bundesstrasse (bus #77 runs in to Südtirolerplatz every 30min between 5.30am and 11pm).

Information

The main **tourist office** is in the heart of the Altstadt at Mozartplatz 5 (May–Oct daily 9am–8pm; Nov–April Mon–Sat 9am–6pm; ☎88987, fax 88987-32), but the first port of call for many new arrivals is the **information kiosk** on platform 2A of the train station (daily: May–Oct 8.30am–9pm; Nov–April 9am–8pm). Both are busy throughout the year, and staff – especially at the station branch – can appear overworked and short-tempered. Information **kiosks** at other likely points of arrival include: at the **airport**, outside the main terminal building in the car park (June–Oct daily 9am–7pm; Easter–May Mon–Sat 9am–6pm); **Salzburg-Mitte**, Münchner Bundesstrasse 1, about 1km south of the Salzburg-Mitte exit from the A1 autobahn on the main road into town (May–Oct daily 9am–8pm; Nov–April Mon–Sat 11am–5pm); and **Salzburg-Süd**, Alpensiedlung-Süd, Alpenstrasse, about 5km north of the Salzburg-Süd exit of the A10 autobahn (same hours as Salzburg-Mitte).

All of the above provide a host of **free brochures** in English (although they charge öS10 for a city map), and will book you into a hotel or pension. They also sell a **Salzburg Card**, which gives free access to the majority of city museums and attractions, as well as unlimited use of city transport (öS190 for 24hr, öS270 for 48hr, öS360 for 72hr) – it's worth the investment if you're visiting more than a couple of attractions a day.

City transport

Most of Salzburg's tourist sights are within walking distance of each other (and the Altstadt is in any case largely pedestrianized), but the municipal **bus network** is a good way of getting to far-flung attractions like Hellbrunn or the Untersberg.

The most important nodal points for public transport are **Südtirolerplatz**, in front of the train station, **Mirabellplatz**, just south of the station, and **F-Hanusch-Platz**, on the left bank on the fringes of the Altstadt. **Tickets** for single journeys cost öS20, but it makes best sense to purchase a **Netzkarte** for 24 hours (öS38) or seven days (öS100), available from automatic vending machines next to major bus stops or from *Tabak* shops. The Salzburg Card, sold at the city's tourist offices (see above), is also worth considering if you're visiting lots of attractions.

Accommodation

Accommodation in Salzburg tends to be more expensive than elsewhere in Austria except for Vienna, and most places fill up fast, especially in July and August. The Altstadt and area around Linzergasse on the opposite side of the river contain any number of comfortable **hotels**, although rates can be exorbitant, especially for those establishments with any kind of historical pedigree. Budget and mid-priced hotels within walking distance of the sights do exist, but it's best to book well in advance to avoid disappointment. Similarly, phone in advance if you possibly can to reserve a place in one of the plentiful, competitively priced **hostel**-type places in town – they're very popular. If you arrive in town without a reservation, any of the tourist offices will find you a hotel room for a fee of öS35, but late arrivals will often find that the only remaining vacancies are a long way from the centre. Tourist offices can also find you a **private room** for around öS300 per person, although most of these are in outlying suburbs, and it's important to check their accessibility by public transport before accepting one of them. Of the **campsites**, *Camping Gnigl*, 2km east of the centre at Parscherstrasse 4 (☎641444; mid-May to mid-Sept), is the easiest to get to by public transport – take bus #27 or #29 from Mirabellplatz to get there. *Camping Kasern*, Carl-Zuckmayer-Strasse 4 (☎50576; open all year), is 4km north of town, just north of the Salzburg-Nord exit of the A1 autobahn. Bus #15 from Mirabellplatz passes by.

△ Vienna, Munich, Innsbruck & Salzburg-Mitte Autobahn Junction

ACCOMMODATION

Adlerhof	3
Auerhahn	2
Bergland	6
Haus Wartenberg	5
Jedermann	7
Jugendgästehaus Salzburg	9
Jugendherberge Aigen	10
Jugendherberge Edward-Heinrich-Haus	11
Jugendherberge Haunspergstrasse	1
Schloss Mönchstein	4
Vienna	8

SALZBURG

N

ELISABETH-
VORSTADT

Bus
Station

Train
Station

SCHALLMOOS

Camping
Gnigl

see 'Central Salzburg'
Map, p312.

Urbanwirt/
Kleines
Theater

Rockhouse

Kapuzinerberg

ZENTRUM

ÄUSSERER
STEIN

Burgl steinstrasse

Freibad Volksgarten

Eishalle skating Rink

Salzach

Kulturgelände
Nonntal

0   500 m

NONNTAL

St Leonhard, Hallein & Salzburg-Süd Autobahn Junction

Hellbrunn & St Leonhard ▽   *Hellbrunn* ▽   *Hellbrunn* ▽   11 ▽ *Hellbrunn,*

Hotels and pensions

Adlerhof, Elisabethstrasse 25 (☎875236, fax 873663-6). Comfortable if unexciting hotel near the train station, offering a mixed bag of rooms – some modern, some quaintly furnished in traditional wood. Most rooms with en-suite facilities (④), but some without (③).

Amadeus, Linzergasse 43–45 (☎871401, fax 876163-7). Popular sightseeing base on the right bank, with modern-furnished rooms in an otherwise historic house. Rooms have en-suite facilities and TV. ⑥.

Auerhahn, Bahnhofstrasse 15 (☎451052, fax 451052-3). In an unfashionable area just north of the train station; therefore not the best sightseeing base, but a comfortable place. ⑤.

Bergland, Rupertgasse 15 (☎872318-0, fax 872318-8). Handy for the Linzergasse area on the right bank, a family-run pension offering generous breakfasts and with a small English-language library. Most rooms come with en-suite shower but shared toilet on the hall (④), though there are some cheaper doubles without either shower or WC (③).

Blaue Gans, Getreidegasse 43 (☎841317, fax 841317-9). A superbly located inn dating from the fifteenth century, with Gothic touches in some of the public rooms but modern and minimalist bedrooms. A choice of rooms with en-suite WC and shower (⑤), or with shared facilities (③).

Goldener Hirsch, Getreidegasse 37 (☎8084-0, fax 843349). Very much the classic address in the Altstadt if you have money to burn (prices start at öS2400 per person); an inn of medieval origin offering plush rooms with antique furnishings. ⑨.

Goldener Krone, Linzergasse 48 (☎872300). A friendly, family-run place on the right bank, whose rather plain rooms are adequate for a comfortable short stay. Most rooms come with en-suite facilities (⑤), though there are some cheaper ones without (④).

Haus Wartenberg, Riedenburgerstrasse 2 (☎844284, fax 848400-5). Good-value pension with a rustic feel, west of the centre on a suburban street behind the Mönchberg. You can choose between rooms with en-suite facilities (④), or smaller ones without (③).

Hinterbrühl, Schanzlgasse 12 (☎846798). Situated at the eastern edge of the city centre just below the Nonnberg, this rather plain pension is nevertheless one of the best deals in Salzburg and therefore fills up quickly. Rooms are with shared facilities. ③.

Jedermann, Rupertgasse 25 (☎873241, fax 873241-9). Cosy, comfortable and friendly pension on the right bank of the Salzach in the Linzergasse area. ⑤.

Markus Sittikus, Markus-Sittikus-Strasse 20 (☎871121-0, fax 871121-58). Big downtown hotel on the right bank near the Mirabell gardens, with modern, functional rooms (⑥), a few with shared bathrooms (④).

Schloss Mönchstein, Mönchsberg-Park 26 (☎848555-0, fax 848589). Hilltop castle offering plush accommodation in idyllic surroundings. Room rates start at öS2400 per person. ⑨.

Schwarzes Rössl, Priesterhausgasse 6 (☎874426, fax 874426-7). Creaky old building in an excellent location on the right bank, serving as student accommodation during the academic year, but offering comfy if plain rooms in July and August. Some rooms with en-suite WC and shower. ④.

Trumer Stube, Bergstrasse 6 (☎874776, fax 874326). Friendly pension on the right bank in the Linzergasse area, with bright, comfortable rooms. ⑤.

Vienna, Gaisbergstrasse 12 (☎643657). Pleasant suburban pension with smallish but adequate rooms, 1.5km east of the centre on the right bank. Bus #6 from the train station or Mirabellplatz. ④.

Weisse Taube, Kaigasse 9 (☎842404, fax 841783). City-centre hotel with medieval roots round the corner from Mozartplatz, offering plush rooms. ⑧.

Wolf, Kaigasse 7 (☎843453-0, fax 842423-4). Perfectly situated on an alleyway just off Mozartplatz, a small family-run place with smallish but characterful rooms. ⑤.

Wolf Dietrich, Wolf-Dietrich-Strasse 7 (☎871275, fax 882320). If you're looking for a top-notch, reasonably central hotel that has indoor pool and sauna on site, then this, expensive though it is, is probably the cheapest. ⑧.

Hostels

Institut St Sebastian, Linzergasse 41 (☎871386, fax 871386-85). A good sightseeing base on the right bank, with an evocative location next to St Sebastian's church. Dorm beds are available throughout the year, and singles and doubles become available in July and August when the local students move out. Reception open Mon–Fri 9am–10pm, Sat & Sun 9am–noon & 3–10pm. Dorm beds öS230, single rooms öS360.

Jugendgästehaus Salzburg, Josef-Preis-Allee 18 (☎842670-0, fax 841101). Large place popular with groups, less than 1km southeast of the Altstadt. Buses #5 or #55 from the train station. Midnight curfew. Dorms (öS160) and some doubles (öS260 per person).

Jugendherberge Aigen, Aignerstrasse 34 (☎623248-14, fax 623848-13). Quiet, suburban location 2km away from the sights. From the train station, take buses #5 or #55 to Rudolfskai then bus #49. Midnight curfew. Mostly dorm accommodation (öS150), but some doubles (öS250 per person).

Jugendherberge Glockengasse, Glockengasse 8 (☎76241). A lovely location at the foot of the Kapuzinerberg. Midnight curfew. Dorm beds only, at öS140.

Jugendherberge Haunspergstrasse, Haunspergstrasse 27 (☎75030). 5min west of the train station. Midnight curfew. Open July & Aug. Dorm accommodation only, öS150.

Naturfreundhaus (aka Gasthaus Bürgerwehr), Mönchsberg 19c (☎841729). Marvellously situated on the hill immediately above the Altstadt, a smallish place that soon fills up – it's a good idea to reserve. Take buses #1 or #2 from the train station to the Mönchsbergaufzug stop, then take the Mönchsberg lift; or walk up the steps from behind the Toscaninihof (not recommended if you're heavily laden). Open May to mid-Oct. A choice of accommodation in either dorms (öS130) or double rooms (öS250 per person).

YO-HO, International Youth Hostel Obermair, Paracelsusstrasse 9 (☎879646, fax 878810). Big place nicely poised between the train station and main sights, very popular with English-speaking backpackers. There's a bar on the premises, and it's probably worth coming here for the social life alone if you want to meet other travellers – but bear in mind that it can be noisy at night. No curfew. Dorm beds öS140, doubles öS200 per person.

The City

Salzburg's central ensemble of archiepiscopal buildings on the left bank of the river forms a tightly woven net of alleys and squares watched over by the sombre grey bastions of the medieval **Hohensalzburg** castle. The bulk of Salzburg's galleries and museums (including **Mozart**'s birthplace) are concentrated in this area, as are many of the city's **cafés**, ideal spots for observing the hordes of vistors that pulse through the streets. From here it's a short hop over the River Salzach to a narrow ribbon of essential sights on the right bank, where another of Mozart's residences, and the flowerbeds of the **Mirabell Gardens**, are the main draws. Both sides of the river add up to a surprisingly compact city centre, and you'll find you can cover a lot of ground in a single day, although you'll need much more time (probably two or three days) if you want to explore the city's sights in any great detail.

The left bank

Salzburg's Altstadt represents one of Europe's best examples of Baroque town planning anywhere in Europe. Archbishop Wolf Dietrich was responsible for initiating the city's transformation, engaging Venetian Vincenzo Scamozzi to draft plans for an ensemble of fountains, squares and public buildings centred on a brand-new cathedral, the building of which was made neccessary by the destruction of the previous church by fire in 1598. Even though the archbishop never lived to see its completion (he was deposed in 1612), the cityscape that greets you is still very much Scamozzi's.

The Getreidegasse and Mozarts Geburtshaus

The Baroque Salzburg of Scamozzi and his successors was grafted onto an earlier, medieval city of narrow streets and squat town houses, and it's this that first hits tourists flowing into the Altstadt over the **Staatsbrücke**, main crossing point over the

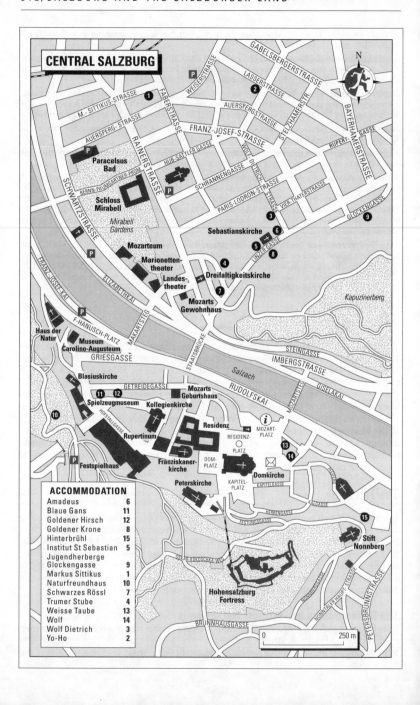

CENTRAL SALZBURG

N

M.-SITTIKUS-STRASSE
FABERSTRASSE
WEISERSTRASSE
GABELSBERGERSTRASSE
LASSERSTRASSE
AUERSPERGSTRASSE
STELZHAMERSTR.
RUPERT-GASSE
BAYERHAMERSTRASSE
AUERSPERG-STRASSE
FRANZ-JOSEF-STRASSE
RAINERSTRASSE
HUR-SATTLER GASSE
WOLF-DIETRICH-STRASSE
SCHRANNENGASSE
SCHWARTZSTRASSE
BERNH.-PAUMGARTNER PROM.
PARIS-LODRON-STRASSE
VIER-THATERSTRASSE
GLOCKENGASSE

Paracelsus Bad

Schloss Mirabell

Mirabell Gardens

Sebastianskirche

LINZER GASSE

Mozarteum

Marionetten-theater

Landes-theater

Dreifaltigkeitskirche

FRANZ-JOSEF-KAI
ELIZABETHKAI

Mozarts Gewohnhaus

Kapuzinerberg

F.-HANUSCH-PLATZ

Haus der Natur

Museum Carolino-Augusteum

GRIESGASSE

MAKARTSTEG
STAATSBRÜCKE

STEINGASSE
IMBERGSTRASSE

Salzach

Blasiuskirche

GETREIDEGASSE

Mozarts Geburtshaus

RUDOLFSKAI

MOZARTSTEG
GISELAKAI

Spielzeugmuseum

Kollegienkirche

HOFSTALLGASSE

Rupertinum

Residenz

RESIDENZ-PLATZ

ℹ MOZART-PLATZ

Franziskaner-kirche

DOM-PLATZ

Festspielhaus

Peterskirche

KAPITEL-PLATZ

KAPITEL GASSE

Domkirche

HERRENGASSE

FESTUNGSGASSE

OSKAR-KOKOSCHKA-WEG

Hohensalzburg Fortress

NONNTALERHAUPT-STRASSE

PETERSBRUNNSTRASSE

Stift Nonnberg

BRUNNHAUSGASSE

ACCOMMODATION

Amadeus	6
Blaue Gans	11
Goldener Hirsch	12
Goldener Krone	8
Hinterbrühl	15
Institut St Sebastian	5
Jugendherberge Glockengasse	9
Markus Sittikus	1
Naturfreundhaus	10
Schwarzes Rössl	7
Trumer Stube	4
Weisse Taube	13
Wolf	14
Wolf Dietrich	3
Yo-Ho	2

0   250 m

Salzach. After passing under the archway of the fifteenth-century **Rathaus**, a right turn leads into the pedestrianized **Getreidegasse**, Salzburg's busiest thoroughfare, lined with opulent boutiques and characterized by overhanging wrought-iron shop signs. At no. 9 is **Mozarts Geburtshaus** (daily: July & Aug 9am–7pm; Sept–June 9am–6pm; öS65, combined tickets for Geburtshaus and Gewohnhaus öS100), where the musical prodigy lived for the first seventeen years of his life. This crowded and rather sterile collection of musical manuscripts, original instruments and family portraits isn't necessarily the best introduction to Mozart (Salzburg's other Mozart museum, the Gewohnhaus, adopts a more thorough, chronological approach to the man and his music), but many people with a strong interest in the composer or musicianship in general will thrill to the sight of some of the artefacts on show here, such as the baby-sized violin Mozart used as a small child.

Mozartplatz and the Residenzplatz

Judengasse, the eastern extension of Getreidegasse, funnels crowds up into the **Mozartplatz**, home to a statue of the composer and overlooked by the **Glockenspiel**, a seventeenth-century musical clock whose chimes attract crowds at 7am, 11am and 6pm. The complex of buildings to the south and west of here exudes the ecclesiastical and temporal power once wielded by Salzburg's archbishops, whose erstwhile living quarters, the **Residenz**, dominate the western side of the **Residenzplatz**. Within, a sequence of bombastic **Prunkräume**, or state rooms, are accessible by guided tour (July & Aug daily 10am–4.30pm, tours every 30min; May, June, Sept, Oct & Dec daily 10am–noon & 2–3pm, tours every hour; Jan–April & Nov Mon–Fri 10am–noon & 2–3pm, tours every hour; öS50): whether the contents merit the fifty minutes taken really depends on your appetite for ageing interiors. Highlights are relatively easy to pick out: the Schöne Galerie has ceilings by Rottmayr and a copy of the mysterious but overhyped Graeco-Roman statue, the Young Man of Magdalensberg (see p.268), while the Audienzsaal is decked with valuable Flemish tapestries.

One floor above, the **Residenzgalerie** (April–Sept daily 10am–5pm; Oct–March 10am–5pm daily except Wed; öS50) offers a fine display of archiepiscopal acquisitions over the centuries, beginning in the entrance hall with Caspar Memberger's mid-sixteenth-century cycle of paintings depicting the Flood. The collection's two most valued works, Rembrandt's small but compelling *Old Woman Praying*, thought to be a portrait of the artist's mother, and Rubens' *Allegory of Charles V as Master of the World* (1664), a blatant piece of Habsburg propaganda showing the (long-deceased) emperor receiving the gift of the globe from a cherub, share wall space with a host of lesser-known landscapes and still lifes that nonetheless provide a useful overview of seventeenth-century Flemish art. Of the Austrian works on display, a Rottmayr *Pietà* and Maulpertsch's *Last Supper* are full of sombre melodrama, while Hans Makart's 1871 portrait of his first wife, Amalie, presents a human side to this normally stuffy, bourgeois painter.

In case all these old masters leave you yearning for a taste of modern art, the **Academia Gallery** (opening hours vary according to exhibition) on the ground floor of the Residenz is probably Salzburg's leading venue for small-scale contemporary art shows – ask at the tourist office to find out what's on.

The Domkirche

Arches link the Residenzplatz with the **Domplatz** to the south, which is dominated by the pale marble facade of Salzburg's cathedral, the **Domkirche St Rupert**. Once the forum of Roman Juvavum, the site has held a succession of churches since Bishop Virgil first built a chapel here in the eighth century. Although initially conceived by Wolf Dietrich as a cathedral to outshine St Peter's in Rome, the current edifice, begun in 1614, reflects the more modest ambitions of his successor Marcus Sitticus and his

MOZART: THE SALZBURG YEARS

It's ironic that such a large part of Salzburg's tourist industry revolves around a man who felt so stifled by his native city that he couldn't wait to leave. Born the son of Leopold Mozart, a member of the archbishop of Salzburg's chamber orchestra and a respected expert on violin technique, **Wolfgang Amadeus Mozart** (1756–91) was recognized early on as a prodigy, learning the piano at the age of 3, going on to teach himself the violin, and embarking on rudimentary compositions by the age of 5 (although these were heavily revised by his father, so we have now way of telling how good they actually were). Mozart's sister Maria-Anna ("Nannerl"), five years older, was equally precocious, providing *père* Leopold with a child-prodigy package with which he could tour the courts of Europe in search of financial reward. Between 1762 and 1771 the family was almost constantly on the road, visiting Munich, Vienna, Pressburg (now Bratislava in Slovakia), Frankfurt, Brussels, Paris and London to perform for princely houses and society figures. Stints back home in Salzburg were largely spent preparing for the next trip abroad. By the time the Mozarts embarked on the first of three trips to Italy in 1770 Wolfgang was developing a reputation as a composer as well as a performer, and was commissioned to write an opera by the ducal theatre in Milan at the age of 14 (*Mitridate, Re di Ponto*).

Initially, many people simply couldn't believe that Mozart was capable of all the feats attributed to him, and subjected him to various tests: both Daines Barrington (a fellow of the Royal Society) in London and Archbishop Sigismund von Schrattenbach in Salzburg shut him up in a room without his father to see whether he could transcribe pieces of music played to him without Leopold there to help. A Neapolitan audience forced him to play without a ring he customarily wore on his finger, which they believed to be a magic charm.

In August 1772, at the age of 16, Wolfgang was appointed Konzertmeister (leader of the court orchestra) by Hieronymous Graf von Colloredo, Schrattenbach's successor as Archbishop of Salzburg. The young composer later became Colloredo's organ master, but the relationship between the Archbishop and the Mozarts was never to be a satisfactory one. Wolfgang's father Leopold was eager to continue touring the courts of Europe, believing that his son would win further commissions, and perhaps be appointed to a top musical post by some foreign prince if only his talents could be showcased as widely as possible. Colloredo, understandably, had misgivings about allowing musicians who were supposedly in his employ to galavant around Europe and take on commissions from other patrons. Wolfgang himself found life at Colloredo's court dull and uninspiring – the archbishop didn't harbour any great passion for music, such that Mozart compared playing for him and his cronies to performing for an audience of table and chairs, and took to calling the archbishop the "arch-oaf" (*Erzlümmel*) in his letters. Court musicians were also treated in much the same way as any other servants – Mozart sat next to the kitchen staff at mealtimes – and this rankled with a young composer who had already tasted a degree of celebrity.

In an attempt to find another job, Mozart spent much of 1777 and 1778 in western Europe, but he re-entered the service of Colloredo on his return to Salzburg in 1779. Relations with the archbishop took a turn for the worse a year later, when Mozart sought six weeks leave in order to supervise the production of *Idomeneo*, an opera he had been commissioned to write for the carnival season in Munich. He ended up staying in Munich for four months. In March 1781, Colloredo summoned Mozart to Vienna (where the prelate was visiting his sick father) in an effort to bring the errant composer back into line. By May, having spent several weeks of inactivity in the archbishop's household, Mozart was ready to cut himself loose: cosmopolitan Vienna not only seemed to offer wider opportunities for a freelance composer, it was also the home of Constanz Weber, with whom he was falling in love. When Mozart tried to give his notice to quit, he was literally kicked out of the building by the archbishop's steward. Mozart married Constanz in 1782 and visited Salzburg with her in 1783, but he was never to reside in the city of his birth again.

favoured architect, Santino Solari. The crests of both Sitticus and Paris Lodron, who occupied the archiepiscopal throne on completion of the forty-year project, adorn the pediment of the harmonious facade; at ground level, modern bronze doors are flanked by monumental statues of saints Rupert, Virgil, Peter and Paul. The interior (donation requested) is impressively cavernous; its dizzying ceiling frescoes may be undistinguished in themselves, but together they form a colourful visual encyclopedia of Christianity. Left of the entrance is the Romanesque font in which Mozart was baptized, a bronze affair resting on four feet in the shape of lions' paws and decorated with reliefs of saints. Below the dome, steps descend to a modern crypt, final resting place of some illustrious prelates, Paris Lodron among them.

The **Dommuseum**, immediately to your right as you enter the cathedral porch (mid-May to mid-Oct daily 10am–5pm; öS50), owes much to the acquisitive habits of mid-seventeenth-century Archbishop Guidobald von Thun, who keenly amassed a collection of wondrous artefacts on the model of the famous Wunderkammer established by Emperor Rudolf II in Prague. What's left of Guidobald's collection (much was moved to Vienna when Salzburg became part of Austria in 1816) is displayed in its original form, a series of cabinets arranged by category: rosaries, minerals, scientific instruments, ivory, things made from goat horn, crystals, seashells and globes. To the modern eye, it looks more like a sale of upmarket bric-a-brac than a serious museum, but contemporaries of Guidobald regarded the sheer variety of objects as a manifestation of God's creative genius. Recurring stylistic motifs such as hourglasses, half-empty goblets, mussel shells and skulls are reminders that mortality and transience were preoccupations of the time. The upper floor of the museum is more conventional, with an impressive array of altarpieces, notably a surreal Temptation of St Anthony by a follower of Hieronymus Bosch. Best of the few Baroque paintings is Rottmayr's fanciful portrayal of a cherubic St Vitus being boiled in a cauldron.

The damp and musty **Grabungen** beneath the cathedral (May–Oct daily 9am–5pm; öS20), accessible via steps outside the cathedral's north wall, expose the modest remains of its predecessors, including St Virgil's eighth-century chapel and the Romanesque basilica that superseded it. Fans of classical archeology will probably benefit most from a visit here – the recently uncovered Roman mosaic fragments are indeed impressive, featuring abstract patterns in vivid colours – but there's little to captivate the non-specialist.

Behind the cathedral to the south, **Kapitelplatz** centres on one of Salzburg's finest fountains, the **Kapitelschwemme**, an eighteenth-century horse-trough magnificently presided over by a trident-wielding statue of Neptune. At the southern end of the square, a steeply ascending pathway and the Festungsbahn funicular railway both provide access to the Hohensalzburg fortress above (see p.317).

The Franziskanerkirche

At the western end of Domplatz an archway leads through to Franziskanergasse and the **Franziskanerkirche**, a thirteenth-century reconstruction of an ancient eighth-century edifice, noted for its high-roofed, semicircular choir. Set into the curve of the choir wall are nine chapels, the interior of each adorned with fussy stucco-work, statuettes and paintings – the result of an eighteenth-century Baroque face-lift courtesy of Fischer von Erlach. Erlach was also responsible for the high altar, although the Madonna that forms its centrepiece is a fine example of late-Gothic sculpture by Tyrolean master Michael Pacher (the Child is a later addition). It's easy to miss the church's oldest artwork, a twelfth-century marble lion guarding the stairway to the pulpit.

The building on the southern side of Franziskanergasse, opposite the church, boasts a fine piece of Renaissance portrait sculpture in a niche above the door, a bust of Wolf Dietrich in the (for him, unlikely) garb of a monk.

The Peterskirche

Opposite the Franziskanerkirche, arches on the south side of Franziskanergasse lead through to the **Peterskirche**, Salzburg's most dazzling Rococo statement. Although occupying a largely Romanesque shell, the church was extensively remodelled in the late eighteenth century, with Philip Hinterseer's elaborate wrought-iron gates separating the porch from a sumptuous visual feast of stucco mouldings in the nave. Among paintings crowding the walls are two dramatic renditions of the Crucifixion by Ignazio Solari and Kaspar Memberger – sombre, extravagantly staged affairs. Behind the church, the eighteenth- and nineteenth-century graves of Salzburg's middle class fill the arcades of the **Petersfriedhof**, lurking beneath the cliffs of the Hohensalzburg. Catacombs cut into the rock face by Christian inhabitants of third-century Juvavum are accessible by brief guided tour (in German with English summary; daily: May–Sept on the hour 10am–5pm; Oct–April at 10.30am, 11.30am, 1.30pm, 2.30pm & 3.30pm; öS15), worth considering more for the atmosphere than any historic sights. Christianity died out after the Roman Empire abandoned the region to Germanic tribes in the fifth century, but was revived by saints Virgil and Rupert.

The Rupertinum

Continuing west along Franziskanergasse, it's not long before you hit Max-Reinhard-Platz and the **Rupertinum** on the corner of Wiener-Philharmoniker-Gasse (mid-July to Sept daily 9am–5pm, Wed until 9pm; Oct to mid-July Tues & Thurs–Sun 10am–5pm, Wed 10am–9pm; öS40), a picture gallery devoted to twentieth-century work and major touring exhibitions of contemporary art. Gustav Klimt's *Unterach am Attersee* is probably the most famous canvas here, a marvellous example of Post-Impressionist landscape painting from an artist more usually known for his florid Jugendstil excesses. Elsewhere are a couple of Kokoschkas, and a picture each by Emil Nolde and Ludwig Kirchner, after which the collection drifts into mediocrity, enlivened only by Robert Zepperl-Sperl's *Gastmahl*, a colourful evocation of Vienna's bohemian artistic elite in the 1960s.

The Universitätsplatz and around

Fischer von Erlach's sizeable but somewhat graceless **Kollegienkirche**, immediately west of the Rupertinum on the **Universitätsplatz**, also holds temporary art exhibitions. Anton Pfaffinger's high altar of 1740, whose classical columns present a rather too literal allegory of the Seven Pillars of Wisdom, seems lost within Ehrlach's lofty interior. Behind the church, Hofstallgasse is dominated by the 1930s **Festspielhaus**, built to provide the Salzburg Festival with a central concert venue. Northeast of here, but still in the shadow of the Mönchberg, is the **Pferdschwemme**, a horse-trough built in 1700 for the archbishop's riding school (which originally stood on the site of the Festspielhaus) and decorated with equine motifs. A couple of hundred metres down Bürgerspitalgasse, the **Bürgerspital** is a sixteenth-century almshouse now containing the **Spielzeugsmuseum** (Tues– Sun 9am–5pm; öS30), an unassuming and badly labelled collection of model railways, puppets and other playthings, which will probably disappoint youngsters.

The Haus der Natur

You'll marvel more at Salzburg's natural history collection, in the **Haus der Natur** (daily 9am–5pm; öS55), a few steps north of the Bürgerspital on Museumsplatz. Five excellently arranged exhibition floors make this one of the city's more fun-filled attractions, a welcome breather from the rather culture-heavy sights on offer elsewhere. Downstairs, the requisite moving dinosaur models (with accompanying sound effects) are joined by fascinating, if incongruous, dioramas detailing life in Tibet, and an aquarium inhabited by piranhas and Red Sea sharks, amongst others. Upstairs floors offer an endless parade of stuffed fauna of all kinds, live snakes and alligators, and a section on space travel featuring the capsule of an American Mercury rocket.

The Carolino-Augusteum

Round the corner from the Haus der Natur at Museumsplatz 1 is the city's main historical museum, the **Museum Carolino-Augusteum** (Tues 9am–8pm, Wed–Sun 9am–5pm; öS40). An excellent place to catch up on the history of Roman-era Salzburg, or Juvavum, its wide range of finds include a number of mosaics (the best, a third-century piece found just east of Mozartplatz depicting Europa's abduction) and the fragmentary remains of a Roman water clock decorated with figures of Andromeda and Perseus. Upstairs are a small folklore section and several dull paintings, and a room devoted to local-born Hans Makart, history painter and society portraitist whose works reflected the stuffy conventions of the late nineteenth-century bourgeoisie. Considerably more interesting are the Gothic wood-sculptures and altar fragments nearby, with a winged altar from the Pinzgau village of Rauris (featuring a relief of the *Pietà*, flanked by panels depicting saints Margaret, Catharine, Dorothy and Barbara), the best of a generally stunning bunch. The next floor up concentrates on Baroque paintings, with the *Beheading of Saint Barbara* (1727) the most notable of a trio of works by Paul Troger. Some reconstructed sixteenth-century interiors display a wealth of intricately inlaid wood surfaces, and there's also a decidedly odd eighteenth-century *Spottofen* (literally "oven of scorn"), a ceramic stove designed – no doubt with a pious Catholic household in mind – in the shape of a library filled with books fit for burning, the works of Luther, Calvin and Zwingli among them.

Hohensalzburg fortress

Surveying the city from its hilltop perch to the south, the **Hohensalzburg fortress** originated in the eleventh century, when Archbishop Gebhard, an ally of the pope in the latter's quarrel with the Holy Roman Empire, needed a strongpoint from which to repel the attacks of the south German princes. Most of the present-day fortress is the result of rebuilding work carried out by Archbishop Leonhard von Keutschach in the early 1500s, who added some sumptuous state apartments.

The quicker of two routes up to the fortress is via the Festungsbahn funicular, from the southern end of Kapitelplatz (daily: May–Sept 9am–9pm; Oct–April 9am–5pm; öS65 one way, öS75 return; ticket includes entrance to the fortress), but the journey on foot isn't as hard or as time-consuming as it looks and offers some excellent views of the city along the way. A roam around the main courtyard of the **fortress** (daily: April–June & Oct 9am–6pm; July–Sept 8am–7pm; Nov–March 9am–5pm; öS35), together with a few of the surrounding bastions and passageways, is enough to gain a feel for the place, though von Keutschach's **state rooms** can be visited as part of a forty-minute **guided tour** for an additional fee (departing on demand; April–June, Sept & Oct, last tour 5pm; July & Aug last tour 5.30pm; Nov–March last tour 4.30pm; öS30). Starting with panoramic views from the castle watchtower, the tour takes in the **Fürstenzimmer**, whose ceiling and doorframes are masterpieces of late-Gothic woodcarving, and a glimpse of *Der Stier* ("The Bull"), a monstrous sixteenth-century organ whose sonorous tones can be heard all over the city centre on the rare occasions when it's played. The tour concludes with a chance to explore two small museums which can't be visited on their own: the **Rainer-Museum** (closed mid-Oct to April), displaying uniforms and weapons of the infantry regiment that was stationed in the castle until 1945; and the **Burgmuseum**, which includes Archbishop Wolf Dietrich's suit of armour, a small collection of Gothic statuary, and instruments of torture, among them grotesque *Schandmasken* ("masks of shame"), which petty criminals were forced to wear by way of punishment.

Paths lead east from the fortress to another example of pre-Baroque Salzburg architecture, the **Nonnberg convent**, whose church is a largely fifteenth-century rebuilding of a Romanesque structure. The convent was founded by St Rupert's niece St Erentrude, who is shown beside John the Baptist and the Virgin on the tympanum above the main doorway, and whose tomb lies in the church crypt. There's a fine collection of marble memorials to other, later abbesses along the north wall of the nave, and, on the right side of the chancel, a fine late-Gothic winged altar showing the Nativity.

The right bank

Streets on the **right bank** of the Salzach zero in on **Platzl**, a small square at the eastern end of the Staatsbrücke. Entering Platzl to the north is Steingasse, originally the route by which the salt traders arrived in the city. Still preserving something of its medieval character, it's a narrow, cobbled alley lined with buildings of medieval origin, many of which now house posh bars. Steps behind no. 9 lead to a museum dedicated to **Joseph Mohr**, one-time assistant pastor in the nearby village of Oberndorf and author of the words to the hymn **Stille Nacht**, or *Silent Night* (Jan–Oct Mon–Sat 11am–5pm; Nov & Dec 11am–8pm; öS30). The most-recorded song in musical history was penned on Christmas Eve 1818, when the Oberndorf church organ broke down just before the midnight service. Mohr decided to improvise a simple song that could be performed with a guitar, enlisting the help of the organist Franz-Xaver Gruber who came up with the chords, and *Stille Nacht* was the result. The limited display of early nineteenth-century mementos inside the museum seems a rather desperate attempt to wring yet more tourist mileage out of Salzburg's musical heritage.

The Linzergasse

Heading east from Platzl is the **Linzergasse**, a busy shopping street skirting the lower slopes of the **Kapuzinerberg**, which is named after the Capuchin monastery that crowns its summit. The hill was fortified by Archbishop Paris Lodron during the Thirty Years' War, and some of the walls are still visible on its southern flanks. The monastery church isn't of great interest, but the view from here of Salzburg's domes and spires warrants the stiff climb. Continuing along Linzergasse, the dour **Sebastianskirche** is less interesting than the pleasant, arcaded **St Sebastian cemetery** (daily 7am–7pm) behind it, which is dominated by the **mausoleum of Archbishop Wolf Dietrich**. The tiled interior, with paintings by Elias Castello (whose own grave, in the arcade to the west, is one of the finest Renaissance monuments in the cemetery), adds delicacy to what is otherwise a pompous and self-regarding monument. The path leading from the cemetery entrance to the mausoleum passes the graves of Mozart's father Leopold and widow Constanz, the latter buried beside her second husband, Georg Nikolaus von Nissen, one of Mozart's first biographers. Elsewhere, innumerable family tombs attest to a uniquely Austrian love of the macabre: skulls abound and, on the von Goldenstein family tomb (under the arcade at the northern end), a fine, emaciated figure of Death holds an hourglass. In the southwestern corner of the cemetery is the **tomb of Paracelsus**, the Renaissance humanist and alchemist who was the founder of modern pharmacology (see box).

Makartplatz and Mozarts Gewohnhaus

Two blocks northwest of Platzl, the **Makartplatz** is presided over by Fischer von Erlach's **Dreifaltigkeitskirche**, or church of the Holy Trinity, notable for the elegant curve of its exterior and the oval plan of its dome, which boasts a crowd of vibrant paintings by Rottmayr. Further along, the house at no. 8 is the site of **Mozarts Gewohnhaus** (daily: July & Aug 9am–6pm; Sept–June 10am–6pm; öS65, combined ticket including the Geburtshaus öS100), where the Mozart family lived between 1773

PARACELSUS

The grandly named Philippus Aureolus Theophrastus Bombastus von Hohenheim (the self-styled "Paracelsus") was born in Einsiedeln, Switzerland, in 1493. He was a pupil of renowned alchemist Abbot Tritheim of Würzburg, and attended various European universities (later claiming, fraudulently, to have received a degree in Medicine from the University of Ferrara), although much of his medical knowledge was obtained in the course of extensive wanderings as an itinerant healer. Crisscrossing Europe between 1517 and 1526, he came to believe that the medical establishment of his day was far too rooted in the ossified theories of ancient Greek and Roman writers, and argued that open-minded enquiry based on close observation of the effects of various medicines was far more important in the development of medical knowledge. However, he was also an arrogant and vain self-publicist, calling himself **Paracelsus** ("the equal of Celsus", a reference to the prodigious first-century compiler of medical encyclopedias), and treating his medical contemporaries with a contempt that was to ensure he remained, for much of his life, a distrusted outsider.

Indeed Paracelsus would probably have remained an unorthodox travelling healer had it not been for his adoption by the intellectual elite of Basel in 1526. It was here that he was engaged as the personal physician of Johannes Froben, a humanist and publisher of Europe-wide renown who went on to recommend Paracelsus to friends, notably among them the esteemed scholar Erasmus. The city fathers of Basel made Paracelsus their municipal doctor, and he was offered a chair in medicine by the local university. He began his university career by publicly burning the works of Galen, the third-century Greek physician who had remained the prime authority on all things medical ever since. Such iconoclasm seriously ruffled the feathers of the local medical elite, and Paracelsus was drummed out of office after two years.

Several parts of Austria boast Paracelsus connections. He lived in Villach as a young man (his father practised medicine here from 1502 to 1532), studied the respiratory ailments of Tyrolean silver-miners, and visited Badgastein, where he was impressed by the curative properties of the local spa waters. Not much is known of Paracelsus's period in Salzburg, save for the fact that he died here in 1541, ostensibly as a result of a wound received in a brawl with one of his medical adversaries. He left behind a huge volume of published writings which, in typical sixteenth-century humanist fashion, tried to combine the discipline of scientific enquiry with a much more esoteric appreciation of the power of mysticism and magic. However many of his ideas were ahead of their time: he emphasized critical observation of the patient, and offered important insights into the psychological side of the healing process, believing that the patient's faith in the power of a particular medicine was often more important than the properties of the medicine itself. More importantly, he challenged the contemporary notion that the human body was governed by the four humours (and the four elements that made them up – choler, blood, phlegm and bile), and placed the role of pharmaceuticals in the treatment of illness on a sound scientific basis. Most peculiarly, he held that ailments should be treated with plants that resembled the afflicted parts of the body (and there are no prizes for guessing which organ he thought would benefit from contact with a cucumber). He was also responsible for introducing the word "gnome" to the lexicon, a creature that he believed dwelt beneath the earth's crust.

and 1787. Though little of the original building survives, courtesy of allied bombing raids in World War II, the museum is a much better introduction to the composer's life and times than the Geburtshaus across the river, largely due to its modern, multimedia approach. Headsets deliver engrossing commentary together with well-chosen excerpts of music, a short video follows Mozart's journeys around Europe, and a small movie theatre screens documentaries on Mozart's career, to booming musical accompaniment. The well-labelled collection of period furniture, original manuscripts and eighteenth-century harpsichords won't disappoint the purists.

The Mirabell Gardens and the Baroque Museum

From Makartplatz, Dreifaltigkeitsgasse leads northwest to **Schloss Mirabell**, which began life as a palace built by Archbishop Wolf Dietrich for his Jewish mistress Salome Alt, with whom the energetic prelate was rumoured to have produced a dozen children. Completely revamped by Lukas von Hildebrandt in the early eighteenth century, and further reconstructed after a fire in the nineteenth, it now houses local government offices and plays host to classical music concerts. Its most outstanding features are the cherub-lined staircase, by Baroque master George Raphael Donner, and the ornate **gardens** behind the building, with the rose-filled high ground of the adjoining Kurgarten offering a much-photographed view back across the city towards the Hohensalzburg. Nestling on the eastern side of the gardens is the **Barockenmuseum** (Tues–Sat 9am–noon & 2–5pm, Sun 9am–noon; öS40), which focuses on Austrian art of that period, although most of the paintings on display are preliminary sketches rather than finished works. While it's a useful insight into how the art of Troger, Donner and Maulpertsch developed, those with limited time should stick to the city's Baroque churches instead.

The outskirts of the city: Schloss Hellbrunn, the Untersberg and the Open-Air Museum

A clutch of worthwhile sights on the southern fringes of the city are easily reached on the municipal bus network. Most important of these are the palace, gardens and zoo at **Schloss Hellbrunn**, 5km south of the Altstadt and accessible via the #55 bus from the train station, Mirabellplatz or Rudolfskai. The Italianate palace was built by Santino Solari between 1613 and 1619 to serve as Archbishop Marcus Sitticus's hunting lodge. Bus #55 continues to St Leonhard just beyond the city's southern suburbs, starting point for the cable-car ascent of the **Untersberg**, an impressively craggy height renowned for its expansive views.

On the road to the Bavarian town of Bad Reichenhall, Styria's excellent **Open-Air Museum** lies 12km to the southwest of Salzburg. You can escape to the museum by bus or cycle – there's a separate cycle path by the side of the road once you leave suburban Salzburg.

Schloss Hellbrunn

For the urbane, Italian-educated Marcus Sitticus, Hellbrunn was a summer retreat where he could relax, enjoy the good things in life and entertain his guests. Foremost among the entertainments devised by the pleasure-loving prelate, the **Wasserspiele** (guided tours in English and German, April & Oct 9am–4.30pm; May, June & Sept 9am–5pm; July & Aug 9am–10pm; öS70) is a themed pocket of the Schloss gardens featuring shell-encrusted grottoes, water-powered clockwork figures, and trick fountains that spurt unexpectedly into life – visitors should come prepared for a soaking.

The **Schloss** itself (same times; 20min guided tours depart at regular intervals; öS30) is filled with reminders of Marcus Sitticus's passion for animals, both those he hunted and those he collected to stock his park: names of some rooms, like the **Fish room**, hint at the decor within. Disturbing to modern eyes, but relatively commonplace to the educated elite of Sitticus's time, are the paintings of the freaks of nature that once filled the archbishop's bizarre private zoo, notably various albino farm animals and an eight-legged horse. More refined tastes are revealed in the **Chinese room**, with hand-painted wallpaper depicting birds and cherry blossom, and in the **Octagon room**, where the archbishop's favoured musicians were invited to perform.

Behind the Schloss stretches an extensive **park** (dawn till dusk), with tree-lined avenues, ornamental flowerbeds and well-stocked fish ponds.

The Volksmuseum and Hellbrunn zoo

Tickets to the Wasserspiele also include entrance to the **Volksmuseum** (April–Oct daily 9am–5pm; öS20 if visited on its own), in the **Monatsschlösschen**, or "month-castle" – so called because it was constructed in a single month. Set on a wooded hill at the far end of the park, it holds a respectable collection of folk costumes and painted wooden furniture, but it's the section on the Salzburger Land's rural festivals that commands most attention. Pride of place goes to the towering effigy of Samson the giant, one of many that used to be hauled through towns during the **Samsonumzug** processions that marked Corpus Christi. In a ritual of ancient origin whose precise meaning remains lost, Samson would have been accompanied by people dressed as the Zwerglmann and Zwerglfrau ("Mr and Mrs Dwarf"). A concerted effort was made to stamp out such practices throughout Austria during the reign of Joseph II, and the custom nowadays survives in only a few towns to the southeast – Tamsweg (see p.333), Mauterndorf and St Michael im Lungau among them. Equally striking are the costumes donned during the **Perchtenlauf** processions, which take place on January 5 in the Pongau (see p.334), incorporating enormous head-dresses onto which mirrors, stuffed birds and other objects are mounted.

Adjoining the park, and stretching along the northern flanks of the hill, are the animal pens of **Hellbrunn Zoo** (daily: March 8.30am–4.30pm; April, May & second half Sept 8.30am–5.30pm; June to mid-Sept 8.30am–7pm; Oct 8.30am–5pm; Nov–Feb 8.30am–4pm; öS70), a well-stocked collection of worldwide fauna, which counts pumas, lions, jaguars, snow leopards and rhinos among its numerous inmates.

The Untersberg

From Hellbrunn, a few of the #55 buses continue to the village of **ST LEONHARD** 7km further south, where a cable car ascends the 1853-metre **Untersberg**. Local legend maintains that the emperor Charlemagne is asleep under the mountain and will awaken when ravens disappear from the skies around the summit. The cable car (9am–5pm; return öS200; closed Nov) provides access to an impressive panorama of the surrounding countryside, with Salzburg laid out to the north and the high Alps to the south.

The Open-Air Museum

The **Salzburger Freilichtsmuseum**, the Salzburger Land's Open-Air Museum (Easter–Oct & Dec 25 to Jan 5 daily except Mon 9am–6pm; öS70), assembles over fifty historic farm buildings from all over the region in a large, partially wooded park. Buildings are grouped by area of origin within the Salzburger Land. The most visible distinction lies between the single-building farmsteads typical of the Flachgau and the Tennengau in the north and east, and the twin-building farmsteads (where animals and hay were kept in a separate building lying parallel to the farmer's house) that once predominated in the Pongau to the southwest. Pongau and Pinzgau farmhouses also tend to have a bell on the roof, usually mounted in a small, intricately carved belfry, and sometimes crowned by a cast-iron weathercock. Demonstrations of rural crafts such as embroidery, smithing and carpentry take place on summer Sundays.

The Open-Air Museum is 5km short of the village of **Grossgmain**, which stands on the Austrian–German border. Hourly buses on the Salzburg–Grossgmain–Bad Reichenhall route drop off at the museum. It's also just about practical to cycle to the museum from Salzburg (head out towards the airport on the Innsbrucker Bundesstrasse and keep going until you see signs for Grossgmain and Bad

Reichenhall). There's little to see in Grossgmain itself, so it's best to avail yourself of the food-and-drink facilities inside the museum (a couple of café-restaurants are housed in some of the traditional wooden buildings) before heading back to the city.

Eating and drinking

There's no shortage of good **restaurants** in Salzburg, many of them dishing out traditional Austrian meat-based fare in atmospheric medieval town houses. Most of these are open for lunch and offer good-value two-course **Mittagsmenüs** as a way of attracting tourist custom – though, as is often the case in Austria, **ethnic restaurants** are best for an inexpensive midday meal. Phone numbers of restaurants where you may need to make a reservation for a weekend evening are included in the listings below. An evening meal in Salzburg need not be any more expensive than in any of Austria's other urban centres.

For **snacks**, the best Würstelstand in town is bang in the centre on the Alter Platz, though there are others on F-Hanusch-Platz, and Platzl on the right bank of the river. *Tresnewski*, Getreidegasse 9, has delicious, if dainty, open sandwiches, while the *Fischkrieg* kiosk on Hanuschplatz is the place to go for local variations on the fish-and-chips theme. *Pizza Quadra* (closed evenings) and *Spaghetti and Co*, both on Getreidegasse, are two fast, filling and cheap sources of pizza and pasta.

Daytime drinkers are well catered for by Salzburg's many elegant cafés. **Night-time drinking** mainly takes place in four zones: the Rudolfskai; the area around Kaigasse and Chiemseegasse just east of the centre; the area around Gstättengasse just west of the centre; and the area around Giselakai, Imbergstrasse and Steingasse over on the right bank of the Salzach.

Restaurants

Altstadtkeller, Rudolfskai 26 (☎849688). Excellent *Wiener Schnitzel* and a range of steaks, though there's little else on the menu. Most people come for the nightly live music: either cocktail-bar jazz or (on Thurs) Austrian folk. Closed Sun & Mon.

An Bing, Goldgasse. Chinese cuisine on the first floor of a city-centre building (so no outdoor seating); one of the cheapest Mittagsmenüs around, from about öS75.

Andreas Hofer, Steingasse 65 (☎872769). Specializing in Tyrolean food, this place has atmospheric, candlelit wood-panelled rooms, low to medium prices and a youngish clientele.

Bella Vita, Vogelweiderstrasse 9 (☎883338). Excellent-value pizza and pasta dishes, plus more pricey examples of classical Italian cuisine, such as *saltimbocca alla Romana*, and a good selection of Italian wines. Just off the Linzergasse. Closed Sun.

Café Hartl, Kaigasse 15. Tempting range of reasonably priced pizzas and crêpes, conveniently located just round the corner from Mozartplatz.

Gäblerbrau, Linzergasse 9. Elegant without being wildly expensive, a big hotel-restaurant with a range of familiar Austrian standards and a couple of vegetarian options.

Humboldt-Stuben, Gstättengasse 6. Inexpensive Austrian cuisine at the northern end of the Altstadt, handy for the Museum Carolino-Augusteum and Haus der Natur. Plenty of outdoor seating, and it's a good place for an evening drink as well.

Krimpelstätter, Müllner Hauptstrasse 31. Set aside from the main tourist routes just north of the old centre, offering a traditional, mid-priced Austrian menu, in some atmospheric rooms of what used to be a sixteenth-century inn. Extensive beer garden at the rear. Closed Sun.

Pitter-Rainerstube, Rainerstrasse 6–8. Solid, inexpensive Austrian fare and a variety of vegetarian selections, but it does get very busy. Closed Sun.

Potatoes & Co, Rudolfskai 26 (☎841465). Baked potatoes, Mexican dishes and big steaks in a snazzy restaurant, off the street in an inner courtyard, which sometimes features Latin American folk music.

Resch & Lieblich, Toscaninihof 1 (☎843675). Good-value Austrian cuisine in a popular restaurant next door to the Festspielhaus, its dining rooms carved out of the cliffs of the Mönchberg. Despite plenty of outdoor seating, it still gets crowded here, especially during the Festival, when it's a popular haunt for musicians and concert-goers.

Rupertihof, Rupertgasse. Restaurant in the Linzergasse area serving all kinds of schnitzels, reasonably priced, as well as fish. There's a large beer garden out the back. Closed Sun.

Soho, Steingasse 61 (☎878060). The menu is limited in this cosy, candlelit bar-restaurant, but the food – usually an Austro-Italian mix – is excellent. It's also a nice place for a drink.

Sternbrau, Getreidegasse 34/Griesgasse 23 (☎840717). Rambling establishment built around a courtyard in the heart of the Altstadt, featuring traditional Austrian restaurant, Italian trattoria, lots of outdoor seating in a beer-garden atmosphere, and there are a couple of vegetarian options on both menus.

Stiftskeller St Peter, St-Peter-Bezirk 4 (☎841268). Medium-priced, traditional Austrian dishes in roomy, atmospheric surroundings, next to the Peterskirche. Abundant outdoor seating nonetheless tends to fill up quickly with tourist parties.

Wasserfall, Linzergasse 10 (☎873331). Smart, gourmet-oriented restaurant offering imaginative variations on traditional Austian fare and delicious sweets. Modern, minimalist decor makes it a nice change from the homely, wooden interiors elsewhere. A three-course meal will set you back öS500–600 per person.

Weisses Kreuz, Bierjodlgasse 6 (☎845641). Specializing in Balkan food, on a cobbled street below the fortress. Dishes range from cheap spicy *ćevapčići* (grilled mincemeat rissoles) to more expensive meat-heavy meals; there's usually also a three-course set menu from around öS150. Closed Sun.

Zur Glocke, Schanzlgasse 2 (☎845391). Homely, cheap, traditional Austrian-food outlet just east of the Altstadt, which fills up quickly.

Cafés and bars

Almrausch, Imbergstrasse 22. A chic designer facade betrays a rustic interior with traditional alpine music on tape and a folk-fixated clientele.

Augustiner Bräu, Augustinergasse 4–6. Although a 15min walk northwest of the centre, this is part of the Salzburg experience for many – a vast, open-air courtyard filled with students, local families and tourists. Beer (brewed on the premises) is served in archaic fashion: you collect a ceramic mug, rinse it under the tap provided, pay a cashier and present the receipt to the barman, who promptly fills your mug.

Bazaar, Schwarzstrasse 3. Classic daytime coffeehouse with a nice terrace overlooking the Salzach, and with notoriously superior waiters.

Bazillus, Imbergstrasse 2a. Bar on the right bank of the river with a slightly more lived-in feel than some of its trendier neighbours, a largely rock-oriented play-list and an outdoor bar in summer.

Bier Amt, Kaigasse 5. A smart, modern bar just off Mozartplatz with a small amount of outdoor seating. Well placed for a post-sightseeing drink.

Chez Roland, Giselakai 15. Posh venue for Austro-yuppies on the right bank of the Salzach; a place to hang out and be seen in more than a riotous evening out.

Chiemsee Pub, Chiemseegasse 5. Not quite as pub-like as the name suggests, but a friendly modern bar on the Altstadt's eastern edges with some outdoor seating.

Flip, Gstättengasse 7. Lively drinking venue on the western edge of the Altstadt with a youngish crowd and 1950s decor, usually open until 3am.

Kaffehäferl, Universitätsplatz 6. One of the nicer small daytime cafés, with tables set out in a courtyard, and a short menu of lunchtime snacks.

Paulusstub'n, Herrengasse 16. Unassuming, studentish bar hiding on the first floor of an old house below the castle (there's no sign outside advertising its presence). You'll either find its down-to-earth atmosphere refreshing after Salzburg's other bars, or be turned off by its obstinate refusal to be anything other than plain.

Pepe Gonzales, Steingasse 3. Bar serving Mexican beer and nibbles to a young and stylish crowd, with Latin American background music. Throbbing with life at weekends, it's more relaxing at other times of the week.

Schnaitl Pub, Bergstrasse 5. Studeny, grungey bar on the right bank with alternative rock on tape – and occasionally live.

Shamrock, Rudolfskai. Popular Irish pub with Guinness and Kilkenny on tap, and regular live music.

Stieglkeller, Festungsgasse 10. Vast beer garden on the way up to the fortress, with outdoor terraces offering excellent views of the city.

Tomasselli, Alte Markt 9. Most renowned of the city's daytime cafés, serving a bewildering array of cakes and pastries. Tends to be deluged by tourists.

Tom's Bierklinik, Judengasse 11. Small, friendly bar with a bewildering array of bottled beers, down a passage accessible from either Judengasse or Rudolfskai. There are two more lively bars next door if you fancy a change of scene.

Vis-à-vis, Rudolfskai. Smart, riverside bar with an attractive grotto-like interior and a relatively upmarket, dressy clientele.

Yeti, Kaigasse 13. Most youthful and raucous of the bars on a street liberally sprinkled with drinking venues.

Zum Fidelen Affen, Priesterhausgasse 8 (☎877361). Small, very popular pub-like place on the right bank of the river, which also does a good line in traditional Austrian cooking. Reserve if you want to eat.

Entertainment

As befits the city of Mozart, **music** is Salzburg's speciality. Most of this is of the classical variety, but a city of such size can't get away without at least a handful of rock venues and clubs. **Theatre** is also serious business here, although challenging German-language drama may not be everyone's cup of tea.

Don't forget **sport**: addresses for activities like swimming and ice skating can be found in "Listings", p.327. The main spectator sport is without doubt **football**. Austrian champions in 1994, 1995 and 1997, local team **Casino Salzburg** play at the Casino Stadion on Schumacherstrasse, 1.5km north of the Altstadt (☎433332-0; buses #49 or #95 from F-Hanusch-Platz to Nelkenstrasse). Most matches are played on Saturday afternoons, and sometimes Saturday evenings.

SOUND OF MUSIC TOURS

Going on a tour of the sights associated with the 1964 film *The Sound of Music* has become an essential part of the Salzburg experience for many visitors, even if only to wallow in kitsch in the company of other English-speaking tourists. The film tells the over-romanticized, but essentially true, story of the Von Trapp family, as related in Maria Von Trapp's 1949 collection of reminiscences *The Story of the Trapp Family Singers*. The book served as the basis for both a Broadway musical and a succesful German film of the 1950s ("Die Trapp Familie") before receiving the attention of Hollywood.

There's little to choose between the two companies currently offering *Sound of Music* tours: Panorama Tours (☎874029) andSalzburg Sightseeing Tours (☎881616). Both have offices on Mirabellplatz, from which the four-hour-long, twice-daily tours depart (although transfers from your hotel are usually included in the price), and both offer a similar itinerary, taking in Nonnberg Nunnery (where the Julie Andrews character was a novice), Schloss Leopoldskron (the exterior of which was used to represent the Von Trapp family home), the gardens of Schloss Hellbrunn (where a summerhouse was used as the setting for the song "Sixteen Going on Seventeen"), and the church at Mondsee, 30km east of Salzburg (used for the wedding scene).

For those who can't get enough, there's a nightly *Sound of Music* show in the Stieglkeller, Festungsgasse 10 (☎832029; öS520 with dinner, öS360 without), which basically involves a band performing songs from the film in perfunctory fashion.

Classical music

As one would expect from the birthplace of **Mozart**, a rich diet of classical music is available in Salzburg all year round. The Salzburg Festival is one of the most prestigious music festivals in the world, and Salzburg's music academy, the Mozarteum, Schwarzstrasse 36 (☎873154, fax 872996), organizes a range of (both Mozart-related and other classical) concerts throughout the year. The Salzburg tourist office will have details of what's on.

Annual festivals

The outstanding event in Salzburg's musical calendar is the **Salzburger Festspiele**, or Salzburg Festival, a five-week celebration of opera, orchestral music and theatre which runs from the last week of July to the end of August. First staged in 1920, the Festival grew out of discussions between the theatre and opera director Max Reinhardt, composer Richard Strauss, conductor Franz Schalk and playwright Hugo von Hoffmannstahl. Their aim was to gather the world's best musicians and performers for a celebration of all that was best in high culture, embracing both the traditional (set-piece performances of Mozart's works have always been a major feature of the festival) and the adventurously modern. This original conception of the Festival is still very much in place, and the main opera and theatre performances are often entrusted to ground-breaking directors, although the event has, over the years, gained a reputation for social exclusivity – tickets are hard to come by and prices high. Major productions take place in the the purpose-built **Festspielhaus**, but other venues around town are pressed into service too. Anyone interested in obtaining tickets should write as far in advance as possible to *Kartenbüro der Salzburger Festspiele*, Postfach 140, A-5020 Salzburg (☎844501, fax 846682), for programme and booking details.

Salzburg's other major festival, the **Mozartwoche**, spotlights Mozart-penned opera, symphonic and chamber music and takes place every year at the end of January at the Mozarteum. For details, contact the Mozarteum direct at Postfach 34, A-5024 Salzburg (☎873154, fax 872996).

Year-round events: church music and tourist-oriented shows

Sunday morning mass in Salzburg's bigger churches often features Mozart's sacral compositions: services at the **Domkirche** (at 10am, featuring full choir and cathedral organ) and the **Franziskanerkirche** (at 9am, sometimes featuring full orchestra) are well worth trying. Many churches, including the Domkirche, also offer **organ recitals** throughout the year. Look out for posters or ask the tourist office if there's anything happening during your stay.

There's a whole host of year-round musical events and concerts aimed primarily at **tourists** drawn to the city by its reputation as musical centre, although this by no means indicates that they're some kind of rip-off – standards of musicianship are invariably high. We've listed a selection below.

TOURIST-ORIENTED SHOWS

Mozart Serenades (☎436870, fax 436970). In the Gothic Hall of the Blasiuskirche on Bürgerspitalgasse or in the Grosser Saal of the Mozarteum, performances of Mozart favourites and pieces by other eminent Austrians, on Fridays and Saturdays throughout the year.

Salzburger Festungskonzerte. A small chamber orchestra plays a Mozart greatest-hits package in the Fürstenzimmer of the Hohensalzburg fortress. Performances all year round, and candle-lit dinners with music (öS550 per head) are sometimes on offer. Contact Direktion der Salzburger Festungskonzerte, A-Adlgasser-Weg 22 (☎825858, fax 825859).

Salzburger Marionettentheater, Schwarzstrasse 24 (☎872406-0, fax 882141). Popular operas and operettas (usually works by Johann Strauss, Offenbach and Mozart) performed by puppets backed by a playback tape. This is one puppet theatre that can be a bit hard going for younger children, but most adults will marvel at the imaginative set designs and dexterous puppeteering.

Schloss Mönchstein. Harp concerts in the café of the *Schloss Mönchstein* hotel every Saturday and Sunday, 3–4pm. Free to café customers.

Schlosskonzerte in the Schloss Mirabell. Chamber music with a strong, though not wholly, Mozartean content, with performances a couple of times a week throughout the year. Salzburger Schlosskonzerte, Griesgasse 6/1 (☎848586, fax 844747).

Popular music, jazz and clubbing

For **rock and pop**, the *Rockhouse*, Schallmooser Hauptstrasse 46 (☎884914; bus #29), is the main venue for medium-sized touring bands. The adjoining *Riff Bar* (same phone number) plays host to smaller acts and occasional club nights. *Kulturgelände Nonntal*, Mühlbacherhofweg 5 (☎848784; bus #5 or #55), also features rock, **world music** and alternative theatre. The **alternative** end of the rock spectrum plays a significant part in the **Sommer Szene Festival** in June and July, which also features contemporary dance and experimental theatre. Advance information is available from *Szene*, Anton-Neumayr-Platz 2, A-5020 Salzburg (☎843448-22).

For **jazz**, the *Urbanwirt*, next door to the *Rockhouse* on Schallmooser Hauptstrasse (☎06212/2077), holds concerts on Fridays throughout the year except July and August. A festival in early November, the **Salzburger Jazz Herbst**, attracts top-ranking performers – advance programme details are available from Viennaentertainment (☎0222/504 8500, fax 504 8333).

The **clubbing** scene in Salzburg is limited and fairly conservative in nature: *Disco Seven*, Gstättengasse 7, and *Cloud*, Anton-Neumayr-Platz 4, purvey mainstream **techno** to a youngish but dressy crowd. The *Riff Bar* adjoining the *Rockhouse* (see above) organizes evenings of cutting-edge techno and jungle, but these are infrequent (call ☎884914 for details).

Theatre

Salzburg has one of Austria's most prestigious dramatic institutions in the shape of the Salzburger Landestheater, the city's main venue for top-quality, serious work. Drama also plays an important part in the **Salzburg Festival** (see "Classical music", p.325), most notably in the annual production of Hugo von Hoffmannsthal's *Jedermann* (an adaptation of the medieval English mystery play *Everyman*) on an outdoor stage in the Domplatz for the duration of the Festival. Seats are usually sold out weeks in advance, but tickets for standing places are sold on the day.

For non-native speakers, the drawback of most drama in Salzburg is that it's in German. Some of the more avant-garde work can be visually interesting enough to make knowledge of the language irrelevant, however. Venues include: the **Kleines Theater**, Schallmooser Hauptstrasse 50 (☎872154; bus #29), for cabaret and comedy; **Kulturgelände Nonntal**, Mühlbacherhofweg 5 (☎848784), for experimental theatre; **Metropolis**, Nonntaler Hauptstrasse 39b (☎872154; bus #5 or #55), for serious fringe and experimental drama; and the **Salzburger Landestheater**, Schwarzstrasse 22 (☎871512), for classic German-language drama in its main auditorium, and smaller productions/fringe in its Kammerspiele studio theatre.

Listings

Airlines Austrian Airlines, at the airport (☎884511); British Airways, Griesgasse 29 (☎842108); Lauda Air, at the airport (☎854533); Lufthansa, Rainbergstrasse 3a (☎809080); Tyrolean Airways, at the airport (☎854533).

Airport information ☎852091.

American Express Mozartplatz 5 (Mon–Fri 9am–5.30pm, Sat 9am–noon; ☎842501, fax 842501-9).

Bike rental At main train station, 24hr at counter #3. Wider range of more expensive bikes from Velo Active, Willibald-Hauthaler-Strasse 10 (☎868827) and the outdoor bike rental stand on Residenzplatz (Easter–Oct only).

Books American Discount, Alter Markt 1, and Bücherei Schneid, Rainerstrasse 24, both have a selection of English-language books.

Car rental Avis, Ferdinand-Porsche-Strasse 7 (☎877278), and at the airport (☎877278); Budget, Rainerstrasse 17 (☎87345); Hertz, Rainerstrasse 17 (☎873452), and at the airport (☎852094).

Cinemas Current international films, usually dubbed into German, are shown at Central, Linzergasse 17–19 (☎872283), and Mozartkino, Kaigasse 33 (☎842222). Filmkulturzentrum, Gisela Kai 11 (☎873100), is the place to go for art-house and cult films.

Consulates Great Britain, Alter Markt 4 (Mon–Fri 9am–noon; ☎848133); USA, Herbert-von-Karajan-Platz 1 (Mon, Wed & Fri 9am–noon; ☎848776). Other nationals should contact their embassy in Vienna.

Dentists Dentistenkammer, Gstättengasse 21 (584377-7), will recommend a dentist.

Exchange Outside normal banking hours, you can try the exchange counter at the main train station (May–Sept 7am–9pm; Oct–April 7.30am–8.30pm); Salzburger Sparkasse at the airport (daily 8am–4pm); or the exchange counter on Alte Markt (July–Oct Mon–Fri 8.30am–4.30pm, Sat 9.30am–1pm; Nov–June Mon–Fri only).

Gay organizations HOSI (Homosexuelle Initiative), Müllner Hauptstrasse 11 (☎435927).

Hospital St Johannsspital, north of the Altstadt at Müllner Hauptstrasse 48 (☎4482).

Ice skating Städtische Kunsteisbahn, on the right bank at Hermann-Bahr-Promenade 2 (open mid-Sept to March; buses #6 or #49 from Rudolfskai).

Laundry Constructa, and Westinghouse, both on Kaiserschützstrasse, opposite the train station; Wegscheid, Paris-Lodron-Strasse 14.

Lost property Fundbüro, Alpenstrasse 90 (Mon–Fri 7.30am–12.30pm).

Motoring organizations ARBÖ ☎433601, emergency service ☎123.

Police The main police station is 4km south of the centre, in the direction of the Salzburg-Süd autobahn junction, at Alpenstrasse 90 (☎63830).

Post office The main post office is at Residenzplatz 9 (Mon–Fri 7am–7pm, Sat 8–10am); the branch at the train station is open 24hr.

Pharmacy Elisabeth-Apotheke, Elisabethstrasse 1 (☎871484). For emergencies, details of duty pharmacies are posted in all pharmacy windows.

Sightseeing tours Horse-drawn fiacres offer sightseeing tours of the Altstadt; a 25min ride should cost öS380–400 per four-person carriage. For coach tours, Panorama Tours, Mirabellplatz, by St Andrä church (☎874029), offer introductory city tours (hourly, lasting 1hr; öS200), tours of the salt mines in Berchtesgaden, Germany (twice daily, lasting 4hr; öS450), and *Sound of Music* tours (twice daily, lasting 4hr; öS330); Salzburg Sightseeing Tours, Mirabellplatz 2 (☎881616), offer city tours (3 daily, lasting 2hr; öS250), tours of the salt mines in Hallein (2 daily, lasting 4hr; öS450) and *Sound of Music* tours (2 daily, lasting 4hr; öS330).

Swimming Paracelsus Bad, Auerspergstrasse 2, is a large, modern indoor pool complete with water jets, water slide and children's section; a solarium, mud baths and a nudist sunbathing terrace are also on the premises. Open-air pools (May–Sept) include Freibad Leopoldskron, 1km south of the centre at Leopoldskronstrasse 50 (bus #55 from Mirabellplatz) and Freibad Volksgarten, on the right bank at Hermann-Bahr-Promenade 2 (buses #6 or #49 from Rudolfskai).

Taxis There are taxi ranks at the main train station, F-Hanusch-Platz, Residenzplatz and Makartplatz. Or phone ☎8111.

Ticket agencies W. Neubaur, Getreidegasse 14 (☎841157); Polzer, Residenzplatz 3 (☎846500 or 84440; Ticket Shop, Getreidegasse 5 (☎847767).

Train information ☎1717.

Travel agents Landesreisebüro, Getreidegasse 24 (☎846846, fax 846151-14); ÖKISTA, Wolf-Dietrich-Strasse 31 (☎883252, fax 881819); Thomas Cook, Rainerstrasse 24 (☎879496, fax 879166); Young Austria, Alpenstrasse 108a (☎625758, fax 625758-2).

Women's organizations Frauenkulturzentrum, Markus-Sittikus-Strasse 17 (☎871639).

THE SALZBURGER LAND

South of Salzburg, most of the attractions in the province that bears its name are of the outdoor variety, providing an alpine counterweight to the urban refinements of the Land capital. Many travellers heading for Innsbruck and the west miss out on this area altogether, following instead the direct route, which cuts through a corner of Germany before re-entering Austria at Kufstein in the Tyrol. An alternative, and worthwhile, road and rail route forges its way south, however, up the **Salzach Valley** through an area of increasingly rugged mountains. The salt mines and Celtic museum at **Hallein**, and the ice caves and castle at **Werfen** are the main destinations here, and both towns' sites can be treated as day-trips from Salzburg. At **Bischofshofen**, the main Salzach Valley route veers west towards **St Johann im Pongau**, an important skiing and hiking centre, before continuing to **Zell am See**, a classic lakes-and-mountains resort that provides the perfect base from which to strike south into the mountains of the **Hohe Tauern**, home to Austria's highest peak, the magisterial **Grossglockner**.

Bischofshofen also provides the gateway to the southeastern corner of the Salzburger Land: if you're en route to Styria, you might consider stopping off at the ski resort of **Radstadt** or the sleepy, folklore-rich village of **Tamsweg**. South of St Johann, the **Gasteinertal** centres on the evocative nineteenth-century spa-resort of **Badgastein**, ideally placed for explorations of the eastern Hohe Tauern.

Accessing the region by rail couldn't be easier: four daily Salzburg–Innsbruck expresses stop at Hallein, St Johann and Zell am See, while an equal number of Salzburg–Villach trains run through the Gasteinertal (otherwise, get a train to Schwarzach-St Veit and change there), and Salzburg–Graz trains go through Radstadt (otherwise, change at Bischofshofen).

Hallein and around

Twenty kilometres south of Salzburg and served by regular bus and train services, the market town of **HALLEIN** has been synonymous with the **salt trade** since the sixth century BC. Celts from Hallstatt in the Salzkammergut opened up the salt mines in the hills around Bad Dürrnberg, immediately west of Hallein and, apart from a period of abandonment following the departure of the Romans from the region in the fifth century, the mines have been the dominant factor in the town's development ever since. While commercial salt extraction came to an end here in 1989, since then tours of the **Bad Dürrnberg show-mine** have constituted one of the biggest tourist attractions in the region. The historic centre of Hallein itself is picturesque enough to warrant a leisurely stroll, and the local museum has one of the country's richest collections of **Celtic artefacts**. Together Hallein and Bad Dürrnberg make a popular day-trip from Salzburg. By the same token, if you prefer a small-town atmosphere, you could stay in Hallein and use it as a base from which to explore its busier northern neighbour.

Arrival, information and accommodation

The main north–south road and rail routes keep to the east bank of the River Salzach; Hallein's historic centre is over on the west bank. From the **train station**, it's a straightforward five-minute walk to the **tourist office** on the central Unterer Markt (Mon–Fri 8am–4.30pm; ☎06245/85394). Here accommodation in **private rooms** can be arranged, a few of which are in Hallein itself, though most are above the town in Bad Dürrnberg, 5km away (and served by bus or cable car from Hallein). As for **hotels and pensions**, *Löwenbräu Scheicher*, Schöndorferplatz 3 (☎06245/80489, fax 80489-22; ③)

is a big, central **hotel** occupying a lovely old building on a picturesque square, with some of Hallein's best-value rooms, with either en-suite bathroom ③; or shared facilities ③. Elsewhere in the centre, *Bockwirt*, Thunstrasse 12 (☎06245/80623, fax 80623-3; ③; closed Nov), has atmospheric rooms in a historic building in the old town, and *Mikl*, Ederstrasse 2 (☎06245/80229; ③), is an adequate pension a block north of the tourist office, near the museum. On the east side of the river, and handy for both the train station and the main north–south route through town, the *Hafnerwirt*, Bundesstrasse Süd 3 (☎06245/80319, fax 80319-45; ③), is good value for a three-star establishment, offering plain rooms with en-suite facilities, and more expensive ones with TV and phone. Up in Bad Dürrnberg near the salt mines, *Hochdürrnberg*, Rumpelgasse 14 (☎06245/75183; ②), is a small pension offering cosy rooms with shared facilities. There's a **youth hostel** at Schloss Wispach, a restored stately home fifteen minutes north of the train station (☎06245/80397, fax 80397-3).

The Town

Hallein's historic importance as a salt processing and distribution point is still in evidence in the centre's charming town houses, which once belonged to the wealthy merchants who controlled the trade. This clutch of tastefully restored seventeenth-century buildings, resplendent in shades of blue, line the compact, pedestrianized squares that form the core of the town – **Unterer Markt**, **Oberer Markt**, **Bayrhamerplatz** and **Kornsteinplatz**.

Hallein's **Celtic heritage** is the main attraction at the **Stadtmuseum** (May–Oct daily 9am–5pm; öS50), a few steps north of Oberer Markt at Pflegerplatz 5. Housed in the former Saltzkammer, from which the salt trade was administered, the museum holds a well-presented collection of earthenware, daggers and bronze jewellery (labelled in German). The star exhibit is undoubtedly the *Schnabelkanne*, or beaked jug, of Dürrnberg, found in a princely grave near the salt mine, and decorated with a stylized leonine beast (a possible representation of the Celtic god Taranis) with a human head in its mouth. The next floor up concentrates on the history of the salt industry from the Middle Ages onwards, with models of the brine pipelines that brought the dissolved salt down from the mountain, the salt-panning workshops, which once stood on an island in the River Salzach, and the boats that ferried the stuff downstream. All stages of the production process feature in a cycle of eighteenth-century paintings, covering the walls of three rooms originally decorated for Sigismund III Graf von Schrattenbach, penultimate Prince-Archbishop of Salzburg.

Bad Dürrnberg

Eight buses a day (hourly in the morning, less frequently mid-afternoon) connect Hallein train station with **BAD DÜRRNBERG**, a hillside village immediately above town to the west. Providing a more direct route than the five-kilometre road journey, the cable car (öS120 return, öS270 including entry to the show-mine) is a five-minute walk to the southwest of Hallein town centre.

Tours of the local **salt mine** (mid-April to Oct daily 10am–5pm; öS180) last about ninety minutes and begin with a ride on the **Grubenhunt**, or underground train, followed by a sound-and-light show introducing the history of the mine, and a descent to lower galleries via wooden slide – a mode of transport characteristic of Austrian mines, rather akin to sitting astride a large banister and letting yourself go (and explaining why the *Arschleder* is such a common feature of traditional Austrian mining uniforms). Further highlights include a trip across an underground lake on a wooden raft, and a glimpse of the "Man in the Salt", the well-kept body of a medieval miner preserved on the spot where it was found.

It's thought that the **Celts** of Hallstatt (see p.368) opened up Dürrnberg as a centre of salt production some 2500 years ago, partly because their Hallstatt mines were increasingly liable to rock falls and floods, but also due to the excellent transport opportunities afforded by the River Salzach in the valley below. Up until the arrival of the Romans, a Celtic community thrived beside the mine workings, now remembered in the open-air **Keltenmuseum** (April–Oct daily 10am–5pm; öS35) outside the mine entrance. Alongside replicas of Iron Age huts and barns is the reconstruction of a princely grave, showing how the sumptuously clad body of the deceased would have been laid out on a chariot and surrounded by the weapons, drinking flasks and food necessary for a journey to the afterlife.

Surrounded by alpine meadows, Bad Dürrnberg is also a good spot for **walking** – a chairlift at the western end of the village ascends to the summit of the local peak, the 1337-metre-high Zinken.

Eating and drinking

Most of the Gasthöfe in the centre of town have perfectly serviceable restaurants, and a couple of foreign-food outlets ensure that **eating** options in Hallein are varied and near at hand. Two centrally located **drinking** venues worth trying are *Café Barock*, Brückhauserplatz, a stylish bar with pleasant outdoor seating in a courtyard just off Unterer Markt, and *Fallschirm*, Oberer Markt, an informal, friendly place that's usually open until 2am.

Restaurants

Café-Bistro Puppet, Griesplatz. Funky, youngish restaurant offering a mixed Austrian–Italian menu and frequent themed evenings (such as fondue nights or old-time dancing). Located in a modern plaza 5min south of Unterer Markt.

Gasthof Unterholzerbräu, Oberhofgasse. A wide range of inexpensive *Knödel* and *Gröstl* dishes, together with slightly more costly schnitzels.

Pizzeria La Grotta, Dr-Albert-Eder-Strasse. A wide range of pizza and pasta dishes, and it's open until 1am.

Stadtkrug, Bayerhamerplatz. A good cross-section of typical Austrian dishes, and a popular lunchtime buffet for around öS100. On the first floor of a downtown building, so there's no outdoor seating.

Sun Ly, Dr-Albert-Eder-Strasse 6. Fairly standard Chinese restaurant offering one of the cheapest Tagesmenüs in town, from just öS65.

Tepito, Salzachtal Bundesstrasse. On the south side of the river (you'll pass it on the way into town from the station), serving Mexican food and steaks in "fun" (as in garish) surroundings.

Werfen and around

Forty kilometres south of Salzburg, the village of **WERFEN** draws day-trippers from the provincial capital to see two very different attractions: the impressive, fanciful Hohenwerfen **fortress** presiding over the village itself, and the **Eisriesenwelt**, giant ice caves in the mountainside to the northeast. Werfen is fairly easy to get to, though not all southbound express trains from Salzburg stop here – check before you travel – and you do need to allow plenty of time to reach the caves if doing the trip by public transport. Provided you set off reasonably early, you should be able to see both the caves and the fortress in the space of a day.

Werfen itself comprises a single street and a clutch of Gasthöfe and shops, but its impressive geographical situation, in a valley wedged between sheer, rocky mountains, makes it an evocative place to stay for a night or two. There's a **tourist office**

(Mon–Fri 8am–noon & 2–5pm, Sat 8am–noon; ☎06468/388) on the main street with a small list of **private rooms**. The nearby *Gasthof Obauer*, Hauptstrasse 46 (☎06486/212-0, fax 212-12; ④), is a medieval house that has modern rooms with en-suite shower and WC. The **restaurant** at the *Obauer* is the place to go for Austrian/modern European gourmet cuisine, while the cheaper *Goldenen Hirschen* nearby has all the usual schnitzels, and the *Alte Post*, also on the Hauptstrasse, offers an acceptable range of pizzas.

Hohenwerfen fortress

Immediately visible from all points of arrival, and a brisk fifteen-minute walk from Werfen train station, the **fortress** of Hohenwerfen dominates the village from a rocky outcrop to the north. Subjected to a cycle of sackings, fires and rebuildings, the fortress has changed immeasurably since Salzburg's Archbishop Gebhard von Felsenstein first fortified the spot as insurance against Bavarian incursions in the eleventh century. The guided tour (in German with English summary, frequency during the following opening hours depends on demand: April & Oct 9am–4.30pm; May, June & Sept 9am–5pm; July & Aug 9am–6pm; öS100) takes you from an impressive inner courtyard to the chapel, where Gothic fresco fragments depicting the Apocalypse are preserved, before passing through state rooms and a torture chamber to the belfry, which offers impressive views of the Salzach Valley and the encroaching craggy peaks. The small **museum of falconry** at the fortress entrance anticipates the bird-of-prey flying displays that take place on the knoll above (mid-July to mid-Aug at 11am, 2pm & 4pm; mid-Aug to Oct & April to mid-July at 11am & 3pm).

The ice caves

Getting to the **Eisriesenwelt** is a scenic excursion in itself, involving a road and cable-car ascent to reach the cave entrance 1641m above the valley floor, and providing views back towards Werfen and the castle. A bus from Werfen train station (currently departing at 8.15am, 10.35am, 12.35pm & 2.35pm; öS70 return; the driver sells a combined ticket covering bus, cable car and cave for öS270) takes you uphill as far as the car park at the road's end (also accessible by private car) 5km above Werfen to the northeast; from there it's a ten-minute walk to the cable-car station (öS110 return). The caves are only accessible by 75-minute guided tour (usually hourly, more frequently at peak periods; May–Oct daily 9–11am & 2–5pm; öS90), which leads past some spectacular ice formations, diving through narrow passageways (involving some steep climbs) before emerging into breathtaking, imaginatively lit galleries. It's cold enough to warrant a sweater or jacket, so come prepared.

Eastern Salzburger Land

Eight kilometres south of Werfen, there's a parting of the ways at Bischofshofen, as one rail line heads westwards to **St Johann im Pongau**, **Zell am See** and the Tyrol, and the other turns eastwards towards Styria, running along the wide valley floor of the Ennstal with the magnificent ridge of the **Niedere Tauern** range rising to the south. Just short of the Styrian border lies **Radstadt**, an attractive historical town and skiing centre. The A10 autobahn also leaves the Salzach Valley near Bischofshofen, veering southeast across the western shoulder of the Niedere Tauern towards the **Tauerntunnel** and Carinthia. Minor roads just before the Carinthian border head into the upper Mur Valley in the far southeastern corner of the Salzburger Land, home to attractive villages squeezed between pasture-covered hillsides such as **Tamsweg**, an alternative starting point for onward routes into Styria.

Radstadt

Midway between Bischofshofen and the Styrian ski resort of Schladming (see p.247), **RADSTADT** was fortified by the archbishops of Salzburg in the sixteenth century to provide a bulwark against the Turks (who, in fact, never got this far) – partly moated walls punctuated by a series of impressive towers still encompass the town centre. With the Tauern ranged imperiously to the south, it's an undeniably pretty spot, and a popular base for winter sports, but unless you're in this part of Austria to ski it probably merits only a brief stop.

The obvious thing to do on arrival is to take the fifteen-minute walk around the town walls. Marking the eastern gateway, the **Kapuzinerturm** (June–Sept Mon–Sat 9.30–11.30am & 2–4pm; öS30) harbours a smallish display of medieval weaponry. West of here is the Romanesque **Pfarrkirche**, with wonderfully expressive postwar stained glass by Josef Wildmoser depicting scenes from the Life of the Virgin. Ten minutes' walk west of the centre, the **Heimatmuseum** in Schloss Lerchen (June to mid-Oct 10am–noon & 3–5pm; late Dec to March 10–11am & 3–4pm; öS40) has the usual collection of local costumes and crafts.

Practicalities

Radstadt's **train station** is five minutes' walk from the town centre: turn left out of the station and take the path that strikes off up the hill to the right. Another left turn at the top of the hill will bring you shortly to the Stadtplatz, where there's a **tourist office** (Mon–Sat 8am–noon & 2–6pm; ☎06452/4305, fax 6702) next to the Rathaus, with touch-screen accommodation information in an outside lobby (7am–midnight). The tourist office also has a list of **private rooms**, though these don't feature among the touch-screen info. Of the local **hotels**, *Gasthof Torwirt*, Hoheneggstrasse 12 (☎06452/5541; ③), is an inexpensive central choice, offering small rooms with en-suite facilities; a step up in price affords the comfort of the *Hotel Post*, Stadtplatz 8 (☎06452/4306; ④), and the *Gründler*, Schlossstrasse 45 (☎06452/590; ⑤), which has indoor pool and sauna.

A couple of Gashöfe on the Stadtplatz offer stolid Austrian lunches, otherwise the best **places to eat** are mostly found along the adjacent Schernbergstrasse, where *Gasthof Stegerbräu* at no. 14 has a wide range of inexpensive Austrian standards, more costly freshwater fish, and its own beer brewed on the premises. *Paradiso* at no. 8 offers tasty pasta dishes and pizzas, while *China-Restaurant Mauer* at no. 17 makes up for a pretty uninspiring line in oriental cuisine by offering the cheapest Mittagsmenü in town, at öS65. Best – and most expensive – of the bunch is *Gasthof Haberstatter*, Schernbergstrasse 12, which serves top-notch meat-heavy dishes such as *Tafelspitz* and *Zwiebelrostbraten*, as well as vegetarian selections like *Spinatstrudel* and *Blattsalat mit gebackenem Schafkäse* (green salad with fried sheep's cheese). Among **places to drink**, the café of the *Hotel Post* is a reasonable daytime venue for coffee as well as cakes, while *3P*, a few steps away from the Stadtplatz at Karl-Berg-Gasse 10, is a lively nighttime bar with pizzeria attached.

Tamsweg

From Radstadt, the Bundesstrasse 99 (served by local buses) and the A10 autobahn follow roughly parallel routes across the **Radstädter Tauern** range towards the Upper Mur Valley, principal vale of the **Lungau**, an isolated corner of the Salzburger Land where archaic folk traditions have survived. The most spectacular of these is the **Samsonumzug**, or Samson procession, which takes place in **TAMSWEG**, 50km south of Radstadt, on several summer feast days, notably Corpus Christi (**Fronleichnam**, in late May), the last weekend in July and the first Sunday in August. An effigy of Samson, accompanied by two dwarfs and the town band, is paraded through the streets. One theory links the Samson effigy to giant figures constructed by sixteenth-century locals in order to frighten off the Turks, but the procession is more likely the Christianized version of some indecipherable pagan ritual.

The town of Tamsweg itself has a pleasant Marktplatz and a pilgrimage church above to the south. There's a **tourist office** (Mon–Fri 9am–noon & 2–5pm, Sat 9am–1pm; ☎06474/416) in the Rathaus on the Marktplatz which will find you a private room or hotel. Tamsweg is at the westernmost end of the Murtalbahn, the railway that provides public transport downstream to Murau in Styria (see Chapter 4) and the main Vienna–Klagenfurt line beyond.

St Johann im Pongau

Main town of the **Pongau**, an area of lush alpine pastures that stretches from Bischofshofen in the north to the mouth of the Gasteinertal in the southwest, **ST JOHANN** has become one of Austria's most popular outdoor holiday centres. Together with **Alpendorf**, the hotel-filled village suburb 3km uphill to the southeast, it offers a wide range of sporting activities year-round, and it's these that constitute the main reason for being here. In wintertime, it's a much-favoured destination among European **skiers** (it features only intermittently in British package-holiday brochures). When the snow has melted, the slopes cater to an influx of **walkers**, while **swimming** and **tennis** are the summertime activities of choice in town.

The Town and around

Stretched along the eastern side of the River Salzach, St Johann is divided into two parts, **Obermarkt**, built on a bluff surmounted by the distinctive twin towers of the Domkirche, and **Untermarkt** on the river bank below it. You might think the place looks comparatively modern and charmless, and that's because it was largely destroyed by fire in 1855, so little of real vintage survives. People from all across the Habsburg monarchy raised money to rebuild the church, hence its current, neo-Gothic appearance.

For those who have come to ski, local passes (one-day öS380; six-day öS1600) cover a large area of interlinked pistes and lifts – known as the Sportwelt Amadé – which encompasses St Johann and nearby villages Wagrain and Flachau. Slopes are best suited to beginners and intermediates. For walkers, the most direct route to the hills above the town is the Hahnbaumbahn chairlift, which begins on the northeast fringes of the centre near the *Sporthotel Prem*, and ascends to the 1200-metre **Hahnbaumalm**, an area of alpine meadow that offers plenty of trails. Hourly buses link St Johann with **Alpendorf** 3km to the south, where a more challenging range of hiking routes are served by a gondola (June & mid-Sept to mid-Oct Wed & Sun 9am–5pm; July to mid-Sept daily 9am–5pm; öS120 return) and a chairlift to the **Gernkogel** (June to mid-Sept 9.30am–4.30pm; öS50 return).

Nestling in a wooded valley 5km south of St Johann, the **Liechtensteinklamm** (mid-May to Oct daily 8am–5pm; öS30) is by virtue of its extreme depth and narrowness one of the most dramatic gorges in the Alps. It's also easy to reach on foot in about an hour: from St Johann head south to the village of Plankenau, where signposted roads and paths bear off to the right; from Alpendorf, a footpath at the southern end of the village leads down to the gorge.

THE PONGAUER PERCHTENLAUF

One of Austria's oddest midwinter folk rituals, the **Pongauer Perchtenlauf** takes place on the night of January 5–6 . It's an annual event that is shared by the Pongau towns of Altenmarkt, Bischofshofen, Badgastein and St Johann, each of which takes a turn hosting the festival on a four-year cycle.

The Perchtenlauf revolves around a procession of young men dressed in the white costumes and masks of the Schiachperchten, kindly spirits who wave birch twigs and jangle cowbells in order to ward off demons and herald a year full of bumper harvests and good fortune. They're accompanied by Schönperchten who wear enormous head-dresses, some of which weigh up to 50kg, their finery designed to bring light to a world subsumed in midwinter darkness. Some head-dresses are decorated with mirrors, to scare away evil spirits afraid of seeing their own reflection. Performances of the Perchtenlauf are traditionally an all-male affair, which – seeing as the Schönperchten are supposed to be accompanied by young wenches – inevitably involves a certain amount of cross-dressing.

The Pongauer Perchtenlauf takes place in Altenmarkt in 1999, Bischofshofen in 2000, St Johann in 2001, and Badgastein in 2002.

Practicalities

Both the main Bundesstrasse and the **train station** are on the west bank of the Salzach, on the opposite side of the river to the town itself. Turn left outside the train station and cross the river to reach the snaking Hauptstrasse, which curls round Untermarkt before climbing into Obermarkt, site of the **tourist office** (Mon–Fri 8.30am–noon & 2–6pm, Sat 9am–noon; ☎06412/6036, fax 6036-74). Both St Johann and Alpendorf have plenty of **private rooms** (available from the tourist office). The tourist office also handles accommodation in farmhouses (①), although you'll probably need your own transport to get to them, and families staying a reasonable length of time (more than three days) are usually preferred.

There are two **youth hostels** in the suburb of **Plankenau** 2km south of town on the way to the **Liechtensteinklamm**: *Plankenauer Hof*, Liechtensteinklammstrasse 126 (☎06412/80766, fax 8076-4); and *Schlosshof*, Liechtensteinklammstrasse 144 (☎06412/6394, fax 6394-4). There's another hostel 1km above Alpendorf in Oberalpendorf: *Jugendgästehaus Weitenmoos*, Oberalpendorf 102 (☎06412/6222, fax 6222-4).St Johann's two well-appointed **campsites** are both open all year round: *Wieshof* (☎06412/8519) is nearest the train station, in Untermarkt just off the road to Plankenau, and *Hirschenwirt* (☎06412/6012) lies at the southern end of town, signposted off the Bundesstrasse. Price categories given for hotels below are for the summer season; expect to pay twice as much in winter.

Hotels and pensions

Brückenwirt-Tennerhof, Hauptstrasse 78 (☎06412/4259, fax 4259-55). Big hotel in traditional Gasthof-style with modern, comfortable rooms in Untermarkt, just across the river from the train station. ④.

Lechner, Kasernstrasse 26 (☎06412/4262, fax 4262-6). Good-value, cosy downtown hotel in Untermarkt, all rooms with en-suite facilities. ③.

Lerch, Liechtensteinklammstrasse 12 (☎06412/4251, fax 4015-13). Use of outdoor pool and children's playground, together with on-site pony-riding, make this a popular choice for young families (⑤). The same family run the *Landhaus Liechtenstein* next door (☎06412/5201, fax 5201-30), offering simple holiday apartments and sharing the same facilities. (②).

Sonnhof, Alpendorf 16 (☎06412/7271, fax 7271-35). Smallish B&B-style hotel up the hill in Alpendorf offering buffet breakfast, plus sauna and solarium facilities. It's a bargain in summer (③).There's also a range of four- and six-person apartments (①).

Sporthotel Prem, Premweg 7 (☎06412/6315, fax 6315-47). Large top-of-the-range hotel in Obermarkt, which offers outdoor pool, indoor and outdoor tennis courts, and tennis courses run by an Australian coaching team. ⑤.

Eating and drinking

Although most of the hotels in St Johann and Alpendorf have good **restaurants** offering a standard range of Austrian food, some of the traditional Gasthöfe or ethnic restaurants in the town centre provide a bit more atmosphere. There's a decent choice of nightlife, too, with the **bars** of St Johann drawing in locals from all over the Pongau.

RESTAURANTS

Bacher, Bundesstrasse. South of the train station on the Schwarzach road, a big family-run Gasthof popular with the locals, serving good-quality Austrian cuisine at a mid-range price.

Bologna, Dr-Untersteiner-Weg 6. Inexpensive Italian with a good selection of pasta dishes and pizzas, midway between Ober- and Untermarkt, signed off the main street.

Braugasthof, Hauptstrasse 22. Good local cuisine at reasonable prices, with rustic wooden tables and chairs lending the place a homely, beer-hall atmosphere. There's a pizzeria attached, but it's not a bad place just to have a drink.

Lotus, Hauptstrasse, Untermarkt. Straightforward Chinese with a good-value Mittagsmenü. *Tao* disco-bar in the basement.

Tiroler Wirt, Hauptstrasse 66. Cosy little place serving Austrian standards, Tyrolean specialities and fondue.

BARS

Baradox, Hauptstrasse, Untermarkt. Perpetually busy bar with youthful clientele and loud, rocky music.

Oberforsthoferalm, Alpendorf village centre. Roomy, pub-like venue, which often features live music (usually folk) and discos, attracting devotees from all over the Salzburger Land.

Titanik, Spitalgasse 4. Small and friendly bar in the town centre, hidden away below the church.

Tschecherl, Wagrainerstrasse 4. Of the bars in Obermarkt, this is the one most popular with the locals, therefore it's reasonably busy all year round. There's a pizzeria attached.

The Gasteinertal

West of St Johann im Pongau, a main road and rail route splits off to head south up the **Gasteinertal**, before tunnelling under the **Hohe Tauern** mountains into Carinthia. Popular with skiers and a paradise for hikers, the Gasteinertal was developed as a centre for tourism early in the last century, when the **hot springs** of Badgastein attracted an influx of wealthy central Europeans eager to take the cure. Still the valley's main centre, **Badgastein** remains one of Austria's most eccentric resorts, a stately cluster of nineteenth-century hotels catering to a strange mixture of mountain-bound outdoors enthusiasts and spa patients. Lower down the valley, the spa town of **Bad Hofgastein** has a more modern feel, while spa-free **Dorfgastein** is small, tranquil and rural by comparison. All three provide access to the surrounding mountains, although Badgastein and its two satellites, **Böckstein** and **Sportgastein**, nestling beneath the eastern spur of the Hohe Tauern, stand closest to the really spectacular alpine terrain. At the entrance to the valley, the cave at **Klammstein** makes for an interesting stop-off.

As far as **winter sports** are concerned, the slopes in the Gasteinertal are more challenging than anywhere else in the Salzburger Land save for Zell am See–Kaprun (see p.342). There's a variety of pistes suitable for advanced and the better intermediate skiers above Bad Hofgastein, Badgastein, Sportgastein and in the Angertal (a side-valley located between Bad Hofgastein and Badgastein). Sportgastein also offers off-piste skiing. Snowboarders are well catered for with half-pipes at Sportgastein, Badgastein and Dorfgastein, and there are snowboarding schools at all the valley's main centres. The **Gastein Super Ski pass** (day pass öS400, six days öS1900) covers all lifts and buses in the Gasteinertal.

Although the main Carinthia-bound **rail line** runs up the Gasteinertal, leaving the main Salzach Valley route at Schwarzach-St Veit, most express trains only stop at Badgastein itself, and **buses** present the best way of getting around once you're here.

Klammstein and Dorfgastein

Regional train services, as well as buses from Badgastein, stop at **KLAMMSTEIN** at the entrance to the valley, where the **Naturhöhle** (guided tours on the hour; Aug 10am–6pm; late March to July & Sept to mid-Oct 11am–3pm; closed Mon; öS100) was once used by local Protestants for clandestine prayer. The chamber where they used to meet has been dubbed the **Fledermaus-Dom**, or bat cathedral. The cave entrance is off the main road to the east, about 45min by foot from the well-signed car park. A visit to the hunting trophies and mineral display at the nearby sixteenth-century **Burg Klammstein** (45min tours at 2pm; closed Mon; öS30) is less interesting, although kids might enjoy the **Gespensterschau**, or ghost show, a series of tableaux illustrating the spirits said to inhabit the nearby cave.

Ten kilometres up the valley, the attractive and quiet village of **DORFGASTEIN** lacks the thermal springs that supply the settlements to the south, and consequently tourism here is relatively low-key. Things liven up slightly in the winter, due the village's nascent reputation as a good snowboarding area. There's a gondola to the heights above the village to the east, a number of small Gasthöfe and a **tourist office** (Mon–Fri 8am–noon & 2–6pm, Sat 8am–noon; ☎06433/7277) in the village centre doling out **private rooms**.

Bad Hofgastein

Lacking both the rural charms of Dorfgastein and the post-imperial splendours of Badgastein, **BAD HOFGASTEIN** is a predominantly modern spa-resort fed by the waters piped down from the head of the valley, its clinic-like hotels grouped around a pedestrianized centre bordered by leafy parks. There's nothing of any vintage save for the late-Gothic **Pfarrkirche** on the main square. Inside, the high altar features an early sixteenth-century Madonna and Child by a follower of Michael Pacher, flanked by contrasting eighteenth-century statuettes – featuring, from left to right, saints Rupert, Dominic, Catherine and Virgil. The whole thing is topped off by an allegory of the Holy Trinity after plans by **Fischer von Erlach** – the Father is on the right holding a globe, the Son on the left, and the Holy Spirit hovering between them in the form of a dove. Note, too, the cherub-bedecked pulpit featuring another traditional piece of symbolism common in areas once strongly Protestant – the outstretched arm holding a crucifix, depicting the triumph of the Catholic Church.

On the western side of the town centre, a direct route into the hills is provided by the **Schlossalmbahn** (June to mid-Oct on the hour 8am–4pm; ascent öS155, return öS180), which climbs in two stages: by funicular to the 1302-metre **Kitzstein Alm**, then by cable car to the 2051-metre **Kleine Scharte** (on the hour 8am–4pm). About 1km south of the funicular station, roads ascend into the **Angertal**, an important skiing area in winter and attractive walking area in summer – but bear in mind the numerous chair-lifts here are only open during the winter season.

Practicalities

The main **train station** is 3km north of town, and most arrivals are met by a local bus into the centre. There's a smaller station, **Bad Hofgastein Haltestelle**, much nearer the town centre, but only regional trains stop here. The town's **bus station**, served by regular Badgastein–Zell am See and Badgastein–Schwarzach services, is just 1km west of the centre on the main road through the valley. The **tourist office** in the pedestrianized zone (Mon–Fri 8am–6pm, Sat 9am–noon; ☎06432/71100) offers a deluge of information on local spa facilities and books visitors into **private rooms**. Of the **hotels and pensions**, *Frühstuckspension Berghof*, Wasserfallgasse 19 (☎06432/6418, fax 6418-3; ③), just north of the town centre, is a big chalet-style building with en-suite facilities in all rooms, and *Schafflinger*, Grünlandstrasse 14 (☎06432/6131-0, fax 6131-4; ②), is an excellent pension ten minutes northwest of the centre in the shadow of the hills. There's no end of more pricey hotels offering spa facilities: the five-star *Grand Park*, Kurgartenstrasse 26 (☎06432/6356-0, fax 8454; ⑨), is bang in the centre and has elegant, balconied rooms together with thermal pool, massage, sauna and solarium facilities, while *Sporthotel Alpina*, Parkstrasse 13 (☎06432/8475-0, fax 8475-70; ⑦), a good mid-price choice, offers the same facilities but without the fin-de-siècle pretensions.

For **eating**, *Café Röck*, on a small square just west of the church, is good for inexpensive daytime pasta dishes; *Kraut & Rüben*, Pirkerstrasse 3, is a mid-priced vegetarian restaurant; and *Gasthof zur Alten Post*, just outside the Pfarrkirche, serves traditional Austrian food including fish and game and at least one vegetarian choice. *Weitmoser Schlössl*, 2km out of town on the Badgastein road, offers top-notch Austrian cuisine in a fifteenth-century castle. Among your choice of **drinking** venues, *Matchbox*, Kirchgasse 10, is a nice café-bar, while *Bel Ami*, on the main road to Badgastein at Erzwiegergasse 5, is the place to go for easy-listening sounds and old-time dancing.

To experience the soothing effect of the **spa waters**, head for the Thermentempel in the centre, a modern indoor pool complex with four thermal spring-fed pools – but it's expensive if all you want is a quick swim (daily 9am–8.30pm; öS150).

Badgastein

Ranged across the head of the valley where the **Gasteiner Ache** descends in a series of cascades, the streets of **BADGASTEIN** gaze down on the Gasteinertal like rows of seating in some ancient amphitheatre. Although known as a **spa** since medieval times, Badgastein didn't really take off until the early nineteenth century, when a stream of

---

TAKING THE CURE: BADGASTEIN

Badgastein owes its reputation as a health resort to an abundant supply of hot spring water rich in **radon**, a radioactive gas reputed to help the human body renew itself by stimulating cell growth. The medical establishment is far from united on the true efficacy of the spa water (it has been promoted as a cure for everything from diabetes to infertility over the years), although its beneficial effect on rheumatism and arthritis is incontrovertible – and, like any good bath, it's a great way to beat stress.

The easiest way to sample the soothing properties of the waters is to head for the town's main swimming pool, the Felsenbad on Bahnhofplatz (daily 9am–8pm; öS150), which has both indoor and outdoor pools fed by spa water. The adjoining Kurhaus (Mon–Fri 8am–noon & 2–5pm) is probably the best place in which to try out some of the more obvious treatments, like a soak in a thermal bath (öS200) or a massage (from öS220).

Numerous other healing institutions exist offering a seemingly endless range of specific therapies involving the spa water – steam baths, radon mud packs and mouthwash treatments being just a few, as well as exposure to radon in the underground Healing Galleries (see p.341). The Badgastein tourist office will happily supply details of these.

society figures – led by Archduke Johann (see p.371), who built the *Meranhaus* here in 1828 – descended on the valley to take the cure. Kaiser Wilhelm I, Emperor Franz-Josef and Bismarck were among those who followed. The town has undergone numerous face-lifts since, and is currently reinventing itself as a chic, "society" resort complete with stylish hotels, modern congress centre and a casino. The languorous, nineteenth-century ambience that still prevails is certainly unique in alpine Austria, however, and you'll find it either appealingly nostalgic or sombrely oppressive. The influx of ski tourists in winter invigorates this strangely ossified place, as do two events in summer that provide an excuse for general partying – the **Sonnwendfeier** on the night of June 21–22, when bonfires are lit on the hills above the valley to mark the summer solstice; and the annual **Strassenfest**, spread over the last weekend in July, featuring food, drink and live music in the streets.

Arrival, information and accommodation

Both **buses** and **trains** come to rest on Bahnhofplatz in the upper part of town; the centre is downhill to the north. Turn left outside the train station and walk down the hill to reach the **tourist office**, at Kaiser-Franz-Josef-Strasse 1 (July–Sept Mon–Fri 8am–6pm, Sat 10am–noon & 4–6pm, Sun 10am–1pm; Oct–June Mon–Fri 8am–6pm; ☎06434/2531, fax 2531-37), where you can buy a local **hiking map** and book into a **private room** in either Badgastein, or **Böckstein** 3km up the valley. The *Adler Jugendhotel*, Kaiser-Franz-Josef-Strasse 36 (☎06434/2369, fax 4064), is a **youth hostel** on the left as you head downhill towards the tourist office.

Many of Badgastein's **hotels** have radon-rich spa waters on the premises (often piped direct to the bath in your room) free of charge, as well as a range of other spa-related services (massages, saunas, mud baths and so on), for which guests pay an extra fee.

HOTELS AND PENSIONS

Grüner Baum, Kötschachtal 25 (☎06434/2516, fax 2516-25). In an idyllic side-valley 3km east of town, this is a luxurious hotel complex grouped around several traditional, chalet-style buildings, and augmented by an open-air pool and tennis courts. Spa waters on site. ⑧.

Haus Freymann, Shareckstrasse 33 (☎06434/2273). Small pension a 10min walk from the train station, on the southern fringes of town. All rooms have en-suite shower and WC. ③.

Haus Hirt, Kaiserhofstrasse 14 (☎06434/2797-0, fax 2797-48). A large villa that was once the favoured retreat of Thomas Mann, offering indoor pool, sauna, solarium. Spa waters on site. ⑧.

Krone, Bahnhofplatz 8 (☎06434/2330-0, fax 2330-86). An old-fashioned cure-oriented hotel with long dark corridoors, 1950s furnishings and en-suite facilities. Spa waters on site. ④.

Landhaus Gletschermühle, Gletschermühlstrasse 7 (☎06434/2097, fax 2380-30). Family-run chalet-style pension in a residential area just east of the train station. All rooms have en-suite facilities and TV. Spa waters on site. ④.

Meranhaus, Kaiser-Franz-Josef-Strasse 11 (☎06434/2328, fax 2386-3). Built in 1828 as the hunting lodge of Archduke Johann (see p.371), an atmospheric old-fashioned place. All rooms have en-suite facilities. Spa waters on site. ④.

Mirabell, Bismarckstrasse 4 (☎06434/3301-0, fax 3967) A venerable downtown spa-hotel, where Bismarck stayed in the 1870s and 1880s. Now rooms are modern with en-suite facilities and TV. Spa waters on site. ⑧.

Pension Bader, Pyrkerhöhenstrasse 17 (☎06434/2031, fax 2031-25). Small, family-run guesthouse in the residential streets east of the train station. All rooms have en-suite shower and WC. ③.

Pension Haussteiner, Shareckstrasse 7 (☎06434/2234). Small pension in residential streets south of the train station. Rooms have shared facilities. ②.

Simader, Shareckstrasse 14 (☎06434/2702, fax 2771-49). Modern chalet-style building in a residential area in the southern end of town, a block west of the main Tauern tunnel-road, and a nice change from the nineteenth-century hotels in the town centre. Advertises itself as a "biker-friendly" hotel. All rooms have en-suite facilities and TV. Spa waters on site. ③.

Villa Solitude, Kaiser-Franz-Josef-Strasse 16 (☎06434/5101-0, fax 5101-3). Small, exclusive hotel with a limited number of rooms decked out in opulent, nineteenth-century style, some with views of the Gastein falls. Residents use the spa facilities of the *Grüner Baum*. ⑨.

Around town

The main attraction of Badgastein is its situation, its streets zigzagging across the hillside and affording a new vista with every turn. **Kongressplatz** provides a focus of sorts, site of the modern Kongresshaus as well as a small museum in **Haus Austria** across the road (mid-May to Sept daily 10.30am–noon & 3.30–6pm; Oct to mid-May Wed 3.30–6pm; öS30), which limits itself to a few stuffed animals and an uninspiring account of gold-mining in Böckstein (see p.340). Bismarckstrasse and Kaiser-Wilhelm-Promenade lead northwards past two churches, the oldest and furthest of which is the fourteenth-century **Nikolaikirche**, the roof of whose short nave is supported by a single pillar. Many of the frescoes, painted in the late fifteenth century – including the image of St Nicholas on the north side of the choir – are badly faded, but look out for the vibrant Day of Judgement in the nave, with sinners being shepherded into hell by club-wielding demons.

Into the mountains

In summer you can scale two local peaks, which are also served by cable car. Just east of Badgastein train station, the Stubnerkogelbahn gondola (on the hour June to mid-Oct 9am–4pm; öS180 return), ascends to the 2230-metre **Stubnerkogel**, a superb vantage point providing glimpses of the three main peaks in the area, with the Grossglockner to the west, the Ankogel to the southeast and the Dachstein to the east. It's also the starting point for numerous hiking trails. On the opposite side of the valley, the Graukogelbahn (on the hour July–Sept 9am–6pm in good weather only; ascent öS155, return öS180) is a two-stage chairlift to the *Graukogelhütte*, on an alpine meadow some 500m below the 2492-metre-high peak of the **Graukogel** itself. It's an evocative place from which to look out over the wilds of the Hohe Tauern.

For walkers, one of two quick routes out of Badgastein and into the mountains is along the **Kaiser-Wilhelm-Promenade**, which leaves the northeastern end of town to work its way along the Kotschachtal, passing the *Grüner Baum* hotel complex before continuing into increasingly desolate alpine territory. The **Prossau** hut, about two and a half hours away, is a reasonable target to aim for. Alternatively, take the **Erzherzog-Johann-Promenade**, which leaves the Bad Hofgastein road about 100m south of the Badgastein tourist office and leads round the northeastern flanks of the Stubnerkogel before arriving in the Angertal, and at the **Angeralm** (where there's a café-restaurant) after about an hour.

Eating and drinking

Many of the hotels offer good-quality (if not always cheap) **food**, while the town's plentiful restaurants widen your choice of venues. There's a good range of bars for a nighttime **drink**, though some of them are only open in the winter season (early Dec to mid-April), and maybe for a couple of months in the summer (typically July & Aug).

RESTAURANTS

Echo, Karl-Heinz-Waggerl-Strasse 21. Serves straightforward Austrian dishes, with an outdoor terrace overlooking the Gasteiner Ache.

Fischerwirt, Karl-Heinz-Waggerl-Strasse 27. In an old wooden house at the southern end of town, specializing in fish and pizzas. Their Mittagsmenü (öS85) is good value.

Jägerhäusl, Kaiser-Franz-Josef-Strasse. Brash city-centre place, serving a wide range of Austrian main dishes and lunchtime snacks in a lively atmosphere.

Prälatur, Kaiser-Franz-Josef-Strasse. Small and stylish restaurant aiming at a smart, youngish crowd, with a limited menu of artfully presented Austrian-international food – not as expensive as its pretensions might suggest.

Straubinger Stüberl, Straubingerplatz 2. A reasonably central place dishing up standard Austrian fare, and usually offering a good-value Tagesmenü.

Villa Solitude, Kaiser-Franz-Josef-Strasse 16. An excellent source of Austrian and modern European cuisine, although the decor verges on kitsch – you can always escape to the outdoor terrace in summer.

CAFÉS AND BARS

Bellevue Alm, on the hill above Kaiser-Franz-Josef-Strasse. A rustic mountain hut-styled venue with accordion-driven folk music and a limited menu of Austrian nibbles.

Eden Pub, Karl-Heinz-Waggerl-Strasse. Best of the central bars, with a convivial, pub atmosphere.

Filou Bier Kneipe, at the northern entrance to town on the main Bad Hofgastein road, near the tourist office. Smart but unpretentious café-bar. Usually open all year-round.

Old El Paso, Kaiser-Franz-Josef-Strasse. Mexican beer and nibbles served to a noisy, youthful crowd.

Schafflinger Schialm, at the south end of town on the Böckstein road. Old-time dancing and folk music, starting (in winter) with a tea dance at 5pm and becoming more rowdy as the evening progresses.

Schuh, Karl-Heinz-Waggerl-Strasse. Best of the places for a daytime coffee, with a tempting range of cakes and pastries and an outdoor terrace offering views down the valley.

Böckstein

Four kilometres south of Badgastein, and an easy walk if you follow the Kaiserin-Elisabeth-Promenade, which starts near the Stubnerkogel gondola station, the village of **BÖCKSTEIN** was once a mining settlement devoted to the extraction of gold from the Radhausberg to the southeast. Tucked away on the western side of the village, **Altböckstein** was founded by eighteenth-century prince-archbishop of Salzburg Sigismund von Schrattenbach as a model community for the workers, complete with tenement-like living quarters, village green, and quaint chapel on a knoll. All the buildings have been tastefully restored, and there's a small **museum** in one of the old storehouses (☎06434/4253; mid-May to Sept daily except Mon 10am–noon & 3–6pm; Oct to mid-May by appointment only; öS30) displaying old mining equipment, ceremonial uniforms and a model of the **Sackzug**, the rudimentary means by which ore was transported to the valley bottom – sacks of the stuff were tied together and then sent down a wooden chute, with a miner riding on the first sack rather like the pilot of a bobsleigh.

Böckstein's numerous **private rooms** can be booked through the tourist office in Badgastein. Of the handful of **hotels**, the *Rader*, Karl-Imhof-Ring 22 (☎06434/2405; ④), is well appointed, modern and near to the Altböckstein; and the *Achenhaus*, Böckstein 438 (☎06434/3212; ④), is a lovely chalet-style pension with balconied rooms a block west of the main road. The *Gasthaus Radhausberg* on the Altböckstein village green serves up excellent mid-priced Austrian **food**, and the *Forellenhof* is a good pizzeria on the road into the village from Badgastein. The *Mühlrad*, at the north end of Böckstein on the Badgastein road, is a wine and beer hall with substantial snack food and occasional live folk music.

Beyond Böckstein: the Heilstollen and Sportgastein

The main road and rail routes head southeast from Böckstein towards the twelve-kilometre-long **Tauern rail tunnel** 1km away, where road vehicles are loaded onto wagons and transported through the tunnel by train. Trains carrying private cars oper-

THE HOHE TAUERN NATIONAL PARK

Established in 1971, the **Hohe Tauern National Park** was mapped out to protect the natural environment around the Hohe Tauern's highest peaks and to keep at bay the zones of human development just below. It embraces 1786 square kilometres and straddles the borders of the Salzburger Land, Carinthia and the Tyrol. Austria's highest mountain, the Grossglockner (see p.346) is within the park, as are the spectacular Krimml Falls (see p.347). The Grossglockner Hochalpenstrasse (see pp.345–346) forges a path straight through the area, but otherwise you're only likely to come across the park if you're out walking in the hills above the towns on its fringes – you'll usually encounter a small sign telling you that you're entering the park, accompanied by a short list of dos and don'ts, the most important of which are to stick to marked paths and take all your litter out with you. Among the wildlife encountered within the park are the elusive *Gemse* (chamois) and the ubiquitous *Mummeltier* (marmot). You're not supposed to feed these cute-looking beasts, although tourists invariably do. There are a few *Hütte* within the park boundaries catering for long-distance hikers..

Tourist offices in Badgastein (see p.338), Zell am See (p.342), Heiligenblut (p.293), Matrei (p.300), Kals (p.299) and other centres bordering the park, usually have a stock of leaflets detailing hiking routes, flora and fauna.

ate from 6.30am to 10.30pm southbound, and from 6am to 10pm northbound; a single journey costs öS190, and a return is öS320. On the other side winds a scenic descent down the **Mölltal** towards Spittal an der Drau in Carinthia (see Chapter 5).

A toll road, the Gasteiner Alpenstrasse (öS50 per person, öS20 for bus passengers) heads southwest from Böckstein up the increasingly narrow valley of the **Nassfelder Ache**, whose steep sides are washed by numerous waterfalls, towards the winter sports area of Sportgastein. One kilometre out of Böckstein, you pass the access road to the **Heilstollen**, or "Healing Galleries", 500m up the hill and hidden among the trees. Inside, an underground train ferries patients to radon-rich tunnels with high degrees of humidity in order to treat a variety of ailments, including respiratory diseases and arthritis. The shafts were first dug in the 1940s in an ultimately unsuccessful attempt to find gold and silver ore; those working on the project soon began to report that the atmosphere underground had a beneficial effect on their aches and pains. Nowadays the network of tunnels form a full-scale medical facility working in tandem with the spa hotels in Badgastein, although it's said that you need at least nine trips down (with at least a day's rest between each one) for it to reap the benefits – thereby discouraging casual visits. If you're interested in trying it, though, a single visit costs öS650, and includes a medical checkup followed by an hour in the tunnels (phone at least a day in advance for an appointment: ☎06434/3753, fax 3753-66), but the humidity coupled with the exposure to radon tends to leave you exhausted. There's one daily **bus** from Badgastein train station to the Heilstollen, leaving around 10.30am and returning around 3.30pm. More frequent Badgastein–Sportgastein services pass by the end of the Heilstollen access road.

Five kilometres beyond the Heilstollen, **SPORTGASTEIN**, on the borders of the Hohe Tauern National Park, is a buzzing ski area in winter; in summer, it's little more than a car park, though facing a truly breathtaking amphitheatre of ravine-scarred mountains. Numerous enticing hiking trails radiate outwards from here, and there are a few Hütte which open their doors in summer to offer refreshments, including the **Nassfeld Alm** twenty minutes' walk south of the car park.

Zell am See and around

ZELL AM SEE is the ultimate Austrian resort, a compact town of picture-postcard perfection, with a lake on one side and an impressive mountain hinterland on the other. A skiing and hiking centre in its own right, Zell is also within easy striking distance of the Glemmtal resorts of **Saalbach** and **Hinterglemm** to the northwest, while the village of **Kaprun** to the south provides access to year-round glacier skiing below the **Kitzsteinhorn**. Other classic alpine excursions within reach are the two mountain reservoirs in the shadow of the Kitzsteinhorn, trips along the **Grossglockner Hochalpenstrasse**, which crosses the Hohe Tauern mountains to the south, and the magnificent **Krimml waterfalls** to the west. Two folk traditions with which Zell is associated are the **Krampusläufen** on December 5, when folk wearing demonic masks take to the streets (see below), and the Hogmoar wrestling competition, a 500-year-old trial of strength for local shepherds that takes place on midsummer's day near the summit of the 2117-metre Hundstein, which rises above the lake to the east.

Arrival, information and accommodation

From the **train station**, at the southern end of Zell's central pedestrian zone, it's a five-minute walk northeast to the **tourist office** at Brucker Bundesstrasse 1 (Mon–Fri 8am–noon & 2–6pm, Sat 8am–noon; ☎06542/770, fax 2032), which is roughly opposite the small **bus station**. The tourist office will help book **private rooms**, either in Zell itself or in the nearby village of Schüttdorf, 2km away at the southern end of the lake. There's an accommodation information board outside for late arrivals. Schüttdorf holds the nearest **youth hostel**, *Haus der Jugend*, at Seespitzstrasse 13 (☎06542/57185, fax 57185-4; to get there from the station, walk southwards along the lakeside path). Best of the **campsites** is *Seecamp*, 3km out of town at Thumersbacherstrasse 34, on the northern shore of the lake (☎06542/72115).

Hotels and pensions

Gasthof Schmittental, Schmittenstrasse 60 (☎06542/72332, fax 72332-8). Chalet-style building 1km west of the town centre on the way to the Schmittenhöhebahn, with a big garden. All rooms have en-suite facilities and TV. ③.

Grand, Esplanade 4 (☎06542/2388, fax 2388-305). A stately nineteenth-century hotel, with its own private stretch of lakefront as well as an indoor pool. ⑨.

YEAR-ROUND ACTIVITIES IN ZELL AM SEE

The **winter** sports area comprising Zell am See and the Kitzsteinhorn Glacier above Kaprun offers a wealth of opportunities for novice and intermediate skiers, although there's not much in the way of advanced runs or off-piste skiing. A one-day ski pass for either Zell am See or the Kitzsteinhorn costs öS400, while a six-day *Europa Sportwelt* pass covering both places costs öS1980. It's an increasingly popular snowboarding centre, with a snowboard park in Zell and a half-pipe on the Kitzsteinhorn, and the presence of snowboarders making use of the snowfields of the Kitzsteinhorn in the summer months helps to keep Zell's nightlife buzzing year-round. The range of **summer** activities on offer is augmented by windsurfing and sailing on the lake, and the chance to try whitewater rafting in the Taxenbach Gorge, 20km to the east of town. Numerous local tour operators arrange trips to Taxenbach (enquire at the Zell am See tourist office for details); expect to pay around öS560 (including transfer to the gorge and a 15km trip in a six- or eight-person dinghy).

Herzog, Saalfeldnerstrasse 20 (☎06542/72503, fax 74509). One of the cheapest places near the lake, a rather anonymous but acceptable pension; some rooms with en-suite facilities. ②.

Hubertus, Gartenstrasse 4 (☎06542/72427, fax 72427-27). A large pension with adequate rooms on the western fringes of the centre, next to the Zellerbergbahn station. ②.

Lebzelter, Dreifaltigkeitsstrasse 7 (☎06542/776, fax 724-11). Traditional, friendly and comfortable downtown hotel with spacious rooms, all with en-suite bath or shower and TV. ⑤.

Zum Hirschen, Dreifaltigkeitsstrasse 1 (☎06542/2447, fax 2447-99). Another comfy town-centre choice; all rooms have en-suite facilities and TV. ⑥.

The Town and local walks

The obvious focus of Zell am See is the **lake** itself, site of a pleasant shoreline promenade and a popular Strandbad, where rowing-boats can be hired. At the height of winter the lake can freeze over, becoming a vast outdoor playground for skating or playing *Eisstockschiessen*, the Austrian version of curling. Just inland from here, the first thing you notice about the **Pfarrkirche** is the impressively sturdy tower, although its claim to fame is the late-Gothic organ loft inside, featuring carved pillars and statuettes of saints Hippolytus and Florian. A few steps to the east of the church, the town's only other real historical sight is the **Vogturm**, a medieval tower that now houses the **Heimatmuseum** (Mon–Fri 1–5pm; öS20), a cramped collection of stuffed animals, minerals, archaic skis and other local oddities – including the devilish, horned *Krampus* masks still made by local craftsmen and worn on the night of December 5 (the eve of St Nicholas' Day), when people run through Zell's streets in the guise of demons. According to folk belief, the *Krampus* is a shadowy counterpart to St Nicholas (the original model for Santa Claus), a hobgoblin figure who torments children who have behaved badly during the year and will therefore not be receiving any Christmas gifts.

A horseshoe of mountains immediately west of town is served by three main lift systems that open for hikers and sightseers in summer; all provide wide-ranging views and an appetizing variety of walks. Nearest at hand is the **Zellerbergbahn** (ascent öS105, descent öS85, return öS135) on the western fringes of the town centre, which involves a two-stage gondola ascent of the Hirschkogel, a peak that can also be approached via the Areitbahn gondola from **Schüttdorf**, 3km south of Zell. Twenty-five minutes' walk further west (and served by a half-hourly bus), the **Schmittenhöhebahn** gondola (return öS110), involves a ten-minute ride to the highland pastures of the 1965-metre Schmittenhöhe. The adjacent **Sonnenalmbahn** (return öS120) climbs in the opposite direction towards the alpine meadows of the Sonnalm, before connecting with the Sonnenkogel chairlift (same price as the Sonnenalmbahn).

Eating and drinking

Innumerable **cafés and restaurants** crowd the streets of Zell's central pedestrianized zone. Most offer standard Austrian dishes at mid-range prices, although ethnic restaurants provide the real bargains. Given the town's favour as a winter resort, there's a reasonable **nightlife** on offer, much of which stays open for the bulk of the year.

Restaurants

Metzgerwirt, Sebastian-Hörl-Gasse. One of the best places to sample traditional Austrian and local Pinzgau food in comfortable surroundings. Moderately expensive, with entrées starting at around öS150.

Pizza Mann, Brucker Hauptstrasse 9. One of the cheapest places to eat, if a bit characterless, with basic pizza and spaghetti dishes.

Pizzeria Giuseppe, Kirchengasse. A tad more expensive than *Pizza Mann*, but with a wider menu – and it's a bit more comfortable for a leisurely sit-down meal.

Schloss Prielau, Hoffmannsthalstrasse, Prielau (☎06542/72609). Located in a castle on the north side of the lake, 3km from the centre of Zell, this is one of the best gourmet restaurants in Austria, and a popular venue for special occasions and business meetings. Main courses start at around öS300. Reservations recommended.

Steinerwirt, Schlossplatz. A 500-year-old Gasthof offering the standard Austrian repertoire at an affordable price.

Strandhotel Bellevue, Seeuferstrasse, Thumersbach (☎06542/73104). Pricey restaurant on the eastern side of the lake (a popular destination by ferry from the Zell am See waterfront) specializing in fresh fish, locally caught. Reservations recommended.

Wang Hai, Bahnhofsplatz. Handily placed Chinese with ridiculously cheap two-course Mittagsmenüs from öS60 – although it might turn out to be spaghetti bolognese rather than something oriental.

Bars

Ampere, Schmittenstrasse. Chic bar with dressy clientele and a smart restaurant with good-quality international food upstairs.

Crazy Daisy, Bruckner Bundesstrasse. Garish, fun pub popular with English-speakers, which also serves good Mexican food.

Evergreen, Seegasse 1. Bar specializing in 1950s and 1960s music and old-time dancing.

Insider, Kirchengasse. Fashionable, European-style bar in the centre of town with plenty of outdoor seating.

Hirschenkeller, Dreifaltigkeitsgasse. Friendly basement bar with rock/techno musical policy.

Lebzeltkeller, Dreifaltigkeitsgasse. Rustic, low-ceilinged cellar-bar beneath the *Lebzelter* hotel.

Kaprun and the Kitzsteinhorn

Sprawling across the plain where the Kapruner Ache joins the Salzach, **KAPRUN**, 5km southwest of Zell, is a modern resort village serving the ski slopes of the **Maiskogel** and the Kitzsteinhorn to the south. Predominantly a winter resort, it's an inoffensive if soulless place at any other time of the year, and anyone thinking of visiting the Kitzsteinhorn in summer (whether for the glacier skiing or the views) would probably do better to use Zell am See as a base. There's an efficient **tourist office** in Kaprun village centre (☎06547/86430) serving up **private rooms**. At the south end of the village at Kaprun 448, a **youth hostel** (☎06547/8507) offers dorm beds, and there's a **campsite** beside the Kapruner Ache, which flows along the western side of the village. Kaprun is only small and places to **eat and drink** are fairly easy to find: the *Dorfstadl* serves good Austrian and regional food in an old stable rustically furnished and decked with animal skins, while *Hielberger's Stadl* is a pub-like place with substantial snacks and good main meals. *Charly's*, a popular Brit-pub, and the *Baum Bar*, a more European-style drinking venue built around a tree, are the places to go if you need a drink.

Buses from Zell am See pass through Kaprun and then climb northwards towards the station of the **Gletscherbahn** 5km beyond, which ascends to the year-round skiing slopes below the 3203-metre **Kitzsteinhorn**. First stage of the climb is via funicular, which passes through a tunnel before arriving at the **Alpincenter** (site of a self-service restaurant and ski hire facilities) at the foot of the pistes, whence a cable car and a couple of chairlifts provide a choice of further uphill routes. There's an extensive panorama of neighbouring mountains, with the Hohe Tauern's second highest peak, the 3674-metre Grossvenediger, to the west, and (in clear conditions) unparalleled views northwest across the ridge of the Kitzbühler Alpen towards the Kaisergebirge 50km distant. Bear in mind that even in midsummer the summit of the Gletscherbahn can be icy underfoot and extremely cold – remember to take the appropriate clothing.

A road continues beyond the Gletscherbahn station towards two reservoirs, the **Wasserfallboden** and the **Mooserboden**, which shelter on the eastern flanks of the Kitzsteinhorn. Leading into an area of eerily desolate beauty, the route promises fine views down the valley at every turn. The full journey can only be made by public transport: the **Kesselfall Alpenhaus**, 2km above the Gletscherbahn station, is the end of the line for private cars. From Kesselfall, a first bus takes you to the **Lärchwand**, where a funicular climbs up from the valley floor to be met by a second bus, which dives through tunnels on the western side of the Wasserfallboden before reaching the **dam** at the northern end of the Mooserboden. Here you'll find a restaurant, trails leading off into the wilderness, and a chance to gaze at snow-clad peaks that crowd in on all sides. Weather permitting, you should also be able to pick out the ridge of the Salzburger Kalkalpen 40km to the northeast.

Saalbach and Hinterglemm

Hourly buses from Zell am See head up the **Glemmtal** immediately to the north, where the twin villages of **SAALBACH** and **HINTERGLEMM** entertain winter-package tourists from the Netherlands, Germany and Britain. Skiing is good for beginners and intermediates throughout the valley, and both villages have plenty of bars and pubs catering to a wide range of tastes, although Saalbach is the rowdier of the two. A **tourist office** (☎06541/7272, fax 7900) on Saalbach's main street will point you in the direction of **private rooms** and **hotels** if you want to stay. The 1794-metre **Kohlmaiskopf** on the mountain ridge north of Saalbach can be reached by gondola; and further up the valley to the west there's a cable car to the 1984-metre **Zwölfer**, most prominent of the peaks south of Hinterglemm.

The Grossglockner Hochalpenstrasse

A deservedly popular excursion from Zell am See, the **Grossglockner Hochalpenstrasse** is one of the most spectacular routes across the Alps, running north–south over a high mountain pass just east of the **Grossglockner**, Austria's highest peak. A toll road for most of its length (cars öS350, motorbikes öS250, bus passengers pay a small toll as a proportion of their ticket price), the route is usually open from mid-May to late October – precise dates depend on weather conditions. **Buses** make the trip to the **Franz-Josefs-Höhe**, main vantage point for sightseers, once a day (three times a day mid-July to early Sept) from both Zell am See to the north and Lienz to the south. The buses stop long enough for you to enjoy the view for a while before embarking on the return journey. They're timed to connect with each other, so you can travel all the way from Zell to Lienz and vice versa.

Leaving the Salzach valley at **Pichl** 5km southeast of Zell am See, the initial stages of the Hochalpenstrasse are leisurely enough, as the road heads up the verdant **Fuschertal**. There's a **campsite** at **Fusch**, 7km up the valley. A **Wildpark** (öS60) at **Ferleiten**, another 7km further, specializes in the chamois, deer and mouflon indigenous to the area. Beyond Ferleiten the toll gate marks the beginning of the road's first truly spectacular stretch, rising via a succession of steep hairpins to the **Fuschertörl**, a popular viewing point, and the start of a sideroad that leads to the **Edelweissspitze**, another spot offering panoramic views, 2km to the northeast.

After negotiating the 2575-metre summit of the pass via the **Hochtor** tunnel, the road descends for a few kilometres before arriving at a junction where the route's most poular side-trip – the **Gletscherstrasse** – forks right towards the Franz-Josefs-Höhe, a lookout point facing the 3798-metre peak of the Grossglockner itself. It's an odd juxtaposition of alpine wilderness and tourist development, with a multistorey car park, two **restaurants** and a **hotel**, the *Alpenhotel Kaiser Franz-Josef*, offering "nostalgia rooms"

A HUT-TO-HUT TOUR OF THE GROSSGLOCKNER

While tens of thousands of tourists "do" the **Grossglockner** each year by car or bus, negotiating the innumerable hairpins of the environmentally insensitive Hochalpenstrasse, the
most rewarding way to approach Austria's highest mountain is on foot. Beginning at
Kaprun, a week's hut-to-hut tour will take you along a scenic route that wanders onto the
south flank of the mountain before descending to **Kals am Grossglockner**, which has
bus links with Matrei, Lienz and other East Tyrol destinations.

From Kaprun, take the Maiskogel cable car to reach a pleasant ridge-walk heading
south to the *Krefelder Hütte* (☎06547/862 1361), set below the graceful Kitzsteinhorn.
The ridge-walk is an uncomplicated one, albeit a little exposed in places, with the big
snow peaks of the Hohe Tauern range, including a preview of Grossglockner, teasing
ahead. Leaving the Krefelder Hütte on day 2, the route continues to the crowded
Alpincenter, with its ski lifts and cableway to the Schmiedinger Grat, crosses the
Kammerscharte on the Kitzsteinhorn's northeast ridge, slopes down to Fürthermoar
Alm then rises over rough pastures to the big dam wall at the northern end of the
Mooserboden. Overnight accommodation is available here in the drab-looking *Dr-Adolf-
Schärf-Haus* (*Berghaus Mooserboden*; advanced booking advisable: ☎06547/827110),
owned by the Touristenverein Naturfreunde. From here you look down the length of the
reservoir towards a rim of snow- and ice-clad mountains effectively concealing the
Grossglockner from view. On day 3, continue along the so-called Austriaweg, which follows the east shore before crossing glacier-fed streams at the far end. Here the trail
climbs through the Wintergasse glen to gain the narrow cleft of the Kapruner Törl, giving access to a wild boulderscape through which a route is waymarked to the large, institutionalized *Rudolfs Hütte* (☎06563/8221), the Austrian Alpine Club's Alpinzentrum,
equipped with sauna, fitness room and climbing wall. A more relaxing half-day's trek follows on day 4. Crossing the 2518-metre Kalser Tauern on the watershed crest, a descent
(which could be tricky in poor visibility) leads to a junction of paths at Erdiges Eck, then
drops down through the Dorfertal to the *Kalser Tauernhaus* (☎04876/283), set among
larches almost due west of the Grossglockner. On day 5, the route continues downval-
ley, through the Dabaklamm to the hamlet of Taurer, then climbs steeply into the
Teischnitztal draining from the northeast. As you gain height, the glaciers adorning the
west and south faces of Grossglockner come into view. The busy Stüdl Hütte
(☎04876/209) occupies the Fanatscharte at the foot of the Luisengrat, a ridge running
south from Grossglockner itself. The final stage, on day 6, descends via the privately
owned *Luckner Hütte* and *Lucknerhaus* (possible to hitch a lift on the road below the
Lucknerhaus) through the Ködnitztal to Kals am Grossglockner, situated at a junction of
green valleys and open pastures, and with plenty of good walks of its own.

Several other trails of varying degrees of difficulty cross the southern flanks of
Grossglockner and link an assortment of huts, some privately owned, the rest belonging
to member clubs of the Alpenverein. It's easy enough to cross from the Dorfertal in the
west to the Mölltal in the east along visually spectacular routes, and continue north-
westwards above the extensive icefield of the Pasterzenkees, the longest glacier in the
Eastern Alps, thereby making a horseshoe round Austria's highest mountain (allow 2–3
days from Kals). But only those with experience of glacier-crossing and with the necessary equipment should attempt to make a full circle round the peak itself.

A recommended map is Freytag & Berndt's *Wanderkarte 122* (Grossglockner, Kaprun,
Zell am See; 1:50,000), covering the whole of the above area.

in nineteenth-century imperial style for öS600 per person and upwards, overlooking the
crevasse-riven wastes of the **Pasterze Glacier**. The Gletscherbahn funicular will take
you down to the glacier surface (öS95 return), although you can make your own
descent via footpath in a couple of minutes.

From the Franz-Josefs-Höhe, it's back to the main road and a highly scenic descent
towards Heiligenblut in Carinthia, and onwards to Lienz (see Chapter 5).

Along the Salzachtal to the Krimml Falls

Fifty kilometres west of Zell am See, situated at the head of the **Salzachtal** in the fertile, cow-strewn **Pinzgau**, the **Krimmler Wasserfälle** are justifiably one of the biggest attractions in this part of Austria – receiving 700,000 visitors a year at the last count. The sight of the Krimmler Ache cascading down from the Hohe Tauern, sending up clouds of spray, which hang suspended above the pine forests, makes for a memorable experience. Hourly **buses** set out from Zell am See to the falls, but a more picturesque way to travel up the valley from Zell is to take one of the six daily trains along the **Pinzgaubahn**, an archetypal rural rail line that winds lazily across barn-dotted meadows.

The Salzachtal harbours a succession of pretty towns and villages, any number of which provide access to scenic alpine side-trips for those who have their own transport. Sixteen kilometres out of Zell, **Uttendorf** stands at the northern end of an attractive route up the tranquil **Stubachtal**, at the head of which a two-stage cable car ascends at **Enzinger Boden** to the **Weiss See**, a high-altitude beauty spot sheltering under the shadow of the 3086-metre **Granatspitze**. Ten kilometres further along the Salzachtal, **Mittersill**, the main tourist centre of the Pinzgau, provides access to the **Thurn Pass**, a panoramic road that heads north over the mountains to Kitzbühel (see p.437). Roughly halfway between Mittersill and Krimml, the small ski resort of **Neukirchen** offers a gondola trip (mid-June to Sept) up the slopes of the **Wildkogel** on the northern side of the valley, and several hiking routes run up the deep, ravine-like side-valleys, such as the Untersulzbach and Obersulzbach, which lead south towards the foot of the 3674-metre **Grossvenediger**, the Hohe Tauern's second highest peak.

Buses (and private cars) arrive at a car park a short distance away from the falls' **ticket booth**. Trains from Zell terminate at Krimml train station 4km short of the falls, entailing a well-signposted fifty-minute walk through woodland. From the ticket booth, a four-kilometre-long trail (April–Oct öS15, Nov–March free) winds its way uphill passing three main sections of **waterfall** (which, starting with the lowest one, drop a distance of 65m, 35m and 60m respectively), eventually reaching the **Krimmlertal**, a starkly beautiful alpine valley, at the top. The path is steep in places, and the full ascent should take about an hour and a half. Even if time is short, you should at least venture part way up the trail for a close-up look at the lower levels of the falls.

There are numerous Gasthöfe offering **food** and refreshment near the car park at the base of the falls, and a small **tourist office** (Mon–Sat 11am–4pm), which has details of **rooms** in local farmhouses, although most visitors come here on a day-trip from Zell am See.

West of Krimml, the main road begins to climb towards the **Gerlos Pass** (a toll road: öS90 per car, öS50 per motorbike), before descending into the Tyrol and the Zillertal (see p.425).

travel details

Trains

Hallein to: Salzburg (16 daily; 25min).

Salzburg to: Attnang-Puchheim (24 daily; 45min–1hr 25min); Bad Hofgastein (10 daily; 1hr 25min); Badgastein (10 daily; 1hr 40min); Bischofshofen (30 daily; 50min–1hr); Graz (3 daily; 4hr 15min); Hallein (16 daily; 25min); Innsbruck via Bischofshofen (5 daily; 3hr 40min); Innsbruck via

Kufstein (7 daily; 2hr); Klagenfurt (3 daily; 3hr 10min); Linz (hourly; 1hr 20min); Radstadt (3 daily; 1hr 15min); St Johann (20 daily; 1hr–1hr 20min); Schwarzach-St Veit (20 daily; 1hr 10min–1hr 30min); Vienna (hourly; 3hr 20min); Villach (10 daily; 2hr 50min); Werfen (12 daily; 55min); Zell am See (8 daily; 1hr 40min).

Zell am See to: Krimml (6 daily; 1hr 40min); Mittersill (6 daily; 1hr).

Buses

Badgastein to: Bad Hofgastein (hourly; 20min); Böckstein (6 daily; 10min); Heilstollen (1 daily; 20min); Sportgastein (6 daily; 30min).

Hallein to: Bad Dürrnberg (8 daily; 25min); Salzburg (8 daily; 35min).

St Johann to: Wagrain (6 daily; 20min); Jägersee (3 daily; 40min).

Radstadt to: Tamsweg (4 daily; 1hr).

Salzburg to: Grossgmain (hourly; 30min); Hallein (8 daily; 35min).

Zell am See to: Franz-Josefs-Höhe (1 daily; 2hr 30min); Hinterglemm (hourly; 30min); Kaprun (hourly; 15min); Krimml (hourly; 1hr 30min); Mittersill (hourly; 50min); Rauris (5 daily; 40min); Saalbach (hourly; 25min); Taxenbach (8 daily; 25min).

THE SALZKAMMERGUT

The peaks of the **Salzkammergut** may not be as lofty as those further west, but they are just as spectacular, hovering above glacier-carved, lake-filled troughs to form a landscape of unique beauty. Shared by Styria, the Salzburger Land and Upper Austria (the last of which encompasses by far the largest portion), Austria's busiest and most compact lake district boasts innumerable stretches of water, among which the **Wolfgangsee**, **Mondsee**, **Traunsee** and **Hallstättersee** are the big four. All the lakeside resorts of any size offer a range of water-based activities; Mondsee, especially, stands out as a good place for windsurfing. The villages of the Salzkammergut are almost impossibly pretty, and there's a great deal of historical interest here, too, with the pilgrimage church of **St Wolfgang**, the abbey church in the **town of Mondsee**, and the Celtic finds at **Hallstatt** likely to prove the highlights of any trip.

Commercial and transport hub of the area is the nineteenth-century spa-town of **Bad Ischl**, 60km east of Salzburg, at the geographical centre of the region. It's not a big place by any means, but a modest menu of tourist sights combined with its proximity to three of the most scenic of the Salzkammergut lakes ensure that you're likely to pass through here at some stage during a tour of the area. Approaching the region from the south you'll pass through **Bad Aussee**, another spa-resort whose unassuming charm provides a good introduction to small-town Salzkammergut life.

The obvious gateway to the region is the city of Salzburg, whence regular **bus** services run to the Mondsee, Wolfgangsee and Bad Ischl – from the latter, you can then catch local buses to most of the places not served directly from Salzburg. In addition, a **rail** line runs through the region on a north–south axis, linking the Traunsee, Bad Ischl, the Hallstättersee and Bad Aussee on the way. To get on it, change at Attnang-Pucheim on the Vienna–Salzburg line or Stainach-Irdning on the Graz–Salzburg line.

Some history

The **salt** from which the area derives its name has been mined since at least 800 BC, when **Hallstatt** emerged as an important focus of **Iron Age culture**. Early miners hacked pure salt from galleries dug deep into the mountains, but the salt was later slowly dissolved in water pumped into the galleries, and the resulting brine channelled down to the valleys where it was evaporated in saltpans. Mercantile centres like Ischl, Gmunden, Ebensee and Aussee grew rich on the resulting trade, giving the Habsburgs and the archbishops of Salzburg occasion to squabble over control of the profits. By the

---

ACCOMMODATION PRICE CODES

All **hotels and pensions** in this book have been graded according to the following price categories. All the codes are based on the rate for the least expensive double room during the **summer season**. In those places where winter is the high season, we've indicated winter room rates in the text. For more on accommodation, see p.30.

① under öS400	④ öS800–1000	⑦ öS1400–1600
② öS400–600	⑤ öS1000–1200	⑧ öS1600–1800
③ öS600–800	⑥ öS1200–1400	⑨ over öS1800

late fifteenth century the Salzburgers enjoyed hegemony over the area around St Wolfgang (and the western half of the Wolfgangsee still forms part of the Salzburger Land), while the rest of the modern Salzkammergut was made an imperial domain under Emperor Maximilian I. It was around this time that the name "Salzkammergut" was coined to describe this imperial territory's new-found status. Life in the area was strictly controlled by the Habsburg court: only people born in the Salzkammergut or involved in the salt trade were allowed to live there, and the purchase or sale of salt was limited to those in receipt of a licence. The salt miners themselves enjoyed some benefits, such as special woodcutting rights and exemption from military service.

Tourism began to challenge salt production as the region's main source of income early in the nineteenth century when the soothing properties of the saline waters were identified, turning places like Ischl and Aussee into high-society **spa-resorts** – and earning them the prefix "Bad" as a result. Franz-Josef's mother, the archduchess Sophie, was an early enthusiast, and the emperor himself spent most of his summers pursuing game (both two-legged and four-legged) in the countryside around Bad Ischl. However, it is the Salzkammergut's lakeland that proved to be the major draw: Wagner, Mahler and Brahms were among those who came here to lose themselves in an inspirational landscape, thus popularizing the area among a burgeoning middle class eager for outdoor recreation. Nowadays the Salzkammergut is one of Austria's busiest spots, attracting long-stay foreign visitors with its dazzling lakes-and-mountains scenery and serving as a buzzing weekend playground for city folk from nearby Salzburg and Linz.

The Wolfgangsee

Nearest of the Salzkammergut lakes to Salzburg, and correspondingly busy, the Wolfgangsee (also known as the Abersee) is also one of the most charming, a fifteen kilometre-long sliver of calm water bordered by odd, sandcastle-shaped mountains. The largest of these, the Schafberg, hovers above **St Wolfgang** on the northern side of the lake. Enchantingly pretty, the village harbours a much-visited Gothic altarpiece in its parish church, but as a traditional summer stomping ground of lakes-and-mountains package tourists, it can get unpleasantly crowded. **St Gilgen** is equally attractive and attracts a younger crowd, while laid-back **Strobl** at the eastern end of the lake is more focused purely on lakeside pursuits. Lake ferries present a leisurely way of exploring the area between May and mid-October, when St Gilgen, St Wolfgang and Strobl are linked by hourly services during the daytime.

The area around the Wolfgangsee is also a popular **skiing** destination, much favoured by weekend crowds from Salzburg, although it rarely features in the major package brochures. The main areas are the **Postalm** (where a popular ski school makes it a good place for beginners) above Ströbl, and the **Zwölferhorn** (with greater range for intermediate skiers) above St Gilgen. A one-day ski pass for either ski area weighs in at about öS250 (children öS180), while a six-day pass valid for both costs öS1500 (children öS1000).

WOLFGANGSEE ACTIVITIES

Bike rental Sport Girbl, Bahnhofstrasse 300, Strobl (☎06137/484). Mountain bikes from around öS150 per day.

Hiking Guided walks organized two or three times a week by St Gilgen tourist office.

Paraskiing Wassersport Zentrum St Gilgen, Seepromenade, St Gilgen (☎06227/7101, fax 7781). Expect to pay around öS650 per trip.

Swimming Outdoor Strandbäder at St Gilgen, St Wolfgang and Strobl. Indoor

pool at Mondseerstrasse 12, St Gilgen (daily 9am–7pm).

Waterskiing Gerd's Wasserskischule, Seepromenade, Strobl (☎06137/484); Wassersport Zentrum St Gilgen (see under "Paraskiing"). Expect to pay around öS120 per round.

Windsurfing Linortner, Seepromenade, Strobl (☎06137/55464), offers board rental; Wassersport Zentrum St Gilgen (see under "Paraskiing") has board rental, in addition to one-day crash courses from öS450, seven-day courses from öS2000.

Salzburg is the obvious gateway to the region if you're approaching from the west. Hourly buses on the Salzburg–Bad Ischl route run along the southern shores of the Wolfgangsee, calling at St Gilgen and Strobl en route. To get to St Wolfgang, disembark at Strobl and pick up a connecting service there. All of the Wolfgangsee settlements are served by direct bus from Bad Ischl.

St Gilgen

In many ways **ST GILGEN** represents the perfect introduction to the Salzkammergut: a combination of quaint country town, modern lakeside resort and ideal base for refreshing walks. The town centres on **Mozartplatz**, site of a fountain dedicated to the composer, although St Gilgen's link with him is rather tenuous (see below). Just off Mozartplatz, the **Heimatmuseum**, on Pichlerplatz (June–Sept daily except Mon 10am–noon & 2–6pm; öS40), occupies what used to be a lace-weaver's house. Inside, displays recall St Gilgen's role in the eighteenth century as an important lace-making centre, aided by a decree of 1776 that forbade the import of foreign lace into Austria,

Ischlerstrasse leads from Mozartplatz down to the lakefront, where the village courthouse, at no. 15, now houses a **Mozart memorial room** (June–Sept Tues–Sun 10am–noon & 2–6pm; öS10), although it's devoted more to the composer's mother, Anna Pertl, who was born in the building on December 25, 1720. There's a limited words-and-pictures display remembering Mozart's grandfather, Wolfgang Nikolaus Pertl, who worked as a magistrate in St Gilgen and dabbled in amateur dramatics, and Mozart's sister Nannerl, who by coincidence married one of Pertl's successors as magistrate (the impressively monikered Johann Baptist von Berchtold zu Sonnenberg) and ended up living in the house in which her mother grew up.

Beyond the courthouse lies the ship station and a pleasant waterfront **promenade**, where most of the boat rental, waterskiing and windsurfing facilities are located.

Local walks

Next to the bus station, the Zwölferhornbahn cable car (June & Sept 9am–5pm; July & Aug 9am–6pm; Dec–May 9am–4pm; return öS180) conveys visitors to the summit of the 1522-metre **Zwölferhorn**, which commands spectacular views of the surrounding area. You can walk back to town from here by a number of routes (allow 2hr–2hr 30min), two of the most popular of which stop off at either the Sausteigalm or the Illingbergalm – both of which boast walk huts offering food and drink.

Another popular three-hour walk heads round the northern end of the lake to St Wolfgang, climbing up along the wooded flanks of the **Falkenstein** hill en route. Leave St Gilgen via Mondseestrasse as far as the *Hotel Fürberg*, and from there follow the signs.

Practicalities

A right turn outside the **bus station**, and a second right, down Schwarzenbrunner-strasse, lead to the central Mozartplatz, site of the **tourist office**, in the Rathaus (Mon–Fri 9am–noon & 2–6pm, Sat 9am–noon; ☎06227/7267, fax 7267-9), which will advise on the availability of **private rooms** – prices depend on how near the lake you want to be. Two atmospheric village inns offer the best **hotel** accommodation: *Kendler*, Kirchenplatz 3 (☎06227/2223, fax 7203-90; ③), and *Hotel zur Post*, Mozartplatz 8 (☎06227/7509, fax 2698; ③). The **youth hostel** at Mondseestrasse 7 (☎06227/365) has beds in large dorms and some attractive doubles (①–②).

For **eating**, the restaurant at the fifteenth-century *Hotel zur Post* serves up all the usual schnitzel dishes, and *Wirt am Gries*, Steinklüftstrasse 6, offers that familiar range of Austrian dishes and boasts a nice garden. On the lakefront, *Seerestaurant Fischer* is a good place to eat fish, while *Pizzeria Papageno*, Ischlerstrasse 16, has a pleasant first-floor terrace. Establishments like *Herold's Pub*, *Café Einstein* and *Podium* are among a string of lively **drinking** venues along Ischlerstrasse near the lake, while the boisterous *Grammophon*, further inland on Steinklüftstrasse, is also worth a try.

Strobl

Although quieter and a good deal less pretty than either St Gilgen or St Wolfgang (see below), **STROBL** is nonetheless a good place to enjoy a beach-oriented lakeside holiday. Comprising a small agglomeration of largely modern houses ranged along the lakefront, it has plenty of places to hire boats and a couple of waterskiing schools. The main bathing area, the **Seebad** (öS20), is in a grassy lakeside park 1km to the northwest of the village centre.

Strobl is also a good base for touring the region, and offers access to some excellent **walks**. Best of the nearby walking destinations is the **Postalm** to the south, which is reached by a twelve-kilometre-long toll road that winds up a sequence of hairpin bends, and is served by a walkers' bus from Ströbl in season (late June to late Sept & late Dec to March currently leaving at 9.30am and 12.45pm; öS100). A large expanse of alpine grazing land raised high above the valley floor, the Postalm offers some excellent views of the surrounding mountains.

Turn left out of Strobl **bus station** and carry straight on for ten minutes to reach the village centre, huddled around a small church. The **tourist office** here (Mon–Fri 9am–noon & 2–6pm, Sat 9am–noon; ☎06137/6255, fax 5958) will check vacancies in **private rooms** for you. Of the moderately priced **hotels**, *Pension Kasberger*, east of the village centre at Salzburgerstrasse 188 (☎06137/249; ②), is a basic but comfortable modern chalet-style building. At the opposite end of the scale, the centrally located *Villa Brandauer*, Strobl 73 (☎06137/205, fax 5903; ⑤), is a lovely nineteenth-century villa with period furnishings and direct access to the lake. The nearest **campsites** are in St Wolfgang (see below) or Geschwendt 3km east of town, just off the St Gilgen road – *Camping Zirlebauer*, at Geschwendt 31 (☎06138/2715; May–Oct), overlooks an evocatively reedy stretch of lakefront, with a large public Strandbad nearby.

For **food**, the *Villa Brandauer*'s restaurant has a good-value Tagesmenü and attractive garden seating, while *Seegasthof Jenisch* has a waterfront terrace and serves excellent fresh fish. Strobl **nightlife** centres on the *Stroblerhof*, at Ischlerstrasse 16, which has a restaurant specializing in steaks, as well as a pub, a disco and an outdoor bar. The *Laimeralm*, in the hills 4km to the southeast and reached by courtesy buses from the centre of Strobl (check with the tourist office whether they're running), is a well-known and enjoyably kitsch folk venue, with live shows on Friday evenings and Sunday afternoons.

St Wolfgang

Four kilometres west of Strobl, on the northern side of the lake, **ST WOLFGANG** owes its existence – and its name – to the tenth-century bishop of Regensburg, who came to this area to reorganize the monastery at Mondsee while enjoying a spot of rural solitude on the shores of the lake that would later bear his name. He built a chapel on a small promontory jutting out into the lake, around which a settlement grew, soon to become a pilgrimage centre devoted to his cult. The village today, with flower-bedecked balconies spilling over narrow thoroughfares, is undeniably pretty, though its fairy-tale good looks can pale after prolonged exposure. Part responsibility for the crowds, and the village's twee, Ruritanian image, goes to Ralph Benatzky and Robert Stolz's 1930 comic opera, *The White Horse Inn*, inspired by the *Im Weissen Rössl* hotel on the lakefront. A stick of musical candy rarely heard outside Austria, it's regularly performed at St Wolfgang's cultural centre, the Michael-Pacher-Haus, on Michael-Pacher-Strasse, in summer.

The **pilgrimage church** of St Wolfgang also plays a part in the town's immense popularity. Tourists flock round the famous high altar by Tyrolean master **Michael Pacher**, one of the high points of Austrian Gothic art. An extravagantly pinnacled structure measuring some 12m high, the altar was probably built with the help of the artist's brother Friedrich, and was completed sometime between 1471 and 1481 in Bruneck (now Brunico in northern Italy) before being carted over the Alps to St Wolfgang. Brightly gilded, sculpted scenes of the Coronation of the Virgin form the altar's centrepiece; St Wolfgang himself is the figure on the left holding a model of the church. The predella is devoted to a depiction of the Adoration, flanked by the Visitation and the Flight into Egypt. Most days only the outer panels of the altar wings are on display, depicting scenes from the Life of St Wolfgang, but on Sundays the wings are opened to allow a glimpse of scenes from the Life of Christ. Providing a contrast to

MICHAEL PACHER

Although nowadays recognized as the leading Austrian painter and sculptor of the fifteenth century, **Michael Pacher** remains a mysterious figure. He was a well-respected artist in his own time, but many of his works were destroyed or broken up during the eighteenth-century enthusiasm for all things Baroque, making it difficult for historians to piece together an accurate picture of Pacher's career. He was born sometime between 1430 and 1435 in or around the South Tyrolean town of Bruneck (now Brunico in Italy), the main settlement of an area known as the Pustertal. Having picked up the rudiments of painting and sculpture, probably as apprentice to a local artist, Pacher went to study in Padua, which was then the main cultural centre of northern Italy and the obvious place for a young artist to perfect his craft. Here, Pacher was able to absorb the artistic traditions of the Italian Renaissance – both from the fine paintings in Padua's churches, and from contact with the many other painters who congregated here at the time, among them Andrea Mantegna, with whom it is thought Pacher was acquainted. Most importantly, Pacher received a thorough grounding in contemporary experiments with perspective and light, giving his subsequent paintings a measure of depth and realism that was unique among the artists of the Austrian lands.

By the late 1460s Pacher had returned to Bruneck and established a workshop turning out altarpieces for local churches. Few of these survive, although individual pieces of sculpture and paintings from them have found their way into museums and galleries. It's unclear when exactly Pacher died, but his last-known works were completed in Salzburg (where a sculpture of the Virgin still survives in the Franziskanerkirche; see p.315) sometime in the early 1490s.

The altar at St Wolfgang is the only one of Pacher's altars to have remained completely intact. It was commissioned in 1471 by Benedict, abbot of Mondsee, for a fee of 1200 Hungarian florins, 50 of which were paid in advance. There was no real deadline for completion of the work because Benedict was still in the process of building the choir of the church for which the altar was intended, and Pacher probably didn't make a start on it until 1478–79. It was a typical piece of workshop-made art, with Pacher himself planning the whole enterprise and executing the most demanding paintings and sculptures, while his assistants were charged with doing the rest. The Adoration of the Magi, on the predella – which hardly displays the same skill and expressiveness as the Coronation of the Virgin, which forms the altar's centrepiece – was probably the work of Pacher's son Hans. Many of the paintings on the altar wings were completed by Friedrich Pacher, another young artist apprenticed to Michael – the name "Pacher" was fairly common in the Pustertal, and he's not thought to be a relation. One of the panels known to be the work of Michael – and indeed one of the highlights of the piece as a whole – is the unsqueamishly graphic Circumcision of Christ, which you can see at the bottom of the wing to your left.

Elsewhere, the best collections of Michael Pacher's art are to be found in the Landesmuseum Ferdinandeum in Innsbruck (see p.411), the Museum mittelalterlicher Kunst in Vienna (see p.108) and the Alte Pinakothek in Munich.

Pacher's work is the seventeenth-century **double altar** halfway up the nave. According to tradition (and such stories are common in places where Gothic altars like Pacher's survive), the artist Thomas Schwanthaler was commissioned to produce a replacement for the Pacher altar, which was due to be trashed, but he deliberately made his own work too big to fit into the space reserved for it.

A lakeside promenade stretches west of the town centre, leading after about 1.5km to the station of the **Schafbergbahn**, a mountain railway operated by antique steam locomotives which ascends to the 1783-metre Schafberg, dominating the lake to the north. There are about nine departures daily (first ascent 8.40am, last ascent 4.40pm, last descent 5.30pm; return öS250), but the trip is vastly (and deservingly) popular, so be prepared to wait for a departure with a seat available. You can also walk from St Wolfgang to the top in about three and a half hours. Once there, you can take in excellent views over the Wolfgangsee, and towards the Mondsee and Attersee to the north. The *Berghotel Schafbergspitze* (☎06138/2232; ③) provides café, restaurant and accommodation should you get stranded at the top.

Practicalities

Buses from Bad Ischl and Strobl stop at the west end of the village centre. Walk back east along Michael-Pacher-Strasse and take a right into Pilgerstrasse to reach the **tourist office**, at no. 28 (Mon–Fri 8am–6pm, Sat 8am–noon; ☎06138/2239, fax 2239-81), which will fix you up with a **private room**. There's no shortage of atmospheric and affordable Gasthöfe grouped around the church in the centre of the village. The *Schwarzes Rössl*, Am Marktplatz 30 (☎06138/2373, fax 3293; ③), offers bright rooms with en-suite facilities, most with access to balconies with wrought-iron fittings. *Haus Erika*, Uferplatz 82 (☎06138/2387; ③), is another traditional building with window boxes, balconies and en-suite rooms overlooking a small harbour. Set a little further back from the lakefront, *Pension Ellmauer*, Michael-Pacher-Strasse 183 (☎06138/2388, fax 3053; ③), is a rather more functional, modern building, but most rooms come with south-facing balconies. Plush rooms with traditional wooden furnishings are the norm at the top-of-the-range, waterfront *Im Weissen Rössl*, Im Stöckl 74 (☎06138/2306, fax 2306-41; ⑦), the hotel that inspired the operetta. There's a **campsite**, the *Appesbach* (☎06138/2206), about 2km out of town along the road to St Gilgen, with its own stretch of lakefront.

There's no end of hotel **restaurants** offering filling Austrian standards to the hordes of tourists prowling the streets, most of them charging very reasonable prices. *Andy's Stehbuffet*, on Markt in the village centre, is the place to go for Wurst-type **snacks**, while the nearby *Wolfgangstub'n* offers more substantial sit-down Austrian fare at low prices. *Pizzeria Mirabella*, Pilgerstrasse, serves inexpensive pizzas and pasta. Moving up in price, the *Hubertuskeller* has game dishes all the year round, while the *Schwarzes Rössl* (☎06138/2306, reservations advised) offers top-quality grub either on a lakefront terrace or in elegant dining rooms. *Lepovino*, Markt 14, has a large selection of Austrian wines, with cold-meat-and-cheese-style accompaniments, while the **bar** at *Disco Shooter*, opposite the Michael-Pacher-Haus, stays open until the early hours.

The Mondsee

With the mountains of the Drachenwand and the Schafberg rising from its southern rim, the **MONDSEE** lends itself equally to an all-out activity holiday or a spot of lazy waterside contemplation. Despite a gaggle of small settlements ranged along the shore, life on the lake revolves around the **town of Mondsee** on the northwestern edge, an engaging huddle of houses that grew up around a Benedictine **monastery** established by the Bavarians in the eighth century. It was here that St Wolfgang, bishop of

Regensburg, arrived in 976 to take a rest cure, embark on monastic reforms, and build the church in what is now the village of St Wolfgang over the hills to the southeast. Mondsee town can be a quiet place, once the day-trippers drawn here by the monastery church pile back onto their coaches – but the proximity of Salzburg ensures a healthy influx of pleasure-seekers on summer weekends. The town is also the site of one of Austria's best **sailing and windsurfing** schools: the placid waters of the lake make it ideal for children and novices, and there are boat- and board-rental facilities for those who no longer need tuition.

Getting to the lake presents few problems: the A1 Salzburg–Vienna autobahn sweeps past the resort, and there are eight daily buses from Salzburg.

The Town

Mondsee's picturesque, café-strewn town centre is set back about 500m from the lake, separated from the waterfront by a small stretch of park. Presiding over a central market square is the impressive twin-domed facade of the **Pfarrkirche St Michael**, originally the church of the former Benedictine monastery, and nowadays known to many as the church used in the wedding scene of the *Sound of Music*. Other visitors are more likely to thrill to the name of **Meinrad Guggenbichler** (1649–1723), the Swiss-born sculptor who spent most of his life working at the monastery, producing seven of the thirteen altars adorning the church. The harmonious combination of columns, arches and attendant statuary that form the surrounds marks Guggenbichler as a master – the paintings that form the centrepieces of the altars were executed by other artists, and are for the most part less spectacular. The Corpus Christi Altar, midway down the nave in the aisle to the left, is probably Guggenbichler's finest, its spiralling, vine-wreathed columns supported by groups of cherubs.

Next to the church, the former monastery buildings house the **Heimatmuseum** (May–Sept daily 9am–6pm; early Oct daily 9am–5pm; late Oct Sat & Sun 9am–5pm; öS30), which features Baroque statuary from the monastery (including a few small-scale pieces by Guggenbichler) and an array of Neolithic finds. Nineteenth-century archeologists working at the eastern end of the Mondsee discovered lake dwellings that had been mounted on stilts dating from around 2500 BC, shedding light on a phase of Neolithic history that has subsequently been dubbed the "Mondsee culture". A selection of beakers and cups decorated with zigzags and circles steal the limelight in a collection otherwise dominated by fragments of functional, unadorned pottery.

Five hundred metres north of the church on a grassy slope overlooking the town centre is the small **Freilichtmuseum** (April Sat & Sun 9am–6pm; May–Sept daily 9am–6pm; öS30), comprised of a few outbuildings and one traditional farmhouse, the eighteenth-century *Rauchhaus* (literally "smoke-house"). One of two open-hearth stoves on the ground floor is usually stoked up and smoking to give visitors an idea of what life might have been like – above it joints of meat would have been hung for home curing. The family living quarters are set to one side, away from the rising fumes, but farm labourers, servants and occasionally guests would have been expected to sleep in the malodorous bedrooms upstairs. Most of the furniture is unadorned and functional: the seeping smoke would have damaged anything more fancy.

A small promenading area and a public bathing beach, the Seebad (öS30), extend along the **lakefront** 500m south of the centre. A couple of huts on the water's edge rent out rowing boats and pedalos, while windsurfing boards can be rented from the Segelschule beside the Seebad. Just inland, the **Lokalbahnmuseum** (mid-May to June Sat & Sun 10am–noon & 2–5pm; July to mid-Sept Fri 2–6pm, Sat & Sun 10am–noon & 2–6pm; öS40) recalls a now-disused narrow-gauge railway that once connected the Mondsee with Salzburg and Bad Ischl, displaying a couple of restored steam locomotives and a model railway.

Practicalities

Mondsee's **bus station** is a block south of the town centre, where the **tourist office**, at Dr-Müller-Strasse 4 (July & Aug Mon–Sat 9am–7pm, Sun 9am–1pm; Sept–June Mon–Fri 9am–1pm & 2–5pm; ☎06232/2270, fax 4470), will fix you up with a **private room**. Of the **hotels**, *Pension Erlinger*, P-Tafner-Strasse 7 (☎06232/2281; ②), is a friendly, family-run place with balconied rooms, most of which share WC and shower, while *Pension Klimesch*, Meinrad-Guggenbichler-Strasse 13 (☎06232/2563; ③), is a larger, comfier place near the lakefront, and *Blaue Traube*, Marktplatz 1 (☎06232/2237, fax 4350; ④), is an atmospheric old inn on the central square. The **youth hostel**, at Krankenhausstrasse 9 (☎06232/2418, fax 2418-75), supplies dorm beds together with a few double rooms, although it soon fills up.

For a quick bite to **eat**, *Karl's Imbiss Stube*, Meinrad-Guggenbichler-Strasse 5, is a good place for a stand-up sausage or sit-down chicken and chips, while *Vini i Panini*, on Marktplatz, is a more upmarket sandwich and pizza bar. The next-door *Mezcal* offers vaguely Mexican snacks on the ground floor, and pasta dishes on the floor above. For more substantial fare, either the *Neue Post*, Rainerstrasse 9, or the restaurant of the *Blaue Traube* hotel, are the best places to sample traditional Austrian cooking. The restaurant of *Hotel Leitnerbräu*, Steinerbachgasse 6, is a good (if pricey) place to sample fresh Mondsee fish.

For **drinking** near the waterfront, the *Lido Café*, Robert-Baum-Promenade, occupies a lakeside pavilion with plenty of outdoor seating. The *Barbados Pub*, next door, has a pleasant waterside terrace that's lively in summer. Further inland, there are several worthwhile bars along Herzog-Odilo-Strasse, the main street heading westwards from Marktplatz: *Café-Bar Tecini*, at no. 6, has a youngish clientele and relaxed feel, and *Mexaderro*s, on the other side of the road, features kitsch decor and Mexican nibbles.

Bad Ischl

Once the centre of the region's salt-processing industry, **BAD ISCHL** became a high society spa-resort in the nineteenth century, and has maintained a refined, well-fed air ever since. The soothing properties of the waters here were first noted in the 1820s by local doctor Josef Götz, who was struck how saltwater baths seemed to relieve the rheumatism suffered by local salt workers. Vienna's big-shot physicians were quick to catch on, and within ten years Bad Ischl had become one of central Europe's most important spas. Emperor Francis's brother, Archduke Rudolph, Bishop of Olmütz, was an early visitor, and Metternich had Ischl saltwater delivered to him in Vienna. The archduchess Sophie ascribed prodigious powers to the Ischl waters after becoming pregnant with the future Emperor Franz-Josef here in 1829, and she proceeded to bring her brood (nicknamed the "salt princes" due to Ischl's role in their conception) on holiday here every summer thereafter. It was a habit that Franz-Josef himself continued,

BAD ISCHL

ACCOMMODATION
Haus Eglmoos 2
Kurhotel 4
Nestroystüberl 1
Sonnenhof 5
Stadlmann 6
Waldesruh 7
Youth Hostel 3

retreating annually to the opulent hunting lodge of the **Kaiservilla**, from where he could walk to the holiday home of his mistress, Katharina Schratt.

A hundred years on, this aura of fin-de-siècle Habsburg gaiety, together with the fact that nineteenth-century waltz-meister **Johann Strauss the Younger** and his spiritual successor **Franz Lehár** spent their summers here (as did musical heavyweights like Bruckner and Brahms), has helped to fashion the town's reputation as **operetta** capital of Austria. It's a musical pedigree remembered in the local operetta season (see p.362), as well as in performances by the Kurorchester (literally "spa orchestra") around town throughout the summer.

Though lakeless itself, Bad Ischl is 12km away from the nearest beach, at either Strobl on the Wolfgangsee or Steeg on the Hallstättersee. The town is a popular day-trip destination for people staying at the lakes, and an important transport hub for the whole Salzkammergut, with regular bus services to most places in the region.

Arrival, information and accommodation

Bad Ischl stands at the confluence of two rivers, with the compact town centre wedged between the Ischl to the north and the Traun to the south. Both the **bus** and **train station** are on the eastern fringes of the town centre, a few steps away from the **tourist office**, at Bahnhofstrasse 6 (Mon–Fri 8am–6pm, Sat 9am–4pm, Sun 10am–noon; ☎06132/235200).

There are plenty of **private rooms**, and there's a modern, functional **youth hostel** near the Kaiservilla at Am Rechensteg 5 (☎06132/26577), with a choice of beds in five-person dorms or in double rooms.

Hotels and pensions

Haus Eglmoos, Eglmoosgasse 14 (☎06132/23154). An ivy-clad, balconied building with clean and comfy rooms, though WC and shower are shared. ②.

Kurhotel, Voglhuberstrasse 10 (☎06132/204, fax 276-82). A modern, glass-and-concrete structure with all imaginable spa and health-cure facilities on site. ⑨.

Nestroystüberl, Brennerstrasse 16 (☎06132/23017). A modern building in a residential area at the bottom of the Kalvarienberg, a wooded hill just west of the centre. All rooms have en-suite shower and TV. ③.

Sonnhof, Bahnhofstrasse 4 (☎06132/23078, fax 252958). One of the nicest (though not the cheapest) pensions in town, in an old villa near the town centre, offering rooms with en suite facilities and elegant modern furnishings. ⑥.

Stadlmann, Mastaliergasse 21 (☎06132/23104). Small pension in a rustic farmhouse about 1km west of the centre. Some rooms with en-suite facilities, most without. ①.

Waldesruh, Kaltenbachstrasse 43 (☎06132/24558). Large, modern chalet-style building 2km southwest of the centre, near the Katrin gondola station. All rooms have balcony and en-suite facilities. ③.

The Town

Spa life traditionally revolves around the **Trinkhalle**, the pump rooms on Auböckplatz, where old folk gather to quaff glasses of the local water and listen to the Kurorchester play. A few steps west of here, the **Esplanade** leads along the banks of the Traun past a sequence of elegant town houses. At no. 10, the **Stadtmuseum** (March Fri–Sun 10am–5pm; April–June & Sept–Dec Tues & Thurs–Sun 10am–5pm, Wed 2–7pm; July & Aug daily 10am–5pm except Wed 2–7pm; öS45) is housed in the former *Hotel Austria*, where the 24-year-old Emperor Franz-Josef became engaged in August 1853 to his cousin, the unfortunate Elisabeth of Bavaria (for whom an unhappy marriage, madness and assassination lay in store). Photographs and mementos of the imperial family understandably dominate the collection, but there's also a colourful section detailing Salzkammergut custom and costume. Among items on show are the enormous star-shaped hats worn by the Ebensee Glöckler (see p.363), as well as more local folk-costume essentials like the curious *Goldhaube*, an embroidered cap of gold-coloured material, gathered into a comb-like protruberance at the back, and the *Schwammerlhut* (literally "spongy hat"), a white, wide-brimmed felt hat, at one time worn by peasants to keep the sun off while working in the fields, but subsequently adopted as a kind of Sunday best.

The Lehárvilla

At the eastern end of the Esplanade, the Elisabethbrücke crosses the Traun to the Lehárkai, site of the **Lehárvilla** (May–Sept daily 9am–noon & 2–5pm; öS50), erstwhile summer home of **Franz Lehár** (see box). The Hungarian-born military bandmaster, who achieved something of a career breakthrough with his 1905 comic opera *The Merry Widow*, spent nearly every summer in the villa from 1910 to his death here in 1948. A few original manuscripts are on display, and the sumptuous furnishings (some belonging to Lehár, but most acquired later) provide an insight into how the opulent holiday retreats of the great and the good were arranged.

FRANZ LEHÁR

Franz Lehár (1870–1948) was the Andrew Lloyd Webber of his day, writing popular music-theatre for a wide audience and making a great deal of money at it. He revitalized the world of Viennese operetta and made himself a dollar millionaire with *Die lustige Witwe* (*The Merry Widow*) in 1905, following it up with several scores which, if not repeating that astonishing success, were hugely popular all round the world.

Born in the Hungarian town of Komáron where his father was a military bandmaster, Lehár was a true product of the Austro-Hungarian empire. He spent his childhood stationed with his father's regiment in various towns across central Europe, and entered the Prague conservatory aged 12 to study the violin. Dvorák, no less, is reputed to have advised him: "Hang up your fiddle and start composing." When called up for military service he followed in his father's footsteps and served as a regimental bandmaster, then in 1902 settled in Vienna and started conducting at the Theater an der Wien, one of the city's principal operetta houses.

Featuring a plot charged with tingling emotional encounters, plenty of misunderstandings and a Ruritanian setting, *Die lustige Witwe* (with a libretto written by Oscar Léon and Leo Stein) became a Viennese sensation and went on to take audiences in Germany, London and New York by storm. The score inaugurated what was to become known as the Silver Age of Viennese operetta, which was epitomized by Lehár and fellow Hungarian Emmerich Kálmán.

After a couple of flops, Lehár scored another success with *Der Graf von Luxemburg* (1909) and *Zigeunerliebe* (*Gypsy Love*) in 1910, both of which won international acclaim. World War I served to dampen the worldwide popularity of Viennese music, but the subsequent downturn in Lehár's career was overcome by his association with the tenor Richard Tauber, who became the most celebrated performer of Lehár's music and gave his name to *Tauberlied*, hugely popular songs which have become more famous than the operettas that spawned them. The most famous of these, *Dein ist mein ganzes Herz* (You are my Heart's Delight), comes from Lehár's last international triumph, *Das Land des Lächelns* (*The Land of Smiles*), 1929.

Despite having married a Jewish woman, Lehár chose to stay in Vienna during World War II. He was one of Adolf Hitler's favourite composers, and prepared a new overture to *Die lustige Witwe*, which he dedicated to the Führer in an attempt to protect himself and his wife. Lehár moved to Switzerland for a few years after the war, before taking up full-time residence in his villa in Bad Ischl, where he died in 1948.

The Kaiservilla and Marmorschlössel

North of the centre on the opposite side of the River Ischl, the **Kaiservilla** (May to mid-Oct daily 9–11.45am & 1–4.45pm; öS100, entrance to park only öS35) was purchased from a Viennese lawyer by the archduchess Sophie as an engagement present for Franz-Josef and Elisabeth of Bavaria. Franz-Josef came here every summer for the next sixty years, though it had soon ceased to be the happy love nest Sophie envisaged. By the 1860s, the unhappy Elisabeth had fixed Franz-Josef up with the actress Katharina Schratt, who remained the emperor's mistress for more than forty years. Conveniently, Schratt's own Ischl retreat, the Villa Felicitas (now the *Restaurant Villa Schratt*) lay only a couple of kilometres upstream from the Kaiservilla. The emperor also liked to relax in the company of local serving girls, who were usually delivered to the mountain huts where he stopped off during hunting trips. Franz-Josef's passion for the hunt sent him roaming the hills around Ischl, Goisern and the Attersee in search of prey – the heads and antlers of his unfortunate victims now crowd the walls of the villa. The imperial apartments are otherwise suprisingly plain and functional, reflecting the disciplined, workaholic habits of this cold and austere Habsburg.

Beyond the villa stretches a park containing the **Marmorschlössel** ("little marble castle"), a neo-Gothic garden retreat built for the empress Elisabeth, and today housing a **museum of photography** (April–Oct daily 9.30am–5pm; öS15). Of no great interest unless you're a big fan of the subject, the collection contains archaic cameras, family albums from the turn of the century, and a section on the history of the Leica (with an English-language voice-over), the prototype for the compact cameras of today.

Katrin and the mining museum

The most direct route to higher planes from Bad Ischl is provided by the Katrinbahn gondola (mid-May to Oct & early Dec to Easter; öS160 return), which commences 2km southwest of the centre and rises to the 1544-metre **Katrin**, the starting point for numerous walks. Bad Ischl–Lauffen buses pass by the gondola station, but they're far from frequent; to get there on foot, walk westwards along the Esplanade and keep going for 25 minutes.

Three kilometres south of the town, the Bad Ischl **Salzbergwerk**, or salt mine (daily: May, June & Sept 9am–3.45pm; July & Aug 10am–4.45pm; öS135), is a show-mine that involves a train ride into the mine and a chance to slide down the wooden slides that conveyed miners from one level of the galleries to another. Bad Ischl–Perneck buses stop nearby, but it's also possible to walk if you follow Grazerstrasse southwards from the Elisabethbrücke.

Eating, drinking and entertainment

There's a plethora of places to **eat**, with most central Gashöfe offering inexpensive Mittagsmenüs to pull in the milling crowds. Among them is the cheap-and-cheerful *Salz-Mühle*, Esplanade, with basic Austrian selections in addition to a good-value two-course set menu most days, and *Goldener Ochs*, Griesgasse, with outdoor garden seating, an emphasis on meat, especially veal, and a good-value Tagesmenü. *Blauer Enzian*, Kaiser-Franz-Josefs-Strasse, also serves inexpensive Austrian standards, in a nice courtyard or a cosy traditional dining room. *Weinhaus Attwenger*, Léharkai 12, is an attractive, riverside chalet-style building with outdoor tables, offering the usual mid-priced Austrian staples. For a change from Austrian fare, the lively *Amigos*, Auböckplatz 9, serves up Tex-Mex food, at reasonable prices. For top-quality dining in period rooms stuffed with hunting trophies, try the *Villa Schratt*, Steinbruch 43 (reservations advised: ☎06132/27647; closed Tues & Wed), housed in the former villa of Franz-Josef's mistress – expect to pay more than öS500 a head.

For daytime **drinking**, the *Café Zauner*, Pfarrgasse 7, is the classic coffeehouse and patisserie in which the cream of nineteenth-century society whiled away the afternoons. There's also a branch of *Zauner* at Hasnerallee 2 (May–Oct only), in a nineteenth-century riverside pavilion with plenty of outdoor seating, and which is the more popular choice in summer. For night-time drinking, there's a string of bars in the narrow lanes behind the church on Auböckplatz: *Tapas* offers trendy imported beers and Spanish nibbles; *Heuriger zum Postgarten* is a good place to sample some Austrian wine and has a large area of outdoor seating; and *Rockcafé K3* features the kind of taped music suggested by the name.

Entertainment

Bad Ischl's **operetta** season runs from early July to the end of August, and its programme almost invariably centres around at least one major work by Johann Strauss the Younger. Tickets (starting at öS180) are available from the Kartenbüro in the Kurhaus, a block west of Auböckplatz on Kurhausstrasse (☎06132/23766; Mon–Sat 9am–noon & 3–6pm).

From late June to early September, waltz music and popular classics are performed by the **Kurorchester** two or three times a day, either in the Kurhaus, the Trinkhalle or the *Café Zauner* on the Esplanade. Bad Ischl also has an annual country music festival over the Whitsun (*Pfingsten*) weekend, attracting top bands from Europe and medium-ranking acts from the USA. The Bad Ischl tourist office will have details.

The Traunsee

One of the Salzkammergut's busiest lakes in summer, the **TRAUNSEE** owes much of its charm to the rugged grey mountains that dominate from the east – the **Erlakogel**, the **Rötelspitze** and, most majestic of all, the 1691-metre **Traunstein**. Focus of the northern shore, bustling **Gmunden** is the biggest lakeside resort in the area, while the smaller resorts, **Traunkirchen** and **Altmünster**, are more village-like alternatives. All

---

TRAUNSEE ACTIVITIES

Bike rental At both Altmünster and Gmunden train stations, from öS90 per day. Bigger range of mountain bikes from around öS140 per day available from Mobil-Tankstelle Esthofer, Bahnhofstrasse 46, or Intersport Höller, Kammerhofgasse, both in Gmunden. Mountain biking maps available from Gmunden tourist office.

Boat rental A profusion of small, electric-powered motorboats, rowing boats and pedalos can be found on the lakefront at each of the Traunsee resorts.

Hang-gliding Flugschule Salzkammergut, Flachbergweg 4, Gmunden (☎07612/73033). Beginners' day including short flight (öS600); longer introductory course of three days (öS3600).

Hiking The *Traunsee-Wanderkarte* hiking map (free) is available from all local tourist offices.

Sailing Boat rental and beginners' courses from Segelschule Gmunden, Traunsteinstrasse 25, Gmunden (☎07612/75100).

Scuba diving Wassersport-Zentrum Ebensee, Strandbadstrasse 12, Ebensee (☎06133/6381). Beginners' courses and equipment rental available. Open May–Sept.

Swimming Outdoor bathing areas at each of the Traunsee resorts; indoor pool at Ebensee, just to the east of the Ebensee-Landungsplatz train station (Mon & Wed–Fri 2–9pm, Sat & Sun 9am–noon & 2–8pm).

Windsurfing Board rental and a range of courses from Hammerschmid, Traunsteinstrasse 141, Gmunden (☎07612/3692).

three resorts are handsomely served by public bathing areas and boat rental facilities (see box). At the southern end of the lake, the town of **Ebensee** is comparatively drab, but offers one of the Salzkammergut's best cable-car rides by way of compensation.

All these settlements are accessible by short hops on the Attnang-Puchheim to Stainach-Irdning **rail** line. Gmunden can also be reached on a privately operated branch line, which leaves the main Vienna–Salzburg route at Lambach.

Ebensee

Embracing both banks of the Traun at the lake's southern end, **EBENSEE** remains an important centre for the salt industry, and looks incongruously workaday when compared to the more attractive resorts further up the lake. There's a perfectly serviceable lakefront, however, with a yachting marina on the west bank of the Traun and a Strandbad on the east. The cable-car ascent to the **Feuerkogel** (May–Oct 8.30am–4.30pm; öS195 return), departing from the western fringes of town, provides access to a hiker-friendly plateau of alpine meadow high above the valley.

Ebensee is enlivened on the night of January 5–6 by the **Glöcklerlaufen**, when the menfolk – clad in white, laden with cowbells and wearing enormous *Lichtkappen* (star-shaped hats made of tissue paper illuminated from within by lanterns) – rush about the town scaring away evil spirits.

Ebensee **train station** is 1km south of the lake – it's better to get off at **Ebensee-Landungsplatz**, the next halt to the north, which is 200m away from the lakefront and virtually next door to the **tourist office** at Hauptstrasse 34 (Mon–Fri 8am–noon & 2–5pm; ☎06133/8016), which will fix you up with a **private room**. The *Seegasthof Rindbach*, just off Rindbachstrasse at Strandbadstrasse 1 (☎ & fax 06133/7187; ③), is a lovely rustic-looking villa, which stands near the main lakeside bathing area. Nearby, there's a good, modern **youth hostel**, 1.5km east of the tourist office, at Rindbachstrasse 15 (☎06133/6698, fax 6698-85).

Traunkirchen

Five kilometres north of Ebensee on the western shores of the lake, the tiny settlement of **TRAUNKIRCHEN** began life as a fishing village grouped around an eleventh-century Benedictine nunnery. On the northernmost of two hillocks overlooking the village, the former nunnery chapel, now the **Pfarrkirche**, is famed for its Baroque **Fischkanzlei**, or fishermen's pulpit, constructed in the form of a fishing boat, a reference to the story of the miraculous draught of fishes. The pulpit is topped by a statue of St Francis-Xavier accompanied by a lobster – recalling the crustacean who retrieved a crucifix that the saint had lost at sea on the way to Japan. Such fishy tales were no doubt popular with a congregation who made their living from the lake. On the festival front, Traunkirchen is the site of an annual **Corpus Christi procession**, when villagers take to the water in small boats festooned with banners, in similar fashion to the much larger affair in Hallstatt (see p.367).

To get to the village, alight at the Traunkirchen-Ort **train station**, rather than at the station marked simply "Traunkirchen", slightly further away. Here you're just uphill from the centre, where there's a **tourist office** on the waterfront (Mon–Fri 8am–noon & 2–4pm; ☎07617/2234, fax 3340) with a small list of **private rooms**. Two **pensions** just south of the tourist office, each occupying a chalet-style house with its own stretch of lakefront, are the *Zimmermann* (☎07617/2371, fax 2360; ②) and the smaller *Hüthmayr* (☎07617/2353; ②). The central *Hotel Post*, Traunkirchen 50 (☎07617/2307, fax 2809; ⑤), is the most characterful of a trio of big hotels. The **restaurant** at the *Post* is the place to go for top-notch Austrian cuisine, while the *Gasthof Goldener Hirsch* on the main road through town has some inexpensive lunchtime options and a traditional schnitzel-type repertoire, with dishes at around the öS100 mark.

Altmünster

Heading north from Traunkirchen, the next settlement of any size is **ALTMÜNSTER**, stretched along the shores of the lake and where virtually every other house is a Gasthof, pension or holiday apartment. It retains a quiet unspoilt atmosphere, however, and the lakeside promenade, site of a big public bathing area in summer, and faced by the towering bulk of the **Traunstein** on the opposite shore, offers vistas as attractive as any the Salzkammergut has to offer. The village revolves around the Gothic **Pfarrkirche**, where the sixteenth-century **Allerheiligenaltar** (All Saints' altar) in the south porch depicts a lively melee of holy men. The church also contains the tomb of Count Herbersdorff, who during the Upper Austrian peasant wars of the 1620s forced Protestant rebels to play dice for their lives after capturing them near Frankenburg – the losers were hanged.

Altmünster's **train station** is 2km southwest of the village centre: follow Maximilianstrasse downhill to get to the centre, where the **tourist office**, Marktstrasse 23 (June–Sept Mon–Fri 9am–noon & 2–6pm, Sat 9am–noon; Oct–May Mon 9am–noon & 2–6pm, Tues–Fri 9am–noon & 2–5pm; ☎07612/87181, fax 87611-34), will fix you up with a **private room**. Good-value **hotels** include the balconied, family-run *Rittertal*, a few steps north of the Pfarrkirche at Lindenstrasse 7 (☎07612/87131, fax 895507; ③), and *Frühstückspension Schlössl am See*, an attractive nineteenth-century villa along the lake south of the centre at Don-Alfonso-Weg 9 (☎07612/87136; open May–Oct; ②). *Campingplatz Altmünster* (☎07612/87276; mid-April to Sept), on the lakeside promenade with good views of the Traunstein across the water, is one of the best places to **camp**. For **food**, the *Kirchenwirt* just by the church on Marktstrasse offers good-value traditional Austrian cuisine in unpretentious surroundings, while the *Gasthof Rieberstorfer*, Maximilianstrasse 2, is slightly more upmarket but without being prohibitively priced, and *Pizzeria Romantica*, Marktstrasse 1, has a range of inexpensive pizzas and pasta dishes. The *Stau* next door is a lively, late place for a **drink**, as is *Nightfly*, Ackerweg 2.

Gmunden

With a prior guest list that includes such august names as Kaiser Wilhelm II, Tsar Nicholas of Russia, Johannes Brahms and Arnold Schönberg, **GMUNDEN** is the only other place in the Salzkammergut that can compete with Bad Ischl for star quality and historical pedigree. Originally a collection centre for the salt trade, the town today is a seething resort where self-confident nineteenth-century urban architecture rubs shoulders with the attractive chalets so typical of rural Austria. It can be oppressive on hot summer days, its traffic-clogged streets leaving you wishing that you'd opted to stay in one of the smaller resorts down the lake, but by evening the benefits of staying become apparent, with a range of good eating options and plenty of places to enjoy an alfresco lakeside drink.

The Town

Gmunden spreads across both banks of the Traun at the point where it flows out of the lake's northern end. The historical centre squats on the high ground to the west of the river, whence a couple of bridges lead over to the quieter east. Focus of attention on the western side of town is the **lakefront**, where the town's long-standing affluence is manifested in the fine Renaissance **Rathaus** with a fanciful, ceramic-tiled clock tower and glockenspiel (chimes at 10am, noon, 2pm, 4pm and 7pm every day). Gmunden's importance as a centre of ceramics production is featured in the **town museum** (Tues–Sat 10am–noon & 2–5pm, Sun 10am–noon; öS20), a fairly undistinguished collection of local

ARCHDUKE JOHANN SALVATOR

A nephew of Emperor Franz-Josef, **Archduke Johann Salvator** (1852–90) was a liberal-minded, romantic and somewhat excitable Habsburg who fell foul of the rule that forbade family members' indulgence in independent political activity (or any activity disapproved of by the manically conservative Kaiser Franz). Salvator's problems started with an article he wrote calling for reform in the imperial artillery. As a result he was sidelined by the Viennese court and sent to run a garrison in the virtual exile of Linz.

Eager to escape from from the anonymity of provincial army life, Salvator suggested himself as a candidate for the Bulgarian throne following the abdication of Alexander Battenberg in 1886. After his candidacy was withdrawn on the orders of his exasperated uncle, Salvator then became involved in promoting the cause of vain German aristo (and future king of Bulgaria) Ferdinand von Saxe-Coburg. Consumed by enthusiasm for the Bulgarian cause (the small Balkan state was at loggerheads with both Turkey and Russia at the time, and under constant threat of invasion), Salvator next attempted to join the Bulgarian army, but was refused on the basis that the enlistment of a member of the Habsburg family would disrupt Austria's cautious diplomatic efforts to bring peace to the region. Salvator, however, saw this as another personal slight engineered by the court, and decided to sever his links with the imperial family, renouncing his title, adopting the name Johann Orth and marrying low-born dancer Milly Stubel, of whom the court strongly disapproved. The death of Crown Prince Rudolf at Mayerling (see p.182) deprived Salvator-Orth of his last real friend and ally at court, precipitating his decision to emigrate. In 1890 he set off with his new bride for South America, in a self-captained sailing ship that went missing somewhere in the South Atlantic.

crafts housed in the **Kammerhof**, the medieval salt exchequer one block east of the Rathaus. From here, several alleys lead uphill into the heart of the medieval town, where the finest of the Baroque altars in the **Pfarrkirche** features a life-size sculptural group representing the Adoration of the Magi, by **Thomas Schwanthaler**, the artist responsible for the unusual double altar at St Wolfgang (see p.355). On the outer walls, late-Gothic frescoes of St Christopher and the Last Judgement have been clumsily restored.

The Esplanade running south from the centre along the lakefront passes a yachting marina before eventually arriving in front of the whitewashed walls of the **Schloss Ort**, built in the seventeenth century by Count Herberstorff (instigator of the notorious Frankenburg dice game; see opposite) and subsequently owned by the endearingly flaky **Archduke Johann Salvator** (see box). A Rococo fountain can be glimpsed in the Schloss courtyard, but most visitors head straight for the wooden footbridge, which leads to the fifteenth-century **Seeschloss** on an island just offshore. There you'll find a small Gothic chapel and a triangular inner courtyard with elegant sgraffito designs on the walls, but it's the romantic location that's the real attraction. South of Schloss Ort, paths continue to Gmunden's main public **Strandbad**.

Main draw on the eastern side of town is the **Grünberg** cable car, which rises to the upper flanks of the 984-metre Grünberg. At the top you're treated to an expansive panorama of the Traunsee. A network of trails can lead you back down the mountain.

Practicalities

Trains on the Attnang-Puchheim to Stainach-Irdning line stop at the **train station** 2km west of the centre; a **tram** runs from here every thirty minutes to Franz-Josefs-Platz, a few steps south of the centre; if you miss it, turn left out of the station, bear right, then carry on for about twenty minutes to reach the centre. Trains from Lambach arrive at the **Seebahnhof** on the eastern bank of the Traun, whence it's a straightforward walk across the Traunbrücke to the centre.

The **tourist office** at Am Graben 2 (Mon–Fri 8am–noon & 2–6pm, Sat 9am–noon; ☎07612/4305, fax 71410) has a list of **private rooms** – an enticing option, since Gmunden's **hotels** are expensive by Salzkammergut standards. Of the town-centre options, the *Goldener Brunnen*, Traungasse 10 (☎07612/4431, fax 4432-55; ④), probably represents the best value, a comfortable if unexciting place whose rooms come with en-suite facilities and TV, while the *Grand Hotel Austria*, Sparkassegasse 1 (☎07612/71925, fax 71927; ⑤), is a stately, nineteenth-century lakeside pile offering all the creature comforts. Some of the most attractive lakeshore hotels are on Traunsteinstrasse, which runs along the eastern side of the lake. Some way out of the centre, but idyllically situated, are the excellent-value *Seepension Neuwirth*, a modern chalet-style building 2km south of the Seebahnhof at Traunsteinstrasse 149 (☎07612/3631; ②), and *Zum Hois'n-Wirt*, a smaller place a kilometre further on at Traunsteinstrasse 277 (☎07612/4598, fax 4598-95; ④; March–Oct).

As far as **food** is concerned, *Reiter*, Rinnholzplatz, is the place to pick up a cheap daytime snack. For more substantial fare, the restaurant at the *Goldener Brunnen* offers excellent-value Austrian food in a cosy, atmospheric dining room, with outdoor seating out the back, and *Pizzeria Amore*, Marktplatz 17, proffers good-value pizzas and pasta dishes. *Mexico Bar La Queva*, Bahnhofstrasse 20, serves Mexican food and sizable steaks, and *Chinatown*, Bahnhofstrasse 16, offers reasonable Far Eastern food in a chic setting. Slightly further afield, the restaurant of *Zum Hois'n Wirt* is the place to eat fresh trout from local streams.

The Rathausplatz, with classic coffee-guzzling venues like the *Kaiser* and the *Rathauscafé*, is a good place to observe the crowds along the lakefront and enjoy a daytime **drink**. Further south along the lakefront, *Gerry's Strandbar* at Dr-Thomas-Strasse 13 is a popular open-air daytime and night-time boozing venue, while *Kulturcafé Villa Lehman*, Esplanade 27, is a stylish café-bar with jazzy, bluesy sounds on tape. Two popular bars in the town centre are *Nobelbeisl zum Blauen Affen*, Kirchengasse 8, and *Café-Bar Salzamt*, Am Graben, a rustic cellar-bar open until 4am.

The Hallstättersee

If you only have time to visit one lake in the Salzkammergut, then the **HALLSTÄTTERSEE**, 12km south of Bad Ischl, would be a worthy choice. Mountains crowd around on all sides, with the Dachstein range to the south, the Sechserkogel to the east; a sheer rock wall to the west provides an eerily sculptural backdrop to the human settlements that cling to its base. The village of **Hallstatt** itself is one of the most appealing and rewarding destinations in the region. Equipped with a couple of worthwhile museums and a famous show-mine, it remains the obvious focus for tourists. **Obertraun** at the southern end of the lake provides access to the **Dachstein caves**, one of the most-visited attractions in the region, and is also a good spot for a swim.

HALLSTÄTTERSEE ACTIVITIES

Bike rental Available at Obertraun train station (öS150 per day, öS90 with train ticket valid for that day).

Hiking An English-language guidebook to local hikes is sold by the Hallstatt tourist office for öS70.

Rafting Sport Zopf, Hauptstrasse 327, Bad Goisern (☎06135/8254), offer trips on the Traun between Hallstättersee and Bad Ischl for around öS550 per person.

Scuba diving Gerhard Zauner, *Gasthof Hallberg*, Seestrasse 113, Hallstatt (☎06134/286, fax 286-5). One-day introductory courses, seven-day courses and equipment rental are available.

About six daily **buses** from Bad Ischl follow the main road down the western side of the lake to Hallstatt (even fewer on Sundays), while more frequent **trains** from Bad Ischl run along the eastern shore of the lake (where boats ferry passengers across to Hallstatt; see below), pausing at Obertraun before hurrying on to Bad Aussee to the east.

Bad Goisern and the Gosausee

Commanding the northern approaches to the lake is the small spa-town of **BAD GOISERN**, although its centre is 3km away from the northern shore and hardly worth a specific stop. Goisern's lakeside suburb of **Steeg** , however, features a couple of public Strandbäder as well as a nudist bathing area. If you want to desport yourself here, the Steeg-Gosau rail halt is nearby. If you're travelling by car, it's worth considering a side-trip along the minor road that heads west from Gosaumühle just south of Steeg towards the **Gosausee**, 15km southwest. A tiny lake hemmed in by mountains, it's famed for the view towards the glacier-pitted Dachstein range, which rises precipitously to the east.

Hallstatt

One of Austria's visually most appealing villages and the real jewel of the Salzkammergut is **HALLSTATT**, occupying a dramatic position on the western shores of the Hallstättersee at the base of a precipitous cliff. Indeed the shoreline is so narrow that the rail line is confined to the opposite side of the lake, and disembarking the train at Hallstatt station and being ferried across to the town itself is one of the most atmospheric and evocative experiences that Austria has to offer. Hallstatt also has a historical pedigree second to none: salt has been mined in the mountains above the lake since at least the arrival of the Celts in the first millennium BC, and the wealth of finds is so great that the name "Hallstatt" has entered archeological terminology – denoting the Celtic culture that blossomed in central Europe during the early Iron Age (800 to 500 BC).

Hallstatt's other main claim to fame is the **Fronleichnahm** (Corpus Christi) procession, which takes place every year at the end of May. The procession begins at the Pfarrkirche, moves down to the main square and then takes to the water as everyone boards boats bound for a small chapel on the eastern side of the lake. All available boats are pressed into service, including one form of lake transport unique to the town – the traditional *Fuhr*, a sharp-prowed boat propelled by a single paddle at the stern, rather like a punt. You can see a few of them still plying the waters, emerging from the characteristic wooden boathouses along the shoreline.

The town can get unpleasantly crowded at times, although the coach parties who mob the resort from mid-May onwards rarely stay the night.

The Town

Many of the Celtic finds that made the town famous can now be seen in the **Prähistorisches Museum** (May–Sept daily 10am–6pm; öS30) next to the tourist office in the centre of the village, where wooden mining implements, pit props and hide rucksacks used by Iron Age miners vie for attention with the delicate jewellery and ornate dagger handles retrieved from the richer graves. The same ticket is valid for the nearby **Heimatmuseum** (May–Sept daily 10am–6pm), which houses the wide-ranging anthropological collection – African masks, Native American head-dresses – of the archeologist who worked on the Celtic sites in the 1930s, inveterate world traveller and hoarder Friedrich Morton. There's also material on the history of salt-mining, with tableaux illustrating working conditions across the centuries.

Hallstatt's **Pfarrkirche**, raised on a terrace above the Marktplatz, has a south portal adorned with Calvary scenes, painted circa 1500. Inside, a late-Gothic altar bears

THE HALLSTATT CULTURE

It's not known precisely when the Celts came to **Hallstatt**, although a settled **salt-mining community** ruled over by a powerful warrior aristocracy certainly existed here by 800 BC, remaining for at least three hundred years. We owe much of our knowledge of the period to the efforts of Dr Johann Georg Ramsauer, an amateur archeologist (he was the works manager at the local salt mine), who began systematic exploration of the grave fields in the Salzbergtal above the town in 1846, uncovering more than a thousand graves in the ensuing eighteen years.

Accompanying the deceased on their journey to the afterlife were foodstuffs, elegantly fashioned pottery, exquisitely wrought bronze horse bits, and iron swords and daggers. Other finds in the Salzbergtal revealed that the salt-miners of the period were using iron picks.

Similar graves were subsequently unearthed throughout Austria, the Rhine Valley, France and northern Spain, demonstrating that an iron-bearing Celtic culture was spreading across much of Europe between the seventh and fifth centuries BC. It's not known what role the rulers of Iron Age Hallstatt played in this period of expansion – although they undoubtedly enjoyed the profits of a salt trade that stretched from the Baltic to the Mediterranean. It's thought that the Celts from Hallstatt relocated to Bad Dürrnberg (near Hallein in the Salzburger Land; see p.329) in the fifth century BC, probably because landslides in the Salzbergtal were making mining unsafe.

Indeed Austria's finest Hallstatt-era relics tend to have been found well outside the area that gave the period its name. The princely graves discovered at Bad Dürrnberg and at Grossgmain, where the bodies of tribal chieftains had been laid out on wagons and enclosed in wooden burial chambers covered with earth, have yielded a host of artefacts – the small archeological museums in both these places are well worth visiting.

scenes from the lives of Mary and Christ on the wings, and a central group of statuettes feature the Madonna and Child flanked by St Catherine (the patron of woodcutters, on the left) and St Barbara (the patron of miners). An adjoining chapel contains the central panel of an earlier, mid-fifteenth-century altar, with a stirring Crucifixion scene. In the graveyard outside stands a small stone structure known as the **Beinhaus**. Due to limited space in the graveyard, the bones of the deceased are recovered from the earth once sufficient time has elapsed for complete decomposition of the body – usually ten years or so. The bones are then stored in the Beinhaus, with skulls arranged on the upper shelves and other bones stacked neatly below like firewood. You can peer at the remains through a grille, but photography is forbidden unless you apply for a permit. The skulls are still painted by the town grave-digger, with male skulls decorated with oak or ivy leaves and female skulls adorned with floral motifs.

The salt mines

Paths behind the graveyard lead up to the **Salzbergtal**, a wooded valley 350m above the lake, where the **salt mines** that provided the area's prosperity are located. The stiff climb takes about an hour, and a much more leisurely way of making the ascent is by funicular from the southern end of town (öS110 return). The entrance to the Salzbergtal is guarded by the **Rudolfsturm**, a tower built in 1284 by Rudolf I's son Duke Albrecht von Habsburg to defend the mine workings. About 800m beyond the tower, a section of eighteenth-century salt workings have now been opened as a **Schaubergwerk**, or show-mine (early May to end May & mid-Sept to late Oct daily 9.30am–3.30pm; June to mid-Sept daily 9.30am–4.30pm; öS140), where an hour-long tour (in German with English summary) involves a rail ride to an underground lake, followed by an exploration of the galleries on foot and the obligatory slither to lower levels of the mine via a wooden slide.

Practicalities

Ferries bearing **train** passengers from the station across the lake arrive just below the central Marktplatz, just north of Hallstatt's **tourist office** at Seestrasse 169 (July & Aug Mon–Fri 8am–6pm, Sat 10am–6pm, Sun 10am–2pm; Sept–June Mon–Fri 9am–noon & 1–5pm; ☎06134/8208, fax 8352). **Buses** drop off at the southern end of the tunnel, from where it's a short walk into the village. The village centre is closed to cars, with the main road that serves the western side of the lake bypassing Hallstatt via a tunnel. Car drivers should leave their vehicle at one of the big car parks (öS50) at either end of the tunnel.

The tourist office will check vacancies in **private rooms** (you might be charged a öS20–30 supplement if you stay less than three nights), most of which are in the suburb of Lahn just south of the centre. *Frühstückspension Sarstein*, Gosaumühlestrasse 83 (☎06134/8271; ②), is a friendly lakeside pension 200m north of the landing stage, while *Gasthof Bergfried*, Echerntalweg 3, Lahn (☎06134/8248, fax 8248-33; ③), offers comfy rooms with en-suite facilities and a gym and sauna on site. Classiest of the village's **hotels** is probably the *Gasthof Zauner-Seewirt*, Marktplatz 51 (☎06134/8246, fax 8246-8; ⑤), an evocative, old central inn, with all rooms featuring WC, shower, TV and phone. There's a good **campsite**, *Camping Höll*, Lahn, near the southern end of the tunnel (☎06134/8322). Of the two **youth hostels** in Hallstatt, the *Jugendherberge* in Lahn (Salzbergstrasse 50; ☎06134/8279) only accepts groups, leaving independent travellers the centrally located, independently run *Gasthaus zur Mühle*, set back from the landing stage at Kirchenweg 36 (☎06134/8318), with dorm beds, as well as some doubles.

There's little to choose between the **restaurants** in the centre of the village – all offer a selection of Austrian regulars augmented by fresh fish, and you only need decide if you want a place with outdoor lakeside seating or not. *Fleischauerei Forstinger*, Seestrasse 139, is a good place to grab a Wurst-type snack, while *Bräu Gasthof*, Seestrasse 120, has a lakeside terrace and a competitively priced range of fresh fish. The *Weisses Lamm*, behind the tourist office, has a tempting selection of Austrian standards, fish and game dishes, served up in the atmospheric if rather touristy *Bergmannskeller*, or miner's cellar. Best of the pizzerias is the *Gasthof Mühle*, just above the main square.

Hallstatt's **drinking** opportunities revolve around the couple of café-bars on the main square, or the folksy *Gaug'n Bar* in the *Gasthof Bergfried*.

Obertraun and around

Though set back slightly from the shore, the village of **OBERTRAUN**, at the southeastern tip of the lake, possesses better beaches than Hallstatt, with an extensive **Strandbad** ten minutes' walk north of the village centre – turn left outside the train station to get there. Obertraun also serves as the departure point for cable-car excursions to the ice caves – the **Rieseneishöhle** and the **Mammuthöle** – located high up on the flanks of the Dachstein, the mountain range that rises above the lake to the south.

There's little else going on in what is essentially a sleepy, rural place, although those in search of rustic tranquillity might fancy one of the **private rooms** offered by the local **tourist office** (Mon–Fri 8am–noon & 2–5pm; turn right outside the train station and carry on for 500m); most of these are in the farmhouses of Winkl, an attractive suburb ranged along the Hallstatt road to the west. There's also a **youth hostel** some way out of town at Winkl 26 (☎06134/360); follow the Hallstatt road westwards then turn left onto the access road to the Dachstein cable car to reach it. Best places to **eat and drink** are the *Gasthof Obertraun* on the main street quite near the train station, and the *Haus am See* by the Strandbad, both offering tasty rustic Austrian dishes.

The Dachstein caves and the Krippenstein

The **Dachstein ice caves** (May to mid-Oct daily 9am–5pm) above Obertraun are one of the most popular excursions in the Salzkammergut.There are two groups of caves to explore – the **Rieseneishöhle**, or giant ice caves, and the **Mammuthöhle**, or mammoth caves (the latter a reference to the system's size rather than the presence of any prehistoric animal) – both of which are reached by a cable car that begins just south of Obertraun village. The cable-car journey is itself a worthwhile excursion, offering stunning views of the Hallstättersee below and providing access to some excellent walks in the pastures below the Dachstein. For those of you driving, the cable-car station is signposted off the Obertraun–Hallstatt road. To reach the Dachsteinseilbahn by foot, turn right outside Obertraun train station and head through the centre of the village for about ten minutes until you see the signposted footpath – the cable-car station is about twenty minutes further.

The first leg of the cable-car journey ascends to a middle station on the **Schönbergeralm** (öS165 return), and stops off for both cave tours, the first of which is the awesome, imaginatively lit Rieseneishöhle (öS85, combined ticket with Mammuthöhle öS125), whose galleries are adorned with strange ice formations. About a fifteen-minute walk from the Schönbergeralm station, the Mammuthöhle (öS85) lacks the ice that characterizes its near-neighbour, but includes the so-called "midnight cathedral", where abstract, psychedelic images are projected onto the cavern walls to dramatic effect.

A second cable car climbs from Schönbergeralm to the 2100-metre **Krippenstein** (öS130 return, combined ticket with the Obertraun–Schönbergeralm section öS255 return), which commands excellent views in all directions – notably towards the 2995-metre summit of the **Dachstein** immediately to the south.

Bad Aussee and around

Sprawling at the foot of lowland hills, **BAD AUSSEE** is another medieval salt-processing town that reinvented itself as a chic spa-resort in the early 1800s. Main settlement in the Styrian corner of the Salzkammergut, it owed much of its nineteenth-century popularity to the regular visits of **Johann, Archduke of Styria**, whose love for the local postmaster's daughter Anna Plöchl (see box) was followed with intense interest by the Austrian public, adding a veneer of romance to the town's otherwise wholesome alpine image. Although not on a lake of its own, Bad Aussee is only a few kilometres away from the **Grundlsee** to the east, a five-kilometre-long expanse backed by the mountains of the Totes Gebirge.

One of Austria's most colourful carnival customs takes place in Bad Aussee on **Faschingsdienstag** (Shrove Tuesday), when the **Flinserln** don sequinned costumes and parade through the town to announce the coming spring. They're accompanied by the top-hatted **Zacherln**, whose job it is to keep the Flinsern in order by waving pigs' bladders on the ends of sticks. Also taking to the streets are the **Drum Women**, men in nightdresses who move from inn to inn banging drums and availing themselves of free food and drink – a misogynistic celebration of men's right to booze in peace without being pestered by their womenfolk. Bad Aussee's other big folk celebration is the **Narzissenfest**, a daffodil festival straddling a weekend at the end of May (check precise dates with the local tourist office), when floats bearing designs made from the flowers course the streets.

The Town

Most life in Bad Aussee revolves around the central **Kurpark**, whose manicured lawns overlook the babbling confluence of the Ausseer Traun and the Grundlseer Traun. A statue in the middle of the park honours the town's great popularizer,

ARCHDUKE JOHANN

It's impossible to visit Bad Aussee without coming across some reminder of **Archduke Johann** (1782–1859), one of the nineteenth century's more likeable Habsburgs, who scandalized the imperial family with his love for **Anna Plöchl**, daughter of Bad Aussee's postmaster. Although the archduke tends to be remembered nowadays as something akin to the romantic lead in a comic operetta, he was a powerful figure at court, whose reformist ideas were ultimately stymied by more cautious rivals. He was considered more capable than his brother the emperor Francis II, who as a consequence had him spied upon and used as a scapegoat for Habsburg failures. Johann was thus blamed for Napoleon's victory at Wagram in 1809, because the troops he was commanding arrived late and missed the battle. Defeat at the hands of the French had a damaging effect on Habsburg prestige among German-speaking peoples, and Johann tried to reinvigorate the empire by encouraging a new, specifically Austrian identity that would unify all its subjects. However, the response to his ideas among ruling circles was less than positive, leaving him increasingly disillusioned. A keen mountaineer who loved nothing better than to hang out in the Styrian countryside in a pair of leather shorts and a huntsman's hat, the archduke preferred provincial life to the backbiting of the capital. His love for the low-born Anna, whom he met in 1818 and whose eyes he somewhat condescendingly described as of the type "which we highlanders compare to chamois", in any case ensured that he was increasingly given the cold shoulder by his fellow Habsburgs.

Johann's relatives didn't really know what to make of his sentimentality: in a family whose male children were expected to marry for dynastic reasons and quench whatever remaining lusts they had with the help of the local serving girls, romantic love was at best seen as a dereliction of duty; at worst, a sign of mental illness. Emperor Francis forbade the marriage on the advice of his chief minister Metternich (a staunch opponent of Johann's liberal-leaning politics), who warned that a wedding to a middle-class girl would only make Johann more popular with the lower orders. Johann himself refused any compromise, moving Anna into his house – his claim that they never shared the same bed seemed to placate a sceptical Catholic hierarchy. In 1829 an exasperated emperor finally gave in, and the couple were married at Brandhof, Johann's palatial hunting lodge near Mariazell.

The archduke continued to stay away from court if at all possible – though he played a key role in persuading Ferdinand I to abdicate in favour of the 17-year-old Franz-Josef (Johann's nephew) in 1848. In the same year, the German assembly in Frankfurt adopted Archduke Johann as its president in the hope that he would serve as a talismanic liberal figurehead, but Franz-Josef persuaded Johann to step down as soon as he felt strong enough to move against him. As a placatory gesture, Franz-Josef gave the hitherto shunned Anna the title of Duchess of Meran in 1850.

Archduke Johann, while the modern **Kurhaus** at the park's northern end houses the main downtown café and a concert hall. Heading north from here along the Hauptstrasse, alleyways lead uphill to **Chlumeckyplatz**, site of most of the town's remaining medieval houses and a pleasant place to stroll. The **Heimatmuseum** (mid-June to Aug daily 10am–noon & 4–6pm; April to mid-June & Oct Tues 3.30–6pm, Fri 9.30am–noon, Sun 10am–noon; öS40) occupies the Kammerhof here, a Gothic building with Renaissance additions, which once housed the administration of the local salt industry. Inside, eclipsing the Flinserln and Zacherln costumes on display, the **Kaisersaal** boasts eighteenth-century frescoes showing vibrant local landscapes framed by floral designs. Downhill from Chlumeckyplatz to the east, on the other side of the Grundlseer Traun, is the **Meranplatz**, site of the Gothic Spitalkirche and the house, at no. 37, where Anna Plöchl grew up, and where she returned after Archduke Johann's death in 1859.

Practicalities

Bad Aussee's **train station** is at the southern end of town, a twenty-minute walk up Bahnhofstrasse to the centre. The **tourist office** (Mon–Fri 8am–noon & 2–6pm, Sat 10am–noon; ☎03622/52323), at the southern end of the Kurpark, will fix you up with **private rooms**, and offers touch-screen accommodation information outside office hours. The *Hotel Post*, on the corner of Kirchengasse and Meranplatz (☎03622/53555; ⑥), is a stylish town-centre Gasthof offering all the creature comforts. There's a **youth hostel** about 400m west of the town centre at Jugendherbergstrasse 148 (☎3622/52238), with beds in four-person dorms.

The best places to **eat** are the *Kirchenwirt* attached to the *Hotel Post*, which has good-quality Austrian food at medium prices, and the slightly more upmarket *Kupfer-Pfanne*, just west of the Kurpark at Ischlerstrasse 70, serving both modern European and traditional Austrian cuisine. Meals are also served at the *Café Meran* on Meranplatz, a good place for a daytime or evening **drink**, which has an Art-Nouveau-influenced interior and a pleasant courtyard. *Diesel*, Chlumeckyplatz, is a lively bar open until the early hours.

The Grundlsee

Four kilometres east of town, the **Grundlsee** can be reached by regular bus from Bad Aussee or by a signposted footpath, which starts at the eastern end of town uphill from Meranplatz and heads off through the woods. Stretching along the western shore of the lake, the village of **GRUNDLSEE** initially played host to nineteenth-century English fishing enthusiasts, though it didn't take long for urban Austrians to be seduced by its tranquil lakeside charm – Sigmund Freud, who loved to go mushroom-picking in the woods above the lake, was one famous Viennese intellectual who used to holiday here before World War I.

The Grundlsee **tourist office** (April–Oct Mon–Fri 9am–noon & 2–4pm), the main road through the village, will sort out **private rooms**. Just opposite the tourist office, *Gasthof Lindlbauer* is a good **restaurant** with a waterside terrace, serving fresh fish from the lake and the usual range of Austrian schnitzels. A similar menu is on offer at the more expensive *Restaurant Seeblick*, on a hill at the western end of the lake about a ten-minute walk from the waterfront.

Buses continue a further 5km to the eastern end of the lake, where the small village of **GÖSSL** squats beside a thin stretch of shingle beach with the usual pedalo- and rowing boat-rental facilities. There are two **campsites** just back from the lakefront, and a **youth hostel** 1km southwest of Gössl centre, where Bad Aussee–Gössl buses terminate. Paths lead from Gössl 1.5km east to the Toplitzsee, beyond which is the smaller Kammersee, source of the River Traun.

A popular excursion on the Grundlsee is the **three-lake tour** (four daily in summer; the return trip takes about 3hr; öS140), which takes in Gründlsee and the two smaller lakes to the east, Toplitzsee and Kammersee. Embarking from a pier next to *Gasthof Lindlbauer* at the west end of Grundlsee village, you're shipped to Gössl, from where you walk overland to the Toplitzsee. There, another boat ferries you past impressive water-falls on the northern side of the lake. Another short walk brings you to the Kammersee; too small for a boat trip, but where you have time to enjoy the view before turning back. Alternatively, a one-hour tour of Grundlsee on its own will set you back öS80.

travel details

Trains

Attnang-Puchheim to: Altmünster (12 daily; 25min); Bad Aussee (10 daily; 1hr 40min); Bad Ischl (12 daily; 1hr); Ebensee (12 daily; 50min); Gmunden (12 daily; 15min); Hallstatt (10 daily; 1hr 25min); Obertraun (10 daily; 1hr 30min); Salzburg (24 daily; 45min–1hr 25min); Stainach-Irdning (8 daily; 2hr–2hr 30min); Traunkirchen (12 daily; 35min); Vienna (hourly; 2hr 35min).

Bad Ischl to: Altmünster (12 daily; 35min); Attnang-Puchheim (12 daily; 1hr); Bad Aussee (10 daily; 40min); Ebensee (12 daily; 10min); Gmunden (12 daily; 45min); Hallstatt (10 daily; 25min); Obertraun (10 daily; 30min); Stainach-Irdning (8 daily; 1hr 30min); Traunkirchen (12 daily; 25min).

Graz to: Stainach-Irdning (8 daily; 2hr 10min–2hr 40min).

Lambach to: Gmunden (8 daily; 1hr 20min; change at Vorchdorf-Eggenberg).

Salzburg to: Attnang-Puchheim (24 daily; 45min–1hr 25min); Lambach (4 daily; 1hr 25min); Vöcklabruck (22 daily; 1hr–1hr 25min); Vöcklamarkt (22 daily; 45min–1hr).

Stainach-Irdning to: Altmünster (8 daily; 2hr 10min); Attnang-Puchheim (8 daily; 2hr–2hr 30min); Bad Aussee (10 daily; 40min); Bad Ischl (8 daily; 1hr 30min); Ebensee (8 daily; 1hr 40min); Gmunden (8 daily; 2hr 15min); Graz (8 daily; 2hr 10min–2hr 40min); Hallstatt (8 daily; 1hr); Obertraun (8 daily; 50min); Traunkirchen (8 daily; 2hr).

Buses

Bad Aussee to: Gössl (7 daily; 30min); Gründlsee (7 daily; 15min).

Bad Ischl to: Gosau (8 daily; 50min); Hallstatt (8 daily; 40min); Salzburg (hourly; 1hr 40min); St Wolfgang (hourly; 45min).

Mondsee to: St Gilgen (4 daily; 25min); Salzburg (8 daily; 55min).

St Gilgen to: Mondsee (4 daily; 25min); Salzburg (hourly; 45min); Strobl (hourly; 15min).

Salzburg to: Bad Ischl (hourly; 1hr 40min); Mondsee (8 daily; 55min); St Gilgen (hourly; 45min); Strobl (hourly; 1hr).

Strobl to: Postalm (2 daily; 40min); St Wolfgang (hourly; 15min).

Lake steamers

Wolfgangsee (May to mid-Oct)

St Gilgen to: St Wolfgang (7 daily; 25min); Strobl (7 daily; 35min).

Traunsee (early May to mid-Oct)

Ebensee to: Altmünster (4 daily; 35min); Gmunden (4 daily; 50min); Traunkirchen (4 daily; 25min).

UPPER AUSTRIA

U pper Austria (Oberösterreich) shares a great deal, both politically and geographically, with neighbouring Lower Austria. Although fought over for centuries by the Bavarians and Habsburgs, it has remained, for the most part, in Habsburg hands since the thirteenth century. Stretching from the Czech border in the north to the alpine foothills of Styria in the south, the landscape is characterized by rich, rolling farmland, which is generally overlooked by tourists, who are drawn more towards Austria's craggy mountainscapes. The few visitors who do find their way here are concentrated in the very south of the province, in the lakeland area known as the Salzkammergut, which is divided between several Länder, and covered separately in Chapter 7. To the Austrians themselves, Upper Austria is seen as something of a rural backwater, with the most provincial of all Austrian cities, **Linz**, as its capital. Paradoxically, Linz is also much maligned because of its all-too-visible industrial baggage, yet it's a place that's full of surprises. At its core, it preserves a very attractive Altstadt, and it boasts one of the country's most **innovative museums**, the Ars Electronica.

Like Lower Austria, Upper Austria is also a region replete with spectacular monasteries, which were transformed into Baroque showpieces during the Counter-Reformation. **St Florian** is the best known thanks to its associations with the composer Anton Bruckner, but the Rococo masterpiece of **Wilhering**, and **Kremsmünster**, with its remarkable fish basins, art collection and observatory, are both equally stunning architecturally – and all three lie within an easy train ride of Linz. Austria's most notorious concentration camp, based in the granite quarries of **Mauthausen**, is also a short journey from the regional capital. The camp was housed in a purpose-built granite fortress, which even the retreating SS couldn't demolish, and it stands today as a salutary reminder of the atrocities committed by the Nazis.

After Linz, Upper Austria has just two other towns of any great size: **Wels**, which has a handsome enough Altstadt and some impressive Roman remains, and **Steyr**, the more compelling of the two, a place of considerable charm, which enjoys a splendid location at the confluence of the Enns and Steyr rivers. Again, you could comfortably see either town on a day-trip from Linz, but Steyr, in particular, makes a pleasant overnight halt, too. There are plenty of picturesque walled towns dotted about the province, none very large but each a minor architectural gem. If you're heading in or out of the Czech Republic, the perfectly preserved fortified town of **Freistadt** is a worthwhile stop-off. Likewise, if you're travelling to or from Germany, you've a choice

---

ACCOMMODATION PRICE CODES

All **hotels and pensions** in this book have been graded according to the following price categories. All the codes are based on the rate for the least expensive double room during the **summer season**. In those places where winter is the high season, we've indicated winter room rates in the text. For more on accommodation, see p.30.

① under öS400   ④ öS800–1000   ⑦ öS1400–1600
② öS400–600   ⑤ öS1000–1200   ⑧ öS1600–1800
③ öS600–800   ⑥ öS1200–1400   ⑨ over öS1800

Vienna

Melk

LOWER

Zwettl

Pöchlarn

AUSTRIA

Gmund

Amstetten

Lunz

Grein

Waidhofen an
der Ybbs

Seitenstetten
Markt

50 km

0

CZECH REPUBLIC

Prague

Freistadt

Kefermarkt

Mauthausen

MÜHLVIERTEL

Linz

Enns

St. Florian

Steyr

Windischgarsten

Wilhering

Kremsmünster

Danube

Eferding

Wels

A9

Schärding

Lambach

Gmunden

Traunsee

SALZKAMMERGUT

Passau

GERMANY

Obernberg

Attersee

Bad Ischl

Ried im
Innkreis

145

INNVIERTEL

Braunau

Wolfgangsee

Regensburg

Danube

Simbach

Burghausen

Salzburg

N

Munich

Munich

of picture-perfect towns along the banks of the Inn, from **Braunau-am-Inn**, Hitler's unreasonably pretty birthplace, to **Schärding**, a short hop across the Inn from the German town of Passau.

Linz

LINZ is definitely the underdog when it comes to Austrian cities. It receives the smallest number of tourists, and is looked down on, even by fellow Austrians, as both deeply provincial and, at the same time, predominantly industrial. By whatever means you approach the city, it's impossible to ignore the chemical plants, steelworks and dockyards ranged along the banks of the Danube. However, in the well-preserved and attractive Altstadt you can still see the core of the much smaller, pre-industrial provincial town. Linz may not bowl you over with its beauty, but it's a place that grows on you – and it does have one remarkable museum, the Ars Electronica, dedicated to the "virtual" arts, that alone justifies a visit here. Finally, as if the city didn't have a big enough PR problem, Linz is also famous for being "Hitler's home town" (see p.382), the place where he spent his "happiest days", and to which he eventually planned to retire.

Some history

Linz began life as the Roman port of Lentia, later becoming a major medieval trading centre, controlled first by the bishops of Passau, and later by the Babenbergs. Apart from its brief stint as imperial capital under the emperor Friedrich III from 1489 to 1493, however, the city was better known for its peasant revolts than anything else. Along with much of Upper Austria, Linz became a bastion of Protestantism following the Reformation, hosting an important Protestant confederation in 1614, and attracting the Lutheran astronomer Johannes Kepler to work in the city. In 1626, an estimated 16,000 local peasants revolted against the Catholicizing policies of Maximilian of Bavaria and besieged Linz. In the end, the Bavarians relieved the city, though at some considerable cost. More than two hundred buildings were destroyed, and the majority of the city's merchant families fled, leaving Linz to languish as a provincial backwater for the next two centuries, and the Counter-Reformation kicked in with a vengeance.

It was the city's strategic position as a bridge over the Danube that ensured its resurgence in the nineteenth century. In 1832, the first horse-drawn railway on the continent was built between Linz and the Bohemian town of Budweis (České Budějovice), and by the end of the century the city had developed into the largest railway junction in the empire. At the same time, Linz became something of a musical centre, thanks to the presence of Anton Bruckner, who took the post of cathedral organist. Like the rest of Austria during the 1920s and 1930s, Linz was torn between paramilitary wings of Left and Right, with violent skirmishes frequently played out on the city's streets. On February 12, 1934, the country was plunged into civil war when a dawn raid by the right-wing *Heimwehr* on a socialist weapons cache in the *Hotel Schiff*, on the corner of Landstrasse and Mozartstrasse, was met with armed resistance. Although widespread, the fighting in Linz was over in a day, ending in defeat for the *Schutzbund*, the paramilitary wing of the socialists.

Despite the delirious reception given to Hitler when he arrived in Linz after the Nazi invasion of March 1938 (it's estimated that five-sixths of the population came out to greet him), Linz had not been a Nazi stronghold during the 1930s. It was, however, a keenly anti-Semitic town, whose persecution of its Jewish population was so thorough that the local stormtroopers found no Jewish property left to destroy on *Kristallnacht*. (The only local-born Jew to survive the war was Hitler's childhood family doctor, Eduard Bloch, who was left unmolested on the Führer's own orders.) Economically, Linz benefited

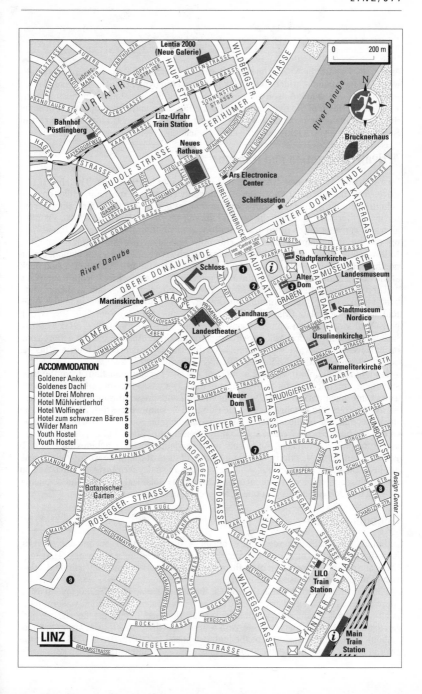

Lentia 2000
(Neue Galerie)

URFAHR

Bahnhof
Pöstlingberg

Linz-Urfahr
Train Station

Neues
Rathaus

Brucknerhaus

RUDOLF STRASSE

Ars Electronica
Center

Schiffsstation

UNTERE DONAULÄNDE

River Danube

OBERE DONAULÄNDE

River Danube

Schloss

Martinskirche

see 'Central Linz'
map, page 380.

Stadtpfarrkirche

① ②

Alter
Dom ③

Landesmuseum

Landhaus

④

Stadtmuseum
Nordico

Landestheater

⑤

Ursulinenkirche

⑥

Karmeliterkirche

Neuer
Dom

ACCOMMODATION

Goldener Anker	1
Goldenes Dachl	7
Hotel Drei Mohren	4
Hotel Mühlviertlerhof	3
Hotel Wolfinger	2
Hotel zum schwarzen Bären	5
Wilder Mann	8
Youth Hostel	6
Youth Hostel	9

⑦

Botanischer
Garten

ROSEGGER- STRASSE

⑧

Design Center

⑨

LINZ

LILO
Train
Station

ⓘ Main
Train
Station

The telephone code for Linz is ☎0732.

enormously under the Nazis. Hermann Göring himself founded the giant iron and steel-works by the Danube, which to this day provides employment for the local population. After the war, Linz found itself on the very border of the Soviet and American sectors, with Urfahr, north of the river, occupied by the Russians, and Linz proper controlled by the US. In 1955, the occupation forces withdrew, and since then Linz, like the rest of Austria, has enjoyed a fairly peaceful and increasingly prosperous existence.

Arrival, information and transport

Linz's **airport** is just over 10km southwest of the city in Hörsching. The airport bus leaves from outside the train station at an ungodly hour in the morning, while the train is hourly, but it's a good half-hour's walk or a short taxi ride to Hörsching station from the airport terminal; a taxi all the way to Linz will set you back around öS300. Virtually all trains arrive at Linz's **main train station**, 2km south of the city centre (buses pull up on the Bahnhofplatz outside). The only exception are slow trains from the Mühlviertel region to the northwest of Linz, which arrive at Linz-Urfahr station, on the north bank of the river. **Boats** chugging along the Danube from either direction dock at the *Schiffsstation* to the east of the Nibelungenbrücke, a short walk from Hauptplatz.

There's a small tourist office (Mon–Fri 8am–6pm, Sat 8am–noon & 3–5pm, Sun 8am–noon) in the Hauptbahnhof, but the city's main **tourist office** is in the Altes Rathaus on Hauptplatz (May–Oct Mon–Fri 7am–7pm, Sat 9am–7pm, Sun 10am–7pm; Nov–April Mon–Fri 8am–6pm, Sat 9am–6pm, Sun 10am–6pm; ☎7070-1777, fax 772873). Either of the above offices will have information on Upper Austria, but, for a more comprehensive rundown on the region, head for the Oberösterreich tourist office at Schillerstrasse 50 (Mon–Fri 9am–12.30pm & 2.30–6pm; ☎771264).

It's a long walk into town (and to most of the city's accommodation) from the train station, so you might prefer to make use of the city's ultra-efficient **public transport**. To get into town, take tram #3, which heads up Landstrasse, through Hauptplatz and across the river into Urfahr. For a single ride (öS18), simply press the "*Midi*" button on the ticket machine by the tram stop. If you're planning on going on more than one tram or bus, it's best to buy a *Netzkarte* (öS35) by pressing the "*Maxi*" button; the "*Mini*" button is for children's tickets. All tickets need validating in the machines on board. If you're planning on staying in Linz for a couple of days, it might be worthwhile investing in a *Linz City Ticket* (öS399), which gives you a two-day *Netzkarte*, a return ride on the Pöstlingbergbahn, entry to one museum and the botanical gardens, and a voucher for öS300 which can be used in one of a selection of the city's restaurants.

Accommodation

Although Linz probably sees more business travellers than out-and-out tourists, **accommodation** is, on the whole, very reasonably priced for a major city. That said, there are no private rooms on offer through the tourist office, and only a limited selection of places to stay close to the centre.

Linz has three **youth hostels**. The one at Kapuzinerstrasse 14 (☎782720, fax 781789-4; March to mid-Nov) is small, friendly and conveniently located, five minutes' walk from the centre. If it's full, head for the youth hostel at Stanglhofweg 3 (☎664434, fax 602164; mid-Jan to mid-Dec), off Roseggerstrasse, 2km southwest of the centre (bus #27 from the train station). Your last choice should be the high-rise hostel (☎237078, fax 237078-15) over the river in Urfahr above the Lentia 2000 shopping centre on Blütenstrasse (tram #3).

The city's main **campsite** (☎305314; March–Nov) is by the Pichlinger See in the suburb of Pichling, 5km southeast of the city centre (on the train to Asten), but it's too close to the autobahn for comfort. For a more peaceful site, for tents only, head to the *Pleschinger See* (☎247870; May–Sept), 3km northeast of the centre, on the north bank of the Danube (bus #33 or #33a from Reindlstrasse in Urfahr).

Hotels and pensions

Goldener Anker, Hofgasse 5 (☎ & fax 771088). Old, family-run Gasthof in the Altstadt. Simplest rooms are a bargain – you pay extra if you want en suite facilities, TV and breakfast. ②.

Goldenes Dachl, Hafnerstrasse 27 (☎675480). Plain but clean rooms over a simple *Gasthaus*, at bargain prices. ②.

Hotel Drei Mohren, Promenade 17 (☎772626, fax 772626-6). Great location and pleasantly modernized interior; all rooms are fully en-suite, and the lounge has a nice balcony overlooking the Promenade. ⑥.

Hotel Mühlviertlerhof, Graben 24 (☎772268, fax 772268-34). Tastefully modernized, fairly swish hotel right in the centre, with en-suite facilities and TV in all rooms. ④.

Hotel Wolfinger, Hauptplatz 19 (☎773191, fax 773291-55). Wonderful old hotel, with creaking parquet floors, a touch of the medieval – it used to be a nunnery – and a lovely balcony at the back. All rooms are en suite with TV, with a tasteful mix of antique and repro furniture. ⑤.

Hotel zum Schwarzen Bären, Herrenstrasse 9–11 (☎772477, fax 772477-47). Simply furnished throughout, but with a bit more character than most, especially in the cheaper rooms with shared facilities. ③.

Wilder Mann, Goethestrasse 14 (☎ & fax 656078). Rooms with or without en-suite facilities in a simple no-frills Gasthof, 5min walk from the train station, and only one block east of Landstrasse. ③.

The City Centre

Linz's main thoroughfare is the kilometre-long **Landstrasse**, traffic-free for the most part, except for trams, and lined on both sides by shops, cafés and department stores. For such a large city, Linz's **Altstadt**, at the far northern end of Landstrasse, is remarkably small: Graben and Promenade now lie along the line of the old city walls. Just about everything of interest on this side of the river lies within easy walking distance of the showpiece main square, **Hauptplatz**.

The Altstadt

Linz's rectangular **Hauptplatz** is one of the finest squares of any Austrian city, with its tall, pastel-coloured facades, and a vast, marble Trinity column, crowned by a gilded sunburst, as the perfect centrepiece. There is, however, something a bit cool and aloof about the whole ensemble – it looks a bit softer and more welcoming when lit up at night. Few of the buildings on the square stand out individually, with the possible exception of the salmon-coloured **Altes Rathaus**, on whose ridiculously small balcony Hitler appeared after his triumphant homecoming in March 1938 (see box, p.382) to greet the delirious crowds.

Rising above the houses in the southeast corner of Hauptplatz are the twin towers of the pea-green Jesuit church, or **Alter Dom** (daily 7am–noon & 3–7pm), where the composer Anton Bruckner was organist from 1855 to 1868. Built by the Jesuits at the zenith of their power in the 1670s, it was taken off them in 1773, and given cathedral status in the following decade, only to be returned to them in 1909 when the cathedral was superseded by the Neuer Dom. The white stucco-work on the barrel-vaulted ceiling of the nave is outstanding, as are the finely carved choirstalls, peppered with grotesques and grimacing cherubs, and the magnificent black and gold pulpit.

Round the corner from the Alter Dom is the much smaller **Stadtpfarrkirche**, a Gothic–Baroque church that's a bit gloomy inside. Its chief claim to fame is the red marble slab stuck into the wall to the right of the high altar, behind which the heart of Emperor Friedrich III is buried (he died in Linz in 1493, but the rest of him was buried in Vienna's Stephansdom). More memorable, though, is the marble-clad chapel in the southwest corner of the church, with its trompe l'oeil dome and statue of St John of Nepomuk by Georg Raphael Donner.

No Austrian city would be complete without its own Mozart plaque, and Linz's is at Klostergasse 20, west off Hauptplatz, now known as the **Mozarthaus**, where the composer stayed with his wife in 1783. He was due to give a concert in the city and, having no other symphony with him, knocked out his 36th (now known as the *Linz*) at breakneck speed – in about four days. On the opposite side of the street is the **Minoritenkirche** (daily 8–11am), its small Rococo interior lined with pinkish side altars culminating in a high altar that positively froths with gilded clouds, cherubs and angels.

Next door stands the regional parliament, or **Landhaus**, a vast complex intended as a Minorite monastery, but bought by the locals in 1564. Very little remains from that period, save for the splendid red-marble entrance portal, on Klostergasse, with its triumphal-arch motif and Dutch gable. The courtyard immediately to the right preserves its triple-decker Renaissance loggia on two sides, and has at its centre the *Planetenbrunnen*, from 1582, a fountain whose figures each represent one of the seven planets then known.

The Schloss and Martinskirche

From the Landhaus, it's a short stroll through the most picturesque of the Altstadt's narrow streets to the city's dour, fortress-like **Schloss** (Tues–Fri 9am–5pm, Sat & Sun 10am–4pm; öS50), built on high ground above the city by Emperor Friedrich III. Having been kicked out of most of eastern Austria by the Hungarian king Matthias Corvinus, Friedrich retreated to Linz in 1489 and, according to the enemies, spent his days collecting mouse droppings and catching flies, before dying here of gout in 1493. Later, the castle was used as a hospital, a prison and a barracks, until it finally became a museum in 1960. Not a lot has changed since those days, and the castle's collection of weapons, musical instruments. paintings and sculptures only really repay selective viewing. The temporary exhibitions on the ground floor are usually interesting enough, but the first floor is better skipped in preference to the second, where, to the left of the stairs, there's a prettily decorated timber-built cottage interior, plus a terrific collection of folk costumes and miniature Passions-in-a-bottle. To the right of the stairs, past the Baroque heaters and the outdoor chess set, the castle's apothecary from 1700 has survived, along with some worrying bygone scientific instruments.

The highlight of the entire museum, though, is the nineteenth- and early twentieth-century picture collection, which begins inauspiciously with a load of mawkish Biedermeier paintings, epitomized by Ferdinand Georg Waldmüller's sentimental depictions of rural folk. Once you've waded through this stuff, though, you'll get to an early, allegorical painting by a pre-Secession Gustav Klimt, along with several works by Egon Schiele, Richard Gerstl and Oskar Kokoschka. Downstairs from here, there's one last room to enjoy, dominated by works by Hans Makart, doyen of the Viennese art scene (until his death from syphilis in 1884), including a wonderfully lugubrious, moody portrait of his long-suffering wife, Amalie. The superb, iridescent Jugenstil and Art-Deco glassware on display here comes mostly from nearby Bohemia, but the samovar, cigarette cases and brooches by Kolo Moser and Josef Hoffmann are pure Wiener Werkstätte.

A short walk west up Römerstrasse from the Schloss is Austria's oldest church, the diminutive **Martinskirche**. Originally a much larger, eighth-century Carolingian construction, built using the ruins of an ancient Roman wall, it's a touch over-restored and really not that impressive. Inside, the bare stone nave features patchy frescoes contemporary with the fifteenth-century choir, and modern stained-glass windows. Unless you either sign up for one of the guided tours of the city organized by the tourist office, or attend a service here, however, you can only peek through the glass doors at the interior.

The Neuer Dom, Stadtmuseum Nordico and Landesmuseum

Away from the Altstadt and the Schloss, there's not much to quicken the heart. The awesome presence of the neo-Gothic **Neuer Dom** is impossible to ignore as you walk around the city. Situated a couple of blocks west of Landstrasse, and topped by a steeple that soars to 134m – just short of Vienna's Stephansdom, as stipulated by the authorities – this massive building is Austria's largest cathedral. It was begun in 1855 under Bishop Franz-Josef Rudigier, a tireless patron of Anton Bruckner, whom he commissioned to write a choral piece to celebrate the laying of the foundation stone. Yet, for all its size, the Neuer Dom is a graceless, academic exercise from the outside; inside, it's slightly more appealing, particularly in the ambulatory, where the sun scatters multicoloured lights through the modern stained-glass windows.

The **Stadtmuseum Nordico** (Mon–Fri 9am–6pm, Sat & Sun 2–5pm; free), a couple of blocks east of Landstrasse down Bethlehemstrasse, houses a model of Linz from 1740 and hosts modern art exhibitions, but that's about it. The building itself was used until 1786 by the Jesuits to train young students from Scandinavia, hence the Nordico suffix. The nearby **Landesmuseum** (Tues–Fri 9am–6pm, Sat & Sun 10am–5pm; öS50) sometimes known as the Francisco-Carolinum Museum, occupies a splendid mustard-coloured building, built in 1887 with red-brick infill, a Neoclassical frieze, and cherub-guarded obelisks on its roof. The interior is equally ornate, but there's no permanent collection, just a series of temporary art and natural history exhibitions.

Urfahr

Urfahr, once a separate town, now a workaday suburb of Linz, lies on the north bank of the River Danube, clearly visible (and a short walk) across the Nibelungenbrücke from Hauptplatz. Dominated by the supremely ugly Neues Rathaus by the riverfront, Urfahr in fact boasts three of the finest sights in Linz: the remarkable **Ars Electronica Center**, the city's top art gallery, the **Neue Galerie**, in the unprepossessing Lentia 2000 shopping centre, and the **Pöstlingbergbahn**, whose cream-coloured trams will lift you high above the city.

HITLER'S HEIMATSTADT

Although **Adolf Hitler** (1890–1945) was born in Braunau-am-Inn (see p.397), he considered Linz to be his *Heimatstadt* or home town, something about which today's tourist authorities are understandably coy. To begin with, the family lived just outside Linz, in the village of Leonding, 5km to the southwest. Hitler commuted to the Linz Realschule from 1900, but was forced to leave in 1904 (the year that philosopher Ludwig Wittgenstein entered the school), after failing his exams twice. Hitler fared little better at the Steyr Realschule, where his first report card was so bad he got drunk and used the document as toilet paper, forcing him to ask for a duplicate to be issued. His father died shortly afterwards, and Hitler left school without graduating, before moving with the rest of the family to Humboldtstrasse 31, in the heart of Linz. The future Führer spent the next couple of years going to the local opera house, sketching and daydreaming.

Some thirty years after leaving Linz for good in an unsuccessful attempt to enter art school in Vienna, Hitler returned in triumph on March 12, 1938. Driving into the Hauptplatz in his open-top Mercedes, the dictator was greeted by such wildly jubilant crowds that he decided, there and then, to go for a full Anschluss, in other words, the incorporation of Austria into the Third Reich; "the cares and troubles of this city are over because I have assumed its personal protection," he declared over dinner at the city's *Hotel Weinzinger*. Two days later, after paying his respects to his parents' grave in Leonding, Hitler continued on his triumphal journey to Vienna.

Though he rarely returned to his home town as Führer, Hitler had elaborate plans for Linz, which he was going to transform into a "Second Budapest", with a new opera house, theatre, concert hall, university, art gallery, museum, park, boulevard – the lot. Within days of the Anschluss, engineers arrived to draw up plans for a new Nibelungen Brücke (designed years before by Hitler himself). Among the Führer's more fanciful proposals were the construction of a gigantic statue of Siegfried on the Freinberg, a hill to the west of the city centre, where Hitler also planned to build his retirement home. The Altstadt was to be left intact, but the riverfront was to be totally transformed with bombastic Neoclassical architecture, and a 160-metre-high tower erected in Urfahr, containing a vaulted crypt for the remains of Hitler's parents, and, in the bell tower where Hitler wished to be buried, a carillon capable of playing passages from Bruckner's *Fourth Symphony*.

An illuminated model of the planned improvements to Linz occupied pride of place in Hitler's Berlin bunker, but very few projects were ever actually realized. Apart from the Nibelungen Brücke, and a few minor buildings, the most significant progress was made in buying, borrowing and appropriating over 5000 priceless artworks ready for the city's new art gallery. Initially, these were stored in Munich, but towards the end of the war the cache was shipped to the salt mines of Alt Aussee in the Salzkammergut, where they were saved in the final days of the war by a group of partisans who blocked the entrance and prevented the local Nazis from carrying out their orders to destroy them.

Ars Electronica

Before you've even reached the end of the Nibelungenbrücke, the starkly modernist building housing the **Ars Electronica Center** (Wed–Sun 11am–7pm; öS80) appears on your right, advertising its *"Museum der Zukunft"* (Museum of the Future). This is a truly remarkable place: a museum dedicated to new technology, in particular to its artistic possibilities. The biggest single attraction is the museum's "CAVE" (Cave Automatic Virtual Environment, and a reference to Plato's "Simile of the Cave"), situated in the basement. A virtual-reality room with 3-D projections on three walls and the floor, this is one of only a handful of such installations in Europe, and the only one open to the public. By standing in the centre of the room, wearing a special 3-D viewfinder, you can navigate your way through a series of virtual spaces, from the solar system to imaginary landscapes and rooms. Although the room is large enough to accommodate a group of ten to twenty people, the full effect of the system only works for the one person wearing the viewfinder/headset.

The other floors of the museum feature a wide range of exhibits, all of which are fun to experiment with, from riding a bicycle across an imaginary landscape, to flying over a computer-generated virtual image of Upper Austria. Even the museum's lift, drolly dubbed Apollo 13, has rear-projected graphics to make you think you're taking off from Linz into outer space, like Charlie in Roald Dahl's *Charlie and the Great Glass Elevator*. Although you're at a definite disadvantage if you don't know any German, most of the staff speak excellent English, and will happily explain and demonstrate any of the exhibits for you. The biggest problem is the museum's popularity, which means it's a good idea to get here early (or late) to avoid the crowds. Also, if you want to see the CAVE, you need to book a place in advance from the ticket desk as you enter. When you're virtually exhausted, you can visit the 1960s-style rooftop cybercafé and enjoy a surf on the Net, or just enjoy views out over the Danube and the Altstadt.

Neue Galerie

It comes as little surprise that the city's **Neue Galerie** (Mon–Wed & Fri 10am–6pm, Thurs 10am–10pm, Sat 10am–1pm; öS60) gets so few visitors, given its location on the first floor of the supremely unattractive shopping centre called Lentia 2000 (the year of its proposed demolition?) on Blütenstrasse. However, it's well worth a visit, since, in addition to hosting temporary exhibitions of twentieth-century artists, alive or dead, the gallery has a small but fairly high-quality permanent collection of nineteenth- and twentieth-century Austrian art. Pride of place goes to **Oskar Kokoschka**'s typically agitated rendition of Linz, painted in 1955 and emphasizing the city's industrial character, while his portrait of the Austrian president Theodor Körner, from the same year, employs an exuberant Fauvist palette. There are several much earlier portraits, too, including the darkly drawn *Die Freunde*, depicting a malevolent-looking bunch of friends, whom you wouldn't wish on your worst enemy. **Egon Schiele,** whose life was as short as Kokoschka's was long, pitches in with two oil paintings: a joyful *Krumau Landscape*, inspired by his brief sojourn in the south Bohemian birthplace of his mother, known today as Český Krumlov; and a striking, almost monochrome double portrait, *Heinrich and Otto Benesch*. Heinrich Benesch (the older of the two) was something of a father figure for Schiele, and a keen collector of the artist's work, pleading with Schiele not to "put any of your sketches, no matter what they are, even the most trivial things, on the fire. Please write on your stove in chalk the following equation: 'Stove equals Benesch.'" Completing the country's most famous trio of artists, there are a couple of unfinished works by **Gustav Klimt**, one of which, the *Portrait of Maria Munk*, is a typical Japanese-influenced late work, in which the gold ornament for which he made his name has been entirely replaced by bright colours and a profusion of plants. The rest of the collection can't quite compete with the works by the above artists, though the demure, but unfinished *Lady in Red* by Hans Makart, Klimt's teacher, and Emil Nolde's splodgy paintings, manage to hold their own.

Pöstlingberg

With an afternoon of fine weather in prospect (or a child or two to entertain), one of the best things to do is take a ride on the narrow-gauge **Pöstlingbergbahn** (Mon–Sat 5.20am–8.20pm, Sun 7.15–11.15am & 11.40am–8.20pm; öS40 return), which departs from the timber and red-brick *Talstation*, just beyond Linz-Urfahr train station. The electrified trains depart every twenty minutes, wind their way up the world's steepest "adhesion" railway, past some swanky villas, to the top of the **Pöstlingberg** (539m), nearly 300m above the Danube.

The views over Linz are pretty spectacular, as is the Baroque **Wallfahrtskirche**, which occupies the crest of the hill. The interior is decorated with an outstanding set of frescoes, and copious rich Rococo stucco-work bristling with gold, but the church's object of greatest veneration is the eighteenth-century carved *Pietà*, which occupies centre stage in the stupendously ornate high altar.

If you have small children, you might consider it necessary to pay a visit to the miniature **Märchenfeld** (Fairy World) and its attendant **Grottenbahn** (March, April & mid-Sept to Oct daily 10am–5pm; May–Aug daily 9am–6pm; Dec Sat & Sun 10am–4pm; öS45), a subterranean railway pulled by a dragon. Everyone else should give the place a wide berth, however, unless they've a penchant for technicolour garden gnomes.

Eating and drinking

Linz's **restaurants** are concentrated in the Altstadt and on and off Landstrasse. The range of cuisines may be modest, though it's a significant improvement on most Austrian towns. The city itself is famous for just one culinary invention, the *Linzertorte*, a raspberry jam tart made with almond pastry, which is available from just about every café and restaurant in Linz, and as a souvenir from the much-esteemed *Philipp Wrann*, Landstrasse 70. Of the cafés, the most famous is *Café Traxlmayr*, which has changed very little over the last century; the *Gelbes Krokodil* is the best of the modern ones. If you need to cut costs and assemble a picnic, the city's main Billa **supermarket** is on the corner of Landstrasse and Mozartstrasse, and there's a smaller Spar store on Steingasse.

Restaurants

Agi's Restaurant, Altstadt 9. Decent Greek restaurant that doesn't try too hard to look Greek; in fact, it looks more like a traditional vaulted *Gasthaus*, which no doubt contributes to its popularity.

Chilli Peppers, Domgasse 5. Passable Tex-Mex food, including meat or veggie enchiladas and burritos, plus ribs, steaks and tequila cocktails. There's a bigger branch called *Los Caballeros*, at Landstrasse 32.

Klosterhof, Landstrasse 30. This place serves standard Austrian fare in the labyrinthine rooms of the former monastery: the *Bierstuben* is a smoky beer hall; the designer *Stieglitz* bar is flashier, with occasional live music; upstairs, there's a traditional wood-panelled and arcaded restaurant; outside is Linz's largest beer garden.

Kremsmünsterer Stuben, Altstadt 10 (☎782111). Imaginative takes on standard Austrian dishes, served up in a lovely Renaissance-era monks' dormitory. More expensive than most places, with main dishes öS200 and over. Closed Mon & Sun.

Levante, Hauptplatz 13. Smart, vaulted Turkish restaurant with a tasty selection of *börek*, kebabs and fish dishes on the menu for öS80 and upwards.

Linzer Stuben, Klammstrasse 7 (☎779028). Eminently *gemütlich* place with capacious armchairs and soft furnishings, specializing in Hungarian food. Closed Mon.

Mangolds, Hauptplatz 6. Despite the sanitized atmosphere, this self-service veggie cafeteria is a popular spot to grab one of the bargain daily hot dishes (öS45–65), or fill up at the giant salad bar. Closed Sun.

Rialto, Rathausgasse 7. Standard Italian job, with bargain weekday, lunchtime two-course menu for öS70, and lots of pizzas for under öS100.

Ursulinenhof, Landstrasse 31 (☎774686). Stylish restaurant with an eclectic menu, situated in a former convent just off Landstrasse, and best visited at lunchtime for the reasonably priced two-course menu for öS100.

Wachauer Weinstube, Pfarrgasse 20. Typical wood-panelled local *Stube* situated just off Hauptplatz, serving hearty Austrian food for under öS100. Closed Sun.

Wein Fassl, Kirchengasse 6. Traditional Urfahr wine-tavern next door to the Ars Electronica, with cheap lunchtime menus from öS65 and outdoor seating. Closed Sat & Sun.

Cafés and bars

The so-called "Bermuda Triangle", one block west of Hauptplatz, is *the* place to go of an evening (the triangle is formed by the streets Hofgasse, Hahnengasse and Altstadt). Quiet and quaint enough by day, these narrow medieval streets provide the most concentrated selection of **late-night bars** in the city, and are usually full of youthful drinkers on a summer evening. It doesn't make a huge difference which place you go for, but as a basic pointer *Aquarium*, Altstadt 22, is a favourite with the older, black-clad crowd, *'s Kistl*, Altstadt 17, serves a range of beers and tasty munchies, while *Smaragd*, next door, is usually good for a spot of live music. In the summer, a similar drinking crowd homes in on the **cafés and wine bars** by the Danube in Urfahr. Again, virtually any one will do, though *Biergartl*, west of the bridge, probably has the nicest beer garden, while *Stadtwerstatt*, Kirchengasse 4, is more of a Bermuda Triangle overspill, with regular, very loud bands. The cafés and bars listed below are more widely dispersed around town, and attract a slightly more discerning crowd.

1. Akt, Klammstrasse 20a. Buzzy, funky wine bar set back from the street in its own cobbled courtyard, and popular with an older, more successful crowd.

Alte Welt, Hauptplatz 4. Sweaty, late-night, cellar wine bar that puts on regular live jazz, folk and world music, plus two upstairs rooms and a nice courtyard, offering a decent range of food. Closed Sun.

Café Ex-Blatt, Waltherstrasse 15. Popular and studenty, but by no means posey, evenings-only café-bar, with just a few snacks and mini-pizzas on offer.

Café Landgraf, Hauptstrasse 12. A cross between a stylish *Kaffeehaus* and a posey cocktail bar, and one of the few places in Urfahr that keeps going of an evening. Food is limited to a two-course daily menu for öS80.

Café Traxlmayr, Promenade 16. A Linz institution, and the city's only real *Kaffeehaus* (in the Viennese tradition), *Traxlmayr* is still very popular with Linz folk of all ages. Coffee, cakes, newspapers, backgammon, chess, cigarette smoke, crystal chandeliers and tuxedoed waiters all guaranteed.

Gelbes Krokodil, Dametzstrasse 30. Superb, stylish café inside the city's Moviemento arts cinema (see p.386). Good enough to spend an evening in, and with an excellent selection of Med-influenced food. Ask a local for directions, as it's difficult to find. Closed Sat & Sun lunchtime.

Kitty Kiernan's, Hessenplatz 19. Every city in the world appears to need an Irish theme pub, and Linz finally got its very own in 1997 – so far, it's proved very popular.

Sassi, Arkade, Landstrasse 12. One of two smart bars in the *Arkade* shopping centre, which attracts a lot of Linz's young urban professionals and features occasional live music.

Entertainment

Linz is big enough to accommodate a wide variety of tastes, but **highbrow culture** still predominates. Full-scale opera goes on at the Grosses Haus in the city's Landestheater, on the Promenade, with straight drama on the theatre's two smaller stages. Children's theatre and puppet shows are staged at *Kuddelmuddel*, Langgasse 13. There are regular concerts at the converted convent of the Ursulinenhof, but the modern Brucknerhaus, by the river, is the main concert hall, and the focus of the annual **Brucknerfest**, which takes place from mid-September to early October. The festival begins with the *Klangwolken-Weekend*, with live transmissions of a Bruckner symphony, a laser show and open-air party by the Danube. The city's most offbeat festival is undoubtedly the **Ars Electronica Festival**, which takes place in early September, and features avant-garde music, installations and a competition for the most innovative piece of art using virtual reality.

Apart from the centrally located places listed above, like *Alte Welt*, *Smaragd* and *Stadtwerstatt*, that regularly feature live music, the best programme of **gigs** is that put on at Posthof, an alternative arts centre at Posthofgasse 43, over by the docks (bus #21 to the Zollfreizone); events range from modern dance to dance DJs. Big-name acts are more likely to be staged at the Stadion der Stadt Linz, up by the botanical gardens (bus #27 to Roseggerstrasse), where you can also watch the local first-division **soccer** team, FC Linz, in action every other Saturday during the football season (and occasionally on Wednesday evenings). A wide selection of films are shown in their original language at Moviemento, the city's main **arts cinema**, at Damtezstrasse 30. For a rundown of the month's events, pick up the *Linz ist los* listings leaflet from the tourist office.

Around Linz

Linz lies within easy reach of two of Upper Austria's finest monasteries, **St Florian**, where Anton Bruckner is buried, and the lesser-known abbey of **Wilhering**, both of which are primarily of interest for their outstanding Baroque and Rococo architecture. Austria's most infamous concentration camp, **Mauthausen**, downriver from Linz, is a chilling reminder of the country's wartime experience, and could be combined with a more light-hearted trip to the small town of **Enns**.

Stift St Florian

The Augustinian **Stift St Florian**, 12km southeast of Linz, is Upper Austria's most illustrious abbey, renowned not simply for its Baroque architecture, but also for its close associations with Anton Bruckner (see box). The composer joined the abbey choir at the age of 11, eventually went on to become organist here, and is buried, according to his wishes, beneath the ornate, and extraordinarily loud, 7000-pipe organ in the **Stiftskirche**, which stands at the northern end of the vast ochre-coloured monastic complex. Begun in 1686 by Carlo Carlone, the church boasts a gleaming-white interior flanked by imposing Corinthian half-columns, crowned with a heavy, stuccoed cornice. Decorated with a continuous band of predominantly golden-brown trompe l'oeil frescoes, the nave's vaulting creates a somewhat lighter atmosphere. Of all the furnishings, the choirstalls are the most playful, with gold-winged cherubs making music, frolicking amongst the carved foliage of the balustrade, and acting as apprentice Atlantes. From mid-May to mid-October you can hear the organ being put through its paces for half an hour, every day except Saturday, at 2.30pm.

To visit the rest of the abbey complex, you must join one of the hourly **guided tours** (April–Oct daily 10 & 11am, 1, 2 & 3pm; öS60), which begin with the **Bibliothek**, lined with undulating bookshelves and balconies and sporting a ceiling fresco by Bartolomeo Altomonte. Next, you get to see Jakob Prandtauer's **Marmorsaal**, a marble extravaganza in patriotic red-and-white Babenberg colours, with a Martino Bartolomeo fresco celebrating the victory over the Turks, who sit around above the cornice dejected, chained and exhausted. A stroll up Prandtauer's monumental staircase, which takes up almost the entire west facade of the main courtyard, brings you to the 200-metre-long corridor, off which are the **imperial apartments**. With their red damask walls, and richly stuccoed ceilings, these VIP guest rooms have remained pretty much unaltered since they fell into disuse in 1782. Prince Eugène of Savoy's four-poster bed (in which the diminutive general never actually slept) is the star attraction: an over-the-top Rococo contraption built in imitation of a Turkish tent, featuring technicolour Turks tied to its corner posts. At the end of the corridor, there's a **Bruckner Gedenkraum**, with yet another bed, this time a special, bouncy, English-sprung brass bedstead bought for the composer by his students, of which Bruckner was especially proud, and in which he died.

Lastly, the abbey owns the world's largest single collection of works by **Albrecht Altdorfer** (1480–1538) of Regensburg, namely fourteen panels from the *Altar of St Sebastian*, painted in 1518 for the old Gothic church of St Florian. Along with Albrecht

Wrought-iron shop signs, Salzburg

Salzburger Land mountainscape

Pasterze Glacier, Grossglockner

Farmhouse near Gosau

Kitzbühel town houses

View from the fortress, Salzburg

Churchyard overlooking lake, Hallstatt

The Goldenes Dachl, Innsbruck

Tyrolean landscape

HERZBERGER, ANTO

"Tales of Hoffman", Bregenz floating stage

MALLAUN, ANTO

Northeastern Tyrol

Dürer and Lucas Cranach the Elder, Altdorfer was a leading figure in the group of painters loosely known as the "Danube School". Danubian scenery features prominently in many of the school's works, particularly in the case of Altdorfer, whose scenes from the Passion are played against luxuriant Upper Austrian landscapes; in the Crown of Thorns scene, the old St Florian church can even be seen in the background. Altdorfer also makes ambitious and unorthodox use of perspective, most noticeably in the Crucifixion scene, where the three crosses are placed at right angles to one another. The tour ends in the Stiftskirche (see opposite), where you get a chance to see Bruckner's tomb in the crypt, set against a mountain of over 6000 bones.

In honour of the town and abbey's namesake, Florian, who is also the patron saint of firefighters, there is a **Feuerwehrmuseum** (Tues–Sun 9am–noon & 2–4pm; öS25) in one of the monastic outbuildings, housing a collection of ancient and modern fire engines and equipment, not to mention one of the trams that used to run to the village from Linz. Florian was the chief Roman official at the nearby town of Lauriacum (Enns), but when he converted to Christianity he was imprisoned, tortured and eventually martyred in 304 AD by being thrown into the River Enns with a millstone around his neck. The story goes that he was washed up and buried at the spot where the abbey was later built. An easy two-kilometre walk west of St Florian, the engaging **Jagdmuseum** (April–Oct Tues–Sun 10am–noon & 1–5pm; öS30) is dedicated to hunting, shooting and fishing. It's housed in the **Schloss Hohenbrunn**, another work by Prandtauer.

If you're in need of **food**, the *Stiftsrestaurant*, off the main courtyard in St Florian, offers main dishes from just öS85.

ANTON BRUCKNER

As a composer, **Anton Bruckner** (1824–95) was a figure of towering stature, his nine symphonies held up with those of Brahms and Mahler as the greatest since Beethoven; but as a person he was seen as figure of fun. In Vienna, he was mocked for his provincial appearance – he liked to wear baggy, black, homespun clothes and a wide-brimmed hat – and caricatured as a country bumpkin because of his regional accent and disingenuousness. The anecdotes attesting to his naïveté are legion. After Hans Richter had conducted the première of the *Eighth Symphony* in 1892, Bruckner is alleged to have waited at the artists' entrance with 48 piping-hot doughnuts and presented them to Richter in gratitude. He was also famous for his lack of success in love: his pursuit of young women in their late teens, and his rejection by them, was a constant theme of his life-long bachelorhood.

The details of his life are relatively mundane. Born in the village of Ansfelden, 10km south of Linz, where his father was a school teacher and organist, Bruckner followed in his father's footsteps until 1855, when he took up the post of cathedral organist in Linz. It was there, in 1862, while studying under Otto Kitzler, a teacher ten years his junior, that Bruckner heard Wagner's *Tannhäuser* for the first time, a revelatory moment that sparked his first compositional masterpieces. In 1868, he became a teacher at the Vienna conservatory, and later a lecturer at the university. It was in the capital that he wrote the bulk of his work, and that he eventually died, though he chose to be buried back at the monastery of St Florian, where he had been a choirboy and, later, teacher.

He was, without doubt, an obsessive man. He took his work very seriously, practising ten hours at the piano, three hours at the organ, then studying into the night. He constantly revised his work, especially towards the end of his life, and suffered from bouts of numeromania (an obsession with counting), keeping a tally of the number of prayers he had said each day, insisting on numbering all the bars in his scores, and, when his condition worsened, even counting the leaves on trees and the stars in the night sky. His other major obsession was with death. He made sure he was present at the exhumation of both Beethoven and Schubert, and apparently visited the mortuary to see for himself the charred remains of the victims of Vienna's Ringtheater fire of 1881. He was buried, according to his own very specific wishes, in the suitably macabre necropolis below the organ in St Florian's Stiftskirche.

Wilhering

The Cistercian monastery at **WILHERING**, 8km upriver from Linz, may not have the associations with Bruckner that St Florian has -- and therefore receives a fraction of the visitors -- but it's an equally alluring prospect. Although founded in the twelfth century, the current abbey was mostly designed by local craftsman Johann Haslinger, after an arson attack by a 12-year-old girl in 1733 destroyed the old monastery. The chief attraction is the remarkable Rococo **Stiftskirche**, which dominates the apricot-coloured complex and overlooks the grassy main courtyard with its circle of conical yew trees and potted palms. Austrian Baroque architecture may be flamboyant, but it only rarely spills over into full-blown Rococo excess -- Wilhering is one such occasion. Such is the wealth of decoration of the stunning interior, designed by Martino Altomonte and his nephew Bartolomeo, it takes a while simply to take in the whole bombastic creation. The visual drama is at its most intoxicating in the ceiling, where the rich colouring of Bartolomeo Altomonte's frescoes is matched in its exceptional detail by the surrounding stucco-work, presided over by acrobatic angels and cherubs in colour-coordinated robes. The organ is also a perfectly executed piece of Rococo art, with its gilded filigree, its music-making putti and, above all, its clock suspended between the organ pipes, which boldly chimes in unison with the church clock every quarter of an hour. You're free to walk round the remaining sections of the old medieval monastery, too, including the **cloisters**, which shelter eighteen more paintings by Altomonte on the life of St Bernhard, one of the founders of the Cistercian order.

Mauthausen

By the end of the war, Hitler's home district of Upper Austria had been endowed with more concentration camps than any other region in the Third Reich. The most notorious of the lot was **KZ Mauthausen** (daily: Feb, March & Oct to mid-Dec 8am–4pm; April–Sept 8am–6pm; öS25), some 20km downriver from Linz, built in August 1938 by prisoners transferred from the concentration camp in Dachau outside Munich. Theoretically, Mauthausen was intended as a slave labour camp, not an extermination camp, its inmates forced to work in the adjacent granite quarries. However, the death toll was such that economic considerations were clearly secondary: of the 200,000 inmates who passed through the camp, around half perished. The life expectancy of the Jewish inmates was shortest of all, but an equal number of those who died were Soviet POWs and Poles.

The most striking thing about Mauthausen is its solidity and its sheer visibility: this is no ad hoc camp, but a huge, granite fortress, and it occupies a commanding position overlooking the Danube. Most of the information within the camp is in German, so it's worth buying a guide in English with a plan to help you get your bearings. Only a few of the 25 flimsy wooden barracks that housed the prisoners have survived. The former **Sick Quarters** now contain a museum detailing life inside the camp. More poignant and affecting, though, are the numerous personal memorials scattered throughout the camp, erected by family and friends of the camp's victims, who hail from countries as far apart as Greece and Great Britain. Underneath the Sick Quarters were the camp's gas chambers, disguised as showers, as at Auschwitz. The cyanide gas Zyklon B was in fact given its first test run in Schloss Hartheim, near Linz, where the Nazis transformed a school for children with special needs into a euthanasia centre. Here, under the guidance of Linz doctor Rudolf Lonauer, 12,000 sick and mentally ill patients, transported there from all over Austria, were gassed and burnt in the castle's crematorium.

The granite quarries themselves lie to the northwest of the camp, beyond the field filled with a vast array of official national memorials. Thousands were literally worked to death on the infamous **Todestiege** (Stairway of Death), the 189 steps that lead out of the granite quarry. En route, you pass what the SS jokingly referred to as the "Parachutists' Jump", a sheer cliff overlooking the quarry, where prisoners were pushed to their deaths. One of the best-known survivors of Mauthausen is **Simon Wiesenthal**, who has since spent his life trying to bring those responsible for Nazi war crimes to justice.

Getting to the camp by public transport is not easy. By train from Linz, you must change at St Valentin, and from Mauthausen train station it's a steep five-kilometre hike up to the camp, although the station does hire out bikes. Alternatively, you can catch the bus from Linz and get off at the bottom of the hill, cutting the walk in half. The village of Mauthausen itself is extremely pretty, but it's difficult to relax there after having been to the camp. The best advice is to hop on a bus or train to Enns.

Enns

The winsome little walled town of **ENNS**, 6km southeast of Mauthausen, makes for an easy day-trip from Linz by train. Situated close to the confluence of the Enns and the Danube, it has been a strategically important site for more than two millennia. Under the Romans, the town was known as Lauriacum, and served as the civil capital of Noricum and military base of the Second Legion, who guarded this section of the imperial frontier. As recently as 1945–55, Enns served as the key entry/exit point between the Soviet and American occupation zones; today, it lies along the border between Lower and Upper Austria.

The town's **Hauptplatz** is very attractive, each side lined with a parade of pastel-coloured Baroque facades, many of which conceal much older, arcaded courtyards. Numerous examples can be clearly seen from the top of the colossal sixteenth-century **Stadtturm**, a lookout tower and belfry which rises to a height of 60m from the centre of the rectangular main square. To examine one of the arcaded courtyards at close quarters, check out the **Alte Burg**, on Wienerstrasse, or no. 4a Bräunerstrasse, which runs parallel with Linzerstrasse, a street that itself boasts a couple of very fine Renaissance houses – one sporting turrets, the other crenellations – facing each other halfway down.

Back on Hauptplatz, the pink, sixteenth-century Altes Rathaus now serves as the **Museum Lauriacum** (April–Oct daily except Mon 10am–noon & 2–4pm; Nov–March Sun only; öS30), housing a modest crop of Roman silverware, statuary and murals. Further archeological remains can be viewed in the Gothic **St Laurenz-Basilika**, situated 1km northwest of the Altstadt, off the road to Linz, on the site of the old Roman civilian town. Here, the high altar has been moved forward, and the chancel floor ripped away to reveal the foundations of a Romano-Celtic temple (180 AD), an early Christian church (370 AD), perhaps founded by St Severin, and a later Carolingian church (740 AD).

Enns **train station** is to the northwest of town, beyond the St Laurenz-Basilika; buses drop you off on the main square. If you want to stay the night, you can get **private rooms** in the Altstadt through the **tourist office**, at Linzerstrasse 1 (Mon–Fri 9am–6pm; ☎07223/3261, fax 6240). Out of office hours, the *Hotel Lauriacum*, Wienerstrasse 5–7 (☎07223/82315, fax 82332-29; ⑤), will help you out with tourist information; if you can't afford to stay there, *Gasthof zum goldenen Schiff* (☎07223/86086, fax 86086-15; ④), on Hauptplatz, is a slightly cheaper alternative. For no-nonsense Austrian **food**, try the specials and fixed-price menus on offer for around öS70 at the *Gasthaus zur Stadt Linz*, at Hauptplatz 4.

Mühlviertel

The **Mühlviertel**, to the north of Linz, between the Danube and the Czech border, is a lost corner of Austria, where few tourists venture. The wonderful sweep and roll of the wooded countryside is more Bohemia than Austria, and holds just two places of compelling interest, **Kefermarkt**, with its remarkable carved altarpiece, and the walled town of **Freistadt**, both reached by the main road and rail line heading north into the Czech Republic.

Kefermarkt

The sole reason for making it out to **KEFERMARKT**, 30km or so northeast of Linz, is to visit the fifteenth-century **Wallfahrtskirche**, clearly visible, and a ten-minute walk up the hill, from the village train station. The church has some attractive lierne vaulting, but it's the enormous winged **altarpiece**, carved entirely out of limewood by an unknown artist around 1490, that is the chief draw. The depth of expression in the faces of the three life-size saints at centre stage is startling, as is the thicket of finials and tracery that reaches to a height of 13m above the main section. Note, too, the two beautifully carved saints in full armour flanking the altarpiece: Florian, casually dousing a tiny fire, and George, nonchalantly dealing with a minuscule dragon.

If you're looking for a bite to eat, walk up the road to **Schloss Weinberg**, a lovely little, double-moated castle with a Baroque keep, which now serves as an art and music school; you can eat hearty fare for under öS100 for main dish at the *Gasthausbrauerei* in the castle's former brewery by the gates.

Freistadt

Surrounded by one of best preserved sets of town fortifications in the country, **FREISTADT**, 17km short of the Czech frontier, is your archetypal medieval border town. The town's moat may be grassed over, but it's clearly visible and still overlooked by several of the original bastions, as well as two imposing gateways, the finest of which is the wedge-shaped Linzer Tor. The current defence system was thrown up around the town during the fourteenth century, as Freistadt grew rich on the salt trade that passed through, and on the privileges heaped upon it by successive Babenberg and Habsburg rulers in order to keep it as a loyal bulwark in the Bohemian borderlands. With both sides of the border in Habsburg hands after 1526, however, Freistadt's strategic significance waned, and not a lot has changed since those days – the town even has a night watchman.

On the central square of **Hauptplatz**, the pale-coloured facades are mostly Baroque, but they hide much older buildings. The most unusual is the pea-green house, two doors down from the Rathaus, which sports an onion dome on one of its two projecting bays. In one corner of the square, the town's fourteenth-century **Schloss** is clearly visible, in its coat of flaking ochre. The castle now houses the local **Heimatmuseum** (May–Oct Tues–Sat 10am & 2pm, Sun 10am; Nov–May Tues–Thurs 10am & 2pm, Fri 10am; öS10), unremarkable except for its collection of *Hinterglasbilder*, pictures painted on the backs of panes of glass, in a technique perfected in the nineteenth century by artists from the nearby village of Sandl. In the opposite corner of the square stands the **Katharinenmünster**, its ostentatious pink and white Baroque tower totally out of keeping with the calm Gothic interior, whose vaulting retains patches of medieval mural. More than any specific sight, though, the back streets of Freistadt are rewarding simply to stroll down, particularly Waaggasse, and along the eastern border of the old town walls.

Practicalities

Be warned that Freistadt's **train station** is 3km southwest of the Altstadt, and buses are infrequent; the alternatives are to take a taxi or hire a bike. You can pick up a plan of the Altstadt from the **tourist office** (Mon–Fri 9am–noon & 2–5pm; also May–Sept Sat 9am–noon ; ☎07942/72974, fax 73207), at Hauptplatz 12. Freistadt is an atmospheric and peaceful town in which to spend the night, with several excellent **hotels** in the heart of the Altstadt, starting with the venerable *Gasthof zum goldenen Hirschen*, Böhmergasse 8–10 (☎07942/72258, fax 72258-40; ④), an old-fashioned family-run inn dating to the fifteenth century and still full of character, followed by *Gasthof zum goldenen Adler*, Salzgasse 1 (☎07942/72112, fax 72112-44; ④), not quite as special but a decent second choice. Other, cheaper possibilities include the simple en-suite rooms at *Pension Pirklbauer*, Höllgasse 2/4 (☎07942/72440, fax 72440-5; ②), and *Gasthof Tröls*, Eisengasse 16 (☎07942/72297, fax 72297-3; ③). The town's **youth hostel** (☎07942/74365; June–Sept) is right by the Schloss, and the nearest **campsite** (☎07942/72624; April–Sept) is a short walk east of the Altstadt, beyond the River Feldaist.

The popular *Lubinger* café by the Schloss is good for a coffee and cake, and *Vis à Vis*, Salzgasse 13 (closed Sun), does hot snacks and a daily two-course lunch for öS90; but for the full monty, you can't beat the aforementioned *Gasthof zum goldenen Hirschen*, or the slightly cheaper *Goldener Adler*. Wherever you decide to eat, be sure to try some of the town's excellent Freistädter Bier, which has been communally owned since 1777.

Steyr

Franz Schubert considered **STEYR** "inconceivably lovely", when he stayed here in 1819 and wrote the famous *Trout Quintet*, and although he was hardly the world's most travelled man he wasn't far wrong. Strategically and dramatically situated at the fast-flowing confluence of two alpine rivers, Steyr is characterized by its picturesque zigzag riverfront of red rooftops. It's a town that grew rich on the trade in iron ore from the Eisenerzer Alps, and then, in the nineteenth century, became one of the most important arms-manufacturing towns in Austria. Even today, it remains a primarily industrial town, though you'd never know it from the beautifully preserved Altstadt.

The Town

The best way to approach the Altstadt from the train station is from the south, through the town's last remaining gateway, Neutor, and past the sgraffitoed Innerberger Stadel, a seventeenth-century granary that now houses the **Heimatmuseum** (Wed–Sun 10am–4pm; free), the usual local history collection, enlivened by a mechanical rod puppet theatre, and a nativity scene with more than four hundred moving figures, though the latter only works during Advent and New Year. Steps by the side of the Innerberger Stadel lead up to the **Stadtpfarrkirche**, built in the late fifteenth century by the architect of Vienna's Stephansdom, but rather crudely re-Gothicized in the 1880s. A more rewarding church interior, decked out with Rococo adornments, can be found in the **Marienkirche**, set back from Grünmarkt.

Steyr's elongated main square, **Stadtplatz**, creates a grand impression, with handsome town houses, three or four storeys high, facing each other across the cobbles. The most famous building on the square is the emblematic **Bummerlhaus**, built in 1497 as an inn and sporting a distinctive triangular gable and first-floor overhang, decorated with intricate tracery and blind arcading. The building now serves as a bank, and during opening hours you're free to wander through to the inner courtyard – one of several hidden behind the houses on the main square – and upstairs to admire the finely painted ceiling from

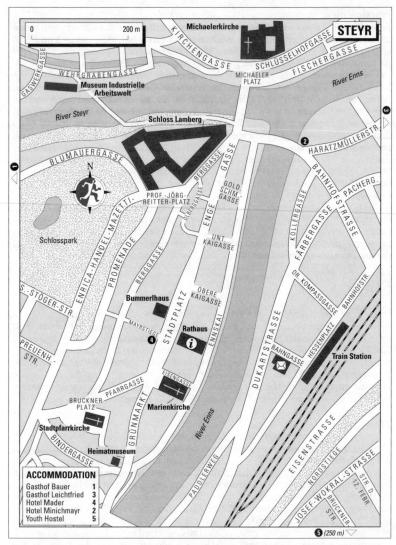

0   200 m

Michaelerkirche

STEYR

KIRCHENGASSE

SCHLÜSSELHOFGASSE

FISCHERGASSE

MICHAELER
PLATZ

GASWERKGASSE

WEHRGRABENGASSE

**Museum Industrielle
Arbeitswelt**

River Enns

River Steyr

Schloss Lamberg

BERGGASSE

ENGE GASSE

GOLD-
SCHM-
GASSE

HARATZMÜLLERSTR.

BLUMAUERGASSE

N

PROF.-JÖRG-
REITTER-PLATZ

OBERGASSE

UNT-
KAIGASSE

BAHNHOFSTRASSE

KOLLERGASSE

PACHERG.

FÄRBERGASSE

Schlosspark

ENRICA-HANDEL-MAZETTI-PROMENADE

BERGGASSE

OBERE
KAIGASSE

DR. KOMPASSGASSE

BAHNHOFSTR.

Bummerlhaus

STADTPLATZ

ENNSKAI

Rathaus
ⓘ

S.-STÖGER-STR.

MAYRSTIEGE

④

DUKARTSTRASSE

BAHNGASSE

HESSENPLATZ

Train Station

PREUENH.-
STR.

PFARRGASSE

EISENGASSE

Marienkirche

GRÜNMARKT

River Enns

BRUCKNER
PLATZ

Stadtpfarrkirche

BINDERGASSE

Heimatmuseum

PADDLERWEG

EISENSTRASSE

NORDSTIEGE

JOSEF-WOKRAL-STRASSE

BRUCKNER-
STR.

STR. D
12. FEBR.

ACCOMMODATION

Gasthof Bauer   1
Gasthof Leichtfried   3
Hotel Mader   4
Hotel Minichmayr   2
Youth Hostel   5

❺ *(250 m)* ▽

1543. The **Rathaus**, on the opposite side of the square, is a suitably imposing edifice, designed by the town mayor with a pink Rococo facade, and flamboyant belfry topped with a pile of copper onion domes and a barley-sugar column. There are several more superb Rococo facades at the north end of Stadtplatz, in particular the **Sternhaus**, from 1768, with its garish sky-blue and yellow colour scheme, fancy stucco-work and posing cherubs in high relief. Stadtplatz eventually funnels into the narrow defile of Engegasse, a busy shopping street lined with yet more brightly painted, overhanging houses.

As you cross the bridge over the River Steyr, to the equally ancient suburb of Steyrdorf, the spectacular facade of the **Michaelerkirche** rises up directly ahead of you. Built by the Jesuits in 1635, its twin towers flank a wonderfully dramatic and colourful gable fresco featuring the Archangel Michael. The picturesque cobbled streets off to the west, up Kirchengasse, are beautifully peaceful and repay a casual wander, or else you can cross over a narrow arm of the Steyr and visit the excellent **Museum Industrielle Arbeitswelt** (daily except Mon 9am–5pm; öS55), housed in a converted factory on Wehrgrabengasse. This is a state-of-the-art museum explaining the fascinating history of the town's industrialization, and in particular the social impact of the advent of steam power and mass production. The nearby pedestrian-only bridge over the Steyr will bring you back to just below the **Schloss Lamberg**, whose two towers – one castellated, one Baroque – barely rise above the castle's barracks-like blank wall. Much of the complex is now used for the town council and police headquarters, but you can wander through the tranquil, triangular courtyard, surrounded by Baroque statues of dwarfs in various poses.

From June to September, steam trains run at the weekend along the narrow-gauge **Steyrtal-Museumsbahn** (Sat & Sun 2–3; öS110 return) to Grünberg, 17km to the southwest. The Lokalbahnhof from which they depart is ten minutes' walk west of Schloss Lamberg, down Blumauergasse. If you continue for another 1.5km upriver, past the train station, you'll come to the Baroque pilgrimage church of **Christkindl**, set high above the river. At Christmas time, more than a million and a half Christmas cards are sent from the church's special post office to philatelists across the globe. Thousands more are sent to the church – each getting a reply – from Austrian kids asking for a present from *Christkind* (Baby Jesus), the traditional giver of Christmas presents in Austria.

Practicalities

The **tourist office** (mid-Jan to Nov Mon–Fri 8.30am–6pm, Sat 9am–noon; Dec to mid-Jan Sat 9am–4pm, Sun 10am–3pm; ☎07252/53229, fax 53229-15) is in the Rathaus, and can help organize **private rooms**. Steyr's finest **hotel** is the *Hotel Mader* (☎07252/533358, fax 53358-6; ⑤), a splendid Renaissance building on Stadtplatz, with an arcaded inner courtyard, and modern en-suite rooms. For spectacular views overlooking the confluence of the Enns and Steyr rivers, head for *Hotel Minichmayr*, Haratzmüllerstrasse 1–3 (☎07252/53410, fax 48202-55; ⑤), or the more modest *Gasthof Leichtfried*, at no. 25 (☎07252/52438-85, fax 47519; ③). All other inexpensive options are well out of the centre, the most convenient being *Gasthof Bauer*, Josefgasse 7, (☎07252/54441; ③), a utilitarian workers' block on one of the river islands. The town's **youth hostel** is at Hafnerstrasse 14 (☎07252/45580; mid-Jan to mid-Dec), a fifteen-minute walk from the train station; turn right out of the station, then right down Damberggasse, under the railway tracks, right again at Arbeiterstrasse, and fourth right down Otto-Glockel-Strasse. The nearest **campsite** is *Campingplatz Forelle* (☎07252/78008; May–Sept), by the River Enns in the woody suburb of Münichholz, 2.5km north (bus #1 from the train station).

Café Werndl, beside the bridge over the Steyr, enjoys fabulous riverside views, while the flagstone-floored *Café Treffpunkt*, down on the Ennskai, is better for an evening drink. For full **meals**, *Gasthof Mader* (closed Sun), at the hotel of the same name, does a very good two-course Tagesmenü for under öS100, and the *Schloss-Restaurant* in Schloss Lamberg is pretty reasonable. If the weather's fine, a table outside at *Pizzeria Michelangelo*, in the Schlosspark, is an enticing option.

Kremsmünster

The Benedictine monastery of **Kremsmünster** is one of the most unsual and rewarding of all Austria's abbeys. It's a huge complex, built on raised ground above the River
Krems, its skyline punctuated not simply by the obligatory twin spires of the monastery
church, but by the strange silo-like bulk of the abbey's observatory, or Sternwarte. In
addition, Kremsmünster boasts a uniquely preserved set of seventeenth-century fish
ponds, as well as the usual feast of Baroque interiors. Although Kremsmünster lies
halfway between Steyr and Wels, it's most easily reached by train direct from Linz, as it
lies on the main line to Graz; the monastery is a fifteen-minute walk west of the station.

The Fischkalter and Stiftskirche

The abbey's most remarkable architectural set piece, its unique Baroque series of
Fischkalter (Fish Basins), is accessible via the abbey's ticket office/shop (daily
9am–noon & 1–5pm; öS10), in the first courtyard. Designed in 1690 by Carlo Carlone,
and expanded by Jakob Prandtauer some thirty years later, the Fischkalter consist of
five perfectly symmetrical ponds surrounded by a set of Italianate arcades held up by
slender Tuscan columns, and originally decorated with frescoes, only patches of which
now survive. Each basin has a mythological or biblical fountain at the centre, and the
cumulative noise of the water echoing round the arcades is quite deafening. If you want
to watch the carp go crazy, you can buy some fish food from the abbey shop. You can
also eat some of the previous inhabitants of the Fischkalter at the *Stiftsschenke* (closed
Mon), across the courtyard.

The **Stiftskirche**, across the moat in the second courtyard, is also the work of Carlo
Carlone, who redesigned much of the abbey in Baroque style from the 1670s onwards.
The interior is coated with a staggering quantity of thick, white stucco, which totally
upstages the ceiling frescoes. The other unusual decoration in the church is the set of
eight seventeenth-century Flemish tapestries wrapped round the pillars of the nave,
depicting the story of Joseph in Egypt. The side altars are refreshingly cherub-free, their
oil paintings flanked only by pairs of finely carved angels by Michael Zürn. The sole
reminder of the original Gothic Stiftskirche is the exquisitely serene, thirteenth-century
tomb of Gunther, which lies in the chapel beneath the south tower. Gunther's death in the
woods hereabouts, at the trotters of a wild boar, prompted his father, Duke Tassilo III of
Bavaria, to found a monastery here in 777. The figure of Gunther lies on his sepulchre
beside the aforementioned boar, with a hunting horn in his hand and his dog by his feet.

The Kunstsammlung and Sternwarte

To see the interior of the monastery, you must sign up for an hour-long guided tour (in
German only) of the **Kunstsammlung** (daily: Easter–Oct 10 & 11am, 2, 3 & 4pm;
Oct–Easter 11am & 2pm; öS45). After a quick visit to the Fischkalter, you get a chance
to wander through the **Kaisersaal**, designed by Carlone in the 1690s as a summer dining room, and so called because of Martino Altomonte's series of imperial portraits set
into the wall, framed by ornate stucco-work. The whitewashed walls contrast sharply
with the colourful and energetic trompe l'oeil ceiling fresco, depicting the triumph of
light over darkness (for which read Habsburgs over Turks). The most precious
medieval *objet d'art* in the monastery's tapestry-lined treasury is the eighth-century
Carolingian **Tassilo-Kelch**, a remarkable gilded copper chalice decorated with portraits of Christ and his disciples, surrounded by what looks remarkably like Celtic inter-
lacing. The decor in the monastery's enormously long **Bibliothek**, again by Carlone, is
reminiscent of the Stiftskirche, with heavy stucco-work framing richly coloured fres-

coes. A bewilderingly large art collection is crammed into several more rooms of the monastery, with works ranging from unkown fifteenth-century Bohemian artists to the likes of Bartolomeo Altomonte and Kremser Schmidt. Finally, there's a small **Kunstkammer**, whose most renowned artefact is the chair made from the bones of the first elephant brought to Austria (in 1552 by crown prince Maximilian II) and a collection of arms and armour.

Without doubt the most unusual building in the entire complex is the **Sternwarte** (May–Oct daily 10am, 2 & 4pm; öS50), a fifty-metre-high, eight-storey tower block completed in 1759. The tower was purpose-built to house a museum that would take visitors from the inanimate world of minerals and fossils on the lower floors, through the animal and plant kingdom, to the human arts and sciences and beyond to the observatory, finishing up with contemplation of God in the rooftop chapel. The collections within the Sternwarte are still arranged pretty much in the above order, with paleontology exhibits down below, and astrology up top. Unfortunately, in order to visit the tower you have to endure a guided tour in German, lasting for an hour and a half. If you persevere, however, you'll be rewarded with a fabulous view over the monastery and the surrounding countryside from the rooftop terrace.

Wels

Despite a history stretching back to Roman times, when it was known as Olivava, **WELS** lacks the drama of Steyr. Situated on the banks of the River Traun, amid the flat landscape to the southwest of Linz, it is, however, the second largest town in Upper Austria, and a place you're almost bound to find yourself passing through. It also has the advantage of being situated on one of the region's most important railway junctions, making it an easy place in which to stop off for an hour or two – just long enough to explore the town's small, but handsome Altstadt.

The Town

The showpiece of the Altstadt is the central **Stadtplatz**, a long, relatively narrow space, closed off at one end by the town's last surviving gateway, or **Ledererturm**, erected in 1376. The square's parade of attractive, mostly Baroque facades features some very fine plasterwork, particularly on the square bulk of the imperial-yellow **Rathaus** from 1748; but by far the most exotic and distinctive single building is the Renaissance **Haus der Salome Alt**, with its rich trompe l'oeil brickwork, patterned with red-and-white diapers and ornate, stone window surrounds. The house was at one time home to Hans Sachs – the most famous of Nürnburg's medieval *Meistersänger*, who wrote his first poems at the school in Wels – but it gets its name from Salome Alt, mistress of the salacious Wolf Dietrich, Prince-Archbishop of Salzburg, who moved here after Dietrich fell from power and was imprisoned in 1612. Directly opposite the Haus der Salome Alt stands the **Stadtpfarrkirche**, Gothic and fairly undistinguished for the most part, but with a finely preserved Romanesque west door and some excellent medieval stained glass hidden away in the chancel.

On the other side of Salome Alt's house is the imperial **Burg Wels** (Tues–Fri 10am–5pm, Sat & Sun 10am–noon; free), where the emperor Maximilian I died in 1519, having been refused bed and board by the folk of Innsbruck, who were fearful that he wouldn't pay his bills. Maximilian was eventually buried in Wiener Neustadt (see p.187), though his tomb remains in Innsbruck (see p.401). In the 1980s, Burg Wels's interior was converted into a cultural centre and local history museum, the latter with a particular emphasis on agriculture and bread-making. The town's best Roman remains are to be found in the **Stadtmuseum und Galerie** (same times as above), housed in a fanciful turn-of-the-century former bank on Pollheimerstrasse. Temporary art exhibitions are held on the ground floor, while the first floor is given over to the museum's permanent collection. Among the Roman finds are the tiny second-century AD bronze *Venus of Wels*, several graves sporting sphinxes and lions, a conical milestone, hoards of coins, and patches of mosaic.

Practicalities

Wels **tourist office** (July & Aug Mon–Fri 9am–7pm, Sat 9am–noon; Sept–June Mon–Fri 9am–6pm; ☎07242/43495, fax 47904), at Hauptplatz 55, publishes a useful series of leaflets, including a bimonthly listings booklet, and can help you find somewhere to stay. Many of the **hotels** in Wels, like comfortable *Hotel Greif*, Kaiser-Josef-Platz 50/51 (☎07242/45361, fax 44629; ⑦), are efficiently run by big hotel chains and cater for the business crowd, but there are less expensive options, such as the excellent *Kremsmünsterhof* (☎07242/46623, fax 46623-44; ④), a converted monastic lodge on Stadtplatz itself, with a fine arcaded courtyard, and the nearby *Goldenes Kreuz* (☎07242/46453, fax 46453-30; ③), a more traditional and characterful inn. Of the town's Gasthöfe, the *Zeilinger*, Ringstrasse 29 (☎ & fax 07242/47440; ②), and *Augustin*, Traungasse 8 (☎07242/46305; ②), enjoy the most central locations. Wels' **youth hostel** (☎07242/235757, fax 235-756; mid-Jan to mid-Dec) is centrally located, at Dragonerstrasse 22, while the nearest **campsite**, *Campingplatz Rosenau* (☎07242/

44195; June–Sept), is a fifteen-minute walk southwest of the Altstadt (bus #16 from out-side the Stadtpfarrkirche).

The *Café Urbann*, Schmidtgasse 20 (closed Sat eve & Sun), is the longest established *Kaffeehaus* in Wels, and a reliable place for a coffee and cake. Another town institution is the old-fashioned self-service café/butcher's *Reiter*, Stadtplatz 62 (closed Sat & Sun). For a more imaginative take on standard Austrian **food**, head further up Stadtplatz to the traditional *Rathaus-Stüberl* (closed Sun) in the *Goldenes Kreuz* hotel. *Da Leone* (closed Sun) is a pizzeria with a pleasant, arcaded *Schanigarten* in narrow Hafnergasse, a street that boasts several decent places to linger over a **drink**, such as *Café Rewü*, which also offers a bargain two-course weekday lunchtime menu for öS60.

Wels is Upper Austria's main cultural centre after Linz, so there's usually a fair selec-tion of **live entertainment** to enjoy. The main stage at the Stadttheater, on the corner of Kaiser-Josef-Platz and Rainerstrasse, plays host to everything from full-scale opera to comedy, while the programme at *Im Kornspeicher*, Freiung 15, is less mainstream, rang-ing from cabaret and dance to jazz. For more details of what's on, pick up the latest list-ings information from the tourist office.

The Innviertel

The River Inn forms the western border between Bavaria and Upper Austria, from just below Braunau to its confluence with the Danube at Passau. The region between the Inn and the Danube, known as the **Innviertel**, is rich, rolling farming country reminiscent of much of Bavaria – indeed, until 1779, and briefly again during the Napoleonic period, the region belonged to the duchy of Bavaria. Inevitably, this gentle landscape can't com-pete with the alpine scenery further south around Salzburg and the Salzkammergut, and most people tend simply to pass through the region, but there are three picturesque bor-der towns that make for a more interesting introduction to Austria, from south to north: **Braunau-am-Inn**, **Obernberg-am-Inn** and, above all, **Schärding**.

Braunau-am-Inn

BRAUNAU-AM-INN, in the western corner of Upper Austria, is saddled with an unfor-tunate legacy, as the birthplace of Adolf Hitler. This rather overshadows the fact that Braunau is also a very handsome border town, worth a quick stop-off whether you're on your way in or out of the country. Lined with pretty, pastel-coloured houses, the town's **Stadtplatz** is stretched out along a north–south axis, its northern end abutting the bridge over the Inn to Germany, while its southern end is closed by the imposing medieval **Torturm**, crowned with a tiny carillon. The town's chief landmark, though, is the spec-tacularly tall stone tower of the fifteenth-century **Stephanskirche**, to the west of the main square, a hybrid affair decorated with blind Gothic tracery and topped by a giant onion dome, which reaches to a height of nearly 100m. The exterior is plastered with finely carved grave slabs, including that of Hans Staininger, whose curly beard reaches down to his toes, while the interior features net vaulting and a series of fine Baroque side chapels, one of which is flanked by a superb pair of grimly reaping skeletons.

Outside **Hitler's birthplace** at Salzburger Vorstadt 15, on the far side of the Torturm, stands a large slab of granite from Mauthausen (see p.388), inscribed with the words "For peace, freedom and democracy/never again fascism/in memory of the millions who died." Hitler's father, Alois, had been a customs inspector in Braunau for eighteen years, and was onto his third marriage (to his niece, and former maid, 23 years his junior) when the future Führer was born in 1889. He was actually born Adolf Schicklgruber, his paternal grandmother's maiden name (see p.173), and only became Adolf Hitler when his father changed his own surname in 1893, shortly after the family had moved to the nearby German border town of Passau. The family eventually settled in Leonding, just outside Linz.

Braunau's **train station** is about 1km east of the Stadtplatz, where you'll find the **tourist office** (May–Sept Mon–Fri 9am–noon & 2.30–5.30pm; Oct–April Mon–Fri 9am–noon; ☎07722/2644, fax 4395) within the *Volksbank* at no. 9. Two **hotels** enjoy the perfect location on Stadtplatz itself: *Hotel Post* (☎07722/63492, fax 63415-2; ③) is the plusher of the two, with all rooms en suite; *Hotel Gann* (☎07722/3206; ②) is simpler, and has some cheaper rooms with shared facilities. Another good option is one of the en-suite rooms at the *Gästezimmer Puchmayr* (☎07722/63273; ②), tucked away in the backstreets of the Altstadt, west of Stadtplatz on Johann-Fischer-Gasse. Braunau has a **youth hostel** (☎07722/81638; mid-Jan to mid-Dec), 1km southwest of the Altstadt, at Osternbergerstrasse 57, and a **campsite** (☎07722/7357; April–Sept) a bit further in the same direction, on the other side of the River Enknach. *Bogner* is a great little place on Stadtplatz that brews its own **beer**, and serves pizzas, toast, coffee and cakes. If you're keen to avoid Austrian **food** for one night, try the Tex-Mex on offer at *Cantina Mexicana* on Kirchenplatz, which also features live music at the weekend, and a regular tequila happy hour in the early evening.

Obernberg-am-Inn

OBERNBERG-AM-INN, 25km downstream from Braunau, is the smallest of the trio of pretty towns that dot the banks of the Inn. The wide expanse of its central **Marktplatz**, lined with boldly coloured Baroque houses sporting beautifully shaped gables, is, if anything, even more attractive than the one at Braunau. Two houses in particular stand out for their exceptional Rococo stucco-work: the bile-green *Café Woerndle*, and the adjacent pastel-pink apothecary, with a statue of the Virgin clad in pink occupying centre stage. Once you've soaked in the prettiness of the town square, there's nothing specific to keep you in Obernberg unless you want to grab a bite to eat at the excellent *Braugasthof zur Post*, on Marktplatz, which has main dishes from öS100 and serves Keller Bräu from the nearby town of Ried. You can also stay the night on Marktplatz at the *Goldenes Kreuz* (☎07758/2202; ②), which has rooms with or without en-suite facilities. There's also the *Panorama* **campsite** (☎07758/2601; open all year), 1km southwest of the Altstadt, off Salzburgerstrasse.

Schärding

SCHÄRDING, 20km downstream of Obernberg, is more picturesque still, with a large and well-preserved Altstadt, surrounded by large swaths of its original fortifications. The sprawling, sloping, central **Stadtplatz** is broken up by two clusters of houses at the centre, but its most distinguished feature is the much-photographed **Silberzeile** – "Silver Row", so called because of its wealthy inhabitants – an uninterrupted, multi-coloured parade of identically shaped gables that form a wave-like roofscape on the north side of the square. The cobbled backstreets of the Altstadt are fun to explore, and the town retains several of its original gate towers, one of which, Burgtor, up Schlossgasse, allows access to the **Schlosspark**, laid out on the site of the town's old moated castle, and from which you get fine views across the Inn over to the German town of Neuhaus-am-Inn.

From Schärding, trains, buses and boats run north to Passau. Boats (May to mid-Sept daily except Mon) leave from the Schiffahrtsstation at the northern tip of the Altstadt; trains and buses from Schärding's **train station**, 1.5km northeast of the Altstadt, beyond the River Pram. There are several **private rooms** in the Altstadt, which you can book through the **tourist office**, Unterer Stadtplatz 19 (Mon–Fri 8am–noon & 1–5pm, ☎07712/4300, fax 4320). Without doubt the finest place to **stay** is the family-run *Förstingers Wirtshaus*, at Unterer Stadtplatz 3 (☎07712/2302, fax 2302-3; ⑤), though there are a couple of less expensive options in the Altstadt, such as *Hotel Scheurecker*, Innsbruckstrasse 6–8 (☎07712/4404, fax 4408; ④), and *Café-Weinstube beim Lachinger*, on the Silberzeile itself (☎07712/2268; ②), where rooms come with shower or bath but no en-suite toilet. The best place to feast on some typical Austrian **food**, washed down with the local Baumgartner Bier, is at the *Wirthaus zur Bums'n*, a traditional pub in the backstreet of Denisgasse.

travel details

Trains

Linz to: Braunau-am-Inn (hourly; 2hr 15min); Freistadt (every 2hr; 1hr 10min); Kefermarkt (every 2hr; 55min); Kremsmünster (every 2hr; 25min); Schärding (hourly; 1hr–1hr 15min); Steyr (every 1–2hr; 40min); Wels (2–3 hourly; 15–25min).

Wels to: Braunau-am-Inn (every 2hr; 1hr 30min–2hr); Passau (every 1–2hr; 1hr–1hr 30min); Schärding (every 1–2hr; 50min–1hr 15min).

Buses

Braunau to: Obernberg-am-Inn (Mon–Fri 1 daily; 45 min); Schärding (Mon–Fri 1 daily; 1hr 35min).

Enns to: Mauthausen (Mon–Fri 1 daily; 25min).

Linz to: St Florian (Mon–Fri every 2hr; 35min); Wilhering (Mon–Sat 5 daily; 20min).

Steyr to: Wels (Mon–Sat 4 daily; 1 hr 30min).

THE TYROL

A spectacular alpine playground filled with craggy peaks, verdant pastures, frothy mountain rivers and onion-domed hilltop chapels, the **Tyrol** (Tirol in German) represents picture-postcard Austria at its most vivid. Apart from a few pockets of industrialization around Innsbruck and Wörgl, hardly a square centimetre of the province is anything but extremely attractive. Although the mountains naturally take centre stage, there's a surprising amount of urban tourism to be savoured here, too: the Tyrolean capital, **Innsbruck**, is a worthy focal point – a lively and attractive place that combines big-city thrills with a wide range of alpine pursuits. To the east, the historic Inn Valley towns of **Hall**, **Schwaz**, **Rattenberg** and **Kufstein** all reward a visit, however brief. An authentic taste of the Tyrolean great outdoors is best gained by a more leisurely approach – though the set-piece alpine valleys feeding into the River Inn (the **Zillertal** and the **Ötztal** are two of the more grandiose) are all perfectly accessible from the more urban centres. Winter sports and a range of summer activities are catered for in cosmopolitan mega-villages like **Kitzbühel**, **Seefeld**, **Mayrhofen** and **St Anton**, and the sheer variety of smaller resort villages and out-of-the-way alpine communities ensures that there's something here for everybody.

Wherever you are in the province, you'll see the imprint of a strong sense of Tyrolean identity. The Tyroleans are proud of their alpine surroundings, cherishing an unspoken belief that the best mountaineers and skiers in Austria come from here. You'll spot traditional dress – lederhosen and feathered huntsmen's hats – in use more widely here than elsewhere in the country, and uniquely Tyrolean dishes like *Gröstl*, *Schlipfkrapfen* and *Tiroler Knödel* (see p.37) dominate local restaurant menus.

Some history

After being settled by Bavarian tribes in the eighth century, the Tyrol began life as a medieval dukedom centred on Meran (now Merano in Italy) on the south side of the Alps. The political centre of gravity gradually shifted northwards, however, with the strengthening of the economic power of Inn Valley towns such as Schwaz (a gold- and silver-mining centre) and Hall (an important salt-producing town). The Tyrol fell into the **Habsburg** orbit in 1363, when Duke Rudolf IV inherited it from his sister Margareta, widow of Meinhard, last of the dukes of Görz-Tirol. For the next century and a half, the Tyrol was home to a regional branch of the Habsburg house, and by the time of **Sigismund the Rich** (1427–96; so named because he had better luck than his father,

---

ACCOMMODATION PRICE CODES

All **hotels and pensions** in this book have been graded according to the following price categories. All the codes are based on the rate for the least expensive double room during the **summer season**. In those places where winter is the high season, we've indicated winter room rates in the text. For more on accommodation, see p.30.

① under öS400	④ öS800–1000	⑦ öS1400–1600
② öS400–600	⑤ öS1000–1200	⑧ öS1600–1800
③ öS600–800	⑥ öS1200–1400	⑨ over öS1800

Friedrich the Penniless), the area had gained a reputation for stability and prosperity, and was coveted by other members of the family as a result. In 1490, a coalition of Tyrolean nobles and Habsburg power-brokers persuaded Sigismund to bequeath the Tyrol to his nephew **Maximilian**, a Habsburg who lacked a significant power base despite being in line for the imperial throne (he became Holy Roman Emperor in 1493). As it turned out, possession of the Tyrol was crucial to Maximilian's fortunes. Using the silver mines of Schwaz as security, he borrowed money from the financiers of Augsburg and set about paying off political opponents, establishing a modern army based on artillery, and assembling a glittering court at his chosen capital, Innsbruck.

During the reign of Maximilian, a piece of legislation known as the **Landlibell** of 1511 made the Tyroleans responsible for defending their own borders, while exempting them from serving anywhere else in the Habsburg lands – an exemption that survived until as late as 1918. As a result, the Tyroleans developed their own defence institutions, with the **Schützen**, or "riflemen", forming a local militia. When the 1805 **Treaty of Pressburg** awarded the Tyrol to Bavaria, the *Schützen* provided local patriot **Andreas Hofer** with a ready-made army with which to lead a revolt against the Bavarians and their French backers. Subsequently dubbed the **Tyrolean War of Independence**, this heroic but doomed escapade was launched with the encouragement of a Viennese court that had no real intention of providing military support. The Tyroleans were left to fight alone, and Andreas Hofer was shot by the French in 1810. Franco-Bavarian control lasted until Napoleon's defeat in 1815, when the province was returned to the Austrian fold. The Schützen rifle associations that formed the backbone of Hofer's army still exist in an amateur capacity, their members turning out in traditional alpine regalia whenever there's a procession, religious feast day, wedding, or other excuse to mount a display of Tyrolean identity.

Tyrolean patriotism was given an added edge this century by a decision to award the **South Tyrol** (Südtirol) to Italy in the aftermath of World War I. It was a decision that paid scant regard to ethnic realities – and the South Tyrol (Alto Adige to the Italians), though within Italy's border, remains to this day a predominantly German-speaking area. The **East Tyrol** (Osttirol; see Chapter 5), meanwhile, was left geographically isolated from the rest of the province.

INNSBRUCK

Sprawling beneath the mountain ridge of the Nordkette, **INNSBRUCK** is the only major urban centre in Austria with an array of high Alps on its own doorstep. If you want to visit museums in the morning, walk up mountains in the afternoon and bar-hop well into the early hours, you'd be hard pushed to find a more convenient place in which to do it. With the Tyrol's largest concentration of mountain resorts in such close proximity, skiing is obviously big news here – and hosting the winter Olympics in 1964 and 1976 provided the city with a wealth of sporting and tourist facilities to call its own. But for those who just want a taste of history, Innsbruck's compact centre – a classic Austrian hybrid of the Gothic and Baroque – invites aimless strolling. It's also a thriving commercial centre that depends on more than just tourism for its living, and supports a range of cultural and nightlife options wide enough to suit most tastes.

Some history

Although an important trading post on the River Inn since Celtic times, Innsbruck was in the shadow of wealthier Tyrolean centres like Hall, Schwaz and Meran until the

The telephone code for Innsbruck is ☎0512.

1380s, when **Duke Leopold III** began to hold court on the spot now occupied by the Hofburg. His great grandson **Maximilian I** made Innsbruck his imperial capital in the 1490s, catapulting a provincial alpine town into the heart of European politics and culture. Maximilian's affections for the place had been founded on material need – Innsbruck stood at the centre of an area whose mining wealth he wanted to exploit – but he soon came to love the city, largely because of the hunting opportunities in the neighbouring mountains. Innsbruck still bears the stamp of Maximilian's era: a fine ensemble of medieval buildings in the centre augmented by the **Goldenes Dachl**

("Golden Roof"), built to add splendour to Maximilian's court, as well as the imperial mausoleum in the **Hofkirche**, an ostentatious shrine to the Habsburg dynasty, and **Schloss Ambras**, home to the eccentric art collection of Maximilian's great-grandson, **Archduke Ferdinand II**, all attest to the Habsburgs' claim to the city. Although the ducal capital of the Tyrol remained at Meran until the 1860s, the dynasty's connection with Innsbruck remained strong. Empress **Maria Theresa** was a frequent visitor, adding a Baroque veneer to the city by rebuilding the **Hofburg**, and erecting the **Triumphpforte** in honour of her son, Archduke Leopold II.

MOUNTAIN RESORTS AROUND INNSBRUCK

There are at least seven major **ski regions** within easy reach of Innsbruck, each of which can be treated as an easily accessible day out from the Tyrolean capital. (One of them, **Seefeld**, is major enough to be dealt with separately on p.440.) Nearest to the city centre is the **Nordkette**, close enough for city dwellers to indulge in a spot of skiing during their lunch hour. South of the city and accessible by municipal transport, the villages of **Igls** and **Patsch** serve the slopes of the **Patscherkofel**. To the southwest, **Mutters** provides access to the popular **Mutterer Alm**, while **Axams** is the starting point for excursions to the varied skiing terrain of the **Axamer Lizum** 9km uphill to the south – also a booming snowboarding centre. Furthest from the city but most versatile is the **Stubai Glacier** 35km to the southwest, where skiing is possible all year round. The Innsbruck tourist office run day-trips for skiers to the glacier in summer for around öS680 per person (including bus transfer, equipment rental and lift pass).

A range of **ski passes** are available, so you can try several of these regions within the space of a week. The Innsbruck Gletcher Ski Pass covers the Innsbruck area (it includes the Stubai Glacier but not Seefeld), and costs around öS1900 for six days. The Innsbruck Super Ski Pass offers a variety of deals combining some of the pistes in the Innsbruck region with those around the Arlberg and Kitzbühel as well – at around öS1800 for five days. Both passes are available from all lift stations or from the Innsbruck tourist office.

For **equipment rental**, try Rental Ski Service, Leopoldstrasse 4 (☎581742), or Schiverlieh Georg Moser, Universitätstrasse 1 (☎589158).

Arrival, information and transport

Innsbruck's **airport** is at Kranebitten, 4km west of the centre. Bus F runs into town every twenty minutes (buy your ticket from the driver or a *Tabak* shop; öS21). A taxi will set you back around öS140. Buses serving **Munich airport** (six daily; öS440 single, öS760 return) arrive and depart from the Olympic Ice Stadium, 2km southeast of the centre on Burgenlandstrasse.

Innsbruck's main **train station** is on Südtirolerplatz on the eastern fringes of the city centre. Turn right outside the main exit, carry on for 100m, then turn left into Museumsstrasse in order to get to the **Altstadt**, at the city's core – a walk of about ten minutes. The **bus station** is immediately south of the train station.

Information

The main **tourist office** is on the fringes of the Altstadt at Burggraben 3 (daily 8am–7pm; ☎5356, fax 5356-43). There's another branch on the train station forecourt (daily 9am–10pm), and an information kiosk at the Innsbruck-Süd exit of the autobahn.

As well as booking rooms, changing money and selling concert tickets, the tourist offices have a wide choice of free **English-language brochures** covering the whole of the Tyrol. They sell **city maps** for öS25, as well as the **Innsbruck card**, a useful investment if you're planning a day or two of heavy-duty sightseeing: it allows free admission to most of the town's attractions, free use of public transport, and the right to one free cable-car journey on either the Nordkette or Patscherkofel (24hr öS200, 48hr öS280, 72hr öS350).

City transport

Innsbruck is easy enough to get around on foot, but the comprehensive tram and bus network comes in handy if you're staying in the suburbs, heading to the airport or visiting Schloss Ambras. The 24-hour ticket (öS30) and seven-day pass (öS105) are better value than a single-journey ticket, which costs öS21 and doesn't allow for changes. Only single and 24-hour tickets can be bought from the driver. All tickets and passes can be bought from *Tabak* shops or from vending machines placed near tram and bus stops, and should be punched in the relevant machines upon boarding.

Accommodation

Both the central tourist office at Burggraben 3 and the branch office at the main train station offer a speedy room-booking service for an öS35 fee and a refundable deposit. **Private rooms** in Innsbruck, or a bus ride away in suburban resorts like Igls (3km south) and Mutters (5km southwest), weigh in at around öS200–250 per person; those in Igls rise to about öS300 in the winter season. There's a shortage of good cheap **hotels** in Innsbruck, but plenty of atmospheric downtown inns cater for the middle of the market. A broad range of **hostel** accommodation is available, although spaces fill up quickly in summer and in school holidays, and there is one well-appointed **campsite**, *Camping Kranebitten*, 5km west of town at Kranebittner Allee 214 (☎284180; April–Oct), equipped with restaurant, laundry facilities and shop, and reached by taking bus LK from Boznerplatz (a block west of the station) to Klammstrasse.

Hotels and pensions

Binder, Dr-Glatz-Strasse 20 (☎33436, fax 33436-99). Clean and friendly if uninspiring inner-city hotel in an unfashionable part of town some 25min walk from the centre (tram #3 runs nearby). Rooms with en-suite facilities (④), or with shared bath and WC (③).

Ferrarihof, Brennerstrasse 8 (☎580969, fax 571062). A large Gasthof 3km south of the city centre just above the suburb of Wilten. Handy for those arriving by car, situated beside the Innsbruck-Süd autobahn exit, its proximity to the junction of the Inntal and Brenner autobahns may put off those intending a long stay. Rooms with en-suite facilities (⑤); without (③).

Goldene Krone, Maria-Theresien-Strasse 46 (☎586160, fax 580189-6). Comfortable downtown hotel with modern, rather cramped rooms at the southern end of Innsbruck's main thoroughfare, just by the Triumphforte. (⑦).

Goldener Adler, Herzog-Friedrich-Strasse 6 (☎586334, fax 584409). Classic city-centre inn with late-medieval pedigree and Gothic feel inside, though rooms are large and have modern furnishings. (⑧).

Helga, Brandlweg 3 (☎261137, fax 261137-6). Some way out, 3km east of the centre, on the main Bundesstrasse to Hall. All rooms have WC, shower and TV, and there's an indoor swimming pool. (⑤).

Innbrücke, Innstrasse 1 (☎281934). Plain but comfortable Gasthof on the west bank of the Inn, just over the bridge from the Altstadt. Some rooms with en-suite facilities (③), although most are without (②).

Innrain, Innrain 38 (☎588981) Small Gasthof within easy walking distance of the Altstadt. Rooms with en-suite facilities and TV (⑤); without (③).

Internationales Studenthaus, Rechengasse 7 (☎501592, fax 501-15). A student hostel open to tourists July–Sept, in the university district 1km southwest of the Altstadt. Accommodation in single or double rooms with en-suite WC and shower (③), or with shared facilities (②). Bus C from the train station.

Pension Paula, Weiherburggasse 15 (☎292262). A long-standing favourite with both Austrian and foreign visitors (so it's worth reserving well in advance), perched attractively on the hillside up towards the Alpenzoo. Rooms with en-suite facilities (③); without (②).

Riese Haymon, Haymongasse 4 (☎589837, fax 586190). Good-value, spacious rooms in a characterful building 2km south of town in the suburb of Wilten, handy for walking on the Bergisel hill. Buses J, K or S to Grassmayrstrasse. (③).

Weisses Kreuz, Herzog-Friedrich-Strasse 31 (☎59479, fax 59479-90). In the Altstadt, an attractive old inn with creaky wooden corridors yet bright, modern rooms; a good way of staying in a classic city-centre hotel without paying exhorbitant prices. Rooms with en-suite facilities (⑥); without (④).

Weisses Rössl, Kiebachgasse 8 (☎583057, fax 583057-5). Cosy, family-run hotel in the Altstadt with fourteen modern, spacious bedrooms. (⑧).

ACCOMMODATION

Binder	16
Ferrarihof	18
Glockenhaus	2
Goldene Krone	15
Goldener Adler	9
Helga	4
Innbrücke	8
Innrain	13
Internationales Studenthaus	14
Jugendherberge Innsbruck	6
Jugendherberge St Nikolaus	5
Jugendzentrum St Paulus	7
MK Jugendzentrum	12
Pension Paula	1
Riese Haymon	17
Torsten-Arneus-Schwedenhaus	3
Weisses Kreuz	11
Weisses Rössl	10

Alpenzoo

Rundgemälde

see 'Central Innsbruck' Map, p409.

Hofgarten

HÖTTING

SCHNEEBURGGASSE
STERNWARTESTR.
Botanischer Garten
BOTANIKERSTR.
SONNENSTR.
HOTTINGER AU

FÜRSTENWEG

AMPFERERSTR.

MITTERWEG

FISCHNALERSTR.

HOHER WEG

RENNWEG

ELISAB

R.WAGNER-STR.

GANSBACH

K. KAPFERER S.

BIENER

SIEBERERST

KAISERJÄGERSTRASSE

FALK

KOCHSTR.

KAPUZINERG

UNIVERSITÄSSTR.

SILLGASSE

VIADUKTBÖGEN

KÖNIG

Landesmuseum Ferdinandeum

MUSEUM STR.

ERLER STR.

MERANER STR.

WILHELM GREIL STR.

BOZNER PLATZ

SÜDTIROLER PLATZ

Train Station

MARIA-THERESIEN-STR.

MAXIMILIAN-STR.

Triumphpforte

Bus Station

WEIHERBURGGASSE
ST-NIKOLAUS S.
INNSTRASSE
HONENSTR.
RIEDGASSE
FRAU-HITT-STR.
HÖTTINGER GASSE
MARIANIFF
River Inn
MARIAGRABEN
INNRAIN
BLASIUS-HEUBER-STR.
BURGSTRASSE
PALMERAYERSTR.
ANICH-STRASSE
BURGGRABEN

Universitätsklinik (Hospital)

MÜLLER-STRASSE
SCHOPF STR.
P. MAYRSTR.
SPECKBACHER STR.
ANDREAS-HOFER-STRASSE
FISCHER-STRASSE
TEMPLSTRASSE
LEOPOLD STR.

I N N R A I N

E G G E R - L I E N Z - S T R.

KONZERTSTR.

Wilten Abbey

Wilten Basilica

PASTORSTR.

KLOSTERGASSE

N

◁ Airport   ◁ Camping Kranebitten

◁ Innsbruck West

▽ Stubai

BERGISEL

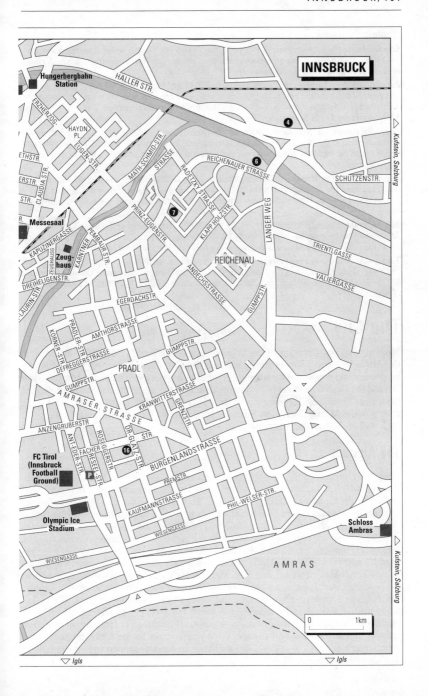

INNSBRUCK

Hungerbergbahn Station

HALLER STR.

ERZHERZOG-

HAYDN PL.

EUGEN-STR.

ETHSTR.

CLAUDIA STR.

ERSTR.

STR.

MATH.-SCHMID-STR.

STRASSE

RAPETZKY STRASSE

REICHENAUER STRASSE

SCHÜTZENSTR.

Messesaal

PRINZ-EUGEN-STR.

KAPUZINERGASSE

ZEUGHAUSG.

Zeug-haus

KARNTNER

PEMBAUR STR.

KLAPPHOLZSTR.

REICHENAU

LANGER WEG

TRIENTLGASSE

VALIERGASSE

DREIHEILIGENSTR.

-LAURIN STR.

ANDECHSSTRASSE

GUMPPSTR.

EGERDACHSTR.

PRADLER-STR.

ANTHORSTRASSE

KORNER-STR.

DEFREGGERSTRASSE

GUMPPSTR.

PRADL

GUMPPSTR.

KRANWITTERSTRASSE

GRENZSTR.

AMRASER STRASSE

ANZENGRUBERSTR.

ROSEGGERSTR.

ANT.-EDER-STR.

FACHER STR.

THERESE-STR.

DR.-GLATZ-STR.

BURGENLANDSTRASSE

FC Tirol (Innsbruck Football Ground)

P

16

PREMSTR.

KAUFMANNSTRASSE

PHIL-WELSER-STR.

Olympic Ice Stadium

WIESENGASSE

Schloss Ambras

WIESENGASSE

AMRAS

4

6

7

Kufstein, Salzburg

Kufstein, Salzburg

0   1km

Igls   Igls

Hostels

Glockenhaus, Weiherburggasse 3 (☎286515, fax 286515-14). Slightly uphill from the River Inn's west bank, within easy walking distance of the town centre. Bus K from the train station. A choice of dorm beds from öS120, or doubles (①).

Jugendherberge Innsbruck, Reichenauerstrasse 147 (☎346179, fax 346179-12). Large, modern and clean, though at 3km east of the Altstadt it's the least convenient of the hostels for city-centre sightseeing. Check-in time is 5–10pm, and there's an 11pm curfew. Take bus O from Museumstrasse. Dorm beds from öS150, doubles (②).

Jugendherberge St Nikolaus, Innstrasse 95 (☎286515, fax 286515-14). Cheap, and therefore crowded, place on the west bank of the Inn, offering beds in dorm rooms for öS120. It's a pretty convenient base for exploring the centre, but not comfortable enough to merit a lengthy stay. Bus K from the train station.

Jugendzentrum St Paulus, Reichenauerstrasse 72 (☎344291). Cheap and friendly, although it's over 2km from the Altstadt, and beds (öS110) are in large eight-person dorms. Check-in time is 5–9pm, and there's an 11pm curfew (key available). Bus O from Museumstrasse. Open mid-June to mid-Aug only.

MK Jugendzentrum, Sillgasse 8a (☎571311, fax 534699). Best placed of the hostels, between the Altstadt and the train station, with a friendly laid-back atmosphere and beds in smallish dorm rooms for around öS160. Check-in time is 5–9pm, with a midnight curfew. Open July to mid-Sept only.

Torsten-Arneus-Schwedenhaus, Rennweg 17b (☎585814, fax 586132). Large, conveniently central hostel about 1km north of the Altstadt by the River Inn. Beds in four-person dorms cost around öS130. Check-in time is 5–10pm, and the 11pm curfew can be avoided by asking for a key. Open July & Aug only.

The City

Most of what you will want to see in Innsbruck is confined to the central precincts of the **Altstadt**. A small area of sturdy medieval houses, many attractively painted in pastel colours and supported by sloping earthquake buttresses, it's bounded by the River Inn and the Graben, a street following the course of the moat that once surrounded the town's medieval core. Leading up to the Altstadt from the south, Innsbruck's main artery is the **Maria-Theresien-Strasse**, famed for its view north towards the great rock wall of the Nordkette range.

The Altstadt

Main thoroughfare of the **Altstadt** is the broad, arcaded strip of **Herzog-Friedrich-Strasse**, which at its northern end opens out into a plaza lined with gift-shops and overlooked by the **Goldenes Dachl**, or "Golden Roof" (though the tiles that give the roof its name are actually copper), built in the 1490s to cover a balcony from which the imperial court could observe the square below. The balcony itself is adorned with a series of reliefs (these are replicas – the originals are in the Landesmuseum Ferdinandeum; see p.411), showing a troupe of Moorish dancers performing for Emperor Maximilian I and his second wife Bianca Maria Sforza – she's the one holding the apple; the woman behind her is Max's beloved first wife, Maria of Burgundy. Part of the building behind the Goldenes Dachl now houses the **Maximilianeum** (daily 10am–6pm; öS60), a museum that puts a modern, show-biz gloss on the city's most famous resident. The collection's main drawback is its small size – there are a couple of original artworks by Maximilian's court painters (including a powerful deathbed portrait by an unknown master), but little else of real vintage. What you're really paying for is the headphone commentary (English available), and a chance to see a pop-video-style documentary film about Maximilian's life.

CENTRAL INNSBRUCK

Hofgarten

INNSTRASSE

INNALLEE

River Inn

HERZOG OTTO-STRASSE

Kongresshaus

HERRENG.

RENNWEG

Tiroler
Landes
Theater

DOMPLATZ

Domkirche
St Jakob

Hofburg

UNIVERSITATSSTRASSE

Goldenes Dachl
and
Maximilianeum

HOFGASSE

HERZOG FRIEDRICHSTRASSE

Volkskunstmuseum

9

Stadtturm

Hofkirche

KIEBACHGASSE

STIFTGASSE

ANGERZELLG

Landesmuseum
Ferdinandeum

11

BURGGRABEN

MUSEUMSTRASSE

10

i

MARKTGRABEN

MARIA THERESIEN-STRASSE

STRASSE

STAINER-STRASSE

SPARKASSEN-
PLATZ

GILMSTRASSE

ADOLF
PICHERPLATZ

ERLER-STRASSE

FALL-MERAYER-STRASSE

N

Rathaus

Annasäule

ANICHSTRASSE

MERANERSTRASSE

WILHELM GREILSTRASSE

ACCOMMODATION
Goldener Adler   9
Weisses Kreuz   11
Weisses Rössl   10

0   100 m

A parade of Gothic-era town houses adds distinction to the western side of Herzog-Friedrich-Strasse, although most are outshone by the **Helblinghaus**, a medieval structure adorned with the swirling encrustations of Rococo, icing-like stucco-work added in the 1730s. Across the road looms the fifteenth-century **Stadtturm** (daily: March–June, Sept & Oct 10am–5pm; July & Aug 10am–6pm; öS25); the viewing platform affords views across neighbouring rooftops towards the Nordkette rearing up to the north.

The Domkirche and the Hofburg

From the Goldenes Dachl, alleys lead north to the Domplatz and the **Domkirche St Jakob**, an unspectacular example of eighteenth-century architecture, which nevertheless conceals a couple of worthwhile artworks. Most renowned is the Madonna and Child by German master Lucas Cranach the Elder, buried amidst the fussy detail of the high altar. To the left is the funerary monument to Archduke Maximilian III (son of Emperor Maximilian II and nephew of Archduke Ferdinand II), whose statue kneels in prayer watched over by St George, the latter accompanied by an expiring dragon. This sculptural ensemble shelters under a canopy embellished with carved birds, caterpillars and snails. Displayed on the walls behind the memorial are the arms of the Teutonic order of knights, of which Maximilian III was a member.

East of the Domkirche, the **Hofburg** marks the spot where Leopold III, the first Habsburg to wield power in Innsbruck, based his rudimentary court, though the whole complex was rebuilt in the eighteenth century on the instructions of Maria Theresa. Within the cavernous, and for the most part unremarkable, Rococo apartments (daily except Mon: May–Oct 9am–5pm; Nov–April 10am–5pm; öS60), monumental wall paintings provide a pictorial guide to Habsburg family history – those in the state ballroom show Maria Theresa, Joseph II and Francis I flanked by lesser members of the imperial family.

The Hofkirche and the Volkskunstmuseum

At the eastern entrance to the Altstadt, at the head of the Rennweg, the outwardly unassuming **Hofkirche** contains the most impressive of Innsbruck's imperial monuments, the **Cenotaph of Emperor Maximilian** (daily: July–Aug 9am–5.30pm; Sept–June 9am–5pm; öS20, combined ticket including the Tiroler Volkskunstmuseum öS50). An extraordinary piece of imperial propaganda, masterminded by Maximilian himself, it was designed both to consummate Maximilian I's special relationship with Innsbruck and to bolster the prestige of the dynasty. Ambitious plans for the emperor's tomb to be flanked by a series of 40 larger-than-life statues, 100 statuettes and the busts of 32 Roman emperors, representing both the real and spiritual ancestors of Maximilian, were never realized, though the resulting ensemble is still impressive – its effect dulled only slightly by the knowledge that the emperor is actually buried at the other end of Austria. Maximilian died in Wels in January 1519 having been refused entry to Innsbruck by burghers fearful that his soldiers wouldn't pay their bills, and his body was interred in Wiener Neustadt (see p.188) far away to the east.

Twenty-eight statues line the emperor's empty **tomb**, including Maximilian's Habsburg ancestors Rudolf I, Albrecht II and Friedrich III, as well as more fanciful antecedents such as Clovis, fifth-century king of the Franks. Sculptor Peter Vischer was responsible for most of the figures, two of which were cast from designs by **Albrecht Dürer**: the quasi-mythical English King Arthur (he's recognizable from the three lions on his shield), and sixth-century leader of the Ostrogoths, Theoderic, the third statue to Arthur's left. The tomb itself is topped by a kneeling statue of Maximilian, and surrounded by marble reliefs depicting the emperor's great victories, all designed by Flemish artist Alexander Colin.

Beside the church entrance, a more modern tomb holds the remains of **Andreas Hofer**, the Tyrolean patriot executed in Mantua on French orders in 1810 (see p.488). Steps at the rear of the nave ascend towards the tomb of **Archduke Ferdinand II**, great-grandson of Maximilian I and Regent of Tyrol (see p.413). It's located in the so-called **Silberkapelle**, or silver chapel – thus named because of the silver-plated Madonna that adorns the far wall. She is faced by Ferdinand's suit of armour, suspended in a kneeling position halfway up the wall. The bones of the man himself are housed in the tomb directly below, topped by a marble effigy that's also the work of Colin. Ferdinand's first wife, the commoner **Philippa Welser** (for whom the chapel was built), is buried nearby.

Next door to the Hofkirche, the **Tiroler Volkskunstmuseum**, or Tyrolean Folklore Museum (July & Aug Mon–Sat 9am–5.30pm, Sun 9am–noon; Sept–June Mon–Sat 9am–5pm, Sun 9am–noon; öS50, ticket includes entrance to the Hofkirche), is replete with traditional woodcraft. Wooden sleds with griffin-like figureheads vie for attention in the courtyard, while the interior boasts painstakingly reconstructed farmhouse interiors dating back to the sixteenth century. Among the many domestic knick-knacks, one marvellous expression of the contemporary fascination with mortality stands out – a wooden towel rack in the form of a figure, half-young woman, half-skeleton. Leading off the courtyard are a couple of rooms devoted to *Krippen*, or nativity scenes, most of them nineteenth-century pieces from the village of Thaur (see p.421) near Hall, where the craft is still practised.

The Landesmuseum Ferdinandeum and Maria-Theresien-Strasse

A short walk south of the Volkskunstmuseum, at Museumstrasse 15, the **Tiroler Landesmuseum Ferdinandeum** (May–Sept daily 10am–5pm plus 7–9pm Thurs; Oct–April Tues–Sat 10am–noon & 2–5pm, Sun 9am–noon; öS50) greets you with a motley collection of archeological fragments, but the unsurpassed range of paintings awaiting inspection upstairs should not be missed. Most space is devoted to the fifteenth-century "Pustertal Painters" based around Bruneck (Brunico) in the South Tyrol, pre-eminent among whom was Michael Pacher (see p.354), who introduced Italian Renaissance techniques into central European painting and sculpture. Michael was in demand all over Austria in the late 1400s, and the gallery here is the best place to get a feel for the evolution of his, and his apprentice Friedrich Pacher's, art. Other highlights point to the unsqueamish nature of contemporary piety: Jakob von Seckau's *Martyrdom of St Ursula* (an entirely fictitious saint but no less popular) portrays the heroine standing in a boat and being shot at by bowmen, while an anonymous fifteenth-century *Martyrdom of St Erasmus* sees the saint being boiled, poked in the eye, disembowelled and having his fingernails torn out all at the same time. The Baroque collection on the upper storey is disappointing, although a few small eighteenth-century pieces are worth dwelling on, among them Simon Troger's sculpture of the Archangel Michael smiting Lucifer, and a house-altar by Stefan Föger – basically a miniature version of a church high altar, encased in a glass jar for the domestic mantelpiece. The odd Klimt and Kokoschka aside, twentieth-century Austrian art is best represented by a couple of brooding canvases from the moody East Tyrolean painter Albin Egger-Lienz (see p.297).

Heading southwards from the Altstadt, **Maria-Theresien-Strasse** cuts a swath through a grid of busy downtown streets. Main focus of the thoroughfare's middle section is the **Annasäule**, a column supporting a statue of the Virgin but named after St Anne, who appears at the base. The column was erected to commemorate the retreat of the Bavarians on St Anne's day, July 26, 1703. Dominating the Maria-Theresien-Strasse's northern end, the **Triumphpforte**, or triumphal arch, was built in advance of celebrations marking the marriage of Maria Theresa's son Leopold in 1756. The sudden death of the empress's husband Franz caused a fundamental rethink of the arch's ornamentation, and macabre symbols were added, including an angel of death on its northern facade. Beyond the arch, Leopoldstrasse continues southwards towards **Wilten**, 1km distant.

Leaving the centre via Universitätstrasse and passing under the railway viaduct brings you shortly to Zeughausgasse and the former imperial arsenal, or **Zeughaus** (same times as the Landesmuseum Ferdinandeum; öS45), built by Maximilian I to provide a secure base for the manufacture of gunpowder and cannon. The building now contains an eminently missable collection of bric-a-brac, ranging from fossils through silver-mining tools to old fire engines.

South of the Altstadt: Wilten and Schloss Ambras

About a kilometre and a half south of the Altstadt, in the shadow of the attractively wooded Bergisel hill, the suburb of **Wilten** offers a brace of Baroque churches and a motley collection of small museums. Dominating the scene is the twin-towered **Wilten Basilica**, whose Rococo edifice, built in the 1750s by the Tyrolean priest-architect Franz de Paula Penz, belies the fact that it occupies a pilgrimage site of long standing. Inside, ceiling scenes by the Augsburg painter Matthäus Gündter include a particularly graphic Salome holding aloft the head of John the Baptist, and are framed by intricate mouldings, rich in leafy fronds and tendrils.

A short distance east of the basilica is the ruddy facade of **Wilten Abbey**, the entrance to which is guarded by statues of giants Thyrsus and Haymon. According to myth, itinerant dragon-slayer Haymon killed local giant Thyrsus in a dispute, and went on to found Wilten Abbey by way of penance. The seventeenth-century **abbey church** within merits a quick peek, even though it lacks the delicacy of the nearby basilica.

Next door to the abbey, the **Kaiserschützenmusem** (May–Sept Mon–Sat 10am–4pm, Sun 9am–noon; free) remembers the imperial Tyrolean militia with displays of ceremonial uniforms and weaponry. Across the road, the tram depot contains a small **transport museum** (May–Oct Sat 9am–5pm; öS30), which is little more than an engine shed containing a few locomotives, but special museum trains run from here to Igls on summer Sundays. Just down the hill from the abbey, on the corner of Leopoldstrasse and Egger-Lienz-Strasse, the Grassmayr **Glockengiesserei**, or bell foundry (Mon–Fri 9am–6pm, Sat 9am–noon; öS40), treats visitors to a short display detailing the history of bell-casting, and a chance to peruse the offerings – models of bells, mostly – in the company's gift-shop.

Immediately to the south of the abbey complex lies the **Bergisel**, scene of the bloody battles between Andreas Hofer's rebels and the French in 1809. At the foot of the hill stands the **Bergisel Museum** (April–Oct 9am–5pm; öS40), honouring the fighters of the Tyrolean War of Independence in suitably reverential mode. Above the museum, paths crisscross the wooded slopes, where it's impossible to miss the takeoff ramp of the **Sprungstadion**, the ski-jump arena used in the 1964 and 1976 Olympics.

Schloss Ambras

Home of Maximilian I's great-grandson Archduke Ferdinand II, **Schloss Ambras** (April–Oct 10am–5pm; Jan–March guided tours only 2–3.30pm; daily except Tues; öS60) is one of the foremost Renaissance palaces in Austria, affording fascinating insight into the courtly culture of the sixteenth century. Situated 2km southeast of the Altstadt, it can be reached by taking tram #6 to the Schloss Ambras stop, or tram #3 to the end of Amraserstrasse before following paths under the autobahn and climbing up the wooded hillock to the Schloss.

ARCHDUKE FERDINAND II OF TYROL (1529–95)

The second son of Emperor Ferdinand I, the future Archduke Ferdinand of Tyrol looked set for a glittering imperial career: appointed governor of Bohemia at the age of 18, he was initially preferred by his father over his elder brother Maximilian (the future Maximilian II, suspected by his father being a closet Protestant) as heir to the throne. Yet Ferdinand disqualified himself from such a high office by falling in love with a commoner, **Philippa Welser**, daughter of an Augsburg banker. The senior Habsburg was expelled from court for not adhering to the correct breeding habits, until, according to one tale, Philippa travelled to Ferdinand I's court in Prague under an assumed name. There she regaled the emperor with a moving story about a wicked father who had disowned his son for falling in love with the wrong woman. Suitably humbled, the august Habsburg dropped his opposition to the match. Whatever the real reason for the change of heart, Ferdinand-*père* sanctioned a **morganatic marriage** between the two in 1557. Ferdinand and Philippa's sons Karl and Andreas were nevertheless given top imperial and ecclesiastical posts, with Andreas ultimately becoming a cardinal. Ferdinand himself was a devout Catholic, and Protestantism made few inroads in the Tyrol under his stewardship of the duchy.

After Welser's death in 1580, Ferdinand married the 16-year-old **Anna Gonzaga of Mantua**, producing three daughters in as many years – the youngest of whom, Anne, in true Habsburg style, married her cousin, the emperor Matthias, in order to keep the archducal lands in the family. However, Ferdinand's marriage to Anna was never really a happy one. He built the Silberkapelle in the Hofkirche (see p.410) as a monument to Philippa, and chose to be buried there himself.

Throughout the 1580s Ferdinand increasingly threw his energies into a mania for collecting that produced the famous **Kunst- und Wunderkammer**, a museum in which works of art are displayed beside bizarre natural phenomena and trinkets from far-flung places. To educated people of the time, such juxtapositions demonstrated the infinite diversity of God's creation. The popularity of such collections survived well into the next century, as demonstrated by the Kunst- und Wunderkammer of the archbishops of Salzburg, together with Archbishop Markus Sitticus's enthusiasm for deformed animals (see p.320). Ferdinand went a step further than many contemporaries by acquiring human exhibits with which to amaze his guests, keeping both a giant and a dwarf at Schloss Ambras in specially made quarters.

On Ferdinand's death, the Ambras collection was sold to Emperor Rudolf II – Ferdinand's great rival in the collecting of oddities. Rudolf never got round to moving the objects out of the Schloss so the collection stayed here in its entirety until 1805, when the most valuable pieces were taken to Vienna to keep them out of the hands of the Bavarians.

Entering the Schloss through the western gateway, you are first directed towards the **Lower Schloss**, comprising an ensemble of outbuildings. First up, the **Rustkammer** flaunts jousting armour from the late fifteenth century, including several suits made for Archduke Ferdinand himself. The collection's most striking piece, however, is the armour worn by Ferdinand's court giant, Bartlmä Bon, at the Vienna tournament of 1560.

Ferdinand's **Kunst- und Wunderkammer** is preserved in something approaching its original form, although many of its most treasured items – including the much-admired golden salt cellar by Benvenuto Cellini – have been removed to the Kunsthistorisches Museum in Vienna (see p.94). Busts of Roman rulers from Julius Caesar to Emperor Theodosius (originally intended for the cenotaph of Maximilian in the Hofkirche) rub shoulders with games and puzzles, Far Eastern porcelain, Turkish hats and an exquisite statuette of Death carved from pearwood. More unsettling to modern eyes, the portrait gallery is filled with the freakish contemporaries who so fascinated Ferdinand: in addition to his court giant and several court dwarfs are Petrus

Gonsalvus of Tenerife, the so-called "Hirsute Man", pictured here with his similarly afflicted son and daughter; and Vlad Tepesch (aka Vlad the Impaler), the fifteenth-century ruler of Transylvania who resurfaced four hundred years later as the inspiration behind Bram Stoker's *Dracula*.

Slightly further uphill, Ferdinand's **Spanische Saal** features a dazzlingly intricate wood-inlay ceiling, and walls decorated with 27 full-length portraits of the rulers of the Tyrol. From here, steps lead to the **Upper Schloss**, where an extensive **portrait gallery** holds the works of artists who are sometimes less interesting than their sitters – a vast array of European rulers and aristocrats across the centuries. The collection also offers a good crash course in Habsburg family history, starting with a portrait of Albrecht III, painted around 1430, and revealing the jutting lower lip and strong jaw that remained a family trademark thereafter. Finally, a room leading off the interior courtyard houses one of the Schloss's most enchanting artworks, an **altar of St George** carved by Sebald Bocksdorfer and painted by Sebastian Scheel about 1500, with a marvellous gilt relief of the saint. The wings portray Maximilian I carrying sheaves of corn – a suggestion linking the knightly warrior-emperor to prosperity and the protection of the harvests.

North of the Altstadt: the Hungerbergbahn and the Alpenzoo

At the northern end of the Rennweg, a large round building houses the **Rundgemälde**, or Panorama (April–Oct daily 9am–4.45pm; öS30), a circular painting portraying the Battle of Bergisel in 1809, when Andreas Hofer's Tyrolean insurgents routed a mixed French-Bavarian force. Just beside the Rundgemälde, the station of the **Hungerbergbahn** funicular presents the most direct route up the flanks of the **Nordkette**, ascending the affluent hillside suburb of Hungerburg before continuing by two-stage cable car to the 1905-metre **Seegrube** and the 2334-metre **Hafelkar**.

Halfway up the Hungerburgbahn, you can alight at a wayside halt in order to visit the **Alpenzoo** (daily 9am–6pm; öS60), also reached by walking up Wieherburggasse from the west bank of the River Inn. The zoo holds a collection of animals indigenous to Europe's mountainous regions, including bears, eagles, pine martens (largely nocturnal, so not much chance of seeing them), ibex, lynx and otter.

Eating, drinking and entertainment

Innsbruck's Altstadt is crowded with establishments offering all manner of food and drink. A constant flow of tourists ensures that not all of them are cheap, but it's extremely rare to be fobbed off with nondescript food or indifferent service wherever you are in town.

There's no shortage of daytime **snack food**, with Würstelstands on both Herzog-Friedrich-Strasse and Maria-Theresien-Strasse. The handy *Panini*, opposite the Goldenes Dachl, and *Subito*, a little further west on the corner of Herzog-Friedrich-Strasse and Kiebachgasse, both offer sandwiches and pizza slices. A little further afield, *Prendi Pizza*, Viaduktbogen 5, and the *Ali Kebab House*, Mariahilferstrasse 12, are popular sources for quick, take-away nosh.

For **daytime drinking**, Innsbruck has a couple of classic coffeehouses that compare favourably with anything Vienna has to offer. A wide range of bars are scattered throughout the centre, and the Viaduktbogen – a line of railway arches ten minutes' walk east of the Altstadt – is home to a string of varied **night-time** venues.

Restaurants

Al Dente, Meranstrasse 7. Popular and youthful pasta joint in the centre of town, with a few vegetarian choices on the menu.

Ali Baba, corner of Tschemmlerstrasse and Dr-Karl-von-Grabmayr-Strasse. Turkish restaurant some way south of the centre on the way to Wilten – worth trying if you're in the area.

Chili's, corner of Boznerplatz and Adamgasse. Large, fun restaurant with Tex-Mex food and booze.

Elferhaus, Herzog-Friedrich-Strasse 11. Crowded, narrow, enduringly popular city-centre place serving solid and inexpensive Austrian standards; also a popular place to drink.

Grotte, Innstrasse 13. Trendy place, decorated to look like a cave, on the west bank of the river with a mid-priced Austrian-Italian menu.

La Cucina, Museumstrasse 26. Fashionable Italian restaurant with a wide range of reasonably priced pizza and pasta dishes, as well as more expensive Italian classics (such as *saltimbocca alla Romana*) and some excellent desserts.

Ottoburg, Herzog-Friedrich-Strasse 1 (☎574652). Bustling establishment in a fifteenth-century town house, with a posh restaurant upstairs (reservations recommended) and a more run-of-the-mill selection of Austrian standards downstairs.

Philippine, Müllerstrasse 9. Eccentrically decorated restaurant with a wide choice of vegetarian dishes, usually featuring an inexpensive Tagesmenü. Closed Sun.

Sahib, Sillgasse 3. Good, medium-priced Indian restaurant round the corner from the Landesmuseum Ferdinandeum. Open till 1am.

Stiegelbräu, Wilhelm-Griel-Strasse 25. A bit antiseptic despite attempts to induce a homely beer-hall atmosphere, but a good centrally located place in which to sample standard Austrian dishes.

Stiftskeller, Stiftgasse 1. A dependable, mid-priced restaurant on the well-trodden route between the Hofkirche and Goldenes Dachl. There's always fresh trout on the menu.

Weisses Rössl, Kiebachgasse 8. First-floor, wood-panelled restaurant with a good mix of tourists and locals, and wide range of Austrian food. A good place for Tyrolean specialities and inexpensive Tagesmenüs.

Bars and cafés

Bierstindl, Klostergasse 6. Cultural centre and café-bar combined, to the south in Wilten, with an attractive beer garden where concerts (mostly rock and world music) take place over the summer.

Café Brazil, Leopoldstrasse 7. Café-patisserie near the Triumphal Arch, decked out in deliberately bohemian style. Lots of comfy chairs, and greenery.

Café Central, Gilmstrasse 5. Venerable coffeehouse with a bewildering array of coffees and mouth-watering cakes, and a mixed clientele.

Filou, Stiftgasse 12. Long-standing city-centre drinking venue for the smart set, featuring late-night basement disco, though recently overtaken in the trendy stakes by many of the places along the Viaduktbogen.

Gartencafé, Hofgarten. A pavilion in the corner of the park opposite the Hofburg, with plenty of outdoor seating in the summer. Popular hangout for an affluent, dressy crowd.

Innkeller, Innstrasse 1. Best of the bars on the west bank of the Inn, with youngish crowds imbibing to a predominantly jungle and trip-hop soundtrack.

Limerick Bill's Irish Pub, Maria-Theresien-Strasse 9. Lively, often crowded, Irish pub with Guinness on tap.

Klappe, Viaduktbogen 21. Dimly lit, club-like bar with minimal decor and predominantly jazz–funk sounds on the turntable.

Krahvogel, Anichstrasse 12. Funky city-centre bar with a good range of draught beers and a nice courtyard at the back.

Nashville, Viaduktbogen 50. Decorated in the style of a Wild West saloon and occasionally featuring live country music – great fun if you like that kind of thing.

Prometheus, Hofgasse 2. Conveniently central place with unpretentious café-bar upstairs, and sweaty cellar disco below.

Stadtcafé, at Universitätstrasse 1. Classic coffeehouse with large outdoor terrace opposite the Hofburg. On the pricey side.

Theresienbräu, Maria-Theresien-Strasse 51–53. Animated beer hall-type place serving ales brewed on the premises.

Treibhaus, Angerzellgasse 8. A cultural centre that doubles as popular weekend drinking venue for the studenty, arty set.

Weli, Viaduktbogen 26. Friendly café-bar with board games, as well as good home-style cooking.

Zappa, Rechengasse 5. Friendly basement bar in the university district southwest of the centre, with studenty clientele (it's underneath a hall of residence) and musical policy that's largely alternative rock.

Entertainment

Although not in the same league as Salzburg or Graz, Innsbruck still serves up a varied cultural diet. For **high culture**, the Tiroler Landestheater, Rennweg 2 (box office Mon–Sat 8.30am–8.30pm; ☎520744), is the main venue for serious drama, opera and ballet; bigger productions sometimes make use of the Congress Centre on Rennweg. Smaller recitals occasionally take place in Schloss Ambras, site of a Festival of Early Music in August – the Innsbrucker Festwochen der Alten Musik – specializing in music of the Baroque and early classical period (advance bookings can be made through the Innsbruck tourist office).

For **rock and pop**, big-name touring bands play at large multipurpose venues like the Olympiastadion or Messehalle. The best places to catch **alternative** bands, local acts, world music or **jazz** are the *Treibhaus*, Angerzellgasse 8, *Utopia*, Tschamlerstrasse 3, or the *Bierstindl*, Klostergasse 6.

The place to go for a show-biz interpretation of **Tyrolean folk music** is Alpenbühne Gundolf (April–Oct nightly), which offers a programme of brass-band music, yodelling and dance. Performances (öS200 including first drink) take place either in the Innsbrucker Messesaal, two blocks east of the Hofgarten at Ingenieur-Etzel-Strasse 35, or the *Gasthaus Sandwirt*, Reichenauerstrasse 151 (bus O from Museumstrasse). Information can be obtained on ☎263263 or from the tourist office; information and tickets for all gigs and cultural events are available from the main tourist office at Burggraben 3.

Listings

Airlines Austrian Airlines, Adamgasse 7a (☎582985); Lufthansa, Südtirolerplatz 1 (☎59800); Tyrolean Airways, at the airport (☎2222-77).

Airport information Innsbruck (☎22525); Munich (☎0049/89/9752 1313).

American Express Brixnerstrasse 3 (☎582491).

Bike rental Limited choice from the train station (☎503/5385); mountain bikes from City-Mountainbikerental, Innstrasse 95 (☎286515).

Books Freytag & Berndt, Wilhelm-Griel-Strasse 15. English-language books and maps.

Car rental Avis, Salurnerstrasse 15 (☎571754); Budget, Michael-Gaismayrstrasse 5–7 (☎588468); Europcar, Salurnerstrasse 8 (☎582060); Herz, Südtirolerplatz 1 (☎580901); Kalal, Leopoldstrasse 54 (☎584544).

Cinema Cinematograph, Museumstrasse 31 (☎578500). Shows art-house films – usually subtitled rather than dubbed into German.

Consulates Great Britain, Matthias-Schmid-Strasse 12/I (☎588320; Mon–Fri 9am–noon). Other nationals should contact their embassies in Vienna.

Exchange Banks are generally open Mon–Fri 7.45am–12.30pm & 2.15–4pm. Outside these hours, try bureaus in the train station (daily 7.30am–8pm); at the tourist office, Burggraben 3 (daily 8am–7pm); or the main post office (24hr), Maximilianstrasse 2.

Football FC Tirol Innsbruck, one of Austria's better provincial sides, play at the Tivoli Stadion on Burgenlandstrasse, southeast of the centre near the Olympiabrücke.

Gay organizations Homosexuelle Initiative Tirol, Innrain 100 (☎562403).

Hiking tours The tourist office runs an extensive programme of guided walks – including nighttime hiking above Igls – from June to early September. They're free to anyone in possession of a Club-Innsbruck card (issued to anyone staying in Innsbruck – get it from the tourist office or your hotel). A hiking pass covering three days' unlimited use of the Hungerburg funicular and the Nordkette and Patscherkofel cable cars costs öS450. The Österreichischer Alpenverein (Austrian Alpine Club), at Wilhelm-Griel-Strasse 15, provides hiking information and sells maps (☎59547, fax 575528; Mon–Fri 9am–1pm, 2–5pm).

Hospital Universitätsklinik, Anichstrasse 35 (☎5040).

Ice skating Indoor (open all year round) and outdoor (open mid-Nov to Feb) rinks at the Eisstadion by the Olympiabrücke (☎33838).

Laundry Waltraud Hell, Amraserstrasse 15 (☎341367; Mon–Fri 8am–6pm).

Lost property At the main police station.

Markets Fresh fruit, veg and rural produce at the Bauernmarkt (farmers' market) in the Markthalle, at the junction of Marktgraben and Innrain. Every morning except Sun.

Police The main police station is at Kaiserjägerstrasse 8 (☎5900).

Post office The main post office, at Maximilianstrasse 2, is open 24hr.

Rafting Contact the tourist office for details of rafting trips up the Inn Valley at Imst (see p.447).

Swimming pools Indoor pool at Amraserstrasse 3 (☎42585); outdoor pool at the Tivoli sports centre, Purtschellerstrasse 1 (☎342344).

Taxis ☎5311; ☎1718.

Tennis In summer, outdoor courts at the Eisstadion (☎33838; öS100 per hour); in winter, Indoor Tennis Courts West, near the airport at Fürstenweg 172 (☎284364; hourly rates from öS160).

Train information ☎1717.

Travel agents ÖKISTA, Andreas-Hofer-Strasse 16 (☎588997); Tiroler Landesreisebüro, Wilhelm-Griel-Strasse (☎59885).

Women's organizations Frauenzentrum Innsbruck, Liebeneggstrasse 15 (☎580839).

EAST OF INNSBRUCK

The eastern part of the Inn Valley, known locally as the **Unterland**, includes many of the Tyrol's most absorbing historical towns – nuggets of late-Gothic culture like **Hall**, **Schwaz** and **Rattenberg**, as well as the fortress town of **Kufstein** on the border with Bavaria. All of these are good bases from which to explore a variety of neighbouring alpine villages, although for a real taste of the mountains you'd do better to plump for **Kitzbühel**, the fashionable society resort in the extreme east, or the **Zillertal**, the most breathtaking of the side-valleys feeding the River Inn from the south. Immediately north of the Zillertal is the **Achensee**, the Tyrol's biggest lake, which in summer offers a lazy waterside alternative to the more strenuous pursuits of the region.

The main autobahn and rail route to Salzburg and Vienna follows the Inn Valley eastwards, through Hall, Schwaz and Rattenberg before entering Germany just beyond Kufstein. The town of **Jenbach**, although of no particular interest in itself, is an important transport hub serving routes to the Zillertal and the Achensee. Further east, **Wörgl** commands another important junction, with road and rail routes branching off towards Kitzbühel.

Hall

At its fifteenth-century peak, **HALL** was the third largest Austrian city after Vienna and Schwaz, an important trading centre that had grown rich on the proceeds of salt mined in the mountains to the north. It was transformed into a major financial centre under Maximilian I's uncle Sigismund the Rich, who moved the Tyrolean mint here from Meran in the 1470s and began production of the *Taler*, a silver coin that became the standard unit of currency in central Europe for a time. (The place it occupied in the popular imagination is today recalled by the monetary unit named after it – the dollar.)

HALL

Schwaz △

Schwaz △

200 m

N

THURNFELDSTRASSE

MILSER STRASSE

Jesuitenkirche

Damenstift

SALZBURGER STRASSE

STIFTSPLATZ

CYCLE PATH

UFER WEG

AUTOBAHN

UNTERE LEND

AGRAMS GASSE

SCHLOSSERG

ROSENGASSE

EUGENSTRASSE

Bergbaumuseum

FORSTER PARK

LEND GASSE

AUSFAHRT N HALL

Inn

STADTGRABEN

BRUCKERGASSE

STRASSE

MAGDALENASTR

WALLPACH GASSE

KIRPGASSE

OB STADTPL.

PFARR.

LANGER GRABEN

UNTERER STADTPLATZ

MÜNZER GASSE

Tulfes △

Innsbruck △

STRAUSS

FÜX MAGEN STRASSE

EILER STRASSE

KATHREINSTRASSE

WALDAUS

BACHLECHNERSTR

PFARRPLATZ

SALVATOR GASSE

SCHMIED GASSE

Burg Hasegg

ZUR AUTOBAHN

Inn

Rathaus

Pfarrkirche
St Nikolaus

STADTGRABEN

BREITWEG SEWERST

SPECKBACHERSTRASSE

FASSER

STOLZSTRASSE

GERBERGASSE

PFANNHAUSER STRASSE

ZUR AUTOBAHN

UFERWEG

SCHILLER STR

REIM MICHL STRASSE

RECHEISTRASSE

SCHWEYGERSTR

AMTSBACH-

GASSE

AUGASSE

Train
Station

BAHNHOF-STR.

BAHNHOFPLATZ

HEILIGKREUZ

BADGASSE

SCHEIDENSTEIN STRASSE

KUGELANGER STRASSE

Campsite △

WEINFELDGASSE

STRASSE

OBERE LEND

MÖSL WEG

ZIEGLWEG

TRIENDLSTRASSE

FASSER GASSE

SÜDTIROLER STR

BRIXNERSTRASSE

TRIENDLSTRASSE

INNSBRUCKER STRASSE

Thaur △

Innsbruck ▽

ACCOMMODATION

Badl   3
Parkhotel   1
Schatz   2

Modern Hall preserves one of the best ensembles of late medieval buildings in the country and is an attractive alternative to Innsbruck – which, only 10km away to the west, makes for an easy day-trip.

The Town

Hall's main attraction is the late-Gothic character of the town centre, a compact grid of medieval alleyways that zero in on a central square, the **Oberer Stadtplatz**. Immediately to the west, a short flight of steps ascends to the **Pfarrkirche St Nikolaus**, a thirteenth-century structure whose interior betrays a curious lack of symmetry, the result of an unfinished fifteenth-century programme of rebuilding that left the choir off-centre. To the left of the high altar, the **Waldaufkapelle** is named after Florian Waldauf, a peasant's son from East Tyrol who rose to become trusted sidekick of Emperor Maximilian I. Waldauf was an obsessive collector of holy relics, and in 1501 arranged delivery of the skulls of numerous minor European saints to the church in a pomp-laden procession. They now occupy the niches along the chapel's northern wall, watched over by a late-Gothic altar to the Virgin Mary, thought to be the work of Tyrolean master Michael Pacher (see p.354).

Behind the church to the east stands the **Magdalenskapelle**, an outwardly featureless grey building, which contains some excellent late-Gothic paintings, including a *Last Judgement* filled with the writhing forms of the damned. In the centre of the chapel an **altar** of 1490 displays some extraordinarily vibrant scenes on the wings, illustrating the Annunciation, Adoration of the Magi and Death of the Virgin, together with images of St Barbara and St Agnes, the latter accompanied by her symbol, the lamb.

Immediately north of the Pfarrkirche, the **Rathaus** was built in the fourteenth century by Henry, King of Bohemia and Duke of Tyrol. It was subsequently used as a hunting lodge by Maximilian I, who would set off into the mountains to indulge in the noble art of *Gemsstecken* – impaling chamoix on 4.5-metre-long pikes. Visitors can usually gain admission to the building's main ceremonial chamber, the Rathausstube, which preserves its sixteenth-century wood ceiling, although its popularity as a venue for weddings ensures that it's rarely accessible to tourists at weekends.

The **Bergbaumuseum**, or mining museum (May–Oct Mon–Sat 9am–noon & 2–5pm; öS30), a block south of Oberer Stadtplatz on the corner of Eugenstrasse, recounts Hall's salt-mining heritage, although the attempt to recreate the atmosphere of underground galleries in the old ducal palace is less than successful. Eugenstrasse heads west from here to the **Stiftsplatz**, where a fine Baroque facade marks the location of the so-called **Damenstift**, the Carmelite convent founded in 1567 by the archduchess Magdalena, sister of Archduke Ferdinand II of Tyrol. One of the strictest of all religious orders, Carmelites observed total silence and slept in their own coffins. Diagonally opposite the convent stands the red and ochre facade of the **Jesuitenkirche**, originally attached to a Jesuit monastery also established by Archduchess Magdalena. Its delicate white and gold stuccoed interior is probably the earliest example of Baroque decoration in the Tyrol.

Burg Hasegg

Hall's famous mint was located within the sturdy walls of **Burg Hasegg**, a largely sixteenth-century strongpoint dominating the lower town south of the centre, and now housing the town **museum** (July–Sept daily 10am–3pm; öS40). The sections on local history and folklore are uninspiring, but the inevitable section on minting features a wide array of Habsburg-era coins and offers you the chance to mint your own *Taler* (for an added charge). Visitors can also see the fortress chapel, where the marriage of Maximilian I and his second wife Bianca Maria Sforza was confirmed (the original marriage, contracted for purely political reasons, had taken place in Milan in the absence of the groom). A small collection of late-Gothic altarpieces is also up for perusal, one of which, painted by local boy Marx Reichlich (whose *Adoration of the Magi* is in Innsbruck's Landesmuseum Ferdinandeum; see p.411), shows Florian Waldauf being knighted by Emperor Maximilian in the right-hand panel (Maximilian is the one in the red jacket and hat), and Waldauf's wife – herself a major donor to local churches – in the left-hand panel.

Those willing to tackle the two hundred steps of the castle's tower, the **Münzerturm**, are rewarded with sweeping views of the urban sprawl of Innsbruck to the west.

Practicalities

Hall's **train station** is on the eastern edges of the town centre. From the station forecourt walk straight ahead to the main road and turn right; five minutes' walk away, Langer Graben heads left uphill to the Oberer Stadtplatz, the main focus of the Old Town. An extremely helpful **tourist office**, just off the Oberer Stadtplatz at Wallpachgasse 5 (Mon–Fri 8am–noon & 1–6pm, Sat 9am–1pm; ☎05223/56269, fax 56220-20), will help book **private rooms**, although most of these are either in the outskirts of town or in the village of Thaur (see below) 3km northeast – an enticing option if you have your own transport. *Schatz*, Innsbrucker Strasse 62 (☎05223/57994, fax 57994-4; ③), is a comfy suburban **Gasthof** on the western fringes of the town, while *Badl*, Haller Innbrücke 4 (☎05223/56784, fax 56784-3; ③), has a pleasant riverside location and bright rooms, some with views towards the old town. The more upmarket *Parkhotel*, Thurnfeldgasse 1a (☎05223/56566, fax 43478; ⑤), is comfortable, modern and very central. There's a **campsite** on Schiedensteinstrasse (☎05223/45464-75) next to the open-air swimming pool, about 1.5km northeast of the centre.

There aren't as many eating and drinking options as you would expect in a town of Hall's size, probably because Innsbruck is so close at hand. For inexpensive **food**, *La Grotta*, beside the Burg Hasegg on Münzergasse, is a good-value pizza and pasta restaurant; the more atmospheric *Geisterburg*, Stadtgraben 18, two blocks north of the Oberer Stadtplatz, offers a popular mixture of Austrian and Italian cuisine, has a nice garden out front and is open until midnight. A small step up in price are *Nagglburg*, Ritter-Waldaufstrasse 11, which specializes in top-quality Tyrolean food, and the *Schwarzer Adler*, Eugenstrasse 3, which has a largely Austrian repertoire and good-value lunchtime Tagesmenüs.

The centrally located *Café Roseneck*, Wallpachgasse 5, serves as a good place for a daytime or night-time **drink**, with outdoor seating and a range of tasty snacks. Alternatively, head for the bars just below the Oberer Stadtplatz on Salvatorgasse: the barrel-vaulted *Haller Kübel*, sometimes featuring live music on Fridays, and the *Salva-Pub*, a touch more garish and attracting a younger crowd, are two good choices.

Around Hall

Hall is a good base from which explore a cluster of attractive villages clinging to the sides of the Inn Valley, among them **Thaur**, **Tulfes** and **Volders**. Popular destinations for Tyroleans, few of them receive English-speaking tourists in any great numbers. Further east, but still within striking distance, the more industrialized town of **Wattens** is home to the **Swarovski Kristallwelt**, a high-tech, multimedia exhibition built around the products of the local crystal factory.

Thaur

Three kilometres northwest of Hall, **THAUR** is an exceedingly pretty village lurking in the shadow of the Nordkette. It's known above all for preserving the kind of authentic **Tyrolean folk traditions** that have died out elsewhere. It's one of the few places that still marks **Palm Sunday** with a procession involving a life-size effigy of Jesus on a donkey, carried through the fields around the village. Originally common throughout Austria, such processions were discouraged during the reign of eighteenth-century rationalist Josef II, and most Jesus-on-a-donkey statues belonging to other villages were destroyed. Festivities in Thaur continue throughout **Holy Week**; a tableau depicting the grave of Christ is placed in the Pfarrkirche, and another procession takes place through the town on **Good Friday**.

Thaur is also an important centre for the making of nativity scenes, or **Krippen**. These painstakingly constructed scenes usually involve a higher degree of craftsmanship than the mass-produced nativity figurines found elsewhere in Europe, their model scenery and painted backdrops investing the craft with the theatricality of the stage set. Such scenes adorned Austrian farmhouses over the Christmas period long before Christmas trees became fashionable, and were promoted by the Catholic Church during the Counter-Reformation as a means of sustaining popular enthusiasm for traditional Christian ritual. In Thaur, the practice of making nativity scenes is continued by several local families, who display their *Krippen* either in the Pfarrkirche or at home between December 26 and January 15. Details of where you can see the *Krippen* are available from the tourist office in Hall – otherwise look out for signs outside private houses reading *"Weihnachtskrippe"* ("Christmas crib").

Thaur doesn't have a tourist office of its own, but **private rooms** here can be procured through the tourist office in Hall. There are also two very plush **hotels** in the centre of the village: the *Strangl*, Kirchgasse 2 (☎05223/492828, fax 492828-56; ⑤), and the *Purner*, Dorfplatz 5 (☎05223/49149, fax 49149-7; ⑤).

Tulfes and Volders

The nearest mountain resort offering winter skiing and summer hiking is the village of **TULFES**, spread across a hillside terrace 6km to the south of Hall. Accessible by minor road, and served by buses from the Unterer Stadtplatz in Hall or from the main bus station in Innsbruck, Tulfes is the starting point for a two-stage gondola ascent to the **Tulfein Alm**, an area of alpine meadow below the area's main peak, the **Glungezer**. The Zirbenweg walk from the top of the Glungezer gondola to the top of the Patscherkofel cable car above Igls is a popular, though strenuous, five-hour hike.

Also on the south side of the Inn, but down on the valley floor some 4km east of Hall, is the village of **VOLDERS** (easily reached from Hall via the foot- and cyclepath that runs along the south bank of the Inn starting from the *Gasthof Badl*), site of the seventeenth-century church of **St Karl Borromäus**. A Baroque masterpiece with a striking red-and-white colour scheme, the building has been blighted by the construction of the adjacent autobahn.

Wattens and the Swarovski Kristallwelt

Eight kilometres east of Hall, and served by numerous local trains, **WATTENS** is home to one of Austria's most popular modern attractions, the **Swarovski Kristallwelt**, or "Crystal World". It was conceived as a high-profile showcase for the nearby Swarovski factory, long-standing producer of high quality optical equipment as well as the ornamental cut-glass animals and figurines regarded as rank kitsch by some, prized collectables by others.

About twenty minutes' walk southeast of Fritzens-Wattens **train station**, the entrance to the Kristallwelt (daily 9am–6pm; öS70) is itself dramatic, hidden beneath an ivy-covered hillside landscaped to form a human face – with a small waterfall emerging from the mouth. Inside, a range of sound-and-light environments created by Viennese installation artist André Heller and others (including ambient music pioneer Brian Eno) aim to induce a sense of wonder or meditative contemplation. The result is both a vastly entertaining futuristic theme park and a staggeringly vulgar monument to corporate vanity (it comes as no surprise to discover that the largest of the exhibition galleries is the gift-shop); but it's one of a kind, and kids will probably love it.

There's little else in Wattens to detain you, and you'd be wise to treat the Kristallwelt as a day-trip from Hall or Innsbruck rather than staying locally.

Schwaz and around

The bustling commercial centre of **SCHWAZ**, 20km east of Hall, bears an equally impressive historical pedigree. Until the closure of the mines some two hundred years ago, Schwaz was the the Tyrol's major producer of **silver**, a resource crucial to the upturn of Habsburg fortunes during the reign of Maximilian I. The old silver workings have been transformed into one of Austria's most popular **show-mines**, on the eastern fringes of town, near the unmissable **Haus der Völker**, an intriguing new ethnographical collection. Schwaz's town centre, by no means as pretty as those of Hall and Innsbruck, nevertheless contains a generous sprinkling of late-Gothic sights. A picturesque gorge at **Stans** and the museum at **Schloss Tratzberg** provide the main out-of-town attractions.

The Town

Schwaz's town centre spreads along the southeastern bank of the River Inn, while the main road and rail routes hug the opposite side of the valley. Bordered to the north by a few remaining portions of medieval wall, its core is marked by the **Pfarrkirche**, with its copper-shingled roof and characteristic crenellated gables. Built during the town's fifteenth-century silver-mining heyday, it was designed to cater for two separate congregations and as a consequence sports two naves: the one on the left was reserved for the burghers, the one on the right for miners. The high altar is twentieth-century neo-Gothic, but the side altar to the left is a fine piece of medieval craftsmanship dating from 1410, featuring a Madonna and Child wearing elaborately jewelled crowns. At the back of the nave near the entrance, don't miss the baptismal font of 1470, with an exquisitely carved relief of John the Baptist at the base, and the Baroque organ case high above, a cherub-and-statuette-laden affair from the 1730s.

From here Franz-Josef-Strasse runs east past a sequence of town houses that betray their medieval origins, most important of which is the **Fuggerhaus**, which has traces of eighteenth-century paintings on the outside. Slightly set back from the main street is the **Franziskanerkirche**, not a source of great interest in itself, but the **cloisters** to the right contain a cycle of paintings illustrating the Passion, painted in the 1520s and currently undergoing restoration.

Burggasse leads uphill from the Franziskanerkirche towards the twelfth-century **Burg Freundsberg**, perched on a knoll about a ten-minute walk away. The small **museum** in the castle keep (mid-April to mid-Oct daily 10am–5pm; öS30) is by no means essential viewing: included are a modest collection of nineteenth-century wooden furniture, wrought-iron crosses from local graveyards, and some late-Gothic wood panelling and wall paintings.

Haus der Völker

Husslstrasse leads northeast from the town centre towards the **Haus der Völker** (daily 8.30am–7pm; öS70), about 1.5km away, a modern museum built to house the private collections of Gert Chesi, a local photojournalist who spent most of his career in Africa and Southeast Asia and collected traditional artefacts along the way. An extensive range of Thai and Burmese wood sculpture, some colourful Yoruba masks and a set-piece grouping of statuettes from Togo representing voodoo deities and fetish figures standing in a ceremonial boat are among the displays. An exhibit of flags made by the Fanti show images of white men crashing in aeroplanes or being eaten by crocodiles, revealing the Ghanaian warriors' hostility towards British colonial authorities. The museum's *Ethno-Café* sometimes has evenings devoted to African or Mexican cuisine.

The silver mine

Another kilometre further on Husslstrasse, the **Silberbergwerk** (May–Oct daily 9am–5pm; öS130) offers an exhilarating kilometre-long train ride into the mine, followed by an hour-long walking tour of the interior. The potted history of mining techniques through the ages won't appeal to everyone, but the imaginatively lit caverns make the experience worthwhile. Tours are in German, although English-language headsets are provided at each stop along the way. Tours depart according to demand and are usually pretty frequent.

Practicalities

From the **train station**, a straightforward ten-minute walk to the southeast, across the Innbrücke, will get you to the centre of town. Most **buses** stop at the train station, some on the other side of the river on Andreas-Hofer-Strasse, just by the Innbrücke. The **tourist office**, at Franz-Josef-Strasse 26 (Mon–Fri 9am–6pm, Sat 9am–1pm; ☎05242/63240, fax 65630), will direct you to **private rooms** in Schwaz or in the village of **Pill** 4km to the west (served by hourly bus from the Innbrücke). If you're travelling in a group or with children, apartments in **farmhouses** (①) are the best bargains, although most of these are out of town, and you'll probably need your own transport to find them. The nearest **campsite** is *Camping Plankenhof* in Pill (☎05242/64195-0).

Pension Heiss, Andreas-Hofer-Strasse 5 (☎05242/73388; ②), is probably the cheapest of the central **hotels**, offering simple rooms with shared facilities, in a modern downtown building. A more tranquil option is the *Pension Clara*, Winterstellergasse 20 (☎05242/63911; ②), a bright, modern suburban house with a small garden, just east of the tourist office. Two bigger hotels immediately north of the centre are the *Goldenes Kreuz*, Falkensteinstrasse 5 (☎05242/62578, fax 64870; ③), offering plain but comfortable rooms with en-suite facilities, and the slightly more upmarket *Goldener Löwe*, Husslstrasse 4 (☎05242/62373-0, fax 62373-44; ③), where you also get TV, phone and access to an indoor pool and sauna.

The centre of town holds a wide range of **restaurants and cafés**. For a quick, cheap meal, *Palazzo*, on Franz-Josef-Strasse opposite the tourist office, is a lively pizza and pasta joint. For something more substantial, *Gasthof Schaller*, on Innsbruckerstrasse, offers the best selection of Tyrolean food, as well as Austrian regulars, in a nice wood-panelled room, while the nearby *Preclarius*, also on Innsbruckerstrasse, specializes in South Tyrolean cuisine – that basically means Tyrolean cuisine with a few Italian recipes thrown in for good measure. A little further afield, the *Goldenes Kreuz* at Falkensteinstrasse 5 is a friendly, unpretentious Gasthof serving the usual range of Austrian favourites, though dishes invariably come garnished with French fries.

Schwaz is far enough away from Innsbruck to have its own **drinking and nightlife** scene; indeed its status as the principal urban centre of the Tyrolean Unterland ensures that there are a couple of clubs pulling in locals from a wide radius. Drawing a younger crowd are *Radio*, a narrow, crowded bar on Stadtplatz, and *Silver City*, Franz-Josef-Strasse, a café-bar decorated in the style of a Western saloon. *Amt*, Josef-Wopfner-Strasse, and *Parterre*, by the river on Andreas-Hofer-Strasse, cater for a dressier, twenty-to-thirty-something clientele. Cosiest and most laid-back drinking hole is *Eremitage*, Innsbruckerstrasse 14, a fashionable first-floor bar with jazz music (occasionally live) and a substantial food menu.

For clubbing, *Giovanni*, Stanser Au 1, in the industrial estate northeast of the centre on the road to Stans, concentrates on the commercial end of techno, while *On-line*, 3km east of town on the road to Jenbach, offers a harder, rave-oriented brand of dance music and the odd alternative-rock night.

Around Schwaz: Stans and Schloss Tratzberg

Travelling eastwards from Schwaz, the autobahn and rail line stay close by the River Inn, while the old Schwaz–Jenbach road (served by regular buses from Schwaz) hugs the northern side of the valley, passing after 3km through the village of **STANS**. The main reason to stop off here is to visit the **Wölfsklamm** (May–Oct daily dawn–dusk; öS20), a small but impressive stretch of gorge spanned by wooden walkways immediately north of the village centre.

Three kilometres east of Stans, an access road ascends to the left towards **Schloss Tratzberg**, another of Maximilian I's former hunting lodges, now containing a small museum (April–Oct daily 10am-4pm; öS40). On the whole, the exhibits – mostly agricultural implements and weapons – are less interesting than their surroundings, with many rooms boasting intricate Renaissance wooden ceilings. The walls of one sixteenth-century room bear frescoes depicting a genealogical tree of the Habsburg dynasty, its branches embellished with portraits of 148 family members, beginning with the first of the family to don the Holy Roman crown, Rudolf I.

The Zillertal

Backed by the impressive wall of the Zillertaler Alps and fed by a succession of deep, picturesque side-valleys (known hereabouts as the *Gründe*), the **ZILLERTAL** is the most versatile alpine vacation area east of Innsbruck. It has long been favoured by the winter package crowd, especially the British, which has led to a high degree of commercialization. Of the valley's principal centres, **Zell am Ziller** retains something of its Austrian character, while **Mayrhofen** is solely a tourist town, above which a certain soullessness perpetually hangs. On the plus side, the scenery is as grandiose as it comes, and all the facilities required for an outdoor alpine holiday are close at hand. Walking opportunities are particularly varied: the Zillertal region is well served by cable cars and chairlifts, most of which operate over the summer, making it easy for the most reluctant of hikers to reach high altitudes with the minimum of effort. Regional **hiking maps** can be purchased at the Zell am Ziller and Mayrhofen tourist offices.

Transport up the valley is provided by the privately owned Zillertalbahn railway, a narrow-gauge line that runs from **Jenbach** in the Inn Valley (all trains on the main Vienna–Salzburg–Innsbruck route stop here) to Mayrhofen, 30km away at the head of the Zillertal. A special steam-hauled train runs twice a day in summer, although tickets for this service don't come cheap (a Jenbach–Mayrhofen return will set you back öS250). From Mayrhofen, buses convey travellers into the highland valleys further south.

Zell am Ziller

Twenty kilometres south of Jenbach, the village of **ZELL AM ZILLER** is the obvious base from which to explore the mountains of the middle Ziller Valley. Cable cars to the **Gerlosstein** and the **Kreuzjoch** are within easy reach of Zell itself, while further lifts in the Gerlos Valley are only a short car or bus ride away. Comparatively free from the package tourism of Mayrhofen further up the valley, it's a quiet little place enlivened each May by a descent into alcohol-fuelled revelry known as the **Gauderfest** (see box, p.427). The village also serves as a good spot from which to observe the **Almabtrieb** (usually the first weekend in October), when the return of the cows from the alpine pastures and end of

---

ZILLERTAL SUMMER AND WINTER LIFT PASSES

For those staying any length of time in **summer** in the Zillertal, it's worth investing in a **Z-Ticket** (available early June to early Oct), which includes free travel on all cable cars, gondolas and chairlifts in the Zillertal region (including the Isskogel cable car at the Gerlos Pass) together with unlimited use of open-air swimming pools in the valley. A standard six-day pass costs öS380, while a six-day pass including free use of Zillertal trains and buses costs öS600 (in both cases, half as much for children). Either can be purchased from tourist offices and railway stations – have a passport-sized photograph ready.

Winter ski passes cost öS350 for one day and can be used on any of the lifts in the Zillertal; öS1995 will buy you a six-day pass that includes the Hintertux Glacier (öS1650 excluding the Hintertux). Resorts are connected by ski buses. Passes can be bought from tourist offices and at some of the lifts – have your photo at the ready.

the summer are marked by a procession and a final bout of merrymaking. In recent years, Zell has enjoyed a growing reputation as Austria's foremost **paragliding** centre.

There's little to actually see or do in the village itself, although the **Pfarrkirche** is worth a quick peek. Ceiling paintings by Franz-Anton Zeiller (another member of the prolific Zeiller brood of Reutte; see p.455) overlook the unusual circular nave, and near the door a sixteenth-century fresco of St Veronica, depicting the cloth that she used to mop Christ's brow and upon which his features subsequently appeared, is worth seeking out.

ZILLERTAL YEAR-ROUND ACTIVITIES

Bike rental Zell am Ziller and Mayrhofen train stations have a limited selection from öS150 per day. Sport Hausberger, Hauptstrasse 415 (☎05285/62400), and Esso-Tankstelle Obermair, Am Marktplatz 213 (☎05285/62308), both in Mayrhofen, and SB-Markt Josef Huber, Gerlosstrasse 30, Zell am Ziller (☎05282/2220), all rent out mountain bikes from öS200 per day. Mayrhofen tourist office also organizes guided mountain-bike tours.

Hiking Both the Mayrhofen and Zell am Ziller tourist offices organize guided walks for non-specialists daily throughout the summer. The Alpinschule Mount Everest (see "Rock climbing") offer more challenging walks, usually involving steeper gradients and crampon-assisted walking on glaciers. Walking maps are on sale at Mayrhofen and Zell tourist offices.

Kayaking Wildwasserschule Mayrhofen, c/o Zillertaler Flugschule, Hauptstrasse 476 (☎0664/180 2483), offers courses for beginners and intermediates either on the Zemmbach immediately south of Mayrhofen, or on the Ziller downstream.

Paragliding Flugtaxi Mayrhofen, Sportplatzstrasse 300 (☎05285/63142), Pizza Air, Zellerbergeben 4, Zell am Ziller (☎05282/2289, fax 2289-4), Pro-Aktiv Zillertal, Zell am Ziller, Stocky Air, Hippach/Ramsau 79a (☎05285/3786), and Zillertaler Flugschule, Hauptstrasse 476, Mayrhofen (☎0664/180 2483), all offer passenger flights, where you'll be strapped in tandem with an experienced pilot, from around öS750. Prices do depend on where the flight starts – departures from higher altitudes obviously stay in the air longer. The Zillertaler Flugschule also offer courses in paragliding, tailored to suit your ability range and how much time you have available.

Rafting Action Club Zillertal, Hauptstrasse 458, Mayrhofen (☎05285/62977), arrange short trips on the River Ziller to Hippach (öS400), or longer trips on the River Inn near Imst (öS770).

Rock climbing Hochgebirgs and Wanderschule Tuxertal, Lanersbach-Juns 424 (☎05287/372, fax 492-22), offer climbing courses on rocks near the Spannagelhaus beside the Hintertux Glacier, as well as climbing in ice crevasses on the glacier itself; Alpinschule Mount Everest, Hauptstrasse 458, Mayrhofen (☎05285/62829, fax 62563-4), organize day courses for intermediate climbers on the Penkenjoch above the village.

Skiing All-year skiing on the Hintertux Glacier is fine for intermediate and advanced skiers. A range of summer ski passes for Hintertux's gondolas and chairlifts is available, from about öS350 per day to öS1900 for seven days. Mayrhofen and Hintertux tourist offices have advice on where to hire equipment.

Swimming Erlebnisbad Mayrhofen, Waldbadstrasse 539 (☎05285/62559), has an outdoor pool with water slides, indoor pool, sauna and solarium (öS40); Freizeitpark, Zell am Ziller, at the south end of town by the river bank (☎05282/4946), sports a large outdoor pool with water slides.

Tennis Freizeitpark, Zell am Ziller (see "Swimming" above), and Tenniscenter Mayrhofen, *Hotel Berghof*, Dursterstrasse 220 (☎05285/62254), both have outdoor and indoor courts for around öS200–250 per hour.

THE GAUDERFEST

Celebrated every year on the first weekend in May, the four-hundred-year-old **Gauderfest** is thought to have been invented by local brewers keen to publicize the local ale, although a whole range of previously existing folk rituals have become associated with the fest over the years. Processions, various sporting contests (including wrestling on the Sunday) and the prodigious consumption of alcohol and food all serve to mark the beginning of the summer cycle of the agricultural year – the **Almabtrieb**, also a big deal in the Zillertal, marks its end. Beware the deceptively strong **Gauder beer**, brewed especially for the occasion.

Most direct route to higher altitudes, the **Kreuzjochbahn** gondola, also known as the Achtergondelbahn (late May to early Oct 8.40am–5pm) rises from the northeastern side of the village to a middle station at the 1039-metre **Wiesenalm** (also accessible by road), followed by a second stage to the 1760-metre **Rosenalm** in the shadow of the Kreuzjoch itself. From here, numerous hiking trails lead back down to the valley or to the various *Hütte* (which are signposted, together with an indication of walking time) offering traditional food and drink in rustic surroundings.

Practicalities

Turn right outside the train station to reach the **tourist office** in the centre of the village at Dorfplatz 3a (Mon–Fri 9am–noon & 2–6pm, Sat 9am–1pm; ☎05282/2281, fax 2281-80), which can fix you up with **private rooms** from around öS170 per person (rising to öS230 per person in winter), many of them in Zellbergeben, the hillside suburb west of town. Among the cheaper **hotels**, *Gästehaus Huditz*, Karl-Platzer-Weg 1 (☎05282/2228; ②), on the eastern fringes of the centre, offers rooms with shared facilities, most of which have access to flower-laden balconies. Another bargain, *Pension Helene*, Talstrasse 46 (☎05282/2169; ②), has plain but bright rooms, 1.5km south of town on the Mayrhofen road. Of the big, central Gasthöfe, *Sporthotel Theresa*, Bahnhofstrasse 15 (☎05282/2286-0, fax 4235; ⑧), is probably the swishest, with indoor pool, sauna and tennis; *Kirchenwirt*, Dorfplatz 4 (☎05282/2280, fax 3388; ④), is a less sporty alternative. *Hotel Garni Maximilian*, Bahnhofstrasse 24 (☎05282/2255, fax 3767; ③), a modern chalet-style building just south of the train station, has balconied rooms with en-suite facilities, as well as the *Piccadilly Pub* on the premises if you need a bit of on-site recreation. Those with their own transport might consider the *Berggasthof Enzianhof*, Gerlosberg 23 (☎05282/2237, fax 3237; ③, dorm beds öS200 per person), a combination hotel and mountain hut located at the top of a winding road on the hillside east of town. *Camping Hofer*, Gerlosstrasse 33 (☎05282/2248), is a **campsite** on the Gerlos Pass road 400m southeast of the centre.

For **eating**, the restaurant at *Hotel Bräu*, Dorfplatz 1, stands out above the rest, with a range of food to suit all pockets, an inexpensive choice of Tyrolean fare, more costly Austrian favourites and excellent fish. The other places on Dorfplatz, the *Tirolerhof* and the *Kirchenwirt*, also offer good-quality, mainstream Austrian fare. For something a bit different, try *Pablo's Pizzeria* in the *Hotel Zellerhof*, near the train station at Bahnhofstrasse 3.

The road to the Gerlos Pass

Zell am Ziller is the western starting point for one of Austria's most scenic cross-mountain road routes (served by five buses a day), over the **Gerlos Pass**. The most fearsome stretch of the route is on the outskirts of Zell itself, as the road zigzags its way out of the valley onto the terrace above, where the seventeenth-century

Wallfahrtskirche Maria Rast (a popular 45min walk from Zell am Ziller) sits on a mountain spur overlooking the valley. A couple of hairpin bends further up the mountain lies the village of **HAINZENBERG**, site of a small **Tierpark**, where examples of the local fauna – goats, mouflon, chamois and deer – are assembled for your inspection. At the eastern end of Hainzenberg starts the Gerlossteinbahn cable car (summer times: early June to late Sept daily 8.30am–12.30pm & 1–5pm), which ascends to the Gerlossteinhütte, overlooked by the rugged face of the 2166-metre **Gerlossteinwand**.

Twenty-five kilometres beyond Zell, the village of **GMUND** is linked by the Fürstalmbahn chairlift (summer times: July–Sept daily 9am–noon & 1–5pm) to the higher slopes on the southern side of the valley. From here it's only 3km to the next village, **Gerlos**, on the far side of which is the Isskogelbahn chairlift (summer times: mid-June to early Oct daily 9am–noon & 1–5pm), serving the alpine meadows above the valley to the north. A steady ten-kilometre climb from Gerlos brings you eventually to the **Durlassboden Reservoir**, where the 1531-metre summit of the Gerlos Pass marks the border between the Tyrol and Salzburg. From here the road descends to the upper reaches of the Salzach Valley and the Krimml Falls (see p.347), before continuing to the Pinzgau towns of Mittersill and Zell am See (p.342).

Mayrhofen

Ten kilometres south of Zell, **MAYRHOFEN** is one of Austria's biggest resort villages. Almost entirely dependent on package tourism, its rustic character lies buried beneath successive layers of fake alpine charm and gift-shop tawdriness. Yet, whatever its shortcomings, Mayrhofen remains the ideal place from which to explore the **Gründe** that fan out to the south, as well as the range of mountains more immediately at hand. The **Penkenbahn** gondola (summer times: mid-May to mid-Oct daily 9am–5pm) climbs the flanks of the Penken from a terminal at the southern end of Mayrhofen Hauptstrasse (the Finkenberger Almbahn approaches the·same uplands from a different direction; see p.430), providing access to numerous **walks**. The **Ahornbahn** gondola (summer times: mid-June to early Oct daily 9am–5pm) on the southeastern fringes of town scales the opposite side of the valley, yielding yet more fine views and hiking opportunities.

The main **skiing** areas are the Ahorn (with plenty of practice slopes for beginners) and the Penken (with numerous short intermediate runs). Longer intermediate runs, and more challenging black runs, are concentrated above Hintertux, 20km to the southwest (see p.430). Skiing on the glacier is possible all year round, making Mayrhofen one of the best places in Austria for advanced skiers to come in summer.

Practicalities

Mayrhofen's **train station** is five minutes west of the **tourist office** (Mon–Fri 8am–6pm, Sat 8am–noon & 3–6pm, Sun 10am–noon; ☎05285/2305, fax 4116-33) in the Europahaus congress centre, which handles **private rooms** of all grades and styles. In Mayrhofen itself, expect to pay around öS220 per person for rooms with en-suite facilities, öS180 for rooms with shared bathrooms; rooms in the slightly more rustic hamlets of Hollenzen and Burgstall 2km north of town are slightly cheaper. Bear in mind that room prices can be thirty percent higher in winter.

There are plenty of **hotels** offering decent-value accommodation, although many of these are block-booked by groups in winter and at the height of summer. Of the smaller Gasthöfe, *Auf der Weise*, Mayrhofen 170 (☎05285/2359; ②), is a nice balconied farmhouse 1km north of town (from the train station, turn left onto the main road) offering cosy rooms with en-suite facilities; *s'Hoamatl*, Dorf Haus, Mayrhofen 758 (☎05285/2749; ②), is a big suburban house at the southwestern end of town with some rooms with shared facilities, others with en-suite WC and shower; while the larger and more central *Haus Eder*, Hauptstrasse 457 (☎05285/2217, fax 3773; ②), has plainer though perfectly acceptable inexpensive rooms, some of which are en suite. Moving up in price, *Haus Robert*, Durst 255 (☎05285/2896, fax 3054; ③), just west of the tourist office, is a modern place where balconied rooms come with en-suite facilities and TV; the large and central *Sporthotel Strass*, Hauptstrasse 470 (☎05285/3477, fax 2205; ⑤), has indoor pool, gym and sauna.

As a rule, **food** in Mayrhofen is more expensive and more mediocre than anywhere else in the Tyrol, although there are a handful of notable exceptions. *Kaiserbründl* on Sternplatz is the place to go for inexpensive, no-nonsense traditional meat dishes like *Schweinshaxe* (leg of pork) and *Selchschopf* (shin of the same animal), while *Mamma Mia* in the *Elisabeth Hotel* on Einfahrt Mitte, just west of the Hauptstrasse, offers a perfectly acceptable range of pizza and pasta favourites. Best for high-quality Tyrolean specialities and the full range of Austrian cuisine are the *Kramerwirt*, Am Marienbrunnen, a traditional Gasthof with wood-panelled rooms, and *Wirtshaus zum Griena*, at the southern end of town at Dorf Haus 768. Consider the *Neuhaus*, Am Marktplatz, if you fancy splashing out on some excellent fish and game dishes.

The best places to **drink** in Mayrhofen change from one season to the next. The *Scotland Yard Pub*, Scheulingstrasse 372, is currently good for an Anglophone night out, while *Movies*, Am Marktplatz, is a kitsch but fun bar next to the cinema.

Beyond Mayrhofen

Immediately south of Mayrhofen, mountain roads provide access to the four side-valleys feeding the Zillertal: the Zillergrund, the Stilluppgrund, the Zemmgrund and the **Tuxertal**. Served by buses that depart from Mayrhofen train station, they all provide excellent walks.

Eight buses a day head up the **Zillergrund**, a narrow valley rising to the east of Mayrhofen with the **Ahornspitze** looming above it to the south. For private cars the road ends at *Gasthof Bärenbad* 15km out of Mayrhofen, while buses climb the extra 2km to the Zillergrund Reservoir. The two-hour trail to *Planauer Hütte* up above the reservoir's northern side is a popular medium-difficulty hike.

Southeast of Mayrhofen, the tranquil **Stilluppgrund** is accessible via toll road (May–Oct; öS80 per vehicle), and is served by a couple of privately operated minibus services (June–Sept; check in the Mayrhofen tourist office for times and pick-up points). One bus goes to the *Gasthof Wasserfälle* on the banks of the **Stillupp Reservoir** 8km up the valley (also the end of the road for private cars); another goes all the way to the *Grüne-Wand-Hütte* a further 7km up the valley. From here you can follow hiking trails that lead further up the valley, or walk back to *Gasthof Wasserfälle* to pick up another bus down to Mayrhofen.

Another route into the mountains from Mayrhofen is the scenic road into the **Zemmgrund** due south of town, for much of the year only passable as far as the *Breitlahnerhütte,* 18km south of Mayrhofen. It's a popular rock-climbing area for the experienced, and the starting point for walks into the upper Zemmgrund, which veers away to the southeast. Southwest of the *Breitlahnerhütte*, a toll road (June–Sept only; cars öS0120, bikes öS60) winds tortuously up another side-valley – the Zamsergrund – to the **Schlegeis reservoir** 6km further on.

The Tuxertal

Of all the valleys south of Mayrhofen, the **Tuxertal** is the most densely touristed, largely due to the popularity of the all-year skiing slopes on the **Tuxer Glacier** at the valley's head. Both the glacier and the resort villages in the valley below are well served by gondolas and chairlifts, providing a wealth of alpine itineraries.

First stop out of Mayrhofen 3km to the west is the village of **FINKENBERG**, where the Finkenberger Almbahn gondola (mid-June to mid-Oct 8.45am–noon & 1–4.30pm) serves the southern approaches to the Penken. Eight kilometres further up the valley is the village of **VORLANERSBACH**, renowned for its traditional wooden farmhouses, closely followed by **LANERSBACH**, where the Eggalmbahn **gondola** (late June to early Oct 8.30am–noon & 1–4.30pm) offers a direct route to the slopes of the Tuxer Alps to the west.

At the head of the valley, the village of **HINTERTUX** is the starting point for the four-section **Zillertaler Gletscherbahn** (open all year round 8.30am–5pm). The first gondola stage ascends to the Sommerbergalm, followed by a second gondola stage to the Tuxer-Ferner-Haus overlooking the **Hintertux Glacier**. After this, a couple of chairlifts bring you to the top station, just below the rocky summit of the 3286-metre **Gefrorne Wand**. From here the highest of the Zillertaler Alps are visible to the south, and the Hintertux Glacier stretches out in front of you to the northwest. Back in Hintertux, the **tourist office** in the village centre (☎05287/8506, fax 8508) will check vacancies in **private rooms** for those who want to stay.

The Achensee

Framed by the Karwendel Mountains to the west and the Rofan range to the east, the **Achensee**, the Tyrol's largest lake, nestles in the **Achental**, a highland valley on the north side of the Inn. The Achensee region is famous for its **Steinöl**, a foul-smelling unguent made from the shale once mined on the shores of the lake and used as a treatment for rheumatism, arthritis, tennis elbow and skin complaints. You'll see it on sale in local pharmacies and gift-shops. There's little to choose between the resort villages edging the shore, **Maurach**, **Pertisau** and **Achenkirch**– all three have plentiful private rooms, good bathing beaches and facilities for lake sports, notably windsurfing. Maurach and Achenkirch have the better lakeside campsites.

Buses from Jenbach and Schwaz are the best way of getting to the lake from the Inn Valley. Jenbach is also the starting point for the **Achenseebahn**, a cog railway served by steam-hauled trains that climbs up to Maurach – though ticket prices for this summer-only service are relatively high (a Jenbach–Maurach return costs öS300).

Maurach

Five kilometres north of Jenbach, the village of **MAURACH** occupies the high ground just short of the lake's southern end, where there are a couple of Strandbäder and a range of boat-rental outlets. The **tourist office** 100m east of the main road (Mon–Fri 8am–noon & 2–6pm, Sat 9am–noon; ☎05243/5340, fax 5297) will help you to find one of the numerous **private rooms** and holiday apartments. A 200-bed **youth hostel** (☎05243/5239, fax 5303) is found on the west side of the village at Lächenwise 120a, with one **campsite** next to it, *Karwendel-Camping*, Maurach 115a (☎05243/6116), and another site, *Seecamping Wimmer*, Buchau 8 (☎05243/5217), just off the northbound Akenkirch road, next to all the lakeside amenities. **Pensions** crowd the streets winding up north from the main road through town: among them, *Haus Rofangarten*, Rofangarten 39 (☎05243/5181; ②), has large, balconied rooms with traditional furnishings.

Pertisau

Six kilometres from Maurach on the eastern side of the lake, **PERTISAU** is perhaps the most commercialized of the Achensee resorts, an agglomeration of souvenir shops and big chalet-style hotels set against the backdrop of the **Karwendel Alps**. The **tourist office**, set back from the lakefront (☎05243/5260, fax 5939), has a list of **private rooms**. *Wirthaus am See*, on the lakefront next to the landing stage

(☎05243/5237, fax 5985-113; ④), is one of the Achensee's best mid-priced **Gasthöfe**, featuring comfy en-suite rooms, all with balconies and some facing the water. Pertisau is the starting point for two scenic **toll roads** (both open May–Oct), heading up into the mountain valleys of the Karwendel massif; one ascends to the **Gramaialm** hut 7km to the southwest; the other to the **Gernalm**, 5km northwest of town.

Achenkirch

Unlike Pertisau, **ACHENKIRCH**, at the northern end of the lake, has preserved something of its traditional village character. The lakefront (site of beach, boat-rental and windsurfing school) is about 2.5km south of the village centre, where the **tourist office** (Mon–Fri 8am–noon & 2–6pm, Sat 9am–noon; ☎05246/6270) by the church just west of the main road will direct you to the best of the **private rooms**. *Gasthof Zillertal*, Achenkirch 104 (☎05246/6396, fax 6993; ②), is a modern chalet-style **hotel** midway between the village centre and the lakefront; most rooms have en-suite facilities and balconies. **Campers** can choose between *Terrassencamping Schwarzenau* (☎05246/6568), on the lakefront at the southern end of town, and *Camping Achensee* (☎05246/6239), which enjoys a similar waterfront position on the other side of the Achental stream to the west. There's a small **Heimatmuseum** on the lakeside (May–Oct daily 1–6pm; öS30), with a display of local costumes and agricultural implements. The eight-kilometre **walk** from Achenkirch to Pertisau along the traffic-free western side of the lake is a popular local excursion. North of Achenkirch, the road climbs to the German frontier 10km distant, from where there's a choice of onward routes (though no public transport) to the Bavarian towns of Tegernsee and Bad Tölz.

Rattenberg and around

East of Jenbach both railway and autobahn continue to plough along the fertile floor of the Inn Valley towards Kufstein and the German border. There are few obvious stop-offs en route save for **RATTENBERG**, a delightful small town that was an important silver-mining centre until the seventeenth century, and retains a core of historic buildings. There are a couple of side-valleys worth exploring, too, most notably the **Alpbachtal** and the **Wildschönau**. Neither can compare with the majesty of the Zillertal, but they're more tranquil and less touristed as a result.

The Town

Paths from Rattenberg's **train station** lead straight down to the **main square**, an extraordinarily photogenic huddle of medieval town houses resplendent in pink, yellow and greenish hues, with a ruined hilltop castle serving as backdrop to the south. Bienerstrasse leads south from the main square towards the fifteenth-century **Pfarrkirche St Virgil**, raised on a bluff below the castle. Like the Pfarrkirche in Schwaz, the church was built with two naves, one for miners (on the right) and the other for the burghers. Heading the right-hand nave is the **St Anna altar**, whose statuary, including the touching group of angels at the base, is by Baroque sculptor Meinrad Guggenbichler, the master of Mondsee church (see p.356). At the back of the Pfarrkirche stands a shrine to **St Notburga** (1265–1313), the Rattenberg-born serving girl who became the centre of a local cult after defending the rights of servants against their rich employers. Her emblem is a sickle, a reminder of her pious refusal to work in the fields on Sundays.

North of the main square, alleyways lead down to the **Augustinermuseum** in the erstwhile Augustinian monastery (daily except Mon; 9am–noon & 2–5pm; öS40), housing a collection especially rich in Gothic wood sculpture. Perhaps the most famous exhibit here, though, is a fourteenth-century gravestone depicting local worthies Johann Kummersbacher and wife, an extraordinarily delicate piece of carving for the period.

Practicalities

Rattenberg is small enough to be treated as a day-trip destination from elsewhere in the Inn Valley, although the **tourist office**, just north of the main square in the Rathaus (Mon–Fri 9am–noon & 2–4.30pm; ☎05337/63321, fax 65417), will try and fix you up with a **private room** should you wish to stay. There are a couple of Gasthöfe on the main square – the *Platzbräu* and the *Schlosskeller* – serving up traditional Austrian **food**, while *Café-Bar Da Vinci*, north of the square on Inngasse, is the place to stop off for a **drink**.

Alpbach

Three kilometres west of Rattenberg, at **Brixlegg**, a minor road heads south up the **Alpbach Valley**, one of the Tyrol's most attractive rural stretches. A relatively quiet ski resort favoured by beginners and intermediates, the village of **ALPBACH** lies some 11km along this road, occupying an extremely picturesque position beneath the western flanks of the Wildschönau range. There's a **tourist office** in the village centre (Mon–Fri 9am–noon & 2–5pm; ☎05336/5211), which has details of **private rooms** in some of the village's large, timber-clad Tyrolean farmhouses, as well as information on local hiking trails. A two-stage **gondola** on the western side of the Alpbach leads up to the Hornboden, an area of mountain pasture just below the 2127-metre **Wiedersberger Horn**.

To reach Alpbach by public transport, catch a train as far as Brixlegg, where ten daily buses depart from the train station, calling at Alpbach village before ending up at Inneralpbach at the head of the valley.

The Wildschönau

Travelling northeast from Rattenberg, the next place of any significance is the industrialized town of **WÖRGL** 20km away, a dull little place with nothing to offer the tourist save for a key **railway junction** – it's here that the line to Kufstein parts company with the line to Bischofshofen, Zell am See and Kitzbühel.

A worthwhile detour from Wörgl, however, is to take the minor road that climbs out of town to the south towards the mountain villages beneath the **Wildschönau** range. The main settlements, served by eight daily buses from Wörgl and attractively situated in an alpine vale, are the resort villages of **NIEDERAU** and **OBERAU**, clusters of modern chalet-hotels that look a little sad once the winter crowds who come here to ski have retreated. Buses terminate at **AUFFACH**, 20km beyond Wörgl, where you can either take the Schatzbergbahn **gondola** to the southern shoulder of the 1903-metre Schatzberg, or walk the remaining 3km south to **Schwarzenau**, a hamlet at the head of the valley hemmed in by a semicircle of peaks.

Kufstein and around

KUFSTEIN was a long-standing bone of contention between Bavaria and the Tyrol until Maximilian I finally brought it into the Habsburg fold in 1504. The man whose possession of modern artillery struck fear into the heart of many a central European monarch placed a cannon nicknamed *Weckauf* ("Wake Up") on one of the nearby hills and bombarded the defenders into submission. Nowadays the hilltop fortress draws a steady stream of visitors, but Kufstein's greatest appeal is as an ideally situated base for exploring the great outdoors. Dominating the countryside east of town are the **Kaisergebirge**, a jagged limestone massif divided into two ridges: the **Zahmer** (or "tame") **Kaiser** lie to the north, and the **Wilder Kaiser** run parallel to the south, their jagged outline providing Kufstein with an impressive backdrop. Several nearby lakes – of which the **Thiersee**, **Hechtsee** and **Hintersteinersee** are the most touristed – provide Kufstein with plenty of sites for summertime bathing; also near at hand are the skiing resorts of **Söll** and **Ellmau**, both nestling beneath the southern slopes of the Wilder Kaiser.

Cycle paths running alongside both banks of the River Inn, and numerous cycling routes towards the neighbouring hills and lakes, combine to make Kufstein and surrounds a **bike-friendly** area, too. Cycling maps can be bought from the tourist office, and bikes hired from the train station or from *Hotel zum Bären* (see below).

Arrival, information and accommodation

Kufstein's **train station** is on the west bank of the Inn; cross the bridge in front of the station forecourt to reach the Unterer Stadtplatz and the **tourist office** at no. 8 (Mon–Fri 8am–noon & 1–5pm, Sat 8am–noon; ☎05372/62207, fax 61455), where you can obtain a limited list of **private rooms**. A **campsite**, *Camping Kufstein*, Salurnerstrasse 36 (☎05372/62229-55, fax 63689), occupies a grassy stretch of river bank next to the *Hotel zum Bären*.

Hotels and pensions

Gander Hof, Weissachstrasse 41 (☎05372/62432). Quiet pension in a residential area south of the centre. All rooms come with en-suite facilities. ③.

Goldener Löwe, Oberer Stadtplatz 14 (☎05372/62181, fax 62181-8). Big, centrally located hotel with comfy rooms. ④.

Hauber, Zellerstrasse 33 (☎05372/63539). Small pension on the western side of the train station, with small but adequate rooms with shared facilities. ①.

Kirchenwirt – Toni Stüberl, Zellerstrasse 17 (☎05372/62512, fax 61430). Big, modern chalet-style building on the western side of the train station, offering small and basic, balconied rooms with en-suite facilities. ②.

Zipferkeller, Marktgasse 14a (☎05372/62396, fax 62396-26). Most reasonably priced of the town-centre establishments, all rooms in this modern building have en-suite facilities and TV. ④.

Zum Bären, Salurnerstrasse 36 (☎05372/62229, fax 636894). Comfortable suburban hotel with TV and en-suite facilities in all rooms, and featuring sauna and free bicycle rental for guests. It's 1.5km south of the centre on the banks of the River Inn (from the train station, cross the river and turn right onto the riverside footpath). ⑤.

The Town

Kufstein's modern suburbs straggle along both sides of the river, but most of what you'll want to see lies huddled below the fortress on the east bank of the Inn, around **Unterer Stadtplatz**, the picturesque main square. Raised on a bluff above the square, the facade of the **Dreifaltigkeitskirche** presents a jumble of Gothic and later architectural styles. The interior, in contrast, is pretty plain, except for a florid Rococo altar with Virgin and Child beneath a crimson canopy and floaty cherubs.

The Heldenorgel

An archway above the church leads to the open-air auditorium for concerts featuring the gargantuan **Heldenorgel**, or Heroes' Organ, completed in 1931 to commemorate the dead of World War I. With its 4307 pipes occupying one of the towers (the Burgerturm) of the fortress above, and the keyboard housed at the foot of the fortress hill, next to the auditorium, it's a very difficult instrument to play – there's a 1.5-second delay between the striking of the keys and the sound of the notes. Atmospheric conditions also wreak havoc with the organ's pitch, and listening to it can be a bizarre experience, with its discordant tones blasting out across the valley. Performances (daily at noon & 6pm) cost öS10 for a seat in the little auditorium – though it can be heard almost everywhere in town – and last about fifteen minutes. They include a couple of pieces of classical organ music (often Bach) followed by a rendition of *Alte Kamaraden*, a mawkish World War I ditty honouring the fallen.

The fortress

From here a covered walkway leads up towards the pale sandstone **fortress** (daily dawn to dusk; öS40, combined ticket including the Heimatmuseum öS65), which can also be approached by lift (daily 9am–5pm; öS20 one way, öS30 return) from Römerhofgasse on the south side of Unterer Stadtplatz. Begun in the thirteenth century, its most impressive features – including the monumental cylindrical **Kaiserturm**, which towers above the central courtyard – date from the sixteenth, when the fortress was extensively modified. Below the Kaiserturm is the entrance to the **Heimatmuseum** (April–Oct daily except Mon 9.30am–4.30pm; öS35), displaying the skeletons of 30,000-year-old cave bears, an unimaginative selection of local furniture and antique weaponry, and, perhaps most compelling, an array of eighteenth-century wooden moulds used for casting wax votive objects – in this case miniature arms and legs intended to represent those parts of the body cured after a period of prayer.

The southern end of the fortress, known as the **Josefsburg** after Josef II, under whose reign it was refortified, is now a grass-carpeted area with several bastions offering views of the valley below. An open-air stage occupies the southern tip of the Josefsburg, where concerts are held in summer.

Into the Wilder Kaiser

At the eastern edge of town attractive parklands merge into the wooded slopes of the **Wilder Kaiser**, a paradise for walking and mountain-biking enthusiasts. The most direct route uphill is the Wilder Kaiser chairlift (June–Sept) 2km northwest of the centre, which ascends to the *Weinbergerhaus* hut and provides access to a plateau of pastureland beneath the rugged, inhospitable peaks that give the range its name. You can also take the Wanderbus (check times with the tourist office; öS65 up, öS45 down, öS100 both ways), which departs from the car park at the end of Pienzenauerstrasse 1km east of the centre and drives up to the starting point for innumerable forest-shrouded hiking trails, at the *Aschenbrenner Hütte*. Run by the family of mountaineer Peter Aschenbrenner, there's a mini-museum recalling his Himalayan expeditions of the 1930s inside.

Walks up the **Kaisertal**, a beautiful alpine valley suspended between the the the peaks of the Wilder Kaiser and the Zahmer Kaiser, begin at a car park 4km north of the centre at the end of Sparchnerstrasse (local Kufstein–Ebbs buses pass by). It's dubbed the "German autobahn" by locals because of its popularity with Bavarian day-trippers.

The lakes

In summer Kufsteiners head out to the string of small lakes hidden away behind the low hills northwest of the River Inn. Biggest of the lakes, and bordered by a flourishing resort that carries its name, is the **Thiersee**, 10km west of Kufstein by road and served by about nine daily buses. There are plenty of small bathing areas, a tourist office in the village centre doling out private rooms, and a campsite on the lake's western shore.

Five kilometres northwest of Kufstein, the small, forest-enclosed and altogether more modest **Hechtsee** has a Strandbad, rowing boat-rental and a popular café-restaurant. Pathways lead round the shore, through the surrounding woods and on into Germany – the border is only a few steps away from the northwestern end of the lake (it's not staffed, but take your passport in case of spot checks). Buses to the Hechtsee may run during high summer; otherwise it's easy enough to cycle there or walk from Kufstein.

Eating and drinking

Finding something to **eat** in Kufstein is rarely a problem. The Römerhofgasse harbours a couple of atmospheric old inns, and there are plenty of places offering standard Austrian fare around Unterer Stadtplatz and its eastward extension, Oberer Stadtplatz.

Inncafé Hell, Unterer Stadtplatz, is the main **daytime café**, with a good choice of lunchtime spaghettis and goulash-style dishes, and an outdoor terrace overlooking the river. Plenty of lively **evening drinking** venues dot the centre; it's really a question of bar-hopping until you find the combination of music and clientele you fit in with best.

Restaurants

Auracher Löchl, Römerhofgasse. A good range of both Tyrolean and standard Austrian fare in atmospheric, wooden-beamed surrounds, which boasts live folk music at weekends.

Batzenhäusl, Römerhofgasse. An affordable range of Tyrolean and Austrian food, in another wooden interior adorned with hunting trophies and assorted curios.

Bräu-Stüberl, Oberer Stadtplatz 5a. Dependable town-centre place with moderately priced Tyrolean and Austrian regulars, and plenty of outdoor seating round the corner on Arkadenplatz.

Weinstadl, Eichenwang, Ebbs. Six kilometres north of the centre on the Ebbs road, this is a bit out of the way for those without transport, but offers solid, unpretentious fare with a generous salad bar. A good place to go in the winter, when there's an open fire in the middle of the dining area.

Bars

Arabia, Franz-Josefs-Platz 15. Roomy and occasionally raucous pub-like venue with youngish crowd, arranged around a large circular bar.

Business, Arkadenplatz. Long thin bar with some outdoor seating catering for a slightly older, more elegant crowd.

Gimlet, Unterer Stadtplatz. Flash, trendy place worth checking out for the modernist interior design.

Kaiser-Tenne, Prof-Schlosser-Strasse 1. Busy disco-bar, 25min walk north of the centre, which caters mostly to mainstream, poppy musical tastes, though with some broader themed nights.

The Old Dutch, Römerhofgasse. Cosy and intimate, with solid, pine furniture and a traditional Austrian feel; it's run by a Dutchman, hence the name.

Söll and around

Southeast of Kufstein, the southern slopes of the Wilder Kaiser are home to the resort villages of **Söll**, **Scheffau** and **Ellmau**. Served by buses working the Kufstein–St Johann and Wörgl–St Johann routes, all three have become especially popular winter-package destinations, though they get their fair share of summer trade seeking the mountains, too.

Söll

Buzzing in winter, resuming a state of rural repose in summer, **SÖLL** is a largely modern village in which newish, chalet-style apartment buildings predominate. In its **Pfarrkirche**, however, Söll possesses the most impressive Baroque monument in the western Tyrol, its riotously stuccoed and gilded interior decked out in vivid ceiling frescoes painted by Christoph Anton Mayr of Schwaz in 1768. Everything focuses on the grandiose red marble pulpit topped by a gilded swan, symbol of Christ. At the southern margins of the village there's a gondola to **Hochsöll**, a mountainside hamlet also accessible by road; from here a cable car ascends to the upper flanks of the 1827-metre **Hohe Salve**, where most of the skiing activity takes place.

The **tourist office** in the village centre (Mon–Fri 8am–noon & 2.30–6pm, Sat 8am–noon; ☎05333/5216, fax 6180) will help book you into **private rooms** from around öS170 per person in summer, considerably more in winter. A surfeit of modern chalet-style **hotels** includes the centrally located *Feldwebel*, Dorf 73 (☎05333/5224, fax 6229; ③), which has more of a traditional Gasthof feel than some of the others, and the equally central but swankier *Postwirt*, Dorf 82 (☎05333/5081, fax 6230; ⑤). The *Postwirt* has a good restaurant serving traditional Tyrolean and Austrian **food**; the *Schindlhaus* a few steps to the south cooks up similar fare. A vibrant après-ski scene tends to attract younger tourists in winter, and there are **drinking** holes aplenty (some only open at weekends over the summer); two of the best known are the *Whiskeymühle*, a disco-bar housed in a building in the shape of a barrel, and *Buffalo's Western Saloon*, a fun pub suitably decked out.

Scheffau and Ellmau

Apart from the cable car up the 1650-metre **Brandstadl**, there's little to detain you in **SCHEFFAU**, 5km to the east of Söll. However, a road heading north out of the village offers an inviting side-trip to the **Hintersteinersee** 4km away, a small lake picturesquely situated in the shadow of the Wilder Kaiser. A Strandbad can be found at the southern end of the lake, as well as some nice walks along the eastern shore.

Five kilometres east of Scheffau, **ELLMAU** is ideally situated for short excursions into the mountains, with the awesome Wilder Kaiser to the north, and the no-less-imposing 1555-metre **Hartkaser** to the south, the latter reached by a funicular at the western end of the village. Several chairlifts to the east, ranged between Ellmau and the next village up the valley, **Going**, provide access to the flanks of the Astberg. Beyond Ellmau, it's another 10km to St Johann in Tirol.

Kitzbühel and around

Centre of a winter sports area that spreads over the easternmost corner of the Tyrol, **KITZBÜHEL** began life as a medieval copper- and silver-mining town. Today, its historic core still looks, at times, like something out of a Gothic fairy-tale. Squat, brightly painted town houses are set against a backdrop of pasture-laden hills that with the first snowfall promise a varied skiing terrain ideal for novices and intermediates. Developed as a ski resort at the turn of the century, the town became a magnet for film stars and central European society figures during the inter-war years (and a recreation centre for Luftwaffe flying aces in the 1940s). Despite the onset of package tourism, Kitzbühel still retains its rich clientele and genteel air. Those coming to Kitzbühel in search of glamour will find it at the peak of the winter season, when hotel prices are at their highest and a bejewelled beau monde descend on the town, but for the rest of the year, the atmosphere in Kitzbühel's restaurants and bars is reasonably egalitarian.

Kitzbühel can't really match St Anton when it comes to challenging the experienced skier. It does, however, possess one classic downhill route, the **Hahnenkamm** (it finishes up just west of the town centre, next to the golf course), which features prominently in the World Cup skiing calendar – usually the last weekend in January for the men, the second to last weekend for the women. Both occasions are major society events.

KITZBÜHEL ACTIVITIES

Bike rental At the train station, or at Kitzsport, Jochbergerstrasse 7 (☎05356/2504), which has a bigger range of mountain bikes.

Golf Kitzbühel is one of Austria's big golfing centres; Golfclub Kitzbühel Schwarzee (☎05356/71645) has an eighteen-hole course, with green fees starting at around öS700. There are a couple of nine-hole courses in the area, together with numerous driving ranges – contact the tourist office for details.

Hiking The tourist office provides regional hiking maps, and organizes free guided walks (Mon–Fri at 8.45am; closed Nov). A summer holiday pass (three days öS340, seven days öS450) covers all cable cars and lifts in Kitzbühel, as well as use of the Aquarena swimming pool (see under "Swimming" for opening times).

Paragliding Hermann's Flying School, Mauringweg 7 (☎ & fax 05356/4389), organizes tandem flights from öS600 upwards, and a range of courses.

Skiing The main skiing areas are on the Hahnenkamm to the west and the Kitzbüheler Horn to the east, both of which are crisscrossed by numerous beginners' and intermediates' runs. A few short black runs are to be found on the Hahnenkamm. In addition, the neighbouring resorts of Kirchberg (10km to the east) and Jochberg (10km south) and the Thurn Pass (20km south) provide access to more slopes, suitable for beginners and intermediates. Intermediate-level skiers should try out the Kitzbühel Ski Safari, an interconnected series of lifts and runs which takes you to the Hahnenkamm, south up the valley to the Thurn Pass, from where a ski bus transports you back to Kitzbühel. There's also a large cross-country skiing area in the valley floor, and a half-pipe on the Horn for snowboarders. One-day ski (öS390), seven-day ski (öS2140) and fourteen-day passes (öS3410) are available from any of the lift stations. Each covers cable cars, lifts and buses for the whole of the Kitzbühel ski region.

Swimming Indoor pool at the Kurhaus Aquarena, Klostergasse 7 (daily 9.30am–7pm; öS80); outdoor swimming at the municipal Strandbad at the Schwarzsee (öS30).

Tennis Indoor and outdoor courts at Tennis Club Kitzbühel, Jochbergstrasse (☎05356/4400).

Arrival, information and accommodation

From the **train station**, head down Bahnhofstrasse and turn left to reach the town centre, which is raised on a small hill about five minutes' walk away. The **tourist office** at Hinterstadt 18 (July–Sept & mid-Dec to mid-April Mon–Fri 8am–6pm, Sat 8am–noon & 4–6pm, Sun 10am–noon & 4–6pm; mid-April to June & Oct to mid-Dec Mon–Fri 8am–noon & 2–6pm; ☎05356/21550, fax 2307) has an array of English-language brochures and a hotel information board for those who arrive outside office hours. Prices for **private rooms** start from around öS190 per person in spring and autumn, öS220 in summer and öS270 in winter. There's a **campsite** at the Schwarzsee, the small lake 2km north of town on the Kirchberg road (☎05356/4479, fax 4479-30).

Hotels and pensions

Astron Sporthotel, Schwarzseestrasse 8 (☎05356/3211, fax 3211-15). Modern hotel with large, comfortable balconied rooms and an outdoor pool. ⑧.

Goldener Greif, Hinterstadt 24 (☎05356/4311, fax 5001). Classic town-centre Gasthof in one of Kitzbühel's oldest houses, which counts film stars and European aristocrats among its guests. Modern furnishings and TV. ⑦.

Hörl, Josef-Pirchler-Strasse 60 (☎ & fax 05356/3144). Conveniently placed between the train station and the centre, this is probably the cheapest place within striking distance of the action, offering cosy doubles, some with en-suite facilities. Single rooms, too, are not that expensive. ②.

Jodlhof, Aschbachweg 17 (☎05356/3004, fax 71997). No-frills pension on the east side of town near the Kitzbüheler Horn gondola station, offering rock-bottom doubles with shared facilities, and some more expensive rooms with en-suite facilities. ②.

Mühlbergerhof, Schwarzseestrasse 6 (☎05356/2835, fax 4488). Pension in a nice suburban house a short distance east of the centre. All rooms have en-suite facilities. ②.

Neuhaus, Franz-Reisch-Strasse 23 (☎ & fax 05356/2200). One of the cheaper options in the centre. Motorbike-friendly, ensuring a healthy influx of leather-clad guests over the summer. ③.

Rosengarten, Maurachfeld 6 (☎05356/2528, fax 72660). Friendly pension just west of the centre, behind the Hahnenkamm gondola station. All rooms come with en-suite shower and WC. ③.

Tennerhof, Griesenauweg 26 (☎05356/3181, fax 3181-70). Attractive timber-clad building with flower-decked balconies, northeast of the centre on the hillside below the Kitzbüheler Horn. Comfortable rooms with TV and en-suite bathrooms, plus a wide range of amenities including sauna and both indoor and outdoor pools. ⑨.

The Town

Downtown Kitzbühel revolves around two elongated squares, **Vorderstadt** and **Hinterstadt**, each boasting a colourful ensemble of medieval merchants' houses. A twelfth-century pile at the southern end of Hinterstadt holds an engaging **Heimatmuseum** (Mon–Sat 9am–noon; öS30), which offers a jumble of folk crafts, skiing mementos and mining artefacts – the latter revealing something of the industrial grit behind the tinseltown of present-day Kitzbühel. Between Hinterstadt and Vorderstadt stands the unassuming **Katharinenkirche**, now used as a memorial chapel honouring the dead of two world wars. Within, the small but exquisite Kupferschmidaltar was carved in 1513 by the Master of Rabenden, surrounding a relief of the Madonna and Child.

Perched on a small plateau at the northern end of Vorderstadt are two more worthwhile churches. The more obvious of the pair, the fifteenth-century **Pfarrkirche**, contains a harmonious ensemble of Baroque altars and statuary, and the Kupferschmids' family grave, a sixteenth-century slab of red marble engraved with scenes from the Passion. Immediately above, the **Liebfrauenkirche** harbours Rococo stucco-work and, in the high altar, a copy of the Cranach Madonna and Child from Innsbruck Cathedral (see p.410).

Into the mountains

Towering above Kitzbühel to the west, the 1655-metre Hahnenkamm can be scaled with the help of the **Hahnenkammbahn** gondola (summer times: early May to mid-Oct daily 8.30am–5pm; öS160 return), which rises from a station about 500m west of the tourist office. Before embarking on one of the many walking trails at the summit, savour the view of the Kitzbüheler Horn on the opposite side of the valley and the jagged ridge of the Wilder Kaiser to the north. The restaurant next to the cable-car station at the top contains a small **museum** (winter and summer only: daily 12.30–4pm; free), which tells the story of alpine sport in the region through an entertaining display of old photographs. The northern shoulder of the Hahnenkamm can also be approached via the **Fleckalmbahn** gondola (daily 8.30am–5pm), which commences just outside the hamlet of **Klausen**, 4km out of Kitzbühel on the Kirchberg road.

On the eastern side of town, the **Kitzbüheler Hornbahn** gondola (summer times: June–Oct daily 8.30am–5pm) ascends to the *Adlerhütte*, where you have the choice of going either to the 1670-metre *Alpenhaus* (also reachable by car) on the southeast shoulder of the Kitzbüheler Horn, or to the 2000-metre summit of the Horn itself.

Eating and drinking

Most of Kitzbühel's **eating and drinking** venues are around the Hinterstadt–Vorderstadt area, although it's worth descending to the lower lying, eastern part of the town centre to seek out a couple of the more interesting bars.

For faster food, a distinct lack of *Würstel* outlets means you may have to make do with *McDonald's* on Franz-Reisch-Strasse, or the *Prima* daytime self-service restaurant at Bichlstrasse 22.

Restaurants

Chizzo, Josef-Herold-Strasse 2. A dependable source of inexpensive Tyrolean dishes and mid-priced Austrian regulars, in attractive wood-panelled rooms or on a pleasant outdoor terrace.

Eggerwirt, Untere Gänsbachstrasse 12. A wide range of good-quality, inexpensive Tyrolean and Austrian food in a nice old inn.

Goldener Greif, Hinterstadt. Top-quality Austrian and international food in refined surroundings, for those prepared to splash out a little.

Huberbräu, Vorderstadt 18. A good place to get no-nonsense Austrian fare, from Wurst-and-chips-type to more substantial dishes, all at a reasonable price.

La Fonda, Hinterstadt 13. Fairly predictable Tex-Mex food, although the lively atmosphere and piped Latin music make this a popular hangout. Also a good place to drink in the evening.

Pizza & Pasta, Hinterstadt 22. Best of the Italians in town, it becomes a loud bar late at night.

Bars and cafés

Big Ben, Vorderstadt. A comfortable pub-cum-café on the main street, with outdoor seating in summer.

Grieserl, Im Gries. A cosy, unpretentious place with a traditional Austrian feel – something of an antidote to the more glitzy international establishments elsewhere.

Highways, Im Gries 20. Roomy, garish bar with a wide range of international beers and a youngish crowd.

Lichtl, Vorderstadt 9. First-floor bar with oldie music on tape, and a slightly older clientele.

The Londoner, Franz-Reisch-Strasse. Lively English-speaking pub with frequent live music and a mixed crowd of Anglophone travellers and young locals.

Olympia, Hinterstadt. One of the more popular discos in town, offering the standard selection of commercial techno.

WEST OF INNSBRUCK

West of Innsbruck, urban tourism takes much more of a back seat to the great outdoors. The attractions of the Inn Valley – the abbey at **Stams**, or small towns like **Imst** and **Landeck** – are worth a fleeting visit, but it's the deep mountain valleys that run north to south through increasingly rugged alpine terrain that merit most attention. The **Ötztal**, the **Oberinntal** and the **Paznauntal** are the main valleys to aim for, all of them offering a wide range of skiing resorts in winter and numerous hiking opportunities in summer. West of the Inn Valley, the **Arlberg** mountain range, home to **St Anton**, among the oldest of Austria's alpine resorts, marks the border between the Tyrol and the Vorarlberg. To the northwest, hard by the German border, the market town of **Reutte** and the resort village of **Ehrwald** are the two most enticing tourist targets. Nearest to Innsbruck, **Seefeld** is a beautifully situated and rather chic alpine resort, easily accessible from the Tyrolean capital.

Despite the obstacles posed by the alpine terrain, **public transport** in the area is pretty comprehensive. The A12 autobahn and main rail line forge westwards along the Inn Valley in the direction of the Vorarlberg and Switzerland, with bus routes branching off to the north and south to serve the communities in the side-valleys. Train stations such as Ötztal, Imst-Pitztal and Landeck are important nodal points, with many bus services either commencing their journeys there or passing through. Connections with the northwest, cut off from the Inn Valley by a formidable mountain barrier, are slightly more problematic. Seefeld, Reutte and Ehrwald are all served by a railway line that heads north from Innsbruck and loops through a corner of Germany before arriving back in the Tyrol. If you're approaching the area from the west, buses from Imst and Nassereith are a better bet.

Seefeld

Occupying a mountain plateau high above the northern side of the Inn Valley, **SEEFELD** offers unrivalled alpine vistas. With low-lying, grassy pastures, forested slopes and rugged peaks in almost every direction, it's hard to think of a better place for an easy-going highland holiday. Seefeld's main drawback is its reputation as a slightly snooty resort for the well-heeled, reflected in accommodation prices that are among the highest in the western Tyrol. The village itself is modern and international rather than quaintly Austrian, featuring big hotels and apartment blocks, expensive boutiques, and horse-drawn fiacres ferrying tourists around the resort.

SEEFELD ACTIVITIES

Bike rental At the train station or from Sport Sailer, Dorfplatz (☎05212/2530).

Paragliding Paragleitschule Ernst Steger (☎05212/3830-0, fax 3830-5) offers tandem flights and beginners' courses, taking off from the upper slopes of the Gschwandt-kopf.

Rafting The nearest rafting centre is at Imst in the Inn Valley (see p.447). The Seefeld tourist office has details of the numerous local firms offering day-trips there.

Swimming Outdoors at Strandbad Wildsee; or indoors at Hallenbad Olympia (daily 9.30am–10pm; ☎05212/3220) just south of the centre, with water slides, whirlpool and sauna.

Tennis Tennisclub Seefeld, Möserer-strasse (☎05212/2888); Olympia (☎05212/3220).

Walking Twice-weekly guided walks are organized by the tourist office.

HUT TO HUT IN THE STUBAI ALPS

The **Stubaier Höhenweg**, a circuit of the Stubaital to the southwest of Innsbruck, away from roads and villages, is arguably one of the finest multi-day tours of the Alps, and a perfect introduction to the Austrian hut system. With at least one pass to cross on each stage, the route is scenically varied, and challenging in places – several sections are laced with wire ropes to safeguard difficult or potentially dangerous steps. Trails are otherwise reasonably straightforward, if occasionally obscured by late-lying snow. Waymarking is mostly good, and each of the huts manned, with meals on offer, making heavy rucksacks unnecessary. Several stages are only about three hours long, so the circuit can feasibly be completed within five or six days by experienced mountain walkers – but the landscape is of such high quality that connoisseurs will allow at least eight.

Usually tackled in a clockwise direction, the tour starts from either Neustift or Neder, with the first day spent walking south through the green and pastoral Pinnistal as far as Karalm, before climbing over the 2380-metre Pinnisjoch to gain the *Innsbrucker Hütte* (☎05276/295) set just below the pass. Across the depths of the nearby Gschnitztal are the limestone Tribulaun peaks, while immediately above the hut to the west rises Habicht (3277m), whose summit is recommended to experienced scramblers. Yet more dramatic country lies ahead on day 2, as you make your way across a series of ridge spurs in order to reach the *Bremer Hütte* (☎0663/57545), simplest and most atmospheric of all the huts on the circuit. Heading west on day 3, the route crosses the Simmingjöchl and skirts below the Feuerstein peaks within sight of the Wilder Freiger (3418m) and its glaciers. Wilder Freiger is usually climbed from the next hut, the four-storey *Nürnberger* (☎05226/2492), while day 4 leads to the *Sulzenau Hütte* (☎05226/2432), passing immediately below it on a day of tarns, moraine ribs and alpine flowers. From Sulzenau to the *Dresdner Hütte*, on day 5, is another short stage, but with two routes to choose from: the most obvious crosses the Peiljoch, but a more challenging way – for experienced climbers with a good head for heights – crosses over the Grosser Trögler (2902m), gaining spectacular views of the region's highest peak, the Zuckerhütl. The *Dresdner Hütte* (☎05226/8112), though comfortable and with good food on offer, is set in a landscape devalued by ski machinery, with tows and cableways marching up to glacial ski-grounds. You leave this behind on day 6 with an eight-hour trek by way of the Grawagrubennieder – at 2881m, the highest crossing on the circuit and with a descent that goes down a loose stony gully – arriving at the next hut, the *Neue Regensberger Hütte* (☎05226/2520), which stands at the mouth of a marshy glen topped by the Ruderhofspitze. Little more than a morning's walk separates Neue Regensberger and the very popular *Franz Senn Hütte* (☎05226/2218) via the rocky Schrimmennieder on day 7, but it's another fine route and with a tempting glen to explore can fill a day. If you've enough time, a second night at *Franz Senn* allows a trip to the beautiful Rinnensee, a climb to the Rinnenspitze or a visit to the narrow notch of the Rinnennieder for its amazing contrasting views. The last full day of the walk (day 8) counts among the best – after an eleven-kilometre-long hillside traverse above the Oberbergtal, the trail shuffles screes at the foot of the dolomitic Kalkkogel massif before arriving at the *Starkenberger Hütte* (☎05226/2867), from where you can see a good portion of the whole Stubai circuit. Your last morning is reserved for the knee-troublingly steep descent back to Neustift.

A recommended map to take on the Stubaier Höhenweg is the *Kompass Wanderkarte* no. 83 (Stubaier Alpen Serleskamm), at 1:50,000. For more on the Austrian hut-to-hut system, see p.33.

Seefeld lies on Bundesstrasse 177, which climbs laboriously out of the Inn Valley at **Zirl** 12km west of Innsbruck and heads north towards the German border. It's a route served by some **buses** from the Tyrolean capital, although **trains** are more frequent, using the rail line that links Innsbruck with Ehrwald and Reutte.

The Town

Little of real vintage survives in Seefeld save for a brace of churches, of which the **Pfarrkirche St Oswald**, dominating the central square, is a real gem. A seventeenth-century king of Northumbria, who died in battle fighting the Welsh, Oswald was canonized for his role in promoting Christianity in the English northeast, and his cult subsequently propagated in central Europe by itinerant English monks. The church has been a pilgrimage centre ever since 1384, when stories circulated of the divine punishment meted out to another Oswald – local magnate Oswald Milser – who insisted that the priest gave him a special Communion wafer traditionally reserved for the clergy. Having scoffed most of the wafer, Milser was swallowed up by a fissure that suddenly appeared in the church floor. Fragments of the wafer snatched from Milser's mouth were found to be stained with the blood of Christ and were henceforth preserved in a reliquary housed in the **Blutskapelle**, accessible by stairs on the north side of the nave. The pinnacled high altar centres on a scene showing the Madonna with St Oswald (the one with curly hair and holding a cup) standing to her right. Other paintings inside the church include scenes from the lives of Mary Magdalene and St Oswald on the north wall of the choir; the death of St Oswald, together with the fate of his namesake Oswald Milser, are the subjects of reliefs on the tympanum above the south door.

At the southeastern end of the village, the small and delightful onion-domed **Seekirche** stands on a grassy knoll against a backdrop of distant mountains – a picture-postcard setting that's more interesting than the interior of the chapel. The only other thing to do in Seefeld is take a wander around the **Wildsee**, 1km south of the centre, a small lake surrounded by rushes and rich in wildfowl. There are a pay-to-enter Strandbad and boat-rental facilities at the southernmost end of the lake.

Into the mountains

East of Seefeld's train station, the *Rosshütte* funicular (daily 9am–5pm) presents the most dramatic route into the mountains, rising to the 1760-metre *Rosshütte*, where there's a great view of the Zugspitze to the northwest and a choice of routes to higher altitudes. The Seefelder Jochbahn cable car (same times) ascends eastwards to the 2064-metre **Seefelder Joch**, an area of meadow beneath the 2220-metre-high **Seefelder Spitze** – to which there's a reasonably easy fifty-minute walk. Alternatively, take the Härmelkopfbahn cable car (same times) southwards from the Rosshütte to the 2050-metre **Harmelkopf**, where there's an attractive walk down to Seefeld via the **Reither Jochalm**, site of a handy refreshment hut, or a relatively easy eighty-minute uphill walk to the 2239-metre *Nördlinger Hütte*. Once here, you can choose to tackle the medium-difficulty ascent of the 2374-metre **Reither Spitze** (1hr). The Reither Spitze and the Seefelder Spitze are connected by a popular medium-difficulty trail, thereby presenting reasonably fit walkers with a tempting circuit, ascending with one cable car, and descending by the other; total time for the circuit would be about three-and-a-half hours.

Over on the southern side of town, a chairlift (daily 9.30am–4.30pm) climbs the slopes of the **Gschwandtkopf**, where the *Ötzihütte* offers refreshments and a small display devoted to "Ötzi", the prehistoric ice man found in the Ötztaler Alps (see p.446), and a farmyard zoo for kids.

Practicalities

Heading out of the **train station**, walk straight ahead for about 200m to find the centrally located **tourist office**, at Klosterstrasse 43 (Mon–Sat 8.30am–6.30pm; ☎05212/2313, fax 3355), where you can pick up handfuls of English-language information and book **private rooms** costing öS180–280 per person in summer, öS300–400 in winter. Virtually every house in the village offers tourist accommodation of some sort, and those who arrive late in the day should be able to find a bed simply by wandering around looking for "*Zimmer Frei*" signs.

The range of **hotel** accommodation is broad enough to suit most pockets, although be aware that price categories quoted below are for summer; expect to pay 25–50 percent more in winter. At the budget end of the scale, *Stark*, Andreas-Hofer-Strasse 144 (☎05212/2104; ①), offers no-frills rooms with shared facilities (some more expensive ones have en-suite WC and shower) one block north of the tourist office. *Försterhäusl*, Hermannstalstrasse 413 (☎ & fax 05212/2779; ②), is a simple pension up by the Seefelderjochbahn station to the east of the village, and *Felseneck*, Kirchwald 309 (☎05212/2540; ②), a small house in the residential streets on the hill west of the centre, offers rooms with en-suite facilities. Stepping upwards in price, *Sonneck*, Klosterstrasse 175 (☎ & fax 05212/2387; ③), is a small, centrally located pension just west of the Pfarrkirche. The top-of-the-range *Hotel Klosterbräu* (☎05212/2621-0, fax 3885; ⑧), behind the Pfarrkirche in an old sixteenth-century monastery with modern, chalet-style additions, features indoor and outdoor pools, and every conceivable comfort.

Despite its reputation as an expensive resort, **eating** out in Seefeld need not be a traumatic experience. Most of the hotels have restaurants offering cheap Tagesmenüs at lunchtime. *Putzi's Grill*, near the tourist office on Münchnerstrasse, is the place to go for Wurst and fried-chicken snacks. The *Alte Stübe* in the Karwendelhof, Bahnhofstrasse, offers inexpensive Tyrolean specialities or more extravagant schnitzels and steaks, while *Luigi and Lois*, Innsbrückerstrasse, is a lively place with plenty of outdoor seating and a mixed Italian-Tyrolean menu. *Südtiroler Stube*, Reiterspitzstrasse 17, serves good, medium to expensive cuisine with local flavour, as well as some Italian dishes, and *Taverna Emilia Romagna*, Leutascherstrasse, has good pizzas and pasta dishes, though tables are packed in tight to fit the cosy dining room.

Of the international-style **bars**, *Café Fledermaus* on Bahnhofstrasse is a nice daytime or evening hangout that also offers good toasted or baguette sandwiches. The slightly dressier *Postbar* in the *Hotel Post* also doubles as a disco. The main Anglophone, pub-like haunts are the *Britannia Inn*, on Klosterstrasse, and *Graham's Pub*, a lively Antipodean-run hangout behind the *Hotel Eden* on Münchnerstrasse. *Le Dome*, Klosterstrasse, is the flashiest of the **discos**.

Stams

Travelling westwards along the Inn Valley from Innsbruck you'll pass by the settlements of **Zirl** and **Telfs**, pleasant enough market towns that nevertheless lack compelling attractions. If you're looking for a stop-off en route to the western Tyrol or the Vorarlberg, you'd do better to carry on as far as the village of **STAMS** 40km out of Innsbruck, site of an abbey that once served as the burial place of the *Landesfürsten*, princes of the Tyrol.

Its stocky ochre towers clearly visible across the meadows from the train station, Stams' Cistercian **abbey** was founded by Meinhard II of Tirol in the thirteenth century. The exquisite interior of the Baroque abbey **church**, its cream stucco-work and gilded altars bathed in light, is nowadays only accessible if you join a tour (May–Oct daily, times vary; öS50), which also takes in the eighteenth-century, fresco-adorned *Fürstensaal*. Sunken in the floor of the nave, the "Prince's Crypt" holds a succession of tombs watched over by statues of those buried here, including Sigismund the Rich's first wife – Scottish princess Eleonore Stuart – and Maximilian I's second wife, Bianca Maria Sforza. Sigmund's father, Duke Friedrich the Penniless, is buried round the corner in the monk's chancel. Visited separately from the guided tour, the **museum** on the first floor of the abbey complex (June–Sept daily except Mon 10–11.30am & 1.30–5pm;

öS30) assembles a small but remarkable collection of Gothic altarpieces. Pride of place goes to the anonymous *Grussitafel* of 1390, depicting the Coronation of the Virgin surrounded by saintly figures, and to the fairy-tale-like *Heuperger Altar* of 1426, in which a diamond-shaped central panel featuring the Virgin and Child is surrounded by twenty vivid scenes of holy men and mythical beasts.

Stams is easily digestible as a day-trip from Innsbruck, but a small **tourist office** just below the train station at the bottom of Bahnhofstrasse (Mon, Tues, Thurs & Fri 8–11.30am; ☎05263/6511) will fix you up with a **private room** should you wish to stay. The restaurant of the *Alte Schmiede*, just west of the abbey in the village centre, is a good place for lunch or a drink.

The Ötztal and around

Probably the most dramatic of the valleys feeding the Inn from the high Alps to the south, the **ÖTZTAL** is a deep, fertile vale that stretches southwards for over 50km to the rugged Ötztaler Alps, which mark Austria's border with Italy. Villages here draw plenty of tourists, but they're not yet the inflated parodies of alpine tourism that you find elsewhere. The main skiing and hiking centres are **Sölden**, a large package resort at the head of the valley, and the three more rustic settlements that lie above it, **Untergurgl**, **Obergurgl** and **Hochgurgl**. Two glaciers above Sölden enable year-round skiing and snowboarding, while a bewildering array of trails draw hikers in summer.

All trains on the main Inn Valley rail line stop at **Bahnhof Ötztal**, the train station at the mouth of the valley, which is now a small town in its own right; about nine buses a day head up the valley from here. There's also a popular cycle path from Bahnhof Ötztal right up the valley to Obergurgl, joining the main road for short stretches but staying apart for most of the way. It's reasonably easy cycling as far as Sölden, after which the path gets considerably steeper – fit mountain bikers might enjoy the challenge.

Even if you don't have the time to explore Ötztal in depth, you should at least try and take the bus up the valley as far as Obergurgl and back down again – a wonderfully scenic ride whatever the season.

ÖTZTAL ACTIVITIES

Mountain climbing An impressive range of high alpine peaks can be tackled as one- or two-day tours in the company of local guides, who can be contacted through Bergführerstelle Vent (☎05254/8106), Bergsport und Erleb-nisschule Sölden (☎05254/2546) and Ski und Hochgebirgsschule Obergurgl (☎05256/305, fax 503).

Rock climbing Bergsport und Erlebnisschule Sölden, Sölden (see above under "Mountain climbing"), offer climbing courses for all abilities, and guided climbs for those with experience. There's an artificial climbing wall at Sölden's main sports centre, the Freizeitarena; and rock-climbing trails can be found at various

points in the valley – Sölden tourist office will provide details.

Skiing All-year skiing is possible on the Rettenbach and Tiefenbach glaciers above Sölden to the west, where there are also a couple of ski schools for beginners. The ski areas are reached via the Gletscher-strasse mountain road.

Swimming There's an indoor pool at the Freizeitarena in Sölden, on the east bank of the river.

Walking Ski und Hochgebirgschule Obergurgl (see "Mountain climbing") offer a weekly programme of guided walks over the summer. Contact them or the Obergurgl tourist office for details.

Sölden

A modern resort village 40km south of Bahnhof Ötztal, **SÖLDEN** straggles along both banks of the Ötztaler Ache. There's not a great deal to the place: the main street, lined with most of the shops and the bigger hotels, runs along the western side of the river, and a chalet settlement of pensions and tourist apartments spreads along the eastern side. Its popularity as a winter resort rests on the fact that it offers a range of pistes suitable for all ability levels. There's also a fair amount of off-piste skiing, and a new snowboard park in the suburb of Giggijoch just north of the centre.

A number of routes lead up to the heights above the western side of the valley, where you'll find most of the ski slopes in winter and a variety of hiking routes in summer. A range of **lift passes** (also including the toll for the Gletscherstrasse; see below) is available to hikers and skiers throughout the year. In **winter**, expect to pay around öS450 for a day pass, öS2100 for six days; in **summer** you'll pay öS350 for one day and öS1600 for six days.

Hochsölden, the mountain suburb located high on a ledge above the town, is accessible by road or via the Hochsölden chairlift from the northern end of Sölden (late June to late Sept 9am–noon & 1–4pm; adult return öS75). From there, another chairlift (same times; adult return öS40) continues uphill to the **Rotkogel**, starting point for numerous walks.

At the southern end of Sölden, the Galatschkogelbahn cable car (late June to late Sept daily 9am–3.30pm; adult return öS210) offers a two-stage ascent to the 3058-metre **Galatschkogel** and access to some stupendous panoramic walks back down into the valley. A free brochure in English, *Cableway Hiking*, details a few of them and is available from the cable-car station.

Just beyond the cable-car station to the south, a right turn brings you onto the **Gletscherstrasse** (open May–Oct; cars öS210, motorbikes öS65, bus passengers öS65), a twelve-kilometre-long road served by five daily buses from Sölden over the summer. It's more of a sightseeing trip than a route to hiking destinations, climbing steeply towards the **Rettenbach Glacier** before traversing a 1.7-kilometre tunnel beneath the Gaislacherkogel to the **Tiefenbach Glacier**. You'll find all-year skiing pistes at both glaciers, and a range of chairlifts to higher altitudes.

Practicalities

Buses stop in the main street close to the **tourist office**, housed in a modern block known as the Rindlhaus (Mon–Sat 8am–noon & 2–6pm; ☎05254/2212-0, fax 3131). The tourist office will give you a list of the innumerable **private rooms** in town, from around öS180 per person in summer, öS230 in winter, though you'll have to make the booking on your own. In summer, a surplus of tourist beds makes finding a room rarely a problem – simply keep your eyes peeled for "*Zimmer Frei*" signs. Of the many family-run **hotels and pensions** on the eastern side of the river, *Jasmin*, Rettenbach 546 (☎05254/2571; ①), *Mina*, Rettenbach 90 (☎05254/2146, fax 2146-10; ②), and *Stefan Prantl*, 1km south of the centre at Kaisers 6 (☎05254/2525, fax 2525; ①), are all cosy, friendly and cheap. The *Hotel Garni Granat*, Rettenbach 171 (☎05254/2283, fax 2807; ③), just across the river from the tourist office, offers stylish balconied rooms with en-suite facilities and TV. At the other end of the scale, the top-of-the-range *Central Hotel*, Hof 418 (☎05254/2260-0, fax 2260-511; ⑨), has roomy apartments and indoor pool, sauna and solarium on site. *Camping Sölden*, at the southern end of town (☎05254/2627, fax 2627-5), is a terraced **campsite** overlooking the valley.

As for most skiing resorts, **eating and drinking** recommendations change from season to season, and many venues close during the spring and autumn. Of the places likely to be open throughout the year, there's not much to choose between the two central pizzerias: flash and loud *Gusto*, on the main street, and *Corso*, on the other side of the river, with a wider variety of Italian dishes and some Austrian, too. *Armin's Törggele Stub'n*, on the eastern side of the river, serves as a café-cum-wine bar with a good range of Tyrolean and general Austrian food. The restaurant of the *Hotel Bergland*, on the main street at Hof 286, is another dependable source of inexpensive Tyrolean staples. *Andy's Stadl*, at the southern end of the main street, is a self-consciously rustic and wood-panelled bar, with Tyrolean music on tape. Next to the tourist office in the Rindlhaus, there's a choice between the lively *Bierhimmel* on the first floor or the more sedate *Café-Bar Rindele* below.

Above Sölden: Vent, Obergurgl and Hochgurgl

South of Sölden, the main road climbs steeply via a succession of hairpin bends to the hamlet of **ZWIESELSTEIN**, where a secondary road up to the Ventertal (served by daily buses from Sölden in summer) bears to the left. Thirteen kilometres further along is the village of **VENT**, dominated by the Tyrol's highest peak, the 3768-metre **Wildspitze**, rising to the northwest. A **tourist office** in the centre of the village (Mon–Fri 9am–noon &

ÖTZI THE ICE MAN

On September 9, 1991, German climbers Erika and Helmut Simon were walking on the Hauslabjoch on the Austrian–Italian border when they noticed a half-exposed human form protruding from the ice of the Similaun Glacier. The couple reported the find to the local police upon their arrival at the nearest alpine hut, and a helicopter was sent to investigate the following day. It took another three days for police and mountain rescue teams to free the body from the ice, during which time it became apparent that this was an extraordinary find. The world-renowned Tyrolean mountaineer Reinhold Messner, who visited the site out of curiosity because he happened to be in the area, immediately declared the corpse to be at least 3000 years old. Such an estimate was considered wildly exaggerated at the time, although it was enough to encourage Austrian state television to send a camera team to film the corpse being airlifted off the mountain – footage that was to be beamed around the world as soon as the true importance of the find became known. Archeologists from Innsbruck University were on the scene within a week to retreive objects found alongside the corpse, although it wasn't until the body had been subjected to carbon dating that the ice man's true age – about 5500 years – was established.

Christened **Ötzi** in honour of the Ötztal above which he was found, the ice man yielded a wealth of new information about Neolithic culture in the region. Not only was the body remarkably well preserved, revealing a dark-haired, blue-eyed individual sporting charcoal tattoos, but he'd also managed to take a wide range of Stone Age artefacts to his grave. He was equipped with well-made shoes featuring separate soles and uppers, a bearskin hat, a flint knife, and a rudimentary rucksack made of skins mounted on a wooden frame. How he came to be on the Hauslabjoch remains the subject of much conjecture, although the idea that the Neolithic population on both sides of the Alps was using the high mountain passes to conduct trade remains an appealing one.

Ötzi soon became a symbol of Austrian, and more specifically Tyrolean, pride, even though it had been common knowledge in the days following Ötzi's discovery that the exact spot on which he was found lay a full 10m on the wrong side of Austria's border with Italy. Despite Ötzi's adoption by a fascinated Austrian public, he technically belonged to the Italians. Notwithstanding the strong local passions aroused, the Austrian and Italian governments just about succeeded in turning the Ötzi case into an example of internationalist cooperation rather than nationalist tub-thumping, allowing Innsbruck University to proceed with their analysis of the body on the understanding that he would ultimately be handed over to the Italians. While most Austrians were resigned to the move, the choice of the Italian city of Bolzano (which, under the name of Bozen, was part of Austria until 1918) as his final resting place rubbed salt into some Tyrolean nationalist wounds, as one group threatened to destroy the corpse should it ever leave Austrian soil. In January 1998, however, Ötzi left Innsbruck complete with police escort to take up residence in Bolzano, where a £6-million museum has been built in his honour.

2–5pm; ☎05254/8193, fax 8174) has a list of **private rooms**, with prices ranging from öS250 per person in summer, öS300 in winter. Though favoured by serious climbers because of the wide choice of mountainscapes within striking distance, there are plenty of opportunities around Vent for the less ambitious, with hiking trails leading up starkly beautiful side-valleys like the **Rofental** to the southwest and the **Niedertal** due south. The head of the Niedertal is overlooked by a high mountain pass known as the Niederjoch, across which shepherds from the Schnaltal on the Italian side of the border drive thousands of sheep every summer in search of grazing land – a practice dating back to the thirteenth century. The timing of the event depends on the weather, so contact the tourist office in Sölden for details. Just west of the Niederjoch is the Hauslabjoch, where the 5500-year-old corpse known as **Ötzi** (rendered somewhat inelegantly into English as "Frozen Fritz") was discovered by German hikers in September 1991 (see box).

Obergurgl and Hochgurgl

After Zwieselstein, the main southbound road continues climbing towards the hamlet of Untergurgl, before ascending above the tree line a few kilometres further on to **OBERGURGL**, the highest village in the Tyrol, its valley girdled by glaciers and hemmed in by ridges and summits well in excess of 3000m. It's a place that revolves largely around winter sports, although a steady stream of hikers are drawn here over the summer by an unparalleled menu of alpine walks (see box on p.448). The local **tourist office** (Mon–Fri 8am–12.30pm & 2–6pm, Sat 8am–noon) is in the village centre – where buses from Sölden stop – and has lists of **private rooms** in Obergurgl and Untergurgl as well as Hochgurgl higher up.

Beyond Obergurgl, the road doubles back on itself to rise to **HOCHGURGL**, the highest of the Gurgl settlements and another winter resort in its own right. From here, a **toll road** (June–Sept; öS200 per car, öS70 per motorbike) ascends to the 2509-metre **Timmelsjoch Pass**, which offers breathtaking panoramas before beginning a tortuous descent into the Italian South Tyrol.

The Landeck region

Beyond Bahnhof Ötztal, the main road and rail routes continue to follow the River Inn as far as **Landeck**, where they leave the valley to begin their slow ascent of the Arlberg Pass. Provincial, workaday Landeck is of no great beauty, but it's a good base from which to visit the adjacent valleys of the **Oberinntal** (or Upper Inn Valley) and the **Paznaun**, the name given to the valley of the **River Trisanna**. The Oberinntal harbours a string of small, low-key alpine resorts – **Ladis**, **Fiss**, **Serfaus**, **Pfunds** and **Nauders** are the places to aim for – while the Paznaun boasts the much ritzier skiing village **Ischgl**, an international package-holiday favourite.

Imst

Travelling west along the main rail line or motorway from Bahnhof Ötztal, you'll pass **IMST**, a small market town lying slightly to the north of the main Inn Valley, best known for its **Schemenlaufen** (or "ghost dance"), held on a Sunday in February every four or five years (the next one is due in the year 2000). Consisting of a large procession of elaborately costumed figures, each with their own lolloping dance, the festivities are rooted in pagan rituals designed to drive away the spirit of winter.

Imst is also renowned as the most important **rafting centre** of the Inn Valley – in fact tourist offices in towns all over the western Tyrol run trips here. The biggest of the local companies offering excursions, during which you'll be challenged to negotiate fast-flowing sections of the river in a large dinghy, is Outdoor-Zentrum Haiming, Alte

HUT TO HUT IN THE ÖTZTALER ALPS

Obergurgl and the Gurglertal

The downhill ski industry has claimed some of the slopes around **Obergurgl**, but there remain plenty of good walks amidst dramatic and unfussed mountain scenery. One of the best of these, which doesn't involve glacier crossing, is that to the *Hochwildehaus* (phone via the *Langtalereck Hütte*: ☎05256/233), a hut set fabulously on the east bank of the Gurglerferner Glacier, at the head of which rise the Hochwilde (3482m), Annakogel (3336m), Mitterkamm (3200m) and Karles-Spitze (3469m), among other peaks. The route is straightforward, takes about **four to five hours** from Obergurgl, and visits both the *Schönwies* and *Langtalereck* huts on the way. Both of these are set in idyllic locations – the first at the mouth of the Rotmoostal glen, the second with a full frontal view of the Gurglerferner's icefall.

On the west flank of the Gurglertal, opposite the Langtalereck Hütte but almost four hundred metres higher, sits the Ramolhaus, another DAV hut wardened in the summer months. A recommended walk to it along the Ötztaler Jungschützenweg takes about three and a half hours from Obergurgl, and makes an excellent introduction to the valley. There is, however, a longer traverse for fit walkers, along a trail that begins at Zwieselstein about 18km from the Ramolhaus (%05256/223), and with a difference in altitude of 1556m. Several small tarns add sparkle to the landscape along the way, and there are a few modest summits accessible to walkers on the ridge above. The most northerly of these is the 3163-metre Nederkogel, from whose summit you can see the snowy masses of the Ötztaler Alps spread in a great arc, while to the east, across the deep Ötztal, the Stubai Alps are equally impressive.

Across the Ötztaler Alps

A reasonably tough three-day crossing of the north flank of the Ötztaler Alps, avoiding glaciers but nudging the highest peaks, gives a first-rate tour amidst outstanding alpine scenery. It starts in the Kaunertal on the district's western fringe, where the rustic *Gepatschhaus* (☎05475/215) provides overnight accommodation at the southern end of the **Gepatschspeicher reservoir** (reached by infrequent bus from Landeck via Prutz). From here a meandering trail climbs eastwards to the 3095-metre Ölgrubenjoch, a bare saddle with stunning views of the Wildspitze ahead to the east. Above to the right the Hinterer Ölgrubenspitze (3296m) is worth an hour's detour if you have the energy. From the *Joch* you descend steeply into a glacial basin below the Sexegertenferner to gain the *Taschach Haus* (☎05413/8239), a DAV hut often used as a base for ice-climbing courses – there's an impressive icefall nearby, which provides an ideal training ground. Day 2 continues down-valley as far as the Riffelsee along the balcony path known as the Fuldaer Höhenweg; you then descend to Mittelberg before starting a demanding ascent to the *Braunschweiger Hütte* (☎05413/8236) set on the edge of a turmoil of glaciers, with the Wildspitze now to the southwest. Day 3, and the final stage of the crossing, scrambles along a ridge above the hut (there's a herd of ibex here), negotiates the Pitztaler Jöchl (2995m) and descends through the wooded Reifenbachtal to Sölden, in the upper reaches of the Ötztal.

A recommended **map** for either of the above tours is the Kompass *Wanderkarte 43* (Ötztaler Alpen), 1:50,000. For more on the Austrian hut-to-hut system, see p.33.

Bundesstrasse 27, Haiming, Imst (☎05266/87188, fax 87311). A short trip on the River Inn costs around öS500, with reductions for children under 13, while a longer, more hair-raising trip on the whiter water stretches of the river (over-13s only) costs around öS600.

Imst-Pitztal **train station** is 3km south of town; regular buses run into the centre. Downtown Imst consists of a long main street (named Kramergasse, Johannesplatz then Pfarrgasse respectively) snaking its way from south to north. Halfway along this main strip, the **tourist office** at Johannesplatz 4 (Mon–Fri 8am–noon & 2–6pm, Sat 9am–1pm; ☎05412/6910-0, fax 6910-8) will help with accommodation. At the northern end of the main street, there's a **Pfarrkirche** with some arresting outer frescoes, notably an animated fifteenth-century scene of local miners at work. The only other reason to linger here is the **Rosengartenschlucht**, a 1.5-kilometre-long gorge accessible via a pathway just opposite the tourist office – a pleasant torrent-side walk through parkland and forest to the hillside suburb of **Hochimst** to the west.

Landeck

Originally a fortress town guarding the eastern aproaches to the Arlberg Pass, **LANDECK** is today a pretty drab, semi-industrialized place, important to travellers as a source of buses into the surrounding mountains rather than as an attraction in its own right. Occupying a hillside above the River Inn to the southeast, central Landeck huddles below the fifteenth-century **Pfarrkirche St Oswald**, a beautifully proportioned late-Gothic structure built by Oswald von Schrofenstein, erstwhile lord of a (now ruined) castle that clings to the hillside on the opposite side of the river. The high altar (the so-called *Schrofensteinaltar* of 1513) centres on a scene of the Adoration; the predella shows St Oswald, together with Oswald von Schrofenstein and his wife, kneeling in prayer. Von Schrofenstein's symbol, a rampant goat, adorns both his tomb, on the south wall of the nave, and his *Totenschild*, or memorial shield, close by the high altar.

Uphill from the church, the thirteenth-century **Schloss Landeck** houses a fairly parochial **folk museum** (daily: June–Sept 10am–5pm; Oct 2–5pm; öS30), proffering the usual range of Tyrolean wooden furniture, and a room devoted to Jakob Prandtauer, the locally born architect responsible for the famous Benedictine abbey at Melk (see p.154). Period rooms upstairs include an example of the *Rauchkuche*, the open-hearthed kitchens common in Tyrolean farmhouses, and a display of the floral head-dresses worn by cows (the better the milk yield, the bigger the head-dress) at the time of the *Almabtrieb*, the mid-September descent from the high alpine pastures.

Practicalities

Landeck **train station** is 2km east of town, whence half-hourly local buses trundle to the **bus station** at the northern end of the main street, Malserstrasse. The **tourist office**, at the southern end of Malserstrasse (Mon–Fri 8am–noon & 2–6pm, Sat 8am–noon; ☎05442/62344), will help you with **private rooms**, although there are more of these in surrounding villages than in Landeck itself (you'll need your own transport). Nicest of the hotels and pensions are in **Perfuchs**, a hillside suburb overlooking the town centre on the west bank of the Inn: *Pension Thialblick*, Burschlweg (☎05442/62261; ②), and the nearby *Pension Paula* on the same road (☎05442/63371; ②), both offer good-value B&B-style accommodation. In the centre of town on the east bank of the Inn, *Gasthof Greif*, Marktplatz (☎05442/62268; ③), is an old-style inn with plain, old-fashioned rooms, while *Hotel Schrofenstein*, Malserstrasse (☎05442/62395, fax 64954-55; ④), is the best of the big business hotels on the main street.

Landeck's two **campsites** are west of the centre on the road towards the Arlberg and the Paznaun: *Sport Camp Tirol*, Bruggen (☎05442/64636, fax 64037), 1km from the centre on the north bank of the river Sanna, organizes a range of rafting, paragliding and biking trips and tends to fill up with large school groups as a result; *Camping Riffler*, Bruggfeldstrasse 2 (☎05442/62477-4, fax 62477-5), on the south bank of the Sanna, is closer to the centre and a bit quieter.

For **eating**, *Prima*, Malserstrasse 36, is a cheap and cheerful self-service place catering for daytime shoppers. The restaurant of the *Gasthof Greif* serves up more substantial, no-nonsense schnitzel-and-chips-style meals, and the *Goldenes Fassl*, up the hill from the tourist office on Malsergasse, offers a higher standard of Tyrolean and Austrian cuisine and usually a couple of vegetarian choices. The best place in which to **drink** away the evening is *KLA4* (pronounced "Klavier") hidden behind a bank at Malserstrasse 11, a fashionable but friendly basement bar, which also does a range of hot meals.

The Oberinntal

Southwest of Landeck, the main road follows the River Inn into the **Oberinntal**, a wide vale surrounded by high Alps. Twelve kilometres out of town the village of **PRUTZ** offers a choice of routes: either straight on towards the Swiss border or uphill westwards to a terrace of highland pastures, and a sequence of three small resort villages. On the lip of the terrace is **Ladis**, a ruined castle at its centre, with excellent views across the valley towards the mountains of the Kaunertal. There's a **tourist office** (Mon–Fri 9am–noon & 2–5pm) on the main road through the village, and a Gasthof on the main road, the *Rose*, which serves good Tyrolean fare. The road continues along rolling pasturelands to **FISS**, dominated by large, modern chalet-style hotels, which again has a **tourist office** on the main road. Four kilometres further on, **SERFAUS** has been equally commercialized, although the core of the village still retains a great deal of character. It's both a resort and a working agricultural village, where chickens strut the back alleys and the smell of dung is never far away. **Buses** from Landeck stop just outside the **tourist office** in the centre (Mon–Fri 8.30am–noon & 1–5.30pm, Sat closes 5pm), which will help with accommodation. Just above the tourist office, the squat, medieval pilgrimage church of **Unsere Liebe Frau** has fragments of fifteenth-century frescoes, including a Last Judgement to the right of the entrance.

Seventeen kilometres south of Prutz, **PFUNDS** is a village that lacks extensive ski slopes of its own but nevertheless serves as a winter resort with access to pistes further up the valley around Nauders. In summer, it's also a good base for hiking. For the less active, the late-Gothic high altar in the village **Pfarrkirche** provides another reason to stop here.

Three kilometres south of Pfunds, a right fork in the road leads up the Schergenbach Valley to the small ski resort of **SAMNAUN**. Although part of Switzerland, Samnaun is only accessible from the Austrian side of the border, and enjoys special, duty-free status – thereby making it a popular day-trip destination for tourists and shoppers.

The main road south of Pfunds continues to follow the upper Inn Valley into Switzerland, where the Oberinntal becomes the Engadine. **Buses** from Landeck and Pfunds run to Scuol, where you can pick up connections to the glitzy resorts of St Moritz and Davos. Alternatively, you can take a southeast-bound road that stays on the Austrian side of the border, climbing over the Finstermünzpass to **Nauders**, another ski-resort village offering hiking opportunities in the summer.

The Paznaun

Narrow and densely wooded, with alpine pastures dotted with log-built barns covering the valley floor, it's easy to see the **Paznaun**'s rustic appeal. **Ischgl** is the valley's main centre, although **Kappl**, in the lower reaches of the valley, and **Galtür**, at the southern end of the valley, are small resorts in their own right. A summer **hiking pass** lasting six days (öS450) is available from Ischgl tourist office, and covers the cable cars and gondolas in Kappl, Ischgl and Galtür, as well as in Samnaun over the mountains to the east.

Ischgl

Sprawled across the eastern slopes of the valley 30km southwest of Landeck, **ISCHGL** is a largely modern village that relies almost exclusively on the winter-package trade and can be relatively quiet in summer. Its reputation as an all-year-round activity centre, however, is growing, with a bit of help from the Ischgl tourist office. Having earned an unrivalled reputation for mixing tourism with showbiz, Ischgl kicks off both the winter and summer seasons (mid-July and early December respectively) with big gala concerts that pull in international pop performers. In addition, the 2300-metre Idalpe above the resort to the southeast plays host to open-air rock concerts on May 1 every year, in what is basically a vast PR exercise designed to put Ischgl on the international tourist map. Putting the glitz aside, summer activities are increasingly well catered for: "Fun Sport City" just below the village in the valley bottom includes ramps for skateboards and BMX bikes, an artificial rock-climbing wall, and beach-volleyball and street-soccer facilities. There are also plenty of possible itineraries for hikers, most immediate of which is to take the gondola, which ascends to the **Idalpe** – you can then walk eastwards and descend by cable car to Samnaun (see opposite) in the next valley, where you can return to Ischgl by bus via Landeck (check the local tourist office for times before attempting this route). The **Fimbertal**, a narrow side-valley running southwards from Ischgl, is also well worth exploring.

Ischgl's **tourist office**, in the centre opposite the main bus stop (Mon–Fri 8am–6pm, Sat 8am–noon & 4–6pm, Sun 8am–noon; ☎05444/5266-0, fax 5636), will help you find a **private room** or **hotel** bed; prices for the former hover around öS180–220 in summer, twice as much in winter. Ischgl is full of restaurants and bars, although trends change from one season to the next, and many of them close in summer.

Beyond Ischgl

Ten kilometres up the Paznaun Valley by road from Ischgl, **GALTÜR** is another small village serving the winter-package trade, though traditionally slightly cheaper than its neighbour and popular with beginners. Above Galtür, the **Silvretta Hochalpenstrasse** toll road (mid-April to mid-Dec; öS100 per vehicle) continues southwestwards, clinging to the side of the increasingly narrow upper Trisanna Valley before arriving at the Bielerhöhe saddle and the Silvretta Reservoir, and descending into the Montafon Valley (see p.476). Buses from Landeck run as far as Bielerhöhe, where you can pick up connections to Schruns on the other side of the pass.

The Arlberg resorts

Straddling the border between the Tyrol and the Vorarlberg, the Arlberg massif is home to some of the most varied skiing terrain in the whole country, and presents both summer and winter visitors with mountainscapes of desolate beauty. The main resorts in the area are **St Anton** and St Christoph on the eastern, Tyrolean, side of the Arlberg summit, and **Zürs** and **Lech**, which fall in the province of Vorarlberg to the west and are covered in Chapter 10. You can stay at any of these resorts and make use of the facilities of the whole region, although generally St Anton and St Christoph offer the most direct access to slopes around the region's highest peak, the 2809-metre **Valluga**. Approaching the region from Landeck, the main westbound road and rail routes follow the Rosanna Valley upstream into the Stanzertal, entering tunnels at St Anton that emerge 10km later on the Vorarlberg side of the 1793-metre **Arlberg Pass**. A minor road from St Anton winds its way over the pass itself (served by local buses working the St Anton–Lech route), passing through the chic skiing hamlet of **ST CHRISTOPH AM ARLBERG**. A small cluster of top-notch holiday dwellings, the resort began life as a fourteenth-century hospice built by local shepherd Heinrich Fidelkind von Kempten. The hospice building survived until 1957 when it was destroyed by fire, and a luxury hotel, the *Hospitz-Alm*, has now been built in its place. It's been a fairly snooty place ever since, and tourist development has been deliberately limited in an attempt to preserve its exclusivity.

Buses continue from St Christoph towards Rauzalpe, 4km beyond, where you can pick up connecting services to Zürs and Lech.

St Anton

A fashionable winter tourism centre since the 1920s, **ST ANTON** rivals Kitzbühel as the Tyrol's swishest society resort. St Anton owes its place on the sporting map to local man **Hannes Schneider**, who started a ski school here in 1907, and together with British winter sports pioneer Sir Arnold Lunn inaugurated the **Kandahar Cup** (named after Lord Roberts of Kandahar, a sponsor of alpine skiing), a classic downhill race that still features in the World Cup calendar every December. For today's skiers, relatively accessible nursery slopes make St Anton a reasonable choice for beginners, although it's the steep descents and off-piste opportunities beloved of the more experienced that make St Anton what it is.

St Anton's reputation for glamour was boosted by future purveyor of Nazi propaganda **Leni Riefenstahl**, who, having given up dancing for a career in the movies, made a name for herself directing and acting in the romantic skiing adventures that were very much in vogue: her 1931 film *Der Weisser Rausch* (*White Frenzy*), a tale of love on the Arlberg pistes, was a landmark of the genre. St Anton still has a reputation for attracting the rich and famous in winter, when its bars and discos throb to the beat of ringing cash registers, although the place can revert to rural tranquillity over the summer, when a less glitzy crowd of hikers and sightseers moves in.

Into the mountains

St Anton itself isn't much more than a pedestrianized strip of hotels, restaurants and boutiques, and it's best to head for higher altitudes as soon as possible. Most of the skiing takes place on the slopes north and west of town, where the main cable-car routes are located. On the western side of town, the Galzigbahn (summer opening: mid-July to late Sept) rises to the 2185-metre **Galzig** (also served by a lift from St Christoph), where a two-stage cable car (same times) continues upwards to the 2650-metre **Vallugagrat** beneath the dramatic **Valluga**. On the north side of St Anton train station, the **Kandaharbahn** funicular (summer opening: early June to late Aug) ascends to the 1846-metre **Gampen**. If you're staying in the region for any length of time in summer, it makes sense to invest in a seven-day **hiking pass**, which covers all cable cars and funiculars at a cost of öS390 – or öS490 with use of St Anton's indoor swimming pool thrown in.

Practicalities

St Anton's **train station** is just north of the largely pedestrianized Hauptstrasse that threads its way through the village. The **tourist office** (Mon–Fri 8am–noon & 2–6pm, Sat 9am–noon, Sun 10am–noon; ☎05446/22690) is at the street's western end, where **buses** also stop. They'll help you to find a **private room** for around the öS200 mark in summer (öS300 in winter).

In winter, **après-ski** begins on the upper slopes at dusk and gradually moves down to the valley below. The *Verwallstüberl* on Galzig is a popular place for a drink and a bite to eat; halfway down the hill from Galzig, two popular bars that also do food are *Krazy Kanguruh* and *Mooserwirt*. Bars in the centre such as *Drop In* and *Piccadilly Pub*, both on the Hauptstrasse, and *Underground*, a block away to the southeast, do a roaring trade in winter and are likely to be open for at least a couple of months in summer.

Northwestern Tyrol: Ehrwald, Reutte and around

The **northwestern Tyrol** lies cut off from the Inn Valley by the Lechtaler Alpen, and presents an alpine environment subtly different to the deep mountain valleys to the south. The lush, open vale of the **Lech Valley** around the market town of **Reutte** makes for a pleasant stop-off en route to the German border just to the north, while the Ehrwald region, a basin of pasture land presided over by the jagged grey mass of the

Zugspitze, presents one of the most dramatic landscapes in the Tyrol. **Ehrwald** itself is the main centre to aim for here, the neighbouring villages of **Lermoos** and **Biberwier** being little more than its package-resort satellites.

The easiest way to get to northwestern Tyrol from the Inn Valley is by train from Innsbruck, although there's also a road over the mountains from Imst (served by buses from either Innsbruck or Imst), which passes through the village of **Nassereith** before climbing over the scenic **Fern Pass**. Nassereith itself doesn't merit a stop, and it's best to press on to **Schloss Fernsteinsee**, the local beauty spot 7km north, where there's an attractive little lake fringed by woods and mountains, a Gasthof with a good (if often busy) restaurant, and a **campsite**. The 1216-metre-high summit of the Fern Pass is only 2km beyond, after which it's only a short distance to the *Gasthof Zugspitzeblick*, site of another roadside restaurant and a marvellous view of the **Zugspitze**. After a steep descent, a minor road heads off for the resort villages of Biberwier and Ehrwald, while the main road continues via tunnel to Lermoos and Reutte.

Ehrwald

Couched in the shadow of the Zugspitze and ringed by a series of similarly rugged mountains, **EHRWALD** is a resort village favoured by German and Dutch tourists, which nevertheless retains a rustic, unhurried atmosphere. It's an excellent base for a range of outdoor activities: the main skiing regions are the **Ehrwalder Alm** immediately east of Ehrwald, the **Marienberg** just above Biberwier, the **Grubigstein** above Lermoos, and the **Zugspitzplatt** below the summit of the Zugspitze – which, despite being on the German side of the border, is accessible from the Austrian side via the

---

EHRWALD ACTIVITIES

Bike rental *Intersport Leitner*, Kirchplatz 13 (☎05673/2371), and *Zweirad Zirknitzer*, Zugspitzstrasse 16 (☎05673/3219), both offer a range of mountain bikes for around öS200–250 per day.

Hiking A selection of hiking trips with local guides (including easier walks for families with children) are organized by Ehrwald tourist office from around öS180 per participant. *Bergsport Total*, Kirchplatz (☎05673/3461), organize more demanding walks (more expensive, but worth considering if you want to attempt mountain paths that you wouldn't try on your own), as well as provide guides for mountaineering expeditions. A couple of local guides offer llama trekking (a day-trip in the mountains with the incongruous beasts serving as baggage-carriers); contact the tourist office for details.

Paragliding Contact *Bergwanderschule Zugspitze*, Unterdorf 23, Lermoos (☎05673/3474).

Rafting *Bergsport Total* (see under "Hiking" above) or Ehrwald tourist office

have details of rafting excursions (from öS500 per trip) to either the Lech Valley to the west, or the Inn Valley to the south.

Riding *Pension Müllerhof*, Biberwier (☎05673/2344), offer a range of guided treks throughout the summer.

Rock climbing The Zugspitze region holds rock-climbing routes for all grades of ability. *Bergsport Total* (see under "Hiking" above) have details, and also offer equipment hire and guided climbs.

Swimming The indoor pool at Familienbad Ehrwald, Hauptstrasse 71 (daily 10am–8pm; öS60; ☎05673/2718), features a children's area, water chutes, sauna and gym. There's an outdoor pool at *Hotel Spielmann*, Wettersteinstrasse 4 (daily 9am–6pm; öS35; ☎05673/2225).

Tennis Indoor courts are available at *Zugspitz-Tennishalle*, Ehrwald (daily 8am–11pm; hourly rates öS120–160 depending on the time of day; ☎05673/3135).

Tiroler Zugspitzbahn cable car and is included in some of the local **ski passes**. Best of these is the Happy Ski Pass (at the time of writing, there's no summer equivalent for hikers), which covers the Ehrwald region as well as Seefeld and the German town of Garmisch-Partenkirchen. The Pass costs öS960 for three days; other durations (six, thirteen and twenty days) are available. There are good nursery slopes just outside Lermoos, a range of intermediate runs on the Zugspitzplatt, and plenty of cross-country skiing tracks in the valley floor.

One of the best times to be in Ehrwald is **Midsummer's Night** (known here as *Bergfeuer*, or "mountain fire"), when bonfires are lit on the mountains ringing the valley.

Into the mountains

Highlight of any trip to Ehrwald is the cable-car ascent of the **Zugspitze**, the inhospitable 2968-metre peak marking the Austro-German border. Buses (5–6 daily) run from Ehrwald's central Kirchplatz to the terminus of the **Tiroler** Zugspitzbahn cable car at **Obermoos**, 5km northeast of town (daily: May–Oct 8.30am–4.30pm; Dec–Easter 9am–4.30pm; öS420 return). In summer, Ehrwald tourist office organizes a weekly walk (usually on Fridays) from the top of the Zugspitze down to Ehrwald itself, using the route known locally as the **Gatterl**. The higher sections of the walk are icy throughout the year, but it's worth considering if you're reasonably fit.

Less spectacular than the Zugspitze, but providing access to a wider range of easy hikes, is the **gondola** to the **Ehrwalder Alm** (May–Oct & Dec–April daily 9am–4pm; öS130 return), which starts about 1km east of Ehrwald's Kirchplatz. There are numerous trails leading across the alpine meadows at the top, most popular of which is the one-hour walk along gravel track to the **Seebenalm** to the southwest. Just above the Seebenalm hut is the small mountain lake, the **Seebensee**, the south end of which provides a classic view back towards the Zugspitze – one of the Tyrol's more famous alpine vistas.

Practicalities

Ehrwald's **train station** is at the northern end of the village about 1km from the centre, while **buses**, more conveniently, drop passengers on the central Kirchplatz, a few steps away from the **tourist office** at Kirchplatz 1 (Mon–Sat 8.30am–noon & 1–6pm; ☎05673/2395, fax 3314). Ask at the tourist office about booking one of the plentiful **private rooms**, at around öS180 per person in summer, öS260 in winter. Of the numerous **hotels**, *Grüner Baum*, Kirchplatz (☎05673/2303, fax 3477; ④), is comfortable and modern with smallish, balconied rooms, while the *Alpin*, Hauptstrasse 29 (☎05673/2279; ③), offers modern rooms, with en-suite facilities and TV, which are heated by traditional *Kachelofen* ceramic stoves.

You shouldn't need to stray too far from Kirchplatz to find decent **food**. For an inexpensive meal, *Pizzeria Al Castagno*, Kirchplatz 22, is the best of the Italians. The restaurant of the *Grüner Baum* has a good range of standard Austrian cuisine, and the *Tiroler Stub'n* in the *Hotel Sonnenspitze* on Kirchplatz has a marginally better choice of traditional Tyrolean dishes. The *Holzerstube*, just off Kirchplatz on Schulweg (☎05673/3323), is the best restaurant in town with an Austrian/international mix – reservations are advised. *Café-Bistro Rainer's* on Kirchplatz is a bright and lively place for a **drink**. Or try the two basement bars on the Hauptstrasse: the friendly and folksy *Kuhalm* in the *Hotel Alpin*, or *Valentin's Bar* a little further north, a much darker, louder affair.

Reutte

Twenty-five kilometres northwest of Ehrwald, **REUTTE** is a pleasant enough market town, which grew rich on the profits of the salt trade between Hall in the Inn Valley and Bavaria to the north. There's not much to the town apart from one long street, which goes by the name of Untermarkt at the northern end and Obermarkt to the south. It's on

Untermarkt that you'll find the most arresting edifice in town, the **Zeillerhaus**, once home to a prolific local family of painters. Paul Zeiller (1658–1738) lived there, and his son Johann-Jakob (1708–83) painted the swirling Baroque designs that adorn the outer walls. There are further reminders of the Zeiller family in the **Heimatmuseum** next door (Mon–Fri 9am–noon & 1–5pm, Sat 9am–noon; öS40), for the most part a very well-presented museum, even if the odd bits of weaponry and traditional wooden furniture on show fail to overwhelm. Highlight of the collection, the *Betrachtungsärgeln*, or "meditation-coffins" – 40cm high with model skeletons inside – were popular in the seventeenth and eighteenth centuries as a means of pondering the transience of earthly life. There's also a corner devoted to local man and forgotten genius **Peter Singer** (1810–82), inventor of the *Pansymphonikon*, a curious piano-type instrument with two keyboards and a wide register of sounds – although sadly, the museum doesn't possess an example.

Practicalities

Reutte's **train station** is at the northern end of town; from the main exit, walk straight ahead to reach the **tourist office** five minutes' away on the corner of Bahnhofstrasse and Untermarkt (Mon–Fri 8am–noon & 2–6pm, Sat 9am–1pm; ☎05672/2336, fax 5422). They can fix you up with a **private room**, most of which are located east of the centre in the hillside suburbs of Breitenwang and Mühl. For a choice of decent **hotels,** you need look no further than Reutte's main street: the *Goldene Krone*, Obermarkt 46 (☎05672/62317; ①), has adequate rooms with shared WC and shower facilities, though no single rooms; the nearby *Schwarzer Adler*, Obermarkt 75 (☎05672/62504; ②), has unadorned rooms, some with en-suite facilities. Moving slightly upmarket, *Hotel-Garni Beck*, Untermarkt 11 (☎05672/62522, fax 62522-5; ③), is a nicely priced source of bright rooms with en-suite facilities, and the four-star *Gasthof zum Mohren*, Untermarkt 26 (☎05672/2345; ④), offers plush, comfortable quarters with en-suite facilities and TV, and some superb four-bed family rooms.

Most **eating** can also be done along the main street, or on Mühlerstrasse just off it. *Prima*, Mühlerstrasse 20, is a cheap daytime self-service, while *Pizzeria Sonnenhof*, Obermarkt 63, has an inexpensive range of pizza and pasta dishes. The restaurant of *Gasthof zum Mohren* (see above) has the best range of Tyrolean food in town, as well as more expensive schnitzels and steaks – the *Goldener Hirsch* on Mühlerstrasse runs a close second. Reutte's main daytime **drinking** venues are the café of *Hotel-Garni Beck* (see above), which also serves excellent pastries in a plant-filled room on the first floor, and *En Vogue*, Untermarkt 25, a café in the daytime, bar by night. Other night-time hot spots include *Pianokeller*, Untermarkt 16, a spacious, friendly cellar bar set back 30m from the road, with a largely youthful clientele, and *Jedermann Stehbeisl*, Lindenstrasse 1, a lively pub catering for a twenty-to-thirty-something crowd.

travel details

Trains

Achensee to: Jenbach (June–Sept: 7 daily; 45min; May & Oct: 3 daily; 45min).

Brixlegg to: Innsbruck (20 daily; 40min); Kufstein (18 daily; 30min).

Hall to: Fritzens-Wattens (20 daily; 8min); Innsbruck (20 daily; 8min); Schwaz (20 daily; 20min).

Innsbruck to: Bregenz (8 daily; 2hr 40min); Brixlegg (20 daily; 40min); Ehrwald (7 daily; 1hr

50min); Fritzens-Wattens (20 daily; 16min); Graz (3 daily; 6hr 15min); Hall (20 daily; 8min); Imst-Pitztal (hourly; 40min–1hr); Jenbach (every 30min; 20–35min); Kitzbühel (10 daily; 1hr 10min); Kufstein (every 30min; 45min–1hr 10min); Landeck (hourly; 45min–1hr 35min); Lermoos (7 daily; 2hr); Ötztal (hourly; 30–50min); Rattenberg (16 daily; 45min); Reutte (7 daily; 2hr 30min); St Anton (hourly; 1hr 30min); Salzburg via Bischofshofen (5 daily; 3hr 40min); Salzburg via Kufstein (7 daily; 2hr); Schwaz (20 daily; 27min);

Seefeld (10 daily; 35min); Stams (hourly; 35min); Vienna via Bischofshofen (4 daily; 7hr 10min); Vienna via Kufstein (6 daily; 5hr 15min); Villach (1 daily; 4hr 10min); Wörgl (every 30min; 35–55min).

Jenbach to: Achensee (June–Sept: 7 daily; 45min; May & Oct: 3 daily; 45min); Innsbruck (every 30min; 20–35min); Mayrhofen (12 daily; 1hr); Zell am Ziller (12 daily; 45min).

Kitzbühel to: Graz (3 daily; 5hr 5min); Innsbruck (10 daily; 1hr 10min); Kirchberg in Tirol (hourly; 10min); St Johann in Tirol (hourly; 10min); Salzburg (11 daily; 2hr 30min–3hr 10min); Vienna (4 daily; 6hr); Wörgl (26 daily; 30min).

Kufstein to: Brixlegg (18 daily; 30min); Innsbruck (every 30min; 45min–1hr 10min); Rattenberg (16 daily; 25min); Salzburg (7 daily; 1hr 15min); Wörgl (20 daily; 15min).

Mayrhofen to: Jenbach (12 daily; 1hr); Zell am Ziller (12 daily; 15min).

Schwaz to: Fritzens-Wattens (20 daily; 10min); Hall (20 daily; 20min); Innsbruck (20 daily; 27min).

Wörgl to: Innsbruck (every 30min; 35–55min); Kitzbühel (26 daily; 30min); Kufstein (20 daily; 15min).

Buses

Axams to: Axamer Lizum (winter & summer only: 6 daily; 20min).

Bahnhof Ötztal to: Hochgurgl (1 daily; 1hr 50min); Obergurgl (8 daily; 1hr 25min); Sölden (9 daily; 1hr 5min); Untergurgl (8 daily; 1hr 15min); Zwieselstein (9 daily; 1hr 10min).

Brixlegg to: Alpbach (10 daily; 30min).

Ehrwald to: Innsbruck (6 daily; 1hr 50min); Lermoos (hourly; 10min); Reutte (hourly; 40min).

Hall to: Tulfes (8 daily; 20min).

Imst to: Landeck (8 daily; 30min); Nassereith (8 daily; 20min).

Innsbruck to: Axams (hourly; 25min); Ehrwald (6 daily; 1hr 50min); Igls (8 daily; 15min); Lermoos (6 daily; 2hr); Nassereith (6 daily; 1hr 15min); Patsch (8 daily; 25min); Reutte (6 daily; 2hr 30min); Tulfes (8 daily; 40min).

Jenbach to: Achenkirch (6 daily; 25min); Maurach (6 daily; 45min).

Kitzbühel to: Ellmau (4 daily; 40min); Jochberg (10 daily; 20min); Mittersill (6 daily; 50min).

Kufstein to: Ebbs (12 daily; 15min); Ellmau (8 daily; 50min); St Johann in Tirol (8 daily; 1hr 15min); Scheffau (8 daily; 40min); Söll (10 daily; 25min); Thiersee (9 daily; 15min).

Landeck to: Fiss (6 daily; 45min); Galtür (12 daily; 1hr 5min); Imst (8 daily; 30min); Ischgl (12 daily; 45min); Ladis (6 daily; 35min); Nauders (7 daily; 1hr 5min); Pfunds (7 daily; 45min); Prutz (hourly; 20min); St Anton (hourly; 50min); Serfaus (6 daily; 1hr).

Mayrhofen to: Brandberg (8 daily; 15min); Gerloss Pass (5 daily; 50min); Hintertux (8 daily; 45min); Krimml (5 daily; 1hr 35min); Schlegeis Stausee (8 daily; 50min); Stillupgrund *Gasthof Wasserfälle* (5 daily; 25min); Stillupgrund *Grüne-Wand-Hütte* (3 daily; 45min); Zillergrund Stausee (4 daily; 55min).

Nassereith to: Ehrwald (6 daily; 35min); Imst (8 daily; 20min); Innsbruck (6 daily; 1hr 15min); Lermoos (6 daily; 45min); Reutte (6 daily; 1hr 15min).

Prutz to: the Weissee Glacier (2 daily; 1hr 10min).

Reutte to: Ehrwald (hourly; 40min); Elbigenalp (3 daily; 1hr); Innsbruck (6 daily; 2hr 30min); Lech (summer only: 2 daily; 2hr 10min); Lermoos (hourly; 30min); Warth (2 daily; 1hr 45min).

St Anton to: Flirsch (hourly; 20min); Landeck (hourly; 50min); Rauzalpe (7 daily; 15min); St Christoph (7 daily; 12min).

St Johann in Tirol to: Ellmau (8 daily; 25min); Kufstein (8 daily; 1hr 15min); Scheffau (8 daily; 35min); Söll (8 daily; 50min).

Schwaz to: Pill (hourly; 5min); Schloss Tratzberg (10 daily; 15min); Stans (12 daily; 10min).

Sölden to: Bahnhof Ötztal (9 daily; 1hr 5min); Hochgurgl (2 daily; 45min); Obergurgl (8 daily; 20min); Tiefenbach Glacier (4 daily; 50min); Untergurgl (8 daily; 10min); Vent (5 daily; 40min); Zwieselstein (9 daily; 5min).

Söll to: Ellmau (14 daily; 25min); Kufstein (10 daily; 25min); St Johann in Tirol (8 daily; 50min); Scheffau (14 daily; 15min); Wörgl (5 daily; 30min).

Wörgl to: Auffach (8 daily; 45min); Ellmau (4 daily; 55min); Niederau (8 daily; 25min); Oberau (8 daily; 35min); Scheffau (4 daily; 45min); Söll (5 daily; 30min).

THE VORARLBERG

ustria's westernmost province, the **Vorarlberg** has since the earliest times led a life slightly separate from the rest of the country. Falling under Habsburg control in the thirteenth century, the area nonetheless remained relatively isolated from the main heartlands of the Empire. This was largely a matter of plain geography: bounded by the **Arlberg** mountain range to the east and the **Rätikon** massif to the south, communication with the rest of Austria was for centuries less than easy. Only with the construction of the Arlbergstrasse highway by Emperor Josef II in the late eighteenth century was the region properly integrated with its eastern neighbours.

Culturally and economically, the Vorarlberg has repeatedly looked towards Switzerland and southern Germany. Like the inhabitants of northern Switzerland, the Vorarlbergers are descended from the **Aleman tribes** who swept through the region during the great migrations of the sixth century AD, and to this day they speak a dialect very close to Swiss German. Indeed, in November 1918 the Vorarlbergers went so far as to declare independence from Austria, seeking union with Switzerland – a request turned down by an international community who feared that any break-up of the infant Austrian state would leave the region prone to future German expansionism. Vorarlberger separatism no longer occupies a prime place on the political agenda, but locals are still likely to view Vienna, more than 600km to the east, as a distant irrelevance. Geographically nearer cities like Munich and Zürich exert greater cultural influence on the Vorarlberg than the Austrian capital does.

Close economic ties with Switzerland and a thriving local economy have ensured that the cost of living in the Vorarlberg is higher than in the rest of Austria. Visitors will find that hotels are more **expensive** here than elsewhere, and budget choices are hard to come by, but there are still plenty of good-value private rooms to be found outside the main urban centres. Restaurants, too, are more expensive, but culinary standards are so high, and international and French-influenced cuisine so greatly valued here, that it's usually well worth paying the extra money. However, archetypal peasant dishes, such as *Kässpätzle*, a combination of cheese and pasta noodles that is very much a local staple, still feature on all restaurant menus.

Shared between Germany, Austria and Switzerland and fed by the waters of the Rhine, the **Bodensee** (known as **Lake Constance** in English-speaking circles), at the northwestern edge of the province, is the main tourist draw in summer, and the lakeside town of **Bregenz** the area's touristic and cultural centre – an obvious

---

ACCOMMODATION PRICE CODES

All **hotels and pensions** in this book have been graded according to the following price categories. All the codes are based on the rate for the least expensive double room during the **summer season**. In those places where winter is the high season, we've indicated winter room rates in the text. For more on accommodation, see p.30.

① under öS400	④ öS800–1000	⑦ öS1400–1600
② öS400–600	⑤ öS1000–1200	⑧ öS1600–1800
③ öS600–800	⑥ öS1200–1400	⑨ over öS1800

△ Innsbruck   △ Ischgl

TYROL

Valluga
2809 m ▲

Zürs •

Lech •

Stuben •

Arlberg Pass

Silvretta Range

Piz Buin
3312 m

Partenen •

Silvretta
Reservoir

Bielerhöhe •

Silvrettahorn
3244 m

Sennigrat
2300 m ▲

St Gallenkirch

188

Gargellen •

316

Schruns •
Tschagguns

Montafon Valley

Muttersberg
1384 m ▲

Bludenz

Nenzing •

SWITZERLAND

10 km

0

LIECHTENSTEIN

Vaduz •

Chur

▽ Lugano

staging post for journeys to and from southern Germany or northern Switzerland. The other towns of the **Rhine Valley** are workaday by comparison, although the medieval market town of **Feldkirch** merits a quick visit. Lying between the Rhine Valley and the Arlberg massif to the east is the **Bregenzerwald**, an attractive area of rolling uplands and picturesque villages, which offers excellent walking opportunities and a relaxing rural atmosphere a world away from Austria's alpine package resorts. South of the Bregenzerwald, the town of **Bludenz** provides access to the **Montafon**, a steeply sided valley at the head of which stands the **Silvretta Reservoir**, a renowned beauty spot surrounded by lofty alpine peaks. East of Bludenz is the equally dramatic mountain region of the **Arlberg**, home to the high-society, high-cost winter resorts of **Zürs** and **Lech**. A combination of challenging downhill runs and extensive off-piste opportunities has helped make the Arlberg into Austria's prime destination for the experienced skier. The Arlberg's largest resort, **St Anton**, is just over the border in the Tyrol, and is dealt with in Chapter 9.

Bregenz

Stretched along the eastern shores of the Bodensee, the Vorarlberg's administrative capital, **BREGENZ**, combines the laid-back gentility of a lakeside resort with the vigour of a booming business and cultural centre. Despite being relatively small for a state capital, with only 25,000 inhabitants, it's an absorbing place offering a wider range of attractions, activities and night-time diversions than anywhere else west of Innsbruck. The town's artistic pedigree is ensured by the **Bregenz Festival** (late July to late Aug), an extravagant celebration of opera and orchestral music involving outdoor performances on a floating stage, which draws in an extra 200,000 visitors every summer. Even though most of these are day-trippers, the sudden influx of festival-goers means that it can be exceedingly difficult to find a room here in August.

Local trains shuttle between Bregenz and Lindau 7km to the north, the most attractive of the German towns on the lake; there's also a lake-steamer service to Lindau, Konstanz and Friedrichshaven over the summer. Good communications with the rest of the Vorarlberg ensure that the town can be used as a touring base from which to explore the Rhine Valley, as well as the nearby Bregenzerwald, a beautiful area worth a day or two of anyone's time. Although about half of all international trains from Switzerland enter Austria at Feldkirch to the south, Bregenz has its own excellent road and rail links with Zürich and Munich.

Bregenz gets its name from the **Brigantes**, a Celtic tribe subdued by the Roman armies of Drusus and Tiberius in around 15 BC. The conquerors placated the locals by naming the settlement that grew up here "Brigantium" in their honour; it evolved into a culturally mixed place, with Roman and Celtic deities worshipped side by side. Destroyed by German tribes in about 260 AD but rebuilt under Diocletian a couple of decades later, Brigantium was finally finished off by the **Alemanni**, who descended on the area in around 450. The Irish missionary Columban (accompanied by Gallus, another major figure in local ecclesiastical history) established a monastery here in 610, although present-day Bregenz really dates from the tenth century, when local aristocrats the Udalrichungs built a castle on the site of the original Roman settlement. Soon after, Feldkirch replaced Bregenz as the region's strategic focal point, and the place settled back into provincial contentment.

The telephone code for Bregenz is ☎05574.

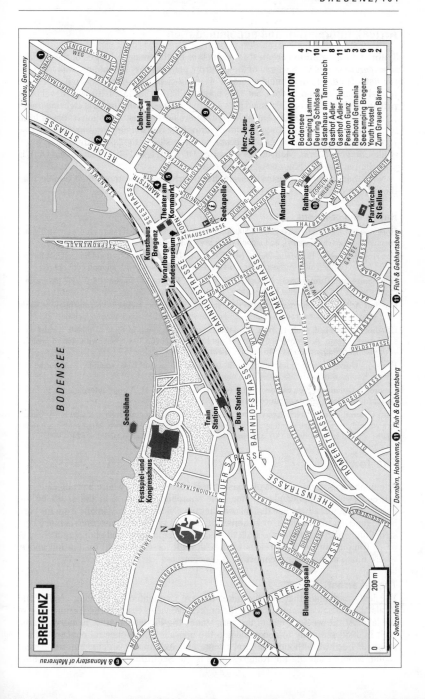

BREGENZ

BODENSEE

Lindau, Germany

Seebühne

Festspiel- und Kongresshaus

Train Station

★ Bus Station

Cable-car terminal

Kunsthaus Bregenz

Vorarlberger Landesmuseum

Theater am Kornmarkt

Seekapelle

Herz-Jesu-Kirche

Martinsturm

Rathaus

Pfarrkirche St Gallus

Blumeneggsaal

Monastery of Mehrerau

Dornbirn, Hohenems, Fluh & Gebhartsberg

Fluh & Gebhartsberg

Switzerland

ACCOMMODATION

Bodensee	4
Camping Lamm	7
Deuring Schlössle	10
Gästehaus am Tannenbach	1
Gasthof Adler	8
Gasthof Adler-Fluh	11
Pension Gunz	5
Radhotel Germania	3
Seecamping Bregenz	6
Youth Hostel	9
Zum Grauen Bären	2

0   200 m

Arrival, information and accommodation

Train and **bus stations** are next to each other on the western fringes of the modern town centre at the western end of the lakefront park, an easy ten-minute walk from the **tourist office**, Anton-Schneider-Strasse 4a (July–Sept Mon–Sat 9am–7pm; Oct–June Mon–Fri 9am–noon & 2–6pm, Sat 9am–noon; ☎43391-0, fax 43391-10), which will book **private rooms** from öS250 a head plus a öS20 fee. The **youth hostel** at Belruptstrasse 16a (☎42867, fax 42867-4; open April–Sept) offers dorm beds; reception is closed from 9am to 5pm. The best of Bregenz's four **campsites**, *Seecamping Bregenz*, Bodengasse 7 (☎71895; mid-May to mid-Sept), occupies a large site by the lake, 3km west of town, while *Camping Lamm*, Mehrerauerstrasse 51 (☎71701, fax 71745-4; May to mid-Oct), is a smaller, urban site 1.5km west of the centre.

Note that during the festival season **hotel prices** can be more than double than those quoted below.

Hotels and pensions

Bodensee, Kornmarktstrasse 22 (☎42300-0, fax 45168). Best of the mid-range choices, with TV and en-suite facilities in all rooms, and a good-value breakfast buffet. ④.

Deuring Schlössle, Ehre-Guta-Platz 4 (☎47800, fax 47800-80). Luxurious hotel housed in a former castle in the Upper Town. Atmospheric, *objet-d'art*-furnished rooms with all mod cons. ⑨.

Gästehaus am Tannenbach, Im Gehren 1 (☎44174). Best of the smaller B&B-style places, in a quiet street a 10min walk east of the centre. Closed Nov–March. ③.

Gasthof Adler, Vorklostergasse 66 (☎71788, fax 61953). A basic, inexpensive guesthouse a 15min walk west of town. Some rooms come with en-suite shower, others have shared facilities. ②.

Gasthof Adler-Fluh, Fluh 11 (☎ & fax 44872). Country-style inn in Fluh, a hillside hamlet 4km southwest of town. A lovely place to stay if you have transport. Cosy rooms with shared facilities (③), plus some bigger rooms with en-suite bathrooms (④).

Pension Gunz, Anton-Schneider-Strasse 38 (☎43657). Cheap and basic stand-by, bang in the city centre. Rooms with shared facilities (②), rooms with showers ③.

Radhotel Germania, Am Steinenbach 9 (☎42766-0, fax 42766-4). A good international business-standard hotel with all the creature comforts. (⑥).

Zum Grauen Bären, Reichsstrasse 8 (☎42823, fax 42823-8). On a main road and a bit noisy, but it's a reasonably inexpensive stand-by if other hotels are full. Closed Dec–Feb. Most rooms are plush affairs with en-suite facilities (④), although there are a few with shared facilities (②).

The Town

The main focus of attention is obviously the **Bodensee** itself, where a promenade and a green swath of parkland run along the shoreline, bordered to the south by the Germany-bound railway line that follows the curve of the lake. Just inland from the park is the modern town centre, or **Innenstadt**, an area of mostly nineteenth-century construction, which witnesses the bulk of Bregenz's commercial and shopping activity. A more tranquil atmosphere reigns in the **Altstadt**, or **Oberstadt**, on the hill above, where much of the older architecture is concentrated.

The lakefront

The leafy parklands that line the **lakefront** are frequented by strolling visitors and locals alike, who've come to savour the impressive views towards the German side of the lake. At the western end of the park stands the **Festspiel- und Kongresshaus**, built in 1980 primarily to accommodate the operatic and orchestral concerts of the Bregenz Festival, although cultural events and exhibitions are held here all year round. Moored outside the Kongresshaus is the **Seebühne**, or sea stage, a floating platform on which the festival's most prestigious performances are held. Seating for 6000 people is provided on the landward side.

West of the Kongresshaus, Strandweg continues along the lakeshore, passing summer bathing areas, open-air swimming pools and a marina before arriving, after about half an hour's walk, at the former Cistercian **monastery of Mehrerau**. The monastery buildings now serve as a school, and the church was rebuilt in 1962 in stark, angular style. Inside the church, however, a wealth of Gothic altarpieces serves as a reminder of the monastery's heyday –, their vibrant colours in dramatic contrast to the austere grey concrete of the interior. The winged high altar alone, painted around 1500 and showing the Crucifixion and Deposition, is striking enough to make the walk here worthwhile.

The Innenstadt

Lying on the landward side of the main road and rail lines that run parallel to the shore, Bregenz's **Innenstadt** presents an unabashedly modern face to the manicured lawns and flowerbeds of the lakefront. Guarding the entrance to the town between Seestrasse and Kornmarkt is the new cultural centre, the **Kunsthaus Bregenz** (Tues, Wed & Fri–Sun 10am–6pm, Thurs till 9pm; öS60), a Mies van der Rohe-inspired cube of light and steel, which houses temporary exhibitions by leading international artists, and a permanent collection of modern Austrian art that devotes special attention to Vorarlberg painters of the inter-war years. Cubist Albert Berchtold and Expressionist Rudolf Wacher are the big local names to look out for.

Just behind the Kunsthaus at Kornmarkt 1 (daily except Mon 9am–noon & 2–5pm; öS40), the **Vorarlberger Landesmuseum** provides an engaging survey of the province's history and folk culture. The first floor presents a fairly routine trot through Stone, Bronze and Iron ages, but things liven up by the time you get to Roman Brigantium, the first-century settlement situated to the west of the modern town centre. There's a model of the Roman town, fragments of mosaics, and a fine sandstone relief of the Romano-Celtic goddess Epona, who, as the patron of equine stock breeding, is always depicted riding a horse. The museum's second floor concentrates on folk crafts, with a range of wooden house interiors and a selection of Vorarlberg costumes. Worth noting here is the range of different hats on display, illustrating that each region within the Vorarlberg has long cultivated its own distinctive look: women of the Grosses Walsertal opted for the bloated, puffball-shaped *Pelzbummera*, while Montafon ladies preferred the *Mässli*, a tall black cylinder capped by a fringe of wool.

The art collection on the third floor is particularly strong on the late-Gothic art plucked from the region's churches. Fifteenth-century Feldkirch painters **Moritz and Jörg Frosch** are represented with a series of *Totentafeln*, or memorial pictures, which usually show some deceased local bigwig kneeling in prayer below a picture of Christ or some other saintly figure, surrounded by family. Another Feldkirch luminary, **Wolf Huber**, is represented by a panel from his St Anne altar, which shows scenes from the life of Christ on the back, and St Joachim and St Anne ascending towards heaven on the front. Also on this floor is a corner devoted to local heroine **Angelika Kauffmann**, the Bregenzerwald craftsman's daughter who became a celebrated painter in late eighteenth-century London (see p.471). Athough her portrait of the Duke of Wellington is probably the best-known work here, her taste for big narrative themes is revealed in mythological subjects, such as the atmospheric *Death of Alcestis*.

From here Rathausstrasse leads into the downtown shopping area, a partly pedestrianized zone grouped around the streets of Deuringstrasse, Maurachgasse and Leutbühel. At the junction of Rathausstrasse and Anton-Schneider-Strasse stands the **Seekapelle**, whose gloomy interior harbours an impressive seventeenth-century altar. A left turn from Deuringstrasse into Belruptstrasse leads to the more interesting **Herz-Jesu-Kirche**, a twentieth-century neo-Gothic affair, which features some wonderfully expressive stained glass designed in the 1950s by **Martin Häusle**. His scenes from

Jesus's parables run along the north side of the nave, while Old Testament stories (such as Cain slaying Abel, Noah offering a sacrifice after surviving the Flood) are ranged along the opposite wall.

The Altstadt

Maurachgasse climbs away from the modern centre towards the **Martinstor**, a fortified gateway that once guarded the entrance to the medieval town. Just around the corner is **Martinsturm**, a medieval tower to which a bulbous wooden dome was added sometime around 1700 and has been a bit of a town landmark ever since. Inside the tower, a small **museum** displays armour and weaponry (May–Sept daily except Mon 9am–6pm; öS30), and there's a chance to enjoy views down towards the lake. The medieval granaries next door were converted into a chapel in the fourteenth century, and frescoes from the period include several figures of Christ and St George. Just up the street from here stands the seventeenth-century **Rathaus** (now a residential building), an imposing half-timbered construction.

Dominating a hillock 300m to the south, the **Pfarrkirche St Gallus** is believed to stand on the site of a chapel built by Irish missionaries Gallus and Columban in the seventh century. The current edifice is the usual mixture of Gothic basics (the main body of the church is fourteenth-century) and Baroque add-ons, remarkable primarily for the excesses of its stuccoed ceiling, across which cherubs vie for space with abstract patterns in pastel greens and pinks. The high altar features statues of four saints: St Gallus, the one on the extreme right, is here depicted in the company of a small bear, which, according to folkloric accounts, was the saint's companion during his wanderings.

The Pfänder and the Gebhartsberg

The most popular local excursion is to the **Pfänder**, a 1062-metre-high peak just northeast of town commanding an excellent panorama of the lake. Served by a cable car from the northern end of Belruptstrasse (daily: May–Sept 9am–7pm; Oct–April 9am–6pm; öS120 return), the Pfänder can also be reached by car by taking the Lindau road and turning right at **Lochau**, the last Austrian settlement before the German frontier. At the summit, there are four Gasthöfe within a two-hundred-metre radius offering food and drink, and a **wildlife park** (free), where Vietnamese pot-bellied pigs and Central African goats rub shoulders with more customary denizens of central Europe such as deer and wild boar.

Several walks radiate outwards from the cable-car terminus, one of the most popular being the two-hour descent into Bregenz itself. Another offers a more gentle descent southwards to the attractive village of **Fluh** (1hr 30min), before heading west to the wooded ridge of the **Gebhartsberg** (40min), former site of the medieval fortress of **Hohenbregenz**. There's little to see of the castle nowadays, except for the pilgrimage chapel of St Gebhard, honouring the tenth-century nobleman's son who is thought to have been born in the fortress. Events from St Gebhard's not particularly dramatic life (relinquishing his inheritance and entering the priesthood, he rose to become Bishop of Constance) feature in a cycle of nineteenth-century paintings inside the church. But most people come here to enjoy the spectacular panorama of the Bodensee and the Rhine Valley, or eat in the *Gasthof Greber* next door to the church, which is fairly expensive, but has a good view from the terrace. Pathways descend from here to the western suburbs of Bregenz (1hr), from where you can make your own way back to the lakefront in fifteen minutes or so.

Eating and drinking

High prices in Bregenz restaurants reflect both the high local cost of living and the constant influx of well-heeled tourists, but standards here are generally outstanding, and budget choices never impossible to find. A fair number of excellent bars are gathered in the modern town centre just inland from the lakefront, with several more drinking spots along Quellenstrasse, in a redeveloped part of the inner city, west of the train station.

Restaurants

Da Li, Anton-Schneider-Strasse 34. Serviceable if unexciting Chinese restaurant, though the lunchtime Mittagsmenü (usually from öS70) is excellent value.

Deuringschlössle, Ehre-Guta-Platz 4 (☎47800). Inventive mix of Austrian and international cuisine in what is one of the country's leading restaurants, with main courses exceeding the öS300 mark. Reserve in advance.

Gasthof Adler-Fluh, Fluh 11 (☎44872). Popular out-of-town restaurant in the chic village suburb of Fluh, offering expertly prepared variations on basic Austrian and Vorarlberg cuisine. Nice outdoor terrace. It's easy to get to if you have your own transport; otherwise you'll have to take a taxi.

Goldener Hirschen, Kirchstrasse 8. An atmospheric old inn with a jovial, pub-like atmosphere and stolid Austrian fare. A nice place for a drink, too.

Gösser Braugastätte, Anton-Schneider-Strasse 1. Standard Austrian fare in an upmarket beer hall. Also a good place for an evening drink.

Gunz, Anton-Schneider-Strasse 38. Probably the cheapest source of traditional Austrian food in town, with main courses (such as *Vorarlberger Kässpätzle*, a local variation on the noodles and cheese sauce combination) from öS80.

Kreuz-Stüb'n, Römerstrasse 5. Standard choice of Austrian food in the rather elegant dining room of the *Wisses Kreuz* hotel. Moderately priced.

Pizzeria Charly, Anton-Schneider-Strasse 19. A large selection of inexpensive pizza and pasta dishes. There's another branch at Quellenstrasse 32.

Rathaus Café, Rathausstrasse. Comfortable if unprepossessing eating venue offering good-value pizzas and noodle dishes.

Wirtshaus am See, Seepromenade. Fairly expensive regional cuisine in a lakeside pavilion; plenty of outdoor seating.

Cafés and bars

Ballhaus, Quellenstrasse 49. Large, modern bar with big outdoor terrace, especially busy on summer weekends. Open till 3am.

Café-Konditorei Rosett, Am Steinenbach 2. A couple of blocks away from the town centre, but still one of the best places to enjoy cakes, pastries and a daytime drink.

Erste Akt, Kornmarktstrasse 24. Popular pub-style bar with relaxing atmosphere and a range of hot meals. Closed Sun.

Finanzamt, Rathausstrasse 27. Chic bar in the town centre catering to a well-heeled, elegant crowd. Friendly, but on the pricey side.

Nachtigall, Rheinstrasse 74. Old-timer music and "proper dancing" in a ballroom-type club aimed at a more mature clientele. Open till 4am; closed Tues.

Neubeck, Anton-Schneider-Strasse 5. Smartish bar with an extensive wine list, serving food right up until 1am. Closed Sun.

Viva, Seestrasse 7. Lively bar with youngish crowd serving a wide range of cocktails, Austrian ales and (rather pricey) Mexican beers. There's a good Mexican restaurant here, too.

Winnie's Pub, Quellenstrasse 17. Housed in a former slaughterhouse, this is a bit too upmarket to really feel like a pub, but it's a nice place for an intimate drink nevertheless.

Entertainment

Bregenz is well served by high culture. Most musical events take place in the Fest- und Kongresshaus, which is also the venue for two major festivals. Running from late July to late August, the **Bregenzer Festspiele** (Bregenz Festival) offers a top-notch programme of opera, involving dramatic outdoor performances on the Seebühne. Usually, a populist programme of familiar favourites (recent choices have included *Fidelio* and *Porgy and Bess*) takes place on the Seebühne, while a more challenging selection of rarely performed or "difficult" operas graces the smaller auditorium indoors. The **Bregenzer Frühling**, or "Bregenz Spring", featuring ballet and orchestral performances, takes place between late March and late April.

Theater am Kornmarkt, Kornmarktstrasse, is the place for classical (German-language) **theatre**, while Blumeneggsaal, Brosswaldengasse 23 (☎43955), has occasional **jazz** concerts.

Details and **bookings** for all events save the Festspiele are available from the Bregenz tourist office (see p.462). For the Festspiele, contact the festival office (Box 311, A-6901 Bregenz; ☎4920-223, fax 4920-228) as early as possible before you intend to travel. Performances are often sold out as much as nine months in advance.

Gig venues tend to be out of town. Local groups and minor touring bands play at the *Altes Kino*, Bahnhofstrasse 30, in Rankweil (☎05522/45387), 30km to the south (see p.469), or at *Jimmy's Palace*, Industriezone 8 (☎05522/82946), in the village of Röthis, 26km south. Local trains stop at both places, but you'll need your own transport or a taxi to get back. For listings of cultural events, you'll have to look out for posters around town or enquire at Bregenz tourist office.

Listings

Bike rental At the train station.

Car rental ARBÖ, Rheinstrasse 86 (☎78100); Herz, Immler Schneeweiss, Am Brand 2 (☎44995).

Consulates Great Britain, 2km south of the centre at Bundesstrasse 110, Lauterach (☎696207). Other nationals should contact their embassy in Vienna.

Exchange Raiffeisenbank, Kornmarktstrasse 14; Sparkasse, Rathausstrasse 29; Volksbank, Bahnhofstrasse 12.

Hospital Landeskrankenhaus, C-Pedenz-Strasse 2 (☎401).

Police Bahnhofstrasse 43 (☎420-21).

Post office, Seestrasse 5 (Mon–Sat 7am–7pm, Sun 9am–noon).

Taxis ☎1718.

The Rhine Valley: Dornbirn to Feldkirch

The Rhine marks the frontier between Austria and Switzerland for 35km, before emptying into the Bodensee just west of Bregenz. The settlements on the Austrian side of the valley form a chain of prosperous, semi-industrialized communities broken up by rich, verdant farmland, dubbed the "garden of the Vorarlberg" by overeager tourist brochures. **Feldkirch**, with its well-preserved historic centre, is the most worthwhile of the Rhine Valley towns to visit, although **Dornbirn**, **Hohenems** and **Rankweil** all merit a brief stop-over – Dornbirn is especially useful as a gateway to the Bregenzerwald region. The main road and rail route from Bregenz links all these towns before wheeling eastwards towards the Arlberg Pass, ensuring that one or more of them could easily be visited from Bregenz as a day-trip.

Dornbirn

Centre of a textile industry from which the Vorarlberg gained much of its nineteenth-century wealth, the sprawling, largely modern town of **DORNBIRN** is not much of a tourist attraction in its own right. The main reasons for coming here are to catch one of the frequent buses to the villages of the Bregenzerwald or to visit the gorge on the outskirts of town.

Central Dornbirn revolves around the **Marktplatz**, a pedestrianized area bordered by the **Rotes Haus**, an attractive half-timbered building from the sixteenth century, and the Neoclassical **Martinskirche**, which boasts nineteenth-century frescoes. Across the way there's a modest **Stadtmuseum**, at Marktplatz 11 (Tues–Fri 9am–noon & 2–5pm; öS20), which documents town life with a display of furnishings and local crafts. Just south of the Marktplatz is the **Vorarlberger Naturschau**, Marktstrasse 33 (July–Sept daily 9am–noon & 2–5pm; Oct–June daily except Mon, same times; öS30), a natural history museum with three floors of stuffed Vorarlberg fauna, as well as local plants (lots of Bregenzerwald fungi) and minerals.

Four kilometres southeast of the centre, the waters of the **Dornbirner Ache** rush down from the heights of the Bregenzerwald through the **Rappenlochschlucht**, or Rappenloch Gorge, an impressive series of cataracts and narrow defiles accessible by wooden walkway. The Dornbirn–Ebnit bus (catch it either at Dornbirn train station or Rathausplatz) goes past the entrance to the gorge, but there are only four services a day. An alternative is to catch municipal bus #5 from Rathausplatz to the Gütlestrasse terminus, and walk the remaining 2km by continuing along Gütlestrasse.

Practicalities

Dornbirn **train** and **bus stations** are northeast of the Marktplatz on Dr-Anton-Schneider-Strasse; it's a straightforward five-minute walk down Bahnhofstrasse to Marktplatz. A block east of here is the **tourist office** at Rathausplatz 1 (☎05572/22188, fax 31233), which will book **private rooms** in town for about öS200–250 per person, or for slightly less in outlying villages. Inexpensive **hotels** are thin on the ground, although *Gasthaus Bären*, Dr-Anton-Schneider-Strasse 17 (☎05572/23067; ③), is an unpretentious but adequate place 1km northeast of the train station; and *Hotel Janner*, Riedgasse 8a (☎05572/23272, fax 24297; ③), is a quiet, family-run pension between the train station and town centre. Higher up the scale, the four-star *Martinspark*, Mozartstrasse 2 (☎05572/3760, fax 3760-376; ⑤), is an excellent, quality business hotel of modernist design, in the heart of the downtown area. There's no youth hostel in town, but a good **campsite**, *In der Enz*, Gütlestrasse (☎05572/29119), occupies a pleasant, partly wooded site on the southeast fringes, on the way to the Rappenloch Gorge. Bus #5 goes past the entrance.

When it comes to **eating and drinking**, *Extrablatt*, Bahnhofstrasse 4, is a good place for a lunchtime snack or daytime drink; *Café-Bar By Pepe*, near the train station at Moosmahdstrasse 2, serves up tasty pasta dishes; *Sloppy Joe's*, Riedgasse 11, is a popular Tex-Mex restaurant and bar; and *Rotes Haus*, an atmospheric old inn at Marktplatz 13, specializes in top-quality regional cuisine, with prices to match. The *Sherlock Holmes Pub*, Marktstrasse 46, is lively, central and open most nights until 2am, while *Roxy*, Klostergasse 16, is a disco-bar with later hours and pricier drinks.

Hohenems

Seven kilometres south of Dornbirn, the small town of **HOHENEMS** sits decoratively beneath the sheer cliffs of the **Schlossberg**, upon which stands the ruined stronghold of the Ems family. Important figures to the town's destiny since the thirteenth century, the Ems brood were extraordinarily well connected in sixteenth-century Catholic circles – Wolf Dietrich von Ems was a brother-in-law of the pope – and it was as prince-archbishop of Salzburg that Wolf Dietrich's son Marcus Sitticus von Ems began construction of the Renaissance **Schloss Hohenems**, which now dominates the town's main square, the Schlossplatz. Today, the Schloss is used for exhibitions, antique fairs and classical recitals, and it's difficult to gain admission outside these events. Marcus's brother Hannibal ordered the construction of the **Pfarrkirche** next door in 1581, and a statue of the benefactor, standing in a niche, is the centrepiece of its fine Renaissance facade. Hannibal's son Kaspar von Ems is buried in a large marble sarcophagus inside, but the highlight of the interior is a carved wooden altarpiece, with a Coronation of the Virgin in the middle, surrounded by various saints, and scenes of the Nativity, Annunciation and Crucifixion stacked above it. The bulk of the altar predates the church – it was made in 1530 – although some of the outer figures were added later.

Marktstrasse heads north from the church towards Schweizer Strasse, where a **Jewish museum** (Wed 10am–9pm, Thurs–Sun 10am–5pm; öS30), at no. 5, documents an intriguing chapter in the history of the Jews who settled in Hohenems in numbers after Karl von Ems issued them with a Charter of Protection in 1617, making the town a reasonably safe haven. The museum nonetheless recounts a sobering picture of the kinds of discrimination, and occasional pogroms, that the local Hebrew community faced. Numbers fell dramatically after 1860, when Jews were allowed to settle anywhere in the empire. Housed in the former villa of the Rosenthal family, who ran the local cotton mill, several rooms of the museum recreate the atmosphere of a nineteenth-century industrialist's house. Another room is dedicated to the Hohenems-born composer Salomon Sulzer, who contributed to the revival of nineteenth-century synagogue music.

Practicalities

The **train station** is an easy ten-minute walk west of the Schlossplatz: from the station, turn left into Angelika-Kauffmann-Strasse and right into Graf-Maximilian-Strasse to get to the square. There's a **tourist office** (Mon–Fri 9am–noon & 2–5pm; ☎05576/74647, fax 76800) opposite the Pfarrkirche on Kirchplatz, which adjoins Schlossplatz. They can refer you to a small number of **private rooms** in town. *Gasthof Hirschen*, Marktstrasse 56 (☎05576/72345; ②), is a reasonable central **hotel** offering rooms with en-suite facilities; *Gästehaus Heim*, Radetzkystrasse 31 (☎05576/72298; ②), is slightly less comfortable for around the same price; *Café-Konditorei Lorenz*, Bahnhofstrasse 17 (☎05576/72332, fax 72332-5; ④), is the best of the mid-range places to stay, as well as being an excellent café.

Most **eating and drinking** takes place on or around Schlossplatz. *Schloss Café*, on the main square at Schlossplatz 10, offers a comfortable setting in which to enjoy a daytime coffee or snack; *Zur alten Post*, Postplatz 1, serves schnitzel-style dishes and vegetarian options; while *Gasthaus Löwen*, Schlossplatz 9, has a range of local specialities. Centrally located *Verrückt*, Schweizer Strasse 25, is a lively bar open until about 2am.

Rankweil

Very much a one-horse town, **RANKWEIL** is primarily known for the **Liebfrauenkirche** (daily: April–Sept till 8pm; Oct–March till 6pm), a pilgrimage church that surveys the town from a nearby crag. Miraculous healing properties are attributed to its thirteenth-century cross, which hangs above the main altar. Bearing a relief of the crucified Christ, the wooden cross was silver-plated in the eighteenth century. Pilgrims are also drawn to the Baroque altar to the Virgin Mary on the left-hand side, which has a Gothic Madonna and Child as its centrepiece. A wooden parapet runs around the outside of the church, offering an excellent panorama of the Rhine Valley and the Swiss Alps, which rise to the west.

Rankweil's **train station** is on the western fringes of the centre, a short walk from the town's main thoroughfare, Ringstrasse, whence a couple of fairly obvious pathways lead up to the church. The **tourist office**, Ringstrasse 27 (Mon–Fri 9am–1pm; ☎05522/404-103, fax 404-33), will sort out private **rooms** for you. *Gasthof Hörnligen*, Bahnhofstrasse 25 (☎05522/44183; ②), looks decrepit, but has a certain elegance within; while *Hotel Hoher Freschen*, just outside the train station at Kreuzlingerstrasse 2 (☎05522/44237; ④), is a reasonably swish, modern establishment. For **food**, *Restaurant schwarzer Adler*, Ringstrasse 3, offers a basic selection of grills and schnitzels and a small vegetarian menu, including such delights as vegetable Strüdel; *Gasthof Mohren*, north of the centre at Stiegstrasse 17, is a much more upmarket restaurant, which draws in a good deal of business from out of town. *Café Freddo*, Ringstrasse 48, has a good selection of ice cream and cakes, and provides a reasonable base to quench an evening thirst; another place for a night-time **drink** is *Patrick's Bombay Bicycle Club*, Alemannenstrasse 49, a popular late bar with a large snooker, billiards and darts playing area. *Altes Kino* on Bahnhofstrasse (☎05522/45387) is a small cultural centre that hosts rock gigs, film shows and cabaret events.

Feldkirch

Even though several international trains enter Austria at **FELDKIRCH**, many travellers speed eastwards to Innsbruck and beyond without sampling the delights of this historic and charming market town. While tourist attractions of any real drama are rather thin on the ground, the largely pedestrianized town centre, richly endowed with a selection of late-Gothic town houses, is a pleasant place in which to amble. A medieval grid-like street plan surrounds two parallel arcaded market squares, **Neustadt** and **Marktgasse**. This area is bounded to the south and west by a succession of medieval towers and gates, reminders of the original town fortifications that were last strengthened at the beginning of the sixteenth century by Emperor Maximilian I. Most impressive of these are the **Churertor**, an ornate fourteenth-century gateway guarding the southwesterly route to Chur, and the elegant, spindly **Katzenturm**, named after the lions' heads that once adorned the cannon housed here. The main attraction in the Gothic **Domkirche St Nikolaus** on the northwestern side of the centre is Wolf Huber's **Pietà** (to the right of the high altar), painted in 1521, the vestige of a much larger altarpiece honouring St Anne (another portion of which is in the Landesmuseum in Bregenz). A native of Feldkirch who spent most of his working life in the Bavarian town of Passau, Huber introduced a new sensitivity towards landscape into the religious painting of the time, visible here in the rolling hills and fields that form the background to the scene. Opinions differ as to whether Martin Häusle's modern stained glass enhances the church; among his lively renditions of various saints is a red-robed St Nicholas, patron of the church, clearly visible above the high altar.

Schlossgraben leads east from the church towards the **Schattenburg**, a hilltop strongpoint that was the seat of the counts of Montfort from the twelfth to the fourteenth centuries, although its current appearance owes much to a subsequent role as courtly residence of the imperial governors of Vorarlberg in the sixteenth century. Inside, the **Heimatmuseum** (March–Oct daily except Mon 9am–noon & 1–5pm; öS25) houses the usual collection of peasant crafts and furnishings.

Practicalities

Feldkirch's **train station** is a ten-minute walk north of the centre. Turn left out of the station forecourt and head down Bahnhofstrasse to reach the **tourist office**, just behind the Katzenturm at Herrengasse 12 (daily 8.30am–noon & 1.30–6pm; ☎05522/23467). The tourist office will provide a small list of **private rooms**, although most are in far-flung residential suburbs like Altenstadt (3km north of town) or Tisis (2km to the south). Cheapest of a generally expensive, though atmospheric, bunch of **hotels** is *Schloss Amberg*, Amberggasse (☎05522/72419; ②), a sixteenth-century castle offering rooms with shared facilities, 1.5km northeast of the train station – turn right into Reichgasse then right into Amberggasse to reach it. *Lingg*, Kreuzgasse 10

(☎05522/72062; ④), is a nice old inn overlooking the Marktplatz, and *Post*, Schlossgraben 5 (☎05522/72820, fax 72820-6; ⑤), is another centrally placed establishment with TV in all rooms. The top-of-the-range *Alpenrose*, Rosengasse 4–6 (☎05522/72175, fax 72175-5; ⑥), is a 500-year-old town house in the centre, many of whose rooms have antique furnishings. Feldkirch's **youth hostel** is in a former medieval hospital, a lovely half-timbered building 1km north of the train station at Reichsstrasse 111 (☎05522/73181, fax 79399; Jan–Oct; buses #1, #2 or #60 from Bahnhofstrasse).

For daytime nibbling, *Imbiss-stube Anatol*, Raffeisenplatz 3, is the best of the numerous Turkish kebab outlets in the centre. For more substantial **eating**, *Johanniter Hof*, Marktplatz, has an inexpensive range of Austrian standards; *Bar Gelateria Italiana*, on the corner of Montfortgasse and Vorstadt, is a basic but serviceable pizzeria; and *Pizzeria la Taverna*, Vorstadt 20, has a wider range of Italian food. *Pancho's*, Gymnasiumgasse 5, is a Mexican restaurant that does a good range in potato skins and is also a popular place to drink. Moving up the price scale, *Schlosswirtschaft*, Burggasse 1, inside Schloss Schattenburg, is an atmospheric place to enjoy local specialities in timber-beamed rooms; *Lingg*, Kreuzgasse, serves excellent Austrian food and offers some good-value lunchtime Tagesmenüs from öS100; and *Dogana*, Neustadt 20, serves expensive, gourmet-style food in a venerable old house beneath the castle.

Two stylish cafés in the old town centre are *Café-Konditorei Fürstin*, Schmiedgasse, and *Café-Konditorei Zanona*, Montfortgasse 3. *Billy's Pub*, Neustadt 4, and *Uwe's Bier Bar*, Zeughausgasse 7a, are good places for night-time **drinking**.

The Montforthaus, a modern concert hall on St-Leonhards-Platz, is the town's main venue for theatre and classical **music**, and hosts the **Schubertiade Festival** during the last two weeks in June. Works by Schubert are performed by top international artists, and tickets are hard to come by unless you book well in advance; contact Schubertiade Feldkirch, Postfach 625, Schubertplatz 1, A-6803 Feldkirch (☎05522/72091, fax 175450). The Saumarkt-Theater, Mühlertorplatz 1, offers jazz concerts and cabaret evenings, as well as a regular diet of German-language drama.

The Bregenzerwald

Although popular with Austrian, Swiss and German trippers, the rural charms of the **Bregenzerwald** remain relatively unknown to the rest of Europe. Far from being the forest that the name suggests, the region is a dense patchwork of dairy-farming villages spread across an undulating landscape of subalpine pasture. Known for its mildly tangy local *Bergkäse*, or "highland cheese", the Bregenzerwald is also famous for its architecture; here more than anywhere else in Austria, traditional wooden farmhouses are still in use, and the age-old techniques used to build them continue to inform modern construction. Using wood from local spruce trees, the typical Bregenzerwald house joins living quarters and animal stalls under a single, shallow roof. Often adorned with intricately carved eaves and balconies, they're almost always shingled – clad in tiny wooden scales that offer the best protection against the bitter winter weather.

Although the villages of the Bregenzerwald are not nearly as developed as the higher-altitude resorts further east, the hills are big enough to provide both alpine and cross-country skiing in the winter (good enough for beginners and intermediates, but there's nothing much to challenge the advanced skier), and a wealth of glorious walking opportunities all year round. The main centres are the rather humdrum Egg, and the more attractive **Bezau** and **Au**, all linked by a main road that heads southeast from Dornbirn towards Warth and the winter resorts of Lech and Zürs. The most characteristic Bregenzerwald villages, Schwarzenberg and **Damüls**, are only a few kilometres off this road. It's ideal touring territory if you have a car, although the local bus network is quite extensive: regular buses from Bregenz and Dornbirn ply the main route through the region, and connecting services (you'll probably have to change at Egg for Schwarzenberg, or at Au for Damüls) ensure that you're never really cut off. One word of warning: buses between the Bregenzerwald and Bludenz to the south are virtually non-existent, so the Bregenz–Dornbirn area remains the only practical gateway to the region.

Entering the region **from Bregenz**, the first settlement of any size you pass through is **EGG** (pronounced "Eck"), a pleasant enough village, even if it lacks the character of the places beyond. It's worth stopping off here to visit the Bregenzerwald **regional tourist office** (Mon–Fri 9am–noon & 2–5pm; ☎05512/2365, fax 3010), which has details of private rooms and other accommodation for the whole area. Buses **from Dornbirn** pass through the hamlet of **Bödele**, a minor skiing resort with five chairlifts and a couple of Gasthöfe, before continuing to **Schwarzenberg**, an all-year-round walking centre and a convenient touring base for the whole region.

Schwarzenberg

Ranged across grassy hillocks and surrounded by pine-clad slopes, **SCHWARZEN-BERG** represents the Bregenzerwald at its most idyllic, with many of the most important examples of the region's traditional architecture found here. It was home to artist **Angelika Kauffmann** (1741–1807), who is remembered in a worthwhile local museum (see box). It's also the site of two of Vorarlberg's best **restaurants**, enhancing the

---

ANGELIKA KAUFFMANN

Born in the Swiss town of **Chur** to a family who hailed from **Schwarzenberg**, and subsequently resident in both England and Italy, **Angelika Kauffmann** has always been a cultural heroine to more than one nation. She picked up the rudiments of painting from her father Johann Josef Kauffmann, a jobbing artist from the Bregenzerwald who worked throughout Switzerland and northern Italy during Angelika's childhood. The family came home to Schwarzenberg briefly in 1757, where father and daughter worked together on the decoration of the village church, thereby giving present-day local tourist authorities sufficient reason to claim her as their own.

When the family returned to Italy, Angelika studied in Florence and Rome, and achieved some local notoriety before becoming the protégée of Lady Wentworth, the wife of the British ambassador in Venice, who took her to London in 1763. Once introduced to London society, Kauffmann went down a storm: the elements of Neoclassicism that she had picked up in Italy were very much in vogue. She certainly knew the demands of the local market, producing large, often sentimental narrative paintings of mythological and historical subjects for wealthy collectors, and dashing off appealing portraits of her high-born circle of friends.

Her private life was the cause of much society gossip, although it's fair to assume that a certain amount of this was malicious. She almost certainly had affairs with English painters Nathaniel Dance and Joshua Reynolds, the Swiss painter Fuseli, and the French revolutionary Jean-Paul Marat, before eventually concluding a disastrous marriage with a gold-digging charmer posing as the Swedish Count de Horn (sic). When he was unmasked as an impostor and bigamist, Kauffmann had to pay out the then exorbitant sum of £300 to persuade him to leave town. He died soon afterwards, leaving Kauffmann free to marry the Venetian painter Antonio Zucchi in 1781, subsequently going to live with him in Rome, where she died.

A founder member of the British Royal Academy of Art, Kauffmann's greatest achievement was to win respect as a female artist working in the male-dominated world of narrative painting. Although much of her work is in private hands, reasonable collections can be found in the Brighton Museum and Art Gallery in England, the Kunstmuseum in Chur, Switzerland, and the Vorarlberger Landesmuseum in Bregenz (see p.463).

village's popularity amongst day-trippers from the urban centres of the Rhine Valley. Extra numbers pour into Schwarzenberg for the **Alpabtrieb** of September 14–15, traditionally the time when the cows come down from the higher pastures for the winter, and nowadays the excuse for a big festival, featuring cheese competitions and a big farm-produce market.

Focal point of Schwarzenberg is the **church of the Holy Trinity** (Dreifaltigkeitskirche), supposedly built over the grave of Ilga, a twelfth-century saint; her bones are concealed in a small Rococo casket inside the church on the left. The 16-year-old Angelika Kauffmann painted the medallions of the apostles adorning the nave, and she later donated the Madonna that hangs above the main altar. The pictures of the Stations of the Cross are by her father, Johann Josef. The Kauffmann heritage can be explored further in the **Heimatmuseum** (May–Sept Tues, Thurs, Sat & Sun 2–4pm; Oct Tues & Sat same times; öS30), in a characteristic Bregenzerwald house just up the hill from the church. The room devoted to Angelika is short on original artworks, but the prints and books on display here provide an adequate summary of her life. The museum's ethnographic collection is strong on local costumes, especially the bizarre range of women's headgear occasionally still worn on feast days: typical of this region are the *Spitzkappe*, a conical black wool hat traditionally worn on Sundays, and the *Brämenkappe* made from otter hide, a big bulbous affair rather like a Russian fur hat. Further rooms contain all manner of agricultural tools and domestic trinkets, of which the most curious are surely the *Flaschenaltäre*, or "bottle altars", which work on the same principle as a ship in a bottle, but feature tiny dolls of saints.

Practicalities

Buses pick up and set down at the crossroads by the church, whence it's a short walk 100m north to the *Gemeindeamt*, or village hall, where the **tourist office** (Mon–Fri 8am–noon; ☎05512/3570, fax 2902) has a list of **private rooms** and holiday **apartments**. *Café Angelikahöhe* (☎05512/2985; ②), just north of the central crossroads, is a small **guesthouse** offering comfortable rooms with shared facilities, while *Gasthof Hirschen* (☎05512/29440; ⑤), immediately next to the crossroads, is in a different league altogether, providing a wealth of creature comforts in a wonderfully restored old inn.

An inexpensive **place to eat** is *Busche* on the Bezau road, which offers standard Vorarlberg cuisine with Tagesmenüs starting at öS120. The highly regarded restaurant in the *Gasthof Hirschen* has a wood-panelled interior and a mixed international/traditional Austrian menu, with main courses starting at öS200. Similar gourmet fare (including fresh fish from the Bodensee) at comparable prices can be found next door at the *Adler*, whose attractive, modern interior plays host to prosperous out-of-towners. The *Rumpelkeller* in the basement of the *Gasthof Hirschen* is a cosy **bar** catering for the village's younger set.

Bezau

It's relatively easy to catch buses from Schwarzenberg onwards to **BEZAU**, the next settlement of any size, 7km to the south. Despite serving as the unofficial capital of the Bregenzerwald, there's not much in Bezau itself save for the plain and largely modernized **Jodokskirche**. The town really comes into its own, however, as a touring base for the Bregenzerwald region or a starting point for local walks. As usual, the best way to begin exploring the highland pastures is to take the gondola from the eastern end of the village to the middle station, **Berghaus Sonderach**, or onwards to the terminus at **Baumgartenhöhe**, a ridge just below the 1711-metre-high Niedere Alpe. From either point, pathways offering panoramic views lead back down to the village.

The **tourist office** (Mon–Fri 8.30am–noon & 2–6pm; ☎05514/2295, fax 3129) in the village centre will direct you to **private rooms** or family-oriented holiday **apartments**.

Gasthof Gams (☎05514/2220, fax 2220-24; ⑤) is an old country inn turned into top-notch **hotel**, featuring tennis courts, outdoor pool and sauna. There's a riverside **campsite** at the western end of the village, just off the main road. You'll find plenty of Gasthöfe in town offering standard Austrian **food**. For something slightly different,*Café-Konditorei Fröwis* has a pizzeria attached; and the *Gams* is a well-known place for traditional Vorarlberg food – although, with main courses starting at around öS200, prices are relatively high.

Mellau

From Bezau the main Bregenz–Warth road follows the valley of the **Bregenzer Ache** through increasingly mountainous terrain, passing a succession of pleasant villages that serve as centres of low-key rural tourism throughout the year. The unassuming village of **MELLAU**, 3km outside of Bezau, is another excellent base for walking. There are a couple of hotels, and most of the householders in the village offer **rooms** or **apartments**. A gondola at the southern end of the village (July & Aug Mon–Sat 8.30am–noon & 1.30–4.45pm, Sun 8.30am–noon & 1–4.45pm; rest of year hours depend on light and weather; öS100 return, seven-day pass öS190) ascends to the Ross-stelle, the 1400-metre-high ridge that looms above the village to the south. From here you can walk back down to the village in just under two hours, or take one of the trails that leads off across the highland pastures. One popular walk ascends to the **Wildguten Alpe**, one hour to the west before descending to *Gasthof Alpenfrieden*, another hour in the same direction, where you can stop for a drink or bite to eat, and then turns northeastwards back to the village; the trip takes about four hours in total. For the more ambitious, a twelve-kilometre hike (one that shouldn't be attempted without a detailed map) leads southwards to the 1882-metre **Bettler Kulm** before skirting the side of the 2095-metre **Damülser Mittagspitze** and descending to the village of Damüls (see p.474) after a total of five or six hours.

Au, Schoppernau and beyond

Nine kilometres beyond Mellau, the village of **AU** was the site of an important guild of craftsmen and builders in the eighteenth century. Relying on the indigenous aptitude for house building as a way out of rural poverty, the craftsmen of Au plied their trade throughout southern Germany, with some of them – such as Michael Beer, architect of the monastery at Kempten in Bavaria – attaining considerable fame. Aside from the usual roundup of photogenic farmhouses, there's little to see of their legacy in Au today, although this prosperous dairy village – together with the adjoining settlement of **SCHOPPERNAU** immediately to the west – is an undeniably attractive spot.

The local gondola, which ascends to the 2090-metre **Diedamskopf** from the valley floor roughly halfway between Au and Schoppernau, is once again an excellent gateway to the dense network of hiking routes on the heights above. A brochure detailing walking routes can be obtained from the **tourist office** in the centre of Au (Mon–Fri 9am–noon & 2–5pm; ☎05515/2288, fax 2955), outside which local buses stop. The tourist office will also direct you to the area's plentiful **private rooms** and **apartments**. *Pension Riedlinger*, Shrecken 392 (☎05515/2385; ①), is a pleasant, small **hotel** midway between Au and Schoppernau. *Gasthof Adler*, Lisse 90 (☎05515/2264, fax 2484; ③), offers rooms with en-suite facilities and TV in an archetypal Bregenzerwald house. There's also a **campsite**, *Köbl*, Au-Neudorf 356 (☎05515/2331), near the gondola terminal. Most of the Gasthöfe in the two villages serve **food**: the *Alte Post* in Au's centre has traditional Vorarlberg dishes with main courses from öS150. For die-hard **drinkers**, the *Adlerhorst Bar* in Au (closed Mon & Tues) and *S'pab* in Schoppernau (closed Mon) are usually open after midnight.

Beyond Schoppernau the main road clambers towards the **Hochtannberg Pass** some 10km beyond, through an area settled by immigrants from the Swiss canton of Valais in the fourteenth century. Villages like **UNTERBODEN** and **SCHRÖCKEN** still bear the imprint of Valaisian architecture, preserving several sturdy wooden houses with painted window frames. Sometimes closed in winter due to risk of avalanche, the road that climbs above Schröcken negotiates a couple of hairpin bends before reaching the 1676-metre summit of the **Hochtannberg**, and descending towards the town of **WARTH**, a sleepy market town dunked beneath the northern foothills of the Arlberg on the other side. From here, one route (frequented in summer by four daily buses from Warth) leads east down the Lech Valley towards the Tyrol and the market town of Reutte (see p.454) 60km away, while another road (closed Dec–March) climbs south, providing low-season access to the renowned winter resorts of Lech and Zürs (see p.479).

Damüls and around

A minor road heads west from Au towards an exceedingly pretty village on a shelf just above the Krumbach Valley, **DAMÜLS**, whose village-centre **Pfarrkirche** boasts a series of Gothic frescoes. Dating from 1484, the cycle are a vivid evocation of late-medieval piety. A lurid Last Judgement covers the chancel arch, while on the left-hand side of the nave are twenty scenes covering Christ's last days, from the entry into Jerusalem to the Crucifixion.

Damüls' proximity to higher altitudes makes it a major centre for **skiing**, with several chairlifts offering immediate access to the slopes. It doesn't feature in any of the winter package-holiday brochures, however, and is much more low-key than the Arlberg resorts further east. It's nevertheless a good place for beginners, with nursery slopes just outside the village, if you're prepared to travel here independently.

In summer, **walkers** can take the chairlift (daily 9am–12.30pm & 1.30–4.45pm; öS105 return) that runs from the valley bottom just north of the village up to **Uga**, a saddle between the peaks of **Eisenkopf** and **Mittagspitze**. The walk back into Damüls from the top of the chairlift takes about two hours. A more strenuous alternative is to head westwards beneath the Mittagspitze towards the 2051-metre-high **Ragazerblanken**, before turning south towards the **Sunsersee**, flanking the 2010-metre **Portlerhorn**, and descending back to the village. Providing access to some excellent views along the way, this particular circuit takes five to six hours.

Practicalities

Most of the houses in Damüls let out **rooms**, with prices starting from öS180 (fifty percent more in winter). The **tourist office** (☎05510/253, fax 549) in the village centre will provide details. Several **pensions** crowd around the Uga chairlift terminal: *Pension Johanna*, Damüls 79 (☎05510/286; ②), is a good budget option. *Gasthof Zimba*, Damüls 202 (☎05510/379, fax 379-7; ③), west of the centre on the road to the Furka Pass, is one of the cheaper **hotels** around, but still fairly comfortable; while down in the valley, *Gasthof Alpenblume*, Damüls 78 (☎05510/265, fax 265-6; ③), is a large, chalet-style place with TV and phone in every room. Top of the range is the *Damülser Hof*, Damüls 147 (☎05510/210, fax 543; ⑥), a chalet complex with indoor swimming pools and a range of traditionally decorated rooms.

Onwards to Faschina and the Grosses Walsertal

The main road through Damüls continues by way of a tunnel to **FASCHINA**, 3km to the southeast (also accessible by a gently ascending footpath from Damüls), another mountain hamlet popular with skiers and walkers. There's a **chairlift** to the 1777-metre **Hahnenkopf**, which looks over Faschina to the west; again, the summit is a good starting point for walks back to Faschina or Damüls. From Faschina, the road descends southwards into the upper reaches of the **Grosses Walsertal**, a picturesque, steep-sided valley that runs southwestwards to **NENZING**, a town on the main road and rail route between Feldkirch and Bludenz. It's a nice trip to make by road, although recent cutbacks in rural public transport mean that bus travel may be more problematic. An occasional bus makes its way from Damüls to Fontanella, Thüringerberg or Thüringen, where there are infrequent onward connections to Bludenz and Feldkirch. It's best to check timings at the Damüls tourist office before setting out.

Bludenz, the Montafon and the Arlberg resorts

East of Feldkirch, both the main Innsbruck-bound railway line and the E60 autobahn follow the Ill Valley as far as Bludenz before ascending through the Klostertal towards the Arlberg Pass, Vorarlberg's border with the Tyrol. As the only town of any size along the route, **Bludenz** is an obvious stop-off point, although it's neither attractive nor historically interesting enough to compete with Vorarlberg's other urban centres. Bludenz does, however, stand conveniently at the entrance to the upper Ill Valley, more commonly known as the **Montafon**, which provides access to the high Alps of the **Silvretta** range. Beyond Bludenz to the east, the gradual climb to the **Arlberg** lacks nothing in terms of grandiose alpine scenery, but the settlements along the route hold too few attractions to necessitate breaking your journey. From the summit of the Arlberg, there's a choice of two routes: onwards into the Tyrol, or northwards over the Flexen Pass to the skiing villages of **Zürs** and **Lech**.

Bludenz

BLUDENZ is the obvious transport hub from which to begin exploring southeastern Vorarlberg, but if you're eager for a taste of the Alps it's probably better to change buses or trains here and press on. That said, the villages of the Montafon can seem a little sleepy at times, especially if you're travelling out of season, and the restaurants and bars of Bludenz provide something of a respite for those needing a fix of urban culture or chocolate. Bludenz's only real claim to fame is the Suchard chocolate factory across the road from the train station, and the Milka Chocolate Festival in mid-July provides an entertaining day out for kids.

The town's paltry collection of sights boils down to the sixteenth-century **Pfarrkirche St Lorenz**, located on a height at the northern end of the town centre and remarkable only for its stately octagonal tower, and the adjacent **Oberer Tor,** a former city gate that now houses the town **museum** (May–Oct Mon–Sat 9am–noon & 3–5pm; öS25), a modest collection of craft implements. Beyond the gate, rows of seventeenth-century town houses with street-level arcading add character to the main shopping area. One kilometre north of the centre, a cable car (every 30min, opening times vary according to season; öS90 return) ascends to the 1384-metre **Muttersberg**, which commands excellent views southwards to the Rätikon and Silvretta mountain ranges.

Practicalities

From the **train station** south of the centre on Bahnhofplatz, a left turn outside the station building followed by a right turn into Bahnhofstrasse will bring you to Bludenz's main street, Mutterstrasse, in about five minutes. From here, a left turn into Werdenbergerstrasse will get you to the **tourist office**, housed in municipal buildings at no. 42 (Mon–Fri 8am–noon & 2–5.30pm, Sat 9am–noon; ☎05552/62170, fax 67597). There are a few **private rooms** in town, a list of which you can obtain from the tourist office. Two mid-range **hotels** located in the hillside suburbs northwest of the centre are

Pension Bergblick, Am Tobel 17 (☎05552/66604; ③), and *Landhaus Muther*, Alemannenstrasse 4 (☎05552/65704; ③), both smallish places offering rooms with en-suite facilities but not much else. Just west of the centre, the 45-room *Hotel-Pension Einhorn*, Alte Landstrasse 62 (☎05552/62130, fax 62130-8; ③), is an attractive modern building with TV and phone in all rooms. Best of the hotels in the centre is the four-star *Schlosshotel Dörflinger*, Schlossplatz 5 (☎05552/63016, fax 63016-8; ④), which surveys the town from a hilltop behind the Pfarrkirche.

There's a Würstelstand opposite the train station for those in search of a quick snack. For more substantial sit-down **eating**, *Café Wichner*, Hermann-Sander-Strasse 4, is probably the cheapest place to enjoy a solid Austrian meal, with main courses from öS80. Slightly more expensive, and offering the standard range of Austrian culinary favourites, are *Fohrenburg*, Werdenbergerstrasse 53, a beer hall-cum-restaurant attatched to the Fohrenburg brewery just west of the town centre; and the more central *Altdeutsche Stuben*, Werdenbergerstrasse 40. Considerably more chic is the *Orangerie*, Wichnerstrasse 2a, with a more international repertoire – most main courses start at around öS200, although there's a selection of cheaper spaghetti and noodle dishes.

Café Dorflinger, Rathausgasse 10, is the best spot for a daytime coffee and cake. Sample the local beer at *Fohrenburg* (see above) or head for *Moccasino*, Bahnhofstrasse, a cosy café-bar and good **drinking** venue at any time of day. *Piccadilly Pub*, Wichnerstrasse 34, offers a friendly pub-like atmosphere and toasted sandwich-type snacks, while *Baragraph*, Bahnhofstrasse 29, with modernist decor and slightly higher prices, is a good place for an intimate late-night drink.

The Montafon Valley

A narrow, high-sided valley presided over by the imperious peaks of the Rätikon and Silvretta ranges, the **MONTAFON** is one of the most dramatic stretches in the Vorarlberg. A string of picturesque villages dot the valley floor, the best of which to aim for are the twin settlements of **Schruns** and **Tschagguns**, situated about 2km apart, 15km up the valley from Bludenz, which together form the centre of a thriving winter sports scene. For much of the rest of the year, things are pretty quiet, although the valley is popular with hikers, and the **Silvretta Hochalpenstrasse** – a road that climbs to the Silvretta dam at the southeastern end of the valley before dropping down to the Paznaun Valley in the Tyrol – is one of Austria's most impressive alpine itineraries. Cycling enthusiasts can take advantage of a macadamed **cycle path** that goes up the Montafon Valley from Bludenz, starting on the north side of the train station (where you can rent bicycles).

Non-Germanic place names like Schruns, Silvretta, Tschagguns – and indeed Montafon itself – point to the **Romansch origins** of the local population, although the Romansch language, a curious descendant of Latin, is no longer spoken here (unlike in the neighbouring Swiss canton of Graubünden, where it has official status alongside German) and any other signs of Romansch culture have largely died out. One surviving Montafon peculiarity is the local breed of **cow**, which sports a distinctive dark tan hide.

For those spending any length of time in the Montafon Valley, a **guest pass** will be a worthwhile investment. The seven-day pass (available from all the region's cable-car and gondola terminals; öS480) entitles you to free travel on all the local cable cars, gondolas and chairlifts, as well as local buses, rail travel between Schruns and Bludenz, and free entry to museums (not that there are many) and swimming pools.

Schruns and Tschagguns

Half-hourly **trains** on the narrow-gauge Montafonerbahn railway make their way from Bludenz to **SCHRUNS**, 12km up the valley. Pressed hard against the flanks of the

Hochjoch, which rises to the southeast, the village clusters around a main square dominated by the **Pfarrkirche St Jodok**, whose elegant onion spire is more interesting than its late nineteenth-century interior. Standing opposite the church, the **Heimatmuseum** (June to mid-Sept Tues–Sat 3–6pm, Sun 10am–noon; mid-Sept to May Tues & Fri 3–6pm; öS30) offers a pretty thorough roundup of Montafon costumes, together with a history of the local dairy industry. At the southern end of the square stands the **Hotel Taube** (see below), where keen skier Ernest Hemingway stayed in winter 1925, dashing off a couple of chapters of *The Sun Also Rises* between trips to the pistes. Nowadays the quickest route to the heights above the town is provided by the three-stage **Hochjochbahn** cable car (summer times: mid-June to Oct daily 8.30am–noon & 1–5pm; öS200 return), which ascends to the 2300-metre **Sennigrat**, whence you can walk back down towards the valley or embark on any number of alternative hiking trails.

Schruns **tourist office**, just south of the main square at Silvrettastrasse 6 (Mon–Fri 8am–noon & 2–6pm, Sat 9am–noon & 4–6pm; ☎72166, fax 72554), has details of **private rooms** starting at around öS200 per person in summer, öS250 in winter. *Gästehaus Hanni Loretz*, Prof-Tschol-Weg 8 (☎05556/73922; ②), is a friendly and cheap pension; while the *Hotel Taube*, Silvrettastrasse 1 (☎05556/72384; ⑤), is a cosy upmarket place with plenty of atmosphere. For **food**, *Café Rocco*, Im Gässle 4, is a daytime café that also functions as a pizza takeaway, while *Don Camillo*, on the same street, has a much wider range of Italian cuisine, including excellent grilled fish (pizzas start from öS90, other main courses from öS150). *Gasthaus zum Kreuz*, Kirchplatz 18, has the usual range of regular Austrian dishes as well as tasty and cheap fondues. You can linger over a daytime **drink** at the pleasant *Café Alpina*, Bahnhofstrasse; across the road, the *Café Astoria* has a late bar and an outdoor terrace overlooking the stream.

About 2km west of Schruns on the opposite side of the valley is the sister settlement of **TSCHAGGUNS**, a smaller, less picturesque place, which nevertheless has its own **tourist office** in the village centre (Mon–Fri 8am–noon & 2–6pm) doling out **private rooms**. A minor road (served by hourly local bus) leads west from Tschagguns to the lakeside settlement of **Latschau** 4km uphill, where there's a gondola to the **Golm** (summer times: June–Sept daily 8.30am–12.30pm & 1.15–4.40pm), which commands an excellent panorama of the surrounding countryside.

The Silvretta Hochalpenstrasse

Between May and October, six daily buses head south from Schruns to tackle the **Silvretta Hochalpenstrasse**, a scenic mountain road that ascends to the Silvretta Reservoir and Bielerhöhe Pass at the southeastern end of the Montafon Valley. From the summit of the pass, it's possible to catch connecting services that descend into the Paznaun Valley in the Tyrol, although you should check times at Schruns tourist office before attempting the trip.

The road begins to climb in earnest just beyond the village of **Partenen**, 20km south of Schruns, rising steeply from the valley floor via a succession of hairpins. A tortuous ascent to the Vermunt Reservoir is followed by another steep climb to the larger Silvretta Reservoir and the 2036-metre summit of the Silvretta Hochalpenstrasse, the **Bielerhöhe** saddle. There you'll find a car park, a café-restaurant in the *Hotel Silvrettasee*, and stupendous views southwards across the reservoir towards the **Silvretta range**, with the 3312-metre **Piz Buin** presiding over a ridge of high Alps that marks the border between Austria and the Swiss canton of Graubünden. On the other side of the Bielerhöhe, the road descends into the Paznaun, one of the Tyrol's most attractive valleys, arriving after 20km in the skiing and hiking resort of **Ischgl** (see p.450).

HUT TO HUT IN THE SILVRETTA ALPS

The Wiesbadener Hütte

A rewarding **one-day circular walk** leaves the summit of the 2036-metre **Bielerhöhe** on the Silvretta Hochalpenstrasse. If you can't get a bed at the nearby *Madlener Haus* mountain hut (☎05558/4234), try the *Berggasthof Piz Buin* (☎05558/4231). The walk heads south alongside the Silvretta Stausee reservoir, then enters the wild-looking Ochsental, with big mountains coming into view as you progress, including Piz Buin and the glaciated peaks that form the Austro-Swiss border. After about two hours the trail reaches the *Wiesbadener Hütte* (2443m; ☎05558/4233), set on a shelf above the moraines of the Vermunt glacier. This is a good place for lunch – a hut with waitress service, which may seem incongruous in such a setting. Excellent views from the terrace overlook a mass of ice and snow and a bevy of attractive peaks, and walkers with alpine experience and the necessary equipment to deal with crevassed glaciers can choose to spend an extra day or two based at the hut in order to scale some of them – Piz Buin, Silvrettahorn and Dreilanderspitze are especially appealing. Walkers not so equipped or experienced should continue on the circuit by returning to the Bielerhöhe along a clear path that rises to the stony Radsattel (2652m), with an option of diverting for a half-hour's easy climb (some mild scrambling involved) to the crown of the Hohes Rad for a far-reaching, 360 degree panorama. From the Radsattel, descend to the Radsee in the Bieltal glen along a trail that spills out at the Bielerhöhe where you began.

Southwest of the Silvretta Stausee (west of the Wiesbadener Hütte) the Klostertal provides access to the uncomplicated 2751-metre Klosterpass on the frontier ridge, a traverse frequently used in a popular cross-border trek between the Saarbrücker Hütte (☎05558/4235) in Austria and Silvretta Hütte (☎083/41306) in Switzerland. East of the Wiesbadener Hütte the lengthy Jamtal digs into the mountains south of Galtür, with the Jamtal Hütte (☎05443/40814) set 10km into the glen. From this hut further routes are possible, connecting with the Heidelberger Hütte (☎05444/5418) via the Kronenjoch, for example, or with the Wiesbadener Hütte by way of the Getschnerscharte (2839m), where the Madlenerferner glacier has all but disappeared.

Silvretta Traverse

A **six-day crossing** of the Silvretta Alps can be achieved by linking a series of huts located in the parallel north-flowing glens that drain the snowbound frontier mountains. On this west to east traverse the Silvretta chain is revealed at its scenic best, while plenty of escape routes are available in case the weather turns bad – which is always possible, especially early in the summer. Start at **St Gallenkirch** in the Montafon Valley and wander south through the Gargellental to Gargellen village or, alternatively, as far as the unwardened *Madrisa Hütte* (get the key from the *Haus Wulfenia*, a Gasthof in the centre of the village) situated about 45 minutes beyond. On day 2 cross the Vergaldnerjoch, which is reached via either the Vergaldatal, or through the more challenging Wintertal and over the Valzifenzer-Joch. The route then crosses the Mittelbergjoch before dropping to the *Tübinger Hütte* (☎05556/2589). On day 3, given good conditions, you can tackle a small crevasse-free glacier below the Plattenjoch (2728m) – from which fine views show the Grosse and Kleine Seehorn – then gain the Schweizerlücke, and descend to the *Saarbrücker Hütte* before continuing to the Bielerhöhe and cutting south to the *Wiesbadener Hütte*. The traverse proceeds on day 4 to the *Jamtal Hütte* over the Radsattel and Getschnerscharte, and day 5 from the *Jamtal* to the *Heidelberger Hütte* by way of the Kronenjoch. The final stage, day 6, crosses the Ritzenjoch, followed by a descent through the Lareintal to **Galtür** – an easier alternative is to amble downstream through the Fimbertal to **Ischgl** in the Paznauntal.

The recommended **map** for the *Wiesbadener Hütte* walk and Silvretta Traverse is *Kompass Wanderkarte* no. 41 (Silvretta Verwallgruppe) at 1:50,000. For more on the Austrian hut-to-hut system, see p.33.

Zürs and Lech

East of Bludenz, the main road and rail route climbs up the Klostertal towards the **Arlberg Pass**, some 30km distant. Near the village of **Langen**, 6km short of the summit of the pass, both railway and main road enter a fourteen-kilometre-long **tunnel**, eventually emerging at the ski resort of St Anton (see p.452) on the Tyrolean side of the Arlberg. A secondary road heads north from Langen over the **Flexen Pass** to Austria's most upmarket alpine resorts, **ZÜRS** and **LECH**, lying 5km apart in a beautiful highland valley formed by the Zürs and Lech streams. Both places are easy to get to by bus either from Bludenz or from Langen train station, where most services on the main line to Innsbruck stop.

Zürs is a largely modern settlement that lives solely from tourism, while Lech is still a working village graced with some attractive alpine houses and a dainty Gothic church; together, they represent Austrian winter tourism at its snobbiest. The area's longstanding reputation as a high-society resort was bolstered in 1993 by a visit from Princess Diana. A range of **skiing** terrain varied enough to cater for all abilities has secured the resorts' popularity, while the policy of closing access to the pistes after a certain number of lift passes for that day have been sold means that overcrowding never cramps your style. In ski season, relatively high accommodation prices help to ensure an air of exclusivity, but outside the season private rooms here are no more expensive than anywhere else in Austria. For the non-skiing tourist, Zürs and Lech can be great places to hang out and observe a pan-European beau monde at winter-play; when the snow melts, though, many bars and restaurants close down, and the essential soullessness of the area soon becomes apparent. Spring and summer hiking opportunities are excellent, but if you want an authentic taste of rural Vorarlberg you'd do better to stay in one of the Bregenzerwald villages to the west.

Practicalities

Quickest routes into the mountains are provided by the cable car to the 2350-metre Rüflikopf, which towers above Lech to the east, and the three-stage cable car and gondola ascent of the 2371-metre Zuger Hochlicht to the west. Lech's **tourist office** (May, June & Sept–Nov Mon–Fri 8am–noon & 2–5pm; July & Aug Mon–Sat 8am–noon & 2–6pm, Sun 10am–noon & 2–5pm; Dec–April Mon–Fri 9am–noon & 2–6pm, Sat 9am–6pm, Sun 10am–noon & 2–5pm; ☎05583/2161, fax 3155), in the village centre just downhill from where the buses stop, will book you into a **private room** (öS350 and above per person in the winter season, öS200–250 outside it) or provide information on hotel vacancies. There's a **hostel**, the *Jugendheim Stubenbach*, 2.5km north of the centre in the suburb of **Stubenbach** (☎05583/2419, fax 2419-4), with beds in dorm rooms for öS280 in winter, öS150–180 in summer. Of the **hotels**, *Tannberghof*, Lech 11 (☎05583/2202; ④), is a large mid-range option with a popular restaurant and bar attached, and *Hotel Elizabeth*, Lech 285 (☎05583/2330; ⑤), a plush establishment with its own swimming pool. For **eating**, *Pizza Charly* at the northern end of Lech is a longstanding favourite where it's possible to have a meal that won't break the bank, while the restaurant of the *Hotel Krone*, between the church and the river, has a reputation for top-quality gourmet food. Nightlife in Lech is almost non-existent in summer, and in winter fashions change pretty quickly: as a general rule, **après-ski** activities kick off at dusk in the bars of **Oberlech**, the hillside suburb above Lech to the west, before moving down to Lech proper as the evening progresses. Popular (if rather snooty) venues currently include the *Pfefferkörndl* **bar** in the *Hotel Pfefferkörn*, Lech 138, and the *Klausur* in the *Hotel Almhof Schneider*, Tannberg 59. The *Zürserl* **disco** up the valley in Zürs is a notoriously dressy place, worth a visit if you fancy sipping expensive drinks and gawping at Eurotrash.

travel details

Trains

Bregenz to: Bludenz (hourly; 1hr–1hr 20min); Dornbirn (every 30min; 12–15min); Feldkirch (every 30min; 30–45min); Hohenems (every 30min; 25min); Innsbruck (8 daily; 2hr 40min); Rankweil (every 30min; 40min).

Bludenz to: Bregenz (hourly; 1hr–1hr 20min); Innsbruck (8 daily; 1hr 40min); Schruns (every 30min; 25min); Tschagguns (every 30min; 22min).

Buses

Au to: Damüls (5 daily; 30min).

Bludenz to: Lech (6 daily; 1hr 20min); Zürs (6 daily; 1hr 10min).

Bregenz to: Bezau (hourly; 1hr); Egg (hourly; 45min).

Dornbirn to: Au (hourly; 1hr 20min); Bezau (hourly; 1hr); Egg (hourly; 50min); Lech (summer only: 3 daily; 2hr 40min); Schwarzenberg (6 daily; 40min); Warth (summer only: 3 daily; 2hr 25min).

Egg to: Schwarzenberg (hourly; 10min).

Langen to: Lech (8 daily; 30min).

Lech to: Bludenz (6 daily; 1hr 20min); Reutte (summer only: 2 daily; 2hr 10min); Warth (summer only: 2 daily; 25min).

Schruns to: the Silvretta dam (May–Oct only: 6 daily; 35min).

Schwarzenberg to: Bezau (6 daily; 20min); Dornbirn (6 daily; 40min); Egg (hourly; 10min).

PART THREE

THE

CONTEXTS

THE HISTORICAL FRAMEWORK

Austria has existed as a state with clearly defined borders only since 1918. Before that the concept of Austria – whether cultural or political – was always a vague one: an agglomeration of lands gradually accumulated and held together by representatives of two remarkable dynasties – the Babenbergs and, more notably, the Habsburgs.

THE CELTS AND THE ROMANS

Reminders of Austria's **prehistoric inhabitants** can occasionally be glimpsed in the country's museums – Vienna's Naturhistorisches Museum holds the Venus of Willendorf, a 25,000-year-old carved fertility figure, while 4000-year-old ceramics left by inhabitants of a lakeland village can be seen in the Salzkammergut town of Mondsee. However, it was only really with the arrival of the **Celts** in the first millennium BC that organized, military and industrial civilization in the Austrian lands began to take off. Initially, Celtic control of a highly lucrative **salt trade** was the key to their wealth and power. Salt mines above the modern-day village of **Hallstatt** in the Salzkammergut (see p.367) were in use from around 1000 to 500 BC. The many Bronze- and Iron Age finds yielded by archeological digs in the region (and on show in Hallstatt's Heimatmusem) reveal a society that combined a high degree of industrial organization in the

mine workings themselves with a pronounced appreciation for the good things in life – as evinced by the many intricate ornaments and ceremonial daggers that have been unearthed. In the eighth century BC, Celts from Hallstatt went on to open salt mines in **Bad Dürrnberg**, above the town of Hallein (see p.329) just south of Salzburg. As at Hallstatt, there's now a popular show-mine in the old mine workings, and an important museum of Celtic culture. The other important concentration of Celtic power was in the southeast, where the kingdom of **Noricum**, centred on present-day Carinthia, established an ascendancy over neighbouring tribes in the second and first centuries BC. Celtic power here was based on the exploitation of the iron ore found deep in the Carinthian valleys around modern-day Hüttenberg. The ruined city on the **Magdalensberg** (see p.268) just north of Klagenfurt is thought to have been Noricum's capital.

Iron from Noricum was particularly valued by the **Romans**, who used it to make javelins, and the growth of trade between Rome and the Celts gradually led to the establishment of Roman economic and cultural hegemony over the region. This culminated in the establishment of Roman political control: the Romans advanced as far as the Danube in 15 BC, and the area was carved up into new administrative units. Western Austria (the Vorarlberg and much of the Tyrol) became the Roman province of **Rhaetia**, most of central and southern Austria was included in a new, reconstituted **Noricum**, while the east became part of **Pannonia**, which also embraced much of present-day Hungary. For the next four centuries, the **Danube** served as the natural military frontier between the empire and the barbarian tribes beyond, with a series of fortifications, or *Limes*, built along the river's banks. Best preserved of the Roman sites in Austria today is **Carnuntum** southeast of Vienna (see p.176), an important military camp on the Danube frontier that went on to flourish as a civilian settlement. Other important centres of Roman power were **Vindobona** (Vienna), **Juvavum** (Salzburg), **Brigantium** (Bregenz), **Flavia Solva** (Leibnitz, in Styria) and **Virunum** (north of Klagenfurt), and museums in each of these places preserve good Roman-era archeological collections.

THE DARK AGES AND THE EARLY MEDIEVAL PERIOD

The Romans finally abandoned the Danube frontier in the 430s, leaving the Austrian lands open to penetration by a succession of **migrating tribes**. The two main groups were German speaking: the **Alemanni**, who settled in the Vorarlberg region as well as neighbouring Switzerland; and the **Bavarians**, who occupied Upper Austria, Lower Austria, Salzburg and the Tyrol. Biggest of the non-German groups were the **Slavs**, who moved into Carinthia and Styria, although the east of the country was periodically subjected to incursions by other races, Huns and Avars among them. Vestiges of the Celto-Roman population, still speaking a Latin dialect, retreated into the high mountain valleys on the south side of the Alps. The period from the seventh to the ninth centuries was marked by the **gradual Germanization** of the Austrian lands, led mostly by Bavarian warrior-aristocrats, a process that often went hand in hand with the missionary activity of the Christian church. **Salzburg** became an important ecclesiastical centre after St Virgil's establishment of a monastery there in around 700, and it was from here that ambitious proselytizing clerics set off to convert the pagan inhabitants of central and southern Austria – many of whom were linguistically and culturally Slav at this point, although they were to lose their distinctive identity as the centuries passed.

THE OSTMARK AND THE RISE OF THE BABENBERGS

A semblance of political order was imposed on central Europe by the Frankish empire of **Charlemagne**, who was crowned Holy Roman Emperor in 800. The Franks established a military colony in what is now Upper and Lower Austria in order to keep disorderly eastern European tribes at bay – carving out a territory referred to by nineteenth-century historians as the *Ostmark*, or "Eastern March". With the collapse of the Frankish empire in 888, the **Ostmark** fell under the sway of Saxon kings Otto the Great and his son Otto II, who contributed to the ongoing Germanization of the area. The Ostmark was handed over to the **Babenberg dynasty** in 976, whose job it was to protect the empire's eastern frontiers, once more marked by the Danube. The Babenbergs

ruled the territory for the next 270 years, first as margraves and later as dukes.

In their search for some kind of official birthday for their country, many twentieth-century Austrian scholars latched onto a Latin parchment from around 996, which contains the first known mention of the name *Ostarrichi*, forerunner of the modern "Österreich". However, there's little evidence to suggest that the term was in common usage at the time, and for most of the Middle Ages the region held by the Babenbergs was known as *provincia orientalis* (or "eastern province", simply a Latin version of the original "Ostmark"). The Babenberg margravate certainly didn't conform to the borders of modern-day Austria. To begin with, it was confined to a small stretch of the Danube centred most probably on Melk, but it gradually expanded eastwards as far as the River Leitha and northwards as far as the River Thaya. Successive Babenbergs founded a number of monasteries in the region, in particular **Leopold III** (1095–1136), who founded Klosterneuburg in Lower Austria (see p.139), and was later canonized for his good works, becoming the country's patron saint.

In 1156, during the reign of **Heinrich II Jasomirgott** (1141–77), the Babenbergs' margravate was at last elevated to the status of a Duchy by the Holy Roman Emperor, with its new capital at Vienna. However, in 1246 the Babenberg male line came to an end with the death of Duke Friedrich II (1230–46) on the battlefield. In 1251, the future Bohemian king, **Otakar II**, took up residence in Vienna and claimed the duchy for himself, shoring up his claim by marrying Friedrich II's widow.

THE EARLY HABSBURGS

While Otakar was laying claim to the Babenbergs' inheritance, he was also putting himself forward as a candidate for the throne of the Holy Roman Empire. In the end, though, the throne was handed in 1273 to **Rudolf of Habsburg**, a little-known count whose ancestral home was the castle of Habichtsburg (hence Habsburg) above the River Reuss in modern-day Switzerland. In 1278 Otakar was defeated (and killed) by Rudolf's forces at the Battle of Marchfeld, to the east of Vienna, allowing Rudolf to lay claim to the Duchy of Austria, as Ostmark was now known. The Viennese, who had backed Otakar, were less than pleased about the outcome of the battle, and weren't easily placated by Rudolf's son, Albrecht, who had been given the duchy by his father.

The Habsburgs, though, were destined to rule over Austria for the next 640 years. At this time, "Austria" still only comprised (roughly) modern Upper Austria, Lower Austria and a southerly province acquired by Rudolf, Styria. Gradually however, the Habsburgs were able to consolidate their Austrian powerbase by annexing surrounding territories (often through marriage treaties rather than military conquest) and appointing family members to rule over them. Much of Carinthia and the Tyrol were acquired by the end of the fourteenth century, although some parts of the Tyrolean northeast remained in Bavarian hands until around 1500. One area that remained immune to Habsburg expansion at this time was the territory of Salzburg (much more than just the city of Salzburg itself, this was an area that roughly corresponds to today's Salzburgerland), which was ruled over by powerful prince-archbishops, and retained its independence until 1815.

The way in which acquired territories were shared out among members of the Habsburg family threatened to dilute the dynasty's power until the emergence of **Friedrich III** (1440–93). Despite numerous setbacks – he was besieged in the Hofburg by one of his own family in 1462 and briefly lost control of Vienna to the Hungarian king Matthias Corvinus in 1485 – Friedrich managed to unite all the Habsburg-held lands under his own control. In 1452, he became the last Holy Roman Emperor to be crowned in Rome, and the following year elevated the family's dukedom to an archdukedom. The Holy Roman Empire, famously dismissed by Matthias Corvinus as "neither holy, Roman, nor an empire", was something of a fantasy, whose emperor, theoretically, ruled over all the German-speaking lands. Though this was far from reality, the position of Holy Roman Emperor gave the Habsburgs enormous prestige, and they persisted with its imperial pretensions, passing the title down the male line, until its eventual dissolution in 1806 (see p.488).

MAXIMILIAN I

In the meantime, the Habsburgs continued to add to their dynastic inheritance through a series of judicious marriages by **Maximilian I** (1459–1519) and his offspring, prompting the oft-quoted maxim, adapted from Ovid: "let others wage war; you, happy Austria, marry." Building on the gains of his father Friedrich III, Maximilian did more than anyone else to turn the Habsburg family possessions into a lasting multinational empire. His 1477 marriage to Mary of Burgundy – the only child of Charles the Bold, she died while hunting in 1482 – won him a belt of territories running through modern Belgium and the Netherlands; the marriage of their son Philip the Fair to princess Juana of Castille (daughter of Ferdinand and Isabella of Spain) ensured that one day a Habsburg would sit on the Spanish throne. Maximilian also consolidated Habsburg control of the Austrian heartland, driving the Bavarians out of northeastern Tyrol and defeating the Hungarians to win back Vienna – which subsequently flourished as a cultural centre under his rule. Maximilian also entered into an alliance with the Hungarian royal house, which stipulated that if the Hungarian throne fell vacant then it would pass to the Habsburg family.

Maximilian's son Philip the Fair died in 1506 (an event that drove his wife insane, and historians have since dubbed her "Juana the Mad"), and it was Maximilian's grandson Karl V who received this vast, painstakingly assembled inheritance. Crowned Holy Roman Emperor in 1519, Karl ruled over an empire on which, it was said, the sun never set, with lands stretching from its Spanish possessions in South America to Vienna itself – bolstered in 1526 by the addition of the kingdoms of Bohemia and Hungary when the childless Hungarian king was killed by the Turks at the Battle of Mohács. Under Karl, Habsburg power was at its zenith, although the French – aided at various times by the north German princes and the English – prevented the Habsburgs from establishing a truly pan-European hegemony.

REFORMATION AND COUNTER-REFORMATION

Such a large territorial unit was too unwieldy to be ruled by one man, and Karl V decided to divide the imperial heritage among his successors. The Habsburgs' Spanish possessions fell to Karl's eldest son Philip II of Spain, while the core central European lands of Austria, Bohemia and Hungary passed to his younger brother **Ferdinand I** (1553–64). The unity of the empire was increasingly threatened by the collapse of traditional Catholicism brought about by the **Reformation**. By the sixteenth century, the population of Austria (excluding the Tyrol) was overwhelmingly Protestant, and the Habsburg dynasty itself increasingly ambiguous in its support for the Catholic Church. Ferdinand I invited the Jesuits to Vienna in 1556 in order to shore up the decaying structures of Catholic belief, even though the atmosphere at his court was one of tolerance, attracting a wide range of European intellectuals – both Catholic and Protestant – to Vienna. The ideas of the Reformation were allowed to flourish further under Ferdinand's son and successor **Maximilian II** (1564–76), who was himself suspected of being a closet Protestant by contemporaries.

It was in the Austrian lands of the empire that the Catholic Church began its fightback. The Jesuits, now established in Vienna, were introduced to Styria in the 1580s by Maximilian II's brother the archduke Karl, while the **Counter-Reformation** gathered momentum. Protestants became alarmed, and began to demand more and more legal rights from an imperial court that was under increasing pressure to put the full weight of its support behind one side or the other. **Rudolf II** (1576–1612), who presided over a remarkably tolerant and humanist court in the Bohemian city of Prague, tried to placate both sides, merely serving to postpone a violent religious conflict that was bound to break out sooner or later. After the brief interregnum of the Protestant-leaning **Matthias I** (1612–19), the accession to the throne of the fanatically Catholic **Ferdinand II** (1619–37) pushed the Protestant nobles of Bohemia towards armed rebellion. The conflict widened to involve neighbouring European states, and in the resulting **Thirty Years' War** the Habsburg court became increasingly identified with the Catholic ideology of the Counter-Reformation. Protestant sympathies were treated as a sign of disloyalty to the dynasty, and Protestants everywhere were subjected to a harsh crackdown. Ferdinand II's devout grandson **Leopold I** (1658–1705), who had initially trained for the priesthood, epitomized the relationship between the dynasty and Catholic piety, a relationship that increasingly relied on showmanship and spectacle – Leopold's endless rounds of praying and fasting, together with his pilgrimage journeys to cult centres like Mariazell (see p.235), were widely publicized.

THE OTTOMAN THREAT

Hardly a competent warrior-king himself, Leopold I was lucky to be on the throne at the time of one of the Habsburg Empire's greatest military victories, the defeat of the **Ottoman Turks** outside Vienna in 1683. Ottoman power had been advancing steadily across Europe from the fourteenth century onwards, and had penetrated as far as Vienna (the "city of the golden apple", as the Turks called it) once before, in 1529. On that occasion, the Turks mysteriously withdrew, despite the fact that the city had been only lightly defended. Ever since, however, the Turks had been a constant threat on the empire's southeastern borders, and the struggle against them was to provide the Habsburgs with a defining sense of historical mission. Grandiose hilltop fortresses like **Hochosterwitz** (see p.269) and **Riegersburg** (see p.232) served to keep the Ottomans at bay, while the Styrian capital **Graz** was for a time a vast armed camp from which Habsburg counteroffensives were launched. The Habsburg–Ottoman border shifted back and forth throughout the sixteenth and much of the seventeenth centuries, with the defeat of the Ottomans at the **Battle of Szentgotthàrd** (1664) finally ushering in a period of apparent stability. However, Ottoman ambitions revived a generation later, and the sudden and unexpected Ottoman advance on Vienna in 1683 led to an Austria-wide panic. At the approach of the Turks, Leopold, and anyone else who had the money, fled to the safety of Linz and Passau.

In their absence, Vienna was confronted by an army of over 200,000. Protected by a garrison of just 10,000 men, the Viennese were understandably ready to make peace with the grand vizier, **Kara Mustafa**. The grand vizier's crucial mistake, however, was that he was overconfident. Loath to share the booty among his army (which would be inevitable if they took the city by force), he orchestrated a two-month siege of the city. By September, however, a relief force of Poles, under their king **Jan Sobieski**, and sundry German troops under the duke of Lorraine, had come to Vienna's aid. On September 12, the papal legate Marco d'Aviano conducted a Mass on the hills above the city and, though outnumbered, the imperial forces managed to roust the Turks, in the process gaining some 20,000 buffaloes, bullocks, camels and mules, 10,000 sheep, corn and flour, sugar, oil and, most famously, coffee. Diamonds, rubies, sapphires and pearls, silver and gold, and "the most beautiful sable furs in the world", belonging to Kara Mustafa, fell into the grateful hands of King Sobieski.

Vienna was quickly followed up by further Habsburg successes, with armies led by one of the heroes of the siege, **Prince Eugene of Savoy**, penetrating deep into Ottoman territory. Victory at the **Battle of Zenta** (now in northern Yugoslavia) in 1697 was followed by the **Peace of Karlowitz**, which granted the Habsburgs control of all of the old kingdom of Hungary, which included Transylvania and much of modern-day Croatia. Prince Eugene's capture of **Belgrade** in 1718 more or less stifled any further Ottoman dreams of expansion in Europe.

THE EIGHTEENTH CENTURY

At the same time that the Ottomans were being pushed back in the east, Austria was engaged in a long-running **war with the French**, who were contesting Habsburg control over much of the Low Countries. A string of victories between 1701 and 1714 (again, mostly presided over by Prince Eugene) re-established Austria as the prime military power on the European mainland, ushering in another (albeit short-lived) period of peace and prosperity. The main beneficiary was Leopold I's second son **Karl VI** (1711–40), a free-spending monarch under whose reign Austrian Baroque art and architecture blossomed. This was especially marked in the capital, where the disappearance of the Ottoman threat provoked a rash of building activity. Damaged churches were repaired, aristocrats built palaces in the suburbs, and Karl undertook various prestigious architectural projects – Vienna's finest Baroque church, the Karlskirche (see p.103), among them.

MARIA THERESA (1740–80)

The area in which Karl VI singularly failed, however, was in producing a male heir to the throne. In the end, he had to accept the fact that his eldest daughter, **Maria Theresa**, was going to have to take over when he died. In an attempt to smooth her accession, Karl introduced the so-called **Pragmatic Sanction** in 1713, which allowed for female succession, and got all the states nominally within the Holy Roman Empire to promise to recognize his daughter's right to the Habsburgs' hereditary lands. Naturally enough, everyone agreed with the emperor while he was alive, and as soon as he died immediately went back on their word.

So it was that Maria Theresa (see p.000) found herself forced to fight the **War of the Austrian Succession** (1740–48) as soon as she took over from her father. For a while, she was even forced to hand over the imperial title to Karl of Bavaria in an attempt to pacify him, though it was eventually regained and handed to her husband, Franz Stephan of Lorraine (she herself, as a woman, could not become Holy Roman Emperor). At the end of the war in 1748, Maria Theresa was forced to cede Silesia to Prussia and, despite an attempt to win it back during the **Seven Years' War** (1756–63), it remained, for the most part, in Prussian hands.

On the domestic front, Maria Theresa's reign signalled the beginning of an **era of reform**, influenced by the ideas of the Enlightenment. The empress created a formidable centralized bureaucracy, taking power away from the provincial diets, in order to ease through her reforms. When the pope abolished the Jesuit order in 1773, Maria Theresa took the opportunity of introducing a state education system. In 1776 she abolished torture, and passed de facto abolition of the death penalty (though hard labour usually killed the convict within a year in any case). Despite her reforms, it would be wrong to get the impression that the empress was some free-thinking democrat. She believed wholeheartedly in absolutism and, as a devout Catholic, ensured Catholic supremacy within the empire with yet more anti-Protestant edicts.

JOSEF II (1780–90)

With the death of her husband in 1765, Maria Theresa appointed her eldest son, **Josef II**, as co-regent. But it wasn't until after the empress's death in 1780 that Josef's reforming zeal could come into its own. His most significant edict was the 1781 *Toleranzpatent*, which allowed freedom of worship to Lutheran, Calvinist and Greek Orthodox groups. Like his mother, Josef was himself a devout Catholic, but was even more determined to curtail church – and particularly papal – power. To this end, he dissolved four hundred contemplative or "idle" monasteries and, as many saw it, was bent on "nationalizing" the church.

Under Josef II all religious processions (previously a daily occurrence on the streets of Vienna, and an important feature of rural life) were banned except the Corpus Christi procession. The blessed sacrament was no longer carried through the streets, causing the faithful to fall to their knees. Pope Pius VI was so concerned, he came to Vienna in person in 1782 to try to change the emperor's mind, but to no avail. With the best of intentions, Josef interfered in every aspect of his citizens' lives, causing widespread resentment. For – again like his mother – despite his enlightened policies, Josef was very much the despot. He was, above all, responsible for creating the Habsburgs' secret police force, which was to become so notorious in the nineteenth century.

THE NAPOLEONIC ERA

The emperor Leopold II, who unenthusiastically succeeded Josef II in 1790, died suddenly of a stroke after a reign of less than two years. As a result, Leopold's eldest son became the emperor **Franz II** (1792–1835). No great military man – his troops had been fighting the French for two years before he bothered to show himself at the front line – Franz was an unlikely candidate to become one of **Napoleon**'s great adversaries.

In his first Italian campaign, Napoleon succeeded in humiliating the Habsburg forces at Mantua, and was within 150km of Vienna when the emperor sued for peace. It was a scenario that was repeated again in 1800 when Napoleon's forces were once more marching on Vienna. By 1803, the Habsburgs had lost their possessions in the Low Countries in addition to several territories in northern Italy to the French. Napoleon added insult to injury by declaring himself emperor the following year, with the clear intention of re-establishing the Holy Roman Empire under French hegemony. In retaliation, Franz II declared himself Emperor Franz I of Austria (a hitherto non-existent title) – ironically, the gesture looked more like an admission of defeat, since Franz was already Holy Roman Emperor.

In 1805, in alliance with Russia and Britain, Austria decided to take on Napoleon again, only to suffer a crushing defeat at **Ulm**. Unable to stop the advance of the *Grande Armée*, the allies decided to regroup further east, leaving Napoleon free to **march on Vienna**, where he arrived on November 13, 1805. The imperial

family had already taken flight to Hungary, carrying the contents of the Hofburg with them. Though there was no fighting, having 34,000 French troops billeted in the city put an enormous strain on the place, and supplies quickly ran short. The French stayed on until January 12, 1806, having exacted taxes and war reparations and appropriated many works of art, including four hundred paintings from the Belvedere. Four days later, Franz II returned to Vienna amid much rejoicing, though in political terms there was little to rejoice about. The **Treaty of Pressburg**, concluded after a defeat at **Austerlitz** in December 1805, had left the Habsburgs without their Italian possessions, the Tyrol and the Voralberg. Further humiliation followed in 1806 when Napoleon established the Confederation of the Rhine and Franz was forced to relinquish his title of Holy Roman Emperor.

For the next few years, there was no hope of the Austrians exacting any revenge. The Habsburgs applauded an **uprising in the Tyrol** (which Napoleon had awarded to his Bavarian allies) led by patriotic innkeeper **Andreas Hofer**, but shied away from offering concrete support. The revolt petered out, and Hofer was captured and shot. In the spring of 1809, however, as Napoleon encountered problems fighting Wellington in Spain, the Austrians seized the moment to reopen hostilities. Although they were once more defeated at Ratisbon, the Austrian forces under the emperor's brother, the Archduke Karl, managed to regroup to the east of Vienna. Once more Napoleon marched on Vienna. As usual, the imperial family had taken flight to Hungary, but this time the city tried to defend itself. Napoleon reached the outskirts on May 10, 1809, and sent two emissaries in to negotiate. They were promptly lynched by the Viennese; the French bombardment started the following evening. It was an uneven battle: the French fired some 1600 shells, and killed 23 civilians; in return, according to one Viennese eyewitness, "our batteries shot off a few shots; they were ineffective". The next day, the city capitulated, its 16,000-strong garrison no match for 100,000 French troops.

Napoleon's *Grande Armée* went on to suffer its first major defeat ten days later at **Aspern**, just east of Vienna. However, the Archduke Karl failed to press home his advantage, and Napoleon succeeded in holding on to Vienna, going on to defeat the Austrians decisively at nearby **Deutsch Wagram** six weeks later, when the Austrians threw in the towel. Vienna was forced to celebrate the new emperor's birthday on August 13 and, in the peace, signed on October 14, the Austrians were forced to give up Galicia and Croatia. Two days later Napoleon left Vienna, but without leaving instruction for his French engineers to blow up the city's defences. On October 29, the French held a farewell ball, and towards the end of the following month, the emperor Franz crept back incognito into the Hofburg.

Clemenz **Metternich** was appointed the chief minister of Austria by Franz, and began to pursue a policy of *rapprochement*. His greatest coup in this direction was getting Napoleon to marry the emperor Franz's 18-year-old daughter, Marie Louise, in March 1810. By 1813, with the tide turning against Napoleon, Metternich even managed to persuade his reluctant emperor to join the latest anti-French grand alliance.

THE CONGRESS OF VIENNA

Following the defeat of Napoleon at Leipzig and his exile to Elba, the victorious powers (Austria, Great Britain, Prussia and Russia) met for the **Congress of Vienna** in autumn 1814. If nothing else, the Congress was a great social success or, as one participant famously put it, *"Le congrès danse, mais il ne marche pas"*. By New Year 1815, most of the foreign delegates and their hangers-on had outstayed their welcome. The congress was costing the emperor a fortune that even he could not afford, forcing him to raise taxes, while many of the participants were living on credit notes. The Congress dragged on, however, until after Napoleon escaped from Elba, finally winding itself up in May 1815, just twelve days before his final defeat at the **Battle of Waterloo**.

The congress nonetheless managed to establish a status quo in Europe. Many of the borders agreed upon in Vienna were to endure for over a century. In the peace deal, Austria won back much of north Italy and Galicia, Croatia, the Tyrol and the Vorarlberg, In addition, the city of **Salzburg** and its attendant territories was brought into Austria for the first time. On Metternich's advice, claims to the Netherlands, and other far-flung territories that would be hard to defend, were relinquished. The Congress also pledged itself to further regular meetings between the heads of the victorious states – at which it was agreed that in order to maintain international peace they would combine to suppress any further revolutionary uprisings within Europe.

THE VORMÄRZ

Following the Congress, Austria enjoyed more than thirty years of peace and stability, a period known retrospectively as the *Vormärz* – literally "pre-March" – because it preceded the March 1848 revolution. In later years, the Austrians would look back on this period through rose-tinted spectacles, as a time of introspective domesticity, played out to the tunes of Johann Strauss the Elder and the melodies of Franz Schubert.

This period was also, however, marked by one of the most oppressive regimes in the history of the Habsburgs. The man most closely associated with the conservative politics of *Vormärz* was Metternich. Under him, and his chief of police Count Josef Sedlnitzky, the vast machinery of the civil service that Josef II had designed to help push through reforms was now used to thwart further reforms. Censorship and the activities of the secret police and its informers did so much to stifle intellectual life that by 1848 the playwright Franz Grillparzer reflected miserably, "Despotism has destroyed my life, at least my literary life".

With the death in 1835 of the emperor Franz I of Austria (former Franz II of the Holy Roman Empire, the title he was forced to relinquish in 1806), the Habsburgs faced something of a crisis, as the heir to the throne, **Ferdinand I** – a victim of Habsburg inbreeding – was, in the vocabulary of the day, an "imbecile", nicknamed Nandl der Trottel (Ferdy the Dotty). He was, in fact, nothing of the sort: he could be perfectly coherent, but suffered badly from epilepsy, which affected his short-term memory. To combat Ferdinand's deficiencies, a Regency Council was established, with Ferdinand as chairman – or, in his absence, his nephew the Archduke Ludwig – and his brother Franz Karl, Count Kolowrat and Metternich as permanent members. Within the council, Metternich had to struggle to maintain his influence.

THE 1848 REVOLUTION

With the deposition of the French king and the outbreak of revolution in Paris in late February 1848, a wave of **revolutionary fervour** spread throughout Europe. Austria, groaning under the weight of an oppressive bureaucracy, was no exception. On March 13, the Estates of Lower Austria, consisting of nobles and senior clergy, were due to meet in the Landhaus on Vienna's Herrengasse. They were pressing for various reforms including the freedom of the press, but top of the agenda was the removal of Metternich. In the morning a crowd gathered outside the Landhaus and, after listening to a German translation of the inflammatory speech given recently by the Hungarian revolutionary Lajos Kossuth in the Hungarian Diet, forced their way into the building. At around 1pm, a detachment of Italian grenadiers fired into the crowd, killing around thirty unarmed protesters, mostly students, and sparking a revolution.

That evening, after playing for time, Metternich finally resigned and fled from the capital (disguised as a washerwoman according to popular legend). The emperor – who, when told of the outbreak of revolution, had apparently said 'But do they have permission?" – immediately made a rapid retreat, declaring, "Tell the people I agree to everything". A National Guard was formed – with Johann Strauss the Younger as *Kapellmeister* – augmented by an academic legion of armed students, with whom they were to man the city in place of the despised imperial troops. In addition a constitution was promised, and a "Responsible Ministry" of bureaucrats formed to produce it. On April 25, a **constitutional monarchy** was proposed, with two chambers elected by limited franchise based on property. This failed to quench the thirst for radical reform, and on May 15 rioting ensued in favour of a single chamber parliament elected by universal suffrage. The emperor and his entourage quickly fled to Innsbruck in a stagecoach, as barricades were erected around the city.

Elections were duly held throughout the empire (with the exception of Italy and Hungary, which were busy with their own revolutions) and the first parliament in Habsburg history met on July 22 in the unlikely surroundings of the Hofburg's Winterreitschule. The deputies were by no means revolutionaries, the majority coming from the educated middle classes, although close to a third were of peasant origin. Hampered throughout by disputes between the various nationalities, the assembly did manage to pass one lasting piece of legislation, the **emancipation of the peasantry**. By August, the court felt secure enough to return to Vienna, bolstered by General Radetzky's military victory over the rebels in Italy and the recapture of Prague by General Windischgrätz.

The spark that lit the final fuse of the Viennese revolution took place on October 6. A battalion, due to be sent to fight against Kossuth's Hungarian revolutionaries, mutinied and joined forces with radicals in the National Guard. Civil war broke out as some within the National Guard fired on the radicals. In the confusion, the war minister, General Latour, was lynched by the mob and the imperial family removed themselves once more, this time to Olomouc in Moravia. As Windischgrätz marched his troops towards the capital, the radicals among the academic legion and the National Guard erected barricades and awaited the final showdown. Their only hope lay in the possibility of a Hungarian relief force, which in the event arrived too late. After several days' bombardment and around two thousand casualties, Windischgrätz flushed out the last of the rebels on October 31.

FRANZ-JOSEF I AND THE END OF THE EMPIRE

Back in Olomouc, the emperor Ferdinand, with his brother Franz Karl, was coerced by the imperial family into renouncing the throne in favour of the latter's 18-year-old nephew, **Franz-Josef**. A new government was formed under the leadership of the arch-conservative Prince Felix Schwarzenberg, while the assembly continued to meet in nearby Moravia to try to thrash out a new constitution. Then, to the astonishment of the assembly, on February 28, 1849, Schwarzenberg announced that as the emperor had himself formulated a new constitution, their services were no longer required. Although the new constitution granted equal rights to all, it was anything but liberal, granting the emperor the power of veto over all legislation, the power to dissolve parliament and rule by decree, and the power to dismiss and appoint ministers as he saw fit. Meanwhile in Hungary, the Austrians were forced to swallow their pride and enlist the help of the Russians in order to defeat Kossuth's Hungarian revolutionaries once and for all.

THE AUSGLEICH

After ten years of relative peace, Franz-Josef suffered his first of many embarrassing military setbacks at the **Battle of Solferino** in 1859 against the French. It was not so much the resultant loss of Lombardy that was the problem, but the opportunity it gave the Hungarians to demand their independence once more. In an attempt to placate them, Franz-Josef agreed in 1861 to establish a two-chamber parliament in Vienna. The Hungarians remained unimpressed and failed to send delegates to fill any of their 85 allotted seats in the lower house.

Five years later, the empire was rocked by an even greater crisis with its army's humiliating defeat at the **Battle of Königgrätz** in the Austro-Prussian War. Not only did the Habsburgs finally lose the battle for hegemony over the rest of Germany, but they were forced to strike a deal with the Hungarians (while studiously ignoring the demands of the empire's other nationalities).

With the 1867 **Ausgleich**, or Compromise, the so-called Dual Monarchy of Austria-Hungary was established. According to this new arrangement, Franz-Josef was to be crowned King of Hungary (he was already Emperor of Austria), and the Hungarians were to get their own parliament in Budapest, with autonomy over everything except defence, foreign affairs and the overall imperial budget. Everything within Hungary was to be prefaced with a *k.* for *königlich* (royal), everything in the rest of the empire was to be prefaced with the initials *k.k.* or *kaiserlich-königlich* (imperial-royal), while everything Austro-Hungarian was prefaced with *k.u.k.* or *kaiserlich-und-königlich*.

At the same time, delegates from the "Austrian" half of the empire met in Vienna's parliament. Among the delegates were Czechs, Poles, Croats, Slovenes, Italians and German -speakers from every corner of the empire, who spent most of their time arguing over language issues, and abusing each other both verbally and physically. The number of people eligible to vote increased gradually until universal male suffrage was finally introduced in 1907, but in reality, the emperor still ruled supreme since he and his ministers could pass any laws they wanted as "emergency measures", not to mention dissolve parliament and rule by decree (which they did on numerous occasions).

FIN-DE-SIÈCLE AUSTRIA

The economy suffered its worst financial crisis ever in the crash of May 1873 – the fault, it was rumoured by some, of Jewish financiers. The Jew had long been a stock Viennese scapegoat, and with the continuing influx of orthodox Jews into the city, **anti-Semitism** began to flourish. It found a spokesman in the figure of the pan-German nationalist **Georg von Schönerer**, whose fanatical followers used to wear the effigy of a hanged Jew on their watch chains. Schönerer's political career faltered, however, after 1888, when he was sent to prison for breaking into the offices of the Jewish-owned newspaper, the *Neues Wiener Tagblatt*.

Anti-Semitism was given a more respectable, populist twist by **Karl Lueger**. This Vienna-born politician became leader of the Christian Social Party, whose combination of Catholicism, anti-Semitism and municipal socialism went down alarmingly well with the Viennese electorate. In 1897, Lueger began a successful spell as mayor of Vienna. (The crowd that turned out for his funeral in 1910 was the largest the city had ever seen – among the mourners was the young Adolf Hitler.)

Most middle-class Jews, understandably, gravitated towards the other side of the political spectrum, dominating the upper echelons of the **Social Democratic Workers' Party** (SDAP) after it was founded in 1889. The party's chief ideologue before World War I was the Prague-born Jew **Viktor Adler**, whose peculiar brand of **Austro-Marxism** was to dominate the party's thinking for the next half-century. As far as Adler was concerned, capitalism was doomed to failure, so the party could afford to adopt a peaceful approach to politics until the time was right for revolution.

In among all the tensions between Right and Left, Jew and gentile, rich and poor, fin-de-siècle Austria – particularly the capital Vienna – succeeded in nurturing an astonishing variety of intellectual and artistic creativity, much of it inspired by assimilated Jews. In music, **Arnold Schönberg** and his followers Alban Berg and Anton Webern changed the face of classical music with their atonal revolution. **Gustav Mahler** turned heads both as a composer and as boss of the Staatsoper. In medicine, **Sigmund Freud** coined the term "psychoanalysis", and expounded on the new discipline in his seminal *On the Interpretation of Dreams*.

In 1897, the artist **Gustav Klimt** led a revolt against the artistic establishment, known as the Secession (see p.102); following in his footsteps were the likes of **Egon Schiele** and **Oskar Kokoschka**. **Otto Wagner** left the most visible legacy of this period, in the Jugendstil and early Modernist buildings that can still be seen on the streets of Vienna today.

WORLD WAR I

Ever since Prince Eugene of Savoy's great military campaigns against the Ottomans, the Austrians had been in possession of considerable territories in the northern Balkans, bringing a large number of **South Slavs** within the borders of the empire. To begin with, most of the Slovenes, Croats and Serbs were loyal to a Habsburg dynasty which seemed to offer them protection against the Turks, but the rise of **nationalism** in the nineteenth century put increasing pressure on Austria's relationship with its non-German subjects. In particular, the emergence of a **Serbian principality** (which had won independence from the Ottoman Empire in 1830) convinced those Slavs living under Habsburg rule that self-government was a realizable political goal. In 1908 Austria's annexation of the hitherto Ottoman province of **Bosnia-Herzegovina** – which contained a mixture of Serbs, Croats and Muslim Slavs – stretched Austrian–Slav relations to breaking point.

In 1914, Franz-Josef's nephew and heir **Archduke Franz-Ferdinand** committed an act of gross political folly in choosing to visit the Bosnian capital **Sarajevo** on June 28, St Vitus' day – a day sacred to the Serbs. Together with his wife Sophie, the archduke was assassinated by Gavrilo Princip, a young Bosnian revolutionary who had been supplied weapons by Serbia's chief of military intelligence. There was little genuine sadness in court circles, for, as Stefan Zweig bluntly put it, the archduke "lacked everything that counts for real popularity in Austria; amiability, personal charm and easygoingness". Even his uncle, the emperor Franz-Josef, was more relieved than anything else, as the two got on notoriously badly.

To begin with, there was also very little action by Austria on the diplomatic front, but eventually on July 23 Franz-Josef and his ministers sent an **ultimatum** to Serbia, with an impossible set of conditions and a 48-hour time limit. Serbia capitulated to almost all the conditions, but Austria-Hungary declared war anyway, without consulting its German or Italian allies. Unwilling to see any further extension of Austrian power in the Balkans, the Russians immediately mobilized, with Britain and France (Russia's allies), following suit. By August 12, the major European powers were at war.

Perhaps surprisingly, the outbreak of war brought patriotic crowds onto the streets of Vienna, and other cities around the empire, with Left and Right alike rallying round the Habsburg cause. Of course, everyone thought the war would be over by Christmas; it was only after several years of military defeats, huge casualties and food shortages that the population began to turn against the war. On October 21, 1916, Viktor Adler's son, Friedrich, took matters into his own hands and assassinated the Austrian Prime Minister, Count Karl Stürgkh. At his trial in May the following year, Friedrich Adler gave such a damning indictment of the war that his execution was postponed so as not to boost the anti-war cause further. On November 21, 1916, Franz-Josef died at the age of 86, leaving the throne to his 29-year-old great-nephew Karl.

The **emperor Karl I** (see p.176) is perhaps best known for his bungled attempt at negotiating a separate peace for his empire with the western allies in March 1917. The approach was rebuffed at the time and a year later became public knowledge, causing huge embarrassment to all concerned. Only victory on the battlefield could now save the dynasty – it was not to come.

In October 1918, the empire began to crumble from within, with **national committees** taking over in the empire's regional capitals. In Vienna, the Social Democrats, who were in favour of self-determination for the empire's various nationalities, set up a provisional government under Karl Renner. On November 2, 1918, with the end of the war in sight, the Hungarian battalion guarding Schönbrunn upped and went, leaving the imperial family and their servants unguarded. The next day an armistice was signed, and eight days later the emperor Karl I agreed to sign away his powers, withdrawing first to Eckartsau outside Vienna, and eventually, in 1919, going into exile in Switzerland.

THE FIRST REPUBLIC

The **Austrian Republic** was proclaimed from the steps of Vienna's parliament on November 12, 1918. Most of the Habsburg Empire's constituent nationalities – whether Hungarians, Czechs, Slovaks, Slovenes or Croats – had by now opted to form their own national states. What was left was a territory composed of the German-speaking parts of the empire, although even here the Austrians had to endure one particularly humiliating territorial loss – the German-speaking **South Tyrol**, for example, was given by the allies to Italy as a reward for the country's participation in the war. Few believed that the new, small-scale Austria would survive as a viable independent state, and there was precious little enthusiasm for the new country among its people. The Christian Socials wanted a constitutional monarchy, the Pan-Germans wanted union with Germany, while the Socialists, more specifically, wanted Anschluss with a Socialist Germany. In the proclamation of November 12, the country was

even described as "a constituent part of the German Republic". In the Länder, both the Tyrol and Salzburg voted overwhelmingly in favour of Anschluss with Germany, while the Vorarlberg voted to join the Swiss.

In February 1919, the first national **elections** took place, creating a coalition government of the SDAP and the Christian Socials under the chancellorship of Social Democrat Karl Renner. Nevertheless, a political vacuum continued until the end of the year, with soldiers' and workers' councils threatening to follow the Soviet revolutionary example of neighbouring Bavaria, which was in the throes of Bolshevik revolution at the time, and Hungary. There were even two unsuccessful attempts by the newly formed Austrian Communist Party (KPÖ) to stage a putsch, in April and June 1919.

The new government's foremost task, however, was to feed the population, particularly that of Vienna. Deprived of its former territories, and hampered by a bad harvest, the country managed it only with the help of the Allied

THE BREAK-UP OF THE
AUSTRO-HUNGARIAN
EMPIRE 1918

Famine Relief programme. The government's next most arduous job was to negotiate the Treaty of St-Germain with the victorious allies. Many in the delegation still hoped for Anschluss with Germany, but it was not to be. The Austrians (along with the Hungarians) were branded an "enemy state", while the rest of the so-called "successor states" like Czechoslovakia were not, and were expressly forbidden ever to undertake Anschluss with Germany.

PARAMILITARY POLITICS

For most of the First Republic, the country remained split between the heavily industrialized Social Democrat-dominated capital of Vienna (nicknamed *Rotes Wien* or "Red Vienna" because of its political affiliations), where some thirty percent of the population lived, and the deeply conservative Catholic rural Länder where the Christian Socials dominated. What made this political polarization all the more dangerous was that by the mid-1920s both sides were backed up by **paramilitary organizations**. The right-wing *Heimwehr*, on the one hand, had their origins in armed groups that had defended Austria's borders in the chaotic early days of the republic. Based on individual Länder and each with their own leader, the *Heimwehr* organizations didn't share a political platform but were united in their opposition to the Left.

The Social Democrats, on the other hand, had created an ad hoc army, the *Volkswehr*, in the last weeks of the war. They continued to dominate the *Volkswehr* until it was replaced by the establishment of the official Austrian army, or *Bundeswehr*. As a result, the SDAP eventually formed its own armed division, the *Schutzbund*, in 1923. Throughout the 1920s the party mouthed the rhetoric of class war, while pursuing moderate, social-democratic policies. In 1926, the party went even further and declared itself ready to use force if necessary to protect the interests of the workers. The bourgeois press interpreted this as a call for revolution, though the slogan coined by Socialist ideologue Otto Bauer was "democratic as long as we can be; dictatorship only if we are forced to it, and insofar as we are forced": To the dismay of many on the Left, however, the SDAP proved itself much less willing to resort to violence than its right-wing foes.

AUSTRO-FASCISM

The onset of the **Great Depression** further destabilized what was already a fragile democracy. In the elections of November 1930, the *Heimwehr*, under Prince Starhemberg, won its first parliamentary seats for its newly formed political wing, the *Heimatblock*. The Social Democrats, meanwhile, emerged for the first time since 1919 as the largest single party, with 41 percent of the vote, but once more it was the Christian Socials who went on to form a series of weak coalition governments. The last of these was formed in May 1932 under the chancellorship of **Engelbert Dollfuss**, with a parliamentary majority of just one.

On March 4, 1933, in an attempt to break a tied vote in parliament, Social Democrat Karl Renner resigned as speaker in order to free himself to vote. When Renner's two deputy speakers from the Christian Social and Pan-German parties both followed suit, Dollfuss seized the opportunity to **dissolve parliament**, claiming it could no longer function properly. The same weekend, Adolf Hitler won an absolute majority in the German parliament. The onset of Nazism had a sobering effect on the majority of Austrians, particularly the SDAP, which immediately dropped their call for Anschluss.

On March 15, Dollfuss sent the police in to prevent parliament from reconvening. In response, the SDAP leadership procrastinated and held back from calling in the *Schutzbund*; two weeks later the latter was outlawed. Dollfuss was determined to combat the threat from Nazi Germany, but instead of agreeing to an anti-Nazi alliance with the SDAP the chancellor threw in his lot with Mussolini, holding the first of many meetings with the Italian dictator in April. On May 21, no doubt prompted by Mussolini, Dollfuss established the Austro-fascist Fatherland Front (VF), under the slogan "Austria Awake!"

In May the Communist Party was banned and in July the Austrian Nazi Party outlawed. A violent showdown with the Social Democrats, who still controlled the Vienna city council, followed in February 1934. The first incident took place in Linz, where the local *Schutzbund* on their own intiative opened fire on police. A three-day battle ensued, with the bloodiest setto in Vienna's. Karl-Marx-Hof housing estate, which Dollfuss eventually ordered the army to bomb into submission. The SDAP had stumbled into civil war, and it was soundly beaten. The party was swiftly outlawed, and its leaders fled abroad or were imprisoned.

Just as it appeared he had successfully established an **Austro-fascist state**, Dollfuss was assassinated on July 25, 1934, during an abortive putsch staged by Austrian Nazis, apparently without the knowledge of Hitler. His successor, **Kurt Schuschnigg**, was forced to rely ever more heavily on Mussolini for support. As a foreign policy this proved disastrous, for in 1935 Hitler and Mussolini began to patch up their differences, and suddenly Schuschnigg found himself being urged by Mussolini to come to an agreement with Hitler. Schuschnigg did just that in the Austro-German agreement of July 11, 1936. In return for Hitler's recognition of Austria's "full sovereignty", Schuschnigg agreed to an amnesty of all Nazi prisoners, and the appointment of various "prominent nationalists" – not Nazis, but authoritarian conservatives with similar leanings – to his government.

In January 1938, the Austrian police raided the apartment of Leopold Tavs, one of Schuschnigg's deputies, and discovered a plan to overthrow the government with German help. As tension between the two countries mounted, the Nazi ambassador, Franz von Papen, suggested Schuschnigg should visit Hitler at his mountain retreat at Berchtesgaden by the Austrian border. At this meeting, Hitler ranted and raved and eventually demanded, among other things, that Schuschnigg hand over yet more key governmental posts to the Austrian Nazi Party. Schuschnigg acquiesced and agreed to appoint the Nazi Dr Arthur Seyss-Inquart as Interior Minister.

As the Austrian Nazis increased their activities, Schuschnigg decided to chance his arm with a **plebiscite** to decide the country's future, reckoning (probably correctly) that the majority would vote against the Anschluss. Hitler was certainly not prepared to risk electoral defeat and swiftly demanded the resignation of Schuschnigg and his entire government. Schuschnigg announced his resignation over the radio, in order to avoid "spilling German blood", and Seyss-Inquart took over the chancellorship. President Wilhelm Miklas refused to agree to the latter's appointment and resigned, and Seyss-Inquart wasted no time in inviting the German army into the country on the pretext of preventing civil war.

ANSCHLUSS AND WORLD WAR II

In the event of the Anschluss, there was no bloodshed: German troops crossed the border into Austria on March 12, 1938, and encountered no resistance whatsoever. Hitler himself began his slow and triumphant journey to the capital in the wake of his troops. First he visited his birthplace of Braunau-am-Inn, then he moved onto his "home town" of Linz, where he was received with such enthusiasm by the locals that he decided there and then to **incorporate Austria into the Greater German Reich**, rather than pursue the more conciliatory path of preserving Austrian autonomy. Eventually, on March 15, Hitler appeared on the balcony of the Hofburg before thousands of jubilant Viennese.

As a propaganda exercise, Hitler also decided to go ahead with Schuschnigg's plebiscite, which took place on April 10. The 99-percent "Yes" vote in favour of the Anschluss came as no surprise. In fact, those known to be opposed to the Nazis, including Schuschnigg and his followers, had already been arrested – some 76,000 by the time Hitler arrived in Vienna – while Jews and other "undesirables" were barred from voting. On the other hand, many whom one would expect to have opposed the Anschluss publicly declared themselves in favour, including the archbishop of Vienna, Cardinal Theodor Innitzer, and the Social Democrat Karl Renner.

Although the Treaty of St-Germain precluded any Anschluss with Germany, only the Soviet Union and Mexico lodged any formal international protest against the invasion. Meanwhile, the very name "Österreich" was wiped off the map, initially replaced by the term "*Ostmark*", but eventually simply divided into seven *Gaue*, or districts, ruled by Nazi *Gauleiter*.

THE FATE OF AUSTRIA'S JEWS

The Anschluss unleashed a "volcanic outburst of popular anti-Semitism", in the words of eyewitness George Clare. Jews were dragged out into the street, and physically assaulted and humiliated. Most anti-Semitic excesses were concentrated in Vienna, where the bulk of Austrian Jewry lived. In one instance, in the well-to-do Viennese suburb of Währing, a group of Nazis urinated on local Jewish women as they forced them to scrub the streets in front of cheering onlookers. A large number of the city's most prominent Jews were arrested, and either sent to the camps or released with orders to leave the country.

In May 1938, without warning, 2000 Jews were arrested and shipped off to Dachau, primarily to encourage still more Jews to emigrate. On the night of November 10–11 – dubbed *Kristallnacht*, or "Crystal Night" – the majority of synagogues in the Reich were torched, and numerous Jewish premises ransacked. Another 7800 Austrian Jews were arrested that night, 4600 of whom were sent to Dachau. By the outbreak of World War II, more than half of Vienna's Jews had emigrated.

Once the Nazis had invaded Poland, their policy towards the Jews changed, with deportation to the camps favoured over forced emigration. The deportations began in earnest in February 1941, while emigration came to a complete standstill in November the same year. Of the 57,000 Jews now left in Austria, more than half had been sent to the death camps by June 1942. By the end of the war, around 200 Austrian Jews had managed to survive in hiding, with just over 2000 returning after the war.

COLLABORATION AND RESISTANCE

Although Hitler preferred to import German Nazis to many positions within Austrian Nazi hierarchy, the Austrians themselves provided more than their ten percent population ratio of concentration-camp guards. The Linz-born Nazi Adolf Eichmann, who ran Vienna's "Central Office for Jewish Emigration" and was one of the architects of the "Final Solution", is probably the most infamous, though the film *Schindler's List* has also increased the infamy of the Vienna-born camp commandant Amon Goeth. Another Linz-born Nazi, Ernst Kaltenbrunner, rose to number two in the SS to Heinrich Himmler, while the Carinthian Odilo Globocnik, with ninety other fellow Austrians on his staff, supervised the death of some two million Jews in the extermination camps of Sobibor, Treblinka and Belzec.

Organized **resistance** to Hitler was, it has to be said, extraordinarily difficult for anti-Nazi Austrians, given the level of collaboration among their fellow citizens and the way in which the Nazis had wiped out their potential leadership. Aside from individual acts of heroism, there was very little significant non-

Communist resistance within Austria. Partisan activity was restricted to a few remote alpine areas, and it wasn't until spring 1944 that an organized home resistance, codenamed 05, began to emerge.

Unlike every other Nazi-occupied country, however, the Austrians had no official government-in-exile. Exiled Austrian politicians spent their time bickering, split between an unlikely alliance between Otto von Habsburg (the son of the last emperor), the Communists and the two mainstream political parties. The most positive diplomatic step took place in November 1943, when the Allied Powers published the Moscow Declaration stating that Austria was a "victim" of Nazi aggression and that it should be re-established as a "free and democratic state".

THE LIBERATION

By April 5, 1945, the Red Army had reached the outskirts of the Austrian capital. The 05 leadership under Major Szokoll had planned to initiate an **uprising** against the Nazis the very next day, but were betrayed by a junior officer, Lieutenant Walter Hanslick. Several of the 05 leaders were arrested, tortured and publicly hanged. The revolt had failed and it took the Russians another three days to reach Vienna's outskirts, and another five days' street fighting to finally win control of the city.

The commander in chief of the Russian troops in Austria, Marshal Tolbukhin, gave his assurances that the Soviets would liberate the country, respect the social order and refrain from appropriating any territory. In reality, Soviet troops spent much of the next few months raping Austrian women and stealing anything they could find. The actions of the Red Army during this period gave rise to the grim Viennese joke that Austria could probably survive a third world war, but it could never endure a second Liberation.

ALLIED OCCUPATION (1945–55)

On April 27, the Soviets sponsored the formation of a **provisional government** under the veteran Social Democrat Karl Renner, causing widespread alarm about Soviet intentions among the Western Allies. Although Renner's cabinet was made up, for the most part, of Socialists and members of the newly founded right-wing People's Party, or ÖVP, the Communists were

Legend:
- British Occupation Zone
- American Occupation Zone
- French Occupation Zone
- Russian Occupation Zone

VIENNA

International Zone

Danube

see inset

Vienna

AUSTRIA 1945–55

given three posts, including the key positions of Interior Minister and Education and Information Minister. As a form of protest at this unilateral action, the Western Allies refused to recognize the Renner government.

Meanwhile, there was continuing confusion over the occupation zones. Although the Moscow Declaration had stated that Austria was a victim of Nazi aggression, the country was nevertheless to be divided just like Germany, with Vienna, like Berlin, lying deep within the Russian sector. However, controversy over the exact zoning of Vienna helped delay the arrival of Western troops in the capital until late August. The Russians took the opportunity of fleecing the capital and eastern Austria of all they could. Vienna, it was agreed, was to be divided between the four Allies, with the Innere Stadt preserved as an international sector, patrolled by one representative of each of the occupying powers. This comical sight on the streets of Vienna became the hallmark of the so-called "four-in-a-jeep" period – and the set-

ting for the famous film *The Third Man* – when, as Karl Renner put it, Vienna was like a small rowing boat in which four elephants sat at the oars pulling in various directions.

ELECTIONS AND DE-NAZIFICATION

In October the Western Allies finally recognized the Renner government, and the Russians, for their part, agreed to free elections. However, whatever hopes they might have had of the Communists gaining power in Austria were dashed by the results of the **November 1945 elections**. The Communists won just 5.4 percent of the vote, up from their previous high of 1.9 percent in 1932, but earning them just four seats in the 165-seat parliament, and the consolation prize of the Ministry of Electrification. In an almost exact repeat of the election results of the 1920s, the country remained split down the middle between Left and Right. Although the ÖVP won almost fifty percent of the vote, it was Renner who headed the new coalition government of the Socialist Party (SPÖ) and the ÖVP.

One of the most pressing and controversial tasks of the postwar era was the **de-Nazification process**. Initially, this was the responsibility of the Allied Powers: the Americans and the British busied themselves by handing out forms in which the respondents were invited to confess; the French, with collaborators of their own back home, were less keen to get involved; the Russians, predictably, were the most assiduous, though they were as concerned to remove political opponents as ex-Nazis. Of the half a million Austrians who were Nazi Party members, only a handful were executed at Nürnberg, mostly for crimes committed outside of Austria. Back in Austria itself, the government took over the de-Nazification process, condemning 38 Nazis to death and depriving the rest of their civil rights for a brief period before an amnesty was agreed in 1948. Some attempt was made to rid the state bureaucracy of its ex-Nazis, but inevitably many – including Eichmann himself ,who fled to South America – slipped through the net.

COMMUNIST AGITATION

When the Red Army liberated Vienna in April 1945, few people thought that the city and the country would remain under Allied occupation for ten years. However, the Soviets were keen to pay back the Austrians for their mass participation in the Nazi armed forces. At the postwar Potsdam conference, the Soviets were granted, instead of cash reparations for war damage, the right to all external German assets in eastern Austria. Over the next ten years, the Russians took this as a carte blanche to asset-strip the entire region of eastern Austria, transporting factories piece by piece back to the Soviet Union.

Soviet control of eastern Austria – the country's agricultural heartland – also gave them considerable political leverage. With the entire country suffering food shortages, the Soviets deliberately hoarded supplies from their sector, supplying them direct to workers in Soviet-run industries. This won them considerable support in the eastern zone, and increased unrest in the western zones. For, despite the Communists' electoral setback, the Russians still had hopes of taking control of Austria. The winter of 1946–47 was particularly harsh, and the Communists took advantage of this by fomenting **food riots** in May 1947. The rioters besieged the Austrian chancellery and called for

a national strike. In the end, the putsch failed, because the the Socialist trade-union leaders refused to support the strike, and the Russians held back from using military force.

While Marshall Plan aid from the West helped ease conditions throughout Austria from the summer of 1947 onwards, the Communist coup in Czechoslovakia in February 1948 and the Berlin blockade (June 1948 to May 1949) only increased political tensions. Despite their recent setbacks, the Communists had high hopes for the **national elections of October 1949**. However, though the ruling coalition lost ground, it wasn't to the Communists, who remained on 5 percent, but to the newly formed extreme right-wing Union of Independents (VdU), who scored 11.6 percent of the vote, attracting the support of the majority of ex-Nazi Party members, who had recently been given back their voting rights.

In autumn 1950, Marshall Plan aid was cut back drastically. With the Austrian government forced to increase sharply the price of food, coal and electricity, strikes broke out among workers in cities across Austria. Seizing the moment, the Communists staged their second and most serious **coup attempt**. Once again, it began with a Communist-inspired mass demonstration outside the chancellery, after which barricades were erected, roads blocked, tram tracks cemented up and bus windows broken. The Russians stopped police reinforcements in their sector from being called up, and it was only with great difficulty that the situation was kept under control. In the end, however, the Socialist trade unions and the government took sufficient steps to stem the tide, and the general strike held on October 4, though heeded by large numbers of workers in the Russian sectors of the city and eastern Austria, was called off the following day.

THE AUSTRIAN STATE TREATY OF 1955

The **withdrawal of the four Allied Powers** from Austria in 1955 – or more specifically the Soviet withdrawal – was a unique event in the otherwise grim history of the Cold War. And something of a surprise, given the previously unscrupulous behaviour of the Soviets in Austria (and elsewhere in Europe).

For nearly ten years, negotiations over a **peace treaty** with Austria were at stalemate, with the Soviets insisting that a German peace treaty be prerequisite to an Austrian treaty. The Soviet threat over the future of Austria was used by them to try and forestall German rearmament. However, with the establishment of the Federal Republic of Germany in 1949, it was clear that this policy had failed. A struggle within the Kremlin then ensued over Soviet policy towards Austria. Following the death of Stalin, this struggle intensified and was eventually won by Khrushchev, who decided to use the Austrian State Treaty as a way of initiating a period of **détente**. Hopes of creating a Communist Austria had died with the failure of the 1950 putsch. The Soviet sector meanwhile had been bled dry and was no longer of any great economic benefit. A neutral Austria, on the other hand, created a convenient buffer that split NATO's northern and southern flanks. And so on May 15, 1955, the **Austrian State Treaty**, or *Staatsvertrag*, was signed by the four powers in Vienna's Belvedere.

CONSENSUS POLITICS: 1955–83

With the popular vote split between Left and Right, the two main parties of the ÖVP and the SPÖ formed a succession of **coalitions** which lasted until 1966. To avoid repeating the mistakes of the past, a system of *Proporz* was established, whereby the ÖVP and the SPÖ shared equally every governmental and state post. In some ways institutionalized political corruption, this process began at the top among the ministries, and continued right down to the local post office. At the same time, various special bodies or chambers representing the various interest groups – the Chamber of Trade, the Chamber of Labour and so on – were established. Like *Proporz*, these new institutions ensured that the country enjoyed an unprecedented period of political and social stability, but left the parliament without an effective opposition and created a system open to widespread abuse. Like the Germans, though, the Austrians enjoyed a period of **economic growth and prosperity**, and there were few voices of complaint.

In the elections of 1966, the People's Party at last achieved an absolute majority and formed the first **one-party government** of the postwar era. Many Austrians feared a repeat of the 1920s, but in practice little changed. The system of *Proporz* and the institutions of the corporate state continued to hand out "jobs for the boys",

and only at the very top level of government were the Socialists excluded from power. However, an economic downturn in the early 1970s increased support for the SPÖ, such that they won an outright majority in the elections of 1971. Under the chancellorship of **Bruno Kreisky**, the Socialists enjoyed thirteen years of power, during which Kreisky carried the SPÖ further away from their radical Marxist past than ever before. The end came in the elections of 1983 when the SPÖ lost its overall majority and was forced into a coalition government with, of all people, the far-right Freedom Party (FPÖ).

THE WALDHEIM AFFAIR

Having struggled to make the headlines of the international press in the 1960s and 1970s, Austria was catapulted onto the world media stage in 1986 during the campaign for the Austrian presidency. The candidate for the ÖVP was **Kurt Waldheim**, a figure of some international stature who had been UN secretary-general for ten years (1972–82). However, during the campaign, Waldheim's war record was called into question. From the summer of 1942 until the end of the war, he had served as a lieutenant in the Balkans with the German army. Waldheim was never a member of the Nazi Party (one of the initial charges) and there was never any clear evidence that he was directly involved in the atrocities committed by the army in the Balkans, though he was formally charged with (but never tried for) **war crimes** by the Yugoslavs after the war. What was more difficult to believe, however, was his claim that he had no knowledge of the deportation of Greek Jews to the death camps, despite being an interpreter for the Italian army in Greece for much of the war.

To the dismay of many around the world, these charges, albeit unproven, did Waldheim's candidacy no harm at all domestically, and he was duly elected to the Austrian presidency with 54 percent of the vote. The international campaign against Waldheim began with the boycott of his swearing-in ceremony by the US ambassador, and culminated in his being put on the US Department of Justice's "Watch List". Waldheim became an international pariah, restricted in his state visits to Arab countries. At Waldheim's suggestion, a commission was set up to investigate the charges against him; however, far from exonerating him, the commission's report found him guilty of "proximity to legally incriminating acts and orders", a somewhat woolly phrase that could be applied to just about any Austrian who'd served in the German army. The British government, meanwhile, followed up the Yugoslav charge that Waldheim had been involved in war crimes against British commandos in the Balkans. The British enquiry concluded that Waldheim's rank was too junior to have had any influence over the fate of the commandos, adding that "knowledge is not itself a crime".

THE 1990S

As if the Waldheim affair were not bad enough, the country has also had to contend with the rise of the Far Right FPÖ under their charismatic leader **Jörg Haider**. In his first stab at the polls, in 1986, Haider won nearly ten percent of the vote, frightening the two main parties back into the grand SPÖ–ÖVP coalition of the postwar years under the Socialist Franz Vranitzky. Unfortunately, this has only played into Haider's hands, increasing popular resentment against the system of *Proporz* (from which the FPÖ is excluded) and thus boosting support for the FPÖ.

Haider also exploited many Austrians' fears over the country's new wave of **immigrants**, who arrived from the former eastern bloc and war-torn Yugoslavia in considerable numbers in the 1990s. Nationalist frustrations were compounded by the country's entry into the European Union in 1994. Although in a referendum sixty percent voted in favour of joining, the austerity measures the country is now having to implement in order to meet the criteria necessary for joining a single European currency have convinced many that it was the wrong decision.

In the national **elections in 1994 and 1995**, popular dissatisfaction was publicly registered with Haider's FPÖ taking a staggering 22 percent of the vote, behind the ÖVP (with 28 percent) and the Socialists (on 38 percent). The biggest shock, though, was in Vienna, where the SPÖ lost its overall majority for the first time, with the FPÖ receiving 27 percent of the vote and becoming the main opposition in the Rathaus, ahead of the ÖVP.

The postwar Austrian republic appears to have overcome the crisis of national identity that plagued the inter-war republic, although celebrations over the country's spurious millennium in 1996 were decidedly muted. The country has also moved away from the polarized politics of the First Republic in favour of consensus, but the rise of FPÖ looks set to upset this cosy setup, with Haider setting his sights on the presidential elections in 1998. It remains to be seen as to whether Vranitzky's successor as chancellor, Viktor Klima, can reverse his party's decline in the polls.

BOOKS

There are a number of books in print about the Habsburgs and various aspects of Austria's glorious past, but precious little written in English about the country in the twentieth century – hence the rather uneven selection below. We've listed a few classics that are currently out of print (o/p), but you you might be able to pick them up in secondhand bookshops. For books in print, we've listed UK publishers first, then US; wherever we've cited a single publisher, it's the same publisher in both territories, unless we've specified UK or US after it.

HISTORY AND SOCIETY

Ilsa Barea, *Vienna: Legend and Reality* (Pimlico, UK). Magisterial overview, by Vienna-born émigré, concentrating mostly on culture and society from Baroque times until the end of the Habsburgs.

Stephen Brook, *The Double Eagle* (Picador, o/p). Taking their shared Habsburg tradition as a starting point, Brook explores the three main cities of the former empire – Vienna, Budapest and Prague – in the 1980s and produces a thoroughly readable and very personal travel journal.

Gordon Brook-Shepherd, *The Austrians* (HarperCollins/Carroll & Graf). Readable, if a little overearnest history – the author refers to himself several times in the third person – which attempts to trace the Austrian-ness (or lack of it) in the country's history from the Babenbergs to entry into the EU in 1994. Brook-Shepherd draws on his experience as a *Telegraph* correspondent and as someone who worked in the Allied High Commission in Vienna after World War II.

George Clare, *Last Waltz in Vienna; The Destruction of a Family 1842–1942* (Pan, o/p). Incredibly moving – and far from bitter – autobiographical account of a Jewish upbringing in inter-war Vienna that ended with the Anschluss.

Edward Crankshaw, *Vienna: The Image of a Culture in Decline* (Macmillan, o/p). Part travel journal, part history, and first published in 1938, this is a nostalgic, but by no means rose-tinted, look at the city.

R.J.W. Evans, *The Making of the Habsburg Monarchy 1550–1700* (OUP, o/p). Masterful overview of politics, culture and society during a formative period in the empire's history.

William M. Johnston, *The Austrian Mind: An Intellectual and Social History 1848–1938* (University of California Press). Johnston knows his stuff, and though this is pretty academic stuff, it's a fascinating insight into fin-de-siècle Vienna.

Robert A. Kann, *History of the Habsburg Empire 1526–1918* (University of California Press). Weighty and wide-ranging 600-page account of the empire, written in the 1970s.

Patrick Leigh Fermor, *A Time of Gifts* (Penguin). The first volume of Leigh Fermor's trilogy based on his epic walk along the Rhine and Danube rivers in 1933–34. Written forty years later in dense, luscious and highly crafted prose, it's an evocative and poignant insight into the culture of *Mitteleuropa* between the wars.

Claudio Magris, *Danube* (Collins Harvill/Farrar, Strauss & Giroux). In this highly readable travel journal from the 1980s, Magris, a wonderfully erudite Trieste-based academic, traces the Danube, passing through Austria along the way.

Frederic Morton, *A Nervous Splendor: Vienna 1888/1889* (Penguin, o/p); *Thunder at Twilight: Vienna 1913–1914* (Penguin). Morton has trawled through the newspapers of the time to produce two very readable dramatized accounts of two critical years in the city's history. The first centres on the Mayerling tragedy; the second, on the Sarajevo assassination.

Carl E. Schorske, *Fin-de-Siècle Vienna* (Cambridge UP, o/p/Random). Fascinating scholarly essays on, among other things, the impact of the building of the Ringstrasse, and of Freud, Klimt, Kokoschka and Schönberg on the city's culture.

A.J.P. Taylor, *The Habsburg Monarchy 1809–1918* (Penguin, o/p). Readable, forthright as ever and thought-provoking account of the demise of the Habsburgs.

Andrew Wheatcroft, *The Habsburgs* (Penguin). Wheatcroft's intriguing history traces the rise and fall of the Habsburgs from their modest origins in Switzerland to their demise at the head of the Austro-Hungarian empire, looking closely at individual family members, and the way the way the family promoted its dynastic image.

Simon Wiesenthal, *Sunflower* (Schocken Books). Wiesenthal relates an instance from his time at Mathausen when an ailing SS guard called him to his bedside and asked for forgiveness. In the second half of the book, Wiesenthal asks leading intellectuals to respond to the dilemma of forgiveness.

Stefan Zweig, *The World of Yesterday* (University of Nebraska Press). Seminal account of fin-de-siècle Vienna written just before Zweig was forced by the Nazis into exile in South America, where he and his wife committed suicide.

BIOGRAPHIES

THE HABSBURGS

Steven Beller, *Franz Joseph* (Longman, o/p). Shortest and most portable of the books on Franz-Josef; more of a political than a biographical account, it's a bit short on personal history.

Jean Paul Bled, *Franz Joseph* (Blackwell). Well-rounded account of the old duffer, with a smattering of the sort of scurrilous gossip missing in some other biographies.

Katerina von Burg, *Elisabeth of Austria* (Windsor Publications, UK). Latest biography of the endlessly fascinating empress who was assassinated by an Italian anarchist in 1898.

Edward Crankshaw, *Maria Theresa* (Constable, UK). Readable account of the "Virgin Empress", though disappointingly short on light touches.

Joan Haslip, *The Emperor and the Actress* (Weidenfeld & Nicolson, o/p). Detailed, steamy account of Franz-Josef's relationship with his long-term mistress, the actress Katharina Schratt.

Alan Palmer, *The Twilight of the Habsburgs: The Life and Times of the Emperor Francis Joseph* and *Metternich* (both Phoenix/Grove-

Atlantic). The first is the latest scholarly and somewhat weighty tome on the emperor; the latter, a solid account of the arch-conservative who ruled the roost in Vienna from 1815 to 1848.

JEWISH HISTORY

Kimberley Cornish, *The Jew of Linz: Hitler, Wittgenstein and their Secret Battle for the Mind* (Century). Utterly wacky book that in effect blames "complex, prickly" Wittgenstein for turning his schoolmate Hitler into an anti-Semite. The philosopher then recruited Kim Philby and his circle for the Russians, to make up for his role in precipitating the Holocaust. The author appears to be serious.

Alan Levy, *The Wiesenthal File* (Constable, UK). Thoroughly entertaining account of the controversial Vienna-based Nazi-hunter and the various Nazis he has helped to pursue, plus an account of the Waldheim affair.

Hella Pick, *Wiesenthal* (Phoenix/Northeastern UP). The most recent of the Wiesenthal biographies, its publication coinciding with another controversy over the octogenarian Nazi-hunter.

ART AND MUSIC

Kurt and Herta Blaukopf, *Mahler: His Life, Work and World* (Thames & Hudson). A selection of letters and quotes by Mahler, plus material by those who knew him.

Malcolm Hayes *Anton von Webern* (Phaidon). Not as well known as Schönberg, or as successful as Berg, Webern is seen by some as a progressive, and accused by others of being a Nazi sympathizer. Hayes, understandably, sits on the fence.

Donald Mitchell, *Gustav Mahler* (Faber/Yale UP). Mitchell's three-volume life of Mahler is a bench-mark biography, as dense and wide-ranging as one of its subject's colossal symphonies.

Elizabeth Norman McKay *Franz Schubert: A Biography* (Clarendon Press). Straightforward biography of Schubert, which does the best it can to unravel the composer's brief life from the limited source material available.

H.C. Robbins Landon, *Mozart, the Golden Years 1781–1791* (Thames & Hudson/Macmillan). Big illustrated romp through the composer's mature, Vienna years; a mixture of biography and musicology.

Alfred Weidinger, *Kokoschka and Alma Mahler: Testimony to a Passionate Relationship* (Prestel Verlag, available in UK). Detailed account of the artist's doomed relationship with Mahler's widow, illustrated with lots of Kokoschka's drawings and paintings from the period.

FREUD

Peter Gay, *Freud* (Papermac/Doubleday). Big tome, a healthy mixture of biography and philosophy, with a bit of spicy drama for good measure.

Michael Jacobs, *Sigmund Freud* (Sage, UK). Brief biography of the bearded one, a quick trot through his ideas and the subsequent criticisms thereof.

Ernest Jones, *Life and Work of Sigmund Freud* (Penguin/Basic). Abridged version of the definitive three-volume biography that Jones – one of Freud's disciples – published in the 1950s just before he died.

WITTGENSTEIN

Ray Monk, *Ludwig Wittgenstein: The Duty of Genius* (Vintage/Viking Penguin). Exhaustive biography of the perplexing philosopher; a model of its kind, Monk's book interweaves Wittgenstein's life and thought into an inseparable entity.

AUSTRIAN FICTION

Thomas Bernhard, *Cutting Timber* (Vintage/Quartet), *Wittgenstein's Nephew* (University of Chicago) and *Extinction* (Penguin/University of Chicago). Dense, stream-of-consciousness ruminations from the leading critic of the hypocrisy and mediocrity of postwar Austria.

Hermann Broch, *The Sleepwalkers* and *The Death of Virgil* (both Vintage). Broch's ambitious trilogy *The Sleepwalkers* outlined his ideas on the gradual breakdown of values in twentieth-century society. With the Anschluss, Broch, who was of Jewish parentage, was briefly interned in a camp, where he began *The Death of Virgil*, which focuses on the last hours of Virgil's life and his questioning of the role his art has given him in society.

Elfriede Jelinek, *Wonderful, Wonderful Times, The Piano Teacher* and *Lust* (all Serpent's Tail). From one of the best writers to come out of Austria for some time, *The Piano Teacher* is an unsentimental look at Vienna from a woman's perspective, while *Wonderful, Wonderful Times*, which takes place in the late 1950s, digs up the city's murky past. *Lust* takes a dark and disturbing look at small-town life in the Austrian provinces.

Robert Musil, *The Man Without Qualities* (Picador/Vintage). Often compared with Joyce and Proust's great works, Musil's 1000-page unfinished novel takes place at the twilight of the Habsburg Empire. This translation, by Sophie Wilkins, includes a massive amount of material that has never appeared in English before; unfortunately, the UK paperback reprint omits this text in order to squeeze the novel into a single volume – so if UK readers want to read the real thing, they have to hunt out the two-volume hardback.

Josef Roth, *Radetsky March* (Penguin/ Overlook Press). Pitifully underrated, this is Roth's finest work – a nostalgic and melancholic portrait of the moribund Vienna of Franz-Josef. Check also the secondhand stores for Roth's masterful short novels *Job, The Emperor's Tomb* and – above all – *Flight Without End*, a heartbreaking tale of dislocation and world-weariness.

Arthur Schnitzler, *Hands Around* (Dover, UK). Schnitzler's play features ten seductions, each of which shares at least one character with the next one until the circle is complete. A classic portrayal of Viennese decadent fin-de-siècle society, it came back to prominence in the 1950s after being filmed as *La Ronde* by Max Ophuls.

Harold B. Segel (ed), *The Vienna Coffeehouse Wits 1890–1938* (Purdue UP). A rare opportunity to read translated snippets of work by *Kaffeehaus* regulars such as Karl Kraus, Peter Altenberg and Felix Salten (the little-known author of *Bambi* and *The Story of a Vienna Whore*, one of which was made into a Disney cartoon).

Stefan Zweig, *The Burning Secret and Other Stories* (Penguin). Exquisitely-wrought tales from fin-de-siècle Vienna, including *Letter from an Unknown Woman*, best and most poignant of Zweig's short stories.

ART AND ARCHITECTURE

Hans Bisanz, *Vienna 1900* (Berghaus Publishing). Full of colour reproductions of drawings and paintings by turn-of-the-century Secession artists.

Gabriele Fahr-Becker, *Wiener Werkstätte 1903–1932* (Taschen) and *Hundertwasser* (Taschen). Two definitive and copiously illustrated volumes, the first showing in colour and in black and white the enormous breadth of WW's output, and the second taking a close look at Hundertwasser's most recent ventures into architecture.

Peter Haiko and Roberto Schezen, *Vienna 1850–1930 Architecture* (Rizzoli). The ultimate coffee-table book on Vienna's most important works of architecture, beautifully photographed (by Schezen) and intelligently discussed.

Ingrid Helsing Almaas, *Vienna: A Guide to Recent Architecture* (Ellipsis, UK). Dinky illustrated pocket guide to Vienna's modern architecture of the last couple of decades, with forthright accompanying critiques and interviews.

Robert Lustenberger, *Adolf Loos* (Birkhauser). One of the Studio Paperback series, cheaper than Schezen's (see below), with more text but black-and-white photos only.

Erwin Mitsch *Egon Schiele* (Phaidon). Nicely produced, with a short introduction, then eighty colour plates and eighty more black-and-white photos.

Gilles Néret *Klimt* (Taschen). Good-value A4-format book, with a fair sprinkling of colour and black-and-white photos, and a succinct text outlining Gustav Klimt's artistic development.

Roberto Schezen, *Adolf Loos Architecture 1903–32* (Monacelli, o/p). Beautiful colour and black-and-white photos of Loos' major works in Vienna and elsewhere.

Patrick Werkner, *Austrian Expressionism: The Formative Years* (SROSS, US). Interesting articles on Schönberg, Schiele, Kokoschka, Gerstl and Kubin; black-and-white illustrations only.

HIKING

Cecil Davies, *Mountain Walking in Austria* (Cicerone Press). Includes a description of a route to the Grossglockner's summit via the *Stüdl* and *Erzherzog-Johann* huts – for experienced and well-equipped walkers – as well as some day-walks in the neighbouring Granatspitz group.

Allan Hartley, *Hut to Hut in the Stubai Alps* (Cicerone Press). Walks you through this region of the Tyrol, with magnificent glacier views along the way.

Jonathan Hurdle, *Walking Austria's Alps, Hut to Hut* (Cordee/The Mountaineers). Includes route information for a week's hut-to-hut tour of the Grossglockner, starting at Kaprun and ending at Kals am Grossglockner.

Kev Reynolds, *Walking in the Alps* (Cicerone Press). Provides detailed route information on the Grossglockner and numerous other Austrian ranges, in clear and authoritative prose.

LANGUAGE

Although a high proportion of Austrians speak some English, any attempts at learning a few phrases of German will be heartily appreciated. That said, German is a highly complex language which you can't hope to master quickly. The biggest problem for English-speakers is that German words can be one of three genders: masculine, feminine or neuter. Each has its own ending and a corresponding ending for any attached adjectives, plus its own definite article.

PRONUNCIATION

Pronunciation (and spelling) is less of a problem, as individual syllables are generally pronounced as they're printed – the trick is learning how to place the stresses in the notoriously lengthy German words. Though Austrians speak German with a distinct accent, and each region has its own dialect, when speaking to a foreigner most folk will switch to standard German.

The following is a rundown of the basics you'll need on a short holiday to Austria. For more detail, check out the *Rough Guide German Phrasebook*, set out dictionary-style for easy access, with English–German and German-English sections, cultural tips for tricky situations and a menu reader.

VOWELS AND UMLAUTS

a as in r**a**ther

e as in g**ay**

i as in f**ee**t

o as in n**o**se

u as in b**oo**t

ä is a combination of a and e, sometimes pronounced like **e** in b**e**t (eg *Länder*) and sometimes like **ai** in p**ai**d (eg *spät*).

ö is a combination of o and e, like the French *eu*

ü is a combination of u and e, like bl**ue**

VOWEL COMBINATIONS

ai as in d**ie**

au as in m**ou**se

ie as in tr**ee**

ei as in tr**i**al

eu as in b**oi**l

CONSONANTS

Consonants are pronounced as they are written, with no silent letters. The differences from English are:

j pronounced similar to an English y

r is given a dry throaty sound, similar to French

s pronounced similar to, but slightly softer than, an English z

v pronounced somewhere between f and v

w pronounced same way as English v

z pronounced ts

The German letter **ß** often replaces **ss** in a word: pronunciation is identical.

CONSONANT COMBINATIONS

ch is a strong back-of-the-throat sound, as in the Scottish loch

sp (at the start of a word) is pronounced shp

st (at the start of a word) is pronounced sht

GERMAN WORDS AND PHRASES

Basics

Ja, Nein	Yes, no	*Jenes*	That one
Bitte	Please or You're welcome	*Gross, Klein*	Large, small
Bitte schön	A more polite form of *Bitte*	*Mehr, Weniger*	More, less
Danke, Danke schön	Thank you, Thank you very much	*Wenig*	A little
		Viel	A lot
Wo, Wann, Warum?	Where, when, why?	*Billig, Teuer*	Cheap, expensive
Wieviel?	How much?	*Gut, Schlecht*	Good, bad
Hier, Da	Here, there	*Heiss, Kalt*	Hot, cold
Geöffnet, Offen, Auf	All mean "open"	*Mit, Ohne*	With, without
Geschlossen, Zu	Both mean "closed"	*Rechts*	Right
Da drüben	Over there	*Links*	Left
Dieses	This one	*Gerade aus*	Straight ahead

Greetings and times

Grüss Gott	Good day	*Vorgestern*	The day before yesterday
Servus	Hi! *or* Goodbye (informal)		
Guten Morgen	Good morning	*Übermorgen*	The day after tomorrow
Guten Abend	Good evening	*Tag*	Day
Gute Nacht	Good night	*Nacht*	Night
Auf Wiedersehen	Goodbye	*Mittag*	Midday
Auf Wiederhören	Goodbye (on the telephone)	*Mitternacht*	Midnight
		Woche	Week
Tschüss	Goodbye (informal)	*Wochenende*	Weekend
Wie geht es Ihnen?	How are you? (polite)	*Monat*	Month
Wie geht es dir?	How are you? (informal)	*Jahr*	Year
Geh weg	Go away	*Am Vormittag/Vormittags*	In the morning
Heute	Today	*Am Nachmittag/Nachmittags*	In the afternoon
Gestern	Yesterday		
Morgen	Tomorrow	*Am Abend*	In the evening

Days, months and dates

Montag	Monday	*Jänner*	January	*Frühling*	Spring
Dienstag	Tuesday	*Februar*	February	*Sommer*	Summer
Mittwoch	Wednesday	*März*	March	*Herbst*	Autumn
Donnerstag	Thursday	*April*	April	*Winter*	Winter
Freitag	Friday	*Mai*	May		
Samstag	Saturday	*Juni*	June	*Montag, der*	Monday, the
Sonntag	Sunday	*Juli*	July	*erste April*	first of April
		August	August	*Der zweite April*	The second of April
Ferien	Holidays	*September*	September		
Feiertag	Bank holiday	*Oktober*	October	*Der dritte April*	The third of April
		November	November		
		Dezember	December		

Some signs

Damen/Frauen	Women's toilets	*Umleitung*	Diversion	*Kein Eingang*	No entrance
Herren/Männer	Men's toilets	*Achtung!*	Attention!	*Drücken*	Push
Eingang	Entrance	*Vorsicht!*	Beware!	*Ziehen*	Pull
Ausgang	Exit	*Not*	Emergency	*Frei*	Vacant
Ankunft	Arrival	*Notausgang*	Emergency exit	*Besetzt*	Occupied
Abfahrt	Departure	*Krankenhaus*	Hospital	*Verboten*	Prohibited
Ausstellung	Exhibition	*Polizei*	Police	*Kasse*	Cash desk/ ticket office
Autobahn	Motorway	*Nicht rauchen*	No smoking		

Questions and requests

All enquiries should start with the phrase *Entschuldigen Sie bitte* (Excuse me, please). Though strictly you should use *Sie*, the polite form of address, with everyone except close friends, young people often don't bother with it. However, the older generation and anyone official will certainly be offended if you address them with the familiar *Du*.

Sprechen Sie Englisch?	Do you speak English?	*Ist der Tisch frei?*	Is that table free?
Ich spreche kein Deutsch	I don't speak German	*Die Speisekarte bitte*	The menu please
Sprechen Sie bitte langsamer	Please speak more slowly	*Fräulein . . . !*	Waitress . . . ! (for attention)
Ich verstehe nicht	I don't understand		
Ich verstehe	I understand	*Herr Ober . . . !*	Waiter . . . ! (for attention)
Wie sagt mann das auf Deutsch?	How do you say that in German?	*Haben Sie etwas billigeres?*	Have you got something cheaper?
Können Sie mir sagen wo . . . ist?	Can you tell me where . . . is?	*Haben Sie Zimmer frei?*	Are there rooms available?
Wo ist . . . ?	Where is . . . ?	*Wo sind die Toiletten bitte?*	Where are the toilets please?
Wieviel kostet das?	How much does that cost?	*Ich hätte gern dieses*	I'd like that one
Wann fährt der nächste Zug?	When does the next train leave?	*Ich hätte gern ein Zimmer für zwei*	I'd like a room for two
Um wieviel Uhr?	At what time?	*Ich hätte gern ein Einzelzimmer*	I'd like a single room
Wieviel Uhr ist es?	What time is it?		
Sind die Plätze noch frei?	Are these seats taken?	*Hat es Dusche, Bad, Toilette?*	Does it have a shower, bath, toilet?
Die Rechnung bitte	The bill please		

Numbers

0	*null*	13	*dreizehn*	60	*sechzig*		
1	*eins*	14	*vierzehn*	70	*siebzig*		
2	*zwei*	15	*fünfzehn*	80	*achtzig*		
3	*drei*	16	*sechszehn*	90	*neunzig*		
4	*vier*	17	*siebzehn*	100	*hundert*		
5	*fünf*	18	*achtzehn*	1000	*tausend*		
6	*sechs*	19	*neunzehn*	1998	*neunzehn-hundert-acht-und-neunzig*		
7	*sieben*	20	*zwanzig*				
8	*acht*	21	*ein-und-zwanzig*	1999	*neunzehn-hundert-neun-und-neunzig*		
9	*neun*	22	*zwei-und-zwanzig*				
10	*zehn*	30	*dreissig*	2000	*zweitausand*		
11	*elf*	40	*vierzig*	2001	*zweitausand-und-eins*		
12	*zwölf*	50	*fünfzig*				

GLOSSARY

German terms

Abtei Abbey

Alm High alpine pasture, meadow.

Ausstellung Exhibition.

Bach Stream.

Bad Spa, bath.

Bahnhof Station.

Bau Building.

Bauernhof Farmhouse.

Beisl Pub.

Berg Mountain, hill.

Bezirk City district.

Brücke Bridge.

Brünn Brno, capital of Moravia (Czech Republic).

Brunnen Fountain.

Burg Castle.

Buschenschank Wine-tavern (see also *Heuriger*).

Bushaltestelle Bus stop.

Denkmal Memorial.

Dom Cathedral.

Donau River Danube.

Dorf Village.

Durchgang Passageway.

Durchhaus Literally a "through-house" – a house whose ground floor is open, allowing access to a street or courtyard.

Einbahnstrasse One-way street.

Erzherzog Archduke.

Fasching Carnival.

Feiertag Holiday.

Flughafen Airport.

Freibad Outdoor swimming pool.

Friedhof Cemetery.

Fussgängerzone Pedestrian zone.

Gasse Alley.

Gehweg Footpath.

Gemälde Painting.

Gemeindeamt Local council offices.

Gemütlich Snug or cosy.

Gletscher Glacier.

Grab Grave.

Gürtel Vienna's outer ring road.

Hallenbad Indoor swimming pool.

Haltestelle Bus/tram stop.

Haus House.

Herzog Duke.

Heuriger Wine-tavern.

Hof Court, courtyard, mansion, housing complex.

Horn Peak.

Hütte Hut, mountain refuge.

Innere Stadt Inner city.

Jugendgästehaus Youth hostel.

Jugendherberge Youth hostel.

Kaffeehaus Café.

Kaiser Emperor.

Kapelle Chapel.

Kärnten Carinthia.

Kaserne Barracks.

Keller Cellar.

Kino Cinema.

Kirche Church.

Kloster Monastery, convent.

König King.

Krippe Crib, Nativity scene.

Kunst Art.

Kunst- und Wunderkammer Cabinet of curios.

Kurort Health resort.

Laibach Ljubljana, capital of Slovenia.

Land (pl *Länder*) Name given to each of the nine federal provinces of Austria.

Langlauf Cross-country skiing.

Loipe Prepared track for cross-country skiing.

Niederösterreich Lower Austria.

Not Emergency.

Oberösterreich Upper Austria.

Palast Palace.

Pfad Path.

Platz Square.

Pressburg Bratislava, capital of Slovakia.

Prinz Prince.

Prunkräume Ceremonial or state rooms in a palace or castle.

Quelle Spring.

Rathaus Town hall.

Reich Empire.

Residenz Palace.

Ring Inner-city ring road, such as the Ringstrasse in Vienna.

Ritter Knight.

Rodelbahn Toboggan run.

Rollstuhl Wheelchair.

Saal Hall.

Sammlung Collection.

Säule Column.

Schanigarten Summer terrace/back yard.

Schatzkammer Treasury.

Schloss Castle.

Schlucht Gorge.

See Lake.

Seilbahn Cable car.

Sesselbahn Chairlift.

Speicher Reservoir.

Spitze Peak.

Stadel, or **Stadl** Barn or stable.

Stadt Town.

Stau Dam.

Stausee Reservoir.

Steiermark Styria.

Stift Collegiate church.

Strand Beach, shore.

Strandbad (pl *Strandbäder*) Outdoor bathing area on a lake or river.

Strasse Street.

Streichelzoo Children's zoo (farm animals and so on).

Tal Valley.

Talsperre Dam.

Tierpark Zoo or wildlife park.

Tor Gate.

Trakt Wing (of a building).

Turm Tower.

Venedig Venice.

Viertel Quarter, district.

Volk People, folk.

Vororte The outer suburbs of Vienna which lie beyond the Gürtel: the tenth to twenty-second districts of the city.

Vorstädte The inner suburbs of Vienna which lie between the Ring and the Gürtel: the third to ninth districts of the city.

Wald Forest.

Wasserfall Waterfall.

Wien Vienna.

Zimmer Room.

Political terms and acronyms

Anschluss Literally a "joining together" or "union" – the euphemism coined by the Nazis for the invasion and annexation of Austria in March 1938.

Austro-fascism Term to describe the one-party state set up by Engelbert Dollfuss in 1934. Dollfuss headed the Fatherland Front (see VF), a non-Nazi clerical-fascist movement that lasted until the Anschluss in 1938.

Austro-Marxism Philosophy expounded by SDAP theorists such as Otto Bauer in the early twentieth century. While still adhering to the language of class war, its programme was essentially revisionist, arguing that the downfall of capitalism was inevitable and didn't have to be brought about by violence.

Babenbergs Dynasty who ruled over Austria from 976 to 1246.

Biedermeier The term (*Bieder* means "upright") derives from the satiric figure of Gottlieb Biedermeier, a Swabian schoolmaster created in 1850 by Ludwig Eichrocht, modelled on Eichrocht's own pious, law-abiding teacher in Baden-Baden, Samuel Sauter. It has been applied retrospectively to the period between 1815 and 1848 when Austria was under the sway of Prince Metternich. The era came to symbolize a safe, bourgeois, cosy lifestyle, and was applied to the history, art and culture of the period.

CSP (Christlichsoziale Partei) The Christian Social Party was founded in the 1890s by Karl Lueger, who later became Mayor of Vienna. The Christian Socials' combination of Catholicism, municipal socialism and anti-Semitism proved popular with the Austrians. They were the main party of government in the 1920s and from their ranks rose Engelbert Dollfuss, who later introduced Austro-fascism in 1933.

FPÖ (Freiheitliche Partei Österreichs) The Austrian Freedom Party was the successor to the postwar VdU (see below). A far-Right party who rose to prominence in the 1980s and scored spectacular electoral success under the charismatic and controversial leadership of Jörg Haider.

Habsburg Royal dynasty whose powerbase was Austria from 1273 to 1918. Successive generations also held the office of Holy Roman Emperor from 1452 to 1806, and by marriage, war and diplomacy acquired territories across Europe.

Heimwehr Right-wing militia whose origins lay in the local armed groups formed after the collapse of the empire in 1918. After 1927, these regional militias joined together and created a political wing, the *Heimatblock*, which supported the onset of Austro-fascism in 1933.

Holy Roman Empire Revived title of the Roman Empire first bestowed by the pope on Charlemagne in 800. The emperor was chosen by the seven electors, and the title was passed around between the Hohenstaufen, Luxembourg and Habsburg families until 1438, when the Habsburgs made it hereditary. It was dissolved on the orders of Napoleon in 1806.

Josephine Of or pertaining to the reign of Emperor Josef II (1780–1790).

KPÖ (Kommunistische Partei Österreichs) Austrian Communist Party.

Kristallnacht Literally "Crystal Night", after the broken glass that was strewn across the streets during the pogrom of November 9–10, 1938. On this one night the majority of Jewish shops and institutions in the Third Reich – and all but one of the synagogues in Vienna – were destroyed by the Nazis.

k.u.k. *kaiserlich und königlich* (imperial and royal) – a title used after 1867 to refer to everything in the Austro-Hungarian empire. Everything within Hungary was prefaced with a "k." for *königlich*, everything in the rest of the empire "k.k." (*kaiserlich-königlich*, imperial-royal).

NSDAP (National Sozialistiche Deutsche Arbeiterpartei) National Socialist German Workers' Party, the official name for the German Nazi Party.

ÖVP (Österreichische Volkspartei) Austrian People's Party, the postwar descendant of the Christian Socials.

Pan-German This adjective covers a whole range of far-Right political parties, who advocated Anschluss with Germany, many of whom came together in the 1920s under the banner of the Greater German People's Party (Grossdeutsche Volkspartei, GDVP).

Red Vienna The period of Socialist municipal government in Vienna which lasted from 1919 to 1934.

Schutzbund SDAP militia founded in 1923.

Schütze The "Tyrolean riflemen", territorial defence units that were used in Andreas Hofer's rebellion against the Tyrol's Franco-Bavarian overlords in 1809.

SDAP (Sozial-Demokratische Arbeiterpartei) Social Democratic Workers' Party, the name given to the Socialist Party, prior to World War II.

SPÖ (Sozialistische Partei Österreichs) The postwar Austrian Socialist Party, later changed to the Sozialdemokratische Partei Österreichs, but keeping the same acronym.

Staatsvertrag The Austrian State Treaty of 1955, which signalled the withdrawal of Allied troops – American, British, French and Soviet – from Austria, in return for Austrian neutrality.

Toleranzpatent The Patent of Tolerance decreed by Josef II in 1782, which allowed freedom of religious observance to Lutherans, Jews and, to a lesser extent, Protestants.

VdU (Verband der Unabhängigen) Union of Independents. Extreme nationalist party formed in 1949 and precursor of the FPÖ.

VF (Vaterländische Front) The Fatherland Front were founded in 1934 by Engelbert Dollfuss, the Christian Social Austrian chancellor who dissolved parliament and introduced Austro-fascism in 1933. The Front was a patriotic, clerico-fascist organization aimed at preventing the Nazis from seizing power.

Art and architectural terms

Ambulatory Passage round the back of a church altar, in continuation of the aisles.

Art Nouveau Sinuous and stylized form of architecture and decorative arts from the 1890s, known as Secession or Jugendstil in Austria.

Atlantes Pillars in the shape of musclemen, named after the Greek god Atlas, whose job it was to hold up the world.

Baldachin A canopy over an altar, tomb, throne or otherwise.

Baroque Expansive, exuberant architectural and sculptural style of the seventeenth and eighteenth centuries, characterized by ornate decoration, complex spatial arrangement and grand vistas.

Biedermeier Simple, often Neoclassical, style of art and architecture popular from 1815 to 1848 (see under "Political terms", p.509) and in part a reaction against the excesses of the Baroque period.

Caryatid Female version of Atlantes (see opposite).

Chancel Part of the church where the main altar is placed, usually at the east end.

Chinoiserie Decorative style drawing on Chinese art and themes.

Diapers Ornamental patterning in brickwork.

Empire Neoclassical style of architecture and decorative arts practised in the first half of the nineteenth century.

Filigree Fanciful delicate ornamental decoration in metal or stone.

Fresco Painting applied to wet plaster, so that the colours immediately soak into the wall.

Glacis Sloping ground outside the outer fortifications of a city.

Gothic Architectural style prevalent from the twelfth to the sixteenth centuries, characterized by pointed arches and ribbed vaulting.

Historicism Style of architecture which apes previous styles – ie neo-Baroque, neo-Renaissance, neo-Gothic.

Jugendstil German/Austrian version of Art Nouveau, literally "youthful style" (see also "Secession" below).

Lierne A short rib that connects the main ribs of a vaulted ceiling.

Loggia Covered area on the side of a building, usually arcaded.

Lunette An oval or semicircular opening to admit light into a dome.

Nave Main body of a church, usually stretching from the western end to the chancel.

Neoclassicism Late eighteenth- and early nineteenth-century style of architecture and design returning to classical Greek and Roman models as a reaction against the excess of Baroque and Rococo.

Oriel A bay window, usually projecting from an upper floor.

Quoins External cornerstones of a wall.

Ringstrasse Pompous, historicist (see above) style of architecture imitating Gothic, Renaissance, Baroque and Classical architecture, used to describe the buildings that line Vienna's Ringstrasse.

Rococo Florid, ornamental style of architecture and design, forming the last phase of Baroque.

Romanesque Solid architectural style of the late tenth to thirteenth centuries, characterized by round-headed arches and geometrical precision.

Secession Movement of artists who split (seceded – hence the term) from the city's Academy of Arts in 1897. Also used more generally as a term synonymous with Art Nouveau and Jugendstil.

Sgraffito Monochrome plaster decoration effected by means of scraping back the first white layer to reveal the black underneath.

Spandrel The surface area between two adjacent arches.

Stucco Plaster used for decorative effects.

Transepts The wings of a cruciform church, placed at right angles to the nave and chancel.

Trompe l'oeil Painting designed to fool the onlooker into thinking that it is three-dimensional.

Wiener Werkstätte (Vienna Workshops) A group of Secession artists founded in 1903.

INDEX

The German "Sankt" has been abbreviated as "St"; names beginning "St" are alphabetized as if the word were spelled out.

Stay in touch with us!

ROUGH*NEWS* is Rough Guides' free newsletter.
In three issues a year we give you news, travel
issues, music reviews, readers' letters and the
latest dispatches from authors on the road.

I would like to receive ROUGH*NEWS*: please put me on your free mailing list.

NAME . . . .

ADDRESS . . . .

Please clip or photocopy and send to: Rough Guides, 1 Mercer Street, London WC2H 9QJ, England
or Rough Guides, 375 Hudson Street, New York, NY 10014, USA.

direct orders from

		UK£	US$	CAN$
Amsterdam	1-85828-218-7	8.99	14.95	19.99
Andalucia	1-85828-219-5	9.99	16.95	22.99
Antigua Mini Guide	1-85828-346-9	5.99	9.95	12.99
Australia	1-85828-220-9	13.99	21.95	29.99
Austria	1-85828-325-6	10.99	17.95	23.99
Bali & Lombok	1-85828-134-2	8.99	14.95	19.99
Bangkok Mini Guide	1-85828-345-0	5.99	9.95	12.99
Barcelona	1-85828-221-7	8.99	14.95	19.99
Belgium & Luxembourg	1-85828-222-5	10.99	17.95	23.99
Belize	1-85828-351-5	9.99	16.95	22.99
Berlin	1-85828-327-2	9.99	16.95	22.99
Boston Mini Guide	1-85828-321-3	5.99	9.95	12.99
Brazil	1-85828-223-3	13.99	21.95	29.99
Britain	1-85828-312-4	14.99	23.95	31.99
Brittany & Normandy	1-85828-224-1	9.99	16.95	22.99
Bulgaria	1-85828-183-0	9.99	16.95	22.99
California	1-85828-330-2	11.99	18.95	24.99
Canada	1-85828-311-6	12.99	19.95	25.99
Central America	1-85828-335-3	14.99	23.95	31.99
China	1-85828-225-X	15.99	24.95	32.99
Corfu & the Ionian Islands	1-85828-226-8	8.99	14.95	19.99
Corsica	1-85828-227-6	9.99	16.95	22.99
Costa Rica	1-85828-136-9	9.99	15.95	21.99
Crete	1-85828-316-7	9.99	16.95	22.99
Cyprus	1-85828-182-2	9.99	16.95	22.99
Czech & Slovak Republics	1-85828-317-5	11.99	18.95	24.99
Dublin Mini Guide	1-85828-294-2	5.99	9.95	12.99
Edinburgh Mini Guide	1-85828-295-0	5.99	9.95	12.99
Egypt	1-85828-188-1	10.99	17.95	23.99
Europe 1998	1-85828-289-6	14.99	19.95	25.99
England	1-85828-301-9	12.99	19.95	25.99
First Time Asia	1-85828-332-9	7.99	9.95	12.99
First Time Europe	1-85828-270-5	7.99	9.95	12.99
Florida	1-85828-184-4	10.99	16.95	22.99
France	1-85828-228-4	12.99	19.95	25.99
Germany	1-85828-309-4	14.99	23.95	31.99
Goa	1-85828-275-6	8.99	14.95	19.99
Greece	1-85828-300-0	12.99	19.95	25.99
Greek Islands	1-85828-310-8	10.99	17.95	23.99
Guatemala	1-85828-323-X	9.99	16.95	22.99
Hawaii: Big Island	1-85828-158-X	8.99	12.95	16.99
Hawaii	1-85828-206-3	10.99	16.95	22.99
Holland	1-85828-229-2	10.99	17.95	23.99
Hong Kong & Macau	1-85828-187-3	8.99	14.95	19.99
Hotels & Restos de France 1998	1-85828-306-X	12.99	19.95	25.99
Hungary	1-85828-123-7	8.99	14.95	19.99
India	1-85828-200-4	14.99	23.95	31.99
Ireland	1-85828-179-2	10.99	17.95	23.99
Israel & the Palestinian Territories	1-85828-248-9	12.99	19.95	25.99
Italy	1-85828-167-9	12.99	19.95	25.99
Jamaica	1-85828-230-6	9.99	16.95	22.99
Japan	1-85828-340-X	14.99	23.95	31.99
Jordan	1-85828-350-7	10.99	17.95	23.99
Kenya	1-85828-192-X	11.99	18.95	24.99
Lisbon Mini Guide	1-85828-297-7	5.99	9.95	12.99
London	1-85828-231-4	9.99	15.95	21.99
Madrid Mini Guide	1-85828-353-1	5.99	9.95	12.99
Mallorca & Menorca	1-85828-165-2	8.99	14.95	19.99
Malaysia, Singapore & Brunei	1-85828-232-2	11.99	18.95	24.99
Mexico	1-85828-044-3	10.99	16.95	22.99
Morocco	1-85828-169-5	11.99	18.95	24.99
Moscow	1-85828-322-1	9.99	16.95	22.99
Nepal	1-85828-190-3	10.99	17.95	23.99
New York	1-85828-296-9	9.99	15.95	21.99
New Zealand	1-85828-233-0	12.99	19.95	25.99
Norway	1-85828-234-9	10.99	17.95	23.99

UK orders: 0181 899 4036

around the world

Pacific Northwest	1-85828-326-4	UK£12.99	US$19.95	CAN$25.99
Paris	1-85828-235-7	8.99	14.95	19.99
Peru	1-85828-142-3	10.99	17.95	23.99
Poland	1-85828-168-7	10.99	17.95	23.99
Portugal	1-85828-313-2	10.99	17.95	23.99
Prague	1-85828-318-3	8.99	14.95	19.99
Provence & the Cote d'Azur	1-85828-127-X	9.99	16.95	22.99
The Pyrenees	1-85828-308-6	10.99	17.95	23.99
Rhodes & the Dodecanese	1-85828-120-2	8.99	14.95	19.99
Romania	1-85828-305-1	10.99	17.95	23.99
San Francisco	1-85828-299-3	8.99	14.95	19.99
Scandinavia	1-85828-236-5	12.99	20.95	27.99
Scotland	1-85828-302-7	9.99	16.95	22.99
Seattle Mini Guide	1-85828-324-8	5.99	9.95	12.99
Sicily	1-85828-178-4	9.99	16.95	22.99
Singapore	1-85828-237-3	8.99	14.95	19.99
South Africa	1-85828-238-1	12.99	19.95	25.99
Southwest USA	1-85828-239-X	10.99	16.95	22.99
Spain	1-85828-240-3	11.99	18.95	24.99
St Petersburg	1-85828-298-5	9.99	16.95	22.99
Sweden	1-85828-241-1	10.99	17.95	23.99
Syria	1-85828-331-0	11.99	18.95	24.99
Thailand	1-85828-140-7	10.99	17.95	24.99
Tunisia	1-85828-139-3	10.99	17.95	24.99
Turkey	1-85828-242-X	12.99	19.95	25.99
Tuscany & Umbria	1-85828-243-8	10.99	17.95	23.99
USA	1-85828-307-8	14.99	19.95	25.99
Venice	1-85828-170-9	8.99	14.95	19.99
Vienna	1-85828-244-6	8.99	14.95	19.99
Vietnam	1-85828-191-1	9.99	15.95	21.99
Wales	1-85828-245-4	10.99	17.95	23.99
Washington DC	1-85828-246-2	8.99	14.95	19.99
West Africa	1-85828-101-6	15.99	24.95	34.99
Zimbabwe & Botswana	1-85828-186-5	11.99	18.95	24.99
Phrasebooks				
Czech	1-85828-148-2	3.50	5.00	7.00
Egyptian Arabic	1-85828-319-1	4.00	6.00	8.00
French	1-85828-144-X	3.50	5.00	7.00
German	1-85828-146-6	3.50	5.00	7.00
Greek	1-85828-145-8	3.50	5.00	7.00
Hindi & Urdu	1-85828-252-7	4.00	6.00	8.00
Hungarian	1-85828-304-3	4.00	6.00	8.00
Indonesian	1-85828-250-0	4.00	6.00	8.00
Italian	1-85828-143-1	3.50	5.00	7.00
Japanese	1-85828-303-5	4.00	6.00	8.00
Mandarin Chinese	1-85828-249-7	4.00	6.00	8.00
Mexican Spanish	1-85828-176-8	3.50	5.00	7.00
Portuguese	1-85828-175-X	3.50	5.00	7.00
Polish	1-85828-174-1	3.50	5.00	7.00
Russian	1-85828-251-9	4.00	6.00	8.00
Spanish	1-85828-147-4	3.50	5.00	7.00
Swahili	1-85828-320-5	4.00	6.00	8.00
Thai	1-85828-177-6	3.50	5.00	7.00
Turkish	1-85828-173-3	3.50	5.00	7.00
Vietnamese	1-85828-172-5	3.50	5.00	7.00
Reference				
Classical Music	1-85828-113-X	12.99	19.95	25.99
European Football	1-85828-256-X	14.99	23.95	31.99
Internet	1-85828-288-8	5.00	8.00	10.00
Jazz	1-85828-137-7	16.99	24.95	34.99
Millennium	1-85828-314-0	5.00	8.95	11.99
More Women Travel	1-85828-098-2	10.99	16.95	22.99
Opera	1-85828-138-5	16.99	24.95	34.99
Reggae	1-85828-247-0	12.99	19.95	25.99
Rock	1-85828-201-2	17.99	26.95	35.00
World Music	1-85828-017-6	16.99	22.95	29.99

US/International orders: 1-800-253-6476

¿Qué pasa?

WHAT'S HAPPENING?
A ROUGH GUIDES SERIES –
ROUGH GUIDES PHRASEBOOKS

Rough Guide Phrasebooks
represent a complete shakeup of
the phrasebook format.
Handy and pocket sized, they
work like a dictionary to get you
straight to the point. With clear
guidelines on pronunciation,
dialogues for typical situations,
and tips on cultural issues, they'll
have you speaking the language
quicker than any other
phrasebook.

Czech, French, German, Greek,
Hindi & Urdu, Italian, Indonesian,
Mandarin Chinese, Mexican
Spanish, Polish, Portuguese,
Russian, Spanish, Thai, Turkish,
Vietnamese
Further titles coming soon...